Gault Millau

The Best of
FRANCE

Editor-in-Chief
Christian Millau

Adaptation and translation
Linda Barrett, Alice Brinton, Timothy Carlson, David Downie, Sheila Mooney,
Edouard Muller, Carinne Propper, Pauline Riddell

International coordination
Sophie Gayot

Edited by
André Gayot

Also available

The Best of Germany

Editorial Staff, French-language Guide
Jean-Louis Perret (Editor)
Jacques Duquesne, Sophie Hagège, Jean Maisonnave, Martine Montémont (Contributing Editors)
Guy Saint-Père (Editorial Director), assisted by Maxime Braquet

Published by RAC Publishing, RAC House, P O Box 100, South Croydon, CR2 6XW

© Gault Millau, Inc. 1991

British Library Cataloguing in Publication Data

The Best of France
1. France. Travel
1. Gayot, André
914.404839

ISBN 0-86211-126-9

International Advertisement Managers: Kingslea Press Limited, 137 Newhall Street, Birmingham B3 1SF. Tel 021-236 8112

Printed and bound in France by Maury

CONTENTS

INTRODUCTION • 5

Read this short chapter before you go any further. How to find your way around *The Best of France* and how to decipher the rankings, prices, symbols and abbreviations.

TOQUE TALLY • 9

An listing of the very best restaurants in France.

PARIS RESTAURANTS • 11

Find out why Paris is unquestionably the restaurant capital of the world. Grand temples of haute cuisine, convivial brasseries, welcoming neighbourhood bistros—here you'll discover hundreds of incisive reviews of Paris's best restaurants.

PARIS HOTELS • 81

You'll find a home-away-from-home in this broad selection of Paris's hotels, whether your budget allows for opulent luxury or modest charm.

PARIS SUBURBS • 95

The best restaurants and hotels in Paris's outlying areas. Includes Versailles.

FRANCE A-Z:
RESTAURANTS & HOTELS • 115

From Abbeville to Wimille, we've scoured France's cities, towns, villages and remote hideaways to uncover the country's best restaurants and hotels. Whether you're looking for a world-famous restaurant, a romantic resort or a charming village inn, you'll find it among these thousands of in-the-know reviews.

INDEX • 509

Places classified by *départements*.

MAP • 514

In and around France.

INTRODUCTION

The Best of France

This book is your key to the 'Best of France'. Crammed with vivid insights and discerning criticism, it will help you open the doors to the pleasures and treasures of thousands of French restaurants and hotels. Armed with this inside information, you will join the select ranks of 'those in the know'.

For more than twenty years we at Gault Millau have scoured the French countryside, from the big cities to the tiniest hamlets, in search of worthwhile places to eat and stay. Today, our guides are synonymous with thorough, honest evaluations written in a witty, entertaining style. Gault Millau is now a household word in France, and respected internationally.

Indeed our guides have influenced the way people cook, eat and think about food. In the early 1970s Gault Millau coined the term 'nouvelle cuisine' to describe the revolutionary recipes and culinary techniques then bubbling up in the pots of a new generation of chefs, like Michel Guérard, Paul Bocuse, and Jean Delaveyne. And today, Gault Millau has joined forces with the RAC, one of Europe's leading motoring organisations, to produce the most comprehensive and authoritative guide to France available in English.

Contributors from every region of France participate each year in a national survey of restaurants and hotels. They work to strict standards, ensuring fairness and continuity of the grading system from Calais to Cannes. For example, when our reviewers spot an exciting new place, they invariably seek a second opinion to confirm that they have come up with a winner.

So you can be confident that by following the famous Gault Millau toques (chefs' hats) you'll find the finest food in France. Black toques denote classic cuisine, based on time-honoured recipes and ingredients. Restaurants that make a concerted effort to maintain regional tradition are awarded our 'Lauriers du Terroir'. But the art of cooking changes and evolves with the times—contemporary 'creative cuisine' takes up where 'nouvelle cuisine' left off. We coif today's inventive chefs with red toques, the bright colour reflecting their lively culinary imagination....

This year, like every year, new talents have been honoured; and a star has become a superstar. Michel Trama, formerly a student of sociology, this year hits the Gault Millau jackpot, scoring a mind-boggling 19.5 out of 20 points. We have no doubt that the young chefs we discover year after year will be celebrated—some day—by the media at large. Among the newcomers we try to eliminate 'forgers' who present their absurd combinations as 'state of the art' cuisine. Nor are we fond of so called 'traditionalists' who lazily trot out the same culinary clichés endlessly.

The purpose of this guide is to help you steer an informed course through the restaurants and hotels of France. Of course, the top restaurants are usually expensive, but we also lead our readers to cosy bistros and family-style 'auberges', where you can indulge your appetite without breaking the bank!

Whether you are a first-time visitor or a frequent traveller to France, let us help you discover these delights—before the crowds get there! We want to share with you the gastronomic joys that France holds out to all who take the time to savour them.

André Gayot

SYMBOL SYSTEMS

RESTAURANTS

Gault Millau ranks restaurants in the same manner that French students are graded: on a scale of zero to twenty, twenty being unattainable perfection. The rankings reflect *only* the quality of the cooking; decor, service, reception and atmosphere do not influence the rating. They are explicitly commented on within the reviews. Restaurants ranked thirteen and above are distinguished with toques (chef's hats), according to the following table:

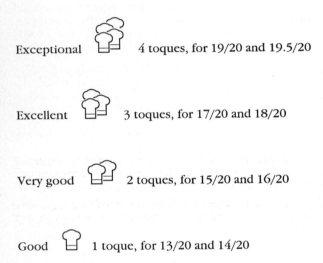

Exceptional   4 toques, for 19/20 and 19.5/20

Excellent   3 toques, for 17/20 and 18/20

Very good   2 toques, for 15/20 and 16/20

Good   1 toque, for 13/20 and 14/20

Toques in red denote restaurants serving modern cuisine; toques in black denote restaurants serving traditional food.

Keep in mind that these ranks are *relative*. One toque for 13/20 is not a very good ranking for a highly reputed (and very expensive) temple of fine dining, but it is quite complimentary for a small place without much pretension.

At the end of each restaurant review, prices are given—either à la carte or menus (fixed-price meals) or both. A la carte prices are those of an average meal (a starter, a main course, and a dessert) for one person, including service and a half bottle of relatively inexpensive wine. Lovers of great Bordeaux, Burgundies and Champagnes will, of course, face stiffer tabs. The menu prices quoted are for a complete multicourse meal for one person, including service but excluding wine (unless otherwise noted). These fixed-price menus often give diners on a budget a chance to sample the cuisine of an otherwise expensive restaurant.

Prices in red denote restaurants that offer particularly good value.

In France, the service charge is always (by law) included in the price of the food. But it is customary to leave a few extra francs as an additional tip.

HOTELS

Our opinion of the comfort level and appeal of each hotel is expressed in a ranking system, as follows:

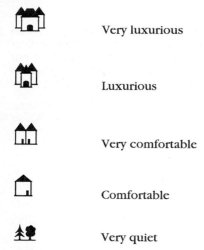

Very luxurious

Luxurious

Very comfortable

Comfortable

Very quiet

Symbols in red denote charm.

Hotel prices listed are for the complete range of rooms, from the smallest singles to the largest doubles; suite prices are also given when possible. These prices are per room, not per person. Half-board and full-board prices, however, are per person.

Sadly, prices continue to creep up, so some places may have become more expensive than our estimates by the time you visit. If you expect to pay a little more—you may end up being pleasantly surprised!

OTHER INFORMATION & ABBREVIATIONS

💮 "Les Lauriers du Terroir': an award given to chefs who prepare noteworthy traditional or regional recipes.

M. (or MM. or Mme. or Mlle.): proprietor's, proprietors' or manager's name

Rms: rooms

Stes: suites

Seas: season

Air cond.: Air conditioning

Half-board: rate per person for room, breakfast and one other meal (lunch or dinner)

Full board: rate per person for room and three meals

Oblig in seas.: obligatory in season

Credit Cards
  V VISA, or Carte Bleue, (also generally includes Mastercard or Eurocard)
  AE American Express
  DC Diners Club

How to read the locations:

ABBEVILLE *(the town)*

280100 Abbeville - (Somme)
(the zip code) (the regional department)
Paris 160 - Amiens 45 - Dieppe 63 - Boulogne-sur-Mer 80
(kilometres to Paris and nearby major cities)

A FINAL NOTE

We have made a Herculean effort to provide as much practical information as possible: phone numbers, proprietors' names, hours, daily, and annual closings, telex numbers, specific amenities and special features, prices, credit cards accepted and more. We've also made a tremendous effort to keep all the information current and correct. But establishments change such things with alarming speed, so please forgive us if you come across incorrect or incomplete information.

TOQUE TALLY

Red Toques: Modern cuisine; Black Toques: Traditional cuisine.

Four Toques (19.5/20)

19.5

Lucas-Carton (Senderens), *Paris 8th*
Robuchon, *Paris 16th*
L'Aubergade, *Puymirol (see Agen)*
Auberge de l'Eridan, *Annecy*
Michel Guérard, *Eugénie-les-Bains*
L'Auberge de l'Ill, *Illhaeusern*
Michel Bras, *Laguiole*
Alain Chapel, *Mionnay (see Lyon)*
Troisgros, *Roanne*
La Côte d'Or, *Saulieu*
Marc Meneau, *Saint-Père-sous-Vézelay (see Vézelay)*
Georges Blanc, *Vonnas*

Four Toques (19/20)

19

Arpège, *Paris 7th*
Vivarois, *Paris 16th*
Guy Savoy, *Paris 17th*
Amat (Saint-James), *Bouliac (see Bordeaux)*
Restaurant de Bricourt, *Cancale*
Le Royal Gray, *Cannes*
La Côte Saint-Jacques, *Joigny*
Le Louis XV, *Monte-Carlo*
Jacques Maximin, *Nice*
Boyer, *Reims*
Grand Hôtel du Lion d'Or, *Romorantin*
Pierre Gagnaire, *Saint-Etienne*
Jean Bardet, *Tours*
Pic, *Valence*

Four Toques (19/20)

19

Taillevent, *Paris 8th*
Paul Bocuse, *Collonges-au-Mont-d'Or (see Lyon)*

Three Toques (18/20)

18

Carré des Feuillants, *Paris 1st*
L'Ambroisie, *Paris 4th*
Jacques Cagna, *Paris 6th*
Le Duc, *Paris 14th*
Faugeron, *Paris 16th*
Apicius, *Paris 17th*
Michel Rostang, *Paris 17th*
La Vieille Fontaine, *Maisons-Laffite*
Les Trois Marches, *Versailles*
L'Oustau de Baumanière, *Les Baux-de-Provence*
Auberge des Templiers, *Les Bézards*
Bernard Robin, *Bracieux*
La Bourride, *Caen*
La Palme d'Or, *Cannes*
Lameloise, *Chagny*
Hôtel Radio, *Chamalières (see Clermont-Ferrand)*
Jean-Pierre Billoux, *Dijon*
Pain, Adour et Fantaisie, *Grenade-sur-l'Adour*
Les Roches, *Aiguebelle (see Le Lavandou)*
Le Flambard, *Lille*
Léon de Lyon, *Lyon 1st*
La Tour Rose, *Lyon 5th*
Le Moulin de Mougins, *Mougins*

Georges Paineau, *Questembert*
Les Pyrénées, *Saint-Jean-Pied-de-Port*
Buerehiesel, *Strasbourg*
Le Crocodile, *Strasbourg*
Chabran, *Pont-de-l'Isère (see Valence)*
La Pyramide, *Vienne*

Three Toques (18/20)

La Tour d'Argent, *Paris 5th*
Le Divellec, *Paris 7th*
Arzak, *San Sebastian (see Hendaye)*

Three Toques (17/20)

Gérard Besson, *Paris 1st*
Drouant, *Paris 2nd*
Le Bourdonnais, *Paris 7th*
Les Ambassadeurs, *Paris 8th*
Au Petit Montmorency, *Paris 8th*
Jean-Claude Ferrero, *Paris 16th*
Patrick Lenôtre, *Paris 16th*
Le Pré Catelan, *Paris 16th*
Amphyclès, *Paris 17th*
Clos Longchamp, *Paris 17th*
Le Manoir de Paris, *Paris 17th*
Sormani, *Paris 17th*
A. Beauvilliers, *Paris 18th*
Duc d'Enghien, *Enghien*
La Tamarissière, *Agde*
La Bonne Auberge, *Antibes*
Jean-Paul Jeunet, *Arbois*
Daguin, *Auch*
Le Goyen, *Audierne*
Les Frères Ibarboure, *Bidart*
Le Chapon Fin, *Bordeaux*
Jean Ramet, *Bordeaux*
Le Rouzic, *Bordeaux*
Le Vieux Moulin, *Bouilland*

Le Bateau Ivre, *Le Bourget-du-Lac*
Moulin de l'Abbaye, *Brantôme*
Le Moulin de Martorey, *Chalon-sur-Saône*
La Bonne Etape, *Château-Arnoux*
Au Fer Rouge, *Colmar*
Le Bateau Ivre, *Courchevel*
Chabichou, *Courchevel*
Restaurant Thibert, *Dijon*
Les Abbesses, *Épinal*
Royal Club, *Evian*
Le Centenaire, *Les Eyzies*
Château *Eza, Eze*
Château de Locguénolé, *Hennebont*
La Cognette, *Issoudun*
La Terrasse, *Juan-les-Pins*
Arabian, *Lille*
Hostellerie du Cerf, *Marlenheim*
Passédat (Le Petit Nice), *Marseille*
Chantecler, *Nice*
Issautier, *Saint-Martin-du-Var (see Nice)*
Auberge Bretonne, *La Roche-Bernard*
Richard Coutanceau, *La Rochelle*
Gill, *Rouen*
Auberge des Cimes, *Saint-Bonnet-le-Froid*
Jean-Jacques Jouteux, *Saint-Jean-Cap-Ferrat*
Chabichou, *Saint-Tropez*
Château de la Messardière, *Saint-Tropez*
Résidence de la Pinède, *Saint-Tropez*
L'Abbaye Saint-Michel, *Tonnerre*
Les Jardins de l'Opéra, *Toulouse*
Régis Mahé, *Vannes*

Three Toques (17/20)

Café de Paris, *Biarritz*
Les Gourmets, *Marsannay-la-Côte (see Dijon)*
Rôtisserie du Chambertin, *Gevrey-Chambertin*
Nandron, *Lyon 2nd*
Greuze, *Tournus*

PARIS
Restaurants

12/20 L'Absinthe
24, pl. du Marché-St-Honoré — 42.60.02.45
*M. Malabard. Closed Sat lunch and Sun. Open until
11.30 pm. Private room: 40. Terrace dining. Parking. V AE DC.*
A charming bistro with turn-of-the-century décor
and a pleasant summer terrace. The cuisine is
costly and rather belaboured (what, pray tell, is
fillet of beef served in a mysterious 'jus' de St-
Estèphe?).
A la carte: 350 F.

10/20 Joe Allen
30, rue P.-Lescot — 42.36.70.13
M. Lesueur. Open every day. Open until 1 am. Terrace dining. Air cond. Telex 215459. V.
This small Franco-American club is a fine place
to knock back a pint and chat up a tall, dark, and
handsome stranger. Try the chef's salad, the chilli
burger, the barbecued pork, and the apple pie.
A la carte: 200 F.

Armand au Palais-Royal
6, rue de Beaujolais
42.60.05.11
*M. Paillat. Closed Sat lunch, Sun and Aug. Open until
1 am. Air cond. V AE DC.*
Chef Jean-Pierre Ferron still merits distinction,
but lack of imagination and unreliable performance have cost this restaurant a point. The setting
is as spectacular as ever: rough-stone former
stables (which once belonged to the maréchal-duc
de Richelieu) facing the gardens of the Palais-Royal.
The salad of foie gras and warm artichoke is excellent, as is the Bresse chicken, and the chocolate
desserts are superb. Less so the service and
hospitality.
A la carte: 450-480 F. Menu: 180 F (lunch only).

Gérard Besson
5, rue Coq-Héron
42.33.14.74
*M. Besson. Closed Sat, Sun and 3 last weeks of July.
Open until 10.30 pm. Air cond. V AE DC.*
A third toque this year for Gérard Besson! He may
not make front-page news like some other chefs,
probably because he is too busy turning out
masterpieces of classic cuisine. A disciple of
Chapel, Garin, and Jamin, Besson has brought his
talent for elegant simplicity to such dishes as oyster
flan with saffron-mussel cream, brioche of
scrambled eggs with prawns, and warm rabbit pâté
in flaky pastry. What might be a pompous exercise
in style in less skilled hands here becomes light,
flavourful, and modern.
With his feet thus solidly set in tradition, Gérard
Besson makes successful sorties into brave new
territory: a morsel of skate with a mousse of
avocado and bell pepper served as an amuse-
bouche alongside a fragrant fumet de coquilles
St-Jacques dotted with plump pasta dumplings;
fabulous sweet-and-sour pigeon (in a reduced
sauce hinting of quince and cardamom); or
sweetbread ragoût in a walnut-bread croûte.
The décor is dignified, despite some coy touches:
bleached-wood furnishings, antique paintings, and
vitrines filled with silver-plated carafes. Excellent
desserts (chocolate sorbet, blanc-manger with
strawberry coulis and almond milk). The service is
less stiff now that Alain Delaveyne supervises the
staff. The wine cellar boasts some 50,000 bottles.
A la carte: 500 F Menus: 250 F (lunch only), 580 F
(menu dégustation).

12/20 Brasserie Munichoise
5, rue D.-Casanova
42.61.47.16
*M. Pouverin. Closed Sat lunch, Sun, 24 Dec-2 Jan
and Aug. Open until 12.30 am. Private room: 20. V.*
A cosy little brasserie that serves famously good
grilled veal sausages and pigs' knuckles, and one of
the best choucroutes in Paris. Excellent Hacker-
Pschorr beer on draught.
A la carte: 180-200 F.

Capeline
18, rue du Louvre
42.86.95.05
*Closed Sat lunch, Sun, 11-25 Feb and 12 Aug-2 Sep.
Open until 10.30 pm. Air cond. V AE DC.*
Out of the old-fashioned, comfortable décor
steps a smiling young Japanese chef. Tetsu Goya,
disciple of Jung and Haeberlin (in Alsace), took
over the kitchen some five years ago. Goya is
diligent in his execution and deserves more attention than he now receives. His cuisine does not
soar, but the dishes are balanced and generously
served (rosette of young rabbit and prawns in a
meat jus, triple filet mignon de bœuf, de veau et
d'agneau).
A la carte: 350-400 F. Menus: 196 F (dinner only),
220 F (lunch only, wine inc), 320 F.

Carré des Feuillants ♻
(Alain Dutournier)
14, rue de Castiglione — 42.86.82.82

M. Dutournier. Closed Sat lunch (and dinner in July-Aug) and Sun. Open until 10.30 pm. Private room: 14. Air cond. V AE DC.

You can take Alain Dutournier out of his native Landes but you cannot take the *landais* out of Dutournier. Together with his wife Nicole, Dutournier regularly nips out to his birthplace in south-west France to sniff the cèpes and stimulate his appetite. Paris? The restaurant's sophisticated setting of stone and pale *trompe-l'œil* woodwork might as well be in Gascony.

Here you spread the terrine of foie gras on a slice of warm cornbread and savour Gascon specialities such as warm pâté of cèpes enhanced by a fresh-tasting parsley jus, garbure with goose confit, range-raised capon with a galette de cèpes, and an exquisite pressed duck bathed in a foie gras sauce. Desserts include an exceptionally fine vanilla ice cream which is handmade to order, and an ethereal feuillantine sablée garnished with hazelnuts and marrons glacés.

We only wish Dutournier would renew his repertoire more often, as we might be tempted to think his imagination is running dry. Jean-Guy Loustau, the able steward of both the dining room and the cellar, dispenses in equal measure smiles, good counsel, and marvellous bottles of wine (with a marked preference for vintages from the Pays d'Oc). Alas, as one might expect, there is nothing rustic about the prices.

A la carte: 500-700 F. Menus: **250 F** (lunch only), 490 F.

Les Cartes Postales
7, rue Gomboust — 42.61.02.93

M. Watanabe. Closed Sun and 4-25 Aug. Open until 10.15 pm. Air cond. V.

Blow-ups of photographs hang on the beige-and-white walls of this small, pretty, flower-filled restaurant. Yoshimasa Watanabe, disciple of the great Robuchon, creates outstanding cuisine with just the right pinch of the exotic at astonishingly low prices. Since his arrival several years ago the restaurant has counted success upon success. Try his deliciously caramelised crab cake with grapefruit vinaigrette, spiced foie gras with broccoli, or the extraordinary Robuchon-style crème brûlée with vanilla and cinnamon. The cellar is improving, but still has a long way to go.

A la carte: 330 F. Menus: **110 F, 180 F, 240 F.**

12/20 Le Caveau du Palais
17-19, pl. Dauphine — 43.26.04.28

M. Dieuleveut. Closed Sat and Sun. Open until 10.30 pm. Private room: 20. Terrace dining. Air cond. V AE.

The good, solid cuisine (grilled andouillette, veal shanks with basil) is served in a charming Place Dauphine cellar divided down the centre by a wine bar.

A la carte: 250-300 F.

Bernard Chirent
28, rue du Mont-Thabor — 42.86.80.05

M. Chirent. Closed Sat lunch and Sun. Open until 10.45 pm. Private room: 16. Air cond. V.

Two years ago Bernard Chirent moved from that high-society haunt, Castel, to open his own restaurant here on the ground floor of the Hôtel du Continent. The sober décor is brightened by a touch of pinkish beige. Famous for his sauces and his peerless prawns in a herbal nage, Chirent also excels with frogs' legs, boned young pigeon per-fumed with tarragon, and an airy millefeuille—all richly deserve a second toque. The wine list is modest but includes several finds (Arbois, Rully, Saumur), some available by the glass. The all-in prix-fixe menu is marvellous.

A la carte: 300 F and up. Menu: **170 F** (wine inc).

12/20 Le Comptoir
37, rue Berger — 40.26.26.66

M. Chiche. Open every day. Open until 1 am. Terrace dining. V.

Sensational prices for tasty tapas (Spanish-style chicken, cold grilled vegetables, spinach-and-ricotta dumplings) served in a lively bistro atmosphere.

A la carte: **100-150 F.**

L'Escargot Montorgueil
38, rue Montorgueil — 42.36.83.51

Mme Saladin-Terrail. Closed Mon, 1 Jan, 1 May and 5-26 Aug. Open until 11 pm. Private room: 20. Terrace dining. V AE DC.

The 1830s décor of moulded ceilings, wrought-iron staircase, and antique mirrors has lost none of its charm. As ever, the elegantly classic cuisine specialises in myriad gastronomical trans-mogrifications of gastropods. Try the 'colimaçon' selection: snails with curry, with saffron, and with Roquefort. The wine list is short, the prices rather steep.

A la carte: 300-350 F. Menus: 160 F (lunch only), 240 F.

L'Espadon
(Hôtel Ritz)
15, pl. Vendôme — 42.60.38.30

M. Klein. Open every day. Open until 11 pm. Private room: 150. Garden dining. Air cond. No pets. Heated pool. Valet parking. Telex 220262. V AE DC.

From the humble ham sandwich at 80 F to the rack of lamb sprinkled with chopped parsley at 420 F (for two, admittedly), the grand Ritz style shines through. As one is entitled to expect, the service is among the finest in the world, the clientele prodigiously prosperous. Owner El Fayed, ever fond of show, is breaking records for 'ritzyness' with his grandiose thermal baths, squash courts, and rooftop heliport (for *deus ex machina* arrivals to the imperial suite—60,000 F a night). From the most sumptuous kitchen in France award-winning chef Guy Legay conjures with increasing grace and inventiveness his delightful dishes, such as veal paillard Coco Chanel and kidneys César Ritz. This year the red mullet with tapenade was delicious and the crispy-skinned sea bass outstanding, but the prawn papillotes were limp and the saddle of lamb had been smothered to death by spongy potato slivers. In short, we were a bit dis-appointed, but such are the ups and downs of *cuisine de palace*. The 120,000-bottle wine cellar is under the direction of virtuoso Georges Lepré.

A la carte: 600-800 F. Menu: 310 F.

La Fermette du Sud-Ouest ♻
31, rue Coquillière — 42.36.73.55

M. Mayer. Closed Sun and Aug. Open until 10 pm. V.

Christian Naulet has returned to his native Périgord, leaving a void behind him. But Jacky Mayer, the Fermette's new owner, has remained faithful to the restaurant's Gascon tradition and has kept the same chef on. Plump for the perfect pork grattons, or excellent boudin with garlicky potatoes. The menu is a bit short, but the welcome is warm.

A la carte: 250 F. Menu: 110 F.

Le Globe d'Or ☘

158, rue St-Honoré — 42.60.23.37
M. Constiaux. Closed Sat, Sun and Aug. Open until 10.30 pm. V AE DC.

The waiters, loaded with trays of cassoulet, confit, and ventre de veau gascon redolent with the flavours of the countryside, do what they can to squeeze between the crowded tables. After dinner, help your digestion along with a tot of superb prune de Souillac.
A la carte: 250 F.

Goumard

17, rue Duphot — 42.60.36.07
M. Goumard. Closed Sun, Mon and Christmas week. Open until 10.30 pm. Private room: 25. Air cond. No pets. V AE DC.

Three times a week Jean-Claude Goumard treks out at 3 am to the Rungis market and nets the very best sole and turbot, the fattest lobsters and prawns, for his chef Georges Landriot—fish and crustaceans so perfect that no flambé nor croûte shall ever be allowed to mar them. A pinch of turmeric to enliven the shellfish fricassée; a drop of veal juice with soy sauce to accompany the braised sole; precious little butter all around: in short, nothing that might denature the marvellously fresh taste of the sea.
Unless of course you prefer the enormous Brittany prawns roasted in their shell, or red mullet dabbed with virgin olive oil and basil. Dessert brings excellent chocolate fondant with coffee sauce. Goumard's elegant two-level restaurant is decorated in a soothing shade of pale yellow, and hung with nineteenth-century paintings.
A la carte: 500-600 F.

12/20 Le Grand Louvre

At the entrance of the museum,
under the pyramid — 40.20.53.41
M. Gauvin. Closed Tue. Open until 10 pm. Air cond. No pets. V AE DC.

Something is cooking under I.M. Pei's glass pyramid. This new restaurant serves country dishes from the South-west at appealingly low prices: poached egg en cassoulet, duck confit with spiced honey, prune nougat glacé. Non-stop service.
Menus: 140 F, 175 F, 260 F.

Le Grand Véfour

17, rue de Beaujolais — 42.96.56.27
Mme Ruggieri. Closed Sat lunch, Sun and Aug. Open until 10.15 pm. Private room: 22. Air cond. No pets. Valet parking. V AE DC.

The More Things Change department: a new chef, Gérard Fouché, has brought a refreshing yet familiar touch to this perennial site of gastronomic pilgrimage. Fouché, a smiling young man of thirty-five, cut his teeth in the kitchens of perfectionist Jacques Cagna and carries in his culinary baggage a taste for modern simplicity wedded to regional—that is: South-western-tradition. Dine on red-mullet minestrone, wild salmon steamed with thyme, chartreuse of young pigeon, a breathtaking chocolate soufflé, or rich frozen nougat with cherries.
As always, the magic of the Grand Véfour also resides in the fact that were every table empty you would still dine in perfect contentment, free to admire the exquisite surroundings that Jean Taittinger's good taste and family fortune have restored to their former glory: carved boiserie ceilings, graceful painted allegories under glass, lush carpeting, tables with white linens among black and gold Directoire chairs. The dining rooms evoke memories of such immortals as Napoleon,

Jean Cocteau, Victor Hugo, and Colette, who once lounged on these red velvet banquettes in the soft glow of the Palais-Royal gardens.
The service, under the expert and charming guidance of Béatrice Ruggieri, is as elegant as the clientele. The à la carte bill is astronomical, but the fixed-price lunch menu—which offers a wide variety of dishes—is excellent value: With a fine Bordeaux for 100 F you'll spend about 400 F all told and walk away with an unforgettable memory.
A la carte: 630-800 F. Menu: 305 F (lunch only).

Serge Granger

36, pl. du Marché-St-Honoré — 42.60.03.00
M. Granger. Closed Sat lunch, Sun and 10-20 Aug. Open until 10.30 pm. Private room: 25. Terrace dining. Air cond. No-smoking section. V AE DC.

At age 49 Serge Granger, a pastry chef and caterer by trade, has just opened his first restaurant. He ships his fish in fresh from St-Malo and creates refined, tasty dishes, to wit: a marvellous red-tunny tartare, or salmon with a tasty mélange of chopped apples, avocado, salmon, onions, and carrots. The desserts are gorgeous, notably the ethereal pear charlotte and the fruit soup with Cointreau sabayon. Sprightly service on a pleasant terrace. The bill, alas, is rather difficult to digest.
A la carte: 400 F and up.

A la Grille Saint-Honoré

15, pl. du Marché-St-Honoré — 42.61.00.93
M. Speyer. Closed Sun, Mon, 4-21 Aug and 24 Dec-3 Jan. Open until 10.30 pm. Private room: 30. Terrace dining. Air cond. V AE DC.

The eyesore (a multiple-storey concrete garage) that currently mars the centre of the Place du Marché St-Honoré will soon be replaced by a glass gallery designed by Riccardo Bofill. Thus transformed, this historic market square will flourish once again.
No surprise then that Jean Speyer, formerly cramped in an eighth-arrondissement basement restaurant, recently took over what was a shabby corner bistro and gave it a new lease of life. In the sparkling pink-and-grey decor Speyer serves tasty, imaginative 'market cuisine': roast veal kidneys with anchovies, pumpkin-mussel soup, crispy mackerel with onion fondue, blanquette of young rabbit. The desserts and affordably priced wines are Speyer's strongest suit.
A la carte: 250-350 F. Menu: 180 F (weekdays only).

12/20 Gros Minet

1, rue des Prouvaires — 42.33.02.62
M. Nocchi. Dinner only. Closed Sun. Open until 1.30 am. V AE DC.

The 1930s-pub décor looks as if it's falling to bits, especially when the thundering crowd of habitués descends elbows bared on Maurice Nocchi's old zinc bar. The food is solid and generously served: magret, cassoulet, veal kidneys. The wine list is short but memorable.
A la carte: 180 F. Menu: 90 F.

12/20 Lescure

7, rue de Mondovi
42.60.18.91
M. Lascaud. Closed Sat dinner, Sun, 1-29 Aug and 23 Dec-1 Jan. Open until 10 pm. Terrace dining. Air cond. V.

Tried-and-true French fare served in a feverishly *gai Paris* bistro atmosphere. Sample the rib-sticking veal sauté.
A la carte: 160-180 F. Menu: 90 F (wine inc).

12/20 Le Louchebem
10, rue des Prouvaires
42.33.12.99

M. Dubois. Closed Sun. Open until 11.30 pm. Terrace dining. V AE DC.

Carnivores can count on satisfaction here: huge portions of grilled or roasted beef, lamb, and pork, tripe, pigs' trotters and the like are served forth in a butcher-shop décor (rather cold, all that tile!). Modest, well-chosen wine list.
A la carte: 200-230 F.

La Main à la Pâte
35, rue St-Honoré – 45.08.85.73

M. Bassano. Closed Sun. Open until 12.30 am. Air cond. V AE DC.

The plastic plants and conservatory décor may be ghastly, but the pasta from Annita Bassano's kitchen (10 eggs per kilo of pasta!) is *squisita*. So too are the rich polenta alla bolognese, the osso buco, and one of the finest Italian wine cellars in Paris.
A la carte: 280 F. Menu: 160 F.

Mercure Galant
15, rue des Petits-Champs
42.96.98.89

M. Caille. Closed Sat lunch, Sun and holidays. Open until 10.30 pm. Private room: 35. V.

The service in this grand old bistro is charming, the décor elegant, and the cuisine better than ever. We are very pleased to award chef Pierre Ferranti a second toque this year. The gratin of just-caught lobster is a perennial favourite. Other specialities include salmon with green apples, pan-fried oysters with chicory fondue, and an exemplary crème brûlée. Appealing fixed-price menus.
A la carte: 500 F. Menus: 230 F (lunch only), 250 F and 370 F (dinner only).

La Passion
41, rue des Petits-Champs
42.97.53.41

M. Zellenwarger. Closed Sat lunch, Sun, holidays and 28 July-27 Aug. Open until 10.30 pm. Private room: 10. Air cond. No pets. V.

Gilles Zellenwarger's *trompe-l'œil* and woodwork décor is rather more elegant than passionate. And his rigorously correct cuisine enhanced by subtle sauces shows great respect for tradition. A well-earned extra point this year for notable progress in the young pigeon with cabbage and foie gras, the truffled blanc de volaille en vessie, and the sole with fresh mint. Excellent fixed-price menus, improved wine list.
A la carte: 300 F. Menus: 150 F, 180 F, 368 F.

Chez Pauline
5, rue Villedo – 42.96.20.70

M. Génin. Closed Sat dinner (and lunch in summer) and Sun. Annual closings not available. Open until 10.30 pm. Private room: 16. Air cond. V.

André Genin has taken over from his father Paul and slapped a fresh coat of paint on this old bistro, with its great mirrors, glowing woodwork, zinc bar, and red velvet banquettes. An almost imperceptible touch of modernity has crept into the menu: old-time specialities like young rabbit in white-wine aspic, or daube of hogs' jowls now flank fresh steamed fish and fresh pasta with truffles and foie gras. The cellar holds memorable Burgundies, and there is an excellent selection of coffees.
A la carte: 350-400 F. Menu: 250 F (lunch only).

12/20 Le Pavillon Baltard
9, rue Coquillière – 42.36.22.00

M. Tissot. Open every day. Open until 1 am. Terrace dining. Air cond. No-smoking section. V AE DC.

This vast brasserie faces the gardens of Les Halles, with a comfortable décor and two pleasant terraces. The cuisine is well-intentioned but sometimes misses the mark: the chef should keep a sharper eye on his sauces and cooking times.
A la carte: 230-250 F. Menu: 148 F.

12/20 Au Pied de Cochon
6, rue Coquillière – 42.36.11.75

M. Blanc. Open every day, 24 hours. Private room: 50. Terrace dining. Air cond. V AE DC.

The atmosphere is at once feverish and euphoric in this Les Halles institution, renowned for trotting out thundering herds of pigs' trotters (85,000 annually) and one tonne of shellfish every blessed day and night of the year.
A la carte: 250 F.

Pierre Traiteur
(Palais-Royal)
10, rue de Richelieu – 42.96.09.17

M. Dez. Closed Sat, Sun, holidays and Aug. Open until 10.15 pm. V DC.

Country delights from the four corners of France fill the lovely handwritten menu of this traditional bistro run by the Dez family. The cuisine is in the reliable hands of Roger Leplu, who uses top-quality ingredients to produce such pillars of French cooking as boudin with onions, mackerel in cider, and bœuf à la ficelle, as well as stuffed cabbage bourguignonne or sheep's tripe and trotters à la marseillaise. Superb home-style desserts.
A la carte: 280-400 F. Menu: 220 F.

12/20 La Pomme
18, pl. Dauphine
43.25.74.93

M. Massé. Closed Sun dinner off-season, Wed and 2 Nov-2 Jan. Open until 10.30 pm. Terrace dining. V.

This restaurant may become the apple of your eye. La Pomme, a modest and charming little establishment on the leafy Place Dauphine, serves good, honest food (fish soup, tête de veau, pot-au-feu).
A la carte: 200-230 F.

Le Poquelin
17, rue Molière
42.96.22.19

M. Guillaumin. Closed Sat lunch, Sun and 1-21 Aug. Open until 10.30 pm. Air cond. V AE DC.

Habitués like us rejoice in the unfailing inventiveness of Michel Guillaumin, a tried-and-true chef renowned for his desserts (the honey ice cream and nougat with apricot coulis are exquisite). Guillaumin lightens and updates traditional recipes such as wild-mushroom feuilleté and fillet of turbot in a spiced croûte. There is an interesting fixed-price menu and many fine wines this side of 100 F.
A la carte: 350 F. Menu: 175 F.

12/20 La Providence
6, rue de la Sourdière
42.60.46.13

Mme Schweitzer. Closed Sat, Sun and holidays. Open until 11 pm. Air cond. V AE DC.

Hearty Alsatian specialities such as presskopf and baeckeoffe are providential for avid appetites. Bustling *winstube* atmosphere.
A la carte: 180 F. Menus: 78 F (lunch only), 109 F.

11/20 Le Samovar
14, rue Sauval — 40.26.77.79
M. Siew. Closed Sun and Aug. Open until 1 am. Air cond. V AE.
Patrick Siew serves up a slice of old Russia in this lively Les Halles bistro, where strolling balalaika players, beef Stroganoff, shashlik, and lots of vodka combine to create an authentic atmosphere.
A la carte: 230-300 F. Menus: 72 F (lunch only), 134 F (weekdays dinner only), and de 190 F à 370 F (dinner only).

Saudade
34, rue des Bourdonnais — 42.36.30.71
M. Simoes. Closed Sun and Aug. Open until 10.30 pm. Private room: 8. Air cond. No pets. V AE DC.
Skilfully prepared Portuguese dishes have a pinch of nostalgia for Old Lusitania: marinated roast suckling pig alentejana, codfish (bacalhau) and robust boiled-beef cozido. Magnificent Portuguese wines and ports.
A la carte: 230 F.

La Terrace Fleurie
(Hôtel Inter-Continental)
3, rue de Castiglione — 42.60.37.80
M. de Roode. Open every day. Open until 11 pm. Terrace dining. No pets. Telex 220114. V AE DC.
Dining amidst flowers year round in the palatial décor of the Inter-Continental Hotel's candle-lit terrace. The service is excellent and the cuisine surprisingly fine. Try chef Jean-Jacques Barbier's lightly smoked lotte in a warm vinaigrette, or the saddle of young rabbit with potato and celery gratin. The prices (unsurprisingly) are pretty stiff.
A la carte: 500 F. Menus: 290 F (lunch only), 400 F (dinner only).

11/20 La Tour de Montlhéry
5, rue des Prouvaires — 42.36.21.82
Mme Benariac. Open 24 hours. Closed Sat, Sun and 14 July-15 Aug. V.
Sawdust spreads underfoot, hams hang from the rafters, and litre-bottles of Côte-de-Brouilly sit on checked tablecloths. The regulars refer to this old-style Les Halles bistro as 'Chez Denise' and come for the terrines, the stuffed cabbage, and bœuf au gros sel.
A la carte: 250 F.

Chez la Vieille
37, rue de l'Arbre-Sec — 42.60.15.78
Mme Biasin. Open for lunch only. Closed Sat, Sun and Aug. No pets.
The obsessive media cult that surrounds chef Adrienne Biasin hasn't corrupted her skilful hand. A regular circle of bankers, press barons, and show-business personalities fill this tiny rustic-kitsch restaurant and worship Adrienne's legendary pot-au-feu, hachis Parmentier, and streaky bacon with lentils.
A la carte: 300 F.

12/20 La Vigne
30, rue de l'Arbre-Sec — 42.60.13.55
Mme Collin. Closed Sat lunch and Sun. Open until midnight. V.
The feminine charm of Sabine Collin pervades this old bistro where the saucisse au couteau, the tarte Tatin au foie gras, and the duck with lentils are homely and delicious. Good regional wines.
A la carte: 220 F. Menu: 117 F.

12/20 Willi's Wine Bar
13, rue des Petits-Champs — 42.61.05.09
M. Williamson. Closed Sun. Open until 11 pm. V.
Mark Williamson, alias Willi, is an extremely knowledgeable British wine expert. He has wisely returned to a low-price policy and simple cuisine. Food here (whiting with olives en croustade, ragoût d'encornets printanier, Stilton served with a glass of cream sherry) now make a better match for the marvellous Côtes-du-Rhônes and other wines on offer. It's elbow-to-elbow at the counter.
A la carte: 200-230 F. Menu: 145 F (wine inc).

PARIS **2nd**

Auberge Perraudin
164, rue Montmartre — 42.36.71.09
M. Perraudin. Closed Sat lunch and Sun. Open until 11 pm. Private room: 14. Air cond. V AE DC.
Classic it was and classic it remains: Claude Perraudin's repertoire of high-quality cuisine is undeniably well-executed, but is as immoveable as a Corinthian column. Perraudin, a pillar of the Paris culinary world, is a disciple of Bocuse, Guérard, and Troisgros. Try his perfect aiguillettes of young rabbit in a truffle vinaigrette, his salmon and lobster carpaccio, and his hot potato tart.
A la carte: 400 F. Menus: 150 F, 250 F.

La Belle Corisande
14, rue L.-Bellan — 42.36.78.79
Closed Sat and Sun. Open until 10.30 pm. V.
Hats off (Basque berets, that is) to Jean-Charles Diehl for bringing us the same generous cuisine and jollity found at his other establishment, Jean-Charles et ses Amis (see eighth arrondissement). Do not be fooled by the dining room done in delicate shades of ivory and grey: the cuisine here is highly seasoned and hearty in the best Basque tradition (tiny squid à la Biscaye, rascasse with fiery Espelette peppers, andouille). The cooling crème catalane with prunes is exquisite. Solid snacks and wine by the glass are available at the bar.
A la carte: 180-250 F. Menu: 98 F.

12/20 Brasserie Gus
157, rue Montmartre — 42.36.68.40
M. Prigent. Lunch only (and dinner Fri until midnight). Closed Sat and Sun. Private room: 20. V.
The original 1870s provincial décor is charmingly down-at-heel. Join the white-collar crowd for oysters, pork with lentils, and grilled meats accompanied by nice little carafe wines.
A la carte: 200-250 F.

12/20 Le Brin de Zinc... et Madame
50, rue Montorgueil — 42.21.10.80
M. Levuslot. Closed Sun. Open until 11 pm. Terrace dining. V AE.
Young, animated Parisians sip Loire wines while watching the comings and goings along the most majestic of the city's old zinc bars. The oxtail in red wine and stuffed pigs' trotters are ably prepared by chef Gilles Guillou, late of Maxim's, but the prices are rather too high.
A la carte: 250-280 F.

12/20 Café Runtz
(ex-Gourmet d'Alsace)
16, rue Favart — 42.96.69.86
M. Leport. Closed Sat, Sun, holidays and 3-25 Aug. Open until 11.30 pm. Private room: 45. V AE.
This is an 1880s Alsatian *winstube* whose classic fare ranges from foie gras to choucroute or potato

salad with pork knuckles. Good French Rhine wines.
A la carte: 180 F.

Le Céladon
(Hôtel Westminster)
15, rue Daunou — 47.03.40.42
M. Corpechot. Closed Sat, Sun, holidays and 27 July-25 Aug. Open until 10 pm. Private room: 45. Air cond. Valet parking. Telex 680035. V AE DC.
Well-lighted, flower-filled, and impeccably elegant dining rooms in what is possibly the loveliest *restaurant de palace* in Paris form the perfect setting for a romantic dinner *à deux*. Le Céladon's remarkable young chef, Joël Boilleaut, former right-hand man to Michel Kérever at the Duc d'Enghien, creates delicious and resolutely refined dishes such as scrambled eggs with sea urchins, grilled coquilles St-Jacques, smoked breast of duck, sweetbreads braised with cumin and chicory, and a marvellously crisp lemon millefeuille.
A la carte: 500-600 F. Menu: 300 F.

La Corbeille
(Hôtel Cyrnos)
154, rue Montmartre — 40.26.30.87
M. Cario. Closed Sat lunch (and dinner 15 Sep-1 March.), Sun, holidays, 1-15 Aug and Christmas week. Open until 10.30 pm. Private room: 18. Air cond. No-smoking section. V AE.
Manneristic touches, 'virtuoso' turns, and an overwhelming penchant for smoke-curing have heavied the skilful hand of chef Jean-Pierre Cario. Nothing too serious as yet, but La Corbeille loses a point this year. Perhaps Cario should try less hard to display his enormous culinary knowledge in the description of each and every dish on the menu ('râble de lièvre encrépiné minute en feuilletage'). On the other hand, Cario excels when it comes to delightfully simple coquilles St-Jacques with coriander, or superb duck terrine with red cabbage, or a perfect filet de bœuf à la ficelle. Comfortable if lavishly lacquered '30s décor. Superb wine cellar.
A la carte: 500-550 F. Menus: 205 F (lunch only), 300 F and 373 F (dinner only, wine inc).

12/20 Coup de Cœur
19, rue St-Augustin — 47.03.45.70
MM. Namura and Oudin. Closed Sat lunch and Sun. Open until 10.30 pm. V AE DC.
The reception, service, and cuisine are thoroughly professional. Appetising entrées (spinach salad with strips of smoked duck breast) lead into tasty 'neo-bourgeois' main courses (pigeon gros sel), and the nice little house Bourgueil is a bargain at 75 F. The atmosphere inclines to the trendy—there are no little grey men in the crowd, despite the monochromatic post-modern décor.
A la carte: 230-250 F. Menu: 125 F.

Delmonico
39, av. de l'Opéra — 42.61.44.26
M. Lindström. Closed Sat, Sun, holidays and Aug. Open until 10 pm. Private room: 14. Air cond. Telex 680217. V AE DC.
The new manager of this old standby has lightened the décor and enlivened the ambience. The menu still encompasses the good (fresh Périgord fettucine with foie gras, confit de canard en potau-feu), the sad (veal chop flamed in Calvados), and the distressing (kidneys cooked in whisky). The service, however, is uniformly charming. And note that a fast pre-theatre supper or business lunch can be served in 45 minutes.
A la carte: 350 F. Menus: 200 F, 290 F.

12/20 Chez Diep
28, rue Louis-le-Grand — 47.42.31.58
See 8th arrondissement

Drouant
18, rue Gaillon — 42.65.15.16
M. Ody. Open every day. Open until 10.30 pm (12.30 am at Le Café). Private room: 50. Air cond. Valet parking. V AE DC.
Louis Grondard has descended from his eyrie at the Jules Verne (second storey of the Eiffel Tower), bringing with him well-deserved laurels and a repertoire of modern gastronomical classics. After his Robuchon-like success on high, Grondard is likely to keep the two hundred seats at Drouant (restaurant, Café, and salons) packed year-round. Appropriately enough, the Goncourt literary prize is awarded here each year, and the monthly literary luncheons of the jury are held in a handsome little dining room, among the charming art deco pastiche of a décor, which features a splendid wrought-iron and marble staircase.
New chef, new menu. But Drouant is still worthy of that third toque we awarded in 1989. The masterly touch of the great sauce-maker is evident in Grondard's belons gratinées au Champagne à la fondue de poireau, the fillet of striped bass with celery and truffles, and the pan-fried fillet of beef with sweet-pepper coulis. Few palates would fail to appreciate desserts like spiced vanilla crème brûlée, croquant aux marrons, and honey and gentian ice cream.
The Grill, rebaptised Le Café, seats 60 and is the haunt of businessmen in search of reasonably priced fare.
The wine cellar's rare bottles at 5,000 F are flanked by a selection of fine wines priced between 100 F and 200 F. Efficient, workmanlike service.
A la carte: 450-600 F. Menus: 290 F (weekdays lunch only), 200 F (at Le Café; dinner only).

12/20 Gallopin
40, rue N.-D.-des-Victoires — 42.36.45.38
M. Wagrez. Closed Sat and Sun. Open until 11 pm. Terrace dining. V AE DC.
The 1876 brassy Victorian décor is a feast for the eyes. The food at Gallopin isn't bad either. Try the house speciality, sole à la crème, a nice, fat fish done to a turn.
A la carte: 250 F. Menu: 150 F (dinner only).

11/20 Le Grand Colbert
2, rue Vivienne — 42.86.87.88
M. Couchet. Open every day. Open until 1 am. V AE.
Classic brasserie cuisine (oysters and shellfish, andouillette ficelle, bœuf gros sel, and poule au pot) served in a freshly restored historic monument, with frescoes and ornate plasterwork, brass railings, and painted glass panels.
A la carte: 200-250 F.

11/20 La Movida
14, rue M.-Stuart — 42.21.98.60
MM. Labat and Teran. Dinner only. Closed Sun, Mon and 12 Aug-21 Sep. Open until 2 am. Air cond. V.
Tattooed guitarists incite wild flamenco dancers barely visible through the fog of cigarette smoke. Unspectacular tapas, astonishingly good Spanish sweets.
A la carte: 200 F. Menu: 150 F.

12/20 Perry Brothers
20, passage des Panoramas
45.08.89.19
M. Perry. Closed Sat, Sun and 10-18 Aug. Private room: 80. V AE.
Welshman Alan Perry creates delightfully fresh and innovative salads, as well as tantalising tandoori chicken rolls and original dishes such as calf's liver with raspberry. Co-owner Jorge Zelaya, a professional graphic designer, has transformed this gorgeous restaurant in the picturesque passage des Panoramas with white linen and a sleek, silvery-grey décor. Good value for money.
A la carte: 250 F. Menu: 170 F.

12/20 Le Petit Coin de la Bourse
16, rue Feydeau — 45.08.00.08
M. Andron. Closed Sat and Sun. Open until 10.30 pm. Private room: 18. V AE DC.
This is a monument of the Belle Epoque whose décor and cuisine have remained faithful to turn-of-the-century bistro tradition: rabbit terrine with pistachios, salmon steak with sorrel, vacherin glacé au nougat.
A la carte: 300-350 F. Menu: 129 F (dinner only).

Pierre
(A la Fontaine Gaillon)
Pl. Gaillon — 42.65.87.04
MM. Boyer. Closed Sat lunch and Sun. Open until 12.30 am. Private room: 40. Terrace dining. Air cond. V AE DC.
The menu is long, but short on ideas. You're better off sticking to the fresh daily specials, which are always ably prepared. Try the grilled sardines, filet de rascasse à l'oseille, or sole des Sables meunière. The delightful old *hôtel particulier* décor was recently restored, and the grand terrace's fountain is spectacular when lit at night. Good set meal on weekdays.
A la carte: 300 F. Menu: 160 F (weekdays dinner only).

Pile ou Face
52 bis, rue N.-D.-des-Victoires
42.33.64.33
MM. Udron, Dumergue and Marquet. Closed Sat, Sun, holidays, Aug and 23 Dec-1 Jan. Open until 10 pm. Private room: 16. Air cond. V.
A pretty, if ruinously expensive, little establishment run by three associates proud of their success and determined to keep standards high. The stockbroker lunch crowd gives way in the evening to a pleasant mix of bourgeois provincials and foreigners. The first floor's red-and gold décor, with *fin de siècle* touches, perfectly matches chef Claude Udron's cuisine. Sometimes slightly off the mark, but mostly on target, Udron scores with delicious duck liver coated with gingerbread crumbs, roast pigeon with truffled oil, and the many other dishes on the 'special' menu, which showcases the restaurant's farm products (rabbit, poultry). A very fine wine cellar.
A la carte: 450 F.

12/20 Le Rond de Serviette
16, rue St-Augustin
49.27.09.90
M. Genin. Closed Sat dinner and Sun. Open until 11 pm. Air cond. V.
Fine bistro cuisine and daily specials are served in a restful décor in shades of bordeaux and cream.
A la carte: 180 F.

12/20 Le Saint-Amour
8, rue de Port-Mahon — 47.42.63.82
Mme Bouché-Pillon. Closed Sat lunch (and dinner in summer), Sun and holidays. Open until 10.30 pm. Air cond. V AE DC.
Impeccable service and a simple, fresh, generous cuisine distinguish Le Saint Amour. The fixed-priced dinner menu is exemplary: salade folle au foie gras, blanquette of young rabbit with wild pleurote mushrooms, dessert, wine, and coffee. It's easy to overlook the unimaginative décor.
A la carte: 300 F. Menus: 165 F (weekdays dinner only, wine inc), 165 F (weekdays only).

12/20 La Taverne du Nil
9, rue du Nil — 42.33.51.82
M. Khalil. Closed Sat lunch, Sun and 1-24 Aug. Open until 11 pm. V.
The setting is rather down-at-heel but lightened and brightened by pink upholstery and *naïf* paintings representing the River Nile. Straightforward Lebanese country dishes (hummous with meat and pine nuts, mezes, keftedes with onions and parsley) at exceptional prices. Belly dancers sometimes shake things up at weekends. An extra point this year for La Taverne du Nil.
A la carte: 150 F. Menus: 60 F (lunch only), 78 F (lunch only, wine inc), 110 F and 165 F (wine inc).

12/20 Le Vaudeville
29, rue Vivienne — 42.33.39.31
M. Bucher. Open every day. Open until 2 am. Terrace dining. Telex 281396. V AE DC.
Heavily laden waiters weave among the tables crowded with merrymakers—a true Vaudeville performance. The décor is grand 1930s art deco, the cuisine classic brasserie: fresh oysters, grilled cod, delicious Pauillac roast lamb, and nice little wines by the carafe.
A la carte: 250 F. Menu: 120 F.

12/20 Vishnou
11 bis, rue Volney — 42.97.56.54
M. Gupta. Closed Sun. Open until 11.30 pm. Private room: 80. Air cond. Telex 670416. V AE DC.
The menu is identical to the Indra's (see 8th arr.), the Gupta family's other fief. Here too the food is becoming 'touristy', although it is still generously served and tasty. The décor is rather more picturesque and exotic than the cuisine.
A la carte: 300 F. Menus: 150 F (lunch only), 220 F, 250 F, 300 F.

Ambassade d'Auvergne
22, rue du Grenier-St-Lazare — 42.72.31.22
M. Petrucci. Closed 2 weeks in July. Open until 11 pm. Private room: 35. No-smoking section. V.
Each visit to this embassy brings the same delightful experience. The Petrucci tribe's hospitality knows no bounds. The décor, with its timbers festooned with hanging hams, is worn but authentic; the atmosphere is marvellously convivial. Authenticity is equally present in the house specialities: real country ham, cabbage and Roquefort soup, boudin with chestnuts, cassoulet of lentils from Le Puy, legendary sausages served with slabs of delicious bread, duck daube with fresh pasta and smoky bacon, and so forth. Good desserts (try the aumônière à l'orange, or the mousseline glacée à la verveine du Velay). The cellar is vast and boasts some little-known Au-

vergnat wines in a wide range of prices.
A la carte: 230-250 F.

⑭ L'Ami Louis
32, rue du Vertbois — 48.87.77.48
*M. De la Brosse. Closed Mon, Tue and 15 July-27 Aug.
Open until 11 pm. V AE DC.*
Despite its improbably shabby décor (note the peeling, brownish walls), l'Ami Louis is probably the world's costliest bistro. It is certainly dear to the hearts of the Americans, tourists, suicidal over-eaters and rail-thin fashion models who battle to book a table at this famous *lieu de mémoire*. The heirs of old Père Magnin carry on the house tradition of huge portions and top-quality ingredients. But nowadays the sauces are sometimes thick and sticky, the chips oily, and the meats overcooked. What a joy, though, to sit down to a Gargantuan serving of foie gras fresh from the Landes, giant escargots de Bourgogne, whole roast chickens, the incomparable gigot of baby Pyrénées lamb. The desserts are insignificant, the cellar respectable.
A la carte: 550-700 F.

12/20 Le Bar à Huîtres
33, bd Beaumarchais — 48.87.98.92
See 14th arrondissement

12/20 La Guirlande de Julie
25, pl. des Vosges — 48.87.94.07
*M. Grolier. Closed Mon, Tue and 18 Dec-20 Jan.
Open until 10 pm. Terrace dining. Air cond. V AE.*
A new chef has taken over and put to rights this lovely little restaurant under the arcades of the Place des Vosges. The cuisine is classic in the style of Coconnas across the square (several delicious versions of pot-au-feu), and also features popular favourites like red-mullet fricassée or duck magret. The coltish service still needs breaking in.
A la carte: 250-300 F. Menu: 150 F.

12/20 Chez Janou
2, rue R.-Verlomme — 42.72.28.41
Mmes Chauvelot. Closed Sat, Sun and holidays. Open until 11 pm. Terrace dining. V.
An honest little old-fashioned bistro with turn-of-the-century décor and a pleasant terrace. The neighbourhood (Place des Vosges/Bastille) has gone up-market and so have Janou's prices, but the country cuisine here (Jerusalem artichokes tossed in hazelnut oil, duck confit) is still authentically homely and good. There are not enough modest wines on the list.
A la carte: 230-250 F.

11/20 Chez Jenny
39, bd du Temple — 42.74.75.75
M. Siljegovic. Open every day. Open until 1 am. Private room: 120. Terrace dining. Air cond. No-smoking section. V DC.
This grand, historical monument of a brasserie, with lovely marquetry upstairs, is on the upswing. Many good 'world-famous' choucroutes and superb Alsatian charcuteries.
A la carte: 200-230 F. Menu: 150 F (wine inc).

12/20 Le Souvré
10, rue des Fontaines-du-Temple
42.72.35.71
MM. Brazilier and Mérien. Closed Sat, Sun and 1-25 Aug. Open until 10 pm. V.
A sombre décor is relieved by lovely candle-lit, lace-covered tables. The cuisine has a regional (South-western) slant and is simple and carefully prepared (foie gras, magret, cassoulet). Try the

copious salmon with dill, or the boned saddle of young rabbit with parsley and garlic, followed by a strawberry pastry brimming with Chantilly cream. Smiling service.
A la carte: 250 F. Menu: 110 F.

PARIS 4th

⑱ L'Ambroisie
9, pl. des Vosges — 42.78.51.45
M. Pacaud. Closed Sun, Mon, Feb school holidays and 3 first weeks of Aug. Open until 10.15 pm. Private room: 12. Air cond. No pets. Valet parking. V.
Bernard and Danièle Pacaud have transformed this former goldsmith's shop under the arcades of the Place des Vosges into the most gracious, charming, and refined salon in the Marais. The dining room is worthy of a château, with high ceilings and inlaid stone and parquet floors, book-lined shelves, and a sumptuous seventeenth-century tapestry adorning the beige walls. Others may find the rigorous and restrained atmosphere rather 'cold'. We don't. It has the lived-in feel of a beautifully maintained private home, of which Danièle is the charming hostess. Don't expect to see much of Bernard, a retiring chef who prefers the sizzling sounds of his kitchen to the applause of an appreciative public. The influence of his mentor, Claude Peyrot, is everywhere felt in Bernard's chiselled, architectural cuisine. We used to find it a bit cool, but recently it has been warmed with sunny spices.
For example, an almost imperceptible touch of aniseed gives a new, needed dimension to a highly concentrated jus of mushrooms and cream, made with baby mousserons, morels, and girolles. Red mullet with cumin and carrots, curried prawns with sesame crêpes, calf's liver with sherry vinegar and a hint of honey have won us over and warmed our hearts.
Vive the new Pacaud! And hats off too for the fantastic profiteroles with vanilla ice cream and warm chocolate sauce, as well as for the florentines napped with a saffron-tinctured crème anglaise. Another round of applause for Pierre Le Moullac, the maître d'hôtel-sommelier, who manages to produce so many magical bottles out of nowhere.
A la carte: 700-900 F.

11/20 Auberge de Jarente
7, rue de Jarente — 42.77.49.35
M. Charriton. Closed Sun, Mon and Aug. Open until 10.30 pm. Terrace dining. Air cond. V AE DC.
Here you'll find unpretentious Basque cuisine served in a charming old Marais atmosphere (skip the prawns cooked in whisky and the sole au Noilly). The fixed-price menu, which includes pipérade de St-Jean, cassoulet, cheese, and gâteau basque, is faultless.
A la carte: 180-200 F. Menus: 120 F (wine inc), 105 F, 160 F.

⑯ Benoit
20, rue St-Martin — 42.72.25.76
M. Petit. Closed Sat, Sun, 25 Feb-3 March and 29 July-19 Aug. Open until 10 pm. Private room: 18. Terrace dining. Air cond.
The more things change, the more Benoît's solid, bourgeois cuisine stays the same. This is the archetypal Parisian bistro, with red- velvet banquettes, brass fixtures, lace curtains, and zinc bar. Sturdy chef Michel Petit continues the lusty tradition begun before the Great War by his

grandfather. His repertoire consists of simple, modest marvels: bœuf mode, foie gras with lentils, beef tongue in port, salt cod with aïoli, accompanied by lush desserts (try the chocolate fondue). An excellent cellar is stacked with reasonably priced bottles from Mâcon, Sancerre, Beaujolais, Saumur-Champigny, and Burgundy. Benoit numbers among Paris's very best—but not least expensive—bistros. An extra point this year.

A la carte: 450 F.

10/20 Brasserie de l'Ile Saint-Louis

55, quai de Bourbon — 43.54.02.59
M. Guepratte. Closed Thu lunch, Wed, 16-25 Feb and Aug. Open until 1 am. Terrace dining.

Choucroute, sausages, and cassoulet terrine washed down with torrents of frothy draught Mutzig. This is a favourite haunt of both islanders and famished punters.

A la carte: 180 F.

 ## Coconnas

2 bis, pl. des Vosges
42.78.58.16
M. Terrail. Closed Mon, Tue and mid-Dec-mid-Jan. Open until 10.15 pm. Terrace dining. V AE DC.

Claude Terrail (La Tour d'Argent) saw a good thing coming when some 35 years ago he bought and transformed this old tourist bistro on the lovely Place des Vosges. The tourists still flock here, but they're on to a good thing. In recent years the cuisine has become reliable and remarkably well-prepared. Sample traditional favourites such as poule au pot with a 'garden of vegetables', salt-cured duck, or tournedos in a gingerbread croûte. The fixed-price lunches offer excellent value.

A la carte: 300 F. Menus: 95 F (weekdays lunch only, wine inc), 130 F (weekdays lunch only).

12/20 Le Coin du Caviar

2, rue de la Bastille — 48.04.82.93
M. Nebot. Closed Sun. Open until midnight. Private room: 12. Air cond. V AE DC.

Greece, Russia, Iran, and France meet here under the sign of the salmon. Upstairs, in the rather precious dining room, choose from among a variety of salmon dishes (raw and smoked). In the less dear, unpretentious downstairs bar, savour bortsch, blini, caviar, and apple strudel.

A la carte: 350 F. Menu: 132 F (lunch only).

 ## Au Franc Pinot

1, quai de Bourbon
43.29.46.98
M. Godillot. Closed Sun and Mon. Open until 11 pm. Air cond. V DC.

Napoleonic iron gates stand guard before this charming *cave* on the Ile St-Louis. New owners maintain the high standards set by their predecessors, and the chef, Patrice Guyader, a disciple of Robuchon, still presides over the kitchen. His polished cuisine is remarkable for its fragrant and subtle sauces: prawn gazpacho with courgette cream, sautéed foie gras with pumpkin and apples, chicken breast with a honeyed touch of Layon wine. The service is as lethargic as ever, and the dining room, though dark, is pleasant nonetheless. The cellar's treasures are also available at the cosy ground-floor wine bar.

A la carte: 350-400 F. Menus: 150 F (lunch only), 185 F.

10/20 Jo Goldenberg

7, rue des Rosiers — 48.87.20.16
M. Goldenberg. Open every day. Open until midnight. Terrace dining. Air cond. V AE DC.

This is the archetypal, and most picturesque, of the Goldenberg restaurants in Paris (see seventeenth arrondissement). The Central European Yiddish cuisine is served in the heart of the Marais's Jewish district. Takeaway boutique on the premises.

A la carte: 180 F.

12/20 Au Gourmet de l'Isle

42, rue St-Louis-en-l'Ile — 43.26.79.27
M. Mestivier. Closed Mon and Tue. Open until 10 pm. V AE.

The reception is charming, the crowd young and cheerful, the stone-and-timber décor suitably rustic. Au Gourmet de l'Isle has enjoyed 40 years of deserved success for one of the city's surest-value fixed-price menus at 110 F: boudin with apples, beef and lentil salad, andouillette with red beans.

A la carte: 180 F. Menu: 110 F.

 ## Miravile

72, quai de l'Hôtel-de-Ville — 42.74.72.22
M. Epié. Closed Sat lunch and Sun. Open until 10.30 pm. Private room: 40. Terrace dining. Air cond. Valet parking. V.

Right, left, right: this remarkable establishment has shifted back and forth over the Seine several times, but is now permanently installed in a beautifully restored building on the quay between the Hôtel de Ville and Châtelet. Terracotta floors, *trompe-l'œil* paintings and warm colours give the surroundings—the comfortable creation of chef/owner Gilles Epié and his wife Muriel—a charming Mediterranean feel. The kitchen has been revamped and expanded, a good thing as the talented young Gilles needs plenty of elbow room. It comes as no surprise that Gilles's cuisine, which was shaped under the tutelage of Alain Passard, is better now than ever. Gilles is determined to join the ranks of the great toque-laden chefs. He's well on his way: Miravile gets an extra point this year. And his further ascent will doubtless be sped by such modern yet nostalgic delights as céleri rémoulade with duck foie gras, grilled red mullet with bitter rocket, hake ratatouille with rouille sauce, roast lotte with mixed wild greens, salt cod with polenta, or rack of lamb with raclette. The desserts are a delight (macaroons with raspberries, chocolate-caramel millefeuille, pistachio-cherry gratin), and the four-course lunch prix-fixe menu is an excellent value.

A la carte: 350-450 F. Menus: 150 F (lunch only), 280 F, 400 F.

 ## Le Monde des Chimères

69, rue St-Louis-en-l'Ile
43.54.45.27
Mme Ibane. Closed Sun, Mon and 15 Feb-1 March. Open until 10.30 pm. V.

A delightful old 'island bistro' now run by former TV personality Cécile Ibane. The cuisine is reminiscent of Sunday dinner *en famille* at its best: terrines with sweet-and-sour quince and cherries, veal paupiettes with tomatoes, chicken sautéed with forty cloves of garlic, and a smooth, creamy brandade de morue gentled with milk and olive oil. Good, homemade desserts and an expertly chosen wine list.

A la carte: 300 F. Menu: 150 F (lunch only).

L'Oulette
38, rue des Tournelles — 42.71.43.33
M. Baudis. Closed Sat, Sun, 3-26 Aug and 21 Dec-2 Jan. Open until 10.15 pm. V.
We feared that success might ruin this marvellous little establishment near the Place des Vosges. We are relieved to report that though the tables are terribly crowded and the chef is the food critics' latest darling, L'Oulette is as smilingly dedicated as ever to authentic cuisine from the French Southwest; what's more, prices are still extremely modest. Marcel Baudis, flanked by his hostess-wife Marie-Noëlle, creates classics from his native Quercy with a personal touch. Sample his brik d'escargots with artichokes and almonds, fresh codfish with walnuts and celery, soupe de fèves fraîches aux gésiers confits, or chartreuse of braised oxtail with foie gras. Baudis also makes an exquisite pastis pastry with prunes, a traditional regional dessert. Wash it all down with a nice little bottle of Coteaux-du-Quercy, a steal at 62 F.
A la carte: 200-230 F. Menu: 120 F.

11/20 La Petite Chaumière
41, rue des Blancs-Manteaux — 42.72.13.90
Mme Parmentier and M. De Turris. Closed Sat lunch, Sun and 15-31 Aug. Open until 11 pm. V.
This is a cheerful, bustling little Marais restaurant. New management, same menu (fish brioche, petites marmites of veal, lamb, or beef).
A la carte: 230 F.

12/20 Au Tibourg
31, rue du Bourg-Tibourg — 42.78.57.44
M. Samarkos. Closed Sun. Open until 11 pm. V AE.
Authentic Greek specialities (djadjik, cabbage stuffed with fish, pan-roasted veal with aubergines) are served in a cosy timbered dining room decorated with eclectic bric-à-brac. An extra point this year.
A la carte: 180-220 F.

Le Vieux Bistro
14, rue du Cloître-Notre-Dame — 43.54.18.95
M. Fleury. Closed at Christmas. Open until 10.45 pm. Terrace dining. V.
Shame on Gault Millau for neglecting this authentic old bistro (perhaps its façade was hidden by a hedge of tour buses). What unexpected pleasures lurk here, among the marble table-tops and velvet banquettes, the shady terrace in the shadow of Notre-Dame! A discovery indeed. The mustachioed owner, Fernand Fleury, late of the much-lamented Boule d'Or, is an old-fashioned host of rare warmth and good humour. Try the andouillette simmered in Sancerre, the beef fillet en papillote with bone marrow, the excellent potatoes au gratin, the succulent kidney in mustard, and, for dessert, chocolate profiteroles. Accompanied by a famously good bottle of Henry Fessy Brouilly, your bill probably won't top 200 F. Be sure to book ahead.
A la carte: 200-250 F.

Wally Saharien
16, rue Le Regrattier — 43.25.01.39
M. Wally. Closed Sun. Open until 11.30 pm. Private room: 20. Air cond. No pets. V AE DC.
Wally's desert empire is expanding (see Moucharabieh, eighteenth arrondissement), bringing with it marvellous Saharan couscous—served dry and sans vegetables—and classic, festive delights such as harira, pigeon pastilla, stuffed sardines, and Oriental pastries.
Menu: 280 F.

Auberge des Deux Signes
46, rue Galande — 43.25.46.56
M. Dhulster. Closed Sun. Open until 10.30 pm. Private room: 30. V AE DC.
A second toque for this marvellous medieval hostelry lovingly restored and run by Georges Dhulster. Solid oak beams, Gothic vaults, and windows that frame Notre-Dame: the setting is nothing short of spectacular (despite the somewhat heavyhanded neo–Louis XIII touches). The new chef is Marc Pralong, formerly of Laurent on the Champs-Elysées. He has brought with him a fresh new menu of delicate, imaginative dishes: boiled-beef ravioli with ginger-scented cabbage, mackerel tart with leek fondue, warm pear croquant laced with Cointreau. Courteous service.
A la carte: 500 F. Menu: 220 F.

10/20 Le Balzar
49, rue des Ecoles — 43.54.13.67
M. Egurreguy. Closed 1-29 Aug and 23 Dec-2 Jan. Open until 12.30 am. V AE.
This Left-Bank/Sorbonne haunt, with its art deco woodwork and mirrors, is ever faithful to tried-and-true brasserie fare (calf's liver, choucroute).
A la carte: 200 F.

11/20 Bénarès
47, rue Gay-Lussac — 43.29.56.04
M. Trivedi. Closed Sun lunch and Mon. Open until 11 pm. No pets. V AE.
The exotic and generously served Indian cuisine features good tandoori butter chicken. Excellent lunch menu.
A la carte: 150 F. Menu: 69 F (weekdays lunch only).

11/20 Le Boute Grill
(Chez Hamadi)
12, rue Boutebrie — 43.54.03.30
M. Bey. Open every day. Open until 1 am. Air cond.
Former owner Hamadi has moved on, but the restaurant continues to serve several varieties of couscous which are all worth queueing for.
A la carte: 120 F. Menu: 72 F (wine inc).

La Bûcherie
41, rue de la Bûcherie — 43.54.78.06
M. Bosque. Open every day. Open until 12.30 am. Terrace dining. Air cond. V AE DC.
Bernard Bosque is built like a Breton buccaneer and has been running his 'Hôtel du Bon Dieu' (the Bûcherie's name back in 1900) for over 30 years with winning talent and great success. Handsome woodwork and good contemporary engravings adorn the walls, and there are views of Notre-Dame through the windows of the comfortable covered terrace. The cuisine is rich and rather too predictable (poached eggs meurette, brandade de morue, lamb sauté with aubergines), but satisfying withal. The wine cellar boasts a magnificent selection of Bordeaux.
A la carte: 350-400 F. Menu: 200 F (wine inc).

Chieng-Mai
12, rue F.-Sauton — 43.25.45.45
M. Takounseun. Closed Sun, 1-15 Aug and 16-31 Dec. Open until 11.30 pm. Air cond. No pets. V AE.
Cool, stylised atmosphere, efficient service, and an increasingly interesting Thai cuisine have won Chieng Mai a toque this year. The repertoire features several delicious new dishes: shrimp and

spiced roe salad, steamed spicy seafood served in a crab shell, and a remarkable coconut-milk flan.

A la carte: 200-230 F. Menus: 91 F (lunch only), 136 F, 159 F and 173 F (dinner only).

Clavel
65, quai de la Tournelle – 46.33.18.65
M. Piras and Mme Clavel. Closed Sun dinner, Mon, Feb school holidays and 5-26 Aug. Open until 10.30 pm. Air cond. V.

Chef Jean-Yves Guichard has brought reliable excellence to the cuisine of this small, quiet restaurant by the Seine. The décor has been newly redone and the soft lights and pleasant service create a cosy, intimate atmosphere. The lunch menu is particularly appealing, the à la carte selections rather dear (especially the entrées). Try the generously served Brittany lobster ravioli with chives, the duck and foie gras tourte, and finish up with the dark, bewitching African chocolate cake. Good choice of wines priced around 100 F.

A la carte: 350 F. Menus: 160 F (weekdays lunch only), 300 F.

Les Colonies
10, rue St-Julien-le-Pauvre – 43.54.31.33
Mme Silly. Dinner only. Closed Sun. Open until 1 am. Private room: 20. Air cond. V.

The decorator of l'Ambroisie took this old building, which faces the church of St-Julien le Pauvre, and transformed it with subtle refinements such as painted woodwork, luxurious fabrics, and fine china. A mild breeze from the colonies stirs certain of chef Philippe Ibert's creations—chicken or lamb curry, pot-au-feu de volaille à la badiane, date parfait with tea-perfumed cream. The performance is somewhat lacking in conviction, but pleasant enough. Charming service and a high-society clientele. Book ahead for late dining.

A la carte: 280 F. Menu: 170 F.

11/20 Délices d'Aphrodite
4, rue Candolle – 43.31.40.39
M. Mavrommatis. Closed Mon. Open until 11.30 pm. Terrace dining. No pets. V.

You'll find a catering service, two takeaway shops, and a small, summery dining room at this likeable Greek spot. The food is hearty and authentic: pan-fried octopus, stuffed cabbage dolmades, moussaka.

A la carte: 180 F.

Diapason
30, rue des Bernardins – 43.54.21.13
M. Olivier. Closed Sat lunch, Sun and 1-15 Aug. Open until 10.30 pm. V AE DC.

A nicely kept, flower-filled establishment crowded with tiny tables pushed up to comfortable banquettes. The cuisine is rigorously classic (warm oysters with lemon butter, sole and salmon à l'orange, grenadin of young pigeon with truffles and foie gras). Good lunch menu, fine Loire wines.

A la carte: 350 F. Menus: 150 F (lunch only), 300 F.

Dodin-Bouffant
25, rue F.-Sauton – 43.25.25.14
Mme Cartier. Closed Sun, 28 July-25 Aug and 22 Dec-3 Jan. Open until midnight. Terrace dining. Air cond. V DC.

Prepare yourself for the sound and the fury of high and not-so-high-society diners jostling for a table in this cigar-box of a bistro. Dodin-Bouffant is renowned for its charming owners (Danièle and Maurice Cartier) and its delicious, no-nonsense cuisine (by chef Philippe Valin, disciple of Jacques

Manière). Two hundred souls feed here daily, enjoying the wonderful oysters and seafood (duo of lotte and lobster with mild garlic), the gutsy bistro fare (daube de joues de bœuf, calf's head) and the many special 'market' dishes (sea bream with peppers). The very fine wine cellar is in the manner of Manière—full of finds at the right price. Roughshod but cheerful service.

A la carte: 350 F. Menu: 165 F (weekdays lunch only).

Les Fontaines
9, rue Soufflot – 43.26.42.80
M. Lacipière. Closed Sun and 8-30 Aug. Open until 10 pm. V.

Roger Lacipière was clever to set aside the back room of his otherwise banal corner café and turn it into a delightful restaurant. Jolly waiters bring on generously robust and reasonably priced dishes like fricasséed young rabbit, Dijon-style kidney, and Bresse pigeon in a sauce thickened with foie gras. Fine selection of Loire and Bordeaux wines, and Beaujolais by the carafe.

A la carte: 180-220 F.

11/20 La Marée Verte
9, rue de Pontoise – 43.25.89.41
M. Thomas. Closed Sun, Mon and 1-27 Aug. Open until 11 pm. Air cond. V AE DC.

New manager (again!), same chef. The prix-fixe, all-in menu (crab salad, lotte with mustard, chocolate gâteau) is good value for money. Friendly service.

Menu: 165 F (wine inc).

Moissonnier
28, rue des Fossés-St-Bernard – 43.29.87.65
M. Moissonnier. Closed Sun dinner, Mon and 29 July-3 Sep. Open until 10 pm. V.

Stick to the ground floor where Jeannine trots to and fro serving the regulars from the university nearby, her arms laden with rib-sticking Lyonnais specialities (tablier de sapeur, quenelles, andouillette au vin blanc) and *pots* of Morgon wine drawn from the barrel. A delightful bistro run by the Moissonnier family for the last thirty years.

A la carte: 250 F.

Au Pactole
44, bd St-Germain – 43.26.92.28
M. Magne. Closed Sat lunch and Sun. Open until 10.45 pm. Terrace dining. No-smoking section. V AE.

Au Pactole is an inexplicably under-appreciated restaurant with a lovely setting (hearth in the centre of the dining room, handsome landscapes hanging on the earth-tone walls) and a skilful chef. Roland Magne, late of Jacques Manière, creates laudably lightened traditional fare at reasonable prices (the fixed-price menu at 145 F is outstanding). Try the excellent beef-jowl terrine with stewed onions, the perfect calf's liver with sage and chives, and one of the best rib steaks in Paris, followed by a tasty apple tart with sabayon sauce for dessert. Nice but pricey wine list.

A la carte: 330-350 F. Menus: 145 F, 280 F.

12/20 Perraudin
157, rue St-Jacques – 46.33.15.75
Mme K'Vella and M. Gloaguen. Closed Sun. Open until 10.15 pm.

This establishment is run by one of the city's top specialists in homely, country-style cookery, formerly of Le Polidor (see sixth arrondissement). Heartwarming Vouvray andouillette, bœuf bourguignon, and confit. Modest but charming

early 1900s décor, mixed crowd.
A la carte: 130-150 F. Menu: 59 F (lunch only).

12/20 Le Petit Navire
14, rue des Fossés-St-Bernard
43.54.22.52
M. Cousty. Closed Sun, Mon, Feb school holidays and week of 15 Aug. Open until 10 pm. Private room: 25. V DC.
For over twenty years regulars have been flocking here for tapenade, garlicky shellfish soup, grilled sardines, and delightful growers' wines that sell for under 70 F.
A la carte: 230-250 F. Menu: 110 F (wine inc).

11/20 Le Petit Prince
12, rue Lanneau – 43.54.77.26
MM. Gobe and Floux. Dinner only. Open until 12.30 am. V AE.
A modest Latin-Quarter restaurant serving classic, honest food (gâteau of young rabbit, leg of lamb, stews) and good little wines at low prices.
Menus: 72 F, 98 F.

10/20 Le Raccard
19, rue Laplace
43.25.27.27
M. Rennard. Dinner only. Closed Mon in summer and 4-19 Aug. Open until 1 am. V AE DC.
Ski chalet atmosphere and food (raclette, fondue) washed down with Swiss and Savoy wines.
A la carte: 160-200 F.

12/20 Chez René
14, bd St-Germain – 43.54.30.23
M. Cinquin. Closed Sat, Sun, 27 July-4 Sep and 23 Dec-3 Jan. Open until 10.15 pm. Terrace dining.
Chez René is the perennial Beaujolais bistro in Parisian garb, run for the last three generations by the convivial, enthusiastic Cinquin family. Try the Swiss chard au gratin, saucisson chaud, and earthy andouillette au vin blanc. The Chénas and Mâcon-Viré wines are bottled by the family.
A la carte: 230-250 F.

Restaurant A
5, rue de Poissy – 46.33.85.54
M. Huynh-Kien. Closed Mon and 17-26 Dec. Open until 11 pm. Air cond. AE.
The young owner Huynh-Kien regales clients with lovely vegetable and rice-paste sculptures while the chef serves up all-but-forgotten Chinese dishes from the imperial court: duck cooked in mustard leaves, sautéed pork with spicy leeks, or the famous imperial chicken.
A la carte: 250 F. Menu: 98 F.

12/20 Rôtisserie du Beaujolais
19, quai de la Tournelle
43.54.17.47
M. Terrail. Closed Tue lunch, Mon and 23 Dec-22 Jan. Open until 11.30 pm. Terrace dining. V.
Claude Terrail of the Tour d'Argent (across the road) opened this traditional Lyonnais bistro in 1989 to great fanfare. It's still a nice little place to spend an animated evening with friends. The gras-double (tripe) baked with onions and white wine is a delight, the saucisson pistaché equally delicious. Exemplary Beaujolais from Dubœuf, impersonal service.
A la carte: 230-250 F.

Sud-Ouest
(L'Escarmouche)
40, rue Montagne-Ste-Geneviève
46.33.30.46
M. Bourgain. Closed Sun and Aug. Open until 10.30 pm. Private room: 20. V AE DC.
Tucked away beneath the stone vaults of an ancient crypt, this is a pretty (though rather dark) little restaurant. But the cuisine is warming and full of regional character: eight varieties of foie gras, magret, cassoulet, and confit washed down with good little *vins de pays*. Two outstanding prix-fixe menus are available. Attentive service.
A la carte: 300 F. Menus: 150 F, 190 F.

La Table d'Harmonie
19, rue du Sommerard – 43.54.59.47
MM. Bertrand. Closed Sat lunch and Sun. Open until 11 pm. Private room: 30. Terrace dining. Air cond. V.
The Bertrand brothers have reduced their menu to artful simplicity: a prix-fixe, two-course lunch offered on weekdays for 95 F (fresh tunny fish tartare, daube de joue de bœuf) and a 165 F prix-fixe evening menu which allows one to choose from a vast selection of dishes. With a nice Mâcon red from Dubœuf, the cheque still won't top 200 F per person. Generous, heartening cuisine: young rabbit ravioli, sole with shellfish and chicory, stuffed lamb chops in pastry. Light and bright Italianate décor.
Menus: 95 F (lunch only), 165 F (dinner only).

La Timonerie
35, quai de la Tournelle – 43.25.44.42
M. de Givenchy. Closed Sun and Mon. Open until 10.30 pm. Air cond. V.
La Timonerie is a handsome, lively little establishment taken over and redecorated a few years ago by Philippe de Givenchy, a disciple of Maximin and Chibois. Givenchy's creations have a sunny southern touch: skate with fennel and black-olive purée, coriander-spiced crab with an orange brunoise, pork and oyster ravioli in bouillon. The tarte fine au chocolat is one of several moreish desserts. Short, oft-changing menu, nice little wine cellar, reasonable prices.
A la carte: 300-330 F. Menu: 110 F (lunch only).

La Tour d'Argent
15-17, quai de la Tournelle – 43.54.23.31
M. Terrail. Closed Mon. Annual closings not available. Open until 10 pm. Private room: 60. Valet parking. V AE DC.
We hope the sight of those sweet little ducks and drakes bobbing on the Seine between the Ile St-Louis and your panoramic table doesn't take away your appetite for the best canard aux cerises you'll ever taste—a pressed duck paddling in a deeply flavourful sauce au sang, which has been the house speciality for one hundred years. Chef Manuel Martinez, now a Tour d'Argent veteran, knows better than anyone how to work wonders with the web-footed fowl.
Don't expect any audacious novelties, or revolutionary changes in the Tour d'Argent tradition. Claude Terrail, eternally youthful, charming, and diplomatic, has chosen his field of honour once and for all. And what better aide-de-camp than Martinez, battle-tested at the Relais Louis XIII? Within the limits of a 'noble'—but not boring—repertoire, he imbues his creations with such flavour and harmony that you might be too delightedly dazed to notice the astronomical bill. But then, who notices the bill when it comes time to buy the Rolls and the diamonds?

You can easily waste 300 F on a ghastly meal elsewhere, and though it might seem galling to spend four or five times that here, you will never call into question the excellence of the repast. It might feature luscious, large prawns with tiny cèpes, tantalising truffled brouillade sauce Périgourdine, lobster-stuffed cabbage escorted by lobster ravioli, or a voluptuously tender double veal chop. And what of the *nec plus ultra* of ice creams, the Tour d'Argent's vanilla or pistachio? A year from now you won't have forgotten it! Nor will you forget the sight of dusk's golden light on Notre-Dame, or the fantastical cityscape spread out before you.

The fabled cellar, skilfully stewarded by David Ridgway, harbours bottles with prices in four and even five digits—but it also holds unsung marvels tariffed at less than 200 F. And do remember: the lunch menu costs only 365 F—put aside a franc each day for a year and there you are! Alas, (and this is our only quibble) there's still no humidor brimming with cigars, a touch that should be *de rigueur* in a restaurant of this calibre!

A la carte: 800 F and up. Menu: 365 F (weekdays lunch only).

12/20 Chez Toutoune
5, rue de Pontoise
43.26.56.81
Mme Dejean. Closed Mon lunch, Sun and 5 Aug-5 Sep. Open until 10.45 pm. Terrace dining. V.

Owner Colette Dejean, alias Toutoune, has put her restaurant right and gets an extra point this year. Charming service and a delicious prix-fixe menu which offers fragrant soups, tasty terrines, duck pot-au-feu, and chocolate soufflé.

Menu: 169 F.

12/20 La Truffière
4, rue Blainville
46.33.29.82
MM. Sainsard. Closed Mon and 1-15 Aug. Open until 10.30 pm. Private room: 48. Air cond. V AE DC.

Succulent specialities of the South-west excite the palate and mask the bitter à la carte prices. The Sainsard brothers serve fine foie gras, good cassoulet, and a nice little prix-fixe menu in their cosy restaurant just off the picturesque Place de la Contrescarpe.

A la carte: 350-450 F. Menus: 92 F (wine inc), 145 F, 320 F.

12/20 Ugarit
41, rue Censier
47.07.90.81
M. Doumid. Closed Sun. Open until 11 pm. Terrace dining. V AE DC.

Here you'll find interesting and original Syrian Lebanese cooking (with occasional forays into Turkish and Armenian territory). The menu is a trove of tasty mezes, flavourful kebabs, rissoles, and fragrantly fresh breads.

A la carte: 180-230 F. Menu: 65 F (weekdays lunch only).

12/20 La Vallée des Bambous
35, rue Gay Lussac
43.54.99.47
M. Tchao. Closed Tue and Aug. Open until 10.30 pm. Air cond.

A friendly family-run Chinese restaurant serving thirty varieties of (mostly) delicious dim sum.

A la carte: 150 F. Menu: 48 F.

12/20 Le Vieux Chêne
69, rue Mouffetard — 43.37.71.51
M. Tartare. Closed Sun and Mon. Open until 11.30 pm. Private room: 22.

This delightful old Parisian haunt is sandwiched between dozens of dismal Greek and Oriental eating-houses on the Rue Mouffetard. The fare is unusual but good: lotte with bell peppers, duck livers with cherries, salad of lamb sweetbreads with capers.

A la carte: 180-200 F. Menu: 125 F.

12/20 Le Vivario
6, rue Cochin — 43.25.08.19
M. Hilaire. Closed Sun, Mon and 2 Sep-2 Oct. Open until 11.45 pm. Terrace dining. V AE DC.

Le Vivario's savoury Corsican and Italian specialities are favoured by neighbourhood habitués and a sprinkling of show-biz personalities.

A la carte: 200-250 F.

PARIS   6th

Allard
41, rue St-André-des-Arts — 43.26.48.23
M. Bouchard. Closed Sat, Sun, Aug and 23 Dec-3 Jan. Open until 10 pm. Air cond. V AE DC.

Fernande Allard would still feel right at home in the enchanting establishment that she and her husband founded several decades ago. For practically nothing has changed, from the décor to the handwritten daily menu of escargots, turbot au beurre blanc, pigeon aux petits pois, duck with olives, and gâteau moka for dessert. The charm and chic of Allard are alive, but the wines are overpriced and the bill often overblown.

A la carte: 350-450 F.

La Bauta
129, bd du Montparnasse — 43.22.52.35
Mlle Lacombe. Closed Sun, Mon, Jan and 1-15 Aug. Open until 11 pm. Terrace dining. Air cond. V.

The 'nouvelle Venetian' creations of chef Marie Lacombe are at once spicy, sophisticated, and solid. Try a surprising dish of octopus sparked with fennel, wholewheat pasta (bigoli) with anchovy sauce, or tagliatelle with bitter cocoa. Equally good are the more traditional black cuttlefish risotto, calf's liver with onions and, for dessert, an exceptional zabaglione. Rustic décor. Some fine Chiantis on the list.

A la carte: 250 F. Menus: 105 F (weekdays lunch only), 250 F (lunch only).

12/20 Le Bélier
(L'Hôtel)
13, rue des Beaux-Arts — 43.25.27.22
M. Duboucheron. Open every day. Open until 12.30 am. Air cond. Telex 270870. V AE DC.

The picturesque, theatrical setting features a tree trunk, a fountain, a huge bouquet of flowers, and an elegant, cosmopolitan clientele. Yet the cuisine, despite many good intentions, leaves much to be desired. No toques this year.

A la carte: 280 F. Menus: 150 F (weekdays lunch only), 170 F (dinner only).

12/20 Bistro de la Grille
14, rue Mabillon — 43.54.16.87
M. Vermot. Open every day. Open until 12.30 am. Terrace dining. V.

Fine shellfish at reasonable prices (offered at dinner only), appealing prix-fixe menus, and good home-style dishes (skate, pot-au-feu) attract a handsome Left-Bank crowd to this bustling bistro hung with photographs of early film stars.

A la carte: 280-300 F. Menus: 75 F (lunch only), 120 F (dinner only).

12/20 Brasserie Lutétia

(Hôtel Lutétia)
23, rue de Sèvres – 45.44.38.10

M. de Margerie. Open every day. Open until midnight. Private room: 400. V AE DC.

The no-nonsense country cooking (whole calf's head, confit, choucroute) is prepared with considerable finesse. The sparkling, comfortable premises were styled by restaurant decorator Slavik, with a boost from fashion designer Sonia Rykiel.

A la carte: 250 F. Menus: 95 F (weekdays lunch only), 160 F.

Jacques Cagna

14, rue des Grands-Augustins
43.26.49.39

M. Cagna and Mme Logereau. Closed Sat (except dinner twice a month), Sun, Aug and Christmas week. Open until 10.30 pm. Private room: 12. Air cond. V AE DC.

Rumour had it last year that Jacques Cagna was fed up with banging pans and was about to hang up his apron. Little chance of that. He had simply changed his right-hand man in the scullery, as is his wont every three or four years. So fear not: The witty, charming Cagna still presides over the prettiest tavern in old Paris, with its ancient oak timbers and woodwork, its Flemish still lifes and discreet lighting. The atmosphere is so elegant you might think twice before raising a fork. Happily, this is not a museum. Food, drink, and—measured—merriment are right at home.

Jacques Cagna's guardian angel is his sister Anny, who glides among the tables dispensing smiles and good counsel. She will not, however, toss angel-dust in your eyes: there is nothing Jacques Cagna likes less than foolery (except, perhaps, fusty cooking). He is at once a Left-Bank sophisticate and a peasant, attached to the solid, lusty fare of his native Normandy. We used to think his classic training had bred in him a secret preference for dark, murky sauces—but we see that in fact his 'jus' are wonderfully clean, light, and sapid. Take for example the deeply flavourful rabbit essence he drizzles over a sea bass meunière with puréed celery and fried celery leaves, or the polished-but-rustic oyster-stuffed brill bathed in a reduction of watercress, or a sensational consommé simmered slowly with a divinely tender veal shin and perfumed with foie gras.

And what happy harmony Sauternes and honey bring to the Brittany pigeon with carrots and sweet onions! Or the sauce of shallots, bone marrow, and limpid meat juices that enhances an incomparable Angus rib steak, hung for a full three weeks and served up with a satisfying side dish of puréed potatoes. Finish with the delightful baba au kirsch topped with whipped cream and cherries, and your palate will have known an hour of unalloyed bliss.... To drink? of course there are ruinously dear bottles of Côte-Rôtie, Hermitage, Burgundy, or Bordeaux. On the other hand, one need not smash one's piggy bank to feast on Cagna's shockingly good fixed-price lunch menu.

A la carte: 550-800 F. Menus: 255 F (lunch only), 480 F.

Le Calvet

165, bd St-Germain – 45.48.93.51

M. Watelet. Closed Aug. Open until 10.30 pm. Private room: 25. Air cond. V AE DC.

Handsome stone walls, great timbers, and the discreet charm of a Louis XIII décor have transformed this former coachman's bistro into a most elegant eating establishment. Often overlooked by food critics, the Calvet team turns out excellent dishes using fresh market ingredients: crab salad, roast lotte with truffled butter, roast chicken with prawns. The strategically situated covered terrace faces the famed Deux Magots and Flore.

A la carte: 300 F and up. Menus: 129 F, 185 F.

12/20 Le Caméléon

6, rue de Chevreuse – 43.20.63.43

M. Faucher. Closed Sun, Mon and Aug. Open until 10.30 pm.

An archetypal Montparnasse bistro dripping with memories and bustling with live, business, Le Caméléon serves simple, fresh cuisine (braised veal with fresh pasta, codfish Provençal, pear clafoutis). Charming service and an excellent list of growers' wines.

A la carte: 180-200 F.

Aux Charpentiers

10, rue Mabillon – 43.26.30.05

M. Bardèche. Closed Sun and holidays. Open until 11.30 pm. Terrace dining. V AE DC.

Pierre Bardèche has opened a new fish restaurant across the street (L'Ecaille de PCB) but continues to serve his renowned home-style cuisine in this former carpenters' guild hall. The menu revolves around sensational daily specials such as codfish aïoli, stuffed cabbage, and veal sauté, accompanied by pleasant little wines.

A la carte: 220-250 F.

Le Chat Grippé

87, rue d'Assas – 43.54.70.00

M. Prunières. Closed Sat lunch and Aug. Open until 10.30 pm. Air cond. No pets. V.

Owner Marc Prunières, an elegant and cordial native of the Quercy region, loves to wander among the tables and chat about the menu or anything else that comes to mind. His presence does much to enliven the dark, mirrored interior of this little establishment (a butcher shop in a former incarnation). The new chef is Eric Thore, trained at Taillevent. He has brought with him a whiff of the sea: delicious fresh codfish minestrone, casserole of shellfish, oysters and crustaceans with ginger. But faithful to the Quercy tradition truffles, warm foie gras with celery and apples, honeyed roast pigeon with spices, cabécous goat cheese, and the robust red wines of Cahors hold a place of honour on the menu.

A la carte: 350 F. Menus: 150 F (weekdays lunch only), 300 F.

12/20 Dominique

19, rue Bréa – 43.27.08.80

M. Wiernik-Aronson. Closed Feb school holidays and 17 July-16 Aug. Open until 10.15 pm. V AE DC.

This famed Montparnasse Russian troika—takeaway shop/bar/restaurant—steadfastly refuses perestroika when it comes to cuisine and décor: purple-and-gold walls, steaming samovars, and goulash Tolstoi. Delicious smoked salmon, bortsch, and blinis.

A la carte: 200-300 F. Menu: 145 F.

11/20 Drugstore Saint-Germain
149, bd St-Germain — 42.22.92.50
M. Boutersky. Open every day. Open until 1.30 am. Air cond. No-smoking section. V AE DC.
The reliable, unpretentious cuisine (salads, grilled sausage, hamburgers) is served in a handsome, comfortable setting designed—wouldn't you know it—by Slavik.
A la carte: 160-180 F.

L'Ecaille de PCB
(Pierre et Colette Bardèche)
5, rue Mabillon — 43.26.73.70
M. Bardèche. Closed Sat lunch, Sun and holidays. Open until 11 pm. Terrace dining. V AE.
Pierre Bardèche, owner of the renowned Charpentiers across the way, recently bought this old Basque *auberge* and transformed it into one of the city's better fish restaurants. Simple dishes, fresh ingredients, and an oft-changing menu spell success. Try the oysters, the baked fish assortment, or the fine fish soup, as well as Brittany lobsters offered here at very low prices. Short but shrewdly chosen wine list.
A la carte: 300 F. Menu: 99 F (weekdays only).

12/20 L'Echaudé Saint-Germain
21, rue de l'Echaudé — 43.54.79.02
M. Layrac. Open every day. Open until 12.30 am. Private room: 30. Air cond. V AE DC.
This charming little old-Paris establishment is run by the Layrac brothers (of Le Petit Zinc and Le Muniche) and frequented primarily by young couples and tourists. A good fixed-price menu is available: feuilleté d'escargots, aiguillettes de canard, and tarte fine.
A la carte: 180 F (lunch only). Menu: 159 F.

11/20 La Fourchette en Habit
75, rue du Cherche-Midi — 45.48.82.74
M. Dufeu. Closed Sat lunch, Mon and Aug. Open until 11 pm. Private room: 25. Terrace dining. V.
Generous servings and low prices come by the forkful. Try the oysters, fresh mackerel, fresh anchovies, and fish soup. The tiny, picturesque dining room features large mirrors and kitsch frescoes.
A la carte: 230-250 F. Menus: 82 F (weekdays lunch only), 148 F (wine inc).

La Foux
2, rue Clément — 43.25.77.66
M. Guini. Closed Mon lunch, Sun and 24 Dec-2 Jan. Open until 10.30 pm. Private room: 14. V AE.
Alex Guini grows stouter, more colourful, and more hospitable as time goes by. Specialities from Nice and Lyon are the centre-piece of his menu: saucisson chaud, cannelloni, tripe. Pleasant modern décor. Alas, the prices are less than heartwarming.
A la carte: 400-450 F. Menus: 135 F and 195 F (weekdays only).

12/20 Guy
6, rue Mabillon — 43.54.87.61
M. Leroux. Dinner only (and lunch Sat). Closed Sun and 8-31 Aug. Open until 12.45 am. Private room: 18. Air cond. No smoking section. V.
This is a Brazilian dinner club with a festive décor and atmosphere (guitars, killer batidas, bossanova...). The cuisine is modest, but portions are generous.
A la carte: 250 F. Menus: 94 F (Wed and Thu), 180 F (Sat lunch).

12/20 Chez Henri
16, rue Princesse
46.33.51.12
M. Poulat. Closed Mon lunch and Sun. Open until 11.30 pm.
Regulars flock here for the sure-value bistro cooking by chef Henri Poulat: calf's liver with creamed onions, range-raised chicken in vinegar, roast lamb, apple clafoutis.
A la carte: 120-150 F. Menu: 150 F (dinner only).

12/20 La Hulotte
29, rue Dauphine
46.33.75.92
M. Güys. Closed Sun, Mon and Aug. Open until 10.30 pm. V AE.
The proof is in the pudding: Bernard Güys is mad about desserts, especially chocolate mousse (he makes it in six delicious variations). Start your meal with tasty grilled meats, coq au vin, and other traditional dishes, made with love and generously apportioned.
A la carte: 180 F. Menu: 140 F (wine inc).

Joséphine
(Chez Dumonet)
117, rue du Cherche-Midi — 45.48.52.40
M. Dumonet. Closed Sat, Sun and July. Open until 10.30 pm. Terrace dining. V.
Joséphine is a right honourable early 1900s bistro frequented by prominent jurists, journalists, and an intellectual theatre crowd. The chummy atmosphere is animated by owner Jean Dumont and fuelled by the perennially popular cuisine, a heady mix of bourgeois and South-western fare. Humble herrings with warm potatoes at 55 F flank truffle feuilleté at 520 F; leg of lamb with beans, or leeks in vinaigrette vie with truffled andouillette in flaky pastry for one's attention. Appropriately, the wine cellar abounds in Bordeaux, both modest and mighty.
A la carte: 400 F.

Lapérouse
51, quai des Grands-Augustins
43.26.68.04
Mme de Bournet. Closed Sun dinner and Mon. Open until 11 pm. Private room: 40. Air cond. No-smoking section. V AE DC.
For years we felt a pinch at our heartstrings each time we strolled along the Left Bank quais past Lapérouse. A landmark restaurant, founded in 1766, it long numbered among the best eating places in Paris. Here Belle Epoque *cocottes* flirted—and more—in ravishing little private salons (and used the diamonds they earned with their naughtiness to scratch their names in the mirrors). But the once-noted cuisine slipped badly in the 1970s, and gourmets abandoned Lapérouse.
What a delight, then, to learn that new owners have restored the décor to its former lustre, and put a brilliant young chef in the kitchen. Gabriel Biscaye, late of the Royal Monceau, has a rare gift for combining tastes and textures in unusual but utterly satisfying ways. A glance at the new *carte* reveals a host of surprising, appetising dishes like tête de veau caramélisée aux huîtres, assiette de poissons à l'encre de seiche, rognon de veau rôti à la moutarde de violette, and a rich array of desserts. Lapérouse is once again an enchanting choice for a romantic dinner by the Seine.
A la carte: 250-300 F.

12/20 Lipp
151, bd St-Germain — 45.48.53.91
M. Perrochon. Closed 10 July-6 Aug. Open until 2 am. Air cond. V AE DC.

The interregnum is over: Lipp has lost both the legendary Roger Cazes and his heir-apparent, Michel Cazes. The new *patron* is an interior architect named Perrichon. Despite the often disappointing food (choucroute, bœuf gros sel) and the cruel whims of fashion, this glossy turn-of-the-century brasserie still manages to serve some 400 to 500 clients a day. Of course, the clientele is not what it was, though one still catches sight of a powerful politico or a beauty queen ensconced at a ground-floor table, admiring the gorgeous décor.

11/20 La Lozère   ❂
4, rue Hautefeuille — 43.54.26.64
Mme Almeras. Closed Sun dinner, Mon, Aug and 24-31 Dec. Open until 10.30 pm. V.

You can taste bracing air of the rural Lozère region in the warm winter soups, herbed sausages, and pâtés served in this charming old-Paris establishment, a combination regional tourist-office, handicrafts shop, and restaurant.

A la carte: 130-150 F. Menus: 79 F (weekdays lunch only, wine inc), 99 F, 121 F.

La Luna
12, rue Dauphine — 46.33.85.85
M. Durand. Open every day. Open until midnight. Air cond. Valet parking. V AE.

Let's be frank: when La Luna opened in 1989 we did not take a shine to the place. The décor seemed too trendy to be true. But on closer inspection we've decided that the rare Portuguese granite and the red-and-blue leather armchairs are stylish—indeed quite handsome. The lighting has also improved. Now all La Luna must do is eliminate—as promised—those annoying video clips (the amusing tellies in the toilets can stay!).

Onwards and upwards—first to the tapas bar serving sherries and tasty titbits of Spanish inspiration. And now—quickly—into the restaurant for fabulous fresh fish. Here come the scaly wonders, transformed into a tiny tartare de saumon, or tunny fish and sea bream, or a salad of warm skate cheeks on a bed of lamb's lettuce, or pan-fried shrimps with a touch of thyme, or oven-roasted miniature black scallops.... We could go on and on.

And we will. About the Andalusian bouillabaisse, for instance, or the formidable turbot à la ficelle simmered in a rich fish fumet, or the 'catch of the day', grilled or fried or braised to order.... Follow these marine marvels with an authentic Catalan flan (made with semolina and vanilla beans) and an aged Calvados... perfect bliss! French and Spanish bottlings dominate the wine list.

A la carte: 300-350 F.

La Marlotte
55, rue du Cherche-Midi — 45.48.86.79
Mme Agaud and M. Bouvier. Closed Sat, Sun and Aug. Open until 11 pm. AE DC.

This old timbered restaurant's pleasant rustic setting is softened by madras upholstery and candlelight in the evening. The cuisine runs to hearty country flavours meticulously prepared. Try the homemade terrines, the veal kidney with mustard sauce, and the delectable chocolate gâteau. Crowded both at lunch and dinner, often with the smart set.

A la carte: 250-300 F.

Le Muniche
27, rue de Buci — 46.33.62.09
MM. Layrac. Open every day. Open until 3 am. Private room: 50. Terrace dining. Air cond. V AE DC.

Count yourself lucky if you can get a 'box' at this, the liveliest, most feverishly overcrowded of Parisian brasseries. Fashionable late-nighters queue for a seat in the dining-car of a *salle* designed by the ubiquitous Slavik, whence they gaze at the scenery. The Layrac brothers and their attentive, smiling staff will regale you with oysters, choucroute garnished with veal knuckle, thick-sliced calf's liver and grilled pigs' ears, washed down with perfect little *pots* of red, white, and rosé.

A la carte: 220 F. Menu: 137 F.

12/20 Le Parc aux Cerfs
50, rue Vavin — 43.54.87.83
M. Hayat. Closed Aug. Open until 11 pm. Terrace dining. Air cond. V.

This was one of the Montparnasse neighbourhood's first 'neo-bistros'—with revisited Lyonnais specialities served in a jovial, youthful atmosphere. Inexpensive lunch menu, and good Rhone wines (by the bottle or carafe).

A la carte: 160-180 F. Menu: 110 F (lunch only).

Paris
(Hôtel Lutétia)
23, rue de Sèvres — 45.48.74.34
M. de Margerie. Closed Sat, Sun, 10-20 Feb and Aug. Open until 10 pm. Private room: 400. Air cond. Valet parking. Telex 270424. V AE DC.

Sonia Rykiel shook this grand hotel restaurant out of a long slumber with her stark, art deco–style dining room, where well-spaced tables help to create a graciously subdued atmosphere. Chef Philippe Renard (who just replaced Jacky Fréon, now at the Grand Hôtel in the ninth arrondissement) lavishes considerable skill on such speciously named but superlative dishes as rose de baudroie—petals of pearly fish arranged with courgettes and tomatoes. Try the perfectly executed soufflé de sandre au Cheverny, the slowly simmered tête de veau, the grilled platter of lamb cutlets and sweetbreads, panaché of beef and veal fillets, or prune and walnut tart. Good lunch menu and wide choice of wines for under 150 F. An extra point this year.

A la carte: 400-500 F. Menu: 280 F (lunch only).

10/20 Le Petit Mabillon
6, rue Mabillon
43.54.08.41
MM. Ruggia. Closed Mon lunch, Sun and 16 Dec-20 Jan. Open until 11 pm. Terrace dining. V AE.

The good Italian home cooking features two daily pasta choices (fusilli, lasagne). Picturesque bistro décor, garden court.

A la carte: 160-180 F. Menu: 72 F.

10/20 Le Petit Saint-Benoît
4, rue St-Benoît
42.60.27.92
M. Gervais. Closed Sat and Sun. Open until 10 pm. Terrace dining.

An unfading coachman's eating-house whose crowded pavement terrace is a refuge for fashionable fast-food haters in search of cheap eats: hachis Parmentier, streaky bacon with lentils.

A la carte: 100 F.

Le Petit Zinc
25, rue de Buci – 46.33.51.66
MM. Layrac. Open every day. Open until 3 am. Terrace dining. Air cond. Telex 201820. V AE DC.
The timeless, slightly uncomfortable, but always cheerful bistro setting designed by Slavik acquires an undeniable charm with wear. Le Petit Zinc shares the same kitchen and country cooking as the equally popular Le Muniche next door, but with an emphasis on South-western specialities: oysters, shellfish, poule au pot, thick-sliced calf's liver, duck thighs with apples. In summer the animated terrace spreads its fluttering tablecloths across the pavement.
A la carte: 250 F. Menu: 137 F.

La Petite Cour
8, rue Mabillon – 43.26.52.26
MM. Larpin and Tellier. Open every day. Open until 11 pm. Garden dining. V.
Owners and chefs may come and go, but the discreet charm of this old restaurant with its garden-court and splashing fountain remains. The dining room's Napoleon III décor is equally appealing and the cuisine, though not terribly ambitious, is fresh and generous: skate with cabbage, beef stew with carrots. Tasty, low-priced Saumur and Valençay wines.
A la carte: 280 F. Menus: 155 F (lunch only), 175 F (dinner only).

11/20 Polidor
41, rue Monsieur-le-Prince – 43.26.95.34
M. Maillet. Open every day. Open until 1 am.
Authentic country fare (boudin with mashed potatoes, rabbit in mustard) and attractive little wines are served in a dining room that has not changed an iota in a hundred years.
A la carte: 100 F. Menu: 50 F (weekdays lunch only).

Princesse
(Castel)
15, rue Princesse – 43.26.90.22
M. Castel. Dinner only. Closed Sun. Private room: 50. Air cond. Telex 203835. V AE DC.
In 1992 owners Jean and Yolande Castel will celebrate 30 years of undisputed success for their exclusive club-restaurant, the Parisian equivalent of Annabel's. Unfortunately, if you aren't a member you probably won't get in, and will therefore have to settle for imagining the Belle Epoque décor and chef Didier Aupetit's succulent home-style cuisine, which features the likes of skate with cabbage and boned saddle of rabbit aux fines herbes.
A la carte: 500-600 F (at the Foyer: 250 F).

11/20 Le Procope
13, rue de l'Ancienne-Comédie
43.26.99.20
MM. Blanc. Open every day. Open until 2 am. Private room: 70. Terrace dining. V AE DC.
The capital's oldest café was recently restored to its original seventeenth-century splendour and now serves good, simple brasserie fare to a clientele in which tourists predominate. Try the oysters (reasonably priced), merlan Colbert, and calf's head.
A la carte: 250 F. Menus: 99 F (lunch only), 289 F (wine inc).

Relais Louis XIII
8, rue des Grands-Augustins
43.26.75.96
M. Poindessault. Closed Mon lunch, Sun and 27 July-27 Aug. Open until 10.15 pm. Air cond. V AE DC.
Louis XIII was proclaimed King of France in this luxurious seventeenth-century tavern whose timbers, polished panelling, and time-worn stones groan with history. Jean Poindessault, the elegant maître d'hôtel, has worked with chef Georges Piron to perfect a timeless and flawless cuisine. This year the menu offers such classics as lobster fricassée, sole and prawns with coriander, and truffled filet de bœuf. In addition to the stupendous and shockingly expensive 1934 Latour (8,750 F) or 1921 Quarts de Chaume (2,000 F), the wine cellar also boasts a few accessibly priced bottlings.
A la carte: 600 F. Menu: 230 F (lunch only).

12/20 La Rotonde
105, bd Montparnasse – 43.26.68.84
M. Tafanel. Open every day. Open until 1 am. Private room: 40. Terrace dining. Air cond. V AE DC.
Along with La Coupole, Le Dôme, and Le Select, La Rotonde belongs to the pantheon of Montparnasse brasseries. No earthshaking food, but the salads are fresh, the steak 'Prince Albert' (with wine sauce and potato cake) delicious, and the Berthillon sorbets splendid, of course.
A la carte: 300 F.

11/20 Chez Claude Sainlouis
(Le Golfe Juan)
27, rue du Dragon – 45.48.29.68
M. Piau. Closed Sat dinner, Sun, Aug and 24 Dec-2 Jan. Open until 11 pm. Air cond.
Reliable salads and steaks are served in an amusing, theatrical décor.
Menu: 92 F.

12/20 La Table de Fès
5, rue Sainte-Beuve – 45.48.07.22
M. Alvès. Dinner only. Closed Sun and 12-31 Aug. Open until 0.15 am. No-smoking section. V.
The same skilful chef has been turning out tasty pastilla, couscous, and tajines for the last 25 years. Fès can get crowded and close in the evening.
A la carte: 200-250 F.

Les Tuffeaux
11, rue Dupin – 42.22.64.56
M. Devaux. Closed Sat lunch, Sun and 4-25 Aug. Open until 10 pm. Terrace dining. V.
This charming, rustic bistro behind the Bon Marché department store is managed by chef Michel Devaux, a long-time globe-trotter who has finally settled down. Devaux is a first-rate chef who knows how to choose his ingredients well. We only wish he would also settle into his own repertoire, preferably that of his native Tours. Try the eels flavoured with puckery purslane, or the sandre with a light beurre blanc and spaghetti squash. The desserts are on the upswing, but so are the prices. Good Loire wines.
A la carte: 350 F. Menu: 165 F (lunch only).

11/20 La Vigneraie
16, rue du Dragon – 45.48.57.04
Mlle Stora and M. Sabatier. Closed Sun lunch. Open until 1 am. Terrace dining. Air cond. V AE DC.
The same good prix-fixe menus (75 F weekdays, lunch; 110 F lunch or dinner) are prepared by a new chef. The salmon fillet is still tasty, the veal kidneys less successful than of yore. Modern,

black-lacquered bistro décor. Many wines are available by the glass.
A la carte: 250 F.

Yugaraj
14, rue Dauphine – 43.26.44.91
M. Meyappen. Closed Mon. Open until 11 pm. Air cond. No pets. Valet parking. V AE DC.
Yugaraj's out-of-the-ordinary Indian cuisine is served in a pleasant, spotless setting reminiscent of a native temple. The generous and warming specialities such as tandoori lamb are flanked by rather disappointing samosas and pastries. Well-chosen wine list. Interesting game dishes in season.
A la carte: 250-300 F. Menus: 95 F (weekdays lunch only), 186 F, 220 F.

PARIS   7th

Chez les Anges
54, bd de Latour-Maubourg – 47.05.89.86
Mme Delmas. Closed Sun dinner. Open until 10.30 pm. Private room: 12. Air cond. V AE DC. •
Former owner Armand Monassier, a winegrower, continues to supply this comfortable Burgundian restaurant with barrels of his delicious Rully. To accompany them ever-reliable chef Bernard Labrosse produces excellent dishes of a classic cast such as ham in parsley aspic (marvellous!), coq au vin, and rosy, thick-sliced calf's liver. The atmosphere and setting are refined, and the menu is expanding with welcome innovations (coquilles St-Jacques au Crémant). Splendid Burgundian wine list, regular clientele studded with MPs.
A la carte: 400 F. Menu: 230 F.

Antoine et Antoinette
16, av. Rapp – 45.51.75.61
M. Pernot. Closed Sat, Sun and Easter school holidays. Open until 10.30 pm. Terrace dining. V AE DC.
Chef Jean-Claude Pernot has no quarrel with classic cuisine, and in the best tradition offers a winter menu and a summer menu. The dependable quality of his cookery accounts for the success of his cushy little restaurant, which sparkles with fine cutlery, crystal, and lovely linens. We recommend the calmars en escabèche, the honeyed roast pigeon, the fish tartare, and kidneys with mustard. Modest bottlings available for around 80 F.
A la carte: 300 F. Menu: 160 F.

Arpège
84, rue de Varenne
45.51.47.33
M. Passard. Closed Sun lunch, Sat and 27 July-21 Aug. Open until 10.15 pm. Air cond. V AE DC.
The 220 F lunch menu is so outstanding that the waiters seem to want to keep it all to themselves. You must ask for it specifically or wind up ordering à la carte—not a bad thing really, as Arpège's talented young chef Alain Passard has earned his four toques for far more than a fine prix-fixe meal. Allow us to harp on a moment: Passard began his career in Reims under Gérard Boyer, then worked as an assistant to Senderens at this same address when it housed L'Archestrate. After proving himself at the Duc d'Enghien, and later at the Carlton in Brussels, he returned here as owner.
At age 35, Passard is a virtuoso. Light though his touch may be, you will never catch him indulging in legerdemain. His inventiveness and imagination are always precisely controlled. Passard's com-

positions, whether variations on well-known themes (sweetbreads with chestnuts and truffles; saddle of hare with walnuts and cèpes), or new symphonies of flavours (crab with mustard butter and cabbage; scallops with citrus and parsley), are uniformly harmonious. We single out the John Dory baked with bay leaves inserted under the skin: a masterpiece.
How to sum up the secret of Passard's success in a word or two? He is blessed with the simple touch of the master which transforms even humble lettuce leaves into gastronomical works of art. Voilà.
Today Alain Passard has a fine wine cellar, a proven staff, and an adoring public (he ministers to many in the neighbourhood's ministries). Now all he needs is a restaurant with decent kitchens and a setting less discordant with his fine-tuned cuisine!
A la carte: 500-800 F. Menus: 220 F (lunch only), 490 F, 520 F.

11/20 Babkine
(Chez Germaine)
30, rue P.-Leroux – 42.73.28.34
M. Babkine. Closed Sat dinner, Sun, Aug and 23 Dec-2 Jan. Open until 9 pm. No-smoking section. No pets.
Just queue up on the pavement and count out your change: here is robust French fare served *sans façon* on an oilcloth! Feast on Babkine's savoury rabbit sauté with polenta, tiny squid braised with olives, or mutton stew, each priced at a bogglingly thrifty 29 F. Add 11 F for the black cherry tart and 12.50 F for a carafe of claret.
A la carte: 60-80 F. Menu: 41 F.

12/20 La Belle France et Le Parisien
Tour Eiffel, Champ-de-Mars – 45.55.20.04
M. Ody. Open every day. Open until 10 pm. Air cond. No pets. Telex 205789. V.
These two establishments belong in the 'Dining Room with a View' department (they're on the Eiffel Tower's first floor facing the fountains of Trocadéro). The lower section, called Le Parisien, is a snack bar. La Belle France serves brasserie fare: good grilled meats, fresh pastries.
A la carte: 250 F (au Parisien : 150 F). Menu: 185 F.

Bellecour
22, rue Surcouf – 45.51.46.93
M. Goutagny. Closed Sat lunch, Sun and 4-27 Aug. Open until 10.30 pm. Terrace dining. V AE DC.
Stéphane Pruvot, the star pupil of Lorain at Joigny, is one of the city's up-and-coming chefs. Over the last two years he has modernised the once fiercely traditional *cuisine lyonnaise* that had made Gérald Goutagny's establishment—a vintage bistro with a vaguely colonial setting—a perennial favourite. Now, after a short eclipse, the Bellecour is again in the limelight. Today the high-society crowd comes less for the old standbys (quenelles de brochet, andouillette au Mâcon, cervelle de canut...) than for the eminently Parisian, mildly exotic fare. Pruvot's technical mastery goes hand in hand with the excellent ingredients he chooses. You will be conveyed to the realm of Happiness by such delicacies as oysters with sweet-pepper mousseline, roast prawns with leeks, spiced skate, or Charollais beef with onion conserve. The ethereal desserts are the handiwork of Gérald Goutagny himself (a former pastry chef), and are among the best to be found in Paris.
A la carte: 350-400 F. Menus: 220 F (lunch only), 320 F.

11/20 Le Bistrot de Breteuil
3, pl. de Breteuil — 43.06.76.78
M. Lemoine. Open every day. Open until 10.30 pm. Terrace dining. V.

An old corner café converted into an up-to-date bistro, the Breteuil serves traditional offerings such as foie gras, smoked salmon, and escargots aux noisettes. The fixed-price menu is a remarkably good deal (it includes an apéritif and coffee as well as wine). Pleasant terrace.
Menu: 162 F (wine inc).

Bistrot de Paris
33, rue de Lille — 42.61.16.83
M. Oliver. Closed Sat lunch and Sun. Open until 11 pm. Private room: 35. V.

Owner Michel Oliver's worldwide renown keeps him busy. So busy that he no longer has time to spend in the kitchen of his old-fashioned bistro decorated by (guess who!) Slavik. Oliver has delegated most kitchen tasks to chef Jean-Pierre Frelet. Now, for years we have turned a blind eye to the uneven quality of Le Bistrot's cuisine. But we can no longer justify awarding two toques to dishes that are pleasant enough, but certainly not memorable (the aubergine terrine with anchovy vinaigrette is overwhelmed by the taste of bell pepper, the saddle of lamb is lost in the turmeric). Several desserts are still up to scratch, the chocolate millefeuille with raspberries and the bitter-chocolate gâteau, for example. Despite its failings, the establishment is perpetually jammed with an arty, society crowd apparently unconcerned with the expense, even at lunch.
A la carte: 250-400 F.

La Boule d'Or
13, bd de Latour-Maubourg — 47.05.50.18
Mme Guinot. Closed Sat lunch and Mon. Open until 10 pm. Private room: 30. Air cond. V AE DC.

Prim and proper provincial décor, a steady clientele, and a charming proprietor: the Boule rolls on. François Le Quillec, the new chef, complicates some dishes unduly, but we have only praise for his truffled young guinea fowl. Stiffish prices.
A la carte: 350-400 F. Menus: 180 F, 300 F.

Le Bourdonnais
113, av. de La Bourdonnais — 47.05.47.96
Mme Coat. Open every day. Open until 11 pm. Private room: 24. Air cond. V AE.

Owner Micheline Coat earns this year's 'Warmest Welcome' award. Never before has her cheerfully redecorated restaurant been so crowded with the chic and powerful. Success has been borne on a south wind, for the keen flavours of Provence pervade chef Philippe Bardau's short but appetising menu. A disciple of Outhier and Maximin, Bardou excels with his tunny gazpacho with grilled artichokes, his sea bass and fennel with a touch of tomato, a pigeon sandwich with celery and Parmesan, a rabbit fillet with cabbage and bacon, and the fig gratin with almond cream. The fixed-price offerings at lunch (220 F) and dinner (250 F) are outstanding values.
A la carte: 370-500 F. Menus: 220 F (lunch only, wine inc), 250 F (dinner only), 380 F.

11/20 Café Bordelais
74, bd de Latour-Maubourg — 45.51.50.58
M. Besnard. Open every day. Open until midnight. Terrace dining. V AE DC.

The wide, sunny terrace with a view of the Invalides fills with a trendy crowd keen on the oysters, foie gras, and rib steak à la bordelaise. Good choice of Bordeaux by the bottle or half-litre carafe.
A la carte: 250 F. Menu: 154 F (weekdays lunch only, wine inc).

12/20 Le Champ de Mars
17, av. de La Motte-Picquet — 47.05.57.99
M. Gellé. Closed Tue dinner, Mon and 15 July-20 Aug. Open until 10.15 pm. Private room: 28. Terrace dining. V AE DC.

Slack service and lacklustre décor are compensated for by a marvellous prix-fixe menu. The cuisine features provincial classics: veal kidney à l'ancienne, turbot with sorrel, charlotte au chocolat. Interesting selection of Burgundy wines.
A la carte: 300 F. Menu: 110 F.

Clémentine
62, av. Bosquet — 45.51.41.16
M. Przybyl. Closed Sat lunch, Sun and 15-30 Aug. Open until 10.30 pm. Private room: 25. Terrace dining. Air cond. V.

Michèle and Bernard Przybyl (you're right, that's Polish) pay homage to the cuisine of their respective/adopted homes: Languedoc (duck cassoulet) and Brittany (skate with capers, lobster à la nage). The rosy décor is dandy, but the tables are still a bit too close for comfort. Pretty people, modest prices, and an ever-expanding wine cellar.
A la carte: 280 F. Menu: 163 F (weekdays only).

11/20 Le Come Bac
16, rue du Bac — 42.61.26.54
M. Combes. Closed 31 Dec, 1 Jan and 1 May. Open until 10.30 pm. Air cond. V AE.

A favourite spot for tourists to chow down after a visit to the nearby Musée d'Orsay (the menu comes in five languages), Le Come Bac features honest French regional classics at reasonable prices. Good red wine available by the carafe.
A la carte: 200-230 F. Menu: 98 F.

Aux Délices de Szechuen
40, av. Duquesne — 43.06.22.55
Mme Lau. Closed Mon, 29 July-27 Aug and 23-31 Dec. Open until 10.30 pm. Terrace dining. Air cond. V AE.

Fresh and tasty Chinese specialities are served here with flair. The chef has a ten-year track record of proven reliability. Try the lacquered duck (in three courses), the grilled won tons served with a ginger-scented sauce, and the beef fillet with orange peel. Elegant décor, excellent service.
A la carte: 200-230 F. Menu: 87 F (weekdays only).

Duquesnoy
6, av. Bosquet — 47.05.96.78
M. Duquesnoy. Closed Sat lunch, Sun and Aug. Open until 10.15 pm. Air cond. V AE.

The Best and the Brightest (in business and TV) flock to Jean-Paul Duquesnoy's comfortable, posh little restaurant, filling both lunch and dinner sittings year round. The light touch extends from the décor and service (directed by the discreet and charming Françoise Duquesnoy) to the cuisine. Jean-Paul steers a skilful course between classicism and novelty, pleasing his elegant patrons with turbot and bacon bathed in a rich veal jus, Bresse chicken in a sauce enlivened with sherry vinegar, or sardines accompanied by lasagne layered with black-olive purée. Luscious desserts include honey-nougat ice cream, walnut crème brûlée, and an assortment of milk and bitter chocolates. Exquisite wines from the Loire, Burgundy, and Côtes-du-Rhône swell the rather stiff à la carte prices. Excellent prix-fixe lunch menu.

A la carte: 450-700 F. Menus: 240 F (lunch only), 490 F.

Ecaille et Plume
[13]
25, rue Duvivier – 45.55.06.72
M. Naël. Closed Sat lunch and Sun. Annual closings not available. Open until 10.30 pm. Private room: 10. No-smoking section. V.

A master matchmaker, Marie Naël puts heart and soul into her innovative cuisine. Seasonal specialities and seafood are her strong point: a vast array of game, crisp salade océane, foie gras marbled with potatoes, Scottish grouse flambéed with single-malt whisky. The décor is cosy, the wines well chosen but oh-so-expensive!

A la carte: 300 F.

La Ferme Saint-Simon
[15]
6, rue Saint-Simon – 45.48.35.74
M. Vandenhende. Closed Sat lunch, Sun and 2-26 Aug. Open until 10.15 pm. Private room: 20. Air cond. V.

MPs, publishing magnates, and food-loving CEOs savour succulent specialities in the intimate little dining rooms of 'the farm' (rustic only in name). Owner Francis Vandenhende dashes like the proverbial chicken from La Ferme to his other, equally renowned restaurant Le Manoir de Paris in the seventeenth arrondissement. The cuisine here is generous and traditional, but with a modern touch: homemade duck foie gras, brill with veal jus, a hearty tourte filled with oxtail and jowls, caramelised almond pastry, and bitter-chocolate tart. Big and little appetites—and thin and thick wallets—will be equally satisfied.

A la carte: 300-400 F. Menu: 190 F (lunch only, wine inc).

12/20 Aux Fins Gourmets
213, bd St-Germain – 42.22.06.57
M. Dupleix. Closed Mon lunch, Sun and 28 July-26 Aug. Open until 10 pm. Terrace dining. Pets allowed.

Hearty Basque/Béarnaise cuisine served in a lively family-run bistro frequented by a smart old-Paris crowd. The charcuteries and confits are good, but skip the desserts. Nice choice of wines from the South-west.

A la carte: 180 F.

La Flamberge
[13]
12, av. Rapp – 47.05.91.37
M. de Saintdo. Closed Sat lunch, Sun, 1 week in May and in Dec, and 3 weeks in Aug. Open until 10.30 pm. Air cond. Valet parking. V AE DC.

The prices are so steep in this pretty little establishment swathed in rosy chintz that soon only millionaires and big-spending MPs will be able to afford them. Perfect oysters, grilled sea bass with fennel (250 F!), baked sea bream. Well-chosen bottlings in a wide range of prices.

A la carte: 550-700 F. Menu: 190 F (lunch only).

Le Florence
[13]
22, rue du Champ-de-Mars – 45.51.52.69
M. Etienne. Closed Sun, Mon and Aug. Open until 10.30 pm. Air cond. V AE DC.

The dining room is rather sombre and so is owner Claude Etienne's welcome. Happily, a fine choice of Italian wines livens things up (especially at night). Chef Alain Morillon's cuisine has been in the doldrums of late, though his carpaccio served on a bed of mixed salad and fried courgettes is up to snuff, as are his classic pasta dishes and tiramisù

dessert. But all things considered... Florence loses a point this year.

A la carte: 350-400 F. Menus: 89 F (lunch only), 220 F.

11/20 La Fontaine de Mars
129, rue St-Dominique – 47.05.46.44
M. Launay. Closed Sat dinner, Sun and Aug. Open until 9.30 pm. Private room: 25. Terrace dining. V.

Checked tablecloths, low prices, and hearty country fare are the perennial attractions of this modest neighbourhood eating-house (andouillette, duck fricassée, Cahors at 50 F a bottle).

A la carte: 160-180 F. Menu: 65 F (weekdays lunch only).

Chez Françoise
[13]
Aérogare des Invalides – 47.05.49.03
MM. Bouillon and Recordon. Closed Sun. Open until midnight. Terrace dining. Parking. V AE DC.

Chez Françoise is an immense subterranean hall decorated in a pseudo-tropical style that has somehow retained its charm, despite 30 years of wear and tear. This is a favourite haunt of hungry MPs. They blithely ignore the excellent fixed-price offering and opt instead for the pricier, equally delicious à la carte fish dishes, grilled lamb, and foie gras.

A la carte: 280-300 F. Menu: 150 F.

Les Glénan
[14]
54, rue de Bourgogne – 45.51.61.09
M. Leroy. Closed Sat lunch, Sun and Aug. Open until 10.30 pm. Private room: 15. Air cond. V AE DC.

In one fell swoop the young and industrious Yann Cadiou has redecorated his dining room (grey with gold highlights), expanded his cellar (lots of whites, superb Médocs), and revamped his menu. Fresh seafood is the Glénan's strongest suit: shellfish fricassée with foie gras, crab soufflé, or fillet of sole with sage-flavoured lentils. The desserts need more work, but we've awarded an extra point this year nonetheless to show how pleased we are with the progress.

A la carte: 450 F. Menu: 200 F (lunch only).

Karlov
[13]
197, rue de Grenelle – 45.51.29.21
M. Maman. Dinner only. Closed Sun. Open until 12.30 am. Private room: 25. Air cond. V AE.

There is more to this (new) address than virtuoso guitarists and gipsy singers: Karlov is a rare example of top-notch Russian cooking. Try the bortsch, zakuski, two versions of shashlik (Uzbek and Caucasian), intoxicating Russian vodkas, and heady Romanian wines.

A la carte: 250-280 F. Menus: 380 F (with caviar), 250 F.

Le Divellec
[18]
107, rue de l'Université – 45.51.91.96
M. Le Divellec. Closed Sun, Mon, 3 Aug-3 Sep and 22 Dec-3 Jan. Open until 10 pm. Air cond. No pets. Valet parking. Telex 270519. V AE DC.

France's *Présidents de la République*—past and present—honour Jacques Le Divellec with their presence, as do press moguls, TV icons, and other high-toned patrons who fill this 'yacht-club' dining room noon and night.

But let's be frank: it's not the big-wigs that make this establishment great: it's the fish! We think Jacques Le Divellec is at the top of his form: he bowled us over on a recent visit with his sublime shrimp in walnut oil with truffle bâtonnets, his flavourful smoked whiting lavished with herbs, and his delectable braised sole napped in a sensational fish-fumet-based hollandaise enhanced with Pouilly-Fuissé and fresh cream. The desserts (vacherin à l'orange, strawberry chaud-froid) are better than ever. Pangloss would be proud: the service is efficient, the wine steward shrewd, and the hostess smiling. In short, all is for the best at Le Divellec.

A la carte: 650 F Menus: 250 F and 350 F (lunch only).

Chez Marius
5, rue de Bourgogne
45.51.79.42

M. Perrodo. Closed Sat lunch, Sun and 5-25 Aug. Open until 10.30 pm. Air cond. V AE DC.

Restaurant pro Michel Perrodo took over this long-lived establishment two years ago, and has no intention of changing a good thing. Intact are the famed 'bouillabaisse Marius', succulent shellfish dishes, and tasty standbys like grilled red mullet or roast saddle of lamb. Mixed crowd, with a sprinkling of MPs. Superb wine cellar.

A la carte: 350 F and up. Menu: 180 F (weekdays only).

12/20 L'Œillade
10, rue St-Simon
42.22.01.60

MM. Huclin and Molto. Closed Sun. Open until 10.45 pm. Air cond. V AE DC.

Things are looking up: the dynamic duo of Huclin and Molto, late of Chez Toutoune, have recently taken over this charming bistro. The prices are as reasonable as ever, the food hearty and unpretentious: mackerel with mustard, calf's liver with gratin dauphinois. Wines are available by the glass.

A la carte: 200 F. Menu: 130 F.

12/20 Le Petit Laurent
38, rue de Varenne – 45.48.79.64

M. Pommier. Closed Sat lunch and Sun. Annual closings not available. Open until 10.30 pm. V AE DC.

Hearty cuisine is served here in an ultraclassic, comfortable Louis XVI décor. Try the terrine of sweetbreads, the skate in truffled butter, or the roast sea bream with mango. The good Loire wines do not come cheap.

A la carte: 300 F. Menu: 180 F.

11/20 La Petite Chaise
36, rue de Grenelle
42.22.13.35

M. Jessel. Open every day. Open until 11 pm. Private room: 33. Terrace dining. V.

This charming little eating-house has been in service since the days of Louis XIV (1680). Sit elbow-to-elbow with university students and publishing people and tuck into the hearty fixed-price menu (Baltic herrings, tripe baked with onions and white wine, and so on).

Menu: 150 F (wine inc).

10/20 Au Pied de Fouet
45, rue de Babylone – 47.05.12.27

M. Persoons. Closed Sat dinner, Sun, holidays, 22 Dec-6 Jan, 24 March-7 April and Aug. Open until 9 pm. Pets allowed.

In an ancient and authentic coachman's bistro, enjoy such simple classics as nicely seasoned lentil salad, blanquette de veau, poule au pot, and clafoutis.

A la carte: 100 F.

12/20 Au Quai d'Orsay
49, quai d'Orsay – 45.51.58.58

M. Richard. Open every day. Open until 11.30 pm. Terrace dining. V AE.

Pleasant décor of hewn stone and tinted glass, home-style cooking (rabbit with tarragon), and grilled meats. But the service has grown lackadaisical, and prices are really too high.

A la carte: 300 F. Menu: 180 F (wine inc).

Le Récamier
4, rue Récamier – 45.48.86.58

M. Cantegrit. Closed Sun. Open until 10.30 pm. Private room: 14. Garden dining. Air cond. V DC.

Martin Cantegrit, the courtly owner of this elegant Empire-style establishment, has been cheek by jowl with chef Robert Chassat for over fifteen years, a most felicitous union. Burgundian classics (game pâtés, jambon persillé, bœuf bourguignon with fresh tagliatelle) flank subtly lightened dishes (tiny scallops with mushrooms, pan-fried tunny with pesto sauce) and moreish desserts. Cantegrit's farm supplies the fresh produce. Le Récamier's clientele—politicos, publishers, and media moguls—also enjoy tapping the 100,000-bottle cellar, surely one of the city's best. In summer the restaurant's lovely terrace spills across a sheltered pedestrian zone (for fume-free outdoor dining).

A la carte: 450-550 F.

Chez Ribe
15, av. de Suffren – 45.66.53.79

M. Pérès. Closed Sun. Open until 10.30 pm. Private room: 30. Terrace dining. V AE DC.

You can still eat here for less than 200 F, including a Bordeaux *primeur* or a tasty little white Saumur. Granted, a 158 F prix-fixe meal is not—yet—any trick to offer even in Paris, but chef Pérès's oft-changing menu is always delicious, well prepared, and generously apportioned. Our last visit yielded a delicate shellfish sauté, a juicy rack of lamb, and a luscious puff-pastry tart, all graciously served in comfortable 1900-style surroundings.

Menu: 158 F.

Tan Dinh
60, rue de Verneuil – 45.44.04.84

M. Vifian. Closed Sun and Aug. Open until 11 pm. Private room: 30. Air cond. Pets allowed.

Tan Dinh's huge wine list (best Pomerols in Paris) has few peers, even among the city's top restaurants, and it far outclasses the menu! One almost suspects that for the Vifian brothers, cuisine is an afterthought, though it was they who twenty years ago introduced Paris to the newest, most refined and creative Vietnamese fare. Alas, that early thrill is gone.... Yet the kitchen's small sins (skimpy portions, dry lamb...) are readily forgiven once the crispy lobster toast, fresh noodles with spicy shrimps, and rosy, subtly herbed beef strips appear on the table. The Vifians, we are sure, can do even better. If one resists the pricier temptations of the wine list, a dinner here amid the select and stylish Left-Bank crowd need not lead to financial disaster.

A la carte: 300 F and up.

11/20 Le Télégraphe
41, rue de Lille – 40.15.06.65

M. Marck. Open every day. Open until 12.30 am. Garden dining. Air cond. V AE.

This immense space of brick and stone (vintage 1900), with its vaulted ceiling, glowing oak woodwork, and Viennese-style mosaics is surely one of the loveliest restaurants in Paris—if still far from the best. But we award an extra point this year to the hard-working new chef for his robust Lyonnais sausage with potato salad, and delicious clams à la marinière.

A la carte: 400 F. Menu: 170 F.

11/20 **Than**
42, rue des Saints-Pères
45.48.36.97
M. Than. Closed Mon lunch, Sun and 10-25 Aug. Open until 11 pm. No pets. V AE DC.

Fried noodles, steamed chicken salad, and mixao—Marie Ta's repertoire appears to be graven in stone. 'Tis tasty enough, withal, and charming Mr Than keeps a benevolent eye on the proceedings in his lively, noisy little restaurant.

A la carte: 150 F. Menu: 53 F (lunch only).

12/20 **Thoumieux**
79, rue St-Dominique — 47.05.49.75
M. Bassalert. Open every day. Open until 11.30 pm. Private room: 120. Air cond. Telex 205635. V.

A busy, successful bistro where you can tuck into the hearty classics of Auvergne and the South-west: terrines, cassoulets, pigs' trotters, etc. Don't overlook the fine calf's head, or the cheap-and-cheerful wine list. The dinner crowd is surprisingly glossy.

A la carte: 180 F. Menu: 52 F.

Jules Verne
Tour Eiffel
(2nd floor) — 45.55.61.44
M. Ody. Open every day. Open until 10.30 pm. Air cond. No pets. Valet parking. Telex 205789. V AE DC.

With a waiting list as long as the restaurant is high (120 metres), chef Alain Bariteau is worry-free. Parisians, provincials, and gastronomic pilgrims are all clamouring to dine where the backdrop is the most beautiful in the world—Paris itself.

The cooking is solidly classical, and we've noted a clear improvement in certain details which were once less than perfect. The salmon gratin scented with thyme butter, the poached turbot sauce mousseline, and tasty little strips of sole with fresh pasta and crab-flavoured butter are all appetising preludes to a pan-roasted chop of milk-fed veal with wild mushrooms, casseroled pigeon à la paysanne, or a lamb tourte of Provençal inspiration. And there is no drop in quality as the feast moves on to crème brûlée flavoured with vanilla and ginger, or Caribbean chocolate cake, and concludes with one of the superb coffees. The high-level (sorry!) service is swift and discreet.

A la carte: 650 F. Menu: 250 F (weekdays lunch only).

Vin sur Vin
20, rue de Monttessuy — 47.05.14.20
M. Vidal. Closed Sat lunch, Sun, 12-28 Aug and 22 Dec-4 Jan. Open until 10 pm. V.

Former sommelier Patrice Vidal has assembled a first-rate cellar made up exclusively of growers' wines, from which he selects a few each week to sell by the glass. The same infectious enthusiasm inspires his brother Marc to concoct inventive dishes to complement the wines: sardines with a tomato custard, roast mullet with fennel, and lamb fricassée with broad beans and artichokes. Too bad the prices are high and climbing, with no prix-fixe relief in sight.

A la carte: 300-350 F.

12/20 **Ajami**
1, rue de Lincoln — 42.25.38.44
Mme Abou Chalback. Open every day. Open until midnight. Terrace dining. Air cond. V.

Fortunately the menu's perfunctory French offerings are outnumbered by authentic dishes from the Lebanese highlands—assorted mezes, chawarma, keftedes, and deliciously sticky pastries. The wines contribute a dash of local colour to the refined, grey-and-blue dining room.

A la carte: 250-300 F. Menus: 99 F and 109 F (weekdays only), 119 F (weekdays dinner only).

12/20 **L'Alsace**
39, av. des Champs-Elysées
43.59.44.24
M. Blanc. Open every day, 24 hours. Terrace dining. Air cond. Telex 280888. V AE DC.

Since this lively brasserie never closes, one can go there any time at all to enjoy perfect oysters, delicious sauerkraut, and the fresh white wines of Alsace.

A la carte: 300 F.

Les Ambassadeurs
(Hôtel de Crillon)
10, pl. de la Concorde — 42.65.11.12
M. Houdre. Open every day. Open until 10.30 pm. Private room: 72. Terrace dining. Air cond. No pets. Valet parking. Telex 290241. V AE DC.

All our wishes have come true! Every detail of a meal in the Crillon's dining room is now fully up to the standards set by the surroundings themselves: a gilt and mirrored salon asparkle with crystal, reminiscent of Versailles in the *Grand Siècle*. What's more, chef Christian Constant (no relation to the famed *chocolatier*) has corrected the small problems (pale flavours, timid seasonings) that occasionally marred his early efforts here.

Classic but modern, vibrant yet harmonious, Constant's cuisine is best represented by such dishes as ragoût of duck with young cress shoots, cured salmon with crisp bouquets of deep-fried celery leaves, sea bream with sweet peppers and sesame in a sapid shellfish broth, casseroled Bresse chicken, and succulent young pigeon slowly stewed in its juices. Desserts do their part to round out a meal that fully merits three toques. The enriched wine list bids fair to make an already stiffish bill rather more hard to swallow, but sommelier Jean-Claude Maitre has charitably included some affordable selections, like Michel Juillot's white Mercurey and a zesty Crozes-Hermitage from Alain Graillot.

A la carte: 600-800 F. Menus: 295 F (weekdays lunch only), 570 F (dinner only).

11/20 **Aux Amis du Beaujolais**
28, rue d'Artois — 45.63.92.21
M. Picolet. Closed Sat (except lunch May-Sep), Sun, holidays, week of 15 Aug and Christmas. Open until 8.30 pm. V.

The full gamut of French home-style and bistro fare is represented here—poule au riz, rabbit in mustard sauce, calf's head, roast beef and chips—washed down with one of the ten tasty *crus* of Beaujolais. Friendly prices, full plates, forgettable décor.

A la carte: 150-180 F.

12/20 Chez André
12, rue Marbeuf – 47.20.59.57
M. Touly. Annual closings not available. Open until midnight. Terrace dining. Air cond. Parking. V.

Hundreds of faithful clients pay homage daily to André's authentic (and immutable) bistro classics. The menu cites calf's head, pigs' trotters, and thick grilled rib steak; these and the excellent wines are served forth by ancient, spiffily marcelled waitresses.

A la carte: 250-280 F.

11/20 Androuët
41, rue d'Amsterdam – 48.74.26.90
M. Blat-Viel. Closed Sun and holidays. Open until 10 pm. Private room: 30. Air cond. No pets. Telex 643093. V AE DC.

Androuët matures some of the city's best cheeses in a labyrinthine cellar below the shop. In the small restaurant upstairs, tyrophiles may sample from a vast selection of cheeses, served in rustic surroundings by an admirably knowledgeable staff. A few hot cheese specialities (more or less successful) are on offer as well.

A la carte: 350 F. Menus: 190 F (weekdays lunch only, wine inc), 200 F.

12/20 L'Artois Isidore
13, rue d'Artois – 42.25.01.10
M. Mendiondo. Closed Sat lunch and Sun. Open until 10.30 pm. Terrace dining. V.

This pre-war restaurant remains faithful to a rustic repertoire of Auvergnat specialities (ham, sausage, tripe, blood pudding) but of late the menu has also listed some less interesting and overpriced oddities. Desserts are skippable, but the cellar is sound.

A la carte: 280 F.

Baumann Marbeuf
15, rue Marbeuf – 47.20.11.11
M. Baumann. Closed 2 weeks in Aug. Open until 1 am. Private room: 22. Terrace dining. Air cond. No-smoking section. V AE DC.

Patrons perch on stools at the bar, or sit at convivial round tables amidst the splendid marbles and mirrors of designer Slavik's décor, to feast on superb shellfish, baroque choucroutes (not all equally successful), and expertly aged meats from Scotland and south-western France. We like the chocolate cake, too, and the thirst-quenching Alsatian wines.

A la carte: 280-300 F.

Bice
6, rue Balzac – 42.89.86.34
M. Ruggeri. Annual closings not available. Open until midnight. Private room: 50. Air cond. Valet parking. V AE DC.

Amiable Italian (or Italian-style) waiters leap and dash among the young, moneyed clientele (St-Tropez, *prêt-à-porter*, the Levant) that forgathers in this refined, blond-wood version of Harry's Bar. Surprise: the food is good–even very good, flavourful, and down-to-earth: lemon-scented tortellini with ricotta and fresh mint, fried squid with white beans, calf's liver with polenta, and heavenly tiramisù for dessert. It's a pricey *pasto*, friends, and the Italian wines are expensive too. The dining room gets terribly crowded after 10 pm.

A la carte: 350 F. Menu: 280 F (weekdays lunch only, wine inc).

11/20 Le Bistrot de Marius
6, av. George-V – 40.70.11.76
M. Richard. Open every day. Open until 12.30 am. Terrace dining. Valet parking. V AE.

Checked table-cloths and stills from Pagnol's film *Marius* provide the Provençal flavour. But the aïoli de morue won't bring back memories of the South of France, and the smoked-haddock salad is sad and dry. Stick to the excellent shellfish, and the fine chocolate mousse. Invariably crowded.

A la carte: 280-300 F.

12/20 Le Bistrot du Sommelier
97, bd Haussmann – 42.65.24.85
M. Faure-Brac. Closed Sat dinner and Sun. Open until 10.30 pm. Private room: 20. Air cond. V AE DC.

Thanks to a new chef, the cuisine is now on par with this bistro's fabled wine cellar: we can recommend the fresh tunny steak with mild garlic, young rabbit with tiny onions and Chablis, and rib steak with red wine (a robust Syrah, in this case). Owner Philippe Faure-Brac is one of the city's most worthy wine wallahs.

A la carte: 250 F. Menu: 350 F (dinner only, wine inc).

12/20 Le Bœuf sur le Toit
34, rue du Colisée – 43.59.83.80
M. Bucher. Open every day. Open until 1.30 am. Air cond. Telex 281396. V AE DC.

From a seat on the mezzanine watch the dazzling swirl of diners and waiters reflected a hundredfold in this mirrored, flower-filled room. But don't get so distracted that you can't enjoy the faultless seafood, copious brasserie fare, or fruity young wines served in *pichets*.

A la carte: 250 F. Menu: 197 F.

Le Bonaventure
35, rue J.-Goujon – 42.25.02.58
MM. Chabannes and Gutrin. Closed Sun. Open until 10.30 pm. Private room: 14. Garden dining. No pets. V AE.

Fashion and media mavens appreciate the subtle tastefulness of this quiet establishment, blessed with a pocket handkerchief garden. The lengthy menu is nicely executed, with fine, fresh ingredients. Try the veal sweetbreads roasted with lime, and any number of rich desserts. Alas, the quality of the service does not always live up to that of the food.

A la carte: 300-350 F. Menu: 200 F (Sat only).

Chez Bosc
7, rue Richepanse – 42.60.10.27
M. Labrousse. Closed Sat lunch, Sun and 1-20 Aug. Open until 10.15 pm. V AE DC.

Yves Labrousse transferred his restaurant last year from the Left Bank to this new, elegant, streamlined setting. Happily, he brought along his penchant for moderate prices (the prix-fixe lunch hasn't inflated in three years) and his careful, classical cuisine. Flawless technique and polished execution produce such delights as a warm salad of sweetbreads and prawns, pan-roasted bass with artichokes and a truffle jus, and cod baked with mild garlic. The pretty tables are graciously served, right through to the bitter-chocolate soufflé for dessert.

A la carte: 350 F. Menus: 160 F (lunch only), 270 F (dinner only).

11/20 La Boutique à Sandwichs
12, rue du Colisée – 43.59.56.69

MM. Schick. Closed Sun and 3 weeks in Aug. Open until 1 am. Air cond. V.

Here is a cramped, lively little 'deli' well known for wonderful sandwiches and varied cold dishes, as well as corned beef, raclette, and Welsh rabbit.

A la carte: 150 F.

10/20 Brasserie Lorraine
2, pl. des Ternes – 42.27.80.04

Mme Faure. Open every day. Open until 2 am. Terrace dining. Valet parking. V AE DC.

Expensive food of uneven quality, and service that can be qualified only as odious distinguish this enormous brasserie, inexplicably adored by wealthy neighbourhood habitués. We grudgingly admit that the seafood assortments and grilled meats are most often of perfectly respectable quality.

A la carte: 300 F.

11/20 Brasserie Löwenbräu
84, av. des Champs-Elysées
45.62.78.63

M. Rath. Open every day. Open until 2 am. Private room: 80. Air cond. V AE DC.

Its namesake *biergarten* in Munich sends four kinds of cool, German beer in barrels to be served on draught here. Where the orchestra (clad in *lederhosen*, no less) hails from is less certain, but the tasty sauerkraut is worth the din.

A la carte: 250 F.

Le Bristol
(Hôtel Bristol)
112, rue du Fg-St-Honoré
42.66.91.45

M. Marcelin. Open every day. Open until 10.30 pm. Private room: 60. Air cond. No pets. Heated pool. Valet parking. Telex 280961. V AE DC.

Few luxury hotels in Paris go this far to convince one of the virtues of being filthy rich. From the solid teak rooftop swimming pool, down to the 1200-square-metre patio garden where meals are served in fine weather amidst birdsong, velvety lawns, and potted orange trees, the intimidating stage is set. The impeccably trained kitchen staff turns out high-toned dishes that perfectly match the imposing environment: oyster and fresh salmon tartare, prawn salad with a crab ragoût, turbot in Sauternes, calf's liver with stuffed lettuce, chicken breast with a suave walnut butter, and a confit of sweetbreads with mushrooms. The desserts, of course, are as sumptuous as the dining room, and the wine list, naturally, is breathtaking.

A la carte: 600-800 F. Menus: 400 F and 480 F (wine inc).

Café Terminus
(Hôtel Concorde St-Lazare)
108, rue St-Lazare – 42.94.22.22

M. Adrian. Open every day. Open until 11 pm. Private room: 200. Air cond. Valet parking. Telex 650442. V AE DC.

This is not only a very pretty spot, with its bevelled mirrors and ebony woodwork, it is also a very good place to eat. A toque this year for chef Gervais Beaulande's light, appealing quatre-quarts de confit de canard aux pistaches, and the skate with chicory and mussels. Interesting cellar. In the evening, a pianist entertains.

A la carte: 250-300 F. Menus: 125 F, 150 F, 180 F.

Le Carpaccio

(Hôtel Royal Monceau)
35-39, av. Hoche – 45.62.76.87

M. Potier. Closed Aug. Open until 10.30 pm. Air cond. No pets. Heated pool. Valet parking. Telex 650351. V AE DC.

When Angelo Paracucchi mans the kitchen, which is visible from the dining room, you can count on fine fare from one of Italy's better chefs. Recently he has beefed up his staff, so that even in his absence the cooking rarely disappoints. Start off with the eponymous carpaccio, paper-thin raw beef further glorified with aged Parmesan, olive oil, and a spritz of lemon juice. And save room for the aged Parma ham, the marvellous fried scampi cloaked in a translucent batter, the raw baby artichokes tossed with warm jumbo shrimps, the house-made pappardelle enhanced with escarole and slivers of guinea fowl, smoky cheese risotto, divine sea bass with boletus mushrooms, herb-crusted rack of lamb and, for dessert, a smooth tiramisù or a pluperfect zuppa inglese. If you still entertain doubts about Italian wines, the Barolos, Brunellos, and Chiantis hunted down by Paracucchi will dispel them. It only remains to scrap the silly 'grand hotel' décor in favour of a more elegant setting to match the spectacular prices.

A la carte: 450-700 F. Menus: 270 F (lunch only), 320 F (dinner only).

12/20 Caviar Kaspia
17, pl. de la Madeleine – 42.65.33.32

M. Dugoujon. Closed Sun. Open until 12.30 am. Private room: 25. Air cond. Telex 642993. V AE DC.

The fine-feathered folk who frequent this dark but charming upper room opposite the Madeleine come to nibble (caviars, salmon roe, smoked sturgeon) rather than feast (smoked fish assortments, bortsch, etc.). But all the offerings, large and small, are quite good, and are courteously served.

A la carte: 250 F (sans caviar).

Le Château de Chine
9, rue de La Trémoille – 47.23.80.90

Mme Ting. Closed Mon and 1-20 Aug. Open until 11 pm. Air cond. V AE DC.

Mme Ting's smiles brighten the boringly high tone of this posh little *chinois*. Her husband's repertoire is absolutely predictable, but scrupulously prepared: steamed dumplings, five-flavour chicken, spiced-beef salad, and so on.

A la carte: 220 F.

Chiberta
3, rue A.-Houssaye – 45.63.77.90

M. Richard. Closed Sat, Sun, 1-26 Aug and Christmas week. Open until 11 pm. Private room: 35. Air cond. V AE DC.

Along with Fouquet's, Chiberta is the only haunt of *le Tout-Paris* left on the Champs-Elysées. Nabobs from the worlds of finance and television forgather here at lunch, relayed by the *beau monde* in the evening. The dining room's discreet, modern décor is ageing gracefully, the floral displays are as sumptuous as ever and—the big news—the food has never been better. Chef Philippe Da Silva was number two here for ten years, but since his recent promotion, he has surpassed himself (and his predecessor!) in the execution of a menu that highlights sublime sauces and a sophisticated use of herbs and seasonings. Examples? Cold crayfish consommé with a crème au caviar; lobster cannelloni with a truffled shellfish fumet; fresh cod sautéed with a coulis of wild mushrooms and chicory; red mullet in a curried Sauternes sauce; veal kidney cooked whole in its juices with horseradish and capers. All these dishes attest to Da Silva's finesse and good taste. Proprietor Louis-Noël Richard's passion for red Burgundies is communicative (but ruinous for the wallet). Remarkable desserts.

A la carte: 550-750 F.

⌂14 Clovis
(Pullman Windsor)
4, av. Bertie-Albrecht — 45.61.15.32
M. Rameau. Closed Sat, Sun, holidays, Aug and 22 Dec-2 Jan. Open until 10.30 pm. Private room: 80. Air cond. Valet parking. Telex 650902. V AE DC.

Dominique Roué, former assistant to the divine Robuchon, is a master of culinary technique. And we are pleased to announce that he seems to have developed an appealing style all his own. Gone are the heavy hand and the *tours de force*; instead, there are bright-tasting dishes such as terrine de jarret de veau à l'orange, pork fillet garnished with a carrot galette, and a sprightly salad of squid and baby artichokes. Clever, tasty desserts, and an interesting wine list. Service is flawless in the pretty pink-and-beige dining room.

A la carte: 450-500 F. Menus: 165 F (dinner only), 235 F (lunch only), 330 F, 360 F.

⌂13 Copenhague et Flora Danica
142, av. des Champs-Elysées — 43.59.20.41
M. Engström. Copenhague : closed Sun, holidays, first week of Jan and 29 July-27 Aug. Flora : closed Christmas and 1 May. Open until 10.30 pm (11 pm Flora). Garden dining. Air cond. V AE DC.

Salmon—smoked, pickled, marinated, or grilled— and delicious tender herring prepared in every imaginable way, are the stars of this limited menu. The other dishes are dull and terribly dear; the Carlsberg draught is badly drawn; the Copenhagen room is stuffy and outdated. If the weather is fine, ask to be seated on the patio behind the Flora Danica.

A la carte: 350 F.

⌂14 La Couronne
(Hôtel Warwick)
5, rue de Berri — 45.63.14.11
M. Muhle. Closed Sun, holidays and Aug. Open until 10.30 pm. Private room: 120. Air cond. Valet parking. Telex 642295. V AE DC.

Covered with international cookery awards, chef Van Gessel has hit his stride once more. We happily grant him another point this year, in particular for the delicious prix-fixe lunch (a bargain compared to the costly à la carte offerings) which might, on a given day, consist of warm daube of lotte and duck liver, sole matelote with onion confit, excellent cheeses, and a moreish apple macaroon. The newly redone dining room will not win any awards for interior decoration, and it is unfortunately stuck into a corner of the Hotel Warwick lobby. Van Gessel's fine work deserves a larger audience than just the hotel guests and business people at lunch.

A la carte: 450-500 F. Menu: 240 F.

12/20 Diep
55, rue P.-Charron — 45.63.52.76
M. Diep. Closed Sun lunch. Open until 11.30 pm. Air cond. V AE DC.

This is the flagship of the Diep family's three-restaurant fleet. The décor is Bangkok swank, and the food is Asian eclectic; the grilled chicken with lemon grass and the garlic pork are successful, but the shrimp and rice crêpes and the heavy fish fritters are not. Desserts are worth a try (we like the sticky-rice cake with coconut), but the wines are too expensive. Other addresses: 22, rue de Ponthieu in the eighth arrondissement, and 28, rue Louis-le-Grand in the second arrondissement.

A la carte: 250-300 F.

10/20 La Dorada
40, av. George-V — 40.70.19.11
M. Coqueblin. Closed Sun. Open until 11 pm. Private room: 70. Air cond. Valet parking. V AE.

Spanish restaurant magnate Félix Cabeza spent a bundle fitting out this behemoth of a seafood restaurant. Nonetheless, early reviews of the cuisine and service were uniformly negative. We hear that a new manager is now on the scene, and that certain shiftless, arrogant waiters were unceremoniously sacked. Indeed, improvements have been noted in the food as well (better deep-fried whitebait, good dorada—sea bream—baked in salt, and grilled fish), but prices remain outrageous.

A la carte: 500-600 F. Menu: 280 F.

11/20 Dragons Elysées
11, rue de Berri — 42.89.85.10
M. Ung. Open every day. Open until 11.30 pm. Private room: 20. Air cond. V AE DC.

Seated between a dark-blue ceiling and an aquarium floor, you may dine on banal Sino-Thai cuisine—unfocused salads, soulless dim-sum, and decent shellfish sautéed on a hot stone griddle.

A la carte: 230 F. Menus: 198 F (for 2 pers) and 70 F (lunch only).

11/20 Drugstore des Champs-Elysées
133, av. des Champs-Elysées — 47.23.54.34
M. Masetti. Open every day. Open until 1.30 am. Terrace dining. Air cond. No-smoking section. Telex 648566. V AE DC.

Believe it or not, the food at this landmark of 1960s chic is not bad at all. The 72 F two-course meal is more than acceptable, and the meal-in-one salads, the grills, and the crisp pommes frites go very well with the vibrant, bustling atmosphere.

A la carte: 160-180 F. Menu: 72 F.

⌂13 Dynastie Thaï
101, rue La Boétie — 42.89.09.05
M. Lang. Open every day. Open until midnight. Private room: 40. Air cond. V AE DC.

Through room after mirrored room decked with orchids, *faux-marbre* columns, and ancient sculptures waiters parade ceremoniously with trays of polished, perfectly spiced Thai dishes. Note the green-curry shrimps, the Thai curry duck, and pork sautéed with garlic and pepper.

A la carte: 250 F. Menu: 85 F (weekdays only).

⌂14 Chez Edgard
4, rue Marbeuf — 47.20.51.15
M. Benmussa. Closed Sun. Open until 12.30 am. Private room: 35. Terrace dining. Telex 640408. V AE DC.

Just because it has often been said that the *gratin* of French politics eats here, don't expect to see Michel Rocard or Laurent Fabius seated across from you. 'Monsieur Paul' serves four to five hundred meals here each day, and in any case the Parisian powers-that-be are always whisked off to the quiet private rooms upstairs. Downstairs, amid the typically Gallic brouhaha, the rest of us may enjoy an eclectic cuisine that runs from fresh thon à la basquaise to onglet à l'échalote, all prepared with care and skill.

A la carte: 300-400 F. Menus: Salons only : from 230 F to 355 F (wine inc).

Elysée-Lenôtre
10, av. des Champs-Elysées
42.65.85.10

M. Lenôtre. Closed Sat lunch and Sun. Open until 10.30 pm. Private room: 150. Terrace dining. Air cond. Valet parking. V AE.

Business was so bad in this Belle Epoque pavilion, once dear to the hearts of Edward VII and Alphonse XIII that proprietor Gaston Lenôtre was rumoured to be on the verge of throwing in the towel. But things began to look up, and now tables are much in demand. It's hard to imagine a better spot for a restaurant: in the middle of gardens in the middle of the city, just over the wall from Mitterrand's flower beds. The 310 F prix-fixe luncheon has been a great success with a select clientele, who choose from among ten first courses (mallard terrine with juniper berries, for example) and ten main dishes (an excellent breast of Loire chicken with chicory is popular). There are cheeses to finish, along with desserts in the grand (though to our palate oversweet) Lenôtre tradition. If you order à la carte, be prepared to pay much more.

A la carte: 500-800 F. Menu: 310 F (lunch only).

Les Elysées du Vernet
(Hôtel Vernet)
25, rue Vernet — 47.23.43.10

M. Lechenet. Closed Sat, Sun and 3-26 Aug. Open until 10 pm. Garden dining. Air cond. No pets. Valet parking. Telex 290347. V AE DC.

Elegantly refurbished at great expense, the dining room of this charming small hotel boasts a fine table. Under the long-distance direction of chef Bruno Cirino, the cooking sparkles with the sunny, precise style that is his signature, legible in dishes like a salad of pigeon and black Niçoise olives, cod fillet in a herb crust, lamb noisettes with garlic, and a bevy of breathtaking desserts. The service is stylish but not stiff (nor is the bill, compared to restaurants of similar quality in the neighbourhood).

A la carte: 400 F. Menu: 220 F.

11/20 Elysées Mandarin
23, rue Washington
42.25.71.20

M. Ung. Closed Sun and Aug. Open until 11.30 pm. Air cond. No-smoking section. No pets. V AE DC.

Book a table in the front room (which is fridge-and-microwave-free, unlike the rear dining room), and enjoy the good Thai food: grilled ravioli, shrimp salad.

A la carte: 230 F. Menus: 85 F (weekdays only), 129 F.

11/20 Les Essais
40, av. Montaigne
47.20.41.16

M. Ruault. Open for lunch only. Closed Sat, Sun, holidays, 27 April-12 May and 3 Aug-2 Sep. Pets allowed.

High-powered Parisian businessmen squeeze into this tiny café day after day for a nostalgic taste of *grand'mère*'s cooking. Try the country charcuterie, one of the excellent meat dishes (they change daily), and a pleasant little wine.

A la carte: 180-230 F.

Fakhr el Dine
3, rue Q.-Bauchart — 47.23.74.24

M. Antoun. Open every day. Open until 12.30 am. Air cond. No pets. Valet parking. V AE DC.

Ignore the insipid décor, and focus instead on the delicious Lebanese mezes, which dazzle the eye as they delight the palate: bone-marrow salad, brains in lemon sauce, spinach rissoles, fried sheep sweetbreads, etc. These titbits are offered in servings of 8, 10, 15 or 20, depending on the size of the company and your appetite.

A la carte: 250 F. Menus: 150 F (lunch only), 160 F.

La Fermette Marbeuf 1900
5, rue Marbeuf — 47.20.63.53

M. Laurent. Open every day. Open until 11.30 pm. Terrace dining. Air cond. V AE DC.

Jean Laurent wisely decided not to send prices skyward after a genuine Belle Epoque décor—now listed by the Beaux-Arts—was discovered during renovations some years ago. Reasonable prices still prevail at the Fermette for superb andouillette, saddle of lamb, and hearty stewed pig's jowls with a hint of ginger, and there is a delicious 150 F prix-fixe dinner, too. Moderation, quality, and affability are the rule here. As a result, customers quickly become regulars, and the staff remains the same—two good signs.

A la carte: 280-350 F. Menu: 150 F (dinner and Sun lunch).

12/20 La Fontana
26, av. des Champs-Elysées — 42.25.14.72

M. Giordani. Closed Sun. Open until 12.15 am. Air cond. No pets. V AE.

This is one of the very few decent restaurants in any of the Champs-Elysées shopping arcades. Enjoy creditable Italian specialities in a vaguely Venetian atmosphere.

A la carte: 250 F. Menu: 115 F (weekdays lunch only).

Fouquet's
99, av. des Champs-Elysées — 47.23.70.60

M. Casanova. Open every day. Open until 12.30 am. Private room: 200. Terrace dining. Valet parking. Telex 648227. V AE DC.

Aesthetically speaking, Fouquet's décor is no great shakes, but in the end the only way to save this nerve centre of Parisian high life was to have it listed. At the same time the management has attracted some of the younger bloods of the film and advertising world, and the tone is once again lively. The menu can be a bit of a minefield, but you won't go far wrong if you order the perennially perfect merlan Colbert, the daube of beef with carrots, or the charcoal-grilled steak. Paradoxically, the food is considerably better at the two new Fouquet's restaurants (at the Bastille and La Défense) than here at the old original.

A la carte: 300-500 F. Menu: 220 F (wine inc).

12/20 Chez Francis
7, pl. de l'Alma — 47.20.86.83

M. Richard. Open every day. Open until 1 am. Terrace dining. V AE.

The smart patrons are reflected and multiplied by rows of engraved mirrors—so much the better for them, since they obviously take more pleasure in who they're seeing than in what they're eating (though the canard en daube au gratin de macaroni is quite good, as are the shellfish).

A la carte: 300-350 F. Menu: 200 F (wine inc).

Les Géorgiques

36, av. George-V – 40.70.10.49

M. Ishimaru. Closed Sat lunch and Sun. Open until 10.30 pm. Private room: 20. Air cond. No pets. V AE.

Twenty years' training with the masters of the old school (Rostang, etc.) have left Katsumaro Ishimaru forever stranded in a culinary time warp, amid tournedos Rossini, turbot stuffed with foie gras in Madeira, and similiar dinosaurs. Too bad that his fine technique is chained to so banal a repertoire. The décor is downright funereal; prices are chilling.

A la carte: 450-550 F. Menus: 180 F (lunch only), 285 F.

11/20 Germain

19, rue Jean-Mermoz – 43.59.29.24

M. Hamou. Closed Sat dinner and Sun. Open until 10.15 pm. V.

One of the last bastions of French home cooking anywhere near the Champs-Elysées, this 30-seat restaurant offers beef bourguignon, coq au vin, etc. at popular prices.

A la carte: 130-160 F. Menus: 90 F, 125 F.

Le Gourmet des Ternes

87, bd de Courcelles – 42.27.43.04

Closed Aug. Open until 10 pm.

Don't saunter in with this book in your hand; the owner has a horror of guidebooks and, it sometimes seems, of the human race. While he won't win our Welcome Award, François Marie does deserve laurels for choosing the finest quality meat, selected on the hoof in Normandy. The sole reason to visit this murky bistro, enlivened (so to speak) by a nineteenth-century ceramic mural celebrating Industry and Commerce, is not the dull hors-d'œuvres, nor the overcooked fish, nor the ordinary desserts, but the juicy red meat: perfectly cooked beef fillet, bœuf miroton, bourguignon and other fricassées all prepared with the finest four-year-old beef. Don't hint that the chips could be fried a bit less—you'll be driven out by the regulars who love them just as they are. And don't ring up at meal times, for the staff is far too busy to answer the telephone.

A la carte: 220 F

Le Grenadin

44-46, rue de Naples – 45.63.28.92

M. Cirotte. Closed Sat, Sun, 1 week in July, in Aug and Christmas. Open until 10.30 pm. Private room: 16. Air cond. V.

A lovely dining room of little nooks and levels, enlarged with mirrors, is a very pleasant setting for Patrick Cirotte's flavourful, adventurous cooking. Ingredients are the key here—they are uniformly first-rate, and handled with respect and simplicity, from the foie gras sautéed without a speck of fat and served with a lentil salad, to the delicious sea bass fillet baked in a salt crust. Desserts are far above average.

A la carte: 400-450 F. Menus: 200 F, 300 F, 360 F.

Hédiard

21, pl. de la Madeleine – 42.66.09.00

Mme Haug. Closed Sun. Open until 10 pm. Private room: 27. V AE DC.

A genteel atmosphere where all is calm, plush, and very staid. The new chef plays in the accustomed grandiloquent key, but occasionally slips a lusty dish onto the menu, for example a cassolette of eel in Sancerre wine, or salmon with red-cabbage confit. Superb cellar and nice view, beyond the heavy curtains, of the Madeleine.

A la carte: 400-500 F.

12/20 Indra

10, rue du Cdt-Rivière – 43.59.46.40

M. Gupta. Closed Sat lunch and Sun. Open until 11.30 pm. Private room: 50. Air cond. Telex 670416. V AE DC.

Perhaps the new décor will inspire the staff to friendliness, and rejuvenate a kitchen that has grown a bit stale (the price of success?). Jumbo shrimp tandoor, marinated salmon, chicken in green spices, all spring from the best tradition of Indian cookery but they are prepared with less care nowadays.

A la carte: 300 F. Menus: 195 F (lunch only), 220 F, 250 F, 300 F.

Au Jardin du Printemps

32, rue de Penthièvre – 43.59.32.91

M. Tan Le-Bieng. Closed Sun and Aug. Open until 11.30 pm. Private room: 50. Air cond. V AE DC.

The three Tan brothers tend to fawn over the political and social celebrities who over the years have come to regard their restaurant as an unofficial clubhouse. Alongside some decent Chinese standards, Tan Le-Huy prepares some very good Vietnamese specialities, many of which are given an appealing personal twist. Try the pho soup, peppery grilled beef fillet, and spareribs in black bean sauce. Shiny lacquer décor.

A la carte: 300 F.

Le Jardin du Royal Monceau

(Hôtel Royal Monceau)

35, av. Hoche – 45.62.96.02

M. Potier. Open every day. Open until 10.30 pm. Terrace dining. Air cond. Heated pool. Valet parking. Telex 650361. V AE DC.

While one doesn't picnic on the manicured lawns of this Jardin, when in fine weather the glass doors are opened wide on a green setting alive with birdsong and fresh breezes, it's as if a bit of countryside had been magically transported to the heart of Paris. Given the opulent silver, Regency furniture, and formal service, the fresh, inventive cooking of Marc Bayon comes as a pleasant surprise.

A Southern accent comes smiling through the prawns with an anchoïade of raw vegetables, stuffed courgette flowers, leek cannelloni stuffed with crab, fish fricassée in pesto cream, lamb chops grilled with thyme flowers, and roast rabbit with figs: attractive fare that titillates even the jaded appetites of Paris's chic and famous.

A la carte: 500-650 F. Menu: 270 F (lunch only).

12/20 Le Jardin Violet

19, rue Bayard – 47.20.55.11

Mlle Yang. Open every day. Open until 11.30 pm. Private room: 20. Air cond. V AE DC.

The short menu is composed of 'Tibetan' this and 'Mongolian' that, presumably in the same spirit as the strange but striking interior design. Unfortunately, despite the mirrors, and exotic nomenclature, and spicy sauces the food is awfully dull.

A la carte: 300 F. Menus: 125 F and 250 F (for 2 pers).

Jean-Charles et ses Amis

10, rue de La Trémoille – 47.23.53.53

M. Diehl. Closed Sat lunch. Open until 11 pm. Private room: 35. Terrace dining. Air cond. V AE.

Happily, Jean-Charles Diehl has found a home again, and even more friends than before. This purebred Basque, abetted by his wife and a young staff, radiates goodwill and fondness for the lusty fare of his native South-west: dried Ustaritz sausage marinated in herbs, duck giblet confit with shallots, salt cod with pimientoes, stuffed pig's tail with beans, Mugron duck confit with cabbage, etc. And it's an affordable feast that won't cost much more than 250 F, with one of the great little wines that Jean-Charles has a real talent for finding.

A la carte: 230-300 F. Menus: 168 F (Sun lunch only), 180 F (weekdays only), 200 F (w-e and holidays only).

Lamazère
23, rue de Ponthieu – 43.59.66.66

M. Lamazère. Closed Sun and Aug. Open until 11 pm. Private room: 35. Air cond. No pets. Garage parking. V AE DC.

Roger Lamazère, an accomplished magician, made all the foie gras and truffles disappear from his menu, only to reappear after the dessert list. This is part of his attempt to branch out from the great classics of South-western cuisine, which made his reputation, into a more creative vein with an emphasis on seafood. The trick took some time to bring off, but before long—presto!—we were enjoying expertly cooked prawns on a bed of mixed greens dressed with olive oil and balsamic vinegar, a delicate trio of salmon, turbot, and lotte lightly poached in a chive-scented broth, and diaphanous shellfish ravioli sparked with a hint of spice. The magic part is that the renowned cassoulet and confits are still marvellous—but the à la carte prices are likely to make customers disappear.

A la carte: 600 F and up. Menu: 270 F (lunch only).

Lasserre
17, av. F.-Roosevelt – 43.59.53.43

M. Lasserre. Closed Mon lunch, Sun and 4 Aug-2 Sep. Open until 10.30 pm. Private room: 50. Air cond. No pets. Valet parking. V.

One of the few surviving examples of *le grand restaurant à la française*, this grandiose establishment merits your attention for the ethnological interest it presents. Nowhere else is the service so minutely choreographed, the atmosphere so festive yet well-bred (piano music, soft lights, glowing silver, silken carpets...). Don't forget to look up as Lasserre's retractable roof brings you (weather and visibility permitting) the stars. As you look back down you'll notice that the menu is a rich American cattleman's dream of French cuisine: duck à l'orange, tournedos béarnaise, and crêpes flambées. Look more closely and you'll find some lighter, more interesting options like freshwater perch with crabs, precisely cooked scallops with asparagus, Bresse chicken in papillote.... But no matter how hard you squint at the wine list, you won't find a bottle of wine for less than 300 F!

A la carte: 600-800 F.

Laurent
41, av. Gabriel – 42.25.00.39

M. Ehrlich. Closed Sat lunch, Sun and holidays. Open until 11 pm. Private room: 60. Garden dining. Air cond. No pets. Valet parking. V AE DC.

Parisians are talking about Laurent's new décor: has Jimmy Goldsmith opened his Scotsman's purse wide enough to restore a gastronomic pleasure dome on the opulent order of Ledoyen and Elysée-Lenôtre? The debate is still open. Joining a team that includes an intelligent manager, a virtuoso maître d'hôtel, and one of the best sommeliers on the planet has been added a talented, technically proficient young chef, Jacques Rolancy. Once the number two man at Laurent, his menu still rests a bit in his predecessor's shadow, but bright new

ideas are coming on quickly: crisp prawns with courgettes and lemon confit, sea bream with black olives, and deliciously simple veal paillard grillé à l'unilatéral.

A la carte: 800 F. Menus: 370 F (lunch only), 760 F and 900 F (dinner only).

Ledoyen
Carré des Champs-Elysées – 47.42.23.23

M. Mollin. Closed Sun. Open until 10.30 pm (Carré 12.30 am). Private room: 250. No pets. Valet parking. Telex 282358. V AE DC.

With what must have been a grand spirit of adventure, 26-year-old Philippe Dorange came up from Nice to take charge of a brigade of 40 cooks who turn out 500 very elegant meals each day. The obviously talented Dorange had been the lieutenant of mega-chef Jacques Maximin in Nice for five years, but the pressure at Ledoyen was great. And from the very start the critics had not been kindly disposed after suffering the indignities of a virtually non-existent welcome, a jolting mishmash of nineteenth-century furnishings, and sky-high, typically Parisian prices.

As for the cuisine, however, Dorange leaves very little ground for carping. We complain only of a few correctable errors such as a sliced (and therefore flavourless) saddle of rabbit, or a bland bouillon of crayfish with chanterelles. But the shellfish soup with leeks, celery, herbs, and macaroni is a marvel of subtlety, and the small white aubergines stuffed with duck liver, or roast lobster with new potatoes, a millefeuille of lobster and polenta, the daube of John Dory with meadow mushrooms, and a risotto of pigeon with truffles are nothing short of thrilling.

After all that, one turns to the talents of the dessert chef, and amazing talents they are: just taste his lavender-scented chocolate soufflé, or a melon-flavoured cream, a frozen confit of mandarin orange, or a celestial assortment of petits-fours and chocolates. All resistance vanishes!

If 10,400 F for a 1929 Cheval Blanc is a bit rich for your blood, rest assured that the cellar boasts plenty of clarets for under 300 F, and Loire wines offered at the usual prices.

A la carte: 700 F and up (Carré : 350 F). Menus: 380 F (lunch only), 700 F and 800 F (dinner only, Guépard), 210 F (Carré).

Lucas-Carton
9, pl. de la Madeleine
42.65.22.90

19.5 *M. Senderens. Closed Sat, Sun, 3-27 Aug and 21 Dec-6 Jan. Open until 10.30 pm. Private room: 14. Air cond. No pets. Valet parking. V.*

Will Alain Senderens be inducted into the Pantheon one day as the inventor of ravioli de pétoncles? It is easy to have fun at the expense of this culinary wizard, as his cultural significance (and pretensions?) continue to grow. His meteoric rise from apprentice to legendary chef has not stopped at the kitchen door; just as Bocuse cast off his apron to become a roving 'ambassador of French cuisine', Senderens bids fair to become the philosopher of Gallic gastronomy.

A literate chef was once as astonishing a rarity as Dr Johnson's woman preacher, but with more and more young *cuisiniers* entering the kitchen from university, the craft of cookery has acquired a cultural dimension. Having said that, however, anyone with normally tuned tastebuds is sufficiently equipped to savour Senderens's extraordinary inventions. So as the French say: *à table*.

Eventhia Senderens's skills as a hostess have greatly improved, but the ambience that reigns in this stunning Belle Epoque dining room, panelled in glowing blond wood, is still awfully chilly. Granted, this is a *Grand Restaurant*, but a warmer, more convivial mood would surely make the food seem more wonderful still. And at its best, Senderens's cooking is wonderful beyond words. Yet as some disgruntled readers have not failed to point out, when one pays 300 F for roast lamb, or 462 F for the famed homard à la vanille, one is not disposed to countenance anything but sheer perfection. And when flaws do occur, it is natural to blame Senderens for straying from his kitchen. In all fairness, though, one ought not to confuse his role with that of his head chef. For even in the master's absence the thoroughly drilled staff, led by Bertrand Guéneron and Philippe Peudenier, delivers pluperfect versions of such Senderens creations as a sublime confit of foie gras with tiny artichokes, or prawns sautéed in tarragon butter served with a heavenly bouillon, or cod cooked in its skin to retain all its juices, accompanied by fragrantly herbal 'crumbled' potatoes, or lapin Isidoria (the saddle roasted with mustard, the hind legs shredded and tossed with foie gras). Not every dish is above criticism: a perfectly cooked sea bream with a bracing touch of vinegar sported a fussy, purely 'decorative' garnish of almonds and cuttlefish ravioli. And pink peppercorns—that plague of nouvelle cuisine—added nothing to a savoury pigeon cressonnière.

Perhaps we are wrong, but it seems that Senderens's creative pace may have slackened somewhat. But our pleasure in his gâteau au chocolat croustillant, or the aumonière au coulis d'abricots, or the sublime vanilla ice cream hasn't diminished a whit. And Lucas-Carton is surely the place where today's most thrilling marriages of food and wine are arranged (Dominique Derozier presides over the unparalleled cellar).

A la carte: 800 F and up. Menus: 350 F and 400 F (lunch only), 750 F and 950 F (wine inc).

12/20 La Maison du Caviar
21, rue Q.-Bauchart – 47.23.53.43
Mme de Lalagade. Closed 1 and 2 May. Open until 2 am. Air cond. Garage parking. Telex 612976. V.

The décor is new and improved—sober, elegant, surely more comfortable—but the menu remains the same: bortsch, salmon, blini, caviar, and cheesecake. A convivial spot, whose popularity hasn't waned in twenty years; ideal for a pre- or post-cinema supper.

A la carte: 300 F and up.

12/20 La Maison du Valais
20, rue Royale – 42.60.22.72
Mme Le Duc. Closed Sun and 1-20 Aug. Open until 11 pm. Private room: 30. Terrace dining. Air cond. V AE DC.

Fake windows open onto an alpine vista, to put patrons in the mood for rustic Swiss specialities: mountain-cured charcuterie, cheese fondue, and grills (including fresh fish shipped direct from Lake Geneva).

A la carte: 250 F. Menus: 190 F and 210 F (wine inc).

Le Manoir Normand
77, bd de Courcelles – 42.27.38.97
M. Pommerai. Closed Sun. Open until 10.30 pm. Terrace dining. V AE DC.

In France, a restaurateur named Pommerai (roughly equivalent to 'apple orchard'), can hardly do otherwise than give his restaurant a Norman accent. But apart from some fish in cream-based sauces and a fine apple tart, the menu is agreeably free from regional chauvinism. Delicious *plats du jour*, and excellent meats grilled in the big fireplace. Glass-enclosed terrace.

A la carte: 300 F. Menu: 135 F.

Le Marcande
52, rue de Miromesnil – 42.65.19.14
M. Pouliquen. Closed Sat, Sun and 2-26 Aug. Open until 10.30 pm. Private room: 35. Garden dining. V AE DC.

With a little extra attention to detail—mind the seasonings and garnishes, spruce up the desserts, and warm up the chilly service—all would be perfect here at Le Marcande. In fine weather the rather glacial dining room may be avoided in favour of the lovely birch-shaded garden, where chef Thierry Lemoine will offer such appetising suggestions as John Dory drizzled with aromatic oil, red mullet simmered in a ginger-scented court bouillon, and beef fillet with calf's foot and bone marrow in a delicate sauce. Superb, costly cellar.

A la carte: 450-500 F. Menu: 210 F.

La Marée
1, rue Daru – 47.63.52.42
M. Trompier. Closed Sat, Sun and 26 July-27 Aug. Open until 10.30 pm. Private room: 32. Air cond. Valet parking. V AE DC.

At a restaurant named for the tide—La Marée—you would naturally expect to eat fish. But the best meal we've ever had here was a juicy saddle of rabbit served whole with small onions, chanterelles, and courgettes. The old-fashioned pâté en croûte is still among the best in Paris and the once-famous pastry selection has regained its former glorious heights.

Beware, however, of the fish. We were dismayed by dried-out red-mullet fillets, and by a so-so turbot masked with an overpowering rosemary cream sauce. This is not what we have come to expect from a restaurant whose praises we have sung for twenty-odd years. Although La Marée is still as charming, warm, convivial, and comfortable in every respect as ever, the kitchen ought, and certainly can, do better.

A la carte: 450-550 F and up.

Marius et Janette
4, av. George-V – 47.23.41.88
M. Richard. Closed Sat, Sun and 21 Dec-1 Jan. Open until 11.30 pm. Private room: 10. Terrace dining. Air cond. Valet parking. V AE.

In warm weather the large, lovely terrace complements the new dining room with its fantastic sport-fishing motif. The nautical theme continues in the kitchen, where truly fine fish are handled, alas, in a rather cavalier fashion—we've noted many failings, large and small, in the cuisine of late. Safe bets include the grilled sea bass, the bouillabaisse, the oysters and other shellfish. Great desserts.

A la carte: 500 F and up. Menu: 250 F (lunch only, wine inc).

Maxim's
3, rue Royale – 42.65.27.94
M. Cardin. Open every day (except Sun in July-Aug). Open until 11.30 pm (1 am Sat). Private room: 90. Air cond. No pets. Valet parking. Telex 210311. V AE DC.

Now that Maxim's once-frightful prices are common currency at many another less glamorous establishment, is this glorious Belle Epoque monument doomed to become just another restaurant? Heaven forfend! The trouble is, times have changed. The chic, sleek Parisians who made Maxim's a legend now keep their jewels locked up in the family safe, and leave revelry to the young and the hoi polloi; the day of the dapper *boulevardier* is long over. But Maxim's remains, its marvellous mahogany, bronzes, and glass sparkle and glow—it's become a mausoleum for an era whose passing it refuses to acknowledge. The ghost of Maxim's former gaiety occasionally returns at lunch, when an urbane crowd fills the place with sophisticated chatter as they pick at their food.

Speaking of the food, chef Michel Menant does a bang-on job, considering the hundreds of meals he is obliged to serve each day. We were enchanted, on a recent visit, by the prawns en gelée, delectable fried baby red mullet, and delicious bœuf mode. A tip of the hat to him (and the invariably stylish, civilised service), and an extra point.

A la carte: 600-700 F (lunch only), 900 F (dinner only).

Jean-Luc Mesline
(Le Vin de Paille)
3, rue du Cdt-Rivière — 43.59.22.85
M. Mesline. Closed Sat lunch, Sun and 11-18 Aug. Open until 10.15 pm. Terrace dining. V AE DC.

Mesline is a self-taught cook (he started out as a cabinet-maker) who acquits himself creditably of a precise, interesting, full-flavoured repertoire. Steep prices are compensated by first-rate ingredients, generous servings and a 185 F all-in dinner that brings wine-braised oxtail terrine, fresh salmon cooked in Vouvray, and vanilla-scented tarte Tatin with crème fraîche, plus wine.

A la carte: 300-350 F. Menu: 185 F (dinner only, wine inc).

Daniel Metery
4, rue de l'Arcade — 42.65.53.13
M. Metery. Closed Sat lunch, Sun, Feb school holidays and 1-20 Aug. Open until 10.15 pm. V.

Metery, a dedicated and hard-working disciple of the renowned Michel Guérard, not long ago took over this pretty pink-and-beige restaurant above the Passage du Madeleine. Though he has yet to realise his full potential, we are delighted with his pigeon salad, his exotically flavoured lamb with vegetable ravioli, and a luscious honey-apricot pastry. The cellar is expanding, and some good wines are offered by the glass.

A la carte: 350 F. Menu: 170 F.

11/20 Mollard
113, rue St-Lazare — 43.87.50.22
M. Gauthier. Open every day. Open until 1 am. Private room: 100. No-smoking section. V AE DC.

An extraordinary turn-of-the-century ceramic mural depicts destinations reached by trains from the Gare St-Lazare across the street. The food is not nearly so enchanting. Safe bets include the chateaubriand and the omelette surprise, but skip the sandre à la vanille. Courteous welcome, discreet service.

A la carte: 200-250 F. Menu: 170 F (wine inc).

11/20 Le Mot de Passe
13, rue Q.-Bauchart — 47.23.05.65
M. Chiere. Closed Sat lunch, Sun and 15 days in Aug. Open until 11 pm. Air cond. V AE.

Vaguely trendy, costly fare: salmon tartare, sole stuffed with oysters, veal kidney with a touch of tarragon vinegar, etc.

A la carte: 280 F. Menus: 135 F (lunch only), 200 F.

12/20 Le Moulin du Village
25, rue Royale — 42.65.08.47
MM. Spurrier and Williamson. Closed Sat and Sun. Open until 10.30 pm. Private room: 35. V.

This charming old bistro, threatened by urban renewal (the terrace is already closed), belongs to the famous British wine specialists Steven Spurrier and Mark Williamson (sumptuous cellar, interesting choice of wines by the glass). The menu features well-prepared seasonal and 'bourgeois' dishes which occasionally lack true Gallic flair; but do try the sea bream and prawn sausages, calf's liver with a touch of sage, and the homemade frozen nougat with fresh fruit.

A la carte: 350 F. Menus: 168 F (dinner only), 180 F (lunch only).

Napoléon
(Hôtel Napoléon)
38, av. de Friedland — 42.27.99.50
M. Baumann. Closed Aug. Open until 10.30 pm. Private room: 25. Air cond. Telex 640609. V AE DC.

Better known as the sauerkraut king, Guy-Pierre Baumann is now branching out into seafood. He has opened for business with a brand-new décor and a Senderens-trained chef. So far, however, the results aren't entirely convincing. The food is delicate and imaginative, yes, but also fussy and complicated. Nicely garnished with Jerusalem artichokes and mangetouts, the skate was more than a shade overcooked; a commendable sea bream baked in a salt crust was needlessly encumbered with vegetable chips. Desserts are quite good, and the cellar is stocked with some wonderful white wines. Stay tuned.

A la carte: 400-500 F.

12/20 L'Obélisque
(Hôtel de Crillon)
10, pl. de la Concorde — 42.65.24.24
M. Houdre. Closed Aug. Open until 10.30 pm. Air cond. No pets. Valet parking. Telex 290241. V AE DC.

Christian Constant, chef of the triple-toque Les Ambassadeurs (see above), also oversees the ably executed (and reasonably priced) menu of the Crillon's other, less formal restaurant. Dazzling service, hearty food: terrine of pig's trotters and jowls, prawn ravioli, braised oxtail with carrots, appealing desserts, tiny wine list.

A la carte: 300-330 F. Menu: 205 F.

Au Petit Montmorency
5, rue Rabelais — 42.25.11.19
M. Bouché. Closed Sat, Sun and Aug. Open until 10.15 pm. Air cond. No pets. V.

Twenty years ago we discovered Daniel Bouché at Le Petit Montmorency, in the Marais district of Paris, and enthralled by the aromas that emanated from his closet-sized kitchen, we predicted a great future for this bold, inventive chef. We later tracked him down to the Rue Rabelais, where Au Petit Montmorency stands surrounded by barricades and soldiers assigned to protect the nearby Israeli embassy.

Inside, the restaurant is pleasantly old-fashioned, with an eclectic décor of culinary prints and bric-a-brac. Eclectic too are Bouché's tastes, but he has successfully struggled to tame his more outlandish fantasies, and now gives disciplined expression to his culinary imagination. The result is a pure, luminous cuisine that fully deserves three toques. Bouché dazzled us not long ago with sublime fresh truffles veiled in a diaphanous crust and heightened by a lightly creamy, boldly spiced truffle jus; afterwards came a sumptuous turbot steak (he fetches the fish himself, in Normandy) simply baked with tomatoes and olive oil. Meat-lovers will go for the rosy, peppery veal kidney, or the beef entrecôte en pot-au-feu, the stuffed rabbit with wild rice, or a sweet-and-sour duck with turnips. Finish with cheese, if you like—you'll rarely encounter a better Livarot or a more expertly aged Cantal—but you really should save room for the marvellous soufflééd lemon crêpes, or a coupe of caramelised honey ice cream with gingerbread croûtons. Nicole Bouché tends the splendid cellar, and greets customers with disarming warmth. Lulled by this deliciousness, your shock may be all the greater when the waiter presents the bill!

A la carte: 400 F and up.

Le Pichet

68, rue P.-Charron — 43.59.50.34
MM. Devergies and Aphecetche. Closed Sat, Sun and Christmas week. Open until midnight. Terrace dining. Air cond. V AE DC.
New owners have scrubbed and polished this old Pichet, which is currently enjoying considerable success with its excellent shellfish assortments, *plats du jour*, and some creditable fish dishes (skate in warm vinaigrette; cod à l'unilatérale). These and other simple dishes play to a sporty but urbane crowd.

A la carte: 300-350 F.

11/20 La Pomme Soufflée

37 bis, rue de Ponthieu — 42.25.07.71
M. Nakad. Closed Sat lunch, Sun and Aug. Open until 10.30 pm. Air cond. V.
Worth a visit for the two prix-fixe menus that offer, for example, a shrimp and chervil bavarois, sea bream with chives, wine, and dessert for just 98 F. Despite all the mirrors, the tiny, tidy dining room is still pretty cramped.

A la carte: 230-280 F. Menus: 98 F and 130 F (wine inc), 150 F.

11/20 La Poularde Landaise

4, rue St-Philippe-du-Roule — 43.59.20.25
Mme Herbomel. Closed Sat, Sun and holidays. Open until 10 pm. Air cond. V AE DC.
An utterly bogus décor that mimics a Southwestern *auberge* is the scene of hearty repasts consisting of wild-mushroom terrine, goose confit, and stuffed goose neck. Jolly service.

A la carte: 300-330 F. Menu: 130 F (dinner only).

Le Prince de Galles

(Marriott-Prince de Galles)
33, av. George-V — 47.23.55.11
M. Douwe Cramer. Open every day. Open until 10.30 pm. Private room: 180. Garden dining. Air cond. No pets. Valet parking. Telex 280627. V AE DC.
The Prince of Wales beats King George (see below) hands down in the culinary arena. Ex-Robuchon disciple (and former chef to the Rothschilds), Dominique Cécillon has emerged from a dry spell and is now back on form, preparing a cuisine laudably free of hotel-dining-room pomposity, but which maintains a suitably high tone. Warm prawns with chanterelles, turbot à la nage, lobster in Sauternes cream, and pot-au-feu of beef fillet are very nearly as delicious as they are dear. In contrast, the set menus are incredible bargains, especially considering the luxurious setting and service. But please, chef Cécillon, do chuck the fussy, precious menu appellations that make your wonderful dishes sound ridiculous!

A la carte: 500 F. Menus: 210 F, 245 F.

Les Princes

(Hôtel George V)
31, av. George-V — 47.23.54.00
M. Bonnetot. Closed 16 July-27 Aug. Open until 10.30 pm. Private room: 396. Garden dining. Air cond. Valet parking. Telex 290776. V AE DC.
This dog-eared hotel dining room is undergoing renovations at last. But the face-lift alone won't lure back the public—chef Pierre Larapidie should consider revamping his menu, which could also do with some grace and style. In fine weather, book a table on the beautiful flower-decked patio. And when the winter winds blow, give the Princes a cold shoulder and head instead for the Grill George-V, a convivial venue where prices are more clement and Larapidie's repertoire shows glimmers of its former verve.

A la carte: 700 F. Menus: 390 F and 550 F (dinner only).

15 Montaigne

(La Maison Blanche)
15, av. Montaigne — 47.23.55.99
Closed Sun. Open until 11 pm. Private room: 50. Terrace dining. Air cond. Valet parking. V.
Parisian gourmets are in mourning for José Lampreia. Sadly, he never had to feel at home in the fabulous ultramodern kitchens of this dazzling contemporary restaurant, whose opening was the gastronomic event of 1990. José Martinez, Lampreia's brother-in-law, has taken over as chef. We'll wait until he's settled into his new position to give him a rating. In the meantime, we wish him the best of luck.

A la carte: 300-400 F. Menu: 270 F (lunch only).

Alain Rayé

49, rue du Colisée — 42.25.66.76
M. Rayé. Closed Sat lunch and Sun. Open until 10.30 pm. Private room: 15. Air cond. Valet parking. V AE DC.
His neighbour, Dalloyau (one of the best pastry shops in town), should be grateful that Alain Rayé doesn't set up a rival operation, for his chocolate millefeuilles, pithiviers, crème brûlée, crêpe with fresh figs, and verbena ice cream would give Dalloyau some serious competition. Not everything Rayé puts his hand to is equally successful. We didn't see the point of his open ravioli garnished with crab, oysters, balm leaves, and lemongrass butter; and the delicate savour of a turbot steak could not stand up to a heavy dose of spices. We wonder too about the wisdom of wedding lobster tails to bone marrow and couscous (in contrast, the marriage of lobster with lime and root vegetables seemed far more promising). Yet Rayé's is a genuine talent, and most of his inventions are spot on: witness his vegetable ragoût enlivened with coriander, the lightly cooked salmon with asparagus and broad beans, roast pigeon stuffed with wild thyme, thick French-fried potatoes with coarse salt, or roast saddle of rabbit escorted by creamy polenta and a salad dressed with a meat-juice vinaigrette. High praise also for the excellent wine list and the generous prix-fixe menu offered in this truly handsome contemporary setting.

A la carte: 450-600 F. Menu: 235 F.

Régence-Plaza

(Hôtel Plaza-Athénée)
25, av. Montaigne — 47.23.78.33
M. Cozzo. Open every day. Open until 10.30 pm. Private room: 96. Garden dining. Air cond. Valet parking. Telex 650092. V AE DC.
More luxury hotel fare: prawns, truffles, lobster soufflé, rack of salt-meadow lamb and so on—all

creditably prepared by Claude Barnier, a former cruise chef who has cast anchor here. Opulent flowers, old-world service, musical luncheons, *et tout le tralala*.

A la carte: 600-800 F. Menu: 330 F (Sun lunch only).

12/20 Le Relais Bellman

(Hôtel Claridge-Bellman)
37, rue François-Ier — 47.23.54.42
M. Plouseau. Closed Sat, Sun, 5 Aug-2 Sep and 25 Dec-1 Jan. Open until 9.30 pm. Air cond. No pets. Telex 641150. V AE DC.

A chef of the old school stands guard over a menu designed for well-heeled patrons who don't mind what they eat so long as it is shrimp cocktail, grilled sole, or rack of lamb.

A la carte: 350 F.

12/20 Relais-Plaza

(Hôtel Plaza-Athénée)
21, av. Montaigne — 47.23.46.36
M. Cozzo. Open every day. Open until 1 am. Air cond. Valet parking. Telex 650092. V AE DC.

Hot croissants from 8 am for Parisian power breakfasts, soothing harp music at tea time, and a pianist in the evening: in short, everything the wealthy international clientele expects, desires, and pays for. The lengthy *carte* promises much, but only really delivers on the bœuf en gelée and a few of the Italian specialities.

A la carte: 300-500 F. Menu: 285 F (dinner only, wine inc).

Le Relais Vermeer

(Hôtel Golden Tulip)
218, rue du Fg-St-Honoré — 49.53.03.03
M. Le Clercq. Closed Sat and Sun. Annual closings not available. Open until 10 pm. Private room: 170. Air cond. No pets. Heated pool. Valet parking. Telex 650657. V AE DC.

A luxurious restaurant for a luxurious hotel, owned by the Dutch Golden Tulip chain. In a restful grey-blue-and-pink dining room, sample Scandinavian fare full of piquant contrasts between sweet and salty flavours: reindeer fillet with an onion and orange confit, smoked eels in puff pastry, and salmon in every possible permutation. Good hot cheese dishes. Chilly service. Steven Spurrier designed the wine list, don't you know.

A la carte: 400 F. Menus: 195 F, 240 F.

11/20 Righi

11, rue de La Trémoille — 47.23.37.32
MM. Benessiano. Open every day. Open until 12.30 am. Private room: 40. Terrace dining. Air cond. V AE DC.

This lively spot is a favourite with the radio and television people who work in the neighbourhood. They enjoy the cheerfully chaotic service of salmon lasagne, skewered chicken with lemon cream sauce, and silken homemade pastas.

A la carte: 250-300 F.

12/20 Le Saint-Germain

74, av. des Champs-Elysées — 45.63.55.45
M. Hasegawa. Closed Sat and Sun. Open until 10 pm. Air cond. No pets. Garage parking. Telex 641566. V AE DC.

Buried beneath the Claridge's shopping arcade, this pleasant establishment boasts a new chef, who offers careful, thoughtful cooking: seafood ragoût with fresh pasta, roast lamb au jus with fresh mint, etc. Appealing pastries, and good set menus.

A la carte: 300 F. Menus: 165 F (weekdays only), 280 F (weekdays only, wine inc).

Saint-Moritz

33, av. de Friedland — 45.61.02.74
M. Raichon. Closed Sat, Sun and holidays. Open until 10.15 pm. Terrace dining. Air cond. V AE DC.

Chef Raichon hails from the Jura, and his cooking too is rooted in that hearty mountain region. Sample his Morteau sausage with warm potato salad, fresh morels and asparagus tips in puff pastry, or sole fillets cooked in Arbois white wine. Fresh seasonal specialities (dilled red-mullet terrine; fig and citrus soup) are featured on the single-price menu, which makes this elegant, wainscotted dining room a popular choice for business luncheons.

Menu: 305 F.

12/20 Savy

23, rue Bayard — 47.23.46.98
M. Savy. Closed Sat, Sun and Aug. Open until 11 pm. V.

Cramped, ill-lit, with ancient imitation-leather banquettes and an even more ancient ceiling fan, Savy has a hard-to-fathom charm that keeps customers (including some of the capital's most noted radio personalities) coming back for robust country cooking: stuffed cabbage, Auvergne-style calf's liver, tripe, and so on.

A la carte: 280-300 F.

Stresa

7, rue de Chambiges — 47.23.51.62
M. Faiola. Closed Sat dinner, Sun, 5-28 Aug and 20 Dec-5 Jan. Open until 10.30 pm. Private room: 12. Terrace dining. AE DC.

This tacky but somehow soothing dining room is always jammed full of press, fashion, and theatre folk who love the antipasti drizzled with fruity Tuscan olive oil, the toothsome osso buco, and the unctuous tiramisù prepared by Marco Faiola. Claudio and Toni seat their guests with a sure social sense of who's up, who's down, who's in, who's out.

A la carte: 350 F.

La Table de l'Astor

(Hôtel Astor)
11, rue d'Astorg — 42.65.80.47
M. Lemarchand. Open for lunch only. Private room: 35. Air cond. No-smoking section. No pets. Telex 642737. V AE DC.

The menu is concise, that's all to the good; it's classic in tone, but that is not meant as a reproach. For Michel Legrand gives every well-made dish a personal touch. Try his sole and scallop fricassée with a hint of ginger, or the veal sweetbreads in scrambled quails' eggs, or grilled veal kidney à l'américaine. The décor is lovely, tables are well spaced, and the service is most stylish.

A la carte: 350-450 F. Menu: 190 F (weekdays only).

Taillevent

15, rue Lamennais
45.63.39.94
M. Vrinat. Closed Sat, Sun, 18-22 Feb and 26 July-26 Aug. Open until 10.30 pm. Private room: 32. Air cond. No pets.

Having narrowly escaped expropriation, Taillevent's proprietor, Jean-Claude Vrinat, can now concentrate on other pressing matters, like enlarging the restaurant's antediluvian kitchens and, even more critically, scouting for a replacement for chef Claude Deligne, scheduled to retire after more than 30 years of brilliant service.

In fact, Vrinat may not have far to look for a new head chef. The rumour is that Philippe Legendre, a Robuchon disciple who is currently number two at Taillevent, may be given the nod. Legendre, as it happens, is behind the menu's recent shift towards new, more subtle dishes, exemplified by a delicious cold cream of rock lobster dotted with minuscule diced vegetables, roast crayfish tails napped with a divine, subtly spiced cream sauce, tiny red mullet with basil in a delicate wine sauce, the suprême de pigeon with its giblets in Médoc wine, and the tender, thick slices of mushroom-stuffed sweetbreads.

The future, it is safe to say, of this noble institution will be guided by Vrinat's policy of grounding the kitchen's innovations in the classics, altering the menu prudently, to suit evolving tastes. It will be interesting to observe how Legendre's meteoric talent accommodates itself to the Taillevent tradition. In short, the good life, the hushed business luncheons, the quiet cosmopolitan soirées will certainly continue here in a setting of rich hangings, wood panelling, and old pictures (we wouldn't shed a tear, however, should the drab blue velvet and the bibelot cabinets suddenly disappear). Didier Bordas guides guests through Taillevent's justly vaunted cellars, and the service functions at the highest level of efficiency and discretion.

A la carte: 660-800 F.

Chez Tante Louise
41, rue Boissy-d'Anglas — 42.65.06.85
Mme Lhiabastres. Closed Sat, Sun and Aug. Open until 10.30 pm. Private room: 14. Air cond. V AE DC.

A regular clientele loves being pampered in this snug little restaurant. The Lhiabastres (from Aveyron) know how to make their guests comfortable, feeding them very good South-western cooking that features (slightly) lightened versions of foie gras, snail fricassée, duck à l'orange, and crêpes Suzette.

A la carte: 320-350 F. Menu: 190 F.

Le Trente
(Fauchon)
30, pl. de La Madeleine — 47.42.56.58
M. Grillon. Closed Sun. Open until 10.30 pm. Garden dining. Air cond. No pets. Valet parking. Telex 210518. V AE DC.

Whoever dreamed up the name (Le Trente—30—is the building's address) of Fauchon's new restaurant won't win any prizes for creativity, but the decorator might do, for his 'Roman fantasy' interior complete with atrium, columns, and *trompe-l'œil* paintings. Bruno Deligne, son of Taillevent's Claude Deligne, has yet to affirm a clear personality in the kitchen. The menu is too timid by half, particularly since Fauchon is (with Hédiard) the city's temple of rare and exotic foodstuffs. The cuisine is skilful, however, and based on superior ingredients. Desserts are superb, and the wine list is surprisingly affordable.

A la carte: 400 F.

12/20 Le Val d'Or
28, av. F.-Roosevelt — 43.59.95.81
M. Rongier. Open for lunch only. Closed Sat, Sun, Aug and Christmas week. V.

Mme Rongier holds firmly to the traditions of French home-cooking, pleasing her patrons with beef in bone-marrow sauce and lapin à la moutarde, escorted by well-chosen wines at reasonable 'bistro' prices. The ground-floor bar stays open at night, serving wine by the glass, charcuterie, and sandwiches.

A la carte: 200-250 F.

12/20 Chez Vong
27, rue du Colisée — 43.59.77.12
M. Vong Vai Lam. Closed Sun. Open until midnight. Private room: 60. Air cond. Valet parking. V AE DC.

Here's everyone's dream of a Chinese restaurant: embroidered silk, furniture inlaid with mother-of-pearl, lots of little nooks, an air of mystery, and dishes named 'dancing eels', or 'plate of the five happinesses'. The cooking is generally well done. Oddly enough, the cellar is rich in fine claret.

A la carte: 280 F.

Yvan
1 bis, rue J.-Mermoz
43.59.18.40
M. Zaplatilek. Closed Sat lunch and Sun. Open until midnight. Air cond. Valet parking. V AE DC.

Yvan Zaplatilek spells it out for his customers on the restaurant's sign: 'Yvan—Cuisine Française'. The food is indeed primarily French, and quite creditably done, with an occasional Belgian touch here and there (sea scallops accompanied by a mousseline flavoured with Gueuze beer; pheasant garnished with chicory). Yvan also has a penchant for exotic seasonings, and turns out an excellent lotte with ginger, and the veal kidneys spiced with cumin. Not the least of this establishment's virtues are the low tariffs, unmatched in this upscale neighbourhood.

A la carte: 280 F. Menus: 158 F (lunch only), 138 F , and from 168 F to 278 F (dinner only).

11/20 Anarkali
4, pl. G.-Toudouze
48.78.39.84
M. Patel. Open every day. Open until 12.30 am. Private room: 35. Terrace dining. V AE DC.

One of the first Indian restaurants in Paris, this little spot on a quiet, shady square is still one of the best. The tandooris and chicken tikka are good, authentic, and inexpensive.

A la carte: 150 F. Menu: 61 F (lunch only).

Auberge Landaise
23, rue Clauzel — 48.78.74.40
M. Morin. Closed Sun and 4-28 Aug. Open until 10 pm. Private room: 35. Parking. V AE DC.

In a rustic atmosphere conducive to a hearty tuck-in, Dominique Morin treats his customers to the best cassoulet in town (served piping hot in an individual earthenware pot), pipérade landaise, braised duck with wild mushrooms, foie gras, and an array of sturdy South-western wines. Do not overlook the collection of Armagnacs, a perfect way to end a meal in this friendly, relaxed restaurant.

A la carte: 280-300 F.

Le Bistrot Blanc
52, rue Blanche — 42.85.05.30
M. Borni. Closed Sat lunch, Sun, 10-17 Feb and Aug. Open until 10.30 pm. Private room: 30. V.

A first toque this year for Bruno Borni, a Marseille native who held the rank of sauce chef at La Tour d'Argent (indeed, his sauces are excellent, well concentrated, light, and fragrant). Recommended are his flavourful cassolette with whisky, pigeon roasted in a salt crust, and citrus fruit 'marvel'. The ambience of this soft-pink dining room manages to be charming, despite the stand-offish service. Limited cellar.

A la carte: 250 F. Menu: 76 F (lunch only).

12/20 La Champagne

10 bis, pl. de Clichy
48.74.44.78

M. Conscience. Open every day. Open until 3 am. Private room: 30. Air cond. No pets. V AE DC.

Until the small hours you can join the carefree, festive crowd that pays high prices for homard flambé, onion soup, oysters, and sauerkraut at this effervescent restaurant. Clever, cheerful staff.

A la carte: 300-400 F.

Charlot

(Roi des Coquillages)
81, bd de Clichy (pl. de Clichy) – 48.74.49.64
MM. Blanc. Open every day. Open until 1 am. Air cond. V AE DC.

A fine view of the Place de Clichy, a warm welcome, and attentive service will take your mind off the overbearing art deco interior. Sparkling fresh oysters, spectacular shellfish assortments, generous bouillabaisse à la marseillaise, and lobsters prepared every possible way are the staples here.

A la carte: 400 F. Menu: 250 F (lunch only, wine inc).

10/20 Chartier

7, rue du Fg-Montmartre – 47.70.86.29
M. Lemaire. Open every day. Open until 9.30 pm. No pets.

Nothing has changed since 1896 at this rigorously preserved bistro, including the classics (roast chicken, calf's head) offered at obstinately philanthropic prices.

A la carte: 60-80 F.

11/20 L'Echiquier

48, rue St-Georges – 48.78.46.09
M. Gaye. Closed Sun, Mon, 26 Jan-6 Feb and 3-27 Aug. Open until 10 pm (11.30 pm w-e). V AE DC.

This is a good spot for after-theatre suppers, so long as your tastes run to simple dishes like terrines, duck breast, confits, and fruit tarts.

A la carte: 200-300 F. Menu: 78 F (until 10 pm only).

Gokado

18, rue Caumartin – 47.42.08.82
M. Hue. Closed Sat lunch, Sun and 1 May. Open until 10.30 pm. Private room: 35. Air cond. V AE.

A restful grey-and-pale-yellow Japanese restaurant, with a menu that goes well beyond sushi. The French manager will explain the subtleties of some of the more complicated dishes like cuttlefish mousse with seaweed, the conger eel grilled with ginger, sea-bream mousse stuffed with pumpkin, or rock lobster poached in a sake court bouillon.

A la carte: 300-350 F. Menus: 90 F, 135 F and 185 F (lunch only), 210 F, 390 F and 590 F (dinner only).

12/20 Le Grand Café Capucines

4, bd des Capucines – 47.42.19.00
MM. Blanc. Open every day, 24 hours. Private room: 30. Terrace dining. Air cond. V AE DC.

The waiter won't pull a face if you order just one course—a shellfish assortment, for example, or a grilled pig's trotter. The extravagant décor is a replica of a Belle Epoque *café boulevardier*.

À la carte: 300 F.

Le Lindbergh

(Hôtel Ambassador)
16, bd Hausmann – 42.46.92.63
M. Claude. Open every day. Open until 9.30 pm. Private room: 130. Air cond. Telex 650912. V AE DC.

Here's yet another Parisian hotel which has been spruced up for a fresh start. The restaurant boasts a new chef, whose market menu is full of pleasant surprises: pan-roasted prawns and vegetables, brill sprinkled with aromatic oil, duck breast with cracklings, and delicious desserts all well worth a toque.

A la carte: 300-350 F. Menus: from 215 F to 275 F.

11/20 Maison de la Franche-Comté

2, bd de la Madeleine – 42.66.26.28
M. Gandemer. Closed Sun and holidays. Open until midnight. Private room: 36. Air cond. V AE.

Opt for the simplest offerings—Jura ham, Morteau sausage, quiche au Comté—and you won't be disappointed. Get dessert elsewhere.

A la carte: 200-250 F. Menus: 69 F, 140 F.

Les Muses

(Hôtel Scribe)
1, rue Scribe – 47.42.03.40
M. Antoine. Closed Sat, Sun, holidays and 1-31 Aug. Open until 10.30 pm. Private room: 80. Air cond. No pets. Valet parking. Telex 214653. V AE DC.

The muse of interior decoration was off duty the day the décor was installed in this basement restaurant. On the other hand, new chef Philippe Renard seems privy to a regular fount of inspiration judging from his technically rigorous, beautifully presented cuisine. He earns a second toque this year for dishes that bear an appealing personal stamp, like a picture-perfect asparagus charlotte, a gelée of crab with broccoli coulis, roast pigeon with braised fresh peas, and ethereal pastries (tarte Tatin, sour-cherry clafoutis, caramelised apple millefeuille). The wine list's virtue is balance rather than length.

A la carte: 400 F. Menus: 210 F (lunch only), 350 F (dinner only).

Opéra Restaurant

(Café de la Paix)
3, pl. de l'Opéra – 40.07.30.10
M. Meyrueis. Closed Aug. Open until 11 pm. Air cond. Telex 220875. V AE DC.

How lucky that the untold sums spent restoring, regilding, re-marbling and reappointing this vast temple of Second Empire opulence did not render it solemn, stuffy, and boring. *Au contraire* the ambience is exuberant, animated by whirling waiters who juggle the Baccarat crystal, fine china, and gilded silver with aplomb. Chef Gil Jouanin carries on imperturbably, producing rich, even ornamental food with admirable brio. A second toque this year in recognition of his roast prawns and tiny scallops seasoned with smoked salt, the turbot braised in an almond crust, the roast pheasant à la Riche, and all his dazzling desserts. The cellar harbours fine bottles at reasonable prices.

A la carte: 450-550 F.

Pagoda

50, rue de Provence – 48.74.81.48
Mme Ek and M. Tan Dinh. Closed Sun and Aug. Open until 10.30 pm (11 pm Sat). Air cond. V.

After a long career in the kitchen, Papa Dinh has taken up his pipe and slippers. His daughter Rosine has enriched the Pagoda's dependable Vietnamese repertoire with some lovely Cambodian specialities, such as green papaya salad, the grilled jumbo blue shrimps, and sautéed lotte with sweet peppers. Excellent Peking duck.

A la carte: 200-230 F. Menus: 75 F (weekdays lunch only), 95 F.

Le Petit Doué
13

65, rue de Douai — 45.96.06.81

M. Via. Closed Sat lunch and Sun. Annual closings not available. Open until 11 pm. V.

Le Petit Doué has a gift for serving fresh, uncomplicated fare based on fine ingredients. Were prices to climb higher, we might view the menu with a more critical eye, but as things stand you can make a good little feast here of crab terrine, lotte with saffron, and kidneys with pasta, washed down with a modest Muscadet or Côtes-de-Bourg.

A la carte: 250 F. Menus: 80 F (lunch only), 130 F.

12/20 Au Petit Riche

25, rue Le Peletier
47.70.68.68

M. Schmidt. Closed Sun. Open until 12.15 am. Private room: 45. V AE DC.

The brass trim, mirrors, and woodwork of this nostalgic bistro are sparkling once again. This everyone's preferred after-theatre spot (an excellent all-in fee procures an orchestra seat in one of eight surrounding theatres, plus dinner), for topnotch pig's trotters, black pudding, rillons, and delicious wines from the Touraine region.

A la carte: 250 F. Menu: 180 F (weekdays only, wine inc).

La Poste
14

34, rue Duperré — 42.80.66.16

MM. Axel and Benamou. Closed Sun and Aug. Open until 1 am. Private room: 20. Air cond. No pets. Valet parking. V AE.

Right in the middle of the seamy Pigalle district stands this listed 1840 town house, where Bizet wrote *Carmen* (the richly restored decoration looks more suited to *La Traviata*). A talented new chef has made this glamorous venture (owned in partnership by fashion designer Michel Axel) a great place for a midnight supper of raw prawn salad, freshwater perch with morels, pigeon pastilla, and a crisp feuillantine aux poires.

A la carte: 500 F.

12/20 Le Quercy   ☺

36, rue Condorcet
48.78.30.61

M. Simon. Closed Sun, holidays and 27 July-27 Aug. Open until 9.40 pm. Private room: 24. V AE DC.

The food, thank heavens, is far more authentic than the rustic décor, which falls just this side of absolute kitsch. Come here for one of the best cassoulets in Paris, for succulent roast goat cheeses, a hearty fricassée de cèpes, and peaches poached with prunes.

A la carte: 260 F. Menu: 138 F.

11/20 Chez Roger

52, rue de Douai — 48.74.77.19

M. Sebban. Closed Sun dinner, Mon, July and Aug. Open until 10.30 pm. Air cond. V.

A jovial host chats up and jokes with his guests, telling improbable stories of colonial life in North Africa. The couscous is decent, the paella fragrant and good, and the pastries are imported from Dalloyau.

A la carte: 250 F.

12/20 Le Saintongeais

62, rue du Fg-Montmartre — 42.80.39.92

M. Chossat. Closed Sat, Sun and 5-25 Aug. Open until 10 pm. Private room: 10. V AE.

The décor is a study in brown (walls, imitation-leather upholstery...); the menu is rather more cheerful, with good mouclade, chowder, and other specialities from the French Atlantic seaboard. Attractive little selection of wines from the Loire.

A la carte: 250 F. Menu: 128 F (dinner only).

12/20 Le Square

6, sq. de l'Opéra — 47.42.78.50

M. Le Glaner. Closed Sat lunch and Sun. Open until 12.30 am. Private room: 40. Terrace dining. Valet parking. V AE.

This famous old bistro is a long-running success, owing to a funky décor and appealing, bountiful dishes like vol-au-vent de pétoncles or perch and salmon with leek coulis. An intelligent wine list, perfect service and, all in all, another point this year.

A la carte: 250 F. Menus: 150 F (lunch only), 180 F (dinner only), 220 F (dinner only, wine inc).

La Table d'Anvers
16

2, pl. d'Anvers — 48.78.35.21

MM. Conticini. Closed Sat lunch, Sun and 5-26 Aug. Open until 10.30 pm. Private room: 40. Air cond. V.

Cooking, as he does, at a remove from the city's more fashionable districts, Christian Conticini perhaps feels freer to flout culinary trends. As ever, his knack for creating novel flavour combinations is nothing short of staggering. But we now find that his technique is more finely honed, and his cuisine is a marvel of balance and character.

So put aside your prejudices, and prepare for a real gastronomic adventure: try Conticini's mould of oysters and bone marrow heightened with smooth balsamic vinegar; or his tart filled with snails, tomato, chanterelles, and spinach, seasoned with a saffron vinaigrette; or a fricassée that brings together morels, tiny peas, asparagus tips, baby broad beans, carrots, and turnips in tarragon and chicken juices (an ode to springtime!). Complicated, you say? Trust us: What looks like a litany of disparate ingredients will burst into a harmony of delicate flavours on the palate.

Conticini is equally adept at bringing out the best of a single, perfect ingredient, witness his roasted foie gras 'steak', well-seared on the outside, very rare within; or the lightly cooked skate, all moist and pearly under a crust of mace-scented hazelnuts.

We could go on about all these exciting new ideas, but we must leave room to mention the fabulous cheeses, and the astonishing desserts of Philippe Conticini. Don't be put off by the latter's imposing waistline: his chocolate-banana-coffee 'combo', his macaron au fromage frais, lait d'amande, et griotte, or mango-rhubarb puff pastry with a hint of cinnamon are all light as a summer breeze.... Now that the dismal service has been overhauled by top professional Serge Calvez, it only remains to revamp the unattractive décor (clumsily camouflaged under an avalanche of plants). While tariffs are well below what this sort of food would command in a more upscale neighbourhood, the cellar tends to be overpriced.

A la carte: 300-400 F. Menus: 250 F (lunch only), 285 F, 310 F (all spices), 380 F (all desserts), 390 F (dégustation, dinner only).

11/20 Taverne Kronenbourg
(L'Ambassade d'Alsace)
24, bd des Italiens — 47.70.16.64
M. Blanc. Open every day. Open until 3 am. Private room: 110. Air cond. V AE.
The last of the *cafés-concerts* on the Grands Boulevards (orchestra nightly) serves robust, unpretentious brasserie fare: shellfish, pork knuckle with cabbage, sauerkraut, and fine Alsatian wines.
A la carte: 200-230 F. Menus: from 98 F to 240 F.

PARIS   10th

12/20 Brasserie Flo
7, cour des Petites-Ecuries
47.70.13.59
M. Bucher. Open every day. Open until 1.30 am. Valet parking. Telex 281396. V AE DC.
The archetypal Alsatian brasserie, Flo is a jewel: nowhere else will you find the atmosphere, the superb décor, the lively patrons, delicious sauerkraut washed down with carafes of sprightly Riesling.... Note the 'night owl' menu, offered after 11 pm: a main dish, dessert, and wine cost only 98 F.
A la carte: 250 F. Menus: 99 F and 139 F (lunch only).

Chez Casimir
6, rue de Belzunce
48.78.32.53
M. Beringer. Closed Sat lunch, Sun and 10 days end Dec. Open until 10 pm. Private room: 20. Terrace dining. V AE DC.
Sea bass with kiwi fruit or lotte à l'infusion de menthe are not the dishes to order in this likeable little provincial restaurant. Stick to the reliable cassoulet, the good andouillette de Troyes, or confit de canard sarladaise, the traditional specialities of the house. The prix-fixe menu including wine is generous and eminently affordable.
A la carte: 300 F. Menu: 170 F (wine inc).

Au Chateaubriant
23, rue de Chabrol
48.24.58.94
M. Bürkli. Closed Sun, Mon and Aug. Open until 10.15 pm. Air cond. No pets. V.
A very cosy, elegant little restaurant decorated with lithos by modern masters (Picasso, Foujita, Chagall...), which offers opulent, no-nonsense Italian cuisine: scampi fritti with tartare sauce, ravioli stuffed with foie gras and truffles, delicious pasta, and fine desserts (zabaglione al Marsala). Lately chef-proprietor Guy Bürkli has been experimenting most successfully in a Mediterranean vein, with dishes that give starring roles to fruits and vegetables: skate with fresh figs in raspberry butter, young rabbit in aspic with fennel and artichokes. Another point this year.
A la carte: 350 F.

12/20 Les Deux Canards
(Chez Catherine)
8, rue du Fg-Poissonnière — 47.70.03.23
M. Faesch. Closed Sat lunch, Sun and 14 July-19 Aug. Open until 10 pm. Air cond. No-smoking section. V AE DC.
The naïve charm of this dining room crammed with bric-a-brac close to the Grands Boulevards will surely win you over. The voluble owner (a former dentist) does not allow smoking—*nous aimons les fumeurs, pas la fumée*—so diners may enjoy the delicious duck terrine, sardines with pesto, Barbary duck à l'orange, and Provençal

mussels in an unpolluted atmosphere. Admirable cellar.
A la carte: 250-280 F.

La Grille
80, rue du Fg-Poissonnière — 47.70.89.73
M. Cullerre. Closed Sat, Sun and holidays. Annual closings not available. Open until 9.15 pm. V DC.
The menu of this charming old bistro, to which time has lent a glowing patina, invariably lists classic mackerel in white wine, tasty terrines and calf's head sauce gribiche. Even more popular is the magnificent whole turbot (for two) served forth with a silken beurre blanc, the pride of chef Yves Cullerre. Geneviève, the *patronne*, greets customers with help from her myna bird.
A la carte: 250-300 F.

12/20 Julien
16, rue du Fg-St-Denis — 47.70.12.06
M. Bucher. Open every day. Open until 1.30 am. Air cond. Valet parking. Telex 281396. V AE DC.
If only for the pleasure of dining in these exuberant, wildly charming surroundings (vintage 1880), we are willing to accept mediocre food; frankly, the kitchen turns out more than its share of botched dishes. But if you stick to the oysters, the cassoulet, or the pig's trotter, you are likely to come away with a pleasant memory.
A la carte: 250 F. Menu: 139 F (weekdays lunch only).

Le Louis XIV
8, bd St-Denis — 42.08.56.56
M. Flottes-Descombes. Closed June, July and Aug. Open until 1 am. Private room: 120. Terrace dining. No-smoking section. Valet parking. V AE DC.
The décor is more Louis XV (Pompadour period!) than Louis XIV, but no one seems to mind. The festive, dressy crowd that dines here is too busy tucking into succulent roast duck, roast lamb, roast pigeon, or juicy ribs of beef—preceded, ideally, by a sparkling assortment of fresh shellfish. Other seafood dishes are systematically overcooked. Jolly atmosphere.
A la carte: 300-350 F. Menu: 195 F.

Chez Michel
10, rue de Belzunce — 48.78.44.14
M. Marzynski. Closed Fri, Sat, Feb school holidays and 29 July-26 Aug. Open until 10 pm. Air cond. Parking. V AE DC.
This Parisian institution was taken over not long ago by Daniel Marzynski, a chef previously unknown to us. It turns out that he is as deft a hand as his predecessor, Michel, whose repertoire he executes with laudable skill. Sauces seem to be his strong suit, witness the wonderful beurre blanc that accompanies chive-steamed turbot, or the sauce diable that adorns grilled Bresse chicken. We were also impressed by the suave salad of foie gras and artichoke bottoms, and a rich lobster omelette. The two toques, therefore, are still solidly in place. Prices are outlandish, but the faithful habitués do not appear to notice or care.
A la carte: 450-500 F. Menu: 170 F (lunch only).

Da Mimmo
39, bd de Magenta — 42.06.44.47
M. Sommella. Closed Sun and Aug. Open until midnight. Terrace dining. V.
Neapolitan Domenico (Mimmo) Sommella serves the best spaghetti in Paris, seasoned with hot-pepper oil, and topped with tender clams. Delicious Italian cold meats, wonderful pizzas, and good tiramisù round out the list of specialities,

which the regulars wash down with carafes of tasty Apulian wine.

A la carte: 180-200 F. Menu: 85 F (wine inc).

Le New Port

[13] 79, rue du Fg-St-Denis — 48.24.19.38
M. Fargeau. Closed Sat lunch, Sun, 22 Dec-2 Jan and 27 July-19 Aug. Open until 10 pm. Private room: 25. V AE.

A pretty, vaguely nautical ambience suits nicely the careful, classic cuisine of chef Didier Muckenhim, based on top ingredients (Pauillac lamb, house-smoked fish, Aberdeen beef). Very fresh fish are sometimes just a bit overcooked (red mullet à l'unilatérale). Worthwhile desserts.

A la carte: 300-350 F. Menus: 89 F and 140 F (weekdays only).

La P'tite Tonkinoise

[13] 56, rue du Fg-Poissonnière — 42.46.85.98
Mme Costa. Closed Sun, Mon, 1 Aug-15 Sep and 22 Dec-5 Jan. Open until 10 pm. V.

Old Indochina hands come regularly for a whiff of the exotic nostalgia that is practically palpable in this quiet establishment. The Costas, who ran a restaurant in Haiphong, have put their son Michel in charge of the kitchen, where he prepares an authentic repertoire of spring rolls, ginger-sautéed crab, and mi-xao with seven vegetables in a crispy rice galette.

A la carte: 230 F.

11/20 Terminus Nord

23, rue de Dunkerque — 42.85.05.15
M. Bucher. Open every day. Open until 12.30 am. Private room: 12. Terrace dining. Telex 281396. V AE DC.

Now part of the brasserie group of which Flo (see above) is the flagship, the Terminus serves exactly the same food as the rest of the fleet. Enjoy the lively atmosphere, the gay 1925 décor, and look no farther than the sauerkraut, the briny oysters, and the steak with chips. Nimble service.

A la carte: 250-280 F.

PARIS **11th**

L'Aiguière

[13] 37 bis, rue de Montreuil — 43.72.42.32
M. Masbatin. Closed Sat lunch and Sun. Open until 10.30 pm. Private room: 40. Air cond. V AE DC.

Elegant down to the last meticulous detail, this little restaurant stays open (relatively) late, serving romantic dinners with candlelight and piano music. The chef spurns simplicity, but his first-rate ingredients are prepared with care: try the prawn ravioli with sweet peppers, or tournedos with sweetbreads and truffles, and finish with a feuillantine de poires en chaud-froid.

A la carte: 300 F and up. Menus: 95 F (lunch only), 165 F.

Astier

[13] 44, rue J.-P.-Timbaud — 43.57.16.35
M. Picquart. Closed Sat, Sun, Aug, 15 days in May and 15 days at the end of the year. Open until 10 pm. Air cond. V.

For just 115 F, choose from a dozen first courses, another dozen main dishes (including several seafood offerings), a huge array of cheeses, and at least six excellent desserts. This is French home-style cooking at its seasonal, market-fresh best: red mullet pan-roasted in olive oil, magret au cidre, skate with capers, rabbit in mustard sauce, yellow-plum clafoutis, and so on. The atmosphere is good-humoured and noisy. Intelligent, far-ranging cellar. Menu: 115 F.

La Belle Epoque

[14] (Holiday Inn)
10, pl. de la République — 43.55.44.34
M. Lutz. Closed Sun and 3 Aug-1 Sep. Open until 10.30 pm. Private room: 200. Air cond. No-smoking section. Telex 210651. V AE DC.

Chef Patrice Trincali's subtle, sure, personal cuisine comes as something of a surprise in the cavernous dining room of a Holiday Inn. We hope that the renovation of the dining room, planned for August 1991, will attract the larger, more attentive public that this valiant young *cuisinier* deserves. You'll echo our praise after a taste of his delicate prawn salad with potatoes and cream, lobster in an aromatic broth with Thai-spiced ravioli, and delectable salmon roasted with honey and spices. Remarkable service; serious cellar.

A la carte: 400-450 F. Menus: 205 F (lunch only), 255 F (dinner only).

11/20 Brasserie Bastille

14, pl. de la Bastille — 43.43.42.76
M. Lassalle. Open every day. Open until 12.45 am. Private room: 10. Terrace dining. Air cond. V AE.

Here's a very pretty spot that offers real brasserie fare at reasonable prices (a boon in this up-and-coming neighbourhood). Affordable oysters, delicious choucroute (excellent pork), first-rate andouillette, and the rare treat of Pilsen Urquell on draught.

A la carte: 200-250 F.

Cartet ✪

[13] 62, rue de Malte — 48.05.17.65
Mme Nouaille. Closed Sat, Sun, holidays and Aug. Open until 9 pm. No pets.

The half-dozen tables and faded furnishings are a throwback to the days of the Front Populaire. The cooking is equally nostalgic, with no concessions made to modern-day calorie-counters: sheep's trotters in sauce poulette, tripe à la lyonnaise flambée, quenelles, croûte aux morilles, and delicious sugar-dusted bugnes (fritters) that go down wonderfully with the wines of Bugey.

A la carte: 250-280 F.

Chardenoux

[13] 1, rue J.-Vallès — 43.71.49.52
M. Souvrain. Closed Sat lunch, Sun and Aug. Open until 10.30 pm. V AE.

In the heart of the old cabinet-makers' district, this graceful (listed) corner bistro displays its charms of marble, mouldings, and etched glass. Chef Marc Souvrain blends country and bourgeois cooking in a most appealing manner: there's a novel salad of boudin and sour cherries, braised leg of lamb Auvergne-style, perfect aligot (garlicky mashed potatoes with cheese), and a wonderfully flaky apple tart. Connoisseur's cellar.

A la carte: 230-250 F.

12/20 Chez Fernand

17, rue de la Fontaine-au-Roi — 43.57.46.25
M. Asselinne. Closed Sun, Mon and Aug. Open until 11.30 pm. V.

This simple little storefront bistro celebrates the culinary glories of Normandy, with (in particular) an astonishing array of Camemberts, lovingly matured by the owner (who also makes his own bread and butter!). An enthusiastic corps of regulars is regaled with tasty terrines, a salad of marinated sardines with crisp vegetables, numerous duck dishes, and apple tart flamed in Calvados. Good wines from the South-west and the Loire, at nice prices.

A la carte: 200-230 F. Menu: 110 F (weekdays lunch only).

Mansouria
11, rue Faidherbe — 43.71.00.16
Mme Hal. Closed Wed lunch, Tue and 8-31 Aug. Open until 11 pm (11.30 pm Sat). No pets. V.
Fatima Hal is a tireless, voluble promoter of Moroccan cookery, but the version prepared by her chef, though authentic, often lacks spark and spice. Decent tajine of chicken with pickled lemons and olives, good couscous with fresh broad beans, and a remarkable pastilla.

A la carte: 260-300 F. Menus: 97 F (lunch only), 142 F.

12/20 Nioullaville
32-34, rue de l'Orillon — 43.38.95.23
M. Couson. Open every day. Open until 12.30 am. Parking. V AE DC.
Most of the hundreds of dishes served to thousands of customers in this huge Chinese food factory are quite good. Dim sum and roast meats are dispensed from trolleys rolled along by rude, glowering waiters. But never mind. The ambience is noisy and effervescent, and there is a dizzying selection of set menus (don't expect much help or advice from the aforementioned waiters).

A la carte: 130-150 F.

Le Péché Mignon
5, rue G.-Bertrand — 43.57.02.51
M. Guyader. Closed Sun and Mon. Annual closings not available. Open until 10 pm. Air cond. V AE.
The new chef of this fussy, overstuffed little dining room has yet to hit his stride. Yet this former student of Robuchon turns out fresh, vivacious fare, to wit: marbré de joues de porc au foie gras et poivron doux, and a delicate stew of lotte and lobster. The prix-fixe 'tasting' menu of several courses is an interesting choice.

A la carte: 300 F and up. Menu: 200 F.

Chez Philippe   🙂
(Auberge Pyrénées-Cévennes)
106, rue de la Folie-Méricourt — 43.57.33.78
M. Serbource. Closed Sat, Sun and Aug. Open until 10.30 pm. Air cond. V.
The menu written in purple ink is nothing if not eclectic: herrings Bismarck, grilled lobster, a monumental cassoulet, paella (the best in Paris), York ham with macaroni au gratin, beef bourgignon, turbot Dugléré, rock lobster in port and an old-fashioned braised hare. Believe it or not, it's all delicious and satisfying. Best of all, these earthy delights are served in the most convivial atmosphere imaginable, complete with a jovial host. Great Burgundies at giveaway prices only add to the gaiety.

A la carte: 300-350 F.

Le Repaire de Cartouche   🙂
99, rue Amelot or
8, bd des Filles-du-Calvaire — 47.00.25.86
MM. Salabert. Closed Sat lunch, Sun and 28 July-25 Aug. Open until 10.30 pm. Private room: 25. V AE DC.
A young chef with a brilliant resumé has recently taken over the kitchen of this shrine of South-western cookery. The prices and repertoire have so far remained stable, but the execution suffers occasional lapses—as does the slowcoach service.

Try the warm foie gras wrapped in cabbage leaves, the lotte stewed in Madiran wine, and the Landais pie laced with Armagnac.

A la carte: 300 F (except Sat dinner). Menus: 150 F (lunch only), 210 F (Sat dinner and holidays only).

11/20 Le Wei-Ya
49, rue de Lappe — 43.57.62.58
Mme Suen. Closed Sun and Aug. Open until 11 pm. No pets. V.
The main attraction here is the spectacle of the owner rolling out his dumplings on a table in a corner of the dining room. The food is not always exciting, but those dumplings are quite good (thin dough, delicious sauce).

A la carte: 130 F. Menu: 49 F (weekdays only).

12/20 La Connivence
1, rue de Cotte — 46.28.46.17
MM. Guetta and Trastour. Closed holidays. Open until 11 pm. V.
The endearingly low prices make the short, seasonal *carte* all that much more appealing: lentil salad with stuffed pig's tail, sautéed mussels with parsley, and a potée of guinea hen, cabbage, and Lyonnais sausage with a spark of cumin are enjoyed by a trendy, slightly bohemian Bastille crowd.

A la carte: 160-180 F.

11/20 L'Européen
2, rue de Lyon — 43.43.99.70
M. Probst. Open every day. Open until 0.45 pm. Private room: 23. Air cond. V AE.
This big, bustling, beautiful brasserie opposite the Gare de Lyon keeps Parisians and out-of-towners alike happy with its excellent shellfish, calf's head, and andouillette.

A la carte: 280 F.

Fouquet's Bastille
130, rue de Lyon — 43.42.18.18
M. Casanova. Closed Sat lunch and Sun. Brasserie Open every day. Open until midnight. Private room: 12. Terrace dining. Air cond. V AE.
Fouquet's new bi-level outpost at the Bastille is not yet in any danger of being stormed by hungry crowds; there are still too many creams, flans, bavarians and other heavy frills on an otherwise light, delicately flavourful menu. Among the better options in the 'gastronomic' restaurant upstairs are a truffled scallop salad, deliciously juicy pigeon à la ficelle, fillet of lamb with mild garlic. A few 'Fouquet's-style' *plats du jour* are offered in the downstairs brasserie, along with good claret in carafes and luminous shellfish.

A la carte: 350 F (restaurant). Menu: 175 F (brasserie).

La Frégate
30, av. Ledru-Rollin — 43.43.90.32
M. Goueffon. Closed Sat, Sun and Aug. Open until 10 pm. V.
The huge menu of this friendly haven for bons vivants is dedicated to seafood. In addition there is an ample list of fresh, bountiful *plats du jour*, marred only by an occasional lapse in execution. We like the prawns served in the shell, the sea bass in Bouzy wine, and the tasty marmite du pêcheur.

A la carte: 350 F and up. Menus: 280 F (dinner only), 180 F.

La Gourmandise
271, av. Daumesnil
43.43.94.41

M. Denoual. Closed Mon dinner, Sat lunch, Sun, 4-26 Aug and 1-7 May. Open until 10.30 pm. Parking. V AE.

Gourmand or gourmet, you'll be tempted to indulge in Alain Denoual's creative cuisine, served in a new, terribly chic décor of beige and blue. We were bowled over by the sheer inventiveness of his steamed sea bream cleverly heightened by black olives in vinaigrette, the duo of foie gras and magret backed up by a potato gratin, and the timbale de lapin aux choux. Cinnamon ice cream with an apple sablé is a dreamy dessert. The cellar (and the prices!) are progressing slowly but surely.

A la carte: 400-450 F. Menus: 180 F (lunch only), 250 F and 330 F (dinner only).

11/20 Les Grandes Marches
6, pl. de la Bastille – 43.42.90.32

M. Solignac. Closed 6-26 Aug. Open until 1.15 am. Terrace dining. Air cond. V AE DC.

Known until recently as La Tour d'Argent (Bastille)—an endless source of irritation to Claude Terrail, owner of the one-and-only Tour, who settled the matter to his satisfaction in the courts—this trap for hungry opera fans serves a lot of expensive, inept food. But if you look no farther than the (good and inexpensive) oysters or the andouillette mâconnaise, your stomach and your wallet will escape intact.

A la carte: 250-300 F.

Le Mange Tout   ۞
24, bd de la Bastille – 43.43.95.15

M. Simon. Closed Sun and 15-31 Aug. Open until 11.30 pm. Terrace dining. V AE.

A refugee from the Latin Quarter, the Mange Tout has transferred its kitchens to the new Eldorado of the Bastille. The move didn't harm Michel Simon's tasty South-western repertoire, which he has extended to include some creditable fish dishes (rascasse à l'orange, grilled salmon béarnaise). Note the good regional wines (Gaillac, Cahors) and the irresistible prix-fixe menus. A toque this year.

A la carte: 230 F. Menus: 90 F (wine inc lunch), 360 F (for 2, wine inc).

12/20 Chez Marcel
(Restaurant Antoine)
7, rue St-Nicolas – 43.43.49.40

M. Trottet. Closed Sat, Sun, holidays and Aug. Open until 9.30 pm. Private room: 14. V.

Neither Marcel—nor Antoine, for that matter—mans the kitchen here any more. Jean-Claude Trottet gets the credit for the classic pig's trotters (served by the pair, if you please!), tripe, charcuterie, and streaky bacon with beans. The décor is tumbledown, but the atmosphere wins one over with its friendly warmth. A wonderful spot!

A la carte: 200-250 F. Menu: 145 F.

La Plantation Paris
5, rue Jules-César
43.07.64.15

M. Delage. Closed Sun. Open until 11 pm. V AE.

This is the Parisian outpost of the Plantation de Gosier, one of Guadeloupe's best restaurants. Frequented by nostalgic Antillais and others who miss the island's soft clime and heady punch, the restaurant is owned by the author of a six-volume opus on Creole cookery who delivers authentic colombo de coq, bonito with hot spices, and saff-ron-scented clams in puff pastry. Prices are heating up.

A la carte: 300 F and up. Menu: 250 F.

Au Pressoir
257, av. Daumesnil – 43.44.38.21

M. Séguin. Closed Sat, Sun, Feb school holidays and Aug. Open until 10 pm. Private room: 40. Air cond. V.

Forgotten by most Parisians since the Colonial Exposition closed 60 years ago, the Porte Dorée district is home to a covey of fine restaurants of which Le Pressoir is no doubt the best. Henri Séguin is a chef unmoved by trends who pursues his search for exciting flavours wherever it may lead us. We quiver with pleasure at the memory of a savoury cassolette of Swiss chard, Jerusalem artichokes, and truffles, a crusty salmon with vegetable marmalade, lotte with split peas and bacon, veal kidneys à l'orange with mushroom mousse, and a capon roasted with asparagus, nor will we ever forget such unprecedented desserts as pan-roasted quince with nougat, or chocolate soup with warm brioche. The décor, which was progressing from dog-eared to dilapidated, is undergoing a face-lift.

A la carte: 500-550 F. Menu: 350 F.

12/20 Le Quincy   ۞
28, av. Ledru-Rollin – 46.28.46.76

M. Bosshard. Closed Sat, Sun, Mon and 10 Aug-10 Sep. Open until 10 pm.

Here is a small, friendly, countrified restaurant that features hearty, simple dishes from rural France, washed down with Loire and Rhône wines.

A la carte: 250 F.

Sipario
69, rue de Charenton – 43.45.70.26

MM. Bolanos and Ferrari. Closed Sat lunch, Sun, 4-19 Aug and 24 Dec-2 Jan. Open until 11 pm. V AE DC.

Not your corner pizzeria, Sipario has pretensions both aesthetic (the cool, airy dining room decorated with giant-vegetable frescoes is most attractive) and culinary. Regional Italian dishes, so hard to find in Paris, are proposed by a chef who claims that they are absolutely authentic versions. But though we salivate as we peruse the menu, we are sometimes disappointed by the reality (an incredibly insipid bollito misto, for example, and a guinea fowl that tasted distinctly of reheating). Yet the crostino al prosciutto is gooey and good, the involtini di vitello are plump and tender, and the tiramisù, for those who like that inexplicably popular dessert, is the best we've encountered hereabouts. The Italian wine list is wonderful.

A la carte: 230-250 F. Menu: 200 F.

La Sologne
164, av. Daumesnil – 43.07.68.97

M. Kaeriyama. Closed Sun. Open until 10.30 pm. Garage parking. V.

Koji Kaeriyama, the Japanese chef who purchased this neighbourhood eating house not long ago, shows touching dedication to tradition: he maintains not only the house repertoire of game dishes offered in autumn and winter, but the restaurant's dated hunting-motif décor as well. The resolutely classic offerings are precisely prepared, with admirably light sauces (jugged hare, venison grand veneur, roast partridge sur canapé). Reasonable prices—particularly for the enticing set menus—and deft, professional service.

A la carte: 300 F. Menus: 120 F, 160 F, 230 F.

12/20 Le Square Trousseau
1, rue A.-Vollon — 43.43.06.00
*M. Damas. Closed Sun, Mon, Aug and 24 Dec-3 Jan.
Open until 11.30 pm. Private room: 20. Terrace dining. Air cond. No-smoking section. No pets. V.*
This lovingly maintained turn-of-the-century
bistro, the haunt of local cabinet-makers, offers
adroitly prepared, seasonal dishes which we find
oddly timid in flavours and seasonings (fine andouillette napped with a pale mustard sauce; foie
gras with Vouvray lacking in rich wine taste). Good
desserts. The cellar is superb, assembled by noted
wine merchant Jacques Mélac.
A la carte: 280 F.

Le Temps des Cerises
216, rue du Fg-St-Antoine — 43.67.52.08
*M. Crouzier. Open every day. Open until 10.30 pm.
Private room: 20. Terrace dining. V.*
A toque this year for Bernard Bergounioux's
sagaciously seasonal cooking, which pays fragrant
homage to the South-west. Order the generously
served and brightly seasoned terrine of young
rabbit and prunes, the duck fillet sprinkled with
sesame or a light navarin of lamb with young
vegetables, and finish up with the delectable
crème brûlée flavoured with roasted chicory root.
The set menu is a bargain.
A la carte: 230 F. Menu: 80 F.

Le Train Bleu
(Gare de Lyon, 1st floor)
20, bd Diderot — 43.43.09.06
*M. Chazal. Open every day. Open until 10 pm. Priv-
ate room: 100. Telex 240788. V AE DC.*
The extravagant, colossal, delirious, dazzling
décor is more than adequate compensation for the
boring, 'standard French' cooking (veal chop
Foyot, quenelles, coquelet Val-de-Saône...) which,
we must admit, is usually quite decent.
A la carte: 300 F and up. Menus: 195 F (weekdays
lunch only, wine inc), 250 F (w-e and holidays
only).

12/20 Le Traversière
40, rue Traversière — 43.44.02.10
*M. Denonain. Closed Sun dinner and Aug. Open
until 9.30 pm. V AE DC.*
Here is the neighbourhood French restaurant of
your dreams: a peaceful, provincial oasis where
charming hosts are happy to serve you their hearty,
delicious cooking. Don't miss the duck terrine, the
leek gratin with lardons, or the young boar with
wine-stewed pears. The cellar features wonderful
Chinons.
A la carte: 260 F. Menu: 140 F.

Au Trou Gascon
40, rue Taine — 43.44.34.26
*Mme Dutournier. Closed Sat, Sun, Aug and 28 Dec-
5 Jan. Open until 10 pm. Air cond. V AE DC.*
As chef Alain Dutournier tells it, a boyhood spent
roaming the Gascon countryside inspired his deep-
rooted devotion to the region's fresh produce.
Though he now spends most of his time at his
three-toque restaurant, Le Carré des Feuillants (see
first arrondissement), Dutournier oversees the
menu of the Trou Gascon, and develops new dishes which are prepared on a daily basis by the
talented Bernard Broux. Even Dutournier's oldest
and most faithful fans would be hard put to say
whether he or Broux is behind the toothsome
medley of asparagus and broad beans with aged
ham, the warm pâté of cèpes with a parsley sauce,
the pan-roasted foie gras, the calf's brains with
morels, or the rich duck and pork cassoulet.

Game dishes are also close to Dutournier's heart
(his spiced saddle of hare is pure magic), and they
are best washed down, as is all this robust fare, by
the cellar's marvellous Madirans and Jurançons.
The lunch-hour set menu (the price hasn't budged
for three years) is a delicious bargain.
A la carte: 350 F. Menus: 190 F (lunch only),
380 F.

12/20 Bœuf Bistrot
4, pl. des Alpes — 45.82.08.09
*MM. Amice and Garnier. Closed Sat lunch, Sun, 15-
23 April and 15-25 Aug. Open until 10.30 pm. Terrace dining. V AE.*
Attention carnivores! A top-drawer selection of
pan-fried, boiled, grilled, and roasted beef awaits
you here in this oxblood-coloured bistro. Between
salad and dessert, admire the enviable collection
of lithos and drawings by Szafran, Giacometti, Van
Velde and others displayed on the walls. The
atmosphere is agreeably relaxed and casual, but
the prices are quite stiff.
A la carte: 350 F. Menus: 100 F (lunch only),
138 F.

Les Marronniers
53 bis, bd Arago — 47.07.58.57
*M. Lorenzati. Closed Sun and 28 July-14 Sep. Open
until 11 pm. Terrace dining. V AE DC.*
In fine weather one can escape from the sadly
ageing provincial interior to the pleasant patio
under the eponymous chestnut trees. The day's
special dishes are usually the best portion of chef
Lorenzati's menu. Look for a good cassolette of
wild mushrooms and shallots, Auvergne-style
turbot, or a rich navarin d'agneau.
A la carte: 300 F. Menu: 200 F (wine inc).

Le Petit Marguery
9, bd de Port-Royal — 43.31.58.59
*MM. Cousin. Closed Sun, Mon, Aug and 23 Dec-2 Jan.
Open until 10.15 pm. Private room: 16. V AE DC.*
Michel and Jacques Cousin cook in a virile vein
(game, offal, fresh fish, regional dishes) for an
appreciative and very faithful public. Their bright,
old-fashioned bistro is a most convivial spot; Alain
Cousin directs fleet-footed waiters who deliver
generous platefuls of pan-roasted wild
mushrooms, gratin of fresh cod with oysters and
asparagus, partridge purée with juniper berries, or
robust bourgeois classics like tête de veau
ménagère and salt-cured duck à la poitevine. Delicious wines, improved desserts.
A la carte: 300-350 F. Menu: 300 F.

12/20 La Pointe aux Piments
14, rue du Jura — 43.31.85.07
*M. Appadoo. Closed Sun and 15-30 Aug. Open until
11 pm. Terrace dining. V.*
The Mauritian *patron* serves a fiery, authentic
Creole repertoire in his exotic—not very attractive,
we're afraid—little dining room. Sample his
smoked tropical fish, crab gratin, beef with ginger,
codfish rougail, and Mauritian lamb curry.
A la carte: 160 F. Menus: 70 F (weekdays lunch
only), 145 F (dinner only).

11/20 Thuy Huong
15, av. de Choisy — 45.86.87.07
M. Liao Yaou. Closed Thu. Open until 10.30 pm.
Original, unusual (even in here in the Chinese
quarter) Cambodian specialities served forth in the

plainest possible surroundings. Try the Angkor shrimp soup, anchovies from Lake Tonle Sap, and steamed fish with coconut sauce.

A la carte: 160 F.

Les Vieux Métiers de France

13, bd A.-Blanqui — 45.88.90.03

M. Moisan. Closed Sun and Mon. Open until 10.30 pm. Private room: 18. Air cond. V AE DC.

Onto an austere modern building chef Michel Moisan (with considerable help from his friends) has grafted the most amazing medieval décor of sculpted wood, stained glass, ancient beams, and antique paintings. What saves all this quaintness from tipping over into kitsch is Moisan's flavourful, personalised cuisine: pig's ear with prawns, seafood minestrone, spiced shoulder of lamb with barley meal, and an array of luscious desserts. The cellar is an oenophile's dream.

A la carte: 350-400 F. Menus: 190 F, 290 F.

PARIS   14th

L'Amuse Bouche

186, rue du Château — 43.35.31.61

M. Lambert. Closed Sat lunch and Sun. Annual closings not available. Open until 10.30 pm. V.

A former bouillabaisse joint has been transformed into an elegant apricot-coloured dining room, where well-heeled patrons enjoy light dishes with clear, definite flavours. We suggest you sample the delicate warm artichokes with vegetables in vinaigrette, freshwater perch bathed in a fragrant prawn coulis, or meltingly tender young pigeon with a Provençal garnish of baby broad beans and tomatoes, then finish with the superb gâteau mousseux au chocolat amer. Succinct, well-designed wine list.

A la carte: 250 F. Menu: 130 F (lunch only).

Les Armes de Bretagne

108, av. du Maine — 43.20.29.50

M. Boyer. Closed Sun dinner, Mon and 29 July-27 Aug. Open until 11 pm. Private room: 40. Air cond. Valet parking. V AE DC.

Roland Boyer maintains old-fashioned traditions of hospitality, service, and French culinary showmanship in his luxurious Second Empire dining room. Top-quality seafood from Brittany stars in the best dishes on the long menu: fresh oysters, sea bass en croûte, abalone fricassée, and grilled lobsters.

A la carte: 400 F.

L'Assiette

181, rue du Château — 43.22.64.86

Mme Rousseau. Closed Mon, Tue and Aug. Open until 10.45 pm. V AE DC.

Lucette Rousseau ('Lulu'), the temperamental proprietress of this pretty, very Parisian spot, is first and foremost a marvellous cook. Behind the bantering charm she applies to her celebrated customers (Françoise Sagan, Karl Lagerfeld...) lies the dedicated soul of an inspired chef. We adore her polished versions of South-western country classics: the salad of duck breast and foie gras, the braised vegetable medley with fresh truffles, the sweetbreads with meadow mushrooms, or the fine Pyrenees lamb.

A la carte: 400 F and up.

12/20 Le Bar à Huîtres

112, bd du Montparnasse — 43.20.71.01

M. Triadou. Open every day. Open until 2 am. Private room: 15. Terrace dining. Air cond. V AE.

Everything's improving, even the service, at this popular oyster bar where, if you wish, you can order and eat just one oyster—but that would be a shame. Six or a dozen belons, fines, or spéciales would surely be more satisfying. Or book a table in the dining room and sample, in addition to the excellent shellfish, some good salt cod with aïoli or salmon with broccoli. Interesting cellar of white wines. Another point this year.

A la carte: 250 F.

12/20 Le Bistrot de la Gaîté

(Mercure)

20, rue de la Gaîté — 43.22.86.46

M. Duquesne. Open every day. Open until 10.30 pm. Air cond. Parking. Telex 201532. V AE DC.

Bistro classics from céleri rémoulade through skate with capers to crème caramel, are all carefully prepared for the Montparnasse crowd that favours this lively little spot.

A la carte: 200-250 F. Menu: 78 F.

Le Bourbonnais

29, rue Delambre — 43.20.61.73

M. Le Meur. Closed Sun and 11-20 Aug. Open until 11 pm. V AE.

The cramped, ill-lit dining room with an ersatz rustic décor is not a worthy setting for Roger Le Meur's creditable *cuisine bourgeoise*. But the food is tasty enough to bring a good crowd to these too-small tables for crab ragoût with fresh pasta, pork knuckle with lentils, sweetbreads with morels, and an adequate nougat glacé. Indifferent cellar, smiling service.

A la carte: 300-350 F. Menu: 110 F (weekdays only).

La Cagouille

12, pl. C.-Brancusi — 43.22.09.01

M. Allemandou. Closed Sun, Mon, 28 April-6 May, 11-26 Aug and 22 Dec-2 Jan. Open until 10.30 pm. Private room: 20. Terrace dining. V.

Gérard Allemandou has a rare talent for drawing hordes of seafood lovers to the most improbable locations. Three years ago, even Parisian taxi drivers had never heard of the Place Brancusi. Now the address is noted in every restaurant guide in the city, thanks to La Cagouille. The décor is a little cool (and awfully noisy), the welcome is lukewarm, and the service often clumsy, but then this is not a grand restaurant—it is a *bistro du port*, where dishes made from the very freshest fish and shellfish (delivered direct from Atlantic ports) are chalked on a blackboard: depending on the day's catch, offerings might include tiny black scallops from Brest, fresh fried anchovies, red mullet with sea salt, cod and cabbage, divinely plump whiting with mustard sauce, steamed gilthead, or thick, juicy sole. If you are content to drink a modest Aligoté or Quincy, your bill will not rise much above 350 F. But beware if you succumb to the temptations of the finest Cognac collection in Paris (or maybe the world)!

A la carte: 350-500 F.

12/20 Le Canard au Pot

2, rue Boulard — 43.22.79.62

M. Feraud. Closed Sat lunch, Wed, Christmas week and July. Open until 10 pm. V.

Here is a reliable neighbourhood bistro, where the speciality of the house is (as the name implies)

duck simmered in a flavourful bouillon with a bouquet of fresh vegetables. The rest of the menu runs to confits, grills, and terrines, and the perfectly drinkable house Cahors costs just 50 F.
A la carte: 200-230 F.

[13] La Chaumière des Gourmets
22, pl. Denfert-Rochereau — 43.21.22.59
M. Huc. Closed Sun and Aug. Open until 10.30 pm. V.
The new owners, Jean-Paul and Nicole Huc, have not altered the cosy provincial décor, but the menu has been instilled with welcome new vigour: tunny carpaccio with fresh truffles, a very successful salad of sweetbreads and turnips, refreshing jellied bouillabaisse with garlic mayonnaise, and a good thin apple tart with bilberry coulis. Attractive list of white wines.
A la carte: 400 F. Menu: 240 F.

12/20 La Coupole
102, bd du Montparnasse — 43.20.14.20
M. Bucher. Closed 24 Dec dinner. Open until 2 am. Private room: 350. Air cond. V AE DC.
This Montparnasse landmark has survived the takeover by the Flo brasserie group with its mystique intact; indeed, improved after a most successful face-lift (layers of grime were removed from the famous murals). La Coupole's traditional lamb curry, fried whiting with tartar sauce, and cassoulet à l'oie are still on offer (and nicely prepared to boot), as are the exemplary shellfish assortments. Carafes of sprightly house Riesling and swift, efficient waiters add to the charm.
A la carte: 180-300 F.

11/20 La Créole
122, bd du Montparnasse — 43.20.62.12
M. Claude. Open every day. Open until 10.30 pm. Terrace dining. Air cond. V AE DC.
Tropical delights spill out onto the pavement from the plant-filled veranda. A warm, smiling staff serves forth rum punches and codfish fritters as preludes to flavourful Creole specialities like stuffed sea urchin, octopus fricassée, and more. Prices are on the rise.
A la carte: 300 F. Menu: 120 F (except holidays).

[15] Le Dôme
108, bd du Montparnasse — 43.35.25.81
M. Bras. Closed Mon. Open until 1 am. Private room: 10. Air cond. V AE DC.
A second toque for Le Dôme, in recognition of chef Franck Graux's wonderful *carte*, which now extends well beyond the traditional house specialities of bouillabaisse and lobster. His prawns wrapped in paper-thin pastry and served with a sapid shellfish bouillon are brilliant; bracing is the word that comes to mind for his tonic tartare of sea bream and salmon with cress; fresh cod with vegetables and garlicky aïoli is superb. Desserts are worth saving room for: we loved the warm citrus baba napped in custard sauce. Service, of late, is more precise and cheerful, and the cellar is filled with bottles that beg one to splurge.
A la carte: 550-650 F.

[18] Le Duc
243, bd Raspail — 43.20.96.30
M. Minchelli. Closed Sat, Sun and Mon. Open until 10.30 pm. Telex 204896.
Although the famed Minchelli brothers, who revolutionised French seafood cookery, have for all intents and purposes disappeared from the scene, their restaurant is every whit as good as when Paul ('le génie du poisson') ran the kitchen in person. It was he who taught Parisians to love raw fish; today his disciple—Tony—continues to prepare raw sea bass fillets rubbed with shallots, cloves, and Cognac, 'petals' of coquilles St-Jacques, tiny clams sautéed with thyme, and red mullet with pesto, and steamed turbot according to the Minchelli method. The classiest crowd in town still graces Le Duc's dining room, where the service is artfully orchestrated by Dominique Turpin. The cellar is a treasure trove of fabulous white wines, from Meursault-Les Charmes to the more modest (but excellent) Muscadet-sur-lie. Did we mention that prices are very high? Or that the chocolate cake is the only decent dessert? In parting, we must warn you that while all of our experiences at Le Duc have been memorable, some readers and colleagues have not always been so lucky....
A la carte: 500-800 F.

12/20 La Ferme Saintongeaise ○
7, rue Boulitte — 45.42.46.02
M. Tourneur. Closed Sun and 20 July-20 Aug. Open until 10 pm. V.
The owner's tales of his native Saintonge in western France are as colourful as ever, but the chef doesn't appear to be listening anymore; the regional offerings have lost their savour, and the restaurant has lost a point.
A la carte: 230-250 F. Menus: 130 F, 150 F, 175 F.

11/20 Au Feu Follet
5, rue R.-Losserand — 43.22.65.72
M. Abellard. Closed Sat lunch, Sun, 5-12 May and 11-18 Aug. Open until 10.30 pm. V.
The chef-proprietor knows his traditional bistro repertoire inside out. The duck confit and the tarte Tatin will never disappoint, nor will the wines or hospitality offered at this modest but attractive little spot.
A la carte: 200 F. Menu: 65 F (weekdays only).

10/20 Giovanna
22, rue E.-Jacques — 43.22.32.09
M. Knafou. Closed Sat lunch, Sun and Aug. Open until 10.30 pm. V AE.
You, your companion, and sixteen other diners can tuck into perfectly wrought fresh pasta and other tasty Italian dishes in this minute *trattoria*. Don't miss the osso buco.
A la carte: 150 F. Menu: 65 F (lunch only).

[14] Aux Iles Marquises
15, rue de la Gaîté — 43.20.93.58
M. Thery. Closed Sat lunch, Sun and 1-16 Aug. Open until midnight. Private room: 15. V AE.
Once a favourite haunt of Edith Piaf and her chums, the Iles Marquises is now decked out with a fresh nautical décor (shrimp-coloured walls with seascape frescoes) which has effectively erased any raffish air that still hung about the place. Chef-proprietor Mathias Thery, a 'disciple', so he claims, of the Troisgros brothers, ought to put a bit more of his own personality into such technically flawless dishes as delicious pan-roasted prawns and courgettes, or the suave biscuit of sweetbreads and morels, or the tender young pigeon roasted with garlic. Dessert brings an outstanding sabayon of pears and citrus fruits. The cellar is rich in fine white wines.
A la carte: 300-350 F. Menus: 130 F, 150 F.

12/20 Le Jéroboam

72, rue Didot — 45.39.39.13
M. Bon. Closed Mon dinner and Sun. Open until 10 pm. Private room: 45. Air cond. V AE.
Brickwork and banquettes make up the décor of this pleasant, spacious spot where lunch centres around a huge and appetising hors-d'œuvre buffet. Daily specials include quail breasts with raisins, pot-au-feu, and salmon steak with mild garlic. Lesser wines can be had by the half-bottle.
A la carte: 150 F. Menus: 150 F (wine inc), 87 F.

12/20 Justine

(Hôtel Méridien-Montparnasse)
19, rue du Cdt-Mouchotte — 43.20.15.51
Mme Blouin. Open every day. Open until 11 pm. Air cond. No section smoking. No pets. Garage parking. Telex 200135. V AE DC.
A gracious winter conservatory facing a green lawn is the backdrop for Raoul Caïga's dandy buffet lunch, which counts as one of Paris's best in the value-for-money league. For 165 F you can help yourself to any amount of soup, crudités, mixed salads, terrines, fish, oyster and crab dishes, not to mention three hot dishes, cheese, pastries, and desserts.
A la carte: 200-250 F.

Lous Landés

157, av. du Maine — 45.43.08.04
M. Rumen. Closed Sat lunch, Sun and 6-27 Aug. Open until 11 pm. Private room: 14. Terrace dining. Air cond. No-smoking section. V AE DC.
Hervé Rumen's South-western specialities range from the frankly robust to more refined versions of country cooking: salad of quail and smoked duck breasts in truffle juice, superb sautéed wild mushrooms, a cassoulet which would be exceptional with less mealy beans, and delicious quail's legs grilled with foie gras (with an odd garnish of raspberries and asparagus tips). Desserts are all you would expect from a former colleague of Christian Constant. A good cellar with a notably excellent Cahors '83 at 160 F a bottle. Pretty green décor, a lovely hostess, and attentive service.
A la carte: 350 F. Menu: 260 F.

Le Moniage Guillaume

88, rue de la Tombe-Issoire
43.22.96.15
M. Garanger. Closed Sun and 1-20 Aug. Open until 10.30 pm. Private room: 25. Terrace dining. Valet parking. V AE DC.
A good address for fish. Prices are steep and the rustic-inn look is not wildly attractive (though the fireside tables and the terrace are quite pleasant), but Nelly Garanger's welcome is wonderful and the dishes prepared by her husband Michel are always top quality. Only good surprises can be had from the fresh shellfish (available year-round), roast turbot, seasonal game, and fine apple tart. Far-ranging cellar.
A la carte: 400 F. Menus: 195 F (weekdays lunch only, wine inc), 240 F, 390 F.

Montparnasse 25

(Hôtel Méridien Montparnasse)
19, rue Cdt-Mouchotte — 43.20.15.51
M. Sabot. Closed Sat, Sun and Aug. Open until 11 pm. Private room: 20. Air cond. No pets. Telex 200135. V AE DC.
Maurice Tapie, who is in charge of the Méridien restaurants, has followed up his success at the Porte Maillot (Clos Longchamp) with a new winner, Montparnasse 25. The art deco interior opens onto a tiny garden, bringing a note of idyllic charm to the surrounding concrete jungle. Chef Jean-Yves Guého, imported from the chain's Hong Kong hotel, entices appetites with turbot with wild mushrooms, succulent duck stew with potato gnocchi, and one of the most remarkable cheese boards in Paris. Delicate desserts round off an elegant and memorable meal. The young sommelier is happy to offer an excellent choice of wines by the glass.
A la carte: 400-500 F. Menus: 240 F (lunch only), 280 F and 400 F (dinner only).

11/20 Natacha

17 bis, rue Campagne-Première
43.20.79.27
Mme Massine. Dinner only. Closed Sun and 10-25 Aug. Open until 1 am. Terrace dining. V AE.
Trendies from the ad, art, and movie world jostle each other under the gaze of the lovely Natacha and her large Italian side-kick. The cuisine has improved of late. Try the ravioli de chèvre, the hachis Parmentier, and the yummy chocolate cake.
A la carte: 300 F.

12/20 L'Olivier-Ouzerie

9, rue Vandamme
43.21.57.58
M. Mavroïdakos. Closed Sun and 28 July-31 Aug. Open until 11.30 pm. V.
A small patio off a quaint stone-and-tile interior is the scene for an authentic repertoire of Greek dishes: squid à la grecque, moussaka, spala, and so on.
A la carte: 180 F. Menus: 54 F (weekdays lunch only, wine inc), 85 F.

Pavillon Montsouris

20, rue Gazan — 45.88.38.52
M. Courault. Open every day. Open until 10.30 pm. Private room: 40. Garden dining. No pets. Valet parking. V DC.
A walk across the Parc Montsouris at sunset will help you work up an appetite for a fine feast in this turn-of-the-century greenhouse overlooking the park, once a favourite rendezvous of Mata Hari. Jean-Michel Bouvier's 235 F menu adds allure to this Parisian charm spot, bringing hordes of people clamouring for his compote of young rabbit with fried vegetables, or a deluxe hachis Parmentier made with duck, truffles and foie gras—every bit as good as Michel Guérard's. The honey-spiced duck served in two courses is a truly great dish, and for dessert, try the triple-chocolate concoction; our only cavil is that the vanilla-pod ice cream with candied oranges tastes very little of vanilla.
Yvan Courault, who used to manage the Grand Véfour, excels in the art of warmly greeting and treating his clients.
Menu: 235 F.

La Perle des Antilles

36, av. J.-Moulin — 45.42.91.25
M. Joseph. Closed Sun. Open until 11 pm. V AE DC.
The charming island atmosphere of this tidy and trim interior is heightened by the chef and the owner, who both hail from Haiti. Their authentic West Indian cuisine is temptingly tasty. Try the exquisite gratin of christophine, the marinated criot de porc, the wickedly spiced tassot de bœuf, and sip a redoubtable coconut-rum punch they call 'la crémasse'.
A la carte: 150-180 F. Menus: 95 F, 148 F, 170 F.

12/20 Les Petites Sorcières

12, rue Liancourt — 43.21.95.68
*M. Teule. Closed Sat lunch and Sun. Open until
10.30 pm. Terrace dining. V.*
Christian Teule is a talented chef of the
Robuchon school. Helped by his wife Carole, he
has worked up a remarkable repertoire of simple
and hearty dishes in his modest bistro: moules
marinière, duck consommé with ravioli, or filet de
rascasse au pistou. Good wines are available by the
carafe.
A la carte: 180 F. Menu: 100 F (lunch only).

11/20 Aux Petits Chandeliers

62, rue Daguerre — 43.20.25.87
*Mme Lakermance. Open every day. Open until
11.30 pm. Private room: 60. V AE DC.*
A Creole décor around a flowered patio where
you can drink a mean rum punch and eat such
sunny dishes as duck curry enhanced with spicy
sauces known as rougails.
A la carte: 150 F.

11/20 Rendez-Vous des Camionneurs

34, rue des Plantes — 45.40.43.36
*M. Huart. Closed Sat, Sun and Aug. Open until
9.30 pm. Air cond.*
We've never actually spotted a lorry driver here,
but all sorts of people crowd this friendly bistro
where a big-hearted *patron* serves up toothsome
pâté de campagne followed by a chunk of streaky
bacon with tasty white beans. Carafes of plonk are
bargain-priced at 4.50 F.
A la carte: 100 F. Menu: 53 F.

11/20 Le Restaurant Bleu

46, rue Didot — 45.43.70.56
*M. Bousquet. Closed Sat, Sun, July and Aug. Open
until 10 pm.*
Hearty and generous fare—pork rillettes, mutton
tripe, confits, and omelette with cèpes—are served
forth here in an all-blue décor.
A la carte: 180-200 F. Menu: 90 F.

Vassanti

3, rue Larochelle
43.21.97.43
*M. Jafaraly. Closed Tue lunch and Mon. Open until
11 pm. Air cond. V AE DC.*
Tucked away in a cul-de-sac, this vintage Indian
eatery has just inaugurated a good-looking Mogul-
style décor. Mother presides at the stove, producing admirably light vegetable samosas, a creditably
moist chicken tikka, and some superb rice dishes.
All would be perfect if the spicing were just a pinch
more bold.... A toque this year.
A la carte: 200 F. Menus: 79 F and 99 F (lunch
only).

Les Vendanges ❍

40, rue Friant
45.39.59.98
Closed Sat lunch, Sun and Aug. Open until 10 pm. V.
Here is a newcomer to the South-western scene.
The enchaud en gelée (pork terrine) merits a
recommendation, as does the filet de saumon au
lard et aux cèpes, the magret aux deux pommes,
and the prunes poached in tea. The Madiran wines
are good (but not cheap), and the old-fashioned
décor is not without charm.
A la carte: 250-300 F.

12/20 Le Vin des Rues ❍

21, rue Boulard — 43.22.19.78
*Mme Rougier and M. Chanrion. Lunch only (and
dinner Wed and Fri upon reservation). Closed Sun,
Mon and Aug. Terrace dining.*
Ex-baker Jean Chanrion's noisy, cramped bistro
offers an exemplary Lyonnais repertoire, ranging
from andouillette to coq au Beaujolais and salt cod
à la lyonnaise. Wines are by the *pichet*, off course.
A la carte: 130-150 F.

L'Aubergade

53, av. de La Motte-Picquet — 47.83.23.85
*M. Moisson. Closed Sun dinner, Mon, 25 March-
4 April, Aug and 22 Dec-3 Jan. Open until 10.30 pm.
Private room: 10. Terrace dining. V.*
Pierre and Rosanna Moisson have shuffled off
their mournful décor for a fresh new one. Jean-
Claude Poulnais is a gifted chef who aims straight
for the taste buds with his salmon with tomato
compote, andouillette de Troyes au Chablis, and a
delicate apple tart. The remarkable all-in business
menu includes kir, wine, and coffee.
A la carte: 350 F. Menu: 150 F (weekdays lunch
only, wine inc).

12/20 Baïa Sardinia

38, bd Garibaldi — 45.66.97.84
*M. Sassu. Closed Sat lunch and Sun. Open until
10.30 pm. Air cond. V.*
This is an authentic trattoria run by Milan AC
supporter Sandro Sassu. Mamma Susana rules the
kitchen, where she makes her own spinach and
ricotta ravioli, malalanu (little gnocchi sauced with
tomato, basil, and fennel) and some twenty different kinds of fettucine, spaghetti, and maccheroni.
Sporting prices.
A la carte: 200 F. Menus: 80 F (lunch only), 150 F,
200 F.

Le Barrail

17, rue Falguière — 43.22.42.61
*M. Magne. Closed Sat, Sun, 1 week at Easter and
3 weeks in Aug. Open until 10 pm. Air cond. No-
smoking section. V.*
An attractive spot done up in soft pink tones. The
cooking is polished but low-key, and the prices
won't cause a heart attack. Alain Magne's superb
langoustines au foie gras, and canard confit aux
haricots retain the succulent savours of the South-
west. Unbeatable prices for lobster and even for
such luxurious dishes as rémoulade de truffes aux
girolles au foie gras cru. Interesting cellar.
A la carte: 250 F. Menus: 126 F (lunch only),
139 F, 180 F.

Bistro 121

121, rue de la Convention
45.57.52.90
*Mmes Moussié. Closed Sun, Mon, 28 July-28 Aug and
22 Dec-1 Jan. Open until 10.30 pm. Air cond. V AE
DC.*
This 30-year-old bistro, founded by Jean Moussié
and decorated by Slavik, faithfully serves the sort
of classic, sauce-heavy fare that will always be
considered by some to be 'real' French cooking.
Hare à la royale and poached stuffed chicken are
two hold-overs from the Bistro's early days, but
current chef André Jalbert now concentrates on a
repertoire of rich, seasonal, mainly seafood dishes:
bay scallops with three sauces, panaché de sole au
homard et langoustines, roast baby lamb with a
(pedestrian) gratin dauphinois. Clients are warmly

greeted by the Moussié mother-daughter team. Prices are steep.

A la carte: 500 F. Menu: 240 F (weekdays only).

11/20 Le Bistro Champêtre
107, rue Saintt-Charles
45.77.85.06

M. Dorr. Open every day. Open until 11 pm (11.30 pm w-e). Terrace dining. Air cond. V.

Green carpeting, potted plants, and lavish bouquets illustrate the bistro's bucolic 'field-and-flower' theme. This is down-to-earth, assembly-line cuisine sold at affordable prices: The lobster terrine and grilled salmon are well made (but skimpily apportioned), and there is decent chocolate bavarian for dessert.

Menu: 155 F (wine inc).

12/20 Le Bivio
101, rue de la Croix-Nivert
48.28.31.88

M. Chioda. Closed Sun. Open until 11 pm. Terrace dining. V.

A broad glass front opens onto a coldly modern interior, but conviviality reigns in this lively Italian restaurant run by the jovial Ermanno. Wonderful hams, pappardelle ai porcini, and sage-scented saltimbocca. Choose from an extensive selection of fine Italian wines.

A la carte: 260 F. Menu: 100 F.

11/20 Brasserie du Pont Mirabeau
(Hôtel Nikko)
61, quai de Grenelle — 40.58.20.00

M. Sekihara. Open every day. Open until 11 pm. Air cond. Heated pool. Valet parking. Telex 260012. V AE DC.

A pity that so few real brasserie dishes are listed on the menu, but Jacques Sénéchal (Les Célébrités) who supervises the menu of this huge establishment facing the Seine has added a few interesting Asian-inspired dishes (fried prawns with Japanese rice) to a menu dominated by excellent grills.

A la carte: 230 F.

Le Caroubier
8, av. du Maine — 45.48.14.38

M. Michel. Closed Sun and 15 July-30 Aug. Open until 10.30 pm. V.

Adrienne, a *pied-noir* from Tunisia has her very own recipe for marvellously light, fragrant lamb couscous—it is one of the best in Paris. Very good pigeon pastilla too.

A la carte: 180-220 F. Menu: 140 F (weekdays only).

12/20 Casa Alcalde
117, bd de Grenelle
47.83.39.71

M. Uranga. Closed Sun dinner, Mon lunch and 22 Dec-5 Jan. Open until 10.15 pm. Terrace dining. Air cond. V.

A folksy, rustic tavern where one eats at blue-tiled tables in a resolutely Spanish décor. Tasty, straightforward fare with strong Hispano-Basque overtones: delicious chistorras (grilled sausages with peppers), confit de canard à l'eskualduna (with ratatouille), paella, and salt cod à la luzienne. Judiciously selected Spanish wines.

A la carte: 200-230 F.

Les Célébrités
(Hôtel Nikko)
61, quai de Grenelle — 40.58.20.00

M. Sekihara. Open every day. Open until 10 pm. Private room: 22. Air cond. Heated pool. Valet parking. Telex 260012. V AE DC.

The Roman emperors who stare down at the perpetual parade of roast lobster and stuffed pigs' trotters passing under their plaster noses don't seem as bored as we now are with them—and with the rest of this pompous, passé décor. Still, there is the view of the Seine beyond the bay window, the comfort of well-spaced tables, soft seating, the attentive, well-trained staff and above all, the artful cuisine of Jacques Sénéchal. This former Tour d'Argent chef has adroitly stepped into the shoes of Joël Robuchon, the Nikko's old star. His repertoire may be a bit static, but we always welcome an opportunity to sample Sénéchal's virtuoso cooking. Prices are steep here, but that's to be expected these days. What counts is the food's irreproachable quality. We cannot speak highly enough of the risotto with prawns, turbot, and a sprightly touch of tomato and basil; or the monumental volaille de Bresse aux morilles et à la crème; or lush sweets like the bright-tasting raspberry clafoutis or unctuous tiramisù.

Surprisingly, the superb cellar is less pricey than one might fear. Note the two worthwhile prix-fixe lunches.

A la carte: 550-800 F. Menus: 230 F and 280 F (lunch only), 565 F, 670 F.

Charly de Bab-el-Oued
215, rue de la Croix-Nivert — 48.28.76.78
See 17th arrondissement

Le Clos Morillons
50, rue des Morillons — 48.28.04.37

MM. Delacourcelle and Leguay. Closed Sat lunch, Sun, 24 Dec-2 Jan and 1-21 Aug. Open until 10.15 pm. Air cond. V.

Since he took over this quiet neighbourhood bistro from Pierre Vedel some years ago, Philippe Delacourcelle has served consistently good food at reasonable prices. His menus, including the more expensive one which includes fine Loire wines (Pierre and his brother Marc are great connoisseurs) offer a selection of clever dishes that combine innovation and tradition in a most satisfying synthesis. To wit: terrine pressée de pommes de terre and foie gras au gros sel, roast salt cod with bacon and a smoky flavoured purée, young pigeon with sesame seeds. The many delectable desserts (Delacourcelle was once a pâtissier at Fauchon) provide instants of pure bliss in a light, charming new décor. Takeaway shop next door.

A la carte: 280-300 F. Menus: 145 F and 185 F (dinner only), 195 F (lunch only), 310 F (wine inc).

Le Croquant
28, rue J.-Maridor — 45.58.50.83

M. Bigot. Closed Sun, Mon, 1 first wk of May and 30 July-27 Aug. Open until 10.30 pm. Air cond. V AE DC.

After a stumbling début, Jean-Yves Bigot has hit his stride. We can recommend his foie gras poached in vegetable bouillon, salmon with bacon and lentils, and really delectable versions of such classic desserts as vanilla-pod ice cream and chocolate soufflé. Well-stocked cellar, good service.

A la carte: 350 F. Menu: 260 F.

10/20 Brasserie Stella

133, av. V.-Hugo — 47.27.60.54

M. Guerlet. Closed Aug. Open until 1.30 am. Terrace dining. V.

An animated meeting-place for the fashionable inhabitants of a fashionable neighbourhood. Omelette Parmentier, streaky bacon with lentils, and andouillette with top-notch pommes frites.

A la carte: 230 F.

12/20 Candido

40, av. de Versailles — 45.27.86.68

M. Boullosa. Closed Sun and 4 Aug-4 Sep. Open until 10.30 pm. Private room: 30. Garden dining. V AE.

For sunny days, there is a flowered courtyard at this Spanish bistro run by a Galician family. All the classics are on hand: Serrano ham, parilladas, zarzuela, and paella.

A la carte: 250-300 F.

Paul Chène

123, rue Lauriston — 47.27.63.17

M. Souffir. Closed Sat, Sun, 28 July-27 Aug and 22 Dec-2 Jan. Open until 10.30 pm. Private room: 35. Air cond. V AE DC.

Paul Chène has turned over his popular restaurant to new owners, but the spirit of his provincial, home-style cuisine is carried on by his long-time chef, Alain Kerfaut. Some improvements have been made, and now the food evinces a lighter touch, and more vigorous flavours. All the more reason, then, to rediscover Kerfaut's marvellous fresh mackerel in Muscadet, flawless breast of duckling with foie gras in a light jelly, or daube de bœuf à l'ancienne. For dessert, there are dainty apple fritters with redcurrant jelly. The cellar boasts a far-ranging, judicious selection, but the tasty house Bordeaux is not to be neglected.

A la carte: 450 F.

Conti

72, rue Lauriston

47.27.74.67

M. Ranvier. Closed Sat, Sun, holidays and 4-26 Aug. Open until 10.30 pm. Private room: 20. Air cond. V AE.

Slavik has refurbished Conti's rather Luciferian décor of mirrors with black and gold highlights. Chef Michel Ranvier took the cue, and has revamped his repertoire of provincial Italian dishes, giving them a vigorous, modern—French!—zest. His puff-pastry tart of fennel and fresh anchovies is the lightest, most ethereal 'pizza' you are likely to encounter; appetising too are the croustillant of asparagus and macaroni, wonderful varations of fresh pastas, and a whole veal kidney roasted in Barolo. The best tiramisù in Paris is to be found right here, along with a superb Italian cellar, excellent service, and a chic, well-bred clientele.

A la carte: 400 F. Menu: 260 F (lunch only, wine inc).

L'Estournel

(Hôtel Baltimore)

1, rue L.-Delibes — 45.53.10.79

Mme Jacob. Closed Sat, Sun, and 15 July-16 Aug. Open until 10 pm. Private room: 90. Air cond. No pets. Telex 611591. V AE DC.

The rotunda dining room has a heady pre-war atmosphere with its crimson walls, gilt, and Decaris paintings, a setting that is particularly seductive at night. This is a perfect spot for a romantic dinner *à deux*—there is even a specially designed 'tête-à-tête' menu, a steal at under 600 F with Champagne thrown in, and the best that chef Henri Boutier can provide: foie gras, fillet of perch with bone marrow, duck à l'orange, dessert, coffee, and sweets.

A la carte: 400 F. Menus: 590 F (dinner only, for 2, champagne inc), 225 F.

Fakhr el Dine

30, rue de Longchamp — 47.27.90.00

M. Antoun. Open every day. Open until 12.30 am. Private room: 12. Air cond. No pets. Valet parking. V AE DC.

Sample Lebanese mezes by the number—8, 10, 15, 20, depending on appetites and the size of your party—in this attractive blond-wood dining room enhanced with a few discreet Levantine touches. Mezes are the must here, but some interesting discoveries can be made amongst the chawarmas and the fish offerings (poisson au piment rouge à la tripolitaine). Interesting local wines.

A la carte: 250-300 F. Menus: 150 F (lunch only), 160 F.

Faugeron

52, rue de Longchamp — 47.04.24.53

M. Faugeron. Closed Sat, Sun, Aug and 23 Dec-3 Jan. Open until 10 pm. Private room: 14. Air cond. No pets. Valet parking. V.

Golden oak panelling now enhances Faugeron's large blue-and-saffron dining room, a décor that some find rather chi-chi, but which everyone finds comfortable. Under the smiling supervision of Gerlinde Faugeron, prize-winning sommelier Jean-Claude Jambon and a whole squadron of courteous (but never obsequious) waiters tend to the patrons, while chef-proprietor Henri Faugeron runs the kitchen. Although he is not obsessed by novelty, Faugeron renews his menu often enough to keep our mouths watering and our curiosity alive. Surely one never tires of such classics as soft-boiled eggs with truffle purée, admirable house-smoked salmon, wild mushrooms with foie gras, Challans duckling with turnips, or tender fillet of beef with bone marrow; yet one is delighted to discover new dishes like fried frogs' legs in basil-scented cream, curried veal shin with Sauternes, or young guinea fowl en cocotte escorted by a salad dressed with the bird's warm juices.

An apple charlotte with vanilla cream (made, incredibly, with no trace of sugar), or pistachio-caramel ice cream are a final thrill to be savoured along with the last drops of a great Bordeaux, a voluptuous Burgundy, or a more modest Chinon or Sancerre. The calm, unruffled ambience attracts a classy clientele; the impressive four-course set lunch has numerous fans.

A la carte: 650 F and up. Menus: 310 F (lunch only), 470 F.

Jean-Claude Ferrero

38, rue Vital — 45.04.42.42

M. Ferrero. Closed Sat lunch and Sun (11 Nov-30 March), 27 April-14 May and 9 Aug-3 Sep. Open until 10.30 pm. Private room: 35. Valet parking. V AE DC.

If you're looking for a winter treat, book a table here when Jean-Claude Ferrero is serving his famous 'all-truffle' menu. Throughout the winter months, this Second Empire *hôtel particulier* welcomes a faithful, very Parisian crowd avid to sample those irresistible, earthy delights. Less expensive and just as lustily flavourful are Ferrero's aïoli with salt cod, blanquette de veau à l'ancienne, and bœuf aux carottes, dishes which regularly feature on the prix-fixe lunch. But the third toque we bestow on Ferrero this year (long withheld 'because of irregularities') is for the more spirited, often ingenious creations that make dining here an adventure. An impulsive, moody chef, Ferrero has gained confidence and consistency as his restaurant has gained in stature, and it is now rare for a dish to disappoint. Allow us to suggest two of our favourite meals. The first would include cold prawns 'Monsieur le Préfet', followed by an assortment of fish sprinkled with saffron pistils, then truffled calf's foot and sweetbreads, rounded off with the dessert *du jour*. A second repast might begin with langoustes aux huiles douces, then proceed to a garlic-studded leg of Pauillac lamb served with a creamy gratin dauphinois. But there are plenty of other marvellous offerings to choose from (bouillabaisse raphaëloise, sea bass à la porquerollaise...). Our sole quibble is that desserts do not always live up to the standards set by the rest.

A la carte: 500 F and up. Menus: 220 F (lunch only), 550 F (all mushrooms), 830 F (all truffle).

12/20 Les Filaos
5, rue G.-de-Maupassant – 45.04.94.53
M. Ruch. Closed Sun and 2 weeks in Aug. Terrace dining. Air cond. V.

The dining room is tidy and neat, the cuisine straight from the islands–it's spicy Creole fare (deliciously fiery rougails) with a strong Indian influence (Madras-style curry). The savoury pork curry with red beans will put tropical sunshine in your veins and fire in your belly!

A la carte: 200 F. Menu: 78 F (lunch only).

La Fontaine d'Auteuil
35 bis, rue La Fontaine – 42.88.04.47
M. Grégoire. Closed Sat lunch, Sun, 10-17 Feb and 4-23 Aug. Open until 10.15 pm. Private room: 15. V AE DC.

Shy, modest Xavier Grégoire, late of the Hilton's Toit de Paris, has spread his wings since he came to this flowery establishment next to the Maison de la Radio. Try his marinated sardines–rollmop style–his pan-fried coquilles St-Jacques sprinkled with chopped nuts and garlic, his luscious vanilla ice cream, and an airy millefeuille made with whipped single cream. An extra point this year, though service is still a bit stand-offish. Good little cellar.

A la carte: 350 F. Menu: 170 F (lunch only).

Chez Géraud
31, rue Vital – 45.20.33.00
M. Rongier. Closed Sat and Sun. Annual closings not available. Open until 10 pm. Air cond. V.

Right across the street from Jean-Claude Ferrero, Gérard Rongier has converted a former bakery into a small neighbourhood restaurant complete with banquettes, Sarreguemines tiles, immaculate napery, and attentive service. Géraud packs in an appreciative audience with his sole aux morilles, raie à la moutarde à l'ancienne, roast rabbit with garlic, and succulent roast Bresse chicken. And they keep coming back for more.

Fans of Côtes-du-Rhône, Savigny-lès-Beaune, or Pineau des Charentes (the latter a golden nectar to sip as an apéritif) will love the wine list. Desserts, though improved, still need work.

A la carte: 300 F.

Le Grand Chinois
6, av. de New-York – 47.23.98.21
Mme Tan. Closed Mon and 29 July-27 Aug. Open until 11 pm. Private room: 30. AE DC.

For a long time now, we've proclaimed this one of Paris's best Chinese restaurants–it is surely the most polished, with the most interesting food.

Colette Tan's huge menu contains some marvels of inventiveness, such as hot oysters with ginger, cabbage stuffed with shrimps and foie gras, minced pigeon, and pork spareribs with a pepper sauce. Or you can try the 398 F menu for two, which features crab claws, spring rolls, huge spicy shrimps, Peking duck, and Cantonese rice. Splendid wines, stylish and courteous service. A second toque.

A la carte: 300 F and up. Menus: 120 F (weekdays lunch only), 398 F (for 2 pers), and from 302 F to 1380 F (for 2 and 4 pers).

La Grande Cascade
Bois de Boulogne
Near the race-track – 45.27.33.51
M. Menut. Closed 20 Dec-20 Jan. Open until 10.30 pm. Private room: 50. Garden dining. Valet parking. V AE DC.

In springtime everyone (it seems) heads to the half-moon terrace of Napoleon III's former pleasure pavilion, shaded by a graceful glass-and-iron marquee. This stylish Belle Epoque establishment offers the reassuring culinary repertoire of Jean Sabine, an enlightened classicist who doesn't mistake tradition for stuffiness. Try his fondant de lapereau au Chablis, roast sea bream with verjuice, sautéed veal kidneys, or rack of lamb with wild thyme. The cellar houses 80,000 bottles, service is formal, and though à la carte prices are anything but rustic, the set lunch is relatively economical.

A la carte: 600-800 F. Menu: 270 F (lunch only).

12/20 Le Jardin
(La Villa Maillot)
143, av. de Malakoff – 45.01.25.22
M. Beherec. Closed Sat, Sun and 3 Aug-2 Sep. Open until 10.30 pm. Private room: 20. Garden dining. Air cond. Valet parking. Telex 649808. V AE DC.

For over twenty years Loulou Bertho was God's gift to fish lovers at his seaside restaurant in Cagnes-sur-Mer. When he retired, a friend persuaded Bertho to come up to Paris to supervise food purchases and preparation at Le Jardin, the restaurant of La Villa Maillot, a former embassy converted into a tranquil, attractive hotel. In the plant-filled courtyard are twenty prettily set tables where the 'catch of the day' is served by a charming, professional staff: rougets en papillote, grilled sole, turbot à l'eau-sel. One or two meat dishes are usually offered as well. A good summer address.

A la carte: 300 F.

12/20 Les Jardins de Bagatelle
Bois de Boulogne
Parc de Bagatelle – 40.67.98.29
M. Bouquet. Closed 23 Dec-15 Jan. Open until 11 pm. Private room: 120. Garden dining. Parking. V.

Under the chestnut trees, a stone's throw from the famous Bagatelle rose garden, this expensive eatery offers (only just) decent, awfully banal dishes (overcooked sea bream with mangoes and–yawn–kiwis, lotte aux petits légumes). For the summertime.

A la carte: 350 F. Menu: 250 F (Sun only).

Patrick Lenôtre
28, rue Duret – 45.00.17.67
M. Lenôtre. Closed Sat lunch and Sun. Open until 11 pm. Air cond. V AE DC.

Patrick Lenôtre won't forget 1990, the year that unsightly scaffolding disfigured his restaurant, and his patrons were serenaded between courses by a pneumatic drill. He might have been tempted to throw in the towel, had it not been for a third toque that brought him a 30 per cent increase in business over 1989. So it was with a light heart that this autumn he opened for the new season with a bright, light, spanking-new décor.

Patrick, a member of the illustrious Lenôtre family (he's Gaston's nephew), juggles adeptly with flavours and comes up with such tantalising innovations as a galette de lapereau aux aromates, ris de veau et foie gras braisés en demi-glace, and saumon caramélisé au jus d'ail et de soja. Beautiful desserts, costly but expertly selected wines. The two less expensive set meals are generous and appealing.

A la carte: 320-550 F. Menus: 220 F (lunch only), 460 F (dinner only), 260 F.

Marius
13
82, bd Murat — 46.51.67.80
MM. Grandjean and Gourbin. Closed Sat lunch, Sun and Aug. Open until 10.30 pm. Terrace dining. V.
Come summer, the bright little dining room is enlarged by a terrace, nicely shaded by a row of spindle-trees. New owners have brought a youthful, energetic tone to this old bouillabaisse institution, and have bucked up the quality considerably (the prices remain reasonable, we are glad to report). Try the wonderfully bracing crab salad, or the simple, satisfying smoked haddock with butter sauce. The delicious desserts win a toque this year. Smiling (but often slow) service.

A la carte: 280-300 F.

12/20 Mexico Café
1, pl. de Mexico — 47.27.96.98
Mme Jabouille. Open every day. Open until midnight. Terrace dining. Valet parking. V.
An amusing retro décor, attentive service, and a pro in the kitchen: fresh pasta salad, andouillette, magret de canard. An extra point for this cheerful spot, beloved of young trendies.

A la carte: 200-250 F. Menu: 125 F (lunch only).

Al Mounia
13
16, rue de Magdebourg — 47.27.57.28
M. Sahri. Closed Sun and 12 July-1 Sep. Open until 11 pm. Private room: 35. Air cond. No pets. V AE.
The owner, his chef, and the sous-chef all hail from Casablanca. They produce some fine tajines and a delectable lamb couscous served in a seductive Moorish setting. A tiny cellar offers the usual Moroccan wines.

A la carte: 300 F.

Passy-Mandarin
13
6, rue Bois-le-Vent — 42.88.12.18
M. Vong Vai Pui. Closed 2 weeks in Aug. Open until 11.15 pm. Air cond. V AE.
Lots of local colour in the three gay, flower-decked dining rooms. Dashing white-coated waiters serve forth dishes prepared by a chef at the top of his form. Highly original stews (cocks' combs, fish...), lotte with soy beans, and flawless lacquered pigeon earn the Mandarin a toque this year.

A la carte: 250-280 F.

Le Pergolèse
13
40, rue Pergolèse — 45.00.21.40
M. Dupré. Closed Sat dinner, Sun and 10-19 Aug. Open until 10.30 pm. Private room: 25. V AE.
The pastel-pink décor of this stylish establishment is as well-bred as the service. A *bon genre* (read: Sloane Ranger) clientele converses in hushed tones while the chef effortlessly trots out agreeable, undemanding fare: crêpe au saumon,

faultless brandade de morue, and a delectably light confection of pears and puff pastry. Excellent house bread.

A la carte: 350 F. Menus: 200 F (wine inc), 158 F, 305 F.

Le Petit Bedon
16
38, rue Pergolèse — 45.00.23.66
M. Marchesseau. Closed Sat, Sun and Aug. Open until 10.15 pm. Air cond. V AE DC.
Chef Pierre Marchesseau is known for his television appearances and as a writer of cookery books. He has won over the chic clientele of Le Petit Bedon's little dining room (the décor is straight out of *House and Garden*) with his spirited renditions of culinary classics: filets de rouget à la fondue de foie gras et d'oignon, duck with lentils, rack of lamb with gratin dauphinois, poularde au vin jaune. His desserts—profiteroles au chocolat, honey-caramel-pistachio ice cream, cherry fondue—will titillate even the most jaded tastebuds. A fine cellar, professional service, dizzying prices.

A la carte: 350-600 F. Menu: 200 F (lunch only).

11/20 Le Petit Victor-Hugo
143, av. V.-Hugo — 45.53.02.68
M. Saul. Closed Sun and Aug. Open until midnight. Terrace dining. V.
Chic neighbourhood, chic crowd. But the food at this bistro is down-to-earth and generous: calf's-head salad, lamb curry, blanquette de veau. Friendly but courteous service.

A la carte: 200-230 F. Menu: 110 F.

La Petite Tour
14
11, rue de la Tour — 45.20.09.31
M. Israël. Closed dim and Aug. Open until 10.30 pm. V AE DC.
This is not the most rollicking spot in town, nor even in the neighbourhood, but the upper-crust clientele likes it well enough. Freddy Israël, a chef who has always preferred seriousness and consistency to flights of fancy, serves a well-made, classic repertoire, including a palatable bœuf à la mode, blanquette de veau, game in season, and some good fish dishes.

A la carte: 350-400 F.

Le Port Alma
15
10, av. de New-York — 47.23.75.11
M. Canal. Closed Sun and Aug. Open until 10.30 pm. Private room: 15. V AE DC.
'Scandalous', we wrote last year, having noticed all the empty seats in one of the finest fish restaurants in town. Luckily, a lot of Parisian seafood aficionados took our protest to heart, for things are definitely looking up in this bright (too bright? maybe even loud?) dining room. Mme Canal's welcome is lovely and warm, and the astonishingly fresh crustaceans and fish are prepared with a light touch by the Dôme's former chef. Sample the engaging crab soup, or scallops and truffles arranged on a 'bouquet' of lamb's lettuce, bonito enlivened with tomato and basil, pan-fried red mullet with courgettes, and for dessert, walnut crème brûlée or a thin apple tart. Wash it all down with a bottle of Roger Neveu's Sancerre or an Hermitage from Guigal, and you'll be in for a real treat from a chef who doesn't skimp on quality ingredients, or mask their flavours with superfluous sauces. For committed carnivores the menu lists just one meat dish, but it is a côte de bœuf de Salers, some of the finest beef in France.

A la carte: 350-450 F. Menu: 230 F (lunch only).

Le Pré Catelan
Bois de Boulogne
Rte de Suresnes — 45.24.55.58

M. Lenôtre. Closed Sun dinner, Mon and Feb school holidays. Open until 10 pm. Private room: 30. Garden dining. Valet parking. Telex 614983. V AE DC.

Why, we wonder, has a certain red-jacketed guidebook given Colette Lenôtre and her young chef, Denis Bernal, such a hard time? The only change at the Pré Catelan is the newly—beautifully—redesigned garden, now one of the most engaging outdoor dining spots in Paris. The welcome, the service, the floral arrangements are all flawless, both in the Belle Epoque dining room and in the charming orangerie.

Denis Bernal, who worked beside Michel Guérard before joining Lenôtre twelve years ago, brought new zest to a repertoire on the brink of tedium. You say that roast prawns with walnut oil and lemon is not the discovery of the century? Granted, but how perfectly they are cooked; how sublimely delicate they taste! The coquilles St-Jacques with pink peppercorns, lobster à la nage de Sauternes, and the sea bass coated with a magical powder of ground spices and mushrooms couldn't be better. Bernal's rognon de veau rosé au pain de poireau, and his golden tourte of sweetbreads with lemon thyme are brimful of flavour. And Colette's papa Gaston has done what we've asked, putting much less sugar in his chocolate. The 'dessert noir intense, crème grains de café' is sheer heaven; and the stuffed crêpes and griottines en coulis should be savoured with bowed head and grateful spirit!. The cellar is large, with manageable prices. But don't fool yourself—depending on how recklessly you order, the bill may add up to more than you can swallow!

A la carte: 600-850 F. Menus: 600 F, 750 F.

11/20 Le Presbourg
3, av. de la Grande-Armée — 45.00.36.40

M. Chaunion. Open every day. Open until 1 am. Private room: 30. Terrace dining. V AE DC.

A large, bright brasserie with a neo-colonial décor and an elegant greenhouse-style terrace that overlooks the Arc de Triomphe. The exorbitantly tariffed cuisine is less edifying than the view, but the shellfish (fresh year round) is reasonable, and the calf's head is decent.

A la carte: 300 F.

Quach
47, av. R.-Poincaré
47.27.98.40

M. Quach. Closed Sat lunch. Open until 11 pm. Air cond. V AE DC.

Aquariums decorate this dining room where Mr Quach prepares some delectable little Cantonese dishes: shrimps grilled with lemon grass, squid with red peppers, and five-flavour grilled lamb. Prices are quite reasonable—for the neighbourhood.

A la carte: 230 F. Menus: 78 F (weekdays only), 99 F.

12/20 Ramponneau
21, av. Marceau
47.20.59.51

M. Bou Antoun. Open every day. Open until 10.15 pm. Terrace dining. Air cond. Valet parking. V AE DC.

Ramponneau's Rabelaisian décor brings to mind those hearty, endless, quintessentially French banquets that had their heyday in the Belle Epoque. Tourists and visitors love the plentiful dishes of foie gras, quenelles de lotte américaine, and magret au poivre vert.

A la carte: 350 F.

Le Relais d'Auteuil
(Patrick Pignol)
31, bd Murat — 46.51.09.54

M. Pignol. Closed Sat lunch, Sun and 10-30 Aug. Open until 10.30 pm. V.

Young Patrick Pignol is a young chef in a hurry, eager to earn recognition for his inventive, resolutely contemporary cuisine. His dishes often combine flavours in provocative, unexpected ways that can perk up the most jaded appetite. Two red toques, then, for Pignol's spirited rougets-barbets au Pinot Noir, suave coquilles St-Jacques with celery essence, and millefeuille of caramelised pears and almond cream. All the dishes are most attractively presented, with painstaking attention to detail; but the menu is mercifully free of overblown descriptions.

A la carte: 400-450 F. Menus: 150 F (lunch only), 330 F.

11/20 Le Relais du Bois
1, rue G.-de-Maupassant — 45.04.27.60

M. Georgelin. Closed Sun dinner, Mon, Aug and 22 Dec-2 Jan. Open until 10.30 pm. Terrace dining. V.

A worthy, sturdy cuisine: moules à la crème, andouillette ardéchoise, escalope à la florentine. The *patron* is charming, the clientele wonderful, the tables set convivially close. Tasty, low-priced wines.

A la carte: 160 F.

12/20 Le Relais du Bois
Bois de Boulogne, Croix-Catelan
Rte de Suresnes — 40.50.19.56

Mme Chipponi. Open every day. Open until 11 pm. Private room: 300. Terrace dining. V.

This rustic rendezvous—an old Napoleon III pavilion where naughty ladies and gents once engaged in rather outrageous behaviour—is now the backdrop for tame family parties and old-boy banquets. The comfortable dining room has its charms, but the huge summer garden is truly delightful. Good—if unexciting—food: fish soup, grilled andouillette, confit de canard.

A la carte: 180-230 F.

Le Relais du Parc
(Hôtel Park Avenue)
55-57, av. R.-Poincaré — 45.53.44.60

M. Pelouard. Closed Sat, Sun and holidays. Open until 10 pm. Private room: 250. Garden dining. Air cond. Telex 643862. V AE DC.

Surprise: the spanking-new façade of this luxury hotel conceals a pretty little park and a lovely terraced *salle à manger* for outdoor dining in fine weather. The decorative, soignée cooking is by Hachemi Mostefaï, whose salade de petite-pêche, duck pot-au-feu, and tournedos au jus de truffe are not exactly adventuresome, but light and fresh as today's tastes demand.

A la carte: 350 F. Menu: 180 F.

Robuchon
32, rue de Longchamp
47.27.12.27

19.5   *M. Robuchon. Closed Sat, Sun and 1-29 July. Open until 10 pm. Private room: 15. Air cond. V.*

Will the Japanese lure Robuchon from Paris? It's no laughing matter. He has always had a soft spot for the land of the Rising Sun, ever since his days at the Hotel Nikko, where we were the first to salute his emerging talent. At Jamin, he hired a Japanese architectural firm to redo the interior decoration, and he is currently involved in a project with his friend Jean-Claude Vrinat of Taillevent, to launch a restaurant in Tokyo, in a little Chambord-style 'château' complete with French gardens.... Rest assured, Robuchon won't actually live in Japan but nevertheless, at 45 this highly organised individual is preparing for the day—still a secret—when he will hang up his apron to write *the* cookbook and become a much-sought-after restaurant consultant.

All the more reason, then, to hurry and put your name on the interminable waiting-list presided over by manager Jean-Jacques Caimant. Do not pretend to be a personal friend of François Mitterrand, or Jacques Chirac's long-lost cousin—it won't get you a table. There's nothing for it but to wait patiently until the day when you too can be one of the 45 privileged people seated in the celadon-coloured dining room or in the charming first-floor private salon that seats fifteen.

We've said everything there is to say about Robuchon's brilliant talent, we've praised his technique, his taste for perfection, and the passion for detail which he dins into his disciples like a drill sergeant. But what stuns us still is this fantastic artisan's (he's too modest to call himself an artist) powers to thrill and surprise us at every visit.

The first time one tastes his crab perfumed with thyme, saffron, and curry, or the sesame sole, or a poulet de Bresse au jus à l'ancienne et aux truffes, one might understandably think that one has reached the summit—but then next time Robuchon astounds us once again with his soupe chaude à la gelée de poule, which the intense tastes of truffle and black pepper push to a paroxysm of flavours. Each mouthful of his spaghetti tossed with prawns and white truffles, his roast milk-fed kid with a persillade of green garlic, or his farm-reared guinea hen set atop a slice of roast foie gras will make you groan with delight.

Frankly, we would love to catch him out just once—but no luck. Neither the tarte aux truffes aux oignons et lard fumé, nor the homard meunière au chou chinois in its delicate saffron-scented bouillon, nor the béatilles de canard aux lentilles, nor the touted mashed potatoes (often imitated, never duplicated!) is open to the slightest criticism, any more than desserts like the turban de pommes à la cannelle, the feuillantine au chocolat, Robuchon's peerless crème brûlée, or the wines chosen with unmatched flair by sommelier Antoine Hernandez.

Gone, however, is the legendary 160 F set lunch. Today's soaring prices may well appal you, but this degree of perfection is necessarily costly. And remember, to serve 45 diners, Joël Robuchon employs a staff of 35.

A la carte: 600-1,000 F. Menus: 950 F (truffles), 790 F.

12/20 Shogun
(Bateau Nomadic)
Port Debilly, av. de New-York
47.20.05.04
M. Kawai. Closed Mon. Open until 10.30 pm. Private room: 12. Air cond. No pets. Parking. Telex 648442. V AE DC.

The Seine flows under foot and the Eiffel Tower glitters beyond the windows—otherwise Shogun's décor is modern and fairly ordinary. The best seats are in the 'grill' area, where chefs prepare dishes to order on their hotplates. Indifferent roast duck, good tempuras and raw fish.

A la carte: 350-550 F. Menus: 210 F (lunch only), 280 F, 380 F, 590 F.

Sous l'Olivier
15, rue Goethe — 47.20.84.81
M. Warnault. Closed Sat, Sun and holidays. Open until 10.30 pm. Terrace dining. V AE.

We aren't wild about the new Nile-green décor and the harsh lighting that does little for patrons' complexions, but summer lunches on the terrace are engagingly lively. The food is uneven, seasonings in particular lack gusto; but the crab pâté with braised leeks, the herring fillets with warm potatoes and bacon, and the chocolate feuillantine are more than creditable.

A la carte: 300-330 F. Menu: 165 F (dinner only).

Le Sully d'Auteuil
78, rue d'Auteuil
46.51.71.18
M. Brunetière. Closed Sat lunch and Sun. Open until 10.45 pm. Private room: 80. Terrace dining. Air cond. V AE.

The exaggeratedly precious nomenclature of the overlong menu has been toned down a bit, but Gyl Bourgeois remains faithful to the spirit of a sauce-rich—technically accomplished—cuisine. The rich note blends in perfectly with the emphatically elegant décor set in place by Michel Brunetière in this idyllic pavilion attached to the Auteuil railway station. There's an attractive summer terrace, and a large clientele which is not put off by staggering bills for sweetbreads sauce ivoire with fresh pasta and asparagus, or bar à la crème d'oursins au Chablis, or calf's head sauce tortue with essence of sherry. Luscious desserts.

A la carte: 500 F.

12/20 La Table d'Hôte
16, rue Lauriston
45.01.68.20
M. Robineau. Closed Sat lunch, Sun, 8 days in Aug and in Dec. Open until 10.30 pm. V DC.

A white ceiling, pink walls, and a light parquet floor lend a slightly chilly air to this otherwise agreeable spot. The menu is well conceived and generously served: we especially recommend the gratinée de tourteau en compote and a tender émincé de bœuf aux cèpes. Excellent wines selected by Jean-Luc Pouteau.

A la carte: 250-300 F. Menu: 135 F.

Le Toit de Passy

94, av. Paul-Doumer
45.24.55.37
M. Jacquot. Closed Sat lunch, Sun, 12-25 Aug and 21 Dec-6 Jan. Open until 10.30 pm. Private room: 25. Terrace dining. Air cond. Valet parking. V.

Check your bank-balance before sitting down to an à la carte meal at Yannick Jacquot's rooftop restaurant. If you're feeling flush, go ahead and treat yourself to a meal in this pleasant, plant-filled dining room, with a large terrace overlooking Paris. Jacquot is not an innovator, but he has a nearly infallible knack for combining flavours. Try his exquisite consommé de langoustines en gelée de petits légumes, his young pigeon baked in a salt crust, or his parfait glacé à la badiane en feuillantine. The cellar holds 45,000 bottles, so the wine list will take some perusing. Good cigars, too.

A la carte: 500 F and up. Menus: 255 F and 295 F (lunch only), 455 F.

12/20 Vi Foc
33, rue de Longchamp
47.04.96.81
M. Té Vépin. Closed 8-23 Aug. Open until 10.45 pm. Air cond. V AE DC.

The red wall hangings have been replaced with white leather, which gives this Thai-Chinese restaurant a luminous, though rather antiseptic look. The welcome and service are not Vi Foc's strong point, but the Peking duck with lemon grass and the crab fritters are worth the trip.

A la carte: 260 F. Menus: 78 F, 98 F and 120 F (lunch only).

Villa Vinci

23, rue Paul-Valéry
45.01.68.18
M. Fayet. Closed Sat, Sun and Aug. Open until 10.30 pm. Air cond. No pets. V.

A business crowd at lunch and an up-market local clientele in the evening frequent this comfortable, luxurious restaurant. Though the pasta is still remarkable, the hors-d'œuvres are ordinary, and the Venetian calf's liver bland and pedestrian. Desserts (like tiramisù) save the day, along with the rich and varied Italian cellar.

A la carte: 360 F. Menu: 170 F (lunch only).

Vivarois
192, av. V.-Hugo
45.04.04.31
M. Peyrot. Closed Sat, Sun and end-July to beg Sep. Open until 9.45 pm. Air cond. Parking. V AE DC.

If we'd known how happy and serene a fourth toque would make chef Claude Peyrot, we would have awarded it sooner. His life has changed, his restaurant is full, and he's no longer talking of retiring to his native Ardèche or of opening a bistro at the North Pole. This marvellous chef sticks faithfully to a concise repertoire enriched daily with dishes created on the spur of the moment. On a given day the maître d'hotel might announce the presence of a terrine chaude de légumes à l'huile d'olive, a fabulous pied de cochon en crépine, or succulent little morsels of calf's head in a crisp, diaphanous pastry that takes one's tastebuds to the limits of lusciousness. Neither classic nor modern, this cuisine is uniquely Peyrot's. An unrivalled technician, he also possesses a sensitivity and grace all his own. To add to the pleasure, there are wines, magnificent and modest, discovered by wine steward extraordinaire Jean-Claude Vinadier, and served under the benevolent but vigilant eye of Mme Peyrot. We are relieved to report that the much-criticised décor is due for a change. Here's hoping that the cold, contemporary furnishings will be replaced by something more sprightly and warm.... Stay tuned.

A la carte: 550-700 F. Menu: 315 F (lunch only, wine inc).

PARIS   17th

11/20 Ahlen
42, rue des Dames
43.87.91.79
M. Ennam-Li. Closed Sun. Open until 11 pm. Terrace dining. Air cond. V.

The décor is less North African than country French. A hospitable chef-proprietor produces generous pigeon pastillas, quail and grape tajines, and tasty couscous with spit-roasted meats.

A la carte: 180 F. Menus: 69 F (lunch only), 119 F.

12/20 Alexandros
18, rue St-Ferdinand — 45.74.75.11
Mme Alexandros. Lunch only (and dinner Thu, Fri and Sat until 10 pm). Closed Sun and 3-26 Aug.

Plain, lusty food—the sort that Greeks thrive upon, but which is so hard to find outside those blessed isles. Try the good pikilias (assorted hors-d'œuvres), the brochette of suckling pig with two vegetables, or the appealing salt cod with olives. Interesting and inexpensive Greek wines.

A la carte: 100-120 F.

Amphyclès
78, av. des Ternes — 40.68.01.01
M. Groult. Closed Sat lunch, Sun and 1-21 Aug. Open until 10.30 pm. Air cond. Parking. V.

As we write, the promised new décor is still under construction. The important thing is that Amphyclès—named after a cook-philosopher of ancient Greece—is currently one of the hottest attractions on the city's gastronomic scene.

Chef Philippe Groult's cuisine resembles its author: strong, full of character, absolutely unaffected, and often diabolically subtle. His deft way with herbs and spices lends extra spark to daring liaisons of textures and tastes. But the couplings are never gratuitous, witness the well-matched ravioli of pigeon and crayfish, admirable dishfellows though one wonders why they're blanketed with a dull veal-based sauce. Groult injects bland perch and potatoes with a jolt of flavour from dill, chives, and shallots touched with vinegar. Divine. And true bliss is assured with the very first forkful of his mitonnée de porcelet aux condiments, or the exemplary canard de Challans à l'orange.

Cheeses are something special here, and desserts are over-the-moon: caramelised apples with almonds, soufflé chaud au chocolat, simple yet sublime vanilla ice cream. The cellar is still young but interesting, overseen by a shrewd young sommelier who trained with Robuchon, Guérard, and Lameloise. A final tip: Groult's set lunch is one of the best deals in town.

A la carte: 450-600 F. Menus: 220 F (lunch only), 380 F.

Apicius
122, av. de Villiers — 43.80.19.66
M. Vigato. Closed Sat, Sun and Aug. Open until 10 pm. Air cond. Valet parking. V AE.

Jean-Pierre Vigato is film-star handsome, but this shy *cuisinier* has eschewed 'stardom', preferring to keep hard at work in his kitchen. Vigato is a master of two distinct but complementary culinary styles: an imaginative, modern, highly refined register, and a heartier, more rustic mode steeped in the traditions of the French countryside. They coexist in harmony, and both bear Vigato's unmistakable stamp, whether it's the robust pâté de lièvre en terrine or the delicate gelée de coquillages et de crustacés à l'eau de mer—the latter invented, barring error, by Marc Meneau—, the light and engaging steamed skate garnished with fruit and capers, or a full-flavoured filet de bœuf napped with a beefy sauce. For our money, Vigato's cooking is better than ever—a recent fabulous meal (lamb carpaccio with Parmesan on a salad of fresh herbs; plump prawns flash-fried in a diaphanous batter of spices, Japanese flour, and egg white; spiced steamed cod; crisp morsels of sweetbreads with a light crumb coating, parsley essence, tarragon, and chervil) has earned him an extra point. In the dessert league, Vigato's crème craquante à la cannelle et aux cerises confits takes top honours. Apicius is usually packed with the Paris carriage trade, who know a good thing when they taste it. Madeleine Vigato supervises the two warmly decorated dining rooms with smiling courtesy, although this year some of our readers have complained of slow service. One last reproach: the prix-fixe lunch is excessively expensive.

A la carte: 450-700 F. Menus: 380 F (lunch only), 450 F (dinner only).

A l'Arcade
18, rue Bayen – 45.72.02.19

M. Albistur. Closed Sat lunch, Sun and 5-31 Aug. Open until 10 pm. Private room: 22. Air cond. V.

In a dainty pink-and-peach décor lavishly bedecked with flowers, Danielle and Louis Albistur entertain the neighbourhood's large business population at lunchtime (given the prices, we reckon that many of the patrons are provided with expense accounts...). What the cuisine lacks in imagination it makes up for in finesse: Treviso lettuce with prawn feuilletés, rognon de veau aux aromates, and a thin hot fruit tart (a former pâtissier, Albistur is a magician with puff pastry).

A la carte: 350-400 F. Menu: 190 F.

Chez Augusta
98, rue de Tocqueville – 47.63.39.97

M. Berton. Closed Sat lunch, Sun, holidays and 3 Aug-2 Sep. Open until 10 pm. Air cond. V.

Scrupulously seasonal, rigorously precise, based on sumptuous, sparkling seafood: Lionel Maître's cuisine is all this and more. Desserts, somewhat neglected in the past, have vastly improved; and the fricassée of sole and prawns scented with summer savory, the saffron-tinctured red mullet and courgettes, the lemony steamed sea bass with chervil, and the monumental house bouillabaisse have hoisted Augusta high into the ranks of the best fish restaurants in Paris. Lionel Maître is still young yet his technique is astonishingly mature. And he is quite a taskmaster too, judging from the choleric commands that resound in the kitchen (and sometimes carry into the slightly fusty blue dining room). The cellar boasts a superb collection of white wines. An extra point for Augusta this year.

A la carte: 450-500 F.

La Barrière de Clichy
1, rue de Paris
92110 Clichy – 47.37.05.18

M. Le Gallès. Closed Sat lunch and Sun. Open until 10 pm. Private room: 15. Air cond. V AE DC.

Superchefs Guy Savoy and Bernard Loiseau cut their milk-teeth here. Now in charge of the Barrière's kitchen is 32-year-old Gilles Le Gallès, who trained with Loiseau.... The establishment suffers from being cut off by the ring road that slices Paris off from Clichy. Confronted with that concrete problem Gilles Le Gallès's preferred weapons are patience—and his talent to surprise. His light, inventive cuisine (he prefers cooking juices to sauces) is marked by interesting marriages: tiny squid stuffed with chicken livers on a bed of courgette fondue, escargots paired with ris de veau, fillets of young rabbit matched with Camembert, or goat cheese with lamb. Most chefs couldn't pull it off, but Le Gallès does—beautifully. The menu lists a few classics too: warm oysters wrapped in spinach leaves and dressed with shallot vinaigrette, salmon steak with sea salt, and pigeonneau aux choux. To finish, bold and conservative tastes alike cast their votes for the tarte fine Verger aux pommes. Warning: some readers

complain of slow service, and a chilly welcome.

A la carte: 350-450 F. Menus: 250 F (lunch only, wine inc), 350 F.

Les Béatilles
127, rue Cardinet – 42.27.95.64

M. Bochaton. Closed Sat lunch, Sun, 29 July-18 Aug and 1 week in winter. Open until 10.15 pm. V DC.

A light, easily digestible, nearly irreproachable cuisine that aims for simplicity. Join the well-heeled neighbourhood crowd that forgathers around pretty tables in the small, sober, white dining rooms for asperges sauce mousseline, pike gâteau with a silken, lemony beurre blanc citronné, and rich tourte de canard feuilletée à la vinaigrette de jus de viande. Come time for pudding, a gingery charlotte aux épices (a sort of crumble) will make you happy you came.

A la carte: 300 F. Menus: 120 F (lunch only), 300 F (dinner only).

Billy Gourmand
20, rue de Tocqueville – 42.27.03.71

M. Billy. Closed Sat lunch and Sun. Annual closings not available. Open until 10.30 pm. Private room: 14. Air cond. V.

Philippe Billy, a young pupil of Jacques Chibois and Claude Deligne, has managed to elbow his way into an already restaurant-saturated *quartier*. Against a backdrop of mirrors and large potted plants you can choose from a classical yet personalised menu: a fragrant ragoût of baby scallops and mussels with fresh herbs, perch with crisp cabbage, fillet of Angus beef, and some pleasing traditional desserts. Good wines by the glass.

A la carte: 300-350 F.

Le Bistrot d'à Côté
10, rue G.-Flaubert – 42.67.05.81

M. Rostang. Closed Sat (lunch only Sep-April) and 1 week in Aug. Open until 11.30 pm. Terrace dining. Telex 649629. V.

All you want from a bistro: hustle, bustle, and cheeky waiters. After a slight falling off this cheery eatery has bounced back to become a perfect Lyonnais-style bistro with a few unexpected dishes—lamb curry mauricienne—thrown in for good measure. The hearty assiette de langue et pied de veau, the galette de maïs au saumon, and the good crème brûlée win back the lost toque this year. But the wines are too expensive for this sort of establishment. Another Bistrot d'à Côté is located at 16, avenue de Villiers, 47.63.25.61.

A la carte: 230 F.

Le Bistrot de l'Etoile
75, av. Niel – 42.27.88.44

MM. Savoy and Gensdarmes. Closed Sat lunch and Sun. Open until midnight. Terrace dining. Air cond. Valet parking. V.

Guy Savoy has gone into partnership with his former pupil, Bruno Gensdarmes, to assure the success of this bistro, now as popular as the one on Rue Troyon. Try the museau ravigote au chou craquant, the gratin d'épaule d'agneau aux aubergines, and some sublime desserts. The house wine, a Merlot, is served 'en pot', Lyonnais-fashion; other choices from the limited cellar are rather pricey.

A la carte: 250 F.

Le Bistrot de l'Etoile
13, rue Troyon – 42.67.25.95

M. Savoy. Closed Sat lunch and Sun. Open until midnight. Air cond. Valet parking. V.

Wonderfully old-fashioned bistro cuisine given a youthful touch by William Ledeuil, who spent three years with Guy Savoy. The latter oversees this successful and busy bistro from his own establishment across the street. Specialities include cuisse de canard aux haricots rouges, thon poêlé, and a pudding aux griottes. Drink the tasty house Merlot served in carafes.

A la carte: 250 F.

12/20 Le Cadre Noir

4, rue Gounod — 40.54.02.29
M. Maman. Closed Sat lunch and Sun. Open until 10.30 pm. Terrace dining. V.

It would be hard to find a more clever or varied menu—85 F for an entrée and a main dish—than the one on offer in this discreetly elegant little restaurant. Too bad the tiny wine list doesn't follow suit. Delectable terrine de tourteau au safran, and a good noisette de veau à la galette d'artichaut. An extra point this year.

A la carte: 180 F.

Charly de Bab-el-Oued

95, bd Gouvion-St-Cyr — 45.74.34.62
M. Driguès. Open every day. Open until midnight. Air cond. No-smoking section. No pets. V AE DC.

An inviting place to dream of the *Arabian Nights'* amidst colourful tiles, cedarwood, and palm trees. Feast on excellent couscous and tajines. The sweet Oriental pastries are made on the spot, and are always fresh. Perfect service.

A la carte: 200-220 F.

Clos Longchamp

(Hôtel Méridien)
81, bd Gouvion-St-Cyr — 40.68.30.40
M. Coulon. Closed Sun. Open until 10.30 pm. Private room: 20. Air cond. No pets. Valet parking. Telex 651952. V AE DC.

As luck would have it, chef Jean-Marie Meulien was away last year when we visited his restaurant; this year, our booking coincided with his day off. Still, his absences prove that whether this excellent fellow is on hand or not, his able team is trained to deliver the goods with admirable consistency. You may thus in full confidence book a table overlooking the new circular garden in the heart of the hulking concrete Hôtel Méridien, and give yourselves over to the joys of a marbré de foie de canard au Beaumes-de-Venise, grenouilles et mousse de brochet en feuille d'épinard in a tangy sauce, a daurade au vin jaune, an étouffée de pigeon en feuilleté, or a whole veal kidney delicately braised in its own juices, a true gastronomic poem. The velouté au chocolat, the gratin d'agrumes, and the impressive bottles collected by sommelier Didier Bureau make a meal here a treat of the first order (but we shall harp on about the ugliness of the strange, banana-shaped dining room until someone decides to do something about it!).

A la carte: 450-700 F. Menus: 240 F (weekdays lunch only), 450 F (weekdays dinner only).

12/20 Le Congrès

80, av. de la Grande-Armée — 45.74.17.24
M. Joulie. Open every day, 24 hours. Air cond. Telex 649538. V AE DC.

A huge barracks-like brasserie, open all day and all night, vigilant about the consistent quality of its battle horses: shellfish (sparkling fresh year round) and large slabs of charcoal-grilled meats: beef fillets, T-bone steaks, and huge ribs of beef. A good tarte Tatin rounds things off nicely. The decent selection of inexpensive house wines will not empty your wallet.

A la carte: 250 F.

La Coquille

6, rue du Débarcadère — 45.72.10.73
M. Lausecker. Closed Sun, Mon, 27 July-3 Sep and 21 Dec-2 Jan. Open until 10.30 pm. Air cond. V AE.

There aren't many restaurants like this well-bred bistro where today's patrons may order exactly the same dishes enjoyed by their parents and grandparents. To wit: the eponymous coquilles St-Jacques au naturel, sea bass Escoffier, jugged hare, boudin grillé aux pommes, and the seemingly immortal hazelnut soufflé. Exceptional cellar.

A la carte: 350-400 F.

12/20 La Cote d'Amour

44, rue des Acacias — 42.67.15.40
M. Mathieu. Closed Sat lunch, Sun and 29 July-19 Aug. Open until 10.30 pm. V.

No real surprises from the young *patrons* whose unadventurous repertoire runs to the likes of tartare aux deux saumons or grilled steaks, with an occasional fashionable dish such as prawns flavoured with vanilla and fresh mint. Pretty dining room, friendly prices.

A la carte: 250 F.

Le Cougar

(Hôtel Centre Ville Etoile)
6-10, rue des Acacias — 47.66.74.14
M. Michaud. Closed Sat lunch and Sun. Open until 10.30 pm. Air cond. Telex 206968. V AE DC.

Taïra Kurihara, a brilliant star in the galaxy of Japanese practitioners of French cuisine, is engaged like many of his colleagues in turning out Gallic dishes influenced by master chefs (in this case, Robuchon, Cagna, Besson). Kurihara's technique has gained authority, and he has developed a knack for creating subtle flavours and vibrant seasonings. In view of all these assets, we shall overlook a few debits (a salad of terribly overcooked prawns), and encourage you to sample the perfect John Dory with rice vinegar and sesame oil, or fresh cod with seaweed and olive oil. The menu is deliberately short on meat dishes. Fine cellar, boring décor.

A la carte: 350 F. Menu: 145 F.

12/20 L'Ecrevisse

212 bis, bd Pereire — 45.72.17.60
M. Diuz. Closed Sat lunch and Sun. Open until 10.30 pm. Air cond. Parking. V AE DC.

The pink, picture-studded walls are the most appetising aspect of this establishment on the wane. We were disappointed by a tepid welcome, indifferent service, and a tarragon cream which appeared on our first-course leeks, then again on the main dish of turbot with nettles and wild mushrooms. The decent pear soufflé is not enough to save the toque.

A la carte: 300 F.

L'Ecrin d'Or

35, rue Legendre — 47.63.83.08
M. Castel. Closed Sat lunch, Mon and 10-27 Aug. Open until 11 pm. Private room: 16. Air cond. V AE.

Huge mirrors, mouldings, Venetian chandeliers, and great swathes of fabric make this a supremely comfortable restaurant, and the cuisine of the young chef, Gilles Cendres, is a pleasant discovery indeed. Alongside some excellent à la carte offerings—salade de jarret de veau, paupiettes de lapin—is a splendid choice of platters and set menus (On weekdays 96 F will buy you an appetiser followed by a main dish). Judicious cellar. A toque this year.

A la carte: 250-300 F. Menu: 140 F.

Epicure 108

108, rue Cardinet — 47.63.50.91
M. Tourette. Closed Sat lunch and Sun. Open until 10.30 pm. Private room: 12. No-smoking section. V.
Here's a quiet little restaurant with a pretty, well-lit interior and a decidedly up-market tone. The oft-changing menu attracts a good lunchtime turnout with consistent, palatable dishes (sometimes a bit shy on seasonings) like filets de rouget poêlés à la basquaise, a decorative panaché de poissons et de langoustines, and rabbit with almonds. Good cellar.
A la carte: 300 F. Menu: 210 F.

L'Etoile d'Or

(Hôtel Concorde-La Fayette)
3, pl. du Gal-Kœnig — 47.58.12.84
M. Blazy. Closed mid-July to mid-Aug. Open until 10.30 pm. Air cond. Valet parking. Telex 650892. V AE DC.
Jean-Claude Lhonneur left the Grand Véfour to take over from Joël Renty in the kitchen of this agreeable hotel restaurant. As always, the food here is perfectly acceptable, if not overflowing with personality. We shall wait and see how the new chef performs before we give our rating.
A la carte: 400-600 F. Menus: 220 F (lunch only), 340 F, 388 F, 543 F.

Faucher

123, av. de Wagram — 42.27.61.50
M. Faucher. Closed Sat lunch and Sun. Open until 10.30 pm. Terrace dining. Valet parking. V.
Gérard and Nicole Faucher have embraced the *beaux quartiers*: they are the proud new proprietors of a very handsome dining room embellished with paintings, sumptuous bouquets, and elegant napery. Nicole welcomes patrons while a bevy of nimble young waiters serve Gérard's clever, exciting cuisine: voluptuous soupe d'escargots au velouté de foie gras, gâteau de pommes Maxim's aux cuisses de grenouilles, homely smoked haddock with lentils, braised short ribs of beef ennobled with a beurre aux truffes. Desserts are equally gorgeous. The cellar is a bit too expensive, but the summer terrace is irresistible.
A la carte: 350-400 F. Menus: 180 F (lunch only, except holidays), 350 F.

12/20 Chez Fred

190 bis, bd Pereire — 45.74.20.48
M. Marc. Closed Sat lunch, Sun and 5-20 Aug. Open until 10.30 pm. Terrace dining. V AE DC.
An influx of trendies has not spoiled the service, the simplicity of the setting, or the heartwarming sincerity of Fred's cuisine: streaky bacon with lentils, pot-au-feu, and blanquette de veau. No-nonsense wines sold by the *pichet*.
A la carte: 200-250 F. Menu: 145 F (weekdays only, wine inc).

La Gazelle

9, rue Rennequin — 42.67.64.18
Mme Koffi. Closed Sat lunch and Sun. Open until midnight. Garage parking. V AE DC.
The prettiest, most distinguished and exotic African restaurant in Paris, La Gazelle boasts a surprising range of intensely flavourful dishes prepared by the *patronne*: n'dolé of dried salt cod with chopped bitter spinach, tender and delicious shrimps in a spicy sauce, marinated kid en papillote with African sweetcorn. Slow-paced service.
A la carte: 220-250 F. Menu: 85 F (lunch only).

Chez Georges

273, bd Pereire — 45.74.31.00
M. Mazarguil. Closed Aug. Open until 11.30 pm. Private room: 30. Terrace dining. V.
The quintessential brasserie-bistro with all its little flaws—some dishes a bit too expensive, appetisers lacking in zest, an upstairs dining room with all the warmth and charm of Siberia—and its immense virtues: an appealingly worn décor (downstairs, of course), an effervescent clientele (tourists, TV personalities, celebrities), and swift, professional waiters who set before one platefuls of picture-perfect bistro fare: heavenly saucisson chaud, juicy roast beef with gratin dauphinois, tête de veau, rare roast lamb with tender beans.
A la carte: 300 F.

12/20 Goldenberg

69, av. de Wagram — 42.27.34.79
M. Goldenberg. Open every day. Open until 11.30 pm. Private room: 80. Terrace dining. V.
Patrick Goldenberg creates a typically Yiddish ambience of good humour and nostalgia, Jewish jokes and anecdotes in which to enjoy delicious pastrami, corned beef, veal sausage, and all the other classics of Central Europe. There's an amusing takeaway delicatessen and a sunny terrace for fine weather....
A la carte: 180-200 F. Menu: 98 F (wine inc).

12/20 Le Gouberville

1, pl. Ch.-Fillion — 46.27.33.37
MM. Pilastre and Bellini. Closed Sun, Mon, 18 Feb-4 March and 4 Aug-2 Sep. Open until 10 pm. Terrace dining. V.
An inviting terrace looks out over the deliciously provincial *place* opposite Ste-Marie des Batignolles. The set menu provides excellent value for money, with duck rillettes and shallots, cassoulet, cheese, and œufs à la neige. A la carte options are more complicated, but nicely handled. Good service.
A la carte: 260-280 F. Menu: 135 F.

Le Gourmand Candide

6, pl. du Mal-Juin — 43.80.01.41
M. Deslot. Closed Sat lunch, Sun and Aug. Open until 10.30 pm. Private room: 50. Terrace dining. Parking. V AE DC.
Annick and Jean-Claude Deslot spare no effort to please their patrons. Jean-Claude turns out French classics that bear the stamp of his own strong personality, like crusty potato and celery galette with mussels and smoked salmon, or succulent queue de bœuf à la berrichonne. Modest but worthwhile wines.
A la carte: 400 F. Menu: 190 F (weekdays only).

La Gourmandine

26, rue d'Armaillé — 45.72.00.82
M. Dumonteil. Closed Sun, Mon and Aug. Open until 10.15 pm. Parking. V AE DC.
It wouldn't take very much to make this dainty pink dining room more cosy (better lighting would help). In the meantime Patrick Dumonteil's cooking is subtle, delicately seasoned, and ably executed. Sample his faultlessly classic salade de haricots verts aux langoustines, or a poêlée de coquilles St-Jacques aux petits légumes enhanced by a luscious crab sauce. Knowledgeably chosen wines.
A la carte: 350 F. Menus: 150 F (lunch only), 210 F (dinner only).

Guyvonne
14, rue de Thann – 42.27.25.43

M. Cros. Closed Sat, Sun, 15-31 July and 20 Dec-6 Jan. Open until 10 pm. Private room: 11. Terrace dining. V.

Guy Cros is a droll and charming chap, a great upholder of the classic culinary tradition. With renewed vigour, he has lately applied his skill to country dishes, updated traditional fare, and 'market-basket' cuisine. A large and faithful clientele flocks to Cros's (rather dreary) beige-and-blue dining room and to the terrace overlooking the Parc Monceau, for Guyvonne is justly considered one of the best seafood restaurants in Paris. No argument from us: we love the prawns with chanterelles and artichokes, the crayfish with chervil root, and the oysters aux 'truffes de Chine' (tasty little violet potatoes). Sweets are moreish, and the cellar is stocked with big Côtes-du-Rhônes.
A la carte: 350-400 F. Menu: 199 F.

L'Impatient
14, passage Geffroy-Didelot
43.87.28.10

MM. Ridard and Blouet. Closed Sat, Sun and 10-25 Aug. Open until 11 pm. V.

The new owners are a hard-working pair: they do everything themselves, from picking flowers to adorn their three comely art deco dining rooms, to gathering fresh fruits and vegetables, and then preparing them in novel, amusing ways: warm sardine terrine with apples, pithiviers de caille aux Granny Smith, gratin de semoule truffé. Good prix-fixe menus, attentive service.
A la carte: 230 F. Menus: 92 F, 112 F.

Chez Laudrin
154, bd Pereire – 43.80.87.40

M. Billaud. Closed Sat, Sun and 1-8 May. Open until 10.30 pm. Air cond. V AE.

Age settles gently but graciously over Jacques Billaud's 'yacht-club' dining room, his regional repertoire, and the moustachioed smile with which he has greeted customers for thirty-odd years. Wines are served by the magnum and tariffed by 'the centimetre' (that is, you pay for what you actually consume). Some of the best tripe dishes in Paris are made in this kitchen, as well as fresh cod with aïoli, and stuffed pigs' trotters with apples.
A la carte: 350-400 F.

12/20 Laurier de Chine
275, bd Pereire – 45.74.33.32

Mme Chik. Closed Sun. Open until 10.45 pm. Terrace dining. Air cond. V AE.

The cosy brown dining room of this charming establishment extends out onto a small terrace where chef Alain Chik shows off his considerable prowess. Try his grilled jumbo shrimps with onions, or the appetising pan-fried Peking dumplings.
A la carte: 180-230 F. Menu: 79 F (weekdays only).

Chez Lee
13, rue Rennequin
43.80.91.48

Mme Lee. Closed Sun and 2 weeks in Aug. Open until 11 pm. Air cond. V AE.

For highly original, light and flavourful Chinese cooking, come to see Mr Lee (and his associate, Mr Lo). Treat yourself to the unusual steamed dumplings, the shrimps with savoury salt, Szechuan duck, and pork in a spicy sauce served by slightly furtive black-garbed waiters in an eleg-ant purple dining room dotted with screens. Not a bad cellar.
A la carte: 160-180 F. Menus: 69 F (lunch only), 83 F (dinner only).

12/20 Chez Léon
32, rue Legendre – 42.27.06.82

M. Saccaro. Closed Sat, Sun, holidays, Feb school holidays and Aug. Open until 9.45 pm. Private room: 20. V DC.

A traditional bistro with the usual robust fare–terrines, tête de veau, and cassoulets. But our old friend Léon had better stop serving tough haricot beans with his gigot d'agneau, and pull the ears of the cook responsible for our unevenly baked apple tart! Service is pleasant, and so are the Beaujolais wines.
A la carte: 250 F. Menu: 155 F.

Le Madigan
22, rue de la Terrasse – 42.27.31.51

M. Lecœur. Closed Sat lunch and Sun. Open until 9.30 pm. Terrace dining. Air cond. No pets. V AE DC.

The owner is a music buff and his chef a fervent disciple of Escoffier. They have combined their talents to launch a perilous enterprise: the musical supper, a rarity in this city. At liqueur time, Le Madigan's sober yet sumptuous dining room is transformed into a concert hall. Hopeful young talents and international prize-winners take their place at the Steinway grand for what are often remarkable recitals. The bearded young chef ably turns out lush, nineteenth-century dishes: poached eggs Rossini, lobster Cardinal, and sweetbreads à la Demidoff. Top-notch ingredients and subtle preparation ensure a harmonious evening on every scale.
A la carte: 400 F. Menus: 250 F (wine inc), 150 F, 200 F.

Maître Corbeau
6, rue d'Armaillé – 42.27.19.20

MM. Giral and Guillet. Closed Sat lunch, Sun, 17-27 Feb and 28 July-21 Aug. Open until 10.30 pm. Private room: 25. Air cond. V AE.

What's new on 'Master Raven's' luxurious perch? More flowers, and candlelight at evening in the splendid, wood-panelled dining room. Owners Paul Giral and Michel Guillet have encouraged their excellent young chef, Julien Vasquez, to overcome his timidity, and let his talent and imagination shine in dishes like a garlicky soup of lobster and tiny squid with fresh fava beans, suckling pig with sage, Pyrenees lamb served in two courses (first the thyme-scented trotter, followed by the roast fillet on a bed of greens), and croustillants de chocolat au whisky. Good set meals.
A la carte: 350-400 F. Menus: 160 F (lunch only), 280 F (wine inc), 210 F.

Le Manoir de Paris
6, rue P.-Demours – 45.72.25.25

M. Vandenhende. Closed Sat lunch (and dinner in summer) and Sun. Open until 10.30 pm. Private room: 50. Air cond. Valet parking. V AE DC.

When chef Philippe Groult left the Manoir to open his own Amphyclès just down the road, Francis Vandenhende and Denise Fabre (the latter a native Niçoise whose heart belongs to the South) encouraged their new chef, Pascal Steffan, to give the menu a Mediterranean slant. And now the Manoir's lavish dining room with its Tiffany-style skylight, mirrored pilasters, intricately carved woodwork, abundant flowers and greenery, is drenched in Provençal sunshine thanks to a menu studded with Southern flavours: langoustines rôties aux blettes et fumet de truffe, herb and mushroom cannelloni napped with a mouthwatering roast veal gravy, an ambrosial pumpkin soup with tiny cheese gnocchi and crisp lardons, roasted lotte with caramelised tomatoes and braised fennel, and pigonneau en cocotte à la polenta with a wild-mushroom sauce.

Desserts include an unctuous tiramisù, and a warm hazelnut-cocoa gâteau accompanied by a glass of Beaumes-de-Venise Domaine de Coyeux from sommelier Remy Aspect's impressive cellar.

As we write, we are informed that a new chef, Gilles Méry, is to head the kitchen staff.

A la carte: 400-600 F. Menus: 265 F (lunch only), 370 F, 445 F.

11/20 Chez la Mère Michel
5, rue Rennequin
47.63.59.80

M. Gaillard. Closed Sat, Sun and Aug. Open until 10 pm. V.

This is the temple of beurre blanc (that voluptuous sauce of butter, white wine, vinegar, and shallots). The atmosphere is welcoming though the dining room is small and plain. The proprietor is charming, but the prices, alas, are becoming exorbitant for turbot, salmon, pike, bass, brill and company, all bathed in the sensational sauce.

A la carte: 300-350 F.

La Niçoise
4, rue Pierre-Demours
45.74.42.41

M. Vandenhende. Closed Sat lunch (and dinner in summer), and Sun. Open until 11 pm. Private room: 50. Air cond. Valet parking. V AE DC.

Honest, simple Niçois specialities. The fresh, flowery décor is reminiscent of Nice at holiday-time, or of a stage set for a turn-of-the-century operetta. An inexplicably tense staff serves robust, full-flavoured ravioli de daube, stuffed sardines, pasta with pistou, and for pudding a pine-nut tart, all dishes which deserve a round of applause—and a toque. Perfect Provençal cellar.

A la carte: 180 F.

12/20 L'Œuf à la Neige
16, rue Salneuve — 47.63.45.43

M. Gérard. Closed Sat lunch, Sun, 1-25 Aug and 24 Dec-2 Jan. Open until 11 pm. V AE DC.

The proprietor is a Nancy native, a fact underscored by his penchant for tasty little finds from the vineyards of eastern France. Excellent lapin en gelée de Gewurztraminer, warm pâté lorrain, ragoût of freshwater fish with Moselle wine, and a generous, aromatic potée lorraine. The setting, reception, and clientele are all warm and friendly.

A la carte: 250-280 F. Menus: 119 F (lunch only, wine inc), 119 F (dinner only).

Paul et France
27, av. Niel — 47.63.04.24

M. Romano. Closed Sat, Sun and 14 July-16 Aug. Open until 10.30 pm. Air cond. No pets. Valet parking. V AE DC.

Stocky Southerner Georges Romano mans the kitchen while his wife, Suzanne, presides over the dining room (blond-wood panelling, *trompe-l'œil* ceiling) where habitués are often greeted with a kiss. These could include Commandant Cousteau back on terra firma, or the Paris-St Germain football team, kicking over the traces between two matches. Romano is a sure-handed chef who eschews contemporary cuisine for generous, classic

fare. Offal is a particular speciality: try the foie de veau à la lyonnaise, for example, or ris de veau aux pâtes fraîches—always magnificent. Fish is another strong suit, witness the delicate rougets with oyster butter. Desserts are good though a bit too sugary; the cellar is rich, with some astounding brandies and eaux-de-vie.

A la carte: 500 F and up. Menus: 250 F (lunch only, wine inc), 380 F.

12/20 Le Petit Champerret
30, rue Vernier — 43.80.01.39

Mlle Bouron. Closed Sat, Sun, 1-15 Jan and 15-31 Aug. Open until 10.30 pm. Terrace dining. V AE.

Some dishes we've tried seem a little slapdash (fricassée de volaille), while others—chou farci and petit salé de canard—are faultless; such are the ups and downs of an old-time bistro. Red-plush banquettes and lots of atmosphere, compliments of Brigitte, the smiling *patronne*. Prices are accommodating too.

A la carte: 160-180 F.

Le Petit Colombier
42, rue des Acacias
43.80.28.54

M. Fournier. Closed Sun lunch, Sat and 28 July-19 Aug. Open until 10.30 pm. Private room: 30. Air cond. Garage parking. V.

Bernard Fournier is a wise restaurateur. When one is lucky enough to inherit a delightful 'provincial' *auberge* from one's father, the sort of place they stopped making in the nineteenth century, one doesn't go messing it about with trendy lacquered ceilings, salmon-coloured fabric, and halogen lighting. In fact, the patrons of Le Petit Colombier (which has just celebrated 60 years of family management) wouldn't stand for it. They come here to tuck a napkin under their chins, make themselves comfortable in the glow of burnished copper and wrought-iron, and discover anew the reassuring flavours of classic French food, a repertoire that will never grow stale in the capable hands of chef Bernard Fournier. For Le Petit Colombier is not a fusty sanctuary of dyspeptic pre-war cuisine. New dishes often slip onto the menu, and a bit of seaweed mixed with pâtes fraîches or a hint of dill in a seafood pot-au-feu doesn't create a ripple among the clientele. But Bernard Fournier's brigade can also instill fresh spirit and zest into a traditional salad of potatoes with fresh truffles, or a gratin de homard à la Newburg, or roast to rosy perfection a young partridge which actually tastes like a partridge and not a chicken raised on fishmeal. And respect for tradition doesn't mean one can't keep up-to-date; air-conditioning, a 'smoking' area, a bilingual staff, and a computer are all part of the mod cons here—as is a business menu which is one of the best (and least known) bargains in the city. And to toast all these delights, there is a fabulous cellar with some 50,000 bottles....

A la carte: 350-450 F. Menu: 200 F (lunch only, wine inc).

11/20 Le Petit Salé
99, av. des Ternes — 45.74.10.57

Mme Laraki. Closed Sun. Open until 11 pm. Terrace dining. V AE DC.

The new 20-year-old chef has changed nothing in the generous house repertoire of petit salé aux lentilles, confits, and tarte Tatin which has made the reputation of this solid old bistro. The dining room is scheduled for a face-lift this year.

A la carte: 180-200 F.

La Petite Auberge

38, rue Laugier – 47.63.85.51
M. Harbonnier. Closed Sun, Mon and 1 July-3 Sep. Open until 11 pm. Private room: 14. V DC.

Léo Harbonnier is a veteran chef who remains young at heart despite decades in the kitchen. His cuisine is traditional (not to say nostalgic), and utterly professional (not to say decorative—perhaps to echo the charming, picture-filled dining room). Taste his escargots Hélène Angot, or the œufs Victor Pagès (with a touch of orange), turbot Camille Renault (with cream and mushrooms), and one of the best and most spectacular millefeuilles that Paris has to offer.

A la carte: 350 F. Menus: 175 F (weekdays lunch only), 230 F, 320 F.

Petrus

12, pl. du Maréchal-Juin
43.80.15.95
Mme Barrie. Open every day. Open until 11 pm. Private room: 20. Air cond. Valet parking. V AE DC.

Petrus has ridden the waves of change through new chefs, new owners, new managers; the excellence and variety of the seafood have remained constant in this luxurious restaurant, with its spacious dining room and terrace. The latest in a line of recent chefs is Jacques Dupont, formerly of the Tour d'Argent. The shellfish selection is one of the most dazzling in Paris, and classic seafood preparations (lightened in keeping with contemporary tastes) are the mainstays of the menu. But some tasty new dishes have come in with the tide: langoustines en bourses de riz, pavé de bourgeois rôti sur ses écailles, and a luscious white-chocolate mousse. Fine cellar.

A la carte: 500 F. Menu: 250 F.

Rech

62, av. des Ternes – 45.72.29.47
M. Meunier. Closed Sun. Open until 11 pm. Terrace dining. Air cond. V AE DC.

A congenial ground-floor dining room leads upstairs to two spacious salons adorned with wood panelling and mirrors, as chic as the upper-crust clientele that graces the elegant tables. The menu sets sail with a few reasonable dishes such as the unexciting but well-crafted terrine de rascasse or the (terribly overcooked!) délices de sole à la vapeur d'algues. The shellfish specialities are absurdly expensive, and watch out for the sea bass flambé and the grilled lobster. On the other hand, the creamy 'double' Camembert is not to be missed, and the pastries (charlotte aux marrons glacés) are yummy.

A la carte: 300-600 F. Menu: 160 F (in summer only).

Michel Rostang

20, rue Rennequin – 47.63.40.77
M. Rostang. Closed Sat lunch (and dinner in sais.), Sun and 1re quinz. d'Aug. Open until 10.15 pm. Private room: 20. Air cond. Valet parking. Telex 649629. V.

Though his serene demeanour doesn't betray the fact, Michel Rostang is a busy man, what with his triumphant New York restaurant, his Bistrots d'à Côte, the luxury hotel in the Caribbean (run by Rostang *père*), la Bonne Auberge in Antibes overseen by his brother, Philippe, and the restaurant that bears his name and occupies most of his time. Nevertheless this youthful 42-year-old manages to keep his composure, even while putting his kitchen brigade through its paces like a veritable ringmaster.

To call a chef 'industrious' may sound like a back-handed sort of compliment. Yet Michel Rostang works hard at his craft, like the skilled artisan he is. And he knows how to improvise too, creating a subtly nuanced, colourful, intensely agreeable cuisine. A menu of ten appetisers and a dozen fish and meat dishes always offers a core of tried-and-true classics (oven-roasted Sisteron lamb with aged wine vinegar and black olives, casseroled veal chop with a coarse-mustard sauce) along with a bouquet of new arrivals. This year's crop includes asparagus tips 'breaded' with a cèpe duxelles, a superlative terrine de langoustines in a vigorously seasoned demi-gelée de crustacés, a delectable Provençal-inspired sea bass with olives and fennel purée, curried saddle of young rabbit cleverly garnished with a purée of spinach and pears. Though Michel's gratin dauphinois is not up to his father's—the benchmark of the genre—his poularde à la crème aux morilles is a monument.

For dessert choose between a clafoutis au pain d'épice, crème brûlée à la vanille, or tarte chaude au chocolat for a taste of pure ecstasy. Alain Ronzatti administers the select, high-priced wine cellar.

A la carte: 650-800 F. Menus: 280 F (lunch only), 485 F, 540 F.

Guy Savoy

18, rue Troyon
43.80.40.61
M. Savoy. Closed Sat lunch (and dinner Easter-mid-Oct), Sun and week of 15 Aug. Open until 10.30 pm. Private room: 30. Air cond. No pets. Valet parking. V.

If a client requested it, we're certain that the ever-so-affable Guy Savoy would provide a chauffeur-driven car to drive him home—free of charge. But who would ever want to leave this beautiful, welcoming establishment, a haven of charm and grace? How marvellous to be a 'regular' *chez* Savoy, with one's special table reserved in the spacious green-and-rosy-beige dining room dotted with lithographs and contemporary paintings—an original, elegant setting, surely one of the most attractive in the city.

For bearded, eternally youthful Guy Savoy life is beautiful—his dining room is full and diners' happy faces bespeak their delight. Routine never casts its pall over Savoy's kitchen—every day he fashions new, exquisite, unexpected flavours into fascinating meals. If we had to pin it down with a single adjective, we would call Savoy's cuisine 'intelligent'. Textures and aromas are brought together with astonishing skill; they are never masked by superfluous sauces, but highlighted by the judicious use of jus, coulis, essences, and spice blends that give each dish its singular style and cachet. Beyond Savoy's technical vigour lies taste, the real taste of a country lad who has never forgotten the savour of fresh garden vegetables, farmyard poultry, or the good smells of country cookery.

Guy Savoy is not out to dazzle his patrons. He pleases himself first, and if others like the results, so much the better. But frankly who wouldn't like his ragoût of crayfish and Chinese artichokes? or the fat, tender prawns with peas, mange-touts, and a tonic touch of celery? or his potée de légumes et de truffes au jus de foie gras? or a succulent little braised turbot napped in a butter-enriched fumet sparked by a hint of fennel? or the sautéed veal kidneys which in a stroke of genius he combines with dandelion leaves and bacon?

We'll stop there. Savoy's imagination works at lightning speed, and we leave it to you to discover the latest marvels on a constantly changing menu.

Desserts are voluptuous (grapefruit terrine with a tea-scented sauce, vanilla millefeuille in a ruby pool of berry coulis), and the wines, delicate or full-bodied, as you prefer, are overseen by young Eric Mancio.

A la carte: 550-800 F. Menu: 600 F (menu dégustation).

Sormani
4, rue du Général-Lanzerac
43.80.13.91

M. Fayet. Closed Sat, Sun, 23 Dec-2 Jan, 1 week at Easter and 1-22 Aug. Open until 10.30 pm. Private room: 14. Terrace dining. Air cond. Valet parking. V.

Indisputably the best Italian restaurant in Paris, Sormani is the first non-French establishment to win three Gault Millau toques. Pascal Fayet hails from Savoie, so he is not, strictly speaking, a 'foreign' chef. He owes his passion for Italian cuisine to his Piedmontese grandmother. Fayet's *cucina italiana* is indisputably Frenchified; for him, the Italian repertoire is more a source of inspiration than a model to be followed to the letter.

This sensitive artist works with flavours and ingredients from Florence, Genoa, and Tuscany but he is never shy about adding his personal signature to a dish. A trickle of truffled oil on the carpaccio with Parmesan, and suddenly a classic dish is reborn. A sea-urchin filling for green ravioli, brandade de morue tucked into tiny gnocchi, or a bed of potatoes for the zesty squid sautéed with chillis and lardons, warm sweetbreads and veal kidneys tossed with Treviso and lamb's lettuce, dressed with truffle-scented oil and your taste buds snap to delighted attention. Fayet's vegetables are uniformly delicious, for he oven-roasts them *à l'italienne* instead of blanching them in the more usual French style. Thoroughly Italian too is his sensual tiramisù, a poem of mascarpone, chocolate, and caramel ice cream. Among the treasures in the cellar are a marvellous Venetian Pinot Grigio, a Peppoli Antinori '86, and other superb Italian wines that the chauvinistic French too often neglect. Aspects of 'go-for-baroque' décor are in dubious taste, but the overall effect of the frescoes and *faux-marbre* is amusing and fun.

A la carte: 400-500 F. Menus: 350 F and 400 F (menu dégustation).

La Soupière
154, av. de Wagram – 42.27.00.73

M. Thuillart. Closed Sat lunch, Sun and 10-18 Aug. Open until 10.30 pm. Private room: 8. Terrace dining. Air cond. V AE.

The pretty new décor is *trompe-l'œil*, but chef Christian Thuillart's cuisine definitely isn't. His straightforward menu shows a distinctive personality at work, as in the nage d'huîtres au coulis de lentilles et aux herbes and the pigeonneau rôti à la fricassée d'asperges et aux fèves. A passionate connoisseur of rare and expensive mushrooms, he has built special menus around truffles and morels. Prices are climbing.

A la carte: 300 F (weekdays only). Menus: 150 F (weekdays only), 185 F (Sat dinner only), 265 F (truffle menu, weekdays only).

Le Timgad
21, rue Brunel – 45.74.23.70

M. Laasri. Open every day. Open until 11 pm. Air cond. No pets. Parking. V AE DC.

With its moulded-plaster arabesques and enamelled tiles, this extravagant palace décor is one of the most successful of its kind in Paris. On his good days, Ahmed Laasri's couscous is perhaps the best in town. But don't neglect his admirable pastilla, the lamb's-brain tajine with preserved lemons, and the out-of-this-world spit-roasted lamb. A very comprehensive cellar of North African wines, curiously all priced the same.

A la carte: 300 F.

La Toque
16, rue de Tocqueville
42.27.97.75

M. Joubert. Closed Sat, Sun, 24 Dec-2 Jan and 20 July-20 Aug. Open until 9.30 pm. Air cond. V.

Jacky Joubert's cuisine is light, refined, seasonal, and highly inventive—though never 'twee' (a failing not infrequent among certain of Michel Guérard's disciples). Laudably low prices add to the pleasure one derives from a terrine de joue de bœuf with tiny vegetables, filets de rougets pan-fried with smoked-salmon butter, and the unusual, powerfully flavourful hot game pie with apricots. Prepare for some elbow-bashing in a tiny dining room swathed in yellow crushed velvet.

A la carte: 280 F. Menus: 160 F, 210 F.

11/20 Toque Noire
73, av. Niel – 42.27.77.33

M. Chapron. Closed Sat lunch and Sun. Open until 11 pm. Private room: 25. Terrace dining. Air cond. No-smoking section. V AE DC.

Fully half the dishes (prawns flamed in pastis, lotte sauce Nantua, etc.) could be booted off this long menu in order to highlight the authentically delicious foie gras, confits, and magrets served in a new, pseudo-sophisticated décor. Prices are too high. Takeaway boutique next door.

A la carte: 250-300 F. Menus: 98 F, 140 F.

12/20 La Truite Vagabonde
17, rue des Batignolles – 43.87.77.80

M. Pagadoy. Closed Sun dinner. Open until 10.30 pm. Terrace dining. V AE.

An agreeably refurbished interior gives onto a terrace opposite the town hall. The food lacks originality but tries to hint at seaside holidays to come with the likes of grilled or flambéed sea bass, bouillabaisse 'du pêcheur', and crêpes Suzette.

A la carte: 300-350 F. Menus: 150 F (weekdays lunch only), 190 F.

PARIS   18th

12/20 L'Assommoir
12, rue Girardon – 42.64.55.01

M. Larue. Closed Sun dinner, Mon and Aug. Open until 11 pm. Terrace dining. V.

Appealingly un-touristic bistro in the heart of Montmartre run by Maria Callas's former photographer. Mainstays of the simple menu are good terrines, grilled fish, confit de canard, and gâteau au chocolat.

A la carte: 250-300 F.

A. Beauvilliers
52, rue Lamarck – 42.54.54.42

M. Carlier. Closed Mon lunch, Sun and 1-17 Sep. Open until 10.45 pm. Private room: 34. Garden dining. Air cond. No pets. V.

Last spring Edouard Carlier, who likes any excuse for a party, decided to celebrate Beauvilliers' fifteenth birthday by inviting small groups of celebrities and friends to add an extra dose of glamour to Montmartre's most ravishing restaurant. If you weren't part of that glitterati, make up for it by heading straight for the Butte and Beauvilliers' three small dining rooms with their Louis-Philippe–era paintings, old prints, damask napery, and phantasmagoric flower displays. And then there's the adorable little 'newlywed' salon with its soft lighting and collection of wedding garlands worn by country brides of yore, pinned like butterflies in glass vitrines.

Michel Deygat who trained with Robuchon and Faugeron has officiated in the kitchen for the last five years. Once a feast chiefly for the eyes, Beauvilliers is now emphatically a feast for the palate as well—the cuisine is truly first-rate without any futile frills. And to accompany it there is a huge selection of rare Champagnes, old port, and some glorious wines. Among the best dishes are the langoustines royales, regally cooked in truffled oil, his terrine aux trois gibiers, a delicate chicken consommé flavoured with sherry vinegar, an incomparable roast grouse with corn crêpes, filet de bœuf stuffed with Ardenne ham, a splendidly rich chocolate cake, and a bittersweet lemon tart.

We are always surprised when others criticise the welcome as 'cold' not to say 'glacial'. His plumpness King Edouard is the cream of hosts. But perhaps he has too many chums to greet, and thus ignores some first-time visitors...?

A la carte: 480-700 F. Menus: 175 F (weekdays lunch only), 300 F (weekdays lunch only, wine inc).

Les Chants du Piano
[14]
10, rue Lambert — 42.62.02.14
M. Derbane. Closed Sun dinner, Mon lunch, 11-18 Feb and 12-27 Aug. Open until 11 pm. Private room: 20. Air cond. Garage parking. V AE DC.

Michel Derbane's cooking is just a bit precious, and the same might be said of his dainty pink-and-green dining room. All the dishes are pretty as a picture, and most are delicious as well, for example the foie-gras sorbet with Sauternes, veal kidneys with toasted coffee beans, and the médaillons of rabbit stuffed with prawns. The clever little cellar is branching out. Super prix-fixe menus.

A la carte: 350 F. Menus: 149 F, 229 F.

Charlot Ier
(Les Merveilles des Mers)
128 bis, bd de Clichy — 45.22.47.08
M. Bessière. Closed for one month for renovation summer '91. Open until 1 am. Air cond. V AE DC.

The new chef, due to arrive last September, promised to liven up this venerable establishment with, of course, the encouragement of proprietor Mr Bessière, who also owns Wepler, the brasserie next door. But while awaiting the arrival of more meat-based and seasonal dishes, you can always count on an out-of-the-ordinary shellfish array followed by some no-nonsense seafood classics: bouillabaisse, rougets Nîmoise, loup flambé.

A la carte: 350-400 F. Menu: 200 F (lunch only).

12/20 Au Clair de la Lune
9, rue Poulbot — 42.58.97.03
M. Roussel and Mme Thullie. Closed Mon lunch, Sun and Fish school holidays. Open until 11 pm. V AE DC.

A downward slide for this little blue bistro with its *naïf* panoramic fresco. Pierrot Roussel's filet de bœuf sauce chevreuil is not exactly a winner, and his scallop salad is too vinegary. A good turbot à la moelle but that wasn't enough to save the toque—one less point this year.

A la carte: 350-400 F. Menu: 185 F.

Clodenis
[13]
57, rue Caulaincourt
46.06.20.26
M. Gentes. Closed Sun and Mon. Open until 10.30 pm. No pets. V.

Some genuine sun-kissed, Provençal specialities distinguish this charming little restaurant set in a highly touristic area of Montmartre. Prices are as steep as the Butte, but the food is first-rate and the brandade de morue, the lapin au thym, or the fleurs de courgettes farcies won't disappoint. Wine prices are climbing up there too.

A la carte: 350-400 F. Menus: 175 F (lunch only), 190 F (dinner only).

12/20 Coin de Rue
88, rue Lepic — 42.58.50.72
Mme Reynac. Dinner only. Closed Tue. Open until 2 am. Terrace dining. V AE.

A late-night spot, and one of the rare ones on the Butte where the music (there's a pianist and the *patronne* sings) doesn't serve chiefly to take tourists' mind off what's in their plates: copious salmon salad, amusing prawns with cinnamon. A warm welcome.

A la carte: 350 F. Menus: 98 F (weekdays only : 7-9.30 pm), 190 F.

Le Cottage Marcadet
151 bis, rue Marcadet — 42.57.71.22
M. Robin. Closed Sun and 1-15 May. Open until 10.15 pm. V.

The location is not exactly a Montmartre charm spot but the Cottage itself is appealing. It will be even more so (attests the owner, Mr Robin) once it has moved into new digs across the street, with a new chef in tow. Watch this space.

A la carte: 300 F. Menu: 180 F (wine inc).

11/20 La Crémaillère 1900
15, pl. du Tertre — 46.06.58.59
M. Bailly. Open every day. Open until 12.30 am. Private room: 80. Garden dining. Telex 200105. V AE DC.

A fairground décor that dates back to the turn of the century, and a cuisine based on simple grills. It's quite decent food in fact, a pleasant surprise so close to the captive tourist public of the Place du Tertre. Pretty summer patio.

A la carte: 280 F. Menus: 100 F (lunch only, wine inc), 180 F, 255 F and 335 F (wine inc).

12/20 Chez Frézet
181, rue Ordener
46.06.64.20
M. Frézet. Closed Sat, Sun, Easter week and Aug. Open until 9.50 pm. V AE.

Christian Marie is the proud new owner of this freshly decorated neighbourhood restaurant which gives onto a minuscule garden. In the evening, people come for the plat du jour (bouillabaisse, gigot en feuilleté) and the rest of the time for generous portions of decent smoked haddock with cabbage, kidneys with mustard sauce, or grilled duck breast.

A la carte: 280-300 F. Menu: 150 F.

Grandgousier
[14]
17, av. Rachel — 43.87.66.12
M. Marzynski. Closed Sat lunch, Sun and 15 days in Aug. Open until 10 pm. V AE DC.

Léon Marzynski and his wife, Renée, have overcome the doldrums of their sleepy corner of Montmartre. The new décor is a success. It is gay, bright, and flower-filled with large, well-spaced tables. The cooking is up to par too. Léon's scrumptious boned quail, pan-fried on fresh foie gras, or his classic fricassée of kidneys with tiny mushrooms, and his desserts (mandarin-chocolate cake) have earned Grandgousier another point this year.

A la carte: 300 F. Menu: 145 F.

12/20 Da Graziano
83, rue Lepic
46.06.84.77
M. Graziano. Closed 3-27 Feb. Open until 12.30 am. Garden dining. Air cond. V.

The success of this historic establishment across from the Moulin de la Galette owes much to its attractive setting: a verdant terrace, tubs of flowers, and an animated Italian *patron*. But the food is too 'Italianate' and fussy and doesn't fulfil its promise. Nevertheless, some good pasta dishes are on offer, alongside a creditable sea bream livornaise, and a smooth tiramisù.

A la carte: 300-350 F. Menus: 60 F (lunch only, wine inc), 163 F (dinner only).

Le Guerlande
(Terrass Hôtel)
12, rue Caulaincourt — 46.06.59.05
M. Hurand. Closed Aug. Open until 10.30 pm. Private room: 25. Terrace dining. Air cond. Valet parking. Telex 280830. V AE DC.

Not too much style, but charm, gaiety, and lots of comfort infuse this hotel dining room. Chef Jacques Guy's rather pricey cuisine is meticulously executed and not devoid of spark. He follows the seasons with his tasty cold cucumber and chervil soup, filets de rougets with tomato and coriander, and papillote de mignon de veau à la sauge. A luxurious brasserie-annexe, the Albaron, serves home-style cooking at affordable prices.

A la carte: 350 F. Menu: 180 F.

Langevin
(Au Poulbot Gourmet)
39, rue Lamarck — 46.06.86.00
M. Langevin. Closed Sun. Open until 10.30 pm. Air cond. V.

This small establishment delivers high quality, but few surprises. Run by Normandy native Jean-Paul Langevin, the cuisine is based on top-notch seasonal ingredients, with a few discreet nods to traditional country cookery. Try the 'tournedos' of salmon with boletus mushrooms, curry de lotte aux galettes de riz, and the oh-so-scrumptious charlotte tiède de pommes au Calvados. Tables are a bit crowded, the background music a little too loud, but the typically Montmartrois décor will delight.

A la carte: 300 F and up.

12/20 Le Maquis
69, rue Caulaincourt
42.59.76.07
M. Lesage. Open every day. Open until 10 pm. Terrace dining. V.

Simple, solid bistro fare, served in copious portions. The tiny terrace is a cheerful, inviting place to tuck into saucisse au chou, poule au riz, or coq au vin escorted by a carafe of hearty red wine from the Costières-du-Gard. Adorable little set menu.

A la carte: 200-250 F. Menu: 59 F (lunch only, wine inc).

12/20 Marie-Louise
52, rue Championnet — 46.06.86.55
M. Coillot. Closed Sun, Mon, holidays, 1 week at Easter and Aug. Open until 10 pm. Private room: 18. V DC.

Kidneys with Madeira, coq au vin du patron, clafoutis of seasonal fruits—here's honest bistro cooking, unchanged for 30 years, served amid copper saucepans and prints of carousing monks.

A la carte: 200 F. Menu: 100 F (weekdays only).

12/20 Aux Négociants
27, rue Lambert — 46.06.15.11
M. Navier. Closed Sat, Sun and Aug. Open until 8 pm (10 pm Tue, Thu and Fri). No pets. Parking.

Jean Navier, winner of the *Meilleur Pot* ('best glass of wine award'), has recently freshened up his bistro, where he serves a wonderful selection of modest but tasty growers' wines, with an emphasis on the Loire. Wine buffs should sample a Jasnières or a Bourgeuil at the bar, but the Rhône wines are velvet on the tongue when married to the hearty home-style offerings simmered by *la patronne*. Forget frills like tablecloths and concentrate instead on robust rillettes, farm-reared veal en cocotte, and cassoulet.

A la carte: 160-200 F.

Oréade
6, rue Caulaincourt — 45.22.55.66
M. Austry. Closed Sun lunch and Sat. Open until 10.30 pm. Air cond. V AE DC.

Just months after its opening, Oréade lost its stellar chef, Bernard Guilhaudin (ex-Laurent). We don't yet know whether his young second-in-command, Cyril Kradolfer will prove able to duplicate Guilhaudin's ambitious repertoire (pied de veau aux lentilles accompanied by bacon-wrapped gambas, raie aux fruits secs et à la pomme 'éclatée', filet de pintade aux épices, exotic desserts...). Co-proprietors Michel Leblanc and Philippe Austry spent a cool six million francs on a soberly elegant sand-coloured décor near (but, thank goodness, far from the noise of) the seamy, steamy Place de Clichy. We wish them and their new chef well. The young sommelier has put together a cellar already chock-a-block with 'reasonable' finds, and the business menu is finding an ever-larger number of takers.

A la carte: 350-400 F. Menus: 195 F (weekdays lunch only), 320 F.

11/20 Palais de Kashmir
77, rue du Poteau — 42.59.40.86
M. Sarfraz. Open every day. Open until 11.30 pm. Air cond. No-smoking section. V.

Exoticism abounds here with fountains, glass, carved wood, and other Kashmiri delights but the Indo-Pakistani cuisine lacks similar brilliance: try a modest butter chicken, rice biryani with 25 spices, Indian hot breads, and refreshing salted lassi.

A la carte: 180 F. Menu: 119 F.

A la Pomponnette
42, rue Lepic — 46.06.08.36
Mme Carteron. Closed Sun dinner, Mon and Aug. Open until 9.30 pm.

A mature, hard-drinking clientele weigh down the long bar of this relic of old Montmartre. The décor is as *vieux jeu* as the regulars, but a lot less convivial. The menu's generous offerings include some good offal dishes such as a foie de veau poêlé and langue de cochon. To drink, carafes of house Beaujolais are your best bet.

A la carte: 300 F.

Le Restaurant

32, rue Véron — 42.23.06.22

M. Peladeau. Closed Sun, Mon and 15 Aug-5 Sep. Open until 11 pm. V.

Yves Peladeau worked his way up from busboy to owner-chef of his dream-place at the foot of the Butte. His Restaurant is as modern, bright, and appetising as the imaginative dishes he concocts: smoky grilled asparagus, luscious bone-marrow tart with wine-stewed onions, and bâtonnets of pork with caramelised spices. Puddings include a yummy pistachio-flavoured charlotte au tapioca. The wine list is short but to the point.

A la carte: 230-250 F. Menu: 98 F (lunch only).

11/20 Wanouchka

28, rue La Vieuville — 42.57.36.15

M. Rybicki. Dinner only. Closed Wed and 15 July-15 Aug. Open until 11 pm.

Raucous rendezvous for vodka lovers and fans of calorific Eastern European fare: sauerkraut, pork knuckle with horseradish, potato pancakes topped with sour cream.

A la carte: 160 F.

12/20 Wepler

14, pl. Clichy — 45.22.53.24

M. Bessière. Open every day. Open until 1 am. Air cond. V AE DC.

A deluxe brasserie with a well-conceived menu and good service. The shellfish is some of the freshest in Paris; other interesting options are pot de fromage de tête, calf's head with a trio of sauces, a matelote of Loire river fish, and a copious choucroute garnie. Fine bouillabaisse, too.

A la carte: 250 F. Menu: 140 F.

PARIS 19th

11/20 Au Bœuf Couronné

188, av. Jean-Jaurès
42.39.44.44

Mme Saquy. Closed Sun. Open until midnight. Private room: 90. V AE DC.

A rallying point for healthy carnivores. The sauces on the steaks leave a lot to be desired but the pommes soufflées are absolutely tops. Tripe and other offal are expertly handled. The bar-brasserie (Au Petit Bœuf) next door is quick and much cheaper.

A la carte: 300 F.

Au Cochon d'Or

192, av. Jean-Jaurès
42.45.46.46

M. Ayral. Open every day. Open until 10.30 pm. Private room: 45. Air cond. Valet parking. V AE DC.

Times have changed since the Ayral family set up shop here in 1924. The nearby slaughterhouses are now defunct; butchers and meat-packers have given way to the cultured, worldly crowd disgorged by the Cité des Sciences at La Villette. In short, the restaurant has evolved along with its clientele. Under René Ayral's management, and with 30 years experience, chef François Médina continues to grill and pan-fry the choicest morsels of beef: filet mignons, prime ribs, and shell steaks. Earthier choices include pigs' trotters served with sauce Choron, boudin and apples, or calf's-head salad. Let's cut the bull: this is the best bet for red meat in town! A crack sommelier oversees the wine cellar.

A la carte: 400 F. Menu: 230 F.

12/20 Dagorno

190, av. J.-Jaurès — 40.40.09.39

M. Abatécola. Open every day. Open until 12.15 am (1 am on w-e). Private room: 80. Air cond. Valet parking. V AE.

Comfortable deluxe brasserie décor with a less-than-brilliant cuisine. But you won't be disappointed by the oysters, the calf's head with lentils, or the enormous côte de bœuf sauce bordelaise. Some original desserts.

A la carte: 300 F. Menu: 160 F (wine inc).

12/20 Ly-Ya

5, rue du Hainaut — 42.08.34.98

Mme Te-Eng. Closed Mon and 12-26 Aug. Open until 10.30 pm. No pets. AE.

A benevolent Buddha, arms upraised, presides over the dining room. In terms of value for money this tasty, fresh, mainly Vietnamese cuisine wins hands down. Try the fritot de crevettes, spicy shrimps soup, stuffed crab, and chicken with lemon grass and ginger.

A la carte: 100 F. Menus: 43 F and 63 F (weekdays lunch only, wine inc).

Le Pavillon Puebla

(Christian Vergès)

Parc des Buttes-Chaumont — 42.08.92.62

M. Vergès. Closed Sun, Mon, 3 weeks in Feb and 2 weeks in Aug. Open until 10 pm. Private room: 30. Garden dining. Valet parking. V.

This stylish Napoleon III hunting lodge, nestled in greenery at the foot of the Buttes de Chaumont park is a joy for all seasons. When the weather is clement, you can sit under leafy trees and parasols on the terrace (the interior décor suffers from a heavy hand). Christian Vergès has been in residence here for four years, always touched by the Catalan spirit that inspires his rich, varied, and vigorous cuisine. Mediterranean flavours and strong colours bring a singular charm to his niçoise de rougets et de saint-pierre au basilic, terrine de tomates au saumon fumé, potée de morue aux lentilles, or galette de pommes de terre et de ris de veau aux épices douces. One of the city's best crème brûlées is made right here and some splendid Banyuls can be found on the extensive wine list.

A la carte: 430-500 F. Menu: 200 F.

12/20 Le Sancerre

13, av. Corentin-Cariou — 40.36.80.44

M. Dauvois. Closed Sat, Sun and Aug. Open until 10.30 pm. Terrace dining. V AE DC.

A new management hasn't changed the nostalgic ambience of this vestige of the old abattoir district of La Villette. But the chef has been ill-advised to introduce a number of Americanised salads. His talent seems surer in traditional dishes such as lamb stew, braised short ribs of beef, and juicy double lamb chops. As for wines, look no further than the wonderful Morgon and Sancerre sold by the centimetre (you pay only for what you drink).

A la carte: 250-280 F. Menu: 180 F (dinner only, wine inc).

PARIS 20th

Aux Becs Fins

44, bd de Ménilmontant
47.97.51.52

Mme Lefèbvre. Closed Sun. Open until 9.30 pm. Private room: 20. Terrace dining. V AE.

This winsome litle bistro runs alongside the Père Lachaise cemetery. Three colourful old ladies (the co-owners) rely on a faithful clientele of regulars who no longer notice the hideous décor (the centrepiece is a ghastly old fridge!). The cuisine sometimes backfires, but the pied et tête de veau sauce gribiche and the terrines and cassoulet 'mère Edith' keep the toque in place... for now.

A la carte: 300 F. Menus: 210 F (wine inc), 170 F.

12/20 Le Bistrot du 20^e
44, rue du Surmelin – 48.97.20.30

M. Bihoues-Lechevallier. Closed Sat and Sun. Open until 10 pm. No pets. V AE DC.

The amusing décor of this former butcher shop has become more high-toned—not necessarily a plus. The cuisine has its ups and downs: a creditable fricassée of oysters and coquilles St-Jacques stands alongside an up-market filet mignon à la mode de Meaux, but many dishes are overcooked and oversauced. Interesting menus. But unless some improvements appear soon, the rating will surely fall.

A la carte: 230 F. Menus: 75 F (lunch only, wine inc), 100 F (lunch only), 180 F (dinner only).

12/20 Le Courtil
15, rue St-Blaise – 43.70.09.32

M. Azincourt. Closed Sun, Mon and 3-31 Aug. Open until 10 pm. Private room: 25. Air cond. V AE.

The sunny dining room gives onto a flowered garden in the rear. On Tuesday evenings a jazz duo enlivens the simple but robust menu, which includes seafood choucroute, and for dessert an intensely chocolaty ganache à la fève de Guanaja.

A la carte: 200 F.

Lao Thaï
34, rue de Belleville
43.58.41.84

Mme Takounseun. Closed Mon. Annual closings not available. Open until 11 pm. Air cond. No pets. V.

The dining room looks more chipper of late: tables are now agreeably well-spaced with comfortable banquettes to persuade one to linger over the pleasures of the table. These are mainly Laotian and Thai: spicy shrimp soup with lemon grass, cuttlefish sautéed with basil, and spicy pork spareribs with coconut milk. Flavours are strong, with no concessions to Western palates. Affordable prices.

A la carte: 140 F. Menus: 47 F (weekdays lunch only), 98 F, 108 F, 118 F.

12/20 Le Vingtième
12 bis, rue de la Chine
43.66.05.54

M. Decelle. Closed Sun dinner, Mon and Aug. Open until 10 pm. Air cond. V DC.

Raffish French bistro cuisine served in copious portions: terrine de lapereau aux olives, beef jowl braised in beer, followed by cheese and a likeable tarte Tatin flambée au Calvados. Smiling service, simple but cosy provincial décor.

A la carte: 230 F. Menu: 180 F.

INDEX OF PARIS RESTAURANTS

> *Red toques signify modern cuisine; black toques signify traditional cuisine.*

PARIS
Hotels

Agora
7, rue de la Cossonnerie – 42.33.46.02
Open year-round. 29 rms 295-550 F. TV. No pets. V.
A smiling reception awaits you at this small hotel in the Les Halles shopping precinct. Soundproofed rooms have modern bathrooms, and something extra like an attractive chest of drawers or Louis-Philippe chair.

Brighton
218, av. de Rivoli – 42.60.30.03
Open year-round. 2 stes 825-935 F. 73 rms 305-627 F. TV. No pets. Telex 217431. V AE DC.
A dream setting opposite the Tuileries gardens, near the Louvre, is offered at very reasonable prices. The large rooms on the Rue de Rivoli have wonderful views, high moulded ceilings, huge brass beds, nineteenth-century furniture, and good-sized bathrooms. The little rooms under the eaves are especially good value.

Britannique
20, av. Victoria – 42.33.74.59
Open year-round. 40 rms 440-570 F. TV. No pets. Telex 230600. V AE DC.
A warm welcome and good service. The rooms are tastefully decorated with pale walls, dark carpeting, minibar, and modern comfortable furniture. Satellite television.

Castille
37, rue Cambon – 42.61.55.20
Open year-round. 14 stes 1,200-3,000 F. 76 rms 750-1,480 F. Restaurant. TV. Telex 213505. V AE DC.
A classic, comfortable hotel opposite the Ritz. Pleasant rooms are decorated in shades of grey, beige, or pink. Air-conditioning would be welcome.

Ducs d'Anjou
1, rue Ste-Opportune – 42.36.92.24
Open year-round. 38 rms 385-550 F. TV. Telex 218681. V AE DC.
Smallish rooms and bathrooms, except for numbers 61 and 62 which will accommodate three people comfortably. Cheap but tiny singles.

Duminy-Vendôme
3, rue du Mont-Thabor – 42.60.32.80
Open year-round. 79 rms 448-786 F. TV. No pets. Telex 213492. V AE DC.
This nineteenth-century building was completely remodelled in the 1920s and renovated in 1984. Comfortable rooms with 1925 furniture and modern bathrooms.

Family Hôtel
35, rue Cambon – 42.61.54.84
Open year-round. 1 ste 1,000 F. 24 rms 375-510 F. TV. V AE.
Situated opposite the Ritz, this hotel charms by its extreme simplicity. Quite small rooms, sometimes with an amusing detail or unusual piece of furniture. The breakfast room is in the basement.

Inter-Continental
3, rue de Castiglione – 44.77.11.19
Open year-round. 70 stes 2,900-10,300 F. 382 rms 1,800-2,400 F. Restaurant. TV. Air cond. Telex 220114. V AE DC.
The architect Garnier, also responsible for the Opéra, designed this huge hotel which is listed as an historic monument but ideally suited to the needs of modern business people. Large, comfortable, relatively quiet rooms, but the bathrooms are often small and out of date.

Hôtel Lotti
7, rue de Castiglione – 42.60.37.34
Open year-round. 5 stes 4,500-6,000 F. 133 rms 1,250-3,000 F. Restaurant. TV. Air cond. Valet parking. Telex 240066. V AE DC.
An elegant hotel much appreciated by old European families and American celebrities. The comfortable rooms have satellite television and minibar, but the ventilation could be better. The pretty attic-rooms are reserved for non-smokers.

Hôtel du Louvre
Pl. A.-Malraux – 42.61.56.01
Open year-round. 21 stes 1,900-3,500 F. 200 rms 950-1,850 F. TV. Air cond. Valet parking. Telex 220412. V AE DC.
Classically comfortable, this hotel between the Louvre and the Palais-Royal has a mixture of rooms: some huge, high-ceilinged and double-glazed, others small and dark. All are pleasantly decorated with good bathrooms.

Meurice

228, rue de Rivoli – 42.60.38.60
Open year-round. 35 stes 4,900-15,000 F. 187 rms 1,850-3,000 F. Restaurant. TV. Air cond 124 rms. Pets allowed.Valet parking. Telex 230673. V AE DC.

No expense has been spared to turn this once again into one of Europe's most prestigious hotels, with exquisite paintings and furniture. The rooms are spacious (especially those on the first and second floors which have higher ceilings) and have either been repainted, or decorated with fine fabrics. Very comfortable beds, marble bathrooms; 22 television channels and double glazing. The hotel offers a free secretarial service.

Montana-Tuileries
12, rue St-Roch – 42.60.35.10
Open year-round. 25 rms 550-850 F. TV. Telex 214404. V AE DC.

This hotel doesn't actually overlook the Tuileries gardens, but they are only a stone's throw away. All double rooms, well equipped. Numbers 50 and 52 have balconies.

Novotel Paris Les Halles
Pl. Marguerite-de-Navarre – 42.21.31.31
Open year-round. 5 stes 1,400 F. 285 rms 690-750 F. Restaurant. TV. Air cond. Telex 216389. V AE DC.

An ultramodern building of stone, zinc, and glass very close to the Pompidou Centre and the Forum des Halles. The huge rooms have small but well-equipped bathrooms. Warm reception and efficient staff. Other services include duty-free shop, travel agency, modern bar open until 2 am, and restaurant (Le Grill) open from 6.30 pm to midnight.

Hôtel de la Place du Louvre

21, rue Pr.-St-Germain-Auxerrois
42.33.78.68
Open year-round. 2 stes 790 F. 18 rms 480-660 F. TV. Telex 213407. V AE DC.

This totally renovated hotel is decorated with paintings and sculptures throughout. Fairly large rooms, all comfortably furnished and with good bathrooms. Breakfast is served in a vaulted cellar. The owner gives a warm welcome.

Régina

2, pl. des Pyramides – 42.60.31.10
Open year-round. 10 stes 1,800-2,500 F. 130 rms 750-1,600 F. Restaurant. TV. Air cond 5 rms. Valet parking. Telex 670834. V AE DC.

A delightful setting that has been the backdrop for many films. All the rooms are different and all but a few boast antique furniture, double beds, and high windows that afford views over Paris. Huge bathrooms.

Ritz

15, pl. Vendôme – 42.60.38.30
Open year-round. 45 stes 3,470-49,000 F. 142 rms 2,100-3,150 F. Restaurant. TV. Air cond. Heated pool. Valet parking. Telex 220262. V AE DC.

The world's most famous hotel is moving into the twenty-first century while losing none of its traditional character. Without leaving your bed or bath with Jacuzzi you can close the windows, change television channels, or make a phone call, none of which detracts from the pleasure of relaxing in an atmosphere of such distinguished luxury that the word 'ritzy' was invented to describe it. An eighteen-metre swimming pool, squash court, and gym have recently been built in the basement, and a heliport has been added on the roof. Superb dining room and the best breakfasts in Paris. The liveried staff know the difference between courtesy and obsequiousness. See 'restaurants': L'Espadon.

Royal Saint-Honoré
13, rue d'Alger – 42.60.32.79
Open year-round. 3 stes 1,200-1,500 F. 74 rms 635-895 F. Restaurant. TV. Telex 680429. V AE.

The quiet rooms vary in size, but all have functional furniture and flowered curtains and bedcovers. Marble bathrooms. The fifth- and sixth-floor rooms have balconies.

Saint-James et Albany
202, rue de Rivoli – 42.60.31.60
Open year-round. 9 stes 1,300-2,000 F. 207 rms 750-1,100 F. Restaurant. TV. No pets. Garage parking. Telex 213031. V AE DC.

The new management is working hard to make this group of buildings worthy of their four-star rating and exceptional setting on the edge of the Tuileries gardens. The plain modern décor is to be refurbished and the self-service system replaced by traditional hotel services. A quiet, comfortable hotel with reasonable prices for the area.

Saint Romain
5-7, rue St-Roch – 42.60.31.70
Open year-round. 1 ste 395-980 F. 33 rms 395-695 F. TV. Telex 217511. V AE DC.

Recently renovated, this small hotel offers services that many of its classier cousins do not, such as typing, photocopying, fax, and telex. Simple, comfortable rooms decorated in pretty colours, and marble baths.

Tuileries
10, rue Saint-Hyacinthe – 42.61.04.17
Open year-round. 4 stes 1,200 F. 26 rms 520-900 F. TV. Telex 240744. V AE DC.

Listed eighteenth-century building. All the rooms are different but with the same degree of comfort. Marble bathrooms. Good soundproofing and many extras (television, minibar, trouser press, hairdryer).

PARIS   2nd

Edouard VII
39, av. de l'Opéra – 42.61.56.90
Open year-round. 4 stes 1,700 F. 80 rms 750-930 F. Restaurant. TV. Telex 680217. V AE DC.

A certain style of 1960s luxury characterises this hotel near the Opera. Half the rooms have been redecorated this year. Well-equipped bathrooms. See 'restaurants': Le Delmonico.

Métropole Opéra
2, rue de Gramont – 42.96.91.03
Open year-round. 24 stes 850-1,300 F. 33 rms 400-1,050 F. TV. Telex 215648. V AE.

A carefully renovated nineteenth-century building houses this comfortable self-service hotel. The flats, from one to six rooms, have kitchens and modern bathrooms.

Westminster
13, rue de la Paix – 42.61.57.46
Open year-round. 18 stes 2,500-4,000 F. 84 rms 1,500-2,250 F. Restaurant. TV. Air cond 55 rms. Valet parking. Telex 680035. V AE DC.

An elegant hotel between the Opera and Place Vendôme. Rooms of various sizes are decorated in pastel shades with pretty fabrics, period furniture, marble fireplaces and a collection of eighteenth-century clocks. Pink or grey marble bathrooms.

Minibar, safe, satellite television. See 'restaurants': Le Céladon.

Hôtel des Chevaliers
30, rue de Turenne — 42.72.73.47
Open year-round. 24 rms 480-500 F. TV. Parking. Telex 211554. V AE DC.
In the heart of the Marais, a small hotel frequented by film people. The rooms are bright and pleasantly furnished; some are perfectly quiet.

Marais
2 bis, rue Commines — 48.87.78.27
Open year-round. 39 rms 280-370 F. TV. Telex 260717. V AE.
A simple, neat hotel between Bastille and République offers small, bright, modern rooms.

Pavillon de la Reine
28, pl. des Vosges — 42.77.96.40
Open year-round. 23 stes 1,300-2,400 F. 30 rms 930-1,080 F. TV. Air cond. Valet parking. Telex 216160. V AE DC.
Set slightly back from the Place des Vosges, part of this hotel dates from the seventeenth-century. An atmosphere of quiet luxury prevails in the comfortable rooms.

Bastille Speria
1, rue de la Bastille — 42.72.04.01
Open year-round. 42 rms 390-460 F. TV. No pets. Telex 214327. V AE DC.
The interior was renovated in a restrained modern style in 1988. The rooms have double glazing. Very pleasant reception and service.

Hôtel de la Bretonnerie
22, rue Ste-Croix-Bretonnerie — 48.87.77.63
Closed July-1 Aug. 1 ste 750 F. 30 rms 470-650 F. TV. V AE DC.
A seventeenth-century town house, tastefully renovated and redecorated. Spacious rooms with beams and antique furniture; modern bathrooms.

Hôtel Saint-Louis Marais
1, rue Charles-V — 48.87.87.04
Open year-round. 15 rms 300-490 F.
Reasonable prices and a delightful reception at this former convent annexe in a quiet street. Each room is different.

Les Deux Iles
59, rue St-Louis-en-l'Ile — 43.26.13.35
Open year-round. 17 rms 550-650 F. TV. Telex 375974.
A particularly welcoming hotel on the Ile St-Louis. The lounge, with its seating covered in flowered chintz, has a family atmosphere. The soundproofed rooms are attractively decorated in pale colours.

Hôtel du Jeu de Paume
54, rue St-Louis-en-l'Ile — 43.26.14.18
Open year-round. 32 rms 680-950 F. TV. Telex 205160. V AE DC.
A splendidly decorated seventeenth-century residence. A glass lift transports you up to the bright, quiet bedrooms. Small, sunny garden.

Lutèce
65, rue St-Louis-en-l'Ile — 43.26.23.52
Open year-round. 23 rms 650-700 F. TV. No pets.
A quiet, comfortable hotel that shows a laudable concern for detail. The rooms are smallish and simply decorated, with modern bathrooms. The new furnishings are in bright, clear colours.

Saint-Louis
75, rue St-Louis-en-l'Ile — 46.34.04.80
Open year-round. 21 rms 490-590 F. Pets allowed.
Simple and elegant with its antique furniture and gorgeous flower arrangements. Small but perfectly soundproofed rooms boast thick carpeting. Modern bathrooms, but no lift.

Saint-Merry
78, rue de la Verrerie — 42.78.14.15
Open year-round. 12 rms 370-750 F. Pets allowed.
A former presbytery, this seventeenth-century building is home to an original collection of Gothic furniture, which the owner has been buying at auction for over 30 years. Unusually large rooms with bathrooms not much bigger than cupboards, and no television. But the charm of the place is such that you have to book well in advance during the summer.

Hôtel du 7ᵉ Art
20, rue St-Paul — 42.77.04.03
Open year-round. 22 rms 240-500 F. Restaurant. TV. V AE DC.
Posters and photographs of the cinema—known in France as the seventh art—paper the walls. Small, comfortable rooms with well-equipped bathrooms. No room service.

Vieux Marais
8, rue du Plâtre — 42.78.47.22
Open year-round. 30 rms 300-450 F. TV. No pets. V.
Small, friendly hotel in a quiet street. The rooms are simply decorated and well equipped.

Agora Saint-Germain
42, rue des Bernardins — 46.34.13.00
Open year-round. 39 rms 440-550 F. TV. No pets. Telex 260881. V AE DC.
A very well-kept establishment which was completely renovated in 1987. Bright rooms with comfortable beds, minibar, radio, and television. Bathrooms with such welcome amenities as hairdryers.

Colbert
7, rue de l'Hôtel-Colbert — 43.25.85.65
Open year-round. 2 stes 1,320-1,595 F. 40 rms 555-870 F. TV. No pets. Telex 260690. V AE.
An elegant hotel in a quiet street. The rooms, decorated in classic style, have double glazing. White tiling and hairdryers in the bathrooms.

Hôtel du Collège de France
7, rue Thénard — 43.26.78.36
Open year-round. 2 stes 930-1,030 F. 29 rms 450-500 F. TV. No pets. AE.
Simple, clean, comfortable rooms, all equipped with radio, television, and direct line telephones.

Elysa
6, rue Gay-Lussac — 43.25.31.74
Open year-round. 30 rms 450-660 F. TV. No pets. Telex 206881. V AE DC.
In the heart of the Latin Quarter, near the Luxembourg Gardens. The pretty pink or blue rooms

with white-lacquered furniture are soundproofed. Buffet breakfast is available at all hours.

Grands Hommes
17, pl. du Panthéon — 46.34.19.60
Open year-round. 32 rms 550-660 F. TV. No pets. Telex 200185. V AE DC.
Opposite the Panthéon. The fairly spacious rooms are decorated with pink, cream, or floral fabric wallcoverings. Room 22 has a four-poster bed. Cable television, minibar. The staff is pleasant and efficient.

Le Jardin des Plantes
5, rue Linné — 47.07.06.20
Open year-round. 33 rms 320-560 F. Restaurant. TV. Telex 203684. V AE DC.
Delightful five-storey hotel in a quiet street behind the botanical gardens. Flowers and floral motifs abound, down to the corridor wall lights. Smallish, well-equipped rooms (minibar, hairdryer). Sauna.

Jardins de Cluny
9, rue du Sommerard — 43.54.22.66
Open year-round. 40 rms 400-620 F. TV. Telex 206975. V AE DC.
A perfectly functional hotel, with comfortable rooms and modern bathrooms.

Hôtel des Nations
54, rue Monge — 43.26.45.24
Open year-round. 38 rms 460-480 F. TV. Telex 200397. V AE DC.
The curtains and bedcovers match the paper or fabric wallcoverings. Tiled bathrooms, double glazing.

Notre-Dame Hôtel
1, quai St-Michel — 43.54.20.43
Open year-round. 3 stes 1,000 F. 26 rms 440-740 F. TV. Telex 206650. V AE DC.
Situated in a noisy area, but the hotel is protected by efficient double glazing. The sixth floor houses three split-level attic rooms with red carpeting, rustic furniture, and a mezzanine that affords superb views over Notre-Dame and the Seine.

Panthéon
19, pl. du Panthéon — 43.54.32.95
Open year-round. 34 rms 550-660 F. TV. No pets. Telex 206435. V AE DC.
A clever use of mirrors makes the entrance and lounge seem bigger. The elegant rooms are quite spacious, decorated in Louis XVI or Louis-Philippe style, with fabric wallcoverings in pale colours. Minibar, cable television.

Select Hôtel
1, pl. de la Sorbonne — 46.34.14.80
Open year-round. 69 rms 390-580 F. TV. Telex 201207. V AE DC.
An atrium with a glass roof has been built at the heart of this hotel. Pleasant, spacious rooms with functional furniture.

PARIS   **6th**

Abbaye Saint-Germain
10, rue Cassette — 45.44.38.11
Open year-round. 4 stes 1,500-1,800 F. 44 rms 690-1,100 F. TV 8 rms. No pets.
A welcoming eighteenth-century residence in a narrow, fairly quiet street. The rooms are well kept and attractively decorated. Number 4 has a terrace leading to the garden.

Angleterre
44, rue Jacob — 42.60.34.72
Open year-round. 3 stes 950-1,200 F. 26 rms 650-950 F. TV. No pets. V AE DC.
Hemingway once lived in this former British embassy built around a patio. The high-ceilinged rooms with beams have recently been renovated. Large double beds and luxurious bathrooms. Lounge with piano. Bar.

Crystal Hôtel
24, rue St-Benoît — 45.48.85.14
Open year-round. 1 ste 600-900 F. 26 rms 350-600 F. TV. Telex 201021. V AE DC.
A charming small hotel with a friendly atmosphere. The rooms are simply decorated with some antique furniture, and thoughtfully equipped bathrooms.

Danemark
21, rue Vavin — 43.26.93.78
Open year-round. 15 rms 520-690 F. TV. Air cond. Telex 202568. V AE DC.
Although recently renovated, the hotel retains the elegance of the 1930s. Rooms are on the small side, entirely decorated in pink. Grey-marble bathrooms.

Ferrandi
92, rue du Cherche-Midi — 42.22.97.40
Open year-round. 1 ste 850-950 F. 41 rms 375-800 F. TV. Parking. Telex 205201. V AE DC.
In a quiet street near Montparnasse, with a reception that matches the charm of the rooms. Some of the guest rooms have four-posterbeds, others a fireplace. All have good bathrooms (hairdryer) and double glazing.

L'Hôtel
13, rue des Beaux-Arts — 43.25.27.22
Open year-round. 3 stes 2,500-3,300 F. 25 rms 900-1,900 F. Restaurant. TV. Air cond. Telex 270870. V AE DC.
Each room has its own character and a story to tell. Number 16 is a copy of the room where Oscar Wilde died in 1900; number 36 houses art deco furniture belonging to the music hall star Mistinguett; number 25 has a huge terrace with rooftop views. Sadly, the décor and furnishings are starting to look rather tired. Minibar, satellite television. See 'restaurants': Le Bélier.

Latitudes Saint-Germain
7-11, rue St-Benoît — 42.61.53.53
Open year-round. 117 rms 700-800 F. TV. Air cond. Telex 213531. V AE DC.
A modern, functional hotel, opened in 1988. The efficiently soundproofed rooms are decorated in pastel tones with large, comfortable beds. Smiling reception.

Hôtel Left Bank
9, rue de l'Ancienne-Comédie — 43.54.01.70
Open year-round. 31 rms 675-750 F. TV. Air cond. No pets. Telex 200502. V AE DC.
Reopened in 1989 after a thorough overhaul. Tasteful but rather repetitive décor features specially made walnut furniture in Louis XIII style, lace bedcovers, brass lamps, and marble bathrooms.

La Louisiane
60, rue de Seine — 43.29.59.30
Open year-round. 1 ste 600 F. 77 rms 300-600 F. No pets. V DC.
An artistic clientele and a warm reception. Rooms are simple and comfortable, either painted or hung with Japanese wallpaper.

Lutétia
45, bd Raspail — 45.44.38.10
Open year-round. 21 stes 2,600-3,500 F. 286 rms 900-1,950 F. Restaurant. TV. Air cond. Valet parking. Telex 270424. V AE DC.
A noteworthy example of art deco furnishing, with marble, gilt, and red velvet gracing the public areas where MPs, top officials, and captains of industry come and go. Leading off the huge entrance are the lounge, bar, brasserie, restaurant, shopping gallery, and conference rooms. Spacious and very expensive suites; comfortable rooms. Efficient service. See 'restaurants': Le Paris and Brasserie Lutétia.

Luxembourg
4, rue de Vaugirard — 43.25.35.90
Open year-round. 34 rms 410-525 F. TV. Telex 270879. V AE DC.
Modernised in 1989. The rooms have minibar, hairdryer, and individual safe; small bathrooms.

Madison
143, bd St-Germain — 43.29.72.50
Open year-round. 55 rms 600-1,050 F. TV. Air cond. Telex 208628. V AE DC.
A comfortable hotel with some antique furniture, and pretty Provençal tiles in the bathrooms. Very well equipped: double glazing, air-conditioning, minibar, satellite television, hairdryer. Smiling service and a generous buffet for breakfast.

Les Marronniers
21, rue Jacob — 43.25.30.60
Open year-round. 37 rms 400-750 F. TV. No pets.
Here is a delightful small hotel in the heart of the St-Germain area with bright, comfortable rooms. Breakfast is served on the veranda overlooking the garden.

Novanox
155, bd du Montparnasse — 46.33.63.60
Open year-round. 27 rms 490-610 F. TV. No pets. Telex 201255. V AE DC.
The owner of this hotel, opened in 1989, has made a judicious mixture of 1920s, 1930s, and 1950s styles for the décor. On the ground floor, a large, cheerful room serves as lounge, bar, and breakfast room.

Odéon Hôtel
3, rue de l'Odéon — 43.25.70.11
Open year-round. 29 rms 460-720 F. TV. Air cond 2 rms. Telex 206731. V AE DC.
In a listed building, the small, pleasant rooms have recently been redecorated. Marble bathrooms.

Perreyve
63, rue Madame — 45.48.35.01
Open year-round. 30 rms 377-500 F. TV. No pets. Telex 205080. V AE.
Near the Luxembourg gardens. Thirty comfortable rooms with tiny but faultless bathrooms.

Quality Inn
92, rue de Vaugirard — 42.22.00.56
Open year-round. 6 stes 850 F. 134 rms 540-800 F. TV. Air cond. Garage parking. Telex 206900.V AE DC.
Part of an American chain with about 1,000 hotels worldwide, this is a quiet, elegant establishment. Well-equipped rooms, some furnished in cruise liner style. Piano bar filled with plants. Substantial breakfasts are served until 11 am. Impeccable service.

Récamier
3 bis, pl. Récamier — 43.26.04.89
Open year-round. 30 rms 210-580 F. No pets.
A simple, quiet hotel near St-Sulpice. Small, attractive rooms are decorated with matching curtains and wallpaper, and cane furniture. Pleasant reception.

Relais Christine
3, rue Christine — 43.26.71.80
Open year-round. 17 stes 1,450-2,100 F. 34 rms 1,100-1,150 F. TV. Air cond. No pets. Valet parking. Telex 202606. V AE DC.
While it has retained some of the peace of the convent that once stood here, the Relais Christine has all the comfort and elegance of the present age, from double glazing to perfect service. The rooms are all different, with multicoloured Provençal bedcovers, period furniture, and pink Portuguese marble bathrooms.

Relais Saint-Germain
9, carrefour de l'Odéon — 43.29.12.05
Open year-round. 1 ste 1,760 F. 10 rms 1,160-1,320 F. TV. Air cond. Telex 201889. V AE DC.
A tiny hotel, unusually quiet for the area. The rooms are big enough and very comfortable, with beams, timbering, and old paintings, as well as marble bathrooms with separate loos. Air-conditioning, double glazing, and individual safe. Excellent reception and service.

Rennes-Montparnasse
151 bis, rue de Rennes — 45.48.97.38
Closed Aug. 4 stes 720-900 F. 41 rms 370-510 F. TV. Telex 250048. V AE DC.
A well-kept hotel with small, neat, comfortable rooms. Those overlooking the courtyard are quieter and more pleasant.

Hôtel de Saint-Germain
50, rue du Four — 45.48.91.64
Open year-round. 2 stes 1,200-1,500 F. 30 rms 450-1,000 F. TV. Air cond 5 rms. No pets. Telex 201144. V AE.
This small hotel with its delightful décor and English furniture offers round-the-clock room service, babysitting, and various tours of Paris (by helicopter, minibus, or on foot).

Saint-Grégoire
43, rue de l'Abbé-Grégoire — 45.48.23.23
Open year-round. 20 rms 650-970 F. TV. Air cond 2 rms. No pets. Telex 205343. V AE DC.
The cosy lounge has a fireplace and there's also a small garden. The rooms are painted in attractive shades of yellow and pink, with matching chintz curtains, white damask bedspreads, and some fine antique furniture. Double glazing and modern bathrooms. Perfect breakfasts.

Sainte-Beuve
9, rue Sainte-Beuve — 45.48.20.07
Open year-round. 1 ste 1,350-1,480 F. 23 rms 630-1,000 F. TV. No pets. Telex 270182. V AE.
A good example of harmonious and comfortable furnishings in a neo-Palladian style. The rooms are modern and the tiled bathrooms have marble floors and washbasins.

Hôtel des Saints-Pères
65, rue des Saints-Pères — 45.44.50.00
Open year-round. 3 stes 1,250 F. 37 rms 400-1,000 F. TV. Air cond 3 rms. No pets. Telex 205424. V.
Situated in two buildings, with all the elegantly furnished rooms overlooking a garden. Professional service.

Sénateur
10, rue de Vaugirard — 43.26.08.83
Open year-round. 5 stes 980-1,080 F. 44 rms 530-680 F. TV. Telex 200091. V AE DC.
A comfortable, modern hotel with a huge mural and plenty of greenery brightening up the ground floor. The rooms, decorated in grey or beige, are rather impersonal. Fine views from the top floor.

Victoria Palace
6, rue B.-Desgoffe — 45.44.38.16
Open year-round. 110 rms 650-1,300 F. Restaurant. TV. No pets. Garage parking. Telex 270557. V AE DC.
A reliable hotel with broad corridors, large, comfortable rooms, and really spacious cupboards.

Welcome Hôtel
66, rue de Seine — 46.34.24.80
Open year-round. 30 rms 280-460 F. TV. No pets.
Cosy little rooms, simply furnished, are offered at very reasonable prices. Double glazing and tiled bathrooms.

PARIS   7th

Bellechasse
8, rue de Bellechasse — 45.51.52.36
Open year-round. 32 rms 530-620 F. TV. Telex 205505. V AE DC.
The rooms are functionally furnished with light fabric wallcoverings, and have a minibar and individual safe. A particularly welcoming reception.

Bersoly's Saint-Germain
28, rue de Lille — 42.60.73.79
Open year-round. 16 rms 440-580 F. TV. Air cond 1 rm. Telex 217505. V AE.
The furniture is largely provided by the nearby 'golden triangle' of antique dealers; reproduction paintings adorn the walls. Breakfast is served in the attractive vaulted basement. Faultless reception.

Cayré
4, bd Raspail – 45.44.38.88
Open year-round. 130 rms 700-750 F. TV. Pool. Telex 270577. V AE DC.
A pink-and-grey marble floor, glass pillars, and red-leather furniture lend an air of luxury to the lobby. The rooms, modern and thoroughly soundproofed, are completely impersonal. Marble bathrooms.

Duc de Saint-Simon
14, rue St-Simon — 45.48.35.66
Open year-round. 5 stes 1,500-1,800 F. 29 rms 950-1,400 F. Air cond 6 rms. No pets. Telex 203277.
Set back from the street, this early-nineteenth-century town house with its small garden is full of understated elegance. Everything, from the reception to the breakfasts, is particularly pleasant. Four lovely rooms on the second floor have terraces overlooking the garden.

Elysées-Maubourg
35, bd de Latour-Maubourg — 45.56.10.78
Open year-round. 2 stes 720 F. 30 rms 500-720 F. TV. Telex 206227. V AE DC.
A hotel for cinema fans, with the television channel that shows many new films, and two videos available every day. The rooms are decorated in shades of green, blue, or beige, with matching curtains and Louis-Philippe or cane furniture. Double glazing, minibar, radio-alarm.

Les Jardins d'Eiffel
8, rue Amélie — 47.05.46.21
Open year-round. 44 rms 435-740 F. TV. Air cond 8 rms. Garage parking. Telex 206582. V AE DC.
Some rooms are awaiting renovation, but 44 have already been redecorated in attractive colours and re-equipped with double glazing, minibar, ten television channels, hairdryer, and trouser press. The upper floors overlook the Eiffel Tower. Sauna. Very pleasant reception.

Lenox
9, rue de l'Université — 42.96.10.95
Open year-round. 2 stes 780 F. 32 rms 430-600 F. TV. No pets. Telex 260745. V AE DC.
An elegant hotel with smallish but pretty rooms, especially those with balconies. There are some suites under the eaves with the beds on a mezzanine. Cold meals are served in the rooms.

Montalembert
3, rue de Montalembert — 45.48.68.11
Open year-round. 5 stes 1,800-2,800 F. 51 rms 1,350-1,550 F. Air cond. V AE.
The new owners have been unstinting in their efforts to restore this 1926 hotel to its former splendour with hardwoods, fine fabrics, marble, and leather. Some of the rooms have retained their 1930s furniture; others have been redecorated in modern style. Really big bath towels and a fine range of guest toiletries.

Saxe-Résidence
9, villa de Saxe — 47.83.98.28
Open year-round. 1 ste 702 F. 52 rms 500-530 F. TV. No pets. Parking. Telex 270139. V AE.
The quiet rooms are kept constantly up to date. 1950s-style bar. Courteous reception.

Solférino
91, rue de Lille — 47.05.85.54
Closed 15 Dec-3 Jan. 1 ste 694 F. 33 rms 231-566 F. TV 520 rms. No pets. Telex 203865. V.
Almost opposite the Orsay Museum, here are small but comfortable rooms with bath or shower. Charming little lounge.

Suède
31, rue Vaneau — 47.05.18.65
Open year-round. 1 ste 910 F. 41 rms 475-525 F. No pets. Telex 200596. V AE.
The Suède is a particularly quiet establishment set among ministries and embassies, with an almost austere decor in refined shades of grey. Choose the more cheerful rooms overlooking the small interior garden.

Université
22, rue de l'Université — 42.61.09.39
Open year-round. 1 ste 1,200 F. 28 rms 400-900 F. No pets. Telex 260717.
Comfortable beds and modern bathrooms are featured in an intelligently renovated nineteenth-century residence with beams, timbering, and period furniture.

Varenne
44, rue de Bourgogne — 45.51.45.55
Open year-round. 24 rms 410-560 F. TV. V AE.
A smiling welcome is always to be had at this small hotel whose provincial air is underscored by a courtyard filled with greenery. Double glazing keeps out traffic noise in rooms facing the street.

PARIS   8th

Alison

21, rue de Surène — 42.65.54.00
*Open year-round. 35 rms 380-630 F. TV. No pets.
Telex 640435. V AE DC.*
Near the Madeleine, the Alison provides airy,
functional rooms with marble washbasins in the
bathrooms. Breakfast is served in the vaulted stone
basement.

Astor L'Horset
11, rue d'Astorg — 42.66.56.56
*Open year-round. 128 rms 820-870 F. Restaurant.
TV. Telex 642737. V AE DC.*
Tastefully furnished rooms above a marble, oak,
and leather lobby with English-style bar. Flowers
all year round.

Atala
10, rue Chateaubriand — 45.62.01.62
*Open year-round. 2 stes 1,200-1,300 F. 47 rms 700-
1,100 F. Restaurant. TV. Telex 640576. V AE DC.*
In a calm setting near the Champs-Elysées, with
satellite TV in all the adequately sized rooms.
Balconies or terraces on the upper floors.

Hôtel Balzac
6, rue Balzac — 45.61.97.22
*Open year-round. 14 stes 3,000-6,000 F. 56 rms
1,280-1,680 F. Restaurant. TV. Air cond. Valet parking. Telex 290298. V AE DC.*
The Balzac is known for modern jet-set luxury, a
discreet staff, and a refined and traditional setting
near the Etoile. The spacious rooms feature deep-
pile wool carpets and superb modern bathrooms.
Room service.

Beverly Hills
35, rue de Berri — 43.59.55.55
*Open year-round. 17 stes 1,600-9,000 F. Restaurant.
TV. Air cond. Parking. Telex 643868. V AE DC.*
This luxury residential hotel is permeated by the
smell of money. Security is a priority, with 24-hour
video surveillance and door code chosen by the
client. A world of marble, subdued lighting, and
antique furniture surmounted by the two-storey
penthouse suite.

Bradford
10, rue St-Philippe-du-Roule — 43.59.24.20
*Open year-round. 2 stes 700 F. 48 rms 550-650 F. TV
2 rms. No pets. Telex 648530. V.*
Slightly faded but elegant, traditional simplicity
off the Champs-Elysées. The really comfortable,
spacious rooms are decorated in discreet Louis XVI
style.

Le Bristol
112, rue du Fg-St-Honoré — 42.66.91.45
*Open year-round. 45 stes 5,600 F. 155 rms 2,100-
3,100 F. Restaurant. TV. Air cond. No pets. Heated
pool. Valet parking. Telex 280961. V AE DC.*
One of the most authentic (and most expensive)
grand hotels in Paris, with its luxurious suites and
matching clientele. Its ultramodern conference
rooms and small heated swimming pool contrast
with the superb Louis XV and XVI furnishings—
some genuine antiques—in the enormous rooms
with marble bathrooms. Friendly, courteous staff,
and an extraordinary restaurant overlooking a
huge garden. See 'restaurants': Le Bristol.

California

16, rue de Berri — 43.59.93.00
*Open year-round. 3 stes 2,200-2,700 F. 177 rms 900-
1,300 F. TV. Telex 644634. V AE DC.*
One hundred metres from the Champs-Elysées.
The California's rooms were recently redecorated.
Smiling service.

Centre Ville Matignon
3, rue de Ponthieu — 42.25.73.01
*Open year-round. 5 stes 1,200 F. 25 rms 800-900 F.
Restaurant. TV. Air cond. Valet parking.
Telex 650343. V AE DC.*
This small 1930s hotel has been renovated with
such care that the rooms still have their mural
paintings behind the beds and the bathrooms their
original mosaics and large white washbasins. Although they are on the small side, the guest rooms
are well equipped (double glazing, minibar, safe,
hairdryer).

Château Frontenac
54, rue P.-Charron — 47.23.55.85
*Open year-round. 4 stes 1,250 F. 106 rms 750-
1,250 F. Restaurant. TV. Air cond 10 rms. No pets.
Telex 644994. V DC.*
Good value considering its setting. The rooms
vary in size, with vaguely Louis XV décor and
comfortable, modern bathrooms.

Claridge-Bellman
37, rue Franois-Ier — 47.23.54.42
*Open year-round. 42 rms 500-1,200 F. Restaurant.
TV. Air cond 2 rms. No pets. Telex 641150. V AE DC.*
The managers of the former Claridge had the
good idea of bringing typical ornaments, paintings,
and furniture with them when they took over this
small, comfortable hotel. Each room has something special: an attractive piece of furniture, a
crystal chandelier, a fireplace. See 'restaurants': Le
Relais Bellman.

Colisée
6, rue du Colisée — 43.59.95.25
*Open year-round. 44 rms 475-570 F. TV. Air cond
11 rms. Telex 643201. V AE DC.*
Unexpectedly quiet and reasonably priced for an
hotel so near the Champs-Elysées. Floral décor and
tiled bathrooms.

Concorde Saint-Lazare
108, rue St-Lazare — 42.94.22.22
*Open year-round. 10 stes 1,800-2,600 F. 324 rms
800-1,400 F. Restaurant. TV. Air cond. Valet parking.
Telex 650442. V AE DC.*
Eiffel—of Tower fame—built this huge hotel with
its impressive three-storey lobby in 1889. Over
three-quarters of the rooms have been renovated,
with pink or beige fabric wallcoverings, painted
panelling, faded chintz for the bedcovers and
curtains, and mahogany furniture. The large
bathrooms are still rather old-fashioned.

Hôtel de Crillon

10, pl. de la Concorde — 42.65.24.24
*Open year-round. 38 stes 4,000-20,000 F. 125 rms
2,000-3,500 F. Restaurant. TV. Air cond. Valet parking. Telex 290204. V AE DC.*
A magnificent hotel, the Crillon has extraordinary eighteenth-century architecture, lavish décor
and amenities. The rooms and suites range from
the sublime to the rather ordinary. Some of the best
have terraces on the Place de la Concorde. The
public areas are particularly striking: the large entrance hall, the dining room of the restaurant Les
Ambassadeurs, with its astonishing painted ceiling, the charming restaurant L'Obélisque and the

winter garden. Relais et Châteaux. See 'restaurants': Les Ambassadeurs.

Elysée
12, rue des Saussaies — 42.65.29.25
Open year-round. 2 stes 1,000-1,250 F. 30 rms 480-800 F. TV. Air cond 2 rms. No pets. Telex 281665. V AE DC.

An intimate, tastefully renovated hotel where you will receive a most pleasant welcome. All the rooms are different; the two suites under the eaves are particularly in demand.

Folkestone
9, rue Castellane — 42.65.73.09
Open year-round. 2 stes 810 F. 49 rms 570-725 F. TV. Telex 290431. V AE EC.

The beamed rooms, decorated with fabric wallcovering or Japanese wallpaper, have art deco armchairs and comfortable beds. Generous buffet breakfasts.

George V
31, av. George-V — 47.23.54.00
Open year-round. 59 stes 3,400-12,400 F. 292 rms 1,930-2,870 F. Restaurant. TV. Air cond. Valet parking. Telex 650082. V AE DC.

An hotel that conjures up magic and memories. Unfortunately, too many of the rooms are still outdated and poorly maintained, and the service is not what we expect from such a prestigious place. The lobby and grill restaurant have been attractively remodelled. See 'restaurants': Les Princes.

Golden Tulip
218-220, rue du Fg-St-Honoré — 49.53.03.03
Open year-round. 20 stes 1,950-3,700 F. 52 rms 1,200-1,600 F. Restaurant. TV. Air cond. Pool. Valet parking. Telex 650657. V AE DC.

Owned by a Dutch chain, this comfortable hotel is decorated in modern style using traditional materials (marble, wood, quality fabrics, *trompe-l'œil* paintings). The spacious rooms offer every amenity; all are air-conditioned, with splendid marble bathrooms. See 'restaurants': Le Relais Vermeer.

Lancaster
7, rue de Berri — 43.59.90.43
Open year-round. 10 stes 3,300-6,900 F. 56 rms 1,495-2,300 F. Restaurant. TV. Air cond 33 rms. Valet parking. Telex 640991. V AE DC.

Constant maintenance keeps the soberly decorated rooms and suites in an excellent state of repair. Persian rugs, fine ornaments, marble fireplaces, and a delightful indoor garden create an atmosphere of discreet luxury. Friendly, efficient service.

Hôtel Lido
4, pass. de la Madeleine — 42.66.27.37
Open year-round. 32 rms 550-750 F. TV. Telex 281039. V AE DC.

Between the Madeleine and the Place de la Concorde. The rooms, decorated in pink, blue, or cream, have comfortable beds with white lace covers. Modern bathrooms, double glazing. The staff is thoughtful and courteous.

Marriott Prince de Galles
33, av. George-V — 47.23.55.11
Open year-round. 30 stes 3,200-6,000 F. 171 rms 1,800-2,400 F. Restaurant. TV. Air cond. Valet parking. Telex 280627. V AE DC.

The colonnaded patio is most pleasant in spring and summer, as is the round Regency Bar at any season. But some of the rooms are outmoded and certain bathrooms are on their last legs. The service can be offhand. See 'restaurants': Prince de Galles.

Napoléon
40, av. de Friedland — 47.66.02.02
Open year-round. 32 stes 1,350-4,500 F. 102 rms 650-1,550 F. Restaurant. TV. Valet parking. Telex 640609. V AE DC.

Near the Arc de Triomphe, this fine hotel has Empire-style décor and spacious (though not very cheery) rooms. Impeccable service. See 'restaurants': Napoléon.

Plaza Athénée
25, av. Montaigne — 47.23.78.33
Open year-round. 50 stes 4,180-8,600 F. 215 rms 1,960-3,770 F. Restaurant. TV. Air cond. Valet parking. Telex 290082. V AE DC.

Its flowers and bright red awnings have added sparkle to the Avenue Montaigne for 90 years. Various styles of décor have been tastefully integrated into this luxurious setting. Most of the rooms have been elegantly modernised. Some deficiencies occasionally appear in the service and reception. See 'restaurants': Régence-Plaza and Relais-Plaza.

Pullman Saint-Honoré
15, rue Boissy-d'Anglas — 42.66.93.62
Open year-round. 8 stes 1,250-1,660 F. 112 rms 620-1,250 F. TV. Telex 240366. V AE DC.

Comfortable and functional, this hotel offers seven storeys of identical rooms with irreproachable bathrooms. The lobby is decorated with marquetry from the trains of the *Compagnie Internationale des Wagons Lits*. There is a bar, and light meals are available round the clock.

Pullman Windsor
14, rue Beaujon — 45.63.04.04
Open year-round. 5 stes 3,000 F. 135 rms 800-1,700 F. Restaurant. TV. Air cond. Valet parking. Telex 650902. V AE DC.

An hotel without much personality, but practical and quiet. Modernisation of the rooms was completed last year. Although relatively large, the bathrooms are rather dismal. See 'restaurants': Le Clovis.

Résidence Maxim's de Paris
42, av. Gabriel — 45.61.96.33
Open year-round. 35 stes 4,000 F. 4 rms 2,250 F. Restaurant. TV. Air cond. Valet parking. Telex 642794. V AE DC.

Couturier Pierre Cardin had the interior of this building demolished and rebuilt to create his dream hotel. Luxurious (oddly eclectic décor), and beyond the bank balance of most ordinary mortals.

Résidence Monceau
85, rue du Rocher — 45.22.75.11
Open year-round. 1 ste 740 F. 51 rms 520 F. TV. No pets. Telex 280671. V AE.

This well-kept, quiet hotel between the Parc Monceau and the Gare Saint-Lazare has rather impersonal rooms, but a very pleasant staff.

Résidence Saint-Honoré
214, rue du Fg-St-Honoré — 42.25.26.27
Open year-round. 91 rms 580-950 F. TV. Air cond 30 rms. Telex 640524. V AE DC.

A surprising range of styles has been used in the gradual renovation of the spacious rooms, which are more comfortable than luxurious. Uncommonly courteous staff.

Royal Hôtel
33, av. de Friedland – 43.59.08.14
Open year-round. 58 rms 775-990 F. TV. Telex 280965. V AE DC.
Comfortable, well-equipped rooms are tastefully furnished in period style. Attentive reception, and limousine service on request.

Royal Monceau
37, av. Hoche – 45.61.98.00
Open year-round. 39 stes 4,000-9,000 F. 180 rms 1,550-2,550 F. Restaurant. TV. Air cond. Heated pool. Valet parking. Telex 650361. V AE DC.
This large, luxurious, and discreet hotel attracts politicians, business people, and show business personalities with spacious rooms, superb comfort, and excellent room service. Among the many amenities are air-conditioning, individual safes, and a deluxe fitness centre. See 'restaurants': Le Carpaccio and Le Jardin.

San Régis
12, rue J.-Goujon – 43.59.41.90
Open year-round. 10 stes 2,100-4,000 F. 34 rms 1,150-2,000 F. Restaurant. TV. Air cond 34 rms. No pets. Telex 643637. V AE DC.
This jewel of an hotel, much appreciated by celebrities from the worlds of show business and *haute couture*, provides a successful mix of traditional comfort and the latest technology. Perfectly kept rooms are decorated in delicate colours that set off the paintings and authentic antiques. Elegant bathrooms. English bar.

La Trémoille
14, rue de La Trémoille – 47.23.34.20
Open year-round. 14 stes 2,400-4,390 F. 96 rms 1,420-2,520 F. Restaurant. TV. Air cond. Valet parking. Telex 640344. V AE DC.
An opulent atmosphere, with period furniture, luxurious bathrooms, and window boxes of bright flowers on the balconies. In winter, the pretty dining room is warmed by a crackling fire.

Hôtel Vernet
25, rue Vernet – 47.23.43.10
Open year-round. 3 stes 2,600 F. 54 rms 1,250-1,750 F. Restaurant. TV. Air cond. Valet parking. Telex 290347. V AE DC.
This is one of the city's finest hotels, combining the best of modern and traditional comforts. The rooms and suites are handsomely decorated with genuine Louis XVI, Directoire, or Empire furniture, and walls are hung with sumptuous blue or green fabric. Jacuzzi in all the bathrooms. See 'restaurants': Les Elysées du Vernet.

Vigny
9, rue Balzac – 40.75.04.39
Open year-round. 11 stes 2,000-6,000 F. 26 rms 1,500-1,900 F. Air cond. Garage parking.
A handsome and brand-new hotel, the Vigny offers English mahogany furniture, comfortable beds, and fine marble bathrooms: the virtues of another age simplified and brought up to date. Excellent service.

Warwick
5, rue de Berri – 45.63.14.11
Open year-round. 21 stes 2,700-8,100 F. 148 rms 1,520-2,270 F. Restaurant. TV. Air cond. Valet parking. Telex 642295. V AE DC.
Luxurious and modern, just off the Champs-Elysées, this hotel boasts spacious rooms (even the singles have double beds) decorated in pastel colours, with double glazing and air conditioning.

Several have terraces. See 'restaurants': La Couronne.

 PARIS **9th**

Ambassador-Concorde
16, bd Haussmann – 42.46.92.63
Open year-round. 2 stes 2,800-3,000 F. 300 rms 1,100-1,800 F. Restaurant. TV. Air cond 100 rms. Valet parking. Telex 650912. V AE DC.
Two of the lounges have new décor and improvements are continuing elsewhere. The rooms, done in art deco, classic, or pastoral style, have built-in furniture and 1930s dressing tables. Views of the Sacré-Cœur from the top floor. Restaurant open from noon to midnight.

Aurore Montmartre
76, rue de Clichy – 48.74.85.56
Open year-round. 24 rms 325-380 F. TV. Telex 280520. V AE DC.
A simple hotel offering smallish rooms, soundproofed and perfectly kept. Minibar.

Bergère
34, rue Bergère – 47.70.34.34
Open year-round. 136 rms 420-730 F. TV. No pets. Telex 290668. V AE DC.
This traditional hotel provides modern, well-equipped rooms. Most overlook a garden-courtyard.

Commodore
12, bd Haussmann – 42.46.72.82
Open year-round. 11 stes 1,800-2,300 F. 153 rms 800-1,300 F. Restaurant. TV. Telex 280601. V AE DC.
Situated close to the new Drouot auction house, the Commodore (built in the 1930s) is about to be modernised. Spacious rooms and attentive service.

Le Grand Hôtel
2, rue Scribe – 42.68.12.13
Open year-round. 30 stes 2,800-11,000 F. 515 rms 1,840-3,040 F. Restaurant. TV. Air cond. Valet parking. Telex 220875. V AE DC.
Major improvements have been going on for several years and are scheduled to end in 1992. Last year saw the completion of a huge central lobby covered with a glass roof, in keeping with the Second Empire style of the building. Work on the rooms and suites is finished: they are bright, spacious, and equipped with everything the modern traveller expects from a luxury hotel. See 'restaurants': Opéra.

Hôtel du Léman
20, rue de Trvise – 42.46.50.66
Open year-round. 24 rms 370-800 F. TV. Telex 281083. V AE DC.
This charming, out-of-the-ordinary small hotel has been tastefully modernised. Tuscany marble inlays enhance the modern décor in the lobby. The rooms are pleasantly decorated with attractive bedside lamps and original drawings. Some have king-size beds. Generous buffet breakfast.

Hôtel du Moulin Rouge
39, rue Fontaine – 42.81.93.25
Open year-round. 2 stes 650-840 F. 50 rms 460-565 F. TV. Parking. Telex 660055. V AE DC.
An oasis of charm and calm near the Place Pigalle. Very spacious rooms are decorated in shades of grey or pink, and some boast a small terrace on the inner courtyards. An excellent buffet breakfast is served until noon.

Hôtel du Pré
10, rue P.-Sémard — 42.81.37.11
Open year-round. 41 rms 350-435 F. TV. No pets. Telex 660549. V AE.
Actually two hotels, comfortable and close to the Gare du Nord and the Gare de l'Est. The rooms have painted wood panelling or Japanese wallpaper, paired with cane and bamboo furniture.

Riboutté-Lafayette
5, rue Riboutté — 47.70.62.36
Open year-round. 24 rms 330-395 F. TV. V.
Bright rooms decorated in pastel colours make this a pleasant small hotel.

Royal Médoc
14, rue G.-Marie — 47.70.37.33
Open year-round. 41 rms 550-680 F. TV. No pets. Telex 660053. V AE DC.
You can taste and buy wines from the Médoc in this modern, functional hotel, with direct telephones and multilingual staff. Located near the department stores on the *grands boulevards.*

Scribe
1, rue Scribe — 47.42.03.40
Open year-round. 11 stes 3,200-6,000 F. 217 rms 1,450-2,300 F. Restaurant. TV. Air cond. Valet parking. Telex 214653. V AE DC.
Completely renovated a few years ago, the rooms and suites all have pretty orange Japanese wallpaper with harmonising brown carpeting. Huge bathrooms. The rooms overlooking the street are double-glazed, with contemporary and Louis XVI-style furniture; those on the courtyard side are very quiet with Louis-Philippe furniture. Other amenities include television with nineteen channels and video, and round-the-clock room service. See 'restaurants': Les Muses.

PARIS 10th

Hôtel Flora
1-3, cour de la Ferme-St-Lazare — 48.24.84.84
Open year-round. 45 rms 525-610 F. TV. Telex 660880. V AE DC.
Near the Gare du Nord and the Gare de l'Est, the Flora offers pleasant, well-equipped modern rooms decorated in pastel shades.

Urbis Paris-Jemmapes
12, rue L.-Blanc — 42.01.21.21
Open year-round. 1 ste 1,100 F. 49 rms 331-366 F. TV. Telex 211734. V.
Near the Canal St-Martin, this well-designed business hotel provides rooms done in a rather cold modern style but with every amenity. Generous buffet breakfast.

PARIS 11th

Holiday Inn République
10, pl. de la République — 43.55.44.34
Open year-round. 8 stes 2,190-3,190 F. 321 rms 1,000-4,000 F. Restaurant. TV. Air cond. No pets. Valet parking. Telex 210651. V AE DC.
The Modern Palace, as it was first called in 1866, now bears the name of the world's biggest chain of hotels. The interior has been totally transformed, while preserving the handsome and historic façade. The pleasant rooms and suites are all well soundproofed. Brasserie with dancing and piano bar. See 'restaurants': La Belle Epoque.

Résidence Trousseau
13, rue Trousseau — 48.05.55.55
Open year-round. 65 rms 450-850 F. TV. Garage parking. Telex 210379. V AE.
Completed in 1989, this self-service hotel is situated in a quiet side street. Pleasant, modern décor and all mod cons: sink, refrigerator, electric hotplates, crockery, coffee machine, and microwave oven.

PARIS 12th

Belle Epoque
66, rue de Charenton — 43.44.06.66
Open year-round. 3 stes 750-1,000 F. 29 rms 440-650 F. TV. Telex 211551. V AE DC.
Not far from the Gare de Lyon, this well-kept hotel is furnished and decorated in 1930s style. Comfortable beds, modern bathrooms, and double glazing throughout.

Claret
44, bd de Bercy — 46.28.41.31
Open year-round. 52 rms 290-380 F. Restaurant. TV. Parking. Telex 217115. V AE DC.
This neat, modernised hotel with a family atmosphere features a wine bar in the basement.

Ibis Paris Bercy
77, rue de Bercy — 43.42.91.91
Open year-round. 368 rms 395-415 F. Restaurant. TV. Parking. Telex 216391. V AE.
This very professional establishment has blue-and-white décor and dark carpeting. One room on each floor is reserved for the disabled. Plain, well-kept bathrooms.

Modern-Hôtel-Lyon
3, rue Parrot — 43.43.41.52
Open year-round. 1 ste 660-760 F. 52 rms 320-510 F. TV. No pets. Telex 230369. V AE.
The location is most convenient (near the Gare de Lyon). Rooms are comfortable, unpretentious, and equipped with minibars. Thoughtful service.

Nouvel Hôtel
24, av. du Bel-Air — 43.43.01.81
Open year-round. 28 rms 270-500 F. TV. Telex 240139. V AE DC.
The small, comfortable rooms are furnished in a rather haphazard style. Pleasant reception.

Novotel Bercy
85, rue de Bercy — 43.42.30.00
Open year-round. 1 ste 990 F. 129 rms 580-615 F. Restaurant. TV. Air cond. Telex 218332. V AEDC.
An ultramodern steel-and-glass building near the Bercy sports complex. The rooms and suites are furnished and equipped to the hotelchain's standards, with direct telephone, minibar, and room service from 6 am to midnight. The only departure from the norms is the combined bath and shower. Conference and meeting rooms for 12 to 300 people. The large terrace is used for receptions in fine weather.

Le Relais de Lyon
64, rue Crozatier — 43.44.22.50
Open year-round. 34 rms 400-460 F. TV. No pets. Garage parking. Telex 216690. V AE DC.
This pleasant hotel provides bright, comfortable, well-equipped rooms. Friendly reception.

PARIS 13th

Mercure Paris-Bercy
6, bd V.-Auriol — 45.82.48.00
Open year-round. 89 rms 500-620 F. Restaurant. TV. Parking. Telex 205010. V AE.
A modern hotel near the Bercy sports complex and the Gare d'Austerlitz, it offers easy access from the *périphérique* (the Paris ring road). Well suited to the needs of business people, the rooms are soundproofed and have a large work surface. Some rooms have a terrace.

Résidence des Gobelins
9, rue des Gobelins — 47.07.26.90
Open year-round. 32 rms 280-370 F. TV. Telex 206566. V AE DC.
A delightful small hotel. The warm welcome of the young owners merits a detour. Rooms are decorated in blue, green or orange, a different colour for each floor.

PARIS 14th

Istria
29, rue Campagne-Première — 43.20.91.82
Open year-round. 26 rms 400-490 F. TV. Telex 203618. V AE.
Elm furniture graces the rooms and bathrooms of this well-kept hotel, modernised in 1988.

Lenox
15, rue Delambre — 43.35.34.50
Open year-round. 6 stes 850 F. 52 rms 430-540 F. TV. Telex 260745. V AE DC.
In the heart of Montparnasse, the Lenox features bright, cheerful rooms and suites with antique furniture and fireplaces.

Mercure
20, rue de la Gaîté — 43.35.28.28
Open year-round. 6 stes 950 F. 185 rms 500-750 F. Restaurant. TV. Aircond. Garage parking. Telex 201532. V AE DC.
The comfortable rooms are just big enough, with double glazing, minibar, direct telephone and ten television channels. Functional bathrooms.

Méridien Montparnasse
19, rue du Cdt-Mouchotte — 43.20.15.51
Open year-round. 33 stes 2,750-5,750 F. 950 rms 990-1,500 F. Restaurant. TV. Air cond. No pets. Telex 200135. V AE DC.
The huge lobby with its marble, mirrors, and greenery recalls grand hotels in the Far East. Along with comfortable beds and air-conditioning, there are many touches of modern luxury: computerised minibar, multi-channel television, direct telephones. See 'restaurants': Justine and Montparnasse 25.

Hôtel du Midi
4, av. R.-Coty — 43.27.23.25
Open year-round. 50 rms 178-288 F. TV 20 rms. Pets allowed.
An hotel from another era, the Midi is rather out of date but has a certain charm. Largish, comfortable rooms with double windows. Minibars.

Orléans Palace Hôtel
185, bd Brune — 45.39.68.50
Open year-round. 92 rms 390-480 F. TV. No pets. Telex 260725. V AE DC.
A quiet and comfortable traditional hotel that offers good value. The well-equipped and soundproofed rooms are in need of redecoration.

Parc Montsouris
4, rue du Parc-Montsouris — 45.89.09.72
Open year-round. 7 stes 450 F. 35 rms 280-450 F. TV. Telex 206670. V AE.
This small, quiet hotel, modernised last year, features plainly furnished white rooms with bright, new bathrooms.

Primavera
147ter, rue d'Alésia — 45.42.06.37
Open year-round. 70 rms 308-480 F. TV. Garage parking. Telex 206831. V AE DC.
Functional rooms cheered up by some *naïf* paintings. Very good reception and numerous services.

Pullman Saint-Jacques
17, bd St-Jacques — 40.78.79.80
Open year-round. 14 stes 1,570-1,750 F. 800 rms 940-1,050 F. Restaurant. TV. Air cond. Parking. Valet parking. Telex 270740. V AE DC.
Quietly situated, with fine views over the city from the sixth floor. Rooms are quite large, and offer air-conditioning, radio alarm, minibar, black-out blinds, and good bathrooms.

PARIS 15th

Beaugrenelle St-Charles
82, rue St-Charles — 45.78.61.63
Open year-round. 51 rms 330-380 F. TV. Telex 270263. V AE DC.
Near the Beaugrenelle shopping complex, this friendly hotel provides modern, well-equipped rooms decorated in restful colours. Breakfast is served in the rooms upon request. Good value.

Hôtel Brancion
105, rue Brancion — 42.50.86.00
Open year-round. 71 rms 400-550 F. TV. Garage parking. Telex 206668. V AE DC.
A brand new seven-storey hotel near the exhibition centre at Porte de Versailles. Spacious, modern rooms are decorated in pale colours. Lounge-bar. Alas, the reception is rather stuffy.

Fondary
30, rue Fondary — 45.75.14.75
Open year-round. 20 rms 330-395 F. TV. Telex 206761. V AE.
Pretty pastel décor, attractive fabrics and plain bamboo furniture make this a pleasant little hotel. Service is warm and efficient. Agreeable lounge-bar.

Frantour Suffren
20, rue J.-Rey — 45.78.61.08
Open year-round. 10 stes 1,700-3,000 F. 397 rms 530-700 F. Restaurant. TV. Air cond. Parking. Telex 204459. V AE DC.
This large, modern hotel near the Seine has well-equipped rooms which are refurbished regularly. There is an attractive, plant-filled restaurant, and meals are served in the garden in summer.

Hilton
18, av. de Suffren — 42.73.92.00
Open year-round. 26 stes 2,900-8,300 F. 455 rms 1,250-2,100 F. Restaurant. TV. Air cond. Valet parking. Telex 200955. V AE DC.
The first modern hotel built in Paris after the last war has spacious rooms, efficient service, and films shown on closed-circuit television. There is no charge for children—whatever their age—sharing a room with their parents. Two bars, hairdresser, luxury boutiques.

Mercure Paris-Vaugirard
69, bd Victor — 45.33.74.63
Open year-round. 91 rms 690-1,350 F. Restaurant. TV. Air cond. Garage parking. Telex 260844. V AE DC.

A good hotel for business people, with spacious, well-equipped rooms, good soundproofing, and a private underground car park.

Nikko de Paris
61, quai de Grenelle — 40.58.20.00
Open year-round. 5 stes 3,400-10,500 F. 779 rms 1,050-1,760 F. Restaurant. TV. Air cond. Heated pool. Garage parking. Telex 260012. V AE DC.

Thirty-one floors piled up to resemble an enormous beehive. Modern, functional rooms with a choice of western or Japanese décor all overlook the Pont Mirabeau from huge, porthole-style windows. The top six floors are reserved for luxury rooms with personalised service. Boutiques, conference rooms, sauna, gym, and massage service are among the Nikko's many amenities. Bar with a view. See 'restaurants': Les Célébrités.

Résidence Saint-Lambert
5, rue E.-Gibez — 48.28.63.14
Open year-round. 48 rms 380-511 F. TV. Telex 205459. V AE DC.

This pleasant, quiet hotel near the exhibition centre at Porte de Versailles has smallish rooms, some overlooking the garden. A laundry and bar are on the premises.

Sofitel Paris
8-12, rue L.-Armand — 40.60.30.30
Open year-round. 16 stes 1,400-2,250 F. 635 rms 700-750 F. Restaurant. TV. Air cond. Heated pool. Valet parking. Telex 200432. V AE DC.

A fine choice for business meetings, the Sofitel boasts 37 conference rooms, with facilities for simultaneous translation in five languages. And for relaxing, there's a gym, sauna, indoor/outdoor heated swimming pool, and a bar with a panoramic view. The modern, comfortable rooms have magnetic locks, but are on the small side. Some have brown marble bathrooms. See 'restaurants': Le Relais de Sèvres.

Wallace
89, rue Fondary — 45.78.83.30
Open year-round. 35 rms 450-490 F. TV. Telex 205277. V AE DC.

This hotel exudes old-fashioned charm. Most of its small but cheerful rooms overlook a quiet garden.

Yllen
196, rue de Vaugirard — 45.67.67.67
Open year-round. 1 ste 800-880 F. 40 rms 420-580 F. TV. Telex 200090. V AE DC.

Yllen's modern, functional rooms have restrained décor and are well soundproofed—but they are very small. Energetic management, friendly reception.

PARIS   16th

Alexander
102, av. V.-Hugo — 45.53.64.65
Open year-round. 3 stes 1,700-2,060 F. 59 rms 690-940 F. TV. No pets. Telex 610373. V AE DC.

This stylish hotel is decorated with slightly outmoded elegance (leaf patterned wallpaper, grey carpeting). Rooms are equipped withdouble glazing and large, modern bathrooms.

Ambassade
79, rue Lauriston
45.53.41.15
Open year-round. 38 rms 370-495 F. TV. No pets. Telex 613643. V AE DC.

The rooms have recently been redecorated with patterned paper on the walls and ceilings, and cane furniture. Small grey-marble bathrooms. Ask for a room overlooking the courtyard and you'll think you're in the country.

Baltimore
88 bis, av. Kléber — 45.53.83.33
Open year-round. 1 ste 1,800 F. 119 rms 1,180-1,480 F. Restaurant. TV. Air cond 20 rms. Telex 611591. V AE DC.

An international business clientele favours the Baltimore's quietly elegant, modernised rooms. Six conference rooms in the basement.

Le Bois
11, rue du Dôme
45.00.31.96
Open year-round. 41 rms 360-465 F. TV. Telex 615453. V AE.

Here is a simple, value-for-money hotel where you will be warmly welcomed. The small, well-kept rooms, were attractively redecorated last year.

Garden Elysée
12, rue St-Didier — 47.55.01.11
Open year-round. 48 rms 800-1,350 F. Restaurant. TV. Air cond. No pets. Parking. Telex 648157. V AE DC.

In a new building set back from the road are elegant, unusually spacious rooms that overlook a pleasant garden where breakfast is served in summer. Décor is 1930s style. Satellite television, Jacuzzi.

Hameau de Passy
48, rue de Passy — 42.88.47.55
Open year-round. 31 rms 420-480 F. Telex 651469.

Tucked away in a flower-filled cul-de-sac, this exceptionally quiet hotel was modernised last year. Plain, comfortable rooms, some connecting, all overlook the garden. Smiling service and reception.

Kléber
7, rue de Belloy — 47.23.80.22
Open year-round. 1 ste 900 F. 21 rms 466-830 F. TV. Parking. Telex 612830. V AE DC.

A charming family hotel that offers neat, well-equipped rooms.

Longchamp
68, rue de Longchamp
47.27.13.48
Open year-round. 23 rms 580-680 F. TV. Telex 610342. V AE DC.

The quiet, comfortable rooms are equipped with minibar, direct telephone, and television with two channels in English. Intimate atmosphere.

Majestic
29, rue Dumont-d'Urville
45.00.83.70
Open year-round. 3 stes 1,000-1,600 F. 27 rms 800-1,050 F. TV. Air cond 11 rms. Telex 640034.V AE DC.

Some rooms are awaiting redecoration but all have comfortable beds, thick carpeting, and television. Friendly reception.

Park Avenue
55-57, av. R.-Poincaré – 45.53.44.60
*Open year-round. 13 stes 1,900-2,500 F. 99 rms
1,180-1,480 F. Restaurant. TV. Air cond. Valet parking. Telex 643862. V AE DC.*
Two hotels with more or less the same amenities.
The Park Avenue is resolutely modern, with
soundproofing and air conditioning. Comfortable,
well-equipped rooms, with 12 television channels
and hairdryer. A few steps away, the Central Park
has similar rooms with lower ceilings. See
'restaurants': Le Relais du Parc.

Passy Eiffel
10, rue de Passy – 45.25.55.66
*Open year-round. 50 rms 440-520 F. TV.
Telex 612753. V AE DC.*
Not all the rooms have views of the Eiffel Tower,
but they are well equipped and have good
soundproofing.

Queen's Hotel
4, rue B.-Lepage – 42.88.89.85
*Open year-round. 22 rms 240-450 F. TV. No pets. V
AE.*
For an 'English' atmosphere and small, confortable rooms, try this modest little hotel. Bathrooms
are equipped with hairdryers.

Raphaël
17, av. Kléber – 45.02.16.00
*Open year-round. 4 stes 2,400-6,000 F. 89 rms
1,500-2,100 F. Restaurant. TV. Air cond 15 rms.
Valet parking. Telex 610356. V AE DC.*
This elegant hotel is decorated with a fine collection of antiques, Oriental carpets, and works of art.
The spacious, richly furnished rooms have huge
wardrobes. Some of the bathrooms have retained
their original 1920s décor. The service is exactly
what you expect in this level of establishment.

Résidence Bassano
15, rue de Bassano – 47.23.78.23
*Open year-round. 3 stes 1,600-1,950 F. 27 rms 650-
1,050 F. Restaurant. TV. Air cond. Valet parking.
Telex 649872. V AE DC.*
Modern, comfortable hotel, popular with business people. The rooms are decorated in pastel
colours with chintz curtains and bedcovers.

Rond-Point de Longchamp
86, rue de Longchamp – 45.05.13.63
*Open year-round. 57 rms 550-780 F. Restaurant. TV.
Air cond. Telex 620653. V AE DC.*
The largish rooms are prettily decorated with
grey carpeting, pale fabrics and burr walnut furniture, and are well equipped with double glazing,
air-conditioning, minibar, and three satellite television channels. Marble bathrooms. Attentive
service.

Saint-James's Club
5, pl. du Chancelier-Adenauer – 47.04.29.29
*Open year-round. 31 stes 2,850-7,450 F. 17 rms
1,450-2,250 F. Restaurant. TV. Air cond. Valet parking. Telex 643850. V AE DC.*
Since its purchase by an hotel group, the hotel
part of this private club has been open to the
public. A staff of 100 looks after the 48 rooms and
suites—a luxury level of attention with prices fixed
accordingly. The good-sized rooms are decorated
in the austere 1930s style, with flowers, plants, and
a basket of fruit adding warmth. Marble
bathrooms.

Hôtel de Sévigné
6, rue de Belloy – 47.20.88.90
*Open year-round. 30 rms 550-650 F. TV. Garage
parking. Telex 610219. V AE DC.*
A classic hotel. The modern, comfortable rooms
have white walls and flowered curtains. Tiled
bathrooms. Expect friendly service and reception.

Trocadéro
21, rue St-Didier – 45.53.01.82
*Open year-round. 23 rms 440-540 F. TV.
Telex 643164. V AE DC.*
Decorated in soft colours, the rooms have
minibar and television. Good bathrooms include a
hairdryer.

La Villa Maillot
143, av. de Malakoff – 45.01.25.22
*Open year-round. 3 stes 1,900-2,100 F. 39 rms 1,300-
1,500 F. Restaurant. TV. Air cond. Valet parking.
Telex 649808. V AE DC.*
Formerly an embassy, this recent conversion has
a warm atmosphere and elegant décor. Spacious
rooms and suites, well soundproofed, and pink
marble bathrooms. See 'restaurants': Le Jardin.

Banville
166, bd Berthier – 42.67.70.16
*Open year-round. 39 rms 500-520 F. TV.
Telex 643025. V AE.*
Flowers at the windows, some of which open to
panoramic views of the city. Bright, cheerful
rooms and good soundproofing. Excellent reception.

Centre Ville Etoile
6, rue des Acacias – 43.80.56.18
*Open year-round. 20 rms 650-900 F. Restaurant. TV.
Air cond. Telex 650343. V AE DC.*
A quiet building, tastefully renovated. The rooms
are furnished in contemporary style, with satellite
television and spotless bathrooms. See
'restaurants': Le Cougar.

Concorde-La Fayette
3, pl. du Gal-Kœnig – 40.68.50.68
*Open year-round. 22 stes 2,800-8,000 F. 1,000 rms
1,100-1,950 F. Restaurant. TV. Air cond. Valet parking. Telex 650892. V AE DC.*
A massive oval tower with fine views. Comfortable, functional rooms, well equipped for
travellers in a hurry. Restaurants, bars, conference
and reception rooms, boutiques, four cinemas,
and a bookshop. See 'restaurants'. L'Etoile d'Or.

Courcelles
184, rue de Courcelles – 47.63.65.30
*Open year-round. 1 ste 1,200 F. 42 rms 495-585 F.
TV. Telex 642252. V AE DC.*
A newly renovated hotel with effective double
glazing. Plain, comfortable rooms are decorated
with pink or green fabric wallcoverings, matching
curtains and bedcovers, and rosy-beige lacquered
furniture.

Eber Monceau-Courcelles
18, rue L.-Jost – 46.22.60.70
*Open year-round. 5 stes 950-1,200 F. 13 rms 500-
550 F. TV. No pets. Telex 649949. V AE DC.*
A clientele drawn from the film and fashion fields
favours this address. The small, attractive rooms
are rather overwhelmed by the large wardrobes.
Good bathrooms.

Etoile
3, rue de l'Etoile — 43.80.36.94
Open year-round. 25 rms 540-590 F. TV. Telex 642028. V AE DC.
The clean, functional rooms are decorated in a pedestrian fashion. Bar.

Etoile Park Hôtel
10, av. Mac-Mahon — 42.67.69.63
Open year-round. 28 rms 415-680 F. TV. Telex 649266. V AE DC.
The tasteful, restrained décor has an 'Italian design' look. Friendly reception.

Etoile-Pereire
146, bd Pereire — 42.67.60.00
Open year-round. 5 stes 900 F. 21 rms 450-650 F. TV. No pets. Telex 305551. V AE DC.
At this welcoming hotel attention to detail is a priority. Particularly quiet rooms, almost all overlooking the courtyard.

Frantour Berthier-Brochant
163 bis, av. de Clichy — 40.25.20.00
Open year-round. 1 ste 800-2,000 F. 648 rms 400-470 F. Restaurant. Half-board 510 F. TV. Parking. Telex 660251. V AE DC.
Probably the country's biggest hotel in its category. The 650 rooms, recently redecorated, are pleasant and well equipped. Magnificent view from the top floor.

Magellan
17, rue J.-B.-Dumas — 45.72.44.51
Open year-round. 75 rms 460-485 F. TV. Parking. Telex 644728. V AE DC.
More functional than luxurious, the Magellan's rooms are quiet and the quality of the service is excellent. Attractive garden.

Méridien
81, bd Gouvion-Saint-Cyr — 40.68.34.34
Open year-round. 15 stes 3,500-7,000 F. 1,012 rms 1,450-1,850 F. Restaurant. TV. Air cond. Valet parking. Telex 290952. V AE DC.
This is the biggest hotel in western Europe and one of the busiest in Paris. The rooms are small but very well equipped. A variety of shops and restaurants liven things up (including the excellent Clos Longchamp—see 'restaurants'), as does the popular bar that presents good jazz in the evenings. Sauna and massage service.

L'Ouest Hôtel
165, rue de Rome — 42.27.50.29
Open year-round. 50 rms 200-300 F. TV. Pets allowed.
Simple hotel overlooking the railway, but soundproofed throughout. The functional rooms vary in size.

Regent's Garden Hotel
6, rue P.-Demours — 45.74.07.30
Open year-round. 40 rms 560-850 F. TV. Parking. Telex 640127. V AE DC.
The nicely proportioned, well-kept rooms are decorated in an occasionally pompous manner, but the building is handsome and the setting most attractive.

Saint-Ferdinand
36, rue St-Ferdinand — 45.72.66.66
Open year-round. 42 rms 610-735 F. TV. Air cond 30 rms. Telex 649565. V AE DC.
This small, functional hotel opened in 1985. The rooms are tiny (the bathrooms even more so), but

they are well equipped with television, minibar, safe, and hairdryer.

Splendid Etoile
1 bis, av. Carnot — 43.80.14.56
Open year-round. 7 stes 1,000 F. 50 rms 650-900 F. Restaurant. TV. Air cond 30 rms. No pets. Telex 280773. V DC.
Right next to the Arc de Triomphe, but protected from the racket by double glazing. Spacious, well-kept rooms.

Ermitage Hôtel
24, rue Lamarck — 42.64.79.22
Open year-round. 12 rms 240-360 F. TV. Pets allowed.
This charming hotel occupies a little white building behind the Sacré-Cœur.

Regyn's Montmartre
18, pl. des Abbesses — 42.54.45.21
Open year-round. 22 rms 310-380 F. TV. Telex 650269. V.
The well-equipped rooms are simply but agreeably decorated. Fine views. Breakfast is served round the clock.

Terrass Hôtel
12, rue J.-de-Maistre — 46.06.72.85
Open year-round. 13 stes 1,200 F. 88 rms 600-930 F. Restaurant. Half-board 590-770 F. TV. Air cond 6 rms. Telex 280830. V AE DC.
These comfortable, well-equipped rooms display fine woodwork and some attractive furniture. The terrace affords panoramic views. Buffet breakfast is available to non-residents as well as guests. See 'restaurants': Le Guerlande.

Utrillo
7, rue A.-Bruant — 42.58.13.44
Open year-round. 30 rms 250-340 F. TV. No pets. Telex 281550. V AE DC.
An excellent renovation behind an old façade. Simple, well-designed rooms.

Le Laumière
4, rue Petit — 42.06.10.77
Open year-round. 54 rms 170-290 F. TV 24 rms. Parking. Telex 212688. V.
Near the La Villette exhibition centre, this meticulously kept, modern hotel with simply decorated rooms is very good value. Cheerful reception.

Europark Hôtel
60, rue des Frères-Flavien — 48.97.92.92
Open year-round. 12 stes 1,100 F. 250 rms 590-680 F. Restaurant. Half-board 730 F. TV. Air cond. Garage parking. Telex 233173. V AE DC.
The fully equipped rooms provide all the usual comforts, including air-conditioning in warm weather. Conference rooms and individual offices are available, as well as round-the-clock room service. Coffee shop.

PARIS

Suburbs

95100 Argenteuil — (Val-d'Oise)
Paris 14 - Pontoise 20 - St-Germain-en-L. 15

La Closerie Périgourdine ❊
85, bd J.-Allemane
39.80.01.28

M. Senot de La Londe. Open every day. Open until 10 pm. V AE DC.

Despite the fussy decor—stone walls, velvet-covered beams and corner fireplace, the menu offers a promising list of specialities: salt-cured duck, escargots aux cèpes, lotte with mustard and thyme, and walnut cake. The wine list includes a good selection of Bordeaux, and more Burgundies.

A la carte: 300-350 F. Menus: 135 F and 170 F (weekdays only, wine inc), 110 F (weekdays only).

12/20 La Ferme d'Argenteuil
2 bis, rue Verte
39.61.00.62

Mlles Claro. Closed Mon dinner, Sun, Feb school holidays and 5-28 Aug. Open until 10 pm. Private room: 20. V AE.

A menu with wine included will give you a relatively painless glimpse of the classic cooking here. Far more expensive are the a la carte dishes, including fondant de langouste sauce grelette, and whole veal kidney with coarse-grain mustard sauce. The décor is due for a face-lift next year.

A la carte: 300-350 F. Menu: 250 F (wine inc).

Le Moulin d'Orgemont
Rue du Clos-des-Moines
34.10.21.47

M. Margana. Closed Sun dinner and Mon. Open until 10.30 pm. Private room: 250. Garden dining. Parking. Telex 611047. V AE DC.

This hilltop windmill overlooking western Paris stopped turning long ago, but the cuisine appears to be taking on a new lease of life. A barrel-organ and nineteenth-century carousel are not the only attractions of this unusual dining room. We recently sampled beef terrine in a delicate pastry crust, roast veal with olives, excellent cheeses, and a cherry dessert. Not all is up to par (insipid red mullet and disastrous crème catalane), but some recipes are original and pleasing to the palate. The quality of the service varies.

A la carte: 350 F. Menus: 330 F (weekdays only, wine inc) 190 F.

92600 Asnières — (Hauts/Seine)
Paris 9 - Argenteuil 6 - Saint-Denis 8 - Pontoise 27

L'Ecurie
4 bis, Grande-Rue-Ch.-de-Gaulle
47.90.91.30

M. Fontaine. Closed Sat dinner, Sun, 16-23 April and 6 Aug-4 Sep. Open until 10 pm. V AE.

An intelligent and generous formula is offered during the week at lunch and dinner (94 F for a starter plus main course, such as a delicious bluecheese tart, and mildly spiced chicken fricassée). One of the good desserts, like the walnut souffl, will cost extra but won't break the bank. The charming *patron*, Andr Fontaine, also makes excellent sole fritters, quick-cooked turbot with citrus fruits, and rognons de veau au Margaux. His desserts are remarkable, which is more than can be said for the heavily rural décor.

A la carte: 260-300 F.

12/20 Le Périgord
3-5, quai Aulagnier — 47.90.19.86

M. Fréville. Closed Sat, Sun and week of 15 Aug. Open until 10 pm. Parking. V AE.

The long *carte* includes a few classic dishes from the Prigord (foie gras, confits, and tournedos Rossini), plus rich, skilfully prepared, market-fresh creations such as pavé de sandre au beurre blanc de Gewurztraminer, or braised duckling with chanterelles. Service is good, prices high.

A la carte: 350 F and up. Menu: 200 F (dinner only, wine inc).

Le Van Gogh
2, quai Aulagnier — 47.91.05.10

M. Daubian. Closed Sat, Sun, week 15 Aug, 2 weeks at Christmas. Open until 10 pm. Private room: 15. Garden dining. No pets. Garage parking. V AE DC.

Robert and Pierrette Daubian have dropped anchor in this ultramodern establishment on Robinson island. The dining room resembles the interior of a luxury liner, with portholes and bay windows offering views of the Seine. The cuisine looks out to sea, with dishes like lobster and prawn feuilleté, and filet de bar royal cooked with the freshest produce. Desserts are superb (try the delicious red-fruit gratin with Champagne), and there are fine wines to wash it all down.

A la carte: 300 F.

91200 Athis-Mons — (Essonne)
Paris 19 - Créteil 15 - Evry 12 - Fontainebleau 50

12/20 Les Jardins de Marrakech
146, rte de Fontainebleau — 60.48.23.55
M. Imakor. Closed Aug. Open until 11 pm. Air cond. Parking. V AE DC.
White stucco walls highlighted with gold provide a glorious setting for the marvellous pastilla, delicate couscous, and the less spectacular lemon chicken tajine. You may find the Oriental pastries too sweet except for the stuffed dates. But do try the boukha (fig brandy) and the honest Moroccan wines. Courteous service.
A la carte: 150 F.

93600 Aulnay-sous-Bois — (Seine-St-D.)
Paris 16 - Senlis 38 - Meaux 30 - Lagny 21

12/20 L'Escargot
40, rte de Bondy — 48.66.64.22
M. Cavallero. Closed Mon (and 2 Sun per month), Christmas week, Feb school holidays and end July-end Aug. Open until 9.30 pm. Private room: 14. V AE DC.
You will be served with a smile in this country cottage. Portions are generous and ingredients excellent: the list includes escargots, of course, followed by rognon de veau St-Lazare or John Dory with sorrel. The wines make the bill even harder to swallow.
A la carte: 300 F.

Novotel
4 km NW on N 370 — 48.66.22.97
Open every day. 139 rms 400-430 F. Restaurant. TV. Air cond. Conference facilities. Pool. Parking. Telex 230121. V AE DC.
This handsome modern hotel is located near the Villepinte exhibition centre. Surrounded by gardens, it is especially suitable for families. Good conference facilities.

Les Relais Bleus
Rue L.-de-Vinci — 48.66.99.46
Open every day. 117 rms 220-295 F. Restaurant. TV. Conference facilities. Telex 233109. V AE.
A stone's throw from the exhibition centre and only minutes from Charles de Gaulle airport, this small hotel has pleasant, convenient rooms.

Hôtel de Strasbourg
43, bd de Strasbourg — 48.66.60.38
Open every day. 2 stes 275-300 F. 22 rms 200-275 F. TV. Telex 212351. V AE DC.
This small suburban hotel offers conventional rooms that are charming, comfortable and now soundproofed as well. Bar.

93170 Bagnolet — (Seine-St-D.)
Paris 6 - Meaux 41 - Lagny 27

Novotel Paris-Bagnolet
1, av. de la République — 43.60.02.10
Open every day. 9 stes 900 F. 611 rms 575-610 F. Restaurant. TV. Air cond. Conference facilities. Heated pool. Parking. Telex 235136. V AE DC.
Just outside Paris, this is a good address for seminars and conferences. The rooms are modern, functional, and well soundproofed. Piano bar.

93150 Blanc-Mesnil (Le) — (Seine-St-D.)
Paris 12 - Le Bourget 3 - Bobigny 6 - Aulnay 3

Novotel Paris-Le Bourget
2, rue J.-Perrin — 48.67.48.88
Open every day. 143 rms 415-450 F. Restaurant. TV. Air cond. Conference facilities. Heated pool. Parking. Telex 230115. V AE DC.
Eight kilometres from the permanent science exhibition at La Villette and close to the Aeronautics and Space Museum. The rooms are bright and functional.

11/20 La Vallière
8, av. Paul-Vaillant-Couturier
48.69.52.01
M. Roméra. Closed Sat lunch, Sun (except lunch upon reserv) and Aug. Open until 9.30 pm. Private room: 20. V AE.
This small, provincial restaurant has rather dreary décor. The food, honest and simple, is fresh and carefully selected: crpes filled with basil-scented escargots, andouillette sausage, salmon with citrus fruit, and banana bavarois with apricot coulis.
A la carte: 200-250 F. Menu: 120 F.

78380 Bougival — (Yvelines)
Paris 18 - Versailles 7 - Saint-Germain-en-Laye 7

Le Bistro du Quai
6, quai Georges-Clemenceau
39.69.18.98
M. Durand. Closed Sat lunch. Open until 10 pm. Private room: 40. V AE DC.
Formerly L'Huître et la Tarte, which Roland Durand has just taken over along with Le Camélia (see below).
A la carte: 150-200 F. Menu: 145 F (weekdays lunch only, wine inc).

Le Camélia
7, quai Georges-Clemenceau
39.18.36.06
M. Durand. Closed Sat lunch and 3-26 Aug. Open until 10 pm. Private room: 14. Garden dining. Air cond. Valet parking. V AE DC.
It was high time Roland Durand found a place of his own, and here it is. The former restaurant director of the Sofitel hotel chain has invested heavily in renovating this venerable culinary institution. We didn't have the opportunity to assess the new Camlia before going to press, but we wish Roland Durand the success he deserves.
A la carte: 400-500 F. Menus: 220 F, 380 F.

92100 Boulogne-Billancourt — (Hauts/Seine)
Paris (Pte de St-Cloud) 10 - Versailles 11

Hôtel Adagio
20-22, rue des Abondances
48.25.80.80
Open every day. 75 rms 640-720 F. Restaurant. TV. Conference facilities. Garage parking. Telex 632189. V AE DC.
This modern, glass-and-concrete hotel has bright, spacious rooms fitted with every convenience and pleasantly furnished. The basement houses a vast complex of conference rooms. Brunch served on Sundays until 3 pm.

L'Auberge
86, av. J.-B.-Clément — 46.05.22.35
M. Veysset. Closed Sun, holidays and 3-26 Aug. Open until 10 pm. Private room: 22. Air cond. V AE DC.
Both the décor and the cooking have undergone a radical change of style in this restaurant once devoted to the Franche-Comt and its food, but the owners and chefs are still the same. Cancoillotte, a soft, pungent cheese spread, and the local sausages have disappeared from the menu to be replaced by galette de pigeon en papillote, a ragot of cockles and squid, and nougat glacé au Grand Marnier (a bit too sweet but nice and creamy). The traditional duck terrine is still available however, and there are Jura wines in the excellent cellar.
A la carte: 350-400 F. Menu: 190 F.

La Bretonnière
120, av. J.-B.-Clément — 46.05.73.56
M. Laurens. Closed Sat and Sun. Open until 9.45 pm. V AE DC.
A former head waiter, Ren Rossignol, has switched to cooking and brought this restaurant back up to standard. Taste the wonderful pickled herring, saddle of lamb with haricot beans, and good, simple desserts like the chocolate mousse with orange sauce. Excellent Loire wines.
A la carte: 300 F. Menus: 110 F (dinner only), 195 F, 280 F.

12/20 La Champagne
(Jean-Pierre Forax)
112, av. V.-Hugo — 48.25.49.20
M. Forax. Closed Sat, Sun and Aug. Open until 10.15 pm. Private room: 20. Garden dining. No-smoking section. V AE DC.
The new décor is extremely elegant and the big round tables popular with business people. You too will appreciate the seafood assortment, larded fillet of veal, and roast rack of lamb. Excellent, varied wines and attentive staff.
A la carte: 250-300 F. Menu: 280 F (champagne inc).

Au Comte de Gascogne
89, av. J.-B.-Clément — 46.03.47.27
M. Charvet. Closed Sat lunch, Sun and 5-20 Aug. Open until 10.30 pm. Garden dining. Air cond. Valet parking. V AE DC.
Three palm trees, a fountain and lots of flowers make it feel like springtime all year round in the delightful courtyard garden. Business lunches actually become enjoyable, while dinner in the suburbs turns into an exotic outing. Grard Vrane, the jovial Gascon who created this tropical greenhouse with its sliding roof, has handed over the kitchen to Henri Charvet, who once served the best meals in Aix-en-Provence. The Gascon flavour lingers on in the seven or eight variations on foie gras, including the wonderful smoked duck foie gras with cucumber and bacon. But it was the sun-kissed Provenal dishes that really captured our attention: prawn fricassée with Sauternes and ginger, sea bass served with artichauts barigoule, and a sweetbread and turnip turnover. The young sommelier, Patrice Marchand, will advise you on the best wines to accompany them.
A la carte: 500-700 F. Menu: 460 F (menu dégustation).

Les Merveilles de l'Océan
117, av. J.-B.-Clément — 48.25.43.88
M. Roubert. Open every day. Open until 10.30 pm. Private room: 25. Air cond. V AE.
Near the Boulogne film studios, the former chef of the luxury liner *France* offers plenty of classic

dishes as well as a few more daring creations: brik de langouste au gingembre, subtly flavoured sturgeon with sweet-pepper coulis, and a light, tasty strawberry tart. Exceptional selection of Armagnacs and Calvados.
A la carte: 400 F. Menus: 190 F (except weekdays lunch, wine inc), 207 F, 300 F.

12/20 Le Petit Vatel
15, rue de Montmorency — 48.25.50.93
M. Perron. Closed Sat lunch and Sun. Open until 11 pm. Private room: 30. V AE DC.
The *carte* has been replaced by two menus offering plenty of choice but slightly stingy portions. The freshness and quality of the ingredients never vary however, and the warm salad of blood sausage, eel stew with Chinon, and chocolate souffl make for an honest meal.
Menus: 140 F (lunch only), 250 F (wine inc).

12/20 Le Poivre Vert
1, pl. B.-Palissy — 46.03.01.63
M. Vérane. Closed at Christmas. Open until 11.30 pm. Air cond. V.
Book early for a top-value meal in this modern, plant-filled setting: the 90 F formula (a starter and main course) is understandably much in demand. Try the salad of smoked duck breast and giblets, excellent leg of lamb with matchstick potatoes, apple tart. Well-chosen wines. The waiters are very efficient, but there just aren't enough of them.
Menu: 90 F.

BUC
78530 Buc — (Yvelines)
Paris 22 - Versailles 5 - Sceaux 8 - Chevreuse 14

Relais de Courlande
2, rue Collin-Mamet — 39.56.24.29
M. Granchamp. Closed Sun dinner, Mon, 16-25 Feb and 5-19 Aug. Open until 10 pm. Private room: 60. Garden dining. Hotel: 10 rms 240-300 F. Parking. V AE.
The newly renovated garden and terrace are becoming popular for business lunches. Besides its central location, this restaurant's success can be attributed to Luc Le Rhin's skilful cooking. Lobster ravioli, delicate crab-filled crpes, and banana and orange sabayon with rum are served by professional, smiling staff.
A la carte: 350 F. Menus: 100 F (weekdays only), 180 F, 220 F.

CELLE-SAINT-CLOUD (LA)
78170 Celle-Saint-Cloud (La) — (Yvelines)
Paris 16 - Saint-Cloud 5 - Bougival 2

12/20 Au Petit Chez Soi
Pl. de l'Eglise — 39.69.69.51
Mlle Berrut. Closed Sun dinner off-season. Open until 10.30 pm. Terrace dining. V.
There's almost a village feel about this restaurant with its warm wood décor and welcoming *patronne*. The cooking is only slightly better than mundane: the warm oysters with Champagne lacking finesse, good grilled fillet steak with sauce barnaise, and well-prepared fruit turnover. Even if it doesn't quite measure up to a toque, the address is still worth noting.
A la carte: 250 F. Menus: 145 F (weekdays lunch only), 155 F (dinner only, and lunch on w-e and holidays).

CERGY

95000 Cergy — (Val-d'Oise)
Paris 30 - Conflans-Sainte-Honorine 7 - Pontoise 4

Novotel
3, av. du Parc — 30.30.39.47
Open every day. 191 rms 405-440 F. Restaurant. TV. Air cond. Conference facilities. Pool. Parking. Telex 607264. V AE DC.
Twenty minutes from Paris and Versailles, this newly renovated hotel has quiet rooms and activities such as table tennis and French billiards. Special weekend rates.

CHÂTEAUFORT

78117 Châteaufort — (Yvelines)
Paris 28 - Versailles 10 - Orsay 11 - Pontchartrain 23

La Belle Epoque
10, pl. de la Mairie — 39.56.21.66
M. Peignaud. Closed Sun dinner, Mon, 12 Aug-6 Sep and 22 Dec-5 Jan. Open until 9.30 pm. Terrace dining. V AE DC.
From the terrace shaded by lime trees, you can enjoy a splendid view of the Mérantaise Valley. Inside, there's a mixture of styles and many souvenirs of the owner's travels. Michel Peignaud also likes to mix cooking styles, and his dishes are a (usually successful) combination of tastes and textures from the Far East, classic French cuisine, and his native Berry. Never have we eaten so well at Peignaud's as during our last visit, so expect a treat when you sample duck foie gras ravioli with mushroom stock, caramelised bass with vinegar, foie gras with soy sauce, and light mango feuilleté with kiwi fruit coulis. Fine wines from Menetou, Quincy, and Sancerre.
A la carte: 400 F.

CHAVILLE

92370 Chaville — (Hauts/Seine)
Paris 13 - Versailles 9 - Meudon 1 - Boulogne 2

La Tonnelle
29, rue Lamennais — 47.50.42.77
M. Tardif. Closed Mon, Feb and Aug. Open until 10.30 pm. Private room: 15. Terrace dining. Air cond. V.
Pretty pink-and-blue curtains and new wallpaper make for an elegant interior, while the garden-terrace with its old wine press is a winner on sunny days. Guy Tardif's cooking is scrupulously classic but lacks the boldness we detected in his early days, especially when it comes to seasonings. We sampled Rocamadour goat cheese in flaky pastry, a generous portion of sautéed calf's liver timidly flavoured with cider vinegar and oyster mushrooms, and an excellent strawberry shortcake. Smiling staff.
Menus: 180 F, 240 F.

CHENNEVIÈRES-SUR-MARNE

94430 Chennevières-sur-Marne — (Val/Marne)
Paris 17 - Lagny 20 - Coulommiers 51

L'Ecu de France
31, rue de Champigny — 45.76.00.03
M. Brousse. Closed Sun dinner and Mon (except holidays), and 2-9 Sep. Open until 9.30 pm. Private room: 12. Terrace dining. No pets. Parking. V.
Were it not for Patrick Gicquel's original, lively cuisine, this restaurant's exceptional location on the River Marne, its rustic décor, lavender tablecloths, and attentive staff would not be enough to fill the huge car park. As it is, you can spot number plates from far and wide. Success hasn't

gone to Gicquel's head, but it might prevent him from devoting all his attention to each dish: prawn and avocado pastries, tasteless scallops (it's hard to believe they were fresh) with tomato and spinach coulis, and an honest strawberry sabayon. Well-balanced choice of wines.
A la carte: 350-400 F.

Au Vieux Clodoche
18, rue de Champigny
45.76.09.39
Mme Huerta. Open every day. Open until 10 pm. Private room: 100. Garden dining. Garage parking. V AE DC.
On the riverside terrace in summer or near the fireplace in winter, Brigitte Huerta's cooking will capture your attention, and not just because of the high prices. The delicate duck foie gras au torchon, marvellous king prawns lightly cooked with butter and garlic, osso buco, cod in a butter sauce, and traditional profiteroles deserve a toque this year. It's a shame the wines are not up to the same standard.
A la carte: 350-400 F.

CLICHY

92110 Clichy — (Hauts/Seine)
Paris 7 - Saint-Germain-en-Laye 17 - Argenteuil 7

La Bonne Table
119, bd J.-Jaurès — 47.37.38.79
M. Berger. Closed Sat lunch, Sun and Aug. Open until 9 pm. Air cond. V.
Gisèle Berger is undoubtedly the star of Clichy, where the competition, to be honest, is modest. Prices are too high for the suburbs, but there's last year's redecoration to pay for as well as the top-quality seafood Gisèle demands for her dishes. You'll enjoy her warm oysters, fish fritters, brandade en aïoli, stuffed cabbage with lobster, and bouillabaisse, and the good white wines chosen by René, the *patron*.

COURBEVOIE

12/20 Les Feuillantines
23, pl. de Seine
Défense 1 — 47.73.88.80
M. Vigouroux. Open for lunch only. (and dinner for groupes upon reserv). Closed Sat and Sun. Private room: 90. Terrace dining. Air cond. V AE DC.
A largely business clientele enjoys a view of the Seine and the Ile de la Jatte from the third-floor terrace. The menu is rather long and expensive, but proposes carefully cooked dishes like sautéed prawns with courgettes, croustillant de bar, and spiced breast of duck. Very good service.
A la carte: 350 F. Menu: 210 F.

Key Largo
45 bis, rue de Bezons — 47.88.00.01
M. de Scitivaux. Closed Mon dinner and Sun. Open until 10 pm. Private room: 25. V DC.
Humphrey Bogart's portrait is one of the many black-and-white snapshots of the stars hanging on the pink walls. Huge mirrors double the size of a dining room decorated with plants and flowers, leading to a garden with sliding roof. The food is hearty and straightforward: blinis with salted mullet roe, delicious grilled salmon steak with fennel sauce, and delicate chocolate mousse with orange. Various choices of just starter and main course, ranging from 79 F to 105 F. Reception and service are satisfactory.
A la carte: 220-300 F.

Le Monarque

(pl. des Reflets - La Défense 2)
48, espl. du Gal-de-Gaulle — 47.78.84.59
M. Perriau. Closed Sat, Sun and holidays. Open until 9.45 pm. Private room: 30. Garden dining. Air cond. Parking. Telex 610050. V AE DC.

The pretentious décor was probably intended for important tête-à-têtes and VIP luncheons. But if you go past the velvet-covered armchairs and Oriental carpets, you'll find a splendid outdoor terrace shaded by young plane trees and looking towards the Arc de Triomphe through the Arche of La Dfense. Whichever setting you choose, you can expect the same faultless service from waiters dressed in wing collars and striped jackets. The cooking of Antoine Gayet is delicate, innovative, and expensive. But tell yourself that luxury doesn't come cheap, and savour the parmentier de sot-l'y-laisse and poached eggs, cod with smoked salmon, sweetbreads with sorrel, and a kirsch-flavoured peach gratin. Search the wine list and you should find a bottle for under 200 F....

A la carte: 500 F. Menus: 250 F, 285 F and 310 F (wine inc), 230 F.

Paris Penta Hotel

18, rue Baudin — 49.04.75.00
Open every day. 494 rms 510-620 F. Restaurant. TV. Conference facilities. Parking. Telex 610470. V AE DC.

This egg-shaped concrete building overlooks a shopping centre. The modern, comfortable rooms have minibar.

La Safranée sur Mer

(La Défense 2)
12, pl. des Reflets — 47.78.75.50
M. Ferreira. Closed Sat, Sun, 26 July-26 Aug and 20 Dec-2 Jan. Open until 10.30 pm. Private room: 35. Terrace dining. Air cond. Valet parking. V AE DC.

Trees are starting to provide a human scale in the huge pedestrian precinct of high-rise buildings. This seafood restaurant uses the finest ingredients, but more care could be taken in preparing them (the sole fillets were slightly undercooked). Other dishes include tunny and sardine tartare, rock lobster casserole with fresh prawns, and basil-scented freshwater perch. Excellent service in the luxurious dining room or outside on the terrace.

A la carte: 500 F. Menus: from 300 F to 400 F.

Les Trois Marmites

215, bd St-Denis — 43.33.25.35
M. Faucheux. Closed Sat, Sun, Aug and 1 week at Easter. Open until 10 pm. Private room: 12. Air cond. V AE DC.

Recently air-conditioned, this restaurant has maintained a traditional bistro décor set off by indirect lighting. Marc Faucheux's honest, seasonal dishes include civet de pied de porc with red beans, stuffed tomatoes with cod, roast pigeon with pommes boulangre, and freshwater perch with leeks. The regional wines are good, but just as pricey as the rest.

A la carte: 300-350 F. Menu: 180 F.

CRÉTEIL

94000 Créteil — (Val/Marne)
Paris 12 - Evry 20 - Melun 35 - Lagny 26 - Bobigny 17

Climat

Rue des Archives — 49.80.08.00
Open every day. 51 rms 280 F. Restaurant. TV. Conference facilities. Parking. Telex 262190. V AE.

This well-kept hotel offers simple but cosy rooms three minutes from the Métro.

Le Cristolien

29, av. P.-Brossolette — 48.98.12.01
M. Donnard. Closed Sat lunch, Sun and 15-30 Aug. Open until 10 pm. Terrace dining. Air cond. Parking. V.

It's no surprise that every senior executive and managing director in Crteil comes here to eat; it's the only good place in this huge, modern suburb. Alain Donnard, who opened here two years ago, delights his customers with carefully prepared and updated bistro specialities: cassoulet toulousain, pot-au-feu grand-mère, freshwater perch in a shallot and wine sauce, and a slightly overcooked turbot fillet souffléed with oysters. The tarte Tatin with caramel sauce is delightful, and the home-baked rolls are a treat. Pleasant but frankly amateurish service.

A la carte: 300-350 F. Menu: 165 F.

Novotel Créteil-le-Lac

N 186, rte de Choisy — 42.07.91.02
Open every day. 2 stes 500 F. 110 rms 410-450 F. Restaurant. TV. Air cond. Conference facilities. Pool. Parking. Telex 264177. V AE DC.

The rooms in this lakeside hotel have recently been modernised. Sports complex with windsurfing nearby.

CROISSY-BEAUBOURG

77183 Croissy-Beaubourg — (Seine/Marne)
Paris 29 - Melun 34 - Meaux 30 - Lagny-sur-Marne 10

Hostellerie de l'Aigle d'Or

8, rue de Paris — 60.05.31.33
M. Giliams. Closed Sun dinner and Mon. Open until 9 pm. Private room: 30. Terrace dining. No-smoking section. Parking. V AE DC.

The Giliams brothers have created a discreet and elegant new décor in pink and white, with a huge fireplace and mezzanine. Herv Giliams carefully tends to his long repertoire of regional dishes: sweetbreads with truffles and chestnuts, baked prawns with bacon on a bed of watercress and baby broad beans, oxtail en crépine, and a scrumptious fruit cake with plum liqueur. High prices.

ENGHIEN

95880 Enghien — (Val-d'Oise)
Paris 18 - Pontoise 20 - Argenteuil 16 - Chantilly 32

Duc d'Enghien

3, av. de Ceinture — 34.12.90.00
M. Kéréver. Closed Sun dinner, Mon, 2-11 Jan and Aug. Open until 10.30 pm. Terrace dining. Parking. Telex 607842. V AE DC.

The nicest spot is outdoors on the lakeside terrace with its geranium beds. In the recently decorated dining room, huge bouquets of flowers do their best to cheer up the ugly airport-style ceiling. Michel Krver regains the three toques he achieved at his Rennes restaurant for ingenious cooking which, unlike the nearby casinos, owes nothing to chance. Among the parade of first courses, you might try warm red mullet on a bed of purslane salad and sweet red peppers in olive oil, or rock lobster with beetroot. Next, there's sea bass on a golden crust of potatoes served with tapenade on toast, delicate prawns with fresh mint and vanilla, superb roast pigeon la goutte de sang, or better still, leg of rabbit on a bed of potatoes, baby onions, and garlic. A selection of some 30 cheeses, divine raspberry cake, and an excellent choice of Bordeaux all add to the pleasure of a meal here. Discreet service.

A la carte: 500-750 F. Menus: 320 F (weekdays lunch only, wine inc), 400 F.

Le Grand Hôtel
85, rue du Gal-de-Gaulle — 34.12.80.00
Open every day. 5 stes 1,200-2,650 F. 46 rms 650-1,100 F. Restaurant. Half-board 580-1,100 F. TV. Air cond. Conference facilities. Parking. Telex 607842. V AE DC.
This bleak building stands in lovely grounds next to the spa. The spacious, comfortable rooms have period furniture.

94120 Fontenay-sous-Bois — (Val/Marne)
Paris 7 - Saint-Mandé 2 - Nogent-sur-Marne 3

La Musardière
61, av. du Mal-Joffre — 48.73.96.13
M. Saumur. Closed Sun, dinner Mon and Tue, and Aug. Open until 9.30 pm. Air cond. V.
This bright, comfortable restaurant lies in the heart of a huge new administrative and shopping centre largely composed of glass and ceramic. The *patron*, formerly of the Savoy Hotel in London, is an attentive host, and his chef, Christian Landier, produces handsome classic dishes with a light touch: saumon au gros sel, smoked haddock and lentils, and kidney with mustard sauce. The excellent fish dishes vary with the market and the set menu is good value.

92250 Garenne-Colombes (La) — (Hauts/Seine)
Paris 12 - Courbevoie 2 - Pontoise 29 - Asnières 4

Auberge du 14-Juillet
9, bd de la République — 42.42.21.79
M. Baillon. Closed Sat, Sun and holidays. Open until 9.30 pm. Private room: 4. V AE DC.
Regular customers are happy to see that this family-run restaurant has new décor. In contrast to the nearby concrete structures of La Dfense, it is a charming, intimate place offering several excellent duck specialities and sumptuous seafood dishes, prepared with increasing confidence by Jean-Pierre Baillon. His son Laurent helps out with the day's catch to make dishes like freshwater perch with Loire wine and bacon, bass quenelles with lemon grass, and salmon with olive oil.

Aux Gourmets Landais
(Hôtel de Paris)
5, av. Joffre — 42.42.22.86
M. Velazco. Closed Sun dinner, Mon and 15 Aug-15 Sep. Open until 10.45 pm. Garden dining. Hotel: 12 rms 180-250 F. V AE DC.
Josette Velazco's South-western hospitality routine contributes to the success of this excellent establishment, which now boasts a small garden with sliding roof. Her husband Alain adds the same regional flavour to his dishes, which include duck carpaccio, sole aux cèpes, five-meat cassoulet, and excellent tourtières (pastries with Armagnac). Good selection of regional wines for under 100 F.
A la carte: 300-350 F. Menus: 110 F (lunch only), 180 F (w-e and holidays only), 140 F.

12/20 Rose
10, pl. J.-Baillet — 42.42.22.07
M. Guérin. Lunch only (and dinner Fri and Sat). Closed 9-23 Aug. Open until 9 pm. Private room: 50. Garden dining. V.
Cosy and full of flowers, this increasingly charming restaurant has recently added tables outside in the courtyard. The prices of the *patron's* rich,

intricate dishes are also on the upswing: napolitain d'escargots and eau-de-vie sorbet, sole souffle aux hutres, sweetbread and kidney casserole with fresh pasta.
A la carte: 350-400 F. Menu: 178 F.

91350 Grigny — (Essonne)
Paris 26 - Versailles 32 - Rungis 7 - Evry 7

Château du Clotay
8, rue du Port — 69.25.89.98
M. Griguer. Open every day. Open until 9.45 pm. Private room: 300. Garden dining. Parking. V AE DC.
After several setbacks, this lakeside restaurant is back on its feet again. Serge Châtelain, a former second-in-command to Roger Vergé, has earned a toque for his balanced cooking: persillade de saumon cru and marinated vegetables, lobster with coral cream, and loup en croûte de sel. The desserts still need a lot of work. Remarkable service.
A la carte: 350-400 F. Menu: 200 F.

Château du Clotay
(See restaurant above)
Open every day. 15 rms 450-600 F. Half-board 545-695 F. TV. Conference facilities. Pool.
This lovely isolated mansion is set in peaceful countryside beside a lake. The fifteen comfortable bedrooms were modernised last year. Pool and solarium.

92130 Issy-les-Moulineaux — (Hauts/Seine)
Paris (Porte de Versailles) 1 - Vanves 1

12/20 L'Auberge d'Armaillé
(La Maisonnette Russe)
42, rue Guynemer — 45.54.70.69
M. Vincendet. Closed Sat lunch, Sun and 28 July-28 Aug. Open until 11.30 pm. Private room: 50. Garden dining. V AE DC.
Evenings are the best time to enjoy the gipsy violinists and the Russian atmosphere. The chef, formerly with Paul Bocuse and Michel Gurard, prepares pricey but authentic specialities like bortsch (beetroot soup), coulibiac (fish pie), and various shashliks (kebabs).
A la carte: 400 F. Menus: 290 F (weekdays dinner only except Fri, wine inc), 580 F (dinner only, vodka inc).

Manufacture
20, espl. de la Manufacture — 40.93.08.98
M. Vigato. Closed Sat lunch, Sun and 1-22 Aug. Open until 10.30 pm. Air cond. V.
Jean-Pierre Vigato, who also runs the three-toque Apicius in Paris, hasn't opened a second restaurant just to make more money; he sees it as an outlet for another aspect of his personality. Unlike Apicius, Manufacture is a hip, bright, spacious restaurant converted from an old tobacco factory. Vigato's former number two, David Van Laer, is the chef, putting his all into making this an exciting, original counterpart to Apicius while maintaining the same quality. If you're lucky enough to catch these dishes before they disappear from the *carte*, try the fricassée de grenouilles et d'escargots aux lentilles, thick cod steak with grilled prawns, and croustillant choco-banane.
A la carte: 250-300 F. Menu: 180 F (lunch only).

JOUY-EN-JOSAS

78350 Jouy-en-Josas — (Yvelines)
Paris 21 - Versailles 4 - Rambouillet 35 - Palaiseau 9

Fondation Cartier
(Restaurant du Château)
3, rue de la Manufacture — 39.56.46.46
Open for lunch only. (and dinner Sat until 10 pm).
Closed 21 Dec-8 Jan and 29 July-20 Aug. Private
room: 180. Garden dining. No pets. Parking.
Telex 696674. V AE DC.

It's probably because he counts cooking as one
of the fine arts that Alain-Dominique Perrin called
on master chef Grard Vi to oversee the kitchens of
this restaurant filled with prestigious works of
modern art by Csar, Garouste, Arman and others.
All Vi has to do in practice is to let the very capable
chef, Olivier Richy, get on with his job. Having
worked with Michel Trama and Marc Meneau, he
is more than equipped to turn out wonderful dishes like poached oysters with cooked lettuce,
duck with turnips and truffles, and feuilleté aux
framboises. Top Bordeaux and Cahors (of which
Perrin is himself a producer) round out the delight
of a meal in the elegant black-white-and-grey
décor. Near the entrance to the restaurant is a caf
with terrace offers a generous 85 F menu.
A la carte: 350 F. Menus: 135 F, 195 F.

KREMLIN-BICÊTRE (LE)

94270 Kremlin-Bicêtre (Le) — (Val/Marne)
Paris 8 - Boulogne-Billancourt 10 - Versailles 22

Les Relais Bleus
6, rue Voltaire — 46.70.15.35
Open every day. 154 rms 320 F. Restaurant. Half-
board 422-500 F. TV. Conference facilities. Garage
parking. Telex 263351. V AE.

This hotel is a stone's throw from the Paris ring
road and the Porte d'Italie. The rooms are welcoming and well equipped.

LEVALLOIS-PERRET

92300 Levallois-Perret — (Hauts/Seine)
Paris (Pte de Champerret) 7.5 - Neuilly 4

Gauvain
11, rue L.-Rouquier — 47.58.51.09
MM. Hude and Guillermou. Closed Sat, Sun, holidays
and 3-18 Aug. Open until 10 pm. Private room: 25.
Air cond. V.

Not a day goes by without business customers
filling this former bakery, with its handsome glass
ceiling. The basement room has a less cheerful
décor but it's just as busy, and the staff are often
unable to keep pace. Jean-Franois Guillermou
offers bright and varied two- or three-course meals,
but avoid the tasteless flan de courgettes
accompanying the prawn terrine. We've deducted
a point, despite the delicious red-mullet fillets with
tarragon. Good wines.
Menus: 185 F, 225 F.

12/20 Le Jardin
9, pl. J. Zay — 47.39.54.02
M. Mouquet. Closed Sat lunch, Sun and 10-28 Aug.
Open until 10 pm. Terrace dining. Garage parking.
V AE DC.

Just off the ring road, a relaxing country
atmosphere has been created here. The *patron*,
who is not above leaving the kitchen to chat with
his customers, prepares rich dishes such as terrine
de confit de canard with fresh foie gras, and sole
in trout mousse.
A la carte: 300 F. Menu: 138 F.

L'Orangerie
56, rue de Villiers
47.58.40.61
M. Bordereau. Closed Sat and Sun. Open until
9.45 pm. Private room: 18. V.

The tiny front garden and intimate atmosphere
of the spacious, wood-panelled dining room offer
a pleasant setting in this drab neighbourhood.
Gilles Bordereau, a conscientious chef, proposes
slightly heavy feuilleté au chèvre chaud, tasty lobster and vegetables, splendidly seasoned bass, and
good nougat glac. Attentive service and a fine
choice of Bordeaux.
A la carte: 350-380 F. Menu: 250 F (dinner only).

12/20 Le Petit Poste
39, rue Rivay
47.37.34.46
M. Leboucher. Closed Sat lunch, Sun and 7-29 Aug.
Open until 10.15 pm. V AE DC.

Fifteen tables crowded around the bar—this is
exactly the type of bistro Brassens used to write
about in his songs. Now it is a favourite among
Levallois office workers, who come to enjoy the
cooking of Pierre Leboucher, formerly of Lucas-
Carton and la Mare: veal sweetbread stew with
honey, young rabbit with cabbage, and fresh cod
casserole, washed down with some good Loire
wines.
A la carte: 220-250 F.

Pointaire
46, rue de Villiers
47.57.44.77
Mme Debonne. Closed Sat and Sun. Open until
9.30 pm. Private room: 17. V AE.

Pre Pointaire remains a legend within the prettily
renovated walls of this rustic bistro, through the
dishes which were his glory: freshwater perch in
butter sauce and beuchelle tourangelle. After eighteen years in the kitchens, the current chef has no
trouble keeping alive the restaurant's tradition of
classic dishes, such as turbot in sorrel sauce, or
roast duckling with turnips. To avoid that sinking
feeling when the bill arrives, take the set menu.
A la carte: 350-400 F. Menu: 150 F.

LINAS

91310 Linas — (Essonne)
Paris 25 - Etampes 23 - Orsay 13 - Montlhéry 2

L'Escargot de Linas
136, rue de la Division-Leclerc
69.01.00.30
M. Comte. Closed Mon dinner, Sun and 10 Aug-2 Sep.
Open until 9.30 pm. Private room: 80. Terrace din-
ing. Parking. V.

Those who love the good old-fashioned style of
careful cooking will delight in this elegant,
mannered Louis XVI restaurant, offering omelette
Curnonsky, fricassée périgourdine, and entrecôte
steak with grapes. But Maurice Comte is capable
of more adventurous fare, using seasonal produce
from nearby Rungis market to produce a wide
selection of handsome dishes such as pan-roasted
cuttlefish and snails, asparagus flan flavoured with
chervil, crispy pig's trotter salad, and pheasant
breasts with juniper berries and buttery cabbage.
If the prices hadn't got so steep, we would come
here every night in summer to dine on the flowery
terrace.
A la carte: 350 F and up. Menu: 200 F.

LIVRY-GARGAN

93190 Livry-Gargan — (Seine-St-D.)
Paris 17 - Meaux 28 - Senlis 42 - Aubervilliers 13

Auberge Saint-Quentinoise
23, bd de la République
43.81.13.08

M. Nicoleau. Closed Sun dinner and Mon. Open until 10 pm. Private room: 130. Garden dining. V.

The courtyard terrace with ivy-covered walls is clearly the star attraction, although the elegant, newly renovated dining room has now come into its own. The classic dishes skilfully prepared by Michel Nicoleau come as a real surprise in this glum suburb: Burgundy snails in parsley cream sauce, tender lamb cooked to perfection (no need for the sauce), and a bland semolina cake saved by the berry coulis. A la carte prices are honest, but that is no reason to be so reluctant to produce the set menus. Satisfactory service and a good wine list.

12/20 La Petite Marmite
8, bd de la République
43.81.29.15

M. Courbis De Oliveira. Closed Wed and 15 Aug-1 Sep. Open until 9.30 pm. Private room: 18. Garden dining. Air cond. No-smoking section. V.

Set in the resolutely suburban shopping district by the railway station, this dim, wood-panelled restaurant has recently changed hands. Fernande, the new *patronne*, keeps busy in the kitchen and though her fish dishes tend to be heavy-handed, her cooking is otherwise enjoyable and well-intentioned: turbot in Champagne sauce, veal tenderloin with oyster mushrooms.

A la carte: 260-280 F.

LOGES-EN-JOSAS (LES)

78350 Loges-en-Josas (Les) — (Yvelines)
Paris 23 - Versailles 5 - Jouy-en-Josas 2

La Ferme des Loges
(Hostellerie des Josas)
Parc de la Porte-des-Loges — 39.56.01.77

M. Woltz. Closed Sun dinner and Mon. Open until 9 pm. Private room: 220. Garden dining. Valet parking. Telex 695152. V AE DC.

This former farmhouse on the Château de Versailles estate has changed more than its name; now its flamboyant Louis XIII–style dining room opens directly on to the grounds and a new chef of Egyptian origin, Tarek Chaker, has been called in to improve the cooking. But he has left behind the brilliant personal style he developed at the Martinez, the Crillon, and the Gray d'Albion. Here you will find more classic dishes, including excellent foie gras salad with over-smoked breast of duck, young rabbit in coarse-grain mustard sauce, and a stingy portion of charlotte au chocolat. We're awarding Tarek Chaker one toque, and who knows what tricks he may still have up his sleeve?

A la carte: 300-350 F. Menus: 170 F, 250 F, 330 F.

La Ferme des Loges
(See restaurant above)

Open every day. 6 stes 820-890 F. 50 rms 390-890 F. Half-board 650-1,200 F. TV. Conference facilities. Tennis.

The rooms in this recently opened hotel are spacious and comfortable. Services include a fitness centre, Turkish baths, sauna, and solarium.

LOUVECIENNES

78430 Louveciennes — (Yvelines)
Paris 24 - Versailles 7 - St-Germain-en-Laye 6

Aux Chandelles
12, pl. de l'Eglise — 39.69.08.40

M. Dohollou. Closed Sat lunch, Wed, and 11-26 Aug. Open until 10 pm. Private room: 20. Terrace dining. V AE.

The upstairs dining room offers a view of the enclosed garden. The young owner-chef, Stphane Dohollou, who studied with Grard Besson, produces dishes that are so delicate you could almost accuse him of pretension. The set menus are excellent value, particularly the 260 F menu which includes wine and features saffron-flavoured perch, and a fine civet de joues de cochon. Perfect service.

A la carte: 300-350 F. Menus: 160 F (weekdays lunch only), 260 F (wine inc).

12/20 La Hulotte
17, rte de Versailles
39.69.05.97

Mmes Roussel and Fedida. Closed Sat lunch and Sun dinner. Open until 10 pm. Private room: 12. Garden dining. Parking. V.

In summer you can eat in the garden and admire the historic bell-tower while savouring os moelle aux grillons de ris de veau, and prawn and prune kebabs.

A la carte: 350 F. Menu: 150 F.

MAISONS-LAFFITTE

78600 Maisons-Laffitte — (Yvelines)
Paris 21 - Pontoise 18 - St-Germain-en-L. 8

Le Laffitte
5, av. de Saint-Germain
39.62.01.53

M. Laurier. Closed Wed, dinner Sun and Tue, and Aug. Open until 9.30 pm. V AE.

Offering good seafood, classic cooking, and a long list of carefully prepared dishes, André Laurier's restaurant is an address worth noting and just the place for hearty appetites. Sample the three-fish terrine, noisette de lotte with pink peppercorns, veal tenderloin en persillade, and dark-chocolate fondant. Splendid wine list, rich in Bordeaux.

A la carte: 350 F. Menus: 200 F, 280 F, 300 F.

Le Tastevin
9, av. Eglé — 39.62.11.67

M. Blanchet. Closed Mon dinner, Tue, Feb school holidays and 15 Aug-9 Sep. Open until 10 pm. Private room: 25. Garden dining. Parking. V AE DC.

Add comfort, lovely surroundings and attentive service to fine cooking and you have all the ingredients of a perfect meal out. Michel Blanchet and his wife Amelia have incorporated them all into their restaurant, making it one of the most pleasant in the Paris suburbs. We hope this serenity will not be threatened by the Blanchets' plans to include some luxury guestrooms in their establishment, and that this bold and generous chef continues to put his heart into his work. Seafood salad with oyster vinaigrette, and pan-roasted lotte with tarragon and wild asparagus are among his balanced and wonderfully prepared fish specialities. The poultry dishes are equally delicious, and the desserts, like the baked pear with honey and spices, are out of this world. Magnificent, costly wines.

A la carte: 500 F.

La Vieille Fontaine
8, av. Grétry — 39.62.01.78
Mme Letourneur and M. Clerc. Closed Sun, Mon and Aug. Open until 10.30 pm. Private room: 60. Garden dining. V AE DC.

Manon Letourneur and Franois Clerc treat all their customers with the same consideration as the many celebrities who come here. Catherine Deneuve is one of the regular visitors. Even with a thriving catering business to take care of, Franois Clerc is always on duty in the kitchen when the restaurant is open. He has finally added some new dishes to his repertoire, such as red mullet accompanied by buttery cabbage, salmon with minced olive pâté, liquorice-scented calf's kidney, and saddle of rabbit with mustard meringue. The 220 F menu, available at lunch and dinner, is excellent value: you might choose mixed salad with rosy cold roast beef, tarragon-flavoured chicken ham, thyme-scented hot goat cheese, and pain perdu aux fruits.
A la carte: 500-700 F. Menu: 220 F.

MALNOUE
77184 Malnoue — (Seine/Marne)
Paris 22 - Noisy-le Grand 2 - Pontault-Combault 6

Au Faisan Doré
5, av. Ch.-Bras — 64.61.71.90
M. Bureau. Closed Sun dinner, Mon and 31 July-20 Aug. Open until 10 pm. Private room: 35. Garden dining. Parking. V AE DC.

Sit by the fireplace in winter, and in summer listen to the birds singing in the garden. This year, despite a few lapses such as imprecise cooking times for fish, this young, conscientious chef has earned one toque for his hard work and good ideas: lambs' tongues in mustardy mayonnaise with crisp salad, John Dory in Saumur served with haricot beans, and sliced duckling breast with the leg grilled and glazed with Sauternes. High prices.
A la carte: 350 F. Menus: 140 F (lunch only, except holidays), 260 F (except holidays).

MARNES-LA-COQUETTE
92430 Marnes-la-Coquette — (Hauts/Seine)
Paris 15 - Versailles 4 - Vaucresson 1

11/20 Les Hirondelles
18, rue G.-et-X.-Schlumberger — 47.41.00.20
Mme Justal. Closed Wed, dinner Sun and holidays, 2 Aug-2 Sep and 24 Dec-2 Jan. Open until 9.30 pm. V.

An unpretentious and amusing little spot where actors and workmen come together to enthuse over the reasonable prices and friendly décor. Try the cèpes à la provençale or the good grilled salmon.
A la carte: 200 F. Menus: 50 F (weekdays only, wine inc), 68 F (w-e and holidays lunch only).

La Tête Noire
6, pl. de la Mairie — 47.41.06.28
M. Thierry. Closed Sun dinner, Mon and 6-20 Aug. Open until 10 pm. Private room: 30. V AE.

The new chef packs a punch and here's a toque for effort, and for the interesting chilled eel salad, the fillet of red mullet (a touch overcooked but served with a delicious eggplant and tomato gratin), and the scrumptious pear charlotte. The well-defined flavours help to excuse minor mistakes in execution. Book a table in the glassed-in terrace, much nicer than the sombre dining room. Service is friendly and the cellar small but select; prices are reasonable.
A la carte: 260-280 F.

MEUDON

92190 Meudon — (Hauts/Seine)
Paris 12 - Clamart 4 - Versailles 10 - Boulogne 3

Relais des Gardes
42, av. du Général-Gallieni
45.34.11.79
M. Oudina. Closed Sun dinner, Sat and 9 Aug-9 Sep. Open until 10 pm. Private room: 70. Terrace dining. V AE DC.

Jean-Claude Cahagnet is in command of the kitchens of this pretty brick house where a classical repertoire and style reign supreme. The atmosphere in the formal beige dining room is certainly too serious and the maître d'hotel positively solemn, but the cooking is well done with no redundant frills: salade gourmande au foie gras, a delicately flavoured noisette of lamb with roast garlic, cooked to order, and a fantastic baba au rhum, rivalled only by the brioche of warm chocolate. The wine list is superb, prices are high, and Mme Oudina is smilingly omnipresent.
A la carte: 400-450 F. Menus: 180 F, 240 F.

12/20 La Terrasse de l'Etang
Etangs de Villebon
Rte de la Patte-d'Oie — 46.26.09.57
M. Godfroi. Closed Sun dinner, Mon and Aug. Open until 9.30 pm. Private room: 70. Terrace dining. Parking. V.

It's in the woods, not far from the motorway, with a lovely terrace overlooking trees and a pond. A good place to bring the family for a salad of freshwater perch fillets, salmon cooked in its skin, or saddle of rabbit with prunes. The cellar is stocked with appealing growers' wines. Take note that things get a bit hectic at weekends.
A la carte: 300 F. Menu: 175 F (weekdays only).

MONTMORENCY
95160 Montmorency — (Val-d'Oise)
Paris 18 - Pontoise 20 - Enghien 3 - St-Denis 8

12/20 Au Cœur de la Forêt
Av. du Repos-de-Diane — 39.64.99.19
M. Touati. Closed Thu, dinner Sun and Mon, and 19-30 Aug. Open until 9.30 pm. Private room: 25. Terrace dining. Parking. V.

Next time you go walking in the Montmorency forest, ferret around until you find this large establishment hidden in the trees. You'll enjoy the family atmosphere and the nicely crafted, clever cuisine, for example a light dish of gently pan-roasted baby squid, a hearty sauté of veal kidneys with a dash of raspberry vinegar, and a good plum tart.
A la carte: 300 F. Menus: 120 F, 180 F.

MORANGIS
91420 Morangis — (Essonne)
Paris 22 - Versailles 24 - Evry 16 - Longjumeau 5

Le Sabayon
15, rue Lavoisier — 69.09.43.80
M. Von Moos. Closed Sat lunch, Mon dinner, Sun and Aug. Open until 9.30 pm. Air cond. Parking. V.

The clientele consists mainly of business people happily gobbling up the somewhat ruinous scallops en secret, the gratin of oysters and winkles with a crayfish coulis or pigeon confit à la graisse de foie gras. Good service.
A la carte: 400-450 F. Menu: 160 F (weekdays only, except Fri dinner).

NANTERRE

92000 Nanterre — (Hauts/Seine)
Paris 13 - Neuilly 5 - St-Germain 8 - Boulogne 7

Ile de France
83, av. du Mal-Joffre — 47.24.10.44
M. Guimard. Closed Sun and Aug. Open until 9.45 pm. Private room: 120. Garden dining. Garage parking. V AE DC.
Don't be put off by appearances! This is not a disused warehouse but a comfortable and serious retaurant catering for business people. It's peaceful and bright, swathed from stem to stern in brown carpeting and dotted with large, well-spaced tables where one can enjoy a light and fresh feuilleté with asparagus tips, a perfectly cooked sole meunière followed by a moreish pear bavarian. Service is adequate, no more.
A la carte: 300 F. Menu: 175 F.

NEUILLY-SUR-SEINE

92200 Neuilly-sur-Seine — (Hauts/Seine)
Paris (Pte de Neuilly) 8 - Argenteuil 9 - Versailles 16

Le Bistrot d'à Côté
4, rue Boutard — 47.45.34.55
See Paris 17th arrondissement

12/20 Brasserie des Arts
2, rue des Huissiers — 46.24.56.17
M. Dureau. Closed Sun. Open until 11 pm. V AE DC.
A simple and unpretentious address often filled with celebrities from this chic neighbourhood. They go for the green-bean salad, artichoke hearts à la ratatouille, filet of beef béarnaise, poached finnan haddock, and yummy profiteroles. Impeccable service.
A la carte: 220 F.

12/20 Café de la Jatte
60, bd Vital-Bouhot — 47.45.04.20
M. Poidevin. Open every day. Open until midnight. Terrace dining. Air cond. Valet parking. V AE DC.
The décor revolves around the giant skeleton of a pterodactyl surrounded by a jungle of plants. Wicker furniture, gay colours, and lots of space and light make up the rest. Young waiters zoom around serving plentiful, fresh, and surprisingly well-presented dishes to family hordes: fish sushi with soy sauce, cod cooked in a salt crust, oven-baked lamb with Provençal-style stuffed vegetables. The cellar could be a little more inventive.
A la carte: 250 F. Menu: 85 F (lunch only).

Carpe Diem
10, rue de l'Eglise — 46.24.95.01
M. Coquoin. Closed Sat Sun, Sun, 1-8 May and 4-28 Aug. Open until 9.30 pm. V DC.
The high prices fully warrant the exigencies of this little bistro's clientele who are obviously drawn to the warm, simple décor, the *patronne*'s gentle attentions, and the diligent service. Chef Coquoin's soigné menu includes a very fine eggplant and prawn mould, grouper grilled with basil, and a delicate pineapple soufflé with cherries. Portions could be larger.
A la carte: 350 F and up. Menu: 150 F (dinner only).

12/20 Le Chalet
14, rue du Cdt-Pilot — 46.24.03.11
M. Brun. Closed Sun. Open until 11 pm. Air cond. V AE.
Après-ski in Neuilly: viande des Grisons (air-dried beef), mountain-cured ham, fondue, and raclette against a backdrop of antique skis and pine panelling. A happy atmosphere and some nice little set menus.
A la carte: 200 F. Menus: 68 F (lunch only, wine inc), 85 F, 110 F and 180 F (dinner only, wine inc).

Jacqueline Fénix
42, av. Charles-de-Gaulle
46.24.42.61
Mme Fénix. Closed Sat, Sun, 3 Aug-4 Sep and 21 Dec-3 Jan. Open until 10 pm. Air cond. V AE.
Jacqueline Fénix's new décor has lightened the business lunch atmosphere and brought buckets of charm to the evening get-togethers of le Tout-Neuilly, with well-spaced, beautifully set tables. Young chef Albert Corre left without a word last summer; his replacement, Christian Hénin, had not, at press time, finished composing a new menu. Thus we've put his toque in parentheses, though we're sure all will go swimmingly if the delicious millefeuille of red mullet en tartare, the terribly tasty snail risotto with chicken gravy, and the pink, meltingly tender lamb with its basil purée were anything to go by.
A la carte: 450-550 F. Menu: 320 F.

Les Feuilles Libres
34, rue Perronet — 46.24.41.41
Mme Guillier-Marcellin. Closed Sat lunch, Sun and 3-20 Aug. Open until 10.30 pm. Private room: 6. Terrace dining. Air cond. V AE DC.
Every second Tuesday of the month, a harpsichord concert adds a tinkling accompaniment to dinners served in this staid, slightly gloomy dining room. On the other hand, the cuisine sparkles with lightness and personality, prepared by an alumnus of the Crillon kitchens. Apart from a dull shark with cabbage, we've thoroughly enjoyed meals of delicate ravioli with snails, fresh shrimps pan-roasted with some wonderful Southern vegetables, and the superb Thursday pot-au-feu. A good cellar also keeps the local clientele happy.
A la carte: 300 F and up. Menus: 150 F (lunch only), 240 F (wine inc).

Foch-An
142, av. Charles-de-Gaulle
47.22.96.46
Mme Ly. Closed 2 weeks in Aug. Open until 10.45 pm. Air cond. V AE DC.
Forget the Chinese-style décor but dig into the Vietnamese assortment of egg rolls, lamb-stuffed samosas, spring rolls filled with shrimp or pork, and grilled shrimp. There's also a highly successful crusty chicken with fresh ginger and a terrific Thai flan. And we wish the welcome were more sincere, and that patrons were given more time to make their choices. An extra point.
A la carte: 200 F and up. Menus: 80 F and 98 F (lunch only).

Focly
79, av. Charles-de-Gaulle
46.24.43.36
Mme Lu Suy Hok. Closed 2nd and 3rd weeks of Aug. Open until 11 pm. Private room: 20. Air cond. V AE.
Monsieur Mach used to cook at the royal palace in Phnom Penh and has just opened a sister establishment in the seventh arrondissement. Try his repertoire of appealing Chinese, Vietnamese, Cambodian, and Thai dishes somewhat confusingly presented on an interminable menu: croquettes of stuffed eggplant, royal crab fritters, Peking duck.
A la carte: 250 F. Menus: 95 F and 115 F (lunch only).

11/20 La Fontaine de Neuilly
(Drugstore de Neuilly)
14, pl. du Marché — 46.37.56.79
MM. Herrero and Jossua. Open every day. Open until 1.30 am. Private room: 40. Garden dining. Air cond. V AE DC.
A gaggle of guests spills on to the market square on summer evenings and a pianist tickles the ivories in the bar until one in the morning. Try the fresh tagliatelle with seafood sauce, or the good and fresh grilled or poached fish.
A la carte: 250-280 F. Menus: 159 F (wine inc), 135 F.

La Guinguette de Neuilly
Ile de la Jatte
12, bd de Levallois — 46.24.25.04
M. Guivarch. Closed at Christmas. Open until 11 pm. Garden dining. V.
Trendy artists are drawn to this old barge and its handful of tables for a cuisine that we think merits a toque: leeks with fresh shrimps, calf's liver, delicious fish wrapped in brik pastry and napped with a saffron-tinctured sauce.
A la carte: 250 F.

Hôtel International de Paris
58, bd V.-Hugo — 47.58.11.00
Closings not available. 3 stes 1,800-3,600 F. 330 rms 700-1,050 F Restaurant. TV. Air cond. Conference facilities. Telex 610971. V AE DC.
A large, imposing hotel which is undergoing full-scale renovations as we go to press.

Jenny Jacquet
(La Truffe Noire)
2, pl. Parmentier — 46.24.94.14
M. Jacquet. Closed Sat, Sun, 1 week in Jan and 3 weeks in Aug. Open until 10 pm. Private room: 14. No pets. Valet parking. V.
A Sloaney, tony clientele has fallen for Jenny Jacquet's seductive powers and his cosy, charming, softly lit décor. The conservative but tasty cuisine runs the gamut of the seasons and is always appetising. Try the authentic œufs en meurette (eggs poached in a red wine sauce) with delicious garlic-flavoured croutons, a thick, tender wedge of skate delicately crusted on top, and a wonderful crème brûlée with Demerara sugar. These are perfect meals at prices that won't make you shudder, particularly if you drink one of the *patron*'s exquisite Loire wines. The youthful service is swift and attentive.
A la carte: 350 F. Menu: 220 F.

12/20 Chez Livio
6, rue de Longchamp — 46.24.81.32
M. Innocenti. Closed Sat and Sun in Aug, 1 May, 15 Aug, and 23 Dec-2 Jan. Open until 10.45 pm. Private room: 16. Garden dining. V.
A real Italian trattoria in the heart of Neuilly, manned by the Innocenti clan. Here is generous and simple cuisine, which features ravioli al magro, gnocchi with basil, pizzas, osso buco and *tutti quanti*. The roof of the dining room rolls back so that you can dine under a canopy of blue sky or stars.
A la carte: 160-200 F.

Neuilly Park Hotel
23, rue M.-Michelis — 46.40.11.15
Open every day. 24 rms 580-680 F. TV. Telex 612087. V AE.
One of the more recent additions Neuilly's clique of fine hotels. This is a luxurious and refined establishment with perfectly appointed rooms, a sober and restful décor, and some super bathrooms.

Hôtel du Parc
4, bd du Parc — 46.24.32.62
Open every day. 71 rms 255-380 F. TV. Telex 615689. V.
Between the Porte de Champerret and the Défense on the Ile de la Jatte facing the Seine is a small 1930s hotel with well-equipped, regularly renovated rooms.

San Valero
209 ter, av. Charles-de-Gaulle
46.24.07.87
M. Valero. Closed Sat lunch, Sun and 23 Dec-1 Jan. Open until 10.30 pm. V AE DC.
Come for a fiesta and a feast at Valero's Spanish restaurant: the menu offers paella of course, but also sardines with basil, a refreshing gaspacho and a delicious dish of tiny fried fish with salt-cod croquettes. Service is sleepy, but there are some good wines from beyond the Pyrenees. A toque this year.
A la carte: 270 F. Menus: 140 F (weekdays only), 180 F.

12/20 Sébillon
(Paris-Bar)
20, av. Ch.-de-Gaulle — 46.24.71.31
M. Joulie. Open every day. Open until midnight. Private room: 20. Air cond. Valet parking. Telex 649538. V AE DC.
The décor changes, the dishes do not. The pride of the house is its famous Sébillon roast lamb and the giant éclair. Add to that the magnificent rib of beef and the tarte Tatin 'à l'ancienne'. There's some good fresh seafood and a thick salmon steak grilled with fennel. Nice Loire wines at affordable prices.
A la carte: 250 F.

11/20 La Tonnelle Saintongeaise
32, bd Vital-Bouhot
46.24.43.15
M. Girodot. Closed Sat, Sun, 2-22 Aug and 21 Dec-6 Jan. Open until 10 pm. Private room: 25. Terrace dining.
Crowds tend to gather under the trees and parasols of this Ile de la Jatte terrace. The cuisine is pleasant but sometimes a trifle clumsy: magret with citrus fruit, steak tartare, marinated fish. Languid service.
A la carte: 250 F.

NOGENT-SUR-MARNE

94130 Nogent-sur-Marne — (Val/Marne)
Paris 11 - Créteil 7 - Lagny 17 - Montreuil 5

Nogentel
8, rue du Port — 48.72.70.00
Open every day. 61 rms 430-460 F. Restaurant. TV. No pets. Telex 264549. V AE DC.
This is a modern hotel in the Nogent marina, well equipped for receptions and seminars (250-seat auditorium). Panoramic restaurant and grill.

We are always interested to hear about your discoveries, and to receive your comments on ours. Please feel free to write to us, stating your opinions clearly.

94396 Orly — (Val/Marne)
Paris 16 - Corbeil 17 - Villeneuve-St-Georges 12

Altea Paris-Orly

Orly-Ouest
94547 Orly-Aérogare — 46.87.23.37
*Open every day. 1 ste 730-890 F. 194 rms 510-580 F.
Restaurant. TV. Air cond. Conference facilities. Parking. Telex 265665. V AE DC.*
The hotel has been recently renovated, and provides soundproof rooms decorated in lively, gay colours. Bathrooms are terrific. Rooms can be rented for the day only (10h-18h) for 230 F. Minigolf and airport shuttle bus.

12/20 La Louisiane

Aérogare d'Orly-Sud — 46.87.33.88
*M. Albrand. Closed Sat, Sun and Aug. Open until
11 pm. Terrace dining. Air cond. Parking.
Telex 265971. V AE DC.*
The hotel's two restaurants, La Louisiane and Le Café du Marché were undergoing full-scale transformations last summer. The cuisine remains tastefully international with a touch of Creole colour: shrimps, rabbit with peanut sauce. The Café serves generous buffets and appetising grilled dishes.
A la carte: 350 F. Menu: 190 F (lunch only).

Hilton International Orly

(See restaurant above)
*Open every day. 366 rms 750-1,120 F. TV. Air cond.
Conference facilities.*
Functional, comfortable rooms near the airport with a free shuttle service. Excellent facilities for conferences or seminars. Twenty-four hour room service. Bar and shops.

Maxim's

Aérogare d'Orly-Ouest — 46.87.16.16
*M. Janisson. Open for lunch only. Grill until 10 pm.
Private room: 25. Air cond. Telex 201389. V AE DC.*
This Maxim's-sur-runway is a favourite eating spot for business people, and as we write these lines, the ersatz décor is being revamped, in part by that ubiquitous restaurant decorator, Slavik. The food is good—chilled lobster bisque, tourtière of ris de veau—but so expensive that lots of diners prefer to be grounded at the Grill, where prices don't soar off into the blue, and there's a set menu with wine included.
A la carte: 450 F (at the Grill: 250-350 F). Menus: 250 F (wine inc, at the Grill), 300 F.

91400 Orsay — (Essonne)
Paris 27 - Versailles 20 - Évry 24

Le Boudin Sauvage

6, rue de Versailles — 69.28.42.93
*Mme de Gennes. Closed Sat, Sun, dinner Mon, Wed
and Thu, and 15 days in Aug. Open until 10.30 pm.
Private room: 20. Garden dining. No-smoking section. V AE DC.*
Alas, the spicy boudin sauvage (black pudding) which gives this establishment its name is served only in winter. But the kitchen has other specialities to offer, giving pride of place to superbly concocted vegetable dishes. Taste the prawns with coriander-scented tomato fondue, the foie gras with fruit, the John Dory with caramel, vinegar, and honey and enjoy the charming décor that looks out on opposite an old garden where you can sit in fine weather.
A la carte: 350-400 F. Menu: 240 F (lunch only).

77330 Ozoir-la-Ferrière — (Seine/Marne)
Paris 34 - Melun 27 - Lagny-sur-Marne 21

12/20 La Gueulardière

66, av. du Gal-de-Gaulle — 60.02.94.56
*M. Bureau. Closed Sat lunch, Sun, Feb school
holidays and Aug. Open until 10 pm. Garden dining.
V.*
It gets better every year. Double glazing has made Alain Bureau's intimate and rustic décor an even quieter and more charming a spot in which to savour a salad of prawns with asparagus, or warm oysters in a Champagne sauce or the rack of lamb with tarragon essence offered on his succinct but appealing menu. The cellar is getting better but prices are on the increase.
A la carte: 350-400 F. Menus: 140 F (weekdays only), 210 F.

94170 Perreux (Le) — (Val/Marne)
Paris 15 - Créteil 11 - Vincennes 6 - Lagny 17

Les Magnolias

48, av. de Bry — 48.72.47.43
*M. Royant. Closed Sat lunch, Sun, holidays, 14 Feb-
4 March, 20 April-6 May and 7-21 Aug. Open until
10 pm. Private room: 16. V.*
Gérard Royant simply won't let the sorry sight of the surrounding suburbs get to him. Each year he does something to improve his cosy décor of oak panelling, red velvet curtains, deep-pile carpeting and well-spaced tables. His cuisine is carefully prepared and refined, in tune with a clientele of top-level executives who have rightly named him best chef in the region. His perfectly poached red mullet en gelée prettily studded with tiny vegetables, his wonderfully cooked fricassée of sole served with remarkable vegetables and his highly original fondant of pears with a delicious chocolate sauce testify to his prowess. Service is faultless and the wine list excellent.
A la carte: 350-400 F. Menu: 270 F (weekdays lunch only).

12/20 Le Palmier

52, av. Pierre-Brossolette
43.24.18.97
*M. Bel Hacel. Open every day. Open until 11 pm.
Garden dining. Garage parking. V DC.*
Algerian couscous is the draw of this garden-terrace on the Marne but the shrimps in brik pastry and the Oriental sweets are equally tasty.
A la carte: 200-250 F.

77340 Pontault-Combault — (Seine/Marne)
Paris 26 - Melun 29 - Lagny 14 - Coulommiers 41

Le Canadel

D 51, aire des Berchères — 60.28.96.20
*Mme Wielemans. Closed Sat, Sun and 27 July-2 Sep.
Open until 10 pm. Private room: 10. Air cond. Parking. Telex 693585. V AE DC.*
Jean-Pierre Riovan's cooking is rich and admirably classical: grilled red mullet with a lemony sabayon, sweetbreads with creamed spinach, chicken pot-au-feu, cold chocolate soufflé. The décor is luscious: chandeliers, murals, stucco columns, comfortable chairs and well-spaced tables. Stylish service; top-notch cellar.
À la carte: 400 F. Menus: 160 F, 220 F.

Saphir Hôtel
(See restaurant above)
Open every day. 6 stes 490-710 F. 105 rms 430-445 F. TV. Air cond. Conference facilities. Heated pool.

A brand new hotel next to the future Euro-Disneyland park. Rooms are airy, pleasant and well equipped. Facilities include conference rooms, sauna, and a superb covered swimming pool. Grill.

95300 Pontoise — (Val-d'Oise)
Paris 34 - Beauvais 55 - Rouen 91 - Mantes 39

In nearby **Méry-sur-Oise**

(5 km E on N 322)
95540 Pontoise — (Val-d'Oise)

Le Chiquito
La Bonneville
30.36.40.23
M. Mihura. Closed Sat lunch, Sun, Aug and 23 Dec-1 Jan. Open until 9.30 pm. Private room: 14. Air cond. Parking. V AE DC.

A pleasant décor topped with painted beams opens out on to a flowered courtyard. Chef Alain Mihura has definitely paid his dues; at barely 30 years of age he has already put together an impressive resumé (he's worked with Savoy and Kéréver among others) and is currently developing a personal style. Exemplary execution marks his braised salmon and vegetables cooked in parchment, his marinière of fish in a delicately flavoured cockle sauce, or the noisettes and paupiettes of lamb with thyme served with a scrumptious vegetable marmalade. Papa Mihura and his children provide the affable welcome and service.
A la carte: 400 F. Menu: 220 F.

78560 Port-Marly (Le) — (Yvelines)
Paris 21 - Versailles 10 - St-Germain 3

Auberge du Relais Breton
27, rue de Paris — 39.58.64.33
M. Chaumont. Closed Sun dinner, Mon, Feb school holidays and 3-27 Aug. Open until 10 pm. Private room: 35. Garden dining. V AE.

Here is a wonderful place for a winter meal when a fire is roaring in the immense fireplace, but not to be overlooked in summer when you can sit in the lovely garden serenaded by little birds whilst enjoying a fricassée of lobster with tiny vegetables, steamed turbot, or a magret with truffle juice. Very nice set menus and reasonable prices.
A la carte: 250-280 F. Menus: 199 F (wine inc), 149 F.

Les Danaïdes
1, rue Jean-Jaurès
39.16.44.88
Mlle Brun and M. Prunier. Closed Sat lunch, Sun dinner and 16-31 Aug. Open until 10.30 pm. Garden dining. V AE DC.

The old Port-Marly post office has taken on a lovely country look thanks to its ravishing garden. The cooking is personal and seasonal and this year a toque is awarded for the lobster Vieux Marly, pig's jowl confit with a Roquefort flan, duck with blackberries, and a thin tart of warm pears with Williamine sorbet.
A la carte: 230-280 F. Menu: 138 F.

Le Lion d'Or
7, rue de Paris — 39.58.44.56
M. Cluzel. Closed Tue, Wed, 1-15 March and 1-15 Sep. Open until 10 pm. Private room: 25. V.

This charming inn seduced the painter Alfred Sisley into immortalising it on canvas in his *Inundation at Port-Marly*. The wood-panelled décor is warmly provincial with a few pieces of antique furniture and well-spaced tables. The *patronne* offers a cheerful greeting, and her husband, the chef, is a rigorous craftsman: sample his duck liver mould, or the herbal lamb tourte, and wind up with a luscious nougat made with Pyrenees honey. An extra point this year.
Menus: 100 F (weekdays lunch only), 137 F.

93310 Pré-Saint-Gervais (Le) — (Seine-St-D.)
Paris (Pte de Pantin) 7 - Lagny 27 - Meaux 38

Le Pouilly-Reuilly
68, rue A.-Joineau — 48.45.14.59
M. Thibault. Closed Sun, holidays and end July-6 Sep. Open until 10 pm. Private room: 25. No pets. V AE DC.

Jovial Jean Thibaut has been at the helm of this authentic and popular suburban bistro-inn for a quarter of a century. You pass through the kitchen full of wonderful aromas to reach the dining room with its yellow tables and zinc-topped bar. Dishes served forth by black-aproned waiters include œufs en meurette, frogs' leg pâté, escargots, andouillette au Pouilly, and tarte Tatin, all washed down by delicious and inexpensive wines.
A la carte: 200-350 F.

92800 Puteaux — (Hauts/Seine)
Paris 10 - Versailles 14 - St-Germain-en-Laye 11

Les Communautés
Paris-la-Défense, in the CNIT
2, pl. de la Défense — 46.92.10.10
M. Boilleaut. Open every day. Open until 10 pm. Private room: 35. Air cond. Valet parking. Telex 613782. V AE DC.

Pierre Miécaze should soon hit his stride at this new Sofitel hotel restaurant at la Défense. For the moment, he is strong on grilled dishes although his Pauillac lamb has a slightly overpowering sauce. But he shows proof of a light touch in his wonderful medley of baby vegetables despite a slightly runny anchoïade. His fruit desserts are terrific. The dining room is full of charm and the service is classy.
A la carte: 400 F. Menu: 360 F (weekdays dinner only, wine inc).

Les Communautés
(See restaurant above)
Open every day. 6 stes 2,350-3,000 F. 141 rms 1,200-1,600 F. TV. Air cond. Conference facilities.

The hotel targets a business clientele with its huge rooms (some boast a view of the Grande Arche), luxurious bathrooms, and 24-hour room service.

Dauphin
45, rue J.-Jaurès — 47.73.71.63
Open every day. 30 rms 395 F. TV. Conference facilities. Tennis. Valet parking. Telex 615989. V AE DC.

The Dauphin stands opposite the Princesse Isabelle, and is run by the same family. Generous buffet breakfasts are set up in the sitting room; guestrooms are comfortable and pretty, with cable television. Some rooms are kept for non-smokers. Free shuttle to the RER station.

Les Deux Arcs
La Défense 10
34, cours Michelet — 47.76.44.43
M. Chevauche. Open every day. Open until 10 pm. Private room: 50. Terrace dining. Air cond. Valet parking. Telex 612189. V AE DC.

Alas, chefs tend to come and go in hotel chains, though newcomer Marc Richard seems to be holding his own. Certainly the clientele of this elegant dining room with its burnished mirrors and old-rose décor can hardly have noticed any changes. The crisp-skinned red mullet with basil, the golden-brown veal with almonds, and the chaud-froid of baked pears with chocolate are certainly worth a little toque. The cellar is growing and service has improved.

A la carte: 350 F. Menu: 295 F (weekdays lunch only).

Sofitel Paris-La Défense
(See restaurant above)
Open every day. 1 ste 2,200 F. 149 rms 1,035 F. TV. Air cond. Conference facilities.

A new link in the chain, warmly decorated with gilt mirrors and pale marble. Rooms are quiet with superb pink marble bathrooms. Service is top-notch and breakfasts are delicious. Good facilities for conferences.

Hôtel de Dion-Bouton
19, quai de Dion-Bouton — 42.04.35.54
Open every day. 33 rms 370-420 F. TV. Telex 612425. V AE DC.

On the Seine with pleasant, English-style rooms. Pretty bathrooms and an indoor patio.

Hubert Gasnier
7, bd R.-Wallace — 45.06.33.63
M. Gasnier. Closed Sat, Sun, holidays, 1 week in Feb and 28 June-5 Aug. Open until 9.45 pm. Air cond. V AE DC.

Hubert Gasnier and his wife Maïté count among the most ardent supporters of South-western cuisine in Paris and the surrounding suburbs. A recent touch-up has only made his delightfully provincial dining room more appealing, and Gasnier's cuisine is still based on superb country ingredients from the Basque and Béarnais regions. If you can resist the fabulous Castelnaudary cassoulet, try the salmon escalope with Jurançon wine, the andouillette of sea bass with truffle essence, or the delicious magret with two kinds of foie gras, before succumbing to the sumptuous old Armagnacs.

A la carte: 400 F. Menu: 200 F.

Princesse Isabelle
72, rue J.-Jaurès — 47.78.80.06
Open every day. 1 ste 850 F. 30 rms 495-570 F. TV. Tennis. Valet parking. Telex 613923. V AE DC.

The rooms of this hotel near la Défense are prettily decorated, and boast Jacuzzi bathtubs or multijet showers. Some give directly on to the flowered patio. There's a free chauffeur service to the RER and the Pont de Neuilly métro station.

Syjac Hôtel
20, quai de Dion-Bouton — 42.04.03.04
Open every day. 7 stes 850-1,400 F. 29 rms 460-680 F. TV. No pets. Conference facilities. Parking. Telex 614164. V AE DC.

A recently built hotel which has managed to shun the concrete solidity of nearby la Défense. Rooms are very pleasing, large, and well appointed. There are some nice duplexes overlooking the Seine.

(with fireplace) and a pretty flowered patio. Free sauna. Meals on trays.

11/20 Le Vercanaille
6, bd R.-Wallace — 45.06.05.24
MM. Robert and Hoffet. Closed Sat lunch and Sun. Open until 11 pm. Private room: 23. Valet parking. V AE DC.

A wine bar where you can drink tasty little wines and enjoy simple but nicely prepared dishes like vegetable terrine, calf's liver with lime, or sweetbreads with prawns. There's a 90 F lunch formula (starter and main course) and a takeaway shop.

A la carte: 250 F. Menus: 100 F, 150 F and 200 F (dinner only).

Le Victoria
85, bd R.-Wallace — 45.06.55.51
Open every day. 32 rms 295-465 F. TV. Telex 615295. V AE DC.

Not far from the Arche de la Défense, this recently opened hotel offers comfortable, well-equipped rooms.

95700 Roissy-en-France — (Val/d'Oise)
Paris 26 - Meaux 36 - Senlis 28 - Chantilly 28

Holiday Inn
1, allée du Verger — 34.29.30.00
Open every day. 240 rms 660-850 F. Restaurant. Half-board 840-1,030 F. TV. Air cond. Conference facilities. Parking. Telex 605143. V AE DC.

It is situated in the old village of Roissy. Rooms are large, bright, and functional. There's a health club for use by hotel guests (sauna, gym, Jacuzzi, etc). Free shuttle to the terminals and the exhibition grounds at Villepinte.

Maxim's
Aéroport Charles-de-Gaulle
48.62.16.16
M. Champagnac. Open every day. Open until 10.30 pm. Air cond. Telex 240270. V AE DC.

For a long time now, we've been waiting for this dull and ageing airport clone of the famous Paris address to revamp itself, get a face-lift, take a health-cure. At last something seems to be happening. As we write, work is under way so we can't yet judge the results. We can, however, predict that this nudge in the right direction will encourage a kitchen crew that works hard and consistently to do honour to the name of Maxim's with conscientious, carefully crafted cuisine. The Grill, with its 220 F all-in menu is particularly good, and is attracting a growing clientele. Try the pot-au-feu salad with a truffle vinaigrette, the medallion of veal with sage, or osso buco with orange zest.

A la carte: 450 F (at the Grill: 350 F). Menus: 220 F (wine inc, at the Grill), 250 F.

Sofitel
Aéroport Charles-de-Gaulle
48.62.23.23
Open every day. 8 stes 1,300 F. 344 rms 690-790 F. Restaurant. TV. Air cond. Conference facilities. Heated pool. Tennis. Parking. Telex 230166. V AE DC.

A comfortable airport hotel with a discothèque, sauna, and coffee shop. Twenty-four hour room service and a free shuttle to the airport. There are two restaurants, one with a panoramic view.

93230 Romainville — (Seine-St-D.)
Paris 10 - Livry-Gargan 9 - Aulnay-sous-Bois 9

Chez Henri
15

72, rte de Noisy — 48.45.26.65
M. Bourgin. Closed Sat lunch, Mon dinner, Sun and holidays. Open until 9.30 pm. Private room: 20. Air cond. Parking. V.

Garages and warehouses are not the ideal environment for a fine restaurant. But Henri Bourgin takes it in his stride, as does his clientele of regulars, who know that behind the sombre, unobtrusive façade lies a comfortable dining room where an instinctive, expert chef is at work. You'll soon forget the charmless surroundings when you tuck into a robust tart made with pig's trotters and creamed morels, or paupiettes of brill filled with foie gras and brightened by a touch of redcurrant wine, or a sauté of lamb with melting potatoes, followed by a luscius walnut, hazlenut, and almond craquelin topped with Sauternes sabayon. A traditional, most flavourful style of cookery. Fine cellar, diligent service.

A la carte: 400 F. Menus: 145 F, 200 F.

92500 Rueil-Malmaison — (Hauts/Seine)
Paris 15 - Versailles 11 - Argenteuil 12

El Chiquito
13

126, av. P.-Doumer — 47.51.00.53
M. Pichois. Closed Sun and 9-19 Aug. Open until 9.45 pm. Garden dining. Air cond. Parking. V AE.

Chefs may come and go, but the kitchen manages to keep on an even keel, producing flashy dishes like sole stuffed with lobster, or rich ones such as a fillet of beef with warm foie gras or blanquette of sole with morels. Prices are constantly on the rise, except at night when the 'little' set menu is served. At the back is a wonderful garden which blots out the traffic.

A la carte: 450-600 F. Menu: 220 F (dinner only).

12/20 Relais de Saint-Cucufa

114, rue du Gal-de-Miribel — 47.49.79.05
Mme Morel. Closed dinner Sun and Mon. Open until 9.45 pm. Private room: 6. Garden dining. V.

A terrace and garden enlarge the rustic dining room in fine weather. Here the *patronne* chooses her ingredients with care, and turns them into generous, delicious dishes. Try her prawn ravioli, the escalope of sweetbreads with morels, and finish up with a bright berry gratin. Small but choice cellar, reasonably priced.

A la carte: 350-400 F.

94150 Rungis — (Val/Marne)
Paris 13 - Corbeil 26 - Longjumeau 10 - Antony 6

Holiday Inn

4, av. Ch.-Lindbergh — 46.87.26.66
Open every day. 168 rms 695-995 F. Restaurant. TV. Air cond. Conference facilities. Heated pool. Tennis. Parking. Telex 265803. V AE DC.

Comfortable and well-kept rooms near Orly airport (free shuttle). A view of the Rungis *halles* (the Paris wholesale food market). Shops.

Red toques signify modern cuisine; black toques signify traditional cuisine.

La Rungisserie
13

20, av. Ch.-Lindbergh — 46.87.36.36
M. Ladeveze. Open every day. Open until 11 pm. Garden dining. Air cond. No pets. Garage parking. Telex 260738. V AE DC.

A huge and happy hotel restaurant with a modern, soothing décor. The good lunch menu (prix-fixe, with wine included) and the large hors-d'œuvre buffet attract a faithful clientele from the Rungis market. The à la carte menu includes some solid offerings such as young rabbit in a saupiquet sauce, andouillette de Troyes, or magret with tarragon and tiny turnips. A good cellar but slightly dour service.

A la carte: 350 F. Menus: 170 F (weekdays only, wine inc), 190 F (weekdays only).

Pullman Paris-Orly

(See restaurant above)
Open every day. 2 stes 1,100 F. 206 rms 595-860 F. TV. Air cond. Conference facilities. Pool.

A reliable, comfortable chain hotel with excellent soundproofing, air-conditioning, colour television, and direct telephone lines. Among the amenities on offer are a non-stop shuttle to and from the airports, a panoramic bar, a sauna, shops, and a swimming pool. There are deluxe rooms ('Privilège') and several lounges.

91400 Saclay — (Essonne)
Paris 21 - Chartres 68 - Versailles 11 - Palaiseau 8

Novotel Saclay

Rue Ch.-Thomassin — 69.41.81.40
Open every day. 136 rms 415-440 F. Restaurant. TV. Air cond. Conference facilities. Pool. Tennis. Parking. Telex 601856. V AE DC.

Part of the Novotel chain with functional, comfortable rooms, recently renovated and air-conditioned. Minigolf, bar. Summer barbecues.

92210 Saint-Cloud — (Hauts/Seine)
Paris 12 - Boulogne 3 - Versailles 10 - Garches 2

La Désirade
13

2, bd de la République
47.71.22.33
M. Blanchet. Open every day. Open until 10 pm. Garden dining. Air cond. Garage parking. Telex 631618. V AE DC.

Colourful fabrics make for a gay, charming décor and Jean-Pierre Anselem's cuisine has definitely progressed enough to earn him a small toque this year for his savoury warm quail salad, his tender casseroled lamb's tongue, the juicy magret roasted with thyme, and a generous fisherman's stew. The choice of desserts could improve, however, and the service lacks zip.

A la carte: 300-330 F. Menu: 120 F (weekdays only).

Hôtel Quorum

(See restaurant above)
Open every day. 58 rms 430-500 F. TV. Conference facilities.

A bright new hotel with simply elegant modern public rooms, and spacious guestrooms with grey marble baths. The best are on the upper floors with a view over the Parc de St-Cloud. The racecourse and St-Cloud golf club are nearby.

Le Florian
14, rue de l'Eglise — 47.71.29.90
M. Calfali. Closed Sat lunch and Sun. Open until 10.30 pm. Parking. V AE DC.
Big, winey sauces with a Florentine touch mark the cooking of Angelo Calfali. He turns out a tasty turbot in Champagne sauce, creditable kidneys in sherry, and a good casserole of prawns and sweetbreads with a duo of sauces. His fresh pasta is delicious, his fish cooked to perfection, and desserts are improving (try the bitter-chocolate cake). Elegant décor.
A la carte: 300 F.

10/20 Le Longchamp
9, av. de Longchamp — 47.71.23.81
M. Darry. Closed Sat dinner, Sun and 26 July-19 Aug. Open until 9 pm (upon reserv). Private room: 20. No pets. V.
The lunchtime crowd pours in from the nearby cinema studios and Dassault industries. The kitchen serves forth a robust South-western repertoire. Service can be a trifle brusque, we've noticed.
A la carte: 200 F. Menus: 52 F (weekdays lunch only, wine inc), 80 F.

11/20 Vanida
6, rue Dailly — 47.71.31.05
Mme Brunie. Closed Sat lunch and Sun, Feb school holidays and 1-20 Aug. Open until 11 pm. V AE DC.
A benevolent Buddha beams out over the fresh, white décor of this establishment which is going off a bit, alas. On our last visit the fish fritters were doughy and the rice sautéed with shrimps definitely lacked its usual flavour. With all due respect to the charming Thai *patronne*, we're removing a point this year.
A la carte: 170-190 F. Menus: 81 F (lunch only), 139 F (weekdays only), 103 F.

Villa Henri IV
43, bd de la République — 46.02.59.30
Open every day. 36 rms 390-470 F. Restaurant. TV. Conference facilities. Garage parking. Telex 631893. V AE DC.
A pleasant address off the boulevard. Rooms are decorated in Louis XVI, Louis-Philippe or Norman style and are huge, bright, and well-equipped.

SAINT-DENIS
93200 Saint-Denis — (Seine-St-D.)
Paris 10 - Argenteuil 10 - Chantilly 30 - Pontoise 24

Mélody
15, rue G.-Péri — 48.20.87.73
M. Balat. Closed Sat, Sun, 9-17 Feb and 4 Aug-1 Sep. Open until 9.30 pm. V.
Last year's highly praised 75 F menu has disappeared, a victim of its own popularity. It has been replaced by starter/main dish/dessert formulas priced between 150 and 180 F. It's hard to know if this modest, honest cuisine—salmon-stuffed ravioli, fresh cod steak in a butter sauce, and lemon tart—will still have quite the same appeal.
A la carte: 150-180 F.

12/20 La Saumonière
1, rue Lanne — 48.20.25.56
M. Bletio. Closed Sun and 1-15 Aug. Open until 10 pm. Air cond. V.
The menu is over-long and the cuisine a trifle fussy, but this is a serious and well-intentioned establishment nonetheless. In a comfortable, slightly overstuffed décor, sample the brochette of grilled grouper with smoked bacon, or the oxtail casserole à l'ancienne.
A la carte: 350 F. Menu: 190 F (weekdays lunch only).

SAINT-GERMAIN-EN-LAYE
78100 Saint-Germain-en-Laye — (Yvelines)
Paris 21 - Chartres 81 - Dreux 70 - Beauvais 69

Cazaudehore
1, av. du Président-Kennedy
34.51.93.80
MM. Cazaudehore. Closed Mon (except holidays). Open until 10 pm. Private room: 130. Terrace dining. Parking. Telex 696055. V.
On the edge of the forest in a wonderful setting of greenery and flowers, sits this ravishing establishment elegantly and luxuriously decorated with old prints and English chintzes; for summer dining, there's a huge terrace that looks out on the trees. It is at this point that the superb and unshakeable 'Cazau' sometimes goes off track, its wonderful cuisine suffering under the pressure of numbers. Still, irregularities are not the rule and you are sure to enjoy some great dishes like the excellent gigot de lotte with sea-urchin coral, or South-western specialities such as a warm foie gras with figs.
A la carte: 400-500 F.

La Forestière
(See restaurant above)
Open every day. 6 stes 860-900 F. 24 rms 605-720 F. TV. Conference facilities.
Thirty rooms and suites have been recently renovated and pleasantly furnished in an old-fashioned style with fresh, spring-like fabrics. The hotel sits on extensive, flower-filled grounds at the edge of the forest. Relais et Châteaux.

12/20 La Feuillantine
10, rue des Louviers
34.51.04.24
M. Chauchereau. Closed at Christmas. Open until 10 pm. V.
Full (and very delicious!) meals at 110 F don't grow on trees in affluent St-Germain. That is why La Feuillantine's dining room is so crowded these days: taste the pan-roasted salmon with tender chicory, a scrumptious chicken with morels, and a flavourful pear gratin. The service remains cheerful, even amid the crush—this spot could well earn a toque very soon.
Menu: 110 F.

Le Pavillon Henri-IV
21, rue Thiers — 34.51.62.62
Open every day. 3 stes 1,900 F. 42 rms 400-1,300 F. Restaurant. Half-board 670 F. TV 30 rms. Conference facilities. Garage parking. Telex 695822. V AE DC.
This is where Louis XIV was born, Alexandre Dumas wrote *The Three Musketeers*, and Offenbach composed a number of operettas. Total comfort inhabits the 45 huge rooms and suites. The public rooms are magnificent and there's a splendid view over the immense park.

RAC Regional Maps of France at 4 miles to 1 inch are the ideal touring companion. Available from RAC offices and all good bookshops.

SAINT-OUEN

93400 Saint-Ouen — (Seine-St-D.)
Paris 7 - Saint-Denis 4 - Pontoise 27 - Chantilly 34

Le Coq
de la Maison Blanche
37, bd J.-Jaurès — 40.11.01.23
M. François. Closed Sun. Open until 10 pm. Private room: 120. Garden dining. V.

The long and lovely menu is handwritten daily to entice diners with jambon persillé, coq au vin, or grilled kidneys. Seasonal dishes also take pride of place and are prepared in grand bistro tradition with a touch of youthful exuberance. The salad of Breton crab's claws, the saddle of lamb with white beans, or the eel sautéed in white wine with spinach and broccoli perfectly suit the convivial atmosphere of this likeable establishment run by a sensational *patron*, Alain François.
A la carte: 300-350 F.

Chez Serge
7, bd J.-Jaurès — 40.11.06.42
M. Cancé. Lunch only (and dinner Tue, Thu and Fri until 8.30 pm 15 Oct-15 April). Closed Sun and Aug. Air cond. V.

Short, simple, and sweet—that sums up chef Serge Cancé's menu. And that policy has brought ongoing success to this bistro set in a bleak *banlieue* north of Paris. Chez Serge is full of demanding clients who bustle in to feast on the marvellous terrines, foie gras with Sauternes, mackerel in white wine, streaky bacon with sauerkraut, salt cod with basil, or lamb with flageolet beans. Washed down with some wonderful wines, expertly chosen (Serge has an award-winning 'nose').
A la carte: 250 F.

SCEAUX

92330 Sceaux — (Hauts/Seine)
Paris 12 - Versailles 16 - Antony 3 - Bagneux 3

L'Orangerie
13, rue M.-Charaire — 43.50.83.00
M. Beaudoin. Closed Sun dinner, Mon and 5 Aug-4 Sep. Open until 9 pm. No pets. V.

The cooking is consistent, the service pleasant, and comfort is assured in this peaceful spot situated on a pedestrian precinct. The prices are not too mad (though we'd like to see a set menu added), and the warm lobster feuilleté, the veal kidneys and sweetbreads with morels, and the farm duck with snails are most pleasing dishes. A reasonable little wine list.
A la carte: 300 F.

SÈVRES

92310 Sèvres — (Hauts/Seine)
Paris 12 - Boulogne 3 - Nanterre 10 - Versailles 8

11/20 Philéas Fogg
5, pl. Pierre-Brossolette
46.26.48.80
Mme Lucarotti. Closed Sun dinner and Mon. Open until 10.30 pm. Terrace dining. V AE DC.

Travel no farther than to the Sèvres railway station to go around the world in eighty dishes. The cooking is nicely handled by (get this) the wife of an ex-script writer for the defunct (but often rerun) television series *The Avengers*: try her tasty jambalaya, curried scampi, or chicken Kiev. A simple décor and a smiling welcome. Superb whiskies.
A la carte: 180-200 F.

SURVILLIERS

95470 Survilliers — (Val-d'Oise)
Paris 30 - Chantilly 14 - Senlis 18 - Lagny 32

Mercure
Rue J.-Moulin
195470 Saint-Witz — 34.68.28.28
Open every day. 112 rms 305-455 F. Restaurant. TV. Conference facilities. Pool. Parking. Telex 695917. V AE DC.

A modern, perfectly maintained hotel in a green setting, the Mercure boasts functional, bright rooms, two of which are equipped for the disabled. Pleasant garden, half-court tennis, and children's playground. Half-pension (580 F) for conference-goers.

Novotel Paris-Survilliers
A 1 then D 16 — 34.68.69.80
Open every day. 2 stes 390 F. 79 rms 390-430 F. Restaurant. TV. Air cond. Conference facilities. Pool. Parking. Telex 605910. V AE DC.

This rather nice modern hotel is set in the middle of a park just five kilometres from the Chantilly forest. Meeting and conference rooms. Bar and grill open from 6 am to midnight.

VARENNE-ST-HILAIRE (LA)

94210 Varenne-St-Hilaire (La) — (Val/Marne)
Paris 16 - Lagny 22 - St-Maur 3 - Chennevières 2

La Bretèche
171, quai de Bonneuil — 48.83.38.73
M. Regnault. Closed Sun dinner, Mon and 5-25 Feb. Open until 10.30 pm. Private room: 18. Garden dining. V.

The chef has a tendency to juggle perilously rich ingredients (turbot with foie gras, chicken breast stuffed with veal sweetbreads and morels cooked in truffled juices). But he also knows how to marry complementary flavours. Witness the plaice salad with ginger and soy-sauce butter, and the veal medallions perfumed with tea. The cellar is well-stocked with bottles in a wide range of prices. And the sunny décor is seductive indeed. But when the weather is fine we opt for the terrace, where the eye wanders over the soothingly verdant banks of the Marne.
A la carte: 350-400 F. Menu: 150 F.

Gargamelle
23, av. Ch.-Péguy — 48.83.11.17
M. Allart. Closed Sun dinner and Mon. Open until 10 pm. Terrace dining. V AE DC.

Simple and flower-filled, the Gargamelle's delightful dining room opens on to a cobbled court used in summer as a terrace. Chef Jean-Yves Delourme is serious and skilful, his cuisine subtle and highly personal. We suggest the freshwater perch with citrus fruit, fillet of beef with grapes, or baudroie ragoût seasoned with saffron. A toque this year for the delicate skate millefeuille with capers, and the perfectly prepared turbot with leeks.
A la carte: 300-350 F. Menus: 120 F, 180 F, 250 F.

Le Pavillon Bleu
66, prom. des Anglais — 48.83.10.56
M. Stumm. Open every day. Open until 11 pm. Private room: 100. Terrace dining. V AE DC.

Once a former suburban dance-café, Le Pavillon Bleu is now a luxurious—and expensive—riverside restaurant boasting elaborate cuisine prepared by talented chef Dominique Stumm. Late of the Vivarois, Stumm's sauces are masterful, and his choice of ingredients is beyond reproach. Sample the tender asparagus feuilleté topped with a suave mousseline, and marvellous lotte medallions with a sublime sauce based on St-Estèphe wine. The desserts leave much to be desired. If the thick carpet and heavy curtains don't thrill you, try the leafy terrace on the water's edge. Opulent wine list.

A la carte: 400-450 F. Menu: 250 F (weekdays lunch only, wine inc).

VARENNES-JARCY

91480 Varennes-Jarcy — (Essonne)
Paris 29 - Corbeil-Essonnes 14 - Evry 13 - Melun 20

Auberge du Moulin de Jarcy

50, rue Boieldieu — 69.00.89.20
Open only Fri, Sat and Sun. Closed 31 July-15 Aug and 24 Dec-16 Jan. 5 rms 150-200 F. Restaurant. No pets. Parking. V.

Located near the Sénart forest, this medieval mill house is set on an island between two forks of the Yerres River. The few rooms are pleasant and comfortable.

12/20 Hostellerie de Varennes

14, rue de Mandres — 69.00.97.03
M. Gautier. Closed Tue dinner, Wed and Aug. Open until 9 pm. Private room: 70. Garden dining. Parking. V AE.

Francis Gautier's gorgeous establishment is graced with a delightful garden full of flowers. The cuisine strikes an intelligent balance between simple (young rabbit terrine, grilled andouillette, and duck confit) and rich dishes.

A la carte: 200-300 F. Menus: 105 F (weekdays lunch only), 185 F.

VÉLIZY

78140 Vélizy — (Yvelines)
Paris 15 - Versailles 7 - Jouy-en-Josas 4 - Antony 11

Holiday Inn

22, av. de l'Europe — 39.46.96.98
Open every day. 1 ste 1,200 F. 182 rms 750-915 F. Restaurant. TV. Air cond. Conference facilities. Heated pool. Parking. Telex 696537. V AE DC.

Situated near a shopping centre, the Holiday Inn offers functional rooms and excellent facilities. Free shuttle to the Pont-de-Sèvres métro station.

VERSAILLES

78000 Versailles — (Yvelines)
Paris 23 - Mantes 44 - Rambouillet 31 - Dreux 61

Bellevue Hôtel

12, av. de Sceaux — 39.50.13.41
Open every day. 3 stes 450-500 F. 25 rms 280-450 F. TV. Telex 695613. V AE DC.

The Bellevue's Louis XV/XVI-style rooms are soundproofed and well equipped (new beds), but rather worn, despite last year's remodelling. Located near the château and conference centre.

12/20 Brasserie du Bœuf à la Mode

4, rue au Pain — 39.50.31.99
M. Vié. Open every day. Open until 0.30 am. Private room: 40. Terrace dining. Air cond. V.

Well-prepared and generously served bistro favourites are on offer here. The chef trained under top chef Gérard Vié (of Les Trois Marches), who also owns this amusing brasserie. There is a fine choice of seafood, mussels marinière, skate with capers, andouillette, calf's head, and bœuf mode. Tasty wines served by the glass or carafe.

A la carte: 180-200 F.

12/20 Au Chapeau Gris

7, rue Hoche — 39.50.10.81
M. Brown. Closed Tue dinner, Wed and July. Open until 10 pm. Private room: 80. V AE DC.

As the ancient exposed beams attest, this is the oldest restaurant in Versailles, and it attracts an extremely well-heeled crowd. The cuisine is honest enough, though not always precise. Traditional dishes are the house speciality: snail omelette, rack of lamb, and caramel ice cream. Exceptional wine list. Classic, thoroughly professional service. Pleasant setting.

A la carte: 300 F. Menu: 150 F.

Eden Hôtel

2, rue Ph.-de-Dangeau — 39.50.68.06
Open every day. 24 rms 190-280 F. TV. V.

Eden lies between the railway station and the château, in a quiet street near the police station. The rooms are regularly refurbished and updated.

12/20 Le Pot-au-Feu

22, rue de Satory — 39.50.57.43
M. Le Falher. Closed Sat lunch, Sun and Aug. Open until 11 pm. Private room: 10. No pets. V.

The dim lighting adds several years to the already well-worn provincial décor. But the Pot-au-Feu's eager new owners have brought in a chef from Marius et Janette. An extra point this year for the light asparagus feuilleté, and flavourful salmon marmite perfumed with olive oil.

A la carte: 250-280 F. Menu: 110 F.

Le Potager du Roy

1, rue du Mal-Joffre — 39.50.35.34
M. Letourneur. Closed Sun and Mon. Open until 10 pm. Air cond. V.

No one comes here for the uncomfortable décor and terrace. The Potager's twin attraction is the animated atmosphere, and chef Philippe Letourneur's delicate, ever-improving cuisine. Formerly with Gérard Vié, Letourneur constantly refines and changes his menu. Whenever possible, he uses simple and fresh ingredients instead of rich items such as foie gras and truffles. And his talent shines through. A second toque this year for the beef-shin salad with exquisite vegetables, oven-baked saddle of lamb, fresh steamed cod, chicken cooked with verjuice and served with fresh pasta, and chocolate tart accompanied by tangy lemon sorbet. The wines are very well chosen but rather expensive. Two exceptionally good fixed-price menus.

A la carte: 300 F. Menus: 115 F, 160 F.

12/20 Le Quai n°1

1, av. de St-Cloud — 39.50.42.26
M. Roche. Closed Sun dinner and Mon. Open until 11 pm. Private room: 40. Terrace dining. Air cond. V.

For the last three years, the Quai's chef, late of Les Trois Marches, has been regaling Versailles with fine seafood and skilfully prepared fish dishes at reasonable prices. Try the exemplary 115 F menu: mussels marinière, tunny provençale, Roquefort with figs and walnuts, and dessert. Amusing, ultramarine-coloured décor.

A la carte: 250-280 F. Menus: 115 F, 160 F.

Rescatore

27, av. de St-Cloud — 39.50.23.60
M. Bagot. Closed Sat lunch and Sun. Open until 10 pm. Private room: 30. Air cond. V AE.

Jacques Bagot has thoroughly refurbished the interior of his handsome, eighteenth-century stone establishment. The magnificent first-floor dining room has been redone in salmon hues, with an elegant grey ceiling. The tables are covered with lace cloths, superbly laid, and crowned with bouquets of flowers. Bagot is a native of the Norman port of Granville; he specialises in vibrant fish and seafood dishes. His cuisine is imaginative and refined. Try the steamed gurnard salad with crispy curly endive, and escalope of sea bream with prunes. The desserts (Madeira cake scented with orange-flower water) are under par, and the cellar could stand a few more bottles of white wine.

A la carte: 350-400 F. Menus: 225 F (lunch only), 245 F (dinner only, wine inc), 345 F.

Trianon Palace
1, bd de la Reine — 30.84.38.00
Open every day. 10 stes 1,960-4,570 F. 110 rms 970-1,750 F. Restaurant. TV 90 rms. Conference facilities. Heated pool. Tennis. Parking. Telex 698863. V AE DC.

A Japanese investment and development corporation has taken over this imposing, extremely comfortable hotel, and is in the process of transforming it into one of its most luxurious European palaces.

Les Trois Marches
18
3, rue Colbert (pl. du Château) — 39.50.13.21
M. Vié. Closed Sun and Mon. Open until 10 pm. Private room: 20. Garden dining. No-smoking section. V AE DC.

Chef and proprietor Gérard Vié feels right at home in the kitchen of his lovely historic townhouse, the hôtel de Gramont, which he has redecorated and refined over the years. But soon he and his crew will move en masse to the Trianon Palace, as part of a programme to upgrade that venerable establishment (see above).

As to Vié's cuisine, we first tasted its pleasures when the chef still toiled in a humble little Versailles restaurant, turning out sophisticated country-style dishes. He hit his stride here, though, just a stone's throw away from the château. Certain of our readers may have complained about uneven performances, but we must say that we've been enchanted each time we've dined at Les Trois Marches in the last few years.

Vié's cuisine has what it takes to thrill and captivate. Witness the warm belon oysters with foie gras, duck liver with strong rancio wine, rabbit gelée with leeks, fillets of sole marinated—almost conserved—in olive oil, roast lobster with thyme, turbot with onions and pommes Anna, braised young pigeon with spices and apricots, and duck with turnips and truffles, simmered for four hours. Even his simple country-style dishes are delicious and full of provincial goodness (beef braised with carrots, cassoulet with Couïza sausages).

The formidable cellar's grand wines push the bill skyward, but prices are not out of line given the quality. There are many fine bottlings at about 100 F, and the fixed-price lunch menu is a marvel.

A la carte: 550-800 F. Menus: 260 F (weekdays lunch only), 450 F, 550 F.

Le Versailles
7, rue Ste-Anne — 39.50.64.65
Open every day. 48 rms 350-450 F. TV. Conference facilities. Parking. Telex 689110. V AE DC.

Conveniently situated near the entrance of the château and facing the convention centre, Le Versailles's modern rooms boast recently refitted bathrooms. Direct access to parking garage by lift. Garden and patio.

And also...
Our selection of places for inexpensive, quick, or late-night meals, and smaller hotels.

Brasserie du Théâtre (39.50.03.21 - 15, rue des Réservoirs. Open until 1 am): Classic brasserie food (head cheese, pepper steak, sauerkraut, tartare), served in a pleasantly smoke-stained décor with great mirrors, woodwork, and leather banquettes (200 F).

La Flotille (39.51.41.58 - in the Château de Versailles parc. Open for lunch only): Set on the edge of the château's Grand Canal, with a marvellous view of Le Nôtre's gardens, the unpretentious cuisine served here is tasty indeed (rabbit cooked with mustard, duck confit, calf's head). Delightful summer terrace (200 F).

Home Saint-Louis (39.50.23.55 - 28, rue St-Louis. 29 rms 140-270 F): This family-style hotel is located in the quiet St-Louis neighbourhood.

Le Lac Hong (30.44.03.71 - 18, rue des Frères-Caudron, 78280 Guyancourt): Fine Chinese-Vietnamese cuisine at low prices (game hen stuffed with rice and mushrooms, duckling à la prune, grilled crab). Exceptionally affordable wines, charming welcome (150 F).

Au Pied de Mouton (39.50.33.00 - 20, rue au Pain. Open until midnight): Fresh fish and seafood are served in this friendly 1950s–style brasserie located inside the old town market hall. Fine daily specials. Starchy prices and service (250 F).

Richaud (39.50.10.42 - 16, rue Richaud. 39 rms 225-365 F): A small, quiet hotel in the centre of the shopping district. The rooms have been remodelled recently.

(4 km N on D 7)
78870 Versailles — (Yvelines)

12/20 La Grille de Maintenon
Rte de Maule — 34.62.90.43
M. Bramas. Closed Sat lunch, Sun dinner, Mon and 15 Aug-12 Sep. Open until 10 pm. Garden dining. Parking. V AE DC.

Set on the edge of the Marly forest, this Maintenon sports a kitsch, rustic décor that is rather heavy-handed. The young chef has had to tone down his bold cooking of late, to please a cautious clientele. Try the refreshing crab chiffonnade, flounder with tasty shrimp, and yummy caramelised œufs à la neige. Attentive, cheerful service.

A la carte: 250-300 F. Menus: 75 F (weekdays lunch only, wine inc), 130 F and 180 F (wine inc).

(NE)
78150 Versailles — (Yvelines)

Le Chesnoy
13
24, rue Pottier — 39.54.01.01
M. Baratin. Closed Sun dinner and Mon. Open until 10 pm. Private room: 20. Garden dining. Air cond. V AE DC.

Bustling and brimming over with *bon vivants*, Le Chesnoy is a welcome oasis in a sea of cement. The sunny dining room opens on to a summer terrace. Late of Les Glénan and Marius et Janette, chef Georges Torrès excels with fish dishes: lightly smoked sea bass with leek sabayon, and crispy salmon cooked in its skin with a salt crust. There are also several fine meat dishes on the menu (veal sweetbreads cooked with rum and nutmeg). Monsieur Baratin, the owner, will guide you ex-

pertly through his cellar.
A la carte: 280-300 F.

Le Connemara

41, rte de Rueil — 39.55.63.07
M. Eynard-Machet. Closed Sun (except lunch 1st and 2nd Sun of the month), Mon and 28 July-20 Aug. Open until 10 pm. Private room: 15. V AE DC.
Ireland features only modestly on the Connemara's menu: succulent smoked salmon, Aran scallop soup, and a dizzying choice of whiskeys. The rest of chef Pascal Eynard-Machet's repertoire plays variations on classic themes, which are tunefully indulged with fruit (sole and salmon served with grapefruit) or vegetables (lamb mignon with fresh white beans, small turbot with a turnip and apple gratin). The handsome décor is done in salmon hues, and the restaurant is set in a swath of greenery.
A la carte: 300 F. Menus: 90 F (weekdays lunch only), 135 F.

L'Etoile de Mer

17, rue des Deux-Frères — 39.54.62.70
M. Pinta. Closed Sun dinner, Mon and 29 July-28 Aug. Open until 9.30 pm. Air cond. Parking. V DC.
L'Etoile de Mer's intimate, modern dining room opens on to the town marketplace. The view features a crowded lobster tank, and beyond it, the fishmonger's shop attached to the restaurant. Whence chef Thierry Corneteau plucks the freshest, best fish and shellfish, and transforms them into spectacular assortments and cooked dishes: superb, lightly grilled scampi, magnificent sea bass, and fresh summer soup made with large prawns. Charming welcome. Negligible wine cellar.
A la carte: 350 F. Menus: 90 F (weekdays lunch only). 180 F.

78110 Vésinet (Le) — (Yvelines)
Paris 18 - Versailles 15 - St-Germain 3 - Pontoise 24

Les Ibis

Ile du Grand Lac — 39.52.17.41
Open every day. 20 rms 360-450 F. Conference facilities. Restaurant.
Just fifteen minutes from central Paris, this turn-of-the-century residence is set in quiet, lovely grounds. The rooms are very comfortable. Conference rooms. Breathtaking view of the lake and landscaped gardens.

91120 Villebon-sur-Yvette — (Essonne)
Paris 23 - Versailles 21 - Evry 22 - Etampes 31

La Morvandelle

86, av. du Général-de-Gaulle
60.10.29.61
M. Blandin. Open every day. Open until 10 pm. Private room: 40. Garden dining. No-smoking section. Garage parking. V AE DC.
A thorough professional recently took over this handsome stone house, and is bending over backwards to prove that he knows how to prepare everything under the sun. His generosity comes through in the perfectly cooked lobster salad, and expertly seasoned, firm and tasty turbot, as well as the outstanding tarte Tatin made with figs instead of apples. The cellar could stand improvement. Sunny, elegant décor, pleasant summer terrace.
A la carte: 350-400 F. Menu: 125 F (weekdays only).

92390 Villeneuve-la-Garenne — (Hauts/Seine)
Paris 11 - St-Denis 2 - Pontoise 22 - St-Germain 18

Les Chanteraines

Av. 8-Mai-1945 — 47.99.31.31
Mme François. Closed Sun dinner. Open until 10 pm. Terrace dining. Parking. V AE.
This smart, spanking-new restaurant is lost in the leaden suburbs north of Paris. The décor has a 1930s feel, and the dining room looks out on the municipal park and pond. Though more modern and less Burgundian, the food here is not unlike that of the Coq de la Maison Blanche (see St-Ouen), which is run by the proprietor's husband. Try the fresh, oft-changing, and honest house specialities: warm sardines with olive oil, thinly sliced lamb seasoned with thyme, and chocolate marjolaine. A toque this year! Interesting wine cellar.
A la carte: 300 F. Menu: 160 F.

93420 Villepinte — (Seine-St-D.)
Paris 24 - Bobigny 10 - St-Denis 21 - Meaux 30

Grilotel

Av. G.-Clemenceau — 49.63.17.30
Open every day. 43 rms 195-210 F. Restaurant. Half-board 270-300 F. TV. Conference facilities. Parking. Telex 262955. V AE DC.
Recently built, and located just a few minutes from the Astérix amusement park and Roissy, this hotel offers functional rooms equipped with television and direct-access telephone. Bar.

91190 Villiers-le-Bâcle — (Essonne)
Paris 24 - Trappes 15 - Chevreuse 11 - Saclay 6

La Petite Forge

1, rte de Gif — 60.19.03.88
M. Ernimo. Closed Sat lunch, Sun, 1-7 April and 5-25 Aug. Open until 9.30 pm. Private room: 70. V.
This charming little stopover at the mouth of the Chevreuse Valley boasts an intimate, roughcast décor with exposed beams. Alas, the frightfully high prices keep all but the wealthiest away. Chef and proprietor Kleber Ernimo nonetheless does his utmost to justify the cost. His cuisine is based on top-quality ingredients and prepared with loving care. The fish are fabulous and fresh, the game delicious, and the farmhouse cheeses remarkable. Taste the asparagus flan, fricasséed fillets of sole, and pink-fleshed sea bream with vegetable ravioli. The impressive cellar houses many excellent Bordeaux.
A la carte: 400 F.

91170 Viry-Châtillon — (Essonne)
Paris 27 - Corbeil-Essonnes 11 - Evry 9 - Versailles 31

La Dariole de Viry

21, rue Pasteur — 69.44.22.40
M. Richard. Closed Sat lunch, Sun, holidays, 14 July-6 Aug and 24 Dec-3 Jan. Open until 10 pm. Private room: 20. Air cond. V AE.
The surroundings are joyless. But the delightful welcome afforded by the *patronne* and young waitresses, and the smart, sky-blue décor, are seductive indeed. Jean-Pierre Richard's cuisine is reliably good, and sometimes excellent and original: ethereal celery and sturgeon millefeuille, John Dory viennoise with bacon, and delicious caramel croustillant. Excellent wine cellar.

RESTAURANTS & HOTELS

Listed Alphabetically

80100 Abbeville — (Somme)
Paris 160 - Amiens 45 - Dieppe 63

Auberge de la Corne
⑬ 32, chaussée du Bois — 22.24.06.34
M. Lematelot. Closed Sun dinner, Mon and 1-15 Feb. Open until 9.30 pm. Private room: 26. Air cond. V AE DC.

Yves Lematelot is a good chef, indeed he might be the best in the region when it comes to simple dishes based on game and fresh market produce. He gets his fish from the Somme bay, and mushrooms from the Crécy forest, and his poultry is always excellent. The dining room, split down the middle by a bar bristling with bottles, is most convivial. This year we enjoyed the red mullet marinated with lime juice and tapenade, sea bass croustillant with glazed onions, and Bresse pigeon chartreuse.

A la carte: 300-350 F. Menus: 120 F, 185 F, 260 F.

Escale en Picardie
⑬ 15, rue des Teinturiers — 22.24.21.51
M. Perron. Closed Mon, dinner Sun and holidays, Feb school holidays and 8-31 Aug. Open until 8.45 pm. V AE DC.

The Perron family's friendly restaurant and oyster bar has been improved of late with comfortable, endearing touches. Ever faithful to Morbihan seafood, Gérard Perron skilfully prepares oysters and coastal fish. Try the oyster chaud-froid perfumed with vermouth and chervil, roasted salt cod with aubergine tian, and turbot with celery compote. The choice of wines is surprisingly vast. Good fixed-price menus, reasonable prices.

A la carte: 300 F. Menus: 135 F, 150 F, 185 F.

Hôtel de France
19, pl. du Pilori — 22.24.00.42
Open every day. 69 rms 195-265 F. Restaurant. TV 52 rms. Conference facilities. Garage parking. Telex 155365. V AE DC.

Conveniently located in the centre of town, the recently renovated rooms are spacious (those at the back are quiet). French billiard table.

Ibis
234, rte d'Amiens — 22.24.80.80
Open every day. 45 rms 232-282 F. Restaurant. TV. Conference facilities. Parking. Telex 145045. V.

Situated on the outskirts of town, the Ibis is set slightly off the main road. The rooms of this chain hotel are well kept, but the service is sometimes lacking. Buffet breakfast on a terrace facing the countryside.

Relais Vauban
4, bd Vauban
22.31.30.35
Open every day. 22 rms 170-255 F. TV. No pets. Garage parking. V.

This family-run hotel was thoroughly remodelled in 1988. The bright, well-kept rooms are fully insulated and soundproofed, and have direct-line telephones. Small bathrooms. Friendly welcome.

74360 Abondance — (H.-Savoie)
Paris 604 - Annecy 100 - Evian 30 - Thonon 28

Bel Air
3 km NE, in Richebourg
50.73.01.71
Closed 20 April-15 May and 30 Sep-20 Dec. 23 rms 115-185 F. Restaurant. Half-board 190-210 F oblig in seas. TV 6 rms. No pets. Parking. V.

Located three kilometres from town, this chalet-style hotel offers quiet, pleasant rooms with balconies overlooking the surrounding mountain landscape.

see Vichy

83600 Adrets (Les) — (Var)
Paris 886 - St-Raphaël 21 - Cannes 28

12/20 Auberge des Adrets
N 7, towards Mandelieu
94.40.36.24
M. Niel. Closed Mon. Open until 10 pm. Private room: 25. Garden dining. Piscine. Garage parking. V.

New proprietors have brightened the once-sombre décor with discreetly romantic touches, and brought in a young chef to stand the cuisine on its head. We only wish he would streamline his style a bit. Nonetheless, we enjoyed the homemade foie gras salad, trout with twin butter sauce, duck confit served on a bed of shallots, and tasty orange salad for dessert.

A la carte: 350 F. Menu: 195 F.

AGAY

83700 Agay — (Var)
Paris 902 - Cannes 30 - Saint-Raphaël 11 - Nice 63

Sol e Mar
2 km SW on N 98
Le Dramont — 94.95.25.60
Closed 15 Oct-29 March. 47 rms 440-590 F. Restaurant. Half-board 390-500 F oblig in seas. TV. Conference facilities. Pool. Parking. V.
Set on the shores of the Mediterranean in relative isolation, this hotel boasts rooms with terraces that afford a sweeping view. Sea-water swimming pools, solarium.

AGDE

34300 Agde — (Hérault)
Paris 818 - Montpellier 57 - Béziers 22 - Sète 23

12/20 Nausicaa
4, pl. de la Marine — 67.94.71.08
M. Kreitmann. Closed Mon dinner and Tue. Open until 10 pm. Private room: 45. Garden dining. V AE DC.
Like Ulysses, the Nausicaa's chef-owner travelled far and wide before dropping anchor in Agde. He has brought with him a certain knowledge of the exotic, which he skilfully blends with regional ingredients and serves in his striking dining room, or on the lovely terrace set on the banks of the Hérault. Sample the succulent fricasséed duck with sweet spices.
A la carte: 200 F. Menus: 92 F, 153 F.

La Tamarissière   ☺
21, quai Th.-Cornu — 67.94.20.87
M. Albano. Closed off-season Sun dinner and Mon, and 15 Nov-15 March. Open until 9.30 pm. Private room: 25. Garden dining. Telex 490225. V AE DC.
Will wonders never cease? Chef Nicolas Albano has recently won renown and respect to match his toques and laurels. Instead of resting on them, or taking a well-deserved rest, he chugs manfully on. Another sort of Southern chef might laze on the banks of the Hérault in this marvellously unspoiled spot, or play at *boules* in the shade of giant sycamores. But Albano is a restless perfectionist. He's constantly improving and updating his restaurant, or redecorating and refitting the rooms of his hotel. As for the cuisine, it encapsulates all the charms of the Midi. Savour, for example, the delicious ragoût of baby Catalan vegetables with fresh fricasséed broad beans, large shrimp sautéed with bacon and flanked by wild artichoke barigoule, spiced and honeyed pigeon, or a thick rabbit steak wrapped in a Swiss chard crépinette. Albano's second-in-command, Patrice Lacroix, joins in with his own specialities, which he gleaned from many years of training with Guérard and Chibois: warm tabbouleh with large prawns and clams seasoned with coriander, John Dory fillet perfumed with dried fennel and green olives, and red mullet in a light crust served with stuffed courgette flowers. Who wouldn't want to spend hours in the lovely dining room, or on the poolside patio? All the more given the seductive prices and the tasty regional wines (Terret white from the Domaine de la Fadèze, Corbières Vieilles Vignes grown by Bérail). The warming presence of Maïté Albano rounds things off nicely. In short, this is a rare find.
A la carte: 360-500 F. Menus: 140 F (weekdays only), 205 F, 305 F.

La Tamarissière
(See restaurant above)
Closed 15 Nov-15 March. 29 rms 400-600 F. Half-board 510-540 F. TV. Conference facilities. Pool.
The new décor is refreshing and smart, and several spacious rooms with sitting rooms and elegant, large bathrooms have been added. They give onto a wide, peaceful terrace. Coming soon: two superb duplex units with views of the sea, river banks, and pine forest. Excellent breakfast and service.

In nearby Cap-d'Agde

(7 km SE on D 32 E)
34300 Agde — (Hérault)

12/20 Le Braséro
Port-Richelieu II — 67.26.24.75
M. Millares. Closed Tue off-season and 7 Jan-26 Feb. Open until 11 pm. Terrace dining. V AE DC.
The delicious meat dishes are earning this restaurant a fine reputation. The fish dishes are worthwhile as well: fresh anchovies with lemon, and turbot en eau-sel. Very reasonable prices for both food and wine.
A la carte: 200-240 F. Menus: 100 F, 130 F.

Capaô
Av. des Corsaires — 67.26.99.44
Closed 31 Oct-1 April. 1 ste 940-1,300 F. 55 rms 310-650 F. Restaurant. Half-board 320-710 F. TV. Air cond. Conference facilities. Heated pool. Parking. Telex 485414. V AE DC.
This seafront hotel was recently built, and blends innocuously into a sports and leisure complex incorporating a fitness club. Narrow but well-designed rooms with terrace-solariums. Sauna, Jacuzzi. Bar.

Hôtel Eve
Av. de la Joliette — 67.26.71.70
Open every day. 37 rms 315-495 F. TV 17 rms. Heated pool. Parking. Telex 490703. V AE DC.
Even Adam and Eve in their birthday suits would be welcome here. In fact, the hotel is a haven for nudists from Easter to October. Off-season special rates: pay for five nights, stay two nights free. Standard, well-soundproofed rooms. Very friendly welcome.

Hôtel du Golf
Ile des Loisirs — 67.26.87.03
Closed 11 Nov-1 March. 2 stes 960-1,200 F. 50 rms 380- 600 F. Restaurant. Half-board 368-463 F. TV. Air cond. Conference facilities. Pool. Garage parking. Telex 480709. V AE DC.
This modern, comfortable hotel complex is quite pleasant, and offers standardised but tastefully decorated rooms. Excellent breakfasts. Private beach. Sea-water cures, tennis, and golf nearby (special rates).

Hôtel du Môle
2, rue du Front-de-Mer — 67.26.75.75
Closed 24 Dec-30 Jan. 2 stes 700-1,200 F. 9 rms 350-650 F. Restaurant. TV. No pets. Pool. Parking. V AE.
Slightly off the madding Cap-d'Agde circuit, this 1930s hotel facing the sea has been remodelled recently in good taste. The comfortable rooms overlook the sea. Cheerful welcome and service. Minimal breakfast. Swimming pool, Jacuzzi, direct beach access.

Saint-Clair
Pl. St-Clair — 67.26.36.44
Closed 1 Nov-1 April. 82 rms 300-530 F. Restaurant. Half-board 320-430 F. TV. Air cond. Conference

facilities. Heated pool. Garage parking. Telex 480464. V AE DC.

Built in the 1970s, this hotel is located just minutes from the harbour. The modern, well-equipped rooms are comfortable. Sauna, Jacuzzi, games room. Shuttle to the beach. Poolside grill-style restaurant.

Les Trois Sergents
Av. des Sergents – 67.26.73.13
M. Boudon. Closed Sun dinner and Mon (except July-Aug), and 2 Nov-15 March. Open until 9.30 pm. Private room: 28. Terrace dining. Heated pool. V AE DC.

The dining room has a squinting view over the port. It is bright and sunny, but the décor is dull as dishwater. Recently arrived new chef Frédéric Schwedt, late of the La Palme d'Or in Cannes, has created an inventive menu based on local ingredients. Try the oyster gelée with fennel in an asparagus feuilleté, warm foie gras touched with hazelnut oil, tiny squid with fresh pasta, veal sweetbreads and tongue seasoned with thyme and served with chanterelles, and calf's brains en salade (he is a virtuoso with offal!). The desserts could stand improvement, but the toque is well earned.

A la carte: 250-340 F. Menus: 100 F, 150 F, 180 F, 250 F.

In nearby Marseillan

(7 km NE on D 51)
34340 Agde – (Hérault)

Hôtel du Château du Port
9, quai de la Résistance – 67.77.65.65
Closed 31 Oct-1 March. 16 rms 160-615 F. Restaurant. Half-board 470-780 F. TV. Conference facilities. Garage parking. Telex 521216. V AE.

An old town house on the quays recently refurbished at great expense in an eighteenth-century style. The rooms have genuine charm and are luxuriously appointed. A truly pleasant stop.

12/20 La Roussette
(Marseillan-Plage)
Av. de la Méditerranée – 67.21.97.63
M. Beltra. Dinner only. Closed 30 Sep-1 June. Open until 11.30 pm. Terrace dining. V.

This summer annexe to the fishmonger next door serves huge seafood platters, some simply cooked shellfish, and very fresh grilled fish, washed down with good regional wines. A simple spot with amazingly moderate prices.

A la carte: 220 F.

11/20 La Table d'Emilie
8, pl. Carnot – 67.77.63.59
M. Boulenc. Closed Wed and 31 Jan-2 March. Open until 11 pm. Private room: 25. Terrace dining. V.

The prices à la carte tend to go through the attractive vaulted roof of this twelfth-century house, but the affordable set menus are representative of the cooking: scallop tart with tomato and basil butter, croustillant de langoustines, curried chicken.

A la carte: 280-350 F. Menus: from 90 F to 220 F.

Some establishments change their closing times without warning. It is always wise to check in advance.

47000 Agen – (Lot/Garonne)
Paris 647 - Bordeaux 142 - Toulouse 108 - Auch 73

L'Absinthe
29 bis, rue Voltaire – 53.66.16.94
M. Geoffroy. Closed Sun. Annual closings not available. Open until 10 pm. Air cond. V.

This cosy, inviting establishment in the old part of Agen has large tables flanked by banquettes which are regularly filled with devoted customers confident of getting a decent meal. The menu doesn't change much but try the salt-cured duck with lentils, cassoulet, and tripe in a white Côtes de Duras. The regionally based wine list is well balanced.

A la carte: 250 F. Menu: 135 F.

L'Aéroport
La Garenne, 3 km SW – 53.96.38.95
M. Pinard. Closed Sun dinner, Sat and Aug. Open until 9.30 pm. Private room: 40. Terrace dining. Air cond. Telex 550225. V AE DC.

The tournedos Rossini and the creamed veal with morels are old favourites, but why not take the plunge and try the gratin of prawns, the salmon cooked on one side, or the rabbit with verjuice and honey for a taste of Patrick Pinard at his most inventive? The modern décor is a bit past its prime.

A la carte: 300 F. Menus: 90 F (weekdays lunch only), 145 F (weekdays only), 165 F (w-e and holidays only).

Château-Hôtel des Jacobins
2, rue Jacob 11 ter, pl. des Jacobins
53.47.03.31
Open every day. 15 rms 250-550 F. TV. Air cond. Valet parking. Telex 571162. V AE.

This imposing early nineteenth-century town house has had a face-lift, and air-conditioning has been installed. The rooms are comfortable, cosily decorated and quiet. Kitchen smells do waft around, though. Supper-trays on request.

La Corne d'Or
1.5 km N on N 113
Rte de Bordeaux, 147450 Colayrac-Saint-Cirq
53.47.02.76
M. Loisillon. Closed Sun dinner and 7-29 July. Open until 9.30 pm. Private room: 80. Air cond. Hotel: 14 rms 220-280 F. Parking. V AE DC.

A breeze of youth has swept through this establishment: the space has been reorganised, the décor lightened, and even the kitchen seems to have awakened from years of slumber. Jean-Louis Loisillon has devised a new menu based on excellent ingredients and with a few flights of fancy such as an astonishing combination of prawns and pig's trotters which is perfectly successful, a delicious craquant de saumon, a fine fisherman's salad, and some superb desserts.

A la carte: 300-350 F. Menus: 90 F and 140 F (weekdays only), 120 F (w-e and holidays only), 190 F.

Ibis
105, bd Carnot – 53.47.31.23
Open every day. 57 rms 240-260 F. Restaurant. Half-board 290 F. TV. Conference facilities. Telex 541331. V.

This hotel is in a residential district of the city centre, near the Garonne. Rooms are small and functional with very basic service.

Lamanguié

66, rue C.-Desmoulins — 53.66.24.35

M. Latrille. Closed Sat lunch and Sun. Open until 10 pm. Air cond. V AE.

A pale-coloured, elegant dining room made larger by clever use of mirrors is the backdrop for chef Michel Latrille's fresh and simple repertoire: various salads, salmon with lemon butter, lamb with thyme. Or try his more ambitious dishes such as a fricassée of prawns with soy butter, scallops with a compote of leeks and truffles, or lotte with garlic and herbs. A lovely welcome by the *patronne*.

A la carte: 300-350 F. Menus: 85 F (lunch only), 160 F, 220 F.

Le Provence

22, cours 14-Juillet
53.47.39.11

Open every day. 1 ste 300-380 F. 25 rms 150-300 F. TV. Air cond 10 rms. Conference facilities. Garage parking. Telex 560800. V AE.

This little hotel in the centre of town has been enlarged and redecorated. Pub-style bar open every night except Sunday.

La Rigalette

2 km N on D 302
at Vérone valley — 53.47.37.44

M. Duprat. Closed Sun dinner off-season and Mon. Open until 9.30 pm. Private room: 80. Garden dining. Hotel: 7 rms 240-300 F. Parking. V AE.

The *patron* offers scrupulous if somewhat unimaginative cooking and his high prices are offset by the quality of the ingredients and his generosity. Try lamprey à la bordelaise, beef with bone marrow, and the crêpes soufflées au citron. The atmosphere of this sixties-built restaurant is cosy, and you can eat in the garden in summer.

A la carte: 350-400 F. Menus: 140 F, 260 F.

In nearby **Bon-Encontre**

(4 km S on N 113)
47240 Agen — (Lot/Garonne)

Le Parc

41, rue de la République
53.96.17.75

M. Mariottat. Closed Sun dinner and Mon. Open until 9.30 pm. Private room: 20. Terrace dining. Air cond. Parking.

Christiane and Eric Mariottat get an extra point for this charming establishment which they've decorated with a great deal of elegance and taste. There's a lovely dining room leading to a terrace, the welcome is warm, the service efficient, and the food very well prepared: perfectly cooked fricassée of scallops, a tasty, pinkly plump young pigeon, and a number of other dishes based on the seasons and the patron's interesting whims. The wine list is improving and there are some excellent Buzets. Prices will keep you happy.

A la carte: 300 F. Menus: 90 F (weekdays only), 190 F (Fri only), 140 F, 220 F.

Le Parc

(See restaurant above)

Open every day. 10 rms 185-250 F. Half-board 285 F. TV. Pets allowed.

Ten well-equipped, perfectly soundproofed simple rooms, recently refurbished with a lot of care.

In nearby **Brax**

6 km W on D 656 and D 119
47310 Agen — (Lot/Garonne)

La Renaissance de l'Etoile

Rte de Mont-de-Marsan — 53.68.69.23

M. Gruel. Closed Mon lunch. Open until 9.30 pm. Private room: 120. Garden dining. Parking. V AE.

Yves Gruel's menus change weekly and the *carte* follows the seasons. His restaurant also boasts an increasingly well-stocked cellar which includes half-bottles and offers wine by the glass. Try the langoustines à la vanille with julienne of leeks, or the farm chicken with mushrooms, port and pine-nuts, followed by a notable cheese board. This worthy cooking has thankfully forsaken a rather heavy classicism to become delicate and light.

A la carte: 250 F. Menus: 89 F (weekdays only), 142 F, 165 F, 260 F.

La Renaissance de l'Etoile

(See restaurant above)

Open every day. 1 ste 290-330 F. 10 rms 190-270 F. Half-board 234-274 F. TV. Conference facilities.

The rooms of this hotel set in a landscape of rare trees are comfortable, largish, and nicely furnished. The décor is pleasant and the atmosphere charming.

In nearby **La Croix-Blanche**

(13 km N on N 21)
47340 Agen — (Lot/Garonne)

La Sauvagère

N 21, Galimas — 53.68.81.21

Closings not available. 12 rms 180-320 F. Restaurant. Half-board 220-280 F. TV. Parking. Telex 560800. V AE DC.

Halfway between Agen and Villeneuve, just off the main road, is a quiet, simple and pleasant country inn covered in Virginia creeper. Nice rooms.

In nearby **Puymirol**

(17 km E on N 113 and D 16)
47270 Agen — (Lot/Garonne)

L'Aubergade

(Michel Trama)
52, rue Royale — 53.95.31.46

19.5 *M. Trama. Closed Mon (Jan-March). Open until 9.30 pm. Private room: 60. Garden dining. Valet parking. Telex 560800. V AE DC.*

A transformed and triumphant Aubergade has scaled the heights to become a pinnacle of gastronomy, thanks to the unquestioned talent of Michel Trama. Together with his wife Maryse and their architect, Yves Boucharlat, they have taken a little hill-top medieval *bastide* built for the Counts of Toulouse in a remote village and, by cleverly mixing the old with the new, have turned it into the very model of a top-class restaurant. The enclosed garden with its bubbling ornamental pond is enough to make anyone swoon with delight and the galleries, terraces and wonderful white stone façades have a Florentine feel which perfectly suits this luminous French-Tuscan landscape. And as for the food! You'd be hard put to believe that the same Michel Trama who once studied sociology and the decorative arts as well as working in a Paris bistro has ended up here to display such a panoply of exquisite and impressive flavours. But the taciturn Trama is loath to divulge the secrets of his cuisine. He is both a perfectionist and an inventor of cooking methods. His approach is almost scientific and he analyses the chemical reactions of ingredients to come up with some stunning dishes. This sort of rigour could become over-fastidious but Trama is also an artist and each dish is a masterpiece of presentation, a sensual mix of flavours which make the tastebuds twitch with pleasure. In short, this extraordinarily elaborate cuisine is whole-heartedly genuine and deeply rooted in the surrounding countryside. Choose a table under the lovely white parasols in the garden or take a seat in the dining room with its great oak beams to try the salad of duck with juniper-flavoured oil, the astounding vegetable 'mushroom', a mixture of all kinds of finely chopped vegetables blended with an aubergine purée flavoured with cumin and herbs, or the daube de cèpes, simmered for three hours and served on a piece of polenta with warm foie gras. Don't stop there; go on to savour the salmon trout which is so tasty it could be wild trout, the lobster lasagne with truffle stock, the quail in a potato crust, and capon in pastry with creamed mushrooms. As for the desserts, the chocolate 'teardrop' with sour red cherries and a Banyuls sauce, jelly made from thyme honey with wild strawberries, and many others deserve to be 'listed' as historic. Add some fine Bordeaux, Buzets and Côtes de Duras, old Armagnacs, nicely aged Havana cigars, a full-flavoured Arabica coffee, the discreet attentions of Maryse Trama and her maître d'hôtel, and your happiness will be complete.

A la carte: 450-700 F. Menus: 150 F (weekdays lunch only), 260 F, 450 F.

Les Loges de l'Aubergade
(See restaurant above)
Closed Mon (Jan-March). 10 rms 700-1,150 F. TV. Conference facilities.

There is definitely an Italian flavour to this hotel, both inside and out. For one thing the Tramas had most of the furniture, lighting fixtures, and various accessories made in Italy and they go beautifully with the bare stone walls of this *bastide*. The huge, bright rooms and the bathrooms have been very well thought out, with a care and attention to detail seldom seen in French hotels. It's no wonder that newcomers often prolong their stay. From the door handles to the specially woven carpets, everything is pretty, original, and impeccably matched. This year a superb and resolutely modern first-floor room has been set aside for conferences and receptions. There are also new loos the like of which don't exist anywhere else! Relais et Château.

AHETZE
See Bidart

AIGLE (L')
61300 Aigle (L') — (Orne)
Paris 141 - Dreux 58 - Argentan 54 - Alençon 65

Le Dauphin
Pl. de la Halle — 33.24.43.12
M. Bernard. Open until 10 pm. Private room: 200. Pets allowed.

The welcome and service in this recently renovated post house are most amiable and the dining room with its well-spaced tables very agreeable. But is the chef neglecting the quality of the ingredients that go into this traditional yet occasionally innovative cuisine? The feuilleté of scrambled eggs and snails is rather bitter, and the roast farm chicken a bit disappointing despite the marvellous mushrooms. The cheese board had a very good Camembert nestling among some more forgettable kinds, and the apples in Calvados served with an iced soufflé were delicious. There is good advice on what wine to order and an exceptional choice of Calvados.

A la carte: 270 F. Menus: from 110 F to 320 F

Le Dauphin
(See restaurant above)
Information not available.

Nice rooms, refurbished with care. A small shop in the hotel sells aged Calvados.

AIGNERVILLE
See Bayeux

AIGUEBELETTE (LAC D')
73610 Aiguebelette (Lac d') — (Savoie)
Paris 551 - Grenoble 53 - Belley 47 - Chambéry 21

Novalaise-Plage
8 km on D 41, Novalaise-Lac
73470 Novalaise — 79.36.02.19
Closed Mon and Tue off-season, and 1 Oct-14 April. 12 rms 130-320 F. Half-board 250-300 F oblig in seas. No pets. Conference facilities. Parking. V.

This hotel on the edge of a lake has a tiny private beach. There's a terrace-restaurant facing the mountains.

AIGUEBELLE
See Lavandou (Le)

AIGUES-MORTES
30220 Aigues-Mortes — (Gard)
Paris 750 - Arles 48 - Montpellier 32 - Nîmes 39

Les Arcades
23, bd Gambetta — 66.53.81.13
M. Merquiol. Closed Mon (except holidays) and 5 Feb-6 March. Open until 10.15 pm (11.15 pm in summer). Terrace dining. V AE DC.

The arcades belong to a lovely restored sixteenth-century house in a quiet corner of Aigues-Mortes. Old beams and stone walls grace the somewhat sombre dining room, which offers a cool respite on a hot summer's day. The menu is eclectic, featuring grilled red peppers with anchovies, a generous fricassée of meadow mushrooms and fresh pasta, bouillabaisse, and a sustaining beef stew. The *patronne* is attentive, the service efficient, the wine list regional, and prices not horrendous. The desserts tend to be boring, apart from a good lemon tart. Definitely not a tourist trap and it deserves a toque this year.

A la carte: 250 F. Menus: 108 F, 185 F.

Les Arcades
(See restaurant above)
Open every day. 6 rms 450-500 F. No pets.

A delightful spot within the walls of the old town. There's a magnificent sixteenth-century staircase and only six huge, comfortable rooms.

Hostellerie des Remparts
6, pl. A.-France — 66.53.82.77
Open every day. 4 stes 560-780 F. 19 rms 260-430 F. Restaurant. Half-board 391-543 F. TV 10 rms. Conference facilities. Garage parking. V AE DC.

An eighteenth-century house in what was once a knight's garrison. The rooms are elegantly furnished and some look out onto the famous ramparts.

Saint-Louis
10, rue Amiral-Courbet — 66.53.72.68
Closed Jan and Feb. 22 rms 295-375 F. Restaurant. Half-board 315-420 F. TV. Conference facilities. Garage parking. Telex 485465. V AE DC.
This hotel has good-sized, well-equipped and comfortable rooms decorated in a somewhat mundane rustic style. The ones on the courtyard are quieter. Smiling service.

AIGUILLON

47190 Aiguillon — (Lot/Garonne)
Paris 670 - Agen 30 - Marmande 28 - Nérac 25

Le Jardin des Cygnes
Rte de Villeneuve — 53.79.60.02
M. Bénito. Closed Sat (except 14 July-25 Aug), 20 Dec-14 Jan and 27 April-6 May. Open until 9.30 pm. Private room: 45. Terrace dining. Parking. Telex 560800. V AE DC.
The setting is so beautiful–a pond surrounded by foliage, an old willow, and a flower-studded garden–that we can't help wondering how Alain Bénito can put up with such a blatantly banal dining room, despite its bright and airy terrace. No matter. His cooking remains a model of lightness and generosity, although it could be more imaginative. The menus are moderately priced: lightly cooked foie gras accompanied by cooked apple slices, grilled salmon with curry, casseroled duck breast with honey and vinegar, prune charlotte spiked with plum brandy.
A la carte: 250-300 F. Menus: 75 F (weekdays only), 105 F, 140 F, 188 F.

Le Jardin des Cygnes
(See restaurant above)
Closed Sat (except 14 July-25 Aug), 20 Dec-14 Jan and 27 April-6 May. 26 rms 160-315 F. Half-board 208-285 F. TV 13 rms. Conference facilities. Pool.
Well-equipped, comfortable, recently refurbished rooms. There's a new swimming pool and special fishing and golf packages.

La Terrasse de l'Etoile
8, cours Alsace-Lorraine — 53.79.64.64
Open every day. 9 rms 200-230 F. Half-board 250-280 F. TV. Pool. Restaurant. V AE.
The hotel is in a pedestrian precinct in the middle of town. Rooms are comfy and in good taste and will attract seekers of peace and quiet. In summer you can dine by the pool.

AINHOA

64250 Aïnhoa — (Pyrénées-A.)
Paris 768 - St-Jean-de-Luz 23 - Bayonne 26

Argi-Eder
Rte Notre-Dame-de-l'Aubépine
59.29.91.04
Closed off-season Sun and Wed, and 15 Nov-22 March. 4 stes 550-650 F. 36 rms 480-600 F. Restaurant. Half-board 520-560 F oblig in seas. TV. Air cond 4 rms. Conference facilities. Pool. Tennis. Parking. Telex 570067. V AE DC.
Just outside the village stands this large Basque chalet with huge grounds and comfortable rooms. The terrace by the swimming pool has been enlarged.

Ithurria
59.29.92.11
M. Isabal. Information not available.
Portions are still appallingly small in this once, memorable establishment where the cooking was becoming over-finicky. But lately things seem to be improving: the piperade with chilli peppers,

steamed hake with a red-pepper coulis, and the salmis of young duck with Madiran show definite promise and indicate that they may be out of the woods. Keep your fingers crossed.
A la carte: 300-350 F. Menus: 130 F, 240 F.

Ithurria
(See restaurant above)
Information not available. 1 ste. 27 rms 350-450 F Heated pool.
Large, pleasant, well-kept rooms with scanty rustic furniture. Sauna and fitness facilities. The breakfasts need improving.

Ohantzea
59.29.90.50
Closed Sun and Mon, and 1 Jan-2 Feb. 10 rms 170-260 F. Restaurant. Half-board 220-240 F oblig in seas. Conference facilities. Parking. V.
A genuine little mountain village inn. The bathrooms have been re-equipped recently. Attractive furniture, a warm welcome, and children's games in the garden.

12/20 Oppoca
59.29.90.72
M. Derungs. Closed Tue off-season, and end Nov to mid-March. Open until 9 pm (9.30 pm in summer). Garden dining. Parking. V. Hotel: 12 rms 140-350 F. Half-board 300-440 F oblig in seas. Conference facilities.
An old stopping place on the way to Compostella situated on the one and only village street. The regional cooking is of good quality and includes superb country ham, 'Oppoca' hake, poached and served with a spicy sauce, and the famous sheep cheese served with cherry jam–an old shepherd's custom. It's a shame that the gâteau Basque, like the bread, is none too fresh. The rustic dining room is in good taste and the welcome cordial.
A la carte: 200 F. Menus: 110 F, 160 F, 220 F.

AIRE-SUR-L'ADOUR

40800 Aire-sur-l'Adour — (Landes)
Paris 708 - Tarbes 69 - Mont-de-Marsan 31 - Pau 31

12/20 Chez l'Ahumat
2, rue des Ecoles — 58.71.82.61
M. Labrouche. Closed Wed, 15 April-2 May and 1-15 Sep. Open until 9.30 pm. Parking. V.
Incredibly low prices–even for the Landes region–explain the surge of tourists and travelling salesmen into the two spick-and-span dining rooms. Try the regional charcuterie, the terrines, snails, confit of grilled duck, and wood pigeon salmis. Local wines cost less than 40 F.
A la carte: 140-160 F. Menus: 120 F (w-e and holidays only), 44 F, 60 F, 75 F.

Chez l'Ahumat
(See restaurant above)
Closed 15 April-2 May and 1-15 Sep. 13 rms 130-150 F (per pers, half-board oblig). No pets.
An unpretentious spot offering cheap, clean, bright rooms with stereotyped décor opening onto small balconies. Pleasant, informal service.

Le Commerce
3, bd des Pyrénées — 58.71.60.06
M. Labadie. Closed Sun, Mon and 2-30 Jan. Open until 9 pm. Private room: 50. Hotel: 20 rms 95-180 F. Parking. V.
Dédé Labadie's bistro façade is not too attractive and the dining room lacks warmth, but the welcome more than compensates. There's a wonderful house terrine and good braised duck foie gras,

but carefully cooked salmon served in a floury Champagne sauce and a rather dull grilled duck breast are putting the toque in danger. The black-currant sorbet is excellent. Regional wines are good and there are some magnificent Armagnacs.

A la carte: 250 F. Menus: 66 F, 125 F, 180 F.

In nearby Ségos

(9 km SW on N 134 and D 260)
32400 Aire-sur-l'Adour — (Landes)

Domaine de Bassibé
62.09.46.71

M. Capelle. Closed off-season Sun dinner and Mon, and 30 Nov-1 May. Open until 9.30 pm. Private room: 30. Garden dining. No pets. Parking. V AE DC.

Following a rough patch, Jean-Pierre Capelle is back in the saddle, giving full rein to his fresh repertoire and winning back his two toques. Try the salad of pork crackling, potatoes, and truffles, the pigeon wing pot-au-feu, the millefeuille of cabbage with foie gras, and scrumptious spit-roast poultry and game. The dining room of this lovely manor house is refined without being ostentatious.

A la carte: 400-500 F. Menus: 180 F, 280 F.

Domaine de Bassibé 🌲🍴
(See restaurant above)

Closed 30 Nov-28 March. 3 stes 850-900 F. 6 rms 580-650 F. Half-board 600-780 F oblig in seas. TV. Pool.

The colourful rooms of this beautiful hotel are ultra-comfortable and have been renovated with a great deal of taste. The welcome is charming and the breakfasts divine. Relais et Châteaux.

See also: Eugénie-les-Bains (Michel Guérard), Plaisance-du-Gers, Villeneuve-de-Marsan

AIRE-SUR-LA-LYS

62120 Aire-sur-la-Lys — (P./Calais)
Paris 236 - Lille 57 - Béthune 25 - Boulogne 60

Les Trois Mousquetaires
Château de la Redoute — 21.39.01.11

M. Venet. Closed Sun dinner, Mon and 15 Dec-15 Jan. Open until 10 pm. Private room: 20. Parking. V AE DC.

The Three Musketeers were actually four and so are the Venets—Mum, Dad, Caroline, and Philippe. The latter is our d'Artagnan in the kitchen and thanks to a lot of family advice he has acquired a very sure touch: fillet of John Dory with a dill and basil sabayon, lamb with sweet-pepper coulis, gratin of cherries with cherry brandy. The pleasant dining room looks out onto wonderful grounds where it would be so nice to eat.

A la carte: 320 F. Menus: 84 F (weekdays only), 132 F, 192 F, 276 F.

Les Trois Mousquetaires 🌲🍴
(See restaurant above)

Closed Sun, Mon and 15 Dec-15 Jan. 26 rms 220-440 F. TV 16 rms. Conference facilities.

Twenty lovingly decorated rooms in a large house dating from the last century. There is a splendid view of the park.

For all the essential motoring information when driving in Europe, refer to the RAC European Motoring Guide.

AIX-EN-OTHE

10160 Aix-en-Othe — (Aube)
Paris 155 - Nogent-sur-Seine 39 - Sens 39 - Troyes 31

Auberge de la Scierie 🌲🍴
3 km on N 60, La Vove — 25.46.71.26

Open every day. 1 ste 330 F. 14 rms 230-330 F. Restaurant. Half-board 320-350 F. TV. Conference facilities. Heated pool. Parking. V AE DC.

A charming establishment in enormous grounds with a river running through, set in the Pays d'Othe. Luxurious rooms furnished in period style, and restaurant with a view.

AIX-EN-PROVENCE

13100 Aix-en-Provence — (B./Rhône)
Paris 760 - Nîmes 105 - Avignon 75 - Marseille 31

Hôtel des Augustins
3, rue de la Masse — 42.27.28.59

Open every day. 3 stes 860-1,200 F. 32 rms 460-960 F. Air cond. No pets. Valet parking. Telex 441052. V AE DC. D4-15

This beautifully restored twelfth-century convent has comfortable, quiet rooms, plainly decorated. Two of them have terraces facing the bell-tower. You may have breakfast in the attractive garden.

11/20 Les Bacchanales
10, rue de la Couronne — 42.27.21.06

M. Poussardin. Open every day. Open until 11 pm. V AE DC. C4-8

The cooking of this friendly spot in one of the narrow streets of Aix's restaurant area mirrors the service: up and down. Nevertheless, the wine list includes some interesting local bottles.

A la carte: 300 F. Menus: 95 F, 150 F.

Le Bistro Latin 🏮
18, rue de la Couronne — 42.38.22.88

M. Ungaro. Closed Sun dinner and Mon. Open until 10.30 pm. Private room: 15. Air cond. V AE DC. C4-2

Behind a little blue entrance hall you'll find a deliciously fresh, old-style décor, and a young, meticulous, and enthusiastic chef, Bruno Ungaro, whose cooking is full of bubbling elegance. You can almost hear the music of Provence in the salted fresh cheese with thyme, chartreuse of mussels and meat with spinach and a saffron cream sauce, or crépinette of young rabbit with basil from his astonishingly good menu of regional dishes. The smiling efficiency of the staff and the prices of his set menus are a welcome bonus.

A la carte: 250 F. Menus: 69 F (weekdays lunch only), 98 F, 145 F, 195 F.

Campanile
ZAC du Jas-de-Bouffan
Rte de Valcros — 42.59.40.73

Open every day. 60 rms 239 F. Restaurant. Half-board 336-359 F. TV. Conference facilities. Parking. V. A6-22

A modern and very quiet hotel near the motorway (and next to the Vasarely Foundation).

La Caravelle
29, bd du Roi-René — 42.21.53.05

Open every day. 33 rms 170-360 F. TV. Conference facilities. Valet parking. V AE DC. F5-23

Half of the rooms (the more expensive ones) give onto a lovely succession of interior gardens. Some have been renovated.

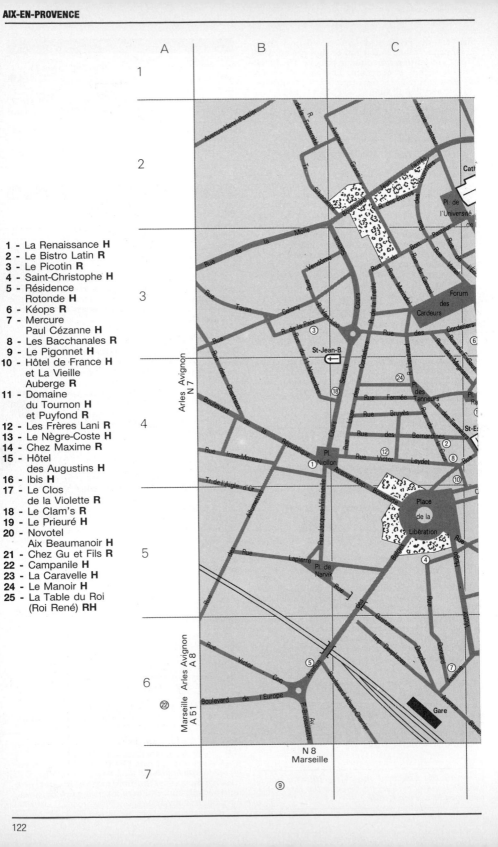

1 - La Renaissance **H**
2 - Le Bistro Latin **R**
3 - Le Picotin **R**
4 - Saint-Christophe **H**
5 - Résidence
    Rotonde **H**
6 - Kéops **R**
7 - Mercure
    Paul Cézanne **H**
8 - Les Bacchanales **R**
9 - Le Pigonnet **H**
10 - Hôtel de France **H**
    et La Vieille
    Auberge **R**
11 - Domaine
    du Tournon **H**
    et Puyfond **R**
12 - Les Frères Lani **R**
13 - Le Nègre-Coste **H**
14 - Chez Maxime **R**
15 - Hôtel
    des Augustins **H**
16 - Ibis **H**
17 - Le Clos
    de la Violette **R**
18 - Le Clam's **R**
19 - Le Prieuré **H**
20 - Novotel
    Aix Beaumanoir **H**
21 - Chez Gu et Fils **R**
22 - Campanile **H**
23 - La Caravelle **H**
24 - Le Manoir **H**
25 - La Table du Roi
    (Roi René) **RH**

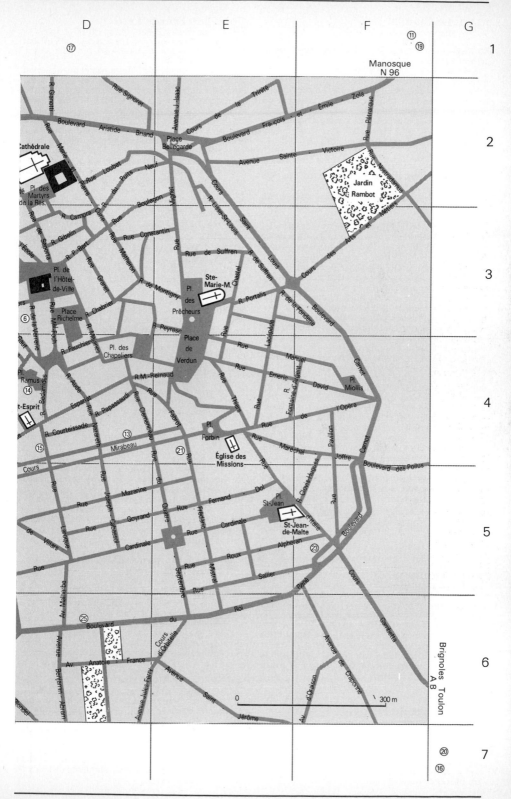

12/20 Le Clam's
22, cours Sextius
42.27.64.78
M. Fredenucci. Closed July and Aug. Open until 10 pm. V AE DC. C4-18

In this well-lit, blue-and-white décor dotted with mirrors, faithful customers enjoy Joseph Fredenucci's excellent repertoire of supremely fresh seafood and fish: good (and expensive) bourrides and bouillabaisse, and an appealing fisherman's menu which varies according to the daily catch.

A la carte: 350 F and up. Menu: 180 F.

Le Clos de la Violette ☺
10, av. de la Violette — 42.23.30.71
M. Banzo. Closed Mon lunch and Sun. Open until 9.30 pm. Private room: 15. Garden dining. Air cond. No pets. V AE. D1-17

Although his restaurant is discreetly tucked away in a residential area, the *patron* of Le Clos de la Violette is no shrinking violet. Indeed, Jean-Marc Banzo has reproached us for not paying enough attention to him. He should understand that it wasn't negligence on our part that kept us from giving a full appreciation of his cooking, but the fact that it lacked certain final touches, perhaps because he spent a little too much time in the dining room. This year, the service was perfect and there's no question that the cooking is among the most intelligent in Provence. Banzo uses extremely high quality regional ingredients, be they oil, vinegar, olives, or rabbit, and flavours are as clear-cut as the grey-and-apricot décor. The seafood on a bed of chopped herbs and salad leaves, the superb stuffed shoulder of young rabbit with its delicately breaded cutlets, the feuilleté of vegetables, or the tian of sole studded with sesame seeds are all fervent celebrations of what must be some of the best regional produce around. For Banzo's cuisine sings of Provence, with all its barely civilised, persuasive flavours, bursting with sensuality. An extra point then for such up-to-date purity and for some complex combinations created by a subtle craftsman. The cellar is also well stocked on classic lines, with lots of Côtes-du-Rhône and Aix wines. The 170 F menu is exceptionally good value though eating à la carte can be costly.

A la carte: 450 F. Menus: 170 F (lunch only), 290 F, 400 F.

Domaine de Tournon
Les Pichinats
42.21.22.05
Open every day. 59 rms 250-400 F. Restaurant. Half-board 420-550 F. TV. Conference facilities. Pool. Tennis. Parking. Telex 441530. V AE DC. F1-11

A quiet and elegant hotel set in five hectares of grounds. The rooms are comfortable and there is a wide range of sports equipment and business services, including interpreting. Sauna, Turkish bath, and French billiards.

Hôtel de France
63, rue Espariat
42.27.90.15
Open every day. 27 rms 170-330 F. TV 15 rms. Conference facilities. V AE. C4-10

This completely refurbished hotel is just a skip and a jump from the Place des Augustins. Rooms are pleasant and well equipped.

Les Frères Lani
22, rue V.-Leydet — 42.27.76.16
MM. Lani. Closed Sun (except holidays lunch) and Mon lunch. Open until 10.30 pm. Air cond. Telex 403639. V AE. C4-12

Behind a plain façade hides a pastel décor set off with wrought-ironwork by a master smith. Here the two Lani brothers have constructed an amusing menu with some successful dishes taken from their family's Bouc-Bel-Air restaurant, and others newly inspired, giving free rein to their imagination and offering a wide range of flavours and prices. The fillets of red mullet with celeriac, fresh lobster salad with soy sauce, the croustillant of pig's trotters with warm duck foie gras, and the pear confit with a spicy crust are dishes which have been finely crafted by these likeable and modest brothers. Bernadette Lani's welcome is delightful and the service formal.

A la carte: 300-370 F. Menus: 120 F, 160 F, 220 F, 280 F.

12/20 Chez Gu et Fils
3, rue F.-Mistral — 42.26.75.12
M. Galasso. Closed Sat lunch, Sun and Aug. Open until midnight. Terrace dining. Air cond. V AE. E4-21

Gu's specialities—hot oysters, pizzas, and thick-cut steaks—are as unchanging as his baseball cap but not as impressive as his handlebar moustache. Still, the rustic décor and convivial atmosphere bring in a well-off crowd who don't quibble at the stiff prices.

A la carte: 300-350 F. Menu: 90 F (lunch only).

Ibis
Ch. des Infirmeries — 42.27.98.20
Open every day. 83 rms 287-310 F. Restaurant. TV. Conference facilities. Parking. Telex 420519. V. G7-16

Since this good-value hotel is near the motorway, the well-kept and fairly small rooms are soundproofed.

11/20 Kéops
28, rue de la Verrerie — 42.96.59.05
M. Fathalah. Closed Mon, 1-25 Nov. Open until midnight. No pets. V AE. D3-6

Leather cushions and low tables in an attractive, air-conditioned cellar are the backdrop for the Egyptian 'peasant menu' proposed by Fathalah Mustapha. Also try the mouchakel, falafel, houra (meat-stuffed crêpes) and some good honey desserts.

A la carte: 130 F. Menus: 60 F (lunch only), 260 F (for 2 pers), 85 F.

Le Manoir
8, rue d'Entrecasteaux — 42.26.27.20
Closed 15 Jan-18 Feb. 43 rms 268-446 F. TV. Conference facilities. Parking. V AE DC. C4-24

You'll get a good night's rest and then your breakfast in the prettily furnished rooms of this perfectly restored fourteenth-century monastery.

11/20 Chez Maxime
12, pl. Ramus — 42.26.28.51
M. Maxime. Closed Mon lunch, Sun and 6-21 Jan. Open until 11 pm. Private room: 25. Terrace dining. Air cond. V. D4-14

An extra-warm welcome and excellent meat dishes draw a jostling crowd of locals to the banquettes of this attractive bistro: delicious home-cooked ham on the bone, beef rib with its marrow, or a braised whole shoulder of lamb. A nice choice of wines.

A la carte: 180-230 F. Menus: 76 F (weekdays lunch only), 110 F and 150 F (dinner only).

Mercure Paul Cézanne
40, av. V.-Hugo — 42.26.34.73
Open every day. 1 ste 1,500 F. 55 rms 480-900 F. TV. Air cond. Valet parking. V AE DC.   C6-7

A remarkable little hotel near the famous fountain with some fairly pretty rooms (nice period furniture), and all of them bright and airy. Plenty of staff ensure that the service is excellent, and the breakfasts are particularly good.

Le Nègre-Coste
33, cours Mirabeau — 42.27.74.22
Open every day. 1 ste 650 F. 37 rms 350-550 F. TV. Garage parking. Telex 440184. V AE DC.   D4-13

The oldest (eighteenth century) of Aix's historic hotels in the town centre. All the rooms have been attractively modernised and soundproofed. It's nicely furnished, there's a wonderful old-fashioned lift and a garage service.

Novotel Aix Beaumanoir
Résidence Beaumanoir — 42.27.47.50
Open every day. 102 rms 390-440 F. Restaurant. TV. Air cond. Conference facilities. Heated pool. Parking. Telex 400244. V AE DC.   G7-20

The hotel is near the motorway, about five kilometres from the city centre. It has all the advantages of the chain: modern, airy, and regularly refurbished rooms. Golf practice. Bar.

12/20 Le Picotin
16, rue de la Paix — 42.27.95.44
M. Emond. Dinner only. Closed Sun, holidays, 1-15 Jan, 1 July-10 Sep. Open until 9.45 pm. V.   B3-3

Here you walk into a corner of Gascony with its Buzets, Madirans, Gaillacs and Cahors. Pierre Emond continues to astonish everyone with his top-quality magrets and their eighteen seasonal accompaniments, summer cassoulet with fresh haricot beans, confits d'oie, a few well-made desserts, and his gentle prices.
A la carte: 300 F. Menus: 149 F, 231 F.

Le Pigonnet
5, av. du Pigonnet — 42.59.02.90
Open every day. 50 rms 500-950 F. Restaurant. Half-board 750-950 F. TV. Air cond 14 rms. Conference facilities. Heated pool. Parking. Telex 410629. V AE DC.   B7-9

A charming Provençal house right in the town centre but surrounded by century-old chestnut trees. There's a splendid, shaded terrace and a flower-filled garden. Pleasing, up-to-date rooms.

Le Prieuré
Rte des Alpes
towards Sisteron — 42.21.05.23
Open every day. 26 rms 145-340 F. No pets.   F1-19

This is an exquisitely comfortable, very well decorated seventeenth-century former priory opposite the clipped box hedges of Lenfant park, designed by Le Nôtre. Solarium.

Puyfond
7 km N on N 96 and D 13
Rte of St-Canadet — 42.92.13.77
Mme Carbonel. Closed Sun dinner, Mon and 28 Aug-17 Sep. Open until 10 pm. Private room: 40. Garden dining. Parking. V AE DC.   F1-11

Anne Carbonel's cooking plays with subtlety on the lusty Provençal flavours that pervade her terrine of snails with lemon-flavoured fennel quenelles, salmon with a mousse of tiny scallops,

or the delectable duck breast with juniper berries and a smoked leek flan. The sunshine in her dishes is best enjoyed under the shade of the chestnut trees or in the calm of the country-house décor with its antique furniture smelling pleasantly of beeswax. The prices are positively angelic.
A la carte: 250 F. Menus: 100 F and 140 F (except Sun), 180 F (Sun only).

La Renaissance
4, bd de la République — 42.26.04.22
Open every day. 35 rms 220-380 F. TV. Conference facilities. Telex 403521. V AE.   B4-1

Well-equipped rooms in an old, recently refurbished house which once belonged to the composer Darius Milhaud.

Résidence Rotonde
15, av. des Belges — 42.26.29.88
Closed 25 Nov-5 Jan. 42 rms 250-400 F. TV. Valet parking. Telex 410777. V AE DC.   B6-5

A modern, functional, and central address with excellent bathrooms and efficiently soundproofed rooms.

Saint-Christophe
2, av. V.-Hugo — 42.26.01.24
Open every day. 56 rms 245-315 F. Restaurant. Half-board 265-300 F. TV. Conference facilities. Valet parking. Telex 403608. V.   C5-4

The hotel is near the Cours Mirabeau, Aix's main axis, and the imposing Rotonde fountain. Rooms are simply decorated but well appointed. Some have a small terrace.

La Table du Roi
22, bd du Roi-René — 42.37.61.00
M. Basciano. Open every day. Open until 10.30 pm. Garden dining. Air cond. No-smoking section. Valet parking. Telex 403328. V AE DC.   D6-25

The newly resuscitated Roi René is luxuriously modern but has lost a lot of charm, with a vast, conventionally decorated dining room opening onto a swimming pool carved out of the courtyard. Though the ambience is less than regal, Jean-Luc L'Hourre's cooking may well be fit for a king. This shy and talented Breton produces warm, colourful dishes in direct contrast to the rather chilling environment. Style and personality come together in his grilled fillet of sea bream with delectable black-radish crisps, sea bass with lavender honey, the superb minute lamb with coriander-flavoured onion sauce and a delicate tarragon essence, and the cold lime soufflé. The wine list is well put together in an effort to keep prices reasonable, but the service needs speeding up.
A la carte: 300-350 F. Menus: 145 F, 180 F, 280 F.

Roi René
(See restaurant above)
Open every day. 3 stes 1,200-1,300 F. 131 rms 590-890 F. TV. Air cond. Conference facilities. Pool.

The rooms are small but highly comfortable and the nicest have a view over the old city. But the décor is somewhat impersonal, despite top-quality fittings. A smiling, youthful welcome and efficient service.

La Vieille Auberge
63, rue Espariat — 42.27.17.41
M. de March. Closed Wed and Thu lunch. Open until 10 pm. V AE DC.   C4-10

Tucked away behind the Cours Mirabeau on one of Aix's most animated streets is a fairly new establishment (it reopened in 1987) with a pretty, white-plastered dining room which somehow manages to be a bit mournful. Daniel Milliner's Provençal cuisine is often well prepared but his inventiveness has fallen by the wayside and too many little mistakes mar certain dishes, such as the over-salted and over-priced turbot with asparagus tips. The frogs' legs with a pistou vinaigrette are fresh and firm, the noisettes of lamb are well cooked, but the strawberry croquant is rather ordinary. Very good wines at reasonable prices. The service is efficient but somewhat distant.

A la carte: 300-350 F. Menus: 95 F (weekdays lunch only), 150 F, 220 F, 270 F.

And also...

Our selection of places for inexpensive, quick, or late-night meals.

Al Dente (42.96.41.03 - 14, rue Constantin. Open until 11 pm): Pasta and sauces are served in generous portions and a friendly atmosphere (80 F).

Bar à Thé (42.33.51.99 - 66, pl. Richelme. Open until 10 pm): You can enjoy simple, fresh cooking at this pocket-sized restaurant in the heart of the old city (100 F).

Les Deux Garçons (42.26.00.51 - 53, cours Mirabeau. Open until 2 am): Expensive brasserie food with Provençal overtones. Recently renovated (200 F).

Chez Malta (42.26.15.53 - 28, pl. des Tanneurs. Open until midnight): Cheap and cheerful classic pizzas and grills keep a chic clientele happy (80 F).

Le Petit Verdot (42.27.30.12 - 7, rue des Entrecasteaux. Open until 10.30 pm): A welcoming wine bar with everyday dishes and meats cooked on the 'hot stone' (130 F).

In nearby **Beaurecueil**

(10 km E on N 7) R13100 Aix-en-Provence — (B./Rhône)

Mas de la Bertrande

Chem. de la Plaine — 42.66.90.09
Closed off-season Sun and Mon (except holidays), and 15 Feb-15 March. 10 rms 300-500 F. Half-board 535 F oblig in seas. Conference facilities. Pool. Parking. Telex 403521. V AE DC.

All the charm is in the grounds with their hidden-away swimming pool. The rooms are pleasant, quiet, and airy. Friendly welcome and pleasant service.

Relais Sainte-Victoire

42.66.94.98
Mme Jugy and M. Bergès. Closed off-season Sun dinner and Mon, seas: Mon lunch, Tue and Wed, 1 week Jan, 10 days in Feb and in Nov. Open until 9 pm. Private room: 20. Terrace dining. Air cond. Parking. V AE.

René Bergès likes to give pleasure and does so most generously in his seasonal menus, on which no two dishes are repeated. His lovely inn in the heart of Cézanne country is constantly filled with customers enjoying fillets of mackerel with white wine from Château Simone, vegetables in mint stock, cod glazed with cumin-flavoured caramel, or farm pigeon in its own juice with herb butter. The large cellar reflects the preferences of a knowledgeable wine lover, the welcome is wonderful and prices absolutely justified.

Menus: 195 F (weekdays only), and from 210 F to 350 F.

Relais Sainte-Victoire

(See restaurant above)
Closed Sun and Mon (except July-Aug), first week of Jan and Feb school holidays and beg Nov. 6 stes

400-600 F. 4 rms 230-300 F. Half-board 380-500 F. TV. Air cond 7 rms. Conference facilities. Pool.

At the foot of the Mont Sainte-Victoire—so often painted by Cézanne—the bedsitting rooms of this hotel are pleasantly decorated and comfortable. There's a large terrace for cosy breakfasts.

In nearby **Bouc-Bel-Air**

(10 km S on N 8 and D 59)
13320 Aix-en-Provence — (B./Rhône)

Restaurant Lani

(L'Etape)
D 6, exit Gardanne on A 51 — 42.22.61.90
M. Lani. Closed Sun dinner, Mon (except hotel clients), 23 -31 Dec and 2 weeks in Aug. Open until 9.30 pm. Private room: 50. Air cond. Hotel: 40 rms 180-260 F. Pool. Garage parking. Telex 403639. V AE DC.

The Lani brothers, who will have to start yo-yoing between this establishment and their new address in Aix, are a humorous duo. Who else would describe a dish as 'flakes of cod in ethereal layers of caviar'? You may laugh, but it is an exquisite dish, as are many in this wonderful provincial establishment: chartreuse de pied de cochon, lamb with olives from les Baux, dreamy desserts, wonderful wines, and perfectly pleasing prices make for a seductive spot.

A la carte: 280-330 F. Menus: 140 F, 190 F, 260 F.

In nearby **Milles**

(2 km SW on D 9)
13290 Aix-en-Provence — (B./Rhône)

L'Alicate aux Champs

Rte de St-Pons, then D 543 — 42.20.05.85
Mme Masserand-Mercier. Closed Sun dinner, Mon, 3 weeks in Feb and 10 days in Sep. Open until 9.30 pm. Garden dining. Pool. Parking. V AE DC.

Nicole Masserand-Mercier sticks faithfully to the menu formula which has made her restaurant a favourite. The cooking is light, bright, and full of flavour. The Coteaux d'Aix wines are admirably suited to a marinière of red mullet with baby broad beans, the fresh goat-cheese ravioli with sweet-pepper coulis, or the mignardise of chicken with leeks. Even if you succumb to all the temptations of this delightful spot, the bill won't be ruinous.

Menus: from 180 F to 280 F.

12/20 Auberge d'Aillane

Plan d'Aillane, rue A.-Mesmer — 42.24.24.49
Mme Curto. Open for lunch only. Closed Sat, Sun and Sep Garden dining. Parking. V AE.

In this verdant garden, the daughters of the house waltz among the guests with dishes of Papa Curto's famous daube and other Southern fare. There are also good, simple desserts.

A la carte: 160-200 F. Menus: 100 F, 250 F.

73100 Aix-les-Bains — (Savoie)
Paris 536 - Annecy 33 - Chambéry 14 - Lyon 112

Adélaïde

Av. de Marlioz — 79.88.08.00
M. Mayu. Open every day. Open until 10.30 pm. Private room: 500. Garden dining. Parking. Telex 980266. V AE DC.

This venerable establishment is over-decorated but highly comfortable. Dishes are expensive and up-market but sometimes inconsistent: melon and smoked salmon pastries, suprême de turbot, lamb with baby vegetables. The terrace is agreeable, the surroundings enchanting, and the service pleasant but a trifle hesitant.

A la carte: 350 F and up. Menus: from 200 F to 310 F.

Ariana
(See restaurant above)

Open every day. 4 stes 1,000-1,800 F. 60 rms 500-950 F. Half-board 500-750 F. TV. Air cond 30 rms. Conference facilities. Heated pool.

Somewhat small, very comfy rooms with individual terraces overlooking the grounds. There are remarkable leisure facilities, and a covered gallery leading to the baths.

Campanile
Av. du Golf — 79.61.30.66

Open every day. 60 rms 239 F. Restaurant. Half-board 198-298 F. TV. Air cond. Conference facilities. Parking. Telex 980090. V.

The hotel is quietly situated in a lush green setting. Well-designed rooms.

12/20 Le Dauphinois
(Dauphinois et Nivollet)
14, av. de Tresserve — 79.61.22.56

M. Cochet. Closed Sun dinner (in Dec, Feb and March), and 15 Dec-15 Feb. Open until 9.30 pm. Private room: 60. Terrace dining. No pets. Hotel: 84 rms 140-260 F. Parking. V AE DC.

This is a large, traditional hotel with a peaceful dining room leading to a pretty garden for summer eating. Prices are reasonable and the repertoire dependable: Savoie hams, lake fish, and fine meat dishes. There are some fine, moderately priced Savoie wines.

A la carte: 230 F. Menus: 105 F (weekdays only), 115 F (w-e and holidays only), 135 F, 175 F.

International Rivollier
18, av. du Général-de-Gaulle
79.35.21.00

Open every day. 58 rms 240-370 F. Restaurant. Half-board 340-370 F. TV 10 rms. Conference facilities. Valet parking. Telex 320903. V AE DC.

A pre-war spa hotel which has withstood the march of time. Rooms have old-fashioned but pleasing furniture and are regularly refurbished. Transport to the baths is free.

12/20 Lille
Le Grand Port — 79.35.04.22

Mme Lille. Closed Wed and 1 Jan-5 March. Open until 9.30 pm. Private room: 20. Garden dining. Parking. V AE DC.

Four generations of the Lille family have helped to establish this lakeside hostelry. The service is precise and the cooking, though unfortunately not the prices, belongs to yesteryear: gelée de ris de veau, pike mousse, beef with morels.

A la carte: 400 F. Menus: from 120 F to 350 F.

Lille
(See restaurant above)

Closed Wed and 1 Jan-5 March. 18 rms 245-370 F. TV. Conference facilities.

The rooms, very quiet and comfortable with television and direct-line telephone, look out over the lake.

12/20 Le Manoir
37, rue George-Ier — 79.61.44.00

M. Pirat. Closed 20 Dec-7 Jan. Open until 9.30 pm. No pets. Garage parking. Telex 980793. V DC.

The outbuildings of two hotels were converted into this luxurious establishment surrounded by flower-filled gardens. The décor is warm, the reception and service professional, and it wouldn't take much to improve the cuisine (more attention to cooking times and a hint of inventiveness). Already worth trying are the marbré of young rabbit, the escalope of salmon with prawns, and the slivered duck breast with honey.

A la carte: 250-300 F. Menus: 125 F, 175 F, 230 F.

Le Manoir
(See restaurant above)

Closed 20 Dec-7 Jan. 73 rms 275-475 F. Half-board 288-438 F oblig in seas. TV. Air cond 11 rms. Conference facilities.

The lovely, recently refurbished rooms are spacious and quiet, with garden views.

12/20 Au Temple de Diane
11, av. d'Annecy — 79.88.16.61

Mme Mattana. Closed Sun dinner, Mon and 15 July-15 Aug. Open until 10 pm. Private room: 50. V.

The décor is oddly picturesque with *trompe-l'œil* paintings and large Bacchic frescoes. A warm welcome and entertaining cooking await you: salad of tiny scallops with grapefruit, fillet of coley en bourride, or confit de porc à l'ancienne.

A la carte: 250-280 F. Menus: 98 F, 148 F, 200 F, 250 F.

AJACCIO

See CORSICA

ALBERTVILLE

73200 Albertville — (Savoie)
Paris 592 - Chambéry 50 - Annecy 45 - Grenoble 86

Eric Guillot
(Chez Uginet)
Pont des Adoubes — 79.32.00.50

M. Guillot. Closed Tue, 25 June-5 July and 12 Nov-5 Dec. Open until 9.30 pm. Private room: 25. Terrace dining. V AE DC.

We're pleased to see that some affordable Savoie wines have made their appearance on the superb wine list. But the stand-offish reception and slapdash service tend to mask Eric Guillot's efforts in the kitchen. His stuffed courgette flowers, marinated tomatoes and sweet pepper, lamb chops with stewed artichokes, and inventive desserts deserve better.

A la carte: 300-350 F. Menus: 110 F (weekdays only), 145 F, 265 F, 315 F.

Million
8, pl. de la Liberté
79.32.25.15

M. Million. Closed Mon (except dinner 14 July-1 Aug), Sun dinner, 22 April-8 May and 16 Sep-1 Oct. Open until 9 pm. Private room: 30. Garden dining. Hotel: 28 rms 400-600 F. Garage parking. Telex 306022. V.

Philippe Million dominates the gastronomic scene of Albertville in his town-centre restaurant with its pleasant terrace and pink dining rooms. The chef takes his inspiration from the repertoire of Edouard Hélouis, a cook at the court of Savoie in the nineteenth century, but his personal interpretation is natural, straightforward, and attractive: cream of herbs with frogs' legs and smoked salmon, ris de veau à la fargette, chocolate cake, and Savoie almond sponge cake. The wine list offers noble wines at impossible prices and the service lacks simplicity. A meal here is a definite treat, but could be ruinous.

A la carte: 500 F. Menus: 170 F (weekdays only), 270 F, 470 F.

Le Roma

N 90 – 79.37.15.56
Open every day. 10 stes 900-1,500 F. 150 rms 260-400 F. Restaurant. Half-board 382 F. TV. Conference facilities. Heated pool. Tennis. V AE DC.

On the way to the Tarentaise and Maurienne ski resorts, this hotel has huge, functional, comfortable rooms. There is a heliport in the grounds.

ALBI

81000 Albi – (Tarn)
Paris 677 - Carcassonne 107 - Rodez 79

Altea

41 bis, rue Porta
63.47.66.66
Open every day. 56 rms 300-450 F. Restaurant. TV. Air cond 28 rms. Conference facilities. Telex 532596. V AE DC.

Situated on the banks of the Tarn, opposite the cathedral, this eighteenth-century mill has charming, air-conditioned, soundproof rooms. Friendly welcome; superb breakfasts.

Hôtel Chiffre

50, rue Séré-de-Rivières
63.54.04.60
Open every day. 40 rms 250-400 F. Restaurant. TV. Conference facilities. Garage parking. Telex 520411. V AE DC.

Centrally located, this good family-style hotel features recently renovated, well-kept rooms. Enclosed brick patio; garden-restaurant; meals served on trays.

Esprit du Vin

11, quai Choiseul – 63.54.60.44
M. Simar. Closed Sat lunch and Sun dinner. Open until 10.30 pm. Private room: 40. Air cond. No pets. V AE DC.

The restaurant has been enlarged and embellished, and the arrival of a new chef (Alain Andreassian, from the Méridien in Paris) has incited the food-loving citizens of Albi to flock here to sample the more daring à la carte listings. Specialities include escargot vol-au-vent, coquilles St-Jacques with Marseillan wine, and an excellent ragoût of choice chicken morsels and cocks' combs with morels. Superb desserts; good cellar; slightly obsequious service. On balance, we think the place deserves a toque.

A la carte: 250 F. Menus: 85 F (weekdays lunch only, wine inc), 125 F, 280 F.

Hostellerie Saint-Antoine

17, rue St-Antoine – 63.54.04.04
MM. Rieux. Closed Sun (except dinner in seas) and Sat lunch. Open until 9 pm. Private room: 100. Air cond. Valet parking. Telex 520850. V AE DC.

The Rieux family has lived within the walls of this ancient hostelry for 250 years; tradition, for them, is bred in the bone. The culinary know-how handed down from father to son is reflected in the mesclun salad with suprême of roast quail, marinated red-mullet fillets infused with thyme, mutton tripe à l'albigeoise, and prune gratin à l'armagnac. The local wines of Gaillac get top billing in the limited cellar. Diligent service.

A la carte: 300 F. Menus: 150 F, 260 F.

Hostellerie Saint-Antoine

(See restaurant above)
Open every day. 6 stes 750-950 F. 50 rms 360-750 F. Half-board 420-750 F. TV. Air cond 30 rms. Conference facilities. Pool. Tennis.

This centrally located, quiet, and very comfortable hotel features elegant rooms and a pleasant interior garden. Other noteworthy amenities are the good breakfasts, and (though they are three kilometres away) a swimming pool and tennis courts.

Le Jardin des Quatre Saisons

19, bd de Strasbourg – 63.60.77.76
M. Bermond. Closed Mon. Open until 10 pm. Private room: 20. Terrace dining. No pets. V AE.

Martine Bermond welcomes guests into an attractive décor strewn with flowers, arbours, and delicate china, while her husband, Georges, prepares spirited dishes in tune with the seasons. A spring dinner might consist of salmon tartare with mushrooms, lightly cooked duck livers with sesame salad, or brill stuffed with crabmeat served with a buttery vegetable ragoût. Their magnificent wine cellar is constantly replenished.

A la carte: 250 F. Menus: 200 F and up (holidays only), 115 F.

Moulin de la Mothe

Rue de la Mothe – 63.60.38.15
M. Pellaprat. Closed Sun dinner and Wed (except July-Aug), and 4-18 Feb. Open until 9.30 pm. Private room: 50. Garden dining. Air cond. Parking. V AE DC.

Set at the foot of the cathedral in lovely green grounds, the Moulin boasts a a tastefully furnished dining room and terrace. Chef Michel Pellaprat, a connoisseur of the Tarn region's traditional dishes, uses the best local produce to prepare freshwater perch fillets poached in crayfish bouillon, perfectly roasted young pigeon with pink garlic and a bouquet of tiny vegetables, and a pleasingly crisp berry turnover. Good wines at unbeatable prices; affable reception.

A la carte: 250 F. Menus: 95 F, 130 F, 190 F.

Hôtel d'Orléans

Place de Stalingrad
63.54.16.56
Closed 15 days end Dec-beg Jan. 2 stes 320-380 F. 60 rms 180-380 F. Restaurant. Half-board 280-420 F. TV 40 rms. Conference facilities. Telex 521605. V AE DC.

A tidy hotel next to the station where a friendly reception and service await. Amenities include conference facilities and a gym.

In nearby **Fonvialane**

(3 km NW)
81000 Albi – (Tarn)

La Réserve

Rte de Cordes – 63.60.79.79
Mmes Rieux and Rieux-Hijosa. Closed 1 Nov-31 March. Open until 9.30 pm. Private room: 200. Garden dining. No pets. Valet parking. Telex 520850. V AE DC.

Chef Jean-François Rieux is a master at blending traditional and creative cuisines. In his riverside restaurant which overlooks a pool and a park, guests are treated to foie gras terrine au naturel, asparagus flan with prawns, ballottines de turbot with a subtly spiced jus, and a truffle-scented sautéed saddle of young rabbit. The cellar harbours a wealth of fine claret. Smiling welcome and service.

A la carte: 330 F. Menus: 160 F, 300 F.

La Réserve
(See restaurant above)
Closed 1 Nov-31 March. 4 stes. 20 rms 650-850 F (per pers, half-board oblig). TV. Air cond. Conference facilities. Pool. Tennis.

A haven of tranquillity on the banks of the Tarn, La Réserve offers variously decorated, comfortable rooms with river views. Guests have use of pedal-boats, canoes, and bicycles. Relais et Châteaux.

ALENÇON
61000 Alençon — (Orne)
Paris 195 - Rouen 145 - Le Mans 49 - Chartres 116

Campanile
ZAT du Londeau, rte de Paris — 33.29.53.85
Open every day. 42 rms 239 F. Restaurant. Half-board 336-359 F. TV. Conference facilities. Parking. Telex 171908. V.

All the rooms in this well-kept hotel are situated on the ground floor. Fireside meals in winter; lovely summer terrace.

Le Chapeau Rouge
1, bd Duchamp — 33.26.20.23
Open every day. 16 rms 140-280 F. TV. Parking. V.

Located away from town's centre, this hotel offers dainty rooms with personalised décor.

12/20 Les Glycines
32, rue St-Blaise — 33.26.41.51
M. Leclere. Closed Sat lunch, Sun and 1-15 Aug. Open until 10 pm. Private room: 10. V.

In a charming stone house with wisteria-blue shutters, this uncommonly charming dining room is the scene of good, generous meals that often have a touch of creativity as well. Among the specialities of the house are a pleasant seafood fricassée, an excellent (and generously apportioned) sirloin steak in a spicy sauce, and a caramelised apple gratin. Limited cellar; gracious service.

A la carte: 220-270 F. Menus: 90 F, 150 F, 180 F.

L'Inattendu
21, rue de Sarthe — 33.26.51.69
M. Lolom. Closed Sat lunch, Sun and 30 July-16 Aug. Open until 10.30 pm. Private room: 25. V AE.

Alain Lolom's concise, nicely balanced menu is interesting indeed, but his attempts to be daring sometimes yield uneven results. For instance, the fresh flavours of the fish bouillabaisse à l'orientale with crisp broad beans is overpowered by an excess of saffron; but the galette of crabmeat and potatoes is wonderfully delicate, as is the lamb baked in a salt crust with a hint of vanilla, and the chocolate-truffle dessert is sensational. The dining room's *faux-marbre* décor is unusual and attractive, punctuated by black-and-white photos from the Roaring Twenties. Alain Lolom has put together a sensational cellar, from which Mme Lolom will help you choose an appropriate bottle.

A la carte: 280 F. Menus: 86 F, 128 F.

The prices quoted in this guide are those which we were given by the restaurants and hotels concerned. Increases in prices are beyond our control.

 30100 Alès — (Gard)
Paris 709 - Albi 230 - Avignon 71 - Nîmes 44

Mercure
18, rue E.-Quinet — 66.52.27.07
Open every day. 75 rms 255-425 F. Restaurant. TV. Air cond. Conference facilities. Garage parking. Telex 480830. V AE DC.

A pleasantly functional, chain-owned hotel.

Robert de la Favède
15 km N on N 106 and D 283
in La Favède
30110 La Grand-Combe — 66.34.12.13
M. Chabaud. Closed 1 Dec-1 March. Open until 9 pm. Garden dining. Parking. Telex 490925. V.

The affable maître d' who takes your order in this pretty little dining room, and who then disappears to the kitchen, is also the chef. Back at his cooker he prepares savoury dishes of escargots in wild herb bouillon, fish croustillant with a creamy ginger sauce, fragrant rabbit crépinettes and other flavourful dishes.

A la carte: 270-330 F. Menus: 160 F, 260 F.

A l'Auberge Cévenole
(See restaurant above)
Closed 1 Dec-1 March. 3 stes 650 F. 17 rms 260-650 F. Half-board 320-500 F oblig in seas. TV 6 rms. No pets. Conference facilities. Pool.

The hotel offers large, comfortable rooms in a cool, peaceful valley setting. Delightfully designed garden.

In nearby **Méjannes-lès-Alès**
(8 km SE)
30340 Alès — (Gard)

Auberge des Voutins
66.61.38.03
M. Turonnet. Closed Sun dinner and Mon (except holidays), 10 days beg Jan and 10 days end Aug. Open until 9.30 pm. Private room: 18. Garden dining. No-smoking section. Parking. V DC.

Housed in a pleasant dwelling surrounded by fields and orchards, René Turonnet's cosy little restaurant offers guests vibrant, beautifully executed dishes. We fell under the spell of his fresh salmon and potato galette flavoured with lime and ginger, lamb escalopes with artichokes and black olives, cheeses expertly matured right on the premises, and a delectable pear croustade à la maur-esque. Gracious reception; somewhat bumbling service.

A la carte: 250-300 F. Menus: 130 F, 160 F, 250 F.

In nearby **Ribaute-les-Tavernes**
(10 km S)
30720 Alès — (Gard)

Château de Ribaute
66.83.01.66
Closings not available. 2 stes 600 F. 4 rms 300-500 F. TV. Conference facilities. Pool. Parking. V DC.

The Chamski's magnificent, listed dwelling features four cosy, antique-filled rooms with every modern convenience. Cordial welcome; copious breakfasts. A table d'hôte is available for guests.

In nearby Saint-Hilaire-de-Brethmas

(8 km S)
30560 Alès — (Gard)

Auberge de Saint-Hilaire
Rte de Nîmes — 66.30.11.42
M. Reymond. Closed Sun dinner and Mon (except holidays), and 15-31 Aug. Open until 9 pm. Private room: 12. Air cond. No pets. Parking. V.

The rhythm of the seasons has a determining influence on the dishes that Alain Reymond chooses to prepare for the patrons of his elegant and appealing restaurant (unluckily situated alongside the main road). Sample the deftly crafted salmon and potato millefeuilles, hearty oxtail crépinettes, a rich sablé with walnuts and caramel. The eminently affordable cellar offers many local bottlings.

A la carte: 300-350 F. Menus: 130 F (weekdays only), 180 F, 250 F.

L'Ecusson
Rte de Nîmes — 66.30.10.52
Closed 20 Dec-10 Jan. 26 rms 145-250 F. Restaurant. Half-board 207-400 F. TV 5 rms. Conference facilities. Pool. Parking. V.

This pleasant Provençal *mas* proposes rooms decorated either in rustic or in Louis XV–style. Comfortable beds; unbeatable prices.

38114 Allemond-en-Oisans — (Isère)
Paris 610 - Grenoble 46 - Bourg-d'Oisans 11

Les Tilleuls
N 526 — 76.80.70.24
Open every day. 22 rms 90-150 F. Restaurant. Half-board 160-195 F. Conference facilities. Garage parking. V.

Located in a park surrounded by venerable trees, this lovely manor offers simple, tidy rooms with views of the mountains. Warm reception; peace and quiet.

38580 Allevard-les-Bains — (Isère)
Paris 595 - Albertville 47 - Grenoble 38

Pic de Belle Etoile
7 km on D 525, in Pinsot — 76.97.53.62
Closed 26 April-6 May and 20 Oct-14 Dec. 34 rms 200-327 F. Restaurant. Half-board 286-308 F. TV 12 rms. Conference facilities. Heated pool. Tennis. Parking. Telex 305551. V.

A family-style hotel, superbly located in the upper Bréda valley, with awe-inspiring views of the glaciers and peaks. A wide range of facilities includes a large park, trout streams, a gym, and a fitness centre (indoor swimming pool, sauna, Turkish baths, etc.).

74350 Allonzier-la-Caille — (H.-Savoie)
Paris 550 - Bellegarde 49 - Genève 30 - Annecy 13

Le Manoir
on A 41 exit Cruseilles
on D 2 — 50.46.81.82
Closed Mon off-season and 1 Nov-20 Dec. 16 rms 275-320 F. Restaurant. Half-board 290-350 F oblig in seas. Conference facilities. Garage parking. Telex 309499. V AE DC.

This hotel offers small but comfortable rooms, and a delightful shaded terrace with a view of the Alps. TV upon request.

See Beaune

38750 Alpe-d'Huez (L') — (Isère)
Paris 625 - Grenoble 63 - Bourg-d'Oisans 13

11/20 L'Ancolie
Rue de la Grenouillère — 76.80.60.91
M. Noseda. Closed 13 May-30 June and 30 Sep-2 Dec. Open until 11.30 pm. Terrace dining. Parking. V AE.

The likeable chef-owner is often right on target (with his juicy pavé de bœuf, for example), though at other times he misses the mark (as with the leaden diplomate aux poires). But the décor is most appealing, the hostess is hospitable, and the prices are quite what one would wish.

A la carte: 250 F. Menu: 85 F.

Le Bel Alpe
76.80.32.33
Closed 28 April-30 June and 25 Aug-1 Dec. 16 rms 245-490 F. TV. Garage parking. V AE.

Here is a centrally located, chalet-style building at the foot of the slopes, featuring sunny rooms (with loggias) that are comfortable and spacious. Copious breakfasts; smiling service.

Au Chamois d'Or
Rte de Fontbelle — 76.80.31.32
MM. Seigle. Closed 3 May-15 Dec. Open until 9 pm. Terrace dining. No pets. Valet parking. V.

Philippe Seigle's tasteful, classic cuisine (buttery local snails with cabbage, breast of Bresse chicken en papillote with truffled butter, etc.), is served both on the restaurant's fabulous panoramic terrace (invariably mobbed at lunch time) or in the sparkling new dining room.

A la carte: 300 F and up. Menus: 150 F and 180 F (lunch only), and from 180 F to 220 F (dinner only).

Au Chamois d'Or
(See restaurant above)
Closed 3 May-15 Dec. 45 rms 520-850 F. Half-board 480-660 F oblig in seas. TV. No pets. Conference facilities. Heated pool.

This hotel offers recently renovated and elegantly styled rooms with loggias, excellent service, and a wealth of amenities (fitness centre, heated swimming pool, hotel shuttle-bus), not the least of which is the wonderfully relaxed atmosphere.

Le Christina
76.80.33.32
Closed 20 April-10 July and 20 Aug-10 Dec. 27 rms 512-577 F. Restaurant. Half-board 463-594 F oblig in seas. TV. Conference facilities. Tennis. Valet parking. V.

Overlooking the resort, at the foot of the slopes, this huge sun-drenched chalet offers impersonal but well-equipped and recently renovated rooms. The reception, however, is downright cold.

Le Dôme
Pl. du Cognet — 76.80.32.11
Closed 28 April-29 June and 25 Aug-7 Dec. 21 rms 320-660 F. Restaurant. Half-board 340-565 F oblig in seas. TV. Conference facilities. Heated pool. Garage parking. V AE DC.

A large and modern chalet next to the slopes, with simply decorated, comfortable rooms facing the Oisans Massif. Family-style atmosphere. One of the resort's most pleasant addresses.

Les Grandes Rousses
76.80.33.11
Closed 2 May-15 June and 1 Sep-1 Dec. 7 stes 550-750 F. 50 rms 450-700 F. Restaurant. Half-board 450-600 F oblig in seas. TV. Conference facilities. Heated pool. Tennis. Valet parking. Telex 308437. V AE.

The managers of this immense chalet at the foot of the slopes are constantly upgrading its comfort. Among the many facilities are a winter garden lounge, fitness centre, billiard room, heated pool, tennis (summers only).

Le Lyonnais
Rte du Coulet — 76.80.68.92
Mme Astic. Closed June, Sep, Oct and Nov. Open until 9.30 pm. Terrace dining. V.

This elegant eating house carries bistro-style cooking to its most refined conclusion, with ably prepared seafood salads, rascasse (scorpion fish) and salmon fillets, calf's liver served with tiny vegetables, creamy white fromage frais, and remarkable tarte Tatin. Lyonnais-style charcuteries are on offer as well as an extraordinary list of Côtes-du-Rhônes. Service is deft and discreet; the set menus are irreproachable.

A la carte: 250-280 F. Menus: 110 F, 150 F.

Le Petit Prince
Rte de la Poste — 76.80.33.51
Closed 7 April-22 Dec. 40 rms 440-590 F (per pers, half-board oblig). Restaurant. Conference facilities. Valet parking. V AE DC.

Most of the hotel's very comfortable and modern rooms face south, allowing guests an exceptional view of the Oisans Massif and valley. The public rooms are delightful, and there is a large, sunny terrace as well. Buffet breakfasts; chilly reception.

Royal Ours Blanc
Av. des Jeux — 76.80.35.50
Closed mid-April-20 Dec. 2 stes 2,200 F. 45 rms 740-1,100 F. Restaurant. TV. Air cond. Conference facilities. Heated pool. Valet parking. Telex 308334. V AE DC.

Considered the resort's most distinguished hotel, the Royal Ours Blanc features 50 luxurious rooms and an outstanding fitness centre (gym, sauna, Turkish baths, Jacuzzi). Bar. You can expect a polite welcome.

La Vallée Blanche
Rte du Siou-Coulet — 76.80.30.51
Closed May. 44 rms 295-920 F. Restaurant. Pension 395-560 F. TV. Conference facilities. Parking. V AE.

This large dwelling, provided with a beautiful terrace, offers bright, spacious and well-equipped rooms with views of the Oisans. Shy reception; billiard room; sauna; nightclub.

ALTHEN-DES-PALUDS

See Avignon

AMBOISE

37400 Amboise — (Indre/Loire)
Paris 206 - Vendôme 50 - Blois 35 - Tours 25

Le Belle-Vue
12, quai Ch. Quinot — 47.57.02.26
Closed 15 Dec-15 March. 34 rms 190-290 F. TV 24 rms. No pets. V.

Set just at the foot of the famed château on the banks of the Loire, Le Belle-Vue offers appealing, comfortable rooms. Charming reception. There is an annexe with additional rooms across the river.

Château de Pray
2 km on D 751 — 47.57.23.67
Closed 31 Dec-15 Feb. 16 rms 300-650 F. Restaurant. Half-board 413-913 F oblig in seas. Garage parking. V AE DC.

Set on a slope overlooking the Loire, this small Louis XIII château is provided with pleasant, quiet rooms.

Le Choiseul
36, quai Ch.-Guinot — 47.30.45.45
M. Traversac. Closed 10 Jan-1 March. Open until 9.30 pm. Garden dining. Parking. Telex 752068. V.

Housed in a late-eighteenth-century mansion, this lovely riverside restaurant is a paragon of understated elegance and ideal service. Gérard Hummel, a talented and imaginative chef whose cuisine faithfully follows the seasons, is forever questing after new harmonies of flavours and aromas. That laudable effort, however, sometimes leads him astray—one can, after all, be *too* modern. Nevertheless, on our last visit we were utterly amazed by his delicious oyster and sea-urchin ravioli, and the beautifully balanced aiguillettes of John Dory with red cabbage and chestnuts.

A la carte: 300-400 F. Menus: 190 F, 240 F, 320 F.

Le Choiseul
(See restaurant above)
Closed 10 Jan-1 March. 3 stes 900-1,250 F. 32 rms 400-850 F. TV 32 rms. Conference facilities. Pool.

For those who revel in luxury and peace, this is the place to be. The hotel offers 32 elegantly furnished rooms with views of an Italian Renaissance-style garden. Lovely swimming pool. Relais et Châteaux.

Le Manoir Saint-Thomas
Pl. Richelieu — 47.57.22.52
M. Le Coz. Closed off-season Sun dinner, Mon (lunch only in seas), and 15 Jan-15 March. Open until 9.30 pm. Private room: 25. Parking. V AE DC.

The sumptuous, stately décor of beamed ceilings, stained glass, antique chests, velvet curtains, and rich table settings is as heady as the sensational cellar of Chinons and Vouvrays. And chef Le Coz's cooking is right in tune with all this 'olde'-style opulence. Sample his subtle, distinctive terrine of lobster and sweetbreads with Newburg sauce, or a thick slice of salmon in port, or the glistening medieval-style lacquered duck fragrant with honey and ginger.

A la carte: 300-350 F. Menus: 190 F, 270 F.

Novotel
17, rue des Sablonnières — 47.57.42.07
Open every day. 121 rms 350-460 F. Restaurant. TV. Conference facilities. Heated pool. Tennis. Parking. Telex 751203. V AE DC.

For calm, comfortable rooms with outstanding views of the Loire and the château. Bar.

AMBONNAY

51150 Ambonnay — (Marne)
Paris 170 - Reims 29 - Châlons-sur-Marne 22

Auberge Saint-Vincent
Rue St-Vincent — 26.57.01.98
M. Pelletier. Closed Sun dinner and Mon. Open until 9 pm. Garage parking. V AE DC.

While Anne-Marie Pelletier ushers guests into a cosy dining room with Louis XIII ceilings and displays of antique china, her husband Jean-Claude keeps busy in the kitchen dreaming up inventive ways to put fine regional ingredients to good use, as in the terrine of sweetbreads with liver mousse and pink lentils, and the savoury stuffed pig's tail.

The cheese tray is generous, but the desserts are overpriced, and the cellar too limited. Nonetheless, we feel that the Pelletiers deserve an extra point this year.

A la carte: 250-350 F. Menus: 100 F, 150 F, 210 F, 260 F, 340 F.

Auberge Saint-Vincent
(See restaurant above)
Closed Sun and Mon. 10 rms 345-375 F (per pers, half-board oblig). TV. No pets.

Situated in the Champagne wine country, this hotel offers spanking-new comfortable, well-equipped rooms. Good hospitality and service.

AMÉLIE-LES-BAINS

66110 Amélie-les-Bains — (Pyrénées-O.)
Paris 950 - Prades 60 - Perpignan 37 - Céret 8

Castel Emeraude
La Petite-Provence — 68.39.02.83
Closed 30 Nov-1 Feb. 59 rms 200-325 F. Restaurant. Half-board 257-294 F. TV 10 rms. Conference facilities. Parking. Telex 506260. V.

A lovely hotel set in a park alongside the river, with comfortable rooms. The numerous amenities include terraces, beach facilities, and a sports centre (swimming pool, tennis) all within easy reach.

Grand Hôtel Reine Amélie
Rte de la Petite-Provence — 68.39.04.38
Open every day. 69 rms 265-380 F. Restaurant. Half-board 285-440 F. TV 40 rms. Conference facilities. Garage parking. V AE DC.

This big, modern hotel enveloped in greenery is provided with constantly renovated rooms and lounges decorated with rustic Spanish furnishings. Guests enjoy a solarium, and may use the hotel shuttle-bus to the nearby thermal springs.

Palm-Tech Hôtel
Quai G.-Bosch — 68.83.98.00
Closed 10 Dec-17 Feb. 56 rms 165-240 F. Restaurant. Half-board 250-280 F. Conference facilities. Garage parking. V.

A recently built hotel by the river, featuring simple, reasonably priced, and perfectly fitted rooms.

In nearby Arles-sur-Tech

(4 km SW on D 115)
66150 Amélie-les-Bains — (Pyrénées-O.)

11/20 Les Glycines
Rue du Jeu-de-Paume — 68.39.10.09
M. Bassole. Closed Jan. Open until 8.45 pm. Terrace dining. Hotel: 34 rms 130-240 F. Parking. V.

In addition to a view of the Canigou massif, this reputable restaurant offers diners an eclectic repertoire (salad topped with a hot goat-cheese feuilleté, snail brochettes, fillet of veal stuffed with foie gras in chive sauce), served in a spacious garden dining room or out on the terrace. Generous portions.

A la carte: 240 F. Menus: 75 F, 88 F and 100 F (weekdays only), 130 F (w-e and holidays only), 190 F.

> *Some establishments change their closing times without warning. It is always wise to check in advance.*

AMIENS

80000 Amiens — (Somme)
Paris 135 - Rouen 116 - Lille 115 - Beauvais 60

12/20 La Couronne
64, rue St-Leu — 22.91.88.57
M. Gravier. Closed Sun dinner, Sat and 14 July-13 Aug. Open until 9.30 pm. V.

Recently enlarged, this pleasant restaurant in the St-Leu quarter draws patrons with its appealing classic cuisine based on fine, fresh ingredients. Of particular interest are the sole fillets with green peppercorns, compote de lapereau à la vieille prune, and frozen nougat.

A la carte: 300 F. Menus: 110 F (weekdays only), 150 F (Sun lunch and holidays).

Ibis
4, rue du Mal-de-Lattre — 22.92.57.33
Open every day. 94 rms 260-280 F. TV. Conference facilities. Garage parking. Telex 140765. V.

Located not far from the Musée de Picardie, this small chain-owned hotel features modern, simply decorated, soundproof rooms.

Les Marissons
68, rue des Marissons — 22.92.96.66
M. Benoit. Closed Sat lunch, Sun dinner, Mon, 30 Dec-8 Jan and 20 July-5 Aug. Open until 10 pm. Private room: 18. Air cond. Parking. V.

Set in the magnificently restored old St-Leu quarter, on the site of a fifteenth-century boatyard on the Somme River, Les Marissons boasts a luxurious dining room and garden. Chef Antoine Benoit is better known for his traditional skill than for any bold creations, but his ingredients are reliably first-rate. We strongly recommend the slivered goose with honey and pears, the freshwater perch with leek confit, salmon in crab coulis, and the moreish quenelles au chocolat à l'orange et aux pistaches. Distinguished reception; stylish service.

A la carte: 300 F and up. Menus: 120 F (weekdays only), 152 F, 185 F.

12/20 Le Petit Chef
8, rue J.-Catelas — 22.92.24.23
M. Bécu. Closed Tue dinner, Wed and 10-31 July. Open until 9.30 pm. V AE.

Order the main course—salmon with mussels, or young pigeon with sage—and the appetiser—skate with asparagus, or duck terrine in aspic—is complimentary, along with the cheese. And you'll have enough change to treat yourself to pudding as well (try the chilled caramel soufflé). Friendly service in a convivial setting. Surprisingly good cellar.

Menus: 67 F (weekdays only), 170 F.

Le Postillon
16, pl. au Feurre — 22.91.46.17
Open every day. 8 stes 450-600 F. 40 rms 250-450 F. TV. Conference facilities. Garage parking. Telex 140754. V AE.

This small hotel occupies a listed building 300 metres from the cathedral. It offers spacious, nicely fitted rooms, but the service and breakfasts are not quite up to scratch. Pub open until 2 am.

Le Prieuré
17, rue Porion — 22.92.27.67
Open every day. 25 rms 200-350 F. Restaurant. Half-board 320-370 F. TV. Conference facilities. Garage parking. Telex 140754. V AE DC.

An hotel with simple, tidy, and very comfortable rooms, some of which look onto the cathedral. Restful atmosphere.

11/20 La Soupe à Cailloux
16, rue des Bondes — 22.91.92.70
Mlle Bultez. Closed Mon and 1-13 Jan. Open until 10.30 pm. Terrace dining. V AE.
Located in the historic Don quarter of Amiens, this engaging little establishment is simply decorated with a dozen blond-wood tables, and provides good, wholesome cuisine. Among the specialities are lotte with basil, blanquette de veau aux asperges, and Maroilles cheese tart.
A la carte: 180 F. Menus: 55 F and 78 F (lunch only).

L'Univers
2, rue de Noyon — 22.91.52.51
Open every day. 41 rms 220-440 F. TV. Conference facilities. Garage parking. Telex 145070. V AE DC.
This large and comfortable residence, conveniently located between the station and the cathedral, offers attractively furnished rooms all the usual amenities, including double windows and a minibar. Half-board arrangements for groups.

And also...
Our selection of places for inexpensive, quick, or late-night meals.
Auberge du Vert Galant (22.91.31.66 - 57, ch. du Halage. Open until 10 pm): An open-air café specialising in regional fare and river-fish dishes. Boat rentals (160-180 F).
Charlie's (22.92.73.64 - 12, rue Flatters. Open until 11 pm): A very trendy spot where the menu focuses on grills and salads (150 F).
L'Himalaya (22.89.32.71 - 8, pl. Longueville. Open 11 pm): Modest, inexpensive Indian food (130-150 F).
Le Khmer (22.91.11.28 - 9, bd d'Alsace-Lorraine. Open until 10.30 pm): A fine place for Cambodian food located next to the railway station (100 F).
La Mangeoire (22.91.11.28 - 3, rue des Sergents. Open 11 pm): Large selection of crêpes and buckwheat galettes (100 F).
Le Saladin (22.92.05.15 - 6, rue des Chaudronniers. Open 9.15 pm): Various hot and cold salads served in a fantasy-garden décor (150 F).
La Taupinière (22.91.27.83 - 12, rue Cormont. Open 11 pm): Fine grilled foods served in a winsome little spot next to the cathedral (170 F).

In nearby Boves

(6 km SE on D 934)
80440 Amiens — (Somme)

Novotel
22.46.22.22
Open every day. 94 rms 380-430 F. Restaurant. TV. Conference facilities. Pool. Parking. Telex 140731. V AE DC.
A very good hotel enveloped in greenery and currently undergoing renovation. Outstanding group facilities; horse-back riding; children's playground.

In nearby Dury-lès-Amiens

(5 km S on N 1)
80480 Amiens — (Somme)

La Bonne Auberge
69, rte Nationale — 22.95.03.33
M. Beaussire. Closed Sun dinner and Mon (except holidays), and 21 Sep-7 Oct. Open until 9.30 pm. Private room: 50. Terrace dining. Air cond. No-smoking section. Parking. Telex 145861. V AE.
Chef Raoul Beaussire's ultraclassic cuisine (tinged with a regional accent) draws in the Sunday

crowd of Amiénois who plump for expertly prepared duck pâté en croûte, ham and cheese pancakes, grilled turbot béarnaise, grilled bass à la sauce nantaise, and Bresse pigeon, all of which are served in a lovely, flower-decked dining room. The fine cellar is ill-served by the badly designed wine list. Youthful, eager service; terrific prix-fixe meals.
A la carte: 350 F and up. Menus: 90 F (weekdays only), 120 F and 159 F (wine inc), 160 F.

See Montargis

68770 Ammerschwihr — (Haut-Rhin)
Paris 438 - Gérardmer 55 - Saint-Dié 49 - Colmar 8

11/20 A l'Arbre Vert
7, rue des Cigognes — 89.47.12.23
M. Gebel. Closed Tue, 15 Feb-25 March and 25 Nov-6 Dec. Open until 9.15 pm. V AE DC.
The lengthy, trilingual menu of this typical Alsatian inn lists the equally typical dishes served in such places: hot foie gras au Pinot, sole fillets à la Roselyne, saddle of rabbit with foie gras, and beef fillet with morels. Generous portions; good wines from local growers.
A la carte: 230-250 F. Menus: from 100 F to 300 F.

A l'Arbre Vert
(See restaurant above)
Closed Tue, 15 Feb-25 March and 25 Nov-6 Dec. 13 rms 100-250 F. Half-board 220-270 F oblig in seas. TV 10 rms. No pets.
This commodious inn stands before the village fountain; it offers pleasant, unpretentious rooms.

Aux Armes de France
1, Grand-Rue — 89.47.10.12
M. Gaertner. Closed Thu lunch, Wed and Jan. Open until 9.30 pm. Private room: 45. Hotel: 2 stes 450 F. 8 rms 300-400 F. Garage parking. V AE DC.
The Gaertners practise an eminently traditional form of Alsatian haute cuisine, never too daring but always precise. Before you set to, be sure to admire the beautiful presentations of the sole fillets with noodles, brochettes of lotte and scampi atop a macaroni gratin, stewed pigeon suprême with cabbage. The desserts are all of the bliss-inducing variety: may we suggest the frozen parfait à la bergamote, or the recklessly caloric variations sur le chocolat, served with a whisky granité. Patrons give themselves over to these rich pleasures in a suitably luxurious dining room with wood-panelled ceilings and light-toned wainscotting. Excellent cellar; astronomical prices.
A la carte: 500-600 F. Menus: 210 F (weekdays lunch only), 330 F, 420 F.

40330 Amou — (Landes)
Paris 741 - Pau 49 - Dax 31 - Mont-de-Marsan 46

Le Commerce
Pl. de la Poste — 58.89.02.28
M. Darracq. Closed Mon off-season, 14-28 Feb and 10-30 Nov. Open until 9.30 pm. Private room: 200. Terrace dining. Hotel: 20 rms 200-250 F. Garage parking. V AE DC.
Local gourmands flock to chef Darracq's large, convivial restaurant to tuck into rigorously prepared regional specialities, like splendid hare terrine, duck kidneys in port, wild-duck confit, magret, duck salmis. Wash down these earthy

delights with sturdy local wines (Tursan and Madiran). Charming and attentive service; bargain prices.

A la carte: 200 F. Menus: 60 F (weekdays only), 98 F, 138 F, 180 F.

AMPHION-LES-BAINS

See Evian

ANCENIS

44150 Ancenis — (Loire-Atl.)
Paris 342 - Angers 53 - Cholet 47 - Nantes 42

Auberge de Bel-Air
[14]
Rte d'Angers — 40.83.02.87
M. Gasnier. Closed Sun dinner and Mon. Open until 9.15 pm. Private room: 16. Parking. V.

Chef Jean-Paul Gasnier's light, imaginative cuisine, combined with Geneviève Gasnier's graciousness, easily make diners forget the restaurant's awkward location between the railway tracks and road. Sample the coquilles St-Jacques à la pêche and pot-au-feu de pigeon fermier à l'ancienne. And follow Gasnier's excellent advice on which of his fine (and inexpensive) Loire wines to order with your meal.

A la carte: 230-250 F. Menus: 90 F (weekdays only), 135 F, 170 F, 235 F.

Val de Loire
2 km E, Le Jarrier-St-Herblon
Rte d'Angers — 40.96.00.03
Open every day. 40 rms 205-258 F. Restaurant. Half-board 189-269 F. Conference facilities. Parking. Telex 711592. V.

A welcoming, recently built hotel surrounded by vineyards and fields. Loire river beaches within easy reach.

ANDELYS (LES)

27700 Andelys (Les) — (Eure)
Paris 92 - Beauvais 63 - Rouen 39 - Evreux 36

La Chaîne d'Or
[14]
27, rue Grande — 32.54.00.31
M. Foucault. Closed Sun dinner, Mon and Jan. Open until 9.30 pm. Private room: 30. Parking. V.

This romantic old restaurant overlooking the Seine features a classic roster of ably crafted dishes (foie gras, seafood pot-au-feu) and a generous, inexpensive prix-fixe menu that offers oyster salad with a creamy chive dressing, skate in an appealingly tart butter sauce with vegetables, cheese, and warm tarte aux pommes. Hospitable welcome. An extra point this year.

A la carte: 300 F. Menus: 120 F (weekdays only), 135 F (w-e and holidays only), 200 F, 320 F.

La Chaîne d'Or
(See restaurant above)
Closed Sun, Mon and Jan. 2 stes 680-740 F. 8 rms 260-460 F. TV. No pets.

A peaceful, typically Norman inn on the banks of the Seine, with soundproof rooms and suites, and thoughtfully appointed bathrooms.

For all the essential motoring information when driving in Europe, refer to the RAC European Motoring Guide.

ANDERNOS-LES-BAINS

33510 Andernos-les-Bains — (Gironde)
Paris 630 - Bordeaux 46 - Arcachon 40 - Dax 137

12/20 La Closerie du Parc
16, rue Pasteur — 56.82.26.49
Mme Latour. Open every day. Open until 10.30 pm. Terrace dining. V.

Brand-new and centrally located, this pricey little spot specialises in market-fresh seafood prepared with a touch of ingenuity. Depending on the season, the menu may offer lotte cheeks atop a salad of marinated vegetables, a ragoût of sole fillets and prawn quenelles, lobster fricassée with spring vegetables, and marvellous desserts (try the original chilled soup of St-Emilion with pears and figs). Excellent cellar, with an emphasis on claret.

A la carte: 350-400 F. Menus: 120 F, 210 F.

11/20 Mer et Golf
Av. F.-Cazenave — 56.26.12.12
M. Dyduch. Open every day. Parking. V.

Though the dining room offers a most captivating view of the sea, the kitchen is not yet up to scratch: our lotte tasted rubbery and the leek fondue was just passable; but the cleverly presented filet mignon forestière was delicious, and the tulipe de fruits rouges was not bad. The small cellar focuses on the region's vinous riches.

A la carte: 150 F. Menus: 110 F, 160 F.

Mer et Golf
(See restaurant above)
Open every day. 100 rms 250-300 F. Half-board 225-345 F oblig in seas. Conference facilities.

The architecture is light and modern, the rooms small and functional. Facilities include an exercise room, steam and whirlpool baths. Expect a pleasant reception from the young staff. Good buffet breakfasts.

ANDON

06750 Andon — (Alpes-Mar.)
Paris 835 - St-Raphaël 76 - Nice 75 - Grasse 35

Hostellerie d'Andon
93.60.45.11
Closed 1 Nov-22 Dec. 18 rms 110-210 F. Restaurant. Half-board 160-215 F. Conference facilities. Pool. Parking. V.

The rooms of this village hostelry are simple and quiet, the cuisine hearty enough to fuel you down the slopes.

ANDORRE (PRINCIPAUTÉ D')

Andorre (Principauté d')
Paris 895 - Toulouse 186 - Perpignan 166 - Foix 103

In nearby **Andorre-la-Vieille**

Andorra Palace
Prat de la Creu — (628) 21.0.72
Open every day. 24 stes 632-737 F. 130 rms 370-474 F. Restaurant. TV. Conference facilities. Heated pool. Tennis. Garage parking. Telex AND208. V AE DC.

This is a small luxury hotel that faces the mountains, with comfortable, modern rooms (minibar/VCR). The outstanding facilities include a sauna and exercise room. Nightclub.

Andorra Park Hotel

(628) 20.9.79

M. Cruz. Open every day. Open until 11 pm. Private room: 30. Garden dining. No pets. Garage parking. Telex 377AND. V AE DC.

The atmosphere is pleasantly relaxed despite the palatial décor and formal service, and there is a delightful garden view. Ricardo Torres' cuisine combines the voluptuously rich and the surprisingly light (goose-liver ravioli with cèpe sauce, hare stew with quince conserves). The outstanding cellar features wines from Spain and Chile.

A la carte: 350-400 F. Menu: 275 F.

Andorra Park Hotel

(See restaurant above)

Open every day. 40 rms 486-926 F. Half-board 655-1,093 F oblig in seas. TV. No pets. Conference facilities. Pool. Tennis.

This luxurious little hotel tucked into a corner of a garden in the upper town has been remodelled from top to bottom; rooms offer refined comfort. Slightly cool but thoroughly professional reception. Marvellous natural swimming pool, tennis, putting and croquet greens.

Sasplugas

15, rue de la Creu Grossa — (628) 20.3.11

Open every day. 26 rms 220-400 F. Restaurant. TV. Garage parking. V AE.

You'll find large, comfortable rooms with balconies in this handsome residence. The pleasant terrace overlooking the valley is ideal for summer dining.

In nearby Les Escaldes

Le 1900

11, carrer de la Unio — (628) 26.7.16

M. Guitard. Closed July. Open until 11 pm. V AE DC.

Owner Serge Guitard and chef Alain Despretz follow the seasons with care, embellishing and refining simple dishes such as prawn cannelloni, sea bass with a concassée of tomatoes, and saddle of lamb with broad beans. Regulars know their way blind-folded to this charming little house tucked away on a quiet square and decorated in pale-green and rose hues. The atmosphere is convivial, and the cellar harbours some fine French and Spanish wines. Prices are on the rise.

A la carte: 350-450 F. Menus: 280 F (wine inc), 350 F.

Roc Blanc

5, pl. des Coprinceps — (628) 21.4.86

Open every day. 4 stes 2,560 F. 236 rms 640-920 F. Restaurant. Half-board 730-895 F oblig in seas. TV. Conference facilities. Heated pool. Valet parking. Telex 224AND. V AE DC.

This is one of the resort's better hotels. It is pleasantly modern with standard rooms; reception and service are adequate. Complete facilities include a hair salon, boutiques, exercise room, and two restaurants.

In nearby La Massana

(5 km NW)

Rutllan

(628) 35.0.00

Open every day. 8 stes 630-800 F. 100 rms 240-400 F. Restaurant. Half-board 290-350 F oblig in

seas. TV. Conference facilities. Heated pool. Tennis. Garage parking. V AE DC.

A large chalet-style hotel four kilometres from Andorre-la-Vieille, the Rutllan has good facilities and pleasant rooms with a view of the valley. Garden, bar.

In nearby Pas-de-la-Case

Refuge des Isards

6, carrer Bernat-III — (628) 55.1.55

Open every day. 48 rms 200-350 F. Restaurant. Half-board 310 F. Conference facilities. Garage parking. V AE DC.

Near the border. Simple, tidy rooms with good beds. Friendly service.

ANDUZE

30140 Anduze — (Gard)
Paris 720 - Montpellier 70 - Nîmes 49 - Alès 13

Les Demeures du Ranquet

in Tornac — 66.77.51.63

M. Majourel. Closed off-season Tue dinner and Wed, 11 Nov-20 Dec and 1 Feb-10 March. Open until 9.30 pm. Private room: 20. Garden dining. No pets. Parking. V AE DC.

Anne Majourel wins an extra point this year for her savoury, sunny cuisine: scallop of salt cod with aïoli and escargots, artichokes with fresh chèvre and chives, mould of young rabbit perfumed with olives. The pleasant ambience is enlivened with piano music; the décor features contemporary works of art. Well-chosen wine list. Though the prix-fixe offerings are reasonably priced, à la carte choices are too expensive.

A la carte: 300-350 F. Menus: 138 F, 180 F, 250 F.

Les Demeures du Ranquet

(See restaurant above)

Closed off-season Tue and Wed, 11 Nov-20 Dec and 1 Feb-10 March. 10 rms 600-800 F. Half-board 750-1,000 F. TV. Air cond 3 rms. Conference facilities. Pool.

The huge, comfortable rooms blend into an oak wood at the foot of the Cévennes mountains. Perfect appointment, original *objets* and paintings, dreamy breakfasts.

Les Trois Barbus

4 km NW on D 129 and D 50 in Générargues 66.61.72.12

M. Marvie. Closed off-season Sun dinner, Mon and Tue, and 2 Jan-15 March. Open until 9 pm. Private room: 60. Terrace dining. No pets. Parking. V AE DC.

This is one of the prettiest sites in the Cévennes, nestled below the Musée du Désert and facing the sublime Camisards valley. Bearded chef Jean-François Marvie (his two brothers are equally bearded, hence the establishment's name) is a skilful and passionate defender of regional cuisine: foie gras marinated in Beaumes-de-Venise, fricassée of lamb sweetbreads, saddle and thigh of rabbit stuffed with woodsy morels. Succulent desserts, affordable fixed-price menus. Warning: the bearded trio's popularity draws mobs in summer and quality sometimes suffers.

A la carte: 300 F and up. Menus: 140 F (weekdays only), 200 F, 240 F, 300 F.

Les Trois Barbus

(See restaurant above)

Closed off-season Sun, Mon and Tue, and 2 Jan-15 March. 38 rms 260-520 F. Half-board 385-475 F oblig in seas. TV 32 rms. Air cond 17 rms. No pets. Conference facilities. Pool.

A comfortable, small, family hotel with an air of splendid isolation, and fine rooms with balconies. There is a grill next to the swimming pool and panoramic terrace, which boasts breathtaking views. Excellent Continental breakfasts.

ANGERS

49000 Angers — (Maine/Loire)
Paris 305 - Rennes 126 - Tours 106 - Nantes 90

Altea Lac de Maine

Rte de Nantes — 41.48.02.12

Open every day. 79 rms 280-450 F. Restaurant. Half-board 330-640 F. TV. Air cond. Conference facilities. Parking. Telex 721111. V AE DC.

In the new Lac de Maine neighbourhood, the hotel's remodelled rooms boast views of the lake or town. Excellent amenities include Jacuzzis and steam baths.

Concorde

18, bd du Mal-Foch — 41.87.37.20

Open every day. 2 stes 780-840 F. 75 rms 380-470 F. Restaurant. TV. Conference facilities. Garage parking. Telex 720923. V AE DC.

You'll find spacious, modern, and quiet lodging here in the centre of Angers. The reception is cordial but the service is somewhat lacking. Good breakfasts.

Continental Hôtel

12-14, rue L.-de-Romain — 41.86.94.94

Open every day. 25 rms 185-270 F. Restaurant. Half-board 225-340 F. TV. Telex 723042. V AE.

A modern and comfortable hotel located near the cathedral, with clean, thoroughly soundproofed rooms, friendly reception, smiling service, and low rates.

Hôtel de France

8, pl. de la Gare — 41.88.49.42

Open every day. 57 rms 280-420 F. Restaurant. TV. Conference facilities. Telex 720895. V AE DC.

This is the best hotel near the railway station, with soundproofed rooms and a charming reception. Brasserie on the premises.

Hôtel d'Iéna

27, rue Marceau — 41.87.52.40

Closed 13-31 July and 25 Dec-7 Jan. 23 rms 170-254 F. TV. Telex 723090. V.

Smallish rooms, fairly quiet, in a provincial hotel located near the château and cathedral.

Mercure

1, pl. P.-Mendès-France — 41.60.34.81

Open every day. 3 stes 290-430 F. 83 rms 290-450 F. Restaurant. TV. Air cond. Conference facilities. Garage parking. Telex 722139. V AE DC.

A large, modern building near the lovely Jardin des Plantes, the Mercure has functional rooms (of which three are equipped for the disabled and thirteen reserved for non-smokers). Good buffet breakfasts. Outstanding service.

Le Progrès

26, rue D.-Papin — 41.88.10.14

Closed 21 Dec-7 Jan. 41 rms 220-330 F. TV. Conference facilities. Telex 720982. V AE DC.

Small, clean, comfortable rooms with kitsch décor. Those facing the rear court are very quiet.

Conveniently situated in centre-city, near the railway station. Charming reception.

La Rose d'Anjou

9, pl. du Ralliement — 41.87.64.94

M. Compain. Closed Sat lunch. Open until 10.30 pm. Air cond. V DC.

Patrice Compain (formerly chef at Lous Landés in Paris) inherited the 1960s motel-style décor from the former owners, the Le Quérés. The least we can say is that the setting doesn't do justice to Compain's repertoire, a happy blend of South-western cuisine and seafood: lobster salad, confit and foie gras in aspic, lotte with oysters, veal kidneys. With a little more finesse and generosity this could become a great address. Nice wine cellar, attentive service.

A la carte: 300 F. Menus: 120 F (weekdays lunch only), 180 F (weekdays only, wine inc), 330 F (wine inc), 240 F.

Saint-Julien

9, pl. du Ralliement — 41.88.41.62

Open every day. 34 rms 160-275 F. TV. Telex 720930. V.

Housed in the same building as La Rose d'Anjou (see above), this is a modest but highly recommended establishment, with spacious, quiet, clean rooms.

La Salamandre

1, bd du Mal-Foch — 41.88.99.55

M. Louboutin. Closed Sun. Open until 9.45 pm. Private room: 24. No pets. Garage parking. Telex 720521. V AE DC.

The sculpted woodwork and stained-glass windows impart a certain neo-Renaissance style to La Salamandre's imposing dining room. Daniel Louboutan consistently turns out delicious fish dishes (meaty turbot, sandre à la nage) and tasty regional specialities such as tarragon-scented crépinette d'agneau. Good choice of desserts, excellent selection of local wines. Very pleasant service.

A la carte: 300-350 F. Menus: 100 F (weekdays only), 140 F, 180 F.

Le Vert d'Eau

9, bd G.-Dumesnil — 41.48.52.31

M. Piers. Closed Sun dinner and Mon. Open until 9.30 pm. Private room: 60. Parking. V AE DC.

New town planning may spell the end in autumn 1991 of this culinary institution, with its 1950s ruby-coloured décor. Before it's too late, try the delicate pan-fried prawns with fresh asparagus, the range-raised lamb, the hearty potato salad with leeks, and wash them down with one of the nice little wines that stock the cellar.

A la carte: 250-280 F. Menus: 85 F (weekdays only), 150 F, 180 F, 220 F.

And also...

Our selection of places for inexpensive, quick, or late-night meals.

Brasserie de la Gare (41.88.48.57 - 7, pl. de la Gare. Open until midnight): Friendly owner, unpretentious cooking and outstanding Anjou wine list (100-150 F).

Chez Clémentineœ (41.87.80.10 - 28, rue Delage. Open until 10.30 pm): A good crêperie in an outlying neighbourhood; reasonable prices (70-100 F).

La Côte de Bœuf (41.66.81.41 - 105, rue de la Madeleine. Open until 10 pm): Excellent and copious portions of grilled meats served in a pleasant setting (100 F).

(5 km NE on N 23)
49480 Angers — (Maine/Loire)

Auberge d'Eventard ♦
Route de Paris, N 23
41.43.74.25

M. Maussion. Closed Sun dinner, Mon and Feb school holidays. Open until 10 pm. Garden dining. No pets. Hotel: 10 rms 280-320 F (per pers, half-board oblig). Parking. Telex 722145. V AE DC.

The motorway has siphoned off the traffic that used to thunder by this nineteenth-century inn on the side of the *route nationale* near the racecourse. Though situated at the gates of Angers it has a decidedly country feel, with its summer terrace, its stunning timbered interior, and pretty flowered chintzes. Owner Jean-Pierre Maussion has slowly but steadily transformed and refined both décor and cuisine. The classic regional dishes have a modern touch: roasted duck foie gras topped with a poached egg, oysters with a winy sabayon sauce, Anjou pigeon with hydromel. Exquisite desserts. The fine selection of Loire wines includes several magnificent finds straight from the growers. The prices are off and running.

A la carte: 350-400 F. Menus: 140 F (weekdays lunch only), 250 F (w-e and holidays only), 175 F, 330 F.

Le Clafoutis
N 23
La Lieue — 41.43.84.71

M. Lebert. Closed Wed, dinner Tue and Sun, 1 May, Feb school holidays, last week of July and 3 first weeks of Aug. Open until 9.30 pm. Private room: 16. Air cond. Parking. V.

Serge Lebert is a native son and thorough professional. He has taken this pretty little restaurant on the outskirts of town and turned it into a serious culinary establishment. The fixed-price menus change weekly and the à la carte selections follow the seasons. Lebert's wife, Violeta, manages the restaurant, serving up delicious dishes such as young rabbit terrine with vegetables, thyme-steamed sandre with beurre blanc, and a satisfying pear and almond-cream clafoutis tart. Good choice of regional wines.

A la carte: 280-300 F. Menus: 80 F and 130 F (weekdays only), 150 F, 240 F.

La Fauvelaie ♣
Route du Parc Expo
41.43.80.10

Open every day. 9 rms 150-250 F. Restaurant. Half-board 200-300 F. TV. Conference facilities. Parking. Telex 720930. V.

A lovely old farm situated in a peaceful park, La Fauvelaie is a fine place to stop if you want to explore Angers and the castles of Anjou.

See Avignon

Some establishments change their closing times without warning. It is always wise to check in advance.

64600 Anglet — (Pyrénées-A.)
Paris 748 - Biarritz 4 - Bayonne 3 - St-Jean-de-Luz 1

Château de Brindos
Rte de l'Aviation — 59.23.17.68

M. Vivensang. Open every day. Open until 10 pm. Private room: 200. Parking. Telex 541428. V AE DC.

The décor of this large Basque-style villa is a bit overblown but the dining room perched on a promontory over a vast and lovely lake has undeniable charm. Albert Bouderba's laudable cuisine fits right in: an exemplary choice of rich foie gras, perfectly prepared brill tartare, fresh and salt cod with sweet peppers, spiced young pigeon. Impeccable service in a luxurious yet relaxed atmosphere.

A la carte: 370-450 F.

Château de Brindos ♣
(See restaurant above)

Open every day. 2 stes. 12 rms 750-1,250 F. Half-board 1,900 F oblig in seas. TV. Conference facilities. Heated pool. Tennis.

Exceptionally comfortable rooms and luxurious suites await you in a quiet setting of timeless beauty near a lake and forest. Superb swimming pool, private fishing. Relais et Châteaux.

Hôtel de Chiberta et du Golf
104, bd des Plages — 59.63.95.56

Open every day. 54 rms 390-860 F. Restaurant. Half-board 380-810 F oblig in seas. TV. Conference facilities. Pool. Tennis. Golf. Parking. Telex 550637. V AE DC.

Nestled between links and lake, not far from the beach, this twin hotel boasts many pretty rooms with salons that open onto the golfing greens. Excellent facilities for conferences, health and slimming cures.

11/20 Le Gulf Stream
153, bd des Plages — 59.52.75.75

M. Pavlovsky. Open every day. Open until 10 pm. Private room: 30. Terrace dining. Air cond. No pets. Parking. Telex 573428. V AE DC.

A boundless view from the sandy terrace embraces the ocean and the mouth of the Adour river. But it cannot make up for the bland cuisine, devoid of vim or vigour. But the marinated raw fish, the veal kidney with tarragon, and the bitter-chocolate cake are worth a try. Impersonal reception and service.

A la carte: 300-350 F. Menus: 160 F (weekdays lunch only, wine inc), 190 F (wine inc).

Atlanthal ♣
(See restaurant above)

Open every day. 99 rms 380-880 F. Half-board 594-1,020 F. TV. Conference facilities. Heated pool. Tennis.

This is a recent construction overlooking the Plage des Cavaliers, between the sea and the Chiberta woods. On the lower level are rooms equipped for health cures and slimming regimes. The spacious, soberly decorated guest rooms offer all the usual amenities. Good breakfasts.

Relais de Parme
Aéroport de Biarritz — 59.23.93.84

M. Laporte. Closed Sat. Open until 10 pm. Air cond. V AE DC.

The classic cuisine of this airport restaurant isn't all that airy but it's reliable and decently done: scallops provençale, sole with foie gras, kidneys with port, vanilla- and honey-flavoured pots de crème. The setting is pleasant and modern. Good service.

A la carte: 300-350 F.

ANGOULÊME

16000 Angoulême — (Charente)
Paris 450 - Bordeaux 116 - Limoges 103

Altea

1, pl. des Halles — 45.95.47.95
Open every day. 90 rms 405-515 F. Restaurant. TV. Air cond 51 rms. Conference facilities. Parking. Telex 793191. V AE DC.

This thoroughly restored grand hotel is in the heart of old Angoulême in a large park above the ramparts. The rooms are small but well equipped and pretty. Perfect breakfasts, attentive reception and service.

Hôtel de Bordeaux

236, rte de Bordeaux — 45.91.60.66
Open every day. 34 rms 205-270 F. Restaurant. Half-board 290-340 F. TV. Conference facilities. Garage parking. Telex 793540. V AE DC.

Here's a modest hotel at the foot of the ramparts. The recently remodelled rooms are tidy, comfortable, and quiet. Friendly reception.

Le Margaux

25, rue de Genève — 45.92.58.98
Mme Pineau. Closed Sun and 20 Dec-6 Jan. Open until 11 pm. Private room: 20. Terrace dining. V.

The two dining rooms—one classic, the other contemporary—present as stark a contrast as chef Francine Pineau's successful dishes (snail risotto with foie gras and prawns, baby boar with quince sauce) do with her oddly banal desserts. Among Le Margaux's assets are a charming setting, affable reception and service, and moderate prices. This is one of the better restaurants in the region and a second toque may be on its way. Some fine wines are available by the glass.

A la carte: 300 F. Menus: 85 F, 125 F, 190 F.

La Ruelle

6, rue des Trois-Notre-Dame — 45.92.94.64
Mme Dauphin. Closed Sat lunch, Sun, 18 Feb-4 March and 12-26 Aug. Open until 10 pm. Private room: 25. V.

Véronique Dauphin and her husband have recently restored this delightful old house with its great timbers and rough-hewn stone walls and fireplace. The delight continues with the creative cuisine: œufs cocotte à la crème et aux truffes fraîches, a thick slice of tender lamb topped with crisp fried potatoes, crab-stuffed cabbage leaves, chocolate and vanilla frozen custards. An extra point this year for the best cuisine in Angoulême.

A la carte: 260 F. Menus: 120 F (lunch only, wine inc), 130 F, 205 F.

In nearby La Vigerie

(8 km W on N 141)
16290 Angoulême — (Charente)

Le Moulin Gourmand

45.90.83.00
Mme Ménager. Closed Sun dinner and Mon (1 Jan-31 March), Nov and Dec. Open until 9.15 pm. Private room: 40. Garden dining. Parking. Telex 791053. V AE DC.

Chef Bruno Nicollet is a skilful brinksman. His rich and complex cuisine teeters on the abyss of preciosity yet never falls in: courgette blossoms stuffed with truffled scrambled eggs and flanked

by caramelised ratatouille, pigeonneau en cocotte with an herbed soufflé and a sauce lightly perfumed with liquorice, and so on. The desserts are interesting though rather contrived (pear pastry and sorbet in a white chocolate croûte). Though the décor is heavy-handed, some fine antiques, fresh flowers, and good service provide that needed touch of lightness.

A la carte: 350-400 F. Menus: 175 F, 280 F, 360 F.

Le Moulin du Maine Brun

(See restaurant above)
Closed Nov and Dec. 2 stes 1,000-1,100 F. 18 rms 485-500 F. Half-board 500-600 F oblig in seas. TV. Conference facilities. Pool.

Picture it: an antiques-filled mill set in a pretty park where deer and ducks roam free. Large, comfortable rooms with well-equipped bathrooms. Expect a friendly reception and service. Relais et Châteaux.

ANNECY

74000 Annecy — (H.-Savoie)
Paris 547 - Lyon 142 - Genève 43 - Aix-les-Bains 34

L'Abbaye

15, ch. de l'Abbaye — 50.23.61.08
Open every day. 3 stes 800-1,100 F. 15 rms 400-700 F. Restaurant. Half-board 380-530 F. TV. Conference facilities. V AE DC.

The seven new rooms equipped for balnéothérapie (bathing cures) are as pretty, comfortable, spacious, and quiet as the rest. Diligent service. Ruinously expensive; generous breakfasts.

L'Amandier

6, av. Mandallaz — 50.51.74.50
MM. Guillot and Cortési. Closed Sat lunch and Sun (Easter- end Sep, except holidays), and 27 July-19 Aug. Open until 9.30 pm. Private room: 16. Parking. V AE DC.

The graceful, marvellously balanced cuisine of partners Nicole Guillot and Alain Cortési enchants us. L'Amandier's young, eager staff, under the direction of the restaurant's third partner, wine connoisseur Jean-François Guillot, ten years' experience now. Their performance is still a joy to watch. Both the fixed-price menus and carte overflow with delicious finds: ravioli with cumin cream, rissoles de grenouilles with a walnut emulsion, millefeuille de pigeonneau aux haricots rouges with truffles, and a bitter-cocoa jus, or a gratin of caramelised spiced pears with cinnamon sauce. The prices are stiff but the food is worth every franc. Jean-François Guillot has stocked the cellar with excellent bottles from his native Bordeaux.

A la carte: 400 F and up. Menus: 150 F (weekdays only), 190 F, 260 F, 390 F.

Auberge de l'Eridan

(Marc Veyrat)
7, av. de Chavoires — 50.66.22.04
19.5 M. Veyrat-Durebex. Closed Sun dinner, Wed, Feb and 15 Aug-8 Sep. Open until 9.30 pm. Private room: 20. Terrace dining. Air cond. Parking. V AE DC.

Lay to rest any doubts you might have had about the influence of the Gault Millau guide: Since Marc Veyrat received his 19.5/20 rating last year, his turnover has increased by 50 per cent! For the first time l'Auberge de l'Eridan was fully booked throughout the season. And to think that without our promotion he might have had to close, depriving the world of his prodigious talent!

Local Savoyards, Swiss, and even Parisians now beat a path to his door with their tongues hanging out. They leave astonished by the exceptional virtuosity of this son of modest farmers from the forsaken Manigod valley.

If all goes as planned Veyrat will soon move his operation from this roadside chalet to a breathtakingly beautiful spot on a nearby mountain slope with a majestic panorama of Lake Annecy. Last century the ubiquitous George Sand dallied here among the forest knolls and wild meadows in the company of her *ami* Eugène Sue. Now a select few will have the chance to savour in the very same spot pleasures not of the flesh but of the table.

It is with great trepidation that we return to restaurants like this *auberge*, which we've singled out as top of the heap. What if we've blundered— much to the pleasure of small minds and envious hearts? Happily there has been no blunder with Marc Veyrat. A naturalist and lover of mountain herbs, he mixes his palette of flavours with a mastery that puts imitators to shame. For only a master could astonish us as he does by adding a red-radish cream to an extraordinary pork gelée with caviar, or wild celery to a sauté of potatoes and smoked trout, or aïli berries—a rare mountain fruit—to a stunningly refined warm foie gras. With Veyrat you'll discover a botanist's dream: wild verbena perfumes both his vegetable soup and his fatless boudin de lotte du lac with a dizzyingly delicious flavour; lemon balm harmonises with the firm flesh of turbot; lait de cresson marries with the incredibly tender grilled pigeon....

No wonder Marc Veyrat and his young staff (Elisabeth, his sous-chef, is 24; Gilles, the sommelier, 25; and Alain, the manager, 29) are now justly considered the region's flagship restaurateurs! The feast continues with a formidable array of Savoie cheeses, and desserts such as crème brûlée made with rich sheep's milk, chocolate millefeuille, and wild-strawberry gâteau. Accompany these rare delicacies with frisky Savoie wines, voluptuous Côtes-du-Rhône, or profound Bordeaux. You may cry when you see the bill, but they'll doubtless be tears of joy. Relais et Châteaux.

A la carte: 500-900 F. Menus: 320 F (weekdays lunch only), 480 F, 900 F.

Le Belvédère

2 km, rte de Semnoz
7, ch. du Belvédère — 50.45.04.90
M. Aubeneau. Closed Sun dinner, Mon, 21 Oct-7 Dec and 2-12 April. Open until 9.30 pm. Terrace dining. No pets. Parking. V.

For over 20 years, Jean-Louis Aubeneau has been offering his clients one of the most spectacular bird's-eye views of Annecy from the leafy terrace or modern dining room of his charming, lively restaurant. The setting perfectly suits the sunny freshness of the cuisine, which is based on Atlantic seafood brought in from Aubeneau's native La Rochelle. His calamars à la chantilly au caviar, his sea bass with wild mushrooms, and his seafood crépinette with garden herbs have convinced us that Aubeneau's Belvédère is the best fish restaurant on the lake. Excellent desserts and an affable welcome from Mme Aubeneau round things off nicely.

A la carte: 400 F.

Remember to reserve your table or your room in advance, and please let the restaurant or hotel know if you cannot honour your reservation.

Le Belvédère

(See restaurant above)
Open every day. 10 rms 140-180 F. Half-board 220-240 F. No pets.

The charm of the large, quiet, tidy rooms lies in their magnificent view of Annecy's lake.

Carlton

5, rue des Glières — 50.45.47.75
Open every day. 55 rms 335-454 F. TV. Garage parking. Telex 309472. V AE DC.

A rosy-pink edifice dating from the 1930s, the Carlton stands just 300 metres from the lake, across from a square in central Annecy. The hotel boasts very comfortable, large, traditional rooms.

La Ciboulette

10, rue Vaugelas — 50.45.74.57
M. Paccard. Closed Sun dinner, Mon and 1-20 July. Open until 9.30 pm. Terrace dining. V.

Set in a pretty courtyard, this smart little restaurant has an inviting air. Accept the invitation! The friendly young owner will escort you into her comfortable, handsomely decorated dining rooms. Chef George Paccard's delicious cuisine changes as often as the variable weather. Try the freshwater char from Lake Annecy with a truffled julienne, saddle of young rabbit stuffed with morels and bacon, and finish up with the caramelised apple feuillantine. The wine list is improving.

A la carte: 300 F. Menus: 160 F (wine inc), 120 F.

Didier Roque

Annecy-le-Vieux
13, rue J.-Mermoz — 50.23.07.90
M. Roque. Closed Tue dinner and Wed. Open until 9.30 pm. Terrace dining. V AE DC.

Fresh ingredients, honest flavours, and a measure of inventiveness mark this restaurant. A generous escalope of liver with puréed lentils and split peas, fillet of féra (a freshwater fish from Lake Annecy), and mousse of pike with fennel are representative of Didier Roque's cuisine. And the charming old restaurant and flower-filled terrace facing the lake grow prettier all the time. Fine wine cellar, excellent fixed-price menus, and a smiling reception.

A la carte: 350 F. Menus: 155 F (weekdays lunch only), 195 F, 285 F, 320 F.

Super-Panorama

7, rte du Semnoz — 50.45.34.86
Closed Mon and Tue, 7 Jan-17 Feb. 5 rms 220 F. Restaurant. Parking. V.

This is an oustanding little hotel situated between lake and mountains, with a restaurant on a panoramic terrace.

12/20 Taverne de Maître Kanter

2, quai Perrière — 50.51.02.65
M. Jacquin. Closed Mon off-season, 1-8 Jan and 1-8 Oct. Open until 10.30 pm. Terrace dining. V.

Seafood, delicious foie gras, choucroute, and sprightly Alsatian wines feature on the menu of this, the best brasserie in town.

A la carte: 160-200 F.

And also...

Our selection of inexpensive restaurants and hotels.

Les Clématites (50.52.84.33 - 19, rue Vaugelas. 19 rms 210-320 F): a nice little family-run hotel in the centre of town.

Le Flamboyant (50.23.61.69 - 52, rue des Mouettes. 2 stes 370 F, 30 rms 220-335 F): a quiet hotel near the lake with pleasant rooms.

Mercure (50.45.09.66 - 3 km S, rte d'Aix-les-Bains, 74600 Annecy Seynod. 1 ste 800 F, 69 rms 300-515 F): this chain hotel is at the gates of town. Well-equipped rooms (one is reserved for the disabled), bar, restaurant with terrace.

Hôtel du Palais de l'Isle (50.45.86.87 - 13, rue Perrière. 23 rms 290-440 F): a recently restored, small-scale hotel in the old part of town. Comfortable rooms with contemporary furnishings.

Le Pré de la Danse (50.23.70.41 - Annecy-le-Vieux, 16, rue J.-Mermoz. Open until 9.30 pm): a charming new restaurant located in Annecy-le-Vieux. Country atmosphere, interesting warm lobster salad with hot cucumbers, spiced filet mignon de veau, and fish dishes. Good wine selection. (150 F).

In nearby Saint-Jorioz

(9 km S on N 508)
74410 Annecy — (H.-Savoie)

🏠 La Cochette 🔺🍴

5 km S, in St-Eustache
La Magne — 50.32.00.08
Closed 15 Dec-15 April. 15 rms 105-175 F. Restaurant. Half-board 165-245 F. Parking. V.

A chalet pretty as a postcard, La Cochette's sunny rooms overlook Lake Annecy.

In nearby Talloires

(13 km SE on N 509)
74290 Annecy — (H.-Savoie)

L'Abbaye de Talloires 🌑

Ch. des Moines — 50.60.77.33
M. Tiffenat. Closed off-season Sun dinner and Mon lunch, and 15 Dec-15 Jan. Open until 9.30 pm. Private room: 86. Garden dining. No-smoking section. Telex 385307. V.

This discreet and serene restaurant never ceases to astonish and seduce its patrons. Despite an occasional blip we've full confidence in the generous, well-prepared cuisine of the Tiffenat family. Savour the foie gras and artichoke marbré, the duck with ginger, and a creamy, old-fashioned St Honoré pastry for dessert.

A la carte: 350-400 F. Menus: from 250 F to 380 F.

L'Abbaye de Talloires 🔺🍴

(See restaurant above)
Closed 15 Dec-15 Jan. 2 stes 1,080-1,470 F. 30 rms 400- 1,290 F. Half-board 425-1,000 F oblig in seas. Conference facilities.

This fief of elegance and good taste sits between lake and mountain, its delightful garden and marvellously appointed rooms flanked by a cloister and large gallery. Whirlpool baths, soundproofing. Relais et Châteaux.

🏠 Beau Site

50.60.71.04
Closed 8 Oct-9 May. 1 ste 750-840 F. 29 rms 250-620 F. Restaurant. Half-board 350-500 F oblig in seas. TV 18 rms. Tennis. Parking. V AE DC.

The two-hectare park includes a private beach and pier. The large and sunny rooms boast a pleasant view of the lake and surrounding countryside.

Le Père Bise

Rte du Port — 50.60.72.01
Mme Bise. Closed off-season Wed lunch and Tue, and 15 Dec-15 March. Open until 9.30 pm. Private room: 25. Garden dining. Valet parking. Telex 385812. V AE.

Things are going so well *chez* the Bise family that they've misplaced their 380 F menu, which no one

dared to order anyway. Chef Sophie Bise promptly invented a 950 F menu featuring truffles (in season) and voilà, the prices are airborne. The bill is indeed horrific but the Père Bise remains one of the great gastronomical institutions of France, loved by well-to-do foreigners and native foodies alike. So look beyond the *addition* and enjoy the view of garden and lake and the taste of Sophie's flawless 'tatin' of truffles and foie gras, her poularde à l'estragon, gratin of crayfish tails, and far-famed chocolate gâteau marjolaine.

A la carte: 600-800 F. Menus: 950 F (truffe), 550 F.

Le Père Bise 🔺🍴

(See restaurant above)
Closed 15 Dec-15 March. 6 stes 2,200-3,500 F. 29 rms 700-1,600 F. Half-board 950-1,600 F. TV. Conference facilities.

Perched on the edge of the lake, this delightfully romantic hotel provides perfect comfort in an ultra-classic setting. Book a room in the beautiful new Villa des Roses annexe. Superb view of the lake. Relais et Châteaux.

74100 Annemasse — (H.-Savoie)
Paris 550 - Genève 7 - Annecy 48 - Evian 39

Hôtel de Genève

in Ambilly, 38, rte de Genève — 50.38.70.66
Open every day. 3 stes 530-600 F. 100 rms 380-460 F. Restaurant. TV. Conference facilities. Garage parking. Telex 385472. V AE DC.

Located one kilometre from Geneva, most of this practical, modern, sunny hotel has been remodelled. The rear rooms are less noisy.

Hôtel du Parc

19, rue de Genève — 50.38.44.60
Closed 22 Dec-10 Jan. 30 rms 200-340 F. TV. Garage parking. Telex 309034. V AE DC.

This classic hotel affords views of the municipal park and Mont Salève and is located only one and a half kilometres from the Swiss border.

In nearby Gaillard

(2 km SW on D 2)
74240 Annemasse — (H.-Savoie)

Mercure

Rue des Jardins — 50.92.05.25
Open every day. 78 rms 300-485 F. Restaurant. TV. Conference facilities. Heated pool. Parking. Telex 385815. V AE DC.

The Mercure is a modern hotel set in a large park on a river bank. The rooms are well equipped (two are accessible for disabled people), the décor light and clean. One floor is reserved for non-smokers. Bar.

07100 Annonay — (Ardèche)
Paris 546 - Le Puy 86 - Valence 53 - Saint-Etienne 43

Marc et Christine 🌑

29, av. M.-Seguin — 75.33.46.97
M. Julliat. Closed Sun dinner and Mon (except holidays), and 2-24 Jan. Open until 9.30 pm. Private room: 50. Garden dining. V.

The crumbling façade has been lifted, the gardens enlarged and beautified, and voilà!—this grand old house is sunnier and cheerier than ever. Christine and Marc Julliat have followed success upon success for over five years now, making their country cuisine sing with lightness and inventiveness.

Half the fixed-price menus are given over to 'revised' Ardèche specialities, the other half to traditional dishes. Try the tarte aux endives renversée enhanced with local bleu cheese, the feuillantine of fresh pasta with crab, goose soup with cèpes and mild garlic, the ris de veau aux salsifis, and finish up with the granité of puckery griotte cherries à l'eau-de-vie. The cellar is magnificent. 'Le Patio' is a bistro annexe.

Menus: 145 F, 185 F, 205 F, 260 F.

Hôtel du Midi

17, pl. des Cordeliers — 75.33.23.77
Closed Sun off-season and 20 Dec-20 Jan. 40 rms 105-225 F. TV 15 rms. Garage parking. V AE DC.

This is a classic hotel in the centre of town with well-maintained rooms.

In nearby Satillieu

(14 km S on D 578 and D 578 A)
07290 Annonay — (Ardèche)

La Gentilhommière

Rte de Lalouvesc — 75.34.94.31
Open every day. 51 rms 250-350 F. Restaurant. Half-board 280-380 F. TV. Conference facilities. Heated pool. Tennis. Parking. Telex 345548. V.

The many facilities (exercise room, putting green, steam bath) and pleasant rooms opening on a large park along the river make this an ideal place for a fitness cure.

11/20 Julliat-Roche

75.34.95.86
M. Julliat. Closed Sun dinner off-season. Open until 9 pm. Private room: 30. Garden dining. Air cond. Hotel: 11 rms 150-270 F. Garage parking. V AE DC.

Generations of the Julliat family have run this inn with a relaxed atmosphere and solid cuisine. The 90 F menu is fine indeed and features trout carpaccio with vegetable julienne, fricassée de volaille aux champignons, cheese, and dessert.

Menus: 60 F (weekdays only), 90 F, 116 F, 160 F.

ANSE

See Villefranche-sur-Saône

ANTHÉOR

83700 Anthéor — (Var)
Paris 890 - Saint-Raphaël 13 - Nice 60 - Cannes 27

11/20 Auberge d'Anthéor

Cap Roux — 94.44.83.89
M. Despocq. Closed 15 Nov-20 Dec. Open until 9.30 pm (11 pm in summer). Terrace dining. Parking. V.

The seaside terrace is enchanting, the rustic dining room pleasantly colourful and the cuisine nicely done, though the *carte* seems to spread in all directions. Several fixed-price menus save the day. Try the classic fresh-fish menu.

A la carte: 240-300 F. Menus: 106 F, 122 F, 156 F, 168 F, 184 F.

Auberge d'Anthéor

(See restaurant above)
Open every day. 3 stes 685-980 F. 23 rms 495-860 F. Half-board 645-1,110 F. TV. Air cond 10 rms. Pool.

Reopened for business after a ten-year hiatus, this 1920s hotel perched over the sea and the red shoals of Esterel offers attractively renovated, well-equipped rooms (some with a kitchenette).

06600 Antibes — (Alpes-Mar.)
Paris 913 - Nice 22 - Cannes 11 - Grasse 2

Bleu Marine

Les Quatre Chemins
93.74.84.84
Open every day. 18 rms 265-330 F. TV. No pets. Parking. V AE DC.

The beach beckons just 500 metres from this modern hotel, with rooms featuring balcony-terraces facing the sea.

La Bonne Auberge

 on N 7, quartier La Brague
93.33.36.65
M. Rostang. Closed off-season except holidays Mon (lunch only in seas), Wed lunch in July-Aug, and 15/11-15/12. Open until 10.30 pm. Private room: 220. Terrace dining. Air cond. No-smoking section. Valet parking. Telex 470989. V AE.

La Bonne Auberge ranks among the finest restaurants on the Côte d'Azur. But with its fusty 1960s 'temple-of-gastronomy' décor, an unfortunate location between the main road and the railway with no garden to compensate for the surroundings, the restaurant faces an uphill struggle. The Rostang family soldiers on, still catering for a smart clientele by providing excellent service and well-thought-out cuisine. Dishes created by Jo Rostang are now prepared by his son, Philippe, who has taken over the kitchen. Jo's is a tough act to follow, and Philippe sometimes falls short. He is at his best with 'simple' dishes (though all are rather elaborate). Try the barely browned Brittany prawns surrounded by squares of polenta and sprinkled with a truffle jus, the breaded tunny fish with a mint béarnaise sauce, or the squab with a perfectly cooked potato galette, as well as the carousel of exquisite desserts.

To pay homage to regional bottlings, the cellar's rich stock now boasts several wines from Provence. Alas, this hasn't lightened the bill—but then the Bonne Auberge crowd doesn't dither over such trifles.

A la carte: 600-700 F and up. Menus: 370 F (lunch only, wine inc, except holidays), 390 F, 500 F and 570 F (except holidays).

12/20 Le Clafoutis

18, rue Thuret — 93.34.66.70
M. Montaron. Dinner only. Closed Tue and 23 Dec-9 Feb. Open until 10.30 pm. Pets allowed.

In his minuscule kitchen chef Gérard Montaron manages to whip up a nice 135 F menu for his youngish clientele: jellied rabbit civet with a fresh herbal sauce, fresh sautéed cod larded with smoked salmon, and an excellent honeyed pear clafoutis tart. Live jazz.

A la carte: 185 F. Menu: 135 F.

La Marguerite

11, rue Sadi-Carnot
93.34.08.27
M. Seguin. Closed Sat lunch and Mon. Open until 10 pm. Air cond. Parking. V AE.

Though the décor is dowdy, the reception and service here are charming. Daniel Seguin's updated regional cuisine highlights frank, straightforward flavours: crayfish and tomato tart, fish panaché with shellfish butter, veal kidney with a pumpkin gâteau. Expensive wines exacerbate an already damaging bill.

A la carte: 350-400 F. Menus: 165 F, 260 F.

Mas de la Pagane ♨

(See restaurant above)
Open every day. 7 rms 250-450 F. Half-board 250-600 F. Conference facilities.
This extremely quiet farmhouse-turned-hotel is a surprising find in bustling Antibes.

Mas Djoliba ♨

29, av. de Provence — 93.34.02.48
Open every day. 1 ste 800 F. 13 rms 350-560 F. Restaurant. Half-board 520-620 F oblig in seas. TV. Pool. Parking. Telex 461686. V AE DC.
Well-situated between beach and centre, the Mas Djoliba sits in a quiet, lovely three-hectare park. The rooms have an appealing personal touch. Minibus excursions may be arranged.

Hôtel Mercator ♨

120, ch. des Groules — 93.33.50.75
Closed 15 Dec-15 Jan. 20 rms 285-345 F. Conference facilities. Pool. Parking. V AE DC.
The studios are extremely well equipped, the country setting perfectly serene.

Au Régal

5, rue Sade — 93.34.11.69
M. Le Hir. Closed off-season Sun dinner and Mon, and 5 Jan-5 Feb. Dinner only in July-Aug. Open until 11.30 pm. Garden dining. Air cond. No-smoking section. Valet parking. V AE DC.
Watercolours and diplomas adorn the roughcast walls of this small restaurant hidden in the heart of the *vieille ville* and managed by a thoroughly professional 26-year-old chef. The delightful summer patio is a perfect place to savour scampi with asparagus and citrus butter, sea bass roasted with saffron, local lamb with ratatouille, and chocolate millefeuille with raspberries. The wine list is slim pickings.
A la carte: 400-450 F. Menus: 130 F (weekdays lunch only), 245 F (dinner only), 165 F.

Restaurant du Bastion

1, av. du Gal-Maizières — 93.34.13.88
M. Hammou. Closed off-season Sun dinner and Mon, 4-21 March and 2-16 Dec. Open until 10.30 pm. Private room: 40. Terrace dining. V AE DC.
The Bastion is a many-splendoured thing: a gorgeous setting on the ramparts of town; a sunny décor; a leafy terrace; and last but not least, a fresh and meticulous cuisine. Try the charlotte de rascasse with a lemony crème de petits pois, medallions of lotte with sea urchin velouté, and young rabbit stuffed with lardons and olives. The wine list boasts a wide-ranging choice of French vintages.
A la carte: 350-400 F. Menus: 130 F, 190 F.

12/20 Le Romarin

28, bd du Mal-Leclerc — 93.61.54.29
M. Boer. Closed Wed and 15 Dec-15 Jan. Open until 10 pm. Terrace dining. Air cond. V.
Prim and proper whitewashed walls, fresh fish, and low prices make this family-style restaurant a winning proposition. Try the thick-sliced salmon au gros sel, bourride provençale, and blanquette des trois poissons.
A la carte: 180-200 F. Menus: 105 F, 130 F.

ANTOIGNY

See Bagnoles-de-l'Orne

ANTONNE-ET-TRIGONANT

See Périgueux

APT

84400 Apt — (Vaucluse)
Paris 732 - Avignon 52 - Aix-en-P. 55 - Carpentras 4

12/20 Peuzin

17, quai L.-Sagy — 90.74.12.50
M. Peuzin. Closed Sun dinner and Mon (except school holidays.), 1-8 July and 15 Nov-15 Dec. Open until 9.30 pm. Private room: 10. Terrace dining. Garage parking. Telex 431369. V AE DC.
Stick to the lower-priced menus, which feature well-chosen regional dishes such as young pigeon, beef with onion conserves, and rich desserts. Pleasant flower-filled terrace under a spreading plane tree.
A la carte: 400-500 F. Menus: 130 F, 195 F, 270 F.

Auberge du Lubéron

(See restaurant above)
Open every day. 1 ste 450-700 F. 16 rms 260-450 F. Half-board 300-425 F. TV 10 rms. Conference facilities.
Near the old town, the rooms of this inn are rather small and simple but well equipped. Good value.

In nearby **Chêne**

(2.5 km E on N 100)
84400 Apt — (Vaucluse)

Bernard Mathys

84400 Gargas — 90.04.84.64
M. Mathys. Closed Wed. Annual closings not available. Open until 10 pm. Private room: 20. Garden dining. Parking. V.
Bernard Mathys's freshly revamped décor now features a pretty dining room with Directoire chairs and an open-air patio. The cuisine is innovative and good-humoured, relying exclusively on ingredients fresh from the *marché*. Mathys underscores their refined flavours in such dishes as terrine of lamb en barigoule de légumes and wild thyme gelée, John Dory cooked in a beetroot-based jus and sweet-and-sour Drôme pigeon with a fig tartelette. The wine cellar boasts many local finds; the service is faultless.
A la carte: 300-350 F. Menus: 160 F, 250 F.

ARBOIS

39600 Arbois — (Jura)
Paris 393 - Lons-le-Saunier 39 - Pontarlier 56

Jean-Paul Jeunet

9, rue de l'Hôtel-de-Ville — 84.66.05.67
M. Jeunet. Closed Wed lunch and Tue (except Sep and school holidays), Dec and Jan. Open until 9.30 pm. Private room: 50. Garage parking. Telex 361033. V DC.
Despite the barbs of some critics, we think Jean-Paul Jeunet's cuisine is subtle and full of nuances, not bland, certainly not flat; to our taste, it recalls the style of superchefs Michel Bras and Marc Veyrat, who also love mountain herbs and country flavours.
After years of effort Jeunet the younger has found his stride, creating vibrant combinations that are complex without being precious. This year we were impressed by his exquisite bouchées of smoked carp flanked by a curried carrot gelée, a wild duck crépinette moistened with goat's-milk whey and crowned by a fragile honey-spice biscuit, roasted prawns with rye galettes and beetroot chips, and truffled tête de veau.
This is one of the most exciting and piquantly harmonious cuisines we know. Take the

sweetbreads served with a light polenta galette, the pigeon suprêmes cooked in goat's milk, or the lobster chaud-froid with a duck gelée and hyssop crème. Shocking at first, then slyly seductive. The same goes for the contrapuntal décor, which combines the rough with the refined. No, bland it is not; for our money, this cuisine is well worth three toques. Even Jeunet the elder, a finicky old fellow, has ceased to criticise his son. The rich cellar is under the able stewardship of a young sommelier. It showcases Jura wines, many at affordable prices. Considering the top-class quality of the food and surroundings, the bill is reasonable.

A la carte: 400 F. Menus: 150 F (weekdays lunch only), 200 F, 250 F, 420 F.

Le Paris
(See restaurant above)
Closed Tue, Wed (except Sep and school holidays), Dec and Jan. 1 ste 450-500 F. 18 rms 280-500 F. TV 12 rms. Conference facilities.
Recently refurbished and intelligently decorated, Le Paris is comfortable, well equipped, and elegantly appointed. Excellent breakfasts.

ARCACHON

33120 Arcachon — (Gironde)
Paris 627 - Biarritz 183 - Bordeaux 60 - Dax 141

Aquamarina
82, bd de la Plage — 56.83.67.70
Open every day. 33 rms 240-520 F. TV. Conference facilities. Garage parking. Telex 570503. V AE DC.
This totally new hotel is located on the seaside *grand boulevard*; the sunny, discreetly decorated rooms are provided with terraces. Room service is available round the clock.

Arc-Hôtel
89, bd de la Plage — 56.83.06.85
Open every day. 3 stes 720-1,780 F. 30 rms 380-850 F. TV. Air cond 26 rms. No pets. Heated pool. Valet parking. Telex 571044. V AE DC.
Beach-resort charm fills this modern, well-maintained hotel. The rooms are luxurious and soundproofed, with terraces overlooking the sea or gardens. Sauna, Jacuzzi.

Grand Hôtel Richelieu
185, bd de la Plage — 56.83.16.50
Closed 3 Nov-15 March. 3 stes 900-1,060 F. 43 rms 250-570 F. TV. Conference facilities. Parking. Telex 540043. V AE DC.
Set in a pedestrian zone in the centre of town, this is a huge, old-fashioned hotel with small, tidy, soundproofed rooms, some with a view of the sea. The reception is courteous, but the service somewhat lacking. Direct beach access.

12/20 Le Miramar
37, bd du Gal-Leclerc — 56.83.33.84
M. Delhomme. Closed Mon off-season, and Jan. Terrace dining. V AE DC.
This brasserie sports a contemporary look, a comfortable terrace, and pretty pink table settings. The fresh, simple dishes available include excellent oysters, expertly seasoned steak tartare, and good gratin dauphinois, as well as a refreshing frozen grapefruit dessert. The choice of wines is limited but judicious.

A la carte: 160 F. Menus: 70 F (weekdays only), 90 F, 130 F.

12/20 L'Ombrière
79, cours Héricart-de-Thury — 56.83.42.52
M. Zorzabalbere. Closed Wed off-season. Open until 11 pm. Terrace dining. Telex 570503. V AE DC.
The large and lovely dining room is spotlessly clean, its décor suspended somewhere between classic and modern. The cuisine is good but rather costly. Stick with the fixed-price menu at 125 F: fish terrine with Champagne mousseline, lotte and salmon cheeks with puréed mushrooms and celery, assorted ice creams for dessert. Friendly, slightly fawning reception. Interesting wine cellar.

A la carte: 300 F. Menus: 125 F, 250 F.

Le Gascogne
(See restaurant above)
Open every day. 24 rms 130-294 F. Half-board 158-258 F oblig in seas. TV. Conference facilities.
Well-kept, comfortable rooms 200 metres from the beach.

Les Ormes
77, bd de la Plage — 56.83.09.27
Open every day. 30 rms 280-640 F. Restaurant. Half-board 380-515 F oblig in seas. TV. Conference facilities. Telex 570503. V AE DC.
Here is a pleasant, unassuming little hotel on the beach (direct access). The rooms are spacious and sunny, with individual terraces.

Le Patio
10, bd de la Plage — 56.83.02.72
M. Falgueirettes. Closed Tue off-season and Feb. Open until 10 pm (11 pm in summer). Private room: 18. Garden dining. V.
Good restaurants are hard to come by on the Bassin d'Arcachon and this one—with its cool and pleasant flower-filled garden—enjoys considerable success. Several dishes merit a toque: asparagus feuilleté with chive butter, vanilla ice cream with flambéed strawberries and green pepper. Others are less brilliant (the duck confit, for example). The service is a bit slow but the owner is irresistibly charming.

A la carte: 250-300 F.

Point France
1, rue Grenier — 56.83.46.74
Closed 15 Nov-15 Feb. 34 rms 250-590 F. TV. Air cond. Conference facilities. Garage parking. Telex 573049. V AE DC.
Point France is a well-designed contemporary hotel facing the beach. Some large rooms have superb bathrooms, and open onto a panoramic terrace that overlooks the Bassin d'Arcachon.

Les Vagues
9, bd de l'Océan — 56.83.03.75
Open every day. 30 rms 310-680 F. Restaurant. Half-board 389-557 F oblig in seas. TV. Air cond 4 rms. Conference facilities. Parking. V AE DC.
This recently built, many-tiered hotel sits astride the beach with its feet in the water. First-floor rooms boast wide terraces; those on the fourth a superb view of the beach through vast windows. The décor is fresh and modern, done in pastel tones, the welcome charming. Very good breakfasts. The restaurant is open to hotel guests only.

And also...
Our selection of inexpensive hotels, or places for quick, or late-night meals.
Le Dauphin (56.83.02.89 - 7, av. Gounod. 43 rms 200-350 F): Well equipped rooms, but rather banal décor, in a pleasant pavilion surrounded by a small

park in a residential neighbourhood. Minibar.
Le Nautic (56.83.01.48 - 20, bd de la Plage. 44 rms
180-380 F): Spacious, comfortable rooms near the
fishing port. Generous breakfasts.
Le Parc (56.83.10.58 - 5-7, av. du Parc. 30 rms
430-490 F): The modern, remodelled rooms are
sunny and face the Parc des Abatilles.
Chez Yvette (56.83.05.11 - 59, bd du Gal-Leclerc.
Open until 9.30 pm): A pleasant seafood brasserie
(oysters, shellfish, sea bream) with a terrace. Warm
welcome, but the service needs attention, and
prices are out of line.

In nearby Pyla-sur-Mer

(4 km SW on D 112)
33115 Arcachon — (Gironde)

La Corniche
in Pilat-Plage
46, av. L.-Gaume — 56.22.72.11
*Closed 23 Oct-23 March. 1 ste 450 F. 15 rms 140-
450 F. Restaurant. Half-board 250-430 F oblig in
seas. TV 9 rms. Air cond 1 rm. V.*
Situated at the foot of the dune de Pilat and facing
the beach, La Corniche has fifteen rooms with
wide balconies opening onto the sea. Tasteful,
comfortable décor.

12/20 La Guitoune
95, bd de l'Océan — 56.22.70.10
*M. Hères. Open every day. Open until 10 pm. Private
room: 50. Garden dining. No-smoking section. Hotel:
21 rms 180-450 F. Valet parking. V AE DC*
The dining room has been revamped but we still
prefer the shady terrace with a view of the Bassin
d'Arcachon. The cuisine isn't exactly audacious
but you can expect to eat fine, fresh seafood:
bouillabaisse, sea bass stuffed with grapes and
leeks, scallops au verjus.
A la carte: 320-350 F. Menus: 125 F, 175 F.

In nearby La Teste

(5 km S)
33260 Arcachon — (Gironde)

12/20 Chez Diego
Centre Captal — 56.54.44.32
*MM. Diego. Open every day. Open until 11 pm. Priv-
ate room: 100. Garden dining. Air cond. Parking. V
AE DC.*
Excellent mussels 'Don Diego', good Arcachon
oysters, and several Spanish specialities
(chipirons, paella) are served here in a colourful
Basque décor. Good île flottante. Only the fine
wine is missing.
A la carte: 200 F. Menu: 85 F (weekdays only).

11/20 Reste-à-Terre
Digue est — 56.54.60.10
*Mme Cameleyre. Closed Mon (except dinner in seas).
Open until 10 pm (midnight in summer). Private
room: 200. Terrace dining. Parking. V.*
The cuisine boasts some good seafood platters
and shellfish, but the desserts are muddled, and the
prices too high.
A la carte: 200-250 F.

ARCANGUES

See Biarritz

ARCINS

33460 Arcins — (Gironde)
Paris 560 - Bordeaux 28 - Margaux 6 - Pauillac 14

12/20 Le Lion d'Or
Pl. de la République — 56.58.96.79
*M. Barbier. Closed Sun dinner, Mon, 2-10 Jan and
July. Open until 9.30 pm. Private room: 14. Terrace
dining. AE.*
Médoc's most picturesque restaurant straddles
the *route des châteaux* between Beychevelle and
Margaux—Mecca for wine-lovers. The food is
famously good but straightforward, and much of
the charm of the place resides in the animated
wine growers who exchange bottles over the
tables. Seasonal dishes are the strong point: wild
duck, cèpes and chanterelles in the autumn, fresh,
roasted or marinated truffles, and jugged hare in
winter. Desserts include fabulous cannelés
bordelais (a sturdy local pastry).
A la carte: 180 F. Menu: 55 F (weekdays only,
wine inc).

ARCS (LES)

73700 Arcs (Les) — (Savoie)
Paris 674 - Bourg-Saint-Maurice 12 - Chambéry 113

Le Green
Arc 1800 — 79.07.25.17
*M. Bumerne. Closed 1 May-15 June and 1 Oct-
15 Dec. Open until 10 pm. Private room: 40. Terrace
dining. No-smoking section. No pets. Parking.
Telex 980404. V AE DC.*
Chef Yasuo Nanuami feels right at home at Les
Arcs, judging by his confident cuisine: moulds of
young rabbit, artichokes and bacon, delicate sea
bass suprême with tomato confit, veal filet mignon
au beaufort, and apricot parfait en feuillantine. We
only wish the décor were lighter and the service
more energetic.
A la carte: 350 F. Menus: 200 F and 350 F (dinner
only).

Hôtel du Golf
(See restaurant above)
*Closed 1 May-15 June and 1 Oct-15 Dec. 7 stes 1,200-
1,500 F. 270 rms 400-1,300 F. Half-board 398-739 F.
TV. Air cond. Conference facilities. Heated pool. Tennis. Golf.*
The reception is perhaps too brisk in winter but
always smiling, but the large rooms are pleasant
and comfortable. Breakfasts lack imagination. Exceptional sports facilities, fitness centre, disco, etc.

Les Trois Arcs
Les Arcs 1600 — 79.07.78.78
*Closed 9 May-27 June and end Sep-15 Dec. 8 stes
40 rms 2,443-4,746 F (per pers, half-board. oblig
weekdays). Restaurant. Air cond. Conference facilities. Tennis. Telex 980016. V.*
This is a modern and well-maintained hotel in the
centre of the resort, with a sunny terrace and a
superb view from the restaurant of Mont Blanc.

ARCS (LES)

83460 Arcs (Lcs) — (Var)
Paris 854 - Draguignan 10 - St-Raphaël 29

11/20 Le Logis du Guetteur
94.73.30.82
*M. Callegari. Closed Fri off-season, and 15 Nov-
15 Dec. Open until 9 pm. Private room: 20. Garden
dining. Parking. V AE DC.*
This old house perches high above a medieval
village, affording a lovely view of the Vallée de
l'Argens and the Massif des Maures. The cuisine is

rather overblown, but the ingredients are good ('rich' salads, salmon carpaccio, chicken legs with morels). The choice of game dishes is impressive (baby boar, venison, pigeon).
A la carte: 250-300 F. Menus: from 78 F to 250 F.

Le Logis du Guetteur 🏕🍽
(See restaurant above)
Closed Fri off-season, and 15 Nov-15 Dec. 10 rms 180-350 F. Half-board 285-355 F. TV. Conference facilities. Pool.
Ten spacious and pleasant rooms (four recently renovated) overlook the plain. Superb view. A swimming pool is under construction.

12/20 Restaurant de la Maison des Vins 🍃
N 7 – 94.47.48.47
M. Bœuf. Closed off-season Sun dinner and Mon. Open until 10 pm. Private room: 160. Garden dining. Parking. V AE.
The traditional gastronomy of the Var region sometimes needs a bit of shaking up. Chef Alain Bœuf is doing just that, by offering 'exotic' dishes such as salmon marinated with basil, seafood salad with saffron, and magret with a wine and grape sauce. The wine list boasts hundreds of different bottlings of Côtes-de-Provence, many at reasonable prices.
A la carte: 180-250 F. Menus: 69 F (weekdays lunch only), 110 F, 155 F, 168 F.

ARGEIN
See Saint-Girons

ARGELÈS-GAZOST

65400 Argelès-Gazost – (H.-Pyrénées)
Paris 812 - Cauterets 17 - Lourdes 13 - Tarbes 33

12/20 Auberge de l'Arrioutou 🍃
15 km SE on D 100
3 km avant Hautacam
65400 Beaucens – 62.97.11.32
Mme Poussy. Open w-e, holidays and school holidays only (open daily 1 July-15 Sep). Open until 9 pm. Terrace dining. Parking.
The view from this marvellous mountain *auberge* is splendid, the cuisine honest and generously served. The best bets are the savoury omelette paysanne, the mutton chops grilled over an open fire, the tasty cheeses, and the delicious crêpes. Unbeatable value for money.
Menus: 75 F, 80 F.

Hostellerie Le Relais
25, rue du Mal-Foch – 62.97.01.27
Mme Hourtal. Closed 10 Oct-1 Feb. Open until 9 pm. Private room: 30. Terrace dining. Hotel: 23 rms 120-230 F. Parking. V.
Jean Hourtal's cuisine is pleasant and satisfying. We could recite the entire menu but... just try the 150 F prix-fixe menu, itself worth the toque and the detour: duck foie gras, salmon steak in Jurançon wine, duck tournedos with black griotte cherries, followed by salad, and walnut fondant with chocolate sauce. The décor is rather austere, but the view takes in a majestic mountain landscape. The nice little Côtes-de-Gascogne at 33 F and Madiran Laplace at 50 F won't hike the bill to the summit.
A la carte: 200-230 F. Menus: 60 F (weekdays only), 85 F, 120 F, 150 F.

Hôtel du Lac d'Estaing 🍃
62.97.06.25
M. Houerie. Closed 11 Nov-1 May. Open until 9.30 pm. Parking.
This grand old hotel-restaurant facing a mountain lake sits some three kilometres from the nearest village, in total isolation. Owner Henri Houerie has kept it from becoming a tourist trap, and the cuisine, served on the large lakefront terrace or in the rustic country dining room, is authentic, full of character and generous. Henri's son Christian is the talented chef, trained at Martinez in Cannes and the Bistro de Paris. Try his savoury warm duck-liver salad with mild garlic, succulent paupiette of duck with foie gras in bilberry sauce, perfect vanilla and honey ice cream, and crème anglaise with strawberry coulis. Family-style welcome. Uninspired wine list.
A la carte: 200-250 F. Menus: 70 F (weekdays only), 130 F.

Hôtel du Lac d'Estaing 🏕🍽
(See restaurant above)
Closed 11 Nov-1 May. 11 rms 150-160 F (per pers, half-board oblig). Pets allowed.
Only two of the eleven modest but charming rooms are equipped with bathrooms. Minimal service.

Thermal 🏕🍽
5 km SE on D 13
in Beaucens-les-Bains – 62.97.04.21
Closed 1 Oct-1 June. 30 rms 150-250 F. Restaurant. Half-board 160-220 F. TV 1 rms. Heated pool. Parking. V.
The Thermal stands in the midst of an eight-hectare park and boasts attractive rooms (some studios with kitchenette), with a fine view of the Pyrenees. Thermal cures.

In nearby Saint-Savin
(3 km S on D 101)
65400 Argelès-Gazost – (H.-Pyrénées)

Viscos
62.97.02.28
M. Saint-Martin. Closed Mon (except school holidays) and 2-26 Dec. Open until 9.30 pm. Terrace dining. Hotel: 16 rms 195-205 F. Parking. V AE.
The modern décor with its bordeaux and rose details, and the flower-filled terrace overlooking the Lavedan, add to the spicy charms of Jean-Pierre Saint-Martin's cuisine. Taste the foie gras au caramel de Banyuls, monkfish en cocotte with diced ham, and panaché of pork and shrimps. Excellent regional wine list, reasonable prices.
A la carte: 220-270 F. Menus: 90 F, 130 F, 200 F.

ARGENTAN

61200 Argentan – (Orne)
Paris 195 - Alençon 45 - Caen 57

La Renaissance
20, av. de la 2e-D.-B. – 33.36.14.20
Mme Moulin. Closed Sun, 21 July-11 Aug and 22 Dec-3 Jan. Open until 9.15 pm. Private room: 45. Hotel: 15 rms 152-290 F. Valet parking. V AE DC.
In this version, the Renaissance is set in the suburbs, in a modern building with Louis XIV décor, and served to you by a rocker waiter. Thankfully, he is competent and attentive, and the setting is comfortable, despite the owner's cool reception. The perfectly fresh, well-prepared fish (turbot with artichoke hearts and sage mousseline) and outstanding desserts (coconut tart, pear and chocolate gâteau) earn La Renaissance an extra

toque this year.

A la carte: 300 F. Menus: 88 F (weekdays only), 145 F, 200 F.

19400 Argentat — (Corrèze)
Paris 510 - Brive 44 - Tulle 29 - Aurillac 54

10/20 Hôtel Fouillade

Pl. Gambetta — 55.28.10.17
M. Fouillade. Closed Mon off-season and 4 Nov-9 Dec. Open until 9.15 pm. Private room: 15. Garden dining. Hotel: 18 rms 100-180 F. Parking. V.

Rustic décor, rustic cuisine, but generous, too, and prepared family-style using good local ingredients. Taste the fricasséed frog's legs, the chanterelle croustade, and the sweetbreads à la limousine.

A la carte: 200 F. Menus: from 58 F to 140 F (weekdays only), and from 65 F to 140 F (w-e and holidays only).

Nouvel Hôtel Gilbert

13, av. J.-Vachal — 55.28.01.62
Closed Fri off-season, and 15 Dec-15 March. 2 stes 285 F. 25 rms 98-240 F. Restaurant. Conference facilities. Parking. V DC.

Fishermen favour this old, traditional inn, whose nicely appointed rooms have been attractively redecorated. Garden, playground.

See Paris Suburbs

74400 Argentière — (H.-Savoie)
Paris 627 - Annecy 103 - Chamonix 8 - Vallorcine 7,5

Les Becs Rouges

2 km NE on N 506 and VO 7
in Montroc-le-Planet — 50.54.01.00
Open every day. 24 rms 175-440 F. Restaurant. Half-board 296-350 F. Conference facilities. Parking. V AE DC.

The forest runs right up to this hotel, which boasts lovely views of the peaks of Chamonix, and soundproofed rooms with loggia. The clever *pension* system allows guests to take away cold lunches or to dine elsewhere with coupons. A shuttle transports guests from the station to the hotel.

Grands Montets

340, ch. des Arberons — 50.54.06.66
Closed 10 May-22 June and 22 Sep-21 Dec. 40 rms 340-520 F. Restaurant. Half-board 267-370 F oblig in seas. TV. Garage parking. V.

Located at the foot of the *téléphérique*, this attractive chalet has large rooms, with some duplexes for the entire family. Ski lessons, tennis, golf, horse-riding are offered. Very good breakfasts. The reception varies from chilly to warm.

13200 Arles — (B./Rhône)
Paris 727 - Marseille 92 - Avignon 40 - Nîmes 31

D'Arlatan

26, rue du Sauvage — 90.93.56.66
Open every day. 8 stes 720-1,250 F. 42 rms 395-610 F. TV 20 rms. Air cond 11 rms. Conference facilities. Telex 441203. V AE DC.

Near the place du Forum, this ancient townhouse groans with history (parts date from the fourth, twelfth, fifteenth, and seventeenth centuries). The rooms are charming and well appointed, with antique Provençal furniture. Garden. Bar.

L'Atrium

Les Lices, 1, rue E.-Fassin — 90.49.92.92
Open every day. 2 stes 980 F. 89 rms 385-580 F. Restaurant. TV. Air cond. Conference facilities. Heated pool. Garage parking. Telex 403903. V AE DC.

Within walking distance of the centre, this recently built hotel with spacious, nicely decorated and air-conditioned rooms, also boasts a rooftop terrace and sun lounge, and an outdoor swimming pool. Fun piano bar. Attentive service. Perfect for conferences or business meetings.

12/20 La Crédence

45, av. Sadi-Carnot — 90.99.40.40
M. Gourdy. Open every day. Open until 11 pm. Private room: 150. Garden dining. Air cond. Parking. Telex 403613. V AE DC.

The menu is short but sweet, and offers excellent value: scallops in saffron broth, duck with olives, îles flottantes. Considerate service. Pleasant summer veranda overlooking a swimming pool.

A la carte: 150-180 F. Menu: 95 F.

Hôtel Réginel

(See restaurant above)
Open every day. 4 stes 300-700 F. 67 rms 300-450 F. TV. Air cond. Conference facilities. Heated pool.

A modern hotel near the motorway, with well-equipped rooms and very professional service.

Grand Hôtel Nord-Pinus

Pl. du Forum — 90.93.44.44
Annual closings not available. 3 stes 1,500 F. 19 rms 650-850 F. TV. Air cond 6 rms. Conference facilities. Valet parking. V AE DC.

Wrought-iron details and Venetian candelabra flank handsome Provençal antiques in this gorgeous hotel, part of which is a listed historical monument. As the many bullfight posters suggest, this is a favourite haunt of matadors. Eclectic yet thoroughly inviting.

Lou Marquès

Bd des Lices — 90.93.43.20
M. Albagnac. Closed 4 Nov-21 Dec. Open until 9.30 pm. Private room: 100. Terrace dining. Air cond. Garage parking. Telex 400239. V AE DC.

The Albagnacs have poured heart, soul, and purse into the complete redecoration of their seventeenth-century, former Carmelite convent in the centre of Arles. The cuisine began its renaissance in 1988 with the arrival of 32-year-old chef Pascal Renaud. Perfect preparation and felicitously wedded flavours mark his fresh codfish with lentils à la crème, John Dory with sweet peppers and tiny squid in a sauce based on the latter's ink, and rib steak with garlic and pastis. Overall, the quality is excellent; we only hope the menu continues to evolve. Thankfully, the prices have slowed their rise after a stiff hike two years ago. The wine list, which features many half-bottles, is faultless. A vast array of whiskies, teas, and coffees has been added of late.

A la carte: 300-400 F. Menus: 185 F, 285 F, 350 F.

Jules César

(See restaurant above)
Closed 4 Nov-21 Dec. 3 stes 1,500-1,650 F. 52 rms 450-900 F. Half-board 543-1,058 F. TV 35 rms. Air cond 25 rms. Conference facilities. Heated pool.

Some fine pieces of Provençal furniture grace the huge, comfortable rooms of this former convent, which sits in a garden on the edge of the old town. Charming reception, service, and hospitality are provided in this Relais et Châteaux establishment.

Mas de la Chapelle
Petite route de Tarascon — 90.93.23.15
Closed off-season Sun and Mon, and Feb. 2 stes 460-660 F. 13 rms 360-460 F. Restaurant. Half-board 540-640 F oblig in seas. TV. Conference facilities. Pool. Tennis. Parking. V AE DC.

This is a charming old farmhouse hidden in a pretty park. The large, comfortable rooms attest to the generous 'tradition camarguaise', and the service and reception are excellent. The restaurant is housed in a sixteenth-century chapel.

Mireille
Quartier de Trinquetaille
2, pl. St-Pierre — 90.93.70.74
Closed 16 Nov-16 Feb. 34 rms 295-490 F. Restaurant. Half-board 299-390 F oblig in seas. TV. Air cond 16 rms. Pool. Valet parking. Telex 440308. V AE DC.

Fully remodelled, functional rooms (those in the annexe near the swimming pool are less grand), and an outstandingly warm welcome make Mireille a pleasant stopover. Dining tables are set up in the patio when the weather is fine. Nearby tennis courts are open to guests.

L'Olivier
1 bis, rue Réattu — 90.49.64.88
M. Cot. Closed Mon lunch, Sun and 1-15 Feb. Open until 9.30 pm. Private room: 25. Terrace dining. Air cond. No pets. V.

Olive branches abound in the rusticated décor and setting—flying buttresses, rough-hewn stones and a glassed-in courtyard—but the chef has made his peace with the ubiquitous fruit. His repertoire includes scallops served with sweet-and-sour carrots, lotte piccata perfumed with vanilla, and stuffed tournedos redolent of mushrooms. Excellent desserts. The rather shallow regional cellar is compensated for by a Cruover machine in good working order. Cheerful service.
A la carte: 320-380 F. Menus: 168 F, 238 F, 340 F.

Le Vaccarès
Pl. du Forum
entrée rue Favorin — 90.96.06.17
M. Dumas. Closed off-season Sun dinner and Mon, and 2-30 Jan. Open until 9.30 pm (10 pm in summer). Private room: 20. Terrace dining. V.

What better neighbour for this delightful restaurant than the quintessentially provincial open market of Arles? It spreads its colourful stands below the balcony of Le Vaccarès and helps fill Bernard Dumas's cuisine with sun and savour. Tradition reigns here, seasoned occasionally with a touch of Dumas's creative zest: red-mullet flan with anchovy butter, marinière de baudroie and gallinette au gingembre, fillet of freshwater perch with artichoke barigoule, medallions of rabbit with rosemary and caviar d'aubergine, and a traditional broufado (slices of highly seasoned marinated beef, an old seaman's recipe). Bottlings include many excellent Côtes-du-Rhône.
A la carte: 300 F. Menus: 160 F, 200 F, 280 F.

And also...
Our selection of inexpensive hotels.
Le Cloître (90.96.29.50 - 18, rue du Cloître. 33 rms 170-250 F): The few, modest rooms here give on the lovely cloister of St-Trophime's. Centrally located but quiet.
Le Montmajor (90.93.98.33 - 84, av. de Stalingrad. 20 rms 215-230 F): A simple, modern, comfortable hotel with good service, run by the owners of Le Rodin (see below).
Primotel-Camargue (90.93.98.80 - av. 1er-Div.-Française-Libre. 147 rms 325-365 F): This rather charmless and under-maintained modern building faces the convention centre, offering functional, soundproofed rooms and a nice outdoor swimming pool.
Le Rodin (90.49.69.10 - 20, rue A.-Rodin. 3 stes 580 F. 26 rms 290-340 F): A motel of recent vintage out of the centre city, each room here has a loggia overlooking the garden and pool (some with kitchenette).

In nearby Raphèle-lès-Arles
(7.5 km SE on N 453)
13280 Arles — (B./Rhône)

12/20 Auberge La Fenière
90.98.47.44
M. Legros. Dinner only Whitsuntide-1 Nov. Closed Sat lunch and 1 Nov-20 Dec. Open until 8.30 pm. Garage parking. Telex 441237. V AE EC.

The décor is rustic, but more in the 'gentleman farmer' than the 'earthy peasant' vein. The proprietress concocts hearty, generous fare for her guests: scallops with pistachios, salmon roulades à la crème, and veal chops in a tarragon-perfumed cream sauce.
A la carte: 200-250 F. Menus: 150 F, 220 F.

Auberge La Fenière
(See restaurant above)
Open every day. 1 ste 552 F. 24 rms 265-433 F. Half-board 285-434 F. TV. Conference facilities.

At the gates of Arles, the décor of this *auberge* is decidedly rustic, its rooms comfortable, outstandingly well kept and equipped.

ARLES-SUR-TECH
See Amélie-les-Bains

ARNAGE
See Mans (Le)

ARNAY-LE-DUC
21230 Arnay-le-Duc — (Côte-d'Or)
Paris 287 - Autun 28 - Dijon 57 - Beaune 34

Chez Camille
1, pl. E.-Herriot — 80.90.01.38
M. Poinsot. Open every day. Open until 9.30 pm. Valet parking. V AE DC.

Professional restaurateurs through and through, Armand and Monique Poinsot have wedded to their merry marriage the happy qualities of humour and good taste. Their Burgundian fief is festive, with a décor fit for an operetta, and superb service with a feminine touch. The cuisine is now under the able stewardship of Pierre Poinsot, who maintains tradition while adding seasonally appropriate innovations to the prix-fixe menus: snail rissoles with minced mushrooms, young rabbit gelée, ham in parsley aspic prepared with Aligoté wine, frog's legs, turban of eels with dill. Reasonably priced and well-designed wine list.
Menus: 122 F (weekdays only, wine inc), 295 F (weekdays only), 160 F, 220 F.

Red toques signify modern cuisine; black toques signify traditional cuisine.

Chez Camille
(See restaurant above)
Open every day. 2 stes 600-800 F. 14 rms 325-380 F. Half-board 460 F. TV. Conference facilities.
The excellent rooms over the restaurant are smartly appointed, with full facilities and modern equipment. Sauna. Outstanding service.

ARPAJON
91290 Arpajon — (Essonne)
Paris 33 - Etampes 19

Le Saint Clément
16, av. Hoche — 64.90.21.01
M. Faure. Closed dinner Sun and Mon, and 1-28 Aug. Open until 9.30 pm. Private room: 25. Air cond. Parking. V.
This impressive, neo-classical building with a spacious, sunny interior is imbued with the happiness of its owners. Their good life filters ever more sweetly into the savoury cuisine, which we have been monitoring for years now. Sample the salad of delicately cooked lobster, the fresh codfish panfried with precision and served in a light, fragrant sauce, the ethereal apple feuilletée in a suave crème anglaise. Not even the brawny selection of Bordeaux and Burgundies will weight down the bill.
A la carte: 350-400 F. Menu: 200 F.

ARRADON
See Vannes

ARRAS
62000 Arras — (P./Calais)
Paris 179 - St-Quentin 75 - Amiens 65 - Lille 51

L'Ambassadeur
Pl. Foch — 21.23.29.80
M. Chaveroche. Closed Sun dinner. Open until 9.45 pm. Private room: 80. Telex 133701. V AE DC.
Comfortable and sunny, this is one of the more streamlined 'railway station buffets' in France. The cuisine avoids the usual freight and offers simple dishes that are right on track: tiny herrings à la flamande, lotte in saffron cream, veal kidney with sweet pepper, and tasty desserts. But watch out or your bill will rise at TGV speed!
A la carte: 300 F. Menus: 110 F (weekdays only), 140 F, 180 F, 260 F.

11/20 L'Antoniolus
2, rue E.-Pottier — 21.51.66.99
M. Antoniazzi. Closed Sun. Open until 9.30 pm. Private room: 50. V.
A smartly decorated, rustic bistro with an inviting veranda. The cuisine makes up with freshness and generosity for what it lacks in imagination: seafood pot-au-feu, veal sweetbreads, Arras andouillette flavoured with juniper.
A la carte: 200 F. Menu: 59 F (weekdays lunch only).

Campanile
Zone d'emploi des Alouettes
62223 St-Nicolas — 21.55.56.30
Closed at Christmas. 39 rms 239 F. Restaurant. Half-board 336-359 F. TV. Conference facilities. Telex 133616. V DC.
Situated at the foot of the flyover, Campanile has simple, functional rooms.

La Faisanderie
45, Grand-Place — 21.48.20.76
M. Dargent. Closed Sun dinner, Mon and Feb school holidays. Open until 9 pm. V AE DC.
Jean-Pierre Dargent has spent lots of *argent* transforming the cellar of this old Grand-Place building into one of the most elegant restaurants in northern France. The marvellous vaulted ceiling and impressive stonework make a match for the superb service, the costly menu, and rich cuisine, which cater for the fortunate: silken asparagus with soft-boiled egg, grilled pigeon breasts with sorrel, lobster estouffade, calf's foot in potato skins with truffle jus. The ingredients are excellent and the preparation is often skilful and daring. Our only regret is the gradual elimination of regional specialities.
A la carte: 400-500 F. Menus: 155 F, 235 F, 335 F.

Inter Hôtel Moderne
1, bd Faidherbe — 21.23.39.57
Closed 24 Dec-2 Jan. 50 rms 190-300 F. TV. Telex 133701. V AE DC.
Located in the centre of Arras, near the railway station, this is a pleasantly modern hotel with comfortable, well-maintained rooms.

11/20 La Rapière
44, Grand-Place — 21.55.09.92
Mme Gœusse. Closed Sun dinner. Open until 9.30 pm. Private room: 28. Air cond. V AE DC.
Chateaubriand steak with Roquefort, veal chops with Camembert.... Meat and cheese marry in a tasty if weighty medley played out under the seventeenth-century vaults of this Grand-Place cellar restaurant.
A la carte: 220 F. Menus: 55 F, 89 F, 95 F, 130 F.

Univers
3, pl. de la Croix-Rouge — 21.71.34.01
Open every day. 3 stes 350 F. 34 rms 285-320 F. Restaurant. Half-board 400-450 F. TV 12 rms. Conference facilities. Garage parking. V AE
In the heart of town, the Univers has risen from the carefully restored ruins of a magnificent eighteenth-century monastery with an indoor garden and cloister. Charming and elegant, it is decorated and furnished with the utmost care. Luxurious rooms, fine salons, and a grand breakfast room.

ARSONVAL
See Bar-sur-Aube

ARTIGUELOUVE
See Pau

ARTZENHEIM
68320 Artzenheim — (Haut-Rhin)
Paris 460 - Sélestat 20 - Colmar 17 - Mulhouse 49

Auberge d'Artzenheim
30, rue du Sponeck — 89.71.60.51
M. Husser-Schmitt. Closed Mon dinner, Tue and 15 Feb-15 March. Open until 9 pm. Private room: 20. Terrace dining. Parking. V.
This pretty Ried *auberge* sits in the wide open countryside of the Rhine. The impeccable, rustic décor features massive open-timbering, and the country setting is pleasant and green. The classic cuisine is equally relaxing: fresh foie gras, fisherman's platter with baby vegetables, and fricasséed veal sweetbreads and kidneys with mustard.

A la carte: 300 F. Menus: 85 F (weekdays lunch only), 145 F, 195 F, 255 F.

▲▲ Auberge d'Artzenheim
(See restaurant above)
Closed Mon, Tue and 15 Feb-15 March. 10 rms 205-295 F. Half-board 195-255 F. No pets.
This is a nice stopover in the Ried, with a few handsomely furnished, pleasant rooms.

17530 Arvert — (Charente-M.)
Paris 510 - Marennes 13 - Royan 21 - La Rochelle 67

▲ Villa Fantaisie　▲♣
46.36.40.09
Closed 15 Jan-15 Feb. 23 rms 280-370 F. Restaurant. Half-board 300-360 F oblig in seas. TV 4 rms. Conference facilities. Garage parking. V AE.
On the edge of the Coubre forest, the bright, quiet rooms look over a leafy park near the sea.

56640 Arzon — (Morbihan)
Paris 485 - Vannes 28 - Muzillac 35 - Sarzeau 11

▲▲ Miramar　▲♣
Port du Crouesty — 97.67.68.00
Open every day. 12 stes 1,500-2,002 F. 108 rms 740-1,075 F. Restaurant. Half-board 940-1,485 F. TV. Conference facilities. Heated pool. Valet parking. Telex 951859. V AE DC.
The Miramar's long building resembles an ocean liner—funnels and all. The rooms are austere but very spacious and well equipped, with views of the sea. The glass-roofed swimming pool is on the 'upper bridge'; the Louison-Bobet *thalassothérapie* (sea cure) institute next door is connected directly to the hotel. Bar.

See CORSICA

See Paris Suburbs

See Bagnères-de-Bigorre

See Paris Suburbs

13400 Aubagne — (B./Rhône)
Paris 791 - Aix-en-P. 36 - Marseille 17 - Toulon 47

Les Fontaines des Creissauds
Le Clos Rufisque — 91.24.84.47
M. D'Agostino. Closed Mon and 10-21 Aug. Open until 10 pm. Private room: 80. Terrace dining. Parking. V AE DC.
Chef René Alloin, late of L'Oursinade in Marseille, is slowly but surely transforming Les Fontaines into a sparkling restaurant-club, with his short yet bubbly *carte* and prix-fixe menus: skate salad with citrus, lamb chops and brains pan-fried with mustard-seed juices, red mullet with thyme, and young rabbit à la tapenade. Excellent service, modest prices.
A la carte: 200-230 F. Menus: 140 F, 180 F.

▲▲ Hostellerie de la Source　▲♣
St-Pierre-les-Aubagne — 42.04.09.92
Open every day. 4 stes 900 F. 25 rms 300-700 F. Restaurant. Half-board 450-1,050 F. TV. Conference facilities. Pool. Tennis. Garage parking. V AE DC.
This seventeenth-century manor was restored inside and out three years ago and offers extremely well-equipped rooms with a discreet modern décor, a bar and salon. Leafy terrace and park.

Manon des Sources
Rte d'Eoures — 42.03.10.31
M. Farjon. Open every day. Open until 10 pm. Private room: 25. Garden dining. Parking. V AE DC.
As in the famous film *Manon des Sources*, good, life-giving things may well lurk below the surface. But for the time being, no toque for Philippe Lerouilly until he caps the prices, restocks the wine cellar, and teaches his staff to smile—the source of success.
A la carte: 300-350 F. Menus: 140 F (weekdays lunch only), 190 F, 350 F.

▲ Manon des Sources　▲♣
(See restaurant above)
Open every day. 5 stes 500 F. 17 rms 250-420 F. Half-board 430-680 F. TV. Conference facilities. Pool. Tennis.
The architecture makes for odd bedfellows when it comes to appointing the large rooms here, which give on a handsome park and pool. The welcome lacks warmth. Sauna, hairdresser, masseur.

10/20　Le Terroir Alsacien
40, av. des Goums — 42.84.90.55
M. Martin. Closed Tue dinner, Sun (except upon reserv.) and Aug. Open until 10 pm. No pets. V.
Meats and fish grilled on stones (*pierrades*), and sauerkraut with pork (in autumn and winter) are served in a chummy Alsatian atmosphere.
A la carte: 150-200 F. Menus: 50 F (weekdays lunch only, wine inc), 75 F, 130 F.

See Nyons

32000 Auch — (Gers)
Paris 716 - Toulouse 77 - Tarbes 72 - Agen 71

Daguin　۞
2, pl. de la Libération — 62.05.00.44
M. Daguin. Closed Sun dinner, Mon and 2-29 Jan. Open until 9.30 pm (10 pm in summer). Private room: 80. Air cond. Valet parking. Telex 520474. V AE DC.
To get mercurial chef André Daguin to stand still you'd have to sink him in goose fat and bottle him once and for all. Always an innovator, his latest move has been to create a regional culinary experimentation centre to make full and better use of local resources, especially the fibre, fat, and flesh of the sainted ducks and geese of Auch. Quackery?
Ducky duckery, more likely. Daguin's restaurant isn't exactly a feather-filled laboratory now, so don't get goose bumps. But he may attempt to feed you some odd concoctions indeed (rillettes of goose fat and shallots, bread made from cotton fibres). These might, someday, find their way onto the shelves of supermarkets. Someday.
Each time we visit he plies us with both nectarous novelties and alarming indigestibles. So be prepared. But goose grease notwithstanding, the

succulent specialities—magret, foie gras, chicken, guinea fowl, etc.—haven't slipped down the slope so far as quality is concerned. So loosen your garments and prepare for a Rabelaisian repast. This year we stuck with the classics, which were faultless: fresh goose and duck foie gras served with a glass of Jurançon; royal duo of magrets en coque de sel served with a lickerishly light goose-grease béarnaise; scrumptious desserts (spiced fruit assortment, saffron-tinctured crème paysanne, and a pistachio-chocolate confection).

Your eyes and tongue will roll with pleasure at the ambrosial wines of the South-west (among others, Daguin's reserve '87 Madiran). Lower-priced, tasty dishes are served at the Côté Jardin terrace or at the Neuvième bar.

A la carte: 500-650 F. Menus: 300 F (weekdays lunch only), 475 F.

Hôtel de France
(See restaurant above)
Open every day. 2 stes 1,300-2,400 F. 28 rms 285-1,100 F. Half-board 795-1,320 F. TV. Air cond 15 rms. Conference facilities.
This old family-run provincial hotel never ceases in its tasteful (if eclectic) transmogrifications towards modernity and comfort. This year a super-luxurious attic suite with sauna and breathtaking view has been added to the hotel's two deluxe suites (one with Jacuzzi). Other facilities include a boutique, regional products, a cookery school, and an eighteen-hole golf course (five kilometres from Auch). Relais et Châteaux.

12/20 Claude Laffitte
38, rue Dessoles — 62.05.04.18
M. Laffitte. Closed Sun dinner and Mon. Open until 10 pm. Private room: 15. Terrace dining. V AE DC.
Laffitte's picturesque boutique-restaurant is an institution of Gascon gastronomy. Try his gargantuan portions of goose magret, duck legs with Tarbais beans, pot-au-feu, and a local cabbage-based soup called garbure. A la carte prices are stiff, but the atmosphere is loose as a goose.
A la carte: 300-400 F. Menus: from 125 F to 350 F.

29770 Audierne — (Finistère)
Paris 588 - Quimper 35 - Pont-l'Abbé 32

Le Cornouaille
in front of the harbour — 98.70.09.13
Closed 25 Sep-1 July. 10 rms 160-300 F. No pets. Garage parking. AE.
Opposite the bustling port, this small hotel has well-maintained, pleasant rooms, and a beach annexe with five studios, all equipped with kitchenette and terrace.

Le Goyen
Pl. J.-Simon — 98.70.08.88
M. Bosser. Closed Mon off-season (except holidays), mid-Nov to mid-Dec and end Feb-beg March. Open until 9 pm. Private room: 25. Terrace dining. No pets. Telex 940422. V.
Close your eyes, count to three, and plunge into the briny splendours of Adolphe Bosser's maritime cuisine. An old salt with the heart of a tender youth, Bosser has been netting piscine perfection for nearly 40 years—he knows a fresh fish or a luscious lobster when he sees one. The ebb and flow of bracing dishes includes sea bass and salmon tartare with caviar, and prawns and lobsters poached in a clam bouillon seasoned with coral. Landlubber specialities are prepared with similar skill: agneau en croûte feuilletée aux girolles, flanked by a fabulous gratin of courgettes with white and black truffles, and an array of astonishingly dainty desserts. Add to Adolphe's culinary triumphs the charming welcome extended by his wife Yvonne Bosser, and the comfort of the grand dining room overlooking the port, and you will agree that Le Goyen has reached high tide.
A la carte: 350-600 F. Menus: 160 F (weekdays only), 165 F (in seas weekdays lunch only, wine inc), and from 210 F to 380 F.

Le Goyen
(See restaurant above)
Closed Mon off-season (except holidays), mid-Nov to mid-Dec and end Feb-beg March. 10 stes 450-1,300 F. 20 rms 270-405 F. Half-board 300-550 F oblig in seas. TV. Conference facilities.
A new and rather grand suite has been added to this solid old establishment above the fishing port, which is attractive without being hugely luxurious. Rooms have been redecorated 'à la provençale', and boast a pleasant view. Charming service, perfect breakfasts, gastronomical picnic baskets, bicycles for rides along the 'route des peintres'.

14250 Audrieu — (Calvados)
Paris 240 - Caen 17 - Bayeux 13 - Deauville 60

Château d'Audrieu
on D 158 — 31.80.21.52
M. Livry-Level. Closed Thu lunch, Wed and 20 Dec-31 Jan. Open until 9.30 pm. Private room: 50. No pets. Parking. Telex 171777. V.
Labours of love have restored this eighteenth-century château to its original splendour. Set in a pretty park dotted with ancient trees, this is Normandy at its best. The Livry-Level clan, nth-generation castle-keepers, have filled their charge with antiques and maintained the painted woodwork, the sculpted stone, and all the other authentic refinements. The dining room is among the most majestic in France. Happily, the smiling staff and vibrant cuisine keep solemnity on the far side of the moat. Chef Alain Cornet, disciple of Senderens, weds aesthetics to the taste of the soil and seasons: duck chaud-froid au pommeau, prawns in sauce vierge with semolina and raisins, lotte with paprika and cider, andouille Parmentier with quail eggs, farmhouse Normandy cheeses, and delicate desserts. Very fine cellar, but the prices are appalling.
A la carte: 400 F. Menus: 140 F (weekdays lunch only), 220 F, 480 F.

Château d'Audrieu
(See restaurant above)
Closed 20 Dec-31 Jan. 7 stes 1,550-1,800 F. 21 rms 450-1,050 F. Half-board 650-1,200 F. Conference facilities. Heated pool.
Seven beautiful suites, furnished with fine family heirlooms, and 21 elegantly appointed rooms grace this magnificent mansion swaddled in a manicured grounds. Golf fifteen kilometres away. Wednesday restaurant service for guests only. Relais et Châteaux.

See Paris Suburbs

AUMONT-AUBRAC

48130 Aumont-Aubrac — (Lozère)
Paris 535 - Espalion 58 - Mende 42 - Marvejols 23

Prouhèze

2, rte du Languedoc — 66.42.80.07
M. Prouhèze. Closed Sun dinner and Mon (except July-Aug), and 1 Nov-15 Feb. Open until 8.45 pm. Private room: 30. Terrace dining. Parking. V.

Chef Guy Prouhèze delves ever deeper into the rich culinary roots of his native Lozère. With astonishing skill, he uses the finest, freshest ingredients to produce dishes of a rare elegance such as gelée of mushrooms with smoked trout, wild morels stuffed with snails and napped with their juices, pot-au-feu de foie gras au bouillon with tiny vegetables, and banana terrine with orange marmalade. The only flaw here resides in the sometimes hasty presentation of dishes, and the heaviness of the atmosphere when the charming Catherine Prouhèze absents herself from the dining room.
Menus: from 135 F to 260 F, 480 F.

Prouhèze

(See restaurant above)
Closed Sun and Mon (except July-Aug), and 1 Nov-15 Feb. 29 rms 200-370 F. Half-board 260-310 F. TV 24 rms. Conference facilities.

The rooms are all comfortable, though unlike the smaller ones in front, the larger rooms at the back (with fine bathrooms) do not have a view of the Aubrac. Opulent breakfasts.

In nearby Fau-de-Peyre

(8 km W on D 10)
48130 Aumont-Aubrac — (Lozère)

Boucharinc-Tichit

(Del Faoû) — 66.31.11.00
Mme Tichit. Closed Sun dinner and 1-20 Jan. Open until 8.30 pm. Private room: 230. Terrace dining. Hotel: 14 rms 200 F. Parking. V DC.

This village bistro's rough-hewn charm is made all the more agreeable by the mouth-watering cuisine of Renée Boucharinc: charcuterie, corn-fed poultry, sturdy mutton tripe, and Aubrac mushrooms with creamy aligot (a garlicky cheese and potato purée). When the bill arrives even the weak of wallet may rejoice.
Menus: 50 F, 75 F, 95 F.

AURAY

56400 Auray — (Morbihan)
Paris 474 - Lorient 36 - Quimper 97 - Vannes 18

La Closerie de Kerdrain

14, rue L.-Billet — 97.56.61.27
M. Corfmat. Closed Tue off-season, and 5-30 Jan. Open until 9.30 pm. Private room: 30. Garden dining. Parking. V AE DC.

During our gastronomical tour of Brittany, we tasted the best scallops—served with wild mushrooms, basil and butter—in this stunning Renaissance mansion. Fernand Corfmat's bold repertoire features warm lobster salad with tomato vinaigrette, lightly cooked sea bass with an oyster béarnaise sauce, flanked by potato gratin with chestnuts, and an incredibly succulent seasonal feuillantine (strawberries, mangoes, and figs). The setting is regal, with eighteenth-century woodwork, an enormous fireplace, and tapestries. Excellent selection of Loire wines at reasonable prices.
A la carte: 300 F. Menus: 90 F (weekdays lunch only), 150 F, 200 F, 350 F.

La Sterne

La Petite-Forêt — 97.56.48.33
M. Claussen. Closed Mon (except July-Aug and hotels clients) and 2 Dec-1 Jan. Open until 9.30 pm. Private room: 60. Terrace dining. No pets. Parking. Telex 951025. V.

What the modern motel architecture lacks in charm, the stellar dining room amends with light, comfort, and warmth. The same may be said for the cooking: seafood gratin, grilled turbot with cabbage and leeks, noisettes of lamb cooked with rosemary, and a generous assortment of clever desserts. Outstanding fixed-price menus, judicious cellar. Friendly, efficient service.
A la carte: 260-300 F. Menus: 80 F and 105 F (weekdays only), 140 F, 220 F.

Hôtel du Loch

(See restaurant above)
Closed 24 Dec-1 Jan. 30 rms 225-260 F. Half-board 250-270 F. TV. No pets. Conference facilities.

The rooms are rather more comfortable than they are attractive (narrow bathrooms, poor soundproofing). Excellent breakfasts. Room service until midnight. Golf course nearby.

In nearby Baden

(9 km E on N 165 and D 101)
56870 Auray — (Morbihan)

12/20 Le Gavrinis

2 km E, in Toul-Broche — 97.57.00.82
M. Justum. Closed off-season Mon. Annual closings not available. Open until 9.30 pm. Private room: 40. Garden dining. Hotel: 19 rms 190-394 F. Parking. V AE DC.

Just minutes from the Baden golf course, this spacious, wood-panelled restaurant serves endearingly familiar dishes such as mackerel poached in Muscadet, croustille de ris d'agneau, red mullet with basil, and dark-chocolate succès. Adequate choice of wines, warm welcome.
A la carte: 210-260 F. Menus: from 126 F to 295 F.

In nearby Sainte-Anne-d'Auray

(6 km NE)
56100 Auray — (Morbihan)

L'Auberge

56, rue de Vannes — 97.57.61.55
M. Larvoir. Closed Tue dinner, Wed, 7-28 Jan and 7-21 Oct. Open until 9.30 pm. Private room: 20. Hotel: 7 rms 84-150 F. Parking. V.

This authentic Breton *auberge* straddles the St-Anne pilgrimage route. The chef's cuisine proves his ability and talent as a sauce-maker: spiced red-mullet feuillantine with mushrooms, lotte with smoked magret, and lobster ragoût à la tête de veau. Yummy desserts, a well-stocked cellar, and the charm of the *patronne* make this a good address.
Menus: 70 F and 115 F (weekdays only), and from 160 F to 270 F.

We are always interested to hear about your discoveries, and to receive your comments on ours. Please feel free to write to us, stating your opinions clearly.

87220 Aureil — (H.-Vienne)
Paris 386 - Saint-Léonard 10 - Limoges 12

Auberge du Bonheur

Gare d'Aureil — 55.00.28.19

M. Samit. Closed Sun dinner and Mon (except holidays), and 12 Aug-15 Sep. Open until 9.30 pm. Private room: 120. Garden dining. Valet parking. V AE DC.

Goodness springs eternal just a few kilometres from Limoges. Speeding down the route towards Eymoutiers you might easily miss this rustic inn, which friendly owners Roxane and Vincent Samit have carefully refurbished. That would be a shame. The fresh 'market cuisine' is worth a stop: snail chaussons with creamy garlic sauce, steamed salmon with a crab-flavoured coulis, lotte paupiette with a Champagne sauce. Fine wine cellar.

A la carte: 200-220 F. Menus: 120 F, 150 F, 250 F.

See Tarbes

06810 Auribeau-sur-Siagne — (Alpes-Mar.)
Paris 926 - Cannes 16 - Grasse 8 - Nice 45

11/20 La Vignette Haute

93.42.20.01

Mme Revel. Closed off-season Mon, 13 Feb-7 March and 12-29 Nov. Open until 10 pm. Garden dining. Air cond. Hotel: 7 rms 375-900 F. Pool. Parking. V AE.

La Vignette is a rustico-luxurious fortified mansion filled with antiques, where diners consume Rabelaisian repasts in a relaxed, candle-light atmosphere. The performance is uneven, however, with some outstanding dishes (tapenade) flanked by flops (mediocre charcuterie, overcooked filet de bœuf). Sprightly service.

Menus: from 220 F to 300 F (weekdays lunch only, wine inc), from 290 F to 400 F (dinner only, wine inc).

31420 Aurignac — (H.-Garonne)
Paris 780 - Toulouse 64 - St-Gaudens 35

Le Cerf Blanc

Rue St-Michel — 61.98.95.76

M. Picard. Closed Mon. Open until 9.30 pm. Private room: 15. Terrace dining. Air cond. Parking. V.

Local food-loving regulars and summer tourists on the Cro-Magnon cave circuit crowd the Cerf Blanc, clamouring for chef Dominique Picard's highly personal, and seasonal, inventive cuisine. A game specialist much respected by his peers, Picard is also a sauce master. Witness the cèpes mousse with scallops and port cream, salmon au Jurançon, and duck escalope with rhubarb. And for dessert, the moreish gâteau opéra. The fine cellar holds some reasonably priced Bordeaux. An extra point this year.

A la carte: 320 F. Menus: 78 F, 156 F, 216 F, 320 F.

Le Cerf Blanc

(See restaurant above)

Closed Mon. 11 rms 120-240 F. Half-board 300-350 F. TV. Conference facilities.

Eleven rather dull, but modern and comfortable rooms.

15000 Aurillac — (Cantal)
Paris 546 - Brive 98 - Clermont-Ferrand 160

Delcher

20, rue des Carmes — 71.48.01.69

Closed Sun, 15 June-1 July and 23-30 Dec. 23 rms 170-230 F. Restaurant. Half-board 175-215 F. TV. Conference facilities. Garage parking. V AE.

All of the 23 smallish rooms of this centrally located hotel have been renovated and soundproofed.

Grand Hôtel de Bordeaux

2, av. de la République
71.48.01.84

Closed 20 Dec-10 Jan. 2 stes 480-580 F. 35 rms 260-392 F. TV. Conference facilities. Garage parking. Telex 990316. V AE DC.

The Grand Hôtel's big white building rises in the city centre near the law courts, just opposite the public gardens. Pleasant, well-kept rooms. Bar, evening meal service.

12/20 Le Pommier d'Amour

Promenade du Gravier
71.48.00.24

Mme Lavergne. Open every day. Open until 10 pm. Private room: 90. Garage parking. Telex 393160. V AE DC.

The chefs change here on a mad merry-go-round, but the cuisine, thanks to the vigilant proprietor, keeps on an even keel: pigeon aux saveurs de Cantal, blanc de volaille au gingembre, pomme soufflée. Art deco setting, appealing and affordable wines.

A la carte: 250 F. Menus: 77 F (weekdays only), 95 F, 180 F.

Grand Hôtel Saint-Pierre

(See restaurant above)

Open every day. 29 rms 200-350 F. TV. Conference facilities.

Ideally situated in the centre of town, the rooms here are comfortable, decorated with restraint, and very well equipped. Free shuttle to the railway station or airport.

11/20 A la Reine Margot

19, rue G.-de-Veyre — 71.48.26.46

M. Dagiral. Closed Mon (except July-Aug). Open until 9 pm. Private room: 40. Terrace dining. Air cond. V.

It's elbow-to-elbow in this old-fashioned, jovial eating house where the robust regional cuisine is simple and good: trout with bacon, fritons, confits, cassoulet.

A la carte: 220-250 F. Menus: 85 F, 165 F, 250 F.

And also...

Our selection of inexpensive hotels.

La Ferraudie (71.48.72.42 - 15, rue de Bel-Air. 22 rms 220-300 F): This small hotel of recent vintage offers good rooms with no surprises, near the Hélitas sports park.

Relax-Hôtel (71.63.60.00 - 113, av. du Gal-Leclerc. 28 rms 195-280 F): Set in green grounds on the outskirts of town; the rooms here are perfectly acceptable.

La Thomasse (71.48.26.47 - rue du Dr-Mallet. 1 ste 400-480 F. 21 rms 290-320 F: A good, functional hotel set in a quiet park above Aurillac, with freshly redecorated rooms. Golf. Bar. Only dinner is served in the restaurant.

06660 Auron — (Alpes-Mar.)
Paris 814 - Nice 97 - Barcelonnette 65

Las Donnas
Grande-Place — 93.23.00.03
*Closed 10 April-30 June and 25 Aug-19 Dec. 48 rms
175-320 F (per pers, half-board oblig). Restaurant.
TV 20 rms. No pets. Conference facilities.
Telex 470300. V.*
The best rooms of this traditional Southern hotel,
set in the centre of the resort, boast pretty terraces.

71400 Autun — (Saône/Loire)
Paris 300 - Dijon 86 - Chalon-sur-Saône 53

Le Chalet Bleu
3, rue Jeannin — 85.86.27.30
*M. Bouché. Closed Mon dinner, Tue and Feb. Open
until 9.30 pm. Private room: 40. V AE DC.*
If ever a façade was misleading, this is it. Behind
the horribly drab exterior you'll find an exuberant
green-white-and-beige dining room, and young
chef Philippe Boucheé's creative—if uneven—cuisine. Late of La Ferme Saint-Simon in Paris, Bouché
impressed us with his persillé de langoustines and
ris d'agneau aux zestes de citron, as well as with
his dreamy desserts. Unbeatable value for money.
The wine list is very short, and shy on Bordeaux.
A la carte: 180 F. Menus: 75 F (weekdays only),
110 F, 140 F, 180 F.

Saint-Louis
6, rue de l'Arbalète — 85.52.21.03
*Closed 20 Dec-28 Jan. 1 ste 435 F. 51 rms 100-320 F.
Restaurant. Half-board 185-383 F. TV 44 rms. Conference facilities. Parking. Telex 801262. V AE DC.*
This seventeenth-century coaching inn is the
archetypal old-fashioned French hostelry; it is well
maintained and spruced up regularly. Flower-filled
patio.

Les Ursulines
14, rue Rivault — 85.52.68.00
*M. Grellet. Open every day. Open until 9.30 pm. Gar-
age parking. V AE DC.*
Red velvet upholstery graces the handsome dining room of this former convent, set in a courtyard
with views of the plain and mountains. A promising new chef has been hired, and is currently
fine-tuning his repertoire. The fresh foie gras was
perfectly cooked, refined and flavourful; the snail
and salmon brochette with curry sauce was somewhat insipid. Superb selection of cheeses; far-ranging cellar. The service is friendly and efficient.
A la carte: 250-300 F. Menus: 140 F, 220 F.

Les Ursulines
(See restaurant above)
*Open every day. 5 stes 430-510 F. 32 rms 300-390 F.
Half-board 380-460 F. TV. Conference facilities.*
Eight of the gaily decorated rooms were
remodelled recently; all are thoughtfully equipped. The supremely quiet setting of this former
convent boasts a fine view of the countryside and
the mountains of the Morvan.

*The prices quoted in this guide are those which
we were given by the restaurants and hotels
concerned. Increases in prices are beyond our
control.*

08260 Auvillers-les-Forges — (Ardennes)
Paris 210 - Laon 70 - Charleville-Mézières 30

Hostellerie Lenoir
Grande-Rue — 24.54.30.11
*M. Lenoir. Closed Fri and 2 Jan-1 March. Open until
9 pm. Private room: 40. Parking. V AE DC.*
Second-generation, 35-year kitchen veterans,
chefs Jean Lenoir and his elder sister Ginette are
perhaps France's fiercest defenders of *la grande
cuisine à l'ancienne*. Their holistic approach to
running a restaurant is akin to a veritable eco-sys-
tem, embracing gastronomy, atmosphere, décor,
reception, service, and wine. And what joy! Jean
and Ginette's cookery is extremely rigorous and
reliable—and absolutely immutable: pigeon
mousse with foie gras, surprise de poissons with
fennel, lobster with asparagus cream, noisettes of
lamb with morels, Périgord truffle sabayon,
poularde au champagne.... Over the years,
sommelier Claude Delaive has amassed an astonishing cellar.
A la carte: 400-500 F. Menus: 220 F and 310 F
(wine inc), 330 F, 410 F.

Hostellerie Lenoir
(See restaurant above)
*Closed Fri and 2 Jan-1 March. 3 stes 390 F. 21 rms
150-320 F. Half-board 265-420 F. Conference facilities.*
The 3 suites and 21 rooms of this rustic yet
luxurious hostelry have been redecorated recently
in fine taste. The hosts' warm welcome, delicious
breakfasts, and quintessentially quiet atmosphere
all year round make this an ideal spot for a weekend
in the country.

89000 Auxerre — (Yonne)
Paris 174 - Dijon 148 - Nevers 112 - Troyes 79

Jean-Luc Barnabet
14, quai de la République — 86.51.68.88
*M. Barnabet. Closed Sun dinner, Mon and 23 Dec-
6 Jan. Open until 9.30 pm. Private room: 50. Garden
dining. Parking. V.*
Jean-Luc and Marie Barnabet, late of La Petite
Auberge in Vaux, joined forces with their maître
d'hôtel and moved recently into this charming
seventeenth-century post house in the heart of old
Auxerre. Jean-Luc's cuisine is of a classic cast, but
extremely precise and professional. With just a
touch more depth of flavour, his artichoke
bottoms with rabbit gelée, the lamb's tongue with
potatoes dressed with vinaigrette, the sea bass
with salmon roe, and the roasted veal kidney
would be perfect. The young sommelier learned
his trade with Loiseau and has stockpiled quite a
cache of Burgundies.
A la carte: 350 F. Menus: 300 F (wine inc), 160 F,
230 F.

Le Jardin Gourmand
56, bd Vauban — 86.51.53.52
*M. Boussereau. Closed Mon (except July-Aug), and
2-30 Dec. Open until 9.30 pm. Private room: 30. Terrace dining. Telex 800997. V.*
How now! Something new is cooking *chez* Pierre
Boussereau. Last year he refitted the winter garden, the flower-filled summer terrace, and the
gracious, intimate dining rooms with their pretty
contemporary pictures. Now he's spent one million francs on a new kitchen, and opened a catering
service and wine bar (at the nearby pleasure-boat-
ing harbour). Fear not, Pierre is still first and
foremost a grand chef, not a business tycoon. His

epicurean cuisine features cuttlefish soup, red-mullet and aubergine millefeuille, fillet of freshwater perch with horseradish, young pigeon with cabbage, cider and apples, veal shin pot-au-feu (with some of the finest vegetables in France!), and a breathtaking raspberry brioche with glacéed fruit. Bogglingly impressive cellar, overflowing with Chablis.

A la carte: 450-500 F. Menus: 120 F, 170 F, 250 F and 320 F (except holidays).

Normandie

41, bd Vauban — 86.52.57.80
Open every day. 47 rms 210-290 F. TV. Conference facilities. Garage parking. V AE DC.

Located on the edge of central Auxerre, Normandie is a handsome dwelling with a small garden-terrace and pleasant, well-equipped rooms. Sauna.

Parc des Maréchaux

6, av. Foch — 86.51.43.77
Open every day. 25 rms 230-350 F. TV. Conference facilities. Garage parking. Telex 800997. V AE.

Near the centre of town, this is an old house with elegant, constantly refurbished rooms, some of which give onto a pretty park.

La Salamandre

84, rue de Paris — 86.52.87.87
M. Colas. Closed Sun dinner and 22 Dec-6 Jan. Open until 10 pm. Air cond. V AE.

Serge Colas's classic (not hugely original) cuisine shows great respect for fine ingredients and boasts the best fish dishes in town. A toque this year for the charlotte of smoked fish on a bed of delicious potato salad, succulent choucroute topped with fish, saumon à la nage. Fine, fresh oysters; attentive, friendly service.

A la carte: 300 F. Menus: 98 F (weekdays only), 138 F, 178 F, 218 F.

And also...

Our selection of inexpensive places to eat or to stay.

Les Clairions (86.46.85.64 - av. de Worms. 62 rms 235-285 F): Two kilometres out of town, near the A 6 motorway to Paris; rather barren setting, but modern, pleasant rooms.
Le Maxime (86.52.04.41 - 3-5, quai de la Marine. Open until 9.30 pm): An old-fashioned restaurant-hotel serving classic cuisine (truffled foie gras, tournedos with grapes) at very stiff prices (200 F).
Le Maxime (86.52.14.19 - 2, quai de la Marine. 25 rms 340-520 F): Rustic hotel rooms on the banks of the Yonne, near the cathedral.
La Primavera (86.51.46.36 - 37, rue du Pont. Open until 10.30 pm): Good pizza and Greek specialities are served in this modest, summery restaurant (150 F).
Le Trou Poinchy (86.52.04.48 - 34-36, bd Vaulabelle. Open until 10.30 pm): Freshly redecorated, this former *pension* serves simple, tasty home cooking (200 F).

The new spiral-bound RAC Atlas France will help you to find your chosen restaurant of hotel, no matter how secluded.

(8 km SW on N 151 and D 1)
89240 Auxerre — (Yonne)

La Chamaille

in La Barbotière
4, rte de Boiloup — 86.41.24.80
M. Siri. Closed Mon, Tue, 2 Jan-1 Feb, 4-11 Sep and Christmas week. Open until 9.15 pm. Air cond. Parking. V AE DC.

Picturesque, bucolic, painterly: the lush green setting, complete with babbling brook by the dining room, makes for utter relaxation. Chef Pierre Siri's cuisine is a celebration of succulent specialities, created with impeccable ingredients whose quality and flavour are underscored, not masked. Try the marinated salmon with cucumber vinaigrette, sole feuilleté with sorrel, pigeon pithiviers prepared with a winy fish stock, and the madeleine baked with orange sugar. Peerless presentation.

A la carte: 300-330 F. Menus: 136 F (except holidays), 240 F.

(4 km N on N 77 and D 84)
89470 Auxerre — (Yonne)

Campanile

Rue d'Athènes — 86.40.71.11
Open every day. 78 rms 239 F. Restaurant. TV. Conference facilities. Parking. Telex 352711. V.

In the countryside just 100 metres off the A 6 motorway, the Campanile's rooms are functional and comfortable.

Monte-Cristo

7a, rue Sommeville — 86.40.77.49
M. Waggoner. Closed Sun dinner, Mon, 15 Dec-15 Jan and 8-15 May. Open until 9.30 pm. Private room: 25. Parking. V AE.

The Count of Monte Cristo would doubtless feel rather out of place in this 1920s pavilion with its décor of brick and wrought iron, chosen by chef-owner Bob Waggoner. But we like it all the same. Late of La Poste in Avallon, Waggoner's refreshingly innovative cuisine has been rolling right along: taste his bracing salad of squid and mackerel with beetroot chips, or braised pike with lentils and bacon, or the delicious lamb noisettes and hot goat cheese served atop a bed of potatoes. All that is lacking now is a decent cellar and an organised staff.

A la carte: 300-350 F. Menus: 110 F (weekdays lunch only), 150 F, 240 F.

89200 Avallon — (Yonne)
Paris 234 - Troyes 103 - Dijon 101 - Auxerre 52

Moulin des Ruats

3.5 km on D 427
Vallée du Cousin — 86.34.07.14
Mme Bobin. Closed off-season Tue lunch and Mon, 19 Nov-19 Dec and 7 Jan-12 Feb. Open until 9 pm. Terrace dining. Parking. V DC.

We used to lament that the cuisine wasn't worthy of the spectacular setting. Now we're tempted to state the reverse. Much money was spent redecorating, but the results (a modern, pink-hued dining room and rustic guest rooms) haven't a whit of charm, gaiety, or elegance! No matter. If you plan to visit the Moulin in fine weather, book a table on the shady terrace, where your ears will be intoxicated by the chirping birds and babbling brook, while your other senses are swept skyward by Gérard Fillaire's up-to-date, original, and savoury cuisine. Sample, for example, the sweetbread salad with hazelnuts, or the hot partridge tourte, dainty fricasséed snails in mushroom soup, and an exceptional dish of salt cod napped with meat juices. For dessert, we recommend you plump for the ginger-perfumed banana tart. Laudable efforts are being made to improve the cellar.

A la carte: 400-450 F. Menus: 150 F (weekdays lunch only), 180 F (weekdays lunch only, wine inc), 220 F, 320 F.

 ### Moulin des Ruats ♠🌲
(See restaurant above)
Closed Mon off-season, 19 Nov-19 Dec and 7 Jan-12 Feb. 1 ste 850 F. 27 rms 280-580 F. Half-board 395-680 F. TV 5 rms. Conference facilities.

On the banks of the enchanting Cousin River, this former mill-house boasts comfortable, rustico-modern rooms which have just been redone (in dubious taste). Terrific terrace on the river. Good breakfasts; uneven service.

 ### La Poste
Pl. Vauban — 86.34.06.12
Closed 30 Nov-15 Feb. 5 stes 650-900 F. 23 rms 150-900 F. Restaurant. TV. Conference facilities. Garage parking. Telex 351806. V DC.

A deluxe stop-over spot since 1707, La Poste is on a slow but sweet decline. Its comfortable rooms give onto a pretty garden, but are decorated with a rather heavy hand.

 ### Le Relais Fleuri
Avallon exit on motorway
in La Cerce — 86.34.02.85
Open every day. 48 rms 300-390 F. TV. Restaurant. Conference facilities. Heated pool. Tennis.

A very fine, cosy coaching inn, with perfectly equipped rooms (ask for those in the rear, near the field). The swimming pool has a sun lounge, and there are tennis courts.

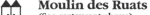
In nearby **Pontaubert**

(5 km W on D 957)
89200 Avallon — (Yonne)

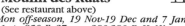 ### Château de Vault-de-Lugny ♠🌲
86.34.07.86
Closed 18 Nov-21 March. 11 rms 650-2,000 F. Restaurant. Half-board 440-1,180 F. TV. Conference facilities. Tennis. Garage parking. V.

This noble, luxurious château sits in a fifteen-hectare park traversed by a river. Rooms and suites are furnished and decorated with refinement, and boast dreamy bathrooms. Horse-riding, fishing. Restaurant for guests only.

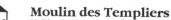 ### Moulin des Templiers ♠🌲
Vallée du Cousin — 86.34.10.80
Closed 31 Oct-15 March. 14 rms 210-320 F. Parking.

On the water's edge, this old mill boasts exquisite rooms, some rather small, but all very comfortable and quiet. Breakfast is served on a delightful terrace.

See also: Saulieu, Vézelay

59440 Avesnes-sur-Helpe — (Nord)
Paris 213 - St-Quentin 66 - Maubeuge 18

 ### La Bretagne en Avesnois
(Le Carillon)
12, pl. Leclerc — 27.61.17.80
M. Lohezic. Closed Sun dinner, Mon and Feb. Open until 9.30 pm. Private room: 35. Air cond. V.

Michel Lohezic has brought a bit of his grandmother's Brittany to 'Little Switzerland', here in the North, where he caters for a mostly Belgian clientele. The recipes and shellfish come from Brittany, as do the little Breton dolls that decorate the otherwise rather sombre dining room. But Lohezic's cuisine also incorporates original—often delicious—dishes, such as crab bisque armoricaine, scallops with black chanterelles, boned and stuffed chicken jambonnette cooked in cider, and veal sweetbreads with fresh foie gras. He has passed on his gift for inventiveness to his daughter Sandrine, who creates some surprising desserts (beer sorbet!). The prices are very reasonable, the wine list rather brief.

A la carte: 260-330 F. Menus: 68 F (weekdays only), 98 F, 148 F, 198 F, 298 F.

La Crémaillère
26, Grand-Place — 27.61.02.30
M. Lelaurain. Closed Mon dinner and Tue. Open until 9 pm. Private room: 45. V AE DC.

Jean-Louis Lelaurain and his son run this friendly rustic *auberge* on the main square, catering for Belgian families (at weekends) and businessmen. The faithful flock here for the 'bouribout'—Picardie duck which is first roasted in the oven, then braised in a flavourful vegetable mirepoix with herbes de Provence. The menu seems rather stuck on tradition of late, and we wonder if these skilful pros are running short on inspiration. But the wine list is long and offers many good deals. Reception and service of a rare warmth!

A la carte: 280 F. Menus: 110 F (weekdays only, wine inc), 280 F (w-e and holidays only, wine inc), 150 F and 230 F.

84000 Avignon — (Vaucluse)
Paris 701 - Valence 128 - Aix 75 - Marseille 100

12/20 L'Arbre à Cannelle
40, bd St-Roch — 90.86.07.71
M. Gabet. Closed Sun dinner. Open until 10 pm. Garden dining. Air cond. V. C6-27

Nostalgia beats its little wings on the shady terrace of this restaurant near the railway station, and you might prefer a cheery table inside instead. The *carte* features scrumptious salmon with morels and seaweed, a perfectly seasoned chicken gigotin (a boned, stuffed leg that looks like a little 'gigot d'agneau'), and alas, a disappointing entremets des îles. Concise wine list with classic bottlings at low prices; charming service.

A la carte: 270 F. Menus: 87 F (lunch only), 180 F.

 ### Brunel
46, rue de la Balance — 90.85.24.83
MM. Brunel. Closed Mon (Jan-Aug), Sun, 1-10 May and 4-20 Aug. Open until 9.15 pm. Private room: 20. Terrace dining. Air cond. Telex 431938. V AE. C3-24

Brunel's location (in a cul-de-sac) ensures that only informed gastronomes and guests at the nearby Mercure hotel enliven the dining room. Locals may love the peace; but a fine line separates 'peaceful' from 'morose'. And chef Robert Brunel's cuisine—intelligent, precise, full of bright, keen

1 - Les Trois Clefs **R**
2 - Mercure **H**
3 - Le Grangousier **R**
4 - Inter Hôtel
du Midi **H**
5 - Xuan **R**
6 - Les Domaines **R**
7 - Hôtel
de Garlande **H**
8 - Le Petit Bedon **R**
9 - Hôtel du Lavarin **H**
10 - Danieli **H**
11 - Notre-Dame **R**
12 - La Vieille Fontaine
(Hôtel d'Europe) **RH**
13 - Café des Artistes **R**
14 - Hiély-Lucullus **R**
15 - Le Saint-Pierre **R**
16 - Christian Etienne **R**
17 - Bristol **H**
18 - Novotel **H**
19 - Cité des Papes **H**
20 - Mercure
Palais des Papes **H**
21 - Primotel Horloge **H**
22 - Novotel
Avignon-Nord **H**
23 - Entrée
des Artistes **R**
24 - Brunel **R**
25 - Hôtel Mignon **H**
26 - Le Jardin
de la Tour **R**
27 - L'Arbre à Cannelle **R**
28 - L'Isle Sonnante **R**
29 - Hôtel Médiéval **H**
30 - Hôtel de la Mirande **RH**

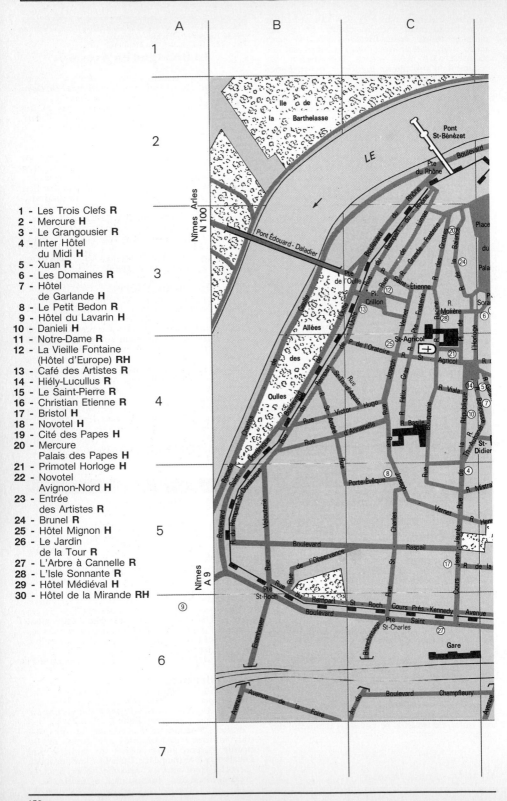

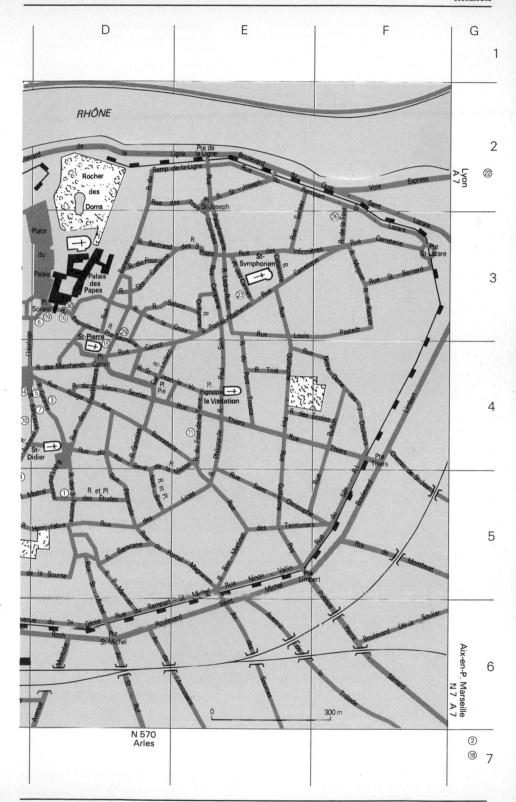

flavours—deserves a proper setting. This should be the most successful restaurant in Avignon. Yet the stoical Brunel seems content to please the 'happy few' with his perfect produce, tasty sauces, and regional specialities spiced with appealing accents: vegetable compote with tapenade, fresh spiced cod, noisettes of lamb with lamb's trotters and artichokes à la barigoule, tiny snails in aniseed-perfumed butter, and divine desserts (what a chocolate feuilleté!) created by sous-chef Roger Hennequin. Superb Côtes-du-Rhône, fine service.
A la carte: 350-400 F. Menus: 150 F (lunch only), 250 F, 330 F.

Cité des Papes
1, rue J.-Vilar — 90.86.22.45
Closed 10 Oct-20 Dec. 65 rms 260-440 F. TV. Air cond. Telex 432734. V AE DC.   D3-19
Situated near the Palais des Papes, this hotel boasts large, comfortable, air-conditioned rooms in a big modern building.

Danieli
17, rue de la République — 90.86.46.82
Open daily. 29 rms 350-370 F. TV. V AE DC.   C4-10
A solid nineteenth-century bourgeois building just a few minutes from the Place de l'Horloge, the Danieli boasts rooms and bathrooms that are pleasantly decorated and well equipped. The reception sometimes borders on the uncivil.

Les Domaines
(ex-Auberge de France)
28, pl. de l'Horloge — 90.82.58.86
M. Tassan. Open every day. Open until 11 pm. Private room: 60. Terrace dining. Air cond. V.   D3-6
The Tassan brothers trio run this anthracite-and-white brasserie in the heart of old Avignon with great aplomb. Frédéric's winning cuisine is simple and generous and perfectly suited to the surroundings, featuring fresh salads, tasty grilled meats, and a mouth-watering andouillette served in sauce charcutière. Finish off with a nectarous nougat glacé with candied fruit. Christophe's cellar brims with Côtes-du-Rhône and Côtes de Provence, with several wines available by the glass. François provides the charming reception and service.
A la carte: 200 F.

Christian Etienne   ○
10-12, rue de Mons — 90.86.16.50
M. Etienne. Closed Sun dinner and Mon. Open until 9.30 pm. Private room: 25. Garden dining. Air cond. V AE DC.   D3-16
Christian Etienne, installed in the former residence of the town bailiff, boasts incontestably the best location in Avignon, facing the Palais des Papes, with a peerless panorama of the eponymous *place*. The bright yellow shutters attracted considerable flak a few years ago, but they have mellowed with time. The flower-filled dining rooms, done in lavender tones, juxtapose delicate, painted woodwork with stern, black metal furniture. Here, and on the splendid terrace, you will savour Christian Etienne's imaginative cuisine, which underscores the flavour of local specialities and first-quality produce: tempting tunny fish millefeuille with aubergines in a garlicky cream sauce, succulent grilled red mullet with tender potatoes heightened with anchovy, a deceptively simple dish of pigeon cooked in fennel bouillon, followed by a superior cheese board and dreamy desserts. Excellent wine cellar, professional and friendly service. An extra point this year!
A la carte: 400-500 F. Menus: 250 F, 400 F.

Hôtel de Garlande
20, rue Galante — 90.85.08.85
Open every day. 12 rms 180-340 F. TV 10 rms. V AE DC.   D4-7
This charming little hotel occupies a well-restored, handsome old house in the centre of town. All rooms have been carefully redecorated. Good bathrooms.

Le Grangousier
17, rue Galante — 90.82.96.60
M. Buisson. Closed Sun and 23 Dec-3 Jan. Open until 10 pm. Private room: 8. V.   D4-3
Chef Philippe Buisson, late of Florentin, recently moved into this singular setting in an old cobbled courtyard under a tall glass roof, near the Place de l'Horloge. The décor has been freshened and streamlined, and so has the cuisine: lamb's-brain salad with capers, savoury biscuit de brandade in a vinaigrette with a touch of truffle, tasty red-mullet fillets, potato and duck tourte, and a banana papillote à la vanille. Fine wine list, interesting fixed-price menus.
A la carte: 280-300 F. Menus: 100 F (weekdays lunch only), 148 F, 190 F.

Hiély-Lucullus
5, rue de la République — 90.86.17.07
M. Hiély. Closed Mon (except 1 July-15 Aug), Tue, 7-30 Jan and 17 June-3 July. Open until 9.30 pm. Air cond. V.   C4-14
The Lucullan repasts of recently retired chef Pierre Hiély—formerly the finest in Avignon—are no longer. Hiély still 'supervises' the menu and runs the restaurant, but until the former sous-chef grows used to running the kitchen on his own (and improves the current level of cooking) we've decided not to rate Hiély at all, as we were rather disappointed on recent visits. Happily, the superb selection of Côtes-du-Rhône, the charming reception by Mme Hiély, and the delightful décor reminiscent of a turn-of-the-century steamship, are all intact. Relais et Châteaux.
Menus: 180 F, 290 F and from 330 F to 413 F.

Hôtel du Lavarin
1715, ch. du Lavarin — 90.89.50.60
Open every day. 44 rms 280-370 F. Restaurant. Half-board 378-398 F. TV 20 rms. Pool. V AE.   A6-9
A recently built hotel located outside the city walls, just off the road to Arles, Lavarin offers well-equipped, modern rooms decorated in soft tones. Pleasant, shady garden.

Hôtel Médiéval
15, rue de la Petite-Saunerie — 90.86.11.06
Closed 1 Jan-28 Feb. 20 rms 165-230 F. TV. Telex 431919. V.   D3-29
Despite the name, this is actually a seventeenth-century townhouse near the Palais des Papes, with smartly turned-out little salons surrounding a flower-filled patio, and spacious, but rather dark, rooms, some with kitchenette. Polite welcome. Average breakfasts.

Mercure Palais des Papes
Quartier de la Balance
Rue Ferruce — 90.85.91.23
Open every day. 3 stes 500 F. 82 rms 350-510 F. TV. Air cond. Conference facilities. Telex 431215. V AE DC.   C3-20
Located inside the city walls, the rooms of this hotel are comfortable, functional, modern, and well soundproofed, and the service is very attentive. Free parking.

Hôtel du Midi
Rue de la République — 90.82.15.56
Open every day. 57 rms 200-300 F. TV 45 rms. Air cond 5 rms. Telex 431074. V AE DC. C5-4

Just 200 metres from the Palais des Papes, the Midi looks drab from the outside but its rooms are perfectly kept and soundproofed (both on the court and street sides). Good service.

Hôtel Mignon
12, rue J.-Vernet — 90.82.17.30
Open every day. 15 rms 130-185 F. V. C4-25

Tiny and sweet as the name suggests, the Mignon offers exceptional services to its guests, including a mini-boutique stocked with newspapers, books, cigarettes. The rooms are small but sunny, soundproofed, and newly refurbished. 200 metres from the Palais des Papes.

12/20 Hôtel de La Mirande
4, pl. de l'Amirande — 90.85.93.93
M. Stein. Open every day. Open until 9.45 pm. Private room: 16. Garden dining. Air cond. No-smoking section. Valet parking. V DC. D3-30

Set in a superb town house restored to life with pride and conviction, La Mirande is one of the most prestigious recent renovation projects in Avignon. Too bad the cuisine is rather pretentious and dull (honest skate, greasy grenadin de veau), the wines pricey, and service flawed.

A la carte: 500 F and up. Menus: 245 F, 430 F.

Hôtel de La Mirande
(See restaurant above)
Open every day. 2 stes 2,500 F. 19 rms 1,200-1,600 F. TV. Air cond. No pets. Conference facilities.

What the restaurant lacks, the hotel compensates. Nestled in the heart of Avignon, this astonishing little 'palace', with a delicious secret garden, boasts richly decorated salons, and good-sized rooms whose décor and refined details evoke the luxury and comfort of centuries gone by. Views embrace the rooftops of the *vieille ville* and the Palais des Papes. Royal bathrooms. Pleasant, professional reception with a feminine touch.

Notre-Dame
34, rue du Four-de-la-Terre — 90.86.69.76
M. Bernadou. Dinner only. Closed week of 15 Aug. Open until 11 pm. V AE DC. E4-11

Monsieur Bernadou, the owner-chef of this baroque eating house, enjoys shuffling from table to table in his clogs and wide trousers, singing and haranguing the regulars, who clamour for the old-fashioned, robust and juicy magret and cassoulet. Bernadou's cuisine may be continuing in grandma's footsteps, but if he isn't careful he might trip on his trousers and lose his toque!

A la carte: 250 F. Menus: 100 F, 150 F, 199 F.

Novotel Avignon nord
Avignon North exit on motorway
84700 Sorgues — 90.31.16.43
Open every day. 2 stes 820-830 F. 100 rms 380-430 F. Restaurant. TV. Air cond. Conference facilities. Pool. Tennis. Parking. V AE DC. G2-22

Situated eight kilometres from the centre of town and only metres from the motorway toll booth, the Novotel's rooms are quiet, extremely well equipped and very comfortable. Excellent reception. Bar.

12/20 Le Petit Bedon
70, rue J.-Vernet — 90.82.33.98
M. Férigoule. Closed Sun and 15-30 June. Open until 10 pm. Private room: 25. Air cond. V AE DC. C5-8

The timeless Provençal verve of owner Jean Férigoule, his reliability, good humour, and generosity have ensured the success of this perennial favourite. Flavourful fixed-price menus include mussel soup with leeks, sheep's tripe and trotters à la marseillaise, lotte stewed in local Gigondas wine, etc.

Menus: 85 F (lunch only), 145 F.

Primotel Horloge
3, rue F.-David — 90.86.88.61
Open every day. 70 rms 235-450 F. TV. Air cond. Conference facilities. V AE DC. C4-21

Watch the location, right on the place de l'Horloge. This tastefully decorated, super-modern hotel tucked among the historic buildings boasts perfectly equipped, soundproofed, air-conditioned rooms with a neo-Louis XVI décor. Multilingual reception.

Les Trois Clefs
26, rue des Trois-Faucons — 90.86.51.53
M. Mergnac. Closed Sun and Feb school holidays and Nov school holidays. Open until 9.30 pm. Air cond. V AE. D5-1

Martine and Laurent Mergnac have found the *clefs* to success by eliminating their outrageously overpriced à la carte menu, and relying on a 170 F prix-fixe formula which is both generous and oft-renewed. It revolves around squash soup with diced foie gras, a thick slice of juicy salmon with bacon sauce, saddle of lamb with truffled juices, local cheeses, and an ethereal pear feuilleté. Wash it all down with a fine Lirac or Tavel, and you won't have spent more than 400 F for two. One of the best deals in town. Pleasant, cool garden setting.

Menu: 170 F.

La Vieille Fontaine
12, pl. Crillon — 90.82.66.92
M. Daire. Open every day. Open until 9.30 pm. Private room: 60. Terrace dining. Air cond. Valet parking. Telex 431965. V AE DC. C3-12

This venerable hotel-restaurant has been in continuous operation since the eighteenth century, making it one of Europe's oldest. It also happens to be Avignon's prettiest. The old fountain never runs dry, though a stream of chefs have flowed through the kitchen of late. If the astonishingly talented Michel Del Burgo stays on, as we hope, La Vieille Fontaine will bubble right along with Avignon's best (Hiély, Brunel, Christian Etienne). Trained by Guérard, Ducasse, and Passard, this gifted youth has mastered the subtleties and seasonings of Provençal cuisine. In a word, Del Burgo's cookery is sunny and bright: just taste his creamy lobster soup infused with sweet red peppers, or the braised shellfish and crustaceans kissed with basil, his ravioli stuffed with local truffles, the grilled scallops in aïoli with garlicky croquettes, the sumptuous pigeon risotto with green wheat, or the juicy saddle of rabbit served complete with its kidneys.... Dessert brings honey and hazelnut parfait, and delicate chocolate and walnut-cream tuiles. These gastronomical delights are especially over-the-top when eaten in the cobbled court, by the splashing fountain and scented wisteria.

The chef works hand-in-hand with maître d'hôtel-sommelier Jacques Napias, a felicitous duo and one we are glad to reward with an extra toque this year. Who knows how many more might be on the way if Del Burgo settles in for a long stay?

A la carte: 350-400 F. Menus: 165 F (weekdays lunch only), 250 F, 350 F.

 ## Hôtel d'Europe
(See restaurant above)

Open every day. 3 stes 1,700-1,750 F. 47 rms 450-1,050 F. TV. Air cond. Conference facilities.

Avignon's most luxurious, seductively splendid hotel is replete with Aubusson tapestries, precious *objets*, and antique paintings and artwork. The rooms are gorgeous and grand, with marble bathrooms. Three elegant, spacious rooftop suites have recently been added, each with a private terrace overlooking the town and the Palais des Papes (which is illuminated by night). Six other rooms have been thoroughly renovated. Patio-terrace.

And also...

Our selection of places for inexpensive hotels, quick, or late-night meals.

Barbotine (90.85.79.93 - 7, rue Racine. Open until 7 pm): Bistro furniture and refreshing décor. Good salads, smoked fish, and daily specials. Delicious scones at tea time (120 F).

Bristol (90.82.21.21 - 44, cours J.-Jaurès. 3 stes 450-600 F, 70 rms 300-450 F): Recently renovated, this is a fine hotel with comfortable rooms.

Café des Artistes (90.82.63.12 - pl. Crillon. Open until 11.30 pm): The animated veranda overlooks one of Avignon's prettiest *places*; the menu offers hearty daily specials, washed down with refreshing carafe wines (200 F).

Le Cintra (90.82.29.80 - 44, cours J.-Jaurès. Open until 11.30 pm): Old-fashioned décor, smiling service, and a good brasserie menu that includes grilled meats, aïoli, choucroute (100 F).

Entrée des Artistes (90.82.46.90 - 1, pl. des Carmes. Open until 10.30 pm): An affordable eating house with a leafy terrace, serving robust cuisine (veal with onions, lamb sautéed with pine-nuts), (100 F).

Le Gourmandin (90.85.88.27 - 18 bis, av. Moulin-Notre-Dame. Open until 10 pm): Hearty Gascon cuisine served in a pleasantly rustic setting (150 F).

L'Isle Sonnante (90.82.56.01 - 7, rue Racine. Open until 9.30 pm): The unpretentious, refined cuisine at extremely low prices, and the warm welcome, make this a favourite with locals (135 F).

Le Jardin de la Tour (90.85.66.50 - 9, rue de la Tour): Both the post-modern, mechanic's-shop décor and the cookery cater for the young and trendy. Good sweetbread salad, turbot with tiny vegetables (250 F).

Mercure (90.88.91.10 - 2, rue M.-de-Médicis. 105 rms 300-450 F): Located at the city's southern end, this hotel has sunny, spacious rooms, some of which give onto a garden.

Novotel (90.87.62.36 - rte de Marseille. 79 rms 370-420 F): Just off the *nationale* 7, with quiet, large, functional rooms.

Le Saint-Pierre (90.82.88.61 - 3, rue F.-David. Open until 11 pm): Low prices and generously served dishes (brandade millefeuille, magret, fig compote), in a pleasant outdoor setting (150 F).

Le Taste Vin (90.86.86.45 - 37, rue St-Michel. Open until 10 pm): Côtes-du-Rhône served by the glass to accompany tasty, robust specialities: andouillettes, tripe (80 F).

(13 km NE on D 942)
84210 Avignon — (Vaucluse)

 ## Moulin de la Roque
Rte de la Roque — 90.62.14.62

M. Chaléon. Closed 10 Nov-15 April. Open until 9.30 pm. Private room: 35. Garden dining. No pets. Parking. Telex 431095. V AE DC.

This magnificent mill-house nestles in a copse of ancient trees, its setting and Italianate décor evoking a sense of timelessness. The endless parade of new chefs, too, seems a study in *déjà vu*, however pleasant. Like his predecessors', Philippe Tur's cuisine is full of fine ideas that don't always work. Sometimes they do, however. Try the ambitious yet successful puff pastry sandwiched with creamy shellfish brandade, or the crisp 'croquant' of baby mackerel with tender, anchovy-flavoured aubergines, and the pink-tinged saddle of rabbit cooked in spiced wine. Inexperienced service.

A la carte: 330-390 F. Menus: 185 F (weekdays dinner only), 220 F (weekdays lunch only, wine inc), 220 F (dinner w-e and holidays only), 290 F.

Moulin de la Roque
(See restaurant above)

Closed 10 Nov-15 April. 2 stes 1,000-1,200 F. 27 rms 350-1,100 F. Half-board 400-700 F. TV. Air cond. Conference facilities. Pool. Tennis.

Guests may fish in the mill-run fed by the Sorgue River. The swimming pool is super, the rooms, decorated with a Provençal touch, are comfortable and well equipped.

(4 km W on N 100)
30133 Avignon — (Vaucluse)

L'Ermitage Meissonnier
Av. de Verdun (rte de Nîmes) — 90.25.41.68

M. Meissonnier. Closed Sun dinner off-season, Mon (except dinner in July-Aug). Open until 10 pm. Private room: 30. Garden dining. Parking. Telex 490715. V AE DC.

The fine old dining rooms and shady veranda have been given a fresh new look to coincide with the definitive retirement of former chef Paul-Louis Meissonnier. He still owns the Hermitage, and visits regularly, but Michel has taken over the kitchen. A tried-and-true chef by now, Michel has incorporated into his cuisine the best of his mentor's dishes and added his own personal, seasonally orientated specialities. Thus the salad of lightly cooked summer truffles served cold with vinegar, the prawn 'beggar's purse' seasoned with poppy and sesame seeds, and the rabbit profiteroles enlivened with wild thyme, followed by dainty desserts. In short, all is well at the Hermitage.

A la carte: 400 F. Menus: 160 F, 230 F, 280 F, 390 F.

Hostellerie L'Ermitage
(See restaurant above)

Closed Jan and Feb. 16 rms 200-380 F. TV 6 rms. Air cond 6 rms. Conference facilities.

Each of the extremely comfortable, soundproofed rooms here has a fine bathroom and minibar. The hotel is separated from the restaurant by a pretty garden, where guests may take breakfast.

(5 km E on D 53)
84140 Avignon – (Vaucluse)

 Climat

35, allée des Fenaisons – 90.88.13.00
Closed at Christmas. 30 rms 260 F. Restaurant. Half-board 300 F. TV. Conference facilities. Parking. Telex 431938. V AE.

Modern and perfectly equipped, the Climat is set in a green section of Avignon's industrial zone. Electronic reception, generous breakfasts.

11/20 La Ferme Saint-Pierre

1551, av. d'Avignon – 90.87.12.86
M. Philip. Dinner only. Closed Sat, Sun, 1 May, 27 July-18 Aug and 21 Dec-5 Jan. Open until 9.30 pm. Private room: 12. Garden dining. Parking. V AE DC.

The comfortable, half-timbered dining room opens onto a pleasant terrace and flower-filled garden. The cuisine is hearty and tasty (rabbit à la tapenade, osso buco, lamb fricassée), the bill modest.

A la carte: 150-200 F. Menu: 120 F.

 Les Frênes

645, av. des Vertes-Rives
90.31.17.93
M. Biancone. Closed 31 Oct-1 April. Open until 9.30 pm. Garden dining. No pets. Valet parking. Telex 431164. V AE DC.

Antoine Biancone, trained by Troisgros and Hiély, has come home to take over from his father Jacques, restoring the excellence of this delightful family-run establishment. We are thoroughly convinced by his cookery: Provençal snail cassolette en croûte, fresh tagliatelle with lobster, freshwater perch with morels, aiguillettes de bœuf à la fondue d'anchois. The desserts, alas, are adequate, but not outstanding. Nonetheless, this is one of the best addresses in Avignon.

A la carte: 350-400 F. Menus: 200 F (weekdays lunch only), 300 F, 360 F.

 Les Frênes

(See restaurant above)
Closed 31 Oct-1 March. 5 stes 1,200-1,900 F. 20 rms 595-1,500 F. Half-board 760-1,115 F oblig in seas. TV. Air cond. Conference facilities. Pool. Tennis.

Major renovation has catapulted this gorgeous, comfortable hotel, set in a leafy park with flower-filled garden and splashing fountains, to the forefront of Avignon's luxury line. The rooms are spread about in various outbuildings set round a superb swimming pool. The décor ranges from Louis XIII, to Restoration, to Empire. Most rooms have been redecorated tastefully and equipped with luxurious baths and *thalassothérapie* facilities. Capacious parking lot, peerless reception and service. Relais et Châteaux.

 Paradou Avignon

Châteaublanc airport
on N 7 – 90.88.29.30
Open every day. 42 rms 340-360 F. Restaurant. Half-board 260-410 F. TV. Air cond. Conference facilities. Pool. Tennis. Parking. Telex 432407. V AE DC.

Located near the motorway in a leafy district, this hotel offers well-soundproofed rooms, and outstanding service (desk open 7 am to 10 pm).

(9 km E on N 100)
84310 Avignon – (Vaucluse)

Le Paradou

Av. Léon-Blum – 90.33.34.15
Closed Sun off-season. 30 rms 280 F. Restaurant. Half-board 250-360 F oblig in seas. TV. Conference facilities. Heated pool. Parking. Telex 432407. V AE DC.

This modern, Provençal-style building is set in a shady park near Avignon and the airport. Comfortable rooms, good service. Complimentary tennis three kilometres away.

(5 km NE on N 7)
84130 Avignon – (Vaucluse)

Auberge de Cassagne

Avignon North exit on motorway
90.31.04.18
MM. Gallon, Trestour and Boucher. Open every day. Open until 9.30 pm. Private room: 60. Garden dining. Air cond. Valet parking. Telex 432997. V AE DC.

Renovation has done much to brighten this luxurious inn, nestled in a pretty, flower-filled park in an otherwise bland suburb of Avignon. The interior is sunny and cheery now, the terrace a treat for the eyes. So too is Philippe Boucher's cuisine, which is both tasty and aesthetically appealing. A graduate of the Blanc et Bocuse school, Boucher is very young but has already created an ambitious menu, which, we are sure, he will soon fine-tune. Taste the harmonious aubergine, courgette, and tomato terrine provençal, the appetising prawns in a tomato and fennel mousseline, or the succulent lotte braised in beef and chanterelle juices. Fine choice of dreamy desserts. Well-managed cellar. Attentive service. The bill, unfortunately, may be a shocker.

A la carte: 500 F. Menus: 190 F (except dinner in seas), 295 F, 405 F.

Auberge de Cassagne

(See restaurant above)
Open every day. 2 stes 980-1,450 F. 22 rms 480-760 F. Half-board 665-805 F oblig in seas. TV. Air cond. Conference facilities. Pool. Tennis.

Hidden in the charmless suburbs of town, this *auberge* is an oasis of luxury and beauty. The rooms are air-conditioned but not terribly spacious, located in a Provençal-style outbuilding opposite the swimming pool. All have been totally redesigned and boast fine furnishings and luxury bathrooms. The reception and service are remarkable. Excellent breakfasts. Access to nearby golf course possible.

 Le Florentin

Le Pigeonnier – 90.32.42.91
MM. Mariani. Closed off-season Sat lunch and Sun, and 1 Jan-20 Feb. Open until 9.30 pm. Private room: 25. Garden dining. Air cond. V AE DC.

Chef Michel Jarry is a retiring sort, so the media have often overlooked him. Not so the Mariani clan, owners of the Florentin, who recognise a rare pearl. Jarry learned the ropes at Nano's and La Flamiche before moving to Avignon. His daring approach to cookery produces surprising marriages of ingredients, which invariably work perfectly: witness his fried mushrooms with a macédoine of roast prawns, the tart green apples and scallops bathed in a vinaigrette, or semolina in meat juices with red sweet peppers flanking a roast fillet of lamb. The desserts are equally astonishing (the pineapple gratin with a rum-and-ginger crêpe is scrumptious). In short, this charming restaurant, set in a pretty garden, has burst onto Avignon's gastronomic scene.

A la carte: 370-430 F. Menus: 195 F (wine inc), 155 F, 230 F, 340 F.

Hôtel des Agassins
(See restaurant above)
Closed 1 Jan-20 Feb. 25 rms 420-780 F. Half-board 475-635 F. TV. Air cond. Conference facilities. Pool.
Agassins's pleasant, spacious rooms have a summery feel owing, no doubt, to the wicker furniture. They give onto the garden and swimming pool via a wide terrace. The reception is absolutely charming.

12/20 Müller's
81, av. d'Avignon – 90.31.02.75
M. Müller. Closed Sat lunch and Sun. Open until 9 pm. Garden dining. Air cond. No pets. Parking.
Herr Müller cut his teeth in Switzerland and Germany and his cuisine sometimes strays into the bizarre (lobster tail in bitter chocolate!). But his summer terrace and cloistered garden are delightful, as are some simple dishes (steamed salmon, filet de bœuf à la ficelle à la moelle).
Menus: 100 F (lunch only), 160 F.

In nearby Villeneuve-lès-Avignon
(3 km NW)
30400 Avignon – (Vaucluse)

L'Atelier
5, rue de la Foire – 90.25.01.84
Open every day. 19 rms 220-375 F. TV 12 rms. Air cond 1 rms. V AE DC.
Set in the heart of sixteenth-century Villeneuve, l'Atelier boasts a pretty patio, and cosy rooms furnished and decorated à l'ancienne.

Les Cèdres
39, bd Pasteur – 90.25.43.92
Closed 15 Nov-15 March. 24 rms 235-315 F. Restaurant. Half-board 235-255 F. TV 13 rms. Air cond 2 rms. Pool. Parking. Telex 432868. V.
A small town house surrounded by ancient cedars, this inn offers some old-style rooms, and others (in bungalows), which are both more up-to-date and comfortable. Restaurant open for dinner only.

Coya
Pont d'Avignon – 90.25.52.29
Open every day. 23 rms 178-297 F. TV. Parking. V.
Modern and rather charmless, half of Coya's rooms have balconies, with views of the Rhône and the Palais des Papes. Meals are served.

Hostellerie du Vieux Moulin
Rue du Vieux-Moulin – 90.25.00.26
Open every day. 20 rms 285-380 F. Restaurant. Half-board 440-700 F. Conference facilities. Parking. V AE DC.
This former mill-house stands in the shadow of the Philippe-le-Bel tower, its cosy rooms facing the Rhône. Breakfast is served on a delightful terrace. Boating excursions may be arranged; moorings are available.

La Magnaneraie
37, rue Camp-de-Bataille – 90.25.11.11
M. Prayal. Open every day. Open until 9.30 pm. Private room: 70. Garden dining. Valet parking. Telex 432640. V AE DC.
Chef Gérard Prayal's classic, refined cuisine is as flavourful as ever, and the opulent dining room opening on a pretty park becomes more charming year by year. Try the dainty feuilletés of foie gras and Ventoux truffles, the shellfish ravioli au beurre de corail, the veal filet mignon with citrus and honey, or the simple yet delicious leg of Alpilles lamb aux herbes. Luscious desserts and a remarkable cellar. The service is attentive, but rather stiff.
A la carte: 400 F and up. Menus: 170 F (weekdays only), 220 F, 300 F.

La Magnaneraie
(See restaurant above)
Open every day. 2 stes 1,000 F. 27 rms 400-850 F. Half-board 500-700 F. TV. Air cond 14 rms. Conference facilities. Pool. Tennis.
Where silkworms once munched mulberries, spacious, freshly decorated rooms with nineteenth-century furniture and a sunny décor now offer modern comfort and the charm of yore. New rooms have been appointed in the same spirit, on the ground floor, and give onto the garden and swimming pool. Particularly fine bathrooms, superb breakfasts.

Le Prieuré
7, pl. du Chapitre – 90.25.18.20
M. Mille. Closed 1 May and 12 Oct-10 March. Open until 9.30 pm. Private room: 80. Garden dining. Air cond. No pets. Parking. Telex 431042. V AE DC.
Thriving under the smiling sun of Provence, chef Serge Chenet's cuisine combines refinement and heartiness in a happy marriage of tradition and modernity. Late of the Château de Rochegude, Chenet excels with lobster and prawn lasagne (prepared with a tarragon-scented fish stock with periwinkles), John Dory flanked by fillets of red mullet marinated with orange, and grilled breast of young pigeon with a foie-gras millefeuille. His ethereal desserts include a triple chocolate confection, and a crisp lime craquelin. Set in a leafy garden, with a cheerful, typically Avignonnais dining room, the Prieuré is a gastronome's godsend.
A la carte: 400-450 F. Menus: 240 F (lunch only), 295 F (dinner only), 400 F.

Le Prieuré
(See restaurant above)
Closed 12 Oct-10 March. 10 stes 1,000-1,600 F. 26 rms 480-1,000 F. TV. Air cond. Conference facilities. Pool. Tennis.
Whether you book in the old priory, next to the church (smallish rooms), or in the new annexe by the swimming pool (large rooms with a fine view of the park or patios), you'll find the same grand style and luxury, far from prying eyes and the madding crowd. Impeccable reception and service. Relais et Châteaux.

See also: **Baux-de-Provence (Les), Noves**

AVORIAZ
See Morzine

AYTRÉ
See Rochelle (La)

37190 Azay-le-Rideau — (Indre/Loire)
Paris 254 - Tours 26 - Saumur 46 - Châtellerault 60

L'Aigle d'Or
10, rue A.-Richer — 47.45.24.58
M. Fèvre. Closed Sun dinner, Wed, 10-20 Dec and 15 Jan-15 Feb. Open until 9 pm. Private room: 40. Garden dining. V.

The pretty new interior in pastels and warm grey seems to have inspired chef Jean-Luc Fèvre to some elegance of his own. A first toque this year for the rabbit in Vouvray, skate with tender artichokes, lamb with a courgette-tomato tian, some expertly selected cheeses, and refreshing fruit desserts. Fine wines, affordably priced. Deft, professional service.

A la carte: 200-250 F. Menus: 78 F (weekdays lunch only), 125 F, 170 F.

L'Automate Gourmand
in La Chapelle-St-Blaise
1, rue du Parc — 47.45.39.07
M. Brisacier. Closed Tue off-season, and 1-15 March. Open until 9.30 pm. Private room: 15. V.

A smiling welcome completes the charm of this simple Loire Valley inn where this year you would do well to sample the soft-boiled eggs with cream and morels, a salad of roast prawns with grapefruit, and freshwater perch in beurre rouge. Excellent all-Loire wine list.

A la carte: 250-280 F. Menus: 80 F (weekdays only), 130 F, 160 F.

Le Grand Monarque
3, pl. de la République — 47.45.40.08
Mme Forest. Closed 6 Nov-15 March. Open until 10 pm. Private room: 40. Garden dining. Garage parking. V AE DC.

Chef Alain Brisacier sports his first toque this year in honour of his delicious prawns in white-wine aspic with a tomato coulis, turbot in saffron with a magnificent oyster butter, and his farm-reared young pigeon confit au porto. The delightful eighteenth-century inn and its lovely grounds add no little enjoyment to the feast. Courteous welcome, professional service with a smile.

A la carte: 250-300 F. Menus: 88 F (weekdays lunch only), 380 F (wine inc), 140 F, 205 F.

Le Grand Monarque
(See restaurant above)
Closed 15 Dec-15 Jan. 2 stes 500-600 F. 29 rms 170-600 F. Half-board 255-400 F oblig in seas. TV 10 rms. Conference facilities. Heated pool.

Charming, well-equipped rooms in a tasteful, quiet, green setting.

(12 km NW on D 17, D 7 and D 119)
37130 Azay-le-Rideau — (Indre/Loire)

10/20 Le Castel de Bray et Monts
47.96.70.47
M. Rochereau. Closed Wed (lunch only in seas.) and 23 Dec-30 Jan. Open until 9.30 pm. Private room: 36. Garden dining. No pets. Parking. V AE.

This striking eighteenth-century mansion which is nicely set off by beautiful grounds, is unfortunately home to a restaurant specialised in serving slapdash meals to unsuspecting tourists. Two points less this year for overcooked fish, dried-out pigeon, and a Camembert with all the flavour and texture of plaster!

A la carte: 260-300 F. Menus: 110 F (weekdays lunch only), 180 F, 245 F, 360 F.

Le Caste de Bray et Monts
(See restaurant above)
Closed Wed off-season and 23 Dec-30 Jan. 2 stes. 8 rms 538-750 F (per pers, half-board oblig). TV. Pets allowed.

All the cosy comforts of a nice private home, plus good breakfasts served under the magnolias.

See Auray

65200 Bagnères-de-Bigorre — (H.-Pyrénées)
Paris 800 - Lourdes 22 - Tarbes 21 - St-Gaudens 57

La Résidence
Parc thermal de Salut — 62.95.03.97
Closed 15 April-1 April. 31 rms 300-310 F (per pers, half-board oblig) Restaurant. No pets. Heated pool. Tennis. Parking. V.

Here you'll find quiet, comfortable rooms in a big establishment facing the mountains and the thermal park.

(3.5 km S on D 935)
65200 Bagnères-de-Bigorre — (H.-Pyrénées)

12/20 Hostellerie d'Asté
D 935 — 62.91.74.27
M. Peyseré. Closings not available. Open until 9 pm. Private room: 30. Garden dining. No pets. Hotel: 23 rms 140-260 F. Tennis. Parking. Telex 530955. V.

Deep in the Basque countryside you'll discover this perfect little holiday spot featuring sports (tennis, biking, table tennis) and entertainment and good seafood dishes served on the terrace: oysters, shellfish platters, sole aux cèpes.

A la carte: 250 F. Menus: 68 F (weekdays only), 115 F (wine inc), 82 F, 190 F.

61140 Bagnoles-de-l'Orne — (Orne)
Paris 234 - Alençon 48 - Argentan 39 - Domfront 19

Lutétia
Bd P.-Chalvet — 33.37.94.77
Closed beg Nov-mid-April. 33 rms 190-420 F. Restaurant. Half-board 310-430 F. TV 26 rms. Conference facilities. Parking. V AE DC.

A solid establishment set in a peaceful garden, near the centre of town, with comfortable, attractively decorated rooms.

Le Manoir du Lys
Rte de Juvigny — 33.37.80.69
M. Quinton. Closed off-season Sun dinner and Mon, and 6 Jan-1 March. Open until 9 pm. Private room: 25. Garden dining. No pets. Garage parking. Telex 170525. V AE DC.

The ultimate Norman manor, complete with flowered balconies and an apple orchard, offers a fine regional menu. Try the duo de boudins de campagne, lotte with pig's trotters, and the salt-meadow lamb baked in a pastry crust.

A la carte: 300 F. Menus: 95 F (weekdays only), 170 F, 190 F, 250 F.

Le Manoir du Lys
(See restaurant above)
Closed off-season Sun and Mon, and 6 Jan-1 March. 1 ste 500-620 F. 10 rms 290-470 F. Half-board 320-620 F. TV. Conference facilities. Tennis. Golf.

This luxuriously renovated nineteenth-century manor house proposes renovated rooms decorated with restraint. Should you tire of golf and tennis, you may learn the sylvan art of mushroom-hunting here.

In nearby Antoigny

(5 km E on D 916 and D 387)
61140 Bagnoles-de-l'Orne — (Orne)

La Vallée de la Cour
33.37.08.90
Closed Wed off-season. 9 rms 130-240 F. Restaurant. Half-board 230-280 F. TV. Conference facilities. Parking. V.

A pleasant spot on a lake in the heart of the forest. Comfortable rooms.

BAGNOLET

See Paris Suburbs

BAGNOLS-SUR-CÈZE

30200 Bagnols-sur-Cèze — (Gard)
Paris 667 - Pont-Saint-Esprit 11 - Avignon 33

Le Florence
14
16, pl. B.-Boissin — 66.89.58.24
M. Rozier. Closed Sun dinner, Mon, Feb school holidays and 1-16 Aug. Open until 9.30 pm. Private room: 30. V AE.

Solange Rozier, the lively, smiling mistress of the house, lavishes attention on her customers and on the service of her husband's superb cooking. The local love of refined cuisine comes shining through in such dishes as the oyster ragoût served atop a watercress mousse, the prawns sautéed in herb butter, red mullet with tiny purple artichokes, and the roast noisettes of lamb.
A la carte: 270-320 F. Menus: 145 F, 220 F, 330 F.

Le Mas de Ventadous
69, rte d'Avignon — 66.89.61.26
Closed 22 Dec-9 Jan. 22 rms 450-650 F. Restaurant. Half-board 550-750 F oblig in seas. TV. Air cond. Conference facilities. Pool. Tennis. Parking. Telex 490949. V AE.

These pleasant, sunny, well-equipped rooms are arranged in bungalows that are surrounded by lawns and border a seventeenth-century pavilion. The latter is available for meetings, conferences, etc.

BAILLY

See Paris Suburbs

BAIX

07210 Baix — (Ardèche)
Paris 591 - Valence 33 - Montélimar 25 - Privas 16

La Cardinale
Quai du Rhône — 75.85.80.40
Closed 1 Nov-31 March. 5 stes 1,250-1,900 F. 9 rms 500-1,205 F. Restaurant. Half-board 850-1725 F. TV. Conference facilities. Heated pool. Parking. Telex 346143. V AE DC.

Luxury and nature are close companions in this lovely seventeenth-century mansion with a superb view of the Rhône valley. Beautiful rooms.

BALDENHEIM

67600 Baldenheim — (Bas-Rhin)
Paris 440 - Marckolsheim 13 - Colmar 28 - Sélestat 9

La Couronne
14
45, rue de Sélestat — 88.85.32.22
M. Trébis. Closed Sun dinner and Mon (except holidays), 24-31 July and 2-8 Jan. Open until 9 pm. Private room: 30. Parking. V AE DC.

The opulence of Alsace is here to taste in this lovely pink house on the edge of the village. From the warm and cosy interior to the first-rate cuisine of Mme Trébis, the treasures of the region are on full display. Lightness, a sure sense of nuance, and the finest ingredients are the hallmarks of such preparations as superb foie gras au naturel, the strudel of frog's legs, Ried River fish stew, and the truffled roast pigeon au jus. The cellar holds a cache of superb local wines.
A la carte: 350 F. Menus: 140 F (weekdays only), 185 F, 260 F, 360 F.

BALEINE (LA)

50450 Baleine (La) — (Manche)
Paris 325 - St-Lô 28 - Villedieu-les-P. 15

Auberge de la Baleine
13
Le Bourg — 33.61.76.77
M. Vezin. Closed Sun dinner, Mon, 18 Feb-5 March and 2-16 Dec. Open until 9.30 pm. Parking. V.

This schoolhouse converted into an exceedingly rustic country inn is Martine and Jean-Charles Vezin's attempt to bring a little tiny hamlet, tucked in a delightful valley. The chef acquits himself nicely of an attractive menu that features salmon tartare, lotte au safran on a bed of onion confit, and an excellent goose breast napped with a lively citrus-butter sauce. Don't neglect the worthwhile prix-fixe meals.
A la carte: 200 F. Menus: 55 F (weekdays lunch only), 75 F (weekdays only), and from 95 F to 135 F.

BANDOL

83150 Bandol — (Var)
Paris 842 - Marseille 49 - Aix-en-Provence 74

Auberge du Port
14
9, allée J.-Moulin — 94.29.42.63
M. Ghiribelli. Open every day. Open until 9.30 pm (11 pm in summer). Terrace dining. V AE DC.

On a stretch of coast not long on good restaurants, this place has what it takes: good shellfish, sparkling fresh fish, and prices well beneath the extravagant average for this part of the world. In a tonic blue-and-white dining room, sample the roast lotte, or salmon with onions, the good local 'catch of the day', tasty rabbit fillets, and one of the appealing desserts. Slow-paced service.
A la carte: 350-450 F. Menus: 128 F (weekdays lunch only), 198 F, 298 F.

Délos
Ile de Bendor — 94.32.22.23
Open every day. 55 rms 410-815 F. Restaurant. Half-board 590-755 F oblig in seas. TV. No pets. Conference facilities. Pool. Tennis. Parking. Telex 404030. V AE DC.

Comfortable rooms, decorated in a variety of styles, enjoy an idyllic view of the sea. Numerous sporting activities.

La Ker Mocotte
Rue Raimu — 94.29.46.53
Closed 25 Oct-28 Feb. 2 stes 472 F. 19 rms 257-367 F. Restaurant. Half-board 333-388 F oblig in seas. TV. No pets. Conference facilities. Parking. V AE.

The former villa of 1930s film star Raimu (remember *Fanny*? or *The Baker's Wife*?) offers very pleasant rooms, a seaside garden, and a private beach. Guests have a choice of many different activities.

12/20 Les Oliviers
17, bd L.-Lumière — 94.29.46.86
M. Barbier. Open every day. Open until 10 pm. Private room: 18. Terrace dining. No pets. Valet parking. Telex 400372. V AE DC.

A huge, undistinguished dining room boasts nevertheless a view of the inlet. The interesting menu (pigeon salad, deftly cooked grouper gratiné, decent desserts) has yet to attract the attention it deserves.

A la carte: 350 F. Menus: 175 F, 200 F, 320 F.

Pullman Ile Rousse
(See restaurant above)
Open every day. 2 stes 875-1,500 F. 53 rms 400-1,180 F. Half-board 645-845 F oblig in seas. TV. Air cond. Conference facilities. Heated pool.

Ideally located between the town and the sea, these comfortable rooms suffer a bit from a décor in need of refreshment. Excellent breakfasts.

12/20 La Réserve
Rte de Sanary — 94.29.42.71
M. Jacquet. Closed off-season Sun dinner and Mon, and 2-22 Jan. Open until 9.30 pm. Terrace dining. Hotel: 16 rms 170-450 F. Parking. V AE DC.

Not necessarily up-to-the-minute, the cooking here is nonetheless a welcome relief for otherwise trapped tourists who flock to this seaside resort region. The tried-and-true repertoire of marinated red mullet, escalope of foie gras with citrus fruits, and a magnificent chocolate pavé spotlights fine fresh ingredients and careful treatment.

A la carte: 300-350 F. Menus: from 130 F to 370 F.

66650 Banyuls-sur-Mer — (Pyrénées-O.)
Paris 960 - Perpignan 37 - Port-Vendres 7

Le Catalan
Rte de Cerbère — 68.88.02.80
Closed 15 Oct-15 April. 36 rms 270-440 F. Restaurant. Half-board 350-430 F oblig in seas. TV 12 rms. Pool. Tennis. Garage parking. Telex 500557. V AE DC.

This bit of modern architecture perches on the rocky coast over the Bay of Banyuls. Every room enjoys the view. Bar. Room service.

11/20 Les Elmes
Plage des Elmes — 68.88.03.12
M. Sannac. Closed Tue and 6 Nov-20 March. Open until 9.30 pm. Private room: 30. Terrace dining. No pets. Parking. V AE.

Simple, heartwarming seafood at modest prices make this pleasant little beach inn a wonderful holiday spot: assortment of home-smoked fish, fish stew, duck confit, nougat glacé. Cheerful service.

A la carte: 200-250 F. Menus: 80 F (weekdays only, wine inc), 105 F, 180 F.

Les Elmes
(See restaurant above)
Closed Tue and 6 Nov-20 March. 21 rms 210-310 F. Half-board 220-280 F oblig in seas. TV. Air cond 8 rms. Conference facilities.

A nice beach hotel, not always as quiet as one might wish, but with a carefree, friendly ambience.

Le Sardinal
Pl. P.-Reig — 68.88.30.07
M. Roméro. Closed Mon and 1 Nov-5 Dec. Open until 9.30 pm. Terrace dining. V DC.

The new owners of this seaside restaurant have wisely left well enough alone, giving free rein to the chef who has a pefect understanding of regional Catalan cuisine, which he prepares with a personal touch. Sample the richly flavoured squid in ink sauce with Catalan boudin, the coquilles St-Jacques and duck liver en papillote, the oven-roasted cod with olive oil, garlic, and meat juices, and the fine desserts. Charming reception, and a new, expanded cellar.

A la carte: 300 F. Menus: 90 F (weekdays only), 150 F, 180 F, 300 F.

77630 Barbizon — (Seine/Marne)
Paris 56 - Melun 11 - Fontainebleau 10 - Etampes 39

Le Bas-Bréau
22, rue Grande — 60.66.40.05
M. Fava. Closed 2 Jan-2 Feb. Open until 9.30 pm. Private room: 40. Garden dining. Valet parking. Telex 690953. V AE.

Better to be very rich and dine here than be a bit less flush and obliged to dine elsewhere: such, it would seem, is the sentiment shared by those who can (and do) leave their expensive automobiles in the car park of this posh eating house on the edge of the Forest of Fontainebleau. Chef Tavernier's cuisine, which makes up what (little) it lacks in imagination with peerless ingredients and expert execution, runs to rich dishes like lobster salad with hazelnut oil, little buckwheat crêpes with prawns, Breton scallops served in the shell, and farm-reared, milk-fed veal chops with asparagus. Even with a modest Bordeaux your bill is sure to top 600 F, but you may take some consolation in the fact that no supplement is charged for the crackling fire (in winter), or the shaded courtyard (in summer), or the distinguished service.

A la carte: 600-800 F. Menus: 290 F and 340 F (weekdays lunch only, wine inc).

Le Bas-Bréau
(See restaurant above)
Closed 2 Jan-2 Feb. 8 stes 1,600-2,700 F. 12 rms 900-1,400 F. TV. Conference facilities. Tennis.

One of the most refined and luxurious inns around Paris, with rose gardens everywhere you look, decorated with delightful simplicity. Relais et Châteaux.

Hostellerie de la Clé d'Or
73, rue Grande — 60.66.40.96
M. Gayer. Closed Sun dinner off-season, and 10-30 Dec. Open until 9 pm. Private room: 12. Garden dining. Parking. Telex 691636. V AE DC.

Like a grand, Ile-de-France dwelling of days gone by, this complex of old outbuildings and stables features a delightful dining room and flower garden wherein to enjoy chef Philippe Gayer's truffle-scented oyster and prawn ragoût, his charlotte of veal kidneys, and a creamy, keen-flavoured lemon

bavarian.
A la carte: 350 F. Menus: 160 F, 220 F.

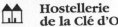

Hostellerie de la Clé d'Or
(See restaurant above)
Closed 10-30 Dec. 1 ste 1,000 F. 15 rms 280-550 F. TV. Conference facilities.
Opposite the Ganne museum, this lovely old inn boasts renovated, quiet rooms.

12/20 Les Pléiades
21, rue Grande — 60.66.40.25
M. Karampournis. Open every day. Open until 9.30 pm. Private room: 50. Garden dining. Garage parking. Telex 691753. Hotel: 1 ste 650 F. 15 rms 260-390 F. Half-board 450-620 F. TV. Conference facilities. V AE DC.
In this former home of the Barbizon School landscape painter Charles Daubigny, a large, luxurious dining room opens onto the gardens. These charming precincts are the stage for somewhat inconsistent cuisine which is based, however, on the best available ingredients (meats in particular are very fine). Try the salad of spring vegetables and salmon or the skate with capers and lemon. The Brie de Meaux is excellent.
A la carte: 250-300 F. Menus: 149 F (weekdays only), 225 F.

12/20 Le Relais
2, av. Ch.-de-Gaulle — 60.66.40.28
M. Pontlevé. Closed Tue, Wed, 2-18 Jan and 19-30 Aug. Open until 9.30 pm. Garden dining. V.
It's hard to waste a glance on the à la carte list when two modestly priced set menus include the best dishes of the house: rabbit terrine, calf's foot with sauce ravigote, coq au Brouilly, and tournedos Bercy. A creditable little restaurant, particularly charming in fine weather when meals are served on the patio.
A la carte: 180-200 F. Menus: 115 F and 145 F (weekdays only), 120 F and 150 F (w-e and holidays only).

BARBOTAN-LES-THERMES
32150 Barbotan-les-Thermes — (Gers)
Paris 686 - Mont-de-Marsan 43 - Condom 37

L'Ambassade Gourmande ✪
62.69.53.75
M. Lamaison. Closed Tue and 30 Nov-31 March. Open until 9.30 pm. Private room: 22. Garden dining. No pets. Hotel: 17 rms 240-300 F. Parking. V AE DC.
Seated on the long terrace of this pleasant villa, you'll enjoy the flavourful inventions of Pierre-Yves Lamaison's personal cuisine. The newly revamped décor complements such market-fresh, regionally rooted dishes as the gratin of oysters and foie gras, a leek and asparagus terrine with walnut vinaigrette, and the pigeon roasted with honey and spices. Attentive service.
A la carte: 280-300 F. Menus: 85 F (weekdays lunch only), 150 F, 180 F, 220 F.

La Bastide Gasconne ✪
62.69.52.09
M. Guérard-Barthélemy. Closed 31 Oct-22 March. Open until 9.30 pm. Private room: 10. Terrace dining. No pets. Valet parking. Telex 521009. V AE.
To our great delight chef Eric Marsanne is still on the scene, as is the superb 190 F fixed-price menu. That winning combination wins another point from us with a flawless array of such dishes as a

'pizza' of asparagus tips and wild mushrooms, a rustic but delicate potato mould, rabbit with tiny browned onions, and a warm chocolate soufflé beautifully presented in a silver timbale. The service is smooth as silk.
A la carte: 350-400 F. Menus: 190 F (weekdays only), 220 F, 280 F.

La Bastide Gasconne ✪
(See restaurant above)
Closed 31 Oct-22 March. 2 stes 700-1,100 F. 36 rms 350-650 F. Half-board 465-655 F. TV 20 rms. Conference facilities. Pool. Tennis.
A truly fine hotel, where the service is as perfectly gracious as the appointments are tasteful and comfortable.

Cante-Grit
Av. des Thermes — 62.69.52.12
Closed 1 Nov-15 April. 23 rms 175-300 F. Restaurant. Half-board 260-440 F. TV 8 rms. Conference facilities. Parking. V AE.
Near the spas, this beautiful vine-covered country house boasts a garden and pretty rooms with views of the countryside.

Château de Bégué ✪
62.69.50.08
Closed 30 Sep-2 May. 9 rms 289-366 F. Restaurant. Half-board 399-419 F. TV 3 rms. Conference facilities. Pool. Garage parking. Telex 531918. V.
Cosy rooms, a lake, lots of trees, and a shady terrace: this is a perfect spot to relax.

In nearby **Cazaubon**

(3 km SW on D 626)
32150 Barbotan-les-Thermes — (Gers)

12/20 Château Bellevue
Rue J.-Cappin — 62.09.51.95
Mme Latreille-Consolaro. Closed off-season Tue dinner and Wed, and 31 Dec-1 March. Open until 9.30 pm. Private room: 50. Garden dining. No pets. Parking. Telex 521429. V AE DC.
The nineteenth century, from the highly polished period furniture to the flower-strewn park, is the setting for this young chef's efforts to bring the cuisine into the twentieth: sample his shrimp ravioli with truffles and herbs, gratin of roast lamb with rosemary and garlic, and escaloped sweetbreads with broad beans and chanterelles. Charming welcome and service.
A la carte: 220-250 F. Menus: 130 F, 160 F, 250 F.

Château Bellevue ✪
(See restaurant above)
Closed off-season Tue and Wed, and 31 Dec-1 March. 2 stes 410 F. 21 rms 175-400 F. Half-board 265-350 F. TV 12 rms. No pets. Conference facilities. Pool.
Some of the spacious, pleasant rooms give onto the pool, others overlook the courtyard. Breakfasts are excellent at this commendable holiday stopover.

BARCELONNETTE
04400 Barcelonnette — (Alpes/H.-P.)
Paris 740 - Gap 69 - Briançon 84 - Nice 209

La Grande Epervière
18, rue des Trois-Frères-Arnaud
92.81.00.70
Open every day. 10 rms 270-350 F. Restaurant. Half-board 290-310 F oblig in seas. TV. Garage parking. V.
This comfortable building is surrounded by spacious grounds which include a large pond. Pretty

mountain views. English-style breakfasts are served.

11/20 La Mangeoire
Pl. des Quatre-Vents — 92.81.01.61
M. Matyja. Closed Tue lunch and Mon (except school holidays), 6 Jan-1 Feb and 9-17 June. Open until 10.30 pm. Terrace dining. V.

A lovely 300-year-old stable, converted into a restaurant where unfortunately the chef seems to wear blinders: tournedos Rossini, côte de veau vallée d'Auge, and the like.
A la carte: 250-300 F. Menus: 69 F, 99 F, 240 F.

10/20 Le Passe-Montagne
2 km S on D 902
in Uvernet, rte de la Cayolle — 92.81.08.58
M. Daneri. Closed Wed, 1-15 June and 1-15 Dec. Open until 9.15 pm. Garden dining. Parking. V AE DC.

At the handful of tables under the trees you may order from a menu of ambitious, costly dishes. Stick to the simplest, and enjoy the mountain view.
A la carte: 250 F. Menus: 100 F, 138 F, 155 F.

In nearby Pra-Loup
(8.5 km S on D 902 and D 109)
04400 Barcelonnette — (Alpes/H.-P.)

Auberge du Clos Sorel
Village de Clos Sorel — 92.84.10.74
Closed 20 April-25 June and 10 Sep-15 Dec. 8 rms 400-600 F. Restaurant. Half-board 480-580 F. TV. Conference facilities. Heated pool. Parking. V.

In a handsomely restored, mountainside farm you'll find this lovely inn with a breathtaking view across the valley. Charming, rustic décor; comfortable rooms.

Le Prieuré de Molanès
92.84.11.43
Closed Oct and Nov 1 ste 350-500 F. 15 rms 250-300 F. Restaurant. Half-board 265-355 F oblig in seas. TV. Conference facilities. Heated pool. Parking. V AE.

A tasteful, rustic interior, and pleasant rooms distinguish this intelligently renovated hotel. Sports enthusiasts may ski in winter, hike, sail, or raft in summer.

In nearby Sauze
(4 km SE on D 900 and D 209)
04400 Barcelonnette — (Alpes/H.-P.)

Alp'Hôtel
92.81.05.04
Closed 13-26 May and 20 Oct-15 Dec. 9 stes 480-1,050 F. 24 rms 390-430 F. Restaurant. Half-board 330-345 F. TV. Conference facilities. Heated pool. Garage parking. Telex 420437. V AE DC.

This modern complex ideally located near the lifts boasts pretty rooms with mountain views, a garden, terrace, and heated pool as well as a bar and a fitness centre. Suites have kitchenettes.

BARJAC
30430 Barjac — (Gard)
Paris 670 - Aubenas 46 - Alès 28 - Pont-St-Esprit 32

Mas de Rivet
66.24.52.18
Closed 1 Oct-30 April. 9 rms 220-290 F. Restaurant. Half-board 230-245 F oblig in seas. Pool. Parking.

The rooms of this refurbished sixteenth-century Provençal homestead are spare but comfortable,

with a view down the valley. Billiard room; solarium. Friendly welcome.

Les Termes
3 km SE on D 901
3 — 66.24.56.31
Closed Jan. 4 stes 500-800 F. 13 rms 250-360 F. Restaurant. Half-board 410-460 F. TV 3 rms. Conference facilities. Pool. Parking. V.

This renovated eighteenth-century Provençal *mas* stands amidst vineyards, and offers modern, comfortable rooms.

BARNEVILLE-CARTERET
50270 Barneville-Carteret — (Manche)
Paris 336 - Coutances 48 - Cherbourg 37

12/20 Les Isles
9, bd Maritime — 33.04.90.76
M. Masson. Closed 18 Nov-9 Feb. Open until 9 pm. V DC.

Here the sea is all around you: from the long strip of beach at your doorstep to the sincere seafood served at table. The 110 F prix-fixe menu offers excellent value: local oysters, pot-au-feu de la mer with horseradish sauce, some good cheeses, and peach diplomate for pudding.
A la carte: 250 F. Menus: 80 F, 110 F, 170 F, 230 F.

Les Isles
(See restaurant above)
Closed 18 Nov-9 Feb. 34 rms 150-285 F. Half-board 195-265 F oblig in seas. Pets allowed.

A pretty little hotel where some of the rooms give onto the beach and the sea. A pleasant stopover.

La Marine
11, rue de Paris — 33.04.91.71
M. Cesne. Closed off-season Sun dinner and Mon, and 6 Nov-1 Feb. Open until 9.30 pm. Terrace dining. Parking. V DC.

The flattering light reflected from the Channel illuminates this dining room, casting a lovely glow on the English period furniture, and on chef Laurent Cesne's many admirers. You too will admire his direct, open style which emphasises fresh ingredients and local traditions. We can recommend the cassolette de langoustines aux petits pois, braised lobster with new potatoes and glazed shallots, and a grand chocolate dessert enhanced with a spicy gingerbread sauce. Sumptuous cellar.
A la carte: 300-350 F. Menus: 99 F (weekdays only), 175 F, 240 F, 350 F.

La Marine
(See restaurant above)
Closed 6 Nov-1 Feb. 2 stes 580-720 F. 30 rms 250-420 F. Half-board 385-425 F. TV. Conference facilities.

One is all but in the drink here at high tide. The comfortable rooms are quiet (double-glazed windows) and well-equipped room. Lovely sea views.

In nearby Carteret
(3 km W)
50270 Barneville-Carteret — (Manche)

12/20 L'Hermitage
(Maison Duhamel)
Prom. Abbé-Lebouteiller — 33.04.96.29
M. Duhamel. Closed Wed dinner, Fri, 10-25 Jan, Feb school holidays and 15 Nov-15 Dec. Open until

*9.15 pm. Terrace dining. Hotel: 6 stes 350-600 F.
1 rm 200 F. V DC.*

The object here is to focus on the commanding view of the harbour and the generous shellfish platters, avoid the overcooked fish dishes, and try to ignore the surly service.

A la carte: 250-300 F. Menus: 74 F, 125 F, 180 F.

BARROUX (LE)

See Carpentras

BARSAC

33720 Barsac — (Gironde)
Paris 608 - Bordeaux 38 - Libourne 45 - Langon 8

11/20 Château de Rolland
N 113 – 56.27.15.75
*Mme Duvillié. Closed Wed lunch (except upon
reserv). Open until 10 pm. Garden dining. Parking.
V AE DC.*

Very château-like are the coats-of-arms, huge beams, and Louis XIII chairs. Meanwhile the cuisine is sincere and well-intentioned, based on prime ingredients, but the execution lacks precision and polish: the quail salad was hearty but messy, the duck in wine sauce was overpowered by onions, the gratin of oranges bountiful but runny). Stiff welcome; charming service.

Menus: 95 F (weekdays lunch only), 200 F (lunch only, wine inc), 150 F, 220 F.

Château de Rolland
(See restaurant above)
*Open every day. 2 stes 470-530 F. 9 rms 350-530 F.
TV. Conference facilities.*

Watch the Sauternes vines grow in perfect tranquillity, from your spacious and comfortable room.

BAR-SUR-AUBE

10200 Bar-sur-Aube — (Aube)
Paris 210 - Troyes 53 - Châtillon-sur-Seine 59

In nearby Arsonval

(6 km NW on N 19)
10200 Bar-sur-Aube — (Aube)

11/20 Hostellerie de la Chaumière
25.27.91.02
*M. Guillerand. Closed Sun dinner and Mon (except
holidays). Annual closings not available. Open until
9 pm. Private room: 30. Garden dining. Hotel: 3 rms
120-160 F. Parking. V AE.*

The riverside garden is a refreshing spot to dine in summer whereas in winter, well, it's the dining room that needs refreshing. In either case, the classic, family-style cooking will make you glad you stopped: try the excellent filet de bœuf périgourdin (the fish offerings are, as a rule, less successful). Cordial welcome and attentive service.

A la carte: 250 F. Menus: 95 F, 155 F.

BARTENHEIM

68870 Bartenheim — (Haut-Rhin)
Paris 552 - Mulhouse 24 - Bâle 15 - Colmar 63

L'Auberge d'Alsace
49, av. de la Gare — 89.68.31.26
*Mme Munck. Closed Wed dinner, Thu, last 2 weeks
of Jan and first 2 weeks of July. Open until 10 pm.
Private room: 40. Terrace dining. Parking. V.*

Taking (quite naturally) Alsatian sauerkraut as its point of departure, the menu of this pretty half-timbered restaurant quickly takes off for such exotic destinations as Polynesian rib steak, Landesstyle tournedos, Chinese slivered pork, Lyonnais rib steak and steak Tartare. This is serious cooking, however, and full of very pleasant surprises. The meats are uniformly outstanding, and the cellar holds all sorts of affordably priced accompaniments. Only the desserts do not measure up to the rest.

A la carte: 260 F. Menus: 80 F, 110 F, 140 F.

BASSE-GOULAINE

See Nantes

BASTELICA

See CORSICA

BASTELICACCIA

See CORSICA

BASTIA

See CORSICA

BATZ-SUR-MER

See Baule (La)

BAULE (LA)

44500 Baule (La) — (Loire-Atl.)
Paris 463 - Rennes 133 - Vannes 72 - Saint-Nazaire 17

Castel Marie-Louise
1, av. Andrieux — 40.60.20.60
*M. Lambert. Open every day. Open until 9.45 pm.
Garden dining. No pets. Valet parking.
Telex 700408. V AE DC.*

Having recently become the only upscale establishment left in La Baule (the others are closing or are in decline), the Castel Marie-Louise can now claim to be the best. Though the hotel is one of the finer places to stay in France, the restaurant is bogged down in an uninventive (though competently executed) repertoire: prawn salad with tomato confit, lotte baked with country ham and meat juices, young pigeon roasted in a sea-salt crust. Fine cellar; professional welcome and service.

A la carte: 400 F. Menus: 195 F (except juil-Aug), 360 F (dinner only), 295 F.

Castel Marie-Louise
(See restaurant above)
*Open every day. 2 stes 1,450-2,200 F. 29 rms 670-
1,820 F. Half-board 965-1,675 F. TV. Conference
facilities. Heated pool. Tennis. Golf.*

The refined, classic décor is regularly spruced up, the rooms are extremely comfortable, the service remarkable, and the whole is situated in a beautiful garden with a sweeping view of the beach. Sea-cure establishment 100 metres from the hotel. Relais et Châteaux.

11/20 Helvetia
65, av. M.-Rigaud — 40.60.25.18
*M. Marion. Closed off-season Tue dinner and Wed,
10-24 Feb and 1-20 Oct. Open until
9.30 pm (10.30 pm in summer). No pets. V.*

No Swiss specialities illustrate the restaurant's name, nor does the menu list many seafood dishes, a rarity at La Baule. Sample the excellent grills (cooked over vine cuttings), the chicken-liver terrine, the rabbit in mustard or the fine tarragon-scented chicken. Diffident reception.

A la carte: 180 F.

L'Hermitage
Espl. F.-André — 40.60.37.00
M. Garnier. Closed 28 Oct-10 April. Open until 10.30 pm. Private room: 450. Garden dining. Air cond. No pets. Valet parking. Telex 710510. V AE DC.

A thorough renovation has considerably refreshed the premises, but chef François Sierra's menu is still staidly classic: langoustines à la grecque, sea bass with truffle and celery 'scales', sweetbreads braised in chicken stock, grape feuilleté with a kirsch-laced sabayon. While the cuisine is well done for the most part, some slips have been noted in the sauces and cooking times. A word to the wise.

A la carte: 400-450 F. Menu: 270 F.

L'Hermitage
(See restaurant above)
Closed 28 Oct-10 April. 9 stes 2,600-4,200 F. 217 rms 900-2,000 F. TV. Air cond. Conference facilities. Heated pool. Tennis. Golf.

An imposing (if not exactly charming) luxury beach hotel, recently renovated. Amenities include a sauna, fitness centre, and children's club in the summer months.

Manoir du Parc
3, allée des Albatros
40.60.24.52
Closed 17 Dec-14 Jan. 18 rms 196-460 F. Restaurant. Half-board 400-450 F oblig in seas. TV. No pets. Parking. V AE.

A charming turn-of-the-century hotel sheltered by pines, just 150 metres from the beach. A recent renovation has made the smallish but nicely appointed rooms even more appealing. Meals are provided for guests in season.

La Marcanderie
5, av. d'Agen — 40.24.03.12
M. Giraud. Closed off-season Sun dinner and Mon (except holidays), and 7 Jan-7 Feb. Open until 9.30 pm. Private room: 12. V AE.

A bright, warm new décor complements chef Jean-Luc Giraud's savoury cooking: potato galette with prawns, shellfish on a bed of jacket potatoes, scallops and chicory in a lightly creamed broth, and a delicate shellfish stew are all worth trying. Charming welcome, friendly (but easily flustered) staff. The cellar could use a few more half-bottles.

A la carte: 350 F. Menus: 135 F (weekdays only), 195 F, 260 F, 360 F.

Hôtel Musset
15, allée des Cygnes
40.60.24.08
Open every day. 2 stes 240-300 F. 11 rms 250-295 F. Restaurant. Half-board 280-330 F oblig in seas. Conference facilities. Parking. V.

This picturesque turn-of-the-century villa with a shady garden offers romantic little rooms. Charming service and reception. Brunch served in the summer months, and on request.

La Palmeraie
7, allée des Cormorans — 40.60.24.41
Closed 1 Oct-end March. 23 rms 250-340 F. Restaurant. Half-board 240-300 F. Full board oblig in seas. TV. V AE DC.

Overrun with flowers, this pink-and-white hotel near the beach offers comfortable rooms, some with English-style furnishings. Inadequate soundproofing. Courteous reception.

12/20 La Pergola
147, av. des Lilas — 40.24.57.61
M. Séguin. Closed Mon lunch in seas, Wed and Fri, off-season Tue lunch and Mon. Open until 10.30 pm. Private room: 12. Terrace dining. Parking. V.

The new chef is trying out a new idea: a single fixed-price menu with several choices for each course. A recent dinner brought us a well-wrought salmon tartare, decent skate in asparagus cream, a selection of cheeses, and a good crème brûlée. The staff has not yet worked out all the kinks, but we're sure all will soon be running smoothly in this pleasant, peach-coloured dining room.

Menu: 105 F.

Royal
Av. P.-Loti — 40.60.33.06
Closed 10 Nov-15 Dec. 6 stes 1,600-2,200 F. 103 rms 660-1,720 F. Restaurant. Half-board 930-1,420 F. TV. Conference facilities. Heated pool. Tennis. Golf. Valet parking. Telex 701135. V AE DC.

A fine seafront hotel that dates from the turn of the century, set in lovely grounds. In addition to bright, inviting rooms, there are three restaurants, a bar, and a night club.

12/20 La Véranda
27, bd de l'Océan — 40.60.28.55
M. Cloërec. Closed Tue off-season, and Feb and Nov school holidays. Open until 9 pm. Air cond. No pets. Parking. Telex 710459. V AE DC.

Brigitte Retailleau welcomes patrons into her two light-filled dining rooms—one facing the sea—where they can enjoy her husband Patrick's seafood cuisine. Some dishes are better than others, but all are based on good ingredients. Sample the salmon tartare, the buckwheat crêpes with crab, and grilled sea bass. Limited cellar.

A la carte: 260-300 F. Menu: 150 F.

Bellevue-Plage
(See restaurant above)
Closed Feb and Nov school holidays. 3 stes 700-800 F. 34 rms 350-680 F. Half-board 370-535 F. TV. Conference facilities.

Here are modern, soundproofed rooms near the sea-cure establishments.

In nearby Batz-sur-Mer
(6 km W on N 771 ou D 45)
44740 Baule (La) — (Loire-Atl.)

12/20 L'Atlantide
59, bd de la Mer — 40.23.92.20
M. Paroux. Closed beg Nov-mid-March. Open until midnight. Private room: 8. Terrace dining. V AE.

This big, newly renovated seafront restaurant now sports a fresh, flower-filled décor. On offer are seafood specialities that are not always perfectly consistent, but the chef's raw materials are reliably high quality. Try the fresh cod, the lotte in a creamy garlic sauce, and the walnut cake. And keep a weather eye on the price column. Concise wine list.

A la carte: 280-300 F. Menus: 140 F, 190 F.

> Remember to reserve your table or your room in advance, and please let the restaurant or hotel know if you cannot honour your reservation.

(3 km W)
44510 Baule (La) — (Loire-Atl.)

La Voile d'Or
Av. de la Plage — 40.42.31.68
M. Arhan. Closed Sun dinner, Mon and Nov. Open until 10 pm. Terrace dining. V AE.
A toque this year for this blue-and-white restaurant beloved by locals for its terrace and good food. We can recommend the nicely seasoned salad of salmon and prawns, perfect butter-roasted coquilles St-Jacques, John Dory fillet with a creamy lettuce sauce, and the excellent sorbets. The welcome is always courteous, but the service often seems harried.
A la carte: 300 F. Menus: 120 F, 160 F, 280 F.

25110 Baume-les-Dames — (Doubs)
Paris 433 - Besançon 30 - Montbéliard 49

Hostellerie du Château d'As
26, rue Château-Gaillard — 81.84.00.66
M. Aubrée. Closed Sun dinner and Mon (except holidays), and mid-Dec-end Feb. Open until 9 pm. Private room: 20. Hotel: 10 rms 100-230 F. Parking. V AE.
The formal, if slightly tumbledown elegance of this provincial hostelry—run with an iron hand by Mme Aubrée—is well suited to chef Henri Aubrée's rigidly classical cooking. Nonetheless, he is a true master of culinary technique, and if you are willing to pay the stiffish prices, we are sure you will enjoy his foie gras terrine, a very delicate sole in beurre blanc sauce with tiny vegetables, and the Bresse hen with morels.
A la carte: 450 F. Menus: 100 F (weekdays only), 195 F, 280 F.

(7 km E on N 83)
25110 Baume-les-Dames — (Doubs)

11/20 La Crémaillère
on N 83 — 81.84.07.88
M. Ziss. Closed Sat lunch (and dinner off-season), 7-29 Oct and 24 Dec-7 Jan. Open until 9.45 pm. Terrace dining. Garage parking. V AE.
This sizable restaurant decorated with neo-rustic copper utensils boasts a large terrace, always mobbed with families enjoying dependably good cooking at very modest prices. Count on rabbit and hazelnut terrine, fried carp, beef tongue in Madeira, and fresh frogs' legs. To drink, try one of the good little clarets.
A la carte: 150-200 F. Menus: 60 F and 70 F (weekdays only), 110 F, 130 F, 150 F, 170 F.

Hôtel Ziss
(See restaurant above)
Closed Sat off-season, 7-29 Oct and 24 Dec-7 Jan. 21 rms 180-270 F. Half-board 240-270 F. TV 5 rms. Pets allowed.
Unadorned, modern, comfortable rooms. Hearty breakfasts.

The prices quoted in this guide are those which we were given by the restaurants and hotels concerned. Increases in prices are beyond our control.

13520 Baux-de-Provence (Les) — (B./Rhône)
Paris 714 - Salon-de-Provence 33 - Avignon 3

Bautezar
Grande-Rue — 90.54.32.09
Closed Mon off-season and 5 Jan-5 March. 10 rms 280-400 F. Restaurant. No pets. V.
A fine little hotel with character, and views across the Val d'Enfer.

La Benvengudo
on D 78F — 90.54.32.54
Closed 1 Nov-10 Feb. 2 stes 750-900 F. 18 rms 385-500 F. Restaurant. TV. Air cond 12 rms. Pool. Tennis. Garage parking. V.
A superb Provençal setting, with magnificent furniture to match, makes this old country manor a delightful stop. Rooms are well equipped and offer excellent value for money.

Bérengère
Rue du Trencat — 90.54.35.63
M. Auzet. Closed Tue dinner, Wed, 1 week in Feb and 2 weeks in Nov. Open until 9 pm. Air cond. V.
The last part of the trip to dinner is on foot, for you must climb to the upper part of the village to reach this warm, attractive restaurant. Seated in the tidy, cosy dining room you may then enjoy Bernard Auzet's varied market-fresh fare: quail eggs with foie gras, noisettes of lamb with a creamy rosemary sauce and stuffed vegetables, game in season, and succulent desserts. The cellar holds some fine regional bottlings.
A la carte: 300-350 F. Menus: 160 F, 240 F.

La Cabro d'Or
in Val d'Enfer — 90.54.33.21
M. Thuilier. Closed off-season Tue lunch and Mon, and 15 Nov-20 Dec. Open until 9.30 pm. Terrace dining. Garage parking. Telex 401810. V AE DC.
The little sister of the grand Oustau de Baumanière (see below) is blessed with a colourful garden and a terrace shaded with mulberry trees. It's a luxurious spot in which to enjoy cookery in the Oustau mode, light and full of natural flavours: sardines marinated in basil, paupiette de sole à la crème and écrevisses, spit-roasted leg of kid, and heavenly frozen chocolate mousse.
A la carte: 350 F. Menus: 150 F, 280 F, 355 F.

La Cabro d'Or
(See restaurant above)
Closed Mon off-season, and 15 Nov-20 Dec. 22 rms 460-740 F. TV. Air cond 11 rms. Conference facilities. Pool. Tennis.
Swaddled in greenery, this hotel features good food, a charming welcome, children's activities and horse-back riding. Rooms vary in size and in quality of equipment and furnishings.

Mas d'Aigret

D 27a — 90.54.33.54
M. Phillips. Closed Wed lunch and 4 Jan-28 Feb. Open until 9 pm. Garden dining. No pets. Parking. V AE DC.
A country jumble of furniture, lace, pictures, and bric-a-brac adds to the charm of this lively Provençal restaurant. Chef Pascal Johnson's passion is the singular flavour of his region, and he balances all the bright Southern savours in a cuisine of great finesse: prawn lasagne with a rosemary honey vinaigrette, lotte stewed in wine lees, pigeon in a sweet-(peach)-and-sour-(redcurrant) sauce, and a verbena sabayon dolloped atop a locally grown melon. We can practically guarantee

you'll be enchanted.
A la carte: 350-400 F. Menus: 160 F, 240 F, 380 F.

Mas d'Aigret
(See restaurant above)
Closed 4 Jan-28 Feb. 1 ste 700 F. 14 rms 410-700 F. Half-board 475-620 F. TV. Conference facilities. Pool.
The lawns, the pool, the friendly greeting, and the terraced olive groves, and the views more than make up for the slightly antiquated rooms, which are soon to be renovated, we hear.

L'Oustau de Baumanière
in Val d'Enfer — 90.54.33.07
M. Thuilier. Closed off-season Thu lunch and Wed, and 14 Jan-1 March. Open until 9.30 pm. Private room: 25. Terrace dining. Garage parking. Telex 420203. V AE DC.
A grandfather himself, Raymond Thuilier is the grandson of a legend, and has become something of a legend in his own right. For over thirty years he has greeted gastronomes from all over the world who make the pilgrimage to this bastion of Provençal tradition, as his grandfather did before him. And when tradition came to weigh too heavily on the cuisine (sometimes tiring it out), Jean-André Charial—Thuilier's grandson—fresh from an impressive round of apprenticeships with major chefs, decided to let the sun of Provence shine into the kitchen of Baumanière. His ambition is clear: to make the Oustau a living conservatory of Provençal flavours and ingredients, where culinary tradition is constantly renewed. In recognition of this aim, and to encourage promising signs of success, we award Thuilier and Charial another point this year.
Indeed only the numbest of palates wouldn't appreciate the keen, bright flavours, the subtle sauces, and the simple country accents in which this cuisine sings of its Southern sources. The tenderest baby vegetables come direct from one of the best-run restaurant gardens in France to play a major role in the menu's best dishes (like the firm, warm prawns with tender fennel; an unctuous asparagus velouté dotted with oysters; miniature broad beans tossed with bits of country ham). The unique savour of Provence fairly bursts forth from the delicate red mullet scented with basil, the scallops simmered with black olives, the little lobsters cooked in Châteauneuf-du-Pape and served atop crisp polenta. Shall we go on? Only to mention the young pigeon fragrant with fresh garlic, or the best saddle of rabbit (baked in a salt crust) that you are likely to encounter.
To complete this blissful tableau, the cellar offers all the best vintages of Condrieu, Côte-Rôtie, Hermitage and the other blessed waters of the Rhône. Naturally, such pleasures do not come cheap; but the enchantment one feels in this exceptional spot is rare—and very nearly priceless.
A la carte: 550-850 F. Menus: 520 F, 640 F.

L'Oustau de Baumanière
(See restaurant above)
Closed Wed off-season, and 14 Jan-1 March. 13 stes 1,250 F. 11 rms 700-900 F. TV. Air cond. Conference facilities. Pool. Tennis.
The captivating beauty of Provence is on full parade here from the swimming pool (which doesn't look like one) surrounded by flowers to the spacious sixteenth-century *mas* itself, with its charming rooms. Tennis and horse-back riding at the nearby Cabro d'Or; nine-hole golf course two kilometres away. Relais et Châteaux.

La Riboto de Taven
au Val d'Enfer — 90.54.34.23
MM. Novi and Thème. Closed Sun dinner off-season, Mon and 15 Jan-15 March. Open until 10 pm. Private room: 25. Garden dining. Parking. V AE DC.
On the edge of this tourists' favourite among Provençal villages, this old country manor stands amidst a riot of colourful flowers. In the antique-furnished dining room Philippe Thème and Jean-Pierre Novi serve their lucky guests light, sophisticated cuisine that lacks only a bit more precision in the seasonings. Be sure to try the truffle ravioli, the lobster lasagne, crispy sea bass with aubergine caviar, or Alpilles lamb studded with anchovies and cooked to a turn. Dessert brings a classic fruit sabayon. An affordable cellar full of fine regional bottlings eases the pain of the otherwise stiff bill.
A la carte: 400-450 F. Menus: 190 F (weekdays lunch only), 550 F (wine inc), 250 F, 390 F.

59570 Bavay — (Nord)
Paris 230 - Lille 76 - Valenciennes 23 - Maubeuge 14

12/20 Le Bagacum
2, rue d'Audignie — 27.66.87.00
M. Lesne. Closed Sun dinner and Mon (except holidays), 2-15 Jan and 2-22 July. Open until 9.15 pm. Private room: 30. Air cond. Parking. V AE DC.
Off with the toque in response—not hommage!—to the continued lack of attention to both cooking and service here. Too much vinegar on the salmon salad, overcooked sandre à l'oseille, and an aggressive sauce on the roast guinea hen underline the need for a fresh start.
A la carte: 300-350 F. Menus: 80 F (weekdays only), 250 F (wine inc), 170 F.

Le Bourgogne
Carrefour de Paris — 27.63.12.58
M. Martin. Closed Mon, dinner Sun and Wed, 11-25 Feb and 29 July-13 Aug. Open until 9.30 pm. Private room: 15. Parking. V AE.
The rich, flavoursome cooking of Claudine Martin and her brother Bernard perfectly suits the rustic elegance of the dining room. The repertoire is heavy on sauces, but deft technique lightens the load. Taste the watercress mousseline with goujonettes de sole in a suave beurre blanc, or prawn ravioli bethed in truffle juice, or the mould of sweetbreads with morels. Owner Jacky Martin presides over the cellar.
A la carte: 260-300 F. Menus: 90 F (weekdays only), 160 F, 300 F.

Hôtel Saint-Maur
1, rue St-Maur — 27.66.90.33
Open every day. 8 rms 195-270 F. Restaurant. Half-board 210-270 F. TV. Conference facilities. V AE DC.
A small, renovated hotel just a few kilometres from the Gallo-Roman archaeological site at Bavay.

See Cabourg

Red toques signify modern cuisine; black toques signify traditional cuisine.

14400 Bayeux — (Calvados)
Paris 251 - Cherbourg 92 - Caen 27 - St-Lô 36

Hôtel d'Argouges

21, rue St-Patrice — 31.92.88.86
Open every day. 2 stes 450-530 F. 23 rms 190-340 F. TV 19 rms. Garage parking. Telex 772402. V AE DC.
The attractive rooms of this eighteenth-century mansion, set in a garden in the centre of town, boast beams and understated décor.

Churchill Hôtel
14-16, rue St-Jean — 31.21.31.80
Closed 15 Nov-1 March. 1 ste 450-600 F. 32 rms 280-390 F. TV. No pets. Conference facilities. Parking. Telex 171755. V AE DC.
This very pretty little hotel in the heart of town offers delightful, well-equipped rooms and satellite television.

Le Lion d'Or
71, av. St-Jean — 31.92.06.90
M. Jouvin-Bessière. Closed 20 Dec-20 Jan. Open until 9.30 pm. Private room: 30. Garage parking. Telex 171143. V AE DC.
Leaded windows, wood panelling, and a cobbled courtyard create a pleasingly elegant setting for expertly prepared (though not terribly inventive) cuisine. We enjoyed a generous portion of sweetbread and kidney terrine in a creamy sauce, tournedos with wild mushrooms (very heavy on the garlic, those last), a tasty suprême de pigeon au foie gras, and an excellent pear feuilleté. A la carte: 260-300 F. Menus: 100 F (weekdays only), 140 F, 190 F, 270 F.

Le Lion d'Or
(See restaurant above)
Closed 20 Dec-20 Jan 28 rms 170-405 F. Half-board 260-370 F oblig in seas. TV. Conference facilities.
The rooms of this spacious mansion in the centre of Bayeux are arranged around a cobbled courtyard alive with flowers.

12/20 Les Quatre Saisons
25, rue des Bouchers — 31.92.00.04
M. Morel. Open every day. Open until 10 pm. Private room: 20. Terrace dining. No pets. Parking. Telex 171663. V AE.
A plush interior brilliantly lit, thick curtains, glowing silver, and soft music are not reason enough to maintain the toque, which the cooking— carelessly done and increasingly expensive—no longer deserves. A la carte: 350-400 F. Menus: from 128 F to 299 F.

Grand Hôtel du Luxembourg
(See restaurant above)
Open every day. 3 stes 850-1,250 F. 19 rms 300-500 F. TV. Conference facilities.
These huge, tasteful rooms done in a pleasing hybrid of styles. Modern amenities; indoor garden; attractive breakfasts.

In nearby Aignerville
(17 km W on N 13 and D 198)
14710 Bayeux — (Calvados)

Manoir de l'Hormette
31.22.51.79
Closed 1 Jan-15 March. 2 stes 730-830 F. 5 rms 430 F. TV 4 rms. No pets. Parking.
Superb rustic antiques add the finishing touch to this restored seventeenth-century farm, now a country hideaway. One outbuilding has been converted to an independent residence, for bucolic weekends *en famille.*

In nearby Crépon
(12 km NE on D 12 and D 112)
14480 Bayeux — (Calvados)

Ferme de la Rançonnière
31.22.21.73
Closed 7 Jan-2 Feb. 23 rms 145-260 F. Restaurant. Half-board 195-215 F. Conference facilities. Parking. V AE DC.
This 500-year-old farm is a listed building, and has been restored with the guidance of the Beaux-Arts commission. The result is a simple, tasteful inn with a family atmosphere near the Landing beaches. Wonderful breakfasts.

In nearby Molay-Littry
(13 km W on D 5)
14330 Bayeux — (Calvados)

Les Comtes de Normandie
4 km N on D 5, rte d'Isigny — 31.22.90.82
M. Jouve. Closed 1 Dec-28 Feb. Open until 10 pm. Terrace dining. No pets. Parking. Telex 171912. V AE DC.
This magnificent eighteenth-century château has been renovated with brilliant success. Every window of the impressive dining room overlooks the vast wooded grounds where deer gambol in plain view. The cuisine is appropriately classical and adroitly done with a welcome light touch. Try the tarte renversée de pommes de terre au foie gras, salmon in beurre blanc, or sweetbreads in Sauternes, and finish up with a cinnamon-scented pear royale. Impeccable service. A la carte: 300 F. Menus: 160 F, 210 F, 300 F.

Château du Molay

(See restaurant above)
Closed 1 Dec-28 Feb. 38 rms 350-700 F. Half-board 410-550 F. TV 19 rms. No pets. Conference facilities. Heated pool. Tennis.
Perfect calm, perfectly fitted rooms, perfect view of the park all around. Amenities include a sauna, and an exercise room.

64100 Bayonne — (Pyrénées-A.)
Paris 744 - Bordeaux 176 - Pau 107 - Biarritz 8

Au Bon Vieux Temps
24, rue des Cordeliers — 59.59.78.94
M. Marcel. Closed off-season Sun dinner and Mon, and 15 Feb-15 March. Open until 10 pm. V.
Set in a picturesque street of old Bayonne, the location and décor both recall the 'good old days' of the restaurant's name. The chef, on the other hand, is resolutely modern. He turns out a deft, well-balanced menu of contemporary dishes like crabmeat in a crêpe 'beggar's purse' napped with prawn coulis, and pork fricasée with orange and almonds. Luscious desserts. The cellar offers slim pickings, but the courteous welcome and diligent service would compensate for far greater shortcomings. A la carte: 180-200 F. Menu: 86 F.

Cheval Blanc ☺

68, rue Bourgneuf — 59.59.01.33
M. Tellechea. Closed Sun dinner and Mon (except July-Aug), and 7 Jan-6 Feb. Open until 10 pm. Private room: 25. Air cond. V AE DC.

Young Jean-Claude Tellechea knows what he is about, as one forkful of his baby lamb pot-au-feu, or his roast hake with chicken juices and browned onions, or the langoustines à la crème de caviar will amply prove. He carefully selects his ingredients from the best of the Basque country's bounty, and draws inspiration from the regional repertoire—he is certainly a chef to watch. The cellar holds some fine local offerings, but we'd like to see some older vintages.

A la carte: 260-320 F. Menus: 132 F (weekdays only), 185 F, 235 F.

Aux Deux Rivières

21, rue Thiers — 59.59.14.61
Open every day. 1 ste 500-600 F. 63 rms 320-520 F. Half-board 300-360 F. TV. Conference facilities. Garage parking. Telex 570794. V AE DC.

Spacious, well-kept, but old-fashioned rooms characterize this comfortable hotel in the centre of town.

La Grande Brasserie

3, pl. de la Liberté — 59.59.09.14
M. Diharce. Closed Sun and holidays. Open until 10 pm. V AE DC.

Bayonne's smart set comes in here for the good food served in a warm, polished setting. Plump for the generously apportioned local ham, or a brochette of duck hearts (cooked to order, and escorted by delicious, puffy pommes dauphine), and finish with the floating island (more like a continent, really...). But skip the scampi.

A la carte: 200-250 F. Menu: 89 F.

11/20 Chez Jacques

17, quai Jauréguiberry
59.25.66.83
M. Sonton. Open for lunch only. Closed Sun and Christmas week. Garden dining. Air cond. Pets allowed.

For good fresh—and cheap!—seafood served by the riverside, eat at Jacques'. Fill up on fish, forget dessert.

A la carte: 130 F.

Mendi-Alde

3 km S on D 932
48, av. 8-Mai-1945 — 59.42.38.44
Open every day. 10 rms 130-175 F. Garage parking. V.

This creditable family hotel with a garden can be found three kilometres from town, in sight of the mountains.

Mercure

Av. J.-Rostand — 59.63.30.90
Open every day. 1 ste 600 F. 109 rms 265-440 F. Restaurant. TV. Air cond. Conference facilities. Parking. Telex 550621. V AE DC.

Practically in the centre of town, this modern structure houses renovated rooms overlooking the River Nive and the wooded towpath.

François Miura

29, rue des Cordeliers — 59.59.49.89
M. Miura. Closed Sun dinner, Wed, 26 June-26 July and 19-31 Dec. Open until 10 pm. V AE DC.

As if in counterpoint to the unsightly stucco décor, the cuisine here is simply beautiful. Every dish, from appetiser to dessert, is skilfully crafted and full of flavour. A case in point is the combination of prawn tails with a courgette galette; another is the local squid (chipirons) with a spirited stuffing based on pigs' trotters; yet another is the crispy Basque-style rabbit. Prices are breathtakingly low.

A la carte: 200-230 F. Menus: 85 F, 130 F.

Le Saint-Simon

1, rue des Basques — 59.59.13.40
M. Carti. Closed Sun dinner, Mon and 25 June-9 July. Open until 10 pm. V AE DC.

In the not-too-far-off future, this restaurant could turn out to be the best table in town. A few improvements are called for, notably in the dessert department, but we have nothing but praise for the grilled lotte with thyme, and the kidneys and sweetbreads with a sauce of coarse-grained mustard. Swift, efficient service in a cosy, rustic dining room.

A la carte: 200-220 F. Menu: 125 F.

La Tanière

53, av. du Cap.-Resplandy — 59.25.53.42
M. Villanova. Closed Mon dinner, Tue, first 2 weeks of March and last 2 weeks of June. Open until 10.30 pm. Private room: 20. V AE DC.

The neighbourhood is not Bayonne's beauty spot, but never mind—once you enter this little Basque 'den', hostess Jackie Villanova will make you feel right at home. Her husband's cooking grows purer and more full of flavour as time goes by. An extra point, then, for his scrambled eggs with foie gras, garlicky pork fricassée with tapenade, and refreshing lime mousse. Sensational list of regional wines.

A la carte: 200-250 F. Menu: 125 F.

In nearby **Urcuit**

(12 km E on D 257)
64990 Bayonne — (Pyrénées-A.)

12/20 Restaurant du Halage

D 261 — 59.42.92.98
Closed Mon. Open until 8.30 pm. Parking. V.

Over the years this riverside inn has found its calling serving a dependable menu of good regional fare to a faithful following of locals and tourists. Best bets are the tender leek tourte, escalope of Adour salmon with sorrel, and the lightly smoked foie gras (it melts in the mouth). Delicious country wines wash it all down.

A la carte: 200 F. Menus: 85 F, 148 F, 178 F.

In nearby **Urt**

(14 km E on D 261)
64240 Bayonne — (Pyrénées-A.)

Auberge de la Galupe ☺

Pl. du Port — 59.56.21.84
Mme Parra. Closed Sun dinner (except July-Aug), Mon, Feb and 15 days in Oct. Open until 9.30 pm. Private room: 30. V.

With its fortunate location within walking distance of some of the finest produce in France (Jurançon wines, Montauzer hams, salmon, shad, and eels from the Adour River...) this fisherman's inn has a head start on fine cuisine. And the brilliant talent of chef-owner Christian Parra does those raw materials proud with dishes like pimientos stuffed with salt cod, pig's trotters and cheeks braised with ginger and sherry, tender Pyrenees lamb with a trio of haricots, and a nougat parfait with dark-chocolate sauce. The set menus are a boon to budget-minded gourmets. Wonderful Bas-Armagnacs; adorable service.

A la carte: 300-370 F. Menus: 150 F (weekdays lunch only), 240 F (dinner only).

L'Estanquet
59.56.24.93

M. Arbulo. Open every day. Open until 10 pm. Private room: 25. Terrace dining. Hotel: 13 rms 200-350 F. V AE DC.

This well-known restaurant has just been transplanted by its owners to a small hotel on Urt's village square, too recently for review. But we look forward to the same level of fresh, open-hearted regional fare for which L'Estanquet is justly renowned.

In nearby **Ustaritz**

(12 km SE on D 932)
64480 Bayonne — (Pyrénées-A.)

La Patoula
59.93.00.56

M. Guilhem. Closed off-season Sun dinner and Mon, and 14 Jan-21 Feb. Open until 10 pm. Private room: 14. Garden dining. Parking. V.

Let's get our sole quibble out of the way at once: we wish that chef Pierre Guilhem would renew his menu more frequently (else his enviable 16/20 rating will be at risk). Having said that, we shall go on to praise his zesty rabbit salad served with a slice of foie gras, the delicious brill with sweet peppers, and the roast baby lamb perfumed with rosemary. Anne-Marie Guilhem extends a lively greeting to guests who enter her charming inn, furnished with handsome local antiques. The wine list is succinct but affordably priced, and the service is most attentive.

A la carte: 250-300 F. Menus: 130 F, 230 F.

La Patoula
(See restaurant above)

Closed 14 Jan-21 Feb. 9 rms 280-420 F. Half-board 280-350 F oblig in seas. TV 1 rm.

The lovely renovated rooms with period furniture are all well equipped. Impeccable service.

In nearby **Villefranque**

(11 km SE on N 636 and D 137)
64990 Bayonne — (Pyrénées-A.)

11/20 Gachouche
Quartier-Bas — 59.44.90.71

M. Auger. Closed off-season Tue dinner and Wed, and Feb school holidays. Open until 9.15 pm. Terrace dining. V.

Gachouche is Basque for 'gracious', and Mme Auger is certainly that. The term also applies to the pretty terrace that opens onto the hilly countryside. And the terrace is where we always ask to be seated (rather than in the sombre dining room) when we come to enjoy the smoked-salmon crêpes, the duck fillets, and the peach gratin with raspberry sauce. The chef's obvious skill is not shown to advantage by the modest repertoire—a pity!

A la carte: 160 F. Menus: 80 F, 100 F.

11/20 Iduzki-Alde
59.44.94.09

M. Vivier. Closed Wed and 1-11 Nov. Open until 9.30 pm. Private room: 16. Garden dining. V.

A pleasant spot dedicated to Basque cuisine, from the tasty rabbit terrine made with Jurançon wine

to the buttery gâteau Basque. The cellar spotlights regional growths.

A la carte: 180 F. Menus: 120 F (weekdays only), 88 F.

See also: **Biarritz**

BAZEILLES

See Sedan

BAZINCOURT

27140 Bazincourt — (Eure)
Paris 70 - Rouen 56 - Gisors 4 - Gournay-en-Bray 20

12/20 La Pommeraie
32.55.11.61

MM. Bergeron. Closed Wed, 15 Jan-1 March and 16 Aug-1 Sep. Open until 9 pm. Private room: 80. Terrace dining. No pets. Parking. Telex 771097. V AE DC.

Book your table in the gallery of this Anglo-Norman manor: the sylvan panorama that gives one the impression of eating out-of-doors may also help to lighten the rich and creamy cuisine: sole paupiettes with prawns, lamb fillet in a pastry crust with aubergines, and crêpes normandes with a Calvados-spiked sabayon sauce.

A la carte: 300 F. Menus: 130 F (weekdays only), 175 F.

Château de la Rapée
(See restaurant above)

Closed Wed, 15 Jan-1 March and 16 Aug-1 Sep. 2 stes 600-800 F. 14 rms 295-420 F. Half-board 540-630 F. No pets. Conference facilities.

The freshly painted rooms are large and comfortable. Peace and quiet are guaranteed on this green hilltop surrounded by rolling countryside.

BEAUCAIRE

30300 Beaucaire — (Gard)
Paris 710 - Alès 67 - Arles 20 - Avignon 25

12/20 Les Doctrinaires
Quai du Gal-de-Gaulle — 66.59.41.32

M. Sauvage-Dijol. Closed Sun dinner off-season. Open until 10 pm. Private room: 80. Garden dining. Parking. Telex 480706. V AE.

Set in an old theological school with a paved terrace and an enclosed courtyard, this restaurant offers traditional fare as solid as the building's vaulted ceiling: sweet-and-sour snail cassolette, ordinairy sea trout, a fine array of nicely chosen cheeses, good homemade desserts. Diligent service.

A la carte: 270 F. Menus: 95 F (weekdays dinner only), 160 F, 210 F.

Les Doctrinaires
(See restaurant above)

Closed Sun off-season. 34 rms 320-370 F. Half-board 350 F oblig in seas. TV. Conference facilities.

A superb old building with lovely views all around and huge, exceedingly comfortable rooms.

BEAUCHASTEL

See Voulte-sur-Rhône (La)

45190 Beaugency — (Loiret)
Paris 150 - Blois 31 - Orléans 25 - Vendôme 48

12/20 L'Abbaye

2, quai de l'Abbaye — 38.44.67.35
M. Aupetit. Open every day. Open until 10 pm. Private room: 40. Terrace dining. Parking. Telex 780038. V AE DC.

This old abbey isn't getting any younger (parts of it are ageing all too visibly), but the dining room with its period furniture and baronial fireplace has a certain charm. While not terribly polished, the food is well prepared. Old favourites include duck with olives, and turbot in hollandaise sauce.

A la carte: 400 F. Menu: 185 F.

L'Abbaye

(See restaurant above)
Open every day. 5 stes 520 F. 13 rms 410-520 F. TV 10 rms. Conference facilities.

A faintly dusty old building with varied, interesting guest rooms.

12/20 Hostellerie de l'Ecu de Bretagne

Pl. du Martroi — 38.44.67.60
M. Michau. Open every day. Open until 10 pm. Garden dining. Air cond. No-smoking section. No pets. Parking. V AE DC.

Now that the dining room has been made much more inviting, only the menu needs improvement—the repertoire is far too fussy and old-fashioned. to wit: sweetbreads and kidneys in sherry, tournedos Rossini, navarin de ris de veau grand-mère. Good cellar of astutely chosen wines from the Loire.

A la carte: 300 F. Menus: from 90 F to 280 F.

Hostellerie de l'Ecu de Bretagne

(See restaurant above)
Open every day. 26 rms 120-240 F. Half-board 230-300 F oblig in seas. Conference facilities.

Nice little rooms in an annexe, giving onto a garden.

Hôtel de la Sologne

Pl. St-Firmin — 38.44.50.27
Closed 20 Dec-1 Feb 16 rms 140-260 F. TV. No pets. V.

A delightful old house at the foot of a monumental eleventh-century tower provides guest rooms that open onto a garden.

(2.5 km SW on N 152)
45190 Beaugency — (Loiret)

12/20 La Tonnellerie

12, rue des Eaux-Bleues — 38.44.68.15
Mme Aulagnon. Closed 13 Oct-29 March. Open until 8.45 pm. Garden dining. No pets. Parking. Telex 782479. V DC.

Reasons to stop at La Tonnellerie are its chic interior, which extends out to a summer terrace and pleasant garden; an outstanding wine list; and service that is eager to please. Reasons to give the place a miss are the stiff à la carte prices, and the uninspired cooking of a kitchen that has gone sound to sleep on its laurels. The indolent chef uses top-drawer ingredients, however, and the desserts are very good.

A la carte: 350 F. Menus: 99 F (weekdays lunch only), 399 F (dinner only), 204 F, 293 F.

La Tonnellerie

(See restaurant above)
Closed 13 Oct-29 March. 4 stes 640-760 F. 21 rms 320-720 F. Half-board 475-610 F oblig in seas. No pets. Conference facilities. Heated pool.

Although some are brighter and more comfortable than others, all the rooms are tastefully decorated and the welcome is warm and friendly. All around is the quiet green countryside of the Loiret.

06310 Beaulieu-sur-Mer — (Alpes-Mar.)
Paris 943 - Menton 20 - Nice 10 - Cannes 43

Carlton

7, av. E.-Cavell — 93.01.14.70
Closed 31 Oct-25 March. 33 rms 500-1,050 F. Restaurant. Half-board 615-890 F. TV. Air cond. Conference facilities. Pool. Garage parking. Telex 970421. V AE DC.

A discreetly luxurious hotel just 200 metres from the beach, with rooms that are pretty and nicely equipped.

Le Métropole

15, bd du Gal-Leclerc — 93.01.00.08
M. Badrutt. Closed end Oct-20 Dec. Open until 10 pm. Private room: 20. Garden dining. Air cond. Valet parking. Telex 470304. V AE.

This is the ideal spot for a salt-air cure. Far from the hordes who invade the Côte d'Azur, Le Métropole provides perfect quiet, beauty, delightfully consistent service and food, an elegant ambience, and wonderful views. Nothing jars the senses, while one's palate is pampered with a familiar but reliably soothing roster of sun-drenched Mediterranean dishes: rockfish soup, prawns and aubergines heightened with virgin olive oil, exquisite rock lobster simmered with basil, and rack of lamb with tiny local vegetables. Pure simplicity—like the bowl of flawless berries offered for dessert—may be the last word in luxury, especially in this palatial setting.

A la carte: 500-800 F. Menus: 420 F, 460 F.

Le Métropole

(See restaurant above)
Closed end Oct-20 Dec. 3 stes 2,740-5,660 F (halh-board for 2). 50 rms 740-1,900 F (per pers, half-board oblig). TV. Air cond. Heated pool.

The air is redolent with the sweet pleasure of living well, in this Italian-style villa where no detail is too small for attention. The quality of the service is exceptional, truly of another age.

La Réserve de Beaulieu

5, bd du Gal-Leclerc — 93.01.00.01
Mme Vendé. Closed 20 Nov-21 Dec. Open until 10 pm. Private room: 60. Garden dining. Valet parking. Telex 470301. V AE DC.

This small but legendary 1950's-style luxury hotel, long favoured by the Hollywood set, was recently purchased by a Parisian antique seller and friends. Great masters' paintings and fine furniture are all part of the effort to bring this old place up to jet-set luxury standards. But it's going to take more than beautiful new fixtures to give La Réserve a soul; we are still awaiting the appointment of a new chef.

A la carte: 600-700 F. Menus: from 340 F to 470 F (except holidays).

La Réserve de Beaulieu
(See restaurant above)
Closed 20 Nov-21 Dec. 3 stes 2,400-4,550 F. 50 rms 700-2,400 F. Half-board oblig in seas. TV. Air cond. Conference facilities. Heated pool.
Even if you don't occupy a room in this luxurious turn-of-the-century villa, you can always pull your boat into the private port to lunch or dine with friends who do. La Réserve boasts a spectacular site, a luxuriant flower garden, and a heated pool overlooking the beach.

La Résidence Carlton
9 bis, av. Albert-Ier — 93.01.06.02
Closed 30 Sep-Easter. 30 rms 400-700 F. TV 23 rms. Air cond 23 rms. Parking. Telex 970421. V AE DC
This modern hotel with a pleasant garden stands just 200 metres from the beach. Laundry service.

See also: **Saint-Jean-Cap-Ferrat**

BEAUMETTES
See Gordes

BEAUMONT-EN-AUGE
See Pont-l'Evêque

BEAUMONT-EN-VÉRON
See Chinon

BEAUNE
21200 Beaune — (Côte-d'Or)
Paris 312 - Dijon 40 - Autun 50 - Chalon-sur-Sâone 31

12/20 Le Bénaton
25, rue du Fg-Bretonnière — 80.22.00.26
M. Monnoir. Closed Thu. Open until 10 pm. Terrace dining. V AE.
A pretty, modern restaurant serves as the setting for Bruno Monnoir's market-fresh cuisine, which is not yet absolutely consistent, but full of promise just the same. We found his salade gourmande au foie gras delicious (and generously served), and though the mussel ravioli were too salty, our rack of lamb en croûte was napped with a perfect sauce.
A la carte: 280-300 F. Menus: 85 F (weekdays only), 130 F, 200 F.

13 Central
2, rue V.-Millot — 80.24.77.24
Mme Cuny. Closed off-season Thu lunch and Wed. Annual closings not available. Open until 9.30 pm. V.
Pretty bouquets punctuate the fresh, dainty ground-floor dining room, while the upstairs décor is more quiet and conservative. The tables are beautifully laid, the service is disciplined, and the business of tourism has not eroded the cuisine. Chef Jean Garcin proposes delicious house-smoked salmon, red mullet fillets in a mussel sabayon, sliced veal kidney in enhanced by a sweet carrot essence. The cellar is costly and not very interesting.
A la carte: 350 F. Menus: from 125 F to 280 F.

Central
(See restaurant above)
Closed Wed off-season. Annual closings not available. 20 rms 310-410 F. Half-board 410 F oblig in seas. TV. Pets allowed.
True to its name, this hotel is centrally located, as well as renovated and maintained with care.

Le Cep
27-29, rue Maufoux — 80.22.35.48
Open every day. 3 stes 1,100-1,500 F. 52 rms 450-850 F. TV. Conference facilities. Valet parking. Telex 351256. V AE DC.
Fifty classy rooms—each one named for a *grand cru* of the Côte d'Or—can be found in this Renaissance mansion located in the heart of Beaune (don't miss the courtyard complete with arcades and a stone stairwell).

11/20 La Ciboulette
69, rue de Lorraine — 80.24.70.72
M. Demougeot. Closed Mon dinner, Tue, 4-19 Feb and 5-20 Aug. Open until 9.30 pm. V.
This tasteful, friendly little restaurant offers a high ground above the tourist floods. The food is simple and unpretentious: snails stewed in red wine, tarragon chicken, confit de canard.
A la carte: 200 F. Menu: 68 F.

La Closerie
61, rte de Pommard — 80.22.15.07
Open every day. 1 ste 650 F. 47 rms 300-475 F. TV. Heated pool. Parking. Telex 351213. V AE DC.
Set between Beaune and the vineyards is this modern, comfortable, and completely equipped hotel with an attractive swimming pool and garden.

14 Dame Tartine
(Alain Billard)
3, rue N.-Rolin — 80.22.64.20
M. Billard. Closed Sun dinner, Mon and Dec. Open until 10 pm (11 pm in seas). Terrace dining. V.
A narrow façade opposite the famous Hospices de Beaune opens into a dainty pink-and-blue restaurant that serves clever, bistro-style fare—a judicious mix of cheap and chic, with something for every budget. Quality ingredients go into the (slightly dry) oxtail terrine, the roast lotte drizzled with truffled oil (a dish that easily deserves two toques), a superb calf's head, and delectable desserts. The cellar is quite eclectic (for these parts) and some wines are available by the glass.
A la carte: 200-350 F. Menus: 79 F, 99 F, 200 F, 300 F.

14 L'Ecusson
Pl. Malmédy — 80.24.03.82
M. Senelet. Closed Mon lunch off-season, Sun and Feb. Open until 9 pm. Garden dining. V AE DC.
The purple-and-beige colour scheme won't bother you at all once the friendly, zealous Mme Senelet begins to ply you with her husband's marvellous cooking. Full of fresh, intelligent ideas, Jean-Pierre Senelet's highly personal cuisine revels in spirited combinations like cauliflower velouté with oysters, roast salmon with a dark coulis of boudin noir, duck sweetbreads sautéed with carrots and a whiff of nutmeg, and a 'foie gras' of chestnuts surrounded by tea-flavoured aspic. Spectacular cellar; prodigal set menus.
A la carte: 250-300 F. Menus: 98 F (weekdays only), 142 F, 184 F, 270 F.

Le Home
138, rte de Dijon — 80.22.16.43
Open every day. 23 rms 245-420 F. TV 6 rms. Garage parking. V.
An intimate little oasis of refinement surrounded by greenery. When the weather is fine, breakfast is served in the garden.

Jacques Lainé
10-12, bd Foch — 80.24.76.10
M. Lainé. Closed off-season Wed lunch and Tue, and 15-28 Feb. Open until 9.30 pm. Private room: 30. Garden dining. No pets. Parking. V AE DC.
This imposing nineteenth-century manor, recently renovated, has become something of an unofficial clubhouse for the upstanding burgermeisters of Beaune. In winter, one may find the dining room a little stuffy (is it the starchy décor? or the company?); but come summer, one can dine in the garden, under a spreading cedar, on Jacques Lainé's expert, rigorously classic fare. And to prove that he isn't getting hidebound, the chef has added some more exotic touches—like bananas with the curry-roasted scallops, or a hint of vanilla with the Bresse pigeon en cocotte. Purists need not fear: the good, garlicky escargots à la bourguignonne are still on hand, as well as the pig's trotter with a truffled potato galette. The wine list is a compendium of sumptuous Burgundies.
A la carte: 400-500 F. Menus: 140 F, 195 F, 260 F, 380 F.

Bernard Morillon
31, rue Maufoux — 80.24.12.06
M. Morillon. Closed Tue lunch, Mon and Feb. Open until 10 pm. Private room: 40. Garden dining. Garage parking. V AE DC.
The opulent setting—no end of silver, candelabra, crystal—is designed to dazzle a moneyed clientele of foreign (and perhaps naive) gastro-tourists. The kitchen delivers predictably elaborate dishes (e.g. pigeonneau Souvarov aux pêches de vigne) served with great flourish. One is nearly startled to discover that the food is quite adeptly prepared, and well worth a toque.
A la carte: 500 F and up. Menus: 160 F, 250 F, 350 F.

La Poste
1, bd Clemenceau — 80.22.08.11
M. Chevillot. Closed 17 Nov-1 April. Open until 10 pm. Garden dining. Valet parking. Telex 350982. V AE DC.
A well-known stop in Burgundy for travellers heading South, where tradition keeps imagination well reined in. But the clientele obviously wants it that way, and it is hard not to enjoy the excellent snails, parslied ham, or poularde aux morilles served in a classic, 'grand hotel' atmosphere. Impeccable service; classic Burgundian cellar.
A la carte: 350-400 F. Menus: 210 F (lunch only), 320 F, 350 F.

La Poste
(See restaurant above)
Closed 17 Nov-1 April. 6 stes. 21 rms 760-770 F (per pers, half-board oblig). TV. Conference facilities.
Kind attention is the watchword of this traditional hotel with a view of both the city and the vineyards.

Relais de Saulx
6, rue L.-Véry — 80.22.01.35
M. Monnoir. Closed Sun dinner, Mon, 15-31 Dec and 15-30 June. Open until 9.30 pm. Air cond. V.
A plush and cosy little spot behind the Hospices that caters for wealthy tourists in quest of creature comforts and hearty Burgundian fare. The chef obliges with nicely done cabbage stuffed with snails, Bresse chicken terrine with foie gras, and Bresse chicken with morels and cream.
A la carte: 350-400 F. Menus: 120 F (weekdays lunch only), 180 F, 240 F, 380 F.

12/20 La Rôtisserie de la Paix
47, rue du Fg-Madeleine — 80.22.33.33
M. Belin. Closed Sun dinner, Mon and end Nov-beg Feb. Open until 10 pm. Garden dining. V AE DC.
We give a provisional rating this year, while waiting to see what becomes of the promising start made by the new owners of this lovely restaurant. Although far from the centre of Beaune, it is fast becoming a meeting point for local connoisseurs who admire chef Jean-Pierre Belin's skill and originality. Sample his fillets of plaice on a bed of cabbage, napped with deftly reduced meat juices, or his lamb noisettes in a subtle sauce. But before we commit ourselves to a toque, we would like to see more generous portions, a worthier wine list, and improved service.
A la carte: 280 F. Menus: 95 F, 250 F.

(5 km N on N 74)
21420 Beaune — (Côte-d'Or)

Clarion
80.26.46.70
Open every day. 10 rms 418-750 F. TV. Conference facilities. Parking. V AE DC.
Set amidst the vineyards, this pretty provincial hotel dates from the seventeenth century. Rooms are spacious, and tastefully decorated; some have individual terraces. Excellent breakfasts.

(4 km NE on N 74)
21200 Beaune — (Côte-d'Or)

Le Bareuzai
N 74, rte de Dijon — 80.22.02.90
M. Voarick. Closed 2-31 Jan. Open until 9.30 pm. Private room: 80. Terrace dining. Air cond. Parking. V AE DC.
The young sous-chef was recently put in charge of the kitchen (his predecessor is off to start a place of his own), and has chosen to stick with the familiar house repertoire: sweetbreads with olives, prawns in an excellent saffron sauce, rack of lamb with vegetables, a good prunelle soufflé. The dining room enjoys a lovely panorama of the wine hills of Beaune, where the proprietors also own a vineyard. Needless to say, claret plays only a cameo role on the wine list!
A la carte: 250-300 F. Menus: 60 F (weekdays only), 125 F, 260 F.

L'Ermitage Corton
N 74 — 80.22.05.28
M. Parra. Closed Sun dinner, Mon and mid-Jan-mid-Feb. Open until 9 pm. Private room: 35. Garden dining. Parking. Telex 351189. V AE DC.
We are still having trouble convincing the owner that it isn't his restaurant we don't like, but the pompous, gimmicky, gilt-encrusted décor. Granted, some may like it, but it is our business to call them as we see them, and this place, to our taste, is tacky, precious, and overdone. The spirit of the décor even creeps onto the plates in the form of little pastry decorations arranged around the food, but fortunately it stops there. The cuisine, as we have always insisted, is adroit, full of flavour, sincere, and based on the very best of ingredients. We have nothing but praise for the trio of truffled foies gras, or the cassis-infused duckling with two sauces, or the quick-sautéed sea bass with truffle butter and assorted mushrooms. Professional service; magnificent cellar; exemplary cheese board.

A la carte: 500 F. Menus: 165 F (weekdays only), 280 F, 380 F, 520 F.

L'Ermitage Corton
(See restaurant above)
Closed mid-Jan-mid-Feb. 10 stes 750-1,250 F. TV. Pets allowed.

Careful: You could lose your dachshund in the thick-pile carpet of these luxurious suites. But the obliging staff would surely find him for you, while you relax in a warm bath in the pharaonic bathroom. Grandiose fittings and furniture, spectacular breakfasts.

In nearby **Ladoix-Serrigny**

(7 km NE on N 74)
21550 Beaune — (Côte-d'Or)

Les Coquines
N 74, in Buisson — 80.26.43.58
M. Juillard. Closed Wed dinner and Thu. Open until 9.30 pm. Private room: 20. Parking. V DC.

This lovely restaurant housed in a wine-grower's residence on the edge of Ladoix has yet another new chef. We hope this one stays on, for his pork sausage in a dense wine sauce, his thick, garlicky cod fillets, and his tête de veau sauce gribiche all showed promise. Fine regional cellar; excellent cheeses. The modern décor of stone and glass is adorned (by the clever proprietress) with masses of fresh flowers.

A la carte: 350 F. Menus: 108 F, 167 F.

Les Paulands
N 74 — 80.26.41.05
Closed 20 Dec-4 Feb. 2 stes 480-680 F. 17 rms 180-340 F. Restaurant. Half-board 345-395 F. TV. Conference facilities. Heated pool. Parking. Telex 351293. V.

Bright, fresh, renovated rooms are on offer in this ivy-covered dwelling just off the main road close to the vineyards of Corton.

In nearby **Levernois**

(5 km SE on D 970 and D 111)
21200 Beaune — (Côte-d'Or)

Jean Crotet
Rte de Combertault — 80.24.73.58
M. Crotet. Closed Wed lunch, Tue, 28 July-13 Aug and 20 Dec-10 Jan. Open until 9.30 pm. Private room: 40. Garden dining. Parking. Telex 351468. V AE DC.

The height of conservative luxury can be savoured in this beautiful residence whose opulently decorated dining room opens onto manicured grounds. The cuisine reflects this serious approach to gastronomy with a concise, perfectly executed menu, which, one can't help regretting, lacks personality, regional accents, and some vivifying imagination. But chef Jean Crotet and his son Christophe are sure to impress with their superior technique, displayed in the duck liver sautéed with sherry vinegar, pigeon sautéed with foie gras, sublime grilled turbot, braised spiced sweetbreads, and a marvellous Bresse chicken roasted with puréed potatoes. Desserts have more verve (thin apple tart with tarragon sorbet). Service is a bit supercilious, and the cellar is costly, very costly.

A la carte: 450 F. Menus: 200 F (lunch only), 350 F, 450 F.

Hostellerie de Levernois
(See restaurant above)
Closed Tue, 28 July-13 Aug and 20 Dec-10 Jan. 12 rms 700-800 F. Half-board 900-1,250 F oblig in seas. TV. No pets. Tennis.

The formal gardens, the nearby river, and the magnificent trees all add to the pleasure of staying in one of the huge guestrooms of this luxuriously renovated establishment. Flawless breakfasts; a tennis court has just been added. Relais et Châteaux.

In nearby **Meursault**

(7 km SW on N 74)
21190 Beaune — (Côte-d'Or)

Les Charmes
10, pl. du Murger — 80.21.63.53
Closed 21-30 Dec and 1-15 Feb. 15 rms 260-450 F. TV. Parking. V AE.

This pleasant stopover on the Burgundy wine road is set in wooded grounds. It offers attractive rooms and—no surprise—a wine bar.

BEAUPOUYET
See Mussidan

BEAURECUEIL
See Aix-en-Provence

BEAUSSET (LE)
83330 Beausset (Le) — (Var)
Paris 822 - Marseille 47 - Aix 64 - Toulon 17

La Cigalière
At La Daby
N 8, rte du Camp — 94.98.64.63
Closed 20-28 Feb and 1-15 Nov. 5 stes 480-580 F. 14 rms 270-360 F. Restaurant. Half-board 275-310 F oblig in seas. No pets. Conference facilities. Pool. Tennis. Parking. V.

A Provençal farmhouse enveloped in greenery offers a warm welcome, pleasant rooms, breakfast (not served in the rooms, but the coffee is excellent), and outdoor dining.

Le Poivre d'Ane
4 km SE on N 8
in Ste-Anne-d'Evenos — 94.90.37.88
M. Billon. Closed Sun dinner and Mon (except holidays). Open until 9.30 pm. Garden dining. Parking. V.

This fine chef from the north of France and his wife couldn't have found a sunnier, prettier place than this Provençal house set in a shady garden. Fitted out with perfect taste, the handsome dining room is a showcase for André Billon's cuisine, which has made a graceful transition South: red mullet in a warm vinaigrette, sea bream with green-pepper coulis, and veal kidneys with fresh coriander are all beautifully done.

A la carte: 260-320 F. Menus: 160 F, 220 F.

12/20 La Vigneraie
(Auberge de la Gruppi)
146, nationale 8 — 94.98.70.18
Mme Viaud and M. Baumgartner. Closed Mon dinner off-season, Tue, 15-28 Feb and 15-30 Nov. Open until 9.30 pm. Hotel: 10 rms 140-240 F. V AE DC.

The heavy-handed neo-rustic décor mars what was doubtless a handsome coaching inn—once upon a time. Fortunately the cooking escapes the pervasive ponderousness of the setting. Try the duck quenelles, skate in beurre rouge or the veal mignon with chanterelles, all best washed down with a good little local Bandol.

A la carte: 150-230 F. Menus: 95 F, 155 F, 200 F.

60000 Beauvais — (Oise)
Paris 76 - Rouen 80 - Amiens 60 - Pontoise 50

12/20 La Belle du Coin
67, rue du Gal-Kœnig — 44.45.07.24
M. Boulanger. Closed Sat lunch. Open until 9 pm. Private room: 12. Parking. V AE.

Rustic beams, hunting trophies, and the provincial Louis XIII décor are at odds with the traffic that zips by on the ring road just outside the door, but the flowers on the table and the creditable classical cooking are pleasant nonetheless. The only fault we can find with the foie gras, the sweetbreads in mustard sauce, and the juicy grilled steak is that they are a bit too dear.

A la carte: 280-300 F. Menus: 90 F, 135 F.

A la Côtelette
8, rue des Jacobins — 44.45.04.42
M. Sérouart. Closed Sun (except holidays). Open until 10 pm. Private room: 50. No-smoking section. V AE.

Local worthies forgather in this modern dining room done in tones of grey, white, and salmon to enjoy the flavourful, attractively presented cuisine of chef-proprietor Denis Sérouart. He seems more keen than ever to procure truly first-rate ingredients for his foie gras, his assortment of lightly cooked fish in a silken cream sauce, and the berry gratin with Champagne sabayon. Prices are stiff, and the reception (we daren't say 'welcome') is often quite chilly. Good cellar, with an emphasis on claret.

A la carte: 400 F. Menu: 160 F (wine inc).

11/20 Le Marignan
1, rue de Malherbe — 44.48.15.15
M. Lelu. Closed Sun dinner and Mon (except holidays), 1-21 Feb and 1-15 Sep. Open until 9 pm. V AE.

Most of the patrons seems to agree that the sauerkraut in the ground floor brasserie is a better bet than the trout with almonds or canard à l'orange served in the more 'stylish' restaurant upstairs.

A la carte: 200-250 F. Menus: 61 F (weekdays only), 99 F, 144 F, 197 F.

36370 Bélâbre — (Indre)
Paris 312 - Châteauroux 57 - Argenton 36

L'Ecu
Pl. de la République — 54.37.60.82
M. Cotar. Closed Sun dinner, Mon, 14 Jan-4 Feb and 16-30 Sep. Open until 9 pm. Private room: 16. Hotel: 6 rms 300-350 F (per pers, half-board oblig). Garage parking. V AE DC.

French provincial life as it should be: a beautiful coaching inn on the village square where one eats very, very well. You'll overlook the mournful, darkly wainscotted rustic décor, chock-a-block with copper pots and pans, when you down your first forkful of Daniel Cotar's generous, open-hearted cooking. From the succinct, seasonal menu you could choose a creative dish, like the crisp hot oysters with leeks, or a pure classic like the fillet of beef in Bourgueil wine. Or opt for a regionally rooted speciality, like foie gras from ducks raised in Bélâbre, or the salmon steak with locally grown lentils, or andouillette bélâbraise à la ficelle. Desserts are often variations on the theme of fruit and puff pastry; the cellar holds intoxicating treasures from the Loire. Now, after all that hearty eating, you may be tempted to stop on and spend the night—six charming guestrooms have been fitted out for the occasion.

A la carte: 350 F. Menus: 130 F (weekdays only), 350 F.

12390 Belcastel — (Aveyron)
Paris 625 - Rodez 27 - Rignac 11 - Decazeville 27

Le Vieux Pont
65.64.52.29
Mmes Fagegaltier. Closed Sun dinner (except July-Aug), Mon and 1 Jan-15 Feb. Open until 9 pm. No pets. V AE.

Deep in the Rouergue region nestles a picture-perfect medieval village where the occasional tourist supposes that he will be fed a good dose of local charcuterie, and a plateful of locally fished, deep-fried whitebait. Well that was how things used to be, when the elder Fagegaltier ran this reputed village restaurant. But with dizzying speed their two daughters have turned the Vieux Pont into a very fine table indeed. The younger was hardly out of hotel school before she began creating fresh, spontaneous dishes like her sea bream cooked with herbs macerated in olive oil, salmon feuillantine with millet seeds, or a crisp gratin of cèpes with a bright parsley coulis. The first-rate desserts betray an undisguised weakness for chocolate. Service is faultless, the cellar is quite fine, but the prices are rising, rising....

A la carte: 300 F. Menus: 100 F (weekdays only), 180 F, 270 F.

90000 Belfort — (T./Belfort)
Paris 424 - Colmar 70 - Bâle 65 - Besançon 90

Altea Hôtel du Lion
2, rue G.-Clemenceau — 84.21.17.00
Open every day. 82 rms 350-550 F. Restaurant. TV. Conference facilities. Garage parking. Telex 360914. V AE DC.

The renovated rooms are comfortable, the location is central and the bar is open late.

Hostellerie du Château Servin
9, rue du Gal-Négrier — 84.21.41.85
Mme Servin. Closed Sun dinner, Fri and Aug. Open until 9.15 pm. Private room: 70. Terrace dining. Air cond. Garage parking. Telex 360724. Hotel: 1 ste 420 F. 10 rms 300-400 F. TV. No pets. V AE DC.

It is no easy feat to play in the classical mode with such lightness of touch, and with nary a slip. Supported by the very best of ingredients, chef Dominique Mathy composes a harmonious menu of foie gras royale with fresh morels, parslied beef jowls with foie gras, duckling and squid stewed in red wine in a blood-thickened sauce, and local lake fish with a frothy beurre mousseux. Desserts like the wild strawberries in Champagne sauce, and the oranges orientales helped Mathy win an extra point this year. Save for a surprising lack of Late Harvest Alsatian Rieslings, the wine list is complete and far-ranging. Superb service.

A la carte: 380-450 F. Menus: from 180 F to 450 F.

Le Pot au Feu

27 bis, Grande-Rue – 84.28.57.84

M. Guyotjeannin. Closed Sun, Mon, first week of Jan and 1-20 Aug. Open until 10 pm. V.

Old boiled-beef barons don't die, they just simmer away. Just when we thought that Mr Guyotjeannin was ripe for retirement, he's added a new 'nineteenth-century pot-au-feu' to his already lengthy roster of boiled dinners. If pot-au-feu is not your meat, try the prime beef from Salers or milk-fed veal from Belfort. Start with sautéed prawns or good foie gras à la compote de figues, and finish up with a tasty fruit gratin. Casual atmosphere.

A la carte: 300 F. Menus: 80 F and 120 F (lunch only), 240 F, 270 F.

In nearby Offemont

(3 km N on D 13 and D 22)
90000 Belfort – (T./Belfort)

Le Sabot d'Annie

5, rue A.-Bria

90300 Valdoie – 84.26.01.71

M. Barbier. Closed Sat lunch, Sun, Feb school holidays and 3 first weeks of Aug. Open until 9 pm. Air cond. Parking. V.

We put up with uncomfortable tables, a tight-lipped greeting, and a waiter who took down our order as if he were citing us for a traffic violation, just to get at the marvellous, purely professional cooking of chef Gérard Barbier. We were so impressed that despite the difficulties, we're giving him an extra point this year for his remarkable frog ravioli in a delicate mushroom fumet, a succulent rabbit terrine in a sapid Riesling gelée, and the fresh, delicious veal kidneys in Jura wine.

A la carte: 320-370 F. Menus: 300 F (dinner only), 150 F, 220 F.

BELLEGARDE-SUR-VALSERINE

01200 Bellegarde-sur-Valserine – (Ain)
Paris 508 - Annecy 41 - Genève 41 - Lyon 121

Auberge de la Fontaine

4 km W on D 101

Rte de Genissiat, in Ochiaz – 50.56.57.23

M. Ripert. Closed Sun dinner, Mon, (Mon lunch only in July- Aug), Jan and 1-10 June. Open until 9 pm. Terrace dining. Hotel: 7 rms 225-295 F (per pers, half-board oblig). Garage parking. V AE DC.

If Colette Ripert could fit another flower into this delightful country dining room she probably would, but instead she's saving room for you to squeeze in and taste the *patron*'s rich, creamy but refined cooking: duck foie gras, turbot in Champagne, sweetbreads in Madeira, raspberry cake spiked with Cointreau.

A la carte: 300 F. Menus: 100 F and 150 F (weekdays only), 235 F, 280 F.

La Belle Epoque

10, pl. Gambetta – 50.48.14.46

M. Sévin. Closed off-season Sun dinner and Mon, 1-17 July and 12 Nov-4 Dec. Open until 9 pm. Garage parking. V.

This pleasant provincial dining room under a soaring ceiling boasts a glassed-in patio with a view of the Place Gambetta. Madame runs the business while Monsieur presides in the kitchen, cooking up sea bream with garden sorrel (whose garden?), stuffed pigeon (stingy portions), and a poached Bresse chicken with morels and cream. A judicious, far-ranging cellar.

A la carte: 300 F. Menus: 120 F (weekdays only), and from 150 F to 260 F.

La Belle Epoque

(See restaurant above)

Closed off-season Sun and Mon, 1-17 July and 12 Nov-4 Dec. 10 rms 220-300 F. Pets allowed.

The ten inviting, cosy rooms, fully renovated, are equipped with fitted carpet, double windows, and pretty accessories.

La Colonne

1, rue J.-Bertola – 50.48.10.45

Closed Sun. 30 rms 120-220 F. Restaurant. Half-board 165 F. TV 15 rms. Conference facilities. Telex 319019. V AE DC.

Thirty well-maintained rooms in the centre of town.

BELLE-ILE-EN-MER

56360 Belle-Ile-en-Mer – (Morbihan)
Boarding in Quiberon (97.31.80.01)

Le Cardinal

in Sauzon – 97.31.61.60

Closed 1 Oct-beg April. 80 rms 250-380 F (per pers, half-board oblig). Restaurant. Conference facilities. Parking. Telex 730750. V.

A rather anonymous contemporary hotel, but the surroundings are sublime: moors, broom plant, and, of course, the sea.

Castel Clara

in Port-Goulphar – 97.31.84.21

M. Goumy. Closed 15 Dec-15 Feb. Open until 9.30 pm. Private room: 25. Garden dining. No pets. Parking. Telex 730750. V.

The hotel's new sea-water spa seems to have rejuvenated the kitchen. Chef Yves Pérous seems to have a lighter touch that respects the simplicity and freshness of his superb ingredients. Test the prawn fricassée with wild fennel, sea bass steamed with seaweed served with beurre blanc, and a pear chaud-froid with local honey. The dining room boasts a ravishing view.

A la carte: 300 F. Menus: 130 F (weekdays lunch only), 290 F (dinner only), 205 F, 195 F.

Castel Clara

(See restaurant above)

Closed 15 Dec-15 Feb. 11 stes 990-1,595 F. 32 rms 780-950 F. Half-board 550-745 F oblig in seas. TV. Conference facilities. Heated pool. Tennis.

Every room and suite has been redone with the installation of a sea-water spa in the hotel. Relais et Châteaux.

La Forge

Rte de Goulphar – 97.31.51.76

Mme Mulon. Closed Wed (except school holidays) and 4 Jan-1 March. Open until 9.30 pm. Garden dining. Parking. V AE DC.

In this adorable décor of stone and wainscotting accented with the shade of blue so typical of Belle-Ile, self-taught chef Marcel Mulon draws his raw materials and inspiration from the briny deep, for simple, generous dishes like shellfish marinière, saffron-scented crustaceans wrapped up in a crêpe 'beggar's purse', and curried cuttlefish ragoût. Expect a smiling welcome.

A la carte: 280-300 F. Menus: 98 F (lunch only), 160 F.

La Désirade

(See restaurant above)

Closed 4 Jan-1 March. 26 rms 420 F. TV. Conference facilities. Heated pool.

A new 'hotel village' offering plush rooms disposed around a swimming pool and garden.

Manoir de Goulphar 🌲🍴

in Port-Goulphar — 97.31.83.95
Closed end Nov-mid-Feb 52 rms 325-380 F (per pers, half-board oblig). Restaurant. TV. Conference facilities. Parking. Telex 730750. V.

Some of the small but comfortable rooms in this beautifully situated hotel offer a balcony on the sea.

11/20 Le Phare

in Sauzon — 97.31.60.36
M. Pacalet. Closed 1 Oct-31 March. Open until 8.30 pm. Terrace dining. No pets. Parking.

You'll see eye-to-eye with the seagulls from your waterside table while you sample some tasty seafood: stuffed clams, turbot in beurre blanc, and sole meunière. Cheap and cheerful.
A la carte: 200 F. Menus: 65 F, 90 F, 150 F.

Le Phare

(See restaurant above)
Closed 1 Oct-31 March. 15 rms 170-190 F (per pers, half-board oblig). Pets allowed.

Small, minimally equipped lodgings behind the lighthouse. Marvellous sea views.

22810 Belle-Isle-en-Terre — (Côtes/Armor)
Paris 503 - St-Brieuc 51 - Morlaix 36 - Lannion 28

Le Relais de l'Argoat

96.43.00.34
M. Marais. Closed Sun dinner, Mon and Feb. Open until 9 pm. Private room: 15. No pets. Hotel: 10 rms 145-185 F. Parking. V.

Passion obviously rules over profit in a restaurant that serves such superb seafood cuisine for so little money in an area famous for crippling prices. The menu changes daily, depending on what looks good at the fish market; it might, for example, offer local bay scallops with asparagus tips, house-smoked salmon with aubergine caviar, or red-mullet terrine on a prawn coulis. Affordable cellar.
A la carte: 200 F. Menus: 70 F (weekdays only), 110 F, 140 F, 220 F.

See Vichy

54940 Belleville — (Meurthe/M.)
Paris 313 - Metz 39 - Toul 28 - Nancy 19

Le Bistroquet

97, rte Nationale — 83.24.90.12
M. Ponsard. Closed Sat lunch, Sun dinner, Mon and 23 Dec-10 Jan. Open until 10.30 pm. Private room: 35. Garden dining. Air cond. Parking. V AE DC.

Regular customers were pleasantly surprised this year by the addition of a new dining terrace overlooking the green countryside behind the Bistroquet. Madame Ponsard, who presides in the kitchen, is rolling up her sleeves to feed the 50 extra customers the expanded premises now hold. Her cooking is rich but in tune with the seasons, conservative but never tedious. You can't go wrong with her potato and salmon galettes, the fatted duck breast with truffles, or a wonderfully herbal fresh cod steak, followed by a delicate apple tart. Jean Ponsard's cellar is splendid, but unmercifully dear.
A la carte: 400 F. Menus: 170 F and 230 F (au Jardin de Marie), 340 F.

12/20 La Moselle

In front of the railway station — 83.24.91.44
M. Laurent. Closed Tue dinner, Wed, 11-27 Feb and 19 Aug-5 Sep. Open until 9.30 pm. Private room: 25. Garden dining. Air cond. Parking. V AE DC.

Love for his work and respect for his customers show in every detail of this good chef's restaurant. Dine outdoors (in fine weather) on foie gras terrine with a bright touch of fennel, escargots en meurette, or a rich chartreuse de pigeon in red-wine sauce.
A la carte: 280 F. Menus: 110 F, 170 F, 240 F.

29118 Bénodet — (Finistère)
Paris 556 - Brest 88 - Concarneau 22 - Quimper 16

Ferme du Letty 🍃

2 km SE, au Letty — 98.57.01.27
M. Guilbault. Closed Thu lunch and Wed (except July-Aug), and mid-Nov-1 March. Open until 10 pm. Private room: 30. Terrace dining. No pets. V AE DC.

Nothing short of blissful are the marriages of flavours, aromas, and tastes so aptly arranged by master chef Jean-Marie Guilbaut. Take for example our most recent meal in this renovated Breton farmhouse: a perfectly balanced (and fat-free!) prawn consommé redolent of coriander and celery, mussels and sole simmered with a zest of orange and a whiff of star anise, turbot cooked in meat juices then layered with crêpes and diced vegetables and spiced with a touch of floral Szechuan pepper, and red mullet with Breton beans and a subtle hint of rosemary. The setting is beautiful and the service never wanting. An extra point this year.
A la carte: 300-350 F. Menus: 138 F (weekdays lunch only), 193 F, 340 F.

12/20 Gwell Kaër

Av. de la Plage — 98.57.04.38
M. Charrettour. Closed off-season Sun dinner and Mon, and 15 Dec-1 Feb. Open until 9 pm. Terrace dining. No pets. Garage parking. V.

The bay windows command a view of the river mouth and the sea, a superb panorama to admire while dining on proficient—if rather simple—cooking. Chef Jean-François Darcillon plans to give the repertoire more zip, but in consideration of his elderly clientele, he is moving slowly. But gourmets of any age are sure to enjoy the beautiful prawns in mayonnaise, plump oysters, and the John Dory with apples in cider.
A la carte: 230-250 F. Menus: 75 F (weekdays only, except dinner in July-Aug), and from 120 F to 350 F.

Gwell Kaër

(See restaurant above)
Closed off-season Sun and Mon, and 15 Dec-1 Feb. 24 rms 200-430 F. Half-board 320-390 F oblig in seas. No pets. Conference facilities.

Most of these blue-and-white rooms have a balcony or a terrace from which to enjoy the ocean view.

Hostellerie Abbatiale

4, av. de l'Odet — 98.57.05.11
Closed Jan and Feb. 58 rms 225-332 F. Restaurant. Half-board 240-330 F. TV. Conference facilities. Tennis. Parking. Telex 941865. V.

This tall historic building near the Gothic church has been entirely renovated. The upper floors especially afford a superb view of the port and the Odet estuary. Pretty rooms, friendly service.

Kastel-Moor et Ker-Moor
Av. de la Plage — 98.57.04.48
Open every day. 83 rms 280-470 F. Restaurant. Half-board 430-460 F oblig in seas. TV. Conference facilities. Heated pool. Tennis. Garage parking. Telex 941182. V.

One of these twins is situated on the beach, while the other stands in verdant grounds. They share squash courts and a wooded park. Both offer large, well-equipped rooms that are oddly devoid of charm.

Le Minaret
Corniche de l'Estuaire
98.57.03.13
Closed 1 Oct-1 April. 21 rms 220-360 F. Restaurant. Half-board 230-340 F oblig in seas. TV. Parking. V.

The name gives away the Moorish motifs that dominate the décor, but you don't have to climb the eponymous prayer tower to admire the superb view. Lovely rooms.

In nearby Clohars-Fouesnant

(3 km NE)
29118 Bénodet — (Finistère)

12/20 La Forge d'Antan
in Pen-Ar-Valannec — 98.54.84.00
M. Bremond. Closed Sun dinner (except July-Aug), Mon and 1-25 March. Open until 9 pm. Private room: 15. Parking. V.

The centrepiece in a bouquet of trees, this perfectly maintained establishment is as delightful as the cooking of chef Jean-Paul Bremond used to be. His fault, however, is inconsistency, so while we found the foie gras terrine to b be remarkable, the salmon tartare with prawns featured a very so-so salmon. The turbot with truffle essence was not at its peak, either, and with the onslaught of lacklustre desserts, we decided we really had to remove the toque this year.

A la carte: 250-300 F. Menus: 120 F (weekdays only), 140 F, 205 F, 300 F.

In nearby Sainte-Marine

(5.5 km W on D 44)
29120 Bénodet — (Finistère)

Le Jeanne-d'Arc
52, rue de la Plage — 98.56.32.70
M. Fargette. Closed Mon dinner and Tue (except July-Aug), and 30 Sep-1 April. Open until 9 pm. Private room: 12. Air cond. Hotel: 9 rms 130-160 F. Parking. V.

René Fargette hails from Burgundy and still evokes a little whimsical homesickness in hybrid dishes like lobster Bresse-style; but for the most part his menu is pure, delightful imagination: crab with maize squares in curry butter, sole in a chervil-scented sauce of eggs and cream, rock lobster royale with lardons, young boned pigeon roasted with lobster butter and served with broad beans. The banal décor serves presumably as contrast to the chef's inventive dishes, which, by the way, do not come cheap. The fine wines carry appalling tariffs.

A la carte: 350-400 F. Menus: 160 F, 240 F, 360 F.

BÉNOUVILLE

See Caen

28560 Berchères-sur-Vesgre — (Eure-et-Loir)
Paris 70 - Evreux 43 - Dreux 29 - Ivry-la-Bataille 9

Château de Berchères
18, rue du Château — 37.82.07.21
Closed Sun and 16 July-13 Aug. 3 stes 935 F. 32 rms 540-685 F. Restaurant. TV. Conference facilities. Tennis. Parking. Telex 780684. V AE DC.

The vast grounds of this pretty eighteenth-century château include a pond. The rooms vary greatly in size and equipment, but all are clean and comfortable.

62600 Berck-Plage — (P./Calais)
Paris 207 - Abbeville 46 - Boulogne-sur-Mer 42

Banque
43, rue de la Division-Leclerc — 21.09.01.09
Open every day. 14 rms 149-235 F. Restaurant. Half-board 225 F. TV. 6 rms. Conference facilities. V AE.

This modest family hotel offers generally agreeable accommodation. Some rooms are quite small.

24100 Bergerac — (Dordogne)
Paris 522 - Bordeaux 92 - Périgueux 47 - Agen 89

Climat
St-Laurent-des-Vignes — 53.57.22.23
Open every day. 46 rms 260 F. Restaurant. Half-board 290 F. TV. Conference facilities. Pool. Parking. Telex 573353. V AE.

A clean, comfortable, impersonal new hotel built on the banks of the Dordogne. Buffet breakfast.

Le Cyrano
2, bd Montaigne — 53.57.02.76
M. Turon. Closed Sun dinner (except July-Aug), Mon, 26 June-10 July and 18-28 Dec. Open until 9 pm. Private room: 15. Air cond. Garage parking. Telex 570418. V AE DC.

A significant price revision—downwards—has brought back some of the clients who found his tariffs off-putting. But Jean-Paul Turon's cooking has remained as dynamic and enthusiastic as ever: tomatoes stuffed with snails, ragoût of duck giblets, sweetbreads in Bergerac wine. And you now can take advantage of an astonishing 120 F prix-fixe feast featuring calf's head in a spicy vinaigrette, salmon wrapped in cabbage leaves, delicious pork jowls with walnuts, and a tempting chocolate dessert. Washed down by a fine Bergerac, it's a meal to leave you happier, but not poorer.

A la carte: 280-300 F. Menus: 85 F (weekdays only), 120 F, 190 F.

Le Cyrano
(See restaurant above)
Closed Sun, 26 June-10 July and 18-28 Dec. 11 rms 210-230 F. Half-board 290-430 F. TV. Pets allowed.

Well-cared-for rooms in a big house with an enclosed veranda.

La Flambée
Rte de Périgueux — 53.57.52.33
M. Bournizel. Closed off-season Sun dinner and Mon, and 2 Jan-2 April. Open until 9.30 pm. Private room: 150. Terrace dining. Parking. V AE DC.

The music played on your palate by this savoury, traditional cuisine will quickly drown out the background buzz of traffic on the main road nearby. To sample the house expertise look no farther than the lovely vegetable terrine with tomato coulis, seafood salad with lime, guinea fowl forestière, followed by beautiful goat cheeses, and a fragrant peach poached in sweet Monbazillac wine with strawberry granité. Interesting regional cellar.

A la carte: 250 F. Menus: 90 F, 130 F, 175 F, 230 F.

La Flambée
(See restaurant above)
Closed 2 Jan-2 April. 1 ste 400-450 F. 21 rms 210-450 F. Half-board 370 F. TV. Conference facilities. Pool. Tennis.

Here's a pretty country manor with perfectly maintained rooms and attractive grounds. In the annexe, some rooms have terraces that overlook a little garden.

Hôtel de France
18, pl. Gambetta — 53.57.11.61
Open every day. 20 rms 190-275 F. TV. Garage parking. Telex 570418. V.

A pleasant little hotel, which new owners are currently renovating. Rooms are modern and good-sized, with a view of the garden.

La Gourmandise
13
10, bd Maine-de-Biran — 53.27.20.95
M. Guilloton. Closed Sun, Mon, and Feb and Nov school holidays. Open until 9.30 pm. Private room: 16. Garden dining. V AE DC.

The self-taught chef has built up a repertoire which he is now polishing to a high sheen. His menu therefore doesn't change a great deal, but the foie gras in port, the perfectly cooked pigeon breast, the tasty grilled pig's trotters, and the hot apple tart are perennially pleasing. A toque this year for technical progress, while we watch for a more personal approach to emerge.

A la carte: 230 F. Menus: 95 F, 125 F, 165 F, 235 F.

Le Terroir
13
38, pl. Gambetta — 53.57.12.83
M. Maury. Closed Jan. Open until 9.45 pm. Private room: 35. Garden dining. Air cond. Garage parking. Telex 550412. V AE DC.

A summer dinner under the garden trellises here is pure enchantment. The regional flavour heralded in the restaurant's name is present only in small, discreet doses, but our pleasure is not diminished for the food is adroitly prepared and ever so savoury: wild-mushroom tart with walnut cream, lotte with jasmine marmalade and fettucine, pigeon and duck breast with spiced pears; for dessert, don't miss the almond pastilla for dessert. The cellar boasts a good range of local bottlings.

A la carte: 250-280 F. Menus: 85 F, 125 F, 190 F.

Hôtel de Bordeaux
(See restaurant above)
Closed Jan 1 ste 360 F. 40 rms 270-320 F. Half-board 300-340 F. TV. Conference facilities. Pool.

The newly renovated rooms of this fine little hotel are simple and modern. Excellent welcome from Bergerac's oldest inn-keeping family.

In nearby Monbazillac
(7 km S on D 13)
24240 Bergerac — (Dordogne)

La Closerie Saint-Jacques
13
Le Bourg — 53.58.37.77
MM. Pingeon and Savignac. Closed off-season Sun dinner and Mon, and 2 Jan-7 Feb. Open until 9.30 pm. Private room: 35. Terrace dining. No-smoking section. Parking. V AE DC.

The thick walls of this long, low, 300-year-old house keep the dining room cool in the summer-

time. Cool customers appreciate the traditional country accents of the deft, creative cooking. Take special note of the 170 F prix-fixe menu—a remarkable value for compote of rabbit with plum eau-de-vie, freshwater perch in Pécharmant (a local wine) butter, grain-fed quail in Monbazillac, cheeses, and prune gâteau with mango purée for dessert.

A la carte: 280-300 F. Menus: 120 F (weekdays lunch only in seas.), 170 F, 215 F.

11/20 La Grappe d'Or
Rte de Marmande
in Peyrat — 53.58.27.67
M. Lachaize. Closed Mon off-season, and 20 Jan-28 Feb. Open until 9.15 pm. Terrace dining. Parking. V AE.

The rich traditions of the Périgord district permeate the owner's honest cooking. The prix-fixe menus are most generous, including the least expensive one: salade de gésiers confits, pollock with sweet red peppers, grilled lamb with a creamy garlic sauce, and dessert. An extra point this year.

A la carte: 250 F. Menus: 88 F, 138 F, 188 F.

Les Ruines
14
53.57.16.37
M. Séguy. Closed Sun dinner and Mon. Annual closings not available. Open until 9.30 pm. Terrace dining. No-smoking section. Parking. V AE.

Chef Philippe Séguy's recent move to this delightful spot in the Périgord seems to have inspired his cooking. A dinner on the veranda overlooking the valley is a lovely introduction to this vivid cuisine, which suffers only from an occasional imbalance of flavours. You'll be pleased by the scallops wrapped in a thin rice crêpe, the red-mullet fillets lightly cooked and served with saffron-spiced chicory, a superb sea bream with virgin olive oil, and moreish desserts like chocolate tart with an oatmeal cream. Appealing cellar.

A la carte: 300 F. Menus: 85 F (weekdays lunch only), 140 F, 230 F, 360 F.

In nearby Saint-Julien-de-Crempse
(12 km N)
24140 Bergerac — (Dordogne)

Manoir
Le Grand Vignoble
53.24.23.18
Closed 22 Dec-10 Jan. 3 stes 750-850 F. 40 rms 300-580 F. Restaurant. Half-board 355-455 F oblig in seas. TV. Conference facilities. Heated pool. Tennis. Parking. Telex 541629. V AE DC.

This handsomely restored sixteenth-century English manor is surrounded by a park where animals roam free (buffalo, yak, horses... nothing too alarming). The magnificent rooms boast rough stone walls, high ceilings, and canopied beds. Beautiful public rooms. Horse-back riding, golf.

In nearby Saint-Nexans
(6 km S on D 19)
24520 Bergerac — (Dordogne)

La Vieille Grange
13
La Petite-Forêt — 53.24.32.21
Mme Cassaresi. Closed Wed, Feb school holidays and 20 Sep-10 Oct. Open until 9.30 pm. Private room: 50. Garden dining. Sal. non- fumeurs. Parking. Telex 570418. V AE DC.

The chef's Italian ancestry must be recent, to judge by the appealing fresh pasta dishes (gnocchi Niçois, tortellini with foie gras) and Marsala cake that ornament an otherwise Gallic repertoire of

soupe d'escargots aux orties (nettles), confits, and
magret de canard au foie gras. The cellar too has
an Italian slant.

A la carte: 250 F. Menus: 95 F, 150 F, 185 F,
190 F.

BERGÈRES-LES-VERTUS

See Vertus

BERGUES

See Dunkerque

BERNAY

27300 Bernay — (Eure)
Paris 150 - Evreux 48 - Lisieux 31 - Rouen 58

 **Hostellerie
du Moulin Fouret**
4 km S
in St-Aubin-le-Vertueux
32.43.19.95

*M. Deduit. Closed Sun dinner and Mon (except
holidays). Open until 9 pm. Private room: 15. Garden dining. Hotel: 8 rms 150-200 F. Parking. V.*

The motto here seems to be: if it can be done
simply, don't do it. François Deduit, an otherwise
talented chef, cannot control his taste for excess.
His technique is precise, his cooking times are
spot-on, he and his charming wife are obviously
eager to please; so it seems a shame that he should
persist in crowding too many incompatible ingredients on a plate. Given his talent, the charm of
his restored mill on a quiet Norman stream, a fine
wine list, and soothing service we look forward to
better.

A la carte: 300-350 F. Menus: 95 F, 145 F,
250 F.

BERRY-AU-BAC

02190 Berry-au-Bac — (Aisne)
Paris 149 - Laon 29 - Reims 19 - Soissons 47

 La Cote 108
N 44 — 23.79.95.04

*M. Courville. Closed Sun dinner, Mon, 14-23 July and
25 Dec-23 Jan. Open until 9.30 pm. Private
room: 25. Air cond. Parking. V AE.*

All the 'big bubbles' of the Champagne district
alight here to partake of Serge Courville's modern,
expert cooking; nor do they fizzle (as we do) at the
sight of the astronomical bill. The dishes are as
consistent as the Greenwich Observatory; count
on an excellent red-mullet fillet with leeks in
vinaigrette, whole grilled sea bass, lobster feuilleté
with fresh pasta, and joint of beef braised in Pinot
with bone marrow. The bright, elegant dining
room is decorated in a pleasing contemporary
style.

A la carte: 400-500 F. Menus: 160 F (weekdays
only), 290 F, 420 F.

BERRY-BOUY

See Bourges

> *We are always interested to hear about your
> discoveries, and to receive your comments on
> ours. Please feel free to write to us, stating your
> opinions clearly.*

BESANÇON

25000 Besançon — (Doubs)
Paris 390 - Nancy 199 - Belfort 90 - Dijon 91

Altea
See restaurant Le Vesontio

 Le Chaland
Bregille bridge
Prom. Micaud — 81.80.61.61

*M. Bertin. Closed Sun dinner, Mon, Feb school
holidays and 25 July-18 Aug. Open until 10 pm.
Private room: 20. Telex 361813. V.*

Stormy weather has hit the galley of this long,
luxurious barge-restaurant moored alongside a
beautiful river-front park, with a magnificent view
of the citadel. The crockery, like everything else
here, is opulently beautiful but the food that adorns them is slipping badly. Chef Bruno Bertin won
a gold medal in Venice for his roast young pigeon
in puff pastry, so that—at least—is a dependable
dish, as is the grilled bass perfumed with anise. But
steer clear of such efforts as the salade gourmande
with its ordinary sauce, the mediocre carpaccio,
and the awful sauce gribiche. The chef had better
get cracking if he wants to keep his two toques,
and make the quality of the food catch up with the
prices, which are headed out to sea.

A la carte: 500 F. Menus: 180 F (weekdays lunch
only, wine inc), and from 150 F to 380 F.

10/20 Charlie Ier
20, rue de Belfort — 81.80.50.43

*M. Gérardot. Closed Sun, Mon and 20 July-19 Aug.
Open until 9.30 pm. V.*

The fish-loving owner had the good idea of opening a little seafood restaurant (decorated, of
course, with fish nets on the walls) that serves
excellent shellfish platters, a delicious fish soup,
and a few dishes based on utterly fresh fish.

A la carte: 200-250 F. Menus: 90 F, 120 F, 140 F.

11/20 Chinatown
23 bis, quai de Strasbourg — 81.82.21.00

*M. Ung. Closed Mon. Open until 11 pm. Terrace din-
ing. Air cond. No pets. V AE DC.*

Red walls punctuated with the usual gold
dragons are the décor in which you can eat your
fill of well-done standard Chinese dishes. Nothing
original, but portions are large.

A la carte: 200 F.

Mercure
4, av. Carnot — 81.80.33.11

*Open every day. 67 rms 290-450 F. Restaurant. TV.
Conference facilities. Parking. Telex 361276. V AE
DC.*

Surprising link in a hotel chain known for its
functional décor; this one is a converted old town
house with a garden, located close to the centre of
town.

Le Mungo Park
11, rue J.-Petit — 81.81.28.01

*Mme Lotz-Choquart. Closed Sat lunch, Sun and 1-
15 Sep. Open until 9.30 pm. Terrace dining. V AE.*

With disconcerting speed, after a brief fling with
exoticism, this establishment has transformed itself into a restaurant of great style and elegance.
The owner is self-taught, and her young chef has
no big-name references to boast of. But the results
are there, and they are convincing. The décor is
both original and wonderfully refined, composed
of African fabrics, beams, stonework, and clever
lighting to provide an imaginative backdrop for the

soaring fancies of Benoît Rotschi's astonishing cuisine. He uses flavours and aromas in unexampled but always successful combinations. The technical skill needed to negotiate this culinary tightrope never fails him. Rotschi highlights regional products in dishes like his oysters and asparagus in a tomato 'milk', or mushroom velouté with a local smoked pork sausage, or crisp fried whiting with potatoes and country bacon, and the veal kidney sliced and served with a delicate ratatouille. Desserts bring perfumed spice cake with a star-anise cream, or a walnut crème brûlée scented with the Jura's famed vin jaune. Gérard Lotz-Choquart has assembled a splendid, eclectic cellar in record time.

A la carte: 450 F. Menus: 150 F, 180 F, 400 F.

Le Poker d'As ♕

14, square Saint-Amour
81.81.42.49

M. Ferreux. Closed Sun dinner, Mon, 8-31 July and 24 Dec-2 Jan. Open until 9.30 pm. V AE.

Don't let the bric-a-brac décor throw you off the scent of one the area's more creative and talented chefs. Eccentricity is all around you except in the continual mastery of both regional themes and sheer invention: pig's ear gratinéed with hazelnut oil set atop a bed of mixed local greens, or mussels perfumed with kirsch and thyme, a fricassée of oysters in vin jaune, Scottish lamb cooked in Pupillin (another local wine) and the best cancoillote (farmer's cheese with butter and white wine) we've ever had. Desserts follow the seasons, and spring brings rhubarb soup with ginger and strawberries.

A la carte: 300 F. Menus: 85 F (weekdays only), 110 F, 140 F, 170 F, 220 F.

Relais de la Mouillère

Parc du Casino
Av. E.-Droz — 81.80.61.01

M. Buys. Closed Tue. Open until 10 pm. Garden dining. Parking. V AE DC.

On the grounds of the former casino, this strange old building houses a restaurant whose kitchen has had ups and downs. Recently, matters have been taken in hand, and owner/chef Jean-Pierre Buys is once again living up to his potential with dishes like snail ravioli, brill wrapped in cabbage leaves, and rich duck pâté. Some excellent bottles from the Jura highlight the wine list.

A la carte: 300 F. Menus: from 100 F to 230 F, 260 F.

12/20 Le Saint-Pierre

104, rue Battant — 81.81.20.99

MM. Eiche and Pône. Closed Sat lunch and Sun (except holidays) and 15-31 Aug. Open until 10 pm. Terrace dining. V AE.

A local Jura native turns out pleasing and clever dishes like snail ravioli scented with the local anise liqueur, and escalope of salmon trout with morels.

A la carte: 250 F. Menus: 85 F (weekdays only), 145 F (wine inc), 150 F, 195 F and 250 F.

12/20 Le Vesontio

3, av. E.-Droz — 81.80.14.44

M. Jacob. Open every day. Open until 10 pm. Private room: 200. Air cond. Parking. Telex 360268. V AE DC.

The dining room is an attractive study in glass that opens onto a pretty garden. Chef Olivier Ramirez keeps things simple and good, but not simple enough still to avoid certain lapses in cooking times, ingredients, and flavour combinations.

Good bread, delicious cherry clafoutis, interesting local wines.

A la carte: 200-250 F. Menus: 176 F (wine inc), 98 F.

Altea Parc Micaud

(See restaurant above)

Open every day. 7 stes 885-985 F. 95 rms 330-520 F. TV. Conference facilities.

Surrounded by the river-front gardens of the former casino, this modern building offers well-maintained rooms. Good breakfasts.

And also...

Our selection of places for inexpensive, quick, or late-night meals.

Chez Barthod (81.82.27.14 - 22, rue Bersot. Open until 11 pm): Here's the place to eat the best local specialities on a little garden-terrace. Wines available by the glass (120 F).

Le Carnot (81.50.17.16 - 1, av. Fontaine-d'Argent. Open until 10 pm): Astonishing value for colourful Provençal cooking (140 F).

Midi Minuit (81.81.12.89 - 13, rue Grande-Rue. Open until midnight): Hearty, filling fare appreciated by the younger set.

Au Pays (81.81.06.81 - 10, rue Mégevand. Open until 10 pm): In the centre of town, tasty cooking is served in a relaxed setting (120 F).

Les Terraces (81.57.05.82 - 40 rte Nationale, Roche-les-Beaupré. Open until 10 pm): Cheap and cheerful family-style meals are served on a shady patio (130 F).

In nearby Ecole-Valentin

(5 km NW on N 57)
25480 Besançon — (Doubs)

Le Valentin

19, rte d'Epinal — 81.80.03.90

Mme Maire. Closed Sun dinner, Mon and 29 July-19 Aug. Open until 9.30 pm. Private room: 18. Garden dining. Parking. V AE DC.

Jean-François Maire is a hard-working, creative chef who will welcome you to this big, plush manse a short distance outside of Besançon. Sample his roast freshwater perch with little vegetables, or his delicious Bresse chicken with prawns. Desserts are excellent.

A la carte: 300-350 F. Menus: 99 F, 178 F, 229 F.

In nearby Montfaucon

(9 km E on N 57 and D 104)
25660 Besançon — (Doubs)

La Cheminée

Rte du Belvédère — 81.81.17.48

M. Gavazzi. Closed Sun dinner, Mon and Feb. Open until 9.30 pm. Terrace dining. Parking. V DC.

In a cosy chalet setting you can enjoy not only a view of the plain, but also the ever-improving cuisine that focuses on regional Franche-Comté specialties prepared with a light touch. We recommend the flavourful artichoke mousseline, the trout fillet in beurre blanc sauce, and the chicken in a curried Comté cheese sauce. A toque of encouragement for the chef.

A la carte: 300 F. Menus: 90 F (weekdays only), and from 110 F to 220 F.

BESSE-EN-CHANDESSE

63610 Besse-en-Chandesse — (Puy-de-Dôme)
Paris 437 - Issoire 35 - Clermont-Ferrand 50

Le Clos
La Villetour — 73.79.52.77
Closed 2-19 April and 28 Sep-21 Dec. 25 rms 145-205 F. Restaurant. Half-board 195-230 F. Conference facilities. Heated pool. Parking. V.
On the edge of town is found this solid, renovated hotel which promises for 1991 a pool, sauna, and whirlpool bath.

Les Mouflons
Rte de Super-Besse — 73.79.51.31
Closed 1 Nov-24 Dec. 50 rms 310-340 F. Restaurant. Half-board 320-410 F. TV. Conference facilities. Garage parking. V AE.
Facing the pretty village of Besse and the mountains, these attractive rooms are quite comfortable. Pleasant welcome and service.

In nearby Super-Besse

(7 km W)
63610 Besse-en-Chandesse — (Puy-de-Dôme)

12/20 La Bergerie
Rte de Vassivières — 73.79.61.06
Mlle Verny. Closed 20 April-15 June and 15 Sep-15 Dec. Open until 10 pm. Terrace dining. Parking. V.
An inviting rustic décor suits the honest, interesting cooking. Madame Verny, the owner and chef, delivers fine if slightly fussy renditions of local specialities: trout with cabbage, sautéed potatoes and cheese with bits of country ham, duck breast with sherry.
A la carte: 180-200 F. Menus: 75 F, 92 F.

Gergovia
1, rue M.-Gauthier — 73.79.60.15
Closed 2-20 April and 13 Oct-20 Dec (except groupes). 53 rms 180-350 F. Restaurant. Half-board 299-594 F. TV. Conference facilities. Parking. Telex 394021. V AE.
This huge modern chalet is perhaps the resort's most inviting, with all kinds of sporting equipment and organised activities.

Le Sabrina
73.79.60.02
Closed 15 April-15 May and 1 Oct-15 Dec. 47 rms 200-280 F. Restaurant. Half-board 190-260 F oblig in seas. TV 5 rms. Conference facilities. Parking. Telex 392217. V.
Smack in the middle of the resort, the Sabrina houses fifty reasonably comfortable rooms. All-in packages for cross-country skiing.

BÉTHUNE

62400 Béthune — (P./Calais)
Paris 213 - Arras 33 - Douai 39 - Dunkerque 67

12/20 La Chartreuse du Val St-Esprit
4 km SW on N 41
1, rue de Fouquières
62199 Gosnay — 21.62.80.00
M. Constant. Open every day. Open until 10 pm. Private room: 80. Parking. Telex 134418. V AE.
The luxurious dining room of this splendid château is the scene of generous, well-intentioned meals that suffers from some minor flaws. Good bets include the prawn and broccoli gratin with the lemon sabayon, the pot-au-feu of quail and foie gras with horseradish, and a nice pear dessert. Fine cellar.
A la carte: 350 F. Menus: 110 F (weekdays only), 190 F, 295 F, 345 F.

La Chartreuse du Val St-Esprit
(See restaurant above)
Open every day. 23 rms 320-430 F. TV. Conference facilities. Tennis.
Perfectly comfortable and spacious rooms look out over extensive grounds. The rooms on the upper floor are cosier than the others.

Marc Meurin
15, pl. de la République — 21.68.88.88
M. Meurin. Closed Sun dinner, Mon and Aug. Open until 10 pm. Private room: 30. V AE.
A peaceful atmosphere prevails in the intimate dining rooms of this imposing house set on a little square. The menu reflects a careful, contemporary style of handling prime ingredients: scallops in a cream of lettuce, noisettes of lamb with broad beans and shallots, gratin of salmon with horseradish, and fromage frais with brown sugar. The friendly, young staff is competent to boot, dispensing reliable advice on the menu and wines.
A la carte: 300-350 F. Menus: 130 F (weekdays only, wine inc), 160 F, 250 F.

Vieux Beffroy
48, Grand-Place — 21.68.15.00
Open every day. 65 rms 100-240 F. Restaurant. Half-board 215-300 F. TV 48 rms. Conference facilities. Telex 134105. V AE DC.
Opposite the eponymous 'old belfrey' stands this reliable hotel which offers simple, fully equipped rooms.

In nearby Beuvry

(4 km SE on N 41)
62660 Béthune — (P./Calais)

France II
on N 41 towards Lille
Rue du Gal-Leclerc — 21.65.11.00
Open every day. 3 stes 470 F. 56 rms 285-380 F. Restaurant. Half-board 370 F. TV. Conference facilities. Garage parking. Telex 110691. V AE DC.
The sunny rooms of this modern hotel afford a view across the spacious grounds. Amenities include a sauna and billiards.

BEUVRON-EN-AUGE

14430 Beuvron-en-Auge — (Calvados)
Paris 224 - Pont-l'Evêque 32 - Caen 30 - Lisieux 28

Le Pavé d'Auge
Pl. du Village — 31.79.26.71
M. Bansard. Closed Mon dinner, Tue, 14-29 Jan and 25 Nov-10 Dec. Open until 9 pm. V.
Jérôme and Susan Bansard, the new owners of this hallowed bit of Normandy, have taken over in all reverence from the famed Odile Engel (now established in Rouen). They have confined themselves to fixing up the tiny kitchen a bit, adding new crockery and such.... The best products of Normandy, treated with great respect and deftness, find their way into dishes like Jérôme's simmered prawns and mussels with cider, turbot with a creamy shellfish sauce, and braised rabbit and tripe sausage with shallot confit. Susan, in the meantime, is an exceptional pastry chef. All in all, the old regulars have nothing to complain about.
A la carte: 300 F. Menus: 125 F (weekdays only), 160 F, 250 F.

See Béthune

BEUZEVILLE

27210 Beuzeville — (Eure)
Paris 185 - Deauville 24 - Honfleur 15

Le Cochon d'Or
Le Petit Castel
Pl. du Gal-de-Gaulle — 32.57.70.46
M. Folleau. Closed Mon and 15 Dec-15 Jan. Open until 9 pm. No pets. Hotel: 21 rms 140-300 F. Parking. V.
By the summer of 1991, the ponderous rustic décor of this grand Norman hall will be a thing of the past. Henceforth guests will be able to focus on Charles Folleau's adroit, regionally rooted dishes, like the suave sole normande, the grilled salmon béarnaise, the farm-reared chicken 'Vallée d'Auge', tripe in Calvados, and chocolate cake with crème fraîche. Even à la carte, the prices for this fresh, generous fare are quite reasonable.
A la carte: 180-280 F. Menus: 70 F and 100 F (weekdays only), 140 F, 195 F.

BÉZARDS (LES)

45290 Bézards (Les) — (Loiret)
Paris 136 - Auxerre 76 - Orléans 69 - Montargis 23

Auberge des Templiers   ❀
N 7 — 38.31.80.01
M. Depée. Closed 15 Jan-15 Feb. Open until 9.30 pm. Private room: 28. Garden dining. Valet parking. Telex 780998. V AE DC.
The Sologne region, lovely land of mists and forest pools, is also the setting for this, one of France's great restaurants. An elegant provincial ambience announces itself immediately in the oaken beams overhead, the antique cupboards and tapestries, the tables adorned with candelabra and beautiful china.
More wonderful still, the mystic elements of the landscape must have seeped into the walls of this magical *auberge*, for every chef who has presided over its kitchen has kept the cooking up to the same superb standard. The rare professionalism of the owners, Philippe and Françoise Depée, keeps this jewel perfectly polished, and most regulars might not even notice the occasional change of chefs if our Guide didn't announce it. That does not mean that we are in any hurry to see the departure of the current incumbent, Bernard Mariller, who for three years now has exercised the skills he acquired during stints with Joël Robuchon, the Troisgros brothers, and Jacques Lamcloise.
Working closely with the Depées (both Monsieur and Madame are accomplished cooks) to bring to daily perfection a tried and true menu, Mariller produces such polished but full-bodied dishes as lamb's trotters with wine-braised artichokes, truffled chicken bouillon, freshwater perch cooked in its skin (it's juicier that way) with Chinon wine and served with a sensational celery purée, a lobster ravigote scented with tarragon, an ethereal woodpigeon pie with a delicate foie gras sauce, and a long-simmered wild rabbit, cooked to melting tenderness and escorted by intensely flavourful carrots. In short, the best local ingredients—especially game, during Sologne's legendary hunting season—are treated to refined but never fussy preparations that will linger long on your palate and in your fondest memories. Desserts? Old-fashioned waffles with berry purée, millefeuille à la gousse de vanille, and hazelnut pastry with dark-chocolate sauce are quite simply the stuff of cloud nine.
Jean-Paul Martin, a most charming sommelier, will help you choose the Burgundy, Loire, or Bordeaux bottling that will make your bliss complete.
A la carte: 450-750 F. Menus: 250 F (weekdays lunch only), 350 F, 520 F.

Auberge des Templiers
(See restaurant above)
Closed 15 Jan-15 Feb. 8 stes 1,450-3,200 F. 22 rms 550-1,200 F. Half-board 680-1,000 F. TV. Conference facilities. Heated pool. Tennis.
The taste and attention to detail lavished on these lodgings—whether in the opulent bungalow on the edge of the park, or in the typically regional cottages that house the rest of the suites—know no limits, nor hardly an equal anywhere. One is transported with delight by the ambience and amenities, including the regal breakfasts. Relais et Châteaux.

BÉZAUDUN-LES-ALPES

06510 Bézaudun-les-Alpes — (Alpes-Mar.)
Paris 952 - Nice 46 - Vence 24 - St-Martin-Vésubie 59

11/20 Auberge Les Lavandes
93.59.11.08
M. Amatteis. Closed Thu and 15 Sep-15 Oct. Open until 8 pm. Hotel: 9 rms 200 F. Garage parking.
A simple prix-fixe menu is all that is available, and all that is necessary to put you back on the trail, restored and refreshed, but not impoverished. Ten francs heavier than last year, the tariff is still as light as the fine salads and local game dishes. To drink, there's a jaunty Côtes de Provence.
Menu: 120 F.

BÉZIERS

34500 Béziers — (Hérault)
Paris 839 - Montpellier 72 - Narbonne 27

L'Ambassade
22, bd de Verdun — 67.76.06.24
Mme Seguin and M. Olry. Closed Mon dinner and Sun. Open until 10 pm. Air cond. V AE.
A good start is getting better, as chef Patrick Olry continues to allow freshness and sunshine to permeate his dishes. We rave on about his scallops and oysters in a shellfish broth, his long-simmered civet of calf's tongue and pig's trotter, and local lake fish with new asparagus. Inspiration has yet to reach to the dessert list. Charming welcome; clever wine list.
A la carte: 270-350 F. Menus: 105 F (weekdays only), 135 F, 175 F, 240 F.

12/20 Le Castelet
Rte de Narbonne — 67.28.82.60
Mme Basti-Duchemin. Open every day. Open until 10 pm. Private room: 200. Garden dining. Valet parking. Telex 485509. V AE DC.
Duck out of the dreary dining rooms for the delights of poolside patio dining. Order the deftly crafted sherry-scented pâté, fresh salmon en papillote and breast of chicken Pauline. The prices go down as easily as the good local wines.
A la carte: 250-280 F. Menus: 75 F (weekdays lunch only), 95 F, 160 F.

Problems with French? The RAC France language pack will help you to converse with confidence.

Le Castelet

(See restaurant above)
Open every day. 2 stes 580 F. 30 rms 180-310 F. Half-board 215-265 F oblig in seas. TV. Conference facilities. Pool.

The period furnishings are sometimes over-powering, but the rooms are comfortable and quiet. The reception is not always the height of urbanity.

Le Framboisier

33, av. du Président-Wilson
67.62.62.57
M. Yagues. Closed Sun, Mon, last 2 weeks of Feb and of Aug. Open until 9.30 pm. Air cond. V AE DC.

This the spot to savour the discreet charm of Béziers' bourgeoisie. Wine growers and other notables dine on conservative (but never heavy) dishes like scallop salad in walnut oil, anglerfish in pesto sauce, and veal noisettes in Armagnac. A wide choice of good, affordably priced wines.

A la carte: 300-350 F. Menus: 320 F (dinner w-e and holidays only), 130 F, 200 F.

Le Jardin

37, av. J.-Moulin – 67.36.41.31
M. Santuré. Closed Sun dinner, Mon, 2 weeks in Feb and first 2 weeks of July. Open until 9.30 pm. Air cond. No-smoking section. V AE DC.

Flowers and friendly smiles are all the garnishes this simple place needs to assure its customers' wellbeing. The highly trained young chef does his part with a cream of oysters punctuated by tiny ravioli, roast sea bass in a brown tarragon sauce, breast of roast guinea hen spiced with cinnamon, and an array of well-wrought desserts. Other attractions include the cellar (fine wines, fine brandies), excellent coffee, and good cigars. Prices permit regular visits. An extra point for Le Jardin this year.

A la carte: 270-320 F. Menus: 100 F (weekdays only), 160 F, 250 F.

L'Olivier

12, rue Boieldieu – 67.28.86.64
M. Leproust. Closed Sun dinner and Mon lunch. Annual closings not available. Open until 10 pm. Private room: 30. Garden dining. Air cond. V AE DC.

Ravioli stuffed with scallops and oyster mushrooms, fresh truffles baked in embers, beef fillet layered with cèpes, and noisettes of lamb's tongue enlivened with sage and truffles will surely win you over to Alain Rességuier's lively, colourful cuisine served in a suitably sunny setting. Attractive cellar.

A la carte: 320-370 F. Menus: 150 F, 200 F, 360 F.

Thélème

63, av. Wilson – 67.62.60.37
M. Bastoul. Open every day. Open until 10 pm. Private room: 60. Air cond. V AE DC.

Owner-chef Jean-Marc Bastoul, who recently completed a training tour through some of the finer kitchens of France, has returned to this comfortably appointed restaurant to prepare tasty regional dishes like roast pigeon with herbs, simmered snails à la biterroise, and airy feuilletés gourmands. The welcome is warm, the cellar appealing.

A la carte: 300-380 F. Menus: 100 F, 180 F, 260 F.

64200 Biarritz — (Pyrénées-A.)
Paris 747 - Pau 115 - Dax 57 - Bayonne 8

12/20 L'Alambic

Pl. Bellevue – 59.24.53.41
M. Laporte. Closed Mon off-season, and 31 Oct-20 Dec. Open until 10 pm. Private room: 150. V.

Annexe of the Café de Paris (see below), the Alambic attracts a chic, sporting set to its large, seaside dining room. These pretty patrons plump for prime rib, paella, and other not-very-special specialities. Prices are on the rise.

A la carte: 200 F. Menu: 115 F.

Auberge du Relais

44, av. de la Marne – 59.24.85.90
M. Lacam. Closed Feb. Open until 9.30 pm. Air cond. Garage parking. V.

The impeccable country décor of this appealing little inn will put you in the mood to enjoy the owner's fresh, precise cooking: scallops and sea urchins, 'catch of the day' in shrimp sauce, baby lamb sweetbreads. The remarkable desserts are as light as what precedes (don't miss the caprice au chocolat amer). Wash it all with a good local wine. Warm welcome, diligent service.

A la carte: 250 F. Menus: 95 F, 220 F.

Auberge du Relais

(See restaurant above)
Closed Feb. 12 rms 126-270 F. Half-board 200-250 F oblig in seas. TV 1 rms. Pets allowed.

The rooms are spare but clean and quiet.

12/20 Le Biarritz

(Le Panoramique)
30, av. de Milady – 59.23.83.03
M. Barrere. Open every day. Open until 9.30 pm. Terrace dining. No pets. Parking. Telex 571808. V AE DC.

The sea and the coast of Spain are the backdrop of this restaurant's flower-decked veranda. Marc Bidegain's cooking still hesitates between the rustic and the sophisticated. The avocado and crab cocktail is less interesting than the hake fillet in a delicious sauce, or the scrumptious gâteau Basque. Wine prices will make a teetotaller of you.

A la carte: 200-250 F. Menus: 145 F, 185 F.

Le Biarritz

(See restaurant above)
Open every day. 50 rms 400-900 F. Half-board 560-1,060 F. TV. Conference facilities.

The haphazard service, the noise, and the measly breakfasts do their utmost to offset the favourable impression made by the modern spacious rooms.

Café de Paris

5, pl. Bellevue – 59.24.19.53
M. Laporte. Opening Easter 91. Open every day. Open until 10 pm. Private room: 150. V AE DC.

Just as everyone was beginning to wonder if the gracefully ageing Pierre Laporte, owner of this Biarritz institution, wasn't perhaps letting it go slack, he has given the place back its youth. The polishing of Le Café de Paris, a jewel of tacky 1960's glory, coincides with the general rejuvenation evident everywhere in Biarritz. Here that translates into a fresh start in the kitchen that fully justifies three toques. While the veranda, alas, still boasts an unsurpassed view of a parking lot by the sea, the grand dining room with its superbly oiled service is a fine place to sample classic cuisine that has abandoned the perilous pursuit of fashion for the safer shores of regional tradition. Witness the terrine of chicken breast and mixed vegetables, the incomparable Bayonne ham sliced thin as tissue paper, a trio of soft-boiled eggs with garnishes of sweet peppers, hot foie gras, and sorrel all bathed in a truffle jus, lobster ravioli with basil (the flavour of lobster is for once brilliant and clear), sea bream cooked to crispness in its skin (to keep in the juices), then napped with sweet-pepper sauce, and intensely sapid Pauillac lamb under a 'crust' of crisped potatoes, with a fresh-tasting medley of onions, courgettes, and mint. The remarkable cheese tray must be followed by the Armagnac-flavored tourte, infinitely preferable to the tasteless chocolate-mint bavaroise.

A treasure trove of magnums, double-magnums, and jeroboams of fine claret awaits those with the means to acquire them. What a pity the wines of the South-west are accorded so small a place on the wine list.

A la carte: 450-800 F. Menus: 230 F, 390 F.

Carlina

Bd Prince-de-Galles — 59.23.03.86
M. Bégué. Closed off-season Tue and 15 Nov-15 April. Open until 11 pm. Terrace dining. Hotel: 1 ste 950 F. 31 rms 450-950 F. Garage parking. Telex 550873. V AE DC.

With its back to the cliffs and its eyes (big bay windows) to the sea, this dining room is a very pleasant place in which to enjoy simple but expert cooking based on fresh, fine ingredients. Try the salmon rillettes with chives or médaillons of lotte in beurre blanc. A toque this year. A wide choice of fine Bordeaux is available.

A la carte: 250 F. Menu: 75 F (lunch only).

Château du Clair de Lune

Rte d'Arbonne
48, av. A.-Seeger — 59.23.45.96
Open every day. 1 ste 600-700 F. 14 rms 350 F. TV 14 rms. Conference facilities. Parking. V AE DC.

A turn-of-the-century manor on large, splendid grounds a mile or so from the centre of Biarritz, offers grand guest rooms where taste and tranquillity reign.

12/20 La Chaumière

4, av. E.-Cavell — 59.03.48.46
M. Rourre. Closed 5 Jan-4 Feb. Open until 11 pm. Garden dining. V.

The young owners have no trouble attracting the nearby golfers onto their shady terrace with a friendly smile, a pretty pastel décor, and good simple cooking. We urge the chef to cook the fish (sea bass in Madiran, Spanish-style cod...) a hair less.

A la carte: 270 F. Menus: 80 F (lunch only), 140 F.

Comfort Inn

19, av. de la Reine-Victoria — 59.22.04.80
Open every day. 3 stes 500-560 F. 40 rms 350-460 F. TV. Air cond. No pets. Conference facilities. Garage parking. V AE DC.

A new hotel in the heart of Biarritz features big, well-outfitted rooms.

Le Galion

17, bd du Gal-de-Gaulle — 59.24.20.32
M. Barbé. Closed Sun dinner, Mon and Feb. Open until 11 pm. Terrace dining. Air cond. V.

Overly solemn though the dining room may be for a seaside restaurant, the cuisine displays a briny, bracing spirit. Monique Lissar has made a fresh start, and the point taken away last year is

restored in honour of her prawn salad with bacon, the lotte with chanterelles, and the melange of sheep's trotters, veal kidneys, and sweetbreads. Youthful, energetic service.

A la carte: 200-250 F. Menu: 135 F.

Le Grand Siècle

1, av. de l'Impératrice — 59.24.09.40
M. Leimbacher. Closed 15 Nov-15 March. Open until 11 pm. Private room: 200. Garden dining. Air cond. No pets. Valet parking. Telex 570000. V AE DC.

Chef Grégoire Sein's illustrious list of masters runs from Michel Guérard to Paul Bocuse; he thus brings considerable experience to bear on the food served in the monumental ballroom where the Empress Eugénie once entertained. He has also brought minute attention to detail, precise cooking times, fresh ideas, and a graceful technique that lends lightness and style to earthy Basque produce. The proof is in the tasting: try Sein's ethereal crab croquettes, his rabbit stuffed with tiny squid, sea bass bathed in an inky squid sauce, roast anglerfish with marinated fresh tomatoes, or the assortment of fish grilled à la plancha, the pan-roasted filet de bœuf béarnaise, or baby lamb from the Pyrenees served with vegetable confit. Prices are still high, but diners are now virtually certain to get their money's worth. Tariffs are lower in the adjoining Rotonde, which affords a view of the sea.

A la carte: 450-700 F (Rotonde: 400-450 F). Menus: 400 F, 600 F (Rotonde: 280 F).

Le Palais

(See restaurant above)
Closed 15 Nov-15 March. 22 stes 2,750-6,000 F. 116 rms 900-2,200 F. Half-board 1,250-1,950 F. TV. Conference facilities. Heated pool.

The Empress Eugénie had this labyrinthine summer palace built in just ten months, and here she and Napoleon III received the nobility of Europe. The palace now belongs to the city of Biarritz, and is run by the Concorde hotel group. Recently refurbished to the tune of millions, its splendour is restored. Period antiques, huge rooms, poolside cabanas to rent for an emperor's ransom, and even eight holes of golf are all designed to draw a glittering, international crowd. Our readers complain, however, of an occasionally glacial reception.

Les Jardins de l'Océan

52, av. de l'Impératrice — 59.41.33.00
M. Touati. Closed 18 Nov-23 Dec. Open until 10 pm. No pets. Parking. Telex 541330. V AE DC.

Young Georges Amestory shows no signs of getting stuck in a boring luxury hotel groove, as he turns out a fresh, imaginative, and tasty menu. The glass-roofed patio is a fine place to tuck into roast prawns with ginger, lotte in a cream sauce spiked with chorizo, foie gras petals and duck breast with celery. To finish, we recommend the short pastry topped with berries and almonds.

A la carte: 300-400 F. Menus: 190 F, 220 F.

Régina et Golf

(See restaurant above)
Closed 18 Nov-23 Dec. 10 stes. 70 rms 500-1,200 F. Half-board 700-1,200 F. TV. Air cond 35 rms. Conference facilities. Heated pool.

A renovated décor now takes full advantage of the superb seascapes visible from every window. A peaceful atmosphere is not the least of the many amenities offered here—others include golf lessons and a sea-water spa.

12/20 L'Operne
17, av. Edouard-VII — 59.24.30.30
M. Carvalho. Closed 8-31 Jan. Open until 10.30 pm. Private room: 16. Terrace dining. Air cond. V AE DC.
A young set favours this Second Empire establishment, which sits in the centre of Biarritz with its feet in the water. They come for the gratin of prawns and leeks, sole stuffed with duck foie gras, or for a platter of fresh, briny shellfish.
A la carte: 250-300 F. Menus: 140 F, 150 F, 170 F.

12/20 Le Petit Doyen
87, av. de la Marne — 59.24.01.61
M. Dagorrette. Closed Mon lunch. Open until 11 pm. Air cond. V AE.
A new décor that plays up the old stonework, handsome fireplace, and pretty crockery is a rousing success. The cooking would rouse more enthusiasm if it shed some of the heavy sauces and garnishes. Try the bright mussel-saffron soup, the tender pigeon with wild mushrooms, and the délice glacé au chocolat amer. Heart-warming reception.
A la carte: 300-350 F. Menus: 120 F, 160 F, 210 F.

Le Petit Hôtel
11, rue Gardères — 59.24.87.00
Closed 10 Jan-10 Feb. 12 rms 300-420 F. TV. V.
Small it is, and tastefully contemporary. Rooms are spacious and well soundproofed. Family atmosphere, delicious breakfasts.

Les Platanes
32, av. Beausoleil — 59.23.13.68
M. Daguin. Closed Tue lunch and Mon. Annual closings not available. Open until 10.30 pm. V.
Chef-owner Arnaud Daguin is a one-man show. All on his own he travels the length and breadth of the markets from Bayonne to the harbour at Ciboure. Back in his kitchen, all by himself, he puts together lovely impromptu menus bursting with freshness and originality. A given day might bring sea bass in a vegetable fondue, maigre (a river fish) with broad beans and mangetouts, guinea hen sautéed with mild garlic and artichokes, and a caramelised banana tart. The repertoire of delicious local wines (Madiran, Jurançon, Pacherenc, Colombard) is most impressive.
A la carte: 230 F. Menus: 150 F (weekdays lunch only), 250 F.

Plaza
Av. Edouard-VII — 59.24.74.00
Open every day. 60 rms 260-605 F. Restaurant. No pets. Conference facilities. Parking. Telex 570048. V AE DC.
The rooms of this luxury hotel that dates from the 1930's have all been refurbished in period style. The beach and the casino are just outside the door. Friendly, competent service.

Le Président
Pl. Clemenceau — 59.24.66.40
Open every day. 64 rms 440-590 F. TV 32 rms. Conference facilities. Telex 573446. V AE DC.
This tall, modern, centrally located hotel features functional rooms, some with a view of the sea. The noise (in summer) and the décor are both a bit discouraging, but should you find yourself in Biarritz with nowhere else to go, this is a perfectly acceptable place to stay.

Relais Miramar
13, rue L.-Bobet — 59.41.30.00
M. Broch. Open every day. Open until 10 pm. Private room: 180. Terrace dining. Air cond. No pets. Valet parking. Telex 540831. V AE DC.
Seated in this heavy, strictly impersonal dining room, one feels a pang of pity for the heroic souls next door, forced to nibble on the 400-calorie slimming menu. Chef André Gaüzère, a rising star on the diet circuit, is obviously a true believer, for even the Miramar's 'regular' menu has been lightened considerably. The crab en gelée, the fricassée of lobster and shellfish with coriander, the spice-lacquered rabbit, the prawns sautéed with tiny artichokes, the turbot with a golden brioche coating, and the duckling fillets cooked in their ginger-scented juices are all light as a feather. Not skimpy we hasten to add—the portions are sumptuous, but thanks to brief cooking times, fat-free sauces, and masterly technique, diners always have plenty of room left for desserts like prune soufflé with Armagnac. Chilly welcome, attentive service.
A la carte: 350-500 F. Menu: 250 F.

Miramar
(See restaurant above)
Open every day. 17 stes 1,230-2,700 F. 126 rms 575-1,935 F. Half-board 755-1,990 F. TV. Air cond. Conference facilities. Heated pool.
The style here is all 'grand hotel' from the glowing rooms to the attentive, stylish service. This is the base camp for Louison Bobet sea-water cures. Low-calorie cooking courses are supervised by chef André Gaüzère.

12/20 Le Vaudeville
5, rue du Centre — 59.24.34.66
M. Erguy. Closed Tue lunch, Mon and Jan. Open until 10.30 pm. Air cond. V.
We'll take a seat in the slightly tired Belle Epoque décor any day to enjoy the wonderful prix-fixe menu that includes, for example, soft-boiled eggs with cèpes, prawns with baby cabbage in sauce américaine, and a chocolate cake with coffee sauce that alone would merit a toque. The cellar is meagrely stocked.
Menu: 145 F.

Windsor
Grande-Plage — 59.24.08.52
Open every day. 53 rms 250-600 F. Restaurant. Half-board 275-450 F oblig in seas. TV. V AE DC.
The charm here is concentrated in the panoramic view from the comfortable rooms. The hotel's exterior is most unprepossessing.

In nearby Arcangues
(7 km S on D 254 and D 3)
64200 Biarritz — (Pyrénées-A.)

Moulin d'Alotz
59.43.04.54
M. Caumont. Closed Tue off-season, Mon and 15 Jan-15 Feb. Open until 10 pm. Private room: 30. Garden dining. V.
In a delightfully furnished converted mill you will enjoy the purity and light touch of chef Jean Caumont's salad of prawns and artichokes with bits of country ham, turbot gratin in Champagne sauce with tiny vegetables, and the delicate feuilleté de poire Belle-Hélène with hot chocolate sauce. Limited cellar.
A la carte: 300 F. Menu: 190 F.

See also: Bayonne, St-Jean-de-Luz

BIDART

64210 Bidart — (Pyrénées-A.)
Paris 755 - Biarritz 6 - Bayonne 12

Bidartéa Best Western

N 10 − 59.54.94.68
Closed off-season Sun and Mon, and 2-9 Jan. 6 stes 560-670 F. 32 rms 296-416 F. Restaurant. Half-board 290-360 F. TV. Conference facilities. Pool. Garage parking. Telex 573441. V AE DC.
A big, Basque chalet one kilometre from the beach. Poolside restaurant.

Les Frères Ibarboure

Chemin de Talienia
59.54.81.64
MM. Ibarboure. Closed Wed off-season, and last 2 weeks of Nov. Open until 9.30 pm. Private room: 35. Garden dining. Air cond. No pets. Parking. V AE DC.

This eighteenth-century manor set on a hillside amid fields and woods is now launched towards gastronomic stardom. The Ibarboure brothers play lovely duets at their kitchen *piano*, producing harmonious, full-flavoured regional fare that bears the stamp of peerless technique. True, the food is not wildly creative, but we are relieved to see that Philippe and Martin have steered away from the precious, mannered style we briefly feared they might adopt. Duck-liver terrine in Jurançon wine aspic, fresh cod ravioli with anchovy butter, salmon straight from the Adour River cooked with coarse salt, olive oil, and balsamic vinegar, or duck-leg confit with a pumpkin custard, or the fillet of lamb with a garlic purée are all brilliant examples of their art. Martin is the family pastry whiz: don't leave before the gingerbread ice cream in chocolate sauce, or the crisp almond pyramid with crushed pralines and caramel ice cream arrive. In any case, your hostesses, Anne-Marie and Marie-Claude Ibarboure, will make you feel so comfortable that you won't be in a hurry to depart. But when you do, the incredibly light bill may leave you feeling like a thief—though a very, very happy one.
A la carte: 330 F. Menus: 190 F, 270 F.

In nearby **Ahetze**

(5 km S on D 655)
64210 Bidart — (Pyrénées-A.)

11/20 L'Epicerie d'Ahetze

Place du Fronton
59.41.94.95
M. Arnault. Closed Wed off-season and 30 Oct-20 Dec. Open until 9 pm. Air cond. V AE.
A pity the new owners of this adorable *épicerie* have turned their backs on the local culinary traditions. All in all, the fish sausage is well made, but the ham steak, though generously served, is heavy; the desserts are skippable. Limited cellar of country wines.
A la carte: 170 F. Menu: 80 F.

BIÈVRES

08370 Bièvres — (Ardennes)
Paris 255 - Sedan 35 - Charleville-Mézières 57

11/20 Relais de Saint-Walfroy

24.22.61.62
M. Vignol. Closed Tue. Open until 8.30 pm. Private room: 25. Parking. V.
Return to the Maginot line to find this spotless country inn, whose smiling hosts will serve you a hearty menu featuring guinea hen and peas, leg of lamb with beans, trout sautéed butter, and coq-au-vin. Just 50 F will buy you a decent bottle of wine.
Menus: from 70 F to 130 F.

BILLIERS

56190 Billiers — (Morbihan)
Paris 458 - Nantes 86 - Redon 37 - Vannes 27

Domaine de Rochevilaine

Pointe de Pen-Lan — 97.41.69.27
Mme Blain. Closed 7 Jan-11 Feb. Open until 9.30 pm. Private room: 70. No pets. Parking. Telex 950570. AE DC.

You need circle the globe no more in search of magic memories; a trip as far as this sea-bound corner of Brittany yields a fifteenth-century manor restored with startling authenticity, from the painted beams to the gorgeous antiques. The bay windows look out onto hydrangeas, the sea and the prettiest sunsets on the south coast of the peninsula. We can imagine no better setting to taste the astute and well-executed cooking of Patrick Caillault: marinated salmon enlivened by the flavours of fennel and courgettes, saffron lasagne accompanying John Dory and crunchy vegetables, lobster fricassée and potatoes with a sauce cardinale. Although fish commands pride of place on the menu, you shouldn't neglect the farm-reared pigeon with Swiss chard and a mushroom fricassée, or the breast of chicken with a truffle-laced stuffing. The fine wine list is rather expensive.
A la carte: 450-500 F. Menus: 750 F (for 2 pers), 245 F.

Domaine de Rochevilaine

(See restaurant above)
Closed 7 Jan-11 Feb. 2 stes 1,500 F. 29 rms 400-990 F. Half-board 510-795 F. TV. Conference facilities. Heated pool.
This manor will accommodate you in individual bungalows or huge rooms, some of which are blessed with a view of the flower gardens and the rocky coast. Assiduous service and delicious breakfasts.

BIOT

06140 Biot — (Alpes-Mar.)
Paris 922 - Antibes 8 - Nice 22 - Cagnes 10

Auberge du Jarrier

30, pass. de la Bourgade — 93.65.11.68
M. Métral. Closed Tue (lunch only in July-Aug), Wed lunch in summer and Mon dinner off-season. Open until 9.15 pm. Private room: 30. Terrace dining. V.
Perhaps the best sort of tribute we can pay to the talents of chef Christian Métral is the observation that on an evening when he was absent, the cooking lacked the master's touch. Which is not to say that along with the warmth of the reception and the joys of a beautifully laid table, we did not also enjoy the stuffed courgette flower with an olive sauce, the perfectly cooked sliced kidney with shallot confit, or the lavender-flavoured crème brûlée. But the baked turbot with olive oil and chanterelles was bland, and the apricot clafoutis with an almond milk sauce was not quite up to the standard of the other desserts. The wines were excellent (try the 1986 St-Baillon rouge) and the bill was up to its accustomed level.
A la carte: 400 F and up. Menus: 180 F, 240 F, 290 F.

Hostellerie du Bois Fleuri

Domaine du Bois-Fleuri
199, bd de la Source — 93.65.68.74
Closed Jan 1 ste 800 F. 65 rms 340-600 F. Restaurant. Half-board 470-630 F. TV. Conference facilities. Pool. Tennis. Parking. Telex 460000. V AE DC.

Come to this pink castle in the woods for attractive, nicely furnished rooms and you'll also find silence and splendid views from your terrace. Perfect service.

11/20 Chez Odile

Ch. des Bachettes — 93.65.15.63
Mlle Rogati. Closed off-season Thu and 15 Nov-11 Dec. Open until 9.30 pm. Garden dining. Pets allowed.

In this friendly inn, Odile and her chef offer simple, hearty fare such as terrine of pheasant with shallot confit, rabbit in aspic, classic Provençal sheep's trotters and tripe, little cheeses in olive oil, and homemade desserts.
Menu: 140 F.

14 Les Terraillers

11, rte du Chemin-Neuf — 93.65.01.59
MM. Fulci and Jacques. Closed Wed and Thu lunch in juil-Aug. Open until 10 pm. Private room: 10. Terrace dining. Parking. V AE DC.

This sixteenth-century pottery with its sunny terrace wins two more points this year. We were impressed by the abrupt about-turn from a simulated grand hotel dining room complete with plain food at fancy prices to a pleasant spot offering some interesting dishes: foie gras ravioli in a very good mushroom sauce, a toothsome pigeon ballottine, and a perfect banana millefeuille. The classic cellar needs more half-bottles. Accomplished but rather frosty service.
A la carte: 350 F. Menus: 150 F, 220 F, 280 F.

BIRIATOU

See Hendaye

BISCARROSSE

40600 Biscarrosse — (Landes)
Paris 660 - Dax 97 - Arcachon 39 - Bayonne 132

Atlantide

Rue J.-de-La Fontaine — 58.78.08.86
Closed 15 Dec-15 Jan. 33 rms 180-360 F. TV. No pets. Conference facilities. Parking. V AE DC.

A brand-new, town-centre hotel which has quiet, practical, modern rooms, but disappointing breakfasts. Courteous reception.

11/20 Le Mille Pâtes

898, av. de la République — 58.78.12.00
M. Dufau. Open every day. Open until 10 pm. Parking. V AE DC.

The huge dining room is divided up by Roman 'ruins' which underscore the simple Italian theme: hearty portions of pasta and pizza served with a smile. The children are kept busy with a film in the games room while you eat. Disappointing desserts.
A la carte: 150-180 F.

10/20 Restaumer

10 km NW on D 146
in Biscarrosse-Plage — 58.78.20.26
M. Pince. Closed Wed off-season and 20 Dec-1 March. Open until 9.30 pm. Terrace dining. V DC.

The high point is the low prices and the low point is everything on the menu except for the fine

shellfish; do as the locals do and stick to that.
A la carte: 150-200 F. Menu: 85 F (off-season only).

BLAGNAC

See Toulouse

BLANC-MESNIL (LE)

See Paris Suburbs

BLOIS

41000 Blois — (Loir/Cher)
Paris 180 - Tours 60 - Orléans 56 - Le Mans 109

15 Le Bocca d'Or

15, rue Haute — 54.78.04.74
M. Galland. Closed Mon lunch, Sun, and 21 Jan-5 March. Open until 9.30 pm. No pets. V AE.

Elegant in its purity, the cuisine of Patrice Galland features nothing unnecessary and everything in perfect balance. The bare stone arches warmed by soft colours and lighting provide a perfect background to such dishes as unshelled prawns with cumin, smoked duck breast served with lentils, pears and walnut oil, slices of sole with ginger and cucumber fumet, and lamb sweetbreads with lemon grass and black radishes. Desserts with more technical perfection than personality won't ruin the memories. Sketchy service.
A la carte: 300-380 F. Menus: 140 F (weekdays lunch only), 185 F (weekdays only).

Campanile

Rue de la Vallée-Maillard
54.74.44.66
Open every day. 51 rms 245 F. Restaurant. TV. Conference facilities. Parking. Telex 751628. V.

This simple hotel has quiet rooms and conference facilities.

10/20 Claude de France

(Le Relais du Château)
22, rue Porte-Côté — 54.78.20.24
M. Raffault. Closed Sat lunch in summer, Sun dinner in winter, Mon and 2-31 Jan. Open until 10 pm (9.30 pm off-season). Private room: 60. Hotel: 42 rms 150-290 F. Telex 752333. V.

An easy flow of tourists from the nearby château has obviously made this place lazy. We subtract two points this year for awful hot oysters and dried-out, overcooked fillet of beef.
A la carte: 250 F. Menus: 100 F (weekdays only), and from 120 F to 250 F.

12/20 L'Espérance

189, quai Ulysse-Besnard — 54.78.09.01
M. Guillot. Closed Sun dinner, Mon, 24 Feb-12 March and 25 Aug-4 Sep. Open until 9.30 pm. Air cond. No pets. Parking. V.

In an admirable move to save the soul of their restaurant before the body, the new owners of this graceless establishment on the Loire have put their energy into the cooking, leaving the pine-panelled ceiling and raspberry-coloured carpeting to be changed later. The carpaccio of salmon and scallops, and the fillet of beef served with fresh goat-cheese ravioli are the highlights of a simple, savoury cuisine, and there's a fine selection of Loire and Touraine wines at moderate prices. Attentive service.
A la carte: 300 F. Menus: 115 F, 150 F, 200 F, 295 F.

L'Horset Blois
26, av. Maunoury — 54.74.19.00
Open every day. 78 rms 400-430 F. Restaurant. TV. Conference facilities. Parking. Telex 752328. V AE DC.
This new, attractive hotel is located opposite the conference centre and has pleasant rooms.

12/20 L'Orangerie du Château
1, av. J.-Laigret — 54.78.05.36
M. Nodot. Closed Sun dinner off-season, Mon and Feb school holidays. Open until 9.30 pm. Private room: 50. Garden dining. Parking. V.
The Renaissance luxury of the building has spilled over into this delightful dining room with its fine china. If a little creativity had spilled over into the conventional but competent cooking of Serge Nodot (hot foie gras with wild mushrooms, baked salmon with a purée of baby crabs), it would have been worth two more points instead of one.
A la carte: 300 F. Menus: 200 F (weekdays only, wine inc), 130 F, 170 F, 280 F.

12/20 La Péniche
Prom. du Mail — 54.74.37.23
M. Bosque. Closed Sun (except holidays). Open until 9.30 pm. Air cond. No pets. V AE DC.
This quay-side barge with its pretty wood ceiling and seawater fish tank is a plush spot to enjoy excellent hot oysters with leeks, good fillet of beef with bone marrow and a Chinon sauce, and a Grand Marnier vacherin with hot chocolate sauce. Good choice of Bordeaux; hardly any Loire wines. The reception is friendly but the service rather stilted.
A la carte: 300-350 F. Menu: 140 F (weekdays only).

12/20 Hôtel de la Poste
9 km W on D 766
11, av. de Blois
41190 Molineuf — 54.70.03.25
M. Poidras. Closed Sun dinner, Wed, Feb and 4-11 Sep. Open until 9 pm. Air cond. Parking. V AE DC.
Follow the gourmets into the simple beauty of this blue-and-yellow dining room full of flowers. A gentle, inviting place, it serves generous if complicated dishes such as simmered tiny scallops with clementines and chicory, a sweet potato, foie gras, and ginger salad, and a white-chocolate mousse with crème caramel.
A la carte: 230 F. Menus: 75 F (weekdays only), 125 F, 170 F.

Au Rendez-Vous des Pêcheurs
27, rue de Foix — 54.74.67.48
M. Jégonday. Open every day. Open until 9.30 pm. Terrace dining. No pets. V.
A modern interpretation of bistro décor provides the background for Laurent Jégonday's clever, youthful, and impossible-to-predict cooking. We can't guarantee you'll be able to try his hot chicken liver terrine with mustard seeds, spinach and cockle salad, fillet of carp with a purée of asparagus tips and peas, or chicken fricassée with mussels and lemon grass.
A la carte: 250 F. Menu: 120 F.

Some establishments change their closing times without warning. It is always wise to check in advance.

Urbis
3, rue Porte-Côté — 54.74.01.17
Open every day. 56 rms 250-310 F. TV. Telex 752287. V AE.
This hotel 100 metres from the château has plainly decorated rooms and an attractive bar with a glass roof.

12/20 Via Vietnam
2, bd Vauban — 54.78.86.99
M. Van Hung. Closed Wed. Open until 10.30 pm. No pets. V.
Ten years ago, the Van Hung clan piled off the boat and went straight to work creating this pretty, Oriental décor. Entirely staffed from within the ranks, the resulting restaurant provides a warm welcome and authentic, full-flavoured Vietnamese fare: a subtle beef and vermicelli salad, perfect chicken with ginger, tender glazed pork.
A la carte: 100-150 F.

In nearby **Ménars**

(8 km NE on N 152)
41500 Blois — (Loir/Cher)

11/20 L'Epoque
23-25, rue G.-Charron — 54.46.81.07
M. Viguier. Closed off-season Tue dinner and Wed, and 10 Jan-1 Feb. Open until 9.30 pm. Private room: 60. V.
The heavy rustic touch results from large doses of wallpaper, printed fabrics, and wood panelling. The prices are also weighty and out of proportion to the modest results: scallops in pastry, beef Sologne-style, liqueur soufflé.
A la carte: 300 F. Menus: 85 F (weekdays only), 115 F, 155 F, 195 F.

BOCOGNANO
See CORSICA

BOIS-DE-LA-CHAIZE (LE)
See Noirmoutier (Ile de)

BOIS-PLAGE-EN-RÉ (LE)
See Ré (Ile de)

BOLLENBERG
See Rouffach

BOLLÈNE-VÉSUBIE (LA)
06450 Bollène-Vésubie (La) — (Alpes-Mar.)
Paris 970 - Nice 54 - Puget-Théniers 58 - Sospel 37

Grand Hôtel du Parc
93.03.01.01
Closed 1 Oct-27 April. 42 rms 140-330 F. Restaurant. Half-board 265-590 F oblig in seas. Parking. AE DC.
A good, traditional hotel with a garden and glorious mountains and forest all around.

BONDUES
See Lille

BON-ENCONTRE
See Agen

BONIFACIO
See CORSICA

25620 Bonnevaux-le-Prieuré — (Doubs)
Paris 414 - Pontarlier 45 - Besançon 26 - Ornans 11

Le Moulin du Prieuré
81.59.21.47

M. Gatez. Closed off-season Sun dinner and Mon, and 15 Nov-10 March. Open until 9 pm (9.30 pm seas.). Parking. V AE DC.

In the heart of Courbet country nestles this charming thirteenth-century mill, whose *patronne* seems to be smiling again (we had received some complaints about the reception). Her husband's cooking can be counted on for precision in its use of fine ingredients, but the flavours can be a little pale: a pleasant snail turnover with walnuts and vin jaune had lost the aroma of the wine. On the other hand, the délice de basse-cour, with duck breast and pigeon, is wonderful. And there is nothing dull about the desserts, the wine list, the brisk service, or the delicate flower arrangements.
A la carte: 350-400 F. Menu: 320 F.

Le Moulin du Prieuré
(See restaurant above)

Closed 15 Nov-10 March. 8 rms 580 F (per pers, half-board oblig). TV. Pets allowed.

The rooms two-to-a-cabin are sprinkled about the grounds and provide adequate comfort and charm, although the soundproofing is imperfect. You make your own breakfast.

74130 Bonneville — (H.-Savoie)
Paris 560 - Chamonix 57 - Annecy 38 - Genève 28

Bellevue
2 km E on D 6
Ayse — 50.97.20.83

Open 15 June-15 Sep. 22 rms 195-230 F. Restaurant. Half-board 185-195 F oblig in seas. Conference facilities. Parking. V.

The quiet rooms are graced with huge balconies overlooking the valley.

Le Capucin Gourmand
N 205, in Vougy — 50.34.03.50

M. Barbin. Closed Sun dinner, Mon and 1-22 Aug. Open until 9.30 pm. Air cond. Parking. V AE DC.

This uninteresting, ill-lit dining room cluttered with artificial flowers and run by a maître d' who doesn't know the wine list is nevertheless where you take a seat for the top-notch, dedicated cooking of Guy Barbin. This would be two-toque fare (excellent red-mullet fillets in olive vinaigrette, prawns sautéed with coriander) were it not for the insipid Provençal lamb with thyme and the leaden pastries.
A la carte: 350 F. Menus: 150 F (weekdays only), 220 F, 260 F, 350 F.

L'Eau Sauvage
Pl. de l'Hôtel-de-Ville — 50.97.20.68

M. Guenon. Closed Sun dinner and Mon (except Aug), 2 first weeks of Jan and of Sep. Open until 9.30 pm. Private room: 50. No-smoking section. No pets. Parking. V AE DC.

After training under Georges Blanc, among others, the son of the household has revamped his family's restaurant with an array of fountains, pools and Greek columns. His cooking is also very decorative, if slightly affected, and wins a toque this year. The gourmandise of smoked salmon and slivered crab is pointlessly accompanied by melon in sweet wine. The hake fillet, however, with its lime butter and Provençal tian, is perfectly cooked,

and the smoked young rabbit in spicy mustard and prunes is faultless. You shouldn't miss the local farmhouse cheeses, but the dessert trolley reverts to the restaurant's habit of favouring the eyes over the tastebuds. Fine wines and excellent coffee.
A la carte: 400 F. Menus: from 200 F to 300 F.

Sapeur Hôtel
(See restaurant above)

Closed Sun and Mon (except Aug), 2 first weeks of Jan and of Sep. 2 stes 300-380 F. 18 rms 230-280 F. Half-board 260-300 F. TV. No pets. Conference facilities.

A pleasant and handy stopover on the ski route from Geneva to Chamonix.

84480 Bonnieux — (Vaucluse)
Paris 727 - Avignon 47 - Apt 13 - Cavaillon 26

L'Aiguebrun
D 943, between Lourmarin and Apt
Domaine de la Tour — 90.74.04.14

MM. Studhalter and Ferraris. Closed Wed, 5 Jan-1 March and 15 Nov-15 Dec. Open until 10 pm. Garden dining. No pets. Parking. V AE.

If your car's suspension can take the abuse, spur it on to this restaurant tucked away in the prettiest part of the Aiguebrun valley. It's become one of the best in the region since Daniel Studhalter took over, regaling us with fresh, fine market cuisine. Perfect salmon marinated in olive oil and coriander, delicate sliced rabbit in a light, creamy sauce, and—a rare treat—a properly cooked crème brûlée (with raspberries) make for a delightful meal under the giant cedar by the river. Excellent local wines and pleasant service.
Menu: 220 F.

L'Aiguebrun
(See restaurant above)

Closed 5 Jan-1 March and 15 Nov-15 Dec. 2 stes 620-640 F. 7 rms 460-500 F. Half-board 510 F.

You're sure of a peaceful stay in simple, pleasant rooms, set in 65 hectares by the river.

11/20 Hostellerie du Prieuré
90.75.80.78

M. Chapotin and Mme Keller. Closed Wed lunch, Tue (in seas Tue lunch, Wed and Thu), and 5 Nov-15 Feb. Open until 9 pm. Private room: 20. Garden dining. Garage parking. V.

Olde worlde charm—by the fireside or in the leafy garden—complements the two short but varied set menus (grilled prawns, roast lamb, perch with sorrel).
Menus: 130 F (except lunch w-e and holidays), 182 F.

Hostellerie du Prieuré
(See restaurant above)

Closed 5 Nov-15 Feb. 10 rms 320-460 F. Half-board 366-386 F oblig in seas. TV 8 rms. Conference facilities.

Delightful buildings at the foot of the ramparts of the medieval village contain antique furniture and some beautiful rooms. Garden.

RAC Regional Maps of France at 4 miles to 1 inch are the ideal touring companion. Available from RAC offices and all good bookshops.

In nearby Buoux

(10 km NE)
84480 Bonnieux — (Vaucluse)

12/20 Auberge de la Loube 🕄
90.74.19.58
M. Leporati. Closed Thu and 2 Jan-2 Feb. Open until 9.30 pm. Garden dining. Parking. V.
This old farmhouse restaurant is devoted heart and soul to the local Provençal traditions: rabbit with cèpes, roast Lubéron lamb with sage, beef brouffade (a casserole with herbs). Not forgetting the tasty little Banon cheeses.
Menu: 135 F.

BONSECOURS
See Rouen

BORDEAUX
33000 Bordeaux — (Gironde)
Paris 566 - Angoulême 116 - Arcachon 60

L'Alhambra
111 bis, rue Judaïque — 56.96.06.91
M. Demazeau. Closed Sat lunch, Sun and 14 July-15 Aug. Open until 9.30 pm. Private room: 20. Air cond. No pets. V.   D2-3
Michel Demazeau is known as Bordeaux' most retiring chef. (The truth is that he is busy cooking and keeping his customers happy). In this attractive, flower-decked restaurant you can share in the rewards of his hard work and persistence. A superb technician dedicated to the rich, provincial classics, Demazeau's skill lies nevertheless in his lightness of touch. His ragoût of cocks'combs and kidneys with mushrooms, the braised medallions of lotte with asparagus, the saddle of young rabbit with bacon, and his subtle desserts, like the orange gratin served with a sorbet of bitter chocolate, command respect as well as a second toque. The *patronne*, Marie-France, personally supervises the cellar of Bordeaux, with a particular passion for Graves.
A la carte: 300 F. Menus: 100 F (lunch only), 200 F (weekdays only).

10/20 Baud et Millet
19, rue Huguerie — 56.79.05.77
M. Baud. Closed Sun and holidays. Open until midnight. Private room: 40. Air cond. V AE DC.   E2-18
You choose your wine in the shop on the way in and after that it is cheese in all its forms (raclette, fondue, welsh rarebit), plus of course the titanic buffet. Dinner and a show at weekends.
A la carte: 130 F and up. Menus: from 88 F to 150 F.

Hôtel de Bayonne
4, rue de Martignac — 56.48.00.88
Closed last 2 weeks of Dec. 36 rms 290-410 F. TV. Air cond 11 rms. No pets. Telex 570362. V.   E3-12
Just reopened after extensive renovations.

11/20 Bistro du Sommelier
167, rue G.-Bonnac — 56.96.71.78
M. Valverde. Closed Sat lunch, Sun and 1-15 Jan. Open until 11 pm. Private room: 70. Terrace dining. Air cond. No-smoking section. V.   D2-41
Nobody beats sommelier Hervé Valverde to the best Bordeaux at the sweetest prices. Sometimes centred around a bottle he has recommended, your meal might include genuine bistro dishes like blanquette de veau and giblet salad.
Menu: 95 F.

12/20 Le Bistrot de Bordeaux
10, rue des Piliers-de-Tutelle — 56.81.35.94
M. Dupuy. Closed Sat lunch and Sun. Open until 10.30 pm. Private room: 20. Air cond. V.   D3-55
Inexplicably, wine bistros are a rare species in Bordeaux. Here's a good selection of the local produce, by the bottle or the glass, including a 1987 Haut-Brion at a remarkable 350 F. As for solids, the dishes are simple, honest and rather expensive: leek and salmon feuilleté, entrecôte steak with shallots, pear and almond tart.
A la carte: 250 F. Menus: 75 F (wine inc), 140 F.

Le Bolchoï
34, cours du Chapeau-Rouge — 56.44.43.50
M. Gautier. Dinner only. Closed Sun. Open until midnight (upon reserv.). V.   E3-27
One floor up from the restaurant Le Rouzic, you'll receive a warm welcome to its Russian little sister. New this year is a bistro-style set menu offering a zaskouskis buffet, the *plat du jour*, and a dessert. It's a good way to sample specialities such as smoked salmon salad, spiced and breaded cutlet Datcha, and the remarkable nalizniki (a fresh cheese and caramel crêpe). Don't forget to try one of the twenty vodkas available.
A la carte: 250-300 F. Menu: 150 F.

Au Bonheur du Palais
74, rue P.-L.-Lande — 56.94.38.63
MM. Shan. Dinner only. Closed Sun and 15 Aug-10 Sep. Open until 11 pm. Private room: 25. No pets. V AE DC.   C3-24
The décor's much-needed revamp ought to be completed by now and you'll be able to enjoy the infinite variety of this Cantonese cuisine in greater comfort. Perfectly steamed mixed ravioli and full-flavoured shrimps sautéed with saté share honours with the spicy chicken full of unusual flavours. Tommy Chan, the chef's enthusiastic and knowledgeable brother, will help you choose. Chinese beer is probably the best thing on the wine list.
A la carte: 250 F. Menus: 148 F, 200 F.

12/20 La Bonne Bouille
7, rue des Bahutiers — 56.48.24.86
M. Gotrand. Closed Sat lunch, Mon, Tue, Nov and 23 Dec-3 Jan. Open until 10.30 pm. V AE DC.   D4-50
Excellent, inexpensive meals and a friendly welcome. Look for the curried oysters in flaky pastry, and cod with pink peppercorns.
Menus: 100 F, 130 F.

Le Buhan
28, rue Buhan — 56.52.80.86
M. Brunel. Closed Mon lunch and Sun. Open until 10 pm. V.   D4-16
Well chosen by Jean-Claude Brunel and simply treated, the ingredients are the stars here. And since his favourites are lobster, foie gras, oysters and salmon, the à la carte prices can soar. Stick to the set menu and you can still sample a soufléed lobster feuillantine or duck foie gras with oysters and spinach.
A la carte: 250-350 F. Menus: 100 F, 175 F.

Hôtel Burdigala
See restaurant Le Jardin de Burdigala

1 - Restaurant
Le Loup **R**
2 - Normandie **H**
3 - L'Alhambra **R**
4 - La Chamade **R**
et Joël D. **R**
5 - Le Musée **R**
6 - Chez Philippe **R**
7 - Le Vieux Bordeaux **R**
8 - Le Chapon Fin **R**
9 - Le Cailhau **R**
et Les Plaisirs d'Ausone **R**
10 - Royal Médoc **H**
11 - Mercure
Pont d'Aquitaine **H**
12 - Hôtel de Bayonne **H**
13 - La Ténarèze **R**
Le Bistrot d'Edouard **R**
et Chez Gilles **R**
14 - Pavillon
des Boulevards **R**
et La Villa Carnot **R**
15 - Hôtel Majestic **H**
16 - Le Buhan **R**
17 - Le Flore (Sofitel
Aquitania) **RH**
18 - Baud et Millet **R**
19 - Les Provinces **R**
et André Thibeaud **R**
20 - El Catador **R**
21 - Campanile **H**
22 - Grand Hôtel
de Bordeaux **H**
23 - Le Cervantès **R**
24 - Le Puits du Roy **R**
25 - Mercure
Bordeaux-le-Lac **H**
26 - La Mamounia **R**
27 - Le Bolchoï **R**
et le Rouzic **R**
28 - La Pelouse **H**
29 - Le Dégustoir **R**
30 - Au Chipiron **R**
31 - La Fortune du Pot **R**
32 - Dubern **R**
33 - Périgord Saint-Jean **R**
34 - Mapotel
Terminus **H**
35 - Chez Dupont **R**
36 - L'Epicerie **R**
37 - La Ferme
Saint-Michel **R**
38 - Le Meriadeck
(Pullman) **RH**
39 - Le Cellier Bordelais **R**
40 - Novotel
Bordeaux-le-Lac **H**

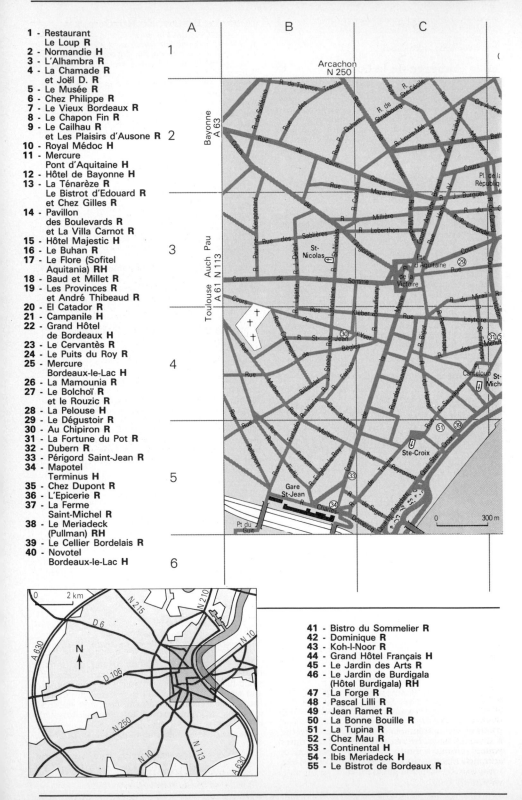

41 - Bistro du Sommelier **R**
42 - Dominique **R**
43 - Koh-I-Noor **R**
44 - Grand Hôtel Français **H**
45 - Le Jardin des Arts **R**
46 - Le Jardin de Burdigala
(Hôtel Burdigala) **RH**
47 - La Forge **R**
48 - Pascal Lilli **R**
49 - Jean Ramet **R**
50 - La Bonne Bouille **R**
51 - La Tupina **R**
52 - Chez Mau **R**
53 - Continental **H**
54 - Ibis Meriadeck **H**
55 - Le Bistrot de Bordeaux **R**

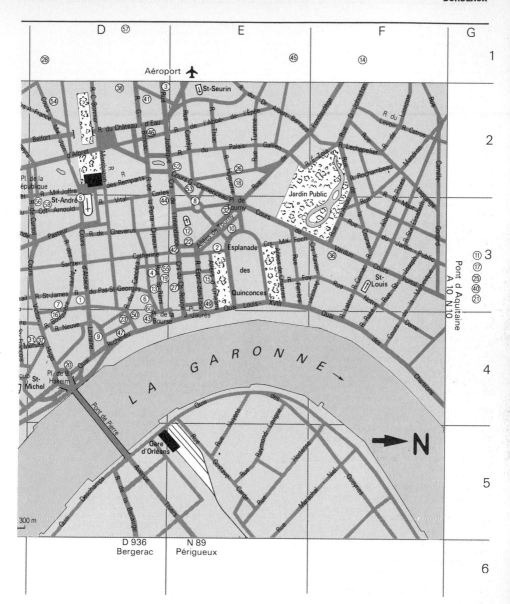

D ⑤⑦ E F G

1

㉘ ⑭ ①

Aéroport ✈ ㊺ ⑭

St-Seurin

2

Jardin Public

㉓
㉗
⑮
Esplanade
des
Quinconces

3

St-Louis

L A   G A R O N N E ⟶

➡ N

4

Pont de Pierre

Gare
d'Orléans

5

300 m

D 936
Bergerac

N 89
Périgueux

6

Le Cailhau

3, pl. du Palais
56.81.79.91

M. Juillard. Closed Sat lunch, Sun and 27 July-
19 Aug. Open until 10.15 pm. Air cond. No pets. V AE
DC.   D4-9

The locals love the witty bistro décor and fine
food. They come for an astonishingly good-value
lunch or a festive dinner featuring Alain Juillard's
simple but beguiling cuisine. The salad of warm
duck foie gras and girolle mushrooms, bass in
pastry with red wine sauce, and baked kidneys in
a thyme sauce are sure to please. The talented
young *sommelière* will advise you on a worthy
accompaniment.

A la carte: 330-380 F. Menus: 145 F (lunch only,
wine inc), 160 F, 220 F.

Campanile

Quartier du Lac – 56.39.54.54
Open every day. 132 rms 239 F. Restaurant. Half-
board 329 F. TV. Conference facilities. Telex 560425.
V AE.   G3-21

This modern, practical hotel overlooks a large
garden with children's amusements.

10/20 El Catador

11, pl. de Bir-Hakeim – 56.52.15.26
M. Blanco. Closed Sun and Mon. Open until 11 pm.
V AE DC.   D4-20

A rainbow of tapas and several Seville specialities
(garlic soup, king prawns, kidneys in sherry) go
well with the Rioja wines.

A la carte: 200 F. Menus: 90 F, 110 F.

12/20 Le Cellier Bordelais
30, quai de la Monnaie — 56.31.30.30
M. Laffargue. Closed Sat, Sun, 22 Dec-2 Jan and mid-July to mid-Aug. Open until 11 pm. V.   C5-39
A couple of score of first-growth Bordeaux displayed amid the wood panelling, columns and mirrors are what attract wine lovers. Food lovers won't mind the eels, squid in its ink, quail with grapes, and oysters. Faultless reception and service.
A la carte: 200-260 F.

10/20 Le Cervantès
17, rue E.-Duployé — 56.52.57.43
M. Biec. Closed Sun, Mon lunch and Sat, 1 week in Aug and 2 weeks in Sep. Open until 0.30 am. Terrace dining. V AE DC.   D4-23
A fine little detour through the Spanish countryside, with stops for calamari, paella, ham and broad beans, and enough funds left to get home.
A la carte: 150-180 F. Menus: 50 F (lunch only), 75 F (wine inc), 105 F.

La Chamade
20, rue des Piliers-de-Tutelle — 56.48.13.74
M. Carrère. Closed 11-18 Aug. Open until 10 pm. Private room: 45. V.   D3-4
The décor alone is a model of elegance and refinement. Add to it the atmosphere created by one of the best teams of serving staff in Bordeaux and the masterly cooking of Michel Carrère, and this vaulted light stone restaurant hung with contemporary art becomes a must. The mixed salad with slivered warm truffles, crunchy mouthfuls of ginger-flavoured oysters and smoked bacon in soy sauce, the stuffed cabbage bundles with veal and a fricassée of sprouted lentils, and the juicy grilled bass all illustrate the dazzling simplicity born of a marriage of skill and audacity. In addition, here is a brilliant seafood chef who —and this is less common—is highly inventive with beast and fowl as well. Excellent Bordeaux.
A la carte: 400 F. Menus: 180 F, 450 F.

Le Chapon Fin
5, rue Montesquieu — 56.79.10.10
M. Garcia. Closed Sun and Mon. Open until 9.30 pm. Air cond. No pets. V AE DC.   E3-8
How's this for a 135 F lunch: saffron and shellfish soup, calf's foot croustillant with capers, and cherry soufflé, served in the historic grotto of Bordeaux' most extravagant restaurant. It would be a godsend in a humbler establishment, but Francis Garcia is one of the city's best chefs and knows just how to harmonise new flavours with traditional tastes. Come back for dinner and start anywhere, for example with the bass escalope with gherkin butter, the salmon steak with garlic confit, or the oyster gratin: they all bear the stamp of a true professional who's not afraid to fight preconceived ideas and the kind of fashions that can all too easily infect an entire menu. The sumptuous desserts and a fine selection of Bordeaux will turn the meal into a feast. Famous folk who have left souvenirs here include Toulouse-Lautrec, Sarah Bernhardt, and Winston Churchill.
A la carte: 450-500 F. Menus: 135 F and 200 F (lunch only), 330 F and 400 F (weekdays only).

The new spiral-bound RAC Atlas France will help you to find your chosen restaurant of hotel, no matter how secluded.

12/20 Au Chipiron
56, cours de l'Yser — 56.92.98.59
M. Etchebest. Closed Sun dinner, Mon and 15 Aug-1 Sep. Open until 9.30 pm. V.   B4-30
The more expensive set menu offers Basques/Landes regional fare, with a mussel and tarragon cream soup, grilled Garonne shad with sorrel, homemade confit de canard, and dessert. An honourable meal.
A la carte: 300 F. Menus: 98 F, 145 F.

Le Clavel Barnabet
44, rue Ch.-Domercq — 56.92.91.52
M. Barnabet. Closed Mon lunch and Sun. Open until 10.30 pm. Private room: 18. Air cond. V.   B5-48
After two years working with Michel and Jean-Michel Lorain at Joigny, Laurent Barnabet, aged 24, has a first toque for his first restaurant. The startlingly good cod steak with garlic purée and delicious, paprika-flavoured hot oysters prove that here is a cook who loves his trade. He still needs to smooth out a few inconsistencies, such as a poor cheese board, and loosen up the serving staff.
A la carte: 250-300 F. Menus: 120 F, 180 F, 230 F.

Clemenceau
4, cours G.-Clemenceau — 56.52.98.98
Open every day. 45 rms 225-265 F. TV. Air cond. Telex 541079. V AE DC.   E2-52
This big corner building houses well-equipped rooms, some of them soundproofed. Shopping gallery.

11/20 La Concorde
50, rue du Mal-Joffre — 56.44.68.97
M. Hosten. Closed Sun and Aug. Open until 11 pm. Private room: 100. Terrace dining. Garage parking. V.   D3-56
A lively brasserie where the strictly classic cooking is popular at lunchtime: tasty if slightly fatty duck terrine, so-so (maybe frozen?) bass in good beurre blanc, and homemade desserts. Relaxed, courteous service.
A la carte: 220 F.

Continental
10, rue Montesquieu — 56.52.66.00
Open every day. 1 ste 600-800 F. 50 rms 210-320 F. TV. Conference facilities. V AE DC.   E2-53
This hotel offers a friendly welcome in a convenient location. The new management is modernising it gradually.

12/20 La Coquille d'Œuf
197, rue G.-Bonnac — 56.93.09.86
Mme Reillat. Closed Sun, Mon and 5-20 Aug. Open until 10.30 pm. Air cond. V.   D1-57
Paintings and decorated eggs provide the backdrop to pleasant, uncomplicated dishes like the brain salad with lime, skate in beurre blanc, fine fillet of beef with Roquefort, and good honey ice cream. Discreet, efficient service.
A la carte: 250 F. Menu: 85 F (weekdays lunch only, wine inc).

10/20 Le Dégustoir
8, rue A.-Dumercq — 56.91.25.06
Mlle Simonet and M. Magnac. Dinner only. Closed Sun, Mon and 28 April-20 May. Open until midnight. V AE.   C3-29
A charming welcome awaits you in this minimalist rustic setting. You choose your wine from one of the 70 selected by Jean-Luc Magnac before turning your attention to his wife Liliane's increasingly

adept dishes: superb duck breast with disappointing foie gras, fine entrecôte steak in red wine sauce, and delicious stuffed prunes.

A la carte: 150-180 F.

11/20 Dominique

2, cours de l'Intendance — 56.52.59.79
M. Train. Open every day. Open until midnight. Private room: 60. No-smoking section. V. E3-42

The set menu includes hot oyster and vegetable gratin, duck fillet in sweet-and-sour sauce, and noisettes of young rabbit with prunes over which to admire the high-class bistro décor. Alternatively, you can order a starter and main course for 95 F.

Menu: 150 F.

12/20 Dubern

42, allées de Tourny — 56.51.67.96
M. Seguin. Open every day. Open until 10.30 pm. Private room: 60. V. E3-32

Modern décor downstairs and seventeenth-century style upstairs: both benefit from the young chef's straightforward and mostly well-executed dishes. The prawns in the seafood salad were slightly overcooked, while the tasty baked lobster with its original potato accompaniment could have stood the heat for a bit longer. The desserts are disappointing, apart from a particularly good crème brûlée. Bordeaux wines only.

A la carte: 330 F. Menus: 150 F (lunch only, except Sun), 200 F, 300 F.

11/20 Chez Dupont

45, rue Notre-Dame — 56.81.49.59
Mmes Lévy and Reiser. Closed Sat lunch, Sun and Aug. Open until 11.15 pm. V. F3-35

The success of this restaurant is an open secret: fresh salad of salmon, asparagus, tomatoes and chives, duck breast and peach kebabs served with a delicious spinach and carrot purée, and a custard-covered chocolate mousse cake. We'd like to see some more dishes on the *carte*. Relaxed service.

A la carte: 200 F. Menu: 59 F (weekdays only).

10/20 L'Epicerie

94, cours de Verdun — 56.44.27.22
M. Lauray. Closed Sat, Sun and Aug. Open until 11 pm. Private room: 55. Terrace dining. No-smoking section. V AE DC. F3-36

The same regular customers and the same inconsistent cooking. The duck breast and leg of lamb grilled on a wood fire are still best value.

A la carte: 200-250 F.

La Ferme Saint-Michel ♧

21, rue des Menuts — 56.91.54.77
M. Rivault. Closed Sat lunch and Sun. Annual closings not available. Open until 10.30 pm. V AE DC. D4-37

Ever popular is this charming bistro which boasts the attractive preparations of Jean-Pierre Rivault. Try for example the oyster and cèpe ravioli, or the superb nougat glacé with Sauternes jelly. The 120 F set menu, once sensational, has slipped a bit: beware of the soggy sea bream.

A la carte: 300 F and up. Menus: 120 F, 180 F, 260 F.

Le Flore

3, bd du Lac — 56.50.83.80
M. Delporte. Open every day. Open until 10 pm. Private room: 800. Terrace dining. Air cond. Parking. Telex 570557. V AE DC. G3-17

Sunshine and reflections from the lake light up the modern, pink-and-green dining room, while the courteous service and honest prices round out the pleasure of a generous style of cooking. The charm of it all draws more than just business customers for the stew of oysters, cockles, and winkles, saffron-flavoured lotte and sweetbreads grilled with sage.

A la carte: 260-300 F.

Sofitel Aquitania

(See restaurant above)
Open every day. 2 stes 1,200 F. 210 rms 545 F. TV. Air cond. Conference facilities. Heated pool.

Since the renovation of this fully equipped hotel, comfort is the watchword. There are conference rooms, a bar, and a discothèque.

11/20 La Forge

8, rue du Chai-des-Farines — 56.81.40.96
M. Pouts. Closed Sun, Mon and 15 Aug-15 Sep. Open until 10.30 pm. V. D4-47

May they brighten the rustic decor without changing the simple dishes based on good, local ingredients: lotte à la bordelaise, cooked country ham with shallots, and delicious sheep's-milk cheese.

A la carte: 170 F. Menus: 70 F, 100 F, 135 F.

12/20 La Fortune du Pot

37, rue des Menuts — 56.92.65.79
M. Rivierre. Closed Sun and Mon. Open until 10.30 pm. Private room: 30. V. D4-31

Anything you want as long as it's duck, from the *carte* built around duck to the duck-only menu. For those of a different feather there's a mussel, prawn and asparagus fricassée, or coq au vin de Bordeaux. The prices of the enlightened choice of wines have been severely trimmed.

A la carte: 180-200 F. Menus: 120 F, 150 F and 170 F (weekdays only).

12/20 Chez Gilles

6, rue des Lauriers — 56.81.17.38
M. Vérin. Closed Sat lunch, Wed and 15-31 Aug. Open until 11.30 pm. Terrace dining. V AE DC. D3-13

Trained in the best restaurants of Bordeaux, the owner-chef offers a selection of dishes at well-judged prices. Try the lotte with Graves mousseline or the veal fillet with caramelised spices.

A la carte: 250 F. Menus: 75 F (weekdays lunch only, wine inc), 110 F (dinner only), 220 F.

Grand Hôtel Français

12, rue du Temple — 56.48.10.35
Open every day. 4 stes 450 F. 35 rms 340-450 F. TV. Telex 550587. V AE DC. D3-44

This traditional hotel in a central, nineteenth-century residence has comfortable rooms.

Ibis Meriadeck

35, cours du Mal-Juin — 56.90.10.33
Open every day. 210 rms 280-335 F. Restaurant. TV. Air cond. Conference facilities. Parking. V. D2-54

Near the town centre, a modern hotel offering comfort at easy prices. Restaurant-brasserie.

Le Jardin de Burdigala

115, rue G.-Bonnac — 56.90.16.16

M. Gaillac. Open every day. Open until 10 pm. Private room: 30. Air cond. Valet parking. Telex 572981. V AE DC.   D2-46

A careful, studied approach to cooking, whose only daring aspect is its cost. The warm foie gras in Sauternes, John Dory fillet with morels and the pithiviers of pigeon and foie gras are just what you might expect. The décor is less conventional, with a glass pyramid letting plenty of light into the huge colonnaded dining room, and a fountain playing gently in the background. Smooth service and good, reliable wines.

A la carte: 350 F. Menus: 120 F (lunch only), 200 F, 300 F.

Hôtel Burdigala

(See restaurant above)

Open every day. 7 stes 980-1,080 F. 71 rms 580-900 F. TV. Air cond. Conference facilities.

A welcome alternative to small, ageing hotels or the big chains, this superb new establishment has varied décor and good soundproofing. Charming reception.

12/20 Le Jardin des Arts

65, av. Carnot — 56.42.26.27

M. Techoire. Closed Sun, Mon and 1-21 Aug. Open until 11.30 pm. Private room: 22. Terrace dining. V AE DC.   E1-45

The bistro version of Philippe Techoire's other restaurant, Chez Philippe. Safe bets include the salmon and sprouted lentils, tournedos steak with bone marrow, and a cinnamon-flavoured crème brûlée, washed down with a smooth Bordeaux.

A la carte: 250 F.

12/20 Koh-I-Noor

3, rue du Puits-Descujols
56.51.17.55

M. Chaudary. Open every day. Open until 11.30 pm. Air cond. No pets. V AE.   D4-43

You will find all your favourite Indian and Pakistani specialities such as chicken tandoori, Madras lamb, fine biryani, and excellent breads cooked in the tandoor. The décor and service are both meticulous.

A la carte: 180 F. Menus: 59 F (lunch only), 109 F (dinner only).

Hôtel Majestic

2, rue de Condé — 56.52.60.44

Open every day. 1 ste 450-550 F. 49 rms 290-400 F. TV. Conference facilities. Valet parking. Telex 572938. V AE DC.   E3-15

This comfortable hotel is conveniently situated.

12/20 La Mamounia

51, rue La Faurie-de-Monbadon
56.81.21.84

M. Benaboud. Open every day. Open until 10.30 pm. Air cond. V DC.   E2-26

It's not hard to fall under the spell of the rich décor with its gold-and-purple wall hangings where you can dine like royalty on, for instance, the richly aromatic couscous of Fes. The wines and desserts are not in the same league.

A la carte: 200-250 F. Menus: 51 F, 120 F.

Mapotel Terminus

Gare St-Jean — 56.92.71.58

Open every day. 81 rms 277-455 F. Restaurant. TV 71 rms. Conference facilities. V AE DC.   B5-34

Close to the Gare St Jean, this plain but well-kept hotel has soundproofed rooms and an underground car park. Meals on a tray available.

Mercure Bordeaux-le-Lac

Quartier du Lac — 56.50.90.30

Open every day. 3 stes 400-500 F. 108 rms 280-480 F. Restaurant. TV. Air cond. Conference facilities. Parking. Telex 540077. V AE DC.   G3-25

The functional, comfortable rooms have been recently modernised. Near the conference centre, and there are special weekend rates for golf lessons and vineyard tours.

Mercure Pont d'Aquitaine

Bordeaux-le-Lac — 56.50.90.14

Open every day. 2 stes 850 F. 100 rms 280-520 F. Restaurant. TV. Air cond. Conference facilities. Pool. Tennis. Parking. Telex 540097. V AE DC.   G3-11

Good business hotel near the convention centre and the trade-fair grounds.

12/20 Le Meriadeck

5, rue R.-Lateulade — 56.56.43.60

M. Marmain. Open every day. Open until 11 pm. Private room: 250. Air cond. No pets. Telex 540565. V AE DC.   D2-38

Chain-hotel dining rooms are not known for their gaiety and charm, and this one is no exception. The cooking unfortunately fits the décor, but if you shun complicated preparations in favour of the simple meat dishes like roast rack of lamb with thyme, or spicy young pigeon, you'll eat reasonably well. Good wines and service.

A la carte: 350 F. Menus: 185 F (wine inc), 110 F.

Pullman

(See restaurant above)

Open every day. 2 stes 1,900-2,100 F. 196 rms 420-820 F. TV. Air cond. Conference facilities.

Ideal business hotel, where function rules over fancy.

11/20 Le Musée

37, pl. Pey-Berland — 56.52.99.69

Mlle Duquesne. Closed Sat and 4-26 Aug. Open until 11 pm. Terrace dining. Telex 571394. V.   D3-5

Good, straightforward food can be enjoyed in the pretty grey-and-pink dining room (fine foie gras, wood pigeon salmis, duck breast in cassis). Downstairs in the vaulted cellar is the 'museum' devoted to Bordeaux wines.

A la carte: 200 F. Menus: 62 F (weekdays lunch only), 98 F.

Normandie

7-9, cours 30-Juillet — 56.52.16.80

Open every day. 100 rms 250-450 F. TV. Telex 570481. V AE DC.   E3-2

This stone corner building provides comfortable rooms and traditional service. Bar.

Le Nouveau Saucier

64, rue du Hâ — 56.81.11.22

M. Ouvrard. Closed Sat lunch (and dinner in summer), Sun, Aug and 1 week in Feb. Open until 10 pm. Garden dining. Air cond. V.   D3-58

This new bistro is already an address to remember. Top marks for the salad of lotte, hazelnuts, and cèpes, a juicy roast young pigeon, and cinnamon parfait. All the dishes are attractively presented, and served with a smile and wonderful breads. Well-chosen wines.

A la carte: 200 F. Menus: 43 F (lunch only), 69 F, 115 F.

Novotel Bordeaux-le-Lac
Quartier du Lac – 56.50.99.70
Open every day. 176 rms 435 F. Restaurant. TV. Air cond. Conference facilities. Pool. Parking. Telex 570274. V AE DC.   G3-40

Well-equipped hotel near the motorway and conference centre, with a lake to go jogging round.

Pavillon des Boulevards
120, rue de la Croix-de-Seguey – 56.81.51.02
M. Franc. Closed Sat lunch, Sun and 10-25 Aug. Open until 10.15 pm. Private room: 18. Garden dining. Air cond. V AE DC.   F1-14

You'll feel at home almost before you cross the threshold of this white stone restaurant with its adorable little garden. And you'll no doubt agree with the locals that the effort to get here from town is immediately soothed by Nelly Franc's warm welcome, the relaxed service, and Denis Franc's inventive cuisine. He does need to be more precise with cooking times and in combining flavours, but it's hard to resist the oysters in lemon aspic served alongside a crépinette of pig's trotters, creamy chanterelle soup accompanied by chicken livers on toast, cod with lentils, or lobster and cabbage in Sauternes sauce. An interesting speciality is the two-course baby pigeon: first the crispy skin with a honey sauce, then the meat in a creamy herb sauce. The desserts are remarkable, and the glories of Bordeaux flow at reasonable prices.

A la carte: 420-500 F. Menus: 200 F (lunch only), 300 F, 400 F.

La Pelouse
65, rue Pelouse-de-Douet – 56.93.17.33
Closed 5-25 Aug and Christmas week. 36 rms 200-290 F. TV. Parking. Telex 699559. V AE DC.   D1-28

Quiet, practical rooms are available in this recent hotel. Easy parking.

Périgord Saint-Jean
202, cours de la Marne – 56.91.42.80
Mme Rebiere. Closed Sat lunch, Sun, Easter school holidays and 3 weeks in Aug. Open until 9.45 pm. Air cond. V AE.   B5-33

Don't let the décor—still a bit drab even after refurbishment—put you off. Mme Rebiere's friendly welcome is the perfect introduction to the generous cooking over which Didier Rebiere takes such evident pains. Mixed fish with chanterelles, guinea fowl with vinegar, and apple tart served with a rum sabayon sauce are among the dishes we enjoyed.

A la carte: 300 F. Menus: 135 F, 210 F.

Chez Philippe
1, pl. du Parlement – 56.81.83.15
M. Techoire. Closed Sun, Mon and Aug. Open until 11 pm. Terrace dining. Air cond. V AE.   D3-6

The modern paintings with which this intimate dining room is hung testify to Philippe Techoire's good taste, and it soon becomes clear that this same sharp eye has been working hard at market and in the kitchen. At lunchtime, choose a table overlooking the magnificent Place du Parlement. Then turn a blind eye to the prices and order the sea bream carpaccio (much tastier than the salmon version), red-mullet fillets lightly grilled and served with tapenade, or the Moroccan version of sea bream with sweet peppers. The desserts are making progress and some moderately priced white

wines have been added to the cellar.

A la carte: 450-500 F. Menu: 160 F (lunch only).

Les Plaisirs d'Ausone
10, rue Ausone – 56.79.30.30
M. Gauffre. Closed Sat lunch and Sun. Annual closings not available. Open until 10.30 pm. Private room: 25. V AE.   D4-9

Another point for Philippe Gauffre, who had achieved three toques in his Paris area restaurant before returning home here. Freshness and imagination shine through in the delicate asparagus flan served with an oyster, slivered salt cod on a bed of warm salad greens, beef fillet with a fresh herb galette, and a bowl of fresh fruit and cream. And that's only the 150 F set menu, including wine. The vaulted stone dining room lacks a touch of warmth, but there's no mistaking the warmth in Nicole Gauffre's smile.

A la carte: 300 F. Menus: 150 F (wine inc), 240 F, 280 F.

10/20 Le Port de la Lune
59, quai de Paludate – 56.49.15.55
M. Bombesin. Closed Sat, Sun and holidays. Open until midnight. No pets. V.   C6-59

A late-night stop near the slaughterhouses for oysters and eels, as well as good duck breasts and a fine sheep's-milk cheese. The service is frosty and the prices won't warm your heart either.

A la carte: 250-300 F.

Les Provinces
41, rue St-Rémi – 56.81.74.30
M. Dumas. Closed Sat lunch and Sun (May to Sep). Open until 10.30 pm. Private room: 100. Air cond. V AE DC.   D3-19

The staff take pains to make you feel comfortable, which shouldn't be too difficult at the big round tables in this flower-filled dining room. Well-chosen local wines and carefully devised set menus all but complete the pleasure of a visit here. The *carte* could be cut down, retaining dishes like the baked trout served with a tomato compote, and the fine Pauillac lamb with spring vegetables.

A la carte: 280-300 F. Menus: 65 F (lunch only), 160 F (wine inc), 90 F, 115 F.

Le Puits Sainte-Catherine
27, rue Parlement-Ste-Catherine
58.81.95.12
Mlle Metz. Closed Sun. Open until 10.30 pm. Air cond. No pets. V AE DC.   D3-60

Well located in the heart of the pedestrian precinct of old Bordeaux, this new restaurant was still working the kinks out when we visited its beautiful pale stone dining room. The pleasing potato and sweetbread pâté with cèpes, the veal fillet with well-seasoned vegetables, and other creative dishes warrant giving the mundane desserts a chance to improve. Rather expensive.

A la carte: 300 F. Menu: 130 F.

Hôtel Sainte-Catherine
(See restaurant above)
Open every day. 82 rms 350-580 F. TV. Air cond 32 rms. Conference facilities.

In the middle of the old quarter, this beautiful eighteenth-century mansion now offers huge, delightful rooms. Perfect service, but the breakfasts are more generous than tasty.

Pullman
See restaurant Le Meriadeck

Hôtel des Quatre Sœurs

6, cours 30-Juillet — 56.48.16.00
Open every day. 35 rms 200-310 F. TV. Air cond
2 rms. Conference facilities. Telex 560334. V AE DC.
Wagner slept here once. Nowadays the comfortable rooms have television and minibar, and there's a dry cleaning service.

17 Jean Ramet

7-8, pl. J.-Jaurès — 56.44.12.51
M. Ramet. Closed Sat, Sun, 31 Dec-6 Jan, 1-8 April
and 5-26 Aug. Open until 10 pm. Air cond. V. E3-49
Thank goodness they heeded our cry over the loud music and turned it down. Now you can hear not only your own conversation but even snatches of your neighbour's, which is sure to be along the lines of 'delicious', 'exquisite', and so on. A former pâtissier who has worked with the Troisgros brothers, Jean Ramet has a simple, sensual style capable of taking the flavours of his ingredients to soaring, lyrical perfection. Taste the seemingly effortless spontaneity of such dishes as steamed sole fillets in a sauce of olive oil, coriander and crushed tomatoes, duck fricassée in a heavenly caramelised lime sauce and accompanied by a potato gratin, and a fruit loaf served with bowls of kiwis, raspberries, and melon. The latter must be tasted sparingly to leave room for the superb petits fours which come with the coffee. In addition, Ramet and his wife Raymonde display an almost mystical ability to make you feel comfortable and well received. There's a long list of fine wines, many of them affordable.
A la carte: 350-450 F. Menu: 200 F (lunch only).

17 Le Rouzic

34, cours du Chapeau-Rouge — 56.44.39.11
M. Gautier. Closed Sat lunch and Sun. Open until
10 pm. Private room: 40. V AE DC. E3-27
Before meeting the lady of the house, Kinette Gautier, known as Zizi, you wouldn't think one individual could overflow with so much enthusiasm and *joie de vivre*. Nor would you think her retiring, bespectacled husband Michel capable of the imagination and boundless inventiveness he pours into his work in the kitchen. In a décor whose exuberance matches that of the hostess, you will be the privileged witness to cooking that presents unexpected flavours in dishes of matchless technical precision. There can be no doubt: this is three-toque fare, from the smoked eel pâté with pears, curried oyster ravioli, and mildly spiced baked prawns with sweetbreads, right through to the lamprey eel in a bordelaise sauce of rare finesse, quick-smoked shad in sorrel sauce, and the impressive saddle of Pauillac lamb served with its kidney. If you have room, don't miss the genuine pithiviers (almond pastries) with warm madeleines and custard. Zizi also harbours a passion for wine which has made the Bordeaux list here a thing of beauty.
A la carte: 400-600 F. Menus: 195 F (lunch only), 250 F (lunch only, wine inc), 280 F, 420 F.

Royal Médoc

3, rue de Sèze — 56.81.72.42
Open every day. 45 rms 200-360 F. TV. Garage park-
ing. Telex 571042. V AE DC. E3-10
This centrally located hotel is clean, friendly and fairly quiet. Bar.

Sofitel Aquitania

See restaurant Le Flore

11/20 Sumo

25, rue du Pas-St-Georges — 56.48.18.72
M. Shindo. Dinner only. Closed Sun. Open until
10.30 pm. No pets. V AE DC. D3-1
Japanese cooking is a novelty in Bordeaux. This restaurant offers a creditable array of sushi, sashimi, tempura, and other classics. Try the tsukidashi moriawase (first course assortment) as an introduction to Japanese food.
A la carte: 200-220 F. Menus: 67 F, 138 F.

12/20 La Ténarèze

18, pl. du Parlement — 56.44.43.29
Mme Dubois. Closed Sun dinner. Open until 10 pm.
Terrace dining. No-smoking section. V. D3-13
Authentic dishes from the Gers region, such as garbure, a stew combining cabbage, ham and preserved goose, as well as a reintroduction to some forgotten vegetables (Jerusalem artichoke gratin, and a salad containing Chinese artichokes, marsh samphire, and baby squash). Good South-west wines.
A la carte: 250-300 F. Menus: 59 F (weekdays lunch only), 95 F, 130 F, 168 F.

14 La Tupina

6, rue de la Porte-de-la-Monnaie
56.91.56.37
M. Xiradakis. Closed Sun and holidays. Open until
11 pm. Private room: 20. Air cond. V AE. C5-51
The new, improved Tupina includes an interior courtyard and a couple of fireplaces to cheer the clientele as well as to spit-roast meat and poultry. What we hope will never change is Jean-Pierre Xiradakis's *carte*, a museum piece containing warming, well-loved dishes of the South-west. There's foie gras of course, in terrines, en papillote, or sliced in salads, duck in every possible form, and garbure, the hearty local stew. Xiradakis' comments on the wine list, which has bottles to suit every pocket, provide a delightful tour of the region.
A la carte: 300 F.

16 Le Vieux Bordeaux

27, rue Buhan — 56.52.94.36
M. Bordage. Closed Sat lunch, Sun, holidays, Feb
school holidays and Aug. Open until 10.15 pm. Priv-
ate room: 20. Garden dining. Air cond. V AE DC. D3-7
This old Bordeaux address for fine food is still getting better, as an old Bordeaux should. Recent improvements include a new, sunlit dining room overlooking the garden pool set among bamboos and ferns. Michel Bordage's menus change frequently and for the better, while the remarkably low prices are hardly changing at all. We enjoyed a delicate lobster and asparagus salad, perfect turbot with potatoes and truffles in a delicious mild sauce, the tasty duck breast with foie gras, and a delectable chocolate tart. Original wines.
A la carte: 350 F. Menus: 140 F, 190 F and 240 F (weekdays only).

13 La Villa Carnot

Corner bd Wilson and 2, av. Carnot
56.08.04.21
M. Belvisotti. Closed Sun, Mon and 24 Aug-15 Sep.
Open until 10.30 pm. Garden dining. No pets. V AE
DC. F1-14
Serge Belvisotti keeps his chic customers happy with luxury cooking centred around foie gras in Sauternes, lobster with leeks and pink peppercorns, duck breast with cherries and fresh pasta, and a moderately priced cellar.
A la carte: 300-350 F. Menus: 150 F, 290 F.

And also...

Our selection of places for inexpensive, quick, or late-night meals.

El Callejon (56.91.71.72 - 3, rue Esmangard. Open until 2 am): Authentic Spanish restaurant and tapas bar (150 F).

Le Casino (56.52.27.58 - 19, cours du Mal-Foch. Lunch only): The huge terrace is always packed. Good *plats du jour* at around 35 F (100 F).

La Côte de Bœuf (56.51.05.52 - 13, rue des Faussets): Lovely wood-grilled cuts of meat like the huge prime rib steaks (150-200 F).

Le Doris (56.39.42.30 - 52, quai de Bacalan. Open until 10.30 pm): Dock-fresh seafood in a dockside bistro (200 F).

Le Jour et Nuit (56.91.66.12 - 45, rue Ch.-Domercq. Open 24 hours): Good for night owl steak tartare and chips, oysters, and onion soup 100-150 F).

Le Mably (56.44.30.10 - 12, rue Mably. Open until 11 pm): Classic brasserie with bench seats, big mirrors, and lunchtime crowds (150-200 F)

.Le Noailles (56.81.94.45 - 12, allées de Tourny. Open until 11.30 pm): This old-style brasserie serves ultra classic dishes at up-to-date prices (200 F).

Le Rital (56.48.16.69 - 64, rue de Hâ. Open until 10.30 pm): A rarity in Bordeaux: good fresh pasta in every guise and sauce (100-130 F).

In nearby Bouliac

(9 km SE on D 10)
33270 Bordeaux — (Gironde)

Amat ❍

(Saint-James)
3, pl. C.-Hosteins — 56.20.52.19
M. Amat. Open every day. Open until 10 pm. Private room: 60. Garden dining. No pets. Valet parking. Telex 573001. V AE DC.

The new non-décor of Jean-Marie Amat's restaurant reflects the current trend for high-consumption nonchalance, like drinking Château Mouton-Rothschild out of paper cups or wearing diamonds with a T-shirt. But why imprison his sensitive, artful cooking in a huge, bare, colourless space that resembles nothing so much as the restaurant of an Albanian airport? We can see that Amat would want a contemporary setting for his creations but surely this visual vacuum is not all there is to current interior design?

But Amat is an artist who thrives in adversity, and although we may not appreciate the setting, his art is flowering as never before. He is at the full flow of his creative powers, the height of his technical mastery. He is in virtually surgical control of every aspect of his remarkable production. A fourth toque is the only possible response to the country pâté composed of duck, chicken livers, pork and foie gras and surrounded by a salad of rosemary, chives, cherry tomatoes, and gherkins, the shad in bordelaise sauce accompanied by its roe, fresh peas, ham, and caramelised shallots, and civet de canard flavoured with cèpes and served alongside thick slices of potato that are utterly delicious. Similarly sublime are the lobster consommé with curry cream, fillets of hake with cockles and asparagus, duckling with cherries, and roast saddle of rabbit in chive sauce.

Nonetheless, we feel constrained to urge Amat to renew his repertoire a little, and to point out that the bread rolls are unpleasantly flabby. Moreover, after the warm reception, the service is evasive to say the least. On the other hand, the wine list is so peppered with lovely surprises that you'll want to come back just to have another crack at it. And the

bill deserves a medal for moderation.

A la carte: 350-400 F and up. Menus: 200 F (weekdays lunch only, wine inc), 250 F (dinner w-e and holidays only, wine inc), 420 F.

Les Jardins de Hauterive

(See restaurant above)
Open every day. 3 stes 600-900 F. 18 rms 400-1,200 F. TV. No pets. Conference facilities.

The architect was allegedly inspired by the sheds where tobacco leaves are hung to dry. You might like it, or at least be intrigued by it. Or you might spend all your time gazing across the vineyards and valleys of the Garonne to avoid the rusted ironwork, the polished concrete floor and the ultra-tech lighting. Huge, soft mattresses and tiny bathrooms.

Auberge du Marais ❍

22, rte de Latresne — 56.20.52.17
M. Paulet. Closed Wed, Feb school holidays and 1-23 Aug. Open until 10 pm. Private room: 25. Terrace dining. Parking. V.

It seems several readers have had disappointing experiences here, but we can only testify, like many other witnesses, to the honest and generous regional food that André Paulet, a self-taught cook who has also worked with Guillot and Lenôtre, prepares so well. For the modest sum of 140 F, try the set menu that includes escalope of tunny in olive oil and crushed tomatoes, canard à l'orange, a fine cheese board, and exquisite pithiviers. The excellent wine list has a heavily local slant.

A la carte: 250-300 F. Menus: 60 F and 100 F (weekdays lunch only), 140 F, 190 F , 230 F.

Le Bistroy

3, pl. C.-Hostein — 56.20.52.19
M. Amat. Closed Sun. Open until 10 pm. Garden dining. Parking. V.

Jean-Marie Amat's cheaper restaurant has décor so cold-with its bare concrete walls, aluminium furniture, and harsh lighting-that it looks nothing like a bistro. But for a tasty plate of South-western food prepared according to the daily markets, you could do much worse. You'll find the chef's signature in such dishes as lentil salad with pig's jowls cheek and cured ham, gratin of sliced boiled beef, cabbage stuffed with ham, and a delightful prune mousse.

A la carte: 150-180 F.

In nearby Carbon-Blanc

(1.5 km Pont-d'Aquitaine)
33560 Bordeaux — (Gironde)

Marc Demund

5, av. de la Gardette — 56.06.14.55
M. Demund. Closed Sun dinner and Mon. Open until 10 pm. Private room: 18. Garden dining. Parking. V AE DC.

There is ample reward in store for the effort it takes to locate this pretty, white stone house in the suburbs. The cooking of Marc Demund improves as relentlessly as the old trees in the garden grow bigger and shadier, providing a perfect spot on a fine summer evening to enjoy the fruit of skills honed under Fredy Girardet and Michel Guérard. Meat and fish of well-chosen quality are treated with equal assurance. The desserts have improved at last, as is only proper for someone with the same name as a famous Bordeaux pâtissier. Smiling, professional service, a good choice of coffees, and an interminable list of good-value Bordeaux. Superb Armagnacs aid digestion, as do the stable prices.

A la carte: 400 F. Menus: 150 F (weekdays only), 220 F, 280 F, 350 F.

(South)
33170 Bordeaux — (Gironde)

Beau Soleil
Ch. du Plantey — 56.89.00.48
Open every day. 32 rms 230-265 F. Restaurant. Half-board 280-340 F. TV. Conference facilities. Garage parking. Telex 540322. V AE DC.
Here is a good place for seminars—15 conference rooms—or for anyone looking for sunny, spacious rooms which suffer only from a contemporary lack of charm. The hotel is set in parkland.

Le Chalet Lyrique
169, cours Gal-de-Gaulle — 56.89.11.59
Open every day. 1 ste 450 F. 40 rms 255-320 F. Restaurant. TV. Conference facilities. Garage parking. V.
This pleasant, recent establishment provides attractive, light rooms in a residential area near Bordeaux. Bar and garden-terrace.

(10 km W on D 106 E)
33700 Bordeaux — (Gironde)

Ibis Aéroport
Av. Kennedy — 56.34.10.19
Open every day. 65 rms 240 F. Restaurant. Half-board 210 F. TV. Conference facilities. Parking. Telex 541430. V.
A free bus takes you to the airport from this hotel with functional, well-soundproofed rooms.

Novotel Aéroport
Av. Kennedy — 56.34.10.25
Open every day. 137 rms 405 F. Restaurant. TV 100 rms. Air cond. Conference facilities. Pool. Parking. Telex 540320. V AE DC.
A shuttle from the airport will convey you to the hotel set in the middle of wooded grounds. The rooms have been modernised and there is a terrace and games area.

(6 km SW)
33600 Bordeaux — (Gironde)

Campanile
Av. du Haut-Lévêque — 56.36.18.56
Open every day. 47 rms 239 F. Restaurant. Half-board 336-360 F. TV. Conference facilities. Telex 571203. V.
All the known advantages of this chain, including conference facilities, plus a verdant setting.

La Réserve
74, av. du Bourgailh — 56.07.13.28
Closed 15 Nov-28 Feb. 1 ste 1,000 F. 20 rms 520-890 F. Restaurant. Half-board 835-1,065 F. TV. Air cond 6 rms. Conference facilities. Pool. Tennis. Garage parking. Telex 560585. V AE DC.
The attraction here, besides the nearness of the airport, is the recent relandscaping of the grounds which include a swan lake. The hotel is well equipped in general but many bathrooms are showing their age. Boring breakfasts.

Royal Brion
10, rue du Pin-Vert — 56.45.07.72
Open every day. 26 rms 260-320 F. TV. Conference facilities. Garage parking. Telex 699559. V AE DC.
This pleasing, modern hotel boasts gardens on every side and very pretty rooms where you can order meals on a tray.

(6 km SW on N 10)
33400 Bordeaux — (Gironde)

Le Jardin de la Truffe
31, bd Franklin-Roosevelt — 56.37.43.56
M. Tougne. Closed Sun dinner and Mon (except upon reserv). Open until 10.30 pm. Private room: 15. Garden dining. Air cond. V AE.
Young Dominique Tougne left the Hôtel Nikko in Paris two years ago with the intention of using truffles in all his sauces—without charging the earth. Generally speaking, this experiment in theme cooking is a success, despite the occasional dish that demonstrates how the glorious tuber should not be used: for example, scallops with truffles and sweet pepper. You will enjoy the prawn salad, the hot oysters, the fillet of lamb, and the omelette, all duly truffled. The cellar is still disappointing.
A la carte: 350 F. Menus: 85 F (weekdays lunch only), 155 F, 210 F.

(10 km S)
33140 Bordeaux — (Gironde)

Hôtel d'Ornon
10, av. du Gal-Leclerc — 56.75.96.47
Open every day. 2 stes 400 F. 50 rms 265-310 F. Restaurant. Half-board 340 F. TV. Conference facilities. Parking. Telex 572270. V AE DC.
A brand-new hotel complex providing very comfortable rooms and various facilities, including gym and sauna.

BORDIGHERA
See Menton

BORGO
See CORSICA

BORMES-LES-MIMOSAS
83230 Bormes-les-Mimosas
Paris 890 - Saint-Tropez 35 - Le Lavandou 5

La Cassole
Ruelle du Moulin — 94.71.14.86
Mme Montanard. Dinner only in seas. (and Sun lunch and holidays). Closed off-season Mon and Tue, and 11 Nov-25 Jan. Open until 9.30 pm. AE.
The simple white stucco décor won't figure on any postcards but you'll take back memories of being thoroughly spoiled by the *patronnes* and the typically Provençal fare that Alain Pasetto enlivens with personal touches. Taste the jellied bouillabaisse, bass in a light wine stock, and the young rabbit in parslied aspic served with an aubergine caviar. The wine list, however, is nothing to write home about.
A la carte: 320-390 F. Menus: 145 F, 260 F.

L'Escoundudo 🔧13 ⚀

2, ruelle du Moulin — 94.71.15.53

M. Dandine. Closed Mon off-season and end Oct-Easter. Open until 11 pm. Private room: 25. Garden dining. Air cond. V.

The name means hidden corner in Provençal, and tucked away here you'll discover Max Dandine's interpretation of Provençal dishes which wins a toque this year. Young rabbit feuilleté, a tasty ragoût redolent of shallots, and the sublime walnut gâteau are among the dishes on offer at moderate prices. Resolutely regional wines and a most pleasant welcome.

A la carte: 250-280 F. Menus: 125 F, 150 F, 200 F.

Le Mirage 🏠

Rte du Stade — 94.71.09.83

Open every day. 3 stes 1,000-1,600 F. 32 rms 580-680 F. Restaurant. Half-board 528-578 F. TV. No pets. Conference facilities. Heated pool. Tennis. Valet parking. Telex 404603. V AE DC.

Despite the name, the delightful views over the bay are no illusion. The rooms with loggia have new décor.

12/20 Les Palmiers

8 km S on D 41, in Cabasson — 94.64.81.94

M. Guinet. Open every day. Open until 10 pm. Private room: 50. Garden dining. Air cond. Parking. Telex 400233. V AE DC.

Enjoy the superb view either from the terrace or the neo-Provençal dining room. The straightforward cooking has no serious flaws: red mullet and fennel with beurre blanc, scallops with bacon and mushrooms. The desserts, however, need attention. Another point this year.

A la carte: 300 F. Menu: 135 F.

Les Palmiers 🏠 🌲

(See restaurant above)

Open every day. 2 stes 1,000 F. 21 rms 250-540 F. Half-board 330-700 F oblig in seas. TV 12 rms.

Surrounded by greenery and five minutes' walk from the sea, this hotel has quiet, attractive rooms.

Paradis 🏠

Mont-des-Roses — 94.71.06.85

Closed 1 Oct-30 March. 20 rms 160-320 F. Restaurant. No pets. Parking.

This is a modest paradise, but it benefits from a fine location and a large garden.

10/20 Chez Sylvia

(Restaurant-Pizzéria Sauveur)
872, av. Lou Mistraou — 94.71.14.10

Mme Giaramidaro. Closed Tue off season, and 15 Nov-27 Dec. Open until 11 pm. Garden dining. Parking. V AE DC.

Sylvia serves Sicilian pizzas and savoury brochettes on the shady terrace.

A la carte: 150 F.

La Tonnelle des Délices

Pl. Gambetta — 94.71.34.84

M. Gigant. Closed 5 Nov-23 March. Open until 10 pm. V.

This delightful *auberge* was a shrine to Provençal cooking when the Gedda brothers were in charge, but we're reserving judgment on Alain Gigart's attempts, praiseworthy as they are, to update traditional dishes. We couldn't see why the panisse (a chickpea-flour pancake) with foie gras, and daube with mediocre pasta deserved all the fuss being made about them.

A la carte: 250-300 F. Menus: 144 F, 179 F, 210 F.

BOUC-BEL-AIR
See Aix-en-Provence

BOUËXIÈRE (LA)
See Rennes

BOUGIVAL
See Paris Suburbs

BOUGUENAIS
See Nantes

BOUILLAND

21420 Bouilland — (Côte-d'Or)
Paris 303 - Autun 55 - Beaune 15 - Dijon 45

Le Vieux Moulin 🔧17 ⚀

on D 2 — 80.21.51.16

M. Silva. Closed Thu lunch and Wed (except holidays), 16 Dec-18 Jan and 20 Feb-9 March. Open until 9 pm. Private room: 30. Garden dining. Air cond. Parking. V.

A family tragedy hit Jean-Pierre Silva hard, but he seems to be gradually regaining his enthusiasm. As if to signal a fresh and determined start, Silva and his wife Isabelle have done up their old mill in a pleasing and original contemporary vein.

Casting his net wide in search of new ingredients, Silva always manages to incorporate them into his cooking with respect for the traditions of the region. A fillet of tombe (a fish similar to lotte) sprinkled with cumin finds itself in the company of a more familiar pig's ear flan; ravioli are introduced alongside farm-reared capon; while grilled kidneys and sweetbreads basted with Beaune mustard make the potatoes in star anise and balsamic vinegar feel at home.

Plenty of other surprises are in store: prawns, frogs' legs and vegetables with tapenade (a black-olive purée), breast of duckling accompanied by dried tomatoes flavoured with hazelnut oil, sliced salmon spread with caviar and served with leeks in sesame jelly. Not everyone will enjoy these taste combinations but they are nearly always the fruit of flawless technique. Silva is also a top pâtissier, as his feuilletés of pears caramelised in grapefruit butter, or millefeuille of crêpes with apricot jam served with chocolate sauce and pistachio ice cream will readily attest. And there is no better guide than Isabelle to the great and small Burgundies that make up one of the most fascinating cellars in the region.

A la carte: 350-400 F. Menus: 190 F, 290 F, 400 F.

Le Vieux Moulin 🏠 🌲

(See restaurant above)

Closed Wed (except holidays), 16 Dec-18 Jan and 20 Feb-9 March. 12 rms 380-800 F. TV. Pets allowed.

A new hotel among the apple trees plus a few rooms in the mill. All your needs are taken care of and only the village rooster is likely to disturb your sleep.

BOUIN

85230 Bouin — (Vendée)
Paris 435 - Noirmoutier 30 - Nantes 51

Hôtel du Martinet 🏠 🌲

Place de la Croix-Blanche — 51.49.08.94

Open every day. 16 rms 170-260 F. TV 11 rms. Parking. V AE DC.

A traditional Vendée residence in a sleepy town offering simple comfort and a pleasant garden. Oyster tasting.

BOULIAC

See Bordeaux

BOULOC

See Toulouse

BOULOGNE-BILLANCOURT

See Paris Suburbs

BOULOGNE-SUR-MER

62200 Boulogne-sur-Mer — (P./Calais)
Paris 242 - Lille 115 - Abbeville 80 - Calais 34

Ibis

Bd Diderot — 21.30.12.40
Open every day. 79 rms 250-270 F. Restaurant. TV. Conference facilities. Telex 160485. V.
You can come straight off the ferry to this hotel with well-kept rooms.

12/20 La Liégeoise

10, rue Monsigny — 21.31.61.15
M. Delpierre. Closed Sun dinner, Wed and 14 July-2 Aug. Open until 9.30 pm. Private room: 30. Telex 110046. V DC.
Flawless reception and service are backed up by Alain Celpierre's cooking, whose only flaw is occasional hesitancy. Try the red-mullet salad with wine vinegar, sole and vegetable terrine with sorrel purée, or the noisettes of lamb venison-style.
A la carte: 300-320 F. Menus: 155 F, 210 F, 310 F.

La Matelote

80, bd Sainte-Beuve — 21.30.17.97
M. Lestienne. Closed Sun dinner, 15-30 June and 23 Dec-15 Jan. Open until 9.30 pm. Private room: 80. V.
In charge of catering at the newly opened National Marine Centre, Tony Lestienne has plenty to keep him busy. But the customers here still receive his full attention, judging from such dishes as the oyster vol-au-vents with foie gras, whiting fillets and leeks served with cod and caper mould, and the chocolate and pistachio fondant with sour cherries.
A la carte: 350-400 F. Menus: 160 F, 335 F.

Métropole

51, rue Thiers — 21.31.54.30
Closed 20 Dec-10 Jan 27 rms 165-294 F. TV. V AE.
Central but fairly quiet, this hotel offers spacious well-maintained rooms. Breakfast served in the garden when the weather permits.

In nearby Pont-de-Briques

(5 km S on D 940)
62360 Boulogne-sur-Mer — (P./Calais)

Hostellerie de la Rivière

17, rue de la Gare — 21.32.22.81
M. Martin. Closed Sun dinner, Mon, Feb school holidays and 16 Aug-12 Sep. Open until 9.15 pm. Hotel: 8 rms 320-380 F (per pers, half-board oblig). Parking. V.
Here you'll find exceptionally fresh fish lovingly prepared by a father and son duo. Their most recent successes include a lobster ans spinach gratin, braised stuffed sole, and salmon baked in cabbage leaves and served with a sweet-and-sour raspberry sauce. Good desserts.
A la carte: 320 F. Menus: 130 F (weekdays lunch only), 195 F (except holidays), 270 F.

In nearby Wimille

5 km N by N 1
62200 Boulogne-sur-Mer — (P./Calais)

Le Relais de la Brocante

2, rue de Ledinghem — 21.83.19.31
MM. Janszen and Laurent. Closed Sun dinner, Mon and 16 Aug-7 Sep. Open until 9.30 pm. Private room: 25. V AE.
Once a school, a presbytery, and a town hall, this old townhouse was tastefully transformed five years ago into a restaurant. Jean-François Laurent's cooking overflows with imagination and reveals passionate dedication to local ingredients. Witness the duck foie gras au torchon with its raisin brioche, lotte with bacon and local garlic, turbot with meat juice and herring fumet, and duck breast with juniper berries. To follow, there are magnificent cheeses from the North of France, and constantly improving desserts. The other half of this partnership, Claude Janszen, is in charge of the service and the cellar, which has a fine choice of wines plus dessert wines available by the glass.
A la carte: 300-400 F. Menus: 145 F (except Sat dinner), 180 F.

BOULON

14220 Boulon — (Calvados)
Paris 229 - Caen 17 - Thury-Harcourt 9 - Vire 56

12/20 La Bonne Auberge

31.79.37.60
M. Gouget. Closed Mon and Tue (except holidays) and first 3 weeks of Sep. Open until 8.30 pm. Private room: 45. Parking. V.
Traditional Norman cooking at its best: poulet à la crème, home-prepared tripe, and the delicious rice pudding with cinnamon called teurgoule. Cider and Calvados flow freely, and the prices are most congenial.
Menus: 55 F (weekdays only), 82 F, 100 F.

BOURBON-LANCY

71140 Bourbon-Lancy — (Saône/Loire)
Paris 308 - Autun 62 - Moulins 36 - Nevers 72

Grand Hôtel

Pl. d'Aligre — 85.89.08.87
Closed 11 Oct-9 April. 1 ste 200-220 F. 30 rms 82-220 F. Restaurant. Half-board 174-292 F. Parking. V AE DC.
Typically sleepy spa-town hotel. Its rooms are old-fashioned but immaculately kept.

Raymond

Allée des Platanes — 85.89.17.39
M.Raymond. Closed Mon off-seas. Annual closings not available. Open until 9.30 pm. Private room: 30. Garden dining. No pets. Garage parking. V AE DC.
This may not be the easiest address to find, but your efforts will be richly rewarded. Suzanne Raymond will give you a friendly welcome as you settle down to enjoy her husband Gérard's adventurous cooking, which has really taken off since they moved here two years ago. We're awarding an extra point for the galette d'escargots, croustillant de langoustines, and the original pastilla of lamb. The desserts uphold their end of the meal admirably, although unfortunately the wine list does not.
A la carte: 350-400 F. Menus: 140 F (weekdays only), 160 F (w-e and holidays only), 180 F, 240 F, and 300 F.

Manoir de Sornat 🏔🌲
(See restaurant above)
*Annual closings not available. 1 ste 600-750 F.
13 rms 300-500 F. Half-board 450-550 F. TV. Conference facilities.*
This charming stop has six beautiful new rooms whose décor might be considered a shade reserved for the setting. Very good breakfasts.

BOURBOULE (LA)
63150 Bourboule (La) — (Puy-de-Dôme)
Paris 438 - Clermont-Ferrand 53 - Le Mont-Dore 7

11/20 Auberge Tournebride
1.5 km N by D 88
Rte de Murat-le-Quaire — 73.81.01.91
Mme Castagnet. Closed Mon off-seas (except holidays), and 15 Nov-15 Jan. Open until 9 pm. Private room: 30. Garden dining. No pets. Parking.
The best of the short *carte* is to be found on the 130F set menu: mountain ham, beef fillet and shallots, salad, Auvergne cheeses, and an almond and chocolate cake. The irresistible charm of the place makes it a bit crowded in summer. Pleasant reception.
A la carte: 250-300 F. Menus: 75 F, 130 F, 180 F.

Auberge Tournebride 🏔🌲
(see above for restaurant)
Closed Mon off-seas (except holidays) and 15 Nov-15 Jan. 8 rms 192-252 F (per pers, half-board oblig). No pets. Conference facilities.
A friendly country establishment whose virtues include generous breakfasts, attractive bedding, and a pleasant view of the wooded valley.

Les Fleurs
Av. Guéneau-Mussy — 73.81.09.44
Closed 7 Oct-31 Dec. 24 rms 90-260 F. Restaurant. Half-board 150-315 F. TV 14 rms. Garage parking. Telex 533933. V.
A delightful welcome awaits you at this chalet overlooking the Dordogne valley. Some of the rooms have balconies.

Les Iles Britanniques
Quai Gambetta — 73.65.52.39
Closed 15 Oct-1 Feb. 12 stes 305-395 F. Restaurant. Half-board 260-378 F. TV. Conference facilities. Garage parking. Telex 393554. V AE DC.
Spa facilities are available here as well as a sauna, gym, and games room. The pleasant rooms are a mixture of modern and old-fashioned décor.

International
Av. d'Angleterre — 73.81.05.82
Closed 4 Nov-20 Dec. 16 rms 200-230 F. Restaurant. Half-board 220-240 F oblig in seas. TV. No pets. Telex 393554. V AE DC.
Close to the cable cars, this hotel offers plain, well-kept rooms.

Le Louvre
Bd G.-Clemenceau — 73.81.01.33
Closed 30 Sep-1 May. 50 rms 150-280 F. Restaurant. Half-board 200-250 F. Conference facilities. Garage parking. Telex 393554. V.
Traditional hotel whose rooms have been meticulously modernised. Excellent service.

BOURBOURG
59630 Bourbourg — (Nord)
Paris 285 - Calais 28 - Lille 83 - Dunkerque 18

13 La Gueulardière
4, pl. de l'Hôtel-de-Ville — 28.22.20.97
M. Philippon. Closed Mon (except holidays). Open until 9.30 pm. Private room: 10. V.
Trained in luxury hotel kitchens, this chef's merit lies in his technical ability and willingness to explore lighter, more personal dishes. Enjoy such innovations as his cream soup of green and red lentils with salt cod, chicken served with a sweetbread mousse, or the superb tarte Tatin with hot chocolate sauce, all of which deserve a toque. Well-stocked cellar.
A la carte: 270 F. Menus: 140 F, 185 F, 280 F.

BOURCEFRANC-LE-CHAPUS
17560 Bourcefran-le-Chapus — (Charente-M.)
Paris 490 - Rochefort 22 - La Rochelle 54

14 Les Claires
1, rue W.-Bertrand — 46.85.08.01
M. Suire. Open every day. Open until 9.30 pm. Private room: 15. Garage parking. V AE DC.
When a restaurant is surrounded by oyster beds you expect the oysters to be superb. But good kitchen technique must also take some credit for the impression of freshness and quality you receive from the dishes served here. Try the well-balanced salad of warm oysters, salmon and pistachio nuts, lotte flavoured with garlic and sage and served with a lentil purée, grilled bass with tomato compote and thyme, and a crunchy strawberry millefeuille. The service is competent, fast and friendly. Another point.
A la carte: 300-350 F. Menus: 150 F, 200 F.

Les Claires
(see above for restaurant)
Open every day. 48 rms 260-390 F. Half-board 300-430 F. TV. Conference facilities. Heated pool. Tennis.
Spacious, comfortable rooms with no special allure. The breakfasts are attractively presented but rather disappointing. Courteous service.

BOURG-EN-BRESSE
01000 Bourg-en-Bresse — (Ain)
Paris 425 - Lyon 61 - Mâcon 34 - Genève 118 - Annecy 122

15 Auberge Bressane
166, bd de Brou — 74.22.22.68
M. Vullin. Closed Mon dinner and Tue. Open until 9.30 pm. Terrace. Parking. V AE DC.
Tradition here means sledgehammer prices, haughty serving staff, and cooking that never varies, but we can hardly blame the owner and chef, Jean-Pierre Vullin, for not wanting to change a winning formula. For it is precisely the unchanging qualities of this provincial institution that have ensured its success for the past twenty years. Nor can we deny the quality of the duck and chicken liver terrines, the lobster gratin, fricassée of Bresse fattened hen with a morel purée, veal kidneys in Madeira, and the fillet of Charollais beef Brillat-Savarin. Marvellous desserts too, but as for the wines... maybe you should stick to water.
A la carte: 500-600 F. Menus: 160 F, 270 F, 330 F, 420 F.

Some establishments change their closing times without warning. It is always wise to check in advance.

Hôtel de France
19, pl. Bernard — 74.45.29.11
Open every day. 1 ste 570 F. 46 rms 180-330 F. TV 30 rms. Conference facilities. Garage. Telex 330740. V AE DC.

An impeccable provincial reception awaits you at this old-fashioned but plush hotel, centrally situated on a shady square, and next door to Jacques Guy's restaurant (see below). The breakfast croissants are excellent.

Jacques Guy
Pl. Bernard — 74.45.29.11
M. Guy. Closed Sun dinner, Mon, 5-18 Feb and 1-15 Oct. Open until 9.30 pm. Private room: 25. Air cond. Garage. V AE DC.

Jacques Guy has been joined in the kitchen by his son Laurent, who had been working with Alain Chapel. The cooking is completely classic and succulently successful: delicious poached Bresse chicken in a light tarragon cream sauce, oxtail terrine enlivened by the zest of citrus fruit, and mixed hors d'oeuvre featuring foie gras, green beans and mangetout peas dressed with hazelnut oil. Desserts are Jacques Guy's speciality: don't miss his heavenly crème brûlée with three kinds of chocolate mousse. The wines are as classic as the rest, but there's a shortage of half-bottles and the wine list is short on information. Attentive service.

A la carte: 280-300 F. Menus: 120 F (weekdays only), 190 F, 270 F, 340 F.

Le Logis de Brou
132, bd de Brou — 74.22.11.55
Open every day. 30 rms 250-350 F. TV. Conference facilities. Valet parking. V AE DC.

All the rooms have balconies in this recently established hotel with garden. Traditional comfort and perfect service.

Le Mail
46, av du Mail — 74.21.00.26
M. Charolles. Closed Sun dinner, Mon, 12-26 July and 23 Dec-14 Jan. Open until 9.30 pm. Air cond. Hotel: 9 rms 180-280 F. Garage parking. V AE DC.

All the provincial virtues are gathered together in this delightful inn: cosy rooms, smiling faces, rustic décor, and generous, uncomplicated fare. Savour the sole in Chiroubles wine, rock lobster ragoût, tournedos steak with morels, and the lovely praline tart. Wide choice of wines.

A la carte: 260-280 F. Menus: from 120 F to 280 F.

12/20 Le Poulet Gourmand
7, rue Teynière — 74.22.49.50
M. Menis. Closed Sat lunch, Sun and 1-21 Aug. Open until 9.30 pm. V.

Wooden beams and a smiling welcome provide a warm introduction to the increasingly polished cooking. Try the saffron-flavoured scallops and leeks, young rabbit stuffed with a duck foie gras mousse, and an interesting dessert with chestnuts and candied oranges.

A la carte: 250-280 F. Menus: 95 F (lunch only), 130 F, 160 F.

Terminus
19, rue A.-Baudin — 74.21.01.21
Open every day. 50 rms 245-330 F. Restaurant. Half-board 265 F. TV. Conference facilities. Garage parking. Telex 380844. V AE DC.

One of the best hotels in town, the Terminus is set in gardens opposite the station and has well-modernised rooms. Excellent reception.

See also: **Vonnas (Georges Blanc)**

18000 Bourges — (Cher)
Paris 226 - Nevers 68 - Dijon 245 - Châteauroux 65

Hôtel d'Angleterre
1, pl. des Quatre-Piliers
48.24.68.51
Open every day. 31 rms 292-359 F. Restaurant. Half-board 270-467 F. TV. Conference facilities. Garage parking. V AE DC.

This traditional town residence has been entirely renovated. Courteous service and faultless breakfasts.

Jacques Cœur
3, pl. J.-Cœur — 48.70.12.72
M. Bernard. Closed Sat dinner, Sun, 22 July-20 Aug and 24 Dec-2 Jan. Open until 9.15 pm. Private room: 12. V AE DC.

New carpeting has softened the medieval look, and although François Bernard's cooking remains rather austere, his competence is beyond reproach. The sautéed scallops, kidneys with cabbage, onions, and chestnuts, or the fresh Loire salmon with béarnaise sauce provide convincing proof. Balanced wine list.

A la carte: 280 F. Menus: 175 F (wine inc), 145 F.

12/20 Le Jardin Gourmand
15 bis, bd E.-Renan — 48.21.35.91
M. Chauveau. Closed Sun dinner, Mon and mid-Dec-mid-Jan. Open until 9.30 pm. Private room: 25. No-smoking section. No pets. V AE.

Warm wood is the highlight of the new décor of this restaurant set in a small, shady garden. It only remains for the chef to put a little backbone into his insipid first courses and pay more attention to the cheese board. The civet of suckling pig, and salmon with curry sauce are good, as are the wines.

A la carte: 250 F. Menus: 90 F, 145 F, 210 F.

In nearby **Berry-Bouy**
8 km NW by D 60
18000 Bourges — (Cher)

La Gueulardière
48.26.81.45
M. Poquet. Closed Mon dinner and Tue. Annual closings not available. Open until 10 pm. Private room: 30. Terrace. V AE DC.

Cheerful fabrics, pretty china, and delightful flower arrangements add to the charm of this popular restaurant. It's rare to see an empty seat and easy to taste why, for example the excellent baked salmon with pistachios and pine-nuts. Nevertheless the chef seems to us a little off his stride this year. Confused perhaps, like the smoked haddock and caviar flan that also includes shrimps, mussels, and foie gras. Friendly welcome and service.

A la carte: 280-350 F. Menus: 100 F (weekday lunch only), 185 F, 220 F, 320 F.

73370 Bourget-du-Lac (Le) — (Savoie)
Paris 527 - Chambéry 11 - Aix-les-Bains 9 - Belley 25

Auberge Lamartine
Rte du Tunnel du Chat
in Bourdeau — 79.25.01.03
M. Marin. Closed Sun dinner and Mon (except holidays), and 1 Dec-20 Jan. Open until 9.30 pm. Private room: 20. Garden dining. Parking. V.

A fine old inn whose bay windows look out over a lake panorama of rarely equalled beauty. Father and son work side by side to turn out fare that is guilty of as few mistakes as flights of fancy. Stuffed omble chevalier (a lake fish), warm foie gras, and prawns with wild rice are all worth a stop. The wine list is brief but discerning.

A la carte: 350 F. Menus: from 200 F to 340 F.

Le Bateau Ivre
79.25.02.66

M. Jacob. Closed end Oct-beg May. Open until 10 pm. Private room: 15. Garden dining. Parking. Telex 309162. V AE DC.

After a Sunday lunch on the terrace during which we were well looked after by the staff, we had no second thoughts about Jean-Pierre Jacob's third toque. What is most impressive about his cooking is its consistently high quality. Everything we tasted was worth three toques, from the appetisers (saffron-flavoured potato stuffed with cod, sardines with céleri rémoulade) to dessert (apricot-stuffed crêpes with pistachio cream, for instance). In between, the Breton lobster with potatoes and a spicy Provençal sauce, crayfish minestrone, and chausson of young pigeon are equally exemplary. Mr Jacob senior oversees details like decanting a 1982 Côte-Rôtie and making sure it's not allowed to get too warm. Other members of the family take care of the service admirably, assisted by René, the faithful maître d'. Fine Savoie wines.

A la carte: 500 F. Menus: 200 F, 340 F, 410 F.

Beaurivage
Bd du Lac
79.25.00.38

Mme Quazzola. Closed Wed and Feb. Open until 9.30 pm. Garden dining. Hotel: 5 rms 180 F. Parking. V.

Although a keen painter, the boss cannot bring himself to paint his dining room; he covers the walls with his canvases instead. None of which alters the splendid view over the lake. His son has taken over in the kitchen and does a conscientious job preparing good, simple dishes occasionally burdened by fancy names. The warm foie gras, grilled steak with tomato sauce, and the freshwater perch salad please regulars and tourists alike, and the friendly service makes them feel at home. There are some bargains to be found on the wine list.

A la carte: 300 F. Menus: 220 F (wine inc), 110 F, 150 F, 300 F.

Ombremont
2 km N on N 504 — 79.25.00.23

M. Carlo. Closed 15 Nov-15 March. Open until 10 pm. Terrace dining. Garage parking. Telex 980832. V AE.

The lakeside terrace and plush dining room are easy on the eye, while the palate is won over by duck foie gras and a salad dressed with walnut oil, lavaret (a lake fish) with braised leeks (tiny portions, alas), and peach crème brûlée served with madeleines. Monique Carlo's welcome is exemplary and the service attentive and efficient. Well-balanced wine list, but the prices will make your head reel.

A la carte: 500-600 F. Menus: 195 F (weekdays only), 310 F, 450 F.

> *The prices quoted in this guide are those which we were given by the restaurants and hotels concerned. Increases in prices are beyond our control.*

Ombremont
(See restaurant above)

Closed 15 Nov-15 March. 2 stes 1,300-1,400 F. 17 rms 550-1,200 F. Half-board oblig in seas. TV. Conference facilities. Heated pool.

The spacious rooms and suites have been recently refurbished and are perfectly comfortable. Enjoy skiing and boating on the lake.

L'Orée du Lac
La Croix-Verte — 79.25.24.19

Closed 20 Nov-20 Jan. 3 stes 890-1,100 F. 9 rms 570-820 F. Restaurant. Half-board 515-885 F. TV. Air cond 3 rms. Conference facilities. Pool. Tennis. Parking. Telex 309773. V AE DC.

A distinguished lakeside hotel set in two hectares of grounds close to Le Bateau Ivre (see above). A restaurant service is available to residents.

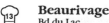

BOURGOIN-JALLIEU

38300 Bourgoin-Jallieu — (Isère)
Paris 503 - Grenoble 66 - Lyon 41

Bruno Chavancy
1, av. Pr-Tixier — 74.93.63.88

M. Chavancy. Closed Aug. Open until 9.15 pm. Private room: 15. Air cond. V AE DC.

Serious-minded, dependable cooking served in a bright, comfortable setting keeps local gourmets happy. Prawn and herb ravioli, scallops with lentil purée, superb cheeses, and chocolate millefeuille are good bets. Conservative choice of wines.

A la carte: 350 F. Menus: 125 F, 190 F, 250 F, 300 F.

Climat
15, rue E.-Branly — 74.28.52.29

Open every day. 42 rms 250 F. Restaurant. Half-board 278 F. TV. Conference facilities. Telex 308152. V AE DC.

This well-designed hotel makes a handy stopover.

In nearby Ruy

(2 km E)
38300 Bourgoin-Jallieu — (Isère)

Laurent Thomas
Vie-de-Boussieu — 74.93.78.00

M. Thomas. Closed Sun dinner, Wed, Feb school holidays and 19 Aug-2 Sep. Open until 9.30 pm. Private room: 20. Terrace dining. Air cond. Parking. V AE DC.

More than once we've seen the setting inspire the chef, and this is a particularly happy instance. From Guy Savoy's stable, Laurent Thomas is bursting with ideas and audacity, especially now that work has been finished on his manor in its own sequoia grove. The pretty grey-and-yellow dining room with its leafy bouquets and modern paintings finds its finishing touch in the beautiful plates of scallops and beetroot in vinaigrette, veal terrine with a creamy mustard sauce, milk-fed veal chops accompanied by a crépine of pig's trotters and truffles. Only the flavour-masking liquorice sauce on the John Dory nearly stopped us from awarding another point. Save room for the grapefruit terrine served with a honey sabayon sauce and a saffron sorbet. Francis takes efficient charge of the service and will share with you his passion for Burgundy.

A la carte: 300-350 F. Menus: 130 F (weekdays only), 180 F, 250 F, 320 F.

Les Séquoias

(See restaurant above)

Closed Sun, Wed, Feb school holidays and 19 Aug-2 Sep. 5 rms 500-700 F. TV. Conference facilities. Pool.

A superb stone staircase leads to huge, remarkably comfortable rooms. Swimming pool and heliport.

73700 Bourg-Saint-Maurice — (Savoie)
Paris 662 - Albertville 54 - Chamonix 83

Le Concorde

Av. du Mal-Leclerc — 79.07.08.90

Closed 15 Oct-25 Nov. 32 rms 300-490 F. Restaurant. Half-board 280-340 F oblig in seas. TV 30 rms. Conference facilities. Garage parking. V.

The lovely mountain views from the terrace will persuade you to overlook the dull décor of the rooms. Jazz evenings in season. Sauna.

BOUSSAC

23600 Boussac — (Creuse)
Paris 335 - Aubusson 47 - Montluçon 34

10/20 Le Bœuf Couronné

Pl. de l'Hôtel-de-Ville — 55.65.15.92

Mme Pinot. Open every day. Open until 8.30 pm. Private room: 70. Garden dining. Hotel: 11 rms 80-190 F. V AE DC.

The substantial meals at featherweight prices are popular with commercial travellers. You too will love the roulade boussaquine (potato pâté), leg of veal with carrots, and the gâteau creusois.

A la carte: 100-120 F. Menus: 44 F (weekdays only), 52 F, 90 F.

Le Relais Creusois

Rte de La Châtre — 55.65.02.20

M. Tulleau. Closed off-season Tue dinner and Wed, 1 week in Feb and 1 week in June. Open until 8.30 pm (9 pm in summer). Private room: 25. Hotel: 4 rms 120 F. V.

Behind this anonymous façade hides a more pleasing, though by no means opulent dining room in shades of salmon pink. The luxury lies in Jean-Jacques Tulleau's expertly prepared dishes. The country pâté with a fruity chutney, stuffed lamb shoulder served with diced celery, the artichoke ragoût with bone marrow, and the handsome array of local cheeses with homemade bread rolls all deserve two toques. Desserts are this chef's speciality: honey-baked pears and ginger biscuits, chocolate cake and chicory ice-cream. Particularly attractive range of Bordeaux. Mme Tulleau is a charming hostess who knows how to present her husband's dishes to best advantage.

A la carte: 230-250 F. Menus: 98 F, 160 F, 198 F, 290 F.

BOUTENAC-TOUVENT

17120 Boutenac-Touvent — (Charente-M.)
Paris 505 - Royan 29 - Pons 23 - Mortagne-sur-G. 5

Le Relais de Touvent

in Touvent — 46.94.13.06

MM. Mairand. Closed Sun dinner, Mon and 15 Oct-5 Nov. Open until 9 pm. Terrace dining. No pets. Hotel: 8 rms 180 F (per pers, half-board oblig). Parking. V.

Surrounded by weeping willows, this restaurant is soon to undergo improvements. Yannick Mairand's cooking can be inconsistent but we liked the marinated salmon in a dozen herbs, and the medallions of lotte with tomato purée. Jacky Mairand, the chef's father, is a cheery host and the wines are well described and not too expensive. A toque this year.

A la carte: 250 F. Menus: 80 F (weekdays only), 120 F, 210 F.

BOUZIGUES

34140 Bouzigues — (Hérault)
Paris 790 - Agde 24 - Montpellier 27 - Béziers 45

Côte Bleue

Av. L.-Tudesq — 67.78.30.87

M. Archimbeau. Closed off-season Tue dinner and Wed, in seas Sun dinner and Mon, and 20 Jan-20 Feb. Open until 9.45 pm. Private room: 18. Terrace dining. Hotel: 32 rms 150-300 F. Pool. Garage parking. V.

The beautiful shellfish, farmed by the owners, can make you spend more than you intended. The best solution might be to choose the excellent 250 F set menu which varies with the market. Or you could splash out on one of the elaborate and brilliantly executed dishes à la carte like the crunchy sesame prawns with Chinese cabbage, or turbot steamed with seaweed and herbs. One of the pleasant and reasonably priced local white wines will help to ease the bill.

A la carte: 400-450 F. Menus: 160 F (weekdays only), 250 F, 450 F.

La Madrague

8, av. L.-Tudesq — 67.78.32.34

M. Martinez. Closed off-season dinner Sun and Mon, and 18 Nov-28 Dec. Open until 9.30 pm. Private room: 20. Terrace dining. V.

The oysters could hop in through the big bay windows onto your plate while you admire the peaceful waters of the Etang de Thau from the first-floor dining room. As if inspired by such fresh ingredients, Eric Martinez prepares a delectable red-mullet salad with anchovy dressing, generous duck breast and apples served with a duck leg preserved in fat, and a perfect pear feuilleté. One black mark for a disastrous preparation of skate with olives, none too fresh and dry as cardboard.

A la carte: 280-300 F. Menus: 98 F (weekdays lunch only), 230 F (weekdays only), 140 F.

BOVES

See Amiens

BOYARDVILLE

See Oléron (Ile d')

BOZOULS

See Espalion

BRACIEUX

41250 Bracieux — (Loir/Cher)
Paris 182 - Romorantin 32 - Blois 18 - Orléans 57

Hôtel de la Bonnheure

54.46.41.57

Open every day. 2 stes 450-500 F. 11 rms 250-300 F. Conference facilities. Garage parking. V.

A modern hotel near the forest, enhanced by lawns and flower beds.

RAC Regional Maps of France at 4 miles to 1 inch are the ideal touring companion. Available from RAC offices and all good bookshops.

Bernard Robin
1, av. de Chambord — 54.46.41.22
M. Robin. Closed Tue dinner, Wed and 23 Dec-30 Jan. Open until 9 pm. Garden dining. Air cond. V AE.

We had been aware for some time of a certain hesitation in the nonetheless commendable cooking of Bernard Robin. Only rarely did he allow his personality to shine through. But this year, inspired perhaps by the thorough renovation of this lovely inn, he has achieved new heights of freedom and character, harmoniously blending tradition and modernity.

While not entirely free of the sin of fashionable complication, the *carte* clearly deserves another point this year. Not one dish lacks interest. Your task will be to choose between young rabbit in aspic with a salad of herbs, a fresh pasta and basil salad complementing veal pâté and leek confit, sardines in tomato sauce and smoked herring arranged on a bed of potato purée, simmered beef tongue, and Loire shad cooked in pastry and served with beurre blanc and mushrooms. Then there are some marvels of highly civilised, country-style dishes like the oxtail in a hachis Parmentier flavoured with truffles, spit-roast leg of lamb cooked with sliced potatoes and onions, or the farm-reared guinea fowl with thyme and braised lettuce. A sumptuous cheese board follows, and the bitter-chocolate ice cream served with an orange sauce provides a perfect end to the meal. A cellar with 170 Loire wines to choose from and the delightful welcome of Mme Robin also contribute to the customers' obvious enjoyment.

A la carte: 400-550 F. Menus: 190 F (weekdays lunch only), 280 F, 380 F, 490 F.

24310 Brantôme — (Dordogne)
Paris 480 - Périgueux 27 - Limoges 90 - Nontron 22

Les Frères Charbonnel
59, rue Gambetta — 53.05.70.15
MM. Charbonnel. Closed off-season Sun dinner and Mon, 5-25 Feb and 15 Nov-15 Dec. Open until 9 pm. Terrace dining. No pets. V AE DC.

Watch the ducks bobbing about on the River Dronne from the best tables. Or simply enjoy the all-duck salad, red-mullet fillets in lobster sauce, and the warm and cold foie gras with one of the many bargain-priced wines.

A la carte: 350 F. Menus: 130 F and 180 F (weekdays only), 265 F, 380 F.

Hôtel Chabrol
(See restaurant above)
Closed off-season Sun and Mon, 5-25 Feb and 15 Nov-15 Dec. 19 rms 240-400 F. TV. No pets.

Old-fashioned comfort here also means old-fashioned plumbing and outdated décor. Good service.

Moulin de l'Abbaye

1, rte de Bourdeilles
53.05.80.22
M. Bulot. Closed Mon (except hotels clients) and 31 Oct-1 May. Open until 10 pm. Garden dining. Valet parking. Telex 560570. V AE DC.

We have said all there is to say about the charm of this delightfully restored watermill on the banks of the Dronne: the lovely garden, elegant dining room, attentive service, and the cellar full of moderately priced Burgundy and Bordeaux. But the purpose of the third toque is to reward the progress made by Christian Ravinel, former number two to the Troisgros brothers. It's hard to choose between his latest creations, but we confess to a weakness for the grilled young rabbit fillet well complemented by a Monbazillac sauce, the grilled turbot with fresh verbena, or bœuf en crépine with mushrooms. For dessert the choice is equally difficult until your eye is caught by the chocolate cake with baked pears, a masterpiece of harmonised flavours. We wish we had space to print the whole menu.

A la carte: 400 F. Menus: 210 F, 280 F, 380 F.

Moulin de l'Abbaye
(See restaurant above)
Closed 31 Oct-1 May. 3 stes 900-950 F. 9 rms 460-800 F. Half-board 560-730 F. TV. Air cond 3 rms.

Redecorated with an eye for detail, this handful of rooms looks out over the river and the unique sixteenth-century bridge. The town boasts an abbey founded by Charlemagne.

See Agen

22870 Bréhat (Île de) — (Côtes/Armor)
St-Quay-Portrieux and Ptc-de-l'Arcouest: 96.55.86.99

11/20 Bellevue
Le Port-Clos
96.20.00.05
Mme Bothorel. Closed 5 Jan-5 Feb. Open until 8.30 pm. Garden dining. V.

The only decent restaurant on the island. Although not stunning, the food is well prepared, with the emphasis on simple, pleasing fish dishes.

A la carte: 220 F. Menus: 100 F, 140 F, 300 F.

Bellevue
(See restaurant above)
Closed 5 Jan-5 Feb. 18 rms 200-300 F. Half-board 300-325 F oblig in seas. Conference facilities.

Well-equipped if tiny rooms right at the water's edge.

La Vieille Auberge
96.20.00.24
Closed 10 Nov-31 March. 15 rms 270-350 F (per pers, half-board oblig). Restaurant. No pets. Conference facilities.

On the edge of town, this pink stone hotel has welcoming, modern rooms.

See Azay-le-Rideau

See Grenoble

29200 Brest — (Finistère)
Paris 590 - Rennes 244 - Saint-Brieuc 145

Continental
Square de La Tour d'Auvergne
98.80.50.40
Open every day. 1 ste 450-600 F. 75 rms 260-450 F. Restaurant. TV. Conference facilities. Telex 940575. V AE DC.

A big, fifties-style hotel with an impressive staircase near the railway station. The rooms are gradually being renovated. Hearty breakfasts.

11/20 Le Florian
164, rue J.-Jaurès — 98.44.96.96
Mme Chemineau. Closed Sat lunch. Open until 11 pm. V AE.
With its turn-of-the-century décor and mouldings, Le Florian resembles a stylish Parisian bistro. Seafood dishes are served with a smile late into the evening.
A la carte: 200-250 F. Menus: 58 F (weekdays lunch only, wine inc), 100 F, 120 F, 190 F.

Le Frère Jacques
15 bis, rue de Lyon — 98.44.38.65
M. Péron. Closed Sat lunch, Sun and 1-15 July. Open until 9.30 pm. Private room: 20. V.
Jacques Péron is still showing the other restaurants of Brest how it's done, from the delightful reception and the big, round tables in the wood-panelled dining room to the daring and successful cuisine. Beautiful presentation enhances the prawns and oysters in warm vinaigrette, salmon in a mild curry sauce served with tiny scallop quenelles, and the sliced duck breast accompanied by a honey and grapefruit gratin. The desserts, hitherto the restaurant's weak point, are gradually improving.
A la carte: 350 F. Menus: 155 F, 205 F, 280 F.

Novotel
6 km N (ZAC de Kergaradec)
Av. du Baron-Lacrosse
29239 Gouesnou — 98.02.32.83
Open every day. 85 rms 370-410 F. Restaurant. Half-board 532 F. TV. Air cond. Conference facilities. Pool. Parking. Telex 940470. V AE DC.
A practical place to stay with free shuttle service to the airport. Plain, comfortable rooms.

Le Rossini
16, rue de l'Amiral-Linois — 98.80.10.00
M. Mevel. Closed Sun dinner, Mon and 25 June-20 Sep. Open until 9.30 pm. Private room: 15. Parking. V AE.
You won't find the tournedos steak of the same name here. Maurice Mevel prefers the clear taste of seasonal ingredients and his cooking is starting to rival that of Le Frère Jacques. The shellfish gâteau with an ultralight crab sauce, the bass and herb galette, the precisely cooked and seasoned cod, and the delicate chicken braised with leeks earn him another point this year. Interesting wines.
A la carte: 300-350 F. Menus: 98 F, 180 F, 290 F.

10/20 Sofitel Océania
82, rue de Siam — 98.80.66.66
M. Bruzac. Open every day. Open until 11 pm. Garage parking. Telex 940951. V AE DC.
It's great to find somewhere open on Sunday evenings. The service is pleasant enough, but was there a chef in the kitchen? (Oysters, steak, sole meunière...)
A la carte: 250 F. Menus: 90 F (wine inc), 140 F.

Sofitel Océania
(See restaurant above)
Open every day. 1 ste 980-1,200 F. 82 rms 420-690 F. TV. Air cond. Conference facilities.
Large, well-equipped, and comfortable rooms, but the décor varies from the dismal to the delightful.

12/20 Le Vatel
23, rue Fautras — 98.44.51.02
M. Le Sann. Closed Sat lunch, Sun, 1-9 May and 4-18 Aug. Open until 10 pm. Private room: 18. V AE DC.
The fish is always excellent and precisely cooked in this attractive restaurant. Note especially the cabbage and rock lobster salad, the catch of the day Creole-style, and the bass in white wine with shellfish. Expensive.
A la carte: 350-400 F. Menus: 75 F (weekdays only), and from 145 F to 280 F.

And also...
Our selection of places for inexpensive, quick, or late-night meals.
La Brocherie (98.44.07.69 - 61, rue L.-Pasteur. Open until 11.30 pm): This good grill stays open late (80-100 F).
La Chaumine (98.45.10.70 - 16, rue J.-Bart. Open until 11 pm:) Breton crêpes, night owls welcome (75 F).
La Choucroutière (98.80.60.03 - 14, rue L.-Blanc. Open until 11 pm): Choucroute of course, plus hearty fondues and late service (55-105 F).
L'Equinoxe (98.41.97.87 - Rue A.-Colas. Open until 10.30 pm): In the new 'Oceanopolis' museum, this restaurant offers inexpensive salads and smoked fish assortments.
La Scala (98.31.11.43 - 30, rue d'Algésiras): Perfect spot for after-theatre pizzas, pasta, and carpaccio (80-100 F).

14130 Breuil-en-Auge — (Calvados)
Paris 204 - Caen 55 - Deauville 20 - Lisieux 9

Le Dauphin
31.65.08.11
M. Lecomte. Closed Sun dinner and Mon. Open until 9 pm. Private room: 50. No pets. V.
Marvellously adept and creative, Régis Lecomte's cooking is gently but surely shaking culinary Normandy out of its rich, creamy torpor. Your tastebuds will awaken to the marvellous salad of prawns, grilled leeks, and tomato sauce, the sole served with julienne vegetables and a green-peppercorn sauce, and the roast young pigeon. By the time the vanilla cream accompanied by a chocolate soufflé arrived, we were happy to award a second toque.
A la carte: 350-400 F. Menus: 160 F and 210 F (except Sat dinner).

See Royan

See Montauban

05100 Briançon — (H.-Alpes)
Paris 693 - Grenoble 116 - Gap 87 - Turin 108

Altea
Grand'Boucle
Av. du Dauphiné — 92.20.11.51
Open every day. 160 rms 360-470 F. Restaurant. Half-board 315-370 F. TV. Conference facilities. Heated pool. Parking. Telex 405937. V AE.
The new décor creates an elegant atmosphere in the small, well-equipped rooms. Relaxed, attentive service.

Le Mont Prorel
5, rue R.-Froger — 92.20.22.88
Open every day. 18 rms 120-350 F. Restaurant. Half-board 230-300 F oblig in seas. TV 15 rms. Conference facilities. Parking. V AE DC.
Pleasant rooms in a chalet next to the cable cars. The Guisame River flows through the large garden.

Le Péché Gourmand
14
2, rte de Gap — 92.20.11.02
MM. Bayrou and Petit. Closed off-season Sun dinner and Mon. Open until 10 pm. Private room: 10. Terrace dining. Parking. V AE.
Leaving the unattractive location behind as you cross the threshold, you'll discover an elegant modern dining room where it's pure pleasure to be at table. Christian Bayrou is a courteous host and the young chef, Laurent Petit, takes infinite pains over dishes such as lentil cream soup with prawns, potato millefeuille with lamb and foie gras, and the yoghurt ice cream served with a quince sauce. It's expensive, but the 180 F set menu is remarkably generous. New this year is an interesting range of wines by the glass.
A la carte: 300-350 F. Menus: 100 F (weekdays lunch only), 180 F, 240 F.

12/20 Vauban
13, av. Gal-de-Gaulle — 92.21.12.11
M. Sémiond. Closed 6 Nov-18 Dec. Open until 9 pm. Private room: 10. Garage parking. V.
No flights of fancy, but the cooking is reliable and service competent. Excellent beurre blanc accompanies the steamed trout, the lamb chops are served with a first-class tarragon butter, and the chocolate soufflé is delicious.
A la carte: 250 F. Menus: 100 F, 110 F, 160 F.

Vauban
(See restaurant above)
Closed 6 Nov-18 Dec. 44 rms 200-380 F. Half-board 230-310 F oblig in seas. TV 12 rms. Conference facilities.
Near the town centre and the ski lifts, this large hotel has small but comfortable modern rooms.

BRIGNOGAN-PLAGE
29890 Brignogan-Plage — (Finistère)
Paris 538 - Morlaix 53 - Brest 37 - Landerneau 26

12/20 Castel-Régis
Plage du Garo — 98.83.40.22
M. Plos. Closed Wed (except hotel clients) and 1 Oct-23 March. Open until 9 pm. Private room: 80. No pets. Garage parking. Telex 940941. V AE.
The view from the dining room plunges down to rocky, wave lashed islands. The cooking is less dramatic, and the prawn and cabbage fricassée, blanquette of scallops and shellfish, and paupiettes de saumon are respectable fare, although the cooking times and seasoning can lack precision.
A la carte: 400 F. Menus: 110 F and 160 F (weekdays only), 170 F and 200 F (w-e and holidays lunch only).

Castel-Régis
(See restaurant above)
Closed 1 Oct-23 March. 21 rms 235-360 F. Half-board 350-420 F. Conference facilities. Heated pool. Tennis.
Most of the rooms are in bungalows and all revel in the superb seascape. Some bathrooms have a Jacuzzi. Smiling reception and service.

BRIGNOLES
83170 Brignoles — (Var)
Paris 815 - Draguignan 53 - Toulon 50 - Aix 57

11/20 Mas de la Cascade
D 554, rte de Toulon, in La Celle
94.69.01.49
M. Gély. Closed Tue dinner and Wed (except July-Aug), and Feb. Open until 9.30 pm. Private room: 28. Garden dining. Parking. V.
The little waterfall in the garden helps drown out the noise of the traffic. The feuilletés of ham, foie gras and truffles, quails 'à la pastourelle', and truffle ravioli in a mushroom sauce are more formal than sophisticated. Regional wines.
A la carte: 300 F. Menus: 100 F, 155 F, 280 F.

Mas de la Cascade
(See restaurant above)
Closed Tue and Wed (except July-Aug), and Feb. 10 rms 250-450 F. Half-board 380-410 F. Conference facilities.
There are views of the garden and river from the agreeable rooms. Generous breakfasts and a smiling reception.

BRIGUE (LA)
06430 Brigue (La) — (Alpes-Mar.)
Paris 883 - Nice 82 - Sospel 39 - Tende 7 - Saorge 13

Mirval
93.04.63.71
Closed 1 Nov-1 April. 18 rms 160-250 F. Restaurant. Half-board 180-230 F oblig in seas. No pets. Parking. V AE DC.
Off the road to the Col de Tende stands this pleasant inn with small, restful rooms. Guided tours of the Vallée des Merveilles are available.

BRIVE-LA-GAILLARDE
19100 Brive-la-Gaillarde — (Corrèze)
Paris 468 - Limoges 96 - Toulouse 212 - Périgueux 73

La Belle Epoque
13
27, av. J.-Jaurès — 55.74.08.75
M. Cherronnet. Closed Sat lunch and Sun dinner. Open until 10.30 pm. Private room: 15. V.
The rising prices are presumably the result of expensive improvements that have provided light and pleasant décor, and an interior garden. Thierry Cherronnet, a native of Lyon, prepares lighter versions of classic dishes: slivered scallops and foie gras in Banyuls, salmon marinated in truffle juice and walnut oil, three-meat sauté with oranges. Wines by the glass and charming service.
A la carte: 300-350 F. Menus: 94 F (weekdays only), 140 F, 149 F, 180 F.

Château de Coutinard
Vicomté de Turenne — 55.85.91.88
Open every day. 3 stes 250-300 F. 10 rms 160-250 F. Restaurant. Half-board 200-300 F. Conference facilities. Valet parking.
This family-run, nineteenth-century château is surrounded by fourteen hectares of grounds.

La Crémaillère
15
53, av. de Paris — 55.74.32.47
M. Reynal. Closed Sun dinner and Mon. Open until 9.30 pm. Private room: 30. Garden dining. No pets. Hotel: 9 rms 160-240 F. V.
Charlou Reynal's interpretation of regional cooking is a combination of culinary memories and modern techniques. Foie gras, cèpes, and truffles are used with restraint and constantly renewed by introducing them to other cuisines. So Reynal does

not hesitate to serve a foie gras terrine and artichoke mousse with a spicy gazpacho, or an aromatic parmentier of morels and cèpes with lobster and saffron-flavoured carrots. A classic duck civet in Cahors rubs shoulders on the *carte* with prawns wrapped in lettuce; tourin, the traditional goose-fat-flavoured onion soup with sorrel appears alongside fillet of lamb roasted with green coffee beans. A set meal, featuring old family recipes like boudin sausage with chestnuts, is also available. The interior garden shaded by a lime tree is a treat in itself come fine weather.

A la carte: 250-300 F. Menus: 185 F, 230 F.

Mercure
5 km W on D 901
Le Griffolet — 55.87.15.03
Open every day. 57 rms 270-440 F. Restaurant. TV. Conference facilities. Pool. Tennis. Parking. Telex 590096. V AE DC.
Near the Château du Griffolet and its lake, this hotel has spacious, quiet, and well-maintained rooms. A restaurant overlooks the swimming pool.

La Périgourdine
15, av. Alsace-Lorraine — 55.24.26.55
M. Husson. Closed holidays (except upon reserv), Sun and 15-30 July. Open until 9.30 pm. Private room: 10. Garden dining. V AE.
The delightful courtyard garden is the high spot of this informally elegant restaurant. The owner-chef steers a simple course veering towards local dishes and ingredients: salad of confit with a walnut dressing, duck breasts in a homemade mustard flavoured with grape juice, poached pears in light syrup. The wine list has some real bargains like the 1969, 1970 and 1971 Musigny Grand Cru at 300 F a bottle. Warm welcome.

A la carte: 350-400 F. Menus: 110 F, 150 F, 275 F.

10/20 Le Régent
3, place W.-Churchill
55.74.09.58
Mme Lignac. Closed Sun dinner and Mon. Open until 9 pm. Private room: 22. Terrace dining. Hotel: 24 rms 150-300 F. V.
A reliable stop which revitalises without impoverishing. Giblet salad, truite meunière, and steak with shallots are served under the parasols on the terrace.

A la carte: 200 F. Menus: 65 F (weekdays only), 90 F, 110 F, 150 F.

Soph'Motel
18 km N on N 20
at La Croix-de-Fer
19270 St-Pardoux-l'Ortigier — 55.84.51.02
Open every day. 26 rms 270-450 F. Restaurant. Half-board 265-360 F. TV. Conference facilities. Pool. Tennis. Garage parking. V AE DC.
A holiday hotel set in lush, green countryside. The well-designed rooms are newly decorated and there's a sauna and solarium. Horseback riding and other sports available.

La Truffe Noire
22, bd A.-France — 55.92.45.00
Open every day. 4 stes 550-650 F. 29 rms 280-650 F. Restaurant. TV. Air cond. Valet parking. V AE DC.
Recently reopened under the control of the local Parveaux group, this central hotel has comfortable, air-conditioned rooms and a restaurant showcasing regional cuisine.

Urbis
32, rue M.-Roche — 55.74.34.70
Open every day. 55 rms 300-330 F. TV. Conference facilities. Parking. Telex 590195. V.
A well-maintained modern hotel five minutes from the town centre.

In nearby Ussac

(5 km N on N 20 and D 57)
19270 Brive-la-Gaillarde — (Corrèze)

La Borderie
at Le Pouret — 55.87.74.45
M. Bordes. Closed Sun dinner and Mon. Annual closings not available. Open until 9.30 pm. Private room: 18. Garden dining. Parking. V.
Lost in the hills overlooking Brive, this superb inn is blessed with two impressive fireplaces and Jean-Claude Bordes's fine cooking. A former pupil of Guy Lenôtre, he renews local dishes with only a hint of pretension: mousseline of foie gras and apples, John Dory with vin paillé, duck parmentier, and some fine desserts. The fish dishes require a little attention and the cellar more half-bottles.

A la carte: 350 F. Menus: 120 F (weekdays only), 165 F, 255 F, 325 F.

La Borderie
(See restaurant above)
Annual closings not available. 1 ste 650 F. 7 rms 400-500 F. Half-board 375-425 F. TV. Conference facilities. Pool.
A haven of peace and refinement in a lovely valley. The new rooms are extremely comfortable and some have a terrace next to the pool. Pleasant staff.

In nearby Varetz

(10 km NW on D 901)
19240 Brive-la-Gaillarde — (Corrèze)

Château de Castel Novel
55.85.00.01
M. Parveaux. Closed mid-Oct-beg May. Open until 9.15 pm. Private room: 80. Valet parking. Telex 590065. V AE DC.
Once a favourite haunt of the writer Colette, this delightful restaurant is the summer setting for Jean-Pierre Faucher's regional cooking. He enjoys preparing tourin, the local onion soup flavoured with goose fat, ragoûts of truffles and foie gras, whole truffles in golden pastry, veal chop casseroled with salsify and Monbazillac, black-cherry clafoutis, and iced chestnut soufflé with walnut sauce as much as his customers enjoy eating them. Our only disappointments here have been when Faucher abandons this cuisine at which he excels and strays in search of pseudo-novelty.

A la carte: 350-400 F. Menus: 205 F, 310 F, 410 F.

Château de Castel Novel
(See restaurant above)
Closed mid-Oct-beg May. 5 stes 1,200-1,450 F. 32 rms 360-1,000 F. Half-board 655-1,125 F. TV. Conference facilities. Heated pool. Tennis.
These 40 hectares include a three-hole golf course and a barbecue. As for the hotel, it has beautifully decorated rooms, fine service and excellent, varied breakfasts. An annexe contains some less luxurious rooms.

BUBRY

56310 Bubry — (Morbihan)
Paris 483 - Lorient 34 - Pontivy 22 - Vannes 53

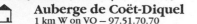

⌂ Auberge de Coët-Diquel ▲♣
1 km W on VO — 97.51.70.70

Closed 1 Dec-15 March. 20 rms 250-300 F. Restaurant. Half-board 265-290 F oblig in seas. Conference facilities. Heated pool. Tennis. Parking. V.

This recent hotel was built in the old style in pleasant grounds bordered by a trout stream. It's well equipped for receptions and groups.

BUC

See PARIS Suburbs

BUISSON-DE-CADOUIN (LE)

See Siorac-en-Périgord

BUOUX

See Bonnieux

BUSCHWILLER

See Saint-Louis

BUSSEAU-SUR-CREUSE

See Guéret

BUSSY-SAINT-GEORGES

See Lagny-sur-Marne

BUXEROLLES

See Poitiers

CABASSE

83340 Cabasse — (Var)
Paris 830 - Draguignan 38 - Le Luc 11 - Brignoles 14

11/20 Le Cabassoir
15, rue Pasteur — 94.80.20.14

M. Kemme. Closed Wed and 10 Jan-28 Feb. Open until 10 pm. Terrace dining. Hotel: 3 stes 180-250 F. V AE.

Wanting to offer something different here in the heart of Provence, Helga Breitling produces a Central European menu featuring stuffed pasta, and 'Leberkäse' (grilled veal with liver and onions). Nothing to get excited about, but it's a change and it's fairly cheap.

A la carte: 150-230 F. Menus: 100 F (weekdays lunch only), 120 F, 165 F.

CABOURG

14390 Cabourg — (Calvados)
Paris 225 - Caen 24 - Deauville 19

⌂⌂ Altea Agora
Av. de l'Hippodrome — 31.24.04.04

Open every day. 1 ste 820-880 F. 81 rms 310-490 F. Restaurant. Half-board 480-660 F. TV. Conference facilities. Heated pool. Parking. Telex 772328. V AE DC.

A pretty half-timbered hotel with small, pleasant rooms. Smiling service and first-rate breakfasts.

12/20 Le Balbec
Prom. M.-Proust — 31.91.01.79

M. Lalanne. Open every day. Open until 10 pm. Terrace dining. Telex 171364. V AE DC.

Turn-of-the-century charm still clings to this seaside hotel but the cooking is starting to show its age. Overcooked sole drowns its sorrows in cream, as does the otherwise excellent mushroom-stuffed chicken, but there are superb shellfish and good desserts to console the customers. Some fairly inexpensive wines are available by the carafe. Rapid, pleasant service.

A la carte: 400 F. Menus: 180 F, 320 F.

⌂⌂ Pullman Grand Hôtel
(See restaurant above)

Open every day. 2 stes 1,800-2,500 F. 68 rms 460-1,200 F. Half-board 680-1420 F. TV. Conference facilities.

This Belle Epoque hotel still pleases with its huge, comfortable rooms (the one where Marcel Proust stayed is much in demand). Big bathrooms too, and the breakfasts are delicious.

⌂⌂ Castel Fleuri
4, av. A.-Piat — 31.91.27.57

Open every day. 1 ste 440 F. 21 rms 290-380 F. TV. V DC.

Recently modernised, this hotel offers small, comfortable rooms and bountiful breakfasts.

⌂ Le Cottage
24, av. du Gal-Leclerc — 31.91.65.61

Open every day. 11 rms 180-340 F. TV. Conference facilities. Parking. V.

Simple, well-equipped rooms and a family atmosphere.

12/20 Le Petit Chaudron
Av. de l'Hippodrome — 31.24.12.34

M. Marchesseau. Open every day. Open until 10.30 pm. Private room: 90. Terrace dining. No-smoking section. Valet parking. V.

Local fare and flair grace this pretty pink dining room where you can sample crab Cabourg-style, fattened hen in apple brandy, and wonderful Normandy cheeses.

A la carte: 300 F. Menus: from 95 F to 280 F.

⌂ Hôtel du Golf ▲♣
(See restaurant above)

Open every day. 40 rms 310-435 F. Half-board 325-410 F. TV. Conference facilities.

Between the golf course and the racecourse, this hotel has bright, quiet, modern rooms.

In nearby Bavent

(7 km SW on D 513 and D 95 A)
14860 Cabourg — (Calvados)

12/20 Hostellerie du Moulin du Pré
Rte de Gonneville-en-Auge — 31.78.83.68

MM. Hamchin and Holtz. Closed Sun dinner and Mon (except holidays and July-Aug), first 2 weeks of March and Oct. Open until 9 pm. Parking. V AE DC.

The dining room with its blazing fire and lace tablecloths promises better, but the cooking, like the millwheel, seems to be going round in circles. The courgette flowers were tasteless, and uninteresting vegetables accompanied the good, fresh red-mullet fillets. Throw in the lifeless apple tart and we have to subtract a point.

A la carte: 300 F. Menus: from 225 F to 260 F.

We are always interested to hear about your discoveries, and to receive your comments on ours. Please feel free to write to us, stating your opinions clearly.

Hostellerie du Moulin du Pré

(See restaurant above)
Closed Sun, and Mon (except holidays and July-Aug), 2 first weeks of March and Oct. 10 rms 170-290 F. No pets.

The pretty and comfortable rooms have attractive views but suffer slightly from tiny bathrooms, noise, and uninteresting furniture.

In nearby Merville-Franceville-Plage

(6 km on D 514)
14810 Cabourg — (Calvados)

Chez Marion

10, pl. de la Plage — 31.24.23.39
MM. Marion. Closed Mon dinner and Tue (except school holidays), and 2-31 Jan. Open until 9.30 pm. Private room: 22. Hotel: 14 rms 290-350 F. Parking. Telex 170234. V AE DC.

The Marion family has run this restaurant for more than 40 years, devoting themselves to the good local seafood. The results include spectacular assortments of shellfish, many ways with lobster (including a lobster-based menu), and perfectly cooked fish. The wine list is respectable, but the pride of the cellar is an astonishing collection of Calvados.

A la carte: 300 F. Menus: 97 F, 175 F, 230 F, 440 F.

CABRERETS

46330 Cabrerets — (Lot)
Paris 566 - St-Céré 64 - Figeac 41 - Cahors 34

La Pescalerie

65.31.22.55
Mme Combette. Closed 1 Nov-1 April. Open until 9 pm. Private room: 15. Terrace dining. Parking. V AE DC.

This manor on the banks of the Célé is run by Hélène and Roger Belcourt, both doctors, from April to October. Roger welcomes you as if you'd been a customer for years, advising you to try one of his excellent Cahors and describing the dishes made of quality produce. Each morning, local farmers and growers deliver the ingredients you'll find on your plate in the evening, transformed into mushroom and walnut tart with a herb and lemon sauce, duck confit and little green cabbages in the company of oyster mushrooms, potatoes, and fresh tomato purée, stuffed goose neck with lentils, remarkable roast chickens, and delicate pastries. The wine list has plenty of fine Cahors but no one will mind if you wish to venture further afield. The service goes without a hitch.

A la carte: 300 F. Menus: 195 F, 230 F.

La Pescalerie

(See restaurant above)
Closed 1 Nov-1 April. 10 rms 450-620 F. TV 5 rms.

These ten rooms are individually decorated, but all have period furniture, good modern paintings, and cut flowers. After a heavenly breakfast, there are many beautiful walks and drives to be taken from here.

CABRIS

See Grasse

CADIÈRE D'AZUR (LA)

83740 Cadière d'Azur (La) — (Var)
Paris 821 - Marseille 46 - Aix-en-Provence 63

Hostellerie Bérard

Rue G.-Péri — 94.90.11.43
Closed 7 Jan-25 Feb. 3 stes 636-1,800 F. 40 rms 387-1,800 F. Restaurant. Half-board 456-630 F. TV. No pets. Conference facilities. Heated pool. Garage parking. Telex 400509. V AE.

Dating from the eleventh century, this hostelry contains carefully decorated rooms. A recent annexe overlooks the garden and swimming pool. Charming reception and service.

CADOUIN

See Beaumont

CAEN

14000 Caen — (Calvados)
Paris 222 - Rouen 124 - Evreux 121 - Cherbourg 119

Altea Malherbe

Pl. du Mal-Foch — 31.84.40.06
Open every day. 2 stes 490-550 F. 46 rms 290-420 F. Restaurant. Half-board 260-330 F. TV. Conference facilities. Telex 170555. V AE DC.

A fine traditional hotel currently undergoing a face-lift.

12/20 Le Bœuf Ferré

10, rue des Croisiers — 31.85.36.40
M. Aparicio. Closed Sat lunch, Sun, 1-15 March and 14-31 July. Open until 9.30 pm. V.

Close attention is paid to cooking fine ingredients and the popular results include turbot braised in Champagne, good smoked salmon, tender rump steak in a real béarnaise sauce, and a delicious nougat vacherin. Less attention is paid to the service.

A la carte: 200-220 F. Menus: 65 F (weekdays lunch only), 90 F, 120 F, 220 F.

La Bourride

15-17, rue du Vaugueux — 31.93.50.76
M. Bruneau. Closed Sun, Mon, 4-25 Jan and 17 Aug-3 Sep. Open until 10 pm. Private room: 16. V AE DC.

We have heard that Michel Bruneau, a passionate ambassador of the cuisine of Normandy, has plans to enlarge his pretty timbered inn. Meanwhile, the beamed, low-ceilinged dining room warmed by the presence of Françoise Bruneau does well enough, especially as you can watch the chef's team beavering away behind a glass partition. Anyone capable of making such delicious andouille sausage—as in the gâteau d'andouille in cider vinegar—deserves a medal. And that's just one of Michel Bruneau's regional masterpieces. Others include foie gras of Normandy duck wrapped in cabbage leaves, mussel soup, snails in poiré (pear cider), John Dory with creamed fresh peas, tender thick turbot in a lentil broth, and local lamb with sage. But it would be a mistake to think of Bruneau as just a culinary curator. His version of Normandy fare is like no one else's, and his personality shines through in the constantly changing *menu découverte* where you might discover a roulade of salmon with broad-bean mousse, or minestrone with scallops, prawns and oysters. The fine wine list is dominated by Bordeaux, but the cider provides a perfect companion to the splendid local cheeses like Camembert, Pont-l'Évêque, and Livarot.

A la carte: 350-500 F. Menus: 187 F (lunch only), 259 F, 351 F, 486 F.

Les Cordeliers
4, rue des Cordeliers — 31.86.37.15
Closed Sun. 1 ste 250-350 F. 21 rms 120-260 F. TV 11 rms. No pets. Telex 170187. V AE DC.
In this very old but refurbished hotel you can smell the furniture polish and the cleanliness. Some rooms face the interior garden, others the pedestrian street.

Le Dauphin ⚙
29, rue Gémare — 31.86.22.26
M. Chabredier. Closed Sat and 15 July-6 Aug. Open until 9.30 pm. Private room: 45. Parking. Telex 171707. V AE DC.
Robert Chabredier's *carte* is short and devoted to market-fresh seafood, while the set menus reflect the same respect for fine ingredients. The dining room is decorated in a rather heavy bourgeois style, but it won't detract from your enjoyment of the fish marinated in cider vinegar, John Dory with bone marrow, and roast saddle of lamb. Fine desserts.
A la carte: 280-350 F. Menus: 85 F (weekdays only), 150 F, 210 F, 320 F.

Le Dauphin
(See restaurant above)
Closed 15 July-6 Aug. 22 rms 260-360 F. TV. Conference facilities.
The thick walls of this former priory maintain the peace and quiet of the unpretentious, comfortable rooms. Pleasant, efficient service.

12/20 L'Ecaille
(Relais des Gourmets)
13, rue de la Geôle — 31.86.49.10
M. Legras. Closed Sat lunch and Mon. Open until 10 pm. Air cond. Garage parking. Telex 171657. V AE DC.
You can always enjoy the view of William the Conqueror's castle, but the cooking has its ups and downs. The oysters, and the duo of salmon and brill, can be superb, but the bread is inexcusably dry and the desserts leaden. Rapid service.
A la carte: 250-300 F. Menu: 130 F (wine inc).

Les Echevins
Le Castel
35, rte de Trouville — 31.84.10.17
M. Régnier. Closed Sun (except holidays), 17 Feb-3 March and 4 Aug-1 Sep. Open until 9.30 pm. Private room: 120. Parking. V.
In just a few years Patrick Régnier's new restaurant has become a success, thanks in part to the huge garden, comfortable dining room, and attentive service. But this chef should pay more attention to the quality of his ingredients and their preparation. The pigeon and foie gras terrine was dull, the fillet of beef with chanterelle lacked finesse, and the profiteroles were a terrible letdown.
A la carte: 350-400 F. Menus: 140 F, 215 F, 285 F.

12/20 Le Gastronome
43, rue St-Sauveur — 31.86.57.75
M. Danet. Closed Sat lunch and Sun dinner. Open until 10 pm. Private room: 25. V AE.
The décor is being renewed here so we'll move straight to the tasty and professional cooking, for instance: calf's foot in salad, lotte with crayfish and fresh pasta, and rabbit stewed in wine. Good, estate-bottled wines.
A la carte: 230 F. Menus: 75 F (weekdays lunch only), 85 F, 135 F.

12/20 Le Jardin Gourmet
21, quai de Juillet — 31.84.64.57
M. Lebrech. Closed Sat lunch, Sun and 19 Aug-10 Sep. Open until 9.30 pm. Private room: 8. Terrace dining. Hotel: 19 rms 260-490 F. V AE DC.
This new restaurant comes close to a toque with its feuilletés of mussels, winkles, and asparagus, the chicken breast with prawns (undercooked but subtly flavoured), and steamed lotte, sole, and turbot. We'd appreciate less familiarity in the reception... and please turn off that radio!
Menus: 89 F (except Sat dinner), 130 F, 140 F, 180 F, 250 F.

Mercure
1, rue de Courtonne — 31.93.07.62
Open every day. 3 stes 395-530 F. 101 rms 330-475 F. Restaurant. Half-board 445-580 F. TV. Air cond. Conference facilities. Parking. Telex 171890. V AE DC.
Comfortable rooms, but rather dark and not too well soundproofed. Centrally located opposite the harbour.

Moderne
116, bd du Mal-Leclerc — 31.86.04.23
Open every day. 40 rms 310-610 F. TV. Garage parking. Telex 171106. V AE DC.
A modern hotel with personalised rooms and good bathrooms. Breakfasts are served on the fifth floor with a panoramic view of the town. Sauna.

10/20 Le Paquebot
7, rue des Croisiers — 31.85.10.10
M. Debelle. Closed Sun. Open until 0.30 am. Private room: 30. V AE DC.
A young and trendy clientele appreciates lamb stuffed with mint, grilled skate with lime sauce, and pistachio nougat glacé. Slow service.
A la carte: 180-220 F. Menus: 70 F (weekdays only), 130 F, 195 F.

La Petite Marmite
43, rue des Jacobins — 31.86.15.20
M. Barthélémy. Closed Sat lunch, Sun, holidays and 3rd week of Aug. Open until 10 pm. Air cond. V AE.
A welcoming, contemporary dining room beckons you to try Jean-Luc Barthélémy's classic cooking with a bent for bistro dishes: fillet of beef with bone marrow, veal kidneys and morels, plus the fish his brother brings off the boat (turbot on a bed of seaweed, or paupiette of sole with prawns). A smiling *patronne* oversees the young, efficient staff.
A la carte: 250 F. Menus: 98 F, 148 F.

12/20 Le Relais des Gourmets
15, rue de la Geôle — 31.86.06.01
M. Legras-Daragon. Closed Sun dinner and 1 May. Open until 9.30 pm. Private room: 35. Garden dining. Parking. Telex 171657. V AE DC.
Tradition lives on in this fine dining room with its white tablecloths, heavy candlesticks, and bay windows opening onto neat flower gardens. The cooking is traditional too, but with a tendency towards inconsistency: the salad of sole, lotte and salmon is well seasoned, but the turbot fillet is overcooked and the desserts heavy. Good wines and impeccable service.
A la carte: ;9300 F. Menus: 130 F (weekdays only), 210 F (wine inc).

Le Relais des Gourmets
(See restaurant above)
Open every day. 5 stes 600-800 F. 28 rms 230-420 F. Half-board 452-642 F. TV. Conference facilities.
Ideally situated near the château, these well-soundproofed rooms have recently been redecorated. Generous breakfasts.

11/20 Saint-Andrew's
9, quai de Juillet – 31.86.26.80
M. Despois. Closed Sun. Open until 10.30 pm. V AE.
Behind the leaded windows nestles a cosy, convivial dining room where you can enjoy good terrines and fresh fish.
A la carte: 250 F. Menus: 100 F (wine inc), 95 F.

15 Daniel Tubœuf
8, rue Buquet – 31.43.64.48
M. Tubœuf. Closed Sun dinner, Mon and 25 July-20 Aug. Open until 9.30 pm. Air cond. No pets. V.
We began to feel last year that Daniel Tubœuf's return to his native region from Paris was helping his talent to take off. After a period of adjustment and experiment, he has focussed his ideas to produce a fine, personal style, and we have no hesitation in awarding a second toque. We enjoyed fillets of sole with rosemary sauce (although it contained a bit too much cream), the calf's liver with raspberry vinegar and crisp chicory, crunchy caramel pigeon, and exquisite desserts. The locals seem to share our enthusiasm now they've recovered from the shock of the theatrical dining room with its stucco and columns. Our only complaint concerns the high cost of the wines.
A la carte: 300-400 F. Menus: 155 F (dinner only), 168 F (lunch only, wine inc, except Sun), 290 F.

And also...
Our selection of places for inexpensive, quick, or late-night meals.
Alcide (31.44.18.06 - pl. Courtonne. Open until 10 pm): A quality bistro serving traditional dishes (80-150 F).
Amalfi (31.85.33.34 - 201, rue Saint-Jean. Open until 11 pm): The best Italian food in Caen, and not at all expensive (50-100 F).
L'Assiette (31.85.29.16 - 2, pl. Fontette. Open until 10 pm): Worth trying especially for the 40 different desserts. Friendly and original (60-80 F)
.La Petite Cale (31.86.29.15 - 18, quai Vendeuvre. Open until 9.45 pm): Very fresh and affordable fish and shellfish (130-180 F).
Les Trois Marches (31.95.21.94 - 15, rue Basse. Open until midnight): Honest menus with good meat dishes (75-120 F).

In nearby Bénouville
(10 km NE)
14970 Caen – (Calvados)

13 Manoir d'Hastings
18, av. de la Côte-de-Nacre – 31.44.62.43
M. Scaviner. Open every day. Open until 9.30 pm. Private room: 60. Parking. Telex 171144. V AE DC.
Much has changed since our enthusiasm of the 1970s over Claude Scaviner's self-taught talents. His son Yves, who for a while provided useful back-up in the kitchen, has left for pastures new. We can't tell if Claude Scaviner's enthusiasm is waning or whether he's simply losing his touch, but our most recent meals here showed a significant decline. As the housing estate gnaws away at the apple orchards, so the regional basis for his cooking has been eroded to the point where most

of the dishes reflect a South-western and occasionally Provençal influence. That is no sin of course, but the imprecise cooking times and shamefully skimpy portions are (our chicken dish totalled five mouthfuls). The ingredients are still first-rate, and the lobster navarin with Beaujolais alone justified keeping the toque.
A la carte: 350 F. Menus: 198 F, 298 F, 420 F.

La Pommeraie
(See restaurant above)
Open every day. 11 rms 520-900 F. Half-board 685-850 F. TV. Conference facilities.
This new white building can't match the charm of the manor housing the restaurant, but the rooms are really comfortable. Remarkable breakfasts.

In nearby Fleury-sur-Orne
(4 km S on D 562)
14000 Caen – (Calvados)

13 L'Ile Enchantée
1, rue St-André – 31.52.15.52
M. Blaize. Closed Sun dinner, Mon, Feb school holidays and 2-22 Sep. Open until 10 pm. Private room: 15. V AE.
The service has improved somewhat in this riverside *auberge*, but it's still pretty slow. Jean-Claude Blaize provides a pleasing interpretation of the local fish dishes. There's an imaginative shellfish assortment, sole soufflé with shrimp sauce, turbot cooked in Sauvignon, and a good apple tart (but give the sorbets a wide berth). Interesting range of wines, but not necessarily the best from each area.
A la carte: 300 F. Menus: 110 F, 130 F, 160 F, 220 F.

In nearby Hérouville-Saint-Clair
(3 km NE)
14200 Caen – (Calvados)

Friendly
2, pl. de Boston – 31.44.05.05
Open every day. 1 ste 450-480 F. 90 rms 350-450 F. Restaurant. TV. Conference facilities. Heated pool. Parking. Telex 772500. V AE DC.
This English hotel, complete with mahogany bar and floral carpeting, is equipped with a sauna, gym, and pool with wave machine.

In nearby Louvigny
(4 km SW on D 212)
14111 Caen – (Calvados)

13 Auberge de l'Hermitage
11, la Haule – 31.73.38.66
M. Grandsire. Closed Sun dinner and Mon (except holidays), Feb school holidays and 3 weeks end Aug-beg Sep. Open until 9.30 pm. Air cond. Parking. V.
On the quiet green banks of the Orne, not far from Caen, Michel Grandsire's professional cooking is making progress. The strong suit of the house is fresh seafood (scallops, mixed fish gratin); the weak suit is the sauces. After the excellent apple croustillant served with a Calvados sabayon sauce, we decided to give a toque of encouragement in the hope that next year's meals will come up trumps.
A la carte: 280-300 F. Menus: 120 F (weekdays only), 150 F, 175 F.

CAGNES-SUR-MER

06800 Cagnes-sur-Mer — (Alpes-Mar.)
Paris 920 - Cannes 22 - Nice 13 - Antibes 11

 ### Le Cagnard
Haut-de-Cagnes
Rue du Pontis-Long — 93.20.73.21
M. Barel. Closed Thu lunch and 1 Nov-15 Dec. Open until 10.30 pm. Private room: 100. Terrace dining. Air cond. Valet parking. Telex 462223. V AE DC.
This delightful fourteenth-century establishment affords a sweeping view of the coast all the way to Antibes and the distant hills. You can now enjoy the panorama from a terrace complete with sliding panelled ceiling which protects you from bad weather or opens to let you admire the stars. Jean-Luc Johany's cooking demonstrates a sure touch which changes the menu slowly but surely. This year be sure to sample the turbot steak in a leek sauce served with a prawn kebab, or the lamb charlotte with mint juice. The prices reflect the luxury of the décor.
A la carte: 550 F. Menus: 370 F, 490 F.

Le Cagnard
(See restaurant above)
Open every day. 12 stes 810-1,300 F. 14 rms 320-780 F. TV. Air cond 7 rms. Conference facilities.
Most of these rooms and suites have a private terrace with glorious views. The décor is luxurious and tasteful.

Les Collettes
Ch. des Collettes — 93.20.80.66
Closed 16 Nov-26 Dec. 13 rms 283-296 F. Pool. Tennis. Parking. V AE DC.
This simple hotel overlooking the sea has plain, pleasantly decorated rooms.

12/20 La Comédie
Haut-de-Cagnes
85, montée de la Bourgade — 93.73.44.64
M. Bellehi. Closed Tue and Feb. Open until 10.30 pm. Air cond. No-smoking section. V AE DC.
Vegetarian food is the young chef's speciality: several clever fruit and vegetable salads, artichoke heart mousse with carrot sauce, and a delicious goat-cheese feuilleté served with a ginger preserve. A few meat and fish dishes are available and the cellar is well stocked.
A la carte: 300 F. Menus: 110 F (vegetarian), 150 F, 220 F.

Josy-Jo
Haut-de-Cagnes
8, pl. du Planastel — 93.20.68.76
M. Bandecchi. Closed Sun and 13 July-15 Aug. Open until 10 pm. Terrace dining. V.
For more than twenty years Jo and Josy Bandecchi have been serving seasonal Provençal food to appreciative customers. There are fresh cèpes en papillote, stuffed sardines, charcoal-grilled meats, and grilled fish. Not to mention friendly service and an adorable terrace covered with flowers.
A la carte: 250 F.

Picadero
3, bd de la Plage — 93.73.57.81
M. Miraglio. Closed Mon (except holidays). Open until 10.30 pm. Air cond. V.
The Miraglios have had a bistro built alongside their busy restaurant, and you may still have to wait for a table to try the fricassée of squid with sea-urchin roe, roast baby lamb served with its tripe, and crêpe of pine-nuts and almond milk. Nicole Miraglio's welcome displays real warmth and the

170 F set menu must be one of the best deals on the Riviera. Good Provençal wines.
A la carte: 320 F. Menus: 170 F, 280 F.

Restaurant des Peintres
Haut-de-Cagnes
71, montée de la Bourgade — 93.20.83.08
M. Lorquet. Closed Wed and 15 Nov-15 Dec. Open until 10 pm. Private room: 25. Air cond. Garage parking. V AE.
The tourists who climb up through the picturesque village to reach this little restaurant probably have no idea that they are approaching one of the best addresses in the area. The lotte with ginger and coriander, fillet of veal with sage, and the cod salad with ratatouille are true Provençal fare.
A la carte: 250-300 F. Menus: 120 F, 165 F.

CAHORS

46000 Cahors — (Lot)
Paris 569 - Rodez 121 - Brive 102 - Montauban 60

Le Balandre
5, av. Ch.-de-Freycinet — 65.30.01.97
M. Marre. Closed off-season Sun dinner and Mon, Sat lunch in seas, 15 days in Feb and 24-30 June. Open until 10 pm. Private room: 15. Terrace dining. No pets. Garage parking. Telex 539000. V AE.
A three-day celebration of sauerkraut and Alsatian wines is held here annually. The rest of the time, this comfortable and immaculate restaurant done up in turn-of-the-century style, offers hearty South-western fare. Chef Gilles Marre is reliably generous with his foie gras and other refined regional dishes, like salmon à la nage with gentian and grapefruit, minced beef in lime, lamb fillet with a gratin of lamb offal sparked with parsley juice, a panaché of homemade foie gras, truffle croustade à la sauce Régence, and warm apple tart with caramelised berries and a touch of ginger. Good selection of Cahors wines; warm reception; efficient service.
A la carte: 300-330 F. Menus: from 100 F to 275 F.

Hôtel Terminus
(See restaurant above)
Open every day. 30 rms 170-295 F. TV. No pets. Conference facilities.
A comfortable establishment, near the station, with calm and tidy rooms. Pleasant terrace; family atmosphere.

France
252, av. J.-Jaurès — 65.35.16.76
Closed 22 Dec-7 Jan. 80 rms 175-300 F. TV 40 rms. Air cond 40 rms. No pets. Conference facilities. Garage parking. Telex 520394. V AE DC.
A very clean and modern hotel, located between the station and Valentré bridge. Lukewarm reception.

11/20 Les Templiers
5 km S on N 20
in Montat — 65.21.01.23
M. Planat. Closed Sun dinner (except July-Aug), Mon, 15-30 Jan and 1-12 July. Open until 9.30 pm. Air cond. V AE.
This wonderful Templar commandery, transformed into a luxurious country inn, now boasts a lovely arched dining hall serving traditional dishes, like lotte à la vigneronne, pigeonneau en cocotte, and a thick slice of juicy veal with morels.
A la carte: 260-300 F. Menus: from 103 F to 235 F.

Wilson
72, rue du Pdt-Wilson — 65.35.41.80
Open every day. 36 rms 251-372 F. TV. Conference facilities. Parking. Telex 533721. V AE.

Modern and centrally located, this small yet well-equipped hotel offers a variety of services: sauna, exercise room, bar. TV dinners served in room.

In nearby Lamagdelaine

(7 km N on D 653)
46090 Cahors — (Lot)

Marco
65.35.30.64
M. Marco. Closed off-season Sun dinner and Mon, 5 Jan-3 March and Nov school holidays. Open until 9.30 pm. Terrace dining. Pool. Parking. V AE DC.

Claude Marco's mastery in the kitchen stems from long experience, endless energy, and a deep love of the land. In the garden-terrace of his gorgeous house, diners are served memorable dishes like foie gras Tatin in truffle juice, oxtail salad with balsamic vinegar, seafood salad with shellfish oil, and rabbit sausage à la royale, garnished with basil-flavoured pasta. Excellent cellar.

A la carte: 300-350 F. Menus: 100 F (weekdays only), 180 F, 260 F.

In nearby Laroque-des-Arcs

(6 km NE on D 653)
46090 Cahors — (Lot)

Les Deux Saisons
65.22.16.28
Mme Augros and M. Fallet. Closed Tue lunch, Mon and 1-27 March. Open until 9.15 pm. Hotel: 1 ste 235-310 F. 15 rms 180-250 F. Parking. V AE.

Don't be put off by the unappealing exterior. Jean-Jacques Fallet's panoramic restaurant, lush with greenery, serves delicious, expertly crafted dishes like a truffled dumpling ('mique') with celery vinaigrette, inspired from an ancient local recipe, and slightly underdone crépinettes of lamb fillet set atop a suave aubergine fondue, and a generous portion of croustillant chocopralin. Warm reception; good wine list. A toque this year.

A la carte: 250-300 F. Menus: from 110 F to 270 F.

In nearby Mercuès

(7 km N on N 20 and D 911)
46090 Cahors — (Lot)

Château de Mercuès
65.20.00.01
M. Buchin. Closed beg Nov to Easter. Open until 9.30 pm. Private room: 300. Terrace dining. Parking. Telex 521307. V AE DC.

The cooking is very conventional at this majestic château overlooking the Lot Valley, and the waiters are suitably stiff as they serve both truffle turnovers à la périgourdine and the aiguillettes de canard au miel et pignons de pin. But the chef seems to be attempting to introduce a few 'market-basket' dishes to the staid repertoire (fricassée of crayfish, bass in a salt crust, fresh fruit gratin, etc.), an effort which merits a toque of encouragement. Superb Cahors wines, including those made on the property.

A la carte: 350-400 F. Menus: 195 F, 285 F.

Remember to reserve your table or your room in advance, and please let the restaurant or hotel know if you cannot honour your reservation.

Château de Mercuès
(See restaurant above)
Closed beg Nov-Easter. 7 stes. 25 rms 540-1,700 F. TV. Conference facilities. Pool. Tennis.

Thirty rooms and suites, entirely redone, overlook a vast and marvellous landscape. Ask for the 'bishop's room' or the 'dungeon' with the sliding glass roof. Relais et Châteaux.

CALAIS
62100 Calais — (P./Calais)
Paris 305 - Amiens 155 - Arras 113 - Dunkerque 39

Bellevue
23-25, place d'Armes
21.34.53.75
Open every day. 2 stes 270-380 F. 54 rms 150-290 F. TV 42 rms. Conference facilities. Garage parking. Telex 136702. V AE DC.

The rooms of this hotel, opposite a watch-tower, are being renovated with admirable restraint.

12/20 Le Channel
3, bd de la Résistance — 21.34.42.30
M. Crespo. Closed Sun dinner, Tue, 20 Dec-18 Jan and 6-12 June. Open until 9.30 pm. Private room: 30. Air cond. V AE DC.

This large harbour-front restaurant offers a respectable seafood repertoire that includes the likes of crusty prawns in Nantais butter and turbot in hollandaise.

A la carte: 260 F. Menus: 70 F (weekdays only), 265 F (wine inc), 116 F, 152 F.

La Diligence
5, rue E.-Roche — 21.96.92.89
M. Coppin. Closed Mon lunch, Sun and 15-31 Aug. Open until 10 pm. Private room: 22. V AE DC.

Located in a quiet district, this elegant little establishment is well known to serious diners from both sides of the Channel. Recently, Patrick Coppin has added a more personal touch to his menu, with excellent dishes like the savoury chicken marinade served with a vegetable terrine, scampi feuilleté with Houlle gin, fillet of beef with a garnish of flavourful stewed oxtail.

A la carte: 300 F. Menus: 98 F, 190 F, 250 F.

Meurice
(See restaurant above)
Open every day. 4 stes 520-700 F. 40 rms 260-350 F. TV.

A blend of modern and 'Meurice'-styled rooms, all very well equipped, comfortable, quiet, and tastefully furnished. Breakfast is served in the winter garden. Hairdresser available; excellent reception.

12/20 La Duchesse
44, rue du Duc-de-Guise
21.97.59.69
M. Leroy. Closed Sat lunch. Open until 11 pm. Private room: 20. V AE DC.

The owner of this dainty little dining spot doubles as an expert sommelier, with a wine cellar that boasts 10,000 bottles and 200 kinds of whisky. The gorgeous fresh scallops in a sauce overladen with butter are a faithful reflection of the rich cuisine—the freshness of the produce deserves a much lighter touch. Extraordinary cheese board.

A la carte: 300 F. Menu: 160 F.

Garden Court
Bd des Alliés — 21.34.69.69
Open every day. 2 stes 590-630 F. 63 rms 340-420 F. Restaurant. TV. Conference facilities. Garage parking. Telex 135655. V AE DC.
A brand-new hotel, centrally located, with all the comforts of a Holiday Inn: modern and superbly equipped rooms; exercise room, sauna.

12/20 George V
36, rue Royale — 21.97.68.00
M. Beauvalot. Closed Sat lunch, Sun dinner and 23 Dec-4 Jan. Open until 9.30 pm. Private room: 60. Parking. Telex 135159. V AE DC.
In the neo-rustic décor of the George, a 'gastronomic' restaurant, the menu consists of a few decent, high-priced specialities: smoked-salmon cutlets with stewed chicory, a thick slice of Angus beef with wine-flavoured butter. Next door, the Petit George offers a varied, generous fixed-price meal of bistro-style fare (64 F for an appetiser and a main course).
A la carte: 300 F. Menus: 245 F (wine inc), 140 F.

George V
(See restaurant above)
Open every day. 45 rms 110-260 F. Half-board 210-280 F. TV 35 rms. Conference facilities.
Centrally located, with tidy, agreeable, soundproofed rooms.

Métropol'Hotel
45, quai du Rhin — 21.97.54.00
Open every day. 40 rms 160-320 F. TV. No pets. Conference facilities. Garage parking. Telex 135219. V AE DC.
Renovated in 1988, this discreet and efficiently run hotel in the centre of town has small, comfortable, well-appointed rooms. English bar.

CALA-ROSSA
See CORSICA: Porto-Vecchio

CALAS
13480 Calas — (B./Rhône)
Paris 770 - Aix-en-Provence 14 - Marseille 17

12/20 Auberge Bourrelly
42.69.13.13
M. Pons. Open every day. Open until 9.30 pm. Private room: 100. Garden dining. Hotel: 1 ste 750-960 F. 11 rms 380-460 F. Pool. Parking. Telex 403706. V AE DC.
Surrounded by trees and flowers, this magnificent country inn has four dining areas fitted out in a modern Provençal-style décor. The young chef does his best, but the cuisine does not rise above the ordinary: panaché of fish (nicely cooked) with small crisp vegetables, an honourable lotte with stewed fennel, pleasant grenadins de veau aux morilles, and a remarkably light pear feuilleté (but the accompanying custard sauce was about as light as the bill!).
A la carte: 350-400 F. Menus: 150 F, 195 F, 300 F.

CALÈS
46200 Calès — (Lot)
Paris 530 - Rocamadour 15 - Souillac 13 - Cahors 57

12/20 Pagès
Rte de Payrac — 65.37.95.87
MM. Pagès. Closed Tue off-season, 3 Jan-3 Feb and 15-30 Oct. Open until 9.30 pm. Private room: 12.
Garden dining. No pets. Hotel: 5 rms 160-260 F. Parking. V.
This lovely typically Quercynoise house boasts picturesque turrets and a park where, weather permitting, tables are laden with savoury regional dishes. An appetising 130 F set menu brings forth homemade truffled duck pâté, country ham, crudités, a delicious coq au vin made with white Cahors wine, local lamb with flageolets, cheeses, and superb fruit tarts. Warm reception and service.
A la carte: 200-250 F. Menus: 80 F, 130 F, 150 F, 170 F.

CALUIRE
See Lyon

CALVI
See CORSICA

CALVINET
15340 Calvinet — (Cantal)
Paris 582 - Aurillac 39 - Rodez 61 - Figeac 39

Le Beauséjour
Rte de Maurs
71.49.91.68
M. Puech. Closed off-season Sun dinner and Mon, and 15 Jan-15 March. Open until 9 pm. Private room: 20. Terrace dining. No pets. Hotel: 10 rms 200-240 F. Parking. V.
Extensive renovations have transformed this charming family-style *auberge* into a small hotel with ten comfortable new rooms. So feel free to linger over a leisurely dinner in the spacious dining room, or on the terrace that overlooks the green countryside of Cantal. Savour the chef's salmon with chanterelle mushrooms, stewed pigeon with blood sauce, perch in red wine with pea purée, and a scrumptious fondant praliné which Louis-Bernard Puech always inscribes on his generous set menus. Nice little cellar.
Menus: 80 F, 125 F, 160 F.

Le Relais de la Châtaigneraie
4 km S on D 19 and D 601
in Cassaniouze — 71.49.90.34
M. Guibert. Closed Wed dinner and 15 Oct-25 March. Open until 9 pm. Garden dining. Parking. V AE.
An elegant décor, a warm welcome, and superbly crafted cuisine more than make up for the undistinguished exterior of this modern village house. This year's specialities include artichokes à la barigoule and prawns with smoky bacon, a copious fricassée of salmon with cabbage and morels, roast pigeon scented with coriander, escorted by a foie-gras-stuffed cabbage leaf. Round out your meal with a smooth lemon-flavoured apple flan with brown sugar. Excellent set menus at unbeatable prices.
A la carte: 200-220 F. Menus: 75 F, 95 F, 145 F.

Le Relais de la Châtaigneraie
(See restaurant above)
Closed Wed (except July-Aug) and 15 Oct-25 March. 10 rms 110-160 F. Half-board 155-170 F.
Ten charming and restful rooms set amid the fields. Rudimentary bathrooms.

Problems with French? The RAC France language pack will help you to converse with confidence.

64250 Cambo-les-Bains — (Pyrénées-A.)
Paris 760 - Bayonne 20 - St-Jean-de-Luz 31

L'Epoque
[13] Allée A.-de-Neubourg — 59.29.25.03
M. Belleau. Closed Wed. Annual closings not available. Open until 10 pm. Garden dining. Parking. V AE.

In a spacious, centrally located Basque house, decorated in shades of blue, Patrick Belleau prepares a masterly salad of pan-fried prawns dressed in honey vinegar, with sweet and sour flavourings, a light and subtle steamed lotte with pink-peppercorn butter, and an intensely flavourful warm pear feuilleté with pear sorbet. Our only quibble: this good food ought really to be more generously apportioned.
A la carte: 250 F. Menus: 65 F, 120 F, 150 F.

Errobia
Av. Chantecler — 59.29.71.26
Closed 30 Oct-Easter. 2 stes 300 F. 15 rms 170-300 F. Parking. V.

A beautiful, family-style Basque house overlooking a valley, with large and rustic rooms (floorboards squeak less on the second floor). Pretty views.

Le Relais de la Poste
Pl. de la Mairie — 59.29.73.03
Closed off-season Sun and Mon, and Jan. 10 rms 230-280 F. Restaurant. Half-board 380 F. TV. No pets. Parking. V AE DC.

Good reception, service, and comfort in this turn-of-the-century family boarding house. Small, quiet rooms.

59400 Cambrai — (Nord)
Paris 170 - Arras 36 - Saint-Quentin 33 - Lille 63

Beatus
718, av. de Paris — 27.81.45.70
Open every day. 26 rms 260-300 F. TV. Garage parking. Telex 820597. V AE DC.

A long one-storey building currently being enlarged. Quiet, dainty rooms done in Louis XV and Louis XVI styles. Agreeable garden; friendly service.

12/20 Château de La Motte Fénelon
Sq. du Château — 27.83.61.38
Mlle Brunet. Closed dinner Sun and holidays. Open until 9.30 pm. Private room: 260. Parking. Telex 120285. V AE DC.

A big and beautiful castle used chiefly for conferences and receptions. The casual trade is assigned tables in the elegantly arched dining room, and is served pomme boulangère gourmande au caviar, or scallops with bone marrow and fresh pasta in wine sauce.
A la carte: 300-350 F. Menus: 170 F (Sun only, wine inc), 140 F, 190 F.

Château de La Motte Fénelon
(See restaurant above)
Open every day. 28 rms 250-470 F. TV. Conference facilities. Tennis.

The six rooms in the château are infinitely more desirable than the ageing, bungalow-style accommodation in the park. The well-maintained wooded grounds boast two tennis courts.

12/20 Le Crabe-Tambour
52, rue de Cantimpré — 27.83.10.18
M. Robinet. Closed Mon, dinner Sun and holidays, 2-10 Jan and 24 July-24 Aug. Open until 9.30 pm. V.

The catch of the day from Boulogne finds its way in a matter of hours into the saucepots and pans of Mr Robinet, who serves his guests, comfortably seated in a pleasant décor of flower-decked tables, such delectable dishes as choucroute aux poissons and grouper fillet in a peppery sabayon sauce. Friendly welcome and service.
A la carte: 250 F. Menus: 95 F, 150 F.

See CORSICA

See Deauville

35260 Cancale — (Ille/Vil.)
Paris 360 - Saint-Malo 14 - Dinan 34 - Rennes 72

12/20 L'Armada
8, quai Thomas — 99.89.60.02
M. Perrigault. Closed Sun dinner and Mon (except July-Aug), Feb and 1-8 June. Lunch only in winter. Open until 8.30 pm. Terrace dining. V.

This newly renovated restaurant overlooking the bay of Mont-St-Michel specialises in seafood. Sample the gorgeous Cancale oysters, nut-sized scallops au beurre blanc, and fillets of sole à la Gaëlle with celery purée. The ingredients are fine and fresh, but the sauces could stand some improvement.
A la carte: 200 F. Menus: 90 F (weekdays only), 110 F, 170 F.

12/20 Le Cancalais
12, quai Gambetta — 99.89.61.93
Mme Bouchard. Closed 10 Dec-18 Jan. Open until 9.15 pm. Hotel: 8 rms 140-240 F. V.

The covered terrace with a view of the port is the most attractive in town. Fresh, somewhat ambitious cuisine: tasty minced salmon boldly seasoned with chives, lotte with pink peppercorns and an overly creamy saffron-flavoured sauce, and a chocolate bavarian awkwardly presented on a plate too small to accommodate the custard sauce.
A la carte: 220 F. Menu: 94 F (weekdays only).

12/20 Le Continental
4, quai A.-Thomas — 99.89.60.16
M. Chouamier. Closed Tue lunch, Mon and 4-21 March. Open until 9.30 pm. Terrace dining. No pets. Hotel: 19 rms 300-570 F. V AE DC.

The chef of this attractive clubhouse-style restaurant opposite Houle harbour uses only first-class ingredients in the preparation of a very classic menu that features a cool smoked-haddock salad, superb traditional sole meunière and generous grilled noisettes of lamb. Fine selection of white wines. Warm welcome, but the service is slow.
A la carte: 250 F. Menus: 132 F, 220 F.

12/20 L'Emeraude
7, quai A.-Thomas — 99.89.61.76
M. Chouamier. Closed Thu off-season, 15 Nov-15 Feb, 11-22 March. Open until 9.30 pm. Terrace dining. V.

The *patron* breeds his own oysters and the seafood is always fresh in this cheerful harbour-front bistro. Enjoy the view from the terrace along

Restaurant de Bacon
Bd de Bacon — 93.61.50.02

M. Sordello. Closed off-season Sun dinner and Mon and 18 Nov-31 Jan. Open until 9 pm (10.30 pm in summer). Air cond. No pets. Valet parking. V AE DC.

For many years now, and for reasons unknown, the Sordello brothers have had access to the best and rarest Mediterrean fish available on the market, and their chef, Serge Philippin, knows exceedingly well how best to prepare them. Simply stated, his bouillabaisse is the best in the world. And then there's the magnificent tarragon-scented fricassée of tiny red-mullet sautéed with raw spinach, crisp green beans, tomatoes, herbs, walnuts, and little fried artichokes. And of course there is the bracing raw-fish salad bright with lemon and herbs, a superb John Dory en papillote, and truffled fish consommé. The freshly painted dining room is lavished with flowers, and the large terrace affords a wonderful view of the mountains and sea.

A la carte: 700 F. Menus: 350 F (weekdays lunch only), 450 F (lunch only).

See also: **Antibes**

CAP-FERRET

33970 Cap-Ferret — (Gironde)
Paris 653 - Bordeaux 71 - Arcachon 69

10/20 Le Mirador
La Pointe — 56.60.64.19

M. Texier. Closed Tue off-season and 1-15 Dec. Open until 9 pm (10 pm in summer). Garden dining. Parking. V.

One comes here for an unparalleled view of the Bassin d'Arcachon, and for decent (if boring) seafood: grilled fish, lotte with sweet peppers, and good shellfish. Drab décor.

A la carte: 200 F. Menus: 65 F, 100 F, 135 F.

10/20 Les Quatre Saisons
Av. de l'Océan — 56.60.68.13

Mlle David. Closed Mon and 30 Nov-1 March. Open until 8.30 pm. Garden dining. Hotel: 15 rms 90-220 F. V.

Unpretentious, reasonably priced seafood served in a tidy boarding-house atmosphere (checked tablecloths...). Among the better bets are the stuffed oysters, mussels quatre saisons, and the bass with fennel.

A la carte: 150-200 F. Menus: 70 F, 85 F, 130 F.

CARANTEC

29660 Carantec — (Finistère)
Paris 546 - Brest 65 - Saint-Pol-de-Léon 10

12/20 La Falaise
Plage du Kélenn — 98.67.00.53

M. Guillerm. Closed 22 Sep-Easter. Open until 8.30 pm. No pets. Parking.

This well-run establishment, with its garden and terrace overlooking Morlaix Bay, primarily features seafood specialities like the croustillant of prawns and lobster, warm shellfish salad, and a seafood pot-au-feu with lemon-flavoured butter. Affordable prices.

A la carte: 200 F. Menus: 90 F, 145 F, 180 F.

La Falaise
(See restaurant above)

sed 22 Sep to Easter. 24 rms 125-205 F. Half-ard 183-225 F oblig in seas. No pets.

Twenty or so rooms periodically upgraded for comfort.

Pors-Pol
7-9, rue Surcouf — 98.67.00.52

Closed 20 Sep-25 March and 10 April-8 May. 30 rms 84-217 F. Restaurant. Half-board 140-201 F. Parking. V.

Restful, family-style accommodation, with renovated rooms overlooking the sea.

CARBON-BLANC

See Bordeaux

CARCASSONNE

11000 Carcassonne — (Aude)
Paris 905 - Perpignan 107 - Toulouse 92 - Albi 107

Auberge du Pont-Levis

near Porte Narbonnaise — 68.25.55.23

M. Pautard. Closed Sun dinner. Annual closings not available. Open until 9.30 pm. Private room: 40. Garden dining. Air cond. No pets. Parking. V AE DC.

Thierry Pautard's son, Olivier, has taken over the kitchen from his dad and is asserting himself with ably prepared regional dishes like parsleyed rabbit with onion marmalade, ragoût de langoustines, lamb with a rich deglazing sauce, all accompanied by splendid desserts. Courteous and attentive service; tempting, well-designed set menus.

A la carte: 280-330 F. Menus: 140 F (weekdays only), 180 F, 250 F.

Château Saint-Martin

(Logis de Trencavel)
4 km NE, in Montredon — 68.71.09.53

M. Rodriguez. Closed Wed. Open until 9.30 pm. Private room: 150. Garden dining. Parking. V AE DC.

Don't order the cassoulet, or like one reader you may leave the château disappointed. Choose instead the coquilles St-Jacques à l'huile de Bize, veal kidney with a fortified wine sauce, or the saupiquet de pigeonneau. Desserts include an exemplary apple cake. Beautiful dining room, splendid garden, reasonable prices.

A la carte: 280-350 F. Menus: 160 F, 200 F, 260 F.

Cité
in La Cité
Pl. de l'Eglise — 68.25.03.34

Open every day. 3 stes 1,200-1,500 F. 52 rms 450-950 F. TV. Air cond. Conference facilities. Heated pool. Valet parking. Telex 505296. V AE DC.

Extensive restoration accounts for the elegant comfort of the rooms and suites in this gorgeous, thoughtfully equipped little luxury hotel. The grand lounge and library are utterly smashing. Uncommonly attentive service. A gastronomic restaurant is planned for the not-too-distant future.

Domaine d'Auriac

4 km SW
in Auriac, rte de St-Hilaire — 68.25.72.22

M. Rigaudis. Closed off-season Sun dinner and Mon lunch, and 14 Jan-3 Feb. Open until 9.15 pm. Private room: 90. Garden dining. Valet parking. Telex 500385. V AE DC.

The elegant dining room of the Rigaudis' large nineteenth-century house, with its view of the mulberry trees that shade the terrace, exudes an aura of friendliness and distinction. Chef Bernard Rigaudis has enlarged his culinary repertoire which, in essence, remains regional though many dishes display a new lightness. Witness a fresh-tasting herbed tartare of sea bream and oysters, marvellous pan-fried John Dory, its juices quickly deglazed with a dash of blueberry wine, a succulent truffled pigeon poached en vessie with rich Banyuls wine, and an exceptional cassoulet.

Among the superb desserts are a fragrant fruit soup laced with Muscat, and an apple soufflé spiked with Armagnac. Remarkable cellar, featuring rare regional bottlings.
A la carte: 400-460 F. Menus: 200 F, 300 F, 380 F.

Domaine d'Auriac
(See restaurant above)
Closed Sun off-season, and 14 Jan-3 Feb. 23 rms 980-1,580 F (per pers, half-board oblig). TV. Air cond 18 rms. Conference facilities. Pool. Tennis. Golf.
The comfortable, stylish rooms are gradually being upgraded for added elegance. Irreproachable breakfasts; delightful reception. Relais et Châteaux.

11/20 Le Donjon
4, rue du Comte-Roger (La Cité)
68.71.08.80
Mme Pujol. Dinner only. Closed Sun. Open until 9.30 pm. Private room: 15. Garden dining. Air cond. No pets. Valet parking. Telex 505012. V AE DC.
Currently under construction in view of enlargement.
A la carte: 250 F. Menus: 110 F, 185 F.

Le Donjon
(See restaurant above)
Open every day. 36 rms 265-420 F. Half-board 417-467 F. TV. Air cond 8 rms. Conference facilities.
A beautiful old building, charmingly restored, with small and very comfortable rooms decorated with restraint. Delightful walled garden.

12/20 Le Languedoc
32, allée d'Iéna – 68.25.22.17
MM. Faugeras. Closed Sun dinner off-season, Mon and 20 Dec-20 Jan. Open until 9.30 pm. Private room: 30. Garden dining. Air cond. Telex 505261. V AE DC.
The Faugeras family takes great care in preparing simple, regional dishes (bourride sétoise, cassoulet au confit, crêpes flambées Languedoc), and are constantly improving the restaurant's décor—the new garden patio is lovely.
A la carte: 280-330 F. Menus: 160 F, 220 F, 280 F.

Le Montmorency
2, rue C.-St-Saëns – 68.25.19.92
Open every day. 1 ste 500 F. 23 rms 200-270 F. TV. Conference facilities. Pool. Valet parking. V AE DC.
Situated just opposite the Cité's main entrance, this hotel has small, tidy and well-appointed rooms, several of which are furnished with antiques. Breakfast is served on the terrace.

Montségur
27, allée d'Iéna – 68.25.31.41
Open every day. 21 rms 260-440 F. Restaurant. Half-board 340-420 F. TV. Air cond 7 rms. Conference facilities. Parking. Telex 505261. V AE DC.
A large nineteenth-century manor house updated for comfort with spacious, soundproof rooms. Round-the-clock service. (For restaurant, see Le Languedoc)

11/20 Le Terminus
(Le Relais de l'Ecluse)
2, av. du Mal-Joffre – 68.25.13.77
M. Tort. Open every day. Open until 9.45 pm. Private room: 200. Parking. Telex 505060. V.
Busloads of tourists flock to this spacious dining room for decent regional dishes, the best of which are the duck liver with grapes and beef fillet Pro-

sper Montagné. Inexpensive local wines.
A la carte: 170-250 F. Menus: from 75 F to 170 F.

Terminus
2, av. du Mal-Joffre – 68.25.25.00
Open every day. 2 stes 510-590 F. 112 rms 230-410 F. TV 78 rms. Air cond 2 rms. Conference facilities. Garage parking. Telex 500198. V AE DC.
A few of the large and constantly renovated rooms in this grand old hotel are furnished with English antiques. Splendid lobby; conference facilities; numerous European TV channels.

La Vicomté
near porte Narbonnaise
18, rue C.-St-Saëns – 68.71.45.45
Open every day. 3 stes 645-845 F. 60 rms 315-420 F. Half-board 350 F. TV. Air cond. Conference facilities. Heated pool. Valet parking. Telex 500303. V AE DC.
The well-appointed rooms (soundproofing, video, safe) afford splendid views of the ramparts.

46110 Carennac — (Lot)
Paris 530 - Cahors 78 - St-Céré 18 - Tulle 58

11/20 Auberge du Vieux Quercy
in Vayrac – 65.38.69.00
M. Chaumeil. Closed Mon off-season, and mid-Nov to mid-Feb. Open until 9 pm. Private room: 10. Garden dining. Parking. V.
A former coaching inn, this charming old house with a large dining room and terrace offers a roster of regional dishes (confit de canard, magret, truffled omelette), as well as some interesting fish dishes, like the excellent marinated halibut with pink peppercorns. The owner's welcome is not notable for its warmth.
A la carte: 200 F. Menus: 60 F, 82 F, 108 F, 145 F, 195 F.

Auberge du Vieux Quercy
(See restaurant above)
Closed mid-Nov to mid-Feb. 3 stes 500 F. 32 rms 200-250 F. TV 14 rms. Conference facilities. Pool.
Located in the heart of this medieval village, the Auberge offers beautiful, sparkling new, soundproof rooms. Generous breakfasts. Courteous reception.

50500 Carentan — (Manche)
Paris 293 - Cherbourg 50 - Bayeux 42 - Caen 69

13 Auberge Normande
17, bd de Verdun – 33.42.02.99
M. Guittard. Closed Sun dinner and Mon. Open until 9.30 pm. Private room: 15. Parking. V AE.
Though it stands right by the main road, this big old red-brick restaurant, dripping with ivy, has undeniable charm. It belongs to a serious chef bent on using only the finest ingredients. Consistent, ably prepared specialities include light, well-balanced scrambled eggs with shrimps, delicious cod stuffed with red-mullet and shrimps, and perfectly cooked sweetbreads with mushrooms. A knowledgeable wine-lover obviously designed the detailed and reasonably priced wine list; charming reception.
A la carte: 300 F and up. Menus: 85 F (weekdays only), and from 130 F to 290 F.

CARGÈSE
See CORSICA

CARNAC
56340 Carnac — (Morbihan)
Paris 481 - Quiberon 18 - Auray 13 - Vannes 31

Le Bateau Ivre
71, bd de la Plage — 97.52.19.55
Open every day. 3 stes 700 F. 20 rms 350-700 F. Restaurant. Half-board 390-520 F oblig in seas. TV. Heated pool. Garage parking. V AE.
A modern seafront hotel with small rooms equipped with kitchenettes, showers, and terraces that face south. Lovely rock garden; decent breakfasts; lukewarm reception.

Le Diana
21, bd de la Plage — 97.52.05.38
Closed mid-Nov to Easter. 1 ste 1,100 F. 32 rms 500-970 F. Restaurant. Half-board 630-775 F oblig in seas. TV. Conference facilities. Heated pool. Tennis. Valet parking. Telex 951035. V DC.
This beachfront hotel features comfortable, regularly renovated rooms, some of which have balconies. Swimming pool and fitness centre.

Novotel Carnac-Plage
Av. de l'Atlantique — 97.52.53.00
Closed Jan. 110 rms 395-620 F. Restaurant. Half-board 390-660 F. TV. Air cond. Conference facilities. Heated pool. Parking. Telex 950324. V AE DC.
A modern, comfortable, functional hotel near the beach, with spacious rooms and tiny, yet well-equipped bathrooms. Thalassotherapy (sea cure) centre.

Le Relais du Sporting
Av. des Druides — 97.52.98.35
Closed 15 Nov-15 March. 8 rms 290-330 F. Restaurant. Half-board 257-277 F oblig in seas. TV 4 rms. Tennis. V.
This hotel, within easy reach of the Beaumer Bay beach has bright, simply furnished rooms. Two tennis courts.

CAROLLES
50740 Carolles — (Manche)
Paris 354 - St-Lô 67 - Avranches 20 - Granville 11

12/20 Le Relai de la Diligence
33.61.86.42
M. Anger. Closed off-season Sun dinner and Mon, 8-22 Jan and 30 Sep-14 Oct. Open until 9.30 pm. Private room: 60. Garden dining No pets. Hotel: 36 rms 90-150 F. Parking. V.
A toque is just within chef Laurent Anger's grasp for the energy he has injected into this delightful old family-style inn, and for his delicate, classic cuisine. Sample the salmon marinated in dill, pollack fillet in a subtle shellfish coulis, and an ethereal yet crisp strawberry feuilleté. Good selection of Burgundies and Bordeaux; warm reception; attentive service.
A la carte: 180-250 F. Menus: 45 F (lunch only, wine inc), 90 F, 120 F, 140 F.

The new spiral-bound RAC Atlas France will help you to find your chosen restaurant of hotel, no matter how secluded.

CARPENTRAS
84200 Carpentras — (Vaucluse)
Paris 683 - Cavaillon 26 - Avignon 23 - Aix 82

Fiacre
153, rue Vigne — 90.63.03.15
Open every day. 20 rms 175-340 F. TV 10 rms. Conference facilities. Valet parking. V AE DC.
Quiet, yet centrally located in an eighteenth-century town house, the Fiacre boasts spacious, stylish rooms that look out on an agreeable patio.

12/20 L'Orangerie
26, rue Duplessis — 90.67.27.23
MM. Trillat and Pala. Closed Sat lunch. Open until 9.45 pm. Private room: 12. Garden dining. Air cond. V AE DC.
A small and charming establishment with a 1930s décor and an attractive garden-courtyard. The young yet quite accomplished chef turns out scrambled eggs studded with local truffles, salmon prepared in beer with fennel, and a pleasing beef fillet with a slight hint of liquorice. He will doubtless recover his predecessor's toque in record time.
A la carte: 250 F. Menus: 74 F (weekdays only), 100 F, 128 F, 188 F.

Safari-Hôtel
Av. J.-H.-Fabre — 90.63.35.35
Open every day. 42 rms 330-350 F. Restaurant. Half-board 310 F oblig in seas. TV. Air cond. Conference facilities. Pool. Tennis. Parking. Telex 431533. V AE DC.
Set in pleasant grounds outside of the town's centre, this hotel offers recently remodelled, perfectly equipped rooms. There are also studios to let with kitchenettes. Fitness centre (gym, body-building gear, etc.).

12/20 Le Vert Galant
12, rue de Clapies — 90.67.15.50
M. Mégean. Closings not available. Open until 10 pm. V.
Some bright watercolours enliven the otherwise plain dining room of this fine old Provençal house. Chef Jacques Mégean's professional touch and penchant for straightforward flavours are evident in the generously served terrine de poularde au foie gras, red-mullet in a delicate curry-scented sauce, and vanilla-flavoured crème brûlée. Service is a bit coltish, and the cellar needs broadening (but both of these slight problems are being attended to, we're told).
Menus: 89 F (weekdays lunch only), 140 F, 190 F.

In nearby Barroux
(11 km N on D 938)
84330 Carpentras — (Vaucluse)

12/20 Les Géraniums
90.62.41.08
M. Roux. Closed Wed off-season, and 3 Jan-15 Feb. Open until 9 pm. Garden dining. Garage parking. V AE DC.
In his immaculate dining room, decked in geranium-red walls and napery, the chef offers good, carefully prepared regional dishes such as rabbit with summer savory, kid roasted with rosemary, and chicken with crayfish. Splendid view of the Carpentras plains.
A la carte: 220-250 F. Menus: 70 F (weekdays only), 120 F, 160 F.

Les Géraniums
(See restaurant above)
Closed Wed off-season, and 3 Jan-15 Feb. 22 rms 170-210 F. Half-board 260-320 F. Conference facilities.

A small and pleasant hotel with impeccably clean rooms and lovely terraces where breakfast is served. Warm reception; friendly service.

In nearby Monteux

(5 km SW on D 942)
84170 Carpentras — (Vaucluse)

Blason de Provence
Rte de Carpentras — 90.66.31.34
Closed 15 Dec-15 Jan. 20 rms 250-350 F. Restaurant. Half-board 280-310 F oblig in seas. TV. Air cond 1 rm. Conference facilities. Pool. Tennis. Parking. Telex 432770. V AE DC.

A pleasant family-style Provençal establishment set in extensive grounds, featuring comfortable rooms of which five have been entirely remodelled.

Le Saule Pleureur
Quartier Beauregard — 90.62.01.35
M. Philibert. Closed Tue dinner (except July-Aug), Wed, 3 weeks in March and 15 days in Oct. Open until 9.30 pm. Private room: 24. Garden dining. Parking. V AE.

The dining room décor is plain though comfortable, but the garden and flowers are lovely, and plans are afoot to build an enclosed veranda so that diners may rejoice in the view. Michel Philibert, a young chef of distinction, presents a concise (but oft-revised) menu that reveals but an inkling of his culinary skills. For a better idea of his talents, one must visit the restaurant often, as do local gourmets who flock here for his 'all-truffle' set menus, his salads flavoured with aniseed, his red-mullet pot-au-feu, in which the lightly grilled fillets are garnished with locally grown vegetables sprinkled with coarse salt, for his veal kidneys and sweetbreads in lavender honey, steamed capon seasoned with a dash of olive oil, roast pigeon in pistou sauce and, among other fabulous desserts, his marvellous crème brûlée with basil and thyme. Excellent cellar of Côtes-du-Rhônes, which perfectly complement this fragrant, lusty cuisine.
A la carte: 400 F. Menus: 178 F, 260 F, 350 F.

In nearby Saint-Didier

(6 km SE on D 4 and D 39)
84210 Carpentras — (Vaucluse)

Les Trois Colombes
Av. des Garrigues — 90.66.07.01
Closed 3 Jan-2 March. 1 ste. 25 rms 260-310 F. Restaurant. Half-board 250-280 F oblig in seas. TV. Conference facilities. Pool. Tennis. Parking. Telex 431067. V AE DC.

Located in a lush green setting, this large, recently built hotel offers comfortable, restful rooms. Covered terrace by the swimming pool.

In nearby Venasque

(11 km SE on D 4)
84210 Carpentras — (Vaucluse)

Auberge La Fontaine
Pl. de la Fontaine — 90.66.02.96
M. Soehlke. Dinner only (and Sun lunch). Closed Wed, Feb school holidays and mid-Nov to mid-Dec. Open until 10 pm. Telex 432770. V.

Housed in a massive eighteenth-century manor in the heart of an old papal village, this charmingly furnished restauant features fresh, full-flavoured dishes in a rustic mode: assiette du pêcheur, sautéed roe deer, and a thin, tasty tarte Tatin baked by the proprietress herself. Excellent wine cellar; somewhat stiff reception.
Menu: 180 F.

Auberge La Fontaine
(See restaurant above)
Closed Feb school holidays. 5 stes 650-750 F. TV. Air cond.

Centrally located and pleasantly furnished, with five new perfectly equipped, air-conditioned suites that include kitchens, dining and living rooms. Fireplaces and terraces add to the charm. Family atmosphere.

83320 Carqueiranne — (Var)
Paris 850 - Toulon 14 - Hyères 10 - Draguignan 82

La Restanque
18, av. J.-Jaurès — 94.58.62.33
M. Doki-Thonon. Closed Tue dinner, Wed and 15-30 Nov. Open until 10 pm. Private room: 15. Terrace dining. V AE.

Serge Doki-Thonon hails from the Réunion Islands. His comfortable dining room, is decked out with artifacts from his homeland, and his cooking has a bright, exotic touch (which we would like to see emphasised). Sample his fresh and generous crab and shrimp salad with ginger, the firm, beautifully cooked grouper fillets served with a fennel-flavoured mousseline and a courgette flan, and farm-bred chicken breast in a good (but banal) spicy sauce of curry and coconut. Astute wine list; the staff is friendly, but shy.
A la carte: 200-250 F. Menus: 79 F, 125 F, 190 F.

CARROZ-D'ARACHES (LES)
74300 Carroz-d'Araches (Les) — (H.-Savoie)
Paris 596 - Annecy 73 - Chamonix 51 - Morzine 33

La Croix de Savoie
50.90.00.26
Closed 15 April-15 June and 15 Sep-15 Dec. 19 rms 190-260 F. Restaurant. Half-board 240-300 F oblig in seas. No pets. Parking. V.

A pleasant Savoyard chalet set amid the pines. Fairly comfortable rooms with with superb terrace-balconies.

Aux Petits Oignons
Résidence L'Edelweiss — 50.90.36.93
M. Plagneux. Closed Tue dinner, Wed and 20 Nov-20 Dec. Open until 10 pm. Private room: 25. No-smoking section. Parking. V.

The dining room in this turn-of-the-century residential chalet is as elegantly refined as Frédéric Benoît's cuisine, which is modern and precisely prepared. Among his subtly conceived dishes are lotte terrine in aspic, scallops fricassée with basil, lotte in rum butter, and a whole range of delicious desserts (assorted sorbets with berry coulis). Professional, rather stiff reception and service.
A la carte: 200 F. Menus: 85 F, 150 F, 200 F.

For all the essential motoring information when driving in Europe, refer to the RAC European Motoring Guide.

CARRY-LE-ROUET

13620 Carry-le-Rouet — (B./Rhône)
Paris 768 - Salon 51 - Aix 40 - Marseille 27

L'Escale

Prom. du Port — 42.45.00.47

M. Clor. Closed Mon (lunch only in July-Aug), Sun dinner and 15 Nov-10 Feb. Open until 9.30 pm. Terrace dining. V.

An occasional slip appears in chef Gérard Clor's otherwise superb repertoire—the stuffed young rabbit in leek coulis literally pales compared to the lamb noisettes with Oriental spices— but it's really the seafood served in this charming art deco setting that accounts for our 16/20 rating. Some of the more attractive offerings have a sunny Southern lilt, like the superbly fragrant canetole (a local fish) de la Côte Bleue, the full-flavoured version of bourride de baudroie, a classic sea bass fillet with spices, or braised turbotin and apples with sautéed sea urchin. Exquisite desserts, superb location. Relais et Châteaux.

A la carte: 450-550 F. Menu: 260 F (weekdays only).

CARTERET

See Barneville-Carteret

CASSEL

59670 Cassel — (Nord)
Paris 253 - Lille 53 - Dunkerque 29 - Saint-Omer 21

Le Sauvage

38, Grand-Place — 28.42.40.88

M. Decaestecker. Closed Wed, dinner Sun and Tue, and 4-25 Feb. Open until 9.30 pm. Private room: 100. Terrace dining. Telex 132182. V AE.

At long last, Willy Decaestecker has committed himself to upgrade the worn décor of his panoramic restaurant atop Mont Cassel. Regional dishes abound on the menu: potjevfleisch (gelée of chicken, veal, pork and rabbit) spiked with gin and garnished with stewed pears, and civet de cuisses de canard à la bière des Trois-Monts. Good cellar; alert service.

A la carte: 250-300 F. Menus: 99 F (weekdays only), 199 F, 275 F.

CASSIS

13260 Cassis — (B./Rhône)
Paris 803 - Toulon 44 - Marseille 23 - Aubagne 14

Le Cassitel

Pl. Clemenceau — 42.01.83.44

Open every day. 32 rms 210-270 F. TV. Garage parking. V AE.

A small, hospitable hotel near the port. Its location is convenient, but the rooms are not absolutely quiet. Direct telephone in the rooms.

Les Jardins du Campanile

Rue A.-Favier — 42.01.84.85

Closed 31 Oct-28 Feb. 1 ste 750-900 F. 35 rms 330-590 F. Restaurant. TV 15 rms. No pets. Conference facilities. Pool. Tennis. Parking. Telex 441390. V AE DC.

This hotel, with its garden and swimming pool, evokes a Provençal summer home, complete with bougainvilleas and lemon trees.

La Presqu'île

Quartier de Port-Miou — 42.01.03.77

Mme Bertolotti. Closed Sun dinner, Mon (except dinner in July-Aug) and 3 Jan-1 March. Open until
10 pm. Private room: 80. Terrace dining. Tennis. Parking. V AE DC.

A victim of last summer's conflagration, this charming house nestled in between the sea, pine forest and cliffs, is to be re-built this spring exactly as before, enabling diners to savour Alain Coulaud's flavourful little farcis provençaux, fresh tunny tartare spiced with coriander, chicken with mildly garlicky tomatoes, rosace of sweetbreads with yams, and his amazing desserts (an exquisite pear pastilla with a sauce that combines honey and lime) which earned him two toques.

A la carte: 300-350 F. Menus: 195 F, 295 F.

Les Roches Blanches

Rte des Calanques — 42.01.09.30

Closed Jan. 35 rms 174-558 F. Restaurant. Half-board 364-744 F oblig in seas. TV. Conference facilities. Heated pool. Valet parking. Telex 441287. V AE DC.

This agreeable, remarkably well-situated establishment on the Cassis headlands offers small, modern, comfortable rooms. Lovely multi-tiered terraces; solarium; private beach.

CASTELLET (LE)

83330 Castellet (Le) — (Var)
Paris 820 - Marseille 45 - Toulon 20 - La Ciotat 18

Castel Lumière

Le Portail — 94.32.62.20

M. Laffargue. Closed Sun dinner, Mon and 2 Nov-2 Dec. Open until 9.30 pm (10.30 pm in summer). Private room: 20. Garden dining. Hotel: 6 rms 350-375 F. V AE DC.

Bernard Laffargue's latest restaurant offers spectacular panoramic views in addition to ably prepared Provençal-inspired cuisine. First-rate ingredients set his estouffade of wild mushrooms, saffron-flavoured seafood medley, and Sisteron lamb in pastry apart from other versions. The sauces, however, could stand some improvement. Desserts are uneven. Stiff but professional service; superb cellar. The prix-fixe meals are worthwhile and affordably priced.

A la carte: 350-450 F. Menus: 160 F (in summer only), 180 F, 220 F, 380 F.

CASTELNAU-LE-LEZ

See Montpellier

CASTILLON-DU-GARD

30210 Castillon-du-Gard — (Gard)
Paris 690 - Nîmes 25 - Avignon 27 - Pont-du-Gard 4

Serge Lanoix

Pl. 8-Mai-1945 — 66.37.05.04

M. Lanoix. Closed off-season Wed lunch and Tue, and 3 Jan-3 March. Open until 10 pm. Terrace dining. Air cond. V AE DC.

After wandering from kitchen to kitchen all over France (including stints at the Rôtisserie du Chambertin in Burgundy and another with pastry guru Gaston Lenôtre), Serge Lanoix has returned to the still unspoiled Provençal village where he spent his youth. A judicious move. Lanoix's formerly heavy, opulent style has lightened considerably, and that's all to the good. We were dazzled by the Southern lightness and freshness of his new repertoire: duck liver quickly seared then enhanced with truffle jus and a spark of redcurrant; barely poached oysters discreetly scented with ginger, a spice that points up the bracing sea-freshness of the shellfish; fat boudinets of Uzès truffles astutely paired with a tarragon-flavoured cream. Even classics like poached lobster in sea-urchin sauce, and a simple saddle of lamb served with its roasting juices have been given a sunny slant. Unfussy but flawless desserts (Lenôtre, remember?) follow superbly matured cheeses (excellent Epoisses). The cellar is rich in Burgundies, somewhat deficient in local bottlings. Service has improved immeasurably, thanks to an able new maître d'hôtel. Just twenty patrons at a sitting can be accommodated in the minuscule dining room (decorated with vividly coloured paintings by Lanoix's godfather), so be sure to book ahead.

A la carte: 320 F. Menus: 130 F (weekdays lunch only), 195 F, 250 F, 295 F.

Le Vieux Castillon
|15| 66.37.00.77
M. Traversac. Closed beg Jan-beg March. Open until 9 pm. Private room: 60. Air cond. Parking. Telex 490946. V.
After the costly restoration of these Huguenot village dwellings with vaulted arches and arcades, diners now enjoy a marvellous setting in which to sample chef Gilles Dauteuil's festival of flavours: try the lemon-sole salad in scented oils, skate in basil with tart tomatoes, roast rabbit with coriander garnished with an aubergine mould, and a crêpe 'beggar's purse' filled with mousse de marc de Châteauneuf. The cellar offers a wide range of Côtes-du-Rhônes to harmonise with the cuisine.

A la carte: 350-400 F. Menus: 260 F, 330 F, 390 F.

Le Vieux Castillon
(See restaurant above)
Closed Jan-beg March. 2 stes 1,230-1,350 F. 33 rms 600-1,230 F. Half-board 670-985 F (for 2 pers) Air cond 13 rms. Conference facilities. Pool. Tennis.
Comfortable, charmingly furnished rooms, with a view of either the Rhône Valley or an indoor garden. Excellent breakfasts; magnificent swimming pool. Relais et Châteaux.

CASTIRLA
See CORSICA: Corte

CAUDEBEC-EN-CAUX
76490 Caudebec-en-Caux — (Seine-Mar.)
Paris 175 - Rouen 36 - Yvetot 12 - Pont-Audemer 28

Manoir de Retival
|14| 2, rue Saint-Clair — 35.96.11.22
M. Tartarin. Closed Tue lunch and Mon. Annual closings not available. Open until 10 pm. Private room: 25. No pets. Hotel: 7 rms 300-600 F. Parking. V AE DC.
Jean-Luc Tartarin's refined, original cuisine has managed to save this nearly abandoned, yet charmingly eccentric building that overlooks the Seine. Worthy of your attention are his crab ravioli in basil, roast lotte paired with prawns in seaweed, John Dory cooked with thyme and bay leaves inserted under its skin, and a feuilleté flavoured with green tea and liquorice. The dining room is to be completely refurbished this year.

A la carte: 350-400 F. Menus: 150 F (weekdays lunch only), 275 F.

12/20 Normotel
(La Marine)
18, quai Guilbaud — 35.96.20.11
Mme Lefebvre. Closed Sun dinner, Mon and 2-28 Jan. Open until 9 pm. Parking. Telex 770404. V.
This formerly famous restaurant by the Seine, with its slightly pompous décor, carries on with dishes like a good salmon bavarois spoiled by a sauce with an overdose of mustard, delicious duck

breast with cranberries, and an exquisite fresh fruit gratin.

A la carte: 270 F. Menus: 58 F (weekdays lunch only), 88 F (weekdays only), 120 F, 158 F, 195 F.

Normotel
(See restaurant above)
Closed Sun and 2-28 Jan. 29 rms 235-295 F. Half-board 310-380 F. TV. Conference facilities.
A new name for this hotel with recently renovated rooms overlooking the Seine.

CAUTERETS
65110 Cauterets — (H.-Pyrénées)
Paris 829 - Tarbes 50 - Lourdes 30

12/20 Les Marmottes
Av. du Gal-Leclerc — 62.92.60.00
M. Wagner. Closed 12 May-1 June and 1 Oct-15 Dec. Open until 9 pm. Private room: 30. No pets. Garage parking. Telex 532951. V DC.
Housed in a modern structure that blends in discreetly with the surrounding landscape, this spacious, attractive dining room decorated in tones of grey, white, and old-rose certainly merits a lighter, more refined cuisine. The lobster civet à la Banyuls is so copious that it's a complete meal by itself; the grilled salmon with basil is a bit dry, and lost amid an excess of vegetables; but the strawberry coupe Melba is yummy—and generously served. Service is swift, but curt.

A la carte: 250 F. Menu: 130 F.

Aladin
(See restaurant above)
Closed 12 May-1 June and 1 Oct-15 Dec. 126 rms 432-644 F. Half-board 330-590 F. TV. Conference facilities. Heated pool.
Recently enlarged, this modern and centrally located complex offers well-furnished, decently equipped rooms with mountain views. The bathrooms are small but cleverly designed. The welcome seems cool, and the service is awkward, but on the plus side are copious breakfasts and such amenities as a sauna, solarium, Turkish baths, and a fitness centre.

CAVAILLON
84300 Cavaillon — (Vaucluse)
Paris 704 - Avignon 27 - Aix-en-Provence 52

Arilys
175, av. du Port — 90.76.11.11
Open every day. 35 rms 230-270 F. Restaurant. Half-board 305 F. Air cond. Conference facilities. Garage parking. Telex 431618. V AE DC.
Located just off the motorway, this new hotel offers bright, simple, soundproof rooms. Friendly reception and service; facilities for the disabled.

Christel
Digue des Grands-Jardins — 90.71.07.79
Open every day. 4 stes 550-650 F. 105 rms 320-420 F. Restaurant. Half-board 310-410 F. TV. Air cond. Conference facilities. Pool. Tennis. Parking. Telex 431547. V AE DC.
Conveniently situated near the motorway, this agreeably modern and functional hotel is fully equipped for conferences. Two billiard rooms; sauna; bar.

Prévot ⍟
353, av. de Verdun — 90.71.32.43
*M. Prévot. Closed Sun dinner and Mon. Open until
9.30 pm. Private room: 30. Garden dining. Air cond.
V.*
Passionately fond of his trade, chef Jacques
Prévot is a perfectionist. Every detail of his spruce
dining room—the fine china, the feminine décor,
the attentive service—reflects the same care that
goes into fragrant, appealing dishes like the
effeuillé of salt cod gratinéed with olives, pâté de
tête d'agneau à la caillette chaude, tian de coquilles
St-Jacques, and the noisettine with honey and candied melon. Excellent wine cellar.
A la carte: 300 F. Menus: 139 F, 187 F, 225 F,
240 F.

Hôtel Toppin
70, cours Gambetta — 90.71.30.42
*Open every day. 32 rms 180-240 F. Restaurant. Half-
board 200-240 F. TV 15 rms. Conference facilities.
Garage parking. Telex 432631. V AE DC.*
This tidy, centrally located establishment, family-
owned since 1890, offers impersonal rooms that
are currently being renovated. Indoor terrace for
sun-bathing.

CAVALAIRE
83240 Cavalaire — (Var)
Paris 900 - Le Lavandou 21 - St-Tropez 18

12/20 Hôtel de la Calanque
Rue de la Calanque — 94.64.04.27
*M. Pantaleo. Closed 7 Oct-15 March. Open until
10 pm. Private room: 50. Terrace dining. Parking.
Telex 400293. V AE DC.*
Clinging to one of the most beautiful rocky inlets
on the Var coast, this modern restaurant opens
onto a stupendous view. The kitchen turns out a
variety of nicely handled culinary classics, the likes
of sea-scallop terrine, garlicky grilled sea bass with
fresh tomatoes, and herb-scented filet de bœuf
poêlé.
A la carte: 300 F. Menus: from 105 F to 210 F.

Hôtel de la Calanque ♠♣
(See restaurant above)
*Closed 7 Oct-15 March. 3 stes 680-740 F. 33 rms 490-
680 F. Half-board 600-740 F oblig in seas. TV. Conference facilities. Pool. Tennis.*
Well-known for its quiet, this gorgeous seafront
hotel features spacious, bright, freshly renovated
rooms with magnificent views of the coast.

CAVALIÈRE
83980 Cavalière — (Var)
Paris 890 - Hyères 30 - Le Lavandou 8 - St-Tropez 31

Le Club
Plage de Cavalière — 94.05.80.14
*M. Buchert. Closed 15 Oct-20 April. Open until
10 pm. Garden dining. Air cond. No pets. Valet parking. Telex 420317. V AE DC.*
Patrick Beekes is out to win a third toque, but his
uneven performance in the kitchen last year keeps
him at two (we had one botched meal in July, a far
better one some months later). He regularly seeks
out the best ingredients money can buy for his
superb foie gras, the crusty galette of barely
cooked tunny (a method that keeps all the fish's
flavours intact), delightful fresh pasta with squid
and pesto, and moreish desserts: puff-pastry tart
with seasonal fruit—apricots, figs, etc., and choc-
ate cake with Bourbon vanilla-flavoured custard.
All these delights are served in a splendid setting
overlooking one of the most beautiful beaches on

the coast. Very good cellar; impeccable service;
warm reception.
A la carte: 450-550 F. Menu: 280 F (dinner only).

Le Club
(See restaurant above)
*Closed 15 Oct-20 April. 6 stes. 27 rms 700-1,200 F
(per pers, half-board oblig). TV. Air cond. Conference
facilities. Heated pool. Tennis.*
The hotel is currently undergoing major
renovations which will make it all the more attractive for beach-loving travellers. Excellent beach
facilities.

CAZAUBON
See Barbotan-les-Thermes

CELLE-SAINT-CLOUD (LA)
See PARIS Suburbs

CENTURI-PORT
See CORSICA

CÉRET
66400 Céret — (Pyrénées-O.)
Paris 945 - Perpignan 30 - Port-Vendres 36

La Châtaigneraie ♠♣
2 km S
Rte de Fontfrède — 68.87.03.19
*Closed 16 Nov-15 March. 8 rms 405-510 F (per pers,
half-board oblig). Restaurant. No pets. Pool. Parking.
V.*
This charming little hotel, set amid cherry,
chestnut, and laurel trees, features comfortable
and pretty rooms with an admirable view of the
Canigou. Warm welcome; sumptuous breakfasts.

Les Feuillants
1, bd La Fayette — 68.87.37.88
*M. Banyols. Closed Sun dinner, Mon and Feb. Open
until 10 pm. Private room: 40. Terrace dining. Air
cond. Garage parking. V AE DC.*
Chef Didier Banyols simply couldn't resist moving into this marvellous, freshly redecorated country house which was offered to him on a silver
platter by a food-loving benefactor. Never has this
talented chef's cooking been more expressive and
filled with obvious joie de vivre than in such
regionally rooted dishes as red bell peppers and
Collioure anchovies served with 'coca', a crisp
bread dough rubbed with garlic and tomatoes, or
his flavourful rockfish soup with lobster ravioli, or
a sublime veal chop accompanied by a truffled
macaroni gratin. Though desserts need improvement, the regional wines are superlative. A well-
deserved extra point this year.
A la carte: 250-300 F. Menus: 200 F, 320 F.

Les Feuillants
(See restaurant above)
*Closed Sun, Mon and Feb. 2 stes 950 F. 1 rm 600 F.
TV. Air cond.*
A charming little hotel with luxury rooms and
suites. Splendid burled-elm furniture.

La Terrace au Soleil
1.5 km on rte de Fontfrède — 68.87.01.94
*M. Leveillé-Nizerolle. Closed 7 Jan-2 March. Open
until 9.30 pm. Private room: 30. Terrace dining.
Parking. V.*
This fine old sun-drenched Catalan dwelling is
slowly being upgraded for comfort, while the
young chef continues to hone his skills, creatively
displayed in such dishes as a gelée de poires au foie

gras, shredded skate with cabbage, poached chicken with lentil purée, a crêpe 'beggar's purse' filled with tart-sweet apples, and a tea-flavoured crème catalane that simply could not be better.

A la carte: 300-350 F. Menus: 120 F (lunch only), 190 F, 320 F.

La Terrace au Soleil

(See restaurant above)
Closed 7 Jan-2 March. 1 ste 780 F. 26 rms 400-780 F. Half-board 425-615 F oblig in seas. TV. Conference facilities. Heated pool. Tennis.

The two modern villas' bright and comfortable rooms, abutting a peaceful little park, offer an outstanding view of the Canigou.

CERGY

See PARIS Suburbs

Le Cheval Blanc

(See restaurant above)
Closed off-season Sat and Sun, and 20 Dec-12 Jan. 25 rms 80-275 F. Half-board 167-327 F oblig in seas. TV 16 rms. Conference facilities.

Simple, modernised, adequately equipped rooms with rudimentary furnishings look out on to a small walled garden.

CERNAY-LA-VILLE

78720 Cernay-la-Ville — (Yvelines)
Paris 48 - Rambouillet 11 - Dampierre 4

Abbaye des Vaux-de-Cernay

34.85.23.00
M. Savry. Open every day. Open until 9.30 pm. Private room: 30. No pets. Parking. Telex 689596. V AE DC.

Philippe Savry, an avid collector of vintage automobiles and exceptional historical sites, has restored and transformed these Cistercian dwellings set in extensive grounds. The Abbaye is now a sought-after site for deluxe receptions and conferences. Beneath the ribbed vaults of the ancient refectory, guests are served ambitious and rather elaborate cooking—lobster and oyster ravioli in lettuce mousse, salmon millefeuille with truffles, and a suprême de pamplemousse au Champagne et aux pralines.

A la carte: 400-450 F. Menus: 195 F (weekdays only), 225 F and 380 F (w-e and holidays only), 270 F.

Abbaye des Vaux-de-Cernay

(See restaurant above)
Open every day. 3 stes 1,800-3,500 F. 60 rms 600-1,760 F. Half-board 670-1,150 F. Conference facilities. Heated pool. Tennis.

The huge, comfortable, ostentatiously decorated rooms are endowed with immense bathrooms and copper bathtubs encased in cane, mosaic, or marble. Marvellous views of the park; impeccable service. More new guestrooms are planned for this year.

CHABLIS

89800 Chablis — (Yonne)
Paris 182 - Auxerre 19 - Tonnerre 16 - Avallon 47

Hostellerie des Clos

(Michel Vignaud)
Rue J.-Rathier — 86.42.10.63
M. Vignaud. Closed off-season Thu lunch and Wed, and 12 Dec-10 Jan. Open until 9.30 pm. Private

room: 35. Air cond. Garage parking. Telex 351752. V.

The fresh pastel tones of this fashionable country inn, its impeccable service and warm reception, outweigh the minor flaws of Michel Vignaud's cooking. If his hot foie gras with apples is indeed succulent, the ocean freshness of his hot oysters is squelched by the garnish of spinach, and though the fish are perfectly cooked, their accompaniments are far too heavy; and his raspberry fondue is so sour that we could eat only a few bites. Thus, if he is to retain his two-toque rating, a little order in the kitchen is urgently called for. Excellent Chablis, skilled sommelier.

A la carte: 400-450 F. Menus: 150 F, 255 F, 370 F.

Hostellerie des Clos

(See restaurant above)
Closed Wed off-season and 12 Dec-10 Jan. 1 ste. 26 rms 420-620 F (per pers, half-board oblig). TV. Air cond. Conference facilities.

Bright, modern, tastefully decorated rooms look out on to flower gardens. Very good breakfasts.

10/20 Au Vrai Chablis

Pl. du Marché — 86.42.11.43
Mme Beucher. Closed dinner Mon, Tue and Wed, and 1 Dec-1 Feb. Open until 9.30 pm. Private room: 25. Terrace dining. V AE DC.

An appealing old bistro with a period zinc bar offers local wines by the glass, along with decent country-style fare: quail with fresh grapes, and délice d'andouillette on a bed of leeks.

A la carte: 150-200 F. Menus: 180 F (wine inc), 72 F.

CHAGNY

71150 Chagny — (Saône/Loire)
Paris 330 - Chalon 17 - Beaune 16 - Mâcon 75

Château de Bellecroix

N 6 — 85.87.13.86
Mme Gautier. Closed Wed and 20 Dec-1 Feb. Open until 9.30 pm. Garden dining. Garage parking. Telex 283155. V AE DC.

Housed in a vine-covered mansion that once belonged to the Order of the Knights of Malta, this spacious, welcoming neo-Gothic dining room features good (if not brilliant) dishes like sea-scallop salad doused in an overdose of hazelnut vinaigrette, a decent truffle-scented turbot, and a fine lamb fillet with a bright touch of lime, garnished with rather ordinary vegetables. Excellent sorbets. Very attentive service.

A la carte: 320 F. Menus: 95 F, 195 F, 295 F.

Château de Bellecroix

(See restaurant above)
Closed Wed and 20 Dec-1 Feb. 19 rms 480-850 F. Half-board 480-680 F oblig in seas. TV. Conference facilities. Heated pool.

Much work has been done to upgrade the level of comfort in this hotel's large, beautiful rooms. Lovely park.

Lameloise

36, pl. d'Armes — 85.87.08.85
M. Lameloise. Closed Thu lunch, Wed, 1 May and 18 Dec-23 Jan. Open until 9.30 pm. Private room: 20. Garage parking. Telex 801086. V.

This excellent family-owned restaurant, with its ancient walls, antique furnishings, and masses of flowers, is now in the hands of Jean Lameloise's son, Jacques, who is slowly, prudently bringing his father's culinary legacy up to date. A pinch of saffron adds contemporary zest to a corolle of frogs' legs; a garnish of caramelised chicory complements pan-fried foie gras; classic ravioli d'escargot get a boost from a sapid garlic bouillon; and a beurre rouge lends a bright touch to freshwater perch baked scales and all, then served forth with a sublime potato purée. Foie gras is something of an obsession with Jacques Lameloise, but who would complain when it produces a divine dish like pigeonneau de Bresse en vessie napped with a sauce au foie gras? Extraordinary desserts include a crisp millefeuille with vanilla cream, le délice caramélisé aux framboises, a superb hot apple tart, and Granny Smith sorbet. The fabulous cellar of legendary Burgundies is administered by the knowledgeable Jean-Pierre Després.

A la carte: 400-600 F. Menu: 310 F.

Lameloise
(See restaurant above)
Closed Wed, 1 May and 18 Dec-23 Jan. 1 ste 1,000 F. 20 rms 320-850 F. TV. Conference facilities.

Standing proudly on the town square, this fifteenth-century dwelling offers rooms and suites of various sizes, agreeably decorated with bright, fresh fabrics. Sumptuous breakfasts. Relais et Châteaux.

See Metz

85300 Challans — (Vendée)
Paris 431 - Nantes 60 - La Roche-sur-Yon 40

Le Dauphin
40, av. Biochaud
51.93.11.52
M. Daraize. Closed Tue off-season. Open until 9.30 pm. Private room: 15. Air cond. Parking. V DC.

In the two years since they purchased this seventeenth-century *auberge* Martine and Thierry Daraize, a youthful and eager-to-please couple, have completely renovated the décor. Thierry has found some good local sources of fresh ingredients for his agreeably light lotte coulibiac, his noisette of stuffed lamb with thyme in an original lentil cream sauce, and his creditable frozen nougat served with two coulis. The least expensive set meal is a remarkable value; the cellar is small but reasonably priced.

A la carte: 250-300 F. Menus: 85 F (weekdays only), 135 F, 190 F.

12/20 Le Pavillon Gourmand
4, rue Saint-Jean-de-Monts
51.49.04.52
M. Pierron. Closed Sun dinner, Mon, Christmas holidays and 1-10 July. Open until 9.30 pm. Private room: 20. Parking. V AE.

Ignore the banal country-style décor of this small establishment, and focus instead on the consistently well-prepared food. Seafood is handled with particular flair, witness the hot oyster ravioli in Champagne, the crab estouffade, and red-mullet fillets in rosemary cream. Attentive service.

A la carte: 200-250 F. Menus: 90 F (weekdays lunch only), 210 F.

See Chambéry

51000 Châlons-sur-Marne — (Marne)
Paris 188 - Troyes 79 - Reims 43 - Bar-le-Duc 72

11/20 Au Carillon Gourmand
15 bis, pl. Mgr-Tissier — 26.64.45.07
M. Perardel. Closed Sun dinner, Mon, 12-25 Feb and 30 July-21 Aug. Open until 10.30 pm. Air cond. Telex 830998. V.

This friendly and simply decorated restaurant, a stone's throw from the towering church of Notre-Dame-en-Vaux, has a faithful clientele for its cleverly prepared and oft-renewed cuisine. We recently sampled an excellent 'Père Duval' andouillette (garnished, alas, with ordinary chips), a tender pie of young pigeon and chicken livers, and a hearty chestnut sweet called marronade napped with vanilla coulis. Excellent cellar of affordable bottles; swift, attentive service.

A la carte: 150 F. Menus: 80 F, 115 F.

Jacky Michel
19, pl. Mgr-Tissier — 26.68.21.51
M. Michel. Closed Sat lunch, Sun, Christmas holidays and 14 July-4 Aug. Open until 9.30 pm. Private room: 20. Terrace dining. Air cond. Parking. Telex 842078. V AE DC.

Every effort has been made to accommodate diners in this beautiful dwelling opposite the church of Notre-Dame-en-Vaux, and though the modern décor is more comfortable than charming, the focal point remains Jacky Michel's skilful, stylish cuisine. He occasionally gives in to the temptation to show off (hence the chartreuse de grenouilles à la fine champagne or the pigeonneau en vessie à l'orge perlé), but they are laudable dishes indeed, as is the Barbary duck caramelised with honey and Chinese spices. The excellent wine list is strong in Burgundies, Bordeaux, and especially Champagnes.

A la carte: 450 F. Menus: 160 F (weekdays only), 205 F (wine inc), 240 F, 300 F, 400 F.

Hôtel d'Angleterre
(See restaurant above)
Closed Sun, Christmas holidays and 14 July-4 Aug. 18 rms 350-500 F. Half-board 550-650 F oblig in seas. TV. No pets. Conference facilities.

A peaceful, constantly modernised and embellished hotel, offering large, comfortable 'decorator'-style rooms. Marble bathrooms; excellent breakfasts.

Pasteur
46, rue Pasteur — 26.68.10.00
Open every day. 29 rms 135-260 F. TV 26 rms. Garage parking. V.

An hotel with spacious, regularly redecorated rooms in what was once a religious community located outside of town.

(10 km E on N 3)
51460 Châlons-sur-Marne — (Marne)

Aux Armes de Champagne
Pl. de la Basilique — 26.66.96.79
M. Pérardel. Closed off-season Sun and Mon, and 6 Jan-11 Feb. Open until 9.30 pm (10 pm in summer). Private room: 80. No pets. Parking. Telex 830998. V.

After five years of extensive renovations, Jean-Pierre Pérardel is now the proud proprietor of a lovely new dining room with a huge bay-window view of Notre-Dame-de-L'Epine, a superb Flamboyant Gothic basilica. Pérardel's cuisine makes the most of his dazzling technical skill and his knack for bringing subtle, yet full-bodied flavours out of prime ingredients. Taste, for example, his 'sous-presse' de lapereau cuite au chardonnay—a terrine in a superbly light aspic accompanied by the rabbit's grilled liver, or the flawless sauté of red-mullet and prawns in a light, slightly tart sauce, or an ethereal citrus-flavoured millefeuille served with a frothy custard and a marmalade of lightly poached citrus fruits. Hervé Pennequin (winner of the Best Young Sommelier award) assists guests with the restaurant's excellent selection of wines. First-class reception and service.

A la carte: 400-500 F. Menus: 100 F (weekdays only), 450 F (w-e and holidays lunch only, wine inc), 195 F, 425 F.

Aux Armes de Champagne
(See restaurant above)
Closed off-season Sun and Mon, and 6 Jan-11 Feb. 39 rms 350-650 F. TV 15 rms. No pets. Conference facilities.
Located in the centre of town, this hotel provides fully renovated, soundproof rooms with all the amenities, and views of either the village or the garden. Impeccable service.

71100 Chalon-sur-Saône — (Saône/Loire)
Paris 346 - Mâcon 57 - Autun 53 - Dijon 68

Le Bourgogne
28, rue de Strasbourg — 85.48.89.18
M. Chemorin-Reniaume. Closed Sun dinner (except July-Aug) and 18 Nov-2 Dec. Open until 9.30 pm. Private room: 60. V AE.
In his comfortable (though not very cheery) dining room, decorated with heavy Louis XIII–style furniture, Stéphane Reniaume presents a creditable salmon carpaccio with artichokes, jambonnette de volaille de Bresse aux foies de volaille—a fine blend of flavours garnished, however, with dreadful rice—, and a perfectly elegant cinnamon-spiced pear with ice cream. The service is charming (as are the prices) but inexperienced.

A la carte: 250 F. Menus: 88 F, 162 F.

Didier Denis
1, rue du Pont — 85.48.81.01
M. Denis. Closed Sun dinner and Mon. Open until 9.45 pm. Private room: 20. Air cond. V.
Didier Denis will soon be wearing a second toque if he continues on his current path of blending classicism and modern tastes with simplicity and skill. His potage de poule aux ravioles de chèvre is a model of balanced flavours; and we admire the technique behind the sublime jus that accompanies his ris de veau. A smooth, fragrant gâteau au chocolat is further proof that this chef is close to the top of his form. Mme Denis welcomes patrons into the understated contemporary dining room. The cellar holds bottles from all over the world.

A la carte: 250 F. Menus: 150 F (weekdays lunch only, wine inc), 120 F, 200 F, 300 F.

12/20 Aux Gourmets
15, av. J.-Jaurès — 85.48.37.25
M. Dervault. Closed Sat and Easter school holidays. Open until 9 pm. V.
While Liliane ushers guests gracefully into the refreshed and flowered décor of the dining room, François works earnestly at his ragoût d'escargots au beurre de graines torréfiées, freshwater perch braised in vermouth, marvellous little goat cheeses fried in wine vinegar, and an improved range of desserts.

A la carte: 250 F. Menus: 78 F, 98 F, 156 F.

Mercure
Av. de l'Europe — 85.46.51.89
Open every day. 1 ste 550 F. 85 rms 300-420 F. Restaurant. TV. Air cond. Conference facilities. Pool. Parking. Telex 800132. V AE DC.
Set in unprepossessing surroundings, this hotel offers renovated, neat, and functional rooms. Warm reception; decent service.

Le Moulin de Martorey
Chalon South exit on A 6
towards Le Creusot
71100 Saint-Rémy — 85.48.12.98
M. Gillot. Closed Sun dinner, Mon, Feb school holidays and 12 Aug-2 Sep. Open until 9.30 pm. Private room: 22. Garden dining. Parking. V.
This former mill on the outskirts of Chalon has been extensively remodelled and is now more in line with the clean, pure, and often quite inventive cuisine of its owner, chef Jean-Pierre Gillot. From his exemplary poulet aux morilles to his creative coquilles St-Jacques à la nage aux rillons de veau et zestes d'orange, from his prawns with lamb jus and chopped black olives to his red-mullet in red wine (with foie gras de canard and a touch of celery salt) every dish is carefully thought out and prepared with precision. Though prices have risen here of late, the Moulin still offers excellent value for cuisine of this calibre. Mme Gillot rules the cellar with discernment and proselytic fervour.

A la carte: 320 F. Menus: 220 F (weekdays lunch only, wine inc), 170 F, 220 F and 350 F.

12/20 Restaurant du Marché
7, place St-Vincent
85.48.62.00
MM. Berthold and Fridrici. Closed Sun dinner, Mon and 18-31 Aug. Open until 9 pm. V AE DC.
The kitchen does its best to execute an over-long, oddly eclectic menu. But the best reasons to visit this narrow little eating house near the cathedral are simple dishes like steamed salmon, andouillette de Troyes, and good, fresh salads. You'll get a very warm reception, and friendly service.

A la carte: 200-230 F. Menus: 74 F (weekdays only), 95 F, 155 F.

Ripert
31, rue St-Georges — 85.48.89.20
M. Ripert. Closed Sun, Mon, 25 Dec-1 Jan and 1-21 Aug. Open until 9 pm. V.
Chef Alain Ripert works in a solid, straightforward vein that takes full advantage of the market's seasonal bounty. Each day brings a new pair of appealing set meals that might feature foie gras, roast magret de canard landais, pan-fried leg of lamb, confit with parsley potatoes, hot raspberry gratin, floating islands, etc. Small but interesting cellar of Burgundies.

Menus: 125 F (Sat dinner only), 75 F, 110 F.

Royal Hôtel Best Western
8, rue du Port-Villiers
85.48.15.86
Open every day. 8 stes 450 F. 50 rms 200-370 F. Restaurant. Half-board 260-350 F. TV. Conference facilities. Garage parking. Telex 801610. V AE DC.
Centrally located, and right near the river, this comfortable hotel offers well-appointed rooms overlooking a peaceful courtyard.

Saint-Georges

32, av. J.-Jaurès — 85.48.27.05
M. Choux. Closed Sat lunch. Open until 10 pm. Private room: 45. Air cond. Garage parking. Telex 800330. V AE DC.

Yves and Claude Chou have taken over their parents' well-known establishment, but they haven't altered the charming, cosily decorated dining room cherished by generations of regular customers. Only the freshest ingredients go into Yves' lightened classic cuisine. Tuck into a tasty ragoût of cockles and sole en marinière, fresh cod 'osso buco' with a hint of orange, and lamb's loin with kidneys. Excellent service; the cellar gets better all the time.

A la carte: 400 F. Menus: 115 F (weekdays only), 180 F, 205 F, 380 F.

Saint-Georges

(See restaurant above)
Open every day. 48 rms 250-400 F. TV. Air cond. Conference facilities.

This charming, provincial hotel opposite the station offers tidy, well-equipped, and recently refreshed rooms. A new indoor garden has been added.

Saint-Régis

22, bd de la République — 85.48.07.28
Open every day. 38 rms 235-420 F. Restaurant. Half-board 280-340 F. TV. Air cond 20 rms. Conference facilities. Garage parking. Telex 801624. V AE DC.

A fine old provincial dwelling, located between the old town and station, with constantly refurbished, nicely equipped rooms decorated in a 1960s style. Lounges; bar.

And also...

Our selection of places for inexpensive, quick, or late-night meals.

Jules (85.48.08.34 - 11, rue de Strasbourg. Open until 10.30 pm): Although their pot-au-feu has been replaced by more ambitious dishes, the 68 F set menu is still a real bargain.

La Réale (85.48.07.21 - 8, pl. de Gaulle. Open until 9.30 pm): Two delightful menus at 68 F and 98 F and a few home-style specialities.

L'Ile Bleue (85.48.39.83 - 7, rue de Strasbourg. Open until 10 pm): Two appealing set menus tariffed at 70 F and 120 F, and well-prepared seafood dishes served behind a pretty, elaborately painted façade.

Le Neptune (85.46.57.57 - 33, pl. de Beaune. Open until 10 pm): A 60 F prix-fixe menu and utterly predictable brasserie-style fare (salads, pizzas, grilled meats and fish, salmon), served forth in a pink-and-grey décor.

In nearby **Saint-Germain-du-Plain**

(14 km SW)
71370 Chalon-sur-Saône — (Saône/Loire)

Le Château

Le Bourg — 85.47.38.13
Closed 5-15 March and 19-29 Nov. 3 stes 900-1,100 F. 7 rms 650-850 F. Restaurant. Half-board 550-650 F. Conference facilities. Valet parking. V AE DC.

An opulent nineteenth-century dwelling set in elegant grounds shaded by hundred-year-old trees. The rooms are stylish and offer every comfort. Training-course facilities (wine-tasting, golf, etc.) are available. Guests are required to dine at the hotel on the evening of their arrival.

In nearby **Saint-Marcel**

(3 km E on N 73 and D 978)
71380 Chalon-sur-Saône — (Saône/Loire)

Hôtel du Commerce

(Jean Bouthenet)
19, rue de Villeneuve — 85.96.56.16
M. Bouthenet. Closed Sun dinner, Mon, Feb school holidays and 6-21 Aug. Open until 9.30 pm. Private room: 45. Terrace dining. Garage parking. V DC.

As soon as he has a few extra francs, Jean Bouthenet plans to redesign his old café. But we find the place warm and likeable just as it is, especially when we're tucking into the robust pigeon terrine à la fine champagne, fresh salmon with chicory, veal with gingered tomatoes, and moreish sweets. Generous portions; good cellar.

A la carte: 350 F. Menus: 90 F (weekdays only), 150 F, 185 F, 280 F.

See also: Chagny

CHAMALIÈRES
See Clermont-Ferrand

CHAMBÉRY

73000 Chambéry — (Savoie)
Paris 560 - Grenoble 57 - Annecy 47 - Lyon 98

Art Hôtel

12, rue Sommeiller
79.62.37.26
Open every day. 36 rms 200-270 F. TV 28 rms. Conference facilities. Garage parking. Telex 319172. V AE DC.

A centrally located hotel featuring spacious, soundproof rooms, all with bathrooms. Cosy bar.

12/20 Le Cul de Bouteille

Rue du Verger — 79.70.04.98
M. Meurier. Closed Sun lunch. Open until midnight. Terrace dining. V AE DC.

Open until midnight, this friendly restaurant in the centre of town offers copious dishes like fisherman's salad, grilled freshwater perch fillets, and (slightly overcooked) magret de canard, all served in a soft décor done in grey, white, and black.

A la carte: 200-250 F. Menus: 75 F, 95 F, 145 F.

Le France

22, fg Reclus — 79.33.51.18
Open every day. 48 rms 260-370 F. TV. Air cond. Conference facilities. Valet parking. Telex 309689. V AE DC.

A modern and functional structure, with recently renovated rooms (all air conditioned and soundproof), some of which boast a mountain view. Bar.

Prince Eugène de Savoie

Esplanade Curial
79.85.06.07
Open every day. 6 stes 540-990 F. 44 rms 260-495 F. Restaurant. Half-board 520-1,400 F. TV. Air cond 1 rm. Conference facilities. Garage parking. Telex 319104. V AE DC.

A pleasant, modern, centrally located hotel, the Eugène de Savoie features elegant, handsomely equipped rooms. The luxurious suites are furnished with canopied beds and marble bathrooms. Amenities include a garden, terrace, conference room, bar, and restaurant (see below under Roubatcheff).

Les Princes

4, rue de Boigne — 79.33.45.36
M. Zorelle. Open every day. Open until 9.30 pm. Private room: 30. Air cond. Garage parking. Telex 319148. V AE DC.

As soon as they renovate their mezzanine dining room, the Zorelles will be ready to welcome the international clientele that the Olympic Games will bring to Chambéry. Already in place are a highly professional staff, an admirable cellar, and a chef (young Alain Zorelle) who knows his ingredients and has mastered a repertoire of updated traditional dishes: salade d'aiguillettes de rouget, grilled fillet of féra (a salmon-like fish) with foie gras and a bright touch of beetroot juice, médaillons de lotte au parfum d'olives, and a tempting parade of light, luscious sweets.

A la carte: 400-500 F. Menus: from 160 F to 390 F.

Les Princes

(See restaurant above)
Open every day. 45 rms 230-370 F. Half-board 400-550 F. TV. Conference facilities.

Situated in downtown Chambéry, this hotel offers 45 entirely renovated, soundproof rooms, with beamed ceilings and fresh, flowery décors.

Roubatcheff

Espl. Curial — 79.33.24.91
M. Roubatcheff. Closings not available. Open until 10 pm. Private room: 50. Garage parking. V AE DC.

The neo-classic décor is bright and comfortable, and chef Jean-Philippe Roubatcheff seems inspired by his new surroundings to perform even better in the kitchen, where he invents (and thoroughly tests) a menu full of delicious surprises. Try his agreeable terrine de pigeon au foie gras, the spirited salmon with lemon grass, warm 'petals' of turbot with an orange-scented julienne, and scrumptious desserts. Mme Roubatcheff welcomes guests warmly, and presides over the attentive, efficient staff.

A la carte: 350 F. Menus: 170 F, 240 F, 420 F.

La Vanoise

44, av. P.-Lanfrey — 79.69.02.78
M. Lenain. Closed Sun (except holidays) and 22 July-4 Aug. Open until 10 pm. Terrace dining. Air cond. V.

Poor Philippe Lenain! Expropriated from his previous establishment, foiled in his attempt to open a new place high up in the mountains, he has returned to his old restaurant in Chambéry, a tiny place that seats just 25 and is desperately in need of renovation. But Lenain is in fine feather nonetheless, judging by the perfect texture and flavour of his rosy terrine de foie gras, the thick, fresh salmon au gros sel, and his battue, a favourite local sweet that resembles a crustless custard pie topped with apples or peaches. The chef is also an avid wine buff, and has accumulated a spectacular cellar.

A la carte: 300 F. Menus: 75 F (weekdays only), 145 F, 220 F, 280 F.

In nearby Challes-les-Eaux

(6 km E on N 6)
73190 Chambéry — (Savoie)

Hôtel du Château

Montée du Château — 79.72.86.71
Open every day. 2 stes 504-614 F. 63 rms 189-498 F. Restaurant. Half-board 315-535 F. TV 33 rms. Conference facilities. Pool. Tennis. Parking. Telex 309756. V AE DC.

This fifteenth-century castle, set in extensive grounds, features superb rooms (33 have

minibars) with views of the Savoie valley and the Dent du Chat peak.

Château de Trivier

79.72.82.87
Open every day. 30 rms 105-422 F. Restaurant. Half-board 167-506 F. TV 5 rms. Conference facilities. Parking. V AE DC.

Located in a large park complete with a pond, this old-fashioned hotel offers nicely equipped rooms furnished with antiques.

In nearby Col de Plainpalais

(16 km NE on N 512)
73230 Chambéry — (Savoie)

Le Plainpalais

73230 La Féclaz — 79.25.81.79
Closed May and 1 Oct-15 Dec. 20 rms 210-230 F. Restaurant. Half-board 191-246 F. Conference facilities. Parking. V.

A chalet at the foot of the ski slopes, with tidy, comfortable rooms and a panoramic lounge. Lovely hiking country all around.

CHAMBRAY

27120 Chambray — (Eure)
Paris 96 - Evreux 18 - Rouen 52 - Pacy 11

Le Vol au Vent

1, pl. de la Mairie — 32.36.70.05
M. Lognon. Closed Sun dinner, Tue lunch, Mon, 7-30 Jan and 10-20 Sep. Open until 9.30 pm. V DC.

This grand old restaurant—a throwback to another culinary age—is run by two veteran professionals who excel at their trade. While Gérard Lognon supervises the dining room and puts the skilled staff through its paces, chef Christian Dupuis devotes himself with utter virtuosity to preparing chausson de crabe, feuilleté de homard, millefeuille de saumon, canard rôti au xérès, tourte de pigeonneau and other rich dishes swathed in layers of pastry and adorned with creamy, alcoholic sauces. The sweets are in the same mould: tarte normande, millefeuille aux fruits.... Nothing light, nothing modern, but every dish is expertly executed in this conservatory of classicism, unique in France. Fine cellar.

A la carte: 300-350 F. Menus: 1,000 F (for 2 pers), 160 F, 190 F.

CHAMONIX

74400 Chamonix — (H.-Savoie)
Paris 619 - Annecy 96 - Genève 86 - Albertville 67

Albert Ier et Milan

119, imp. du Montenvers — 50.53.05.09
M. Carrier. Closed Wed lunch, 13-31 May and 21 Oct-5 Dec. Open until 9.30 pm. Private room: 40. Air cond. No pets. Garage parking. Telex 380779. V AE DC.

From his spanking-new basement kitchens chef Pierre Carrier sends up to his bright, panelled dining room the most ravishingly beautiful food, prepared with keen precision and an infallible knack for harmonising spices and flavours. Examples? Try his Val d'Aoste trout à la fleur de sel, or the bouillon of crayfish and Lake Geneva féra tinted with saffron, or fillet of freshwater char gratiné scented with wild thyme, or Bresse chicken breast in a peppery vanilla sauce with prawns, or saddle of lamb en rognonnade. Uncommonly attentive service; excellent far-ranging wine cellar with an emphasis on local Savoie wines.

A la carte: 400 F. Menus: 165 F (weekdays only), 180 F (w-e and holidays only), 260 F, 390 F.

Albert Ier et Milan

(See restaurant above)
Closed 13-31 May and 21 Oct-5 Dec. 9 stes 710-865 F. 23 rms 400-600 F. Half-board 430-612 F. TV. No pets. Conference facilities. Heated pool.

A friendly, family-style hotel that stands out among Chamonix's finest, with a recently renovated Tyrolean look. The rooms are rather small, though charming and remarkably well equipped, the reception is warm, and the breakfasts (hot Viennese pastries, homemade yoghurt, mountain honey) are simply delicious. Relaxation room with sauna and Jacuzzi; driving-range with putting-green; lovely flowered grounds.

Atmosphères

113, pl. Balmat — 50.55.97.97
Open every day. Open until 11 pm. V AE DC.

If you can tear your attention away from the splendid view of the Mont Blanc, beyond the bay window of this warm, intimate dining room, you will see that the cuisine is worth your notice. Good bets are the magnificent house-smoked salmon, an original and very good croustillant of sea bream with fresh tomatoes and pesto sauce, garnished with al dente vegetables, and an adequate crème brûlée à la cassonade (desserts need improvement). Appealing wine list; occasional live music in the evenings.

A la carte: 250-300 F. Menus: 90 F (weekdays only), 119 F.

12/20 Auberge du Bois Prin

Les Moussoux — 50.53.33.51
M. Carrier. Closed Wed lunch, 21 May-6 June and 14 Oct-12 Dec. Open until 9.30 pm. Garden dining. Air cond. Garage parking. V AE DC.

Among the solid, deftly prepared offerings on Denis Carrier's menu are a fondue of cabbage and smoked salmon with chive butter, roast rack of lamb with wild thyme, and rhubarb tart, all served in a sweet little mountain chalet (the terrace boasts a view of Mont Blanc). Delightful service from waiters in Savoyard costume. The cellar holds an ample selection of half-bottles.

A la carte: 320 F. Menus: 160 F (weekdays only), 210 F (w-e and holidays only), 220 F, 350 F.

Auberge du Bois Prin

(See restaurant above)
Closed 21 May-6 June and 14 Oct-12 Dec. 11 rms 610-1,000 F. Half-board 535-915 F. TV. Air cond. Conference facilities.

This attractive little family-style hotel features warm, personalised rooms with splendid mountain views. Charming reception; Relais et Châteaux.

Beausoleil

5 km NE (N 506)
Le Lavancher
60, allée des Peupliers — 50.54.00.78
Closed 20 Sep-20 Dec. 15 rms 250-380 F. Restaurant. Half-board 270-310 F oblig in seas. TV. Tennis. Garage parking. V.

A friendly hotel, set in pastures a few minutes' walk from Chamonix. The owner is a mountain guide.

Eden

2.5 km N, in Praz — 50.53.06.40
M. Lesage. Closed Tue off-season, 1-15 June and 5 Nov-15 Dec. Open until 9.30 pm. Parking. V AE DC.

In addition to the tournedos Rossini and seafood choucroute, the owner of this delightfully decorated restaurant offers a more personalised cuisine with such dishes as rabbit in red-wine aspic, petit sâlé de poisson aux lentilles, and fruit terrine with almond cream. Appealing regional wine list (good Crépys).

A la carte: 350-400 F. Menus: from 150 F to 350 F.

Eden

(See restaurant above)
Closed 1-15 June and 5 Nov-15 Dec. 2 stes 500-600 F. 10 rms 350-600 F. Half-board 360-390 F. TV. No pets. Conference facilities.

This hotel has tiny but astutely equipped rooms, recently refurbished in pastel tones. Minimal service.

Le Labrador

in Praz, rte du Golf — 50.53.23.27
Open every day. 4 stes 1,260-2,500 F. 32 rms 350-680 F. Restaurant. Half-board 425-490 F. TV. Conference facilities. Parking. Telex 319222. V AE DC.

Situated right on the Chamonix golf course and opposite Mont Blanc, this unusual wooden house features lovely, cosy rooms with comfortable beds and well-designed bathrooms.

Le Matafan

Pl. de l'Eglise — 50.53.05.64
M. Morand. Closed 15 Oct-15 Dec. Open until 10 pm. Private room: 30. Garden dining. No-smoking section. Garage parking. Telex 385614. V AE DC.

His handsome new dining room is spacious and well-lit, the service and reception are perceptibly warmer, and Jean-Michel Morand is more adroit than ever at preparing his regionally rooted repertoire: ravioles de rave aux coquilles St-Jacques à l'anis vert, attriaux de truite et féra à l'essence de verveine, grenadin de veau Amédée VIII et sa deigne aux bourgeons de pin. Good local wines accompany these unusual dishes.

A la carte: 350 F. Menus: 150 F, 250 F, 350 F.

Le Mont-Blanc

(See restaurant above)
Closed 15 Oct-15 Dec. 15 stes 1,014-1,432 F. 29 rms 427-1,032 F. Half-board 607-816 F. TV. Heated pool. Tennis.

A beautiful hotel that is regularly updated, located in the centre of Chamonix. In addition to renovated rooms and lovely suites, there is a pretty garden, a swimming pool, sauna, and tennis courts.

Le Prieuré

Allée du Recteur-Payot — 50.53.20.72
Closed 29 April-15 May and 15 Oct-15 Dec. 14 stes 434-623 F. 77 rms 320-626 F. Restaurant. Half-board 320-433 F. TV. Conference facilities. Garage parking. Telex 385614. V AE DC.

This elegant chalet overlooking Chamonix offers bright, spacious rooms with balconies that face Mont Blanc. Free shuttle-bus to ski slopes; friendly reception.

La Sapinière-Montana

102, rue Mummery — 50.53.07.63
Closed 15 April-10 June and 22 Sep-20 Dec. 30 rms 410-500 F. Restaurant. Half-board 335-360 F oblig

in seas. TV. No pets. Conference facilities. Garage parking. Telex 305551. V AE DC.

A large, quiet house with a garden, this hotel is located a few minutes from the centre of town and the Brévent lift. The rooms are comfortable and decorated with restraint, and most have a balcony facing Mont Blanc. Sauna; billiard room.

CHAMPAGNAC-DE-BÉLAIR

24530 Champagnac-de-Bélair — (Dordogne)
Paris 464 - Périgueux 33 - Brantôme 6 - Nontron 22

Moulin du Roc
[16] Lieu-dit Moulin du Roc — 53.54.80.36
M. Gardillou. Closed Wed lunch, Tue, 15 Jan-15 Feb and 15 Nov-15 Dec. Open until 9.30 pm. Private room: 20. Garden dining. Garage parking. Telex 571555. V AE DC.

An old ivy-covered millhouse set in an exuberantly lush green garden by the River Dronne, the Moulin du Roc is the most eccentrically baroque restaurant imaginable. Past the first shock, one inevitably succumbs to the charm of Lucien Gardillou's welcome, and even more willingly to the charms of the cuisine, the work of mother and son Alain and Solange Gardillou. Their precise technique and unerring instinct produce wonderful dishes with a regional accent: cassolette of truffled potatoes, steamed foie gras, freshwater perch drizzled with tomato- and sweet-pepper-flavoured oils, a tender fricassée de pintade, and a simple, pleasant pear croustillant. Young François Gardillou administers a cellar rich in Bordeaux.

A la carte: 350-400 F. Menus: 200 F, 280 F, 350 F.

Moulin du Roc
(See restaurant above)
Closed 15 Jan-15 Feb and 15 Nov-15 Dec. 4 stes 650-700 F. 10 rms 380-600 F. Half-board 700-950 F. TV. Conference facilities. Heated pool. Tennis.

Beneath the beautiful beams and antiquated gears of this converted walnut-oil mill, guests are lodged in dainty and exceptionally comfortable rooms furnished with antiques. Gorgeous breakfasts.

CHAMPAGNE-AU-MONT-D'OR

See Lyon

CHAMPIGNY

See Reims

CHAMPILLON

See Epernay

CHAMPTOCEAUX

49270 Champtoceaux — (Maine/Loire)
Paris 367 - Cholet 48 - Angers 62 - Nantes 31

Les Jardins de la Forge
[15] 1 bis, pl. des Piliers — 40.83.56.23
M. Pauvert. Closed Wed, dinner Sun and Tue, 5-27 Feb and 8-23 Oct. Open until 9.15 pm. Private room: 20. V AE DC.

Like good wine, Paul Pauvert's rigorously classic cuisine improves with the years. His quaint old smithy is now one of the best eating houses from Angers to Nantes. In a dining room done in tender tones of pale pink and green, sample his salad of baby eels in a tart and tasty sauce, a perfectly wrought feuilleté of freshwater perch in a subtle sauce based on sweet Anjou wine, a thick slice of turbot and a garnish of eels in a sauce of Bonnezeaux wine, veal kidneys à la goutte de sang served with remarkably fresh vegetables. Among the sweets, the Opéra chocolate cake is outstanding. The cellar holds some splendid Loire vintages at most attractive prices. Two toques this year.

A la carte: 350 F. Menus: 135 F (weekdays only), 198 F, 315 F.

CHAMROUSSE

38410 Chamrousse — (Isère)
Paris 596 - Chambéry 80 - Grenoble 29 - Allevard 59

L'Hermitage
opposite the cable cars — 76.89.93.21
Closed 15 April-15 Dec. 2 stes 420-450 F. 48 rms 295-440 F. Restaurant. Half-board 345-430 F. TV 15 rms. Conference facilities. Garage parking. V AE.

Short on charm, long on comfort, this traditional hotel is decorated in rustic style.

CHANGÉ

See Mans (Le)

CHANTEMERLE

See Serre-Chevalier

CHANTILLY

60500 Chantilly — (Oise)
Paris 42 - Compiègne 45 - Pontoise 36 - Senlis 10

Le Relais Condé
[13] 42, av. du Mal-Joffre — 44.57.05.75
M. Kermorgant. Closed off-season Sun dinner and Mon. Open until 9.30 pm. Private room: 12. Terrace dining. V AE DC.

Lodged in a charming white dwelling surrounded by trees, this restaurant has several little dining rooms decorated with glowing wood panelling, with pink and green fabrics on the walls. Despite his youth (all of 26 years), the chef is stuck in a culinary rut, with no thought of moving beyond the house repertoire of cassolette d'escargots à la crème d'ail, délice du Périgord (hot foie gras with a creamy sauce), sole meunière, and sea bass with fennel. Good cellar, but the prices are fearsome.

A la carte: 350 F. Menus: 150 F (wine inc), 240 F.

Relais du Coq Chantant
[13] 21, rte de Creil — 44.57.01.28
M. Dautry. Open every day. Open until 9.45 pm. Private room: 50. Parking. V AE DC.

Well-heeled pensioners and Sunday golfers swear by this address. The atmosphere is terribly *bon ton*, but—surprise!—the kitchen has its moments of inspiration, for dishes like dariole of frogs' legs with ham, yellow potatoes, spicy sauté of lotte, or lapereau farci à la picarde. Exceptional cheeses, tempting desserts. The décor needs a face-lift.

A la carte: 350-400 F. Menus: 98 F (weekdays only), 164 F and 305 F (w-e and holidays only), 175 F.

Le Tipperary
[13] 6, av. du Mal-Joffre — 44.57.00.48
M. Greffe. Open every day. Open until 10 pm. Private room: 16. Terrace dining. Air cond. V AE DC.

The stylish English décor is seen in its most brilliant light when the horsey set shows up to celebrate the various *grands prix* held at nearby Chantilly racecourse. The food is reliably decent (though the seasonings are often too tame): lightly cooked leeks in puff pastry with a touch of chervil, (over) grilled tunny sauced with a mere spoonful of vinaigrette, delicious frozen nougat with an even smaller spoonful of berry coulis. An ample choice of affordable wines is available.

A la carte: 300 F. Menus: 145 F (weekdays only), 170 F (w-e and holidays only), 250 F.

In nearby Gouvieux

(3 km W on D 909)
60270 Chantilly — (Oise)

Château de la Tour
Ch. de la Chaussée — 44.57.07.39
Closed 22 July-11 Aug. 15 rms 270-480 F. Restaurant. Half-board 250-310 F. Conference facilities. Tennis. Parking. Telex 155014. V AE.
A large turn-of-the-century dwelling, set in a five-hectare park, with comfortable lodgings and public rooms with tall windows and lovely hardwood floors.

In nearby Lamorlaye

(7 km S on N 16)
60260 Chantilly — (Oise)

Hostellerie du Lys
in Lys-Chantilly
63, 7e-Avenue — 44.21.26.19
Open every day. 35 rms 290-440 F. Restaurant. Half-board 295-575 F. TV. Conference facilities. Parking. Telex 150298. V AE DC.
Situated in a large park, this opulent country inn boasts comfortable rooms in a friendly, restful atmosphere. Tennis courts, golf course, and swimming pool are all within easy reach.

In nearby Montgrésin

(8 km SE on D 924)
60560 Chantilly — (Oise)

12/20 Relais d'Aumale
37, pl. des Fêtes — 44.54.61.31
M. Hofheinz. Closed 22 Dec-2 Jan. Open until 10 pm. Private room: 70. Terrace dining. Parking. Telex 155103. V AE DC.
Much in favour with the racing set, this bright and comely restaurant features rich, caloric cuisine: poached egg in puff pastry with salmon, mixed greens topped with grilled foie gras, and lobster ragoût with fresh pasta. Lovely terrace.
A la carte: 280-300 F. Menus: 170 F (weekdays only), 190 F (w-e and holidays only).

Relais d'Aumale
(See restaurant above)
Open every day. 2 stes 800-850 F. 22 rms 390-450 F. Half-board 400-580 F. TV. Conference facilities. Tennis.
Recently opened for business, this spacious hotel provides restful, bright, thoughtfully equipped rooms.

CHAPELLE-D'ABONDANCE (LA)

74360 Chapelle-d'Abondance (La) — (H.-Savoie)
Paris 590 - Annecy 106 - Evian 34 - Morzine 45

Le Chabi
50.73.50.14
Closed 15 April-15 June and 15 Sep-15 Dec. 21 rms 190-310 F. Restaurant. Half-board 220-290 F. TV. Conference facilities. Heated pool. Parking. V.
Set in the middle of verdant pastures, this handsome, modern hotel has nicely fitted-out rooms, a sauna, and a spa.

CHARITÉ-SUR-LOIRE (LA)

58400 Charité-sur-Loire (La) — (Nièvre)
Paris 216 - Autun 127 - Auxerre 95 - Bourges 51

A la Bonne Foi
91, rue C.-Barrère — 86.70.15.77
M. Guyot. Closed Sun dinner, Mon and Feb. Open until 9 pm. Private room: 11. V DC.
He may not be the region's boldest chef, but Didier Guyot's light, deft touch brings forth a marvellous lamb's head ravigote, a faultless chicken-liver mould with prawns en surprise, and honey-roasted grain-fed pigeon with tiny onions. Appealing cheese board, delicious desserts. The restaurant is comfortable, despite a drab décor.
A la carte: 300-350 F. Menus: 90 F (weekdays only), 135 F, 180 F, 230 F.

Le Grand Monarque
33, quai Clemenceau — 86.70.21.73
Closed Fri off-season, and Feb school holidays. 9 rms 150-260 F. Restaurant. Half-board 320 F oblig in seas. TV 5 rms.
A tiny hotel with nicely appointed rooms, currently under renovation.

CHARLEVILLE-MÉZIÈRES

08000 Charleville-Mézières — (Ardennes)
Paris 235 - Metz 160 - Nancy 205 - Reims 82

Abbaye de Sept Fontaines
in Fagnon — 24.37.38.24
MM. de Mérode and Saint-Lô. Closed Sun dinner and 22-30 Dec. Open until 10 pm. Private room: 80. Garden dining. Parking. V AE DC.
This commodious, charming seventeenth-century castle stands proudly on the sunny slope of a hill, remembering the eminent figures who have graced its halls: Kaiser Wilhelm II, Field Marshal Joffre, and President Charles de Gaulle. Now much in demand as a luxurious conference site, the Abbaye serves classic cuisine made with the finest quality raw materials: shellfish and cabbage sauté, prawns roasted with herbs, truffled chicken, paupiette de sandre au lard. The magnificent English-style grounds boast a golf course.
A la carte: 300-350 F. Menus: 250 F (wine inc), 120 F, 160 F.

Abbaye de Sept Fontaines
(See restaurant above)
Closed 22-30 Dec. 1 ste 750 F. 23 rms 365-750 F. Half-board 440-520 F. TV. Conference facilities. Golf.
This two-storey hotel offers spacious, handsomely decorated rooms with the most sophisticated amenities. Those on the upper floor are smaller, but very pretty. Stiff service; gargantuan breakfasts.

Le Château Bleu
3, bd L.-Pierquin-Warcq — 24.56.18.19
M. Belloir. Closed Sun dinner and Mon. Open until 10 pm. Private room: 20. Garden dining. No-smoking section. Parking. Telex 842835. V AE DC.
This so-called 'château' (it does boast a few turrets) is in fact a large nineteenth-century dwelling done up to look like a Florentine mansion: pink-and-pale-blue décor, heavy curtains, marble floors, crystal chandeliers.... Chef Max Belloir, formerly of Lucas-Carton, ably prepares ambitious, high-priced dishes such as a delicious combination of tomatoes and Breton lobster, lamb fillets with a garlicky cream sauce, and an array of lovely desserts. The cheese board is exceptional, the cellar judiciously stocked, and the service discreet but vigilant. An extra point this year.
A la carte: 400 F. Menus: 130 F, 175 F, 270 F.

Le Château Bleu

(See restaurant above)
Closed Aug. 13 rms 250-500 F. Half-board 410-650 F. TV. Conference facilities.
An Italianate ambience pervades the hotel's thirteen rooms. Splendid view of the park; excellent breakfasts; efficient service.

11/20 La Cigogne

40, rue Dubois-Crancé — 24.33.25.39
Mme Tabouret. Closed Sun dinner, Mon and 30 July-6 Aug. Open until 10 pm. Private room: 35. Air cond. V.
A pleasant, homely atmosphere, a cosy, provincial décor, and honestly prepared traditional dishes make this a most soothing place to stop. Try the chicken ballottine with morels, veal sweetbreads with sorrel, and profiteroles.
A la carte: 230 F. Menus: 70 F (weekdays only), 100 F and 130 F (except holidays).

Le Clèves

43, rue de l'Arquebuse — 24.33.10.75
Open every day. 48 rms 210-330 F. Restaurant. Half-board 280 F. TV. Conference facilities. Garage parking. Telex 841164. V AE DC.
Located between the railway station and Place Ducale, this hotel offers fairly quiet, modernised rooms. Groups welcome. Pub on the premises.

La Côte à l'Os

11, cours A.-Briand — 24.59.20.16
M. Durmois. Open every day. Open until 11 pm. Private room: 40. Terrace dining. V AE.
The name of this friendly, eccentrically decorated restaurant would naturally lead one to expect a hefty rib steak to be the speciality, but in fact the chef leans more to seafood: shellfish, matelote (freshwater fish stew), and fish soups. The copious 160 F set menu (wine and coffee included) comprises a vol-au-vent of sweetbreads in Pinot Noir, stewed salmon à l'ardennaise, warm goat cheese and frozen nougat.
A la carte: 250 F. Menus: 160 F (wine inc), 73 F, 135 F.

CHARTRES

28000 Chartres — (Eure-et-Loir)
Paris 96 - Orléans 72 - Dreux 35 - Evreux 77

Le Buisson Ardent

10, rue au Lait — 37.34.04.66
M. Geins. Closed Wed, and dinner Sun and Tue. Open until 9.30 pm. V AE DC.
Chef-proprietor Claude Geins has handed his popular establishment over to a young chef with solid references. As of press time we had not yet been able to sample his baked salmon in a warm vinaigrette, fresh cod with a touch of coriander and a parsley flan, or fricassée of lamb's sweetbreads with morels. The attractive two-tiered restaurant is located in the old part of Chartres, with a splendid view of the cathedral.
A la carte: 250 F. Menus: 85 F (weekdays only), 138 F, 198 F.

L'Estocade

1, rue Porte-Guillaume — 37.34.27.17
Mme Boizard. Closed Sun dinner and Mon. Open until 9.30 pm. Private room: 30. V AE DC.
Nestled within the old district's labyrinth of mills and tanneries, close to the small stone bridge that leads up to the cathedral, this restaurant is decorated with rather unwieldy Louis XIII furnishings and a profusion of plants. Our only

regret is that chef Bruno Letartre has yet to demonstrate the true scope of his skills here, although he has added some interesting new dishes to the menu, for example a smoked salmon tartare with crisp cucumbers, and escalopines of warm foie gras with an apple-prune galette.
A la carte: 300-350 F. Menus: 90 F, 140 F, 200 F, 280 F.

Le Grand Monarque

22, pl. des Epars — 37.21.00.72
M. Jallerat. Open every day. Open until 9.30 pm. Private room: 100. Terrace dining. Valet parking. Telex 760777. V AE DC.
Although Michel Menier's cuisine is never really daring, he always uses the freshest ingredients, enhancing them through skilful combinations, subtle sauces, and precision timing. We highly recommend the salad of lamb's lettuce with morsels of warm sole, the lotte in Chenonceaux wine, warm foie gras with a dash of apricot vinegar and nasturtium blossoms, sweetbreads prepared with garden vegetables and fragrant chanterelles, and the pâté de Chartres en croûte au canard. The grilled sole, however, and the grilled rib steak béarnaise verge on the commonplace. The affordably priced cellar is absolutely first-rate with particular strengths in wines from the Loire, Côtes-du-Rhône, and Champagne. Adroit, affable service.
A la carte: 350 F. Menus: 186 F, 278 F.

Le Grand Monarque

(See restaurant above)
Open every day. 5 stes 620-970 F. 49 rms 300-600 F. TV. Conference facilities.
Undisputably the best hotel in Chartres, with charming, very quiet new rooms in two adjoining turn-of-the-century pavilions that overlook a garden. Also, five superb and modern suites. The abundant breakfast buffets are served on an indoor patio.

Henri IV

31-33, rue du Soleil-d'Or — 37.36.01.55
Mme Cazalis. Closed Mon dinner and Tue. Annual closings not available. Open until 8.45 pm. Private room: 18. V AE DC.
It would not take much to convert this drab restaurant into a museum of Third-Republic furnishing; the cuisine is not very lively either, running to such time-tested specialities as pâté chartrain (young partridge and pistachio nuts), veal sweetbreads des Carnutes, and tournedos Rossini. Amusing old-fashioned service; superb cellar. One point less this year.
A la carte: 300-350 F. Menus: 165 F (except w-e and holidays lunch, wine inc), 220 F, 275 F.

Mercure

6, av. Jehan-de-Beauce — 37.21.78.00
Open every day. 48 rms 340-415 F. TV. Conference facilities. Garage parking. Telex 780728. V AE DC.
Situated next to the railway station, some 300 metres from the cathedral, this hotel offers comfortable rooms, most of which look on to an indoor garden. The owners run a restaurant behind the hotel.

Novotel

Av. M.-Proust — 37.34.80.30
Open every day. 78 rms 380-420 F. Restaurant. TV. Conference facilities. Pool. Parking. Telex 781298. V AE DC.
This modern, functional hotel is located in a leafy setting and offers 30 recently renovated rooms. Bar.

La Vieille Maison

15

5, rue au Lait — 37.34.10.67

M. Roger. Closed dinner Sun and Mon. Open until 9.15 pm. Private room: 15. V AE DC.

This venerable house stands in the old town, at the foot of the cathedral. An elegant new décor shows off its beamed ceilings and centuries' old stones to excellent advantage. Chef Bernard Roger relies on the freshest regional produce (vegetables, escargots, Beauce lamb, etc.) for his precise, generous cuisine. Savour his rich chicken and mushroom pie, or prawns sautéed with sweet spices, or his flavourful cabbage galette with tiny snails. Sweets are uniformly excellent.

A la carte: 400-450 F. Menus: 190 F (except holidays, wine inc), 250 F, 360 F.

In nearby Nogent-le-Phaye

(8 km E on D 4)
28630 Chartres — (Eure-et-Loir)

12/20 Relais de la Tour

N 10, Le Bois-Paris — 37.31.69.79

M. Noris. Closed dinner Sun, Mon and Tue, 2-13 Aug and 23-30 Dec. Open until 9.30 pm. Air cond. Parking. V.

Just off the Nationale 10, this vivid pink dining room features surprisingly good, carefully made dishes (salmon tartare with spicy sauces, tiny scallops in saffron-flavoured butter, a fine cheese board, decent crème brûlée). Good grilled meats, and unexpectedly swift, smiling service.

A la carte: 200 F. Menus: 72 F (weekdays only), 102 F, 155 F, 170 F.

CHASSENEUIL-DU-POITOU

See Poitiers

CHÂTEAU-ARNOUX

04160 Château-Arnoux — (Alpes/H.-P.)
Paris 717 - Digne 25 - Sisteron 14 - Manosque 38

La Bonne Etape

17

Chemin du Lac — 92.64.00.09

M. Gleize. Closed off-season Sun dinner and Mon, 5 Jan-12 Feb and 1-9 Dec. Open until 9.30 pm. Private room: 20. Air cond. Garage parking. Telex 430605. V AE DC.

President François Mitterrand chose this elegant little Provençal 'château' to entertain his G-7 partners at dinner not too long ago. We understand why. Chef Jany Gleize is extremely demanding in his choice of fresh regional ingredients, whether its Gavot lamb from the nearby mountains, unblemished courgette blossoms from local gardens, or sparkling, firm-fleshed Mediterranean fish. On our last visit we sampled a delightful salad of marinated calf's head, served with bits of tongue, liver, salted veal breast and pine-nuts; tender bonito with fresh anchovies in a jus spiced with coriander, pepper and cinammon; rabbit stuffed with bulghur-like épeautre, napped with wild-thyme-scented cooking juices, and accompanied by an olive purée; locally raised pigeon cooked en cocotte with cardamom and quince; and bitter-almond macaroons filled with caramel ice cream and drizzled with a sweet pistachio sauce. A superb cellar features sumptuous Côtes-du-Rhône and fine Provençal wines. You can count on a warm reception from the Gleize family.

A la carte: 400-500 F. Menus: 190 F, 360 F, 390 F, 440 F.

La Bonne Etape

(See restaurant above)

Closed off-season Sun and Mon, 5 Jan-12 Feb and 1-9 Dec. 7 stes. 11 rms 800-950 F (per pers, half-board oblig). TV. Air cond. Conference facilities. Heated pool.

Pretty, quiet rooms with period furnishings overlook a swimming pool and trees. A new car park across the street is planned for this year. Relais et Châteaux.

CHÂTEAUBOURG

35220 Châteaubourg — (Ille/Vil.)
Paris 330 - Laval 50 - Rennes 20 - Vitré 15

Ar Milin'

13

30, rue de Paris — 99.00.30.91

M. Burel. Closed Sun off-season (dinner only in Oct, March and April) and 20 Dec-2 Jan. Open until 9.15 pm. Private room: 40. Terrace dining. Parking. Telex 740083. V AE DC.

A big old mill, an immense park with a river running through it, a bright veranda dining room served by an experienced staff: such is the setting for pleasant meals that may, on a given day, feature young rabbit with foie gras, saffron-flavoured lotte with mushrooms, or roast wild duck bathed in its reduced cooking juices. The affordably priced set menus are most worthwhile. Excellent reception; conference facilities.

A la carte: 250-300 F. Menus: 90 F, 120 F, 162 F.

Ar Milin'

(See restaurant above)

Closed Sun off-season and 20 Dec-2 Jan. 4 stes 468 F. 30 rms 238-468 F. Half-board 343 F. TV. Conference facilities. Tennis.

The more charming among the hotel's well-kept rooms are in the mill and have a view of the river. The others, recently renovated in 'modern motel' style, are set in the park.

In nearby Saint-Didier

(5 km E on N 157)
35220 Châteaubourg — (Ille/Vil.)

Pen'Roc

14

La Peinière — 99.00.33.02

M. Froc. Closed Sun dinner and Feb school holidays. Open until 9 pm. Private room: 90. Terrace dining. Parking. Telex 741457. V AE DC.

There's nothing quaint or picturesque about the surroundings or the gawky modern structure that houses this restaurant. But food-lovers come from miles around to tuck into Joseph Froc's light, delicate prawn salad with avocados and walnut oil, his beautifully cooked, juicy salmon steak, his 'croustillant' of lobster with sesame, and delicious chocolate-based desserts. Mireille Froc greets guests with singular warmth in a new dining room furnished with attractive antiques. An extra point this year.

A la carte: 250-300 F. Menus: 125 F (weekdays only), 135 F and 190 F (w-e and holidays only), 223 F.

Pen'Roc

(See restaurant above)

Closed Feb school holidays. 1 ste 450 F. 33 rms 218-275 F. Half-board 275-378 F. TV. Conference facilities.

Pilgrims come to town to honour Notre-Dame de la Peinière, and many choose to stay at this fine hotel, with its modern, nicely equipped rooms. Excellent reception.

CHÂTEAU-DU-LOIR

72500 Château-du-Loir — (Sarthe)
Paris 235 - Tours 42 - Le Mans 40 - Vendôme 59

Manoir du Riablay
Rte St-Jean — 43.79.45.86

Open every day. 1 ste 890 F. 9 rms 650-750 F. Restaurant. Half-board 900-1,300 F. TV. Heated pool. Tennis. Parking. Telex 722172. V AE DC.

This listed sixteenth-century dwelling, poised atop a cliff, offers large, extremely comfortable rooms with beautiful appointments in a magnificent country setting. Relaxation is assured in this elegant hotel. Generous breakfasts; warm reception.

CHÂTEAUFORT

See PARIS Suburbs

CHÂTEAULIN

29150 Châteaulin — (Finistère)
Paris 549 - Brest 51 - Quimper 28 - Douarnenez 27

12/20 Auberge des Ducs de Lin
La Pointe-de-St-Coulitz — 98.86.04.20

Mme Corlay. Closed 2-7 Jan. Open until 9 pm (10 pm in summer). Private room: 25. Terrace dining. Hotel: 6 rms 300 F. Parking. V.

The view of the Aulne River is simply beautiful when seen through the bay windows of this beamed, wainscotted dining room. The quality of the cooking, however, is uneven: the fragrant fisherman's soup with seaweed and the generous prawn croustade are honourable dishes, but our portion of leg of lamb roasted in the inn's fireplace was tough, with a meagre garnish of steamed potatoes, carrots, and tomatoes. And the fruit compote we were served for pudding came right out of a tin! For shame! We found the reception and service rather curt.

A la carte: 250 F. Menus: 110 F (weekdays lunch only), 145 F, 160 F, 250 F , 310 F.

In nearby Lopérec

(13.5 km N on N 170 and D 121)
29117 Châteaulin — (Finistère)

10/20 Auberge Bretonne
5, pl. de l'Eglise — 98.81.11.11

Mme Avan. Open for lunch only. Closed Mon. Private room: 24. Air cond. V.

Decent, simple meals are served in this restaurant's sparkling new décor. Of particular interest are the nicely cooked prawns and the leg of lamb. The cheese tray is not bad, and the cellar holds some very good, reasonably priced claret.

Menus: 68 F, 98 F, 150 F, 188 F, 250 F.

In nearby Pont-de-Buis-lès-Quimerch

(8 km N)
29590 Châteaulin — (Finistère)

Château du Bot
98.26.93.90

M. Le Bihan. Closed off-season Sun dinner and Mon, and 24 Feb-10 March. Open until 9.30 pm. Private room: 81. Garden dining. Hotel: 6 rms 170-350 F. Tennis. Parking. V AE.

Happily for chef Jean Le Bihan, increasing numbers of locals and tourists are discovering his fine restaurant, an eighteenth-century manor house set in a huge park. A warm, exotic note permeates Le Bihan's cuisine, which is based on fresh local ingredients touched with West Indian spices and fruits. His chaud-froid of John Dory with pumpkin blossoms and a cauliflower cream, his lobster braisé à l'absinthe, his rosemary-scented roasted veal chop are all beautifully balanced dishes. The cellar is being gradually fleshed out (more half-bottles would be welcome). Speaking of welcome, like the service here it is uncommonly warm. Several spacious, lovely rooms are available in the château (the bathrooms need improvement).

A la carte: 400 F. Menus: 98 F (weekdays lunch only), 150 F (weekdays only), 250 F, 400 F.

CHÂTEAUNEUF

71740 Châteauneuf — (Saône/Loire)
Paris 390 - Roanne 30 - Charolles 30 - La Clayette 11

La Fontaine
85.26.26.87

M. Jury. Closed Tue dinner, Wed, Feb and 10-19 June. Open until 9.30 pm. Parking. V.

Behind the banal exterior of this village restaurant lies an extravagant décor of pink-and-pistachio-coloured mosaics capped by a pyramidal glass skylight. Therein chef Yves Jury serves an ever-changing array of inventive, full-flavoured dishes inspired by his mood and by what looks good at the market. Treat yourself to his pig's trotter en crépinette with lentil salad, or the terrine of kid's sweetbreads with wild mushrooms, or oxtail soup with fresh white beans and cabbage, his sautéed sweetbreads with salsify, or the salmon with a zesty jus of shallots, and finish up with a liquorice-scented crème brûlée. The prices are the very soul of charity.

A la carte: 250 F. Menus: 98 F (weekdays only), 170 F, 230 F.

CHÂTEAUNEUF-DU-PAPE

84230 Châteauneuf-du-Pape — (Vaucluse)
Paris 673 - Avignon 17 - Orange 13 - Carpentras 24

Château Fines Roches
2 km on D 17, towards Avignon
90.83.70.23

M. Estevenin. Closed off-season dinner Sun and Mon, and 23 Dec-14 Feb. Open until 9 pm. Private room: 40. Air cond. No pets. Hotel: 7 rms 390-750 F. Parking. V.

In a neo-Gothic castle surrounded by vineyards, the Estevenin brothers concoct such creditable dishes as red-mullet escabèche with vegetables, juicy roast salmon, and tender young pigeon with whole garlic cloves. The dessert offerings are uniformly excellent, while the cellar is a treasure-house of local vintages.

A la carte: 350-400 F. Menus: 195 F, 250 F.

CHÂTEAUNEUF-EN-THYMERAIS

28170 Châteauneuf-en-Thymerais — (Eure-et-Loir)
Paris 104 - Chartres 25 - Dreux 21 - Châteaudun 64

Saint-Jean
4 km N on D 928
St-Jean-de-Rebervilliers — 37.51.62.83

Mme Aubry. Closed Thu dinner, Fri, 7 Feb-1 March and 12 Sep-4 Oct. Open until 9 pm. Private room: 16. Garden dining. Telex 760189. V AE DC.

A venerable country *auberge*, with its large open fireplace and beamed ceilings is a soothing setting indeed in which to savour traditional, highly polished cuisine prepared by master *saucier* Pierre Aubry. An extra point this year, to reward him for his 'anges en caleçon' (exquisite paupiettes of smoked salmon enveloping huge oysters, set on a pool of sea-salty sabayon), lobster fricassée with chanterelles and seaweed, and an exemplary lamb navarin 'minute' with lightly cooked spring vegetables. Round off the meal with a delectable crisp pear tart, then sit back and enjoy the fire. Prompt service.

A la carte: 350 F. Menu: 195 F.

CHÂTEAUROUX

36000 Châteauroux — (Indre)
Paris 250 - Tours 109 - Bourges 65 - Vierzon 57

12/20 La Ciboulette

42, rue Grande — 54.27.66.28
M. Garnier. Closed Sun, Mon, holidays, 6-31 Jan and 4-21 Aug. Open until 10 pm. Private room: 15. V.
Wine enthusiast Maurice Garnier is a master at unearthing little-known, bargain-priced vintages, but his cellar also boasts some high-class rarities which he magnanimously pours by the glass (Beychevelle '74, Lafaurie-Peyraguey '79, Champagnes, etc.). To keep them company, he also proposes a few choice dishes, always served in copious portions: salade de jambon de canard, feuilleté de sole au foie gras, minted pears with almond syrup.

A la carte: 200-250 F. Menus: 125 F (wine inc), 59 F, 95 F, 145 F.

[13] Jean-Louis Dumonet

1, rue J.-J.-Rousseau — 54.34.82.69
M. Dumonet. Closed Sun dinner, Mon, 1 May and 5-20 Aug. Open until 10 pm. Private room: 40. V AE DC.
From the moment he took over Jean Bardet's far-famed restaurant, Jean-Louis Dumonet has striven to live up to its fabled reputation. Alas, his cuisine is inconsistent, and mistakes are not rare: our meagre portion of mussels with vegetables literally swam in an oversalted broth; perfectly cooked lamb noisettes came with burned (burned!) spinach; and a salad of lamb's sweetbreads was unpleasantly greasy. The desserts, however, are quite good, the cellar is well stocked, and the reception and service brim over with warmth. Nonetheless, we are obliged to take away two points, and the second toque.

A la carte: 350-400 F. Menus: 165 F (weekdays only), 185 F (w-e and holidays only), 220 F (wine inc), 250 F, 330 F.

Elysée Hôtel

2, rue de la République — 54.22.33.66
Closed Sun (except upon reserv). 18 rms 250-350 F. TV. No pets. V AE DC.
A fine, small hotel that features comfortable, constantly renovated rooms. Bar.

12/20 Le Manoir du Colombier

232, rte de Châtellerault — 54.29.30.01
M. Moineau. Closed Sun dinner and Mon (except holidays). Open until 9.30 pm. Private room: 40. Garden dining. Garage parking. V AE DC.
This large country dwelling presents an elegantly decorated dining room, an agreeable garden, and cuisine that tries hard to please. The excellent prix-fixe luncheon (served on weekdays) includes marinated sea bream with crunchy cabbage, duck breast with pink peppercorns, cheese, dessert, and wine. An extra point for their efforts this year.

A la carte: 300 F and up. Menus: 150 F (weekdays lunch only, wine inc), 150 F (weekdays dinner only), 180 F, 295 F.

Le Manoir du Colombier

(See restaurant above)
Open every day. 11 rms 280-450 F. Half-board 400-450 F. TV. Conference facilities.
Châteauroux's best hotel, offering bright, spacious, and well-equipped rooms furnished with wicker and pretty fabrics. Copious breakfasts.

12/20 Relais Saint-Jacques

N 20 — 54.22.87.10
M. Jeanrot. Closed Sun and 20 Dec-4 Jan. Open until 9.30 pm. Private room: 100. Air cond. Parking. Telex 751176. V AE DC.
It's easy enough to forget the charmless surroundings (an awkward building opposite an airfield) when you taste your first forkful of Pierre Jeanrot's bass fillet with tiny vegetables, his generous rabbit aiguillettes with thyme, and his gorgeous caramelised apple tartlets in Calvados cream. Good cellar, with a fine choice of half-bottles at unbeatable prices. Friendly service.

A la carte: 300 F. Menus: 90 F and 100 F (weekdays only), 250 F (w-e and holidays only), 220 F.

Relais Saint-Jacques

(See restaurant above)
Closed 20 Dec-4 Jan. 46 rms 280-310 F. TV. Conference facilities.
A good, functional hotel, with nicely equipped, soundproof rooms.

CHÂTELAILLON-PLAGE

17340 Châtelaillon-Plage — (Charente-M.)
Paris 472 - La Rochelle 12 - Niort 60 - Rochefort 21

Domaine des Trois Iles

La Falaise — 46.56.14.14
Open every day. 61 rms 380-480 F. Restaurant. Half-board 520-550 F. TV. Conference facilities. Pool. Tennis. Parking. Telex 791813. V AE DC.
This new seafront complex is the region's most beautiful hotel, splendidly situated, with very comfortable rooms that look out over the islands. In addition, there are 17 studios and 20 duplexes which are let by the week. Numerous sports facilities, including a golf green.

11/20 Saint-Victor

35, bd de la Mer — 46.56.25.13
M. Blaineau. Closed off-season Sun dinner and Mon, 7-26 Jan and 7-26 Oct. Open until 9 pm. Private room: 25. Terrace dining. Telex 793227. V AE.
The best to be had at this big seaside establishment is the 135 F set menu, which offers shellfish or foie gras (15 F extra), duck aiguillettes, cheese, and dessert. A la carte choices are less reliable.

A la carte: 220 F. Menus: 80 F (weekdays only), 98 F, 135 F, 175 F.

Saint-Victor

(See restaurant above)
Closed off-season Sun and Mon, 7-26 Jan and 7-26 Oct. 12 rms 195-230 F. Half-board 210-240 F. TV. Conference facilities.
Small, recently renovated rooms with sea views.

Remember to reserve your table or your room in advance, and please let the restaurant or hotel know if you cannot honour your reservation.

63140 Châtelguyon — (Puy-de-Dôme)
Paris 375 - Clermont-Ferrand 21 - Vichy 47

11/20 La Grilloute
33, av. Baraduc — 73.86.04.17
Mme Brandibat. Closed Tue and 5 Oct-5 May. Open until 9.30 pm. Terrace dining. V.

In a friendly, relaxed atmosphere, guests are served a singular blend of exotic and traditional fare that runs the gamut from Mexican omelettes to Indian-style grilled chicken and heaty local charcuterie.

A la carte: 150-200 F. Menus: 90 F (weekdays only), 120 F (w-e and holidays only), 100 F, 110 F.

International
Rue Punett — 73.86.06.72
Closed 3 Oct-26 April. 68 rms 190-335 F. Restaurant. Half-board 290-410 F. TV. V AE DC.

A traditional hotel decorated in 1930s–style. The surroundings are blessedly peaceful (magnificent trees), and the rooms are irreproachably tidy. Free shuttle to town's centre.

Manoir Fleuri
Rte de Chazeron — 73.86.01.27
Closed Mon and 15 Oct-25 April. 15 rms 170-260 F. Restaurant. Half-board 230-280 F. TV 7 rms. Conference facilities. Garage parking. V.

A large, eccentric building set among the trees, with an outstanding view of the Auvergne mountains.

Pullman Splendid
5-7, rue d'Angleterre — 73.86.04.80
Closed 1 Nov-30 March. 1 ste 700-1,020 F. 80 rms 333-1,060 F. Restaurant. Half-board 470-1,020 F. TV. Conference facilities. Heated pool. Parking. Telex 990585. V AE DC.

This immense, very formal hotel set amid lawns and flower gardens provides constantly upgraded rooms. Among the amenities and facilities on the premises are a spa, a fitness centre, sauna, excursions, and a nightclub.

86100 Châtellerault — (Vienne)
Paris 305 - Cholet 128 - Tours 69 - Poitiers 34

La Charmille
74, bd Blossac — 49.21.30.11
M. Proust. Closed Wed, 20 Jan-20 Feb and 10 days in Oct. Open until 9.30 pm. Private room: 25. Garden dining. Air cond. Garage parking. Telex 791801. V AE DC.

It was in 1970 that Christian and Marie-Jeanne Proust bought this rambling turn-of-the-century establishment—called the Hôtel Moderne for the very good reason that it was not modern at all. Within a few years they had succeeded in putting some sparkle back into the hotel, and now Christian's cooking is an added attraction. He took charge in the kitchen after a succession of chefs failed to share his culinary views, and his talent shone forth instantly. The short but harmonious menu changes frequently because it is based on what is best at market, cooked with skilful simplicity. This year's delights include a blanquette of vegetables and green asparagus, cod glazed with spices and strips of fried leek, prawns en papillote with asparagus, saddle of young rabbit stuffed with foie gras and cooked in Chinon, and veal sweetbreads with diced prawns. There is a fine wine list, with an obvious leaning towards the region's quality names, such as Chinon, Saumur-

Champigny, and Vouvray. But the biggest change this year is the total and tasteful transformation of the premises, with the kitchen moved to new quarters. Cascading plants, beige marble floors, and walls in tones of peach and salmon-pink give a feeling of peace and luxury to both the renovated dining room and the new garden restaurant.

A la carte: 300-350 F. Menus: 140 F, 220 F.

Grand Hôtel Moderne
(See restaurant above)
Open every day. 30 rms 220-500 F. TV. Conference facilities.

Comfortable rooms, carefully and tastefully decorated. You are assured of a warm welcome from Marie-Jeanne Proust and her young staff and of fairly quiet nights, despite the hotel's central location.

Château de la Borde
N10 — 49.93.39.40
Mme Balzano. Open every day. Open until 10 pm. Private room: 40. Garden dining. No pets. Parking. V.

This captivating nineteenth-century residence has been stylishly renovated, and the cooking is worthy of the surroundings. Try oysters poached in a frothy sabayon sauce flavoured with sweet pepper, young roast pigeon, its juices thickened with foie gras, feather-light orange pastries. Attentive if somewhat inexperienced service in the grey-and-wine-coloured dining room, and Joguet and Olga Raffault's wonderful Chinon.

A la carte: 280-320 F. Menus: 98 F, 175 F, 240 F.

Château de la Borde
(See restaurant above)
Open every day. 1 ste 650 F. 9 rms 240-700 F. Half-board 370 F oblig in seas. TV. Conference facilities. Heated pool.

Peaceful and very romantic rooms. Service with a smile.

39130 Châtillon — (Jura)
Paris 421 - Lons-le-Saunier 18 - Champagnole 23

Chez Yvonne
2.5 km E on D 39 — 84.25.70.82
Closed Wed off-season and 30 Nov-15 March. 8 rms 160-180 F. Restaurant. Half-board 230-240 F. Conference facilities. Garage parking. V.

Pretty and unassuming, this *auberge* perched above the River Ain has the bonus of trout fishing nearby. Shady riverside terrace.

36400 Châtre (La) — (Indre)
Paris 301 - Bourges 71 - Châteauroux 36 - Guéret 53

12/20 Château de la Vallée Bleue
Rte de Verneuil, in St-Chartier — 54.31.01.91
M. Gasquet. Closed off-season Sun dinner and Mon, and 28 Jan-5 March. Open until 9.30 pm. Garden dining. Parking. V AE.

A charming nineteenth-century château, simply and tastefully furnished. Good cooking and liberal portions (osso buco of lotte with vegetables, veal steak with morels). Probably on the expensive side, especially if you let yourself be tempted by the extensive and carefully chosen wine list. Another point.

A la carte: 280-300 F. Menus: 98 F (weekdays only), 160 F, 245 F, 295 F.

Château de la Vallée Bleue
(See restaurant above)
Closed off-season Sun and Mon, and 28 Jan-5 March. 14 rms 140-390 F. Half-board 260-325 F. TV. Conference facilities.

Surrounded by grounds featuring hundred-year-old trees. Pleasant and peaceful rooms. Various refurbishments this year.

Le Lion d'Argent
2, av. du Lion-d'Argent — 54.48.11.69
Open every day. 34 rms 220-250 F. Half-board 220-300 F. Restaurant. TV 24 rms. Conference facilities. V AE DC.

Soft beige décor and small but cosy rooms. An hotel that is gradually becoming more attractive.

12/20 Les Tanneries
Pont du Lion-d'Argent — 54.48.06.82
M. Audebert. Closed Thu lunch, Wed, 15 Nov-20 Dec and 3 Jan-15 Feb. Open until 9.30 pm. Terrace dining. Parking. Telex 751650. V AE DC.

Bright décor and open views from the upper floor onto gardens and the river. The atmosphere is relaxed, and the cooking reflects praiseworthy but often over-complicated efforts to be different. The cheapest menu is excellent.
A la carte: 300 F. Menus: 100 F, 150 F, 300 F.

Les Tanneries
(See restaurant above)
Closed 15 Nov-20 Dec and 3 Jan-15 Feb. 10 rms 240-300 F. Half-board 245-340 F. TV.

Bright, spacious rooms, all overlooking the lawn and with pleasant views over the former tanneries and the old prison, now converted into a George Sand museum. Perfect reception and service.

In nearby **Pouligny-Notre-Dame**

(12 km S)
36160 Châtre (La) — (Indre)

Les Dryades
54.30.28.00
M. Vedy. Open every day. Open until 9.30 pm. Terrace dining. Air cond. Valet parking. Telex 750945. V AE DC.

The promoters of this dismal concrete wall towering over the gentle surrounding countryside can begin to breathe more easily: the vast sums sunk into the project might not be wasted. Since the arrival of Philippe Larmat, who was Jean Bardet's second-in-command at Châteauroux, this up-market health centre has turned into one of the region's best restaurants. And word seems to have got round, judging by the way customers fill the huge neo-classical dining room overlooking an eighteen-hole golf course. Taste the elegant fillet of freshwater perch with tarragon, saddle of young rabbit with foie gras and grapes, baked fillet of bass with oysters, and a cinnamon-spiced baked pear served with melting warm nougat, and you'll forget the architecture in no time. The finest cellar in the Berry region at keen prices.
A la carte. 350 F. Menus: 180 F, 240 F, 295 F.

Les Dryades
(See restaurant above)
Open every day. 5 stes 1,300 F. 80 rms 600-700 F. Half-board 550-775 F. TV. Air cond. Conference facilities. Heated pool. Tennis. Golf.

An astonishing building reminiscent of a Le Corbusier church, or even a specimen of Soviet architecture. But many harassed executives appreciate its understated luxury, with huge, well-equipped rooms decorated in gentle colours. The hotel's strong point is the superb golf course, and there's also a health club. Pleasant, helpful staff.

CHAUDES-AIGUES

15110 Chaudes-Aigues — (Cantal)
Paris 527 - St-Flour 32 - Aurillac 92 - Espalion 56

Auberge du Pont de Lanau
4 km N on D 921
15260 Lanau — 71.23.57.76
M. Cornut. Closed Tue dinner, Wed and Jan. Open until 9.30 pm. Private room: 25. Garden dining. No pets. Garage parking. V.

In this stone-roofed *auberge* covered with vines on the banks of the Truyère, Jean-Michel Cornut's cooking reflects his love of his native region. His popular millefeuille with bleu d'Auvergne cheese is as light and delicate as ever, and you should also try the trout fritters with bacon and buttery cabbage, tripoux (an Auvergne speciality similar to faggots) on a bed of green lentils, and rolled pork with bay leaves and white beans. Dessert sees the return of the flaky pastries, filled with fruit in season. Josette Cornut is welcoming and attentive.
A la carte: 150-200 F. Menus: 130 F, 160 F, 180 F, 240 F.

Auberge du Pont de Lanau
(See restaurant above)
Closed Tue, Wed and Jan. 8 rms 230-320 F. Half-board 220-245 F. TV. Conference facilities.

Eight quiet, attractive rooms. The family make the croissants and other breakfast pastries, and ensure guests feel at home.

12/20 Aux Bouillons d'Or
10, quai du Remontalou — 71.23.51.42
Mme Cornut. Closed off-season Mon dinner and Tue, and 10 Nov-Easter. Open until 9 pm. Private room: 20. Terrace dining. No pets. V AE DC.

You are greeted with a smile at this pretty restaurant and treated to skilfully cooked regional dishes: salmon tart, aligot (a potato purée with cheese and garlic), fillet of lamb with potatoes and onions. Good Bordeaux at reasonable prices.
A la carte: 210-250 F. Menus: 75 F, 110 F, 175 F.

Aux Bouillons d'Or
(See restaurant above)
Closed off-season Mon and Tue, and 10 Nov-Easter. 12 rms 210-230 F. No pets.

Very pleasant rooms: small, but quiet and well kept. All have bathrooms and are furnished in Regency style. Double glazing. Excellent reception and hearty breakfasts.

Thermal du Ban
27, av. du Pdt-Pompidou — 71.23.51.06
Closed 21 Oct-25 April. 46 rms 160-250 F. TV. Parking. V.

Bright, well-equipped rooms with direct access to the adjoining spa. The hotel also has a gym

Les Thermes
21, av. du Pdt-Pompidou — 71.23.51.18
Closed 20 Oct-25 April. 35 rms 115-230 F. Restaurant. Garage parking. V.

A quiet hotel with plain, well-kept rooms, a stone's throw from the spa.

CHAVILLE
See PARIS Suburbs

49330 Cheffes-sur-Sarthe — (Maine/Loire)
Paris 288 - Angers 19 - Château-Gontier 33

12/20 Château de Teildras
41.42.61.08

M. de Bernard du Breil. Closed Tue lunch and 1 Dec-1 March. Open until 9.30 pm. Private room: 25. No pets. Parking. Telex 722268. V AE DC.

The rather outdated décor is the main attraction, but the chef knows how to choose and cook top-quality ingredients: freshwater perch in red Anjou wine, pike mousse with marinated mushrooms, roast pigeon with a blood-thickened sauce. Good Bordeaux at high prices.

A la carte: 350 F. Menus: 195 F, 250 F.

Château de Teildras
(See restaurant above)

Closed 1 Dec-1 March (open 1 Jan). 11 rms 440-950 F. Half-board 645-935 F. TV.

Pretty and comfortable rooms (although not always quiet) in a magnificent sixteenth-century manor house. Rather off-hand service.

69840 Chénas — (Rhône)
Paris 415 - Lyon 62 - Mâcon 17 - Juliénas 5

Robin
in Deschamps — 85.36.72.67

M. Robin. Lunch only Sun, Tue and Thu. Closed Wed and mid-Feb to mid-March. Open until 9 pm. Private room: 35. Garden dining. Telex 351004. V AE DC.

It's best not to be in a hurry during summer weekends because the superb garden-terrace overlooking vineyards is always packed. Sample well-loved dishes like andouillette sausage, roast Bresse chicken, and a beef joint cooked in Burgundy, or some less familiar but finely crafted fare: clear snail soup with truffle juice or a fish fresh from the market baked in sweet-and-sour sauce. All the best Beaujolais, and a good Chénas as house wine.

A la carte: 350 F. Menus: 285 F and 335 F (w-e and holidays only), 185 F, 240 F.

See Apt

See Saumur

See PARIS Suburbs

37150 Chenonceaux — (Indre/Loire)
Paris 213 - Bourges 113 - Tours 35 - Amboise 11

11/20 Le Bon Laboureur
et Château
6, rue du Dr-Bretonneau — 47.23.90.02

M. Jeudi. Closed 30 Nov-15 March. Open until 9.30 pm. Private room: 60. Garden dining. Garage parking. V AE DC.

A million tourists come to Chenonceaux every year so the Jeudi family hardly need make an effort to attract customers. They could, however, put more into polishing their dishes: good raw salmon but the toast served alongside is awful, the perch and the lamb are overcooked, nondescript desserts. Indifferent service. Elegant décor.

A la carte: 300 F. Menus: 175 F, 225 F, 300 F.

Le Bon Laboureur
et Château
(See restaurant above)

Closed 30 Nov-15 March. 30 rms 250-480 F. Half-board 450-680 F oblig in seas. TV 8 rms. Conference facilities. Heated pool.

Vine-covered *auberge* with pleasant rooms overlooking a flower-filled inner courtyard.

50100 Cherbourg — (Manche)
Paris 360 - Caen 119 - Bayeux 92 - Avranches 134

12/20 Le Clipper
Gare maritime — 33.44.01.11

M. Larbi. Open every day. Open until 10.30 pm. Terrace dining. Telex 170613. V AE DC.

The dining room looking out over the harbour is modern and comfortable but lacking in charm. Unpretentious cooking with good fresh produce: nicely prepared timbale of oysters with samphire, tasty grilled bass with fennel, respectable apple tart Tatin. Rapid service. A few more good bottles would not hurt the wine list.

A la carte: 220-250 F. Menus: 98 F, 120 F.

Mercure
(See restaurant above)

Open every day. 84 rms 240-490 F. TV. Conference facilities.

Extensive views over the harbour. Pleasant service and good breakfasts. One of the floors is reserved for non-smokers.

12/20 Le Faitout
Rue Tour-Carrée — 33.04.25.04

M. Pain. Closed Sun lunch and Mon. Annual closings not available. Open until 10.30 pm. Terrace dining. V.

Homely dishes (pot-au-feu, blanquette, calf's head), good portions, low prices, pay-as-you-drink wine on the tables: Jacky Pain, who also runs Le Plouc, has found the formula to draw the crowds. Relaxed atmosphere.

A la carte: 120-180 F. Menu: 100 F.

Le Louvre
2, rue H.-Dunant — 33.53.02.28

Closed 24 Dec-1 Jan. 42 rms 155-200 F. TV. Garage parking. Telex 171132. V.

Near the marina. Spacious rooms with good soundproofing, tiny bathrooms. Pleasant staff.

Chez Pain
(Le Plouc)
59, rue au Blé — 33.53.67.64

M. Pain. Closed Sat lunch and Sun. Annual closings not available. Open until 10 pm. V AE.

Businessmen at lunchtime, a refined clientele for dinner, and English tourists in summer keep the two dining rooms busy. Mme Pain has a pleasant greeting for them all while her husband, who formerly worked at Ledoyen in Paris, is the experienced and reliable but not over-imaginative cook. His latest offerings include marinated fresh sardines on hot toast, rolled and baked lotte. Good wines, competitively priced.

A la carte: 280-300 F. Menus: 95 F, 130 F, 190 F, 250 F.

See PARIS Suburbs: Versailles

CHEVANNES

See Auxerre

CHEVREUSE

78460 Chevreuse — (Yvelines)
Paris 32 - Rambouillet 19 - Versailles 16 - Etampes 45

In nearby Saint-Lambert-des-Bois

(5 km NW on D 46)
78470 Chevreuse — (Yvelines)

Les Hauts de Port-Royal
2, rue de Vaumurier — 30.44.10.21
M. Poirier. Closed off-season dinner Sun and Tue, Mon, Nov school holidays and Feb school holidays. Open until 9.30 pm. Private room: 18. Terrace dining. Parking. V AE.

The predominantly pink décor, tasteful if slightly affected, is designed to appeal to those who flock to the area every weekend to ride horses and play golf. This charming half-timbered establishment also boasts a glorious terrace, but we were not overwhelmed by the cooking this year, except for an avocado mousse with smoked salmon perfectly partnered by a tomato sorbet. Among the disappointments: ordinary, crumbly prawn ravioli, a soufflé stingily garnished with lobster and a few crayfish, turbot en papillote with an overbearing taste of smoked bacon. The crêpes with orange butter are good.
A la carte: 350-400 F.

CHINON

37500 Chinon — (Indre/Loire)
Paris 282 - Tours 47 - Poitiers 95 - Angers 80

Cheops
Centre St-Jacques — 47.98.46.46
Closed 1-10 Jan. 55 rms 320-385 F. Restaurant. Half-board 332-434 F. TV. Conference facilities. Parking. Telex 752547. V AE DC.

A modern pyramidal building opposite the Château de Chinon. The rooms are bright and comfortable and all have balconies. Equipped for conferences.

Chris'Hôtel
12, pl. Jeanne-d'Arc — 47.93.36.92
Open every day. 40 rms 180-300 F. TV 20 rms. Garage parking. V AE DC.

Overlooking the château and the river, with pleasant rooms furnished in period style.

Hostellerie Gargantua
73, rue Haute-St-Maurice — 47.93.04.71
M. Fossé. Closed Wed off-season, and 15 Nov-15 March. Open until 10 pm. Terrace dining. No pets. Garage parking. V AE DC.

Attentive hosts greet you amid chunks of Loire chalk and old furniture redolent of wax polish. The chef's omelette Gargamelle, with cheese, mushrooms and herbs, is a must, and his steamed freshwater perch with citrus and walnut tart with acacia honey deserve a toque of encouragement: to find a good baker and vary his menus more, for instance.
A la carte: 280 F. Menus: 150 F, 180 F.

Hostellerie Gargantua
(See restaurant above)
Closed Wed off-season, and 15 Nov-15 March. 10 rms 200-500 F. Half-board 330-630 F. No pets. Conference facilities.

Ten rooms with beamed ceilings and old-fashioned charm. Welcoming, homely atmosphere.

Au Plaisir Gourmand
2, rue Parmentier — 47.93.20.48
M. Rigollet. Closed Sun dinner, Mon, 11-28 Feb and 12-29 Nov. Open until 9.15 pm. Private room: 20. Air cond. V.

Jean-Claude Rigollet is no publicity seeker, and his restaurant built of chalk at the foot of the château will never attract those who go out to see and be seen. Just as well. His faithful customers and the odd tourist in the know will better be able to appreciate the elegant setting, breathtakingly low prices, and the studied simplicity that stands out both in the cooking and in the welcome provided by Danielle Rigollet. Jean-Claude works diligently and quietly all year round, producing such delights as suprême of freshwater perch in a buttery wine sauce, strips of pike with walnuts, coquilles St-Jacques in Vouvray, stuffed pigs' trotters, and ox-tail braised in Chinon, a wine of which this restaurant has a wonderful collection.
A la carte: 280-300 F. Menus: 165 F, 210 F.

In nearby Beaumont-en-Véron

(5 km on D 749)
37420 Chinon — (Indre/Loire)

Château de Danzay
47.58.46.86
Closed 10 Nov-25 March. 2 stes 1,000-1,200 F. 10 rms 600-1,000 F. Restaurant. Conference facilities. Parking. V.

This lovely fifteenth-century manor has been completely restored. Spacious rooms with exposed beams and a warm atmosphere.

La Giraudière
47.58.40.36
Closed Jan. 1 ste 350 F. 25 rms 150-350 F. Restaurant. TV 14 rms. Conference facilities. Parking. V AE DC.

An elegant seventeenth-century residence set in three hectares of grounds. Comfortable rooms, but only half have kitchenettes.

In nearby Marçay

(6 km S on D 749 and D 116)
37500 Chinon — (Indre/Loire)

Château de Marçay
47.93.03.47
M. Ponsard. Closed 6 Jan-23 Feb. Open until 9.30 pm. Private room: 80. Garden dining. Valet parking. Telex 751475. V.

Surrounded by vineyards and gardens, this château with its turrets, steep roofs, and fine views will give you a taste of real French hospitality. Old beams, fine tableware, and lavish flower arrangements contribute to the atmosphere of relaxed luxury. The chef, Gérard Côme, contributes well-balanced sauces, and dishes such as crisp prawns in Vouvray, freshwater perch with oysters and bone marrow cooked in Chinon, pigeon pastries, and a perfect lime-sparked crème brûlée. Corinne, the young *sommelière*, will give you expert advice on choosing from the 10,000 bottles that make up one of the finest cellars in Touraine.
A la carte: 400-500 F. Menus: 140 F (weekdays lunch only), 230 F, 360 F.

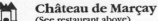

Château de Marçay

(See restaurant above)
Closed 6 Jan-23 Feb. 6 stes 1,195-1,530 F. 38 rms 495-1,230 F. Half-board 655-1,035 F. TV 30 rms. Conference facilities. Heated pool. Tennis.

Huge, bright rooms with elegant tapestry wall hangings. Spacious bathrooms, some with Jacuzzi. Peaceful and luxurious surroundings in which your every need is efficiently attended to. The home-produced Touraine Vieilles Vignes is sold on the premises.

CHISSAY-EN-TOURAINE

See Montrichard

CHOLET

49300 Cholet – (Maine/Loire)
Paris 350 - Angers 61 - Nantes 61 - Niort 106

Le Belvédère

5 km SE on D 20, lac de Ribou – 41.62.14.02
MM. Thepaut and Inagaki. Closed Sun dinner, Mon lunch, Feb school holidays and 22 July-21 Aug. Open until 9 pm. Private room: 12. Terrace dining. No pets. Parking. V AE DC.

Set in green countryside and overlooking Lake Ribou, this restaurant has a dining room enhanced with beams and a magnificent fireplace, plus a pleasant terrace. Daisuke Inagaki continues to come up with original combinations like navarin of snails with fresh pasta, strips of sole with smoked duck breast and spicy prawns, and young pigeon with star anise.
A la carte: 300-350 F. Menus: 110 F and 190 F (weekdays only), 170 F and 220 F (w-e and holidays only).

Le Belvédère

(See restaurant above)
Closed Sun, Feb school holidays and 22 July-21 Aug. 8 rms 275-320 F. TV.

Eight perfectly quiet rooms. Faultless reception.

Fimotel

Av. des Sables-d'Olonne – 41.62.45.45
Open every day. 42 rms 220-270 F. Restaurant. Half-board 270-295 F. TV. Conference facilities. Parking. Telex 722298. V AE DC.

A modern hotel five minutes from the town centre. Ordinary, well-equipped rooms with soundproofing.

Arnaud Vallée

Rue Ch.-Lindbergh – 41.62.03.14
M. Vallée. Closed Sun dinner and Sat. Open until 10 pm. Terrace dining. Parking. V.

Tall plants frame the tables that cluster round a grand piano and look out over a small aerodrome. The owners are charming and Arnaud Vallée's careful preparation of quality ingredients wins a toque this year. Try the Loire sandre with butter sauce, or boned, glazed pigeon. Chocolate soufflé and pistachio ice cream are good desserts.
A la carte: 300 F and up. Menus: 98 F, 158 F, 250 F.

CHONAS-L'AMBALLAN

See Vienne

CHOREY-LÈS-BEAUNE

See Beaune

CHOUZÉ-SUR-LOIRE

See Bourgueil

CHOUZY-SUR-CISSE

See Onzain

CIBOURE

See Saint-Jean-de-Luz

CIOTAT (LA)

13600 Ciotat (La) — (B./Rhône)
Paris 805 - Aix 49 - Toulon 37 - Marseille 32

L'Orchidée

3, bd Beaurivage – 42.83.09.54
MM. Mary. Open every day. Open until 10 pm. Terrace dining. Air cond. Parking. Telex 420425. V AE DC.

The Sciaris have handed their business over to a new young couple and nothing seems to have changed in this seaside restaurant. The cooking is still skilful, although the flavours are sometimes blurry. Good choices are the terrine of aubergine with anchovies, Barbary duck with Provençal walnut-flavoured wine, and caramelised pear pastries. High prices if you eat à la carte and the wine list has room for improvement. Professional but rather slow service.
A la carte: 350-400 F. Menus: 95 F (weekdays lunch only), 155 F, 260 F.

Miramar

(See restaurant above)
Open every day. 25 rms 420-750 F. Half-board 360-425 F. TV. Air cond. Conference facilities.

An old hotel set between the pine trees and the sea. The rooms have been re-equipped and redecorated to suit modern tastes with wicker furniture.

12/20 Le Séréno

6 km E, corniche du Liouquet – 42.83.90.30
M. Boissi. Closed Sun dinner. Open until 9.30 pm. Terrace dining. Air cond. No pets. Parking. Telex 441390. V AE DC.

The poolside terrace and bright dining room are more immediately enticing than the cooking, which calls for a tighter technique: marinated duck with an olive and caper purée, spatchcocked red-mullet, fricassée of young rabbit with rosemary. The desserts are better than last year, and the wine list full but rather expensive.
A la carte: 280-330 F. Menus: 145 F, 195 F, 295 F.

Ciotel Le Cap

(See restaurant above)
Open every day. 43 rms 365-690 F. TV. Conference facilities. Pool. Tennis.

Quiet, recently decorated bungalows scattered through pretty grounds planted with flowers. Secretarial services, baby-sitting, and tennis lessons are available.

CLAIX

See Grenoble

CLAMECY

58500 Clamecy — (Nièvre)
Paris 210 - Auxerre 43 - Dijon 143 - Nevers 69

L'Angelus

11, pl. St-Jean – 86.27.23.25
M. Etienne. Closed off-season Wed dinner and Thu. Open until 10.30 pm. Private room: 25. Terrace dining. Parking. V AE DC.

Pascal Choppin, the 25-year-old chef, has a bright future but his cooking needs to be more consistent. His classic meat dishes, such as duck breast with almond sauce, are not up to scratch. For a better idea of his talents, choose the salade gourmande (tasty foie gras, smoked duck, and breast of chicken with multi-coloured salad and an excellent raspberry-vinegar dressing), expertly baked John Dory with meat essence, or blanquette of perch with orange. Good desserts and a wine list that, oddly (given the location), contains more Bordeaux than Burgundies. The timbered restaurant is a listed building.

A la carte: 250 F. Menus: 90 F, 140 F, 200 F.

CLÉCY

14570 Clécy — (Calvados)
Paris 249 - Falaise 31 - Condé-sur-Noireau 10

11/20 Auberge du Chalet de Cantepie
31.69.71.10
M. Charpentier. Closed Sun dinner and 15 Nov-15 Dec. Open until 9 pm. Garden dining. Parking. V AE DC.

Serving staff in Norman costume enhance the décor of this eighteenth-century forge. The cooking is classic and consistent, with some local specialities: tripe with cider, duck in cider sauce, braised Normandy ham, excellent regional cheeses, and a worthy apple tart.

A la carte: 250 F. Menus: 85 F (weekdays only), 135 F, 165 F, 220 F.

11/20 Moulin du Vey
1 km E on D 133a, Le Vey — 31.69.71.08
Mme Leduc. Closed 30 Nov-28 Dec. Open until 9.30 pm. Private room: 280. Garden dining. No pets. Parking. V AE DC.

A delightful former grain mill covered in ivy. Heavily rustic décor and a riverside terrace provide the setting for lacklustre but conscientious cooking. Too much vinegar in the salad of (large) prawns, and a rather ordinary chicken with foie gras, but the fresh and smoked salmon in a light creamy sauce is good. Slow service.

A la carte: 300-350 F. Menus: 125 F, 210 F, 350 F.

Moulin du Vey
(See restaurant above)
Closed 30 Nov-28 Dec. 12 rms 350-500 F. Half-board 410-450 F. TV 7 rms. Conference facilities.

Peaceful rooms in the mill itself, which is surrounded by greenery, plus an annexe whose accommodation is less pleasant and badly soundproofed. The breakfasts are reliable.

CLEDER

29221 Cleder — (Finistère)
Paris 570 · Plouescat 6 · Brest 49 · St-Pol-de-Léon 9

Le Baladin
9, rue de l'Armorique — 98.69.42.48
M. Queffelec. Closed Tue dinner, Mon and 15-31 Jan. Open until 9.30 pm. Private room: 30. V AE.

A smiling welcome awaits you in the cheerful dining room, while in the kitchen Pierre Queffelec is gradually establishing a personal style. Eating à la carte is quite costly (turbot baked with thyme, sole and prawn soufflé) but the 98 F menu includes gratin of oysters with winkles, jambonette of duck studded with green peppercorns served with a classic but well-prepared potato gratin, salad with hot goat cheese, and an acacia-honey frozen mousse.

A la carte: 300 F. Menus: 55 F (weekdays only), 98 F, 138 F, 195 F, 245 F.

CLÈRES

76690 Clères — (Seine/Mar.)
Paris 150 - Rouen 23 - Dieppe 44 - Yvetot 34

Au Souper Fin
in Frichemesnil
Pl. de l'Eglise — 35.33.33.88
M. Buisset. Closed Wed dinner, Thu and 30 Aug-28 Sep. Open until 9 pm. V.

A cosy blue dining room nestles behind the geraniums that crowd round the windows. A delightful reception and skilful cooking from Eric Buisset, who is working hard to perfect his sauces and blends of flavours. Delicate roast duck breast with chanterelle mushrooms, red-mullet flavoured with olive oil, and a fresh fig dessert that would be better without the mandarine liqueur.

A la carte: 300 F. Menus: 80 F (weekdays lunch only), 150 F, 200 F.

CLERMONT-FERRAND

63000 Clermont-Ferrand — (Puy-de-Dôme)
Paris 389 - Limoges 191 - Lyon 183 - Moulins 96

Jean-Yves Bath
Pl. du Marché-St-Pierre — 73.31.23.23
M. Bath. Closed Mon lunch, Sun, holidays, Feb and Nov school holidays. Open until 10 pm. Terrace dining. Air cond. V.

Not everyone appreciates the ultra-modern décor but Jean-Yves Bath, a former pupil of Senderens, is not trying to impress anybody: it's just his personal taste. The same could be said of his surprising and sometimes disconcerting cuisine. This year his quest for originality is reflected by roast calf's head, lobster vinaigrette, cabbage stuffed with lobster in Waleska sauce, and prawn ravioli with herb essence. There are also dishes with a local flavour: sausage salad with coq au vin, Cantal cheese ravioli with meat and herb essence, perch with fresh herbs. Jean-Yves Bath often comes out of the kitchen to charm his customers. Those in search of cheaper and simpler fare will like Le Clos Saint-Pierre next door, which he also owns.

A la carte: 300 F. Menus: 160 F (weekdays lunch only, wine inc), 260 F.

12/20 Le Charade
51, rue Bonnabaud — 73.93.59.69
M. Fest. Closed Sat and Sun. Open until 10 pm. Private room: 135. Air cond. Garage parking. Telex 392779. V AE DC.

Jacques Debord, the new chef, is hitting his stride. There's a light, tasty Landes salad, slightly too-sweet duck breast with cranberries, a selection of cheeses that could be improved, and a generous medley of desserts.

A la carte: 250 F. Menus: 105 F (wine inc), 145 F, 190 F.

Gallieni
(See restaurant above)
Open every day. 80 rms 210-395 F. Half-board 300-350 F. TV. Conference facilities.

Near the town centre and with as many parking spaces as modern, comfortable rooms. Hairdresser, bookshop.

Clavé
10-12, rue St-Adjutor — 73.36.46.30
M. Clavé. Closed 14 July-15 Aug. Open until 10.30 pm. Private room: 30. Valet parking. V.

The new law courts nearby seem set to change the atmosphere of this street, which used to be on the seamy side, leaving a different clientele to discover the cuisine of Jean-Claude Gérard, one of the best chefs in Clermont-Ferrand. A former pupil at Maxim's, he makes excellent sauces and pays tribute to this region with young rabbit on a bed of shredded salad, salmon steak with Chanturgue (a local red wine), and timbale of salt cod. Alain Clavé gives attentive and expert service.

A la carte: 300-350 F. Menus: 105 F, 160 F, 210 F, 300 F.

Le Clos Saint-Pierre

Pl. du Marché-St-Pierre — 73.31.23.22
M. Bath. Closed Mon dinner, Sun, holidays, Feb and Nov school holidays. Open until 11 pm. Terrace dining. V.

Just right for a relaxed evening with friends that won't break the bank. Gilles Paulet, formerly of the Royal Monceau and Les Mouflons in nearby Besse, proposes a terrine of coq au vin, salmon with shellfish purée, and pig's tail with Le Puy lentils. Good local wines by the bottle or the glass.

A la carte: 180 F.

Le Connétable

13, rue. Terrace dining — 73.90.92.81
M. Pierson. Closed Sat lunch, Sun and Aug. Open until 10 pm. Private room: 30. Valet parking. V AE.

Yves Pierson, who once worked on the cruise liner *France*, may well be the only chef in the country who has his customers' cars washed while they relax in the majestic setting of this thirteenth-century vaulted chapel. More reliable than original, his cooking still deserves praise and a toque. New dishes include home-produced duck foie gras (slightly overcooked) and firm-fleshed John Dory with a good butter sauce. Classic desserts and a fine wine list.

A la carte: 250 F. Menus: 130 F, 230 F.

Le Lyon

16, pl. de Jaude — 73.93.32.55
Open every day. 32 rms 235-295 F. Restaurant. TV. Garage parking. V.

A 200-year-old establishment near the cathedral. Half-board for groups. Crêperie. Pub.

Mercure Arverne

16, pl. Delille — 73.91.92.06
Open every day. 57 rms 325-385 F. Restaurant. Half-board 240 F. TV. Conference facilities. Garage parking. Telex 392741. V AE DC.

Modern, functional, and central, with spacious rooms. Bar.

12/20 La Retirade

82, bd Gergovia — 73.93.05.75
M. Ganancia. Closed Sat lunch. Open until 10 pm. Private room: 240. Terrace dining. Air cond. Parking. Telex 392658. V AE DC.

The chefs change so often here you can hardly remember their names, let alone their cooking. The latest offers an ambitious range of dishes with a good regional menu that should rekindle interest in this establishment with its splendid new décor.

A la carte: 260-300 F. Menus: 132 F, 151 F and 200 F (weekdays only), 165 F (w-e and holidays only).

Altea

(See restaurant above)
Open every day. 2 stes 850 F. 124 rms 300-550 F. TV. Conference facilities.

Central and facing the mountains. Pretty fabrics enliven the quiet, spacious and air-conditioned rooms. Interesting buffet-style breakfasts. Conference rooms.

12/20 Le Saint-Emilion

97, av. de la République — 73.91.92.92
M. Joubert. Open every day. Open until 10.30 pm. Private room: 100. Terrace dining. Garage parking. V.

Bare walls and yellow tablecloths provide an uninspired setting in this brand- new restaurant. André Joubert's cooking is equally hesitant: ordinary duck terrine, plainly but perfectly grilled salmon with chanterelles, varied cheese including a sheep cheese from Thiers. The chef visits the Bordeaux growers in person to buy his interesting wines.

A la carte: 200-250 F. Menus: 80 F, 125 F, 160 F.

Le Saint-Emilion

(See restaurant above)
Open every day. 55 rms 180-280 F. Half-board 330-350 F. TV. Conference facilities.

Comfortable beds and perfect soundproofing at this functional hotel in a rather drab industrial area.

12/20 La Table à Poissons

16, rue Claussmann — 73.91.95.69
M. Berdu. Closed Sun, Mon and 15 Aug-15 Sep. Open until 10 pm. Air cond. V AE.

Fresh seafood prepared with a pleasing simplicity: assortment of seafood, grilled lobster, paella, bouillabaisse (order in advance), and local-style sauerkraut. Pretty décor.

A la carte: 180-220 F. Menus: 89 F and 140 F (except holidays).

Gérard Truchetet

Rond-Point de la Pardieu — 73.27.74.17
M. Truchetet. Closed Sat lunch, Sun, 1 week of Jan and mid-July to mid-Aug. Open until 9.30 pm. Private room: 40. No pets. V.

An experienced chef who spent many years at the Altea, Gérard Truchetet laid a new table last year at this bright, functional establishment. Plain, honest, cooking at very reasonable prices. The 140 F regional menu deserves a mention: salad of pigs' trotters with lentils, trout with creamed morels, quick-cooked beef with bone marrow and Châteaugay, warm goat cheese, and frozen nougat with Auvergne honey.

A la carte: 200 F. Menus: 110 F (weekdays lunch only), 145 F, 196 F.

La Truffe d'Argent

17, rue Lamartine — 73.93.52.25
M. Anglard. Closed Mon lunch, Sun, holidays, 23 Dec-1 Jan, 5-12 May and 4-20 Aug. Open until 10 pm. Private room: 20. Terrace dining. Air cond. V AE DC.

Gérard Anglard has been forced to set his sights lower after a spell at Montaigut-le-Blanc, a delightful village in summer but often inaccessible in winter. He moved here in the autumn and is practising the honest and refined style of cooking that earned him 16/20 at Le Rivalet. His new menu includes: duck liver with apples and sherry, marinated salmon with herbs, pigeon with a purée of leeks and foie gras, cinnamon ice cream with caramelised apples.

A la carte: 250-300 F.

12/20 Vacher

69, bd Gergovia — 73.93.13.32
M. Vacher. Closed Fri dinner and Sat (en July-Aug). Open until 10 pm. Private room: 80. Terrace dining. Air cond. V AE DC.

A brasserie on the ground floor and huge restaurant upstairs. Reliable, well-prepared food but the menu is far too long. Try the sweetbread salad with toasted almonds, steamed lotte with olive oil, and young pigeon in a pastry crust.

A la carte: 250-300 F. Menus: 150 F (weekdays only), 160 F (w-e and holidays only), 220 F.

And also...

Our selection of places for inexpensive, quick, or late-night meals.

L'Auberge Auvergnate (73.37.82.68 - 37, rue des Vieillards. Open for lunch onlt): Bistro in an area under renovation. Delicious stews and choucroute for lunch; dinner to order (70 F).

L'Auvergnat (73.91.40.40 - 27, av. de l'Union-Soviétique. Open until 9 pm): The Hôtel Saint-André's restaurant. Blue-cheese salad, hearty stews, and other regional dishes (120 F).

La Grolle (73.36.19.87 - 60, rue Fontgiève. Open until 10 pm): Fine grilled red meats. There is a 70 F menu and you can eat à la carte for 100 F to 120 F.

La Passerelle (73.91.62.12 - 24, rue A.-France. Open until 9 pm): A varied clientele appreciates the 50 F menu and accordion music.

Rimbaud (73.34.21.39 - pl. Aragon. Open until 11 pm): Honest food and a friendly atmosphere. Service on the terrace in summer (150 F).

La Rue (73.37.78.74 - 62, rue Fontgiève. Open until 11 pm): A variety of grilled meats plus assortments of Nordic specialities, dishes from the Landes, and desserts. Wine by the glass (100 F).

Le Steak Barbare (73.37.15.51 - 3, rue de la Michodière. Open until 9 pm): An impressive and tender chunk of beef for two, various salads, and good young Bordeaux (90 F).

Le Vaudeville (73.35.22.51 - Centre Jaude. Open until 10.30 pm): Good, plain cooking taken over by François Joubert from his brother (200 F).

In nearby **Chamalières**

(3 km W)
63400 Clermont-Ferrand — (Puy-de-Dôme)

Hôtel Radio
43, av. P.-Curie — 73.30.87.83
M. Mioche. Closed Sun dinner, Mon and 30 Nov-1 March. Open until 9.30 pm. Private room: 30. Air cond. Garage parking. Telex 530955. V AE DC.

The next time you drive from Paris to Cannes, why not leave the traffic jams behind and make a detour through the Auvergne countryside to Clermont-Ferrand? Not such a crazy idea as it sounds—not only is it easier on the nerves but it's an ideal opportunity to make the acquaintance of this restaurant we've been telling you about for years.

The rather odd name pays tribute to the early days of the wireless, of which Michel Mioche's father was a fan. Set on a residential hillside, it is a vast, welcoming place with a pre-war charm that belies its brand-new art deco furnishings. And the entire staff—as well as the dog—shares our view that Yvette Mioche is a delightful hostess.

The couple won't tell you how they struggled to renovate and then to fill their establishment; they prefer to look to the future, which glitters with promise. Michel Mioche's cooking, served in an attractive if unconventional dining room hung with pleated curtains, has improved enough to earn an extra point. He steers a skilful course between the rich, earthy tastes of his native Auvergne and the subtler flavours of the sea.

On the hearty side, there's foie gras, served either with green beans with chervil and beetroot in julienne strips, or hot on an artichoke bottom and covered with a delicious truffle purée, roast young

rabbit with a winy cream sauce, boudin (blood sausage) with apple, salmon with green lentils, marinated and sautéed beef garlanded with potatoes sprinkled with coarse sea salt, duckling with buttery cabbage, and a monumental potée auvergnate. On the lighter side, you will discover salmon 'petals' with grapefruit and poppy seeds (a particularly successful combination), lobster in wine sauce with angelica, leek, and celery, mousse of salt cod with fresh tomato sauce, 'Chinese-style' jumbo prawns with fresh pasta, and the chef's masterpiece, ravioli of Bresse chicken with celery leaves. The finest mature Cantal and St-Nectaire cheeses imaginable, and a dessert worth a fourth toque—Auvergne pudding, made with rye breadcrumbs and citron, napped with a vanilla sauce enlivened by saffron, rum, and coriander. To accompany all this, try a white Graves that tastes of roses, or one of the local wines, which deserve to be better known.

A la carte: 350-500 F. Menus: 200 F (weekdays only), 350 F, 450 F.

Hôtel Radio
(See restaurant above)
Closed 30 Nov-1 March. 1 ste 750-950 F. 27 rms 380-680 F. Half-board 630-800 F. TV. Conference facilities.

Between the mountains and the roofs of the town. Tranquillity guaranteed in the 27 rooms and one suite. Exemplary service.

In nearby **Durtol**

(5 km NW on D 941)
63830 Clermont-Ferrand — (Puy-de-Dôme)

Bernard Andrieux
(Auberge des Touristes)
Rte de la Baraque, on D 941 — 73.37.00.26
M. Andrieux. Closed Sat lunch, Sun, Feb school holidays and mid-July-beg Aug. Open until 9.30 pm. Private room: 20. No pets. Parking. V AE.

If he wants to fly higher than the surrounding mountains, Bernard Andrieux should concentrate on refining his style rather than exaggerating it. With his sound training, he is perfectly capable of doing so, but at the moment he is too in tune with his new décor, whose huge net curtains recall a palace out of the *Arabian Nights' Entertainments.* A sampler of dishes: hot breaded cheese with (unnecessary) beetroot juice, excellent vegetable tempura, succulent foie gras cooked with hazelnuts, gâteau de crabe with a flavoursome vegetable mousse scented with virgin olive oil (alas, taste of cucumber dominated the rest). The prawn brochettes with cauliflower cream are offered with a blue-cheese sauce, wild mushrooms and baby broad beans, and the freshwater perch fillet with duck is cleverly rolled in a jacket potato. Divine chocolate cake would be better without the vanilla-flavoured whipped cream. The young hostess and the rest of the staff display a rare professionalism. Superb wine list.

A la carte: 350-450 F. Menus: 160 F, 270 F, 390 F.

L'Aubergade
on D 941, rte de la Baraque — 73.37.84.64
MM. Defix and Zimmermann. Closed Sun dinner, Mon, 4-25 March and 2-23 Sep. Open until 9.30 pm. Garden dining. Parking. V.

Don't miss this attractive building tucked away on a bend in the road. The owners will welcome you with a smile to their comfortable floral interior and serve you excellent and reliable regional food. The cheapest menu is faultless and if you venture à la carte you'll have fond memories of the prawn salad with foie gras, turbot with tarragon cream sauce, and young pigeon with cabbage. Well-stocked cellar and good service.

A la carte: 260-280 F. Menus: 110 F (weekdays only), 170 F, 230 F.

In nearby Orcines

(8 km W on D 941A and D 941B)
63870 Clermont-Ferrand — (Puy-de-Dôme)

Pichon
Rte de Limoges — 73.62.10.05

MM. Ray and Lille. Closed Sun dinner, Mon, Jan and first week of Sep. Open until 9.30 pm. Private room: 35. No pets. Hotel: 2 stes 310 F. 13 rms 195-250 F. Tennis. Golf. Garage parking. Telex 530955. V AE DC.

The young joint owner and chef, who trained with Troisgros, Guérard, and Rostang, is an aware and imaginative cook who never strays from the path of honesty and simplicity. So the recently decorated dining room attracts more and more customers, despite rather high prices à la carte (the set menus are good value). Young curly kale with prawns, cockscombs and kidney salad with truffles, braised burbot with raw shallots, and sweetbreads with diced courgettes. Good wines, precise service.

A la carte: 300 F. Menus: 90 F (weekdays lunch only), 150 F (except holidays), 220 F, 280 F.

In nearby Pérignat-lès-Sarliève

(4 km SE)
63170 Clermont-Ferrand — (Puy-de-Dôme)

12/20 Le Petit Bonneval
73.79.11.11

M. Henrich. Closed dinner Wed and Sun, 1-8 April, 22 July-11 Aug and Christmas week. Open until 9 pm. Private room: 26. Garden dining. Hotel: 6 rms 160-220 F. Parking. V.

The large terrace draws customers on sunny days but the charming owners and careful cooking are attractions whatever the weather. Particularly good meat and poultry: duck breast in parsley jelly, Bresse pigeon in flaky pastry, duck and goose confits, grilled meats. Appealing wine list.

A la carte: 200-220 F. Menus: 90 F and 115 F (except holidays), 155 F, 205 F.

In nearby Royat

(3.5 km W)
63130 Clermont-Ferrand — (Puy-de-Dôme)

La Belle Meunière ✪
25, av. de la Vallée — 73.35.80.17

M. Bon. Closed Sun dinner, Wed, 15 days in Feb and 3 weeks in Nov. Open until 9.30 pm. Private room: 30. Terrace dining. Hotel: 2 stes 260 F. 8 rms 195-260 F. Garage parking. V AE DC.

Every year Jean-Claude Bon tries to give a bit more character to his excellent repertoire of regional dishes. The classics such as moulded chicken livers, carp with Chanturgue, and salmon with lentils have been joined by cabbage stuffed with pigs' trotters, snail-filled crêpes, and pigeon in red wine. Charming décor.

A la carte: 350 F. Menus: 145 F (weekdays lunch only, wine inc), 130 F, 180 F, 210 F, 320 F.

Some establishments change their closing times without warning. It is always wise to check in advance.

Métropole
2, bd Vaquez — 73.35.80.18

Closed 1 Oct-1 May. 5 stes 750-920 F. 76 rms 190-550 F. Restaurant. Half-board 360-600 F. TV. Conference facilities. Valet parking. V.

A few metres from the hot springs, this turn-of-the-century spa hotel was updated in the 1950s. Large, comfortable rooms with mismatched furniture. Some have views over the park.

12/20 Le Paradis
Av. du Paradis — 73.35.85.46

M. Blanc. Closed Sun dinner, Mon, 2-31 Jan and 2-12 Oct. Open until 9.30 pm. Private room: 100. Terrace dining. Parking. V AE.

Worth a visit for the view over the Limagne plain and Auvergne's volcanic summits from this high-perched grey stone fort. The food is less striking: nondescript avocado mousse with tomato purée, rather tough salt-cured duck, and dull desserts. A good cheese board, however, with the emphasis on local foodstuffs, and the wines are good value (excellent St-Estèphe '86). Pleasant but inexperienced service.

A la carte: 300 F. Menus: 140 F, 180 F, 230 F.

In nearby Saulzet-le-Chaud

(8 km S on N 89)
63540 Clermont-Ferrand — (Puy-de-Dôme)

Auberge de Montrognon
73.61.30.51

M. Bettiol. Closed Sun dinner, Wed and 5-20 Jan. Open until 10 pm. Private room: 40. Terrace dining. Air cond. Parking. V.

Gilles Bettiol, formerly of Le Charade, has done wonders since taking over here two years ago. Tasty cooking and excellent value. Sweetbread salad with lardons, perch meunière with braised cabbage, red-mullet with basil, and baby veal kidneys sautéed with fresh mint. Modern salmon-pink décor reflected in a mirrored ceiling.

A la carte: 230 F. Menus: 95 F, 145 F, 190 F, 250 F.

CLICHY

See PARIS Suburbs

CLISSON

44190 Clisson — (Loire-Atl.)
Paris 377 - Nantes 28 - Niort 124 - Poitiers 150

La Bonne Auberge
1, rue O.-de-Clisson — 40.54.01.90

M. Poiron. Closed Sun dinner, Mon, 10-26 Feb and 11-31 Aug. Open until 9.30 pm. Private room: 40. Garden dining. V AE.

Old tiles, attractive furniture and tableware grace this elegant restaurant with veranda and flower-filled garden. Serge Poiron renews his menus according to the seasons, the market, and his fancy, which leans towards fine, expensive ingredients (foie gras, lobster, turbot) which he handles with skill and generosity. Fine regional wine list.

A la carte: 400 F. Menus: 85 F (weekdays only), 150 F, 200 F, 320 F.

CLOHARS-FOUESNANT

See Bénodet

CLUNY
71250 Cluny — (Saône/Loire)
Paris 396 - Autun 83 - Mâcon 24 - Tournus 38

Bourgogne
⑬ Pl. de l'Abbaye — 85.59.00.58
M. Gosse. Closed Wed lunch, Tue (except dinner in seas) and 8 Dec-2 Feb. Open until 9 pm. No pets. Valet parking. V AE DC.

We leave the owner to tell you the story of his *auberge* opposite the magnificent abbey. The poet Lamartine was an early visitor, and French and foreign tourists have since followed in his footsteps. The cooking is of consistently good quality, despite a succession of chefs. There is a tendency to overcook some dishes, but the rabbit or duck terrines are good and the truffle-flavoured chicken consommé extraordinary. Fine cheeses and desserts and a well-constructed wine list that should nevertheless offer more Bordeaux. Very friendly service.

A la carte: 400 F. Menus: 110 F (lunch only), 190 F (w-e and holidays only), 280 F, 360 F.

Bourgogne
(See restaurant above)
Closed Tue off-season and 8 Dec-2 Feb. 3 stes 800-980 F. 15 rms 420-465 F (per pers, half-board oblig). TV 3 rms.

Quiet, comfortable rooms with attractive old furniture. The shutters open onto a view of the abbey and stables.

Hermitage
Les Cras, rte de Cormatin — 85.59.27.20
M. Bernigaud. Closed Thu dinner and Wed vous.

Monsieur Bernigaud and his team (see Moderne, below) were set to move into this comfortable establishment in March 1991. Their success seems assured.

Moderne
⑬ Pont-de-l'Etang — 85.59.05.65
M. Bernigaud. Closed Sun dinner off-season, Mon (lunch in seas), 20 Jan-15 Feb and 11 Nov-5 Dec. Open until 9 pm. Private room: 90. Parking. V AE DC.

Lionel Febvre's fine cooking was scheduled for transfer two kilometres to the north in March 1991 (see Hermitage above).

A la carte: 300 F. Menus: 80 F (lunch only), 150 F (wine inc), 120 F, 190 F.

Moderne
(See restaurant above)
Open every day. 15 rms 140-260 F. Half-board 370-480 F oblig in seas. TV 8 rms. Conference facilities.
Large, well-kept rooms.

11/20 Le Potin Gourmand
4, pl. du Champ-de-Foire — 85.59.02.06
M. Ripert. Closed Sun dinner off-season, Mon, 3 Jan-5 Feb and 25-29 June. Open until 9 pm. Private room: 15. Garden dining. Parking. V.

A warm, welcoming décor of beams and stone, with simple, homely fare: veal with chive sauce, beef salad, honey nougat with blackcurrant sauce.
A la carte: 200 F. Menus: 68 F, 100 F, 130 F.

Hôtel Saint Odilon
in Belle-Croix — 85.59.25.00
Closed 20 Dec-5 Jan. 36 rms 240 F. TV. Conference facilities. Parking. V AE.
A modern hotel, 300 metres from the abbey, with functional rooms overlooking open country.

CLUSAZ (LA)
74220 Clusaz (La) — (H.-Savoie)
Paris 579 - Saint-Gervais 40 - Annecy 36 - Megève 29

11/20 Le Coin du Feu
La Perrière — 50.02.52.25
Mme Fernandez. Closed Wed (except school holidays), end April to June and 1-28 Oct. Open until 10.30 pm. V.

A staggering range of fondues, grills, and crêpes, served in a cheerful chalet-style setting. Glassed-in terrace overlooking the slopes.
A la carte: 180-200 F.

Le Cythéria
50.02.41.81
Closed 20 June-15 Sep. 30 rms 180-300 F Restaurant. Half-board 250-300 F TV. V.

A three-storey chalet with balconies and large, comfortable rooms with country-style furniture. Sunny terrace.

11/20 L'Ecuelle
50.02.42.03
M. Charpin. Closed lunch in seas Mon and Tue, off-season Tue and Wed, and June. Open until 10 pm. Terrace dining. V AE DC.

Trout straight from the fishtank are the speciality, along with fondue and other dishes made from Reblochon, the mild local cheese, served by staff in regional costume.
A la carte: 200 F. Menus: 115 F and 145 F (winter only), 60 F, 98 F.

11/20 L'Ourson
50.02.49.80
M. Cornillon. Closed Tue off-season, 27 May-20 June and 30 Sep-28 Oct. Open until 9.30 pm. V AE DC.

A huge poster depicting mountains brightens the end of the dining room. Reblochon cheese in flaky pastry, John Dory with tiny vegetables, and fondues, with prices as pleasant as the service.
A la carte: 100-120 F. Menus: 55 F (lunch only), 72 F, 90 F, 140 F.

Le Panorama
50.02.42.12
Closed 5 April-1 July and 1 Sep-22 Dec. 13 stes 1,700-4,600 F. 14 rms 200-380 F. TV. Garage parking. V.

One of the resort's biggest hotels, overlooking the village and the slopes. Each room has its own little balcony and there are flats to let by the week.

11/20 Hôtel de Savoie
50.02.40.51
M. Perillat. Closed 3-20 June. Open until 9.30 pm. No pets. Hotel: 14 rms 170-300 F. V DC.

A huge fireplace and warm atmosphere at this central establishment. Leg of lamb and potato gratin, perfect trout cooked in butter, plus numerous Savoie specialities. Short wine list.
A la carte: 150 F. Menus: 73 F, 94 F, 145 F.

Le Vieux Chalet
⑬ 1 km NE, Les Tollets — 50.02.41.53
Mme Faber. Closed off-season Tue dinner, Wed and Thu, 12-29 June and 15-30 Oct. Open until 8.45 pm. Terrace dining. Parking. V.

Pretty chalet-style décor more reminiscent of good-value fondues than costly and elaborate cooking, but the latter is what you'll find at Jean-Michel Faber's old Savoie farm. With unusual personal creations like shellfish in kirsch, fillets of red-mullet with vinegar butter accompanied by small scallops, or the delicious 'épigramme' of goose (the breast with a blood-thickened sauce, leg in white sauce, and the neck stuffed). Some good desserts and reasonably priced local wines. Sunny terrace.

A la carte: 300-350 F. Menus: 90 F (lunch only), 180 F, 225 F.

Le Vieux Chalet
(See restaurant above)

Closed off-season Tue, Wed and Thu, 12-29 June and 15 -30 Oct. 7 rms 210-300 F. Pension 340 F oblig in seas. No pets. ·

Typical and attractive hotel. Some rooms are prettier than others.

Vitahotel
50.02.58.96

Closed May and 1 Oct-15 Dec. 103 rms 251-750 F. Restaurant. Half-board 270-594 F oblig in seas. TV. Conference facilities. Heated pool. Garage parking. V AE DC.

Looking out over the slopes at the heart of the resort, a fashionable hotel with fitness centre (gym, sauna, steam baths). Warm reception.

COARAZE

06390 Coaraze — (Alpes-Mar.)
Paris 970 - Nice 28 - Contes 10 - Lucéram 19

12/20 Auberge du Soleil
93.79.08.11

M. Jacquet. Closed 15 Nov-15 March. Open until 9 pm. Terrace dining. V DC.

It's a steep climb to this delightful *auberge* with magnificent views, but you'll feel you deserve the simple, generous meals prepared by the *patronne*. Try her homemade flan, rabbit cooked in wine, and prune dessert, served in a relaxed, family atmosphere.

A la carte: 160-180 F. Menu: 105 F.

Auberge du Soleil
(See restaurant above)

Closed 15 Nov-15 March. 2 stes 340-820 F. 8 rms 240-420 F. Half-board 260-415 F oblig in seas. Conference facilities. Pool.

In the heart of the village far from the noise of traffic, ten elegantly modernised rooms with fairytale mountain views. One of the region's most peaceful and charming hotels.

COCHEREL

See Pacy-sur-Eure

COGNAC

16100 Cognac — (Charente)
Paris 465 - Angoulême 42 - Niort 80 - Saintes 26

11/20 Le Coq d'Or
33, pl. François-Ier — 45.82.02.56

M. Luzié. Closed Fri dinner off-season, Sun and school holidays, 1 Nov. Open until 10 pm. Private room: 90. Terrace dining. V AE DC.

Pleasant, modern décor downstairs and a first-floor dining room catering for groups. Good cooking: prawn omelette, sole aux cèpes, calf's liver à la mandarine.

A la carte: 200 F. Menus: 75 F, 90 F and 130 F (weekdays only), 190 F (w-e and holidays only).

> *Red toques signify modern cuisine; black toques signify traditional cuisine.*

L'Echassier

2 km S on rte de St-Brice
72, rue de Bellevue
16100 Cognac-Châtaubernard
45.32.29.04

MM. Lambert and Goern. Closed Sun. Open until 9.30 pm. Private room: 20. Terrace dining. Parking. Telex 790798. V AE DC.

This modern white building set among lawns and tall trees has a distinctly colonial air and an atmosphere of relaxed professionalism. The cooking of Bernard Lambert, a former pupil of the Troisgros brothers, is precise and varied, seeking simplicity and definite flavours: snail ravioli with herbs, shellfish assortment in peach wine, veal sweetbreads with prawns and Roquefort butter, pigeon with caramelised onions, sea bass cooked in St-Emilion, and craquelines au chocolat amer. Martine Lambert will give you an excellent reception, and it's wise to book. Improved service.

A la carte: 300-350 F. Menus: 130 F, 165 F.

L'Echassier
(See restaurant above)

Closed Sun off-season. 2 stes 590-690 F. 17 rms 345-445 F. Half-board 450 F. TV. Conference facilities. Heated pool.

New and totally quiet rooms with pretty floral furnishings and grey marble bathrooms. Wonderful breakfasts.

Les Pigeons Blancs
110, rue J.-Brisson — 45.82.16.36

MM. Tachet. Closed Sun dinner and 8-31 Jan. Open until 9.30 pm. Private room: 12. Garden dining. Hotel: 7 rms 230-400 F. Parking. V AE DC.

This former post house has been owned by the Tachet family since the seventeenth century. The latest generation has turned it into a restaurant warmly decorated with wood and stone and surrounded by attractive grounds. Jacques Tachet is in the kitchen, producing tasty lobster in Pineau (a local apéritif wine) and fennel with foie gras with a perfect, slightly tart sauce. His brother Jean-Michel presides over a fine wine list while their sister Catherine provides efficient service.

A la carte: 350 F. Menus: 118 F, 155 F, 295 F.

11/20 La Rôtisserie
2 km S, in Châteaubernard
Carrefour de la Trache — 45.35.42.00

MM. Belliot and Dupeyroux. Open every day. Open until 10.30 pm. Private room: 110. Terrace dining. Air cond. Parking. Telex 790615. V AE DC.

Different cuts of grilled steak are the specialities, served in a huge dining room overlooking the swimming pool. Excellent service and good-value Bordeaux.

A la carte: 200-250 F. Menus: 75 F (weekdays only), 145 F (w-e and holidays only), 105 F.

Les Relais Bleus
(See restaurant above)

Open every day. 55 rms 270-290 F. Half-board 235-265 F. TV. Conference facilities. Heated pool.

Bright, functional new rooms with ultra-modern bathrooms. Minimal service. Good breakfasts.

Le Valois
35, rue 14-Juillet — 45.82.76.00

Closed 20 Dec-2 Jan. 1 ste 450 F. 45 rms 330-360 F. TV. Air cond. Conference facilities. Garage parking. Telex 790987. V AE DC.

Recently renovated hotel with pleasant and spacious rooms. Sauna, solarium, bar.

In nearby **Saint-Fort-sur-le-Né**

(14 km S on D 731)
16130 Cognac — (Charente)

Le Moulin de Cierzac
45.83.01.32

M. Labouly. Closed 25 Jan-28 Feb. Open until 9.45 pm. Private room: 50. Garden dining. Hotel: 10 rms 250-490 F. Garage parking. V DC.

Daniel Barret may win you over with his oyster pastries with foie gras, shad with leeks, or his astonishing escargots scented with liquorice, only to produce quite shameful salmon in honey vinegar and give his desserts minimal attention. This is still one of the most attractive addresses in the area, despite bills that take your breath away. An extra point.

A la carte: 380-450 F. Menus: 150 F and 200 F (weekdays only).

COGOLIN (PLAGE)

83310 Cogolin (Plage) — (Var)
Paris 880 - Ste-Maxime 8 - St-Tropez 7 - Cogolin 8

Port-Diffa
Les Trois-Ponts on la Giscle
La Foux (N 98) — 94.56.29.07

M. Sibony. Closed 7 Jan-29 March. Open until 10 pm. Terrace dining. Air cond. No pets. Parking. AE DC.

Low tables, soft sofas, and Moroccan cooking as tasty as in Marrakesh. Pastilla with pigeon (and not guinea fowl, which is becoming the norm), little meat pastries, wonderfully light couscous, lemon chicken, and sticky sweet pastries. Charming service, and the bill is reasonable.

A la carte: 300-350 F. Menu: 149 F.

COGOLIN (VILLAGE)

83310 Cogolin (Village) — (Var)
Paris 870 - St-Tropez 9 - Ste-Maxime 13 - Hyères 42

11/20 La Ferme de Magnan
4 km on N 98, to La Môle — 94.49.57.54

M. Campanile. Closed Tue and 28 Jan-1 March. Open until 10 pm. Garden dining. Parking.

An old farmhouse overlooking vineyards where everything comes grilled over vine cuttings—meat, mussels, blood sausage, jumbo prawns. Both the cooking and the service have their ups and downs.

A la carte: 250 F. Menus: from 142 F to 250 F.

Hôtel Jasmin
Parc Bellevue, N 98 — 94.56.43.43

Closed 15 Jan-15 Feb. 48 rms 395-760 F. Restaurant. Half-board 560-820 F. TV 20 rms. Conference facilities. Pool. Tennis. Garage parking. Telex 461930. V AE DC.

A recent, functional building looking out over the Bay of St-Tropez. Bright, modern rooms with terraces.

COIGNIÈRES

78310 Coignières — (Yvelines)
Paris 40 - Versailles 18 - Rambouillet 13

Auberge d'Angèle
296, rte Nationale 10 — 34.61.64.39

M. Charrault. Closed Sun dinner and Mon. Open until 10 pm. Garden dining. V.

Inside, beams and a rather dark décor brightened with flowers and Delft-style tiles; outside, a paved garden under the trees. Whatever the setting, you'll enjoy classic, reliable food: hot oysters with pumpkin purée, John Dory flavoured with truffles,

filet de bœuf aux deux poivres.
A la carte: 400 F. Menus: 150 F, 246 F, 315 F.

Auberge du Capucin Gourmand
170, N 10 — 34.61.46.06

M. Lebrault. Closed Sun (except holidays). Open until 9.30 pm. Private room: 8. Garden dining. Parking. V AE DC.

Visitors are surprised to find this pretty *auberge* in the middle of a soulless shopping centre near a busy main road. Some think it might be a tourist trap but they need not worry: Michel Lebrault's cooking is honest and reliable. Fillet of lamb with tarragon, lotte in sabayon sauce (made rather sickly by too much vanilla), and an oyster and mussel soup with a pastry lid which seems closely related to Paul Bocuse's famous creation for Valéry Giscard d'Estaing. Sadly there are few new dishes, while prices soar skywards (especially on the impressive wine list), so this year we feel obliged to subtract a point from this talented chef.

A la carte: 450-550 F. Menu: 230 F (dinner only and Sat lunch).

COLLE-SUR-LOUP (LA)

See Saint-Paul-de-Vence

COLLIAS

See Uzès

COLLIOURE

66190 Collioure — (Pyrénées-O.)
Paris 955 - Perpignan 27 - Céret 32 - Port-Vendres 4

La Balette
Rte de Port-Vendres — 68.82.05.07

M. De Gelder. Open every day. Open until 10 pm (10.30 pm in summer). Private room: 60. Terrace dining. Air cond. Parking. Telex 506112. V.

Eric Vincens' deft cooking and well-finished sauces bring a ray of sunshine to the rather bare dining room. Squid with saffron butter and garlic purée, galinette (a Mediterranean fish) in broth, baked lotte and anchovy 'sausages' with a herbal tomato sauce. Remarkable desserts. Views over the harbour from the terrace. The young maître d'hôtel makes a valiant effort to speed up the service.

A la carte: 300 F and up. Menus: 165 F, 245 F, 295 F.

Relais des Trois Mas
(See restaurant above)

Open every day. 4 stes 980 F. 19 rms 280-880 F. Half-board 485-735 F. TV. Air cond. Conference facilities. Heated pool.

We reserve judgment until the ambitious improvements are finally completed.

Boramar
Rue J.-Bart — 68.82.07.06

Closed 6 Nov-23 March. 14 rms 168-275 F.

Pleasant little hotel by the beach, opposite the harbour.

Les Caranques
Rte de Port-Vendres — 68.82.06.68

Closed 10 Oct-1 April. 16 rms 210-280 F (per pers, half-board oblig). Restaurant. No pets. Parking. V.

Small hotel at the water's edge. Plain but well-kept rooms, all with loggias overlooking the bay.

Casa Païral
Impasse des Palmiers
68.82.05.81
Closed 5 Nov-Easter. 2 stes 650-790 F. 26 rms 300-620 F. TV. Pool. Parking. Telex 505220. V.
A delightful Catalan residence in the town centre with large, quiet, attractively furnished rooms.

12/20 La Frégate
24, quai de l'Amirauté — 68.82.06.05
M. Costa. Closed Fri. Open until 10 pm. Terrace dining. Hotel: 24 rms 350-490 F. Telex 505072. V.
Thirty minutes before anyone took our order ('not all that long', said the maître d'hôtel facetiously), followed by endless waits between courses. That was last summer. If he wants his toque back, Monsieur Costa had better restrict the number of customers or employ more kitchen staff. How else can we appreciate his salmon with clams, marinated anchovies, or suckling pig roasted with Banyuls (the local fortified wine)?
A la carte: 300 F. Menus: 110 F (weekdays only), 190 F.

Madeloc
Rue R.-Rolland — 68.82.07.56
Closed 15 Oct-Easter. 21 rms 220-330 F. Parking. V AE DC.
A modern and well-planned hotel facing the surrounding mountains and 500 metres from the beach. Lovely rooms with superb terraces.

12/20 La Marinade
14, pl. 18-Juin — 68.82.09.76
M. Trux. Closed off-season Sun dinner and Wed, and 4 Jan-5 Feb. Open until 9.30 pm. Terrace dining. Air cond. V.
The new chef has granted the owner's wish to make the fish dishes more consistent. The mussel soup with orange zest, fish soup, and mackerel and red-mullet with cuttlefish fricassée are all good and tasty.
A la carte: 230-280 F. Menus: 98 F, 165 F.

12/20 Pa i Trago
1, rue Arago — 68.82.20.44
M. Riera. Closings not available. Open until 10.30 pm.
The fishing boats never net enough for all those who flock to the Rieras' tiny house to devour fresh anchovies, sardine fritters, and lotte with herbs. The restaurant closes when the day's catch is poor.
A la carte: 200 F.

12/20 Les Templiers
Quai de l'Amirauté — 68.82.05.58
M. Pous. Closed Sun dinner, Mon and 15 Nov-15 Feb. Open until 10.30 pm. Private room: 30. Terrace dining. Hotel: 52 rms 150-350 F. V.
Enjoy the young chef's red sculpin (a local fish) with morels, rockfish, or bouillabaisse in a rather fussy décor filled with paintings by the owner's famous friends.
A la carte: 300 F. Menu: 140 F.

Triton
1, rue J.-Bart — 68.82.06.52
Open every day. 20 rms 148-245 F. TV. V AE.
Nice but quite noisy hotel by the harbour. Sun-terrace and impeccable rooms.

83610 Collobrières — (Var)
Paris 902 - Bormes-les-M. 24 - Grimaud 24

12/20 La Petite Fontaine
1, pl. de la République — 94.48.00.12
Mme Fontana. Closed Sun dinner. Annual closings not available. Open until 9 pm. Terrace dining.
Kid and game in season, and tables on the village square from spring onwards. All year round you'll appreciate guinea fowl with cabbage, garlicky chicken fricassée, daubes, and goat cheese from the owner's farm, washed down with wines from the local co-operative.

See Lyon

68000 Colmar — (Haut-Rhin)
Paris 445 - Strasbourg 69 - Nancy 141 - Bâle 68

Altea Champ de Mars
2, av. de la Marne — 89.41.54.54
Open every day. 75 rms 350-440 F. TV. Conference facilities. Garage parking. Telex 880928. V AE DC.
Modern and pleasantly situated in the municipal park. Spacious and well-equipped rooms.

Hôtel Amiral
11a, bd du Champs-de-Mars — 89.23.26.25
Open every day. 1 ste 500 F. 44 rms 295-500 F. Restaurant. Half-board 320-430 F. TV. Conference facilities. Garage parking. Telex 880852. V AE DC.
A restored maltings on the edge of the old town. Most of the rooms overlook a quiet courtyard. The décor is slightly too functional. Piano bar.

12/20 Le Chaudron
5, pl. du Marché-aux-Fruits — 89.24.56.18
M. Olivieri. Dinner only. Closed Sun. Open until midnight. Air cond. V AE.
Honest if rather pretentious food with well-sauced dishes served on lace tablecloths: raw salmon charlotte with pepper, good portions of veal tenderloin with Banyuls wine, frozen coffee mousse.
A la carte: 250-290 F. Menus: 119 F, 155 F.

12/20 A L'Echevin
5, pl. des Six-Montagnes-Noires
89.41.60.32
M. Bomo. Open every day. Open until 10 pm. Private room: 30. Garden dining. Air cond. Parking. Telex 880949. V AE.
Delightful pink timbered building with a terrace on the River Lauch. The two dining rooms are decorated in neo-Renaissance and neo-Louis XV style. Quality ingredients, but some dishes seem unnecessarily complicated: minced smoked salmon and oysters, (over)-fried red-mullet with sweet peppers and aubergines, a good fruit gratin with sabayon sauce.
A la carte: 350 F. Menus: from 150 F to 400 F.

Le Maréchal
(See restaurant above)
Open every day. 5 stes 900-1,200 F. 26 rms 300-750 F. Half-board 450-650 F. TV. Air cond. Conference facilities.
Lovely spacious rooms with fine furniture in this superb sixteenth-century establishment. Some have views over the Lauch.

Europe

3 km E on N 415
15, rte de Neuf-Brisach
68180 Horbourg-Wihr — 89.41.26.27
Open every day. 3 stes 400-550 F. 86 rms 240-420 F. Restaurant. Half-board 425 F. TV. Conference facilities. Heated pool. Tennis. Parking. Telex 870242. V AE.

An hotel of recent vintage, with comfortable rooms. Well equipped for conferences.

Au Fer Rouge

52, Grand-Rue — 89.41.37.24
M. Fulgraff. Closed Sun dinner, Mon, 6 Jan-4 Feb and 1-12 Aug. Open until 9.30 pm. Private room: 33. Telex 880400. V AE DC.

Patrick Fulgraff has spent 14 of his 36 years in the kitchens of this fine old family establishment in the heart of historic Colmar and he's still improving. One more point last year, another this, for his intelligent revival of regional cooking. By way of example: an ultra-light ballottine of quail and foie gras, brik with mustardy pigs' trotters and napped with a marvellous sauce, braised sole and lobster with chicory in red-wine sauce, perfectly cooked perch with sauerkraut and another wonderful sauce, this one hinting of bacon. One small fault: the fine fillet of venison was served almost cold— and there may be a touch too much cream in those sauces.

A good choice of reasonably priced Alsace wines presented by a talented young sommelier, Bernard Didier. Patrick's mother takes care of the service with infinite grace.

A la carte: 350-500 F. Menus: 210 F (weekdays only), 320 F, 450 F.

11/20 Garbo

15, rue Berthe-Molly — 89.24.48.55
M. Parlato. Closed Sat lunch and Sun. Open until 11 pm. V AE DC.

Pleasant and overcrowded (especially in the evenings), a good address in the centre of town where you can try a fresh-tasting salad of prawn and citrus fruit, salmon with vermouth, and a berry charlotte.

A la carte: 260 F. Menus: from 75 F to 140 F.

12/20 La Maison des Têtes

19, rue des Têtes — 89.24.43.43
M. Rohfritsch. Closed Sun dinner, Mon, 1 week of July and mid-Jan to mid-Feb. Open until 9.30 pm. Terrace dining. V AE DC.

The fine Gothic façade decorated with strange carved heads opens into a wood-panelled dining room presided over by the spirited Carmen Rohfritsch. Her husband Marc prepares classic, honest dishes slightly lacking in sparkle: plentiful but dull poultry terrine, good fillet of beef stuffed with foie gras and sauerkraut, rather heavy chocolate cake.

A la carte: 280 F. Menus: from 95 F to 264 F.

Mercure

Rue Golbery — 89.41.71.71
Open every day. 4 stes 650-700 F. 72 rms 340-480 F. Restaurant. TV. Air cond. Conference facilities. Garage parking. Telex 870398. V AE DC.

Near the Unterlinden museum and the old town. The rooms, are in delicate colours, but on the small side: three are reserved for disabled people and six for non-smokers.

Le Rendez-Vous de Chasse

7, pl. de la Gare — 89.41.10.10
M. Riehm. Closed Tue (except holidays). Open until 10 pm. Private room: 50. Telex 880248. V AE DC.

Avant-garde, temperamental, perfectionist— Serge Burkel is not at all the sort of chef you expect to find in a staid station hotel like this. But with the encouragement of the owner, Mme Riehm, he has swept away the past with scintillating cooking. The décor has also been changed and simplified, bringing an end to fifteen years of peaceful ticking over. Burkel still needs to learn more consistency but one thing is sure: Colmar has acquired another great chef with his wonderful fleischnakkas (a kind of cannelloni) with crab, leek stuffed with rabbit offal and flavoured with olives and balsamic vinegar, frogs' legs baeckeoffe, a transfigured choucroute, pork chops stuffed with foie gras, gratin of turbot with chopped herbs. Another point.

As we go to press, we have just learned that both Serge Burkel and Mme Riehm are due to leave the restaurant.

A la carte: 400 F. Menus: 175 F (lunch only), 185 F, 300 F and 400 F (dinner only).

Terminus Bristol

(See restaurant above)
Open every day. 12 stes 650-800 F. 70 rms 300-500 F. Half-board 450-600 F. TV. Conference facilities.

A fine traditional hotel, quiet despite its central position. The rooms have recently been modernised.

Saint-Martin

38, Grand-Rue — 89.24.11.51
Closed 20 Nov-10 March (except w-e). 24 rms 240-520 F. TV. V AE DC.

Sober, rustic décor for this attractive hotel in the old town. Mostly quiet rooms, attractively furnished. Charming reception but the breakfasts are disappointing.

Schillinger

16, rue Stanislas — 89.41.43.17
M. Schillinger. Closed Sun dinner, Mon and July. Open until 9.30 pm. Private room: 35. V AE DC.

The menu has received a youthful boost since Jean Schillinger's son, Jean-Yves, returned from training under Boyer and Robuchon to join him in the kitchen. The exquisite foie gras with Pinot-Noir jelly and the lobster gratin are still on the menu, but they are now kept company by fillet of freshwater perch with grapes, cucumber and raw prawns marinated in caviar, the amazing, amusing, and delicious chilled broccoli soup with caviar-flavoured beaten egg white, and frogs' legs and snails dressed in sea urchins. The wine list is magnificent, with many fine old Alsace vintages. The L-shaped dining room (book a table near the door— there's more space) is luxurious but rather ostentatious. On the minus side, the cheese board contained two disappointing Munsters, and the desserts are rather ordinary. We had been hoping to award a third toque, but we'll wait... with confidence.

A la carte: 500 F. Menus: 250 F, 320 F, 450 F.

The prices quoted in this guide are those which we were given by the restaurants and hotels concerned. Increases in prices are beyond our control.

12/20 La Taverne Alsacienne
Ingersheim
4 km NW on N 415
99, rue de la République — 89.27.08.41
M. Guggenbuhl. Closed Mon and 2 last weeks of July. Open until 9.30 pm. Private room: 12. No-smoking section. Parking. V.

A large family busy themselves in the plush dining room with its cane chairs and damask table linen. The son, trained in the region's best restaurants, produces ambitious and careful cooking. Highlights include freshwater perch with parsley and clams, and sliced duck breast with honey and spices. Fine local wines.

A la carte: 300 F and up. Menus: 65 F (weekdays lunch only), 85 F (weekdays only), and from 135 F to 250 F.

In nearby Eguisheim
(7 km S on N 83 and D 14)
68420 Colmar — (Haut-Rhin)

 ### Le Caveau d'Eguisheim   ✿
3, place du Château
89.41.08.89
M. Schubnel. Closed Tue dinner, Wed, 15 Jan-1 March and 1-12 July. Open until 9.15 pm. Air cond. V AE DC.

Situated on the Place du Château where a fountain plays, this is one of the most attractive restaurants in this fortified town. Pascal Schubnel specialises in traditional cooking (choucroute, escargots, baeckeoffe), adding a few more original dishes of his own such as salt-cured poultry with foie gras and terrine with pistachios. Pretty floral décor and a delightful reception.

A la carte: 340 F. Menus: 130 F, 210 F, 310 F.

In nearby Husseren-les-Châteaux
(9 km S)
68420 Colmar — (Haut-Rhin)

 ### Husseren-les-Châteaux
Rue du Schlossberg
89.49.22.93
Open every day. 6 stes 560-890 F. 38 rms 340-890 F. Restaurant. Half-board 368-618 F. TV. Conference facilities. Heated pool. Tennis. Garage parking. V AE DC.

Six kilometres south of Colmar, this hillside hotel has views of the Vosges countryside and vineyards. Bright, comfortable rooms. Indoor swimming pool, sauna, solarium, table tennis, and children's games room.

See also: Ammerschwihr, Illhaeusern (Auberge de l'Ill)

COLOMARS
06670 Colomars — (Alpes-Mar.)
Paris 945 - Nice 17 - Vence 22 - Cannes 43

 ### Auberge du Rédier
93.37.94.37
Closed 2 Jan-2 Feb. 28 rms 280-320 F. Restaurant. Half-board 340 F oblig in seas. TV. Conference facilities. Pool. Tennis. Parking. Telex 470330. V AE DC.

Set among lemon trees, orange trees, and mimosas 300 metres above sea level. The nicest rooms are in front of the swimming pool.

COLOMBEY-LES-DEUX-EGLISES
52330 Colombey-les-Deux-Eglises — (Haute-Marne)
Paris 226 - Chaumont 27 - Bar-sur-Aube 15

Les Dhuits
N 19 — 25.01.50.10
Closed 20 Dec-5 Jan. 42 rms 230-300 F. Restaurant. Half-board 250-300 F. TV 20 rms. Conference facilities. Garage parking. Telex 840920. V AE DC.

A large, recently built hotel set back from the main road. Spacious, comfortable, well-equipped rooms, hunting and fishing breaks a possibility. The breakfasts could be improved.

COLROY-LA-ROCHE
67420 Colroy-la-Roche — (Bas-Rhin)
Paris 402 - Sélestat 30 - Saint-Dié 30 - Obernai 41

La Cheneaudière
88.97.61.64
M. François. Closed 3 Jan-1 March. Open until 9 pm. Terrace dining. Air cond. Parking. Telex 870438. V AE DC.

A luxurious dining room in beige and dark wood and a terrace overlooking the Vosges forest. The meticulous cooking deserves another toque this year: generous servings of foie gras, Munster ravioli with Roquefort sauce, tender and tasty lamb fillet served with ratatouille in a crêpe 'beggar's purse'. Lovely desserts and an extensive wine list.

A la carte: 500 F and up. Menus: 280 F (weekdays only), 500 F.

La Cheneaudière
(See restaurant above)
Closed 3 Jan-1 March. 6 stes 1,250-1,700 F. 27 rms 900 F. Half-board 700-900 F. TV. Conference facilities. Heated pool. Tennis.

A large, especially quiet hotel. The luxurious rooms have terraces overlooking the mountains and forest. The reception could be warmer. Good breakfasts. Private hunting.

COMBLOUX
74920 Combloux — (H.-Savoie)
Paris 610 - Annecy 65 - Chamonix 33 - Megève 5

Au Cœur des Prés
50.93.36.55
Closed 15 April-1 June and 25 Sep-20 Dec. 34 rms 250-360 F. Restaurant. Half-board 315 F. TV 15 rms. Conference facilities. Tennis. Garage parking. V.

Green in summer, white in winter, and attractive all year round. Cosy rooms with balconies, 1,050 metres up. You can see Mont Blanc from the restaurant.

Le Coin Savoyard
near the church — 50.58.60.27
Closed Mon off-season, 20 April-5 June and 15 Sep-1 Nov. 10 rms 260 F. Restaurant. Half-board 220-250 F. Parking. V.

Family atmosphere and simple, renovated, soundproofed rooms. Shady garden.

Aux Ducs de Savoie
Le Bouchet — 50.58.61.43
Closed 22 April-8 June and 30 Sep-18 Dec. 50 rms 360-460 F. Restaurant. Half-board 330-390 F. TV 24 rms. Conference facilities. Heated pool. Garage parking. Telex 319244. V AE DC.

A large, modern chalet across from the mountains. Swimming pool in summer and ski tow 100 metres away in winter.

Rond-Point des Pistes 🌲🍴
Le Rond-Point des Pistes
Le Haut-Combloux — 50.58.68.55
Closed 15 April-20 June and 15 Sep-20 Dec. 29 rms 300-450 F. Restaurant. Half-board 255-410 F. TV 22 rms. Conference facilities. Parking. Telex 385550. V.
Near the ski lifts and cross-country trails. Intelligently equipped rooms, some with balcony and views of Mont Blanc. Sauna.

COMMENTRY
03600 Commentry — (Allier)
Paris 330 - Moulins 67 - Montluçon 15 - Riom 68

Michel Rubod
47, rue J.-J.-Rousseau — 70.64.45.31
M. Rubod. Closed Sun dinner, Mon, Feb school holidays, 1-14 Aug and 25 Nov-15 Dec. Open until 10 pm. Private room: 35. V.
Some tables near the kitchen let you overhear lively exchanges between the owner, Michel Rubod, and his staff. Luckily, Mme Rubod is there to smooth things over and the excellent food keeps the customers happy. Dishes like grilled red-mullet and aubergine, baby beetroot and prawn salad, and sweetbreads with garlic come and go at the whim of the chef. The wines are on the young side but there is an intelligent selection.
A la carte: 350-400 F. Menus: 120 F, 170 F, 198 F, 295 F.

COMPIÈGNE
60200 Compiègne — (Oise)
Paris 82 - Amiens 77 - St-Quentin 64 - Senlis 32

11/20 Le Bistrot de Flandre
2, rue d'Amiens — 44.83.26.35
M. Chudant. Closed 1-16 Jan. Open until 10.30 pm. Private room: 55. Terrace dining. V AE DC.
The terrace is more pleasant than the gaudy dining room for tasting a Breton shrimp salad, lotte with tagliatelle, and pear charlotte. Some good Beaujolais.
A la carte: 240 F. Menus: 78 F (weekdays only), 92 F (Sun and holidays only).

Hôtel de Flandre
16, quai de la République — 44.83.24.06
Open every day. 44 rms 140-250 F. Garage parking. V DC.
A modest establishment on the banks of the Oise that boasts large, clean rooms. Courteous reception, plentiful breakfasts with good croissants, and very reasonable prices.

Hostellerie du Royal-Lieu 🌲🍴
9, rue de Senlis — 44.20.10.24
Open every day. 3 stes 450 F. 18 rms 345 F. Restaurant. TV. No pets. Conference facilities. Parking. V AE DC.
Here is a timbered *auberge* in a quiet suburb, with pleasant, smallish rooms decorated in different styles, overlooking wooded parkland.

11/20 Les Jardins d'Eugénie
23, pl. de l'Hôtel-de-Ville — 44.40.00.88
M. Cahors. Open every day. Open until 11 pm. Private room: 100. V.
This corner brasserie serves carefully grilled meats, good chips, and casseroles. Pleasant glassed-in terrace.
A la carte: 200-250 F. Menus: 71 F (weekdays only), 98 F.

12/20 Hôtel du Nord
(René Laudigeois)
1, pl. de la Gare — 44.83.22.30
M. Laudigeois. Closed Sun dinner and Aug. Open until 10 pm. Garage parking. V.
The enormous prices on an endless menu probably help pay for the recent redecoration, which included sliding frosted-glass doors looking onto the River Oise. But then good seafood never comes cheap. Try the prawn sauté with tarragon butter and the grilled fish with sauce béarnaise. Extensive wine list.
A la carte: 400 F. Menus: 190 F (weekdays only), 240 F.

Hôtel du Nord
(See restaurant above)
Closed Aug. 20 rms 240-285 F. TV.
Practical and fairly quiet, although near the station. Undistinguished but well-equipped rooms. Pleasant service.

12/20 Rôtisserie du Chat qui Tourne
17, rue E.-Floquet — 44.40.02.74
Mme Robert. Open every day. Open until 9.45 pm. Private room: 30. Telex 150211. V.
This seventeenth-century timbered building in a narrow street of the old town has lost none of its charm; nor has the restaurant with its varnished beams, floral curtains and lace tablecloths. But the cooking has become sluggish: fresh but scanty coquilles St-Jacques, tasteless lamb fillet with good vegetables. The wine list has plenty of half-bottles. The offhand reception and service need to be smartened up. No toque this year.
A la carte: 300 F. Menus: 90 F (weekdays only), 175 F (weekdays lunch only, wine inc), 125 F, 190 F.

Hôtel de France
(See restaurant above)
Open every day. 21 rms 110-300 F. Half-board 249-338 F. TV. Conference facilities.
Well located in a quiet street. Comfortable, reasonably priced rooms.

12/20 Vivenel
30, rue Vivenel — 44.86.10.15
M. Hauterville. Closed Sat lunch, Sun dinner, Mon and 27 July-17 Aug. Open until 9.30 pm. V AE.
Bold, original cooking by a young chef from Martinique: papaya choucroute with simmered fish, fricassée of lamb with coconut milk, gratin of christophine (a nutty Caribbean vegetable), and delicious desserts.
A la carte: 200 F. Menus: 105 F, 139 F.

In nearby Elincourt-Ste-Marguerite
(14 km N on D 142)
60157 Compiègne — (Oise)

Château de Bellinglise
Route de Lassigny
44.76.04.76
M. Colin. Open every day. Open until 9.30 pm. Private room: 30. No pets. Parking. Telex 155048. V AE DC.
A majestic L-shaped Renaissance château reflected in a lake and surrounded by 260 hectares of wooded parkland. The new young chef has a more positive style of cooking, with wonderfully subtle sauces. Salad of lotte (slightly overcooked) with tasty sweet-pepper marmalade, John Dory (also overcooked) with a delicious shellfish sauce,

and good fresh fruit pastries. Fine wines and professional reception.

A la carte: 450 F. Menus: 185 F (weekdays only), 295 F, 420 F.

Château de Bellinglise

(See restaurant above)

Open every day. 2 stes 1,180-1,390 F. 50 rms 495-1,390 F. Half-board 700-1,040 F. TV. No pets. Conference facilities. Tennis.

A remarkably preserved and restored sixteenth-century château in extensive grounds. Beautiful rooms, riding stables, facilities for conferences.

In nearby Rethondes

(8 km E on N 31)
60153 Compiègne – (Oise)

Alain Blot

(Auberge du Pont)
21, rue du Mal-Foch – 44.85.60.24

M. Blot. Closed Sat lunch, Sun dinner and Mon. Open until 9.15 pm. Private room: 30. V DC.

The cooking of Alain Blot merits a pilgrimage to this charming village, famous for its memories of two armistices (1918 and 1940). As you read these lines, he will be revamping the pretty pink décor, so we'll just mention the happy atmosphere, attractive garden, pleasant reception, and especially the light and masterful cooking, from lobster and scallop salad through to frozen nougat with berries. You could also sample slices of roast wild duck breast with pepper and spices, a thick chunk of salmon with crispy skin, or fillet of young rabbit with wild mushrooms and artichokes in a white wine sauce. Good cellar.

A la carte: 350-400 F. Menus: 180 F (weekdays only), 420 F (avec homard), 300 F, 340 F.

In nearby Saint-Jean-aux-Bois

(11 km SW on D 332 and D 85)
60350 Compiègne – (Oise)

A la Bonne Idée

5, rue des Meuniers – 44.42.84.09

M. Royer. Closed 15 Jan-20 Feb. Open until 9.30 pm. Private room: 25. Air cond. Parking. Telex 155026. V.

Perfect for peaceful weekends, the old monastery town of Saint-Jean-aux-Bois, surrounded by forest, was once called La Solitude. This *auberge* has been redecorated in a rather graceless luxury style, with Louis XIII armchairs, beams, and stone walls. At first Michel Royer's menu looks long and confusing, but good, classic dishes, expertly prepared and presented, can be uncovered with patience and the help of the attentive staff. Beware, however, of the 'menu suggestion' at 260 F; its most enticing suggestions carry hefty (though clearly marked) supplements.

A la carte: 400 F. Menus: 160 F (weekdays only), 260 F, 360 F, 390 F.

A la Bonne Idée

(See restaurant above)

Closed 15 Jan-15 Feb. 1 ste 390-490 F. 24 rms 330-390 F. Half-board 450 F. TV 23 rms. Conference facilities.

Small, simple, cosy rooms. Perfect for country weekends spent walking, cycling, or horse riding.

Problems with French? The RAC France language pack will help you to converse with confidence.

In nearby Vaudrampont

(10 km SE on D 332)
60127 Compiègne – (Oise)

12/20 Auberge du Bon Accueil

Carrefour de Vaudrampont – 44.42.84.04

M. Delacroix. Closed Mon dinner, Tue, 28 Jan-23 Feb and 16-23 Aug. Open until 9.30 pm. Hotel: 7 rms 110-310 F. Parking. V.

Living up to its name, this peaceful family establishment will certainly give you a cordial welcome. The décor is on the sombre side but the pleasant garden helps to justify the bill, which doesn't go with the owner's good but plain cooking: lotte with prawn coulis, andouillette sausage with Muscadet, game in season.

A la carte: 350 F. Menus: 175 F, 310 F.

CONCARNEAU

29110 Concarneau – (Finistère)
Paris 537 - Quimper 23 - Saint-Brieuc 130

12/20 La Coquille

1, rue du Moros – 98.97.08.52

M. Le Maître. Closed Sun dinner off-season, Mon and 2-23 Jan. Open until 9.30 pm. Private room: 25. Terrace dining. V AE DC.

This fish and seafood restaurant also provides a feast for the eyes with a stone wall covered with pictures on one side and views over the harbour on the other. Dishes to try include the stuffed clams, cod with crab mousse, and seafood blanquette.

A la carte: 300 F. Menus: 90 F (lunch only), 140 F, 160 F, 250 F.

Le Galion

15, rue St-Guénolé (ville close) – 98.97.30.16

M. Gaonac'h. Closed off-season Sun dinner and Mon, 20 Jan-15 Feb and 17-29 Nov. Open until 9.30 pm. Private room: 35. Telex 940336. V AE DC.

You'll want to return to this enchanted place that is so obviously the object of daily care and attention. Flowers inside and out, elegantly laid tables, and old Breton décor provide an enticing backdrop for the talents of chef Henri Goanac'h. They show best in the oyster soup with diced vegetables and lentils, blanquette of asparagus and prawns, John Dory with rhubarb sauce, calf's head and tongue in a tasty vinaigrette, and bourdaloue (an almond-flavoured dessert) with pears and Calvados.

A la carte: 350-400 F. Menus: 150 F, 185 F, 235 F, 330 F.

La Résidence des Iles

(See restaurant above)

Closed off-season Sun and Mon, 20 Jan-15 Feb and 17-29 Nov. 5 rms 290-400 F. TV.

A friendly atmosphere reigns in the five simply decorated rooms. Very pleasant service.

Modern

5, rue du Lin – 98.97.03.36

Open every day. 17 rms 180-300 F. No pets. Garage parking.

Near the fishing port, a small, well-kept hotel with an annexe on a nearby inlet.

L'Océan

Plage des Sables-Blancs – 98.50.53.50

Open every day. 40 rms 290-420 F. Restaurant. Half-board 300-350 F. TV. Conference facilities. Heated pool. Parking. V AE.

A new, somewhat impersonal hotel from which to admire the sea. The beige and pink rooms have double glazing and there are two-floor flats for families. Out of season, two children can stay in their parents' room free from the third night. Restaurant with a panoramic view.

Restaurant de la Douane

[14]
71, av. A.-Le Lay – 98.97.30.27
M. Péron. Closed Sun off-season and 15 Nov-15 Dec. Open until 9.30 pm. Air cond. V.
The infectious laughter of Jean-Marie Péron (a friend and disciple of Jean Delaveyne) and his wife Josée make this an unusually cheerful restaurant. The market oriented cooking, which varies almost every day, will delight your purse as well as your palate. Space is restricted so it's best to book.
A la carte: 300 F. Menus: 165 F (wine inc), 100 F.

12/20 Les Sables Blancs

Plage des Sables-Blancs
98.97.01.39
M. Chabrier. Closed 10 Nov-20 March. Open until 9.30 pm. Private room: 60. Terrace dining. V AE DC.
Here you can gaze at the sea as you sample some of its finest, freshest products, simply prepared: lobster 'ty houlen', shellfish, grilled turbot with lime butter.
A la carte: 250 F. Menus: 175 F (wine inc), 68 F, 85 F, 115 F.

Les Sables Blancs

(See restaurant above)
Closed 10 Nov-20 March. 48 rms 140-275 F. Half-board 205-320 F oblig in seas. TV 4 rms. Conference facilities.
A graceless modern building on the beach. Superb views and small, neat rooms. A rather stiff reception.

Ty Chupen Gwenn

Plage des Sables-Blancs – 98.97.01.43
Closed Sun off-season, 29 April-5 May and Dec 15 rms 230-365 F. TV. V DC.
Set on the beach at the edge of the town. The rooms are well-kept with splendid views; avoid the noisy rooms overlooking the street.

27190 Conches – (Eure)
Paris 119 - Rouen 60 - Dreux 47 - Evreux 18

La Toque Blanche ✿

[13]
18, pl. Carnot – 32.30.01.54
Mme Bachet. Closed Tue dinner and Mon. Open until 9 pm. V AE.
Cider, perry (a pear drink), and staff in regional costume provide plenty of local colour in this Norman inn devoted to showing the best of the region. Careful cooking with the personal touch by a self-taught chef: pastries of pétoncles and seaweed, duck breast cooked in perry, Norman sweetbreads. And you can buy a bottle of the 100-year-old Calvados to take away.
A la carte: 300 F. Menus: 60 F (weekdays lunch only), 98 F (weekdays only), 157 F, 187 F.

32100 Condom – (Gers)
Paris 680 - Auch 43 - Agen 38 - Toulouse 110

Le Logis des Cordeliers 🌲🌹

Rue de la Paix
62.28.03.68
Open every day. 21 rms 200-350 F. TV. Pool. Garage parking. V.
A very quiet hotel in a walled garden with well equipped, functional rooms.

12/20 L'Origan

4, rue Cadeot – 62.68.24.84
M. Cano. Closed Sun, Mon, 2 weeks in Feb and 3 weeks in Sep. Open until 11 pm. Terrace dining. V AE DC.
A convivial setting in shades of Italian red and green, where the quality of the reception is echoed in the kitchen, even if the cooking is still rather timid. Fresh salad of escarole and mussels, good-sized entrecôte steak with cream and mushrooms, and superb chocolate profiteroles. Efficient service. Rustic Italian wines lacking in charm.
A la carte: 120-150 F.

Hôtel des Trois Lys 🌲🌹

38, rue Gambetta – 62.28.33.33
Open every day. 10 rms 250-500 F. TV. Conference facilities. Pool. Parking. V AE.
Recently and tastefully restored, a superb eighteenth-century residence that now contains ten spacious and comfortable rooms. Friendly service and perfect breakfasts. Unbeatable value.

69420 Condrieu – (Rhône)
Paris 514 - Lyon 41 - Annonay 34 - Vienne 11

Beau Rivage

[14]
2, rue Beau-Rivage
74.59.52.24
M. Humann. Open every day. Open until 9.15 pm. Private room: 30. Garden dining. Air cond. Garage parking. Telex 308946. V AE DC.
Let's make one thing quite clear to the Humanns and their chef Reynald Donet: all we and our readers can't swallow is their prices. The fillet of freshwater perch with Côte-Rôtie is successful (the accompanying vegetables less so) and the saddle of young rabbit stuffed with chicken liver mousse is an accomplishment that easily deserves two toques, but the Condrieu rigotte cheese and salad, like the unoriginal sweet trolley, isn't even worth one. The wines are still marvellous and the setting on the banks of the Rhône has lost none of its charm. Another point then—to encourage lower prices.
A la carte: 500-600 F. Menus: 180 F (weekdays lunch only), 260 F, 385 F.

Beau Rivage 🌲🌹

(See restaurant above)
Open every day. 4 stes 790 F. 20 rms 500-720 F. TV. Air cond 6 rms.
The new owners have made improvements to some of the bathrooms and put in air-conditioning here and there, but this fine establishment amid vineyards looks just the same.

12320 Conques – (Aveyron)
Paris 603 - Espalion 50 - Figeac 54 - Rodez 37

Hôtel Sainte-Foy

Rue Principale – 65.69.84.03
Closed 1 Dec-15 March. 1 ste 650 F. 35 rms 220-550 F. Restaurant. Half-board 285-330 F. Conference facilities. Parking. V AE.
A seventeenth-century building next to the abbey in the heart of this lovely village. The adjoining former convent houses an annexe. Heated indoor swimming pool.

CORSICA

20000 Ajaccio — Corse
Bastia 153 - Bonifacio 140 - Calvi 163 - Porto 83

Albion
15, av. du Général-Leclerc
95.21.66.70
Closed Feb and March. 63 rms 324-438 F. TV. Air cond. Parking. Telex 460846. V AE DC.
A classic modern building in a residential area a stone's throw from the centre. Rooms are comfortable, well equipped, with carefully thought-out décor. Warm welcome and cosy bar.

12/20 L'Alta Rocca
7, rue Mal-d'Ornano — 95.51.22.46
Mme Santoni. Closed Sun, 4-10 July and 1-15 Dec. Open until 10.30 pm. Air cond. V AE DC.
Solange Santoni seeks out the best local ingredients for her menu, which she prefers to keep simple until her clientele's tastes evolve. Sample her fresh, seasonal seafood salad, perfectly cooked sole fillets, pear delight (fruit slices and sorbet), and red Patrimonio wine from Jacques-François Devichi with a surprising hint of Muscat. Friendly welcome and service. The décor, alas, is ponderously petit bourgeois.
A la carte: 220 F. Menus: 60 F (weekdays lunch only, wine inc), 90 F (weekdays lunch only), 130 F, and 500 F.

L'Amore Piattu
at Diamant II
8, pl. du Gal-de-Gaulle — 95.51.00.53
Mme Maestracci. Closed Sat lunch, Sun and Oct. Open until 10 pm. Terrace dining. Air cond. V.
Brand-new is the elegantly feminine pink-and-grey décor, and the terrace is a recent addition too, though it affords the same stunning view of the sea. Marie-Louise Maestracci plays to the hilt her favourite role of 'mistress of the house': going to market each day, adding her own touch to her finds, and sometimes delving into her grandmother's cookery book (whence the savoury leg of lamb and aubergine mould). At lunchtime she goes round the tables reciting the menu to enchanted guests: octopus salad, skate, mussels with grilled peppers, sardines stuffed with broccio (local sheep's-milk cheese) and mint, Oriental chicken fricassée, lemon tart or marquise au chocolat. The usual tipple is wine from the Ajaccio or Sartène hills. For our money, this is the most charming restaurant in Ajaccio.
Menu: 220 F.

Arcade
115, cours Napoléon — 95.20.43.09
Open every day. 49 rms 300-360 F. TV. Air cond. Conference facilities. Parking. Telex 460992. V AE.
Functional building on the edge of town (coming from the airport). Clean, but awfully austere rooms. Lounge bar.

Campo dell'Oro
(See restaurant above)
Open every day. 1 ste 830-1,535 F. 130 rms 350-1,300 F. Half-board 445-850 F oblig in seas. TV. Air cond 76 rms. Conference facilities. Pool. Tennis.
We've been told a new swimming pool and a huge terrace were installed during the winter.

Rooms overlook the sea and garden (the view is their best feature).

Cala di Sole
5 km SW on N 193b
Rte des Sanguinaires — 95.52.01.36
Closed 15 Oct-31 March. 31 rms 440-610 F (per pers, half-board oblig). Restaurant. TV. Air cond. Conference facilities. Heated pool. Tennis. V AE DC.
Rooms in this holiday hotel are sparsely furnished, but they are light and airy, opening onto small balconies and a large lawn overlooking the sea. The bathrooms are adequate.

Costa
2, rue Colomba — 95.21.43.02
Open every day. 53 rms 287-397 F. TV. No pets. Telex 468080. V AE DC.
Modern and well-kept hotel with a garden, right near the sea (the beach is just 100 metres away). Spacious rooms, where breakfast is served with no time limit.

Côte d'Azur
12, cours Napoléon — 95.21.50.24
M. Lamic. Closed Sun and 20 June-20 July. Open until 9.30 pm. Air cond. V AE DC.
Local government officers have astutely made this their regular canteen. The management has achieved a perfect balance between undying tradition (Empire décor) and the kind of classic, fresh cooking of which one never tires. Daily specials include plump rabbit with wild mushrooms, baked local sea bass in a light sauce. We also recommend the marvellous stuffed capon, and the glazed strawberries. Good Corsican wines from Sartène and delicious bottles from Patrimonio.
A la carte: 220 F. Menus: 95 F, 125 F, 145 F, 175 F.

Eden-Roc
Rte des Iles-Sanguinaires — 95.52.01.47
Open every day. 6 stes 870-2,040 F. 40 rms 390-1,840 F. Restaurant. Half-board 490-1,070 F oblig in seas. TV. Air cond. Conference facilities. Heated pool. Valet parking. Telex 460486. V AE DC.
An imposing building on a hillside overlooking the sea; bright, carefully furnished rooms done in modern style, with pretty geranium-filled balconies facing the golf course. Charming welcome and smiling service. Sea-water spa, all water sports (private beach), and a variety of games equipment.

Fesch
7, rue Fesch — 95.21.50.52
Closed 16 Dec-16 Jan. 77 rms 260-365 F. TV. Telex 460640. V AE DC.
Double-glazed windows make for peaceful nights in the small but cosy and comfortable rooms, in the heart of the old city.

La Mer
8 km W, rte des Sanguinaires — 95.52.00.93
M. Federici. Closed Nov-March. Open until 10 pm. Private room: 40. Terrace dining. No pets. Parking. Telex 460854. V AE DC.
After passing the pretentious entrance to the Dolce Vita, go quickly through the dining room with its old-fashioned 1950s décor, and out onto the vast seafront terrace to admire the marvellous sunset. The cooking lacks originality but is

nevertheless well executed and on the upturn. A toque this year for the rock lobster ravioli (diaphanous pasta), pot-au-feu de la mer (poached fillets of red mullet, lotte, etc.) garnished with al dente vegetables, and an iced rum nougat. The waitresses' severe uniforms and the ever-present gold-epauletted waiters reinforce the impression of living in another era. Classic and expensive wine list.

A la carte: 300 F. Menu: 195 F.

Dolce Vita

(See restaurant above)

Closed Nov-March. 34 rms 430-835 F. Half-board 725-840 F oblig in seas. TV. Air cond. Pool. Tennis.

Rooms are rather small but functional, bright, and well furnished. Some open right onto the pine-shaded lawn facing the beach. Warm welcome, very good service.

Les Mouettes

9, cours L.-Bonaparte — 95.21.44.38

Closed 5 Nov-31 March. 22 rms 490-790 F (per pers, half-board oblig). Restaurant. TV. Air cond. Conference facilities. Pool. Parking. Telex 468397. V AE DC.

In a flower-decked setting away from the city centre (1.5 kilometres), this is one of the most pleasant places in the area. Welcoming, well-equipped rooms. Superb terrace right over the sea (a stone's throw away).

Point U

59 bis, rue Fesch — 95.21.59.92

Mme Nocera and M. Malaclet. Closed Sun and Christmas week. Open until 11 pm. Terrace dining. Air cond. V AE DC.

Crowds rush to this charming, low-beamed restaurant to savour the completely unstereotyped regional cooking, prepared by Alain Malaclet and served under the attentive eye of Marie-Madeleine Nocera: rabbit in myrtle wine, stuffatu (Corsican stew) and fiadone (Corsican cheese and orange flan), but also to enjoy some dishes of a more original stamp, like stuffed capon ballottine, lobster ravioli, and turbot with pears. To drink, order Corsican wines such as Clos Nicrosi white and Peraldi from the Ajaccio hills.

A la carte: 250-300 F. Menus: 100 F, 150 F.

10/20 U Scalone

2, rue du Roi-de-Rome
95.21.50.05

M. Richez. Closed Sat lunch, Sun and 1 Dec-7 Jan. Open until 9.30 pm. Terrace dining. V.

The warm welcome and impressive collection of cigarette lighters cannot distract one from the irregularity of the cooking. Best bet is the beef in Roquefort sauce; other options include Corsican charcuterie, trout with broccio cheese, and tarte Tatin.

A la carte: 250 F.

In nearby Cuttoli-Corticchiato

(18 km NE)
20167 Cuttoli-Corticchiato — (Corse)

12/20 U Licettu

Plaine de Cuttoli
Rte de Bastelicaccia — 95.25.61.57

M. Catellagi. Closed Mon and Nov. Open until 9.30 pm. Terrace dining. Pool. Parking. V.

A single menu, with all you can eat and drink, served in an ordinary but cordial setting warmed (in season) by a large fireplace. The jovial owner fusses about, and worries you are not eating en-

ough. Good, hearty terrines, fabulous ham, country bread, and Corsican wine in abundance, traditional spit-roast suckling pig, local cheese and broccio to finish. Whew!

Menu: 170 F (wine inc).

12/20 Chez Pascal

At Pedi-Morella — 95.25.65.73

Mme Torre. Dinner only. Closed Mon and 30 Sep-5 Nov. Open until 10 pm. Terrace dining. Hotel: 4 rms 200 F.

Thick country soup, roast lamb, tender broccio cannelloni, aged sheep's-milk cheese: the island repertoire doesn't change much at Angela's. But since it's straightforward, generous, and inexpensive, hordes of locals from Ajaccio are attracted to this small mountain village to fill their stomachs while trying to find elbow room.

Menu: 150 F.

In nearby Valle-di-Mezzana

(20 km N on N 193 and D 1)
20167 Valle-di-Mezzana — (Corse)

A Vignarella

At Ondella — 95.25.69.95

M. Hulot. Dinner only. Closed Sun dinner off-season and Wed. Open until 10.30 pm. Terrace dining. V.

After a delightful walk, you will find the Hulot's place nestled in a mountain hamlet. Regulars are surprised by the constant inventions of the skilful, discriminating chef, despite his occasional excesses (cider-braised coquilles St-Jacques, sea bass in tarragon cream sauce). The wine list favours reasonably priced island vintages, and the hostess's welcoming smile makes you want to linger watching the sunset and savouring her husband's seafood delicacies.

Menu: 200 F.

ASCO

20276 Asco — Corse
Ajaccio 125 - Bastia 64 - Corte 42

Le Chalet

12 km SW on D 1
in Haut-Asco — 95.47.81.08

Closed 1 June-30 Sep. 22 rms 140-260 F. Restaurant. Half-board 240-260 F. Parking.

Lovely view over the Cinto mountains from certain rooms, which are simple but well kept.

BASTELICA

20119 Bastelica — Corse
Ajaccio 41 - Cauro 19 - Porticcio 34 - Corte 62

12/20 U Castagnetu

95.28.70.71

MM. Brassens and Folacci. Closed Tue off-season, Nov and Dec. Open until 9.30 pm. Terrace dining. Parking. Telex 460918. V AE.

Dine on the little terrace overlooking the village, or in the cool, inviting dining room. Two outstanding set menus are offered: the *Montagnard* ('Mountaineer'), for example, brings house charcuterie, broccio cheese omelette, a thick slice of lamb, cheese, and dessert. The food is traditional, but Andrée Folacci is adept at adding new flavours to her finely wrought Corsican classics. Charming welcome and service.

A la carte: 200 F. Menus: 80 F (weekdays only), 150 F.

🏠 U Castagnetu 🎋🌲
(See restaurant above)
Closed Tue off-season, Nov and Dec. 15 rms 150-300 F. Half-board 240-260 F oblig in seas. Conference facilities.

A simple rustic hotel next to a chestnut grove, beautifully kept, with rooms overlooking the old basilica. Warm welcome, super breakfasts, inexpensive.

11/20 Chez Paul
95.28.71.59
M. Mocanetti. Open every day. Open until 11 pm. Private room: 80. Terrace dining. V.

Overlooking the old village, surrounded by chestnut groves, this mountain bistro concentrates on its own charcuterie (pigs are raised and butchered right there), filling broccio cheese omelettes and delicious sheep's-milk cheeses, washed down with good local wines.
Menus: 55 F, 65 F, 85 F.

BASTELICACCIA

20166 Bastelicaccia — Corse
Ajaccio 20 - Porticcio 10 - Cauro 14

12/20 Auberge Seta
95.20.00.16
M. Seta. Closed Wed. Open until 10.30 pm. Private room: 120. Parking. V AE DC.

The voluble, charming owner, Paul Seta, supervises a staff of uncommonly courteous waiters in this dining room overlooking the Gulf of Ajaccio. The generous mussel and beer fricassée could have done with less salt to bring out the aroma of the shellfish, and the platter of assorted fish brought a confusing compilation of flavours. The cooking is generous, and full of bright ideas, but the execution still leaves something to be desired.
A la carte: 300 F. Menu: 150 F (weekdays only, wine inc).

BASTIA

20200 Bastia — (Corse)
Ajaccio 153 - Porto 135 - Calvi 93 - Bonifacio 170

🍴 La Citadelle
5, rue du Dragon — 95.31.44.70
M. Mattei. Closed Mon. Annual closings not available. Open until 10.30 pm. Terrace dining. Air cond. V AE.

A rising star, despite the desperately passé—but very Mediterranean—surroundings. François Mattei, a former Lenôtre pastry cook, has talents that extend well beyond desserts, witness his lobster salad sparked with fresh mint (and served in generous portions), or his lotte with smoky bacon and broad beans; excellent too are the cinnamon-spiced pear gratin, and his version of fiadone, a Corsican cheese and orange flan. The cellar is still rather weak. Urbane welcome and service overseen by Jean-François Rocchi.
A la carte: 300-320 F. Menu: 130 F (lunch only).

🏠 Piétracap
3 km N, rte de San Martino
in Pietranera — 95.31.64.63
Open every day. 43 rms 330-570 F. TV. Conference facilities. Pool. Parking. V AE DC.

In an olive grove overlooking the sea, spacious rooms (some recently added), very well equipped. The décor, however, is rather cold and the soundproofing is not very effective.

🍴 Le Romantique
4 bis, rue du Pontetto — 95.32.30.85
M. Roncaglia. Closed Sun (Sat lunch and Sun in seas), and Feb. Open until 11 pm. Private room: 8. Garden dining. V AE DC.

Be romantic at any time of year at this restaurant in the old port, where Marie-Thérèse Roncaglia serves an appealing repertoire of sea scallops in puff pastry, baby chicken grilled with Corsican wild honey, profiteroles, and the famous fiadone. Concise, classic wine list with a good Patrimonio at 45 F. Always delightful welcome and service at this reliable address.
A la carte: 280-300 F. Menus: 95 F, 120 F, 138 F.

In nearby Erbalunga

(10 km N on D 80)
20222 Erbalunga — (Corse)

11/20 Le Pirate
in Brando — 95.33.24.20
M. Moioli. Closed Mon and 15 Oct-Easter. Open until 10.30 pm. Terrace dining. V AE.

Le Pirate stands out in this neck of the woods, not known as a gastronome's paradise. Nothing dazzlingly original here, but ingredients are well chosen (fish soup, carpaccio, fisherman's catch of the day). Some good vintages with a native tang. Irregular service.
A la carte: 270 F.

In nearby Palagaccio

(2.5 km N)
20200 Palagaccio — (Corse)

🏠 L'Alivi
Rte du Cap — 95.31.61.85
Open every day. 37 rms 380-595 F. TV 25 rms. Conference facilities. Parking. Telex 468349. V.

Here's a comfortable, modern, well-equipped hotel just above a pebble beach facing the Tuscan islands. Rooms with loggias. Garden.

BOCOGNANO

20136 Bocognano — (Corse)
Ajaccio 40 - Corte 43

12/20 L'Ustaria
95.27.41.10
Mme Alberdi. Closed off-season Sun dinner and Mon, and 15-28 Feb. Open until 10.30 pm. Private room: 8. Garden dining. No-smoking section. No pets. Parking.

Mementos abound in this charming family's cosy stone house. The son's adroit cooking (homemade terrine, petals of sea trout in red Corsican wine, prune 'soup' with ice cream) is diligently served in the restaurant's two dining rooms, one a bistro and the other 'gastronomic'.
A la carte: 300 F. Menus: 98 F (weekdays only; at the bistrot), 168 F, 210 F, 250 F.

BONIFACIO

20169 Bonifacio — Corse
Ajaccio 140 - Bastia 170 - Porto-Vecchio 27

🍴 La Caravelle
at the harbour — 95.73.06.47
M. Filippeddu. Closed 1 Oct-15 March. Open until 11.30 pm. Terrace dining. Air cond. Hotel: 22 rms 486-956 F. V AE DC.

La Caravelle is on hold while waiting for chef Jean-Claude Hérin to strike out on his own. It's a difficult situation for the restaurant's owners, who continue to insist that Hérin prepare a menu that they have designed. Not every dish is successful, but you are sure to be pleased with the light, subtly flavoured lobster ravioli soup, a dish that shows the potential of this chef, who is sure to become one of the island's best when he sets up on his own. La Caravelle's façade is the loveliest in this over-built port, where the pavement is being extended to accommodate even more tourists. The pretty dining room boasts delicate Byzantine-style frescoes, a most soothing décor (and you will need soothing, once you get a load of the exorbitant bill!).

A la carte: 430-450 F. Menu: 150 F (wine inc).

Hôtel Genovese
Haute Ville – 95.73.12.34
Open every day. 14 rms 600-1,500 F. TV. Air cond. No pets. Conference facilities. Parking. V AE.

The former legionnaires' barracks in the old city overlooking the bay and port is now a deluxe hotel complex. Refined modern décor with opulent rooms and suites. Decent breakfasts.

12/20 Stella d'Oro
7, rue du Gal-de-Gaulle – 95.73.03.63
M. Filippeddu. Open every day. Open until 11 pm. Air cond. V AE DC.

Pleasant local atmosphere. Try the fish dishes cooked by Jules' mother in this venerable institution, where the prices are steeper than the town's twisting streets: aubergines à la bonifacienne, baked capon, grilled red mullet, and fruit gratins.

A la carte: 300 F. Menus: 90 F and 150 F (lunch only).

BORGO
20290 Borgo – (Corse)
Bastia 18 - Aéroport de Poretta 6.5 - Casamozza 7

11/20 Les Espaces Verts
Rte de la Plage – 95.33.13.24
M. Soriano. Closed Mon and 1 Jan-15 Feb. Open until 10.30 pm. Garden dining. Pool. Tennis. Parking. V AE DC.

This lovely modern building, light and well decorated, stands between the sea and a swimming pool. Prices are rather stiff for the creditable cooking based on well-chosen ingredients: rabbit terrine, honey-lemon duck breast, and fresh grilled fish. Good welcome, classic wines.

A la carte: 300 F. Menus: 120 F, 250 F.

Isola
Cordon lagunaire – 95.33.19.60
Closed 20 Nov-10 March. 70 rms 220-550 F. Restaurant. Half-board 245-450 F oblig in seas. No pets. Conference facilities. Pool. Tennis. Parking. Telex 460695. V AE DC.

A modern, well-situated establishment in a garden 250 metres from the beach. Functional rooms with loggia.

CALVI
20260 Calvi – (Corse)
Ajaccio 163 - Bastia 93 - Porto 80 - Corte 96

L'Abbaye
Rte de Santore – 95.65.04.27
Closed 30 Oct-1 March. 46 rms 350-700 F. Restaurant. TV 30 rms. Air cond 30 rms. Conference facilities. Parking. Telex 460533. V DC.

In a pastoral setting 100 metres from sea and port, the former St François abbey has been artfully converted; it offers unusual, comfortable, ad-

equately equipped rooms. Panoramic terrace over the sea. Pleasant welcome.

Les Aloès
1.5 km SW, quartier Donatéo – 95.65.01.46
Closed 1 Oct-30 April. 26 rms 170-400 F. Parking. Telex 460540. V AE DC.

Hidden in leafy calm not far from the beach, this hotel offers lovely views of the gulf and the citadel of Calvi.

Hôtel Balanéa
6, rue Clemenceau – 95.65.00.45
Open every day. 37 rms 310-1,100 F. TV. Air cond. Telex 460540. V AE DC.

Pleasant renovated old house. All rooms are air-conditioned and soundproofed, most open onto the port. Nearby restaurant, L'Abri Côtier, is under the same management.

11/20 Comme Chez Soi
Quai Landry – 95.65.00.59
M. Blondeau. Closed Thu off-season, and 25 Feb-31 March. Open until 10.30 pm. Terrace dining. V AE DC.

For some reason there's always a queue at this restaurant, where the owner's cooking is ordinary in every respect save the high prices he charges for it. However portions are generous, and the ingredients are of good quality (skate with capers, fish soup). Smiling welcome and service.

A la carte: 350 F.

L'Ile de Beauté
Quai Landry – 95.65.00.46
M. Caumeil. Closed Wed lunch (except July-Aug) and 1 Oct-1 May. Open until 10 pm (11 pm in summer). Terrace dining. Air cond. No pets. V AE DC.

This restaurant on the Calvi quayside has recruited a new young chef, Yvan Vautier a cook with an impressive pedigree. Seafood, not surprisingly, dominates the menu: warm oysters with fresh lime, rock lobster in a creamy white-wine sauce, stunning shellfish platters, flawlessly grilled fresh fish, all sold at crippling prices.

A la carte: 400-500 F. Menus: 95 F (lunch only), 350 F.

Le Magnolia
Place du Marché
95.65.19.16
Open every day. 12 rms 380-750 F. Restaurant. Half-board 450-750 F. TV. Air cond. No pets. V AE DC.

An adorable all white nineteenth-century manor house set in a garden between the church and the marketplace in the old district of Calvi. Rooms are well equipped and decorated with infinite taste.

12/20 La Signoria
Route de l'Aéroport
95.65.23.73
MM. Ceccaldi. Dinner only in July-Aug. Closed 31 Oct-30 March. Open until 10.30 pm. Private room: 12. Terrace dining. No pets. Parking. Telex 460551. V AE.

This handsome seventeenth-century residence stands nobly in a eucalyptus grove. The chef (who has his own vegetable garden and spends his winters *chez* Robuchon) should cultivate the regional roots of his repertoire, for his best successes highlight fine Corsican produce: the star of his truffled turbot salad is neither the fish nor the tuber, but a fragrant olive oil used in the dressing! We were unimpressed by his foie gras and melon, and by a bland vegetable fondant. The service is classy, and the Corsican cellar is most worthwhile, but the chef will have to do better to reconquer the toque.

A la carte: 350 F. Menus: 180 F (lunch only), 290 F (dinner only).

🏠🏠 La Signoria
(See restaurant above)
Closed 31 Oct-30 March. 1 ste 1,400-2,000 F. 10 rms 450-960 F. TV. Pool.

Absolutely delightful rooms looking out on the mountain beyond the trees and swimming pool. Hire of motor and sailboats, tennis.

12/20 U Spuntinu 🄲
Rte de Bonifato — 95.65.07.06
M. Apparu. Closed Nov-May. Open until 11 pm. Parking. DC.

This modest *auberge* set in a magnificent landscape is owned by a farmer, who cooks with the freshest produce from his own fields. He charges most reasonable prices for his traditional island recipes: scrambled eggs with broccio, veal stew with wild boletus mushrooms, tender young kid sautéed with lemon and garlic.

A la carte: 250 F. Menu: 165 F.

20230 Canale-di-Verde — (Corse)
Ajaccio 152 - Corte 69 - Aléria 21

12/20 Le Roc
95.38.83.16
M. Policicchio. Dinner only (and lunch on Sun and holidays). Closed 15 Nov-15 Jan. Open until 10.30 pm. Garden dining. Air cond. Parking. V.

The superb terrace encircled by rocks, close to a meadow overlooking the Alistro bay, is a well-known beauty spot. Ernesto Policicchio's cooking is conservative but skilfully done: sample his duck breast in rasberry vinegar, carpaccio, or lotte 'ambassadeur'.

A la carte: 220 F. Menu: 160 F.

20130 Cargèse — (Corse)
Ajaccio 50 - Calvi 108 - Porto 32 - Sagone 14

🏠 Thalassa
Plage du Péro — 95.26.40.08
Closed 15 Oct-20 May. 22 rms 200-260 F. Restaurant. Half-board 250-265 F oblig in seas. Parking.

Two buildings right on the beach offer bright rooms overlooking the sea or mountainside.

20238 Centuri-Port — (Corse)
Ajaccio 210 - St-Florent 60 - Bastia 55 - Rogliano 15

12/20 Le Vieux Moulin
95.35.60.15
M. Alessandrini. Closed 30 Oct-25 Feb. Open until 11 pm. Private room: 35. Garden dining. Hotel: 14 rms 195-250 F. Tennis. Parking. V AE DC.

In a wonderful little port town at the tip of the Corsican cape, on a quiet, shaded terrace, enjoy well-crafted cooking with the tang of the Corsican sea and soil: fish carpaccio, broccio cheese ravioli, bouillabaisse, boar with wild mushrooms, and Corsican cheeses. An extra point this year.

A la carte: 300 F. Menus: 120 F, 215 F, 245 F.

> *Red toques signify modern cuisine; black toques signify traditional cuisine.*

20250 Corte — (Corse)
Ajaccio 83 - Bastia 70 - Calvi 96 - Porto 86

12/20 Auberge de la Restonica
95.46.09.58
M. Colonna. Closed Mon, Jan and Feb. Open until 9.30 pm. Private room: 50. Garden dining. Hotel: 6 rms, rates not available. Pool. Parking. V AE.

This rural hillside inn is run by Pascal Colonna, an ex-international footballer. The very rustic dining room opens to terrace and forest, and the food is simple, straightforward stuff: lapin farci à la corse, cannelloni au broccio, trout with garlic.

A la carte: 200 F. Menus: 78 F, 80 F and 120 F (weekdays only), 145 F.

(12 km N on D 18)
20218 Castirla — (Corse)

11/20 Chez Jacqueline 🄲
2 km N, at Castirla bridge — 95.47.42.04
Mme Costa. Closed Feb. Open until 8.30 pm. Terrace dining. No pets. Parking.

Merry bands of noisy tourists often invade the shaded terrace of this little bistro, which stands alongside a small road deep in the *maquis*. And with good reason: the single, bargain-priced set menu features tasty, genuine boar terrine, light cheese and spinach cannelloni, and a delicious dessert of fresh, mild broccio (sheep's-milk cheese) drizzled with brandy and sprinkled with sugar. To drink, a tasty little Patrimonio is offered.

Menu: 120 F.

20126 Evisa — (Corse)
Ajaccio 70 - Calvi 100 - Corte 63 - Piana 33 - Porto 23

10/20 L'Aïtone
Rte principale — 95.26.20.04
M. Ceccaldi. Closed 10 Nov-Jan. Open until 9.30 pm. Private room: 20. Air cond. No pets. Hotel: 32 rms 180-500 F. Pool. V AE.

Splendid view over the valley from this quiet inn with hearty cooking: Corsican charcuterie, veal in Roquefort sauce, omelette garnished with broccio and mint.

A la carte: 200 F. Menus: 85 F, 120 F.

20260 Ferayola — (Corse)
Ajaccio 144 - Calvi 24 - Porto 65 - Galéria 15

🏠 Auberge de Ferayola 🌲
95.65.25.25
Closed 1 Oct-25 May. 10 rms 160-275 F. Restaurant. Half-board 250-275 F oblig in seas. No pets. Tennis. Parking. V.

Here in the midst of the *maquis*, rest and relaxation are guaranteed. The sea is not far away.

20220 Ile-Rousse (I.') — (Corse)
Ajaccio 165 - Bastia 68 - Calvi 24 - Corte 72

12/20 La Bergerie
Rte de Monticcello — 95.60.01.28
M. Caumer. Closed Mon off-season, and 15 Nov-15 March. Open until 10 pm. Private room: 60. Garden dining. Hotel: 18 rms 332 F. Parking. V.

An eclectic roster of solid, mostly seafood dishes is offered at this cosily converted old Corsican farmhouse. Seated in the pleasant, shady garden, sample the unusual sea-urchin omelette or a Moroccan fish tajine, and break open a bottle of reasonably priced Corsican wine. Courteous welcome.

A la carte: 220 F.

La Pietra
Rte du Port — 95.60.01.45
Closed 1 Nov-31 March. 40 rms 250-500 F. TV 22 rms. Air cond 20 rms. Conference facilities. Parking. V AE DC.
This modern hotel stands perched on the rocks of Ile-Rousse. The spare, contemporary, comfortable rooms have loggias that open to a view of the sea. Smiling welcome.

Santa Maria
Rte du port — 95.60.13.49
Open every day. 56 rms 200-460 F. TV 12 rms. No pets. Conference facilities. Parking. Telex 468145. V AE DC.
At the entrance to the causeway that leads to Ile de la Petra, this recent hotel is admirably situated between two beaches. The small rooms with balconies are light, comfortable and very well kept. Billiard room. Meals on a tray are served upon request.

In nearby Monticello

(4 km SE on D 63)
20220 Ile-Rousse (L') — (Corse)

11/20 A Pasturella
95.60.05.65
M. Martini. Closed Sun dinner off-season, and Nov. Open until 11.30 pm. Air cond. Hotel: 14 rms 180-260 F. V DC.
This large and lively village bistro overlooking the scrubland and valley owes its rousing success to Jean-Paul Tronchet's simple, appetising cuisine, which makes the most of superb local ingredients: grilled local fish, river trout, sole stuffed with lotte. Other bonuses are the owner's smiling welcome and his reasonable prices.
A la carte: 220 F. Menu: 100 F.

LISCIA (GOLFE DE LA LA)

20111 Liscia (Golfe de la) — (Corse)
Ajaccio 26 - Cargèse 25 - Vico 26 - Calcatoggio 4

Les Sables de la Liscia
Rte de Tiuccia
20111 Calcatoggio — 95.52.21.40
Closed 1 Oct-31 March. 10 stes 510-800 F. 25 rms 220-400 F. Restaurant. Half-board 230-315 F. Pool. Parking. V.
A group of Moorish-style buildings stand at the water's edge on a fine sandy beach. They offer rooms or bedsitting rooms (fifteen of them for three to five people) with kitchenettes. Sauna, underwater diving, wind-surfing, and evening babysitting service available. New rooms are planned.

LUCCIANA

20290 Lucciana — (Corse)
Bastia 19 - Aéroport de Poretta 5 - Casamozza 5

Hôtel Poretta
Rte de l'aéroport — 95.36.09.54
Open every day. 34 rms 220-400 F. TV. Air cond. No pets. Garage parking. V AE.
An anonymous modern building practically situated, with the airport just a stone's throw away.

Rooms are pleasant, functional, and well equipped.

MACINAGGIO

20248 Macinaggio — (Corse)
Bastia 38 - Barcaggio 19 - Rogliano 6

11/20 Marina Pizzeria
95.35.44.87
M. Filippi. Closed Jan. Open until midnight. Parking. AE DC.
A friendly pizzeria with a concise menu and moderate prices, facing the port and the sea. Good pizzas, fresh salads, fish, and paella, all well prepared.
A la carte: 170 F.

NONZA

20217 Nonza — (Corse)
Ajaccio 195 - Bastia 32 - St-Florent 19

11/20 Auberge Patrizi
95.37.82.16
Mme Patrizi. Closed 1 Nov-1 March. Open until 10 pm. Terrace dining. Hotel: 15 rms 220-350 F. V.
Situated in the main square of this marvellous village on Corsica's northern cape, a cordial, rustic dining room where you can share heartwarming food prepared with a feminine touch: Corsican charcuterie (superb saucisson), fragrant cannelloni with fresh broccio, hearty sautéed boar, and fiadone (orange-flavoured cheese flan). Affable welcome.
Menu: 85 F (wine inc).

OLETTA

20232 Oletta — (Corse)
Ajaccio 170 - Bastia 19 - St-Florent 9 - Murato 9

10/20 A Maggina
95.39.01.01
M. Jacobelli. Closed Tue and 15 Jan-15 March. Open until 9.30 pm (10.30 pm in summer). Garden dining. V.
The extraordinary view over the Nebbio plain and St-Laurent bay upstages the classic, carefully crafted cooking (fish soup, salmon with leeks in flaky pastry, orange-scented cheese flan). The concise wine list offers some inexpensive Corsican vintages. Cordial reception.
A la carte: 180 F. Menus: 90 F, 120 F.

PIEDICROCE

20229 Piedicroce — (Corse)
Ajaccio 137 - Corte 54 - Bastia 56

10/20 Le Refuge
95.35.82.65
M. Raffalli. Closed Dec. Open until 9.30 pm. Garden dining. No pets. Hotel: 20 rms 160-280 F. V AE DC.
The décor is rather scanty, but the view over the valleys, hills and chestnut groves is just grand. Tuck into sturdy Corsican charcuterie and island specialities, followed by lovely local cheeses, all served with charm and simplicity at agreeably low prices.
Menus: 70 F (weekdays lunch only, wine inc), 95 F, 120 F, 150 F.

> *Some establishments change their closing times without warning. It is always wise to check in advance.*

20259 Pioggiola — (Corse)
Calvi 48 - Belgodère 20 - Olmi-Capella 4

12/20 Auberge Aghjola ⊙
95.61.90.48

M. Albertini. Closed Mon off-season, and 15 Oct-15 March. Open until 11 pm. Terrace dining. No pets. Parking. V AE DC.

The Corsican image is important in this hamlet, perched at an altitude of 1,000 metres right in the heart of the island. The owner concocts some very successful versions of local dishes, at sensible prices. Taste one (or several) of his delicious terrines, or roast baby lamb, or a flavourful ragoût of goat, or thrush, or or pigeon served on a bed of wild mushrooms. All these delights may be sampled in a warm, neo-rustic dining room, or on a beautiful shady terrace.
A la carte: 180 F.

Auberge Aghjola ♣♥
(See restaurant above)
Closed 15 Oct-15 March. 12 rms 300-350 F (per pers, half-board oblig). Pool.

Far, far away from the crowds. Simple but very comfortable rooms with perfectly decent plumbing.

20237 Porta (La) — (Corse)
Ajaccio 150 - Bastia 60 - Piedicroce 15 - Corte 47

12/20 Restaurant
de l'Ampugnani ⊙
(Chez Elisabeth)
95.39.22.00

M. Mattei. Dinner upon reserv. Closed Mon (May-June), and end Nov-end April (except w-e lunch). Open until 10 pm. V.

Mme Mattei is serious about orthodox Corsican cookery (charcuterie, deep-fried broccio cheese, cannelloni, stuffed courgettes, aubergines, and potatoes). The house wine is lip-smacking good, too, but we hate to see the tourists descending en masse from their coach to invade the large veranda overlooking the valley, where one could be so comfortable.
Menus: 95 F and 120 F (wine inc).

20166 Porticcio — (Corse)
Ajaccio 19 - Sartène 80 - Bastia 153 - Calvi 163

[14] L'Arbousier
95.25.05.55

Mme Salini. Open every day. Open until 9.45 pm. Garden dining. Air cond. No pets. Valet parking. Telex 460597. V AE DC.

Amid a host of rather ill-assorted buildings, you come upon a delightful old house haloed with multi-coloured flowers and the sea spread out in front. Pure charm is dispensed by the *patronne*, Catherine Salini, whose son, Gérard Lorenzoni was trained at the Negresco and the Carlton, making this one of the island's best restaurants. Book a table on the large terrace, and savour the delicate scrambled eggs with sea urchins, a superb lotte fricassée with grapes and a buttery sauce studded with al dente vegetables; a fragrant fruit cup topped with vanilla ice cream illustrates the kitchen's decided lack of imagination in the dessert line. The décor is luxurious—antique woodwork and precious bibelots—and the deep, comfortable armchairs will support you when you take a look

at the bill. Service is pleasant, but more flurried than efficient.
A la carte: 400 F and up. Menu: 220 F (dinner only).

Le Maquis ♣♥
(See restaurant above)
Open every day. 4 stes 1,550-5,000 F. 26 rms 330-2,140 F. Half-board 980-1,320 F oblig in seas. TV. Air cond. Conference facilities. Heated pool. Tennis.

A delightful place to stay, indeed a voluptuous one, owing to the service and exceptional attentions lavished on guests (baskets of fresh fruit are placed in the rooms each afternoon...). Spacious rooms, perfectly equipped, decorated and furnished with exquisite taste, boast balconies that open, naturally, over the sea. Other amenities include a private beach, tennis, an exercise room, and a recently added indoor pool, enshrined in an extraordinary winter garden filled with tropical plants.

12/20 Le Caroubier
Pointe de Porticcio — 95.25.00.34
M. Ernandorena. Closed 30 Nov-31 Dec. Open until 10.15 pm. Terrace dining. No pets. Parking. Telex 460708. V AE DC.

Le Caroubier is completely encircled by greenery in a marvellous setting on a headland in the Gulf of Ajaccio, with a swimming pool that juts out above the rocks and numerous hidden coves below. Getting into shape here is helped along by a slimming menu, offered alongside a more gastronomic *carte*. The latter has made laudable progress of late, under the watchful eye of chef Éric Corailler: we can recommend the smoked-salmon roll filled with cream of caviar (some black, but too much red); cream of lentil soup with oysters and bone-marrow croutons, rosemary-scented pigeon with a carrot gratin, and tea-flavoured crème brûlée. The terrace is too hot (even in the evening, and in April) and the wrought-iron tables and chairs give the place a slightly decadent look. The waiters are quick and professional, but there are too many of them.
A la carte: 300 F. Menu: 245 F.

Sofitel Porticcio
(See restaurant above)
Open every day. 4 stes 1,020-3,420 F. 98 rms 700-2,150 F. Half-board 700-1,750 F oblig in seas. TV. Conference facilities. Heated pool. Tennis.

The 1960s architecture seems to have grown on people, and is now more or less accepted. Comfortable rooms boast terrace-solaria and sea views. This was one of the first hotels to offer thalassotherapy (sea-water spa); the proximity to Campo dell'Oro airport is not always an advantage.

In nearby Pisciatello
(7 km NE on D 55 and N 196)
20129 Pisciatello — (Corse)

12/20 Auberge du Prunelli ⊙
old Sartène road
95.20.02.75

Mme Pittiloni. Dinner in summer. Closed Tue and 30 Sep-20 Nov. Open until 9.30 pm. Private room: 12. Terrace dining. Parking.

In this quiet, commodious *auberge* with an airy terrace right on the water, tradition is a by-word. The sole, immutable, exceedingly generous set menu is known throughout the region: start with charcuterie, follow with broccio cheese omelette, then proceed on to trout, kid, and then perfect sheep's-milk cheeses, including a brandy-soaked broccio sprinkled with sugar. A heady local wine washes it all down.

Menu: 138 F (wine inc).

(12 km S on D 55)
20138 Verghia — (Corse)

Le Iéna
[13] 95.25.47.41
M. Gaggioli. Closed Mon lunch and 30 Dec-1 April. Open until 11.30 pm. Terrace dining. Parking. V AE.

The terrace offers a vista of the gulf of Ajaccio; the air is scented with the heady perfume of a profusion of roses. Philippe Schekenburger creates uncommonly fresh, keenly flavoured cuisine that is in perfect harmony with these surroundings: fish couscous, a sumptuous bouillabaisse, roast lotte with lobster bisque, capon paupiette spiced with saffron, and an apple tart perfumed with rosemary. Responsive to guests' needs, the owners give advice on geographic and historical tours.

A la carte: 300-350 F. Menus: 230 F (w-e and holidays only), 135 F, 150 F.

PORTICCIOLO

20228 Porticciolo — (Corse)
Ajaccio 178 - Bastia 25 - Barcaggio 32

Caribou
95.35.02.33
Closed 30 Sep-10 June. 3 stes 800-1,200 F. 35 rms 300-700 F. Restaurant. Half-board 500-700 F oblig in seas. TV 8 rms. Conference facilities. Pool. Tennis. Parking. V AE DC.

A pleasant waterside hotel offering bungalows and comfortable rooms. Superb view over the sea, the cove, the fine sandy beach, and the isle of Elba.

12/20 Torra Marina
95.35.00.80
M. Mattei. Closed 1 Oct-31 March. Open until 10 pm. Garden dining. Hotel: 4 rms 250-350 F. Parking. V AE DC.

Fish fresh from local waters form the basis of this simple, deftly wrought cuisine, served in the cool of the inn's beamed cellar or on the garden terrace. Choose from among the best vintages of upper Corsica to accompany your grilled lobster, red mullet, and mostelle fillets with shellfish.

A la carte: 300 F.

PORTO

20150 Porto — (Corse)
Ajaccio 83 - Bastia 135 - Corte 86 - Calvi 76 - Evisa 23

Les Flots Bleus
Marine de Porto — 95.26.11.26
Closed 30 Sep-1 April. 20 rms 295-340 F. Restaurant. Half-board 270-300 F oblig in seas. Parking. V.

This long building leans up against the mountain, tucked into a cleft in the rock; marvellous views of the coast and the gulf of Porto. Rooms are comfortable and functional.

10/20 Le Soleil Couchant
95.26.10.12
M. Mardeni. Closed end Oct-beg March. Open until 10.30 pm. Garden dining. V AE DC.

The terrace, adorned with masses of (artificial!) flowers, affords a superb view over the marina. The food is rudimentary, but of good quality: Corsican charcuterie (excellent coppa), daube à la

corse, and remarkable sheep's-milk cheeses.
A la carte: 200 F. Menus: from 70 F to 270 F.

(10 km SW on D 81)
20115 Piana — (Corse)

11/20 Hôtel Capo Rosso
Rte des Calanches — 95.27.82.40
MM. Camilli and Ollivier. Closed 15 Oct-1 April. Open until 11 pm. Parking. Telex 460178. V AE DC.

Admire the breathtaking view from this hillside hotel over the swimming pool, the coves, and the sea, while you enjoy sparkling fresh local fish and shellfish: bonito, wrasse, mostelle, rock lobster... be sure to ask that they be lightly cooked.

A la carte: 250 F. Menus: 110 F, 160 F, 260 F.

Hôtel Capo Rosso
(See restaurant above)
Closed 15 Oct-1 April. 57 rms 350-550 F. Half-board 410-480 F oblig in seas. TV. No pets. Conference facilities. Pool.

The exceptional view makes up for the charmless décor in this 1960s–style crescent-shaped structure overlooking a swimming pool and the sea. The rooms have balconies and are well equipped, but breakfasts are mediocre (limp croissants), and guests are barely accorded a greeting.

(3.5 km N on D 81)
20147 Serriera — (Corse)

L'Aiglon
Plage de Bussaglia — 95.26.10.65
Closed 30 Sep-1 May. 18 rms 200-300 F. Restaurant. Half-board 200-250 F. No pets. Parking. V.

A wide stone house encircled by holm oaks and pines set amidst the *maquis*, 800 metres from the Gulf of Porto. Bright rooms.

Eden Park
Plage de Bussaglia — 95.26.10.60
Closed 30 Oct-1 May. 1 ste 800-1,500 F. 35 rms 300-700 F. Restaurant. Half-board 380-700 F oblig in seas. Conference facilities. Pool. Tennis. Parking. V AE DC.

These beautifully decorated bungalows with pleasant, well-equipped rooms open onto a view of oleanders and a pine forest. Dine in the lovely rotunda room by the swimming pool.

PORTO-POLLO

20140 Porto-Pollo — (Corse)
Ajaccio 133 - Sartène 33 - Propriano 20

Les Eucalyptus
95.74.01.52
Closed 8 Oct-15 May. 27 rms 225-280 F. Restaurant. Half-board 220-270 F oblig in seas. No pets. Tennis. Parking. V AE DC.

Simple, light rooms in a modern building overlooking the Gulf of Valinco. Panoramic restaurant.

PORTO-VECCHIO

20137 Porto-Vecchio — (Corse)
Ajaccio 133 - Sartène 63 - Bonifacio 27 - Bastia 143

12/20 Auberge du Maquis
Rte de l'Ospédale — 95.70.20.39
M. Branca. Dinner only. Closed 30 Oct-1 June. Open until 10 pm. Terrace dining. Parking.

Simplicity is the keyword here: it characterises the bistro décor, the short menu, the sweet straw-roofed terrace, and the generous Corsican cooking: homemade charcuterie, island soup, terrine of wild boar, trout, homemade ravioli, and grilled kid with herbs.

A la carte: 220 F. Menu: 140 F.

Le Baladin
13, rue du Gal-Leclerc — 95.70.08.62
M. Toussaint-Mattei. Dinner only in seas. Closed off-season Sat lunch and Sun, and 15 Dec-15 Feb. Open until 11.30 pm. Air cond. V AE DC.

Newly redecorated in pastel colours, with a new chef from Lenôtre, Pierrick Berthier, Le Baladin has been charming people for eighteen years with a menu that features delicate fish soup, veal sweetbreads and kidneys in pastry, and warm rasberry millefeuille. Very gracious welcome and service.

A la carte: 300 F. Menu: 150 F.

Le Bistrot du Port
Quai Paoli — 95.70.22.96
Mme Serre-Guiducci. Closed Sun off-season. Open until 11 pm. Garden dining. Air cond. V AE DC.

At any time of year you can take yourself (and your well-stuffed wallet) to this reliable establishment. In either of the two dining rooms, or on the terrace overlooking the port, you'll partake of fresh, mostly seafood dishes prepared by an experienced chef from first-rate ingredients. Try his delicious prawns with courgettes, fish broth perfumed with basil, red-mullet fillets spiced with saffron and served with fresh pasta, and a refreshing orange and grapefuit aspic for dessert. The welcome is unfailingly cordial, and the cellar holds some good local wines.

A la carte: 300 F and up. Menus: 85 F, 135 F, 155 F.

12/20 Le Flamboyant
Rte de Bonifacio — 95.70.12.06
M. Terrazzoni. Closed Mon off-season, and 15 Jan-28 Feb. Open until 10 pm. Garden dining. Parking. V AE DC.

Although rather conventional, the white-and-green décor is fresh and inviting, and the service here is genuinely friendly. Stick to the seafood offerings, and you'll be happy you came: there's turbot in sabayon sauce, John Dory julienne, and sea bream with crab coulis. Desserts are honourable, and prices are reasonable.

A la carte: 250-300 F. Menu: 105 F.

11/20 Le Lucullus
17, rue du Gal-de-Gaulle — 95.70.10.17
M. Baggioni. Lunch only off-season. Closed in seas Mon lunch and Sun, and 15 Jan-17 Feb. Open until 10.30 pm. Air cond. V AE DC.

You must climb right to the top of the town to seek out this unusual bistro. Clients in the know choose what the house does best: home-cured ham, kid, and baked fresh fish.

A la carte: 280 F. Menu: 95 F (off-season weekdays only).

Regina
3 km on N 198
Rte de Bastia — 95.70.14.94
M. Gantner. Dinner only. Closed 18 Nov-1 Feb. Open until 10.30 pm. Private room: 80. Garden dining. No pets. Parking. Telex 460023. V AE DC.

The restaurant of the Roi Théodore hotel aims to be the island's most regal; chef Dominique Frérard is accorded princely sums to purchase the very finest raw materials, which he prepares quite well, though with many a superfluous—dare we say

pompous?—flourish: salad of fresh pasta tossed with pan-roasted scampi and duck foie gras dressed with red-mullet vinaigrette (whew!); a light and luscious crab gratin with a marinière of oysters; lobster lasagne with a ratatouille cooked to jam-like consistency in chicken juices; and veal mignon served with a crisp cocks' comb and sweetbread pie in a truffled sauce (no less). It's enough to convince one that simplicity is the only true luxury. And indeed, perhaps the most appealing dish on this baroque menu is grilled local fish drizzled with Muratello virgin olive oil. Desserts, predictably, are elaborate concoctions, and the bill, as you may expect, is not simple either! Wine buffs take note: the Regina's cellar is hands down the best on the island.

A la carte: 400 F. Menus: 195 F, 340 F.

Hôtel du Roi Théodore
(See restaurant above)
Closed 18 Nov-1 Feb. 2 stes 580-1,320 F. 37 rms 380-920 F. Half-board 600-940 F. TV. Conference facilities. Heated pool. Tennis.

Set well back from the road, the hotel offers rooms that are pleasant, cool, and well equipped, with views of a garden and a swimming pool surrounded by luxuriant oleanders. The décor is an improbable mix of Corsican and Bavarian styles. Pleasant welcome and very professional service. Excursions by boat are available.

La Rivière
6 km W on D 368, VO and D 159
Rte de Muratello — 95.70.10.21
Closed 30 Oct-5 May. 30 rms 295 F. Restaurant. Half-board 415 F oblig in seas. Conference facilities. Pool. Tennis. Parking. V AE DC.

Simple rooms in a quiet park between sea and mountains.

San Giovanni
Rte d'Arca, 3 km SW on D 659 — 95.70.22.25
Closed 30 Oct-31 March. 1 ste 1,270-1,905 F. 29 rms 263-430 F. Restaurant. Half-board 383-446 F oblig in seas. No pets. Heated pool. Tennis. Parking. V AE DC.

Situated in a large park with masses of flowers five kilometres from the sea, this hotel provides fairly large, simple but pleasant rooms. Amenities include sauna, table tennis and bike-riding.

In nearby Cala-Rossa
(10 km NE on N 198, D 568 and D 468)
20137 Cala-Rossa — (Corse)

Grand Hôtel de Cala Rossa
Rte de Cala-Rossa — 95.71.61.51
M. Canarelli. Closed 15 Nov-1 April. Open until 10 pm. Garden dining. Air cond. No pets. Parking. Telex 460394. V AE DC.

Chef Georges Billon, a native of Lyon, has had seven years to familiarise himself with Corsica's bounty, starting with local seafood taken straight from the boat to the kitchen: he makes a lovely rock lobster salad dressed with fragrant olive oil, steamed red mullet with Mediterranean herbs, fillet of John Dory, also steamed to perfection, chapon de mer (another local fish) stuffed and braised à la bonifacienne. Meals are served in the spacious white dining room or on the shady terrace of this heavenly estate nearly hidden under luxuriant pines, oleander, and bamboo. Owner Toussaint Canarelli oversees the relaxed but very professional service. The wine list is extensive, but the best bests are Corsican vintages, like the superb Domaine de Torraccia or the Fiumicicli from Sartène. A well-deserved extra point is theirs this year.

A la carte: 400 F. Menus: 150 F (lunch only), 200 F (dinner only), 300 F.

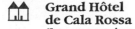

Grand Hôtel de Cala Rossa

(See restaurant above)
Closed 15 Nov-1 April. 3 stes 900-1,600 F. 50 rms 450-1,400 F. Half-board 650-1,250 F oblig in seas. TV 50 rms. Air cond 15 rms. No pets. Conference facilities. Tennis.

Renovations are in progress and the wooden interior architecture is so beautiful that one almost forgets about the beach. Perfect soundproofing; yummy breakfasts with croissants, rolls, fresh bread, and homemade jams. Private beach with Polynesian straw huts, excursion boats, water-skiing, sailing, deep-sea fishing....

In nearby La Trinité-de-Porto-Vecchio

(7 km N on N 198 and D 468)
20137 La Trinité-de-Porto-Vecchio — (Corse)

L'Orée du Maquis

Rte de la Lézardière — 95.70.22.21
Mme Carteaud. Dinner (upon reserv). Closed Sun and Feb. Open until 9.30 pm. Terrace dining. Pool. Parking. V AE DC.

Danielle Carteaud entertains at home in her villa, which she has transformed into a restaurant that serves a maximum of 12 people in winter and 25 in summer. Her guests are encouraged to enjoy the garden and its cork-oak trees, set right in the midst of the *maquis* with a view out to sea. The menu changes every day according to what the market offers. Our last meal: delicious sweet-and-sour rock lobster on a bed of sliced turnips, perfect scallops in port butter with asparagus tips, rosemary-scented red mullet on a bed of wild mushrooms, an excellent apple feuilleté with a zesty touch of blue cheese, and the sort of big, delectable chocolate profiteroles that one rarely sees anymore. The food is a little showy, a little ostentatious—so are the prices—but nevertheless this one of the best tables in southern Corsica.

Menus: 280 F, 350 F.

U Stagnolu

Rte de Cala-Rossa — 95.70.02.07
Closed 15 Oct-Easter. 26 rms 240-580 F. Restaurant. Half-board 260-370 F oblig in seas. Conference facilities. Parking. V AE DC.

A handful of little houses scattered among the cork oaks, offering classic rooms or studios and suites with kitchenettes, and balconies overlooking the gulf.

PROPRIANO

20110 Propriano — (Corse)
Ajaccio 74 - Corte 138 - Sartène 13 - Bonifacio 67

Grand Hôtel Miramar

Route de la Corniche — 95.76.06.13
Open every day. 30 rms 400-800 F. Restaurant. Half-board 580-1,500 F. TV 25 rms. Air cond. No pets. Conference facilities. Heated pool. Valet parking. Telex 460907. V AE DC.

Completely renovated this year, the Miramar now boasts a sauna. Huge, bright, and airy rooms have balconies over the sea. Situated in a pleasant one-hectare park with a magnificent view over the Gulf of Valinco.

12/20 Le Lido

95.76.06.37
M. Pittilloni. Closed Sep-May. Open until 10.30 pm. Garden dining. Garage parking. V AE DC.

The terrace faces the cirque of white rocks that dominates Propriano—an eternally enchanting Mediterranean scene. More interesting, certainly, than the short menu with its immutable fennel-steamed capon, baked rock lobster, pineapple à la tahitienne. The food is fresh and flavourful, but so boring—and so dear!

A la carte: 350 F and up.

Le Lido

(See restaurant above)
Closed Sep-May. 17 rms 265-285 F. Half-board 300 F oblig in seas. No pets.

Encircling a beach patio, adequately comfortable rooms for those who ask nothing more than sea and sun. Very reasonable prices.

11/20 Le Rescator

11, av. Napoléon — 95.76.08.46
M. Gaggioli. Closed 1 Oct-15 March. Open until 10.30 pm. Terrace dining. V AE DC.

When summer comes, everyone rushes for the shade of the terrace awning to tuck into scallops with sea-urchin butter, tasty little rock mullets, and—especially—the young chef's excellent desserts. Friendly service and prices.

A la carte: 180-220 F. Menus: 95 F, 110 F.

SAGONE

20118 Sagone — (Corse)
Ajaccio 38 - Piana 33 - Porto 45

10/20 U Libbiu

95.28.06.06
M. Lepetit. Closed 4 Jan-15 March. Open until 9.30 pm. Private room: 30. Garden dining. Parking. V AE.

For an uncommonly warm welcome, a pleasant poolside terrace, luxuriant greenery, and simple, honest cooking, this is the place. Try the homemade starling pâté, a fine, juicy rib steak, and delicious crêpes.

A la carte: 250 F. Menu: 130 F.

U Libbiu

(See restaurant above)
Closed 4 Jan-15 March. 22 rms 270-530 F. Half-board 255-390 F. TV. Conference facilities. Pool.

Here's a handsome, completely new hotel a stone's throw from the beach; with bright, well-decorated, nicely furnished rooms and a terrace that gives onto the garden. Charming welcome.

SAINT-FLORENT

20217 Saint-Florent — (Corse)
Ajaccio 176 - Bastia 23 - Calvi 70 - L'Ile-Rousse 46

Hôtel Bellevue

95.37.00.06
Closed end Sep-beg April. 27 rms 270-600 F. Restaurant. Half-board 315-705 F. TV. Conference facilities. Heated pool. Tennis. Parking. Telex 460296. V AE DC.

An attractive modern building set in a huge park that dominates the bay. Welcoming, practical rooms.

Hôtel Dolce Notte
95.37.06.65

Closed 30 Oct-30 March. 1 ste 330-490 F. 25 rms 195-490 F. TV 5 rms. Garage parking. V DC.

Away from the village (and its noise) but right on the sea, this is a likeable building of recent vintage. The studio-style rooms boast spacious, modern bathrooms and private balconies or loggias from which to admire the view. The genuinely attentive welcome is endearing.

12/20 La Gaffe
Port de St-Florent — 95.37.00.12

Mlle Bourneuf. Closed Mon and 15 Nov-15 Jan. Open until 11 pm. Terrace dining. V AE DC.

Sheltered from the sun by the terrace's inviting blue awning, you can watch the boats sail by while savouring fresh, appetising food (a rare commodity in most of the island's port-side restaurants). An extra point this year for the large, lightly cooked mussels, the rock lobster in a spirited lemon-mint sauce, and a refreshing myrtle-scented orange salad. Excellent Corsican wines, pleasant welcome and service.

A la carte: 200 F. Menus: 105 F, 145 F, 165 F.

10/20 Ind'e Lucia
Pl. Doria — 95.37.04.15

M. Costa. Open every day. Open until 10.30 pm. Terrace dining. V.

Local specialities served forth in a rustic dining room (reminiscent of a hunting lodge) or on the shady terrace. The set menu often features broccio cheese omelette, Corsican soup, herbed meat cannelloni, excellent Corsican cheeses, and ice cream.

A la carte: 170-200 F. Menu: 100 F.

11/20 La Marinuccia
Pl. de l'Ancienne-Poste — 95.37.04.36

M. Panzani. Closed Mon and 30 Oct-20 March. Open until 10.30 pm (midnight in seas). Terrace dining. No pets. Hotel: 4 stes 380-650 F. 34 rms 200-420 F. V AE.

The attractive dining room sports pink-brick arches and extends out onto a raised terrace opposite a pretty cove. The menu is wholly devoted to seafood (salmon, chapon de mer...) freshly caught, served grilled or in a sauce, washed down with a lively white Corsican wine.

A la carte: 200-250 F. Menus: 95 F (lunch only), 110 F (dinner only), 140 F (w-e and holidays only).

Motel Treperi
95.37.02.75

Closed 30 Oct-1 April. 4 stes 600 F. 20 rms 160-350 F. Pool. Tennis. Parking. AE.

Simple, well-kept rooms in bungalows overlooking either the Golfe de St Florent or the mountains. Pleasant, extensive grounds. Affable welcome.

12/20 La Rascasse
Espl. du Port — 95.37.06.99

M. Schneider. Closed Mon off-season, and 31 Oct-1 April. Open until 11 pm. Terrace dining. Air cond. V AE DC.

The terrace overlooks the port, source of the prime ingredients for this restaurant's fresh (if slightly affected) cooking: shellfish, sea bream, chapon de mer, etc. which are best simply grilled. Charming welcome and service.

A la carte: 200-250 F.

20100 Sartène — (Corse)
Ajaccio 86 - Bastia 178 - Corte 141 - Bonifacio 54

Auberge Santa Barbara
95.77.09.06

Mme Lovichi. Closed 30 Oct-Easter. Open until 10 pm. Private room: 120. Garden dining. Parking. V AE.

Nothing to do with the interminable American soap opera of the same name, the huge garden terrace with a superb view of old Sartène is more conducive to relaxation and conviviality than revenge, passion, and shady dealing. Gisèle Lovichi, a committed and enthusiastic cook, is full of ideas and talent; she has now moved beyond her grandmother's traditional repertoire (Sartène-style tripe, broccio cheese omelette), and asserts her own personality in fresh, spontaneous dishes like lightly cooked rock lobster salad, lotte with citrus butter, rack of lamb with tiny stuffed vegetables, or fillet of beef in pastry with mushrooms, all served by a charming female staff.

A la carte: 250-300 F. Menus: 145 F, 280 F.

10/20 La Chaumière
39, rue du Cap.-L.-Benedetti — 95.77.07.13

Mme Bianchini. Closed off-season Mon and 4 Jan-10 March. Open until 10 pm. Terrace dining. V AE DC.

This typically Corsican inn is carved out of the granite hillside; just as typical is the traditional island cooking: homemade charcuterie, Sartène-style tripe, and pasta with wild boar, escorted by delicious local wines.

A la carte: 180 F. Menu: 75 F.

Villa Piana
Rte de Propriano — 95.77.07.04

Closed 25 Sep-20 April. 32 rms 260-300 F. No pets. Tennis. Parking. V AE DC.

From the balconies of this large Provençal-style villa set among oaks and olive trees, you have a superb view of old Sartène, the mountains, and the *maquis*. Look forward to a friendly welcome, bright and pleasant rooms with rustic décor. Floodlit tennis courts.

20145 Solenzara — (Corse)
Ajaccio 131 - Bastia 103 - Bonifacio 67 - Sartène 77

In nearby Sari-di-Porto-Vecchio

(8 km SO on D 68)
20145 Sari-di-Porto-Vecchio — (Corse)

U Dragulinu
in Favone — 95.73.20.30

Closed 15 Oct-15 April. 32 rms 350-450 F. Restaurant. Half-board 290-390 F oblig in seas. No pets. Conference facilities. Parking. V AE.

A long building right on the beach, with the forest behind and the mountains beyond. The simple rooms are well disposed and fairly comfortable. Ideal for quiet family holidays.

20281 Speloncato — (Corse)
Ajaccio 150 - Calvi 32 - L'Ile-Rousse 19

A Spelunca
95.61.50.38

Closed 1 Oct-31 May. 18 rms 170-240 F. V DC.

Here you have the former palace of Cardinal Savelli and the quiet calm of a Corsican village.

CORTE
See CORSICA

COTEAU (LE)
See Roanne

COTINIÈRE (LA)
See Oléron (Ile d')

COUARDE-SUR-MER (LA)
See Ré (Ile de)

COULON
See Niort

COURBEVOIE
See PARIS Suburbs

COURÇAY
See Cormery

COURCHEVEL
73120 Courchevel — (Savoie)
Paris 653 - Chambéry 99 - Annecy 96 - Albertville 51

 Les Airelles
Jardin Alpin — 79.08.02.11
Closed 20 April-20 Dec. 6 stes. 50 rms 950-1,900 F (per pers, half-board oblig). Restaurant. TV. Conference facilities. Heated pool. Valet parking. Telex 980190. V AE DC.

André and Raymonde Fenestraz have completely remodelled this gorgeous Jardin Alpin hotel in a cheery Austrian style (painted wood, old tiles...). Its reopening was *the* event of this winter season at Courchevel. Sauna, Jacuzzi, and heated garage.

 Annapurna
Courchevel 1850
Rte de l'Altiport — 79.08.04.60
Closed 22 April-15 Dec. 4 stes 3,900-4,820 F. 57 rms 500-2,370 F. Restaurant. Half-board 1,010-1,450 F. TV. Air cond. Conference facilities. Heated pool. Valet parking. Telex 980324. V AE DC.

This is one of the best hotels of the resort, indeed in all the French Alps. The terraced rooms were completely redone between 1989 and summer 1990. They are spacious, remarkably well appointed and face full south towards the mountains and the slopes. Amenities and services galore, including a fitness club, masseur, swimming instructor, manicurist, and a piano-bar.

 Le Bateau Ivre
79.08.02.46
M. Jacob. Closed 15 April-20 Dec. Open until 10 pm. Terrace dining. Air cond. Valet parking. Telex 309162. V AE DC.

Now that young Jean-Pierre Jacob has brightened the dining room and let waves of light wash over his Bateau Ivre, he has no intention of being anchored down. This inventive, self-assured, and remarkably consistent young chef can nail a third toque to his mast this year. Time and again in the past months he has impressed us with a cuisine redolent of Savoie's culinary riches. In a word, we are wild about his moreish *beurrecks au beaufort,* tiny pastries filled with mountain cheese, served as an amuse-bouche; and his huge briny oysters served hot with intensely flavourful shallots; and the spiced prawns with fried onions, for their subtle Oriental touch; and of course his sublimely simple sea bass fillet with braised lettuces and savoury meat juices. Oh and the sweets! Do not under any circumstances miss Jacob's mousse au chocolat soufflée served with orange ice cream, a true litle masterpiece! Welcome and service are top-notch.

A la carte: 500 F and up. Menus: 340 F, 410 F.

 La Pomme de Pin
(See restaurant above)
Closed 15 April-10 Dec. 50 rms 860-925 F (per pers, half-board oblig). TV. Conference facilities.

After the recent redecoration, rooms are spacious, bright, and well equipped. Comfortable beds and super breakfasts.

Bellecôte
79.08.10.19
Closed 13 April-1 Dec. 6 stes. 55 rms 825-3,100 F (per pers, half-board oblig). Restaurant. TV. Air cond 9 rms. No pets. Conference facilities. Heated pool. Valet parking. Telex 980421. V AE DC.

Alongside the Bellecôte run, this luxurious chalet has spacious, pretty wood-panelled rooms looking out onto the mountains. Public rooms are inviting and comfortable, and there are lots of high-quality amenities (hairdresser, sauna, and more).

12/20 La Bergerie
79.08.24.70
M. Sauvanet. Closed Easter-Dec. Open until 10.30 pm. Terrace dining. V AE DC.

Apart from eating the world's most expensive raclette here, you can indulge in Russian evenings complete with generous portions of caviar and beef Stroganoff (better than the original, which definitely wasn't made with steak of this quality!). This is where Courchevel's café society gathers for a Friday night frenzy... there's a Russian orchestra too.

A la carte: 300-350 F and up.

12/20 Le Bistrot du Praz
Courchevel 1300
Le Praz — 79.08.41.33
M. Renaudie. Information not available.

The chef's quirks include some overpriced specialities from the South-west: cassoulet Landais, magret, marmite Gasconne. Incredibly there are also some twenty set menus centred around raclettes, fondues, and rich classics padded out with lobster and foie gras. A happy, friendly clientele.

A la carte: 350 F.

12/20 Byblos des Neiges
(La Clairière and Les Arches)
Jardin Alpin — 79.08.12.12
M. Virot. Closed 14 April-18 Dec. Open until 10 pm. Terrace dining. No pets. Valet parking. Telex 980580. V AE DC.

Expensive, 'grand hotel'-style cooking. The basil-scented sea bass and saddle of lamb en croûte with wild mushrooms and potatoes are much less astounding than the prices charged for them, or the strange and other-worldly décor in which they are served.

A la carte: 500 F and up. Menus: La Clairière: 270 F (lunch only), 310 F (dinner only). Les Arches: 340 F (dinner only).

For all the essential motoring information when driving in Europe, refer to the RAC European Motoring Guide.

Byblos des Neiges
(See restaurant above)
Closed 14 April-18 Dec. 8 stes. 61 rms 1,370-2,000 F (per pers, half-board oblig). TV. Conference facilities. Heated pool. cheminée.

A real snow palace with sinfully luxurious rooms, saunas, Jacuzzi, Turkish baths, gym, and pool, a piano-bar, and lots of restaurants. Sunny terraces and spectacular interiors.

Caravelle
Jardin Alpin — 79.08.02.42
Closed 1 May-20 Dec. 13 stes. 70 rms 515-1220 F (per pers, half-board oblig). Restaurant. TV. No pets. Conference facilities. Heated pool. Valet parking. Telex 980821. V DC.

Here's an attractive and welcoming chalet, recently transformed for the better. Rooms have been cosily decorated and there are lots of extras: sauna, massage, squash courts, gym, and games room.

Carlina
Courchevel 1850 — 79.08.00.30
Closed 20 Dec-15 April. 4 stes 1,190-1,900 F. 50 rms 770-1,800 F (per pers, half-board oblig). Restaurant. TV. Conference facilities. Heated pool. Valet parking. Telex 980248. V AE DC.

Magnificent resort hotel with untold comfort and every imaginable service: sauna, massage, UVA, and lots more.

Chabichou
Courchevel 1850
Quartier Les Chenus — 79.08.00.55
M. Rochedy. Closed end April-beg Dec. Open until 10.30 pm. Terrace dining. Valet parking. Telex 980416. V AE DC.

Rumour has it that the owners—the Rochedy family—are in financial difficulty. Whatever the truth may be, Michel Rochedy's immense talent in the kitchen is obviously impervious to his bankers' demands. He continues to produce a delicately imaginative cuisine inspired by the two regions he calls home: the Mediterranean at St-Tropez, and the Alps at Courchevel. Rochedy's soufflé au Beaufort is incomparably light, but how can one resist his escalope de foie gras chaud with lentil salad, or deceptively simple lake char baked in a salt crust? The latter, a freshwater fish of the trout family, is perfectly cooked and subtly flavoured with the essence of fresh thyme, fennel, and chive-scented mashed potatoes—a heavenly dish. Desserts are equally ambrosial: what can one say about the cinnamon-scented date and walnut fritters served with a passion fruit sorbet, an indescribably unctuous rum cream, or a gentle pistachio jelly with chocolate ice cream? We devoutly hope that the day won't come when we cannot sit down to one of Rochedy's fabulous meals under the dining room's spectacular glass roof, or enjoy Maryse Rochedy's warm welcome and the multifarious charms of Chabichou (not the least of which is the sensational wine list).

A la carte: 500 F and up. Menus: 200 F (lunch only), 280 F, 480 F.

Chabichou
(See restaurant above)
Closed end April-beg Dec. 18 stes 1,010-2,002 F. 22 rms 700-1,640 F. Half-board 650-1,400 F. TV. Conference facilities. Heated pool.

The Rochedy's gingerbread chalet is even prettier under snow. The rooms have forsaken their gloomy look for a bolder, brighter décor, and they are now spacious and comfortable. The buffet-

style breakfasts will enable you to skip lunch and save up for a dinner at Chabichou.

12/20 Le Chalet de Pierres
Courchevel 1850 — 79.08.18.61
Mme Saxe. Open every day. Open until 10 pm. Terrace dining. V.

Every night this ski-slope setting is jammed with Courchevel's *beau monde*. The menu is written in six languages and offers a concise repertoire of excellent *plats du jour*, country charcuterie, good grilled dishes, and adequate pastries.

A la carte: 250-280 F.

Crystal 2000
Rte de l'Altiport — 79.08.28.22
Closed 7 April-20 Dec. 5 stes. 46 rms 495-865 F (per pers, half-board oblig). Restaurant. TV. Conference facilities. Garage parking. Telex 309170. V AE DC.

This vast and agreeable modern chalet is perched above Courchevel. There's a large south-facing terrace, and all rooms have video. Organised activities, sauna.

Les Ducs de Savoie
Jardin Alpin — 79.08.03.00
Closed 15 April-20 Dec. 70 rms 550-950 F (per pers, half-board oblig). Restaurant. TV. No pets. Conference facilities. Heated pool. Garage parking. Telex 980360. V AE DC.

Rooms facing the mountains boast pleasant nice terraces in this large and peaceful chalet of recent vintage, set in the Jardin Alpin residential quarter of Courchevel. Great service, saunas, gym, billiard club, and more.

Gd Hôtel Rond-Point des Pistes
Courchevel 1850 — 79.08.02.69
Closed April-Dec. 4 stes. 54 rms 745-995 F (per pers, half-board oblig). Restaurant. TV. Conference facilities. Valet parking. Telex 980847. V AE DC discothèque.

A classic address with large, quiet rooms facing the mountains. The terrace faces south, there are huge lounges, and a club-discothèque.

Le Lana
Courchevel 1850 — 79.08.01.10
Closed 15 April-15 Dec. 6 stes 1,480-1,730 F. 70 rms 930-1,730 F (per pers, half-board oblig). Restaurant. TV. Conference facilities. Heated pool. Valet parking. Telex 980014. V AE DC.

In the centre of Courchevel 1850 with a view of the valley, stands this superb, huge hotel with large, attractive rooms. Services include sauna, massage, gym, Jacuzzi, and Turkish bath.

Mercure
Jardin Alpin — 79.08.11.23
Closed 4 May-1 July and 20 Sep-10 Dec. 5 stes 800-1,200 F. 121 rms 550-1,000 F. Restaurant. Half-board 295-756 F oblig in seas. TV. Conference facilities. Heated pool. Parking. Telex 980127. V AE DC.

A long wood-fronted building, pleasantly situated in the Jardin Alpin. It has spacious, inviting rooms and a loggia. The view of the mountain tops is spectacular. Friendly welcome and service.

Hôtel des Neiges
Courchevel 1850 — 79.08.03.77
Closed 15 April-15 Dec. 3 stes. 47 rms 875-2,130 F (per pers, half-board oblig). Restaurant. TV. No pets.

Conference facilities. Valet parking. Telex 980463. V AE DC.

This large and immensely comfortable chalet is situated at the foot of the slopes. A lively atmosphere is assured thanks to the film-world clientele. Entertainment nightly in the piano-bar.

La Poule au Pot
Courchevel 1650 – 79.08.33.97
M. Rochedy. Closed April-June and Sep-Dec. Open until 10.30 pm. Telex 980416. V DC.

The Rochedy touch is evident in the colourful, painted wood setting. The service is agreeably informal, and the cooking simple and generous. Good surprises include a warm salad of tender chicken livers, poule au pot of course, and in keeping with local culinary traditions, braserade, fondue savoyarde, and raclette.

A la carte: 200-250 F. Menus: 98 F (lunch only), 115 F.

Pralong 2000
Rte de l'Altiport – 79.08.24.82
M. Parveaux. Closed 7 April-20 Dec. Open until 9 pm. Private room: 25. Terrace dining. Valet parking. Telex 980231. V AE DC.

For the last ten years, chef Jean-Pierre Faucher has spent his winters in the kitchen of this mountain restaurant on the Pralong slope. Its terrace is one of the most sought-after for the lunch buffet. From the rustic traditions of Périgord cookery Faucher draws the inspiration for his fresh truffle in a fragrant, golden crust, the rabbit civet with mashed potatoes perfumed with chives, and a divine Gascon pear flan with a bright apricot coulis. Good wines from the South-west, and impeccable service. A second toque this year.

A la carte: 350-400 F. Menus: 260 F (lunch only), 330 F (dinner only).

Pralong 2000
(See restaurant above)
Closed 7 April-20 Dec. 4 stes. 68 rms 485-1,385 F (per pers, half-board oblig). TV. Conference facilities. Heated pool.

A very special hotel set atop Courchevel 1850 opposite the ski lifts. Rooms are huge, comfortable, and attractively decorated. There's a superb buffet breakfast. Also an indoor swimming pool, a leisure centre, golf practice green, and a hairdresser. Lots of television channels too!

La Sivolière
Courchevel 1850 – 79.08.08.33
Mme Cattelin. Closed 1 May-1 Dec. Open until 10.30 pm. Private room: 20. No pets. Garage parking. Telex 309169. V.

Owner Mado Cattelin makes guests feel right at home. A roaring fire blazes in the fireplace, and huge bouquets of fresh flowers dot this cosy panelled interior, which has won over many of the celebrities who frequent the resort. They (and we) prefer this quiet atmosphere and the honest home cooking to the tarradiddle of the grander hotel dining rooms. Especially when chef Xavier Palmieri offers his pumpkin gratin, his salad of local air-dried beef, and his huge rib of prime beef grilled to a turn over a wood fire.

A la carte: 280 F. Menus: from 120 F to 240 F (weekdays only).

La Sivolière
(See restaurant above)
Closed 1 May-1 Dec. 25 rms 300-1,390 F. TV. No pets. Conference facilities.

This wonderful and elegant hotel is set among some pine trees near the slopes. Rooms are both intimate and functional, and all enjoy a splendid view of the mountains. Numerous leisure activities.

Les Trois Vallées
Courchevel 1850 – 79.08.00.12
Closed 20 April-1 Dec. 4 stes. 30 rms 900 F. Restaurant. Half-board 850-1,200 F oblig in seas. TV. No pets. Conference facilities. Valet parking. Telex 309194. V AE.

A superb chalet of recent date that juts out over la Croisette. Rooms are large and cosy, full of light wood and pretty fabrics, with furniture painted in the Austrian manner. In addition to bathrooms clad in marble, the hotel offers every conceivable mod con: sauna, Turkish bath, and much, much more. Service is a bit amateurish, but full of enthusiasm. Sumptuous breakfasts can be had in the rooms at any hour.

COURLANS
See Lons-le-Saunier

COURSEULLES-SUR-MER
14470 Courseulles-sur-Mer — (Calvados)
Paris 260 - Bayeux 20 - Caen 18 - Arromanches 13

La Belle Aurore
32, rue du Mal-Foch – 31.37.46.23
Closed off-season Sun and Mon, and 3 Feb-4 March. 7 rms 190-280 F. Restaurant. Half-board 210-310 F. TV. Conference facilities. V DC.

A modern building facing the marina with cosy, well-equipped rooms (some with terraces), all entirely refurbished last winter.

La Crémaillère et Le Gytan
Bd de la Plage – 31.37.95.96
Open every day. 1 ste 330-495 F. 50 rms 138-330 F. Restaurant. Half-board 195-330 F oblig in seas. TV 35 rms. Conference facilities. Parking. Telex 171952. V DC.

Pleasant rooms give onto the sea beyond the beach (La Crémaillère) or the garden (Le Gytan).

COURTENAY
45320 Courtenay — (Loiret)
Paris 120 - Sens 26 - Montargis 25 - Orléans 96

La Clé des Champs
2 km SE on D 32, towards Joigny
Les Quatre-Croix – 38.97.42.68
M. Delion. Closed Tue dinner, Wed, 14 Jan-6 Feb and 16 Sep-3 Oct. Open until 9 pm. Parking. V.

This large, rustic dining room with well-spaced tables features skilful cuisine by Marc Delion. His menu contains some classics (grilled andouillette, duck à l'orange), as well as some appealing innovations: cromesquis d'escargots, turbot with cardamom. Luscious desserts and some nice regional wines. Good service, but steep prices.

A la carte: 350-400 F. Menus: 160 F, 260 F, 360 F.

COURTILS
50220 Courtils — (Manche)
Paris 307 - Rennes 61 - Fougères 37 - Avranches 12

Le Manoir de la Roche Torin
Rte du Mont-St-Michel – 33.70.96.55
Closed 15 Nov-15 March. 1 ste 600 F. 12 rms 320-450 F. Restaurant. Half-board 360-400 F oblig in

seas. TV 11 rms. Conference facilities. Parking. Telex 170380. V AE DC.

A nineteenth-century edifice with a dozen well-appointed rooms set in spacious, quiet grounds along the shores of the Mont-Saint-Michel.

COUTAINVILLE

50230 Coutainville — (Manche)
Paris 343 - St-Lô 40 - Coutances 13 - Cherbourg 77

12/20 Hardy
Pl. 28-Juillet — 33.47.04.11
M. Hardy. Closed off-season Sun dinner and Mon (except school holidays and holidays), and 10 Jan-10 Feb. Open until 9 pm. Private room: 40. Terrace dining. V AE DC.

Quality ingredients and generous servings are still by-words here, but we must admit that we have known the house of Hardy in better form. The pan-roasted prawns with Muscadet and chives were excellent, but we burned our fingers trying to shell them. Braised sole fillets adorned with a light caviar cream sauce were nicely cooked, but there was nothing tantalising about their bland flavour. We were burned again (tongue, this time) at dessert by the soft (even runny, in spots) strawberry clafoutis.... Better luck next time! However, the décor is as attractive as ever, the magnificent wine list is affordably priced, and Mme Hardy offers the usual warm welcome to her guests.

A la carte: 350 F. Menus: 100 F (weekdays only), 160 F, 230 F, 330 F.

Hardy
(See restaurant above)
Closed off-season Sun and Mon (except school holidays and holidays), and 10 Jan-10 Feb. 17 rms 200-380 F. Half-board 280-350 F oblig in seas. TV 14 rms. Conference facilities.

The rooms vary in quality. Four of them are prettily furnished in an old-fashioned style, the others are more modern. Good breakfasts, but the coffee is too bitter.

COUTANCES

50200 Coutances — (Manche)
Paris 330 - Cherbourg 75 - Avranches 46 - St-Lô 27

Cositel
Rte de Coutainville — 33.07.51.64
Open every day. 1 ste 400-540 F. 55 rms 230-305 F. Restaurant. Half-board 240-260 F. TV. Conference facilities. Garage parking. Telex 772003. V AE DC.

A modern establishment on the outskirts of town. Rooms are impersonal but have all mod cons, along with a view of the cathedral. Nice service. Bar.

CRÉPON

See Bayeux

CREST-VOLAND

73590 Crest-Voland — (Savoie)
Paris 579 - Albertville 27 - Megève 14 - Annecy 56

Les Aravis
Le Cernix — 79.31.63.81
Closed 15 April-10 July and 25 Aug-20 Dec. 17 rms 210-230 F. Restaurant. Half-board 210-226 F. Parking.

A tiny chalet in the middle of mountain pastures. Rooms with big balconies face the valley and summits.

CRÉTEIL

See PARIS Suburbs

CRILLON-LE-BRAVE

84410 Crillon-le-Brave — (Vaucluse)
Paris 690 - Carpentras 14 - Vaison-la-Romaine 19

Hostellerie de Crillon le Brave
Place de l'Eglise — 90.65.61.61
M. Chittick. Closed Jan. Open until 9.30 pm. Garden dining. Valet parking. V AE.

The abbot of this hamlet at the foot of Mt Ventoux was surely not a man to be pitied. His presbytery is still the village's most beautiful and dignified establishment; now it is a Provençal hostelry charmingly run by a Canadian proprietor, Peter Chittick. Christian Watteau, a journeyman chef, is right at home in the wonderful vaulted dining room, where he serves a personalised and down-to-earth cuisine: his freshwater perch with a lemony butter sauce, and pan-roasted lamb bergerette could earn him two toques, if he'll just bring the desserts were up to scratch. Service is good, but the cellar is small and banal.

A la carte: 350 F. Menus: 195 F, 240 F.

Hostellerie de Crillon le Brave
(See restaurant above)
Open every day. 4 stes 1,150-1,450 F. 20 rms 650-850 F. No pets. Conference facilities. Pool.

Overlooking Mt Ventoux and the Comtat vineyards, these rooms are decorated with pretty fabrics and superb caned Provençal chairs. Beautiful bathrooms and expensive but exceptional breakfasts. Terrific welcome.

CRISOLLES

See Noyon

CROISIC (LE)

44490 Croisic (Le) — (Loire-Atl.)
Paris 460 - Nantes 84 - La Baule 10 - Guérande 10

Le Bretagne
11, quai de la Petite-Chambre — 40.23.00.51
M. Coïc. Closed off-season Tue dinner and Wed, Mon lunch in seas, Jan and Feb (except w-e) and 15 Nov-15 Dec. Open until 10 pm. V AE DC.

This is Croisic's number one restaurant in all respects—not only is it the best, it's also the first you come upon—since Yves Gravelier, who worked with Senderens, joined his godmother Michèle Coïc in the kitchen. She will no doubt be inspired by her godson's impeccable salad of prawns and sweetbreads, and his immaculately fresh turbot fillet with tiny vegetables to liven up her own tasty but more homely cuisine. Pierre Coïc always welcomes patrons warmly into the rustic Breton dining room overlooking the fish market.

A la carte: 300-360 F. Menus: 140 F, 200 F, 350 F.

11/20 Le Pornic
4, quai du Port-Ciguet
40.23.18.56
M. Guillard. Closed Mon dinner and Tue (except July-Aug), and 12 Nov-15 March. Open until 9.30 pm (11.30 pm seas). V AE DC.

This portside restaurant chalks up its daily dishes on a blackboard after the kitchen decides what to do with the daily catch. On a given day, that might include warm steamed prawns, fricassée of clams, and fresh shellfish platters. The pretty blue-and-white dining room is bedecked with flowers. Expect a lovely family welcome. Don't miss the the selection of growers' Gros-Plant and Muscadet.

A la carte: 250-300 F. Menu: 160 F (lunch only).

CROISSY-BEAUBOURG

See PARIS Suburbs

CROIX-BLANCHE (LA) 47

See Agen

CROIX-BLANCHE (LA) 71

See Mâcon

CROIX-MARE

See Yvetot

CROIX-VALMER (LA)

83420 Croix-Valmer (La) — (Var)
Paris 879 - Toulon 62 - St-Tropez 12 - Grimaud 12

12/20 La Brigantine
Bd de la Mer — 94.79.67.16
M. Guth. Closed 1 Oct-15 May. Open until 10.30 pm. Garden dining. Parking. Telex 970987. V DC.

Enjoy a lazy, holiday atmosphere on a patio shaded by pines along the edge of the Gigaro beach, with a restful view of beach umbrellas and the Cavalaire bay. This is summery country cooking at its most casual and relaxing: terrine de lotte, turbot with artichokes, roast chicken with sorrel sauce, at prices that won't give you sunstroke.

Menus: 78 F (lunch only), 195 F (dinner only).

Les Moulins de Paillas
(See restaurant above)
Closed 1 Oct-15 May. 30 rms 430-560 F (per pers, half-board oblig). TV. Air cond. Pool. Tennis.

A freshly coloured décor for bright, comfortable rooms overlooking some pine trees, a private beach, and the sailing club.

Hôtel de Gigaro
Plage de Gigaro — 94.79.60.35
Closed 15 Oct-15 May. 38 rms 480-700 F. Restaurant. Half-board 430-560 F oblig in seas. TV. Conference facilities. Pool. Tennis. Parking. Telex 970987. V.

Airy, comfortable rooms in a pleasant new hotel swathed in greenery. The leisure centre includes both a bar and a reading room. Just 150 metres away is a private beach for games, windsurfing and a grill. The La Brigantine restaurant (see above) is part of the Moulins de Paillas under the same management.

La Pinède
Rte de Gigaro — 94.54.31.23
Closed 31 Oct-15 April. 40 rms 370-1,000 F. Restaurant. Half-board 500-750 F oblig in seas. TV. Heated pool. Tennis. Parking. V AE DC.

A recently built and very pleasant hotel by the sea, well situated among eucalyptus trees and parasol pines. Rooms are bright, light and modern. There's a lovely terrace from which to gaze out to sea. Private beach.

Souleias
Plage de Gigaro — 94.79.61.91
M. Yvon. Closed 5 Nov-15 March. Open until 10 pm. Garden dining. No pets. Parking. Telex 970032. V.

What a gorgeous place this is: a totally isolated *mas* perched in the middle of a circle of bun-galows. And what a success story for the owner, a former chemical engineer who in record time has turned it into one of the most sought-after hotels on the Var coast. On the stunning terrace which juts out over the Gigaro beach, chef Georges Coquin will serve you affordably priced, deliciously fresh cuisine. For pure pleasure, try his herb-infused prawns, or the Provençal soup, or a marinière de moules, an excellent turbot à la crème de lentilles, or the young pigeon with mild garlic, before the crisp chocolate pastry with local strawberries. Hotel guests have a magnificent catamaran at their disposal.

A la carte: 300-400 F. Menus: 190 F (lunch only), 205 F, 295 F.

Souleias
(See restaurant above)
Closed 5 Nov-15 March. 6 stes 1,300-1,900 F. 45 rms 530-1,300 F. Half-board 560-980 F. TV. Air cond 20 rms. Conference facilities. Heated pool. Tennis.

A superb neo-Provençal edifice, nestled in foliage and flowers with an eye-catching view of the sea and coastline. Take a sailboat to the îles d'Or. Rooms are large, sunny, and amazingly comfortable.

Thalotel
(L'Hôtel de la Mer)
4, bd de la Mer (D 559) — 94.79.56.15
Open every day. 35 stes 470-1,190 F. 32 rms 290-750 F. Restaurant. Half-board 300-570 F oblig in seas. TV 18 rms. Conference facilities. Heated pool. Parking. V AE DC.

About 300 metres from the beach, set in a huge wooded area, this Provençal-style hotel has been entirely refurbished as part of a vast complex. Rooms are well appointed, most have terraces or a private balcony. There's a gym and a sauna, and tennis courts are in the offing. A restaurant for the evening and a grill for lunchtime, in front of the swimming pools.

CROUTELLE

See Poitiers

CROZANT

23160 Crozant — (Creuse)
Paris 334 - Argenton-sur-Creuse 32 - Guéret 40

Auberge de la Vallée
55.89.80.03
M. Guilleminot. Closed off-season Mon dinner and Tue, and 2 Jan-2 Feb. Open until 9 pm (10 pm in summer). V.

A somewhat naive gaiety enlivens this bijou décor of crushed velvet where old cart wheels have been recycled as chandeliers. Waiters wear costume and clogs, and the folkloric click-clack of the service takes place against a musical background. But the keen tourist in search of local colour won't be cheated; Jean Guilleminot bends over backwards to keep prices down and to serve some splendid little dishes such as a salade de coquilles St-Jacques with orange butter, a turbot fillet with seaweed, and fresh pasta with foie gras.

A la carte: 180-220 F. Menus: 65 F (weekdays only), 95 F, 125 F, 250 F.

CUERS

See Toulon

CUTTOLI-CORTICCHIATO

See CORSICA: Ajaccio

DAMPIERRE-EN-YVELINES
78720 Dampierre-en-Yvelines – (Yvelines)
Paris 44 - Versailles 18 - Rambouillet 16

Les Ecuries du Château
Château de Dampierre – 30.52.52.99
M. de Luynes. Closed Tue off-season. Open until 9.30 pm. Parking. V DC.

The charming old outbuildings of the château have been tastefully transformed into a comfortable, pleasant restaurant decorated in tones of beige and pink. Christian Deluchey is a capable chef who treats seasonal produce with care in classic, technically perfect dishes such as hot oysters with braised leeks, joint of beef with a ragoût of morels, and mandarine-orange gratin. Splendid game dishes in winter.

A la carte: 350-400 F. Menus: 190 F, 260 F.

DARDILLY

See Lyon

DAX

40100 Dax – (Landes)
Paris 706 - Biarritz 57 - Mont-de-Marsan 52 - Pau 78

Climat
NE on N 124 in St-Paul-lès-Dax
Allées de Christus – 58.91.70.70
Open every day. 42 rms 245-265 F. Restaurant. Half-board 288-300 F. TV. Conference facilities. Parking. Telex 573634. V AE.

Forty rooms are available in this brand-new hotel not far from the Lac de Christus. Buses welcomed.

Grand Hôtel
Rue de la Source – 58.74.15.03
Open every day. 7 stes 344-401 F. 131 rms 179-273 F. Restaurant. Half-board 257-333 F. TV. Conference facilities. Heated pool. Parking. Telex 540516. V AE.

Part of the thermal spa. Bright, spacious rooms in a huge, charmless yet well-appointed edifice. Lots of services, and conference rooms available.

Le Parc
Pl. Thiers – 58.74.86.17
Closed 15 Dec-15 Jan. 40 rms 260-400 F. Restaurant. Half-board 280-350 F. TV 20 rms. Telex 540481. V AE DC.

Spa hotel with an inviting décor and comfortable rooms, magnificently situated on the Adour River.

Régina
Bd des Sports – 58.74.84.58
Closed 1 Dec-1 March. 169 rms 149-329 F. Restaurant. Half-board 206-362 F. TV 26 rms. Conference facilities. Heated pool. Parking. Telex 540516. V AE.

A quiet, modern, comfy hotel linked to the spa by a heated gallery. Most rooms have balconies, and the 25 well-equipped studios have terraces.

12/20 Restaurant du Bois de Boulogne
Allée du Bois-de-Boulogne – 58.74.23.32
Mme Lafaurie. Closed Sun dinner and Mon, and Jan. Open until 10 pm. Garden dining. Garage parking. V.

The members of the Notre-Dame-de-Fatima community have decamped, and now this handsome structure is an attractively decorated restaurant. But the cooking needs some attention, the menu needs filling out, and the chef could use an extra dose of self-confidence. The coquilles St-Jacques au champagne are fresh but a bit dull, the scampi with mushrooms pretty but uninteresting; yet we were

won over by the dessert, an exquisite tarte fine aux pommes. Warm welcome, discreet and attentive service.

A la carte: 220 F. Menu: 145 F.

11/20 Le Richelieu
13, av. V.-Hugo – 58.74.81.81
M. Darc. Closed Sat off-season. Open until 9.30 pm. Private room: 30. Garden dining. Hotel: 18 rms 200-250 F. V AE DC.

Basic, solid fare: warm foie gras de canard, poule au pot stuffed with foie gras, rabbit with acacia honey. The Darc family's repertoire is one of the most 'serious' in town.

A la carte: 300 F. Menus: 100 F, 145 F, 300 F.

Splendid Hôtel
2, cours de Verdun – 58.56.70.70
Closed 3 Dec-3 March. 20 stes 450-520 F. 168 rms 350-530 F. Restaurant. Half-board 230-680 F. TV. Conference facilities. Heated pool. Telex 573616. V AE DC.

This cleverly modernised old luxury hotel has not surrendered its enormous rooms, impressive bathrooms, and art deco furniture. Thermal cure, fitness classes, and more.

In nearby **Pontonx-sur-l'Adour**
(13 km NE on N 124)
40465 Dax – (Landes)

12/20 Le Val Fleuri
58.57.20.75
M. Pozuelo. Closed Tue dinner, Wed and mid-Dec to mid-Jan. Open until 10 pm. Private room: 25. No pets. Parking. V.

The pretty dining room with its big fireplace, tiled floor, and copper knick-knacks has been nicely revamped. José Pozuelo has his own classic way of preparing dishes such as a scrumptious feuilleté of asparagus, or a copious and tasty ragoût fin made with truffles, foie gras, sweetbreads, et al. The crêpes au pralin are pretty divine too. And the prices are aimed to keep you happy.

A la carte: 160-200 F. Menu: 60 F (weekdays only).

DEAUVILLE
14800 Deauville – (Calvados)
Paris 206 - Le Havre 72 - Caen 43 - Lisieux 30

Altea Deauville
in Port-Deauville, bd E.-Cornuché
31.88.62.62
Open every day. 70 rms 350-740 F. TV. Conference facilities. Telex 170364. V AE DC.

Situated in the centre of the Port-Deauville marinas, the hotel has excellent, well-equipped rooms on two levels with balconies facing the port and the beaches. Room service.

12/20 L'Ambassade d'Auvergne
109, av. de la République – 31.88.74.78
M. Cayla. Closed Wed (except July-Aug) and 15 Nov-15 Dec. Open until 9.30 pm. Garden dining. V AE DC.

A real slice of Auvergne in Deauville with charcuterie from Aubrac and tripe from Rouergue. The 155 F set menu offers lightly cooked foie gras, plentiful and tender confit de canard with potatoes sautéed in duck fat, well-ripened cheeses, and a decent tarte Tatin. To wash it down there's a more-than-drinkable Marcillac. Cosy décor, informal service.

A la carte: 150-200 F. Menus: 79 F, 96 F, 155 F.

11/20 Augusto

27, rue D.-Le Hoc — 31.88.34.49
M. Lebreton. Closed off-season Mon and Tue. Open until 11 pm. Private room: 20. Terrace dining. Air cond. V AE DC.

The restored façade and refreshed décor of this Deauville establishment have not improved the kitchen's sometimes sloppy technique: scallops with celery and truffles, and turbot in Champagne or with ginger are systematically overcooked; the adequate feuilleté au pralin has less to do with this spot's success than the high-fashion, high-society patrons.

A la carte: 500 F and up. Menus: 155 F (weekdays only), 295 F.

12/20 Bagdad Café

23, rue Fossorier — 31.98.25.45
Mme Boulenger. Closed Wed, Thu and 7 Jan-8 Feb. Open until 11.30 pm. Terrace dining. V.

Dominique Boulenger haunted antique shops to find the remains of a Spanish mansion, which she has cleverly turned into a Moroccan restaurant. The menu offers pigeon pastilla, fish tajine, rabbit with prunes, and an exotic Bagdad sundae complete with vanilla ice cream, figs, pine-nuts, and almonds. A friendly welcome.

A la carte: 250 F.

Le Ciro's

Bd de la Mer — 31.88.18.10
M. Barrière. Open every day. Open until 9.30 pm. Terrace dining. Telex 772532. V AE DC.

Patrick Durant has replaced Christian Girault in the kitchen of Deauville's most fashionable and gossipy institution. The terrace has been redone and so has the immense rosy-beige dining room. Pretty women and dashing gents seem to like the changes and they're right. Despite a salad of sole en goujonettes which was a bit over-fried, and an overcooked pigeon with potatoes and truffle juice, the cuisine does show promise. The 'mini-pomme', an ethereal apple mousse garnished with tiny poached apples scented with Calvados, is a magnificent way to end a meal. Fine wines and Calvados, and exceptional service.

A la carte: 350-450 F. Menus: 175 F, 290 F.

11/20 Le Drakkar

77, rue E.-Colas — 31.88.71.24
M. Ciavatta. Closed Tue, Wed and 8 Jan-9 Feb. Open until midnight. Terrace dining. Air cond. V AE DC.

During the *festival du cinéma*, the film-world rubs shoulders in this English pub-style brasserie divided into booths . But native Deavillians also appreciate Thierry Lerat's simple, fresh cuisine: coquilles St-Jacques sautéed to perfection, or a tasty rib steak with a light Roquefort sauce. Proprietor Philippe Ciavatta is a dab hand with a shaker, and his cocktails are in great demand. Lively, competent service.

A la carte: 180-250 F.

L'Etrier

(Hôtel Royal)
Bd E.-Cornuché — 31.98.66.33
M. Sionneau. Closed 12 Nov-beg March. Open until 10.30 pm. Private room: 180. Garden dining. No pets. Heated pool. Tennis. Valet parking. Telex 170549. V AE DC.

The Royal's other restaurant has shaken off its staidness with the arrival last year of Pascal Auger, a young chef whose only fault is a penchant for rich (though ably crafted) dishes like lobster with warm foie gras in a tart sauce aigrelette, gratinéed sole

with a shellfish broth scented with star anise, a savoury tartelette of lamb with Swiss chard and garlic cream, and sautéed pears with caramelised pistachios and hazelnuts. The décor is gilt and old-rose and the service is formal, but with no trace of obsequiousness. Take note: a good 150 F set menu brings a main dish, cheese or dessert, and a glass of wine.

A la carte: 350-400 F. Menu: 200 F.

Hélios Hôtel

10, rue Fossorier — 31.88.28.26
Open every day. 44 rms 270-410 F. TV. No pets. Heated pool. V AE DC.

Between the beach, the casino, and the race course, this modern, Norman-style hotel offers pleasant rooms and a little pool in a garden courtyard. Bar.

Le Kraal

Pl. du Marché — 31.88.30.58
M. Chauvin. Open every day. Open until 10 pm. Private room: 25. Terrace dining. Air cond. V AE DC.

Jean Chauvin plans to totally revamp his establishment this year and to become, once more, one of Deauville's top addresses. It's already the most reliable, notably for its seafood platters, lobsters, and langoustes. But you can also enjoy cod with cider and green apples, or a bouillabaisse of fish and shellfish while watching the colourful life of the little market below. Free parking guaranteed by the restaurant!

A la carte: 450-500 F. Menus: 150 F (weekdays lunch only), 270 F.

Parc Hôtel

81, av. de la République — 31.88.09.71
Open every day. 21 rms 300-600 F. TV. Parking. V AE DC.

Fairly large, well-kept rooms, simply but tastefully decorated in a large, centrally located villa, typical of the kind found in old seaside resorts.

Hôtel du Pavillon de la Poste

25, rue Fossorier — 31.88.38.29
Open every day. 16 rms 310-350 F. TV. V DC.

Situated right in the middle of town, this charming pavilion is just right for lovers' trysts: small rooms decorated with floral fabric or rustic wallpaper, furnished with exquisite taste. Attentive service.

La Pommeraie

3 km S on D 278 — 31.88.19.01
M. Scotto. Closed 19 Nov-1 March. Open until 10.15 pm. Private room: 300. Terrace dining. Parking. Telex 170448. V AE DC.

This large, half-timbered house overlooking Deauville and the sea has seen a lot of renovation this year. André Plunian's menu still includes old favourites such as his good prawn ravioli with shellfish coulis, along with a lamb fillet with mild garlic, and a silken crème brûlée which hints at the old dash and flair of Plunian's former style.

A la carte: 350 F. Menu: 175 F.

Hôtel du Golf

(See restaurant above)
Closed 19 Nov-1 March. 10 stes 1,100-1,840 F. 165 rms 440-920 F. TV. Conference facilities. Heated pool. Tennis. Golf.

This grand hotel overlooks the sea and offers golf as a major attraction. The amazingly comfortable rooms have been redone in pastel shades which reflect the serenity of the spot. Service is a bit impersonal, and breakfasts could be more generous. All sporting activites, except for golf, are free.

12/20 Chez Pommier
6, rue Hoche – 31.88.64.64
M. Pommier. Closed off-season Wed, Thu, 3-21 March and 2-19 Dec. Open until 10.30 pm. Private room: 40. Terrace dining. V AE DC.

Pommier's décor is as fresh and invigorating as a draught of sparkling cider. Everyone in Deauville is mad for this attractive bistro with its tasty, unpretentious cooking: eggs cocotte with morels, sea bass with butter-stewed leeks, and for dessert, some ambrosial crêpes or a Calvados coffee. Katy Pommier greets guests enthusiastically.
A la carte: 250-280 F. Menus: 175 F, 210 F, 260 F.

La Potinière
38, rue J.-Mermoz – 31.98.66.22
M. Cagnon. Open every day. Open until 10.30 pm. No pets. Valet parking. Telex 170617. V AE DC.

A restaurant in a grand hotel doesn't necessarily have to go in for pomp and circumstance. Here the setting—on two levels—has a slightly English cast with its honey-coloured panelling and windows emblazoned with coats-of-arms. And there is nothing particularly pompous or conventional about Gérard Sallé's cuisine. Try his plump Brionne chicken stuffed with foie gras, an impeccably cooked turbot de Honfleur with apples and cider, lamb chops with wild thyme and mild garlic, and his excellent fruit tart. The set menu is exceptional, and the Calvados selection one of the region's best. Service is professional, and performed with a smile.
A la carte: 350-400 F. Menu: 200 F.

Normandy
(See restaurant above)
Open every day. 26 stes 1,600-7,500 F. 320 rms 880-1,500 F. TV. Conference facilities. Heated pool.

Despite their modernisation, many of the rooms of this turn-of-the-century pile hark back nostalgically to Deauville's heyday. Nothing can alter the seductive charm of this most cosy, fashionable, and lively hotel. The seaside façade has been entirely redone. Sunday brunch is served under the apple trees of the Norman courtyard, but breakfasts are terribly ordinary.

12/20 Le Royal
Bd E.-Cornuché – 31.98.66.33
M. Sionneau. Closed 30 Nov-1 March. Open until 10.30 pm. Private room: 180. Garden dining. Valet parking. Telex 170549. V AE DC.

A solemn, pale-green décor graces this vast dining room with huge bay windows looking out to sea. Service is a bit starchy, and the food is rich and pricey, though creditably prepared: salade de langoustines, langouste à la nage. Wine tariffs are prohibitive, but you can expect a warm welcome.
A la carte: 400-450 F. Menu: 200 F.

Le Royal
(See restaurant above)
Closed 30 Nov-1 March. 24 stes 1,700-5,000 F. 300 rms 880-1,500 F. TV. Conference facilities. Heated pool. Tennis. Golf.

This monumental, old-fashioned luxury hotel faces the sea near the casino. The comfortable and cosy classic-style rooms are being renovated slowly but surely. Ask to be put on the top floors for a wonderful sea view. There are facilities for tennis, golf, and swimming, as well as a health club.

Le Spinnaker
52, rue Mirabeau – 31.88.24.40
M. Angenard. Closed Thu off-season, Wed and 15 Nov-15 Dec. Open until 9.30 pm. No pets. V.

A tiny little address between the port and the marketplace where tables are a bit on top of each other. The shy and serious chef does produce a generous 150 F menu, and a few specialities on the à la carte menu merit a try: a soup of local shellfish, tripe-sausage terrine with butter-stewed cabbage and white-bean cream, and a white-and-black chocolate dessert with a hint of chicory.
A la carte: 320-350 F. Menu: 150 F.

Le Trophée
81, rue du Gal-Leclerc – 31.88.45.86
Open every day. 2 stes 590-800 F. 22 rms 290-500 F. Restaurant. TV. Telex 306022. V AE DC.

A recently built hotel quite near the beach, with bright, modern, and well-soundproofed rooms. Family run.

In nearby Canapville
(6 km S on N 177)
14800 Deauville – (Calvados)

Jarrasse
N 177 – 31.65.21.80
M. Jarrasse. Closed off-season (except holidays) Tue (and 12 July-30 Aug) and Wed, 15 March and 24 June-12 July. Open until 9 pm. Garden dining. Parking. V.

A quaint, typically Norman house set in a flower-filled garden is the backdrop for François Jarasse's personal style of country cooking. Try his fresh and generous foie gras maison, farm-reared chicken with morels, crêpes soufflées, and a moreish apple puff pastry.
A la carte: 250-300 F. Menu: 150 F (wine inc).

In nearby Saint-Arnoult
(3 km SE on D 218)
14800 Deauville – (Calvados)

Campanile
Rte de Deauville – 31.87.54.54
Open every day. 43 rms 239-275 F. Restaurant. TV. Conference facilities. Parking. Telex 171962. V DC.

This chain offers a high degree of comfort for reasonable prices. The hotel is between the golf course and the race track. Good lunch buffet.

In nearby St-Martin-aux-Chartrains
(8 km SE)
14130 Deauville – (Calvados)

Auberge de la Truite
31.65.21.64
M. Lebon. Closed Sun dinner, Mon and 15 Nov-15 Dec. Open until 9.30 pm. Private room: 40. Parking. V AE DC.

Jean-Michel Lebon's menu could do with the touch of spring that refreshed this dear little Norman inn last year. For as time marches on, each year finds one contemplating the same dishes on his menu—marinière de poissons et huîtres chaudes, turbot with a potato crust, stuffed chicken leg with prawns, and a medley of apple sweets with cinnamon ice cream. The ingredients are of superb quality, but sometimes suffer from over- or undercooking. Françoise Lebon remains a wonderful hostess and prices are affordable.
A la carte: 350 F. Menus: 98 F, 160 F and 280 F (weekdays only).

Manoir de Roncheville
31.65.14.14
M. Vola. Closed Jan. Open until 10 pm. Private room: 25. Terrace dining. Parking. V.

Michel and Ghislaine Vola run this amusing 'Belle Epoque resort'- style brick pavilion set plumb in the Norman countryside. It's still hard to gauge the clientele that drifts through these extraordinary dining rooms, decorated with Louis XIII panelling and turn-of-the-century tapestries. Suffice it to say that the cuisine of Patrick Bignon shows a strong commitment to excellent ingredients, witness his thick and succulent slice of calf's liver with onion compote, médaillon de lotte cooked with sweet spices, and a few original creations like an unctuous chocolate terrine with a sour-cherry coulis. The cellar is rich in good claret. Friendly welcome.
A la carte: 320-350 F. Menu: 170 F.

Manoir de Roncheville
(See restaurant above)
Closed Jan. 8 rms 450-600 F. Half-board 370-470 F. TV. Conference facilities.

The rooms come in every size, but all are equipped with amenities like hair dryers, safes, and what have you. The view encompasses either a trout stream or the park, which has a garden where vegetables and herbs are grown for in-house use.

In nearby Touques

(3 km SE on N 834)
14800 Deauville — (Calvados)

L'Amirauté
31.88.90.62
Open every day. 6 stes 995 F. 115 rms 595 F. Restaurant. TV. Conference facilities. Heated pool. Tennis. Parking. Telex 171665. V AE DC.

Surrounded by a leisure park on the edge of the Touques River, this functional and pleasant hotel is ideal for meetings or business conferences. Located three kilometres from the sea, it offers helicopter service upon request, a fitness club, billiard room, and a sports complex.

11/20 Aux Landiers
90, rue Louvel-et-Brières — 31.88.00.39
M. Salmon. Closed Tue dinner, Wed and 14-28 Feb. Open until 9.30 pm. No pets. V.

A simple little wooden house at the foot of the church with un-Deauville-like prices for a soupe du littoral (basically a fish soup) expertly roasted beef, and simple sorbets. Very warm atmosphere.
A la carte: 200 F. Menus: 80 F, 120 F, 170 F.

12/20 Le Relais du Haras
23, rue Louvel-et-Brière — 31.88.43.98
M. Gaumont. Open every day. Open until midnight. Private room: 25. Garden dining. V AE DC.

A most disappointing experience last year caused us to withdraw Le Relais, a three-storyed restaurant with a tiny garden, from our guide. But the Gaumont family has since bounced back and we recently had a perfectly honourable meal in the beamed dining room: a good scallop flan, a tasty crème de langoustines, and well-cooked salmon with a delicate tarragon sauce. The cellar could be improved, however, and the son of the house does take himself rather seriously. There's a little bistro annexe on the garden.
A la carte: 300-350 F. Menus: 160 F, 210 F, 250 F.

Le Relais du Haras
(See restaurant above)
Open every day. 1 ste 690-820 F. 8 rms 200-460 F. TV. Conference facilities.

Brand-new rooms give onto an appealing orchard. Family run.

In nearby Tourgeville

(8 km S on D 27)
14800 Deauville — (Calvados)

Hostellerie de Tourgeville
Ch. de l'Orgueil — 31.88.63.40
Open every day. 19 stes 1,420-2,250 F. 6 rms 980-1,400 F. Restaurant. Half-board 680-1,600 F. TV. Conference facilities. Heated pool. Tennis. Valet parking. Telex 171189. V AE.

A dream spot for high-level seminar-goers: marvellous big, bright rooms on two or three levels in a pleasant set of buildings laid out like a modern cloister, and luxuriously equipped with a jogging track, a fitness centre, and a cinema.

DECAZEVILLE

12300 Decazeville — (Aveyron)
Paris 605 - Aurillac 68 - Figeac 28 - Rodez 37

Hôtel de France
Pl. Cabrol — 65.43.00.07
Open every day. 24 rms 190-250 F. Restaurant. Half-board 170-220 F. TV. Conference facilities. Valet parking. Telex 533655. V.

A solid, cosy hotel with quiet, comfortable rooms facing the surrounding hills. Cordial welcome.

DEUX-ALPES (LES)

38860 Deux-Alpes (Les) — (Isère)
Paris 641 - Grenoble 74 - Le Bourg-d'Oisans 25

Hôtel Ariane
1, prom. des Écrins — 76.79.29.29
Open every day. 101 rms 250-950 F. Restaurant. Half-board 360-650 F. TV. Conference facilities. Pool. Tennis. Parking. Telex 308315. V AE DC.

A recent hotel in the new Deux-Alpes village. There's a superb view over l'Oisans or la Muzelle from the hundred or so rooms, half of which have loggias. Other amenities include a sauna, Turkish bath, Jacuzzi, and a discothèque.

La Bérangère
76.79.24.11
M. Lherm. Closed 12 May-29 June and 1 Sep-15 Dec. Open until 9 pm. Terrace dining. No pets. Garage parking. Telex 320878. V AE.

The only charms that the dining room of this vast edifice has to offer are views of the snowy slopes and the skiers filing past the swimming pool beyond the bay windows. A moneyed clientele sits down to a similarly rich, high-priced cuisine based on fine, luxurious ingredients. To wit: duck foie gras with truffles and quails' eggs, sea bass with asparagus tips, pigeon in puff pastry bathed with reduced cooking juices. The proprietress welcomes guests warmly.
A la carte: 350 F. Menus: 190 F, 275 F.

La Bérangère
(See restaurant above)
Closed 12 May-29 June and 1 Sep-15 Dec. 59 rms 420-600 F. Half-board 450-600 F oblig in seas. TV. Conference facilities. Heated pool.

The hotel stands at the foot of the slopes, and offers all-around comfort and lots of equipment: two swimming pools, a solarium, hot tubs, and games rooms. Relais et Châteaux.

11/20 Chalet Hôtel Mounier
(P'tit Polyte)
76.80.56.90

M. Mounier. Closed 13 May-22 June and 10 Sep-14 Dec. Open until 9 pm. Private room: 25. No pets. Garage parking. Telex 308411. V.

It's all sweetness and light at the doyen of this resort's hotels. The dining room looks out across the mountain, and serves a few unexciting but well-wrought salads, timbale of shrimps, grilled steaks, etc. A piano-bar adjoins the restaurant.

Menus: 115 F (weekdays only), 125 F (w-e and holidays only), 180 F, 220 F.

Chalet Hôtel Mounier
(See restaurant above)

Closed 13 May-22 June and 10 Sep-14 Dec. 48 rms 250-600 F. Half-board 225-450 F oblig in seas. TV. Conference facilities. Heated pool. Tennis.

A handsome chalet, decorated with great attention to detail, and with some terrific extras such as a hammam, sauna, Jacuzzi, solarium, billiards, and more. The atmosphere is intimate, welcoming, and lively. A few of the rooms are rather basic, others are huge and well equipped.

La Farandole
76.80.50.45

Closed 12 May-22 June and 8 Sep-30 Nov. 14 stes 1,000-1,900 F. 46 rms 400-1,000 F. Restaurant. Half-board 530-730 F. TV. Conference facilities. Heated pool. Valet parking. Telex 320029. V AE DC.

Ideally situated with a view of the glaciers (depending on which side your room is on), this large chalet is splendidly kitted out with satellite television, a fitness centre, and a piano-bar. Large sums have been earmarked for additional furnishings and improvements.

12/20 Les Marmottes
76.79.21.91

M. Degret. Closed 13 April-20 June and 10 Sep-20 Dec. Open until 9 pm. Private room: 80. No pets. Parking. Telex 320700. V.

The ten round tables facing the bay window are the nicest part of this otherwise rather large, dull dining room. Waiters in dinner jackets serve forth salmon and artichokes in puff pastry, or filet mignon with oysters, prepared with method and rigour by chef Yves Degret.

À la carte: 300 F. Menus: 130 F (lunch only), 170 F (dinner only), 220 F (w-e and holidays dinner only), 190 F.

Les Marmottes
(See restaurant above)

Closed 13 April-20 June and 10 Sep-20 Dec. 40 rms 350-450 F. Half-board 390-590 F oblig in seas. TV. Conference facilities. Heated pool. Tennis.

Very large and rather noisy rooms in a chalet well equipped for sport and leisure (two pools, golf, and squash). The new public rooms are oak panelled.

68780 Diefmatten — (Haut-Rhin)
Paris 521 - Belfort 24 - Mulhouse 23 - Thann 17

Au Cheval Blanc
17, rue Hecken — 89.26.91.08

M. Schlienger. Closed Mon, Tue and 16-31 July. Open until 9 pm. Private room: 30. Garden dining. Parking. V AE DC.

The flower-bedecked tables, nicely spaced, laid with pretty china and silverware, are set in an airy, bright décor hung with white curtains. In what he terms his 'up-dated, seasonal, gastronomic cuisine' chef Patrick Schlienger blends tradition, authentic regional ingredients, and a healthy dose of imagination. High praise for the salade gourmande with foie gras and poached fillets of trout, the lotte and lobster medallions with red-wine butter, and for his ethereal sour-cherry tart. The regional wine list also offers some good Chablis.

À la carte: 350-400 F. Menus: 140 F (weekdays only), 190 F, 260 F, 380 F.

DIEPPE
76200 Dieppe — (Seine-Mar.)
Paris 185 - Rouen 58 - Abbeville 63 - Le Havre 103

Aguado
30, bd de Verdun — 35.84.27.00

Open every day. 56 rms 210-390 F. TV. No pets. Conference facilities. V.

A good, modern, family-run hotel facing the sea. Rooms have been redone in an English style. Terrific breakfasts.

12/20 L'Armorique
17, quai Henri-IV — 35.84.28.14

Mme Guinot. Closed Sun dinner and Mon (except holidays), 15 Aug and 15-29 Oct. Open until 9 pm. V.

The outside looks like the hull of a boat and the interior is pleasantly and tastefully decorated with nautical paraphernalia, portholes, nets, and fish tanks. Of Dieppe's many portside establishments that afford views of ferries chugging to and fro, this is the most highly recommended—so long as you choose the best, not surprisingly the simplest, dishes: soupe de poissons and extraordinarily fresh seafood and shellfish.

À la carte: 250-300 F.

Ibis
Le Val-Druel — 35.82.65.30

Open every day. 45 rms 240-265 F. Restaurant. TV. Conference facilities. Parking. Telex 180067. V.

Situated in the 'supermarket zone' on the edge of town (from the direction of Paris), this chain hotel offers modern, well-appointed rooms which have been entirely refurbished.

12/20 A la Marmite Dieppoise
8, rue Saint-Jean
35.84.24.26

M. Toussat. Closed Thu dinner off-season, Sun dinner, Mon, 20 June-1 July and 31 Dec-15 Jan. Open until 9.15 pm. Private room: 50. V.

The undisputed specialist of the famed local speciality commemorated in its name (a creamy fish and shellfish soup), this establishment also offers some other creditable seafood dishes: salmon 'brawn' with tomato coulis, red-mullet mousseline with beurre blanc sauce. At night, candlelight flickers over the somewhat gloomy décor of bricks and plants.

À la carte: 250 F. Menus: 80 F (weekdays lunch only), 115 F (weekdays only), 190 F.

La Mélie
2, Grande-Rue du Pollet
35.84.21.19

M. Brachais. Closed Sun dinner, Mon, 5-25 March and 10 Sep-10 Oct. Open until 9.30 pm. V AE DC.

From the recently revamped little dining room, you can watch the boats glide in and out of port under the Colbert Bridge. Fresh, uncomplicated fare is the stock in trade here: try the light, crisp prawn feuilleté flavoured with port, the marmite

polletaise (a sort of local bouillabaisse), and finish up with a satisfying apple crêpe for dessert.
A la carte: 230-250 F. Menus: 200 F (wine inc), 150 F.

12/20 Le Panoramic
1, bd de Verdun — 35.84.31.31
M. Urbin. Open every day. Open until 1 am. Private room: 40. Air cond. Garage parking. Telex 180865. V AE DC.
You might have to do battle to win a seat in front of the great bay windows facing the sea, but once you do, you'll not be disappointed with the affordable, ably prepared Norman specialities like saffron-tinctured mussel soup, salmon tournedos aux deux poivres with vegetable lasagne, and grenadins de veau with a sinfully unctuous cider sauce.
A la carte: 280-320 F.

La Présidence
(See restaurant above)
Open every day. 1 ste 750-850 F. 88 rms 320-515 F. TV. Conference facilities.
Only some of the rooms have views out to sea, but they're all comfortably well equipped. English bar.

Le Saint-Jacques
12, rue de l'Oranger — 35.84.52.04
M. Maget. Closed Thu lunch, Wed and 10 Oct-9 Nov. Open until 10 pm. V.
This adorable little eighteenth-century house has a welcoming and prettily furnished dining room, where a fire blazes in the fireplace in the colder months. Chef Benoist Carteret is a rigorously academic, no-nonsense cook who produces impeccable dishes with light, fragrant sauces. Try his salmon 'won ton' rolled around tiny sautéed vegetables, his feuilleté de filet de bœuf with crunchy vegetables, and a warm thin apple tart served with a little pot of thick cream. The cheese board includes Normandy's best: Camembert, Livarot, and Neufchâtel.
A la carte: 200-250 F. Menus: 110 F, 145 F, 175 F, 245 F.

In nearby Martin-Eglise

(7 km SE on D 1)
76370 Dieppe — (Seine-Mar.)

11/20 Auberge du Clos Normand
22, rue Henri-IV — 35.82.71.01
M. Hauchecorne. Closed Mon dinner, Tue and 15 Dec-15 Jan. Open until 9 pm. Private room: 40. Garden dining. Parking. V AE DC.
This fifteenth-century Norman house boasts a splendid beamed ceiling. The cuisine is traditional and creamy-rich: mussel tart, sole Dieppoise, lotte au poivre, hot apple tart.
A la carte: 200-250 F.

Auberge du Clos Normand
(See restaurant above)
Closed Mon, Tue and 15 Dec-15 Jan. 9 rms 280-340 F (per pers, half-board oblig). TV. Pets allowed.
Ten comfortable rooms in an annexe of the Clos.

The new spiral-bound RAC Atlas France will help you to find your chosen restaurant of hotel, no matter how secluded.

DIEULEFIT

26220 Dieulefit — (Drôme)
Paris 633 - Montélimar 27 - Valence 72 - Nyons 31

In nearby Poët-Laval

(4 km on D 540)
26160 Dieulefit — (Drôme)

Les Hospitaliers
in Vieux-Village — 75.46.22.32
M. Morin. Closed 15 Nov-1 March. Open until 9 pm. Terrace dining. Parking. V AE DC.
From the vantage point of this ancient perched village, the Knights of Malta used to survey the valley below; the huddle of venerable buildings at the summit of the town counts among the most enchanting sites of this rugged Provençal countryside. The Morins, father and son, have assiduously assembled all the elements necessary to create a captivating setting of peace, quiet, good taste, and charming atmosphere. On the terrace shaded by a majestic almond tree or in the dining rooms with views across the wooded hills and valley, diners delight in Bernard Morin's vigorous, inventive, and regionally rooted cuisine. We urge you to taste his warm trout salad with red cabbage and Côtes-du-Rhône, or the warm fresh goat cheese with St-Péray wine and fresh local truffles, a locally reared guinea hen braised in Palette wine, or even a simple yet delicious hazelnut mousse. The cellar is exceptional and judiciously priced.
A la carte: 300-400 F. Menus: from 200 F to 440 F.

Les Hospitaliers
(See restaurant above)
Closed 15 Nov-1 March. 2 stes 1,500-2,300 F. 23 rms 480-780 F. Conference facilities. Pool.
Beautiful old furniture graces rooms decorated in perfect taste. The building has undergone some wonderful renovations. This is a magical hotel.

DIGNE

04000 Digne — (Alpes/H.-P.)
Paris 760 - Aix-en-Provence 110 - Sisteron 40

12/20 Hôtel de Bourgogne
Av. de Verdun — 92.31.00.19
M. Petit. Closed Mon off-season, and 20 Dec-20 Feb. Open until 10 pm. Private room: 30. Hotel: 11 rms 140-250 F. Parking. V DC.
The alert young owner is an earnest chef who takes his work to heart. He's come up with some interesting concoctions lately (hence the extra point), among them salmon with an ethereal mousse d'escargots, and saddle of rabbit stuffed with its liver and mild garlic.
A la carte: 280-300 F. Menus: 80 F, 120 F, 250 F.

Central
26, bd Gassendi — 92.31.31.91
Open every day. 20 rms 110-250 F. TV. V.
Provençal-style rooms in a nicely restored old house near the pedestrian precinct, between the post office and the cathedral.

Le Grand Paris
19, bd Thiers — 92.31.11.15
M. Ricaud. Closed off-season Sun dinner and Mon, and 20 Dec-1 March. Open until 9.30 pm. Private room: 20. Garden dining. Garage parking. V AE DC.
Jean-Jacques Ricaud's menu continues to offer his star dishes: lotte with pink peppercorns, poached salmon with a hint of soy, oxtail gelée, and pan-roasted duck breast with shallots. For diners just passing through Digne, that is all well and good, for the food is most professionally pre-

pared. And for regulars who'd like a change, the *carte* offers a few new options, like the frothy leek soup, or the escalope of salmon with fresh pasta. Everyone likes the large, rustic dining room and the terrace with its venerable shade trees. Service and welcome are impeccable—in short, one feels quite happy at the Grand Paris. Especially as the cheeses are carefully chosen, desserts are faultless, and the cellar is interesting. A la carte prices seem to be on the rise.

A la carte: 350-400 F. Menus: from 150 F to 330 F.

▲▲ Le Grand Paris
(See restaurant above)
Open every day. 5 stes 530-640 F. 31 rms 252-410 F. Half-board 390-480 F oblig in seas. TV 27 rms. Pets allowed.

The hotel is housed in a seventeenth-century convent once the home of the Frères de la Trinité. It's centrally located and the rooms, some of which were just redone, are spacious, well equipped, and protected from street noise by the terrace's leafy plane trees. The lovely breakfasts are served in antique silver services. An eighteen-hole golf course is nearby.

12/20 Mistre
63, bd Gassendi — 92.31.00.16
M. Comte. Closed Sat (except July-Aug), and 10 Dec-10 Jan. Open until 9.15 pm. Private room: 80. Garage parking. V AE.

When the chef is on form, he puts regional specialities to good use. Try a more-than-honourable local sausage served hot with lentils, or the grilled tuna with lime, or the red-mullet 'sausage' en bouillabaisse. The big dining room seems a bit cold under its glass ceiling.

A la carte: 250 F. Menus: 140 F, 195 F, 285 F.

▲▲ Mistre
(See restaurant above)
Closed 10 Dec-10 Jan. 19 rms 295-420 F. Half-board 400-500 F. TV 10 rms. Conference facilities.

In the heart of town, this hotel's twenty rooms have been recently refurbished in a somewhat impersonal style, with modest fittings. Prices are reasonable.

Origan
6, rue Pied-de-Ville — 92.31.62.13
M. Cochet. Closed Sun, 1-18 Nov and 25-31 March. Open until 9.15 pm. Terrace dining. Hotel: 9 rms 90-140 F. V AE.

The whole family joins in to run this cheerful establishment. Mme Cochet and her daughter oversee the dining room, all smiles and natural charm, while papa Cochet mans the kitchen. Together they make a highly professional team. Order the thick slices of juicy duck, the pork fillet with Reblochon and mustard, the superb cheeses, and traditional desserts. This is serious eating in a comfortable, rustic atmosphere.

A la carte: 240-300 F. Menus: 95 F, 148 F, 210 F.

See also: Château-Arnoux

> *Red toques signify modern cuisine; black toques signify traditional cuisine.*

71160 Digoin — (Saône/Loire)
Paris 337 - Roanne 54 - Autun 67 - Moulins 59

Diligences et Commerce
14, rue Nationale — 85.53.06.31
M. Soujaeff. Closed Mon dinner and Tue (except July-Aug), and 18 Nov-10 Dec. Open until 9.30 pm. Terrace dining. No pets. Hotel: 9 rms 120 F. V AE DC.

Only the sign and the old façade recall the glorious era of nineteenth-century coaching inns. The youthful new owners are renovating the property methodically. The dining room is spick-and-span, the courtyard terrace inviting, and the cooking adroitly done in a classical style: poached foie gras, freshwater perch with tiny vegetables, veal fillet with morels and fresh pasta. A la carte prices are pretty stiff, but you can soften the bill by drinking the good little house Mâcon.

A la carte: 300-350 F. Menus: 90 F (weekdays only), 120 F, 190 F, 285 F.

Jean-Pierre Mathieu
79, av. du Gal-de-Gaulle — 85.53.03.04
M. Mathieu. Closed Wed (except July-Aug) and 14 Jan-11 Feb. Open until 9.30 pm. Private room: 15. Air cond. Hotel: 14 rms 180-350 F. V DC.

The décor definitely needs sprucing up, but that doesn't stop Jacqueline Mathieu from being the most welcoming of hostesses, nor does it prevent her husband Jean-Pierre from showing off his classic, consistent skill in the kitchen. Presentations are admirable, but we'd like slightly more generous portions of the lobster salad, the expertly cooked hare with myrtle berries, and the fillet of freshwater perch in Burgundy wine.

A la carte: 280-300 F. Menus: 90 F (weekdays only), 116 F, 190 F, 285 F.

21000 Dijon — (Côte-d'Or)
Paris 310 - Reims 283 - Lyon 192 - Besançon 94

Altea
See restaurant Château Bourgogne

11/20 L'Amandier
23, rue Crébillon — 80.30.36.00
M. Minchella. Closed Mon dinner, Sun, 10-17 Feb and 4 Aug-2 Sep. Open until 10 pm. Air cond. V AE DC. C4-6

In the picturesque old Berbisey quarter, this long, narrow dining room with an intimate atmosphere and rough stone walls proposes an affordable repertoire of well-crafted modern dishes: crisp morsels of deep-fried fish, fragrant and flavourful rabbit pot-au-feu, and a silken crème brûlée. Concise wine list.

A la carte: 120-150 F. Menus: 65 F (weekdays lunch only, wine inc), 300 F (champagne inc), 90 F, 155 F.

10/20 L'Aromate
20, rue des Godrans
80.30.86.89
M. Meseguer. Closed Sat lunch, Sun and 13 Aug-1 Sep. Open until 10 pm. V. C3-29

Small, spartan spot near the market, where good, unpretentious cooking—sweetbread salad, suprême de volaille, strawberry soup—is served with a smile.

A la carte: 220 F.

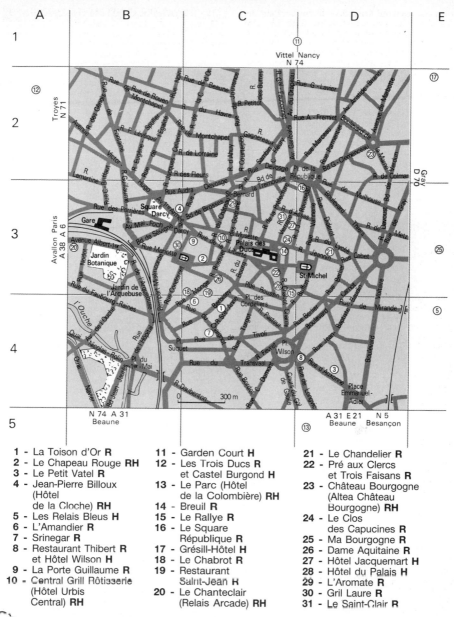

1 - La Toison d'Or **R**	11 - Garden Court **H**	21 - Le Chandelier **R**
2 - Le Chapeau Rouge **RH**	12 - Les Trois Ducs **R**	22 - Pré aux Clercs
3 - Le Petit Vatel **R**	et Castel Burgond **H**	et Trois Faisans **R**
4 - Jean-Pierre Billoux	13 - Le Parc (Hôtel	23 - Château Bourgogne
(Hôtel	de la Colombière) **RH**	(Altea Château
de la Cloche) **RH**	14 - Breuil **R**	Bourgogne) **RH**
5 - Les Relais Bleus **H**	15 - Le Rallye **R**	24 - Le Clos
6 - L'Amandier **R**	16 - Le Square	des Capucines **R**
7 - Srinegar **R**	République **R**	25 - Ma Bourgogne **R**
8 - Restaurant Thibert **R**	17 - Grésill-Hôtel **H**	26 - Dame Aquitaine **R**
et Hôtel Wilson **H**	18 - Le Chabrot **R**	27 - Hôtel Jacquemart **H**
9 - La Porte Guillaume **R**	19 - Restaurant	28 - Hôtel du Palais **H**
10 - Central Grill Rôtisserie	Saint-Jean **R**	29 - L'Aromate **R**
(Hôtel Urbis	20 - Le Chanteclair	30 - Gril Laure **R**
Central) **RH**	(Relais Arcade) **RH**	31 - Le Saint-Clair **R**

Jean-Pierre Billoux

14, pl. Darcy – 80.30.11.00
M. Billoux. Closed Sun dinner, Mon, Feb school holidays and 2 first weeks of Aug. Open until 9.30 pm. Terrace dining. Air cond. Valet parking. Telex 351445. V. D3-4

Despite the complaints of some disgruntled Belgian clients, for our money Jean-Pierre Billoux's pure and inspired cuisine ranks among the most rigorous and exacting we know. The cornerstone of the Billoux style is precision timing, something that many chefs, side-tracked by their enthusiasm for inventing novel compositions, often neglect. Billoux's cuisine is also characterised by highly defined flavours, sometimes cleverly juxtaposed but never confused, and, especially, a most original approach to vegetables. We're thinking of his meltingly tender fondant de saumon with tiny fried vegetables, or the lightly caramelised fennel that accompanies a John Dory in rapeseed oil, or the tart fruit chutney the adds tang to rock lobster spiced with a touch of curry.

Billoux is sensitive to contemporary trends, but his true inspiration springs from a more rustic, 'close to the land' style of cooking. He makes a real feast out of a simple farm chicken, and his classic breast of guinea hen, sliced and sandwiched with foie gras and a few capers, is a truly brilliant dish. Behind the scenes a real team spirit reigns, with Marie-Françoise Billoux in the dining room, second-in-command Roland Surdol in the kitchen, and sommelier Patrice Gillard who has put together a magnificent and highly personal cellar. Prices are not low, but are absolutely worth the quality and care which has gone into the cooking, the superb service, and the beautiful Napoleon III setting. Relais et Châteaux.

A la carte: 470 F. Menus: 240 F (weekdays only), 450 F.

Hôtel de la Cloche

(See restaurant above)

Open every day. 4 stes 1,050-1,150 F. 76 rms 360-550 F. TV. Air cond. Conference facilities.

A majestic old edifice with marvellous fittings and a pleasantly modern, elegant décor. Ask for a duplex room on the second floor. They're ravishing. Others are smaller.

12/20 Ma Bourgogne

1, bd P.-Doumer — 80.65.48.06

M. Minot. Closed Sun dinner, Mon, 1-15 Feb, 12-25 Aug. Open until 10 pm. Terrace dining. V. E3-25

Bernard Minot, the offspring of an illustrious family of chefs, cooks with consummate skill and a deliberately simple approach which has won the hearts of the good citizens of Dijon. In the sober modern dining room, or in summer on the inviting terrace, try Minot's cool rabbit in chervil aspic, salmon with tiny scallops, and the lovely chaud-froid de pommes à la pistache. The cellar holds a judicious selection of modest Burgundy wines.

A la carte: 230-250 F. Menus: 95 F (weekdays only), 145 F.

Breuil

(La Chouette)

1, rue de la Chouette — 80.30.18.10

M. Breuil. Closed Mon dinner, Tue, 15-31 Jan and 25 June-10 July. Open until 10 pm. Private room: 15. V AE DC. C3-14

Year in, year out, you'll encounter a solidly professional, top-quality cuisine that illustrates what's best about the French provincial table. Lucette and Christian Breuil's cosy establishment is situated in a pretty part of town filled with antique shops. In the dining room the atmosphere is intimate and informal, the décor tasteful and luxurious. Don't expect any great sparks from the kitchen. Yet Christian Breuil is an accomplished technician of the old school who does know how to embroider a traditional repertoire. Taste his frogs' legs salad with kale in a mustard-spiked cream, or the juicy salmon steak cooked in its skin and served with an epicurean sauce made with red Burgundy and butter-stewed leeks. To finish there's a delectable millefeuille au chocolat with a mouthwatering ginger sauce. A huge and highly respectable Burgundian cellar to boot.

A la carte: 450 F. Menus: 145 F, 220 F and 380 F (except holidays).

Castel Burgond

2 km NW on N 71, in Daix

3, rte de Troyes

21121 Fontaine-les-Dijon — 80.56.59.72

Open every day. 38 rms 220-260 F. TV. Conference facilities. Parking. V AE DC. A2-12

An enormous geometric block above Dijon. Rooms are functional, with lots of space and light. Restaurant (see Les Trois Ducs).

Central Grill Rôtisserie

3, pl. Grangier — 80.30.44.00

Mme Belin. Closed Sun. Open until midnight. Private room: 50. Terrace dining. Air cond. V AE DC. C3-10

A good address, slap-bang in the nerve centre of Dijon. The large dining room has no windows but is well lit, inviting, and peaceful. The cuisine is simple, fresh, generous, and adroitly prepared: curried chicken-wing salad, salmon tartare with paprika, spit-roasted rack of lamb, and soufflé glacé aux fruits rouges. A modest but well-chosen, reasonably priced wine list. Diligent but informal service; the grill is open until late at night.

A la carte: 250-300 F.

Hôtel Urbis Central

(See restaurant above)

Open every day. 90 rms 255-305 F. Half-board 380-465 F. TV. Conference facilities.

Definitely superior to its two-star classification, this old house in the city centre has been entirely modernised, and its rooms were refurbished last winter. Breakfast is not served in the rooms.

Le Chabrot

36, rue Monge — 80.30.69.61

M. Bouy. Closed Mon lunch, Sun and Aug. Open until 10.30 pm. No-smoking section. V. C3-18

The narrow, pink-and-black interior of this popular establishment fills up quickly owing to the attractive set meals, the good wines poured by the glass, and a jovial owner (he's the one sporting a handlebar moustache). We prefer the less elegant but more inviting basement dining room, where an essentially fish-based cuisine is served: the food is delicious when chef Joël Guillaud is on form. A la carte, order one of some twenty salmon variations, or a good sweet-and-sour duck breast. Tempting desserts.

A la carte: 300 F. Menus: 69 F (lunch only), 280 F (wine inc), 92 F.

11/20 Le Chandelier

65, rue Jeannin — 80.66.15.82

M. Fedel. Closed Sun dinner. Open until 11.30 pm. Air cond. V AE. D3-21

What it lacks in originality, this cuisine makes up for in freshness, simplicity, and low prices: lotte with stewed chicory, duck breast with cranberries, pork fillet à la Dijonnaise. Appealing provincial décor.

A la carte: 200 F. Menus: 62 F (weekdays lunch only), 75 F, 95 F, 130 F.

11/20 Le Chanteclair

15, av. Albert-Ier — 80.43.01.12

M. Jacquier. Open every day. Open until 11.30 pm. Private room: 180. Terrace dining. Air cond. Parking. Telex 350315. V. B3-20

A boringly modern dining room with an inviting terrace-cum-garden where you can get easy-going, affordably priced dishes such as poached eggs in red wine, pan-roasted lamb, and chocolate tart. Very friendly service.

A la carte: 170 F. Menus: 85 F (weekdays dinner only, wine inc), 125 F (w-e and holidays only, wine inc).

Relais Arcade

(See restaurant above)

Open every day. 128 rms 280-320 F. TV. Conference facilities.

A stone's throw from the station and the new Grévin-Bourgogne complex. Quiet, comfortable little rooms and a decent breakfast buffet. Well-equipped conference rooms.

Le Chapeau Rouge
5, rue Michelet — 80.30.28.10
M. Lagrange. Open every day. Open until 9.45 pm. Private room: 50. Air cond. No pets. Telex 350535. V AE DC. C3-2

A lot of effort and expense has gone into rejuvenating this restaurant. The new proprietor is a true professional, and has given Le Chapeau Rouge a more youthful, vigorous image. It's now a question of infusing some zest into the good but impersonal cuisine: œufs en meurette with bacon and celery, croustades d'escargots with a basil cream, stuffed pigeon stewed à la bourguignonne, veal noisettes with whole-grain mustard sauce. We'll leave the rating as it is, to encourage the kitchen.

A la carte: 400 F. Menus: 210 F (lunch only, wine inc), 180 F.

Le Chapeau Rouge
(See restaurant above)
Open every day. 2 stes 1,000-1,350 F. 29 rms 420-650 F. Half-board 435-520 F. TV. Air cond 10 rms. Conference facilities.

Renovations have definitely improved this comfortable family hotel. Half the rooms have been modernised with Jacuzzis in some of the bathrooms. The good soundproofing is appreciated, given the location in the centre of town. Service is impeccable.

Château Bourgogne
22, bd de la Marne — 80.72.31.13
M. Thenard. Open every day. Open until 10 pm. Private room: 80. Garden dining. Air cond. No-smoking section. Garage parking. V AE DC. D2-23

Great value for money, appealing set menus, and fast-moving, efficient service keep this hotel restaurant going full tilt. In a vaguely 'Chinese-style' décor you can indulge in a tasty chausson d'escargots, turbot fillet with fresh lasagne, or a succulent though slightly overcooked hare with raisins. Pastries are splendid (much improved), and the cellar boasts a good choice of Burgundies.

A la carte: 280-300 F. Menus: 155 F and 178 F (wine inc), 220 F.

Altea Château Bourgogne
(See restaurant above)
Open every day. 7 stes 520-550 F. 123 rms 360-500 F. TV. Air cond. Conference facilities. Pool.

Here's an excellent, American-style hotel situated in the new, slightly gloomy Palais de la Foire area, ten minutes from the centre. Rooms are big and modern, well-ventilated, and recently refurbished. Conference rooms are thoughtfully equipped. Swimming pool.

Hôtel de la Cloche
See restaurant Jean-Pierre Billoux

12/20 Le Clos des Capucines
3, rue Jeannin — 80.65.83.03
Mme Fresse. Closed Feb school holidays. Open until 10 pm. Private room: 30. Terrace dining. Air cond. V AE DC. C3-24

A very pretty fourteenth-century house in the old part of Dijon, with a small interior courtyard, a terrace, and a fireplace in the lovely old dining room. Sample the serious, nicely presented cuisine: poached prawns with a hint of vanilla, duck in wine with redcurrants, and gingerbread charlotte.

Concise but interesting wine list. Cellar attached for tasting and purchasing wine.

A la carte: 200 F. Menus: 230 F (wine inc), 79 F, 107 F, 157 F.

Hôtel de la Colombière
See restaurant Le Parc

Dame Aquitaine   🕄
23, pl. Bossuet — 80.30.36.23
Mme Saléra. Closed Sun. Open until 11.30 pm. V AE DC. C3-26

A former crypt with medieval ribbed vaulting opens onto an eighteenth-century courtyard right in the heart of Dijon—it's now one of the most attractive spots in town. The décor has been refreshed; the kitchens too have had a face-lift, and proprietress Monique Saléra should take advantage of the general spruce-up to polish her Southwestern specialities. Of the four foie gras on our *dégustation* plate, two were up to par, and our duck breast with sour cherries was cloying. The menu lists an abundance of confits and cassoulets. Good wine list.

A la carte: 350 F. Menus: 95 F (weekdays lunch only), 125 F, 168 F, 195 F.

Garden Court
(Holiday Inn)
1, pl. Marie-de-Bourgogne — 80.72.20.72
Open every day. 104 rms 340-430 F. Restaurant. Half-board 525-615 F. TV. Conference facilities. Parking. Telex 352180. V AE DC. C1-11

A nice, new hotel in the equally new commercial complex of the Toison d'Or. Standardised but luxurious comfort in the modern rooms, which are superbly outfitted (video, trouser-press, coffee machine) and soundproofed. They give onto the pool of the water-sports centre next door.

Grésill'Hôtel
16, av. R.-Poincaré — 80.71.10.56
Open every day. 47 rms 225-280 F. Restaurant. TV. Conference facilities. Parking. Telex 350549. V AE DC. E2-17

A charmless modern construction near the Palais des Congrès et des Sports, but with functional and well-kept rooms. Bar and pub.

10/20 Gril Laure
8, pl. St-Bénigne — 80.41.86.76
M. Damidot. Closed Sun lunch. Open until 11 pm. Garden dining. Air cond. V. B3-30

Artfully simple, decently priced cuisine: a good assiette gourmande with foie gras and salmon, and an agreeable though somewhat overcooked lake char (omble chevalier). Honest wines served in carafes. Pleasant but oh so slow service.

A la carte: 200 F.

Hôtel Jacquemart
32, rue de la Verrerie — 80.73.39.74
Open every day. 2 stes 280-360 F. 32 rms 136-285 F. TV. V. C3-27

This old, comfortable hotel is situated in the antiquarian quarter of medieval Dijon. A warm, family welcome.

Hôtel du Palais
23, rue du Palais — 80.67.16.26
Closed 24 Dec-1 Jan. 15 rms 160-240 F. TV. V. C3-28

An appealingly renovated small hotel, which offers excellent value for money, located off the centre of town between the library and the Palais de Justice. Courteous welcome and an cosy atmosphere.

12/20 Le Parc

49, cours du Parc — 80.65.18.41
M. Petit. Open every day. Open until 10 pm. Private room: 200. Garden dining. Parking. Telex 351482. V. D5-13

Granted, this is Dijon's pleasantest covered terrace, but otherwise the exceptional surroundings—wide paths leading to the Colombière park, a favourite with the Dijonnais—have not been made sufficient use of. In a modern dining room with an unexciting décor, you can tuck into an ambitious and imaginative cuisine: rabbit terrine (a bit dry) served with an excellent herbal oil, calf's head with nicely cooked vegetables, and an indifferent mousse au chocolat et sauce pistache. In terms of quality, prices are good. But service is slow, and the cellar mediocre at best.

A la carte: 280 F. Menus: 89 F (weekdays lunch only), 145 F, 195 F.

Hôtel de la Colombière
(See restaurant above)
Open every day. 2 stes 460 F. 39 rms 280-330 F. TV. Conference facilities.

Overlooking the greenery of the Colombière park, the hotel's forty rooms have been entirely modernised in a bright, functional style.

12/20 Le Petit Vatel

73, rue d'Auxonne — 80.65.80.64
M. Lespagnol. Closed Sat lunch and Sun (except holidays), and 14 July-20 Aug. Open until 10 pm. Air cond. No pets. V. D4-3

The décor falls somewhere between the modern (bright colours) and the rustic (bare stone). Though earnest and attentive, the proprietress lacks enthusiasm, and her quality ingredients are prepared without an ounce of imagination. Ably cooked prawns are paired in a salad with fairly unappetising foie gras; fillet of freshwater perch with smoked cod roe is marred by a lacklustre sauce. Dessert—a pear roasted with honey—saved the meal. Tiny wine list, and alas, no more wines by the glass.

A la carte: 250 F. Menus: 85 F (lunch only), 120 F.

12/20 La Porte Guillaume

(Hôtel du Nord)
Pl. Darcy — 80.30.58.58
M. Frachot. Closed 24 Dec-10 Jan. Open until 10.45 pm. Private room: 50. Hotel: 29 rms 155-330 F. Telex 351554. V AE DC. C3-9

A country-style restaurant in the centre of Dijon, where the kitchen is firmly set in its ways. An immutable menu proposes eggs poached in red wine, coq au vin, fillet of beef with peppercorns. The grilled scampi are exceptionally good, desserts are forgettable. Wines by the glass. Efficient service.

A la carte: 250 F. Menus: 98 F, 120 F, 190 F.

12/20 Pré aux Clercs et Trois Faisans

11-13, pl. de la Libération — 80.67.11.33
M. Fillion. Open every day. Open until 11 pm. Private room: 100. Air cond. V AE DC. C3-22

The décor of beams and bare stone looks out onto the wonderful Place de la Libération. The classic cuisine buries itself in indifferent sauces (escargots en cocotte with a chive-flavoured cream, panaché de poissons with an artificial sauce) and any spectacular sleight-of-hand is aimed above all at the passing tourist. A good cellar, and discreet, hard-working staff in a magnificent spot.

A la carte: 300 F. Menus: 98 F (weekdays only), 150 F, 170 F, 300 F.

Le Rallye

39, rue Chabot-Charny — 80.67.11.55
M. Roncin. Closed Sun, holidays, mid-Feb-beg March and end July-16 Aug. Open until 9.30 pm. Private room: 20. V AE DC. C3-15

The Rallye deserves an award for virtue. Twenty years after helping to shake up Dijon's slumbering, self-satisfied cuisine it continues quietly and consistently on its course. This despite frequent changes of chefs (all trained, however, by the knowledgeable François Minot) and thanks to the hard work of the owners, who run the comfortable dining room and ensure the smooth functioning of their establishment. The cuisine moves skilfully between lightened traditional fare, and neo-regional dishes. Good bets include a lentil salad adorned with fillets of goose breast, a ridiculously simple but good andouillette with mashed potatoes, capably cooked calf's head or liver. This is tasty food with few frills at pleasing prices.

A la carte: 260 F. Menus: 90 F, 145 F, 195 F.

Relais Arcade
See restaurant Le Chanteclair

Les Relais Bleus

Parc de Mirande
12, rue P.-de-Coubertin — 80.66.32.40
Open every day. 45 rms 270 F. Restaurant. Half-board 330-380 F. TV. Conference facilities. Parking. Telex 352117. V AE. E4-5

A fairly recent hotel built on the by-pass. Rooms are modern and bright. Wine bar. Reductions for those holding a Relais Bleus membership card.

11/20 Restaurant Saint-Jean

13, rue Monge — 80.30.06.64
M. Zingerlé. Closed Wed and 19-26 Aug. Open until 2 am. Private room: 50. Air cond. V AE DC. C3-19

Despite a mediocre wine list and a tired décor, this is one of Dijon's few late-night spots, where a body can get decent, honest country-inn fare: good salmon feuilleté, nice fish fillet with crab coulis, and an excellent soupe d'oranges à la menthe.

A la carte: 200 F. Menus: 59 F (lunch only), 80 F, 100 F.

Restaurant Thibert

10, pl. du Pdt-Wilson — 80.67.74.64
M. Thibert. Closed Mon lunch, Sun, Feb school holidays and 29 July-19 Aug. Open until 9.45 pm. Private room: 20. Air cond. V. D4-8

The shy natures of both Jean-Paul Thibert and his wife Maryse are something to be thankful for. It leaves them unspoiled by their sudden fame, and so unsure about what tomorrow will bring that they put their heart and soul into the present. Bravo, and thanks for this genuine modesty (another form, perhaps, of respect for their guests), which proves that honest craftsmanship is the real foundation of the chef's profession, something too easily forgotten in these media-mad times.

Thibert puts all his daring and imagination into his bold cooking, a daily defiance of his retiring nature. This culinary adventurer is constantly exploring, and more often than not comes up with incredible discoveries. This time, for example, we were bowled over by crisply sautéed morsels of sweetbreads in a subtle rhubarb sauce, by pigeon bathed in a sublime shallot and bone-marrow jus, by a wonderfully balanced potato cake spiced with cumin, and by the delectable green-pea jus that escorted a freshwater char.

Pure dazzlement, great gustatory thrills, all this and a cellar of divine Burgundies too. Such delights help us ignore the rudimentary décor and service, as well as (we had better warn you) the sudden surge in prices. For the rest, the unexpected here is almost always better than the expected. We almost died of pleasure over a vanilla ice cream drizzled with a cardamom-scented strawberry compote.

A la carte: 380 F. Menus: 95 F, 180 F, 240 F, 350 F.

12/20 Le Saint-Clair
52, rue de la Verrerie — 80.72.30.50
M. Medjekane. Closed Sun, 1-12 Aug and 23 Oct-15 Nov. Open until 10.30 pm. Private room: 45. Terrace dining. V DC. C3-31

Somewhat lost in the warren of Dijon's medieval streets, this daintily rustic dining room with large bay windows offers a warm welcome and fresh, straightforward cuisine: yummy escargots en cassolette, scrumptious paupiette of trout, and a delicately flavoured suckling pig dressed with fragrant vinaigrette. A great little address.

A la carte: 150-200 F. Menus: 50 F (weekdays lunch only), 60 F, 75 F, 110 F.

Le Square République
10-12, pl. de la République — 80.74.39.55
MM. Novack and Thibaut. Closed Sat lunch, Sun and 23-31 Dec. Open until 10 pm. Garden dining. V AE DC. D3-16

When he gives himself the trouble, as he does quite often, Serge Thibaut will serve you some delectable little dishes, like his snail chowder with garlic cream, a nicely crafted nage de poissons flavoured with basil, or salmon baked in coarse salt and napped with a silken beurre blanc.

A la carte: 260 F. Menus: 92 F, 122 F, 162 F.

10/20 Srinegar
36, rue du Chaignot — 80.50.16.26
M. Kirar. Open every day. Open until 11 pm. No-smoking section. V AE DC. C4-7

Good, orthodox Indian cuisine: a classic chicken curry, generous chicken biryani with rice and spices, and an excellent lamb korma.

A la carte: 200 F. Menus: 59 F (weekdays lunch only, wine inc), 89 F, 150 F.

La Toison d'Or
18, rue Ste-Anne — 80.30.73.52
M. Glorion. Closed Sun dinner. Open until 9.30 pm. Private room: 130. Parking. V AE DC. C4-1

The wine company that runs this luxurious old Burgundian establishment has announced the imminent opening of a thirty-room hotel, which will doubtless make the Toison d'Or one of Dijon's charm spots. Until then, groups and conference-members continue to pour into the fabulous salons and dining rooms of this Gothic house, restored from top to bottom in best Burgundian style. Candlelight dinners under the beams are romantic indeed, and the chef, Daniel Broyer, when he is not being pressed by sheer numbers, produces some magnificent dishes such as a salade gourmande au foie gras, with smoked salmon and quail's eggs, or sweetbreads simmered with truffle cream and smoked bacon, a thick slice of turbot baked with bone marrow, and a refreshing hot-and-cold citrus soup. There is an expectedly good

cellar (many young growers' wines), and a small wine museum which you can visit.

A la carte: 400 F. Menus: 120 F, 180 F, 230 F.

Les Trois Ducs

2 km NW on N 71
5, rte de Troyes
21121 Daix — 80.56.59.75
M. Piganiol. Closed Sun dinner, Mon, 3-19 Feb and 4-27 Aug. Open until 9.45 pm. Private room: 60. Terrace dining. Parking. V AE DC. A2-12

One doesn't come here for the architecture or the décor, although Emmanuel Joinville, who runs this roadside establishment, has promised improvements in that sector. Right now, a stop here is motivated by the quality of the cuisine, also in the hands of Emmanuel. It is neat, precise, and constantly changing. There is the touch of the true professional in his prawn colombo with apples, the duck breast confit with a remarkable garnish of pommes Anna, and an exceptional frozen nougat, accompanied by a ginger sorbet. Some very nice menus, two of which have been conceived for people watching their weight. A good choice of wines.

A la carte: 350 F. Menus: 135 F (weekdays only, wine inc), 145 F, 190 F, 250 F.

Hôtel Urbis Central
See restaurant Central Grill

Hôtel Wilson
1, rue de Longvic — 80.66.82.50
Open every day. 27 rms 300-400 F. TV. Garage parking. V. D4-8

Situated on the square of the same name, next to the Restaurant Thibert, this comfortable seventeenth-century coaching inn has been entirely renovated. Rooms are personalised with rather opulent rustic furnishings. The welcome could be warmer.

And also...
L'Armstrong (80.30.74.06 - 42, rue Berbisey. Open until 11.30 pm): Decent, not too imaginative cuisine with jazz some nights.
Bistingo (80.30.61.38 - pass. Darcy. Open until 11 pm): Centrally located, casual little bistro serving hearty dishes (140 F).
Les Congrès (80.72.17.22 - 16, av. R.-Poincaré. Open until 11 pm): Pleasant grill with a new terrace. Seafood in season (150 F).
Le Dôme (80.30.58.92 - 16 bis, rue Quentin. Open until 9.45 pm): Alongside the central food market, this animated café serves good, honest bistro cooking (150 F).
Les Nouveaux Abattoirs (80.66.71.42 - 34, rue E.-Petit. Lunch only): Meat, offal, and a generous little 39 F menu (60-100 F).
La Table Marocaine (80.30.46.20 - 4, rue J.-Prévert. Open until 11 pm): Couscous, tajines, and other Moroccan dishes, meticulously prepared and served (100-150 F).
Villa Tan (80.43.23.40 - 16, rue des Perrières. Open until 10 pm): The town's best Chinese restaurant, with Cambodian specialities. Not too much monosodium glutamate in the food (130 F).

The new spiral-bound RAC Atlas France will help you to find your chosen restaurant of hotel, no matter how secluded.

In nearby Marsannay-la-Côte

(7 km SW on D 122)
21160 Dijon — (Côte-d'Or)

Les Gourmets

8, rue du Puits-de-Têt — 80.52.16.32
M. Perreaut. Closed Sun dinner, Mon, 7-31 Jan and 30 July-13 Aug. Open until 9.30 pm. Private room: 15. Garden dining. Telex 352113. V AE.

Joël Perreaut believes in the essentials, which form the basis of his culinary credo: pure, clean ingredients, split-second cooking times, and concise sauces.

His progress in those areas amply justify today's third toque. Perreaut's sauces are succinct—almost essences, really, full of intense flavours and refined nuances. They leave one feeling light but with sharpened senses. A case in point, the osso buco de lotte, cooked on the bone and served under a very fine layer of diced vegetables and citrus fruits; another example: a marvellous, winy rabbit daube with lasagne; or the thick codfish steak with juices and balsamic vinegar which we were served this year. A great ray of sunshine has swept through this chef's repertoire, banishing some of the more anonymous dishes from the menu. Look instead for a splendid tarte fine au saumon fumé, or roast red mullet with its croûton spread with tapenade, or a keen-flavoured saddle of lamb with black olives. The décor too has been brightened, and a summer treat is to lunch on the terrace under the graceful plum tree. The wine list is one of the area's best—it will help you to discover the underestimated wines of Marsannay and Fixin. Having said that, however, we would like to see the cellar range a bit farther afield. Nicole Perreaut supervises the professional service.

À la carte: 350-400 F. Menus: 135 F (weekdays lunch only), 200 F, 310 F, 420 F.

In nearby Neuilly-lès-Dijon

(7 km SE on N 5)
21800 Dijon — (Côte-d'Or)

La Flambée

Ancienne rte de Genève — 80.47.35.35
Open every day. 1 ste 600-700 F. 23 rms 285-450 F. Restaurant. TV. Air cond. Conference facilities. Parking. Telex 350273. V AE DC.

Quiet, renovated, well-equipped rooms in a luxurious country cottage (the peasants never had it so good!).

In nearby Val-Suzon

(16 km NW on N 71)
21121 Dijon — (Côte-d'Or)

Hostellerie du Val-Suzon

N 71 — 80.35.60.15
M. Perreau. Closed Thu lunch, Wed and 15 Dec-15 Jan. Open until 9.30 pm. Private room: 18. Garden dining. No pets. Parking. Telex 351454. V AE DC.

How could one resist this attractive inn nestled in a profusion of greenery in a small valley that scores of birds have elected for their habitat? Mme Perreau is warm and welcoming, and the service is on its toes. But what about the cooking? Well.... In 1989 we were happy to give Yves Perreau his second toque to reward the spirit and skill of his cuisine. His soft-boiled eggs with lobster and foie gras, the morel ravioli with foie gras cream, or the pan-roasted pigeon breast with confit are still fixtures on the menu. Their very richness illustrates a generous, flavourful style of cookery.

Trouble is, the execution sometimes suffers from hiccups: our portion of home-smoked salmon was too salty, and the John Dory with verjuice was expertly cooked, but the sauce was strewn with grape pips. These are mistakes which Yves Perreau could easily correct. The wine list is rich (so are the prices) and offers lots of half-bottles. A few vintages, though not the best, are available by the glass.

À la carte: 350-400 F. Menus: 180 F (weekdays only), 250 F, 350 F.

Hostellerie du Val-Suzon

(See restaurant above)
Closed Wed and 15 Dec-15 Jan. 1 ste. 17 rms 370-510 F (per pers, half-board oblig). TV 10 rms. Conference facilities.

Comfortable, rustic-style hotel with a chalet-annexe, totally renovated in 1990. Attractive bathrooms, and a very handsome suite.

DINAN

22100 Dinan — (Côtes/Armor)
Paris 370 - St-Brieuc 59 - St-Malo 29 - Rennes 51

Avaugour

1, place du Champ
cd96.39.07.49
M. Quinton. Closed 15 Jan-15 Feb. Open until 9.30 pm. Private room: 25. Garden dining. Telex 950415. V AE DC.

A luxurious, though rather bland provincial décor characterises this restaurant, which at the back opens onto the old ramparts and a flower-decked garden. In the vast, vaulted fifteenth-century dining room, Georges Quinton caters regally for tourists with sumptuous grilled dishes cooked before your eyes in the Cyclopean fireplace. His second-in-command is left to his own devices in the kitchen where he turns out successful, sunny dishes like little red mullet with citrus-scented prawn fritters, warm lobster salad with marinated vegetables, or turbot with pickled lemons and dill, and sweetbreads with capers and tagliatelle.

À la carte: 300-350 F. Menus: 70 F (weekdays lunch only), 130 F, 200 F, 320 F.

Avaugour

(See restaurant above)
Open every day. 27 rms 320-420 F. Half-board 380-450 F oblig in seas. TV. Conference facilities.

Gisèle Quinton lavishes time and effort on this large, attractive establishment. Rooms are comfortable and regularly renovated; some give onto the ramparts and garden.

La Caravelle

14, pl. Duclos
96.39.00.11
M. Marmion. Closed off-season Sun dinner and Wed, and 12 Nov-4 Dec. Open until 9.30 pm. Garage parking. V AE DC.

The mouldings, marble, and beams are all fake in this new, obviously expensive, oddly unappealing décor. No matter. Cordiality abounds, and Jean-Claude Marmion's cuisine, when it is good, is very, very good indeed. Having tasted the huge oysters with black pepper combined with red mullet in a deftly reduced sauce, the John Dory with sea salt and wine-stewed onions, the young pigeon with sweetcorn cakes and a hint of bacon, and an array of divine desserts, we had no choice but to confirm Marmion's two toques (and write off a previously unsuccessful repast as a fluke).

À la carte: 350 F and up. Menus: 110 F, 160 F and 250 F (weekdays only).

Marguerite

29, pl. Du Guesclin – 96.39.47.65
Closed Sun and Mon (15 Jan-31 March), and 15 Oct-15 Jan. 19 rms 140-300 F. Restaurant. Half-board 210-250 F oblig in seas. TV 5 rms. Conference facilities. V.
A small, well-run, traditional hotel right behind the castle on the large car park. Bar.

12/20 Chez la Mère Pourcel

3, pl. des Merciers – 96.39.03.80
M. Danjou. Closed Sun dinner and Mon (except July-Aug). Annual closings not available. Open until 9.45 pm. Terrace dining. V.
The setting is wonderful, with bare stone walls, beams, and wood panelling. The quality of the food is not always top-notch, unfortunately—dishes are occasionally too fussy. The chanterelle ravioli with crab coulis are tasty (though a bit spongy), the thick slice of turbot braised in cider is undermined by a strong taste of onions, but the peach poached in a tarragon syrup is refreshing. Nice, affordable wines.
A la carte: 300 F. Menus: 85 F (weekdays only), 145 F, 250 F, 350 F.

DINARD

35800 Dinard — (Ille/Vil.)
Paris 370 - Rennes 72 - Dinan 22 - Lamballe 47

Altaïr

18, bd Féart – 99.46.13.58
Mme Leménager. Closed Sun dinner, Mon and 5 Nov-9 Dec. Open until 9 pm. Private room: 20. Terrace dining. Hotel: 21 rms 200-320 F. V AE DC.
At a hop and a skip from the beach is this comfy, country-style establishment, made cosy with pitch-pine furnishings and flowered carpet. Patrick Leménager's cuisine grows more proficient every day, and his set menus are most edifying and generous. Try the warm fish terrine with sweet red peppers, or the savoury combo of braised and grilled chicken lavished with fresh herbs, and finish with the pear gratin embellished with praline ice cream—perfection. The cellar needs building, but it's coming along.
A la carte: 280-300 F. Menus: 80 F (weekdays only), 110 F, 140 F, 180 F.

Grand Hôtel

46, av. George-V – 99.46.10.28
Open every day. 3 stes 1,320-3,000 F. 93 rms 330-1,300 F. Restaurant. Half-board 550-1,250 F. TV. Conference facilities. Heated pool. Valet parking. Telex 740522. V AE DC.
A fine example of the last century's grand hotels, facing the St-Servan bay. Rooms are spacious, and some have been recently refurbished with period furniture. Great bathrooms. Breakfast is expensive—and disappointing.

La Plage

3, bd Féart – 99.46.14.87
Closed 6 Jan-14 Feb and 5-24 March. 18 rms 375 F. Restaurant. Half-board 230-300 F. TV. Telex 740802. V AE DC.
Neat, pleasant, comfortable rooms not far from the beach. Some boast sea views.

Reine Hortense

19, rue de la Malouine – 99.46.54.31
Closed 15 Nov-25 March. 4 stes 1,200-1,800 F. 10 rms 750-1,200 F. TV. Valet parking. Telex 740802. V AE DC.
A few souvenirs of Queen Hortense have been preserved along with some highly picturesque furniture. The superb turn-of-the-century salon has a Versailles parquet floor. Don't miss the fantastic silver bathtub in the 'Reine Hortense' room. Direct access to the beach.

In nearby Pleurtuit

(5 km S on D 266)
35730 Dinard — (Ille/Vil.)

Manoir de la Rance

Château de Jouvente – 99.88.53.76
Closed 3 Jan-10 March. 3 stes 600-900 F. 10 rms 330-600 F. TV 5 rms. Parking. V AE.
Ten kilometres from Dinan stands this large, charming hotel perched above the Rance River. Rooms are furnished with period pieces; they are quiet, well equipped, and have lots of character. Breakfasts are delicious, and there is a pretty terrace, a garden, a bar, and tea room for your pleasure. Smiling service.

DIVONNE-LES-BAINS

01220 Divonne-les-Bains — (Ain)
Paris 502 - Genève 19 - Nyon 13 - Gex 9 - Bourg 120

Le Champagne

Av. de Genève – 50.20.13.13
M. Carrier. Closed Thu lunch, Wed, 23 Dec-15 Jan, 10 days end June and beg Oct. Open until 9.30 pm. Garden dining. Parking. V.
Charcuterie, grilled meat, and delicious home-baked tart for dessert sums up the menu. Basic perhaps, but Suzanne and Roger Carrier's restaurant is always crowded with customers who appreciate the warm atmosphere and no-frills cuisine. Excellent terrines, fresh fish from Brittany (grilled red mullet and baked sea bream), and tasty meat (charcoal-grilled andouillette, steaks, and duck breast).
A la carte: 250 F.

Duchesse de Vendôme

Rte de Gex – 50.20.00.32
M. Martin. Closed off-season Wed lunch and Tue, and beg Jan-beg March. Open until 9.30 pm. Private room: 65. Terrace dining. Air cond. Parking. Telex 309033. V.
It would be hard to find a chef more passionate about his work than Guy Martin. For seven years, as chef and manager of this nineteenth-century château overlooking Lake Geneva, he has worked for its success as devotedly as if he were the owner. What this establishment lacks, in common with René Traversac's other hotels, is charm. The façade is superb, the rooms spacious and the décor acceptable, but when you compare it with what Michel and Christine Guérard have done at Eugénie-les-Bains with a much less promising building, you realise that an opportunity has been wasted here. Although it hasn't stemmed the flow of visitors, we believe business could be better without the sterile atmosphere.
Luckily, Guy Martin's cuisine makes the pill easier to swallow. The *carte* includes a selection of recipes dating from the royal court of Savoie: mosaïque de langue et oreilles de veau with a salad of celery and smoked bone marrow, kidney with bacon, coarse-grain mustard, and a polenta pancake, lotte ragoût with crayfish and sweetbreads, or a casserole of fattened hen, duck, and oxtail, served with risotto. Interesting certainly, but we would rather recommend the sweetbreads with broad beans and truffle juice, omble chevalier (a lake fish) accompanied by vermicelli moistened with fish fumet, and saddle of young rabbit in aniseed-flavoured pastry with a

sauce of vin jaune. Don't pass over the ginger sponge cake served with a coffee sabayon sauce, iced pear soufflé, and Gex blue cheese served in stoneware pots, not to mention charming Savoie wines and the finest Juras.
A la carte: 450-600 F. Menus: 250 F (weekdays lunch only, wine inc), 240 F, 330 F, 470 F.

Château de Divonne
(See restaurant above)
Closed beg Jan-beg March. 5 stes 1,000-1,550 F. 27 rms 400-1,020 F. Half-board 685-1,145 F. TV. Conference facilities. Tennis.
Enjoy a gorgeous view of Lake Geneva and the Mont Blanc range from an early nineteenth-century estate situated on 22 wooded hectares. The interior design is nothing special, but you'll love the spacious rooms, modern bathrooms, exquisite breakfasts and perfect service. There's an eighteen-hole golf course, casino, sailing, and music festivals in summer. And if all this activity gives you aches and pains, you can call on a young Vietnamese osteopath who knows just how to soothe them. Relais et Châteaux.

Les Grands Hôtels
Rue de Plan – 50.40.34.39
Open every day. 6 stes 1,000-1,500 F. 150 rms 475-1,050 F. Restaurant. Half-board 720-1,195 F. TV. Conference facilities. Heated pool. Tennis. Golf. Parking. Telex 385716. V AE DC.
A slightly outdated grand hotel from the turn of the century. You can choose between a view of the grounds and Jura mountains, or Lake Geneva and the Alps. Special rates for weekends and fitness breaks. Three restaurants.

35120 Dol-de-Bretagne – (Ille/Vil.)
Paris 373 - St-Malo 24 - Rennes 54 - Dinan 26

La Bresche Arthur
36, bd Derminiac – 99.48.01.44
M. Martel. Closed off-season Sun dinner and Mon, 15-31 Jan and 15-30 Nov. Open until 10 pm. Hotel: 24 rms 220-240 F. Parking. V.
This tourist town was in need of a quality restaurant and Philippe Martel, formerly with Gérard Boyer in Reims, fills the bill admirably with La Bresche Arthur. A warmly decorated dining room with terrace, and quick, professional service enhance the simple but generous food: salmon carpaccio with basil vinegar on a bed of vegetables, or chicken breast with prawns and fresh pasta in a light, creamy shellfish sauce. Handsome cheese board and well-chosen wines.
A la carte: 250 F. Menus: 75 F (weekdays lunch only), 115 F, 160 F.

See Oléron (Ile d')

24250 Domme – (Dordogne)
Paris 530 - Gourdon 26 - Sarlat 12 - Cahors 52

L'Esplanade
53.28.31.41
M. Gillard. Closed off-season Sun dinner and Mon, and 12 Nov-15 Feb. Open until 9 pm. Air cond. V AE.
A marvellous panoramic view stretches across the Dordogne from this huge yellow-and-blue dining room. Nothing new where service is concerned: unlike her amiable staff, the *patronne* is as cantankerous as ever. But the fearful prices have risen even higher this year, even if you avoid

truffles, lobster and caviar. Play it safe and stick to the delicate coussin de saumon à la mousseline de truite, or good, herb-seasoned rack of lamb.
A la carte: 400 F. Menus: 135 F, 190 F, 220 F.

L'Esplanade
(See restaurant above)
Closed off-season Sun and Mon, and 12 Nov-15 Feb. 1 ste 420 F. 19 rms 220-450 F. Half-board 300-500 F. Conference facilities.
Well-renovated, quiet rooms. Some offer beautiful views over the Dordogne Valley.

26290 Donzère – (Drôme)
Paris 620 - Orange 39 - Montélimar 13 - Aubenas 47

Hostellerie du Mas des Sources
75.51.74.18
M. Picard. Closed Wed off-season, Tue dinner, 2 Jan-28 Feb and first week of Nov. Open until 9.30 pm. Garden dining. Parking. V.
Is fear of heights the reason for the high turnover of young chefs in Jean-Marie Picard's kitchen? Not to worry; this old farmhouse overhanging the Donzère gorge seems to keep attracting good ones. The latest, Ludovic Sinz, had already worked with Chibois, Loiseau, and Robuchon before arriving in this far corner of Provence, and he's still only 23. He has turned his talents to the local fare with such flair and finesse that you would think he was a native. Soupe d'escargots au jus de persil et ail confit, salmon and artichoke pastries with tomato coulis, skate with olive oil and garlic-scented aubergines, rack of lamb with stuffed vegetables, and nougat glacé with prune coulis provide ample proof. When the mistral dies down, you can eat outside on the terrace and enjoy the impressive view of the Rhône Valley.
A la carte: 350-400 F. Menus: 160 F (weekdays lunch only), 200 F, 250 F.

Hostellerie du Mas des Sources
(See restaurant above)
Closed Wed off-season, Tue, 2 Jan-28 Feb and first week of Nov. 2 stes 600-700 F. 3 rms 300-450 F. TV. Pets allowed.
The attractive rooms with breathtaking views are currently being renovated. Breakfasts are excellent. The hotel has tennis courts and a swimming pool, and there's a golf course nearby.

59500 Douai – (Nord)
Paris 203 - Lille 37 - Valenciennes 37 – Cambrai 26

La Terrasse
36, terrasse St-Pierre
27.88.70.04
M. Hanique. Open every day. Open until 9.30 pm. Private room: 70. Air cond. V.
Emile and Muriel Hanique are always trying to make their town-centre establishment even more welcoming and comfortable. The cooking is costly but remarkably consistent, with generous portions and well thought-out vegetable accompaniments: filet de sandre aux oignons confits and rosemary butter, jambonneau de lotte en crépine de lard, breast of duck with fresh figs. Wide selection of desserts, and a somewhat intimidating cellar with 800 wines.
A la carte: 350 F and up. Menus: 164 F, 300 F, 375 F.

▲▲ La Terrasse
(See restaurant above)
Open every day. 2 stes 530-660 F. 24 rms 295-600 F. TV. Conference facilities.

Just across the way from the St Pierre collegiate church, this hotel has cosy rooms with soundproofing, period furniture, and satellite television. Excellent breakfasts with home-baked breads and pastries.

12/20 Au Turbotin
9, rue de la Massue — 27.87.04.16
M. Mené. Closed Mon, dinner Sun and holidays, Feb school holidays and Aug. Open until 10 pm. Private room: 18. V AE DC.

The dining rooms have high ceilings and tastefully laid tables, although the reception lacks charm. The owner's cooking is generally dextrous but he needs to work on presentation and blending flavours. Good chicken liver terrine, not-so-hot curried mussel casserole, and delicious baked sole with basil and tomato coulis.

A la carte: 300-400 F. Menus: 85 F (weekdays only), 135 F, 165 F, 250 F.

In nearby Corbehem
(5 km S on N 50 and D 45))
62112 Douai — (Nord)

12/20 Manoir de Fourcy
48, rue de la Gare — 27.96.44.90
M. Barbier. Closed Sun dinner. Open until 10 pm. Private room: 180. Garden dining. Parking. V.

This newcomer is worth noting. The warm fondant de foie gras with lentils, and lotte with braised leeks are interesting, but don't fulfil their promise. Prices are steep.

A la carte: 300-320 F. Menus: 430 F (wine inc), 130 F, 180 F, 230 F.

▲▲ Manoir de Fourcy
(See restaurant above)
Open every day. 8 rms 290-380 F. TV. Conference facilities.

Peacefully located in a hectare of grounds, with well-equipped rooms.

DOUAINS
See Pacy-sur-Eure

▲▲ Hostellerie Blanche de Castille
(See restaurant above)
Open every day. 1 ste 590 F. 40 rms 330-480 F. TV. Conference facilities.

Near the forests of Dourdan and Rambouillet, this inn is set in the heart of the old town. Garden and pleasant rooms.

DOUVRES-LA-DÉLIVRANDE
14440 Douvres-la-Délivrande — (Calvados)
Paris 250 - Caen 13 - Bayeux 27 - St-Aubin-sur-Mer 5

12/20 Auberge du Relais
11, rte de Caen — 31.37.29.82
M. Berthault and Mme Richard. Closed Sun dinner and Mon. Annual closings not available. Open until 9.30 pm. V.

Martine Richard's cooking is simple and generous: vanilla-flavoured salmon escalope, confit d'oie normande with cabbage, and chocolate cake. Her partner, Vincent Berthault, is a charming host.

A la carte: 250 F. Menus: 75 F, 140 F, 170 F.

DRAGUIGNAN
83300 Draguignan — (Var)
Paris 876 - Aix-en-Provence 106 - Toulon 81

▲▲ Col de l'Ange
3 km on D 557, rte de Lorgues — 94.68.23.01
Open every day. 30 rms 299-351 F. Restaurant. Half-board 320 F. TV. Conference facilities. Pool. Parking. Telex 970423. V AE DC.

Exceptionally situated between the sea and the mountains and surrounded by greenery, this modern hotel looks out over the town. Large rooms, all with terrace. The grill house by the pool is a pleasant spot in summer.

12/20 Lou Galoubet
23, bd J.-Jaurès — 94.68.08.50
Mme Michel. Closed dinner Sun and Mon, and 25 July-5 Sep. Open until 10 pm. V AE.

The seafood here is so fresh you'll forget the seriously outdated red leatherette seating and forgive the heavy chive cream sauce served with the oysters. The town's favourite fish restaurant.

A la carte: 300 F. Menu: 98 F (weekdays only).

Restaurant Arménien Ohaness
15, av. du Mal-Juin — 94.47.18.88
Mlle Ohanessian. Closed Mon. Open until 9.30 pm. Pets allowed.

Brigitte Ohanessian offers a varying selection of mezes (easier to eat than to translate!) after her daily trip to market: soudjouk, tarama, stuffed mussels, lentil kefté, cheese- and meat-filled pastries. The appropriate drink is raki, but if you don't like the taste of aniseed you could choose a Lebanese or Cypriot wine.

Menu: 130 F.

▲ Hostellerie du Moulin de la Foux
Quartier de la Foux — 94.68.55.33
Open every day. 29 rms 240 F. Half-board 315 F. Restaurant. TV. Conference facilities.

Excellent little inn with neat, functional rooms overlooking the terrace and trees. Prices are reasonable and service, led by the *patronne*, pleasant.

⌂ Le Victoria
52-54, bd Carnot — 94.47.24.12
M. Lucisano. Open every day. Open until 9 pm. Private room: 25. Garden dining. Air cond. No-smoking section. Parking. V.

The young chef demonstrates a light, modern touch throughout the three intelligently composed set menus. Try the scallop mousseline, sole in a port-flavoured sauce, and medallions of veal with orange and lime. The desserts lack originality, but the service in this brand-new décor is remarkable.

Menus: 85 F, 135 F, 220 F.

▲▲ Victoria Hotel
(See restaurant above)
Open every day. 2 stes 800-1,500 F. 22 rms 220-400 F. Half-board 280 F oblig in seas. TV. Air cond. Conference facilities.

This big, turn-of-the-century hotel has been entirely renovated. The rooms are spacious, soundproofed, and well equipped (18 television channels). Extremely pleasant reception.

28100 Dreux — (Eure-et-Loir)
Paris 84 - Chartres 35 - Verneuil 34 - Rouen 97

 Le Beffroi
12, pl. Métézeau — 37.50.02.03
Open every day. 16 rms 247-348 F. TV 10 rms. V AE DC.
By the river and opposite the thirteenth-century St Pierre church, this hotel has comfortable, well-kept rooms, all of them modernised.

In nearby Montreuil

(4.5 km N on D 928 and D 116)
28500 Dreux — (Eure-et-Loir)

 Auberge du Gué des Grues
Le Gué des Grues — 37.43.50.25
M. Caillault. Dinner upon reserv. Closed Mon dinner and Tue. Private room: 20. Terrace dining. Parking. V AE DC.
Don't all rush to this cosy establishment expecting adventurous cooking, or even something different from your last visit. Robert Caillaul knows nothing but consistency and conscientiousness—a style well suited to the relaxing floral décor. We enjoyed asparagus and fresh truffle salad, red-mullet fillets with coral butter, and fricassée d'escargots aux chanterelles.
A la carte: 350 F. Menus: 150 F, 230 F.

In nearby Ste-Gemme-Moronval

(3 km E)
28500 Dreux — (Eure-et-Loir)

L'Escapade
37.43.72.05
M. Aubry. Closed dinner Sun and Tue, 7 Feb-1 March and 18 July-1 Aug. Open until 9.15 pm. Private room: 20. Telex 760189. V AE.
The customer is someone special for Lucia and Paolo Gomez, and their staff will attend to your every need. The cooking won't dazzle with its novelty, but you'll appreciate the excellent shellfish, seafood blanquette, and smoked Barbary duck with green cabbage.
A la carte: 300-350 F. Menu: 150 F.

DUNKERQUE

59140 Dunkerque — (Nord)
Paris 292 - Amiens 144 - Lille 73 - Calais 40

Altea
Tour du Reuze, rue J.-Jaurès — 28.59.11.11
Open every day. 2 stes 700 F. 122 rms 315-575 F. TV. Conference facilities. Parking. Telex 110587. V AE DC.
These rooms, located on the twelfth through twentieth floors of a well-situated building, provide fantastic view of the harbour, out to sea and the Plaine de Flandres. They are comfortable and practical; half of them were redecorated last year. The service is excellent, and the hotel can accommodate seminars; it boasts fully equipped offices for business meetings. This is by far the best hotel in the region. New restaurant and bar on the ground floor.

12/20 Au Bon Coin
49, av. Kléber, in Malo-les-Bains
59240 Dunkerque — 28.69.12.63
M. Loywyck. Closed 23 Dec-4 Jan. Open until 10 pm. Air cond. Hotel: 4 rms 160-210 F. V AE DC.
Mundane brasserie décor is the backdrop to fresh seafood dishes and a wide choice of shellfish. The day's catch is best served simply grilled. Good selection of white wines.
A la carte: 250-300 F. Menu: 60 F (weekdays only).

 Borel
6, rue l'Hermitte — 28.66.51.80
Open every day. 48 rms 280-330 F. TV. Telex 820050. V AE DC.
Some rooms in this excellent little hotel overlook the harbour, but all of them are large, clean, and bright. Extra pleasant service and reception.

12/20 L'Islandais
46, rue Belle-Vue — 28.63.37.05
M. Van-Autryve. Closed Sun and 14 July-15 Aug. Open until 10 pm. Private room: 10. V AE.
Regular customers rarely look at the menu. They trust Bernard Van-Autryve, known as the Icelander, to recommend the best and freshest fish, which he cooks to order: North Sea cod with aïoli (garlic mayonnaise), grilled sole with pasta, potjevfleisch.
A la carte: 250-280 F. Menus: 90 F (dinner only), 120 F and 150 F (wine inc).

12/20 Le Mareyeur
83, rue H.-Terquem — 28.66.29.07
M. Rougeaux. Closed Sun dinner and Mon. Open until 11 pm. Private room: 300. Air cond. No pets. Hotel: 4 stes 363-424 F. 124 rms 264-336 F. Garage parking. Telex 120084. V AE DC.
This hotel-restaurant with its bright, elegant décor serves classically prepared fresh seafood like bouillabaisse, waterzoï, poached or grilled turbot, and sole fillets with a shallot cream sauce. Good, reasonably priced oysters, an honest set menu, and well-chosen white wines. There's also a brasserie.
A la carte: 300 F. Menu: 110 F.

12/20 Le Métropole
28, rue Thiers — 28.66.85.01
M. Bisiaux. Closed 15 July-10 Aug. Open until 10 pm. Private room: 25. V AE.
New décor awaits the faithful business clientele, who need no convincing about the quality of the cuisine. The salmon and asparagus gratin, sweetbreads with cider and green apples, and fillet of beef served with a ragoût d'escargots come in generous portions.
A la carte: 250 F. Menus: 75 F (weekdays only, wine inc), 175 F (wine inc), 100 F, 135 F.

12/20 Le Soubise
49, rte de Bergues
59210 Coudekerque-Branche — 28.64.66.00
M. Hazebroucq. Closed Sat lunch and Sun dinner. Open until 10 pm. Private room: 40. Parking. V AE DC.
This former farm and coaching inn, dating from 1761, stands opposite a 30-hectare public garden. The chef, who uses first-class ingredients, has updated his menu. Try the fine smoked salmon and pot-roasted baby pigeon.
A la carte: 280 F. Menus: from 95 F to 240 F.

Welcome Hotel
37, rue Poincaré — 28.59.20.70
Open every day. 40 rms 302-352 F. Restaurant. TV. Garage parking. Telex 132263. V DC.
This new hotel in the town centre has small, well-designed rooms.

In nearby **Bergues**

(8 km S on D 916)
59380 Dunkerque – (Nord)

13 **Au Cornet d'Or**
26, rue Espagnole – 28.68.66.27
M. Tasserit. Closed Sun dinner, Mon and mid-June to mid-July. Open until 9.45 pm. Private room: 25. Parking. V.
Last year's couscous with sole has been replaced by couscous with prawns, but elsewhere on the menu Jean-Claude Tasserit shows greater inventiveness. We appreciate his efforts to update classic recipes such as rabbit compote, or salmon rolls with shrimps. You might also like to sample young partridge pot-au-feu, the good local cheeses, and the chicory-flavoured vacherin. The service could be more spirited and the atmosphere cosier in the opulent, beamed dining room.
A la carte: 300 F. Menus: 165 F, 210 F, 265 F.

Mercure
in Armbouts-Cappel
Bordure du Lac – 28.60.70.60
Open every day. 64 rms 195-410 F. Restaurant. TV. Conference facilities. Heated pool. Parking. Telex 820916. V AE DC.
The lake view will help you forget the industrial surroundings of this comfortable, modern establishment just off the motorway.

In nearby **Teteghem**

(3 km SE on D 4)
59229 Dunkerque – (Nord)

16 **La Meunerie**
174, rue des Pierres – 28.26.14.30
M. Delbé. Closed Sun dinner, Mon and 23 Dec-20 Jan. Open until 9.30 pm. Private room: 25. Air cond. Valet parking. Telex 132253. V.
This carefully restored mill embodies a certain idea of style, from the statues in the garden to the carefully arranged vegetables on your plate. Well looked after by the attentive staff, you'll feel you have come much further from the smoke and bustle of Dunkirk. The quality of the cooking hasn't changed since our last visit. You can expect the same top-quality ingredients—the best fish on the coast, excellent roast Challans duck, and rich, classic sauces, for Jean-Pierre Delbé is first and foremost an expert sauce chef. His filet de bar au jus de truffe, young guinea fowl with broad beans, tasty sweetbreads in port sauce, and beef with morels are more noteworthy for their careful preparation than their originality. The desserts, on the other hand, are as creative as they are skilfully cooked. We almost awarded a third toque this year. With more than 500 wines from all parts of France and even abroad, you should find a bottle to suit your taste. Just ten kilometres from Belgium, La Meunerie is popular with customers from across the border who find it a fine example of *la cuisine française*. And the bill provides a high point in this lowland region!
A la carte: 500 F and up. Menus: 220 F, 350 F, 450 F.

La Meunerie
(See restaurant above)
Closed 23 Dec-20 Jan. 1 ste 1,250 F. 8 rms 450-750 F. TV. Conference facilities.
In the heart of peaceful countryside, this charming hotel has just nine rooms overlooking the courtyard garden—so remember to book. Each is decorated in a different style but all share the same comfort and amenities.

DURTOL
See Clermont-Ferrand

DURY-LÈS-AMIENS
See Amiens

ECHETS (LES)
01700 Echets (Les) – (Ain)
Paris 445 - Bourg-en-Bresse 45 - Lyon 16

14 **Douillé**
983, rte de Strasbourg – 78.91.80.05
M. Douillé. Closed Mon dinner, Tue, Feb school holidays and 5-28 Aug. Open until 9.30 pm. Private room: 80. Garden dining. Hotel: 8 rms 260-320 F. Garage parking. V.
You might not be tempted to stop off at this restaurant with its huge sign, but you'd be wrong. Roger Douillé's cooking is as light and generous as it was when he started here in 1959. The salad of sweetbreads and warm foie gras, and poached pigeon with tender young vegetables may not be the most original of dishes, but they are beyond reproach. Brigitte, the daughter of the house, is in charge of the fine wines. Prices shot up last year but seem to have stabilised since.
A la carte: 350-400 F. Menus: 160 F, 210 F, 300 F.

14 **Marguin**
916, rte de Strasbourg – 78.91.80.04
M. Marguin. Closed 3-19 Jan and 3-14 Sep. Open until 9.30 pm. Private room: 30. Terrace dining. Hotel: 9 rms 145-310 F. Garage parking. V AE DC.
If it were up to them, the Marguins would take a break from investing in new technology, and be content to keep their country restaurant just outside Lyon ticking over comfortably. But then there's their son Christophe, who is learning the trade with the best chefs and hopes to inherit a top establishment. So Jacky Marguin continues his efforts in the kitchen, producing original tomates farcies aux grenouilles, superb grilled saddle of lamb accompanied by a macaroni gratin with truffle juice and foie gras (not for dieters), and steamed Norwegian salmon with a lentil purée. Accomplished reception and service by Adrienne Marguin add to the pleasure of your visit, as do the excellent Burgundies and Bordeaux. The bill can sting a bit.
A la carte: 350 F. Menus: 150 F, 195 F, 295 F.

ECOLE-VALENTIN
See Besançon

ECRENNES (LES)
77820 Ecrennes (Les) – (Seine/Marne)
Paris 70 - Melun 15 - Fontainebleau 20 - Nangis 14

14 **Auberge Briarde**
60.69.47.32
M. Guichard. Closed Mon, dinner Sun and Wed, 15 days in Feb and 3 weeks in Aug. Open until 9.30 pm. V AE DC.
Since he took over this rustic yet refined restaurant, Jean-Alain Guichard's cooking has been improving steadily. Our latest visit turned up an original sweetbread and lobster soup with a light pastry crust, excellent breast of duck accompanied by a purée of split peas, and wonderful turbot à l'oseille. With the region's best cheeses and delightful desserts to follow, the meal deserved another point. Monique Guichard makes sure the service runs smoothly. Good wines.
A la carte: 350 F. Menus: 190 F (weekdays only), 255 F, 330 F, 385 F.

EGUISHEIM

See Colmar

ELBEUF

76500 Elbeuf — (Seine-Mar.)
Paris 125 - Le Havre 82 - Rouen 20 - Louviers 15

11/20 Naudin
1, rue du Mal-Gallieni — 35.77.06.94
M. Dubois. Closed Sat dinner, Sun and 5-31 Aug. Open until 8.45 pm. Private room: 15. Air cond. Hotel: 3 rms 80-110 F. V.

Simple cuisine at humble prices: stuffed mussels, filets de sole d'Antin, veal cutlet, and strawberry tart.

A la carte: 160 F.

ELINCOURT-STE-MARGUERITE

See Compiègne

ENGHIEN

See PARIS Suburbs

ENTRECHAUX

See Vaison-la-Romaine

EPERNAY

51200 Epernay — (Marne)
Paris 140 - Châlons-sur-Marne 32 - Reims 27

Les Berceaux
13, rue des Berceaux — 26.55.28.84
M. Maillard. Closed Sun dinner. Open until 9.30 pm. Private room: 30. Hotel: 29 rms 310-400 F. Telex 842717. V AE DC.

This century-old coach house is both a restaurant and wine bar, offering a large selection of magnificent wines, some by the glass. The décor is pleasantly rustic, the reception cool, and Luc Maillard's cooking rich and rather complicated: cassolette d'escargots au champagne, sole soufflé, and game dishes. Splendid cellar.

A la carte: 300-400 F. Menus: 160 F, 200 F, 320 F.

Champagne
30, rue E.-Mercier — 26.55.30.22
Open every day. 32 rms 235-250 F. TV. Conference facilities. Garage parking. Telex 842068. V AE DC.

Modern little hotel with bright, practical rooms and buffet breakfasts.

In nearby Champillon

(5 km N on N 51)
51160 Epernay — (Marne)

Royal Champagne
26.52.87.11
M. Dellinger. Closed 2-24 Jan. Open until 9.30 pm. Private room: 50. Garage parking. Telex 830111. V AE DC.

Marc Dach's impressive collection of Champagne is one of the many charms of this former post house. His cooking is back on form this year, as befits a chef who has worked with Michel Guérard and Gérard Boyer. The spicy sautéed prawns and apple crisps, sea bream with thyme and chilli sauce, and the basil-scented poached fillet of veal show what he can accomplish when he tries.

A la carte: 450-550 F. Menus: 230 F (lunch only), 370 F (dinner only), 310 F.

Royal Champagne
(See restaurant above)
Closed 2-24 Jan. 1 ste 1,500 F. 24 rms 580-1,100 F. TV. Conference facilities.

Charming, ultra-comfortable bungalows offer a splendid view of the hillside vineyards and the Marne Valley. Relais et Châteaux.

In nearby Vinay

(7 km S on N 51)
51200 Epernay — (Marne)

La Briqueterie
4, rte de Sézanne — 26.59.99.99.
M. Guillon. Closed at Christmas. Open until 9.30 pm. Private room: 40. Garage parking. Telex 842007. V AE DC.

Four months of work and a major investment have restored this inn to its former charm. The dining room still has its beams and huge fireplace, but fresh new décor echoes Lieven Vercouteren's enthusiastic cooking. Always in search of new ideas, he came up with lamb's brains enlivened by a sharp vinaigrette, young rabbit and chanterelles in a crêpe parcel topped with crispy prawns, and a splendid Paris-Brest (choux pastry ring with cream and almonds) during our recent visit, persuading us to award an extra point and a second toque. Remarkable selection of Champagnes and Burgundies, and professional service.

A la carte: 400 F. Menus: 165 F (weekdays lunch only), 290 F (Sun and holidays lunch only), 350 F and 380 F.

La Briqueterie
(See restaurant above)
Closed at Christmas. 2 stes 1,370 F. 40 rms 710-820 F. TV. Conference facilities. Heated pool.

This handsome, entirely renovated house, now with an additional wing, offers quiet, spacious rooms with deep-pile carpeting and bathrooms in pale marble. Buffet breakfasts are served in the new dining room opening onto the garden. Smiling service.

EPINAL

88000 Epinal — (Vosges)
Paris 365 - Nancy 69 - Colmar 92 - Vesoul 82

Les Abbesses
(Jean-Claude Aiguier)
23, rue de la Louvière — 29.82.53.69
M. Aiguier. Closed Sun dinner and Mon. Open until 9.30 pm. Private room: 40. Garden dining. V AE.

Everyone loves the story of the chef who gets up at the crack of dawn to go to market. Jean-Claude Aiguier is one such—and he drives from Epinal to Strasbourg (about 100 kilometres) to select top-quality oysters, glistening tender prawns, and the ingredients for his excellent all-lobster menu. If you're really ravenous and the sugar-pink curtains haven't spoiled your appetite, try the *menu dégustation* which offers Marennes oysters with vegetable purée, a warm salad of lobster and leek with truffles, red mullet cooked in Graves and accompanied by excellent pommes dauphine, bone marrow, and coarse salt, and buttery prawns in puff pastry served with fresh asparagus and morels. The rest of the meal is less good: fatty and bland stuffed cabbage with smoked goose foie gras, quail with chanterelles on a dry potato pancake. The three cheeses accompanied by three wines are just too much to follow all that, not to mention the crème brûlée with hazelnuts. Our basic objection to Jean-Claude Aiguier's cooking is that he offers too much; while others often charge more for tiny portions. The service is satisfactory in general, but the 1985 Riesling de Lorentz suggested to accompany the whole meal was not robust enough for some of the dishes. Inconsistent reception by Francine Aiguier, who seems to give regular customers more attention.

A la carte: 400 F. Menus: 220 F, 260 F, 320 F, 360 F.

Les Ducs de Lorraine
16, quai du Col.-Sérot – 29.34.39.87
M. Obriot. Closed 5-12 March and 12 Aug-1 Sep. Open until 9.30 pm. Air cond. V.
Forgotten herbs, surprising, tantalising tastes, and colourful vegetables have been making their appearance in Claudy Obriot's cooking lately. His quest for perfection is backed up by sound technique and reflected in the comfortable dining room with bay windows overlooking the River Moselle and in the smooth service supervised by Agnès Obriot. The foie gras en gelée de poivre served with a compote of honey and sherry-flavoured prunes, rosemary-scented salmon, smoked trout tart with celery, braised sweetbreads topped with a potato crust, and mirabelle plum soufflé are unforgettable. Thoroughly justified prices.

A la carte: 350 F. Menus: 175 F, 260 F, 330 F.

Mercure
13, pl. E.-Stein – 29.35.18.68
Open every day. 2 stes 400-600 F. 46 rms 280-440 F. Restaurant. Half-board 405-475 F. TV. Conference facilities. Garage parking. Telex 960277. V AE DC.
A newly renovated building with spacious, comfortable rooms. The reception is excellent.

EPINE (L')

See Châlons-sur-Marne

ERBALUNGA

See CORSICA: Bastia

ERDEVEN

56410 Erdeven – (Morbihan)
Paris 490 - Lorient 28 - Carnac 9 - Quiberon 21

Château de Kéravéon
1.8 km NE on D 105
97.55.68.55
Closed Mon off-season and 15 Sep-1 May. 19 rms 660-770 F. Restaurant. Half-board 550-620 F oblig in seas. Conference facilities. Pool. Parking. V AE DC.
This huge, handsome residence dating from the sixteenth and eighteenth centuries has a moat, keep, and dovecote. The spacious rooms are thoughtfully decorated. Four kilometres away is the St Laurent international golf course.

ERNÉE

53500 Ernée – (Mayenne)
Paris 300 - Laval 30 - Mayenne 24 - Fougères 20

Le Grand Cerf
17-19, rue A.-Briand – 43.05.13.09
Mme Sémerie. Closed off-season Sun dinner and Mon, and 15-31 Jan. Open until 9 pm. Private room: 60. Air cond. Valet parking. Telex 723412. V.
Brothers Hugues and Laurent Sémerie, who share the cooking with obvious enthusiasm and increasing confidence, deserve your encouragement. Fresh, seasonal dishes make up a menu that relies more on good ideas than luxury ingredients. Try the tunny tartare with sesame seeds, iced shellfish soup with mint, grilled carp with asparagus, and tender lamb with fresh broad beans. Attractive décor and a delightful garden.

A la carte: 200-230 F. Menus: 68 F (weekdays only), 98 F, 139 F, 210 F.

Le Grand Cerf
(See restaurant above)
Closed off-season Sun and Mon, and 15-31 Jan. 8 rms 169-209 F. TV. No pets. Conference facilities.
An abundance of flowers and smiling service add to the pleasure of a stay in this well-modernised hotel.

ERQUY

22430 Erquy – (Côtes/Armor)
Paris 450 - Dinan 47 - Dinard 40 - St-Brieuc 35

Le Brigantin
Sq. de l'Hôtel-de-Ville – 96.72.32.14
Open every day. 22 rms 130-260 F. Restaurant. Half-board 220-240 F. TV 8 rms. Conference facilities. Heated pool. V AE.
Just 200 metres from the beach, this hotel makes a good base for fishing trips. Pleasant, well-kept rooms.

L'Escurial
Bd de la Mer – 96.72.31.56
M. Bernard. Closed Tue dinner and Wed (except July-Aug), Feb school holidays and 30 Sep-17 Oct. Open until 9.30 pm. V AE DC.
The comfortable dining room overlooks the harbour and bay. In the kitchen, Véronique Bernard's search for new flavours sometimes results in dishes that don't quite work, like the nonetheless interesting brill with seaweed containing too much seaweed and a bit too much pepper. Sometimes, however, she succeeds admirably, as with the wonderful lightly poached scallops, tasty baked lotte with garlic-flavoured ormers (a highly prized shellfish), and scallop and prawn fricassée with crabmeat marred only by a slightly over-rich sauce. The wine list is short but varied, offering Graves, Listrac, and Loire wines at affordable prices. Friendly reception by the *patron*, who won't mind chatting while you wait, sometimes too long, for your food.

A la carte: 280 F. Menus: 350 F (wine inc), 110 F, 180 F, 250 F.

LES ESCALDES

See Andorre (Principauté d')

ESCRINET (COL DE L')

07200 Escrinet (Col de l') – (Ardèche)
Paris 615 - Aubenas 17 - Privas 13 - Montélimar 60

12/20 Col de l'Escrinet
(Le Panoramic Escrinet)
75.87.10.11
M. Rojon. Closed Sun dinner and Mon lunch off-season, and 16 Nov-15 March. Open until 9 pm. Private room: 35. No pets. Hotel: 3 stes 420 F. 17 rms 250-300 F. Heated pool. Garage parking. V AE DC.
You can admire magnificent views from the newly decorated dining room. The *carte* is divided into two sections: one featuring classic dishes, the other more adventurous fare. All are carefully prepared: try the traditional caillette (a pork and green vegetable sausage) or the unusual queue de lotte au safran. The small cellar has a few good Côtes-du-Rhônes. Hesitant reception and service.

A la carte: 250 F. Menus: 100 F, 160 F, 200 F.

ESCURES

See Port-en-Bessin

ESPALION

12500 Espalion — (Aveyron)
Paris 583 - Figeac 94 - Millau 79 - Aurillac 76

 L'Eau Vive
(Hôtel Moderne)
27, bd de Guizard — 65.44.05.11
M. Raulhac. Closed Sun dinner and Mon (except July-Aug), and 10 Nov-10 Dec. Open until 9.30 pm. Hotel: 28 rms 190-300 F. Garage parking. V.
The Raulhacs, a father-and-son-team, take care to pamper their guests. Should you happen to be a fishermen, they will be happy to show you their favourite fishing spots, but everyone benefits from their passion for freshwater specialities like fried baby trout, freshwater perch salads, and crayfish tartlets. Excellent local cheeses and homemade desserts complete the pleasure of a meal in this really warm, friendly restaurant.
A la carte: 200-220 F. Menus: 300 F (w-e and holidays only), 90 F, 150 F, 250 F.

 Le Méjane
near the old bridge
8, rue Méjane — 65.48.22.37
M. Caralp. Closed Sun dinner, Wed (except Aug), 14 Jan-14 Feb, 24-30 June. Open until 9 pm. V AE..
The Caralps' plans to move to a new restaurant have fallen through for the moment so they're making do with the tired décor here. But don't worry—Philippe Caralp's cooking is as vivacious as ever, and you'll be enchanted by imaginative dishes like smoked salmon with sliced avocado and beetroot mousse, scallop 'sausage' with herb butter, and ham-flavoured baked salmon. Prices have gone up slightly, but are still incredibly cheap.
A la carte: 220 F. Menus: 70 F (weekdays lunch only), 90 F, 150 F, 210 F.

In nearby **Bozouls**

(11 km S on D 920)
12340 Espalion — (Aveyron)

 Le Belvédère
65.44.92.66
Closed Sat, Sun and 24 Dec-15 Jan. 11 rms 160-230 F. Restaurant. Half-board 180-200 F oblig in seas. TV. V AE.
Admire the famous 'Trou de Bozouls', a deep gorge, from this pleasant traditional hotel that has recently been modernised.

ESPELETTE

64250 Espelette — (Pyrénées-A.)
Paris 761 - Bayonne 22 - St-Jean-de-Luz 25

 Euzkadi   ♥
Rue Principale — 59.93.91.88
M. Darraidou. Closed Tue off-season, Mon, 15-25 Feb and 15 Nov-15 Dec. Open until 9 pm. Private room: 25. Hotel: 32 rms 160-200 F. Pool. V.
Here in the mountains where wild horses roam and sweet peppers grow, you can immerse yourself in Basque tradition, food, and song. A wide selection of regional specialities is available in the huge dining room: axoa (veal with chilli peppers), ttoro (fish soup), tripoxa (a mutton and veal sausage). Not to mention a salade gourmande au foie gras, superb breast of duck, and good Basque cake which merit another point. Jocular service and rock-bottom prices.
A la carte: 170 F. Menus: 75 F, 110 F, 130 F, 160 F.

ETAMPES

91150 Etampes — (Essonne)
Paris 49 - Orléans 66 - Melun 47 - Versailles 54

12/20 Auberge de Courpain
7 km S, at Court-Pain
in Fontaine-la-Rivière
91690 Saclas — 64.95.67.04
Mlle Tewe. Open every day. Open until 9.45 pm. Private room: 80. Garden dining. Parking. V AE DC.
This ivy-covered former post house stands amid cornfields in the Beauce region. Fine but pricey cuisine, served in a darkish neo-rustic dining room and veranda: lobster salad (with more shrimp than lobster but flavourful nonetheless), good lotte fillets with slightly tough leeks, and a delicious caramelised pear tart. More than enough staff, all very competent.
A la carte: 350 F. Menus: 125 F (weekdays only), 170 F.

 Auberge de Courpain
(See restaurant above)
Open every day. 3 stes 400-550 F. 17 rms 220-300 F. Half-board 480-550 F. TV 3 rms. Conference facilities.
Ten minutes from Etampes and surrounded by green countryside, this inn has comfortable, attractively furnished rooms.

In nearby **Morigny**

(3 km N)
91150 Etampes — (Essonne)

 Hostellerie de Villemartin   🌲🌳
4, allée des Marronniers — 64.94.63.54
Closed Sun, Mon (except holidays) and 29 July-27 Aug. 14 rms 260-390 F. Restaurant. TV. Conference facilities. Tennis. Parking. V AE DC.
A truly lovely estate in wooded grounds by the River Juine. The rooms are immaculate, with classic décor and superb views. Polite, helpful staff.

ETRÉAUPONT

02580 Etréaupont — (Aisne)
Paris 182 - Laon 44 - St-Quentin 51 - Hirson 15

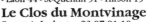 **Le Clos du Montvinage**   🌲🌳
8, rue A.-Ledent — 23.97.91.10
Closed Sun, 16-30 Aug and 22-27 Dec. 20 rms 195-380 F. Restaurant. Half-board 350-500 F. TV. Air cond. No pets. Conference facilities. Tennis. Garage parking. Telex 150529. V AE DC.
This beautiful nineteenth-century residence has comfortable rooms with Louis-Philippe furniture. Bar.

ETRETAT

76790 Etretat — (Seine-Mar.)
Paris 220 - Le Havre 28 - Rouen 86 - Fécamp 17

11/20 Le Belvédère
Falaise d'Antifer, 11 km S
76280 St-Jouin-Bruneval — 35.20.13.76
Mme Cabillic. Closed Sun dinner, Mon and 30 Dec-27 Jan. Open until 8.30 pm (9.30 pm in summer). V.
You can order excellent prawns, crabs and whelks with mayonnaise while watching the supertankers in the bay below. The fish dishes are generally overcooked.
A la carte: 200 F. Menus: 70 F, 115 F, 155 F.

12/20 Le Donjon
Ch. de St-Clair
35.27.08.23
M. Abo-Dib. Open every day. Open until 10 pm. Private room: 60. Garden dining. Parking. V AE DC.
In this ivy-covered manor, Claire Baudouin prepares honest dishes with a marked preference for seafood and especially oysters, which she serves six different ways. Stiffish steep prices.
A la carte: 350 F. Menus: from 95 F to 260 F.

Le Donjon
(See restaurant above)
Closings not available. 8 rms 500-800 F (per pers, half-board oblig). TV. Conference facilities. Pool.
Major renovations have added greatly to the comfort of this hotel overlooking the sea and cliffs.

Dormy-House
Route du Havre
35.27.07.88
Closed 29 Oct-Easter. 94 rms 350-510 F. Restaurant. Half-board 450-575 F. TV. Conference facilities. Heated pool. Parking. V.
An extension is being built at this very well run hotel. A few rooms offer an exceptional view of the cliffs.

EU
76260 Eu — (Seine-Mar.)
Paris 167 - Dieppe 31 - Abbeville 32 - Le Tréport 5

12/20 La Gare
20, av. de la Gare
35.86.16.64
M. Maine. Closed Sun dinner. Open until 10 pm. Terrace dining. Parking. V AE.
In these well-lit, elegantly decorated rooms you will find prettily laid tables and classic, deftly-prepared dishes. High points include the Roquefort terrine, noisettes of lamb larded with ham, the excellent fillet of beef, and the chocolate and orange meringue cake.
A la carte: 200-250 F. Menus: 75 F (weekdays only), 90 F, 150 F.

La Gare
(See restaurant above)
Closed Sun. 22 rms 195-250 F. Half-board 280-310 F oblig in seas. TV. Pets allowed.
A nineteenth-century hotel with very comfortable rooms, overlooking a quiet square.

12/20 Le Moulin du Becquerel
8 km S on D 1314 and D 258
in St-Martin-le-Gaillard — 35.86.74.94
M. Tessal. Closed Mon and Feb. Open until 9 pm. Private room: 80. Garden dining. V.
The fifteen-hectare grounds surrounding this delightful Norman house include the vegetable and herb garden which supplies the kitchen. Ask to be seated in the first and much more attractive dining room, and order the skewered snails and smoked salmon with saffron sauce, the turbot fillet with leeks and truffle juice, and the good apple tart.
A la carte: 250-280 F. Menu: 160 F.

Pavillon Joinville
Rte du Tréport — 35.86.24.03
Open every day. 2 stes 660-790 F. 24 rms 340-660 F. Restaurant. Half-board 340-475 F oblig in seas. TV. Conference facilities. Heated pool. Tennis. Parking. Telex 172151. V AE DC.
This used to be Louis-Philippe's hunting lodge. The perfectly comfortable rooms evoke a grander

era, and look out over the superb grounds. Good breakfasts, but the welcome could be warmer. Fitness centre.

EUGÉNIE-LES-BAINS
40320 Eugénie-les-Bains — (Landes)
Paris 726 - Pau 53 - Mont-de-Marsan 25 - Dax 69

Michel Guérard
58.51.19.50
19.5 *M. Guérard. Closed 2 Dec-14 Feb. Open until 10 pm. Private room: 12. No pets. Valet parking. Telex 540470. V AE DC.*
The passing years have left no trace on the Michel Guérard miracle. His undertaking is enormous: the hotel, the annexes, the restaurant, the spa, the slimming cures—yet all are continually improving and evolving. The man behind the miracle also seems to be ageless. Twenty years after setting up in this tiny village to which the whole world now beats a path, Guérard has earned the right to a short rest. But no, new projects unfold, new enthusiasm surfaces, and the intense creativity of this modest individual continues to find form.
And, most surprisingly, he continues to produce fresh, spontaneous cooking year after year, firmly rooted in the Landes region but taking flight on the wings of imagination. We can still taste the flavours of farm and garden in the game pâté in a golden crust, the cream of green vegetables with a hot sheep cheese soufflé, the featherlight pastries filled with meadow and morels as well as truffles, the astonishing mixed salad with grilled prawns and foie gras, the ragoût of wild mushrooms and small scallops, and the light and subtle (believe it or not) duck, quail, and foie gras pie. There's pleasure just in reciting the litany of dishes, which must also include the young rabbit in claret aspic, hachis Parmentier of goose and sweetbreads with truffles, and especially the lobster à l'américaine so exquisitely refined we may soon be wondering if it wasn't Guérard who invented the dish. On the dessert menu, good old-fashioned pain perdu rubs shoulders with newer entries like the crunchy croque-miettes aux pommes. The wine list ranges from the finest Bordeaux to a full-flavoured Jurançon, and now features the wonderful white Tursan 'Baron de Bachen' from the Guérards' own vineyards. The restaurant is also a feast for the eyes with its old paintings, gleaming silver, and the uniforms of the serving staff which change every year.
A la carte: 480-700 F. Menus: 390 F, 550 F.

Les Prés d'Eugénie
(See restaurant above)
Closed 2 Dec-14 Feb. 9 stes 1,564 1,679 F. 34 rms 900-1,380 F. TV. No pets. Conference facilities. Heated pool. Tennis.
The latest and most breathtaking addition to this fairyland of quiet taste and luxury is the eighteenth-century Couvent des Herbes, which has been restored with refined taste. It contains eight enormous rooms opening onto the grounds of the herb garden. There's already a long waiting list.... Work is continuing on even more luxurious spa facilities which will be for the exclusive use of guests of Les Prés d'Eugénie. At the other end of the grounds the Résidence Maison Rose has been redecorated and still offers excellent value (especially the seven-day package deal that includes a slimming cure and a gala dinner chez Michel Guérard). Other amenities include a beauty salon, sauna, and cookery school. Relais et Châteaux.

EVIAN

74500 Evian — (H.-Savoie)
Paris 589 - Annecy 81 - Genève 42 - Montreux 38

Les Prés Fleuris
in St-Paul — 50.75.29.14

*M. Frossard. Closed beg Oct-beg May. Open until
8.30 pm. Private room: 10. Garden dining. No pets.
Parking. Telex 309545. V AE.*

A fairytale view over Lake Geneva with mountain
pastures in the foreground is not the main attraction: that honour falls to Roger Frossard's
reassuringly changeless ability to choose only perfect ingredients and prepare them with a pure
classicism that never palls. Taste for example the
fricassée of meadow mushrooms, lake fish
meunière, trout in butter sauce, and the chicken
with tarragon—which are much more palatable
than the bill.
A la carte: 400-500 F. Menus: 220 F, 280 F, 350 F.

Les Prés Fleuris
(See restaurant above)

*Closed beg Oct-beg May. 5 stes 1,300 F. 12 rms 800-
1,200 F. Half-board 750-1,000 F oblig in seas. TV.
Pets allowed.*

A delightfully relaxed atmosphere pervades the
quiet, huge, comfortable rooms of this hotel perched high above Lake Geneva. Relais et Châteaux.

Royal Club Evian
(Casino Royal)
South shore of lake Geneva — 50.75.03.78

*M. Novatin. Open every day. Open until 10.30 pm.
Private room: 100. Air cond. No pets. Valet parking.
Telex 385759. V AE DC.*

Showing himself to be a star organiser as well as
a three-toque chef, Michel Lentz now manages all
the restaurants of the Royal Club Evian. Starting by
the shores of the lake at La Toque Royale, we
notice no change in quality or style now that a
close colleague has taken over production of the
cold soup of crayfish and nettles, omble chevalier
(a lake fish) meunière, saddle of rabbit with caramelised onions, and the slow-cooked kid with
mountain herbs. Country traditions and modernity
still intermingle, under the close supervision of
Lentz.
Up on the slopes we turn our attention to the
opulent Royal Hotel. Here Lentz has revamped
everything, starting with the set menu which now
proposes 25 dishes and changes daily. The emphasis is on excellent ingredients, carefully and simply
cooked: very fresh fish, grilled meat, classic
desserts. In a separate dining room, calorie-con-
trolled meals are served to those on the slimming
programme. (Early reports indicate that it is worth
putting on some weight for.)
We also ought to mention the poolside buffet
lunches, the simple light meals at the golf club, and
finally the new restaurant of the Hôtel Hermitage,
aimed at a younger, sporty set with more limited
means. This herculean undertaking naturally
leaves Lentz in the role of grand supervisor of fine
kitchens. He's good at it, there's no denying, but
his first love and greatest talent is still cooking.
Word has it that in two years he will open a
restaurant where he will be the chef. Until then we
are more than happy to grant him the three toques
that he has so clearly earned in the past.
A la carte: 350-550 F. Menus: 160 F (lunch only,
except holidays), 220 F, 310 F (dinner only, except holidays).

Royal Hôtel
(See restaurant above)

*Closed 15 Dec-10 Feb. 29 stes 2,100-5,660 F.
129 rms 500-2,420 F. Half-board 620-1,430 F. TV.
Conference facilities. Heated pool. Tennis. Golf.*

The new goal is to make this luxury hotel one of
the best in Europe. Not a modest ambition, but a
realistic one, considering the peerless setting on
the wooded mountain slopes above Lake Geneva,
the superb hotel with its art nouveau frescoes, and
the open, corporate purse that finances it all. Other
advantages include lovely, thoroughly equipped
rooms, one of the most effective health and beauty
institutes in Europe, an indoor and an outdoor
swimming pool, world-renowned eighteen-hole
golf course, six tennis courts, a heliport, myriad
planned excursions, the casino of course, and the
famous spring chamber music festival, directed by
Russian cellist and composer Mstislav
Rostropovich.

La Verniaz
Neuvecelle-Eglise — 50.75.04.90

*MM. Verdier. Closed 24 Nov-9 Feb. Open until
9.30 pm. Private room: 40. Garden dining. Garage
parking. Telex 385715. V AE DC.*

On the slopes above Evian, this large mansion
dominates grounds dotted with chalets and outbuildings. When you finally find the immense dining room you could imagine you're still in the
garden as you luxuriate in the light and the flowers.
The total lack of originality in the kitchen is compensated for by marvellous ingredients cooked
with care and precision. Try the foie gras, sea bass
with squid, fillet of lamb in a parsley-flecked crust,
and all the spit-roasts. Another point this year.
A la carte: 450 F. Menus: 200 F, 260 F, 350 F.

La Verniaz
(See restaurant above)

*Closed 24 Nov-9 Feb. 5 stes 800-1,500 F. 35 rms 350-
850 F. Half-board 545-700 F. TV. Conference facilities. Heated pool. Tennis.*

The pleasant chalet rooms scattered around the
peaceful grounds command a view of Lake Geneva
and an Alp or two. Relais et Châteaux.

In nearby Amphion-les-Bains

(4 km E on N 37)
74500 Evian — (H.-Savoie)

Le Chablais
1 km S on D 111, in Publier — 50.75.28.06

*Closed 24 Dec-24 Jan. 22 rms 126-250 F. Restaur-
ant. Half-board 130-215 F. TV 14 rms. V.*

Some of the cosy rooms look straight down at
Lake Geneva. Half-board allows you to try other
local restaurants belonging to the same hotel
group.

EVISA

See CORSICA

EVREUX

27000 Evreux — (Eure)
Paris 100 - Rouen 51 - Mantes 44 - Dreux 44

Auberge de Parville
4 km W on N 13, in Parville
27180 St-Sébastien-de-Morsent
32.39.36.63

*M. Barrande. Closed Sun dinner and Mon. Open
until 9.30 pm. Private room: 42. Garden dining.
Parking. V.*

This former post house has been converted into
a charming Norman inn, popular for weekend

breaks. In fine weather, be sure to reserve a table on the flowered patio. You'll be joined by other adepts of chef Wilfried Travet's impulsive, personal style to enjoy the salad of crisp rabbit giblets, roast young pigeon, and peppered pineapple tart, chocolate and raspberry croquettes, and hot prune soufflé with Armagnac sauce. The reception and service are perfect, but we'd appreciate a fuller wine list including some cheaper bottles.

A la carte: 350 F. Menus: 145 F, 180 F, 230 F, 260 F.

Hôtel de France
29, rue St-Thomas — 32.39.09.25
M. Meyruey. Closed Sun (except holidays). Open until 10 pm. Private room: 12. Garage parking. Hotel: 1 ste 400-450 F. 16 rms 150-295 F. V.

The new owners found a three-toque chef, Raymond Brochard, to appoint to the kitchen, where he has already managed to secure two toques. This former pupil of Joël Robuchon has not yet matched the creativity he displayed at Le Président de Saint-Quentin, but his asparagus and prawn fricassée, juicy duck in Pomerol, and sweetbread and scallops with celery and truffle juice are highly promising. The desserts in particular need more work. The long wine list offers a good choice of Bordeaux at moderate prices, and Michelle and Bernard Meyruey ensure a warm welcome to their revamped rustic restaurant.

A la carte: 400 F. Menus: 160 F, 220 F, 260 F.

13810 Eygalières — (B./Rhône)
Paris 715 - Avignon 28 - Cavaillon 13 - Marseille 81

Mas de la Brune
90.95.90.77
M. Gagg. Closed Wed lunch, Tue and 3 Nov-21 March. Open until 9 pm. Garden dining. No-smoking section. No pets. Valet parking. V.

You have to pass a sort of oral exam by intercom at the gate to this lovely sixteenth-century consul's residence barely touched by the passage of time. But as long as you booked before 7.30 pm, a charming welcome awaits you in the vaulted dining room or on the shady terrace. The cooking is a trifle fussy, but the bass with lemon butter and fennel, medallions of veal cooked in mint tea, and excellent desserts will keep you happy—at least until you get the bill.

Menus: 195 F (weekdays lunch only), 285 F, 370 F.

Mas de la Brune
(See restaurant above)
Closed 3 Nov-21 March. 1 ste. 9 rms 660-770 F (per pers, half-board oblig). TV 5 rms. Air cond. Heated pool.

Behind the mullioned windows, the ten rooms of this listed château have meticulous décor, air-conditioning, and sumptuous bathrooms.

24620 Eyzies (Les) — (Dordogne)
Paris 521 - Périgueux 45 - Sarlat 22 - Bergerac 57

Le Centenaire
Le Rocher de la Penne
53.06.97.18
MM. Scholly and Mazère. Closed Tue lunch and beg Nov-beg April. Open until 9.30 pm. Private room: 30. Garden dining. Garage parking. Telex 541921. V.

The art of the can opener is much too popular in this region swarming with tourists, but here is an enclave of elegance and imaginative cooking

hidden behind high walls. Attention to detail underlines the charms of the dining room and veranda, where Alain Scholly will welcome you with a smile. In the kitchen, Roland Mazère explores the full flavours of regional food to produce resolutely modern dishes like raw prawns lightly marinated in a truffle vinaigrette and accompanied by an asparagus croquant, quail and lamprey roll simmered with chestnuts and beans, salmon which would have been perfect even without the astonishing gentian sabayon sauce, the classic roast stuffed and truffled capon, and, among the exquisite desserts, the poached pear coated with strawberry purée and served with a chocolate sorbet. The set menus are excellent value. All we find lacking here is a choice of good regional wines to join the fine Bordeaux and Burgundies.

A la carte: 400-500 F. Menus: 220 F, 320 F, 450 F.

Le Centenaire
(See restaurant above)
Closed beg Nov-beg April. 4 stes 700-1,000 F. 21 rms 350-500 F. TV. Heated pool.

A team of attentive staff ensures pleasant service in the very comfortable and cheery rooms. Swimming pool, gym, and sauna. Relais et Châteaux.

06360 Eze — (Alpes-Mar.)
Paris 959 - Nice 11 - Menton 18 - Monaco 7

Auberge du Troubadour
Rue du Brec — 93.41.19.03
M. Vuille. Closed Sun dinner (except July-Aug), Wed, Feb school holidays and 24 Nov-24 Dec. Open until 9.30 pm. Private room: 6. V.

The evident charm of this pretty inn means it can be crowded with tourists in season, but this has no adverse effects in the kitchen where they know just how to make the most of the finest ingredients. We're awarding a toque this year for the fresh duck foie gras (one of the best in the area), the beautiful fillet of beef with cèpes, John Dory and an artichoke gratin, and the apple feuilleté with Calvados. Capable service.

A la carte: 270-320 F. Menus: 105 F (weekdays lunch only), 160 F.

11/20 La Bergerie
Grande Corniche — 93.41.03.67
M. Senfftleben. Closed Wed. Open until 10 pm. Terrace dining. Parking. V.

The young rabbit in aspic, lotte kebabs, and seafood tagliatelle haven't changed for ten years, and the customers show no signs of complaining. It must be pointed out that the dishes are well prepared and served on a charming terrace in fine weather.

A la carte: 250 F.

Richard Borfiga
Place du Gal-de-Gaulle
93.41.05.23
M. Borfiga. Closed Mon off-season, and 10 Jan-10 Feb. Open until 10 pm. V AE DC.

Despite the pleasant, floral décor and the gorgeous view from the bay windows, this handy halt has rather a starchy atmosphere. But there's nothing reticent about Richard Borfiga's fresh, flavourful cooking. The red-mullet, mushroom, and sweet potato salad, the baked bass with basil, and roast pigeon with garlic are the kind of classic dishes you never tire of when adroitly are well prepared.

A la carte: 350-400 F. Menus: 180 F, 250 F, 350 F.

Cap Estel
Eze-Bord-de-Mer — 93.01.50.44
Closed 1 Nov-28 Feb. 8 stes. 35 rms rates not availabe. Restaurant. Half-board 1,000-1,500 F oblig in seas. Air cond. Conference facilities. Heated pool. Valet parking. Telex 470305. V AE.

Film-star luxury is the rule in this grand hotel set on a rocky promontory jutting out to sea. All the rooms have sea views and there's a private beach, sauna, and two hectares of grounds.

 ### Château de la Chèvre d'Or
Moyenne-Corniche, rue du Barri
93.41.12.12
M. De Daeniken. Closed Wed in March, and 3 Dec-2 March. Open until 10.15 pm. Air cond. Valet parking. Telex 970839. V AE DC.

Nature has provided a breathtaking panorama from this eagle's nest location and the man-made décor, once so strikingly conventional, has been greatly improved by bigger windows, pastel walls, and new furniture. It is now an unmitigated pleasure to sit here and sample the prawn salad and crunchy potatoes, red mullet with a citrus fruit sauce, roast duckling, and croustillant au chocolat, all professionally prepared by Elie Mazot. The superb cellar includes some most affordable regional wines.
A la carte: 500-800 F. Menu: 350 F (lunch only).

 ### Château de la Chèvre d'Or
(See restaurant above)
Closed 3 Dec-2 March. 3 stes 2,200-2,800 F. 12 rms 950-2,500 F. TV. Air cond. Conference facilities. Pool.

A helicopter was needed to transport the building materials, but several new rooms are finally ready to receive the jet set who make up the clientele of this neo-medieval refuge, built in the 1920s. Superb swimming pools, simple meals at the Café du Jardin, and a new private car park. Relais et Châteaux.

 ### Château Eza
93.41.12.24
M. Rochat. Closed Nov-March. Open until 10 pm. Private room: 15. Terrace dining. Valet parking. Telex 470382. V AE DC.

Chef Bruno Cirino is on the threshold of Côte d'Azur stardom, and we expect the third toque to be only the beginning. We would have awarded it last year, had we been sure then that this young native of Nice, trained by Jacques Maximin, Roger Vergé, and Alain Ducasse, was going to stay put. As Cirino seems to be well installed, along with a well-balanced menu and a short *carte* that gets straight to the point, we're happy to keep our word. A typical feast here might start with baked crayfish and garlic surrounded by a bouquet of baby onions, local asparagus, and new potatoes in their skins, or perhaps the exquisite vegetables mixed with slivered rock lobster and crispy bacon, tossed in a well-seasoned vinaigrette and served on a bed of baby potatoes. You might continue to the intense flavours of turbot with crayfish and skinned red beans simmered in bacon broth, or lobster given new meaning by truffled macaroni and baby peas. Next comes the masterpiece: a saddle of young rabbit cooked two ways, a thick fillet simply grilled with artichokes, and the breast stuffed with the giblets and slow-cooked in truffle stock. It shows the sublime heights to which peasant dishes can be taken!
You won't be able to resist the cheeses, and even

less the desserts, like the baked cherries stuffed with pistachios in a syrup scented with spices and orange water. And to make the meal complete there's an array of Bandols, Cassis, and Côtes-du-Rhônes in the capable hands of the young sommelier, Angel Plata. Alain Moser, in charge of the service, is civility personified. The high-perched terrace is a better place to appreciate all this than the dining room, where a gloomy still life reminds you that you are not yet in heaven.
A la carte: 500 F and up. Menus: 250 F (lunch only), 490 F.

 ### Château Eza
(See restaurant above)
Closed Nov-March. 3 stes 2,500-3,500 F. 5 rms 1,000-2,500 F. TV. Air cond.

A cluster of medieval dwellings made into a 'château' by Prince William of Sweden, and completely restored a few years ago by a former International Red Cross executive. The décor is strongly medieval, the view timeless, and the prices in line with present-day luxury.

Eze Country Club
Route de La Turbie
93.41.24.64
M. Cremilleux. Open every day. Open until 10 pm. Private room: 120. Terrace dining. Air cond. Valet parking. Telex 461301. V AE DC.

Dominique Nouvian's capable and consistent cuisine has earned a toque this year. The discreetly luxurious modern décor provides a pleasant place to enjoy oysters on a pastry shell, prawn salad with aubergines, fricassée of sweetbreads and sorrel, and some original desserts.
A la carte: 350 F and up. Menus: 220 F, 310 F.

 ### Eze Country Club
(See restaurant above)
Open every day. 6 stes 1,500-2,500 F. 80 rms 900-1,300 F. Half-board 1,200-1,400 F. TV. Air cond. Conference facilities. Pool. Tennis.

The ultra-comfortable rooms have sunny balconies and wide terraces overlooking the sea. Electronic golf practice, fitness centre, and helipad.

12/20 Le Grill du Château
(La Taverne)
Rue du Barri — 93.41.00.17
M. De Daeniken. Closed Mon. Open until 10 pm. Private room: 25. Terrace dining. Air cond. Telex 970839. V AE.

The terrace of this annexe to the Château de la Chèvre d'Or affords views of the village, sea and hills, while the chef supplies simple and delicious terrines, seafood salads, sea bream, and tarte Tatin.
A la carte: 250-270 F. Menu: 140 F (lunch only).

27530 Ezy-sur-Eure — (Eure)
Paris 82 - Evreux 30 - Dreux 18 - Mantes 29 - Anet 2

 ### Maître Corbeau
15, rue M.-Elect
37.64.73.29
M. Blondeau. Open every day. Open until 9.30 pm. Private room: 25. Garden dining. No-smoking section. Parking. V AE DC.

This comfortable, attractive restaurant deserves more custom during the week, especially in winter. The owner-chef offers delicious wines and masterly cooking at fair but not giveaway prices. And the snail fricassée with shrimps and oyster mushrooms, turbot stuffed with spinach, blanquette of veal offal, basil, and black olives, and the pear gratin with vanilla cream ought to attract a wider audience.

A la carte: 300 F. Menus: 120 F and 300 F (weekdays only), 160 F, 200 F.

FAU-DE-PEYRE

See Aumont-Aubrac

FAYENCE

83440 Fayence — (Var)
Paris 910 - Draguignan 34 - Grasse 27 - St-Raphaël 37

Le Castellaras
Rte de Banégon — 94.76.13.80
M. Carro. Closed Wed, off-season dinner Mon and Tue, Feb school holidays and 13-27 Nov. Open until 9.30 pm. Private room: 25. Garden dining. Pool. Parking. V AE.

Unexpected varieties of tree—birch, beech, and weeping cedar—grace the garden of this Provençal villa. In the tranquillity of the Fayence hills, Alain Carro has found the perfect setting for his finely crafted cuisine: prawns and asparagus tips with orange butter, his own pot-au-feu, and constantly improving desserts. Good wines too.

A la carte: 300-370 F. Menus: 165 F, 250 F.

12/20 Moulin de la Camandoule
Ch. Notre-Dame-des-Cyprès — 94.76.00.84
M. Rilla. Closed Tue lunch, 2 Jan-25 March and 1 Nov-23 Dec (except w-e and hotels clients). Open until 10 pm. Garden dining. Parking. V.

The English owners of this old mill have created an elegant restaurant with the original oil-press as the star feature. It serves good French food like a young rabbit and almond terrine, salmon and stuffed baby vegetables, and roast fillet of lamb with Swiss chard and haricot beans. Friendly welcome; rather more formal service.

A la carte: 300 F. Menu: 190 F.

Moulin de la Camandoule
(See restaurant above)
Open every day. 2 stes 540 F. 11 rms 190-540 F. Half-board 385-490 F oblig in seas. TV 9 rms. Pool.

Each room is unique but they share a view of the cherry orchard and the Fayence hills.

12/20 Le Relais du Castel
Quartier St-Eloi — 94.76.07.48
Mme Carro. Closed Mon. Open until 9.30 pm. Terrace dining. V.

Traditional décor with a Provençal air is the setting for light, careful cooking: smoked salmon bavarois with a chive sauce, grouper in a perfect green-peppercorn sauce, and friandine aux fruits. Can the toque be far away?

A la carte: 150-180 F. Menus: 76 F (weekdays lunch only), 150 F.

FÉCAMP

76400 Fécamp — (Seine-Mar.)
Paris 215 - Rouen 71 - Le Havre 40 - Dieppe 64

12/20 Auberge de la Rouge
2 km S on D 940, in St-Léonard — 35.28.07.59
M. Guyot. Closed off-season Sun dinner and Mon, and Feb school holidays. Open until 9.30 pm. Private room: 14. Garden dining. No-smoking section. Hotel: 8 rms 260-310 F. Garage parking. V AE DC.

Dining around the new fountain in the garden would be a delight were it not for the drone of the nearby road. New also are several fine dishes such as the crêpes stuffed with frogs' legs in a Madeira and cream sauce, young pigeon Rouen-style, and the warm feuilleté of fresh fruit with acacia honey.

A la carte: 280-300 F. Menus: 90 F (weekdays only), 170 F, 240 F.

12/20 Le Viking
63, bd Albert-Ier — 35.29.22.92
M. Benoit. Closed Mon. Open until 9.30 pm. Private room: 35. V.

Alain Dublanchet, a former pupil of Marc Meneau, applies his talents to the omnipresent cod: in rillettes with onion confit, braised with potatoes and meat stock. For a change, try the equally fine duck fricassée. And enjoy the beautiful seascape.

A la carte: 300 F. Menus: 98 F (weekdays only), 135 F, 195 F, 250 F.

FEGERSHEIM

See Strasbourg

FERAYOLA

See CORSICA

FÈRE-EN-TARDENOIS

02130 Fère-en-Tardenois — (Aisne)
Paris 110 - Soissons 26 - Reims 46 - Laon 54

Hostellerie du Château
3 km N on N 967 — 23.82.21.13
M. Fremiot. Open every day. Open until 9 pm. Private room: 40. Valet parking. Telex 145526. V AE DC.

The grounds of this country manor include some magnificent medieval ruins. The three dining rooms are havens of harmony, with meticulous attention to detail evident in the silverware, engraved glass, wood panelling and chandeliers. The cooking may not be all it used to be, but it is still excellent: leek and smoked salmon terrine with caviar, turbot cooked in a salt crust, or the grilled, truffled lamb's tongue. The fine wines include some magnificent Champagnes, and the service is friendly.

A la carte: 450 F. Menus: 290 F (weekdays lunch only, wine inc), 290 F, 430 F.

Hostellerie du Château
(See restaurant above)
Open every day. 9 stes. 14 rms 830-1,305 F (per pers, half-board oblig). TV. Conference facilities. Tennis.

The rooms come in varying styles and sizes, but all are luxuriously comfortable. They overlook either the royal ruins in the grounds or the meadows. The service can be offhand.

FERNEY-VOLTAIRE

01210 Ferney-Voltaire — (Ain)
Paris 510 - Bellegarde 36 - Genève 7 - Gex 10

Le Chanteclair
13, rue Versoix — 50.40.79.55
M. Garcin. Closed Sun, Mon, 25 Feb-8 March and 8-25 July. Open until 9.30 pm. Terrace dining. V.

Trained by Emile Jung and the Troigros brothers and full of enthusiasm, Jacques Garcin turns out inventive, intelligent cooking that is starting to attract an appreciative clientele. His prawn-studded poultry sausage, the extraordinary chaud-froid of foie gras glazed with Beaumes-de-Venise, mildly spiced pigeon pastilla, and the exquisite desserts are all moderately priced.

A la carte: 250-300 F. Menus: 85 F (weekdays lunch only), 210 F (dinner only).

Le Pirate
Av. de Genève — 50.40.63.52
M. Bechis. Closed Mon lunch, Sun, 10 July-1 Aug and 20 Dec-2 Jan. Open until 10 pm. Private room: 15. Garden dining. Garage parking. V AE DC.

The clean modern décor bears no resemblance to a galleon, but Alain Bechis's fish specialities justify the maritime theme. Avoid the ruinous *carte* and choose the good-value lunchtime menu featuring fresh pasta and shellfish, lotte with fennel, and luscious desserts. The cellar offers only the best-known and most expensive wines.

A la carte: 400 F and up. Menus: 200 F (lunch only, wine inc), 260 F, 300 F.

12/20 Le Voltaire
Av. du Jura — 50.40.77.90
M. Gantelet. Open every day. Open until 10.30 pm. Private room: 100. Garden dining. Air cond. Garage parking. Telex 309071. V AE DC.

A bright, modern hotel where the chef works hard to make the most of quality ingredients. Prices à la carte are high, but the business set lunch offers oysters, a mixed grill with lemon, cheese, and dessert, and includes wine.

A la carte: 350 F. Menus: 115 F (weekdays lunch only), 175 F (lunch only, wine inc), 250 F (dinner only).

Pullman Ferney-Genève
(See restaurant above)
Open every day. 2 stes 1,300 F. 120 rms 570-645 F. TV. Conference facilities. Heated pool.

A perfect business hotel whose small, soundproofed rooms have views of Mont Blanc or the Jura range. Pleasing buffet breakfasts.

61450 Ferrière-aux-Etangs (La) — (Orne)
Paris 230 - Alençon 61 - Domfront 14 - Flers 10

Auberge de la Mine
Le Gué-Plat — 33.66.91.10
M. Denis. Closed Sun dinner, Wed, 6-27 Feb and 1-8 Aug. Open until 9 pm. Private room: 20. Parking. V.

This long, ivy-covered building hides two lovely flower-filled dining rooms. The *patronne*'s welcome is relaxed and cheerful, and her husband's cooking makes honest if timid use of first-rate ingredients: young rabbit in a tomato vinaigrette that could be tastier, pork discreetly spiced with curry and ginger, good cheeses, and a rich chocolate fondant unfortunately paired with an over-sharp cherry sauce. We'd appreciate better advice on choosing from the short wine list.

A la carte: 200-240 F. Menus: 78 F (weekdays only), 110 F, 145 F.

77260 Ferté-sous-Jouarre (La) — (Seine/Marne)
Paris 64 - Château-Thierry 26 - Meaux 20 - Melun 63

Auberge de Condé
1, av. de Montmirail — 60.22.00.07
M. Tingaud. Closed Mon dinner and Tue. Open until 9.30 pm. Private room: 100. Garage parking. V AE DC.

Several years have passed since Pascal Tingaud, who trained in the Troisgros' restaurant and at Pic in Valence, took over as chef from his famous grandfather, but he still maintains some of the richest, heaviest elements of the previous menu. Is he a prisoner of tradition, of his regular customers' expectations, or of the women of the family who handle the reception and service?

Recently however, he seems to be making an effort to lighten his cooking. The Brie hen, once served with cheese ravioli, is now cooked in pink Champagne, and there's less cream in the sauces. But the greatest progress has been made with the desserts, such as the pineapple croustillant. We're giving back the point we took away last year to encourage the trend. The wines are exceptional and, like the rest, expensive. And you may not appreciate the maître d' treating you like a philistine if you don't happen to be a regular customer.

A la carte: 550-750 F. Menus: 200 F (weekdays only), 250 F (weekdays only, wine inc), 550 F (Champagne inc), 295 F.

46100 Figeac — (Lot)
Paris 559 - Cahors 71 - Aurillac 67 - Tulle 103

Hôtel des Carmes
Enclos des Carmes — 65.34.20.78
M. Tillet. Closed off-season Sun dinner and Sat, and 15 Dec-15 Jan. Open until 9 pm. Private room: 45. Terrace dining. Parking. Telex 520794. V AE DC.

A little flair wouldn't hurt this big, modern, bay-windowed dining room, just as a spark of inspiration would make a difference to the otherwise well-executed cuisine. Which doesn't mean the regional specialities are not already excellent: tomato tourin (onion soup with goose fat), local charcuterie, foie gras with capers, and the tarragon-stuffed saddle of rabbit. At lunchtime you can order a green salad and *plat du jour* for 55 F.

A la carte: 300 F. Menus: 98 F, 175 F, 265 F.

Hôtel des Carmes
(See restaurant above)
Closed off-season Sat and Sun, and 15 Dec-15 Jan. 40 rms 260-350 F. TV. Conference facilities. Pool. Tennis.

Modern, functional rooms near the town centre but shielded from the noise of traffic.

74300 Flaine — (H.-Savoie)
Paris 596 - Annecy 79 - Megève 49 - Bonneville 42

Le Totem
50.90.80.64
M. Miradoli. Closed 11 May-29 June and 1 Sep-20 Dec. Open until 9 pm. Terrace dining. Telex 670512. V AE DC.

Forget the ski resort concrete architecture by taking a seat in this huge dining room and enjoying the mountain view. Then turn your attention to the quality cooking: grilled freshwater perch with red cabbage and creamed horseradish, Charollais tournedos steak in truffle stock, and mountain honey bavarois served with fruit and nut jelly. The reception is warm and the *patron* is an expert on wines, especially Châteauneuf-du-Pape.

A la carte: 350 F. Menus: 160 F (lunch only), 240 F and 300 F (dinner only).

Le Totem
(See restaurant above)
Closed 11 May-29 June and 1 Sep-20 Dec. 54 rms 330-620 F. Half-board 315-645 F oblig in seas. TV. Conference facilities. Tennis. Golf.

The rooms, with a fine view over the mountains, are well equipped, but the soundproofing is poor. A pool, sauna, and gym are available and a golf course appears when the snow melts.

See Nancy

61100 Flers — (Orne)
Paris 240 - Caen 57 - Laval 87 - Alençon 71 - Vire 31

[13] Au Bout de la Rue
60, rue de la Gare — 33.65.31.53
M. Lebouleux. Closed Sun, holidays, 1-9 Jan and 4-19 Aug. Open until 10 pm. Private room: 20. No-smoking section. V AE.

Marie-Noëlle and Jacky Lebouleux offer such creative dishes as prawns sautéed with sea salt, steamed Scottish salmon and mussels in white wine, a curry of sliced chicken breast served with basmati rice, and a tender beef fillet with three kinds of pepper.
A la carte: 150-200 F. Menus: 78 F, 98 F, 158 F.

69820 Fleurie — (Rhône)
Paris 420 - Lyon 58 - Belleville 12 - Mâcon 21

[16] Auberge du Cep
Pl. de l'Eglise — 74.04.10.77
Mme Cortembert. Closed Sun dinner, Tue lunch, Mon, 5-12 March, 1-8 Aug and 17 Dec-9 Jan. Open until 9 pm. Air cond. V AE.

Chantal Cortembert bought this bistro before she met Gérard, who became its chef and her husband for twenty years. When he died on the job last year, she decided to carry on his work, admirably helped by a tightly knit team whom they had trained over the years. Former second-in-command Michel Guérin has taken over in the kitchen and now it is his cooking that we enjoy here: pike quenelles in the traditional style, frogs' legs in a crayfish fumet, farm chicken cooked in Fleurie, and veal kidneys in their cooking juice, prepared in the Cortembert tradition of precision cooking which respects natural flavours. Daughter Hélène has rallied round to help with the service, leaving her mother free to bake, shop, and welcome customers. We have full confidence in the future of the Cep.
A la carte: 400 F. Menus: 275 F, 390 F, 500 F.

See Caen

34510 Florensac — (Hérault)
Paris 810 - Montpellier 50 - Béziers 24 - Agde 10

[16] Léonce
8, pl. de la République — 67.77.03.05
M. Fabre. Closed Sun dinner, Mon, 2 weeks end Sep-beg Oct and mid-Feb to mid-March. Open until 9.15 pm. Private room: 25. Air cond. No pets. Hotel: 12 rms 180-220 F. V AE DC.

Jean-Claude Fabre has to steer a course between modernity and tradition to satisfy the tourists who flock here as much as the conservative locals. Keeping alive the memory of his grandfather Léonce and his grandmother's cooking, this former sauce chef with Jacques Maximin manages to delight them all with dishes like capelletti with ham and celeriac, baked prawns and artichokes served with a brown-butter sauce, and fabulous chocolate desserts. The choice of local wines is limited but reliable, and Josette Fabre's relaxed reception makes you feel at home in this former café with its limestone walls and pastel décor.
A la carte: 300-380 F. Menus: 110 F (weekdays only), 200 F, 280 F.

See Ré (Ile de)

09000 Foix — (Ariège)
Paris 763 - Toulouse 82 - Carcassonne 81

12/20 Le Médiéval
42, rue des Chapeliers
61.02.81.50
M. Merlin. Closed Sat lunch, Sun dinner and Wed. Open until 11 pm. Private room: 40. V AE DC.

A pleasant inn with beamed ceilings, stucco walls, and big bay windows featuring lively, aromatic local fare. Try the powerful garlic soup, meat and winter vegetables in the *azinat* and *rouzole*, an interesting Bethmale cheese, and an honest apple croustade. There's a superb choice of whiskies.
A la carte: 200 F. Menus: 65 F, 90 F, 115 F.

Pyrène
1.5 km S on N 20
Le Vignoble, rue S.-Denis — 61.65.51.12
Closed 15 Dec-15 Jan. 21 rms 225-300 F. TV. Pool. Tennis. Garage parking. V.

A small modern hotel on the edge of town with a garden and good sports facilities.

77300 Fontainebleau — (Seine/Marne)
Paris 65 - Melun 16 - Nemours 16 - Orléans 88

[14] L'Aigle Noir
(Le Beauharnais)
27, pl. Napoléon-Bonaparte — 64.22.32.65
M. Duvauchelle. Closed 28 July-25 Aug, and 21-29 Dec. Open until 9.30 pm. Private room: 80. Garden dining. No-smoking section. Valet parking. Telex 694080. V AE DC.

The Dukes of Retz, to mark their precedence at court, built their residence right in front of the Château de Fontainebleau—which gives customers at this restaurant a privileged view while savouring the astute and artistic cooking of Bernard Bordaries. Fresh from Toulouse, he intertwines South-western influences, everyday dishes, and his own creations: coriander-flavoured prawn chaud-froid, fried pigs' trotters with cèpes, gratin of sorrel and fennel butter, and light desserts like pineapple millefeuille and fresh fruit gratin with honey. As soon as his flavours have regained the freshness they had in the South, Bordaries will get his second toque back. There are many fine wines in the cellar.
A la carte: 400 F and up. Menus: 200 F, 290 F.

L'Aigle Noir
(See restaurant above)
Open every day. 2 stes 1,200-2,000 F. 57 rms 800 F. Half-board 1,075-2,275 F. TV. Conference facilities. Heated pool.

The recently renovated luxurious rooms with period décor and dream fittings overlook the château and gardens. A covered pool, sauna, gym, and indoor putting green are being built.

12/20 Chez Arrighi
53, rue de France
64.22.29.43
Mme Amprou. Closed Mon and Feb school holidays. Open until 10 pm. V AE DC.

Despite the name and the blue-fabric Empire décor, there is nothing from Corsica here. Attentive and thoroughly uninventive cooking produces such dependable favourites as the snail and chanterelle ragoût, warm smoked salmon with sorrel, and lamb chop gratinée with foie gras.
A la carte: 250-300 F. Menus: 89 F, 139 F, 189 F.

Hôtel Legris et Parc
36, rue du Parc — 64.22.24.24
Closed Sun and Mon off-season, and 22 Dec-28 Jan.
5 stes 475-500 F. 26 rms 270-500 F. Restaurant.
Half-board 360-450 F. TV. Conference facilities. V.
Period-furnished, very comfortable rooms, some of which open onto the interior flower garden.

Napoléon
9, rue Grande — 64.22.20.39
Open every day. 1 ste 990 F. 57 rms 580-790 F.
Restaurant. Half-board 690-850 F. TV. Conference
facilities. Valet parking. Telex 691652. V AE DC.
This beautiful hotel in the town centre has good service, excellent bathrooms, and disappointing breakfasts. The rooms facing the courtyard are bigger and quieter.

In nearby Thomery

(8 km E)
77810 Fontainebleau — (Seine/Marne)

Le Vieux Logis
5, rue S.-Carnot — 60.96.44.77
M. Plouvier. Open every day. Open until 9.30 pm.
Private room: 40. Garden dining. Parking.
Telex 692772. V AE.
Young Jean-Luc Daligault is making his mark from the word go in this refined, glass-roofed dining room which opens onto a wonderful patio. He gets another point for his tender sliced raw beef perfumed with olive oil and pistou (pounded basil and garlic), roast pigeon and a salad seasoned with pineapple vinegar, and a slightly crisp roast guinea fowl stuffed with tarragon which is really remarkable. A strawberry and cinamon souffléed tart represents good progress among the desserts.
A la carte: 300 F. Menus: 120 F, 220 F.

Le Vieux Logis
(See restaurant above)
Open every day. 14 rms 350 F. Half-board 480 F. TV.
Conference facilities. Tennis.
A perfect stop with its elegant décor, luxurious bedlinen, friendly service, and absolute peace. As a bonus, the breakfasts are out of this world.

See also: Barbizon

76740 Fontaine-le-Dun — (Seine-Mar.)
Paris 188 - Dieppe 24 - St-Valéry-en-Caux 16

Auberge du Dun
5 km N on D 237
in Bourg-Dun — 35.83.05.84
M. Chrétien. Closed Sun dinner and Mon (except
holidays), 20 Jan-3 Feb and 10-31 Oct. Open until
9 pm. No pets. Parking. V.
A very short *carte* which changes frequently reflects Pierre Chrétien's devotion to fresh ingredients and meticulous preparation. From the dining room you can watch him cook everything to order, such as the tartlets of asparagus and baby oysters, John Dory in a creamy crab sauce, sweetbreads en croûte, and the delicious rhubarb crème brûlée.
A la carte: 300 F. Menus: 266 F (wine inc), 90 F, 165 F.

> *Red toques signify modern cuisine; black*
> *toques signify traditional cuisine.*

41250 Fontaines-en-Sologne — (Loir/Cher)
Paris 190 - Blois 23 - Chambord 13 - Romorantin 27

Auberge
de la Fontaine aux Muses

7 km on D 765
La Gaucherie — 54.79.98.80
M. Soyer. Closed Tue dinner, Wed and Feb school
holidays. Open until 9 pm. Garden dining. V.
Time to reflect has helped Alain Soyer distil his efforts and produce an inspired, cohesive menu worthy of his great talent: freshwater perch in olive oil, leeks and coriander, braised calf's head and sweetbreads, foie gras pot-au-feu. The desserts are less fussy than in the past.
A la carte: 250-350 F. Menus: from 150 F to 280 F.

See PARIS Suburbs

See Montargis

77610 Fontenay-Trésigny — (Seine/Marne)
Paris 45 - Meaux 30 - Melun 26 - Coulommiers 23

Le Manoir
Rte de Coulommiers — 64.25.91.17
M. Sourisseau. Closed Tue and 15 Nov-23 March.
Open until 9 pm. Private room: 150. Terrace dining.
Garage parking. Telex 690635. V AE DC.
This luxurious little manor, perfect for weekend breaks, has its own airfield and a marvellous swimming pool. The classic silk, velvet, and wood-panelled elegance of the dining room is matched by high standards in the kitchen: traditional home-prepared charcuterie, and young pigeon à la française.
A la carte: ;8350-400 F. Menu: 230 F (weekdays lunch only, wine inc).

Le Manoir
(See restaurant above)
Closed Tue and 15 Nov-23 March. 2 stes 900 F.
12 rms 430-720 F. Half-board 660-720 F. TV. Confer-
ence facilities. Heated pool. Tennis.
The spacious rooms are furnished in a variety of styles but there is only one level of creature comforts—high. Rolling lawns and a swimming pool surrounded by trees tempt you outside. Relais et Châteaux.

49590 Fontevraud-l'Abbaye — (Maine/Loire)
Paris 306 - Angers 70 - Chinon 23 - Saumur 16

La Licorne

Allée Sainte-Catherine
41.51.72.49
M. Criton. Closed Sun dinner. Annual closings not
available. Open until 9 pm. Garden dining. V AE DC.
Step off the well-marked paths leading to the abbey and discover behind this elegant eighteenth-century façade a beautiful, limestone-walled dining room with a handful of tables. The generous, full flavours of Michel Lecomte's cooking reflect his training *chez* Robuchon, Taillevent, Apicius, and L'Ambroisie. Try the oyster tart, casserole of prawns and chicken breast with tapioca, and turbot in meat juice. The cellar is well stocked with wines from the Loire and Burgundy.
A la carte: 300 F. Menu: 170 F (weekdays lunch only).

13990 Fontvieille — (B./Rhône)
Paris 711 - Tarascon 11 - Avignon 30 - Arles 10

🍴[14] La Cuisine au Planet
144, Grand-Rue — 90.54.63.97

M. Ferary. Closed Sun dinner off-season, Mon, 1-15 March and 15-30 Nov. Open until 10.30 pm. Private room: 20. Terrace dining. V AE.

The exquisite terrace shaded by Virginia creeper next to the pretty dining room is a delightfully cool spot to appreciate set menus featuring the light, seasonal cooking of Hervé Ferary, who studied under Jacques Manière. You can sample prettily presented dishes such as little sausages of pig's trotters and foie gras with potato salad, sea bream in local wine, and cinnamon-scented duck breast. The short wine list is well put together.

Menus: 150 F, 185 F, 195 F, 240 F.

🍴[13] Le Patio   ۞
117, rte du Nord — 90.54.73.10

Mme Remy. Closed Tue dinner, Wed and 2 Jan-6 Feb. Open until 9.30 pm. Terrace dining. V AE DC.

The interior resembles hastily erected television scenery and the décor is overdone, but the charming *patronne* and the fine cooking of her young chef make the pill easier to swallow. Try his authentic Provençal menu (a tart of salt cod purée, and tasty, wood-grilled mountain lamb), and turn a blind eye to culinary relics like the millefeuille of scallops with a cream and crayfish sauce.

A la carte: 240-300 F. Menus: 110 F (weekdays only), 145 F, 185 F.

🏠 La Peiriero
Av. des Baux — 90.97.76.10

Closed 30 Oct-20 Dec and 5 Jan-1 April. 3 stes 480-600 F. 37 rms 330-410 F. TV. Conference facilities. Pool. Garage parking. V AE DC.

A traditional Provençal homestead with big rooms facing the hills.

🍴[13] La Régalido   ۞
Rue F.-Mistral — 90.54.60.22

M. Michel. Closed Tue lunch, Mon (except dinner in seas), Dec and Jan. Open until 9 pm. Private room: 18. Garden dining. Valet parking. Telex 441150. V AE DC.

The pleasures for which one pays here—and one does pay—are provided by competently crafted perennial favourites, rather than by any invention or novelty. Sample such familiar fare as aubergine mould with fresh tomato and grilled peppers, or sea bass simmered with olive oil and tomatos, or a thick slice of leg of lamb stewed with garlic. We are always entranced by the charming vaulted dining room and the garden of this former olive-oil mill.

A la carte: 300-370 F. Menus: 220 F (weekdays only), 270 F, 290 F, 390 F.

🏠 La Régalido
(See restaurant above)

Closed Dec and Jan. 14 rms 550-1,200 F. Half-board 650-950 F. TV. Air cond. Conference facilities.

The delightful rooms of this turn-of-the-century hostelry look out over the Alpilles.

🏠 Le Saint Victor
Ch. des Fourques — 90.54.66.00

Open every day. 1 ste 960-1,020 F. 10 rms 370-530 F. TV. Air cond 2 rms. Pool. Garage parking. Telex 410777. V AE DC.

A new residence, handsomely landscaped, offers nicely furnished accommodation.

See Albi

57600 Forbach — (Moselle)
Paris 385 - Metz 60 - Sarreguemines 19 - St-Avold 23

🍴[15] La Bonne Auberge
15, rue Nationale
57350 Stiring-Wendel — 87.87.52.78

Mlles Egloff. Closed Mon dinner and Tue. Annual closings not available. Open until 9.15 pm. Private room: 12. Air cond. Parking. V.

Follow the procession of posh German automobiles up to Isabelle's door. She will welcome you warmly, then introduce you to the fragrant, generous cooking of her sister Lydia, and to the treasures of a wine cellar she capably (and enthusiastically) oversees. A few slips (a cold dish here, an inaccurately timed one there) are easily forgiven after a taste of the prawn and potato vinaigrette, the fricassée of John Dory and chanterelles served with poppyseed noodles, old-fashioned calf's head tortue, and a souffléed gratin of tiny yellow plums. A faithful German clientele regularly crosses the border to enjoy the sisters' hospitality in their pretty, modern dining room decorated in luminous shades of grey.

A la carte: 400 F and up. Menus: 210 F (weekdays lunch only), 240 F, 360 F.

In nearby **Rosbruck**

(6 km SW on N 3)
57800 Forbach — (Moselle)

🍴[13] Auberge Albert-Marie
1, rue Nationale — 87.04.70.76

M. Sternjacob. Closed Sun dinner and Mon. Open until 9.30 pm. Private room: 30. Parking. V.

A bilingual hostess greets the German customers loyal to this traditional inn, graced with elegant table settings and flower arrangements. The prices tend to soar higher than the chef's inspiration, but new dishes occasionally appear alongside the marinated salmon, breast of guinea hen and sauerkraut, and the quail ballotine with veal kidneys.

A la carte: 350 F. Menus: 200 F (weekdays lunch only), 280 F and 350 F (w-e and holidays lunch only).

76440 Forges-les-Eaux — (Seine-Mar.)
Paris 113 - Dieppe 54 - Beauvais 50 - Rouen 42

🍴[15] Auberge du Beau Lieu   ۞
Le Fossé   35.90.50.36

M. Ramelet. Closed off-season dinner Sun and Wed, and 16-30 Jan. Open until 9.30 pm. Private room: 8. Garden dining. No-smoking section. Parking. V AE DC.

Patrick Ramelet is a self-taught cook who could teach many pedigreed professionals a thing or two. After a season in the kitchen of the great Marc Meneau, he is back home busily preserving and restoring such local culinary traditions as andouille gâteau with apples and cider, andouillettes manufactured by his neighbourhood *charcutier*, and marvellous farmhouse Neufchâtel cheeses. His respect for tradition does not prevent him from developing some creations of his own, like lobster tail minestrone, wine-roasted bass, or duck tartare.

A la carte: 370-420 F. Menus: 125 F (weekdays lunch only), 235 F (wine inc), 220 F, 270 F.

▲▲ Auberge du Beau Lieu
(See restaurant above)
Closed off-season Sun and Wed, and 16-30 Jan. 3 rms 260-320 F. TV. Conference facilities.
It's hard to leave these handsomely decorated and furnished rooms, which open on to manicured lawns and gardens.

29170 Fouesnant — (Finistère)
Paris 560 - Quimper 15 - Concarneau 13

12/20 La Pointe du Cap Coz
in Cap-Coz
81, av. de la Pointe — 98.56.01.63
Mme Le Torc'h. Closed Wed and 2 Jan-Feb school holidays. Open until 8.30 pm. No pets. V.
The dining room at the back of this Breton establishment set on a spit of land is surrounded by the sea, giving one the impression of eating aboard a ship. Sample the young chef's shellfish ragoût, hake with smoky bacon, and bitter-chocolate crème. And order a bottle of the excellent cidre de Fouesnant.
A la carte: 230 F. Menus: 86 F, 155 F.

🏠 La Pointe du Cap Coz
(See restaurant above)
Closed Wed and 2 Jan-Feb school holidays. 19 rms 190-350 F. Half-board 210-290 F. Conference facilities.
Here is a simple, family-style establishment with a magnificent view.

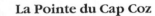
In nearby Forêt-Fouesnant

(4 km NE on D 44)
29940 Fouesnant — (Finistère)

🏠 L'Espérance
6, rue de la Baie — 98.56.96.58
Closed 15 Nov-30 March. 30 rms 124-265 F. Restaurant. Half-board 176-246 F. Parking. V.
A perfect little holiday hotel by the sea, with a modest restaurant.

70220 Fougerolles — (Haute-Saône)
Paris 363 - Épinal 43 - Vesoul 38 - Luxeuil-les-B. 9

🍴 Au Père Rota
8, Grande-Rue — 84.49.12.11
M. Kuentz. Closed Sun dinner and Mon (except holidays) and 23 Dec-18 Jan. Open until 9 pm. Air cond. Parking. V AE DC.
Fougerolles may be the kirsch capital of France, but a rollicking spot it emphatically is not. Jean-Pierre Kuentz fights off the morose influence of his surroundings with a bright, quietly elegant dining room and a cuisine that is light, precise, and discreetly inventive. He ably underscores the regional accents of dishes like turbot simmered in vin jaune and ginger, river perch in Château-Chalon wine, sweetbreads with locally cured gammon, and cherry millefeuille with mint sauce. The cellar's fine Burgundies and Bordeaux would benefit from the services of a professional sommelier.
A la carte: 320-380 F. Menus: 142 F and 220 F (weekdays only), 185 F (w-e and holidays only), 275 F.

See Najac

17450 Fouras — (Charente-M.)
Paris 482 - La Rochelle 26 - Rochefort 13

🏠 Grand Hôtel des Bains
15, rue du Général-Bruncher
46.84.03.44
Closed 31 Oct-26 March. 35 rms 185-260 F. Restaurant. Half-board 210-260 F oblig in seas. Conference facilities. Garage parking. V.
This renovated coaching inn near the seaside offers comfortable, pleasant accommodation (book a room overlooking the enclosed garden).

11/20 La Jetée
Pointe de la Fumée
46.84.60.43
M. Bichaud. Closed Tue off-season, 3-15 Dec and 4 Jan-4 Feb. Open until 9.30 pm. Terrace dining. Parking. V AE DC.
A cheerful seaside spot with a view of the isle of Aix. The Bichaud family specialises in gigantic portions of simple seafood. Plump for the generous shellfish platters, conger-eel soup, chowder, and galettes Charentaises.
A la carte: 280 F. Menus: 80 F, 110 F, 210 F.

22240 Fréhel — (Côtes/Armor)
Paris 420 - Dinan 50 - St-Brieuc 49

🏠 Relais de Fréhel
96.41.43.02
Closed 5 Nov-24 March. 13 rms 150-240 F. Restaurant. Half-board 230-280 F. No pets. Tennis. Parking. V.
The warm and friendly atmosphere of this nineteenth-century Breton inn make it an ideal place to relax, either in salon by the fireside or in the pleasant garden.

🍴 Le Victorine
Pl. de la Mairie — 96.41.55.55
M. Blandin. Closed Sun dinner, Wed, 15 Jan-15 Feb and 15-30 Nov. Open until 9 pm. Garden dining. V DC.
A young chef has taken over old Aunt Victorine's upstanding establishment, where he serves forth generous portions of (rather complicated, not to say fey) dishes like steamed duet of sole and salmon, frivolité de fruits de mer en salade, and a caramelised pear feuillantine. The freshened-up dining room is an agreeable place to enjoy lunch, dinner, or tea.
A la carte: 300 F and up. Menus: 59 F (weekdays lunch only), 145 F, 180 F, 250 F.

83600 Fréjus — (Var)
Paris 890 - Cannes 40 - Ste-Maxime 21 - Hyères 76

▲▲ Résidences du Colombier
Rte de Bagnols — 94.51.45.92
Open every day. 60 rms 315-460 F. Restaurant. Half-board 455-600 F. TV. Conference facilities. Heated pool. Tennis. Parking. Telex 470328. V AE DC.
Guestrooms are situated in bungalows scattered over three hectares of pine groves. On the grounds are private gardens, volley-ball, and children's amusements.

La Toque Blanche
in Fréjus-plage
365, av. V.-Hugo — 94.52.06.14
M. Collin. Closed Sun dinner off-season, Mon and 15 Nov-15 Dec. Open until 10 pm. Air cond. V AE DC.
Chef Jacky Collins employs his intelligence and technical skills to keep his classic specialities (lobster ravioli américaine, veal kidneys and sweetbreads with whole-grain mustard, young pigeon stuffed with foie gras) from paling alongside newer entries like foie gras aux fruits, and ravioli d'escargots aux orties. Fine cellar, smooth service.
A la carte: 300-350 F. Menus: 145 F, 200 F, 250 F.

44580 Fresnay-en-Retz — (Loire-Atl.)
Paris 416 - Nantes 39 - La Roche-sur-Yon 58

 ### Le Colvert
Route de Pornic
40.21.46.79
M. Boulestreau. Closed Wed, dinner Sun and Tue, and Feb school holidays and Christmas. Open until 9 pm. Private room: 18. No pets. V AE DC.
She makes you perfectly comfortable in the pretty peach-and-almond-green dining room, while he keeps busy in the kitchen preparing scallop galettes in truffle-scented oil, river perch in a buttery sauce flavoured with cedar liqueur, and Creole tart with caramelised spices. The cellar is improving.
A la carte: 250 F. Menus: 115 F (weekdays lunch only, wine inc), 97 F, 147 F, 210 F.

See Hendaye

See Manosque

See Annemasse

See PARIS Suburbs

See Nîmes

83580 Gassin — (Var)
Paris 877 - Le Lavandou 33 - St-Tropez 8

La Verdoyante
866, VC de Coste Brigade
94.56.16.23
M. Mouret. Closed Wed (except dinner in July-Aug) and 5 Nov-20 March. Open until 9.30 pm. Garden dining. Parking. V.
Soft vineyard breezes and the gentle rhythm of yesteryear stir this exquisite terrace where yesterday, today, and—we are certain—tomorrow patrons feed on an unvarying menu of Provençal daube, rabbit liver tartinettes, and other perennial favourites.
A la carte: 200-280 F. Menu: 130 F.

The prices quoted in this guide are those which we were given by the restaurants and hotels concerned. Increases in prices are beyond our control.

88400 Gérardmer — (Vosges)
Paris 421 - Colmar 52 - Epinal 40 - Saint-Dié 30

 ### Les Bas Rupts et Chalet Fleuri
3 km on D 486
29.63.09.25
M. Philippe. Open every day. Open until 9.30 pm. Private room: 40. Garden dining. Garage parking. Telex 960992. V AE DC.
There is no finer place to take in the beauty of the fir-covered Vosges mountains than in this big, perfectly run chalet. Family traditions provide the backbone, constant renovations the pretty face of this comfortable establishment. Similarly, a classic sauce-based cuisine of the highest order is renewed by the seasons and the *air du temps*. The addition of a skilled pastry chef to the staff has brought the desserts up to the uniformly superb level of the sliced scallops with dandelion greens and pistachios, crunchy potatoes with truffled sweetbreads, duck breast stuffed with goose liver, local frogs' legs sautéed with garlic and parsley, and salmon ravioli with caviar, broad beans, and lime.
A la carte: 400 F. Menus: 120 F (weekdays only), 180 F, 240 F, 280 F.

 ### Les Bas Rupts et Chalet Fleuri
(See restaurant above)
Open every day. 1 ste 800 F. 32 rms 280-580 F. Half-board 400-540 F oblig in seas. TV 20 rms. Conference facilities. Tennis.
A modern mountain chalet featuring bright, pretty, spacious rooms whose tasteful décor reflects the beauty of the surroundings. Discreet service, terrific breakfasts.

74260 Gets (Les) — (H.-Savoie)
Paris 595 - Bonneville 37 - Morzine 7 - Genève 52

 ### Chalet-Hôtel Crychar
50.79.72.84
Closed 11 May-30 June and 10 Sep-20 Dec. 12 rms 300-518 F. TV. No pets. Heated pool. Garage parking. Telex 385026. V AE DC.
Off by itself above the rest of the resort, this small chalet-hotel boasts large rooms and a pretty terrace.

21220 Gevrey-Chambertin — (Côte-d'Or)
Paris 310 - Beaune 26 - Dijon 13 - Besançon 46

 ### Les Grands Crus
Route des Grands-Crus
80.34.34.15
Closed 1 Dec-25 Feb. 24 rms 275-365 F. Garage parking. V.
A peaceful establishment with neat, renovated rooms situated in the celebrated vineyard opposite a twelfth-century church. There's a pretty flowered garden where breakfast is served.

Les Millésimes
25, rue de l'Eglise
80.51.84.24
Mme Sangoy. Closed Wed lunch, Tue and Jan. Open until 9.30 pm. Private room: 20. Air cond. Parking. V DC.
It's all in the family: father and sons are at the stoves, another son is in charge of the cellar, and Mme Sangoy and her daughter receive guests and

oversee the service. Thanks to them, this pretty winemaker's house perched on the village heights is one of the region's gastronomic Meccas. Prices, alas, are verging on the unholy (the kitchen is prodigal with caviar, truffles, lobster and the like). Yet the sauces are lighter than ever, flavours are clear and sharp, and dishes are timed with admirable accuracy. The elder Sangoy favours high-quality ingredients and his offerings include a Barbary duck with honey and spices, a salad of pan-roasted foie gras, and a papillote de pêche au poivre vert. The cellar, predictably, is mind-boggling.

A la carte: 550 F. Menus: 195 F (lunch only), 275 F, 370 F, 470 F.

 ### Rôtisserie du Chambertin 🕸
Rue du Chambertin
80.34.33.20

M. Menneveau. Closed Sun dinner and Mon, Feb and first week of Aug. Open until 9 pm. Private room: 150. Air cond. Parking. V.

This is Burgundy's heartland at its most sensual and opulent. Take the time to admire the Rôtisserie's beautiful stonework and the staircase that winds its way down to the cool *caves*, before crossing the small kitchens to the vaulted, panelled dining room. Here is a restaurant that could qualify as a sort of repository of Burgundian tradition—had it not been one of the first to shake up that tradition with a style of cooking based on absolutely authentic ingredients.

Today the Rôtisserie is one of the best restaurants of the Côte d'Or; owner Pierre Menneveau urbanely greets visitors from all over the world. Working beside him is chef Jean-Pierre Nicolas (longtime second of maestro Louis Outhier at la Napoule) who has adapted his personal style and know-how to this region of France. Some dishes are particularly rich—homardine de pommes de terre, pan-roasted duck liver à la bigarade, or gigot de poulette aux morilles—but the menu also includes lighter offerings, like the exquisite frogs' legs with parsley coulis, fillet of carp with sorrel, and a sterling coq au vin (the best of its kind around), dishes which gently embrace Burgundian traditions without putting a damper on Nicolas's masterly creations: fillet of turbot with ginger or fillet of freshwater perch cooked in powerful, golden vin jaune from the Jura. This is first-rate Burgundian cooking which just manages not to overdo the calories.

A la carte: 450 F. Menus: 260 F, 330 F, 410 F.

 ### La Sommellerie
7, rue Souvert
80.34.31.48

MM. Simon. Closed Sun (except holidays), 1-24 Feb and 22-31 Dec. Open until 9.30 pm. Private room: 15. V DC.

Two brothers filled with laudable ambitions run this village establishment. Philippe supervises the stylish service in a rather dull wine-coloured dining room on the first floor, while François gives himself wholeheartedly to a contemporary, personal, and well-prepared cuisine with keen, distinctive flavours. Try his snail ravioli in a garlic bouillon, his frogs' legs salad with olive oil, or the red-mullet soufflé with celeriac. The wine list offers some wonderful Côte-de-Nuits.

A la carte: 350-400 F. Menus: 140 F (weekdays only), 190 F, 250 F, 310 F.

Red toques signify modern cuisine; black toques signify traditional cuisine.

GIEN

45500 Gien — (Loiret)
Paris 154 - Orléans 64 - Bourges 76 - Cosne 41

Le Rivage
1, quai de Nice — 38.67.20.53

M. Gaillard. Closed 10 Feb-15 March. Open until 9.15 pm. Private room: 30. Air cond. No-smoking section. Parking. V AE DC.

A team of true professionals welcomes you with a smile into the chic and comfortable dining room or onto the flowered terrace bordering the Loire. Under owner Christian Gaillard's eagle eye, a trio of chefs labours away to produce a rich and tasty cuisine: effeuillé of lotte with a tart shallot butter, tender aiguillette of beef with watercress and an artichoke mousse, superb cheeses, and a succulent gratin de poires. Interesting wines. Top-notch service.

A la carte: 300-350 F. Menus: 145 F, 200 F, 295 F.

Le Rivage
(See restaurant above)

Closed 10 Feb-15 March. 3 stes 430-630 F. 19 rms 260-315 F. Half-board oblig in seas. TV. Conference facilities.

On the quay by the old Anne de Beaujeu bridge. Some of the rooms are simple and well furnished, others definitely more luxurious. Jolly nice bathrooms, first-rate breakfasts, and a flawless welcome.

GIGNAC

34150 Gignac — (Hérault)
Paris 790 - Montpellier 30 - Sète 44 - Lodève 24

Capion
3, bd de l'Esplanade — 67.57.50.83

Mme Capion. Closed off-season Sun dinner and Mon, and Feb. Open until 9.30 pm. Private room: 80. Terrace dining. Air cond. No-smoking section. Hotel: 8 rms 180-320 F. V AE DC.

Too bad! Renovation projects for this Louis XIII-provincial décor have obviously been shelved. But the elegant tables, Jacqueline Capion's charming welcome, and the efforts of the son of this old Languedoc house to lighten his menu and widen his sources of inspiration make this spot a traditional favourite for Sunday outings or family feasts: truffled chicken croquettes, grilled morsels of lamb's sweetbreads with a lively parsley coulis, crisp sea bream in a red-wine infusion, and nougat glacé with raspberry coulis. An exceptional cellar.

A la carte: 300 F. Menu: 150 F (weekdays only).

GIGONDAS

84190 Gigondas — (Vaucluse)
Paris 677 - Orange 18 - Avignon 37 - Vaison 15

Les Florets
Rte des Dentelles-de-Montmirail
90.65.85.01

Mmes Germano and Bernard. Closed Tue off-season, Wed, Jan and Feb. Open until 9 pm. Private room: 30. Garden dining. Parking. Hotel: 15 rms 300 F (per pers, half-board oblig). V AE DC.

The lovely terrace is overhung with plane trees, acacias, and chestnuts. The cuisine is tasty and fresh and faithfully regional, an ideal companion for the wines of Gigondas. Join the habitués for the pleasures of quail Provençal, aïoli of fresh cod, or a tian d'agneau. Prices are always reasonable.

A la carte: 200-250 F. Menus: 130 F, 180 F.

GILLY-LÈS-CÎTEAUX

See Nuits-Saint-Georges

32200 Gimont — (Gers)
Paris 699 - Toulouse 51 - Agen 85 - Montauban 70

Château de Larroque   ♟
Rte de Toulouse — 62.67.77.44
M. Fagedet. Closed off-season Sun dinner and Mon lunch, and 2-24 Jan. Open until 9.30 pm. Private room: 200. Garden dining. Garage parking. Telex 531135. V AE DC.

This outsized château set in the middle of extensive grounds and built the year Napoleon was crowned emperor, takes one's breath away. So does the Gers landscape stretching out towards infinity from the wide terrace. The welcome and décor are warm and appealing, as is André Fagedet's cuisine; in fact, the food here is better than ever (hence the extra point this year). Try the confit de canard in a stew of tender broad beans delicately flavoured with fresh thyme. The ris de canard en persillade is a real find and the charlotte of cèpes with foie gras is a dream. The wine list has good regional wines and Bordeaux at affordable prices. Efficient, friendly service.
A la carte: 300 F. Menus: 125 F (weekdays only), 185 F, 245 F.

Château de Larroque   🌲🍴
(See restaurant above)
Closed Sun off-season and 2-24 Jan. 1 ste 1,250-1,350 F. 14 rms 360-800 F. Half-board 490-610 F. TV. Conference facilities. Pool. Tennis.
A delicious Relais et Châteaux in the opulent Gascon countryside. Rooms are first-rate and have all mod cons including big, marble bathrooms. Breakfast is served on a pretty terrace. Fishing.

06350 Golfe-Juan — (Alpes-Mar.)
Paris 929 - Nice 27 - Cannes 6 - Antibes 5 - Grasse 21

12/20 Le Bistrot du Port
53, bd des Frères-Roustan — 93.63.70.64
M. Druffin. Closed off-season Sun dinner and Mon, Dec and Jan. Open until 10 pm. Air cond. No pets. V.
The draw here is a series of small glassed-in rooms overlooking the port, an enjoyable summer terrace, and simple cuisine based on fresh ingredients: an unctuous and delicious gratin d'aubergines, very fresh sea bass with a decent hollandaise sauce, and a perfectly acceptable apple tart. Succinct wine list.
A la carte: 300-350 F. Menu: 210 F.

11/20 Chez Claude
162, av. de la Liberté — 93.63.71.30
M. Fugairon. Closed Tue off-season, and 15 Dec-15 Jan. Open until 11 pm. Garden dining. Hotel: 10 rms 180-230 F. Garage parking. V AE DC.
Uninventive but generous and conscientious cooking: salade niçoise, grilled striped bass with fennel. The dear little dining room gives onto a wonderful garden.
A la carte: 150-200 F. Menus: 98 F, 150 F, 180 F.

84220 Gordes — (Vaucluse)
Paris 717 - Apt 20 - Avignon 38 - Cavaillon 17

La Bastide de Gordes
Le Village — 90.72.12.12
Mlle Mazet. Closed Mon and 12 Nov-22 Dec. Open until 10 pm. Private room: 30. Terrace dining. Air cond. Valet parking. Telex 432025. V AE.
Originally a convent, then a police station, now an elegant hotel on the ramparts of Gordes, the

Bastide de Gordes enjoys a view over the entire Lubéron chain. The proprietor, Mr Mazet, and his daughter have succeeded in making this one of the region's most charming 'town houses'. They even secured the collaboration of top chef Alain Ducasse, who sent them one of his best pupils, Alain Solivères, to preside over the kitchen. Solivères's talent is keen and sure, and he possesses a deep understanding of Provençal flavours.
He scrupulously reproduces Ducasse's specialities, but it may be time for this star pupil to spread his wings and let his own personality soar. In the meantime there is a great deal of pleasure to be had from his pot-au-feu de légumes en vinaigrette et au jus de truffe, the pan-roasted rockfish fillets with caramelised tomatoes and crisp fried herbs, the baby duck stuffed with garlic, or the admirable côte de veau en cocotte with tiny stuffed vegetables, as well as the many other dishes for which Alain Ducasse provides (via telex) meticulous recipes.
Desserts are as scrumptious as what precedes them. Finish up with a palet au chocolat et noisettes, or the tambourin Provençal, a mould of almond praline and caramel ice cream. The cellar contains some excellent Provençal wines, and service is charming and efficient. The second toque is awarded in hopes of something even better.
A la carte: 400 F. Menus: 225 F (lunch only), 285 F (dinner only).

La Bastide de Gordes
(See restaurant above)
Closed 12 Nov-22 Dec. 1 ste 1,300-1,450 F. 18 rms 490-1,250 F. TV. Air cond. Conference facilities. Heated pool. Tennis.
Twenty spacious and inviting rooms which make you feel you're visiting friends. They're totally comfortable and unostentatious, with lovely Provençal fabrics and whopping great bathrooms. Gym, sauna, and a little swimming pool on the terrace that faces a splendid view.

Les Bories   🌲🍴
2 km NW on D 177
Rte de l'abbaye de Sénanque — 90.72.00.51
Closed 1 Dec-15 Jan. 18 rms 450-1,450 F. Restaurant. Half-board 500-1,700 F. TV. Heated pool. Tennis. Parking. V AE DC.
A marvellous spot in a magical corner of Provence. Ten new rooms (in a little *mas*) have been added to the old rooms set in authentic dry-stone bungalows. There's a well-kept garden with a lovely covered pool. New access road since last summer.

Comptoir du Victuailler   ♟
Pl. du Château — 90.72.01.31
M. Schmitt. Closed Wed off-season, Tue (except dinner in July-Aug), 16 Nov-16 Dec and 16 Jan-16 March. Open until 8.30 pm (9.30 pm in summer). Terrace dining. V.
In the heart of the village, opposite the Renaissance château which houses the Vasarely foundation, Joëlle Chaudat prepares a version of French home cooking so unfashionable that it may soon be considered avant-garde. A strictly limited number of patrons may enjoy her turbot with seaweed, Mediterranean fish with basil, or guinea fowl with raspberries. Clever wine list, long on Côtes-du-Rhônes, but short on everything else. Wine and prepared food may be purchased to take away.
A la carte: 300 F.

Domaine de l'Enclos
Rte de Sénanque — 90.72.08.22

M. Sibourg. Open every day. Open until 9.30 pm (10 pm in summer). Private room: 30. Garden dining. No pets. Parking. Telex 432119. V AE.

Just as we were getting tired of the ups and downs of this establishment, we've had a very good surprise. There's a new team on board, as well as a young and serious chef, José Martinez, armed with a lively talent, remarkable technical skills, and a plethora of good ideas. Try the extraordinary quails' eggs en gelée de caviar, or the aïoli of salt cod with saffron-flavoured potatoes. Desserts are a shade less dazzling, but we hope these two toques will spur him on to even greater things.

A la carte: 380-450 F. Menus: 270 F, 480 F.

Domaine de l'Enclos
(See restaurant above)

Open every day. 6 stes 600-2,200 F. 10 rms 400-1,200 F. Half-board 480-780 F. TV. Air cond. Conference facilities. Heated pool. Tennis.

Some important renovations will no doubt put the charm back into the comfortable rooms, which open out onto a large garden and a unique view. A pleasant, professional welcome.

Le Gordos
Rte de Cavaillon — 90.72.00.75

Closed 13 Nov-1 March. 19 rms 425-525 F. TV. Pool. Tennis. Parking. V AE.

The hotel is totally surrounded by an oak-dotted landscape and was entirely renovated this year by the owners of the Bastide de Gordes (see above). There's lots of stone and red tile, and rooms have showers only but are prettily done up. Terraces enjoy a view either of a patio or the Lubéron. The swimming pool has been enlarged.

Le Mas Tourteron
Les Imberts — 90.72.00.16

Mme Bourgeois-Baique. Closed Sun dinner and Mon (except July- Aug), 15 Nov-10 Dec and 15 Jan-6 Feb. Open until 9.30 pm. Private room: 6. Garden dining. Parking. V AE.

Our readers are enthusiastic and so are we. Everyone loves the presbytery garden with its immense lime tree and the little salon which unaffectedly affords a view of Elisabeth Bourgeois and her brigade moving around the gleaming kitchen. This talented amateur of fast cars and planes has gained in finesse and intelligence, without losing any of her fetching personality. Her seafood minestrone with pistou, salad of squid and lamb's trotters, daube of red tunny with open-face ravioli, or her charlotte of Lubéron lamb with aubergines are full of inspiration and superbly cooked and presented. The cellar is well looked after by Philippe Baïque, the affable and attentive host.

Menus: 215 F, 295 F.

12/20 La Mayanelle
Rue de la Combe — 90.72.00.28

M. Mayard. Closed Tue, Jan and Feb. Open until 9 pm. Private room: 30. Terrace dining. Hotel: 10 rms 230-330 F. V AE DC.

From the panoramic terrace, the splendid Lubéron valley stretches out as far as the eye can see. Come here for a simple, well-made meal at very reasonable prices: salads, terrines aux herbes. Nice ambience and regional wines.

A la carte: 200-250 F.

In nearby **Beaumettes**

(7 km S on D 2 and D 103)
84220 Gordes — (Vaucluse)

12/20 Le Moulin Blanc
Ch. du Moulin — 90.72.34.50

Mlle Diez. Open every day. Open until 9 pm. Private room: 20. Garden dining. No pets. Parking. Telex 432926. V AE DC.

This old coaching inn was a flour mill before it was converted into a fine hotel with vaulted ceilings, imposing fireplaces, and Louis XIII furniture. On a summer's day head for the superb terrace looking over the leafy park, and enjoy the 190 F menu: amuse-bouche, warm salad of skate with citrus, filet de rascasse in a basil-scented beurre blanc, farmhouse goat cheese, and a tartelette aux épices.

Menus: 190 F, 300 F.

Le Moulin Blanc
(See restaurant above)

Open every day. 2 stes 800-1,000 F. 16 rms 410-830 F. Half-board 420-670 F. TV. Conference facilities. Heated pool. Tennis.

An old fifteenth-century mill in the heart of the Lubéron. Pretty rooms and comfortably equipped, nicely furnished, some with four-poster beds. Choose one on the garden.

In nearby **Joucas**

(6 km E on D 2 and D 102)
84220 Gordes — (Vaucluse)

Le Mas des Herbes Blanches
90.05.79.79

M. Juillard. Closed 4 Jan-8 March. Open until 9.15 pm. Private room: 20. Terrace dining. Garage parking. Telex 432045. V AE.

This exquisite dry-stone *mas* is on a slope facing the sombre mass of the Lubéron. A tasteful, unostentatious décor is perfectly suited to the luminous and wild beauty of this remote landscape. Patrick Deschamps's cuisine too is without frills or fantasy, strict and precise in its execution. Try his rouleau of smoked salmon with fresh salmon tartare, his millefeuille of foie gras with a truffle jus, or his lamb with vegetables, dishes which are absolutely fresh with big, strong flavours. Expensive, but worth it.

A la carte: 350-500 F. Menu: 240 F (lunch only).

Le Mas des Herbes Blanches
(See restaurant above)

Closed 4 Jan-8 March. 1 ste 1,320-1,630 F. 18 rms 770-1,320 F. Half-board 725-1,155 F. TV. Air cond 6 rms. Conference facilities. Heated pool. Tennis.

The twenty rooms have been ravishingly renovated. Most of them give onto the Lubéron mountain and the large park where the stipas—the 'white grasses' which gave the hotel its name—grow in profusion. Relais et Châteaux.

Le Phébus
Rte de Murs — 90.05.78.83

Closed 15 Nov-15 March. 2 stes 730-770 F. 17 rms 660-730 F. Half-board 597-631 F. Restaurant. TV. Conference facilities. Heated pool. Tennis.

Lovely, large rooms facing a dream-like perspective. Period furniture, pretty floral arrangements, an attractive terrace, smiling welcome, and excellent service.

In nearby **Murs**

(8 km NE on D 15)
84220 Gordes — (Vaucluse)

Mas du Loriot
Rte de Joucas — 90.72.62.62
M. Revel. Dinner only. Open until 9.30 pm. Garden dining. Hotel: 5 rms 450-520 F. Pool. Parking. V.

This doll's house stands lost in the garrigue, atop a hill that juts out over the village of Joucas. Rooms are small but pretty with tiny bathrooms and terraces overlooking the Lubéron. There's a swimming pool in which to work up an appetite. The Revels should have no trouble earning back the toque they had at their last establishment in Dourdan, near Paris, for Mme Revel is an excellent cook with a light, precise touch and a knack for choosing first-rate ingredients.

Menu: 150 F.

22570 Gouarec — (Côtes/Armor)
Paris 470 - Saint-Brieuc 50 - Carhaix 31

Hôtel du Blavet
N 164 bis — 96.24.90.03
M. Le Loir. Closed Sun dinner and Mon (except July-Aug), 29 Jan-25 Feb and 20-26 Dec. Open until 9 pm. Private room: 40. Hotel: 15 rms 140-350 F. Parking. V.

This appealing, family-run hotel nestles in greenery right in the middle of Brittany. The peaceful Blavet River, which runs in front of the terrace off the large dining room with its beautiful Breton furniture, inspires Louis Le Loir to produce a consistent yet unoriginal cuisine based on excellent ingredients. This year, try the escalopines of fresh salmon marinated in pistachio oil, or veal fillets with morels. A good little cellar.

A la carte: 280-320 F. Menus: 75 F (weekdays only), 140 F, 200 F, 300 F.

25470 Goumois — (Doubs)
Paris 485 - Besançon 93 - Bienne 44 - Maîche 19

12/20 Taillard
81.44.20.75
M. Taillard. Closed Wed off-season, and 15 Nov-1 March. Open until 9 pm. Private room: 30. Garden dining. Garage parking. V AE DC.

From the comfortable dining room of this large Franc-Comtois chalet you look out onto the gorges, mountains, and forests of the Doubs. The cuisine is based on cream and country recipes: foie gras with Fougerolles cherries, a fondue of morels with double cream, Bresse poultry with vin jaune.

A la carte: 350 F. Menus: from 120 F to 295 F.

Taillard
(See restaurant above)
Closed Wed off-season and 15 Nov-1 March. 5 stes 390 F. 12 rms 250-280 F. Half-board 320-340 F oblig in seas. TV. Conference facilities. Heated pool.

An ideal stop for those in search of bucolic delights and tranquil dreams. Half the rooms were redone this year. Good breakfasts.

See Chantilly

See Bordeaux

46500 Gramat — (Lot)
Paris 524 - Figeac 35 - Cahors 57 - Brive 56

(5 km NW on N 140)
46500 Gramat — (Lot)

Château de Roumégouse 😊
65.33.63.81
Mme Lainé. Closed 4 Nov-1 April. Open until 9 pm. Private room: 20. Garden dining. Valet parking. Telex 532592. V AE DC.

This miniature castle with its pointed roofs, dungeon and transom windows dominates the Rocamadour causse, and is in fact a most inviting place to stop, despite its rather forbidding medieval air. Luce and Jean-Louis Lainé have opted for an impeccably high-class décor to make this an ideal spot from which to tour this wonderful region. For his part, chef Yannick Bruneau produces generous country-style dishes such as foie gras flavoured with raspberry vinegar or veal kidneys Rocamadour with a mouthwatering foie gras and juniper sauce. Lots of good Cahors wines, though not enough half-bottles. Prices are rising steeply.

A la carte: 350-400 F. Menus: 100 F (weekdays lunch only), 150 F, 200 F, 300 F.

Château de Roumégouse
(See restaurant above)
Closed 4 Nov-1 April. 3 stes 880-1,400 F. 12 rms 400-780 F. Half-board 600-750 F oblig in seas. TV. Pool.

The rooms all have a great deal of charm (there's a new one this year with a private garden), and they are elegant, comfortable, and neat as can be. Wonderful breakfasts. Also a boutique, video library, and music room. Picnics can be arranged. Relais et Châteaux.

34280 Grande-Motte (La) — (Hérault)
Paris 747 - Nîmes 44 - Montpellier 20 - Palavas 15

Alexandre
Espl. de la Capitainerie — 67.56.63.63
M. Alexandre. Closed Sun dinner, Mon, 8 Jan-15 Feb and 28 Oct-8 Nov. Open until 10 pm. Private room: 45. Terrace dining. Air cond. No pets. Parking. V.

Working in resorts does indeed have its drawbacks, and off-seasons can be profoundly discouraging; but that's not a good enough excuse for the botched meal served to us by Michel Alexandre on a very slow day, while his dining room slumbered under the weight of its fussy period décor. We know how precise and intelligent a chef he normally is, and how he harmonises the elements of ingenious little dishes like his stuffed vegetables à la languedocienne with mussels, or his lamb fricassée in a thyme-flavoured cream sauce, or his delicate roast pigeon with cardamom.

A la carte: 350 F. Menus: from 190 F to 330 F.

Hôtel Azur
Presqu'île du Port — 67.56.56.00
Closed 30 Nov-6 Jan. 3 stes 695-800 F. 20 rms 390-560 F. TV. Air cond. No pets. Conference facilities. Pool. Parking. V DC.

Away from the madding crowd, but near the quays, the boats, and the casino. Nice rooms with pretty furniture look out to sea.

11/20 La Brasserie de la Mer

(Chez Fabrice)
Quai d'Honneur — 67.56.75.93
M. Soliveres. Open every day. Open until 11 pm. Garden dining. V AE DC.

On a terrace facing the sea, guests tuck into plates of shellfish, grilled fish, and bouillabaisse. Tasty, fresh, generous, and not too dear.
A la carte: 180-400 F. Menus: 60 F, 145 F.

Le Quetzal

Allée des Jardins — 67.56.61.10
Open every day. 52 rms 295-495 F. Restaurant. TV. Conference facilities. Heated pool. Garage parking. Telex 485385. V AE DC.

The sweet little rooms with large loggias are a sunbather's dream. The hotel is a modern construction set in a pine forest, though near the centre and port. Charming service.

37350 Grand-Pressigny (Le) — (Indre/Loire)
Paris 293 - Tours 58 - Loches 33 - Châtellerault 29

⑬ Auberge Savoie Villars

47.94.96.86
MM. Gatault and Richard. Closed Mon dinner, Tue, 4-18 Feb and 7-21 Oct. Open until 9.30 pm. Private room: 30. Hotel: 7 rms 105-170 F. V.

Ignore the slightly drab dining room of this old inn, and focus instead on the *carte*, which is tiny and whimsical, or on the marvellously prodigal set menus, and you will enjoy one of the cleverest, most flavourful meals in the region: sample the pan-roasted chicory and shellfish with chicken juices, a rich stew of pork and duck gizzards with fresh pasta, and a frangipane de pommes à l'orange. This team of youngsters is going places! Nice little cellar.
A la carte: 220 F. Menus: 58 F (weekdays only), 95 F, 120 F, 155 F.

⑬ L'Espérance

Pl. du Carroir-des-Robins — 47.94.90.12
Mme Bernard. Closed Mon and 6 Jan-6 Feb. Open until 10 pm. Air cond. Hotel: 10 rms 130-160 F. Garage parking. V AE DC.

Fresh market produce and his own vegetable garden are the indispensable elements of chef Bernard Torset's repertoire, typical of Touraine in its traditionalism touched with modernity: escalope of sea bass roasted in its skin, marinated fillet of beef sauce Grand Veneur, wild-strawberry gratin. The décor is as rosy as life becomes after a few glasses of the regional wine!
A la carte: 280-300 F. Menus: 80 F (weekdays only), 120 F, 160 F, 180 F.

In nearby Petit-Pressigny

(9 km E on D 103)
37350 Grand-Pressigny (Le) — (Indre/Loire)

⑯ La Promenade

47.94.93.52
M. Dallais. Closed Sun dinner, Mon, 2-21 Jan and 23 Sep-8 Oct. Open until 9.30 pm. Air cond. V.

This old country bistro has been touched with grace since Jacky Dallais set up his kitchen in this spiffingly modern, airy restaurant, filled daily with fresh flowers by a youthful, dynamic staff. Thankfully, success has not spoiled this young establishment nor fuelled its prices. Dallais's enthusiasm is intact, and he manages to stun us at each visit with dishes like marvellous marjoram-scented prawns wrapped in leek leaves, a cream of broccoli soup with oysters and salmon roe, or

baby pigeon, its juices enhanced with a hint of bitter cocoa, served with a croustillant of fresh cabbage, or his duck liver roasted with lime-flavoured chicory. Exquisite!
A la carte: 270-340 F. Menus: 96 F (weekdays only), 165 F, 220 F, 285 F.

GRANE

26400 Grane — (Drôme)
Paris 598 - Valence 29 - Privas 28 - Montélimar 31

⑮ Giffon

Place de l'Eglise
75.62.60.64
M. Giffon. Closed Sun dinner off-season, Mon (except holidays) and Feb. Open until 9.30 pm. Private room: 20. Terrace dining. Air cond. Parking. Hotel: 9 rms 180-280 F, half-board 320 F. V AE DC.

Grane is no great tourist Mecca, nor is it a river port. But to give it a miss would be to neglect an adorable family inn run by the Giffon family. Son Patrick is in charge of the kitchen, and has all the virtues of a fine chef: he's careful, conscientious, and consistent on the one hand, and respectful of seasons and regional recipes on the other. The second toque is awarded for the little stuffed courgettes with snails and garlic cream, the duck liver with verbena jelly, the charlotte of young rabbit with thyme, and the splendid fruit desserts. A plush velvet décor gives way to a superb terrace under a huge plane tree.
A la carte: 300 F and up. Menus: 120 F (weekdays only), 160 F, 200 F, 280 F.

GRANGES-LES-BEAUMONT

See Romans-sur-Isère

GRANVILLE

50400 Granville — (Manche)
Paris 350 - Cherbourg 104 - Coutances 29

⑬ La Gentilhommière

152, rue Couraye
33.50.17.99
M. Poude. Closed Sun dinner, Mon, 23 Feb-11 March, 3-10 June and 23 Sep-7 Oct. Open until 9.30 pm. V.

A promising newcomer who fills a gap, René Poude has set up shop on the outskirts of Granville in a comfortable and intimate little dining room with overhead beams. Try the foie gras flan with morels and a fragrant artichoke cream sauce, a first-rate croustillant aux langoustines, or the (slightly overcooked) baked red mullet. The cellar holds a good stock of claret, and also offers Loire wines at under 80 F.
A la carte: 350 F. Menus: 125 F, 250 F.

GRANZAY-GRIPT

See Niort

GRASSE

06130 Grasse — (Alpes-Mar.)
Paris 938 - Nice 39 - Draguignan 56 - Cannes 17

12/20 L'Amphitryon

16, bd Victor-Hugo
93.36.58.73
M. André. Closed Sun, 23 Dec-3 Jan and Aug. Open until 9.30 pm. Air cond. Telex 470871. V AE DC.

Grey, not gay, is the décor of this establishment which offers very conscientiously crafted dishes, such as tasty warm oysters with spinach and pine-nuts, a good fish stew in red wine with mushrooms, and floating island (which seemed in imminent danger of sinking into its custard). A

courteous, though somewhat listless welcome. Prices, in contrast, are full of vigour.
A la carte: 300 F. Menus: 108 F, 145 F, 222 F.

 Campanile
5 km E on D 2085
in Pré-du-Lac
06740 Châteauneuf – 93.42.55.55
Open every day. 36 rms 239 F. Restaurant. TV. Conference facilities. Parking. Telex 470092. V DC.
Good functional rooms off the Nice road. Bar.

 Ibis Grasse
Rue M.-Carol – 93.70.70.70
Open every day. 65 rms 280-360 F. Restaurant. TV. Air cond. Conference facilities. Pool. Tennis. Parking. Telex 462682. V AE.
A recently built hotel set in green countryside on the Grasse to Cannes road. Modern, spacious, and bright rooms. Pretty sitting room. Bar.

11/20 Maître Boscq 🔾
13, rue de la Fontette – 93.36.45.76
M. Boscq. Closed off-season Sun and Mon, and 27 Oct-11 Nov. Open until 8.30 pm. V AE.
Follow the warren of narrow streets in the old town until you come to this bistro where Maître Boscq will serve you aïgo boulido—a garlic and sage-flavoured soup—fassum grassois, aïoli (advance notice required), and prunes in peppered wine.
A la carte: 180-200 F. Menu: 103 F.

 Panorama
2, pl. du Cours – 93.36.80.80
Open every day. 36 rms 285-400 F. TV. Air cond 20 rms. Conference facilities. Telex 970908. V.
A well-appointed, agreeably modern hotel with smiling service. Tray meals available upon request.

 Hôtel du Patti
Pl. du Patti – 93.36.01.00
Open every day. 50 rms 290-460 F. Restaurant. Half-board 275-375 F. TV. Air cond. Garage parking. Telex 460126. V AE DC.
Marvellously situated in the heart of the old town, this hotel is exceptional for its rating. The attractive, recently renovated rooms are most comfortable, with individual heating and superb bathrooms. Pleasing service and full breakfasts.

In nearby **Cabris**

(5 km SW on D 4)
06530 Grasse – (Alpes-Mar.)

 L'Horizon 🌲🍴
93.60.51.69
Closed 15 Oct-15 March. 22 rms 250-350 F. Half-board 250-300 F. TV. No pets. Conference facilities. Pool. AE DC.
This little Provençal house is situated in a typical hinterland village, overlooking the lovely countryside around Grasse. Rooms are simple but comfortable, and regularly refurbished. Family-run.

12/20 Le Petit Prince
15, rue F.-Mistral – 93.60.51.40
M. Massot. Closed Thu dinner off-season, Fri and 1 Nov-18 Dec. Open until 9.45 pm. Terrace dining. V AE DC.
A nice place to stop in the hills behind Cannes. A simple, warm welcome is the prelude to a meal in the somewhat ordinary dining room or (even better) on the terrace, which on a summer day is lush with greenery. We recommend the millefeuille of smoked salmon, the noisettes of

duck with foie gras and morels, and the délice of mango with tarragon. Friendly, unpretentious service.
A la carte: 250-300 F. Menus: 98 F and 138 F (weekdays only), 140 F, 180 F.

 In nearby **Spéracèdes**

(6 km W)
06530 Grasse – (Alpes-Mar.)

 **Lou Pitchoun Casteou** 🌲🍴
61, ch. des Basses-Molières – 93.66.01.65
Closed Wed. 2 stes 700 F. 12 rms 265-700 F. Restaurant. Half-board 380-950 F. TV. Conference facilities. Parking. V AE.
This recently built Provençal-style family house stands at the end of a narrow road set plumb in the middle of the countryside. It offers good-sized, impeccably clean, imaginatively decorated rooms. The new swimming pool should be finished by this edition.

11/20 La Soleillade
Rue des Orangers – 93.60.58.46
M. Forest. Closed Wed and 15 Oct-15 Dec. Open until 9 pm. Terrace dining. Hotel: 10 rms 115-185 F.
An appealing, friendly spot complete with garden and a talkative proprietor. The food doesn't vary much, but it's fresh and there's always plenty of it. The farmhouse tourte, good charcuterie, and charcoal-grilled beef will ensure a pleasant meal at most reasonable prices for the region.
A la carte: 180-200 F. Menus: 75 F (weekdays lunch only), 120 F, 160 F.

***See also:* Mougins**

30240 Grau-du-Roi (Le) – (Gard)
Paris 755 - Nîmes 47 - Arles 53 - Aigues-Mortes 6

In nearby **Port-Camargue**

(3 km S on D 62b)
30240 Grau-du-Roi (Le) – (Gard)

 Hôtel du Cap
66.73.60.60
Closed 9 Dec-31 Jan. 94 rms 360-500 F. Restaurant. Half-board 295-610 F. TV. Air cond. Conference facilities. Pool. Tennis. Garage parking. Telex 480806. V AE DC.
This modern, prestigious beach resort boasts comfortable rooms with large terraces where sun-worshippers can cultivate a tan while watching the tide roll in. The hotel is part of a vast residential complex complete with sporting and leisure facilities, as well a salt-water cure centre.

👨‍🍳 **La Datcha des Sables**
15
U-turn at roundabout, and 9 km SE
by the private road (Domaine Capelude)
66.51.43.19
Mme Gomez. Closed Wed off-season, 3-29 Jan and 4 Nov-21 Dec. Open until 10 pm. Private room: 50. Garden dining. Air cond. Valet parking. V AE.
Recent municipal upheavals may upset Francine Gomez's hotel project on these 200 hectares of wild Camargue flanked by two kilometres of beach. In the meantime, the well-heeled continue to drop in by boat, chopper, or fancy car to taste Bruno Ménard's light-hearted, sunny cuisine. His concise menu is rooted in the Provençal *terroir*, with a croustillant of large prawns, quenelles of pélardon (local goat cheese) with black-olive purée, and cumin-spiced lamb fillet escorted by a

luscious ratatouille. Ménard, the son of a pastry chef, fashions some delectable desserts: try his gentian sorbet, warm chocolate cake with tart cherries, or a peach croustillant. The service, supervised by Isabelle Ménard, is charming and helps one swallow the rather stiff prices. The wine list is minute.

A la carte: 600 F. Menus: 200 F (lunch only), 220 F, 280 F.

La Datcha des Sables
(See restaurant above)
Closed 3 Jan-29 March and 4 Nov-21 Dec. 1 ste 2,260-2,800 F. 14 rms 520-2,560 F. Half-board 600-1,600 F oblig in seas. TV. Air cond 5 rms.

Several small, traditional *mas* nestle in a paradisaical setting of dunes and reeds. Rooms are small, though each is different and tastefully decorated.

Relais de l'Oustau Camarguen
3, route des Marines
66.51.51.65
Closed 30 Sep-28 March. 2 stes 590-650 F. 40 rms 320-430 F. Restaurant. Half-board 347-402 F oblig in seas. TV. Air cond 5 rms. Conference facilities. Pool. Garage parking. V AE DC.

Set on the edge of the marinas, the comfortable rooms of this authentic Camargue *mas* are all well appointed and give out onto the garden and swimming pool. Fitness centre.

Le Spinaker
Rte du Môle — 66.53.33.33
Mme Cazals. Closed off-season Sun dinner and Mon, and 7 Jan-14 Feb. Open until 9.15 pm. Private room: 60. Garden dining. Air cond. Parking. V.

This is an airy, sun-kissed site in the Camargue, where Jean-Pierre Cazals presents, with seemingly effortless flair, a vibrant, technically expert cuisine full of *joie de vivre* and bright Southern flavours. A second toque, then, for his unctuous foie gras marbled with artichoke and celeriac, roasted red-mullet fillets combined with a brunoise of tiny diced courgette skins, and a scrumptious little crépinette (a small sausage patty) of oxtail and beef jowls. Desserts are by a remarkable young pastry chef, Stéphane Maréchal. Mme Cazals's welcome is warm and elegant, but the service is a mite too coolly classic.

A la carte: 300-400 F. Menus: 170 F (weekdays lunch only, wine inc), 245 F, 335 F.

Le Spinaker
(See restaurant above)
Closed 7 Jan-14 Feb. 21 rms 410 F. Half-board 468 F oblig in seas. TV. Conference facilities. Pool.

Pleasant rooms are set among the piers, clustered around the swimming pool. All have nice sunny terraces, but the slightly dull interior décors are due for a face-lift.

70100 Gray — (Haute-Saône)
Paris 342 - Besançon 45 - Dijon 48 - Langres 54

12/20 Château de Rigny
5 km NE on D 2 — 84.65.25.01
M. Maupin. Closed 6-30 Jan. Open until 9.30 pm. No pets. Garage parking. Telex 362926. V AE DC.

We're sorry, but we must take back the toque we had awarded to this little château's restaurant. The setting is lovely and so is the welcome. But the cooking is not up to scratch: médaillon of veal which tasted as if it had been reheated, and a

Chavignol goat cheese which hadn't been properly grilled. Prices are outlandish.

A la carte: 350-400 F. Menus: 180 F, 280 F.

Château de Rigny
(See restaurant above)
Closed 6-30 Jan. 24 rms 290-480 F. Half-board oblig in seas. TV. Conference facilities. Heated pool. Tennis.

Gracious château set in a quiet, comfortable spot with a lot of atmosphere and character. Huge rooms and very copious breakfasts.

Relais de Nantilly
4 km W on D 2, in Nantilly — 84.65.20.12
Closed Mon off-season, and 31 Oct-1 March. 2 stes 750-900 F. 12 rms 450-650 F. Restaurant. Half-board 675-875 F. TV. Conference facilities. Pool. Tennis. Parking. Telex 362888. V AE DC.

This old hunting pavilion is set in a huge wooded park complete with a babbling brook. The rooms are comfortable, and each is decorated in an individual style. Some attractive pieces of period furniture help create a cosy atmosphere, and the prevailing peace and quiet make this an ideal address for a weekend break or a low-key business conference.

40270 Grenade-sur-l'Adour — (Landes)
Paris 720 - Aire-sur-l'Adour 18 - Mont-de-Marsan 15

Pain Adour et Fantaisie
7, pl. des Tilleuls — 58.45.18.80
M. Oudill. Closed off-season Sun dinner and Mon (except holidays), and 24 Feb-15 March. Open until 10.30 pm. Private room: 35. Terrace dining. Hotel: 12 rms 380-680 F. V DC.

Ever since he settled in this ravishing eighteenth-century house on the ancient village square of Grenade, clients have exclaimed to Didier Oudill: 'What a pity you don't have any guestrooms!' Well, by the time you read these lines, some dozen rooms will have been added, making this noble establishment on the banks of the Adour River one of the region's most desirable stopovers. Long a close collaborator of Michel Guérard (and still a close friend), Didier Oudill has certainly captured and distilled Guérard's influence, but he is not in thrall to it. The disciple is too talented to plagiarise the master; Oudill's personality comes through in every dish he creates. This consummate artist works with a palette of rustic flavours, which he combines in his own inimitable way: take, for example his pipérade of succulent lamb given depth and tone with hot chutney and cool essence of cucumber; or a garlic-studded salmon cooked slowly in goose fat (like a confit), and served on a bed of asparagus tips with a tart meat jus; or eel fresh from the river grilled and served in a wine-laced crayfish bouillon; or a ragoût of sweetbreads with macaroni, broad beans, and morels. Each dish is more clever than the next, so it's no wonder we've awarded an extra point this year.

Didier Oudill cooks with inexpensive ingredients, a strategy that has won him the loyalty of local food lovers, unused to paying Parisian-style bills. Lest we forget, Oudill also offers Gabriel Bachelet's beautifully aged cheeses, and an array of ambrosial desserts: liquorice parfait with caramelised pears, or a lace-like croustillant with tropical-fruit marmalade. And the cellar is stocked with a tremendous collection of great South-western wines as well as some high-flying Bordeaux.

A la carte: 350 F. Menus: 185 F (weekdays lunch only, wine inc), 150 F (weekdays only), 250 F, 350 F.

GRENOBLE
38000 Grenoble — (Isère)
Paris 562 - Lyon 104 - Chambéry 57 - Bourg 142

Alpazur
59, av. d'Alsace-Lorraine — 76.46.42.80
Open every day. 30 rms 130-240 F. TV 2 rms. Telex 980651. V AE.
This hotel is situated in the pedestrian district of the city centre. Well-appointed rooms. Covered and supervised car park nearby.

Les Alpes
45, av. F.-Viallet — 76.87.00.71
Open every day. 67 rms 198-264 F. TV. Garage parking. V.
Between the railway station and the Isère River, this is one of Grenoble's best two-star establishments.

Alpotel-Mercure
12, bd du Mal-Joffre — 76.87.88.41
Open every day. 88 rms 300-485 F. Restaurant. TV. Air cond. Conference facilities. Garage parking. Telex 320884. V AE DC.
All the pluses of a large international hotel right in the city centre.

Angleterre
5, pl. V.-Hugo — 76.87.37.21
Open every day. 70 rms 300-410 F. TV. Air cond. Telex 320297. V AE DC.
A modern and regularly renovated hotel, admirably situated on the edge of Grenoble's largest square, looking out over the Vercors massif.

Le Berlioz
4, rue de Strasbourg — 76.56.22.39
Mlle Legras. Closed Sat lunch, Sun, 29 April-4 May and 22 July-19 Aug. Open until 10.15 pm. V AE.
A favourite of greedy Grenoblois who like to be surprised without being fleeced. The *patronne* has a nose for appealing little wines from good producers, and the new chef has a fertile imagination. Try his cressonière of oysters, marinated halibut with a touch of ginger, the pan-roasted turbot with celery confit and meaty wild mushrooms, or fork-tender lamb cooked for seven hours. Some superb regional set menus are offered.
À la carte: 300 F. Menus: 83 F (lunch only), 112 F, 165 F, 270 F.

11/20 Café Victor
Parc Europe, rue du Gal-Mangin — 76.56.26.56
M. Fritsch. Open every day. Open until midnight. Private room: 300. Air cond. Garage parking. Telex 308393. V AE DC.
Bruno Lechêne used to be at Lamelloise and is a dab hand at fish cookery, but his restaurant is not yet up to par with the hotel (we are sure it could be). Try the scrambled eggs with shrimps, the (dry) rabbit with basil, and some topping house pastries. Competent service.
À la carte: 250 F. Menu: 160 F.

Hôtel Président
(See restaurant above)
Open every day. 3 stes 680-790 F. 102 rms 410-510 F. TV. Air cond. Conference facilities.
A long-awaited modern hotel which the region lacked: 102 rooms and three suites, comfortable, nicely equipped, and elegantly decorated in 1930s style. Good breakfasts. The atmosphere is a bit austere, but the reception and service are fine.

L'Escalier
6, pl. de Lavalette — 76.54.66.16
M. Girod. Closed Sat lunch and Sun. Open until 10 pm. V AE DC.
A fashionably contemporary, clean-lined dining room in Grenoble's old quarter is the rendezvous for an equally fashionable crowd who likes to be recognised and greeted (audibly) by name, before sitting down to smart, up-to-date dishes. The proprietor, Alain Girod, acts like one of the gang, but he keeps an eagle eye on the quality of his ingredients and the constancy of chef Gilbert Grandsire's cuisine. The engaging low-calorie menu is low-priced as well, but if you prefer, you could also gorge on large prawns in filo pastry, sea bream with a garlicky bourride sauce, a puff-pastry tart of lamb's brains and oyster essence, and a marvellous croquant au chocolat. The cellar offers a few finds and the bill when it comes will be a happy surprise.
À la carte: 280-300 F. Menu: 120 F (lunch only except holidays).

Gallia
7, bd du Mal-Joffre — 76.87.39.21
Open every day. 35 rms 115-240 F. TV 28 rms. Garage parking. V AE DC.
A simple hotel with well-kept rooms near the centre and the North-South line of the new tramway.

Le Grand Hôtel
5, rue de la République — 76.44.49.36
Open every day. 73 rms 240-490 F. TV. Air cond. Conference facilities. Telex 980918. V AE DC.
This venerable establishment in the city centre is a nineteenth-century hotel currently under renovation. A fast-food outlet on the ground floor has cost it some of its former prestige. The comfortable rooms are well appointed, and there's a small inner courtyard. Billiards.

Lesdiguières
122, cours de la Libération — 76.96.55.36
Closed 15 Dec-2 Jan and 1 Aug-2 Sep. 36 rms 275-435 F. Restaurant. Half-board 290-360 F. TV. Conference facilities. Garage parking. Telex 320306. V AE DC.
This excellent establishment is a training ground for students from the local hotel school. Rooms are pleasant and give onto the large park. There's a lift for the disabled.

11/20 La Madelon
55, av. d'Alsace-Lorraine — 76.46.36.90
M. Cartillier. Closed Sat lunch and Sun. Open until 10 pm. Private room: 15. Terrace dining. V AE DC.
A modern, deluxe litle brasserie where one comes to sip delicious northern Côtes-du-Rhône vintages discovered by the wine-buff proprietor, and to eat fairly pricey but well-crafted cuisine: fresh salt cod with ravioli, pan-roasted beef steak, and crème brûlée with demerara sugar.
À la carte: 260-300 F. Menus: 98 F, 148 F, 192 F.

Mercure
1, av. d'Innsbruck — 76.33.02.02
Open every day. 2 stes 700-900 F. 100 rms 350-500 F. Restaurant. TV. Air cond. Conference facilities. Pool. Garage parking. Telex 980470. V AE DC.
This is a modern hotel with about a hundred rooms near the Summum and the Palais des Congrès. It has all the accoutrements you would expect from this chain. Some rooms look over the Dauphiné countryside.

327

Patrick Hôtel
116, cours de la Libération — 76.21.26.63
Open every day. 4 stes 550-650 F. 59 rms 280-650 F.
Restaurant. TV. Conference facilities. Garage park-
ing. Telex 320320. V AE DC.
A modern hotel in which all rooms have
bathrooms en suite, satellite television and video,
radio-alarms and direct phone lines. Light meals in
the rooms.

La Poularde Bressane
[13]
12, pl. P.-Mistral — 76.87.08.90
M. Piccinini. Closed Sat lunch and Sun (except
holidays). Open until 9.45 pm. Private room: 50. Air
cond. Parking. V AE DC.
The colonnaded dining room of this restaurant
opposite the Parc Paul-Mistral is not really conducive to good service or conviviality. But it draws a
sleek local crowd that appreciates Jean-Charles
Piccinini's generous cuisine. His repertoire seems
to hesitate between reassuring classicism and
something a little more daring: try the fresh salmon
grilled with apples and truffle juice, the plump
poularde Albuféra, and the light-as-a-feather
feuillantine of pears. A capital cheese board proposes many regional specialities. The friendly staff
occasionally becomes flustered, making for rather
hilarious scenes.
A la carte: 300 F. Menus: 118 F, 178 F.

Restaurant de l'Arche
[13]
4, rue P.-Duclot — 76.44.22.62
M. Slama. Closed Sun, Mon lunch, 1-15 May and
1-15 Nov. Open until 10 pm. Terrace dining. V DC.
A young team runs this restaurant in a well-pre-
served eighteenth-century house with a pleasant
shaded terrace, in the heart of Grenoble's antiques
district. Alaya Slama presides over a generous and
fairly traditional repertoire based on top-quality
ingredients, for example: well-prepared foie gras,
fillet of beef with scallops, and soufflé glacé à la
chartreuse. The wine list is adequate, the
atmosphere most convivial.
A la carte: 300 F. Menus: 85 F (weekdays only),
165 F.

Hôtel Rive Droite
20, quai de France — 76.87.61.11
Closed 23 Dec-2 Jan. 2 stes 330-520 F. 56 rms 250-
300 F. Restaurant. Half-board 300-335 F. TV. Confer-
ence facilities. Garage parking. V AE DC.
This is a large wood-shuttered house on the quay
near the centre. A simple, cosy décor and small but
comfortable rooms.

A Ma Table
[13]
92, cours J.-Jaurès — 76.96.77.04
M. Martin. Closed Sat lunch, Sun, Mon and Aug.
Open until 9.30 pm. V.
Everything here is on a small scale: the dining
room with six tables, the astutely composed wine
list, the bustling and smiling hostess, and the simple, down-to-earth menu of market dishes prepared by chef Michel Martin: grilled salmon with
an infusion of fresh tarragon, confit of duck, and
real profiteroles with hot-chocolate sauce.
A la carte: 250 F.

11/20 Taverne de Ripaille
10, pl. P.-Mistral — 76.87.29.11
M. Ducret. Closed Sun lunch, 27 July-18 Aug and
24 Dec-2 Jan. Open until midnight. Private
room: 52. Air cond. Garage parking. Telex 320767.
V AE DC.
A favourite Grenoblois meeting-place, very
fashionable with a jolly ambience. The food,

though, is hit-or-miss; our last visit yielded generous portions of doughy ravioli, overcooked sole
meunière, and excellent Beaufort cheese.
A la carte: 250 F.

Park Hôtel
(See restaurant above)
Closed 27 July-18 Aug and 24 Dec-2 Jan. 10 stes
1485 F. 50 rms 610-995 F. TV. Air cond. Conference
facilities.
An exemplary, well-outfitted hotel with highly
trained personnel and comfortable rooms. Conference facilities and fitness centre. Private rooms for
business lunches.

Terminus
10, pl. de la Gare — 76.87.24.33
Open every day. 50 rms 160-295 F. TV 33 rms. Con-
ference facilities. Telex 980904. V AE DC.
The hotel faces the railway station and is well
kept and quiet. Up-to-date facilities.

And also...
L'As de Pique (76.87.32.91 - 14, rue du Lt-Chana-
ron. Open until 11.30 pm): Dishes for slimmers
and good little wines. Fashionable (120 F).
Le Brûleur de Loups (76.51.82.18 - 4, rue A.-
Chevalier. Open until 11 pm): A good old-
fashioned bistro in the old city (100 F lunch, 160 F
dinner).
Café des Promeneurs (76.90.76.23 - 1, Grande-Rue,
in la Tronche. Open until 11 pm): More for the
summer garden and terrace than for the food
(100 F).
Le Couscous (76.47.92.93 - 19, rue de la Poste.
Open until 10 pm): One of the better bets for
couscous (44-60 F).
Le Malassis (76.54.75.93 - 9, rue Bayard. Open until
10 pm): Fireside dinners in winter, excellent
desserts in all seasons (100 F).
La Panse (76.54.09.54 - 2, rue de la Paix. Open until
10 pm): Copious home-style cooking served with
a smile (menus from 85 F to 130 F).

In nearby Bresson
(7 km S on D 5 and D 264)
38320 Grenoble — (Isère)

Chavant
[14]
Rte Napoléon — 76.25.15.14
M. Chavant. Closed Sun and Mon (except in
summer), and 25-31 Dec. Open until 9.30 pm. Priv-
ate room: 25. Garden dining. Air cond. Parking.
Telex 980882. V AE DC.
You'll need a compass to find this old regional-
style house surrounded by the sprawl of suburbia.
There's a charming terrace as well as a Gothic-style
dining room in which to partake of the traditional,
serious, and seasonal cooking of Jean-Pierre Chavant. On offer: quail Emile Chavant (created by his
grandfather), and fillet of beef with foie gras, but
also the more modern roast thyme-scented turbot
with fig marmalade, and the perennial (but delicious) crêpes Suzette au Grand Marnier and hot
soufflé Grande-Chartreuse. Fine cellar, stylish
service.
A la carte: 400-450 F. Menu: 178 F.

Chavant
(See restaurant above)
Closed Mon and 25-31 Dec. 2 stes 750 F. 7 rms 550-
750 F. TV. Air cond. Conference facilities. Pool.
Ten lovely rooms for breathing lungfuls of fresh
mountain air. Charming countryside nearby.

In nearby **Claix**

(10.5 km on D 269)
38640 Grenoble – (Isère)

 Le Manoir des Matitis
76.98.84.55
Open every day. 1 ste 900-1210 F. 12 rms 495-900 F.
Restaurant. Half-board 720-900 F. TV. Air cond. Con-
ference facilities. Heated pool. Parking.
Telex 320161. V AE.
    A luxury hotel housed in a cosy turn-of-the-cen-
tury manor near the motorway exit at Claix. Large
rooms all have bathrooms and television. Limousine hire and special weekend holiday packages.
See below Les Matitis at Varces.

Les Oiseaux
Ch. des Pérouses – 76.98.07.74
Closed Sun off-season and 20 Dec-20 Jan. 20 rms
251-356 F. Restaurant. Half-board 229-404 F. TV.
Conference facilities. Pool. V AE.
    Near Claix, with terraces for a view of the Alps.
The hotel is set in extensive grounds, and the
rooms have been entirely renovated to allow
guests peace and quiet.

In nearby **Corenc**

(3 km)
38700 Grenoble – (Isère)

Les Trois Roses
32, av. du Grésivaudan – 76.90.35.09
Closed 24 Dec-2 Jan. 50 rms 379-447 F. TV. Confer-
ence facilities. Parking. Telex 980593. V AE DC.
    A modern hotel in spacious grounds in a residen-
tial suburb. Rooms are pristine, soberly decorated,
and well fitted. A charming welcome from the
proprietors.

In nearby **Meylan**

(3 km NE on N 90)
38240 Grenoble – (Isère)

Alpha
34, av. de Verdun – 76.90.63.09
Open every day. 86 rms 410-430 F. Restaurant. TV.
Conference facilities. Pool. Garage parking.
Telex 980444. V AE DC.
    This is a modern, recently built hotel on the
Geneva road. Some of the huge rooms have
kitchenettes. Good facilities for groups.

In nearby **Saint-Martin-le-Vinoux**

(2 km NW)
38950 Grenoble – (Isère)

Pique-Pierre
(Jacques Douvier)
1, rue C.-Kilian – 76.46.12.88
M. Douvier. Closed Sun dinner, Mon and 22 July-
19 Aug. Open until 9.30 pm. Private room: 50. Gar-
den dining. Air cond. Parking. V AE.
    Winter or summer, this is where the Grenoblois
come when they want great blasts of fresh mountain air and a good tuck-in. In fine weather clients
make a beeline for the flowered terrace; otherwise
it's indoors to be served by an impeccable and
smiling personnel in a provincial décor of wood
panelling, fine crystal and silverware. Jacques
Douvier treats patrons to salmon with dill and
coarse salt, fresh, tender tunny Antibes-style, an
opulent cheese board, and a good fresh-fruit gratin.
Some nice prix-fixe offerings, particularly the business menu which includes wine.
    A la carte: 350 F and up. Menus: 180 F (weekdays
lunch only, wine inc), 148 F, 180 F, 250 F, 360 F.

In nearby **Saint-Paul-de-Varces**

(17 km S)
38760 Grenoble – (Isère)

12/20 Auberge Messidor
76.72.80.64
M. Perret. Closed Tue dinner, Wed and Feb. Open
until 9.15 pm. Terrace dining. Parking. V.
    This old village coaching inn has been in the
Perret family for years. André Perret combines
contemporary touches with his Dauphinois herit-
age to produce a solid, classic repertoire. Depending upon whether your tastes are traditional or
contemporary, choose a coulibiac of salmon or an
airy feuilleté of crab and avocado. Attentive service
and a remarkable wine list contribute to the inn's
renown.
    A la carte: 220-270 F. Menus: 120 F and 150 F
(except holidays), 180 F and 260 F (except w-e).

In nearby **Sappey-en-Chartreuse**

(15 km N)
38700 Grenoble – (Isère)

12/20 Le Pudding
D 512 – 76.88.80.26
M. Borrel. Closed Sun dinner, Mon, 15 Aug-15 Sep.
Open until 9.30 pm. Garden dining. No pets. V.
    This little inn has forsaken the pseudo-rustic
décor of yore in favour of a slightly kitsch new
look. Two generations of Borrels cooperate in the
kitchen to produce prawns with a coulis of
mangetouts, noisette of pan-roasted veal with a
Thai sauce, and some marvellous desserts. Good
wines and efficient service.
    A la carte: 250-280 F. Menus: 115 F (weekdays
only), 160 F, 250 F, 280 F.

Rogier
4.5 km N on D 512
at Porte pass – 76.88.82.04
Closed Thu and Fri (except school holidays), and
12 Nov-20 Dec. 15 rms 140-195 F. Restaurant. Half-
board 170-210 F. TV 8 rms. Conference facilities.
Parking. V AE.
    A large edifice high up in the mountains, sur-
rounded by fir trees, not far from the Charterhouse, the original home of the Carthusian monks.
Dainty, well-tended rooms.

In nearby **Varces**

(13 km SW on N 75)
38760 Grenoble – (Isère)

L'Escale
Place de la République
76.72.80.19
M. Buntinx. Closed in winter Sun dinner and Mon,
Tue in summer, and 2 Jan-3 Feb. Open until 9 pm.
Private room: 20. Garden dining. Parking.
Telex 306254. V.
    Frédéric Buntinx has judiciously brought his pri-
ces to heel by introducing a few 'affordable' dishes
(which are far from being the least interesting
items on the menu), to wit: pumpkin mousseline
with mussels, rockfish ragoût with saffron and tiny
ravioli, and pot-au-feu of duck with rosemary.
There are two terrific set menus, and a large garden
under the trees serves as a luxurious sitting room
in summer.
    A la carte: 300-350 F. Menus: 98 F (weekdays
lunch only), 150 F, 230 F, 298 F.

Les Matitis
Allée des Chênes — 76.98.15.46
M. Gonzalez. Closed Sun dinner, Mon and 9 Aug-9 Sep. Open until 10 pm. Private room: 18. Garden dining. Valet parking. Telex 320161. V AE DC.

After surviving a few imprudent ventures, restaurateur Jean-Pierre Gonzalez has had the good judgment to procure the services of Gilles Hubert, a remarkable young chef who has turned this lovely stone house into one of Grenoble's most exciting gastronomic addresses. The savarin of carp spiced with saffron, the salad of lotte with watercress and walnuts, or red mullet enhanced by virgin olive oil flavoured with Chinese anise, and suckling pig with polenta all testify to Hubert's bold way with flavours and his technical prowess. Superb cellar.

À la carte: 350 F. Menus: 145 F (lunch only), 170 F, 230 F, 320 F.

In nearby Voreppe

(10 km N Lyons motorway)
38340 Grenoble — (Isère)

Novotel
76.50.81.44
Open every day. 114 rms 370-430 F. Restaurant. Half-board 520-600 F. TV. Air cond. Conference facilities. Pool. Parking. Telex 320273. V AE DC.

A fantastic setting at the foot of the Vercors mountains and the Charterhouse. Very comfortable rooms.

12/20 La Petite Auberge
2.5 km S, in Chevalon
76.50.08.03
M. Berger. Closed Sun dinner, Mon, 8-15 Jan and 6-27 Aug. Open until 9.30 pm. Private room: 15. Garden dining. Parking. V.

Stop by in the summer for an alfresco meal and you'd hardly know the sea wasn't just beyond the garden wall of this lovely roadside establishment. The superlative shellfish and oysters come straight from Marennes, Riec-sur-Belon and Audierne. The rest of the menu is just as resolutely turned to the sea: try the turbot with oysters, or the roast sea bass with oyster mushrooms. Good white wines.

À la carte: 300-350 F. Menus: 120 F (weekdays lunch only), 185 F (w-e and holidays only), 240 F.

GRÉOUX-LES-BAINS

04800 Gréoux-les-Bains — (Alpes/H.-P.)
Paris 786 - Digne 62 - Aix-en-P. 50 - Manosque 15

La Crémaillère
Rte de Riez — 92.74.22.29
M. Montoya. Closed 1 Dec-28 Feb. Open until 9.30 pm. Private room: 16. No pets. Parking. Telex 420347. V AE DC.

A new management is at the helm of La Crémaillère, where chef Gilles Chiriat has been chosen to head the kitchen. His cuisine has great taste and personality, and having experienced his wild-mushroom polenta with pan-fried foie gras and a splash of verjuice, his sage-scented grenadin of veal, his ragoût of prawns with sweet curry and shellfish butter, and his frozen apricot soufflé, we saw every reason to leave the rating and the red toque in place.

À la carte: 300-350 F. Menus: 170 F, 210 F, 320 F.

For all the essential motoring information when driving in Europe, refer to the RAC European Motoring Guide.

La Crémaillère
(See restaurant above)
Closed 1 Dec-28 Feb. 54 rms 320-360 F. Half-board 435-485 F. TV. Conference facilities. Pool. Tennis.

Comfortable, functional rooms open onto a patio. The bathrooms are minute. Golf practice green.

Lou San Peyre
Avenue des Thermes
92.78.01.14
Closed 30 Nov-1 March. 47 rms 290 F. Restaurant. Half-board 258-398 F. TV. Conference facilities. Pool. Tennis. Parking. V AE DC.

Relaxation is the name of the game. Pretty, renovated rooms in a flower-filled landscape. Golf practice green.

Villa Borghèse
Avenue des Thermes
92.78.00.91
Closed 26 Nov-10 March. 1 ste 660-1040 F. 70 rms 200-520 F. Restaurant. Half-board 340-660 F oblig en seas. TV. Air cond 36 rms. Conference facilities. Heated pool. Tennis. Golf. Garage parking. Telex 401513. V AE DC.

A fine modern hotel set against a backdrop of greenery. Rooms are tastefully decorated. Special fitness packages available. Guests may use the neighbouring golf course free of charge. Bridge classes.

GRIGNY
See PARIS Suburbs

GRIMALDI INFERIORE
See Menton

GRIMAUD
83310 Grimaud — (Var)
Paris 857 - Hyères 45 - Saint-Tropez 10

La Boulangerie
Rte de Collobrières — 94.43.23.16
Closed 10 Oct-1 April. 1 ste 900-1,200 F. 10 rms 490-770 F. Restaurant. TV 2 rms. Air cond 1 rm. Conference facilities. Pool. Tennis. Parking. V.

An attractive and cosy hotel with a capital view of the Massif des Maures. Video library. In fine weather, lunch is served to residents around the superb swimming pool.

10/20 Le Café de France
Pl. Neuve — 94.43.20.05
M. Darras. Closed Tue and 25 Oct-1 Feb. Open until 10 pm. Terrace dining. V.

A shaded terrace in a Provençal setting. No comment on the cuisine except to say that it won't break the bank.

A la carte: 180-220 F. Menu: 105 F.

Le Coteau Fleuri
Place des Pénitents
94.43.20.17
M. Minard. Closed 2 Jan-1 Feb and 2-20 Dec. Open until 9.30 pm. Terrace dining. No pets. V AE DC.

Flowers, flowers everywhere, and greenery too engulf this wonderful villa next to the Penitents' Chapel. The terrace looks out onto a mind-blowing view of the Massif des Maures and the Provençal hill country. The young chef, formerly with Troisgros, works in a refined, delicate vein, with a marked preference for local produce: foie gras de canard served with a glass of Jurançon wine, salmon baked with lardoons, prawn and leek tart, red mullet with pistou, rack of lamb with tiny vegetables. Attractive array of regional wines.

A la carte: 300-350 F. Menus: 130 F (lunch only), 190 F.

Le Coteau Fleuri

(See restaurant above)

Closed 2 Jan-1 Feb and 4-20 Dec. 14 rms 300-450 F. Conference facilities.

Rooms differ in size, comfort, and price but they all share in the tranquillity of this hotel built in the 1930s, ensconced in a lush green setting.

12/20 Le Jardin d'Antinéa

Quartier le Brusquet — 94.43.21.97

M. Decoster. Closed off-season Sun dinner and Mon, and 1-26 Dec. Open until 10 pm. Private room: 25. Garden dining. Parking. V.

A pleasant open-air dining room, perched on a hill, which would be even more agreeable were the chef to lower his sights a bit, and make better use of home-grown Provençal ingredients. Lobster with celery, and somewhat wizened red mullet in a vanilla sauce are to be avoided in favour of the more down-to-earth duck leg with garlic confit, snails with wild thyme and vegetables, or the herbed lamb with olive compote.

A la carte: 250-350 F. Menus: 160 F, 230 F.

Les Santons

Route nationale
94.43.21.02

M. Girard. Closed Wed (except dinner in summer), 2 Nov-23 Dec and 2 Jan-15 March. Open until 10.30 pm. Air cond. V DC.

Santons—those little painted terra-cotta Provençal figures which adorn the Christmas crèche—fill this Provençal dining room, the fief of gentle giant Claude Girard. Here's a chef who goes in for classic cuisine with lots of Mediterranean flavour and fervour. Sample his moist pâté de lapereau aux pistaches, his salad of spiny lobster and baby vegetables drizzled with a wonderfully aromatic olive oil, a suprême of sea bream cooked in its juices à la provençale, or a remarkable saddle of Alpine lamb roasted with thyme blossoms. For dessert there is an apple tart with an almond-custard filling or caramel ice cream with a crisp praline pastry. Good regional and non-regional wines from between 100 F and 150 F.

A la carte: 400-500 F. Menus: 200 F, 280 F, 400 F.

12/20 Le Verger

Route de Collobrières
94.43.25.93

Mme Zachary. Closed 12 Nov-20 Dec and 2 Jan-22 March. Open until 11 pm. Terrace dining. Hotel: 5 rms 550-680 F. Pool. Parking. V.

An attractive spot in a verdant garden. The chef takes few risks, but he does a creditable job with courgette flowers in mousseline sauce, sea bream in a delicate olive sauce, duck confit, honeyed rack of lamb. Lots of regulars.

A la carte: 250 F.

See also: **Port-Grimaud**

Some establishments change their closing times without warning. It is always wise to check in advance.

07120 Groix (Ile de) — (Morbihan)
access in Lorient

12/20 Hôtel de la Marine

7, rue du Gal-de-Gaulle — 97.86.80.05

M. Hubert. Closed off-season Sun dinner and Mon, and Jan. Open until 10 pm. Terrace dining. Hotel: 22 rms 156-328 F. V.

For a seafood 'cure' that will set you right up (but won't set your finances on their ear), try the Huberts' simple, fresh, unassuming cuisine. Sailing and deep-sea fishing fanatics blow in en masse for meals. Rooms are available, half of which face the Atlantic Ocean.

A la carte: 130-150 F. Menus: 62 F, 95 F, 110 F.

44350 Guérande — (Loire-Atl.)
Paris 445 - Nantes 77 - La Baule 6 - Vannes 65

La Collégiale

63, fg Bizienne — 40.24.97.29

M. Portner. Closed Wed lunch, Tue and Feb. Open until 11 pm. Private room: 25. Garden dining. AE DC.

The two Christians have an almost religious approach to running a restaurant. Christian Portner soldiers on in the dining room while Christian Mimault attempts to create miracles in the kitchen with his elegant (occasionally fussy), reliably good cuisine. Try the veal loin and kidney salad, the fresh cod with vanilla, the mignon of veal with orange-flavoured mustard, and the paradisaical desserts. The food is a bit expensive, but the veranda dining room is a joy, and the garden a hymn.

A la carte: 400 F. Menus: 150 F (weekdays only), 350 F.

Manoir Le Cardinal

2.5 km N, near Miroux — 40.24.72.56

M. Louvrier. Closed Mon and Tue (except July-Aug), and 1 Oct-Easter. Open until 11 pm. Private room: 35. Garden dining. DC.

Thick beams, a beautiful fireplace, rush-bottomed chairs, and meadow flowers make up the charm of this inviting dining room in a pretty little fourteenth-century Breton manor. The cooking is based on fresh, seasonal, carefully selected ingredients; sample the fresh feuilleté of firm prawns, a fine escalope of lotte with two types of pear and a delicate sauce, and a tasty chocolate cake. Limited wine list, amiable service.

A la carte: 250-300 F. Menu: 150 F.

12/20 Les Remparts

15, bd du Nord — 40.24.90.69

M. Cariou. Closed dinner off-season, and 1 Dec-2 Jan. Open until 9 pm. Private room: 10. V.

A small, unpretentious hotel restaurant decorated with Quimper chandeliers. Simple, deftly prepared dishes include fillets of sole with scallops, duck leg stuffed with foie gras, and chocolate feuilleté with a coffee-flavoured sauce. Adorable welcome and service.

A la carte: 250-270 F. Menus: 90 F (weekdays only), 130 F, 180 F.

Les Remparts

(See restaurant above)

Open every day. 8 rms 220-260 F. Half-board 260-270 F oblig in seas.

A typical little provincial inn with attractive, regularly refurbished rooms.

GUÉRET

23000 Guéret — (Creuse)
Paris 351 - Bourges 122 - Poitiers 142 - Limoges 82

Auclair

19, av. de la Sénatorerie — 55.52.01.26
Closed 15 Dec-20 Jan. 32 rms 135-295 F. Restaurant. Half-board 235-310 F. TV. Conference facilities. Garage parking. V.

This fairly central, well-kept hotel offers simple, agreeable rooms. Tennis, horse-back riding, and fishing pond nearby.

In nearby Busseau-sur-Creuse

(18 km SE)
23150 Guéret — (Creuse)

12/20 Le Viaduc

55.62.40.62
M. Le Mestre. Closed Sun dinner, Mon and 2-31 Jan. Open until 9 pm. Terrace dining. Hotel: 7 rms 180-200 F. V.

A few impeccably tidy little rooms and a panoramic terrace jutting out over the valley of the River Creuse. Take in the view of the Eiffel viaduct while you tuck into freshwater perch with beurre nantais, roast young pigeon with wild-mushroom caviar, and moist lamb chops cooked in caul fat. Delicious little wines and a warm welcome.

A la carte: 230 F. Menus: 75 F (weekdays only), 135 F, 185 F, 235 F.

GUÉRINIÈRE (LA)

See Noirmoutier (Ile de)

GUINGAMP

22200 Guingamp — (Côtes/Armor)
Paris 479 - Saint-Brieuc 32 - Brest 114 - Lannion 32

Le Goéland

2 km SE on N 12
on La Chesnaye
22970 Ploumagoar — 96.21.09.41
Closed Christmas holidays. 30 rms 198-255 F. Restaurant. Half-board 198 F. TV. Conference facilities. Garage parking. V.

A modern edifice on the outskirts of town. Pretty, bright rooms, four of which have been equipped for the disabled. Resident restaurant from Monday to Thursday.

Le Relais du Roy

42, pl. du Centre — 96.43.76.62
Closed Christmas holidays and last week Aug. 7 rms 350-450 F. Half-board 780 F (2 pers oblig in summer). Restaurant. TV. Conference facilities.

This small, centrally located hotel is a restored (and listed) sixteenth-century house with period rooms.

GUJAN-MESTRAS

33470 Gujan-Mestras — (Gironde)
Paris 616 - Bordeaux 48 - Arcachon 12

La Guérinière

Rte d'Arcachon — 56.66.08.78
MM. Daisson and Malvaës. Open every day. Open until 10.30 pm. Private room: 120. Garden dining. Parking. Telex 541270. V AE DC.

A ritzy holiday resort complex complete with piano-bar, swimming pool, and discothèque. But prices are climbing. Marc Roussel's cuisine, however, retains its peculiar appeal, evident in such dishes as red mullet in an aromatic broth with tiny vegetables, veal kidneys with Sauternes and a

celeriac custard, warm bitter-chocolate tart. There's a well-endowed cellar, but the service is somewhat inattentive.

A la carte: 300-350 F. Menus: 100 F (weekdays only, wine inc), 150 F, 185 F, 250 F.

La Guérinière

(See restaurant above)
Open every day. 2 stes 390-560 F. 25 rms 285-390 F. Half-board 310-475 F. TV. Conference facilities. Pool.

HAGUENAU

67500 Haguenau — (Bas-Rhin)
Paris 479 - Strasbourg 29 - Sarreguemines 76

13 Relais Princesse Maria Leczinska

1, rue de Rothbach — 88.93.70.39
M. Immelé. Closed Sun dinner, Mon, Feb school holidays and 9-23 Sep. Open until 9.30 pm. Garden dining. Air cond. Heated pool. Parking. V AE.

Young Jean-Marc Mader, a pupil of Haeberlin, has pumped new blood into this once flagging establishment. The décor is cosily rustic, perhaps a bit fussy, but not entirely lacking in charm. The cooking is solid and classic, just as the local patrons prefer it, though flashes of an independent spirit shine through in dishes such as an avocado mould with a salpicon of shrimps, a croustade of finnan haddock on a bed of sauerkraut, or a frozen rhubarb soufflé. Good Alsace wines.

A la carte: 280-300 F. Menus: 80 F (weekdays lunch only, wine inc), 125 F (weekdays only), 155 F, 185 F, 285 F.

HAIE-FOUASSIÈRE (LA)

See Nantes

HALLES (LES)

69610 Halles (Les) — (Rhône)
Paris 485 - Lyon 47 - Feurs 23 - Montrond 23

13 Auberge des Charreton

La Pontanerie — 74.26.16.31
M. Charreton. Closed Wed. Open until 9.30 pm. Private room: 12. Hotel: 5 rms 250-350 F. Parking. V.

Country comfort is the hallmark of this large establishment facing the Lyonnais hills. Pierre Charreton is an old pro who goes in for classic—though personal—expertly crafted, richly flavourful cuisine. Try his mould of pike with a red-wine and crayfish butter, the compote d'agneau, or tiny scallops with garlic confit, and finish with a fruit gratin napped with raspberry sabayon. Interesting cellar.

Menus: 100 F, 150 F, 220 F.

HAM

80400 Ham — (Somme)
Paris 122 - Amiens 66 - St-Quentin 20 - Péronne 24

14 Le France

5, place de l'Hôtel-de-Ville
23.81.00.22
M. Mailliez. Closed Sun dinner, Feb school holidays and 3 weeks en Aug. Open until 9 pm. Hotel: 6 rms 200-250 F. Garage parking. V.

Chandeliers, imposing mirrors, and impeccably set, well-spaced tables create a formal, but very comfortable setting of provincial elegance. A fleet, attentive staff directed by the charming *patronne* serves rabbit pie with onion marmalade, paupiette of salmon with cabbage, sweetbreads with watercress coulis, and a good chocolate cake signed by the young owner, Jean-Pierre Mailliez. There are a few delicious and reasonably priced

wines to go with this generous and honest fare.
A la carte: 300 F. Menus: 90 F (weekdays only),
170 F (except holidays), 230 F (w-e only), 240 F
(holidays only).

HARFLEUR

See Havre (Le)

HASPARREN

64240 Hasparren — (Pyrénées-A.)
Paris 764 - Bayonne 25 - Cambo-les-Bains 10

In nearby Saint-Esteben

(11 km SE on D 14)
64640 Hasparren — (Pyrénées-A.)

 Chez Onésime
2 km from Oxocelhaya caves
59.29.65.51

*M. Salles. Closed Wed and 15 Nov-7 Dec. Open until
9.30 pm. No pets. V.*
The bright, gaily decorated dining room of this
village inn certainly belies its boring exterior. As
for the cuisine, it continues to make slow but sure
progress, owing to a judicious choice of very fresh,
often local ingredients: a beautifully seasoned salad
with marinated anchovies, the assiette Landaise,
and sea bass braised in Jurançon wine all deserve
a toque. Desserts, however, would benefit from a
more critical approach. The wine list is remarkably
precise.
A la carte: 250 F. Menus: 130 F, 220 F.

HAULCHIN

See Valenciennes

HAVRE (LE)

76600 Havre (Le) — (Seine-Mar.)
Paris 204 - Amiens 179 - Rouen 86

 Astoria
13, cours de la République
35.25.00.03
*Open every day. 1 ste 300 F. 37 rms 160-300 F. Half-
board 240 F. TV. Air cond. Conference facilities. Garage parking. Telex 190075. V AE DC.*
Here's a handy hotel with well-equipped rooms
in front of the railway station. A smiling and amiable welcome awaits.

Bordeaux
147, rue L.-Brindeau — 35.22.69.44
*Open every day. 31 rms 270-446 F. TV.
Telex 190428. V AE DC.*
Right in the centre of town, facing the winter
yacht basin, this hotel offers modern, comfortable
rooms. The new proprietors plan some important
refurbishments.

La Chaumette
17, rue Racine — 35.43.66.80
*Mme Fréchet. Closed Sat lunch, Sun, 24 Dec-3 Jan,
1-9 May and 8 Aug-2 Sep. Open until 9.30 pm. V AE
DC.*
A pinch of Brittany—that's where Christine
Fréchet hails from—a zest of Normandy, and a whiff
of Périgord go into the delicious pain perdu with slivers
of finnan haddock, the tatin of scallops, the skate
with beetroot vinegar and celery purée, to say
nothing of the delicious pain perdu de pain d'épice
(gingerbread French toast!) with a cassis sorbet.
Her cooking is right on the mark, precise, and
imaginative, and there's nothing else quite like it
in Le Havre. Prices, alas, are on their way up.
A la carte: 350-400 F. Menu: 149 F.

Hôtel Foch
4, rue de Caligny — 35.42.50.69
*Open every day. 33 rms 165-260 F. TV. Garage park-
ing. Telex 190369. V AE DC.*
A quiet, centrally located hotel in the shadow of
the belfry of St-Joseph church and just 300 metres
from the marina. All the rooms have been entirely
renovated by the new management, and are very
comfortable. Supper-trays at night, from Monday
to Friday.

12/20 La Manche
18, bd Albert-Ier — 35.41.20.13
*M. Duchemin. Closed Sun dinner and Mon. Open
until 9.30 pm. Private room: 30. V AE DC.*
A new management and a new chef now occupy
this bright décor with a stunning sea view. The
cuisine is carefully prepared, if a bit confused, and
shellfish are inexplicably given short shrift. The
Channel prawns lack flavour, and the matelote of
fish direct from the market is very fresh, but uninteresting and certainly not worth a toque. A good
cellar, a courteous welcome, and efficient service.
A la carte: 300 F. Menus: from 95 F to 215 F.

12/20 La Marine Marchande
27, bd de l'Amiral-Mouchez — 35.25.11.77
*M. Radenac. Closed Sat, Sun, holidays and Aug. Open
until 10.30 pm. V.*
A bistro not far from the docks, where the good
citizens of Le Havre like to take in the waterfront
atmosphere and tuck into steak and chips, along
with shellfish, fresh prawns, and seafood *plats du
jour.*
A la carte: 250 F. Menu: 90 F (wine inc).

Le Marly
121, rue de Paris — 35.41.72.48
*Open every day. 37 rms 250-340 F. TV.
Telex 190369. V AE DC.*
A handy, functional hotel near the car-ferry
embarkation point.

Le Montagné
50-52, quai M.-Féré — 35.42.77.44
*M. Barboux. Closed Sat lunch, Wed, 10-16 Feb and
Aug. Open until 10.30 pm. V.*
Young Bruno Barboux has occupied this sleek,
comfortable establishment in the historic St-
François district of Le Havre for the last two years.
And the local gentry quickly adopted this talented
chef, and his light, sophisticated cuisine. Alongside
some great classic dishes like pan-roasted veal
kidneys or bœuf aux trois poivres, his *carte* includes more original offerings such as the
gourmand de volaille served with a sauce based on
mussel cooking juices, or sweetbreads in puff
pastry set in a pool of haricot vert cream. For
dessert try the delectable chaud-froid of caramelised apples with orange butter. The composi-
tion of each dish is carefully described on the
menu, so there should be no strange surprises. The
cellar features good clarets and wines from the
Loire.
A la carte: 250 F. Menu: 130 F.

12/20 La Petite Auberge
32, rue de Ste-Adresse — 35.46.27.32
*M. Douillet. Closed Sun dinner and Mon (except
holidays), Feb school holidays and 3 weeks en Aug.
Open until 9.30 pm. Private room: 24. Air cond. V
AE.*
Good news: new seating and a refreshed décor
echo some new dishes that highlight the menu,
like millefeuille of snails and oysters with saffron,

noisette of veal with honey and spices, and a gratin of citrus fruits with almonds. The à la carte menu is expensive, but the set menus are terrific.

A la carte: 280 F. Menus: 100 F (weekdays only), 115 F (w-e and holidays only), 135 F, 170 F.

12/20 Le Trois-Mâts

Chaussée d'Angoulême – 35.21.23.45
M. Hossin. Open every day. Open until 10.30 pm. Private room: 200. Terrace dining. Air cond. Garage parking. Telex 190749. V AE DC.

A small open-air terrace protected by glass affords a magnificent view of the port. The welcome is wonderful, the cellar astonishing, and the cuisine excellent on the whole: paupiettes of salmon and scallops, fillet of brill with cider. Regional gastronomic weeks.

A la carte: 230 F. Menus: 110 F (weekdays lunch only), 135 F (dinner only, wine inc), 145 F (w-e and holidays only, wine inc).

Mercure

(See restaurant above)
Open every day. 24 stes 505-550 F. 96 rms 330-570 F. TV. Conference facilities.

Architecturally light-hearted when compared to the austerity of Auguste Perret's Le Havre (he redesigned it after the war), the hotel has a superb view of the Commerce docks. Rooms have been redone and are large and pleasant. Service is simple and breakfasts are satisfying.

And also...

Our selection of places for inexpensive, quick, or late-night meals.

Les Abattoirs (35.25.07.12 - 17, rue G.-Buffon. Open 9 pm): Good grilled meat and *plats du jour* (140 F).

La Taverne Basque (35.41.74.93 - 73, av. Foch. Open until 10 pm): Centrally located and always full. Tasty grilled dishes in a relaxed brasserie ambience (100 F).

Taverne de Maître Kanter (35.41.31.50 - 22, rue G.-Braque. Open until 11.30 pm): Also known as 'Chez Paillette', this is an amusing brasserie with good Alsace wines (100-150 F).

In nearby **Harfleur**

(3 km E)
76700 Havre (Le) – (Seine-Mar.)

12/20 Auberge du Prieuré

52, av. de la République – 35.45.02.20
M. Legros. Closed Sun dinner and Mon. Open until 9.30 pm. Private room: 10. Garden dining. V AE.

This appealing inn, just steps away from Harfleur's magnificent priory-museum, occupies an old apothecary's shop. In winter, meats are grilled in the huge central fireplace of the elegant dining room, while in summer tables are set out on the wide lawns, where patrons are served deftly prepared fish, or calf's liver with a creamy bacon sauce.

A la carte: 300 F. Menus: 145 F, 210 F.

We are always interested to hear about your discoveries, and to receive your comments on ours. Please feel free to write to us, stating your opinions clearly.

In nearby **Hode**

(18 km E on D 982)
76430 Havre (Le) – (Seine-Mar.)

Dubuc

on D 982 – 35.20.06.97
M. Dubuc. Closed Sun dinner, Mon, 10-18 March and 11-26 Aug. Open until 9.15 pm. Private room: 16. Parking. V AE DC.

No, this is certainly not a charm spot, but Dubuc is nonetheless one of the region's best restaurants. Louis-Philippe Dubuc is a master chef who specialises in serious, slightly old-fashioned, often achingly rich cuisine (roast prawns with fried leeks and garlic cream, ris de veau aux champignons et jus de truffe, divine apple tart with cinnamon ice cream). Rich too are the captains of Le Havre's industry and the local oil magnates who compose his clientele.

A la carte: 450-550 F. Menus: 220 F and 325 F (except holidays).

In nearby **Sainte-Adresse**

(1 km NW)
76310 Havre (Le) – (Seine-Mar.)

Le Nice Havrais

6, pl. F.-Sauvage – 35.46.14.59
M. Caillet. Closed dinner Sun and Mon. Open until 8.45 pm. V AE.

A large building overlooking the estuary and the Côte Fleurie, where chef Jean-Pierre Nys has officiated for more than sixteen years. His cooking is in fact less complicated and sauce-rich than would appear from the menu. Sole delight, turbot with stuffed prunes, beef fillet with oyster sauce, and crêpes flamed with B & B are ultraclassic, but beautifully crafted, delicately flavoured dishes. The owner welcomes guests charmingly in his immense blue dining room, which opens onto the bay.

A la carte: 320-350 F. Menus: 85 F, 160 F, 280 F.

Yves Page

7, pl. Clemenceau – 35.46.06.09
M. Page. Closed Sun dinner, Mon, 10-22 Feb and 15 Aug-6 Oct. Open until 10 pm. Private room: 14. Terrace dining. V AE DC.

A few tables in prime position have a marvellous view of the sea and Le Havre harbour. Others are well-spaced with soft lighting. Quality is evident everywhere, from the perfectly fresh ingredients to Yves Page's generous, intelligent cooking: exquisite and copious lobster salad with orange butter, scallops with wild mushrooms, their flavour enhanced by a Noilly sauce, perfectly grilled sole in a light butter sauce. Short but astute wine list; young, efficient service.

A la carte: 300-350 F. Menus: 148 F, 270 F.

HENDAYE

64700 Hendaye – (Pyrénées-A.)
Paris 777 - Biarritz 28 - St-Jean-de-Luz 13 - Pau 141

In nearby **Biriatou**

(4 km SE on D 258)
64700 Hendaye – (Pyrénées-A.)

Bakéa

59.20.76.36
Mme François. Closed 1 Oct-1 May. Open until 10 pm. Terrace dining. Hotel: 15 rms 160-400 F. Parking. V AE DC.

The pace here is as unchanging as the course of the Bidassoa River that flows lazily round the islands below the terrace. And while chef François lingers in California, we pine for his crayfish in aromatic broth, Armagnac-spiked pâté, poached young turbot, plump chicken sautéed in port, his spicy pipérade, tunny with tomato fondue, and other lusty dishes he has prepared for us for 30 years, always for eminently reasonable prices.

A la carte: 270-350 F. Menus: 130 F, 200 F.

In nearby **Fuenterrabia**

(2 km W, in Spain)
20280 Hendaye — (Pyrénées-A.)

Ramon Roteta
Calle Irun
(43) 64.16.93

M. Roteta. Closed 11 Feb-1 March and 14 Oct-1 Nov. Open until 11 pm. Private room: 20. Garden dining. No pets. Parking. V AE.

This pleasant villa on the Spanish side of the Bidassoa River attracts a faithful clientele of trendy international gourmets. Welcomed by the gracious Se7Enorita Roteta on the terrace or in the elegantly furnished dining room, they appreciate this blend of modern and traditional cooking based on beautiful foodstuffs deftly prepared. Fish here is particularly fine. Savour, for example, prawn tails with spring mushrooms, fresh clam salad, and delicious homemade pastries. The wine list is predominantly Spanish.

A la carte: 300-400 F.

In nearby **Oyarzun**

(10 km SW, in Spain)
20180 Hendaye — (Pyrénées-A.)

Zuberoa
Barrio de Iturriotz
(43) 49.12.28

MM. Arbelaitz. Closed Sun dinner, Mon, 15-31 May and 15-31 Oct. Open until 11 pm. Private room: 80. Terrace dining. Parking. V AE DC.

The three Arbelaitz brothers have created an enchantingly tranquil haven at their venerable family farm set amid flowers, fields, and apple trees. Trained by his mother, Hilario finds his inspiration in the regional repertoire, to which he adds his own subtle touch: sample his oyster and shellfish soup, or the cod, green pepper, and tomato tartlets, or his duck liver with port and apples, and an extraordinary selection of chocolates. The cellar is worth exploring.

A la carte: 250-350 F. Menus: 200 F, 350 F.

In nearby **San Sebastian**

(19 km W in Spain)
20015 Hendaye — (Pyrénées-A.)

Akelare
Barrio de Igueldo
Paseo del Padre Orcolaga 56 — (43) 21.20.52

M. Subijana. Closed Sun dinner, Mon, 3-18 June and 2 Dec-14 Jan. Open until 11 pm. Private room: 28. Air cond. No pets. Parking. V AE DC.

The Spanish would have you believe that a real *akelare*, or witches' sabbath is in full swing in this modern, mostly grey, décor with a view extending as far as Guipuzcoa; their reasons are Pedro Subijana's cheeky creations, his culinary boldness that borders on the shocking. Subijana transforms fine, traditional Basque cookery with his powerful personal style, to wit: an intensely tasty asparagus and truffle ragoût, turbot in Swiss chard and carrot sauce, an exceptional lobster salad, and a caramelised pineapple puff pastry. Charming femin-

ine service, well-acquainted with the good wine list and the phenomenal liqueur selection.

A la carte: 350-450 F. Menu: 260 F.

Arzak
21, alto de Miracruz — (43) 27.84.65

M. Arzak. Closed Sun dinner, Mon, 16 June-3 July and 3-27 Nov. Open until 11 pm. Private room: 40. Air cond. No pets. Valet parking. V AE DC.

This large, welcoming bistro, just 25 minutes by motorway from Bayonne, is the place to discover the delicious, updated Basque cooking of Juan Maria Arzak. Try his extraordinary little prawns sautéed with prunes and sweet peppers, or delicate hake cheeks with bulghur, or lobster cooked in fruit juice with green asparagus, unctuous escalopes of foie gras with honey-glazed carrots, wild duck in pineapple juice, or his ethereal chocolate-mandarin soufflé escorted by hot bitter-orange crêpes. There are more rustic dishes as well—take the delectable chorizo sausage with red beans, for example—to warm your stomach and heart. From start to finish, it's a symphony of marvellous flavours and brilliant ideas. If your knowledge of Spanish wines is limited, this is the place to perfect it: Arzak's cellar is incredibly rich, but not chauvinistic. If your prefer, charming se7Enoritas, dressed in black with white lace aprons, will also uncork one of the great Bordeaux.

A la carte: 400-550 F. Menu: 360 F.

Maria Christina Cigahotels
Paseo Republica Argentina, 4 — (43) 42.49.00

Open every day. 30 stes 2,573-5,092 F. 109 rms 912-1,608 F Restaurant. TV. Air cond. No pets. Conference facilities. Valet parking. Telex 38195. V AE DC.

The atmosphere, fittings, and comfort of a superb palace. Magnificent lounges with marble columns and huge, perfect rooms. Unfortunately, the welcome, service, and breakfasts are unworthy of such an establishment. Conference rooms and piano-bar.

HENNEBONT
56700 Hennebont — (Morbihan)
Paris 482 - Vannes 56 - Concarneau 55 - Lorient 10

Château de Locguénolé
5 km S on D 781
Rte de Port-Louis — 97.76.29.04

Mme de La Sablière. Closed Mon (except July-Aug and holidays) and 2 Jan-8 Feb. Open until 9.30 pm. Private room: 170. Garden dining. No pets. Parking. Telex 950636. V AE DC.

A dynamic chatelaine, who by dint of circumstance became a great hotel professional, Alyette de La Sablière has never been one to have complexes—at least until now. She has just equipped her château with a fabulous fitness complex: saunas, solarium, Jacuzzi, Turkish baths, exercise gym—the works. While she's at it, may we suggest that she also add a windowed terrace to her restaurant, which looks over a meadow sloping down to the Blavet estuary, one of the most romantic vistas in all of Brittany. The present décor is quite charming in its way but rather stuffy, really just begging for a spectacular view.

And a more luminous dining room would make a dream setting for Denis Le Cadre's imaginative cuisine. Supplied with Brittany's choicest foodstuffs, this talented chef creates vibrant, intelligent dishes in the spirit of today's *renaissance culinaire bretonne*. Alongside his now classic (still stellar) crab millefeuille with Noirmoutier potates, you'll find a cold shellfish minestrone brightened with lemon thyme; hot foie gras with a crisp, spiced semolina galette; an exquisite mackerel terrine with red Anjou-wine jelly; sardine and artichoke coulibiac with coriander-scented oil; pristinely fresh prawns barely roasted, then served with shallot butter or with celery and truffles; sea bass cooked with grape juice and ginger; or licorice-flavoured duck breast with browned new potatoes. The desserts (ah! that pain perdu à la vanille! that briar-honey ice cream!) and the cellar are equally brilliant—making this one of the most enticing establishments in South Brittany (or anywhere else!).

A la carte: 400-700 F. Menus: 130 F (lunch only), 190 F (weekdays only), 280 F, 460 F.

Château de Locguénolé
(See restaurant above)

Closed 2 Jan-8 Feb. 4 stes 950-1,800 F. 31 rms 380-1,160 F. Half-board 512-918 F oblig in seas. TV. Conference facilities. Heated pool. Tennis.

In this admirable 100-hectare domain made for endless strolls, Alyette de La Sablière has patiently created an exceptional hotel complex. A ravishing Renaissance pavilion contains conference rooms, next door to the new relaxation centre with large bay windows that overlook an open-air swimming pool. Finally, the large nineteenth-century residence stands atop a grassy knoll; within are stately drawing rooms, suites, and rooms furnished with antiques but with all modern conveniences. A motor launch is available for sea excursions (the Ile de Groix is nearby), visits to Port-Louis (superb museum of the eighteenth-century mercenaries, La Compagnie des Indes), trips to Quiberon, or outings on the Blavet. Relais et Châteaux.

HERBAUDIÈRE (L')
See Noirmoutier (Ile de)

HÉROUVILLE-SAINT-CLAIR
See Caen

HEYRIEUX
38540 Heyrieux — (Isère)
Paris 487 - Lyon 24 - Vienne 24 - Bourgoin-Jallieu 20

L'Alouette
3 km SE on D 518
at L'Alouette — 78.40.06.08

M. Marlhins. Closed Sun dinner, Mon, 1 week in May and 15 Aug-15 Sep. Open until 9.30 pm. Private room: 20. Air cond. Parking. V.

The old country bistro where the Marlhins settled a few years ago is now a spiffing little restaurant. The cooking is simple, but fragrant and full of verve, as in the terrine of calf's liver, sweetbreads, and foie gras scented with floral Beaumes-de-Venise wine, or salmon in oyster essence. The owners regard stocking a cellar as a serious undertaking.

A la carte: 300 F. Menus: 95 F (weekdays lunch only), 125 F (weekdays only), 155 F, 180 F.

HODE (LE)
See Havre (Le)

HONFLEUR
14600 Honfleur — (Calvados)
Paris 192 - Le Havre 57 - Caen 60 - Lisieux 34

L'Assiette Gourmande
8, pl. Ste-Catherine — 31.89.24.88

M. Bonnefoy. Closed Mon dinner, Tue and 15 Jan-15 Feb. Open until 10 pm. Terrace dining. Air cond. V AE DC.

Opposite the church on the Place Ste-Catherine, this beautiful house with terrace is Gérard Bonnefoy's new restaurant. His wife, Anne-Marie, welcomes you gaily into the new décor done in shades of red from top to bottom, alternating with bricks, stone, and timber. This vivid new setting has inspired Gérard to surpass himself in the kitchen, where he works at turning out inventive and subtle dishes like prawns marinated in caviar (a surprising blend of sweet and salt), or sea bass with bone marrow in a spirited sauce of wine and meat glaze, or pigeon in carrot jus with Calvados sorbet, and for dessert, a typically Norman caramelised apple confit. Speaking of Normandy, Gérard goes against regional tradition by deliberately avoiding cream in his sauces. Honfleur can congratulate itself on its acquisition of a great new chef!

A la carte: 350 F. Menus: from 130 F to 350 F.

Castel Albertine
19, cours A.-Manuel — 31.98.85.56

Open every day. 12 rms 264-514 F. TV. Conference facilities. Garage parking. Telex 171439. V AE DC.

Charming large residence in a garden full of huge trees. Pretty, English-style rooms with new, well-fitted bathrooms. The welcome is delightful and breakfasts are good. There is also a sauna and billiards.

Le Cheval Blanc
2, quai des Passagers — 31.89.39.87

M. Bouvachon. Closed Wed dinner, Thu and 2 Jan-15 Feb. Open until 9.30 pm. V.

Enjoy a view overlooking the port while savouring one of Christian Bouvachon's clever set menus; they are lively and oft-renewed, with an emphasis on seafood (and an occasional excess of cream!). On a given day, offerings might include scrambled eggs with finnan haddock, crab soup laced with Calvados, stuffed squid, and chicken sautéed with foie gras. An array of moreish desserts rounds off a very pleasant meal.

A la carte: 270-350 F. Menus: 130 F, 175 F, 250 F.

Le Cheval Blanc
(See restaurant above)

Closed 2-26 Jan. 35 rms 314-600 F. Conference facilities.

Good-sized rooms with rather conventional décor; not all offer the same level of comfort, but all overlook the port and the old town. Charming welcome and good breakfasts.

L'Ecrin
19, rue E.-Boudin — 31.89.32.39

Open every day. 1 ste 600-850 F. 20 rms 280-520 F. TV. No pets. Conference facilities. Parking. Telex 772153. V AE DC.

Astonishing manor house and park in the town centre with mad furnishings and a neo-medieval décor. The huge rooms are very comfortable and boast canopied beds. The trendy clientele relaxes in the games room, with billiards, or in the sauna.

La Ferme Saint-Siméon

Rue A.-Marais — 31.89.23.61
M. Boelen. Open every day. Open until 9.30 pm. Private room: 60. Garden dining. Parking. Telex 171031. V.

A string of truly beautiful Norman houses dominating the Seine estuary, where Monet, Courbet, Sisley and others came to seek inspiration—it's the superb setting for a very (perhaps excessively) luxurious stopover. Naturally, the kitchen works with first-rate—very expensive—ingredients, as evinced by the escalope of foie gras with apples, but one could wish for more harmony in dishes like the brill (a bit overcooked) with sorrel, and more modesty in the prices (apple tart is tariffed at 90 F). The meat offerings, however, are more enticing, witness the calf's feet and kidneys cooked to rosy perfection. The plethoric, starchy staff steps crisply through flower-decked dining rooms with low beamed ceilings.

A la carte: 650 F and up. Menus: 230 F (weekdays lunch only), 390 F.

La Ferme Saint-Siméon

(See restaurant above)
Open every day. 4 stes 1,910-3,600 F. 34 rms 690-2,120 F. Half-board 1,070-1,635 F. TV. No pets. Conference facilities. Heated pool. Tennis.

Seventeen luxurious rooms with sea view have been added in a Norman-style building next to the delightful seventeenth century farm. Bathing treatments are available in the marble bathrooms; other facilities include a swimming pool, Finnish sauna, Turkish bath, fitness room, solarium, whirlpool, and massages. Opulent décor and irreproachable service. Relais et Châteaux.

Hostellerie Lechat

Pl. Ste-Catherine — 31.89.23.85
Open every day. 23 rms 300-450 F. Restaurant. Half-board 320-580 F oblig in seas. TV. Conference facilities. Telex 772153. V AE DC.

Large ivy-covered building facing the delightful Ste-Catherine church. Comfortable beamed rooms with pleasant views, but the fittings are rather old. Satisfactory service.

12/20 Le Vieux Clocher

9, rue de l'Homme-de-Bois — 31.89.12.06
M. Rivière. Closed Thu, 26 Nov-7 Dec and 4-16 Feb. Open until 9.30 pm. V AE

Two bright little dining rooms serving modest, well-prepared prix-fixe menus which change regularly: we enjoyed a crisp, fragrant seafood feuilleté, lotte (slightly overcooked) with a savoury crab coulis, and a refreshing coupe Normande (ice cream, sautéed apples, and Calvados). Short, balanced wine list. Smiling service. Prices are headed upwards.

A la carte: 250 F. Menus: 88 F (weekdays only), 149 F, 189 F.

40150 Hossegor — (Landes)
Paris 726 - Biarritz 28 - Bayonne 20

Beauséjour

Av. du Tour-du-Lac — 58.43.51.07
Closed 31 Oct-26 April. 1 ste 900-1,200 F. 45 rms 310-690 F. Restaurant. Half-board 396-588 F oblig in seas. TV. Conference facilities. Heated pool. Garage parking. V AE DC.

Deep in the forest, this beautiful building with a spacious terrace stands next to a saltwater lake. The comfortable, tidy rooms have been redecorated, and offer views of the swimming pool or lake. Plenty of efficient staff.

Les Huîtrières du Lac

1187, av. du Touring-Club — 58.43.51.48
Mme Eychenne-Cotis. Closed Wed off-season (except holidays and school holidays), Dec, Jan and Feb. Open until 10 pm. Private room: 30. Terrace dining. Parking. V.

This popular spot is blessed with an impressive lake view. A good address for oysters and shellfish, but also for the novel baked sea bream stuffed with smoked ham, good brill meunière with wild mushrooms, or curried cod steak. Engaging little wines from the South-west.

A la carte: 270-300 F. Menus: from 100 F to 260 F.

Les Huîtrières du Lac

(See restaurant above)
Closed Wed off-season (except holidays and school holidays), Dec, Jan and Feb. 10 rms 200-230 F. Half-board 250-270 F oblig in seas.

Some rooms have a lake view and all are cosy, well kept, and regularly renovated.

See Colmar

83400 Hyères — (Var)
Paris 866 - Fréjus 76 - Toulon 18 - Aix 99

12/20 La Colombe

La Bayorre — 94.65.02.15
M. Bonamy. Dinner only July-Aug. Closed Sat lunch and Sun dinner. Open until 10 pm. V.

This roadside house does not have much character, but inside the décor is fresh and inviting (doves are much in evidence). The youthful chef chooses the foodstuffs for his short menu judiciously, and offers an excellent seafood soup, an assortment of fish in a morel broth, and a very tender beef fillet spiced with green peppercorns, but in general we think the seasonings could be better balanced. Service is provided by a young, bashful staff.

A la carte: 300 F. Menu: 130 F.

Les Jardins de Bacchus

32, av. Gambetta — 94.65.77.63
M. Santioni. Closed Sat lunch in summer and Sun dinner in winter. Open until 10 pm. Air cond. V AE

Jean-Claude Santioni's tasty repertoire is a blend of rich Lyonnais cookery and sunny Provençal fare. The result is a distinctive style that highlights strong, clearly defined flavours: sample the red-mullet with tapenade, lotte stuffed with tabbouleh, salmon with lemon and caper cream, or mascarpone cake, and you'll see what we mean. It's a pity that the décor, which glorifies Bacchus, didn't influence the oddly ordinary wine list.

A la carte: 250-350 F. Menus: 110 F, 150 F, 220 F.

Mercure

19, av. A.-Thomas — 94.65.03.04
Open every day. 84 rms 295-480 F. Restaurant. TV. Air cond. Conference facilities. Pool. Parking. Telex 404508. V AE DC.

Set in a huge residential and commercial complex along the bypass, this functional new hotel features bright rooms with balconies and perfectly fitted bathrooms. Buffet-style breakfasts and a noisy swimming pool.

See Baume-les-Dames

IGÉ

71960 Igé — (Saône/Loire)
Paris 394 - Tournus 30 - Mâcon 14 - Cluny 11

Château d'Igé
13
85.33.33.99
M. Jadot. Closed 1 Dec-1 March. Open until 9.30 pm. Private room: 120. Garden dining. No-smoking section. No pets. Garage parking. Telex 351915. V AE DC.

This little château, once the home of the Counts of Mâcon, now opens its elegant little Gothic dining rooms to a mostly well-heeled clientele. Classic cooking, lavishly napped with sophisticated sauces, dominates Frédéric Barbier's menu. Taste his delicious croustillant d'escargots, a warm frogs' legs salad with chives and a watercress custard, or a delicate ragoût of kidneys, cocks' combs, and sweetbreads. Excellent but expensive selection of Mâcon wines. Affable, professional service.
A la carte: 320 F. Menus: 190 F, 295 F, 365 F.

Château d'Igé
(See restaurant above)
Closed 1 Dec-1 March. 6 stes 700 F. 6 rms 420-625 F. TV. Conference facilities.

Charming château and park in a Mâcon village surrounded by vineyards. Attractive, comfortable rooms are tastefully furnished in authentic rustic style. The breakfasts are well prepared, and the service is pleasant indeed.

ILE-ROUSSE (L')

See CORSICA

ILLHAEUSERN

68150 Illhaeusern — (Haut-Rhin)
Paris 448 - Colmar 17 - Sélestat 12 - Strasbourg 60

L'Auberge de l'Ill
Rue de Collonges
89.71.83.23
19.5
MM. Haeberlin. Closed Mon (dinner only in seas), Tue, Feb and first week of July. Open until 9 pm. Private room: 50. Air cond. Heated pool. Parking. Telex 871289. V AE DC.

The Haeberlins talk of expanding, but being Alsatian, it is their way to move slowly. Slowly—but surely: this quiet but determined family always does what it sets out to do, and the hotel may well materialise before the year 2000.
Meanwhile the pleasure of discovering this extraordinary inn needs no other enhancement. Set on the banks of the Ill, the Auberge overflows with talent, *joie de vivre*, and Alsatian cordiality. Jean-Pierre Haeberlin welcomes guests into the large almond-green dining room above the garden, while in his spanking-bright kitchen young Marc Haeberlin, under the benevolent eye of his father, Paul, works magic with the fragrant, flavourful bounty of the Alsatian *terroir*. He enchanted us with a prawn velouté with bits of bacon, and red and white beans; equally spell-binding were a fillet of young rabbit in aspic with goose foie gras, a splendid truffle in a potato crust, and the fillet of sturgeon (from the Gironde River) pan-roasted on a bed of crisp cabbage and sauerkraut (which didn't really need the further fillip of caviar cream...).
Nor was that all: we marvelled at his salad of scallops napped with herring cream atop a mélange of potatoes and trout roe; and applauded the appearance of the suckling pig—its trotter stuffed and its ribs glazed, accompanied by a salad of beetroot and lentils spiced with ginger—which

would rouse an anorexic's appetite. A draught of Rhine forest-mushroom and verbena consommé clears the palate for the cheese (hot or cold Munster), and then on come the desserts! gingerbread charlotte with Sauternes sabayon, cherry-filled crêpes, rhubarb délice, or frozen macaroon with mocha and caramel parfait, with an intensely vanilla-flavoured sauce.
If you are unfamiliar with Alsatian wines, Serge Dubs (voted the world's best sommelier in 1989) will convert you with Rieslings from Trimbach or Théo Faller, Léon Beyer's Tokay, Lorentz's Gewurztraminer, or Hugel's Vendanges Tardives.
A la carte: 500-800 F. Menus: 400 F (weekdays lunch only), 500 F (w-e and holidays lunch only), 560 F.

La Clairière
46, rte d'Illhaeusern
68970 Guémar — 89.71.80.80
Closed Jan and Feb. 2 stes 1,200-1,400 F. 25 rms 430-800 F. TV. Tennis. Parking. V.

On the edge of the Ill forest, comfortable, pleasantly decorated rooms favoured by clients of the Auberge de l'Ill. Book well in advance.

ILLZACH

See Mulhouse

ISLE-SUR-LA-SORGUE (L')

84800 Isle-sur-la-Sorgue (L') — (Vaucluse)
Paris 698 - Avignon 23 - Apt 32 - Carpentras 17

Mas de Cure Bourse
14
Rte de Caumont-sur-Durance — 90.38.16.58
Mme Donzé. Closed off-season Sun dinner and Mon. Open until 9.30 pm. Private room: 60. Garden dining. No-smoking section. Parking. V.

Francine Donzé simmers the most delicious Provençal dishes in these inspiring surroundings (a former eighteenth-century coaching inn, hidden among the trees). Savour her bright-flavoured fresh cod with orange butter, lamb brawn with red-pepper coulis, and pan-roasted quail with two kinds of cabbage. Host Jean-François Donzé proffers a charming welcome and a tempting wine list packed with good Côtes-du-Rhône. An extra point this year.
A la carte: 300 F. Menus: 164 F, 188 F, 220 F and 248 F (except holidays).

Mas de Cure Bourse
(See restaurant above)
Open every day. 1 ste 440-460 F. 10 rms 260-460 F. Half-board 450-590 F. TV 10 rms. Conference facilities. Pool.

Opening onto orchards, these few cosy and elegant rooms are decorated in a spare, fresh, Provençal style. Pleasant service and a sunny swimming pool set in greenery.

ISOLA 2000

06420 Isola 2000 — (Alpes-Mar.)
Paris 830 - Nice 94 - St-Martin-Vésubie 60

Le Chastillon
93.23.10.60
Closed 16 April-15 Dec. 3 stes 1,400-3,000 F. 54 rms 290-1,200 F. Restaurant. Half-board 390-1,100 F oblig in seas. TV. Conference facilities. Valet parking. Telex 970507. V AE DC.

Smack in front of the ski runs, this comfortable hotel offers large terraces, good plumbing, and entertainment in season (nightclub).

Le Diva
93.23.17.71
Closed 5 May to mid-Dec. 5 stes. 23 rms 990-2,490 F (per pers, half-board oblig). Restaurant. TV. No pets. Heated pool. Valet parking. Telex 460322. V AE DC.
A luxurious, chalet-style hotel overlooking the resort, with a splendid terrace. Personalised, spacious rooms with English furniture (two rooms are accessible for the disabled). Two saunas, Jacuzzi, and a piano bar.

ISSAMBRES (LES)
83380 Issambres (Les) — (Var)
Paris 899 - Toulon 83 - Fréjus 11 - Ste-Maxime 10

Chante-Mer
Village provençal — 94.96.93.23
M. Battaglia. Closed Sun dinner and Mon (except July-Aug), and 15 Dec-31 Jan. Open until 9 pm. Terrace dining. Air cond. DC.
Seated on the sunny terrace, relax and enjoy Mario Battaglia's good, unpretentious cooking: sole fillet with noodles, fennel-perfumed sea bass, spicy mussel stew and bouillabaisse (order in advance). The desserts are delicious, notably the flaky pear tart with hot caramel sauce. Prices are reasonable and the welcome warm.
A la carte: 250 F. Menus: 100 F, 150 F, 200 F.

La Réserve
N 98 — 94.96.90.41
M. Gayrard. Closed Wed and 30 Sep-1 April. Open until 9 pm. Garden dining. Parking. Hotel: 8 rms 275-380 F, half-board 400-450 F oblig in seas.V.
There's a beautiful view over the gulf of St-Tropez from the delightful waterside terrace. What's on your plate is not bad either, for it is simple, fresh, and appetising: basil and garlic soup, fresh pasta with basil butter, and bouillabaisse. Sip a cool Provençal vintage, and bask in the sunny, smiling service.
A la carte: 350-400 F. Menus: 180 F, 200 F, 240 F.

Le Saint-Pierre
N 98 — 94.96.89.67
M. Loudet. Closed Tue (except dinner in seas) and 15 Dec-1 Feb. Open until 9.30 pm. Terrace dining. Parking. V AE DC.
Set atop a rocky spur among the coves, this beautiful, luminous restaurant is blessed with a huge terrace that looks out to sea. In these splendid natural surroundings, savour Néné Loudet's enticing shellfish assortments, seafood lasagne, and simply prepared, uncommonly fresh fish. Attentive service; expensive local wines; high prices both à la carte and for the prix-fixe menus.
A la carte: 350 F. Menus: 220 F, 300 F.

Villa Saint-Elme
N 98, L'Arpillon — 94.49.52.52
Mme Chbib. Closed Wed off-season (except hotel clients), and Jan. Open until 10 pm. Terrace dining. Air cond. No-smoking section. Hotel: 6 stes 1,600 F, 8 rms 800-1,300 F. Pool. Parking. V AE DC.
A 1920s seaside villa has become the latest luxury hotel on the Côte d'Azur. A distinguished and charming young couple is the dynamic force behind this magical establishment, set on the rocks right by the sea, with a swimming pool dug into a huge platform, and below it a beautiful terrace, where handsomely laid tables are shaded with Italian parasols. Inside, the supremely elegant dining room successfully (and discreetly) recreates a Twenties' atmosphere.
Filled with enthusiasm for the cuisine of Marc Veyrat, Annecy's great chef, the owners of the Villa St-Elme decided to lure him to the coast to set up a team and establish a menu. Veyrat's pupil, Julien Valéro, now follows in his master's footsteps, using herbs and wild plants freshly picked from the Provençal hills to scent his red-mullet and leek salad, sea bream fillet, and rack of Alpine lamb. The cooking is truly inspired—hot foie gras with caramelised melon is simply sensational; similar sentiments are elicited by salt cod pan-roasted in olive oil with onions and potatoes; chicken breast with walnut juices; thyme-scented rabbit; incredibly sapid pigeon pot-au-feu with truffles; and extraordinary desserts by a young pastry chef we are bound to hear more of (his chrysanthemum ice cream, his mango-stuffed figs, his croquant au chocolat are big, big news). How then—we ask you—could we do otherwise than award a pair of toques right off the bat for this colourful, uncommonly flavourful food? Gourmets take note: St-Elme's owners have taken the calculated risk of remaining open virtually year round.
A la carte: 350-500 F. Menus: 220 F, 450 F.

ISSOUDUN
36100 Issoudun — (Indre)
Paris 229 - Bourges 38 - Châteauroux 27 - Vierzon 34

La Cognette
2, bd Stalingrad — 54.21.21.83
M. Nonnet. Closed Sun dinner, Mon and 7-18 Jan. Open until 10 pm. Private room: 30. Air cond. Garage parking. V AE DC.
Nicole Nonnet and her daughter welcome guests warmly into their stately (save for the frivolous curtains) dining room. Chef Alain Nonnet and his son-in-law Jean-Jacques Daumy man the kitchen of this venerable provincial inn (described by Balzac, no less). The repertoire piously preserves certain regional specialities (duck pâté in flaky pastry, pike with nettles, chicken in a blood-thickened sauce), but is chiefly given over to Nonnet's personal, masterly version of *la grande cuisine bourgeoise.* He is capable of bold touches (filet mignon au thé), but his true penchant is for wonderful fish dishes (prawn croquant with meadow mushrooms, spiced cod) and for game. As soon as the first autumnal fogs envelop the region, Nonnet's many local fans book tables to get their fair share of hare à la royale (Périgord-style), and Flemish-style venison in a bitter-cocoa sauce. Desserts too are sumptuous, and range from a simple cherry-brandy baba to pralin au noisette with hot toffee sauce, and an incomparable dark-chocolate marquise. The wine list is equally remarkable, with premium Loire Valley wines, and some great local whites (Reuilly, Quincy, and Sancerre). A sophisticated choice of coffee, liqueurs and cigars is offered to round off a marvellous meal at La Cognette.
A la carte: 400-500 F. Menus: 200 F (weekdays only, wine inc), 310 F, 370 F, 450 F.

La Cognette
(See restaurant above)
Closed 7-18 Jan. 3 stes 800-900 F. 11 rms 300-600 F. Half-board 420-620 F. TV. Conference facilities.
Set in a delightful garden a hundred metres from the restaurant via ancient, narrow streets, fourteen rooms and three suites await, beautifully maintained and equipped with a romantic décor. Excellent breakfasts with marvellous jam.

ISSY-LES-MOULINEAUX
See PARIS Suburbs

13800 Istres — (B./Rhône)
Paris 742 - Marseille 57 - Arles 41 - Salon-de-Provence 20

Le Mazet de Pépi
Rue des Baumes — 42.55.42.43
M. Hoffalt. Closed Sun dinner, Mon, 2-9 Jan and 22 July-12 Aug. Open until 10 pm. Terrace dining. Air cond. No pets. Parking. V AE DC.
A lovingly restored sheepfold is where Xavier Hoffalt practises the art of classic cuisine. Taste his finely wrought 'petals' of salmon and John Dory, his sweetbreads in Armagnac, his profiteroles au chocolat. Pieds et paquets à la marseillaise (sheep's tripe and trotters, an earthy local dish) is also a house speciality.
A la carte: 300 F. Menu: 145 F.

JARD-SUR-MER

85520 Jard-sur-Mer — (Vendée)
Paris 450 - Les Sables-d'Olonne 20

Le Parc de la Grange
Rte de l'Abbaye — 51.33.44.88
Closed end Dec-beg March. 19 stes 500-1,287 F. 41 rms 278-865 F. Restaurant. Half-board 510-543 F oblig in seas. TV. Conference facilities. Heated pool. Tennis. Telex 700898. V AE DC.
A nice modern complex placed in a 22-hectare park by the sea, with light, comfortable rooms and good conference facilities. Exercise club, billiards, discothèque, and other amenities.

JARNAC

16200 Jarnac — (Charente)
Paris 454 - Angoulême 29 - Cognac 15

Restaurant du Château
Pl. du Château — 45.81.07.17
M. Destrieux. Closed Sat lunch, Sun dinner, Mon, 7-22 Feb and 7-28 Aug. Open until 9 pm. Private room: 40. V.
The charming owners have been attending to every detail of their delightful, traditional Charentais establishment for the past twenty years. For nearly as long, chef Daniel Chapon has been regaling local gourmands (who have precious few good restaurants in the vicinity) with his conservative but flavourful cuisine; his strict, classic technique turns fresh market produce into prawn and garden-vegetable salad, sea bass stuffed with cèpes, rabbit wrapped in a cabbage leaf napped with morel juice.
A la carte: 230 F. Menus: 130 F and 170 F (except holidays).

JOIGNY

89300 Joigny — (Yonne)
Paris 148 - Sens 30 - Auxerre 27 - Troyes 75

La Côte Saint-Jacques
14, faubourg de Paris
86.62.09.70
M. Lorain. Closed 2-31 Jan. Open until 9.45 pm. Private room: 60. Air cond. Valet parking. Telex 801458. V AE DC.
Not satisfied with linking their two buildings on either side of the main road with a sumptuous underground passage, installing Hollywood-style suites over the swimming pool and garden on the banks of the Yonne, the Lorains have just renovated a nearby old villa and doubled the size of the garden. More spectacularly, across the river they have built a tennis court, dug a little lake, and planted an arboretum. For their guests' pleasure, a motorboat is available, as well as a ten-seater

launch for 'apéritif' cruises and small parties. That's not all. Rooms in the old building have been enlarged and agreeably remodelled, and the Lorains' guests are now admitted free of charge to play at a superb golf course just ten kilometres away.
Michel Lorain has turned the kitchen over to his fabulously talented 31-year-old son, Jean-Michel, who recently served us an unforgettable meal. Among the highlights were local snails with lentils and spring onions, a sort of risotto of Basmati rice with sole meunière in a splendid duck-liver sauce, an original and highly successful croustillant of pig's trotter and crab with fresh basil-scented pasta, and a sensational bouillon de pigeon 'façon bortsch'. There followed all manner of ambrosial desserts: millefeuille with a trio of cream fillings, pithiviers with cherries and rhubarb, iced wild strawberry soup topped with meringue eggs.... We watered this gargantuan repast (incredibly light, we might add) with two sensational Burgundies, scented out by Jacqueline Lorain, one of the most discerning 'noses' in France: the illustrious Ramonet's Chassagne-Montrachet Morgeot '86 and Lafarge's Volnay Clos-des-Chênes '80.
A la carte: 500-800 F. Menus: 300 F (weekdays lunch only), 560 F.

La Côte Saint-Jacques
(See restaurant above)
Closed 2-31 Jan. 4 stes 1,550-2,450 F. 25 rms 600-1,800 F. TV. Air cond 15 rms. Conference facilities. Heated pool. Tennis. Golf.
The main building now has been pleasantly renovated, with large, very well-equipped, soundproofed rooms (most are air-conditioned). But the ultimate luxury are the suites on the other side of the road; despite a rather flashy décor, they are divinely comfortable, with perhaps the best bathrooms of any French hotel. There is also a piano-bar for post-prandial entertainment. Dogs are welcome. Relais and Châteaux.

JOUCAS

See Gordes

JOUY-EN-JOSAS

See PARIS Suburbs

JUAN-LES-PINS

06160 Juan-les-Pins — (Alpes-Mar.)
Paris 920 - Nice 22 - Cannes 9 - Antibes 2 - Aix 160

Beauséjour
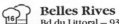
Av. Saramartel — 93.61.07.82
Closed mid-Oct to mid-April. 1 ste 1,500-1,950 F. 30 rms 550-1,100 F. Restaurant. TV. Air cond. Conference facilities. Pool. Parking. Telex 470673. V AE.
A hotel with the atmosphere of a private house, very well situated in the green part of Juan-les-Pins. Recently renovated rooms are light, with shady balconies. Nice garden and barbecue by the swimming pool.

Belles Rives
Bd du Littoral — 93.61.02.79
M. Estene. Closed 10 Sep to Easter. Open until 10 pm. Garden dining. Air cond. No pets. Valet parking. Telex 470984. V AE.
Everything is different here, a refreshing change from the host of lookalike restaurants and hotels that line the French Riviera. Formerly a holiday villa occupied by the likes of Scott and Zelda Fitzgerald, for the last 60 years Belles Rives has been a family-run luxury hotel, with a guest regis-

ter signed by the Windsors, Edith Piaf, Josephine Baker, Miles Davis and loads of other celebrities. A talented young chef, Bernard Mathis, now commands the kitchen of this inspired setting. His cooking is energetic and unpredictable: we loved the Spanish-style sole and sea scallops pan-roasted with chick peas, chorizo, peppers, and tomatoes, as well as the John Dory and artichokes wrapped in diaphanous pastry, and the goat-cheese ravioli in a bright carrot jus. The desserts do not attain the same exhilarating heights, and the wine list (we complain once again) is just not up to scratch. The service is oddly irrational, but on balance the staff is most enthusiastic, and is sure to evolve well. For waterside meals, a simple (but varied) beach menu is available.

A la carte: 450-500 F. Menus: 280 F, 380 F and 480 F (dinner only).

Belles Rives
(See restaurant above)

Closed 10 Sep-Easter. 4 stes 2,100-4,620 F. 41 rms 790-2,310 F. Half-board 945-1,630 F oblig in seas. TV. Air cond. Conference facilities.

With superb views over the entire bay of Antibes, the 1930s-style rooms are all different and extra comfortable. Business services available, as well as a private beach and landing dock.

Bijou-Plage
Bd Ch.-Guillaumont — 93.61.39.07

M. Ariza. Open every day. Open until 10.30 pm. Terrace dining. Air cond. V AE DC.

Here's a rarity: a real 'bijou' of a Riviera beach restaurant, set just opposite the Lérins islands, and open year round to boot. The Japanese chef deftly selects and prepares utterly fresh fish for a gilt-edged clientele: exquisite sea capon in bouillabaisse sauce, grilled John Dory fillet napped with vinaigrette, and sea bass steamed over fennel. An otherwise well-stocked cellar is deficient in half-bottles. Rather a long wait between courses; high prices; and the cheaper set menu doesn't include the most appealing dishes.

A la carte: 400 F. Menus: 158 F, 250 F.

La Frégate
La Pinède
15-17, bd Baudoin — 93.67.25.25

M. Roche. Open every day (dinner only July-Aug). Open until 10.30 pm. Terrace dining. Air cond. No pets. Garage parking. Telex 470888. V AE DC.

A luxurious hostelry all of marble and tinted glass, wedged between the beach and the pines. At the helm of Le Frégate's kitchen is chef Georges Pelissier. This pupil of Outhier and Ducasse turns out imaginative cooking full of keen local flavours, witness a very refined médaillon de rascasse served as an amuse-bouche, or red-mullet fillets on a bed of al dente vegetables, or young pigeon roasted with whole garlic cloves, served with silken braised cabbage. It's a pity the desserts are not all up to standard. Good cellar. Stylish service; high prices.

A la carte: 400-450 F. Menu: 250 F.

Garden Beach Hôtel
(See restaurant above)

Open every day. 17 stes 1,550-4,200 F. 158 rms 500-1,950 F. Half-board 810-2,010 F. TV. Air cond. Conference facilities.

Housed in a modernist cube constructed on the site of the former casino, this luxurious hotel offers every comfort and service. The rather chill décor of red and black marble and granite is warmed by the omnipresent photos of jazz greats who have graced the local festival. Impeccable service.

Hélios
3, av. du Dr-Dautheville — 93.61.55.25

Closed 30 Oct-30 March. 5 stes 2,500-4,000 F. 70 rms 650-1,900 F. Restaurant. Half-board 700-1,250 F oblig in seas. TV. Air cond. Conference facilities. Valet parking. Telex 970906. V AE DC.

Another luxurious hotel, this one with its own private beach (meals are served by the water). Some of the lovely, large, modern rooms have splendid balconies, while others are smaller with characterless furniture and only the merest sliver of a sea view. Piano-bar.

Les Mimosas
Rue Pauline — 93.61.04.16

Closed 1 Oct-1 April. 34 rms 420-590 F. TV 8 rms. No pets. Pool. Garage parking.

An agreeable white house and garden in a residential area 500 metres from the sea. The bright rooms all have balconies, and are pleasantly decorated.

Le Pré Catelan
22, av. des Lauriers — 93.61.05.11

Open every day. 20 rms 220-420 F. Restaurant. Half-board 350-400 F oblig in seas. Parking. V AE.

A little house in a quiet, palm-shaded garden 200 metres from the sea. It has its own private beach with restaurant.

La Terrasse
La Pinède
Av. G.-Gallice — 93.61.20.37

MM. Barache. Dinner only in July-Aug. Closed end Oct to April. Open until 10 pm (10.30 pm in summer). Private room: 20. Garden dining. Valet parking. Telex 470778.

There's magic in the air of this very special spot, where fortunate guests take their ease on a terrace surrounded by masses of flowers and palm trees. The atmosphere of this art deco villa is reminiscent of more gracious days, when Scott Fitzgerald, Cocteau, and Chanel spent leisurely holidays at Juan-les-Pins. A perusal of Christian Morisset's menu makes one's taste buds quiver in anticipation of such sunny, colourful fare as fresh scampi ravioli in shellfish broth, or an assortment of vegetables perfumed with coriander, or a salad of shellfish and violet asparagus, or a premium sea bass baked in its juices with olive oil, or lobster risotto, or milk-fed lamb fillet served with its kidneys and sweetbreads and stuffed courgette flowers. To finish, there are bright, light desserts like wild-strawberry cake, and the basket of lemon 'merveilles'. But then, just as a mood of mellow indolence settles over one (helped by a delicious Bandol form Pibarnon, or Pradeaux), the bill arrives.... Less costly than the à la carte options is the generous 480 F set menu.

A la carte: 600-800 F. Menus: 380 F (lunch only), 480 F, 550 F.

Hôtel Juana
(See restaurant above)

Closed end Oct-April. 5 stes 2,200-4,400 F. 45 rms 750-2,500 F. Half-board 1,130-2,880 F. TV. Air cond. Conference facilities. Heated pool.

Apart from the rather sad brown-hued bar, this art deco hotel has been excellently remodelled. Thanks to its great class, comfort, charming flowered terrace, and lovely swimming pool, the new Juana has contributed to the rebirth of elegance at Juan-les-Pins. Alas, there is no sea view, but the hotel overlooks the beautiful casino gardens.

33890 Juillac — (Gironde)
Paris 560 - Bordeaux 56 - Libourne 30 - La Réole 34

 Le Belvédère
4 km E on D 130 — 57.40.40.33
*M. Pestel. Closed Tue dinner, Wed and Oct. Open until
9 pm. Private room: 30. Terrace dining. Parking. V
AE DC.*

The terrace of the Pestels' chalet dominates the
majestic sweep of the Dordogne Rivier from a
height of 60 metres. The panorama is also visible
from the dining room, where the staff takes the
time to look after the guests. Light and tasty cooking is in store, with offerings like half a dozen warm
oysters in delicious leek fondue (with a glass of
Entre-Deux-Mers), warm sea-trout mousse, and
chicken drumstick stuffed with succulent wild
mushrooms. Good Bordeaux wines, and exceptionally kind welcome and service.
A la carte: 250-300 F. Menus: 120 F, 180 F, 280 F.

JUILLAN
See Tarbes

JUMIÈGES
76118 Jumièges — (Seine-Mar.)
Paris 165 - Rouen 28 - Caudebec-en-Caux 15

Auberge des Ruines
Pl. de la Mairie — 35.37.24.05
*M. Henry. Open every day. Open until 9.30 pm. Ter-
race dining. Hotel: 4 rms 100-130 F. V.*

Facing the most imposing ruins in the region is a
lively little abode run by a young, friendly crew. In
summer, you can eat on the quiet terrace—lobster
vinaigrette with corn salad, herb-scented bass with
chanterelles, boned pigeon with vanilla butter, and
berry croquant all prepared by 23-year-old Loïc
Henry and his equally youthful assistant. Good
Loire Valley wines.
A la carte: 300-350 F. Menus: 72 F (weekdays
only), 135 F, 185 F, 235 F.

JURANÇON
See Pau

KAYSERSBERG
68240 Kaysersberg — (Haut-Rhin)
Paris 434 - Colmar 10 - Munster 25 - Sélestat 26

Chambard
9-11, rue du Gal-de-Gaulle — 89.47.10.17
*M. Irrmann. Closed Tue lunch, Mon, 1-21 March and
22 Dec-4 Jan. Open until 9.30 pm. Private room: 30.
Air cond. Parking. Telex 880272. V AE DC.*

Chambard is a well-known Alsatian restaurant
reputed for its quietly refined décor, its huge wine
cellar, and the remarkable cooking of owner-chef
Pierre Irrmann. He certainly lives up to his billing
with dishes like an admirable pot-au-feu d'oie
minute au gros sel, lobster simmered in a spicy,
aromatic broth, sweet Breton prawns with fried
ginger, and some fabulous desserts (apple strudel
with vanilla sauce; hot figs with almond ice cream)
Quality service; high prices.
A la carte: 450-500 F. Menus: 220 F, 300 F, 380 F.

Chambard
(See restaurant above)
*Closed 1-21 March and 22 Dec-4 Jan. 2 stes 650-
700 F. 18 rms 450-500 F. TV. Conference facilities.*
Pretty little hotel with twenty handsomely
decorated, extremely comfortable rooms. The bar
is in the old wine cellar.

KINGERSHEIM
See Mulhouse

KREMLIN-BICÊTRE (LE)
See PARIS Suburbs

LABARTHE-SUR-LÈZE
See Toulouse

LABATUT
40300 Labatut — (Landes)
Paris 739 - Mont-de-Marsan 73 - Bayonne 46 - Dax 27

Auberge du Bousquet
N 117 — 58.98.18.24
*M. Lacarrau. Closed Mon dinner. Open until
9.30 pm. Private room: 18. Terrace dining. Parking.
V AE DC.*

For nearly two centuries successive generations
of the Laccarau family have run this inn, famous for
its seasonal cooking and game dishes. Young
Bernard Lacarrau has left off experimenting with
new-fangled styles, and now practises a satisfying
brand of lightened traditional cuisine: pheasant
pâté in cabbage leaves, roast Basque turbot, and
local palombes (wood doves).
A la carte: 250-350 F. Menus: 90 F, 150 F, 240 F.

LACAVE
46200 Lacave — (Lot)
Paris 540 - Cahors 65 - Rocamadour 10 - Souillac 10

Château de la Treyne
65.32.66.66
*Mme Gombert-Devals. Closed 15 Nov-Easter. Open
until 9 pm. Private room: 40. Garden dining. Parking. Telex 531427. V AE DC.*

An aristocratic establishment with an unchanging menu that gives talented Bernard Darcissac
only limited opportunity to realise his potential.
His occasional flights of fancy prove that he is
capable of more challenging dishes than trout en
papillote with basil, or lamb with thyme butter.
Good selection of Cahors wines, young and enthusiastic service, and a wonderful setting.
A la carte: 350 F. Menus: 150 F, 240 F.

Château de la Treyne
(See restaurant above)
*Closed 15 Nov-Easter. 13 rms 1,500-2,200 F (for
2 pers, half-board oblig). TV. Conference facilities.
Heated pool. Tennis.*
The Dordogne flows lazily by, the furniture,
hangings, and decorations are beautiful, the rooms
are elegant, and breakfast on the terrace overlooking the river is a rare pleasure.

Pont de l'Ouysse
65.37.87.04
*M. Chambon. Closed Mon off-season and 11 Nov-1
March. Open until 9 pm. Private room: 20. Garden
dining. Parking. V AE DC.*

Tucked below the Château de Belcastel, this
long, low, handsomely renovated house, which
one reaches across a little bridge, is set in paradisaical surroundings, where the murmur of the river
soothes one on the shady terrace in summer, and
the fireplace in the apricot-coloured dining room
warms one in winter. Both are perfect spots for
savouring Daniel Chambon's imaginative interpretations of regional dishes. We applaud his crayfish bouillon with tiny vegetables, roast pigeon
wing with a pastilla of truffled pig's trotter, lamb
fillet with a herb crepinette, rabbit roulade with
baby vegetables, and invariably remarkable

desserts. The cellar is astutely composed, with a good selection of half-bottles. Young, efficient service.

A la carte: 350-400 F. Menus: 150 F, 250 F, 300 F.

Pont de l'Ouysse

(See restaurant above)

Closed Mon off-season and 11 Nov-1 March. 1 ste 700 F. 12 rms 400-500 F. Half-board 450-500 F. TV. Heated pool.

A dozen ravishing bedrooms, with cosy country décor and white wicker furniture. Breakfast is served in the garden.

LADOIX-SERRIGNY

See Beaune

LAGNY-SUR-MARNE

77400 Lagny-sur-Marne — (Seine/Marne)
Paris 33 - Meaux 21 - Senlis 51 - Melun 42

Egleny

13, av. du Gal-Leclerc — 64.30.52.69

M. Gaudet. Closed Sun dinner, Mon, 24 Feb-4 March and 28 July-26 Aug. Open until 9.30 pm. Private room: 20. Terrace dining. Parking. V AE DC.

The road to Lagny takes one through traffic jams, past beetroot fields and monstrous concrete amusement parks.... But in the old village there stands this lovely old mason's house, with three small adjoining rooms that open onto a delicious garden. Here, for the last three years, Yves Gaudet (a chef of disarming modesty) has been creating wonderful, truly exciting food. His very personal cuisine is full of allusions to the *bourgeois* tradition, as in his vol-au-vent d'une maison bourgeoise, or the stuffed saddle of lamb 'à la reine'. Just as fine, but more modern in spirit, are his extremely light, flavourful crab aspic perfumed with star anise, sea bass with olive coulis and fried courgettes, and miraculous desserts, like millefeuille aux fruits d'été, caramelised melon feuillantine, or roasted apples with walnuts. The welcome is cordial, the atmosphere is relaxed, and the prices are reasonable (note the tempting prix-fixe menu served on weekdays).

A la carte: 400 F. Menus: 200 F (weekdays lunch only), 340 F.

In nearby Bussy-Saint-Georges

(4 km S)
77600 Lagny-sur-Marne — (Seine/Marne)

Le Clos Saint-Georges

15, av. du Golf — 64.66.30.30

M. Révil. Open every day. Open until 10 pm. Garden dining. Parking. Telex 693322. V AE DC.

A long, low concrete construction, more suited to commercial travellers than romantic weekends. Yet the dining room is bright and modern, and extends out to a garden terrace; and chef Raymond Beck's engaging cuisine is based on superb ingredients. We were impressed with his fresh, perfectly seasoned salad of sea trout and green beans, a superbly cooked bonito ragoût with crushed tomatoes, and a light, tasty quail pot-au-feu. Courteous welcome and smiling, efficient service. The cellar provides lots of good, affordable wines.

A la carte: 250 F. Menu: 145 F.

RAC Regional Maps of France at 4 miles to 1 inch are the ideal touring companion. Available from RAC offices and all good bookshops.

Le Clos Saint-Georges

(See restaurant above)

Open every day. 1 ste 550 F. 95 rms 395-450 F. TV. Conference facilities. Tennis.

Classic businessman's hotel, not lacking in charm. The good-sized rooms are ultramodern and impeccably tidy, with perfect soundproofing.

LAGUIOLE

12210 Laguiole — (Aveyron)
Paris 552 - Aurillac 82 - Rodez 56 - Espalion 24

Michel Bras

(Lou Mazuc)
65.44.32.24

19.5 *M. Bras. Closed Sun dinner (except July-Aug), Mon and 21 Oct-26 March. Open until 9 pm. No pets. Valet parking. V AE.*

Each day Michel Bras climbs to the top of 'his' hill to gather wild herbs and survey the progress on his new hotel. Practically hidden in the rock, to harmonise perfectly with the rugged landscape, the structure will be blessed with a fantastic panorama over the Aubrac mountains. The design is quite extraordinary, and bears little resemblance to the common run of hotel projects. When Bras's dream is realised (spring 1992 perhaps?), he will at last have a setting worthy of his talents. For this man is a real artist, a poet, a herborist, a philosopher, and an uncommonly talented photographer. As we write, however, he is still cooking in the old family inn, with its cramped, enclosed dining room. Yet with the first taste of Bras's dazzling dishes, one pays little attention to the surroundings, for all one's senses are occupied with savouring their glorious flavours and feasting on their visual beauty.

Michel Bras's knowledge and use of herbs is unparalleled. He combines and contrasts their fresh vegetal flavours to create a cuisine that is highly personal, utterly unlike any other: wild anise seeds and basil enliven a creamy crab soup; Douglas fir needles lend a forest fragrance to foie gras de canard; lamb sweetbreads are paired with exquisitely sweet wild onions; crayfish jus, along with blue and white borage, heighten the mild sweetness of prawns with orange confit; turbot is stuffed with ham and green anise. Desserts share the same wild yet refined, natural yet sophisticated flavours (gentian perfumes the cherry and almond pastries, for example).

Ginette Bras has put together a cellar of wines, brandies, and other spirits that could make a professional sommelier pale with envy. And though service may occasionally be slow, at least one can be sure that the food is worth waiting for!

A la carte: 420-600 F. Menus: 180 F (weekdays only), 330 F, 490 F.

Lou Mazuc

(See restaurant above)

Closed Sun (except July-Aug), Mon and 21 Oct-26 March. 13 rms 240-540 F. TV. No pets.

Until the new hotel is finished on the hillside, the refurbished family inn offers thirteen little rooms with a lovely fresh mountain smell. The beds are not as comfortable as they might be, but you will forget that minor detail when you taste the excellent breakfast. No tennis, no golf course, no heliport, but Michel Bras has put together careful itineraries for some beautiful walks.

LAMAGDELAINE

See Cahors

LAMALOU-LES-BAINS

34240 Lamalou-les-Bains — (Hérault)
Paris 840 - Montpellier 80 - Lodève 38 - St-Pons 37

[13] Mas
25, av. Charcot — 67.95.62.22
M. Bitsch. Open every day. Open until 9.30 pm. Private room: 150. Terrace dining. Parking. V AE DC.

Emile Bitsch has found an excellent chef in young Gérard Galinier, a hard-working lad whose culinary style is light and fresh. His varied repertoire of regional dishes includes scallops in Faugères wine, lotte feuilleté with oyster mushrooms, gratin de pigeon aux figues fraîches. A sprightly young staff zips about the tastefully updated nineteenth-century dining room.

A la carte: 230 F. Menus: 68 F and 78 F (brasserie), 98 F, 138 F, 175 F.

Mas
(See restaurant above)
Open every day. 39 rms 100-210 F. Half-board 195-300 F. TV 8 rms. Conference facilities.

The huge traditional bedrooms are slowly being renovated to their former early twentieth-century splendour. Charming welcome.

LAMASTRE

07270 Lamastre — (Ardèche)
Paris 582 - Le Puy 73 - Privas 56 - Valence 40

[14] Barattéro
(Bernard Perrier)
Pl. Seignobos — 75.06.41.50
M. Perrier. Closed Sun dinner and Mon (except July-Aug and holidays), and 15 Dec-1 March. Open until 9 pm. Private room: 35. Garage parking. Hotel: 13 rms 250-330 F, half-board 300-340 F oblig in seas. V AE DC.

Nothing could be simpler than the cool, flowery dining room, nor calmer than the garden under the bay trees, where one sips an apéritif before choosing from Bernard Perrier's interesting menu. His cooking is careful, conservative, but flavourful and fresh: crusty sea bream with shredded chicory, poularde truffée en vessie, lamb fillet with tarragon jus, and iced chestnut soufflé. A good choice of Côtes-du-Rhône, and swift, attentive service.

A la carte: 350-400 F. Menus: from 160 F to 340 F.

Château d'Urbilhac
2 km, rte de Vernoux — 75.06.42.11
M. Xompero. Closed Thu lunch and 10 Oct-30 April. Open until 9 pm. Private room: 25. Garden dining. No pets. Garage parking. V AE DC.

Ignore the architecture, and feast your eyes instead on the wondrous, sublimely peaceful wild beauty—unequalled in the region. The huge nineteenth-century manor looks down on the verandas and swimming pool, over a breathtaking view of mountains and forests. A glass-enclosed terrace that opens onto the scenery affords relief from the solemn 'château' dining room. As for the cooking (13/20 in our last guide), we cannot comment this year for the new chef had not taken up his duties at press time.

Menus: 160 F, 195 F, 250 F.

Château d'Urbilhac
(See restaurant above)
Closed 10 Oct-30 April. 13 rms 350-600 F. Half-board 425-500 F oblig in seas. Heated pool. Tennis. ments superbes, and une patronne aux petits soins (petits déjeuners délicieux).

This Renaissance-style nineteenth-century château is perched at an altitude of 500 metres in a 60-hectare park. A shaded tennis court and panoramic swimming pool are just two of the many facilities. Rooms are spacious and prettily furnished, with charm and personality. Delicious breakfasts; perfect service.

LAMBERSART
See Lille

LAMORLAYE
See Chantilly

LANDERNEAU

29220 Landerneau — (Finistère)
Paris 571 - Morlaix 39 - Brest 20 - Quimper 70

[13] Le Clos du Pontic
Rue du Pontic — 98.21.50.91
M. SAug. Closed Sat lunch, Sun dinner and Mon. Open until 9 pm. Private room: 40. Parking. Telex 941572. Hotel: 38 rms 200-270 F, half-board 210-240 F. V.

Things are looking up at this rambling mansion swathed in greenery. Patrons are greeted warmly in a dining room that affords a tranquil view of the grounds; and though the cooking is still not as consistent as we might wish, it surely deserves the toque we suspended last year: copious warm cod salad, crisp skate with baby vegetables, decent sea bass in puff pastry (swamped, however, by an aggressive bouillabaisse sauce), and delicious chocolate tart with a too-sweet vanilla sauce.

A la carte: 250-350 F. Menus: 85 F (lunch only), 150 F, 190 F, 280 F.

LANDERSHEIM

67700 Landersheim — (Bas-Rhin)
Paris 433 - Strasbourg 24 - Saverne 14 - Haguenau 31

[14] Auberge du Kochersberg ۞
Rue de Saessolsheim — 88.69.91.58
M. Klipfel. Closed Mon, Tue, dinner Sun and holidays, 25 Feb-13 March and 29 July-21 Aug. Open until 9.30 pm. Private room: 45. Air cond. Tennis. Parking. Telex 870974. V AE DC.

This huge Alsatian dining room regularly performs a quick-change act: it serves successively as a canteen for the staff of the Adidas factory opposite, and as a luxury restaurant with lace tablecloths and pretty table settings. Chef Armand Roth has trained with all the greats of French cooking, as is manifest in his up-to-date dishes made with top-quality ingredients: prawn salad with foie gras slivers, freshwater perch fillet with bone-marrow dumplings, and pigeon in a puff-pastry tourte with a ragoût of baby vegetables. Good cheese board. Among the succulent desserts we chose a poached pear in mocha sabayon with honey ice cream. Exceptional wine list.

A la carte: 400-450 F. Menus: 200 F, 300 F, 380 F.

LANFROICOURT

54760 Lanfroicourt — (Meurthe/M.)
Paris 327 - Nancy 20 - Metz 43 - Custines 16

[13] Auberge des Capucines
12, rue des Capucines — 83.31.81.18
M. Gérardin. Closed Tue, Wed, 14-28 Feb and 1-15 Aug. Open until 9 pm. Private room: 25. Garden dining. Parking. V.

Here's a pretty establishment in a hard-to-find little village in the suburbs of Nancy, where a professional father-and-son team turn out honest, classic cooking—sometimes with a flash of adventurous originality. Taste, for example, sole fillet with fresh mint, feuillantine of rabbit with chanterelles, or mignon de poularde et ris de veau. Large (in every sense) wine list. Guests are charmingly welcomed into a comfortable dining room, luxuriously decorated and well furnished.

A la carte: 300-350 F. Menus: 180 F, 280 F.

37130 Langeais — (Indre/Loire)
Paris 258 - Angers 83 - Chinon 31 - Tours 25

In nearby Saint-Patrice

(9 km SW on N 152)
37130 Langeais — (Indre/Loire)

Château de Rochecotte
14
47.96.91.28
Mme Pasquier. Closed Feb. Open until 9 pm. Private room: 90. Garage parking. V AE DC.

What could be more enchanting than to linger in the luxurious surroundings of this beautifully restored Renaissance château, or in the idyllic garden that slopes down to the Loire? Mme Pasquier, the owner of this jewel, has solved the problem of keeping her chefs at the end of the season by placing her daughter in charge of the kitchen. Fresh from the Blois hotel school, Emmanuelle Pasquier was apprenticed under the château's last three chefs; her evident talent is a joy to see—and taste! Her short (high-priced) menu offers a finely wrought salade folle à l'oiseau, salmon paupiette stuffed with minced pig's trotter and napped with lentil cream, roasted prawns with a hint of vanilla, and for dessert, a bright-flavoured strawberry and glazed grapefruit shortbread.

A la carte: 400 F. Menu: 190 F.

Château de Rochecotte ♠♥
(See restaurant above)
Closed Feb. 2 stes 950 F. 22 rms 360-790 F. Half-board 560-1,190 F. TV. Conference facilities.

Set on a hillside overlooking the valley, the very comfortable rooms and suites are thoughtfully equipped in contemporary style, with a felicitous mixture of antique and modern furniture. An atmosphere of delicate refinement reigns throughout the magnificent drawing rooms, the admirable terrace and gardens. A charming, cultivated hostess capably runs this, one of the most enticing hotels in Touraine.

33210 Langon — (Gironde)
Paris 604 - Bordeaux 47 - Marmande 37

Claude Darroze
15
95, cours du Gal-Leclerc — 56.63.00.48
M. Darroze. Closed 7-21 Jan and 2-10 Oct-5 Nov. Open until 9.30 pm. Private room: 60. Terrace dining. Air cond. Hotel: 17 rms 250-420 F. Valet parking. V AE DC.

Certain fans of this restaurant won't let a year go by without a visit, swear they adore the trompe-l'œil décor of the large dining room and the club-like atmosphere of the other. We don't wish to wound any sensibilities, but were we (Heaven forbid!) to open a restaurant, Darroze's decorator would be last on our list! But when it comes to food, how well we know and love Claude Darroze's knack of bringing out the best in his remarkable ingredients. This generous, traditional regional cooking is made to measure for an élite, no-nonsense clientele: baby eel salad with a garlicky dressing, wild lamb's lettuce with truffles and foie gras, lamprey with leeks, olive-stuffed duck, wood doves flamed with ham fat, sublime local

lamb, and 'bachelor's jam' served with cinnamon ice cream. We recommend you do as the food-loving locals do, and wash down this hearty fare with a premium claret, the best you can afford!

A la carte: 350-400 F. Menus: 165 F, 260 F, 360 F, 450 F.

52200 Langres — (Haute-Marne)
Paris 294 - Auxerre 155 - Dijon 68 - Vittel 72

12/20 Grand Hôtel de l'Europe
23-25, rue Diderot — 25.87.10.88
M. Jossinet. Closed Mon (except dinner in seas), Sun dinner, 2 weeks in April and 3 weeks in Oct. Open until 9 pm. Private room: 15. Hotel: 28 rms 100-270 F. Garage parking. V AE DC.

Steeped in tradition, this seventeenth-century hostelry offers seriously good cooking (smoked-salmon bavarois, freshwater perch with bacon) in a charming setting, as well as several simple, comfortable rooms perfectly suited for overnight guests or explorers of the old fortified town of Langres.

A la carte: 220 F. Menus: 60 F and 150 F (weekdays only), 90 F.

22300 Lannion — (Côtes/Armor)
Paris 515 - Brest 96 - St-Brieuc 63 - Morlaix 38

Le Manoir de Crec'h Goulifen ♠♥
Rte de Beg-Leguer Servel — 96.47.26.17
Closed 30 Sep-1 March. 7 rms 230-350 F. Tennis. Parking.

Nestled in lush grounds just three kilometres from the sea, this Breton manor promises a quiet night's sleep.

Le Serpolet
13
1, rue F.-le-Dantec — 96.46.50.23
M. Le Balc'h. Closed off-season Sun dinner and Mon, 20-31 Jan and 2-10 Oct. Open until 9.30 pm. V.

The exposed-beam ceiling and crackling fireplace help to create an intimate atmosphere in this old house in the centre of town. The cuisine is flavourful, fresh and skilfully prepared: scallops perfumed with tarragon, foie gras with grape confit, brill steamed in thyme with beurre blanc, or the astonishing cotriade fish stew seasoned with tarragon and chives. Some fine bottles are on offer at moderate prices. Smiling welcome, flustered service, modest bill.

A la carte: 250 F. Menus: 62 F (weekdays lunch only), 80 F, 110 F, 155 F, 170 F.

In nearby La Ville-Blanche

(4 km E on D 786)
22300 Lannion — (Côtes/Armor)

La Ville Blanche
13
96.37.04.28
M. Jaguin. Closed Sun dinner and Mon (except July-Aug), and 28 Jan-28 Feb. Open until 9.15 pm (9.45 pm in summer). Parking. V AE DC.

Chef Daniel Jaguin, late of Michel Guérard, faces a daunting challenge in trying to turn this rather charmless former lorry-drivers' stop into a gastronomic restaurant. He's freshened up the décor with shades of blue and Breton objets, and his cooking is sincere, intelligent and well-presented: luscious Landes duck foie gras, delicate lotte in a coulis perfumed with aromatic herbs, and robust pigeon ragoût with bacon in a savoury wine sauce.

Smiling, family-style welcome, and attentive service.

A la carte: 230 F. Menus: 95 F (weekdays lunch only), 160 F, 215 F, 270 F.

02000 Laon — (Aisne)
Paris 139 - Saint-Quentin 46 - Reims 47

Angleterre

10, bd de Lyon — 23.23.04.62
Open every day. 30 rms 150-320 F. Restaurant. TV 10 rms. Conference facilities. Garage parking. Telex 145580. V AE DC.

Located in the lower town, this fine hotel has recently been redecorated. Some rooms overlook a park setting.

La Petite Auberge

45, bd P.-Brossolette — 23.23.02.38
M. Zorn. Closed Sat lunch, Sun and 1-15 Aug. Open until 9.30 pm. Private room: 15. No pets. V AE DC.

Young chef Willy-Marc Zorn took over from his parents and has thrust this rustic restaurant into the gastronomic limelight. Bold, and with an excellent knowledge of ingredients and technique, Zorn-the-younger turns out dishes such as salmon with boned pig's trotters, skate steamed in a cumin-perfumed fish stock, and jugged hare. Dreamy desserts, and a cellar brimming with finds straight from the growers.

A la carte: 400 F. Menus: 139 F, 195 F.

03120 Lapalisse — (Allier)
Paris 340 - Moulins 50 - Digoin 45 - St-Pourçain 31

In nearby **Sanssat**

(12 km W on N 7 and D 125)
03150 Lapalisse — (Allier)

Château de Theillat

70.99.86.70
M. Boche. Open every day. Open until 10 pm. Private room: 150. Garden dining. Parking. Telex 393007. V AE.

A bold hand was needed to undertake the restoration of this handsome eighteenth-century mansion, which used to be a state-run boarding school. Its three elegant dining rooms open onto a leafy, 15-hectare park. Jacques Muller's enthusiastic cooking features chanterelle salad with foie gras, scallops cooked in a creamy vermouth sauce, pig's trotters with wild mushrooms and a succulent truffle jus, and peach flambée with vanilla ice cream. The service is sometimes hesitant; the wine cellar is particularly rich in Burgundies.

A la carte: 450 F. Menus: 260 F, 350 F, 420 F.

Château de Theillat

(See restaurant above)
Open every day. 18 rms 650-1,100 F. Half-board 1,020-1,430 F. TV. Conference facilities. Heated pool. Tennis.

The eighteen spacious, well-equipped rooms are decorated in classic style, and boast perfect bathrooms. The welcome is friendly, but the staff is too small.

See Lorient

See Cahors

84360 Lauris-sur-Durance — (Vaucluse)
Paris 732 - Avignon 54 - Cavaillon 27 - Aix 33

La Chaumière

Place du Portail
90.08.20.25
Mme Diamant and M. Corcinos. Closed Tue and 15 Nov-15 Dec. Open until 10 pm. Private room: 25. Garden dining. No-smoking section. Garage parking. V AE DC.

The Chaumière's delightful dining room affords a lovely view of the Durance valley. Here you'll be regaled with robust regional fare such as young rabbit compote with wild purslane and cherries in vinegar, prawns and scallops cooked in a leek and truffle bouillon, and roast kid stuffed with savory. Desserts revolve around local fruit.

Menus: 145 F (weekdays lunch only), 198 F, 245 F.

La Chaumière

(See restaurant above)
Closed 15 Nov-15 Dec. 1 ste 700 F. 14 rms 375-650 F. Half-board 380-550 F oblig in seas. TV. Conference facilities.

Tastefully appointed, the rooms here are comfortable and quiet, and overlook the Durance Valley. Fine breakfasts, charming welcome.

53000 Laval — (Mayenne)
Paris 291 - Tours 140 - Le Mans 75 - Angers 73

Le Bistro de Paris

67, rue du Val-de-Mayenne — 43.56.98.29
M. Lemercier. Closed Sat lunch, Sun and 5-26 Aug. Open until 9.45 pm. Private room: 18. No pets. V.

Universally hated and envied by other restaurateurs in the region, award-winning chef Guy Lemercier continues to create flawless meals at frustratingly low prices (100 to 115 F!). His smart little establishment on the banks of the Mayenne, with its delicious southern feel, presided over by his smiling wife, is perpetually booked solid. No wonder they wish he would take it elsewhere! We, on the other hand, have been thoroughly and consistently delighted by the superb, savoury, succulent cuisine: rillettes of semid-smoked sea bream, raw sardines with sea salt, crab and aubergines on a bed of tomatoes and aubergines, lamb sweetbreads and chicken braised with pistachios, foie gras flanked by cod poached in a vanilla-perfumed infusion (marvellous!), and, for dessert, a dreamy chocolate feuille à feuille with caramel sorbet. All this for a pittance! Envy, in the case of Lemercier, is the sincerest form of flattery.

A la carte: 250 F. Menus: 100 F, 115 F, 200 F.

La Gerbe de Blé

83, rue V.-Boissel — 43.53.14.10
Open every day. 2 stes 500-590 F. 8 rms 325-460 F. Half-board 495-686 F. Restaurant. TV. Conference facilites. No pets.

The huge, nicely decorated rooms are well equipped and have fine bathrooms. They are rather noisy, however, as they overlook a busy street. Good Continental or English breakfasts. Slack staff, friendly owner.

Some establishments change their closing times without warning. It is always wise to check in advance.

LAVANDOU (LE)

83980 Lavandou (Le) — (Var)
Paris 887 - Toulon 41 - Saint-Tropez 38 - Cannes 104

L'Algue Bleue
62, av. du Gal-de-Gaulle — 94.71.01.95
*M. Dal Sasso. Closed Wed and 15 Oct-15 March.
Open until 10.30 pm. Private room: 15. Terrace dining. V AE DC.*

The lovely port-side setting, with a view of the Hyères islands, the leafy terrace and fresh new décor are a perfect match for René Théveniot's formal, flavourful cuisine. Taste the refreshing fish cheek tartare with savory, and the novel purée of red mullet accompanying a fillet of sea bass, followed by a delicious génoise au café. One more point.
A la carte: 400 F. Menus: 195 F, 240 F, 400 F.

La Calanque
(See restaurant above)
Closed 15 Oct-15 March. 2 stes 900-1,100 F. 36 rms 500-600 F. Half-board 700-1,076 F oblig in seas. TV. Conference facilities.

This handsome, post-war building, set before the moorings, has just received a face-lift. The rooms have been updated in good taste and all have sea views. Boat trips and tuna fishing can be arranged.

Belle Vue
in Saint-Clair — 94.71.01.06
Closed Nov-March. 19 rms 300-600 F. Restaurant. Half-board 400-600 F oblig in seas. No pets. Conference facilities. Parking. Telex 400555. V AE.

Overlooking the sea and coast, this charming hotel offers rustic, rather dull, but comfortable rooms.

L'Orangeraie
1.5 km on N 559
Av. A.-Gide, in St-Clair — 94.71.04.25
Closed 7 Oct-22 March. 20 rms 210-420 F. TV 14 rms. Air cond 19 rms. Parking. V.

Expect a very warm welcome at this beachfront hotel. The modern, air-conditioned, soundproofed rooms (some with kitchenette) boast excellently equipped bathrooms.

Au Vieux Port
Quai G.-Péri — 94.71.00.21
M. Lambert. Closed Wed off-season, and 29 Oct-16 March. Open until 10.30 pm. Terrace dining. Air cond. V AE DC.

Either you eat outside, on the terrace facing the port, and breathe in the exhaust fumes of the countless cars and motorbikes of teenagers showing off. Or you take refuge in the uninspiring dining room. It's a problem. Pity, for chef Philippe Durandeau is a serious craftsman, especially good with local ingredients: prawn croustillant with tartare sauce and fresh vegetables in brik pastry, fillet of weever with creamed lentils, and grapefruit crème légère. The rosé is served over-chilled and the staff tends to stand on ceremony.
A la carte: 350-400 F. Menus: 90 F (weekdays lunch only), 130 F, 190 F, 260 F.

Hervé Vinrich
(Auberge Provençale)
11, rue Patron-Ravello — 94.71.00.44
M. Vinrich. Open every day. Open until 9 pm (11 pm in seas). Terrace dining. Air cond. Hotel: 13 rms 190-300 F. V AE DC.

Sadly, like many a Provençal restaurant, this one is a marvel out of season, and a frenetic factory in summer. Still, this year we've awarded Vinrich a toque for his excellent red-mullet brandade, young

rabbit stuffed with shallots, red mullet with a wine and anchovy sauce, and seafood medley (salmon, lotte, large prawns, sole). The wine cellar and desserts could both be improved, as could the lead-footed service.
A la carte: 300 F. Menus: 145 F, 300 F.

In nearby Aiguebelle
(4.5 km E on D 559)
83980 Lavandou (Le) — (Var)

Les Roches
1, av. des Trois-Dauphins — 94.71.05.05
M. Tarridec. Closed 2 Jan-15 March and 18 Nov-13 Dec. Open until 10.30 pm. Private room: 60. Terrace dining. Valet parking. Telex 430023. V AE DC.

If the expression weren't so shopworn we'd be tempted to call this seafront restaurant—huddling behind hibiscus hedges and bougainvilleas, with a sweeping view of the cap Bénat and île du Levant—a paradise. Well, so be it! This is now one of the Riviera's most luxurious establishments, the fief of chef Laurent Tarridec, late of Rochedy and Rostang. At 32, Tarridec is both imaginative and possessed of a delicate hand, and has managed to marry the perfumes of the Provençal soil to the savours of the sea. Witness, for example, the paradisiacal pumpkin soup with chicken jelly served with bacon-flavoured toast, prawn or sardine beignets with puréed sweet peppers, roast rabbit served cold with lightly charred aubergines, and baby artichoke and fennel barigoule bathed in clam juices. Or the John Dory sprinkled with perfumed oil and cooked in a lemon-grass bouillon, the baby lobster with a semolina croustillant seasoned with spicy curry and cooled with coconut. And so on.
From the homemade bread to the heavenly desserts (gratin of sour cherries with brown sugar and liquorice parfait, for instance) and chocolates, you will be assailed by tempting creations. And nowhere else has a sommelier so diligently amassed scores of the best wines of Provence and Corsica (including an ambrosial 1973 Bandol from Château Vannières). Time slips by like warmed honey when you settle in for a few hours on the dining room-terrace. So if this isn't heaven, please don't tell us. Three toques and eighteen points to salute the arrival of one of the coast's best, and most inventive, restaurants.
A la carte: 550-700 F. Menus: 280 F, 360 F, 420 F.

Les Roches

(See restaurant above)
Closed 2 Jan-15 March and 18 Nov-13 Dec. 5 stes 1,320-1,370 F. 42 rms 725-1,500 F. TV. Air cond. Conference facilities. Pool.

This *petit palace* is unquestionably one of the most refined of recent constructions on this stretch of coast, unexpected but welcome. The sunny, antique-filled rooms, with terraces overlooking the sea, are furnished with taste, the bathrooms equipped with marble and Salernes porcelain. Shady footpaths wind through a garden studded with cactus and rare trees, leading to the private beach and freshwater swimming pool. Tennis and boating facilities are close at hand, and there's a golf course nearby.

See also: **Bormes-les-Mimosas, Porquerolles (Ile de), Port-Cros (Ile de)**

LECTOURE

32700 Lectoure — (Gers)
Paris 700 - Agen 36 - Condom 23 - Toulouse 94 - Auch 35

Hôtel de Bastard
Rue Lagrange — 62.68.82.44

M. Arnaud. Closed Sat lunch, dinner Fri and Sun, 15 Jan-28 Feb and 22-28 Dec. Open until 9.30 pm. Private room: 20. Terrace dining. Garage parking. V AE DC.

This eighteenth-century burgher's residence sits in a gorgeous little village, yet opens onto the countryside. The dining rooms are spacious, comfortable and discreetly elegant, the quality cooking solid and well thought-out: terrine of duck confit with mild garlic, grilled salmon au beurre rouge, thinly sliced beef with fried foie gras. Short but well-chosen wine list; courteous, efficient service.

A la carte: 280-300 F. Menus: 75 F (weekdays only, wine inc), 140 F, 190 F, 260 F.

Hôtel de Bastard
(See restaurant above)

Closed 15 Jan-28 Feb and 22-28 Dec. 29 rms 170-285 F. Half-board 240-280 F. TV. Conference facilities. Heated pool.

A superb townhouse with well-equipped rooms, decorated with taste. Good Continental or Gascon breakfasts. Unostentatious, polished service.

LEMBACH

67510 Lembach — (Bas-Rhin)
Paris 460 - Strasbourg 56 - Wissenbourg 15

Auberge du Cheval Blanc   ○
4, rue de Wissembourg — 88.94.41.86

M. Mischler. Closed Mon, Tue, 4-22 Feb and 8-26 July. Open until 9 pm. Private room: 25. No pets. Parking. V AE.

Opulence and splendour envelop you as you cross the threshold of this enormous, eighteenth-century coaching inn, operated for untold generations by the Mischler clan. The book-lined, carved-wood dining room, with its stained-glass windows and stone fireplace, is animated by the nightly crush of some 200 eager gastronomes from both banks of the Rhine. Waiters got up in old-style livery dash about, serving the fresh, high-quality cuisine: guinea fowl and sweetbread terrine with smoked foie gras, sea-bass wine stew seasoned with lemon grass and star anise, quail millefeuille, and lime soufflé with wild strawberries. Sumptuously stocked cellar.

A la carte: 350 F. Menus: from 140 F to 330 F.

Gimbelhof
9 km N on D 3 and RF — 88.94.43.58

Closed 11 Nov-26 Dec. 8 rms 66-166 F. Restaurant. Half-board 115-135 F. Parking. V.

Lost in a magnificent wood, this quiet, modest little hostelry has cosy rooms at unbelievably low prices.

LENS

62300 Lens — (P./Calais)
Paris 203 - Arras 18 - Lille 34 - St-Omer 73

Lensotel
3.5 km N
Centre commercial Lens II
62880 Vendin-le-Vieil — 21.78.64.53

Open every day. 1 ste 320 F. 70 rms 270-300 F. Restaurant. Half-board 320 F. TV. Conference facilities. Pool. Parking. Telex 120324. V AE DC.

This hotel, of curious architectural design, houses comfortable, pleasant rooms on the ground floor, overlooking a garden and swimming pool.

LESQUIN (AIRPORT DE)

See Lille

LESTELLE-BÉTHARRAM

64800 Lestelle-Bétharram — (Pyrénées-A.)
Paris 790 - Pau 23 - Lourdes 16 - Laruns 35 - Nay 9

Le Vieux Logis   ○
Rte des Grottes — 59.71.94.87

M. Gaye. Closed 15 Jan-1 March. Open until 9 pm. Private room: 120. Terrace dining. Parking. Hotel: 12 rms 160-220 F, half-board 260-300 F oblig in seas. V AE.

Between Béarn and Bigorre in an island of greenery, this charming old farmhouse offers a warm, family-style welcome, and generous cooking that springs from the region's fertile soil: trout and scallop terrine, duck civet cooked in Madiran, and the famed 'all-duck' salad (gizzards, foie gras, breast, neck). The service lacks polish.

A la carte: 250-300 F. Menus: 90 F, 140 F, 180 F.

LEVALLOIS-PERRET

See PARIS Suburbs

LEVANT (ILE DU)

83 Levant (Ile du) — (Var)
Boarding: Cavalaire, Le Lavandou, Hyères

La Brise Marine
Pl. du Village — 94.05.91.15

Closed 15 Oct-1 May. 23 rms 230-375 F. Restaurant. Half-board 387-455 F oblig in seas. Conference facilities. Heated pool. V.

Situated at the high point of the island, overlooking the sea, the Brise boasts handsome, comfortable, well-equipped rooms set round a delightful, flower-filled patio. Superb swimming pool and sun-terrace.

Hôtel Gaétan
94.05.91.78

Closed 15 Oct-1 April. 13 rms 220-250 F. Restaurant. Half-board 270-290 F oblig in seas. No pets. V.

Set in a pleasant garden, the Gaétan's rooms are very simple but well kept. Solarium, bar.

Héliotel
94.05.90.63

Closed 30 Sep-Easter. 2 stes. 18 rms. Rates not available. Restaurant. No pets. Conference facilities. Pool. Telex 400555. V AE.

Facing the îles d'Or and hidden in the greenery between the nearby village and Héliopolis, this hotel offers a piano bar and video room well isolated from the bedrooms. Salads and grilled meat are served for lunch by the pool. Change of management under way.

LEVERNOIS

See Beaune

LEZOUX

63190 Lezoux — (Puy-de-Dôme)
Paris 390 - Clermont-Ferrand 27 - Thiers 16 - Vichy 42

Château de Codignat   ♣♥
8 km SE on D 223 and D 115e
in Bort-l'Etang — 73.68.43.03

Closed 4 Nov-15 March. 4 stes 1,100-1,600 F. 10 rms 550-1,100 F. Restaurant. Half-board 710-1,150 F oblig in seas. TV. Air cond 4 rms. Conference facilities. Heated pool. Parking. Telex 990606. V AE DC.

This fifteenth-century château, complete with weathered wrought iron, armour, and parapets, sits in a vast country park. There are four luxurious suites, as well as ten very large rooms, all decorated in the rather heavy Haute Epoque style. Some bathrooms are equipped with Jacuzzi. Relais et Châteaux.

LILLE

59000 Lille — (Nord)
Paris 219 - Dunkerque 80 - Bruxelles 116 - Strasbourg 526

Alliance
17, quai du Wault — 20.30.62.62
Open every day. 8 stes 1,400 F. 75 rms 450-640 F. Restaurant. Half-board 640-820 F. TV. Conference facilities. Valet parking. V AE DC.
This centrally located luxury hotel, tucked behind seventeenth-century brick-and-stone walls, has just been built into the former Minimes convent. A glass roof covers the cloisters. The rooms are superb, equipped with all modern conveniences, including magnetised cards instead of keys.

Arabian

(Le Restaurant)
1, pl. de Sébastopol — 20.57.05.05
M. Arabian. Closed Sat lunch, Sun, holidays, 24 Dec-6 Jan, 29 March-7 April and 5-18 Aug. Open until 10 pm. Private room: 40. Valet parking. V AE DC.
Talented young Flemish chef Ghislaine Arabian is so at home in her kitchen that we doubt she would abandon her stove for an instant, even if all the guide book gurus of France arrived at once and demanded her attention. And don't expect to ever see her in the dining rooms. She's a retiring sort. We spotted her several years ago but could not have imagined such a meteoric rise. Though she came from a food-loving family and had a certain talent for pâtisserie, she never planned nor studied to become a professional chef. But then she met and married Jean-Paul Arabian, former maître d'hôtel at L'Oasis and Maxim's, and together they transformed this former café, located in the otherwise charmless Place de Sébastopol, into Lille's most talked-about restaurant. Unsatisfied with the chefs they hired, Ghislaine donned a toque and took over herself. Now she wears three! Her epicurean repertoire is eclectic and highly original, blending Flemish, coastal, and even southern French influences to produce harmonious dishes. Taste her mouthwatering cooking and you'll agree with us that her ascent has probably just begun: vegetable compote sprinkled with olive oil, open-faced prawn ravioli with wild mushrooms, flamiche (cheese and vegetable tart), tiny shrimp croquettes with fried parsley, grilled kippers and potatoes in their skins, baked turbot in beer with fried onions, and so forth. The divine desserts are the work of Philippe Bénot (Belgian waffles with ice cream, warm chocolate mousse, rhubarb strudel with caramel sauce). The service and excellent wine cellar are under the able stewardship of Jean-Paul Arabian. Lille's *beau monde* settles happily into the cheerful art deco décor.
A la carte: 550-750 F. Menus: 180 F (lunch only), 300 F, 450 F.

Le Baan Thaï
(Cuisine Royale Thaïlandaise)
22, bd J.-B.-Lebas — 20.86.06.01
M. Barthelemi. Closed Sat lunch, Sun and 4-25 Aug. Open until 10.30 pm. V.
This extremely successful Thai restaurant serves royal specialities such as lemon grass-flavoured scampi soup, fish cooked in banana leaves and flavoured with coconut, and beef curry with Thai aubergines. Outstanding service.
A la carte: 180-230 F. Menu: 180 F.

Bellevue
5, rue J.-Roisin — 20.57.45.64
Open every day. 80 rms 199-650 F. TV. Conference facilities. Telex 120790. V AE DC.
The wistful charm of a pre-war provincial hotel hangs in the spacious, comfortable, well-soundproofed rooms of the Bellevue, with their 1930s furniture and excellent bathrooms. The reception is rather solemn. American bar, room service.

Carlton
3, rue de Paris — 20.55.24.11
Open every day. 3 stes 700-1,500 F. 60 rms 410-750 F. TV. Air cond 7 rms. Conference facilities. Parking. Telex 110400. V AE DC.
Across the road from the opera house and just 200 metres from the railway station. The recently remodelled rooms are large and comfortable, with well-equipped working areas. The famous Brasserie Jean is in the building.

12/20 Le Champlain
13, rue N.-Leblanc — 20.54.01.38
M. Gaboriau. Closed Sun dinner and 15-31 Aug. Open until 9 pm. Private room: 50. Garden dining. No pets. V AE DC.
Tall windows open onto a shady courtyard-garden. The quiet, comfortable dining room is embellished with bourgeois touches, and the cooking reflects the owner's love of seafood. For 180 F you get hot oysters, lobster ravioli, piccata de lotte, cheese, and dessert. The homemade bread is a delight.
Menus: 130 F (weekdays lunch only, wine inc), 148 F, 180 F, 210 F.

Le Club Clément Marot
16, rue de Pas — 20.57.01.10
M. Marot. Closed Mon dinner, Sun, 5 Aug-1 Sep and 1 week in winter. Open until 10 pm. Private room: 36. Terrace dining. V AE DC.
Claire and Clément Marot's cosy little establishment is indeed like a club—comfortable and convivial. The finest ingredients go into the meticulous cooking, which produces some excellent dishes, such as rabbit tartlets with puréed onions, turbot and fresh pasta, and rack of lamb seasoned with thyme. Hearty wines.
A la carte: 300-350 F. Menus: 125 F, 192 F.

La Coquille
60, rue St-Etienne — 20.54.29.82
M. Deleval. Closed Sat lunch, Sun and 1-20 Aug. Open until 10.30 pm. Private room: 30. Terrace dining. V.
Fine food and pleasant décor make this a good address—one of the nicest in Lille. The flower-filled dining room, with its ancient timbers, is ideal for a romantic dinner *à deux*. Feast on smoked-salmon boudin with crispy cabbage, sea bass with mild spices, and artichoke mousseline, followed by a white-chocolate and caramel marquise.
A la carte: 300 F. Menus: 160 F (weekdays lunch only), 190 F (dinner only), 120 F.

La Devinière
61, bd Louis-XIV — 20.52.74.64
M. Waterlot. Closed week 15 Aug. Open until 9.30 pm. Private room: 40. Air cond. V DC.
Bernard Waterlot is wild about wine, and he'll take off across the country at the merest whiff of a discovery for his cellar. His collection of Chinon is particularly fine. The classic-to-a-fault cuisine—still worth two toques, but barely—is enlivened by seasonal specialities and market-based dishes. Try

the salmon roll stuffed with prawns, foie gras and tiny turnips, and smoked tongue.

A la carte: 300-400 F. Menus: 149 F (weekdays only), 278 F.

Le Flambard

79, rue d'Angleterre — 20.51.00.06
M. Bardot. Closed Sun dinner and Aug. Open until 9.30 pm. Private room: 35. V AE DC.

Vermeer would have liked to paint this magnificent, seventeenth-century Flemish dwelling. Owner-chef Robert Bardot has restored it with great enthusiasm and at great expense (in collaboration with the *Monuments historiques*). Enlarged by the addition of two old houses flanking the original, Le Flambard is now unquestionably the most handsome—and best—restaurant in Lille, with two dining rooms, five lounges, a private business club, catering service, sumptuous cellar, and capacious car park.

Bardot, 55, seems to have taken on a new lease of life in the process. His award-winning cuisine is as learned, full-flavoured, and imaginative as ever. His repertoire includes cold shellfish soup with caviar and parsley, lobster royale in cockle fumet, salmon cooked on its skin and potatoes with garlic mayonnaise, prawn ravioli and a spicy West Indian sauce, and pigeon with vanilla-seasoned salt, honey and lemon grass. After sampling the tasty Northern cheeses, you have the difficult task of choosing among some twenty dreamy desserts (warm coconut-cream millefeuille, pear with almonds, liquorice-flavoured ice cream with mango). The cellar boasts wines from all over the country. Efficient service, well-rounded bill (the 240 F menu, featuring lobster, fish and meat courses, desserts and petits fours is good value). Relais et Châteaux.

A la carte: 500-700 F. Menus: 240 F, 380 F, 480 F, 520 F.

La Fringale

141, rue de Solférino — 20.42.02.80
M. Coopman. Closed Sat lunch, Sun, 1 week in Feb and 15 July-15 Aug. Open until 9.30 pm. V AE DC.

Chef Christian Coopman and his wife Jeanine run this jewel-box of a restaurant (it seats only eighteen), offering tasty, carefully crafted dishes and a frequently changing menu: king prawns with black radish and mead, lobster with Jerusalem-artichoke purée, or roast farm pigeon with celeriac and Banyuls. Lovely chocolate desserts.

A la carte: 350 F. Menus: 160 F (lunch only), 210 F, 290 F.

12/20 Le Hochepot

6, rue du Nouveau-Siècle — 20.54.17.59
M. Coquelet. Closed Sat lunch and Sun. Open until 10 pm. V.

You'll discover lipsmacking, locally brewed beers and the best juniper-flavoured Dutch gin in the region, in this absolutely authentic Flemish restaurant, with a smart brick décor. Taste the potjevfleisch, poultry waterzoï, Belgian oxtail hotpot, and coq à la bière.

A la carte: 230 F. Menus: 115 F, 135 F, 170 F.

L'Huîtrière

3, rue des Chats-Bossus — 20.55.43.41
M. Proye. Closed Sun dinner and 22 July-31 Aug. Open until 9.30 pm. Private room: 40. Air cond. V AE DC.

Customers continue to flock to this classic, rigorous restaurant, whose elegant dining room is upholstered in red, panelled with warm wood, and illuminated by crystal sconces. Before settling in, though, guests must walk through what is doubtless the most impressive fishmonger's in France, with turn-of-the-century décor and ceramics. It comes as no surprise then that the fish and seafood items on the menu are fabulously fresh, and we found the preparation faultless this year. Try the red mullet baked in a basil vinaigrette with baby vegetables, and the fillets of sole with asparagus tips and morels. For dessert, indulge in the delicious strawberry gratin. From 15 May-15 June don't fail to taste the maatjes (baby herrings) served with green beans, onions, and chopped parsley in a mustard vinaigrette. The cellar brims with 40,000 bottles, attended to by three accomplished sommeliers. Extremely pleasant service.

A la carte: 400 F. Menus: from 380 F to 500 F.

12/20 Lino

1, rue des Trois-Couronnes
20.31.12.17
M. Barmio. Closed Sun dinner, Mon and week 15 Aug. Open until 9.30 pm. V.

Sunny Italian specialities are served in this doll's house of a restaurant: fresh lasagne, osso buco, zabaglione alla Marsala. Reasonably priced Italian wines, and smiling, sprightly service.

A la carte: 200 F.

Novotel Lille Centre

116, rue de l'Hôpital-Militaire
20.30.65.26
Open every day. 2 stes 1,150 F. 102 rms 520-550 F. Restaurant. TV. Air cond. Conference facilities. Garage parking. Telex 160859. V AE DC.

This modern hotel is strategically located behind the Grand Place, and offers sunny, comfortable, functional and totally soundproofed rooms. Friendly welcome. Bar.

Le Paris

52 bis, rue Esquermoise
20.55.29.41
M. Martin. Closed Sun dinner and beg Aug-beg Sep. Open until 9.30 pm. Private room: 90. V AE DC.

Proprietor Loïc Martin has skilfully piloted this dignified restaurant through 30 years of changing fashions. The classic décor, velvet banquettes, and silverware make for a peaceful provincial atmosphere. Ever serious, Martin goes to market himself, passing on the perfect produce to his chef Gérard Chamoley, whose cooking pays tribute to tradition. Taste the salmon with bone marrow, grilled lotte with lemon, andouillette à la ficelle and a red-wine sauce, and the many splendid game dishes in season. The cellar houses some appealing little wines and good Armagnacs.

A la carte: 350-400 F. Menus: 186 F, 290 F.

Royal Hôtel

2, bd Carnot — 20.51.05.11
Open every day. 102 rms 290-580 F. TV. Conference facilities. Telex 820575. V AE DC.

This early 1900s corner hotel, located near the opera house, has recently been renovated, and the rooms are very comfortable and quiet. Seven office-rooms. Easy access for the disabled.

La Salle à Manger

91, rue de la Monnaie — 20.06.44.25
Mme Hemar. Closed Sat lunch and Sun. Open until 9.30 pm. Private room: 17. V.

The almond-green, flower-filled dining room is appealing, as is the pretty inner courtyard. Plate-glass windows allow you to look into the spotless kitchen. This year we've awarded chef Marie-Madeleine Hemar a toque for her delicious, updated country dishes: veal shin stew with gribiche sauce, quail salad, freshwater perch in butter sauce, poule au pot, marvellous Maroilles cheese, and chocolate tarte.

A la carte: 350 F. Menus: 105 F (lunch only), 170 F.

Hôtel de Strasbourg
7, rue J.-Roisin
20.57.05.46
Open every day. 48 rms 170-280 F. TV. Conference facilities. V AE DC.

This good little hotel in the centre of town is regularly refurbished. The rooms on the inner courtyard are quiet.

Le Varbet
2, rue de Pas — 20.54.81.40
M. Vartanian. Closed Sun, Mon, holidays, 12 July-20 Aug and 24 Dec-3 Jan. Open until 9.30 pm. Private room: 14. V AE DC.

Gilles Vartanian makes sure that his menu changes every two months, so you're sure to find more than just fabulous foie gras and hearty veal kidneys (always listed) to choose from. In response, faithful regulars crowd Le Varbet's unremarkable dining room, clamouring for Vartanian's imaginative and generous cuisine: fillet of beef with smoked garlic, sea bass and woodland mushrooms, or partridge with a blackberry-flavoured sauce. Customers sometimes complain that the welcome could be warmer. The wine list is rich, especially in Burgundies, and very reasonably priced.

A la carte: 350 F. Menus: 300 F (dinner only), 140 F.

And also...
Our selection of places for inexpensive, quick, or late-night meals.

Bar de la Cloche (20.55.35.34 - 13, pl. du Théâtre. Open until 10 pm): At this wine bar you'll find regional dishes and cheery service (130-150 F).

Brasserie de la Paix (20.54.70.41 - 25, pl. Rihour. Open until midnight): A favourite late-night spot, this classic brasserie serves shellfish, choucroute, and carafe wines (180 F.

La Chicorée (20.40.19.44 - 15, pl. Rihour. Open until 4 am): Tasty brasserie food served until the wee small hours (excellent onion soup) (150 F).

Le Compostelle (20.54.02.49 - 4, pl. Rihour. Open until 10 pm): Overly elaborate cuisine at stiff prices (pigeon stuffed with mushrooms and truffles), (200 F).

La Déesse-La Houblonnière-Les Messageries (Pl. du Gal-de-Gaulle): Three restaurants side by side serving local specialities on outdoor terraces (150 F).

Lakson (20.31.21.96 - 21, rue du Curé-St-Etienne. Open until 10.45 pm): This Scandinavian caterer offers salmon, herrings, eels, and sturgeon eggs at rustic wooden tables (100 F).

Christian Leclercq (20.74.17.05 - 9, rue Lepelletier. Open until 10 pm): A master *maître-fromager* purveys his wares at three tiny tables (fondue, raclette) (100 F).

Le Lion Bossu (20.06.06.88 - 1, rue St-Jacques. Open until 10 pm): Simple and classic cuisine and a crowded setting (salmon steak au beurre blanc, lamb chops, île flottante), (160 F).

The Queen Victoria (20.54.51.28 - 10, rue de Pas. Open until 1 am): A lively pub offering oysters, shellfish, and hearty meat dishes to young night-owls (150 F).

In nearby Bondues
(9 km N on N 17)
59910 Lille — (Nord)

12/20   Le Val d'Auge
44, route nationale — 20.46.26.87
Mme Capliez. Closed Wed, dinner Tue and Sun, Aug and 1 week at Easter. Open until 9.30 pm. Parking. V AE.

The décor of this rustic old coaching inn is slightly down-at-heel. But the atmosphere is warm, the cooking solid and savoury, and made from fine ingredients: chicken liver terrine, salmon marinated in lime juice, turbot with apples. Wise choice of wines.

A la carte: 250 F. Menus: 98 F (weekdays only), 170 F.

In nearby Lambersart
(2 km NW)
59130 Lille — (Nord)

La Laiterie
138, av. de l'Hippodrome — 20.92.79.73
M. Vantours. Closed Sun dinner and Mon. Open until 10.30 pm. Private room: 50. Garden dining. Parking. V AE DC.

When the weather is fine you can dine in the garden of this old café just outside Lille, in a delightful country atmosphere. In winter, the glassed-in dining room is so bright and light that it feels as if you're sitting out of doors! Do not think that the relaxed, family-style manner of the young proprietors means they are unprofessional. The service is peerless. And Ludovic Vantours's cooking is inventive, up-to-date, light, yet lusciously traditional: smoked haddock with cabbage, baked prawns seasoned with curry, stuffed salmon with warm oysters and seaweed, and Flemish-style tête de veau. The interesting wine cellar is under the stewardship of award-winning sommelier Eric Dugardin. Perfect all-inclusive business-lunch menu.

A la carte: 350 F. Menus: 200 F (weekdays lunch only, wine inc), 200 F, 320 F.

In nearby Lesquin
(12 km SE)
59810 Lille — (Nord)

Mercure
110, rue J.-Jaurès — 20.97.92.02
Open every day. 213 rms 400-600 F. Restaurant. TV. Air cond. Conference facilities. Heated pool. Parking. Telex 132051. V AE DC.

A recent face-lift has transformed this vast hotel complex into an American-style establishment, with spacious, very comfortable rooms, and a sauna. Shuttle service to the airport.

In nearby Loos
(4 km SW on D 941)
59120 Lille — (Nord)

L'Enfant Terrible
25, rue du Mal-Foch — 20.07.22.11
M. Desplanques. Closed Sun dinner and Mon. Open until 9.30 pm. Private room: 20. Terrace dining. V.

The décor of this suburban café isn't terribly cheery, with its dark colours and blow-ups of old postcards. But the owner's cooking is bold and original (with just the occasional error). Try the scrumptious crab gratin with mustard seeds, or the top-quality guinea fowl breast served with a mussel cream sauce. With a delectable dessert like the chicory crêpe gâteau, it all adds up to another point. Skittish service.

A la carte: 300 F. Menus: 90 F, 340 F.

In nearby Marcq-en-Barœul

(5 km NE on N 350)
59700 Lille — (Nord)

Holiday Inn
Avenue de la Marne
20.72.17.30

Open every day. 125 rms 480 F. Restaurant. Conference facilities. Heated pool. Parking. Telex 132785. V AE DC.

This mammoth of a hotel has undergone a major face-lift, and now has functional rooms, and the biggest conference halls in the region. Sauna, bar, and two restaurants.

Le Septentrion   ۞
Ferme des Marguerites
Parc du château du Vert-Bois — 20.46.26.98

M. Lelaurain. Closed Mon (except holidays), 2 weeks in Feb and 3 weeks in Aug. Open until 9.30 pm. Private room: 80. Parking. V AE DC.

The rustic décor is rather cold, but the setting is brightened by gorgeous greenery. The cooking can be hesitant, but chef Gilbert Lelaurain's enthusiasm is unfailing. Stick with the traditional regional offerings, such as seafood waterzoï, veal kidneys sautéed with juniper berries, and homemade honey and chicory ice creams. Intelligent selection of wines.

A la carte: 300 F. Menus: 140 F (weekdays lunch only), 240 F.

In nearby La Neuville

(18 km S on D549, 925 and C62 and C3)
59239 Lille — (Nord)

Au Leu Pindu
Forêt de Phalempin
1, rue du Gal-de-Gaulle — 20.86.57.59

M. Bardot. Closed Sun, dinner Mon, Tue and Wed (except groupes), and Aug. Open until 9.30 pm. Private room: 70. Parking. V.

Robert Bardot, the three-toque chef of Le Flambard in Lille, owns this fortified forest mansion with its rustic décor and huge fireplace. He has installed a young, talented chef in the kitchen, who turns out plain but carefully prepared dishes: magnificent terrines, York ham, salmon with tarragon butter, daube of ox jowl, and attractive desserts. All generously, and politely, served.

A la carte: 250 F. Menus: 95 F (weekdays only), 165 F.

See also: Roubaix, Tourcoing

LIMOGES

87000 Limoges — (Haute-Vienne)
Paris 374 - Poitiers 118 - Angoulême 103 - Niort 161

L'Amphitryon
26, rue de la Boucherie
55.33.36.39

M. Robert. Closed Mon lunch, Sun, 11-17 Feb and 29 July-19 Aug. Open until 10.30 pm. Private room: 14. Terrace dining. No pets. V.

Bouquets of flowers, fresh linen, and classic tableware fill the comfortable, sunny Amphitryon, which is set in a pretty street in the town centre. The reception is as convincingly charming as Pascal Robert's hearty, flavourful fare: salmon millefeuille with chives, sea-bass fillet with lemon,

or tournedos du Limousin. Few, but well-chosen, wines.

A la carte: 250-280 F. Menus: 95 F (weekdays lunch only), 125 F.

Cantaut
10, rue Rafilhoux — 55.33.34.68

M. Cantaut. Open every day. Open until 9.30 pm (except reserv). Private room: 18. Hotel: 12 rms 95-250 F. V AE DC.

Owner-chef Patrice Cantaut bends over backwards to please his customers, and obviously succeeds with his charming, split-level restaurant that drips with medieval décor. On offer: wonderful wine and several succulent dishes (galette de saumon, foie gras parmentier with a sweet-pepper coulis, and scallops and red mullet with artichokes).

A la carte: 280-300 F. Menus: from 90 F to 300 F (except holidays).

Caravelle
21, rue A.-Barbès — 55.77.75.29

Open every day. 39 rms 190-325 F. TV 32 rms. Garage parking. Telex 580733. V.

A comfortable hotel, some of whose rooms overlook the wooded Champ-de-Juillet. Warm welcome. Bar.

Le Champlevé
1, pl. Wilson — 55.34.43.34

M. Amardeilh. Closed in seas Sun dinner, off-season Sat lunch, Wed, 2-10 Jan and 16 Aug-8 Sep. Open until 10 pm (9.30 pm Sun). Air cond. V.

Fabrice Amardeilh wanted to enlarge and redecorate his restaurant, and work should be completed by the time you read this. The pretty tables needed room to breathe! Amardeilh's top-quality cuisine is impeccable as ever: prawns, coconut and soya wrapped in filo pastry, lobster ravioli in vanilla-flavoured sauce, lamb with shallots, and dark-chocolate millefeuille with pistachios. The prices are still rising.

A la carte: 300-380 F. Menus: 150 F (weekdays only), 195 F, 280 F, 410 F.

Jeanne d'Arc
17, av. du Gal-de-Gaulle — 55.77.67.77

Closed 21 Dec-2 Jan. 55 rms 140-380 F. TV 38 rms. Conference facilities. Parking. Telex 580011. V AE DC.

An excellent stopover, well equipped and just 50 metres from the Bénédictins railway station.

Luk Hôtel
29, pl. Jourdan — 55.33.44.00

Closed Feb school holidays. 55 rms 180-380 F. Restaurant. Half-board 270-480 F. TV. Conference facilities. Telex 580704. V AE DC.

Located in the town centre, the Luk has luxurious, rather overblown décor, but is an unquestionably comfortable hotel, renovated this year.

Philippe Redon
3, rue d'Aguesseau — 55.34.66.22

M. Redon. Closed Mon lunch and Sun. Annual closings not available. Open until 10 pm. Private room: 20. V.

Locals have been flocking to Philippe Redon's 1930s-style restaurant since it opened last year. And for good reason. Formerly of the Gray d'Albion in Cannes and La Radio at Chamalières, Redon is a true professional, and his cooking is very good indeed. It will doubtless be great once he settles in and sorts out his sauces. Try the duck pie with garlic, skate with creamed green lentils, and good desserts. The cheeses are worthy of a top restaurant. The wine list offers dozens of good-value bottles (especially the Bordeaux). The service is polished.

A la carte: 220 F. Menus: 90 F (lunch only), 130 F.

Le Richelieu
40, av. Baudin – 55.34.22.82

Open every day. 35 rms 170-335 F. TV 26 rms. Conference facilities. Garage parking. Telex 580705. V.

This quiet hotel in the town centre has sunny, well-soundproofed rooms. Warm welcome and a pleasant bar. Meals on trays available.

Royal Limousin
1, pl. de la République – 55.34.65.30

Open every day. 5 stes 600-990 F. 70 rms 360-480 F. TV. Air cond 7 rms. Conference facilities. Telex 580771. V AE DC.

A modern, well-situated hotel which offers many facilities and services. The well-maintained rooms are spacious and sunny, and some are luxurious. Meals for groups available.

Le Trou Normand
1, rue F.-Chénieux – 55.77.53.24

M. Métais. Closed Sun dinner, Mon and 14 July-15 Aug. Open until 10 pm. Air cond. V AE DC.

We haven't seen the new décor in this luxurious seafood restaurant, but we're confident they will perfectly reflect the ambitious prices you'll pay for the fresh, faultlessly prepared shellfish, salmon perfumed with ginger, sole with morels, and lotte aux cèpes. The *patronne* and her Pekingese offer a distinguished welcome.

A la carte: 300-400 F.

And also...
Our selection of places for inexpensive, quick, or late-night meals.

Le Grillon (55.34.64.36 - 18, rue Ch.-Michels. Open until 9.30 pm): Frequented by the young and trendy, this new restaurant serves low-priced, ultraclassic food (150-200 F).

L'Orangeraie (55.32.33.89 - 14, rue E.-Berthet. Open until 9.30 pm): The amusing décor features multiple mirrors. The cooking is traditional, the service polite (150-200 F).

Les Petits Ventres (55.33.34.02 - 20, rue de la Boucherie. Open until 10 pm): Robust 'pavement' fare (offal, tripe, grilled meats), served rather slowly in a picturesque, timbered house (150 F).

Pirana (55.34.58.55 - 17, rue Ch.-Michels. Open until 10 pm): Spanish specialities politely served at modest prices: Madrid-style mussels, squid fritters, kidneys with sherry (120-150 F).

Les Temps Modernes (55.32.30.79 - 8, rue Ch.-Michels. Open until 10.45 pm): Try the simple, pleasant cooking either in the tiny back courtyard or the updated bistro-style dining room (150 F).

In nearby **Saint-Martin-du-Fault**

(11 km NW)
87510 Limoges – (Haute-Vienne)

Chapelle Saint-Martin
55.75.80.17

M. Dudognon. Closed Mon, Jan and Feb. Open until 10 pm. Private room: 50. Garden dining. No-smoking section. No pets. Garage parking. V.

This lovely old mansion's weakest point is still the moody reception, which upsets some guests. But you'll like the grand, classic park, the sophisticated bourgeois décor, and the cooking of Gilles Dudognon, the son of the house. His dishes

are rigorously prepared and lively, like the mackerel tartare and black-radish salad, cod fillet and curried lentils, pig's trotter sausage, and young pigeon in sweet-and-sour sauce. The rich and generally costly cellar also offers some fine, reasonably priced bottles. Efficient service.

A la carte: 300-400 F. Menus: 190 F (lunch only), 360 F.

Chapelle Saint-Martin
(See restaurant above)

Closed Mon, Jan and Feb. 3 stes 1,100-1,250 F. 10 rms 490-890 F. Half-board 700-850 F. TV. Conference facilities. Tennis.

The first floor has been totally reorganised and now boasts several rooms and suites that are even more comfortable and elegant than before. The rooms afford a restful vista over the wooded park. A covered, heated pool is being built. Relais et Châteaux.

In nearby **Séreilhac**

(18 km SW on N 21)
87620 Limoges – (Haute-Vienne)

La Meule
N 21 – 55.39.10.08

Mme Jouhaud. Closed off-season Sun dinner and Tue, and 20 days in Jan. Open until 9 pm. Terrace dining. Garage parking. Hotel: 10 rms 200-420 F. V AE DC.

This big old building set on a busy road, with a garden at the back, is rather uninviting and so is the solid but comfortable, rustic décor. It's just as well chef Nicole Jouhaud's generous cooking is so fresh and tasty; it almost allows us to forget the dizzying prices. Taste the prawns and chopped foie gras spread on a bed of fresh pasta steamed with mint, or the fillet steak grilled with roast chicory root. Good sorbets, especially the cherry, and a range of teas and coffees, but too few reasonably priced wines. Another point this year.

A la carte: 350-400 F. Menus: 100 F and 130 F (weekdays lunch only), 190 F, 340 F.

LINAS
See PARIS Suburbs

LISCIA (GOLFE DE LA)
See CORSICA

LISIEUX
14100 Lisieux – (Calvados)
Paris 173 - Evreux 72 - Caen 49 - Deauville 28

12/20 La Coupe d'Or
49, rue Pont-Mortain
31.31.16.84

M. Lion. Open every day. Open until 9.15 pm. Hotel: 18 rms 140-295 F. Telex 772163. V AE DC.

As always, you'll find many varied set menus, each built around a theme, and tempting carafe wines, all at low prices. The cooking is uneven, however. Try the fish soup, skate with mustard sauce, and nougat glacé.

A la carte: 220 F. Menus: 140 F (wine inc), 88 F, 170 F, 210 F.

Hôtel de la Place

67, rue H.-Chéron
31.31.17.44
Open every day. 3 stes 840-960 F. 33 rms 250-380 F. TV 27 rms. Valet parking. Telex 171862. V AE.
The thoroughly restored, spacious, soundproofed rooms overlook St Pierre's cathedral. Good service. Four rooms are equipped for the disabled.

In nearby **Ouilly-du-Houley**

(11 km NE on N 13 and D 137)
14590 Lisieux — (Calvados)

Auberge de la Paquine

31.63.63.80
M. Champion. Closed Tue (except lunch in seas), Wed and 13 Nov-16 Dec. Open until 9 pm. Garden dining. No pets. Parking. V.
This delightful little Norman inn nestles in the green landscape of the Pays d'Auge. When the weather is fine, you can eat outside on the banks of a stream; in winter you're welcomed into a handsome, rustic dining room. The staff is overwhelmingly friendly, the cuisine innovative and based on quality produce. Try the sea bass with thyme, crispy lamb with baby vegetables, and little flaky pastries filled with fresh strawberries and custard.
A la carte: 300 F. Menu: 130 F.

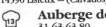
LIVERDUN

54460 Liverdun — (Meurthe/M.)
Paris 306 - Toul 20 - Nancy 15 - Pont-à-Mousson 25

Les Vannes
et sa Résidence

6, rue Porte-Haute — 83.24.46.01
M. Fonderflick. Closed Mon (except holidays) and Feb. Open until 10 pm. Private room: 70. Parking. V AE DC.
We suspect that this glorious, rather pompously decorated old mansion overlooking a meander of the Moselle is finally finding its feet again. After a whirlwind of cooks and owners, Denis Cros, late of Michel Guérard at Eugénie-les-Bains and Arabian in Lille, has taken over the kitchen. He's both a tireless pro and a devotee of fresh ingredients, and has proved adept at creating new taste combinations. Witness the red mullet in black-olive purée with artichoke hearts, and the lobster and shellfish in a cold velouté of peas and marjoram. Of course, we'd appreciate them all the more if they were served more swiftly on busy days. The wine list is outstanding, the service deferential.
A la carte: 450-500 F. Menus: 160 F, 250 F, 360 F.

Les Vannes
et sa Résidence

(See restaurant above)
Closed Feb. 2 stes 480 F. 11 rms 250-480 F. Half-board 360-500 F. Conference facilities.
Huge, slightly tatty but charming rooms overlook either the Moselle Valley or a small village square. Diligent reception, and good value for money.

LIVRY-GARGAN

See PARIS Suburbs

LOGES-EN-JOSAS (LES)

See PARIS Suburbs

LONGUYON

54260 Longuyon — (Meurthe/M.)
Paris 315 - Metz 69 - Verdun 48 - Thionville 54

Le Mas

(Hôtel de Lorraine)
Pl. de la Gare — 82.26.50.07
M. Tisserant. Closed Mon off-season, and 7 Jan-9 Feb. Open until 9.30 pm. Private room: 200. Hotel: 15 rms 100-235 F. V AE DC.
There's no pine wood around this 'farmhouse' set on the station square, but the perfumes of Provence waft up to the timbers of the dining room all the same. Alas, fine ingredients do not always a perfect cuisine make. But Gérard Tisserant's prawns with vegetable spaghetti and sautéed aubergines, red mullet in wine sauce, and duck sotl'y-laisse with olives and foie gras, are delicious. Good range of desserts and very pleasant service.
A la carte: 350-400 F. Menus: 160 F (weekdays lunch only), 320 F.

LONS-LE-SAUNIER

39000 Lons-le-Saunier — (Jura)
Paris 407 - Besançon 88 - Bourg-en-Bresse 61 - Dijon 102

La Comédie

Pl. de la Comédie — 84.24.20.66
M. Hemery. Closed Mon dinner, Sun, Feb school holidays and 4-27 Aug. Open until 9.30 pm. Air cond. V.
The setting is dull and the dining room slightly cramped. But the cooking is sunny and full of the fresh flavours of the sea. Taste the succulent salad of grilled prawns with potatoes, the excellent red mullet with (not enough) fennel and black-olive purée, and the sublime crème brûlée with vanilla pods and brown sugar. Average wines and unremarkable cheese board. The reception is rather distant.
A la carte: 300 F. Menu: 90 F.

Hôtel Parenthèse

in Chillé — 84.47.55.44
Closed 2-16 Jan. 21 rms 170-280 F. Half-board 315-385 F. Restaurant. TV. Conference facilities.
This large country hotel provides modern, comfortable rooms at reasonable rates. The setting is very quiet, with views of the village.

In nearby **Courlans**

(6 km W on N 78)
39000 Lons-le-Saunier — (Jura)

Auberge de Chavannes

84.47.05.52
M. Carpentier. Closed Sun dinner, Mon, 11 Feb-11 March and 9-16 Sep. Open until 9 pm. Garden dining. Air cond. Parking. V.
A third toque hovers over the curly head of Pierre Carpentier, whose cooking is authentic, reliable, and discerning. These three qualities permeate everything in this roadside *auberge*, from the rustic elegance of the apricot-and-lime décor, to the pleasant garden dining area.
Carpentier gets his impeccable ingredients from a farmer friend, and transforms them into succulent dishes such as duck fillet in Château-Chalon, served with a tangy potato chutney, and prawns sautéed in mild spices. His seasonal specialities include fresh egg with asparagus tips, pigeon confit with foie gras served on a flavourful lentil salad, chicken neck stuffed with morels and calf's foot, or chicken breasts with stuffed morels.
The repertoire is somewhat limited, yet is always bountiful. Witness, for example, the fabulous sole

with pasta and mushrooms. In short, minor masterpieces, writ small—as are the prices! The elegant, maternal Monique Carpentier directs the attentive staff. The cellar is stocked with the best Jura wines, including some from little-known southern growers, as well as fine Burgundies.

A la carte: 320 F. Menus: 160 F and 280 F (wine inc).

LOOS

See Lille

LOPÉREC

See Châteaulin

LORGUES

83510 Lorgues — (Var)
Paris 850 - Draguignan 13 - Brignoles 33 - St-Raphaël 43

Chez Bruno
Rte de Vidauban — 94.73.92.19
M. Bruno. Closed Mon and Jan. Open until 8.30 pm (9 pm in summer). Private room: 18. Garden dining. Parking. V AE.

Clément Bruno, a thoroughly accomplished chef, serves but one menu inspired by the best of the day's market produce. He and his wife Nicole manage to maintain a guest-house atmosphere in their welcoming *bastide*. On a given day the menu might include ravioli of cèpes and foie gras, lamb sweetbreads with truffle coulis, and countless other dishes that attract gourmets from all over Provence. One toque this year.

Menu: 230 F.

LORIENT

56100 Lorient — (Morbihan)
Paris 491 - Quimper 68 - Vannes 56 - Rennes 145

L'Amphitryon
127, rue du Col.-Müller — 97.83.34.04
M. Abadie. Closed Sat lunch and Sun, 26 Aug-12 Sep and 23 Dec-4 Jan. Open until 11 pm. Air cond. No pets. V AE DC.

Jean-Paul Abadie's cooking joins the traditions of his native Gers and those of his wife Véronique's Brittany, and has improved consistently over the last five years. His foie gras is as expertly prepared as the savoury mackerel terrine and braised lobster with baby vegetables. The cheese tray and desserts are superb, and we were also impressed by the wines, which are chosen and presented by Véronique. We're awarding a second toque.

A la carte: 320-350 F. Menus: 95 F (weekdays lunch only), 140 F (weekdays only), 200 F, 300 F.

Mercure
31, pl. J.-Ferry — 97.21.35.73
Open every day. 58 rms 285-450 F. TV. Conference facilities. Telex 950810. V AE DC.

This hotel offers large, constantly updated, and well-equipped rooms, all within easy reach of the conference centre and wet dock. Conference facilities, bar.

Novotel Lorient
5 km NE on N 24 - Centre hôtelier de Kerpont-Bellevue
56850 Caudan — 97.76.02.16
Open every day. 88 rms 380-420 F. Restaurant. TV. Conference facilities. Heated pool. Parking. Telex 950026. V AE DC.

A pleasant hotel set in two hectares of wooded grounds, with simply decorated, comfortable rooms. Beaches within easy reach.

Le Pic

2, bd Franchet-d'Esperey
97.21.18.29
M. Le Bourhis. Closed Sun (except if holidays Mon), Sat lunch, 1 week in March, 2 weeks in June and 2 weeks at Christmas. Open until midnight. Private room: 30. V.

This friendly, generous, and unaffected restaurant ranks among Lorient's best. The young chef continues to delight customers with lively dishes like the fricassée of small scallops à la bretonne, and pig's trotters stuffed with lentils. The wines are superb and the set menus excellent value. Our only complaint would concern the décor, and it seems the owner is planning some changes.

A la carte: 300 F. Menus: 85 F, 150 F.

Le Poisson d'Or

1, rue Maître-Esvelin
97.21.57.06
M. Rio. Closed Sun and Nov school holidays. Open until 10 pm. V AE DC.

Despite a few culinary flaws, Hervé Rio's centrally located and comfortable restaurant attracts many of the local worthies. This smiling owner-chef prepares a hot lotte tart (which could have more flavour), baked prawns, marinated salmon on a bed of (particularly bitter) chicory, and good pâtisserie. Interesting wines. Ill-designed lighting makes for a rather gloomy atmosphere.

A la carte: 320 F. Menus: from 95 F to 300 F.

12/20 La Sardegna
28-30, rue P.-Guieysse — 97.64.13.05
Mme Posadinu. Open every day. Open until 11.30 pm. Private room: 16. V AE DC.

Delicate Italian aromas permeate the rustic Spanish décor of this friendly late-night restaurant next to the station. Specialities include a large selection of pizzas, silken homemade pasta, lasagne, seafood turnovers, and Italian charcuterie. Friendly service.

A la carte: 120-140 F. Menu: 48 F (weekdays lunch only).

In nearby **Larmor-Plage**

(6 km S on D 29)
56260 Lorient — (Morbihan)

12/20 Beau Rivage
Plage de Toulhars — 97.65.50.11
M. Roig. Closed Sun dinner, Mon and 25 Oct-5 Dec. Open until 10 pm. Private room: 25. Parking. V AE DC.

There's a choice of 80 dishes on the *carte* of this drably decorated seafront restaurant known for its fresh, well-prepared, and expensive seafood. Excellent wine cellar, well-stocked with Bordeaux and Burgundies.

A la carte: 270 F. Menus: 82 F (weekdays only), 110 F, 175 F, 285 F.

Beau Rivage
(See restaurant above)
Open every day. 19 rms 100-225 F. Half-board 180-225 F oblig in seas. TV 9 rms. Conference facilities.

Despite its lacklustre appearance, this hotel features cosy, comfortable, and modern rooms. Pleasant service.

See also: **Hennebont**

and duck foie gras with fresh fruit.
A la carte: 350 F. Menu: 160 F.

Laurent
11, rue de la Libération — 43.88.40.03
M. Laurent. Closed Tue lunch off-season and Wed (except holidays), and 3 Jan-8 March. Open until 9.30 pm. Private room: 30. Garden dining. No pets. Valet parking. Telex 722013. V AE DC.

Gilbert Laurent's cooking varies from fairly good and traditional to very good and creative. When we last visited his superb restaurant by the river, we were both enchanted and disappointed. Enchanted by his exquisite oysters in seaweed aspic, perfectly cooked cabbage stuffed with lobster and scallops with caviar butter, and his classic chicken in cream with morels. Disappointed by the conventional fish stew, and the slightly heavy soufflé au Grand Marnier with crystallised oranges.

A la carte: 550 F. Menus: 190 F (weekdays lunch only), 280 F, 400 F, 520 F.

Laurent
(See restaurant above)
Closed 5 Jan-5 March. 6 stes 700-1,200 F. 16 rms 280-700 F. Half-board 550-950 F oblig in seas. TV. Conference facilities. Heated pool.

Sixteen rooms and six suites in a dream setting. The redesigned garden is superb and you can take boats on the river. Excellent breakfasts, and a perfect welcome and service. Relais et Châteaux.

Galilée-Windsor
10-12, av. Peyramale — 62.94.21.55
Closed 15 Oct-10 April. 169 rms 400 F. Restaurant. Half-board 350-400 F. TV. Valet parking. Telex 521424. V AE.

Located next to the grotto, this large and recently renovated establishment features traditional rooms, some of which have views over the Pyrenees.

Gallia-Londres
26, av. B.-Soubirous — 62.94.35.44
Closed 15 Oct-10 April. 90 rms 650 F. Restaurant. Half-board 550 F oblig in seas. TV. Conference facilities. Valet parking. Telex 521424. V AE.

A classic grand hotel offering period rooms with balconies above the pilgrimage route. Lovely garden, bar, and pub.

Hôtel de la Grotte
66, rue de la Grotte — 62.94.58.87
Closed 20 Oct-1 April. 3 stes 1,200-1,600 F. 84 rms 330-550 F. Restaurant. Half-board 300-660 F. TV. Garage parking. Telex 531937. V AE DC.

From the upper storeys, one of the best views in Lourdes takes in the river, sanctuaries, and the Pyrenees. Attractive garden by the Adour.

Le Relais de Saux
(ex-Relais Pyrénéen)
Hameau de Saux — 62.94.29.61
Mme Héres. Open every day. Open until 9.30 pm. Private room: 20. Garden dining. No pets. Parking. V AE.

Delightful gardens surround this peaceful restaurant, far from the madding crowd of pilgrims. At the elegant round tables you'll be served costly dishes made from luxury ingredients: warm lobster salad with a sea-urchin purée, turbot in butter sauce with an upside-down celery tart,

Le Relais de Saux
(See restaurant above)
Open every day. 8 rms 230-390 F (per pers, half-board oblig). TV 3 rms. No pets.

This hotel features beautiful, high-ceilinged rooms that are charming, comfortable, and quiet. Limited service. Good breakfasts. Special rates are available for Lourdes golf course.

Le Tara
6, av. Peyramale — 62.94.22.33
Closed 1 Jan-10 Feb, 13 Feb-1 April and 1 Nov-1 Dec. 73 rms 180-200 F. Restaurant. Half-board 240-260 F. Telex 531937. V AE DC.

Within easy reach of the sanctuaries, this newly built riverside hotel offers nine storeys of bright, simply decorated, and functional rooms.

La Fenière
9, rue du Grand-Pré — 90.68.11.79
M. Sammut. Closed Sun dinner (except July-Aug), Mon (except holidays), 2-31 Jan, 24-3 June and 1-7 July. Open until 9.30 pm. Private room: 30. Terrace dining. Air cond. V AE DC.

Miles Davis's trumpet wafts through this converted barn dining room, along with the perfumes of Provençal cooking and the aromas of local wines that Guy Sammut has a talent for tracking down. Such subtle harmonies sum up the style of his restaurant with its white stone walls and elegant décor. In the kitchen his wife Reine combines a love of the traditional with a taste for adventure to create new dishes like the John Dory with vanilla and olive oil, escabèche de moules (intensely flavourful), and the red-mullet fillets in mullet-roe sauce (almost worthy of four toques). From the typically regional 135 F set menu, you might choose soupe au pistou, ox jowl daube, and crème brûlée à la vanille. Reine gave up her medical studies a few years ago and has now become the best *cuisinière* in Provence. We celebrate her continuing progress with two more points.

A la carte: 350 F. Menu: 135 F.

Le Moulin de Lourmarin
Rue du Temple — 90.68.06.69
M. Cahez. Closed 15 Nov-20 Dec. Open until 11 pm. Private room: 25. Terrace dining. Air cond. Valet parking. Telex 431704. V AE.

This beautifully restored oil mill is now an elegantly decorated restaurant. The 160 F set menu includes artichokes à la barigoule, fresh salmon with coriander-flavoured vinaigrette, lovely farm-fresh cheeses, and a selection of seasonal fruit sorbets. Gorgeous terrace.

A la carte: 350-400 F. Menus: 160 F, 260 F.

Le Moulin de Lourmarin
(See restaurant above)
Closed 15 Nov-20 Dec. 4 stes 1,200-1,800 F. 23 rms 460-950 F. Half-board 680-2,000 F. TV. Air cond. Conference facilities.

A covered footbridge leads from the mill to this restored house offering fully equipped rooms (one with terrace) and attractive bathrooms. The breakfasts need improving, but the welcome is faultless and prices reasonable. Sauna.

See PARIS Suburbs

See Caen

01800 Loyettes — (Ain)
Paris 468 - Lyon 33 - Vienne 48 - Bourgoin-Jallieu 28

La Terrasse
10, pl. des Mariniers — 78.32.70.13
M. Antonin. Closed Sun dinner, Mon and 10-28 Feb. Open until 9.30 pm. Garden dining. V AE.
You'll love this riverside restaurant for its charming terrace on the Rhône and for Gérard Antonin's well-prepared regional dishes such as frogs' leg and mussel soup, paupiette de raie en marinière, and breaded veal kidneys and duck breast with cider butter. Superb but costly wines. We found the service better organised this year.
A la carte: 350-400 F. Menus: from 160 F to 370 F.

See CORSICA

31110 Luchon — (H.-Garonne)
Paris 816 - Tarbes 90 - St-Gaudens 46

12/20 Le Gipsy
5, av. A.-Dumas — 61.79.36.22
Mme Candel. Closed 20 Oct-1 April. Open until 9 pm. Private room: 24. Garden dining. No pets. Parking. Telex 520347. V AE DC.
Ample portions of honest food are served by the pleasant staff in the intimate dining room. Order the salade commingeoise, trout à la luchonnaise, and duck breast. You'll receive good advice on choosing from the limited wine list.
A la carte: 250 F. Menus: 120 F, 180 F.

Hôtel Corneille
(See restaurant above)
Closed 20 Oct-1 April. 3 stes 780 F. 58 rms 220-520 F. Half-board 280-500 F. TV.
A quiet hotel in a residential area, with attractive Napoleon III furnishings. Impeccable reception.

62380 Lumbres — (P./Calais)
Paris 266 - Arras 86 - Boulogne 40 - St-Omer 13

Moulin de Mombreux
Rte de Bayenghem — 21.39.62.44
M. Gaudry. Closed 20-29 Dec. Open until 9.15 pm. Private room: 80. Parking. Telex 133486. V AE DC.
You can admire this former watermill's impressive wooden workings while sipping an apéritif in the lounge before going up to the first-floor dining room. The food is better than ever and we're awarding another point, despite the steep prices. Try the asparagus in a highly scented truffle vinaigrette, young pigeon roast with thyme, superb local poultry, and a souffléed apple tart. Impeccable welcome and service.
A la carte: 400 F. Menus: 230 F, 286 F, 370 F.

Moulin de Mombreux
(See restaurant above)
Closed 20-29 Dec. 24 rms 450-570 F. TV. Conference facilities.
This peaceful hotel offers several small, neat, and well-decorated rooms with views of the river and ducks.

54300 Lunéville — (Meurthe/M.)
Paris 340 - Strasbourg 124 - Metz 92 - Nancy 35

Château d'Adoménil
in Réhainviller-Adoménil — 83.74.04.81
M. Million. Closed Sun dinner, Mon and Feb. Open until 9.30 pm. Private room: 40. Garden dining. Garage parking. V AE DC.
Set in a splendid park, this graceful nineteenth-century mansion houses ornate, theatrically decorated dining rooms where the affable Bernadette Million and her team of efficient staff will make you glad you came to this little-known corner of Lorraine. And Michel Million's cooking, simple and light at heart, never disappoints. The feast begins with varied cocktail snacks, and might continue to a salad of perfect baked prawns, a snail and split-pea soup flavoured with bacon, a deftly prepared lamb en croûte (rosy pink meat, light pastry), and a marvellous croustillant of seasonal fruit with a delectable caramel sauce. Wide choice of wines.
A la carte: 400-500 F. Menus: 190 F (weekdays only), 280 F, 340 F, 400 F.

Château d'Adoménil
(See restaurant above)
Closed Feb. 7 rms 400-650 F. TV. Conference facilities.
Seven comfortable, very luxurious rooms in a huge and magnificent park. Superb breakfasts. A railway passes nearby and a peacock screeches on the roof, but overall atmosphere is restful and the prices almost reasonable. Relais et Châteaux.

64660 Lurbe-Saint-Christau — (Pyrénées-A.)
Paris 795 - Lourdes 60 - Pau 42 - Oloron-Ste-Marie 9

Au Bon Coin
59.34.40.12
M. Lassala. Closed Mon off-season, and 1-24 Nov. Open until 9 pm. Hotel: 14 rms 120-160 F. V AE.
The flickering firelight is reflected in the copper, pewter, and silverware, giving a restful, homely air to this isolated inn. The dishes, unfortunately, vary in quality: the foie gras and salmon with citrus-flavoured butter are excellent, but the prawn ravioli are limp, and the chocolate and pear charlotte is far less satisfying than the delicate hot apple pie. Friendly welcome and efficient service.
A la carte: 220 F. Menus: 55 F, 80 F, 125 F, 170 F.

Relais de la Poste et du Parc

in Saint-Christau
59.34.40.04
Closed 28 Oct-31 March. 3 stes 400-620 F. 43 rms 210-550 F. Restaurant. Half-board 310-500 F. TV 28 rms. Conference facilities. Pool. Tennis. Parking. Telex 550656. V.
Near the large white buildings with green shutters, you'll find a small boating lake. The quiet setting ensures a relaxing stay, and there's a gym for the more active.

37230 Luynes — (Indre/Loire)
Paris 248 - Tours 13 - Langeais 14 - Chinon 45

Domaine de Beauvois
2 km NW on D 49 — 47.55.50.11
M. Taupin. Closed 6 Jan-23 March. Open until 9.15 pm. Private room: 25. Terrace dining. No pets. Valet parking. Telex 750204. V AE DC.
This country manor with its fifteenth-century tower and 150 hectares of wooded grounds ranks

among the most luxurious establishments in the Touraine region. Its restaurant features seasonal dishes like spring vegetables with tomato coulis, freshwater perch baked in Chinon, pigeon cooked in a salt crust with artichoke and onion ragoût, and a crisp prune feuilleté. Fearsomely expensive.

A la carte: 400-500 F. Menus: 160 F and 230 F (weekdays lunch only), 220 F and 340 F (dinner only).

Domaine de Beauvois ⚔🌲

(See restaurant above)

Closed 6 Jan-23 March. 5 stes 1,410-2,160 F. 35 rms 490-1,240 F. Half-board 785-1,000 F oblig in seas. TV. Air cond 2 rms. Conference facilities. Heated pool. Tennis.

Ideally situated for a break visiting the nearby Châteaux de la Loire, this fine hotel has huge, frequently updated and delightfully furnished rooms with marble bathrooms. Fishing and horse riding are available, and visits to local wine growers are organised after the *vendanges*.

LYON

69000 Lyon — (Rhône)
Paris 462 - Grenoble 106 - Valence 100 - Genève 190

Lyon's establishments are classified by arrondissement. An alphabetical index on page 372 enables you to find the correct arrondissement (or nearby town or village) for all the establishments mentioned here.

And also...

Our selection of places for inexpensive, quick, or late-night meals.

L'Assiette en Douce (78.92.93.54 - 31, rue Ste-Hélène, 2e. Open until 11 pm): Fine and often imaginative cooking, reasonably priced, and a friendly atmosphere (150 F).

Bar du Passage (78.28.11.16 - 8, rue du Plâtre, 1er. Open until midnight): Daniel Ancel's bistro-style fare is served in a theatrical décor. Wines by the jug (100 F).

Bernachon (78.24.37.98 - 42, cours Franklin-Roosevelt, 6e. Lunch only): Always crowded, this tea room offers *plats du jour*, cakes, and a selection of teas, plus jugs of hot chocolate (100 F).

Le Bistrot de la Minaudière (78.37.32.96 - 7, rue de la Poulaillerie, 2e. Lunch only except w-e): The prototype bistro. The excellent 57 F set menu changes every day.

Le Blandan (78.28.76.43 - 28, rue Sergent-Blandan, 1er. Open until 9.30 pm): Patronised by young customers, this pleasant spot features Lyonnais dishes with the occasional excursion into *nouvelle cuisine* (150 F).

Brasserie de Bondy (78.28.37.34 - 16, quai de Bondy, 5e. Open until 1 am): Lyon's best choucroute, as well as pretzels, quetsch plum tarts, and Alsace beer and wine (150 F).

Le Café du Jura (78.42.20.57 - 25, rue Tupin, 2e. Open until 10.30 pm): You can sample typical local fare at the bistro tables with bench seats (160 F).

Café de la Mairie (78.28.55.92 - 44, quai P.-Scize, 5e. Dinner only): Homely cooking in a patriotic décor.

Café du Musée (78.37.71.54 - 2, rue des Forces, 1er. Lunch only): A tiny bistro huddling in a tiny street. Classic Lyonnais cooking (120 F).

Comptoir de Gastronomie (78.24.64.00 - 125, rue de Séze, 6e. Open until 10 pm): Vacuum-cooked lunches. You might prefer foie gras and Poilâne bread (made from stone-ground flour and natural yeast), (150 F).

Le Coquemar (78.25.83.32 - 23, montée de Fourvière, 5e. Lunch only): These well-prepared family dishes won't break the bank (100 F).

La Conciergerie (78.83.23.39 - 12, quai P.-Scize, 5e. Open until 11 pm): Trendy atmosphere, jovial service, and good home cooking (120-150 F).

La Corbeille (78.27.74.50 - 21, rue du Bât-d'Argent, 1er. Open until 10 pm): The cheapest set menus fill you up for well under 100 F. Excellent desserts too (150 F).

La Daudon Médée (78.39.36.01 - 120, bd de la Croix-Rousse, 4e. Open every day, dinner only): This is the place to go for succulent meat dishes (150 F).

Le Gouliot (78.42.77.35 - 49, rue de la Charité, 2e. Open until 10 pm): Updated traditional cooking in the antique dealers' district. Inexpensive (two set menus at less than 100 F).

Hugon (78.28.10.94 - 12, rue Pizay, 1er. Lunch only): A dozen first courses, *plats du jour*, and typical Lyonnais desserts, prepared practically before your eyes by Arlette Hugon (150 F).

La Minaudière (78.68.11.11 - 41, av. H.-Barbusse, Villeurbane. Lunch only): A simple meal downstairs can be had for less than 100 F, or you may prefer the 'gastronomic' restaurant on the first floor. Both are open for lunch only.

Chez Mounier (78.37.79.26 - 3, rue des Marronniers, 2e. Open until 11.30 pm): All the classics of Lyonnais cuisine, plus wine by the carafe (100 F).

Le Neuf (78.42.07.59 - 7, pl. Bellecour, 2e. Open until 7 pm): Breakfast à la carte, *plats du jour* at lunchtime, and pastries for tea (100-150 F).

Le Petit Léon (72.00.08.10 - 3, rue Pléney, 1er. Lunch only; and dinner only upon reserv and groups): Well-prepared set meals and inexpensive local wines (100 F).

Le P'tit Garioud (78.37.76.27 - 26, rue Ferrandière, 2e. Open until midnight): Guy Garioud's 'annexe' offers moderately priced menus (150 F).

Pignol (78.37.39.61 - 17, rue E.-Zola, 2e. Lunch only): Just the place to meet for a *plat du jour* or *pâtisserie* (120 F).

La Rose des Vins (78.28.48.22 - 5, rue de la Fromagerie, 1er. Open until 1 am): Good wines sold by the glass, family cooking, and assortments of regional cheeses. Sometimes you'll find live jazz in the evenings (150 F).

Le Shalimar (78.42.18.20 - 39, quai Gailleton, 2e. Open until 11 pm): A pleasing Indian restaurant with a *menu-dégustation* at around 100 F.

Sofishop (78.42.72.50 - 20, quai Gailleton, 2e. Open until 2 am): The Sofitel's late-night snack-bar serves American-style hamburgers alongside typical Lyonnais dishes (100-150 F).

Sorey (78.27.95.56 - 10, pl. F.-Rey, 4e. Open until 11.30 pm): Featuring fresh cooking in a Provençal décor, this restaurant is popular with the theatre crowd.

Tapas des Loges (78.42.75.75 - 6, rue du Bœuf, 5e. Open until midnight): Salads and *plats du jour* are served at the counter (150 F).

Le Tonnelier (78.28.05.48 - 10, rue Mulet, 1er. Open until 9.30 pm): Enjoy the quenelles (pike dumplings), and Lyon sausage with a bottle of Beaujolais wine. The cheapest menu's only 45 F.

Le Val d'Isère (78.71.09.39 - 64, rue de Bonnel, 6e. Lunch only): Go here at the crack of dawn and watch the chefs tuck in when they return from market (120 F).

Le 21 (78.37.34.19 - 21, quai R.-Rolland, 5e. Open until 2 am): A late-night establishment on the banks of the Saône offering typical meals (180-200 F).

Les Visiteurs du Soir (78.37.22.23 - 34, rue des Remparts-d'Ainay, 2e. Open until 10 pm): Elaborate cooking with prices to match (200 F).

Woerhlé (78.60.66.53 - 156, rue de Créqui, 6e. Lunch only): Choucroute and other Alsace specialities have been dished up here for 60 years (150 F).

LYON   1st

12/20 L'Assiette Lyonnaise
19, pl. Tolozan — 78.28.35.77
M. Gros. Closed Sat lunch and Sun. Open until 11.30 pm. Private room: 14. Terrace dining. Air cond. Valet parking. V AE DC. Z1-24

The new-look Assiette has 1930s–style brasserie décor, air-conditioning, and a man to park your car (quite a novelty in Lyon). But the prices and cuisine are much the same, with carefully crafted dishes like escargots with tarragon, pig's trotters à la lyonnaise, and skate in brown butter. To go with them, try Georges Dubœuf's excellent Regnié (a Beaujolais village).

A la carte: 200-230 F. Menus: 98 F, 150 F.

12/20 Boname
5, Grande-Rue des Feuillants — 78.30.83.93
M. Boname. Closed Mon off-season, Sat in seas, Sun, 1-21 Aug. Open until midnight. Air cond. V. Z1-53

Jean-Paul Boname's bistro cooking ventures beyond the scope of classic Lyon fare. He likes to surprise his trendy clientele with intriguing dishes like shellfish with red wine and cinnamon, salade de cervelles aux câpres, and mussel soup with watercress.

A la carte: 230 F. Menu: 98 F.

12/20 Café des Fédérations
8, rue du Major-Martin — 78.28.26.00
M. Fulchiron. Closed Sat, Sun and Aug. Open until 9.45 pm. AE. Y1-33

Despite the unappealing décor, food lovers flock here for the chef's single menu featuring Lyonnais charcuterie, cervelle de canut (soft cheese whipped with shallots, wine, and herbs), tablier de sapeur (egg-and-breadcrumbed tripe), and homemade tarts. Côtes-du-Rhône and Beaujolais to drink, and it's all at reasonable prices.

Menu: 120 F.

13 Le Champier
10, rue des Fantasques — 78.28.41.33
M. Cantat. Closed Sun dinner, Mon and 1-15 Aug. Open until 9.30 pm. V DC. C2-43

Ask for a seat near the windows to enjoy the breathtaking views of Lyon that compensate for the restaurant's drab interior. Daniel Cantat's cooking, however, is fresh and individual: a tasty terrine of young rabbit (not boned, unfortunately), perfectly cooked salmon with chive sauce, excellent tarte Tatin, and an interesting peach sorbet. Good regional wines. Inexplicably slow service.

Menus: 100 F (weekdays only), 155 F, 210 F, 260 F.

12/20 Chevallier
40, rue du Sg.-Blandan — 78.28.19.83
MM. Coutant and Tuset. Closed Tue, Wed, 18-28 Feb and 8 July-1 Aug. Open until 10 pm. Private room: 30. Air cond. V AE DC. X1-47

This restaurant's subdued beige tones contrast with its cheerful specialities of hot sausage, egg-and-breadcrumbed tripe, hare dumplings in

vinegar sauce, and other copiously served Lyonnais dishes.

A la carte: 200-300 F. Menus: 78 F (weekdays lunch only), 105 F, 155 F, 185 F.

12/20 L'Estragon
27, quai St-Vincent — 78.28.14.51
M. Lauro. Closed Sun and 24 Dec-3 Jan. Open until 11 pm. Terrace dining. V. B3-49

A relaxed atmosphere prevails in this popular restaurant on the banks of the Saône. *Patron* Christian Lauro keeps a watchful eye on the quality of dishes like lamb's lettuce with foie gras, hearty fish and potato soup, and beef with bone marrow.

A la carte: 180 F. Menu: 98 F.

12/20 Le Garet
7, rue du Garet — 78.28.16.94
M. Laurent. Closed Sat, Sun, 20 July-20 Aug and 23 Dec-2 Jan. Open until 10 pm. Private room: 15. Air cond. V. Z1-48

Typical Lyonnais bistro, offering salads, potato feuilletés, tablier de sapeur, and *plats du jour*. Côtes-du-Rhône and Beaujolais by the jug, easy on the palate and the purse.

A la carte: 100-130 F.

12/20 La Gousse d'Ail
20, rue du Sg.-Blandan — 78.30.40.44
M. Carpentier. Dinner only (except Sun and holidays). Closed Mon and 15 Aug-15 Sep. Open until midnight. V. X1-42

A 'clone' of this popular bistro has just opened in the second arrondissement. The young *patron*'s winning formula is based on a friendly atmosphere, reasonable prices, and dishes that everyone enjoys. Fillet of lamb en croûte, rabbit with thyme and olives, and red mullet with buttery leeks are examples. The wine list includes a potent Syrah from the Ardèche at only 65 F.

A la carte: 200 F. Menus: 87 F, 110 F, 145 F.

14 Henry
27, rue de la Martinière — 78.28.26.08
M. Balladone. Closed Mon. Open until midnight. Terrace dining. Air cond. V AE DC. Y1-29

The new décor, warm and inviting, does nothing to prepare you for the stand-offish reception and brusque service. And although the food is prepared with as much care as ever, we detected a certain banality, a certain soullessness, creeping into the chef's repertoire: artichokes and shrimps à la barigoule, hastily put-together rascasse mousseline with lobster sauce, and an over-sweet nougat glacé. Balanced but expensive wine list.

A la carte: 350-400 F. Menus: 160 F, 230 F.

18 Léon de Lyon ۞
1, rue Pléney — 78.28.11.33
M. Lacombe. Closed Mon lunch, Sun and 4-26 Aug. Open until 10 pm. Private room: 30. Air cond. No-smoking section. Valet parking. V. Y2-22

This culinary landmark now features a calorie-conscious 'menu-dînette' that casts a shadow on our enthusiasm. The price hasn't been trimmed in line with the portions and we weren't exactly overwhelmed by the hors d'œuvre composed of three leek leaves and two scampi, hot foie gras with crisp potatoes, and calf's liver steamed with savory, thyme, rosemary, and sage but still almost tasteless. Luckily there followed a delicious dessert of praline, ice cream, and tart, garnished with chocolate and berry sorbets. This kind of cooking may be fashionable, but unfortunately it's not what

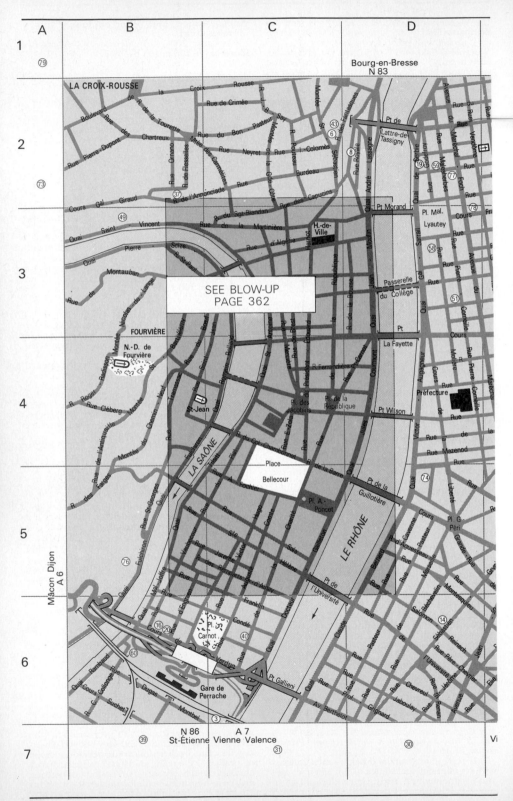

SEE BLOW-UP
PAGE 362

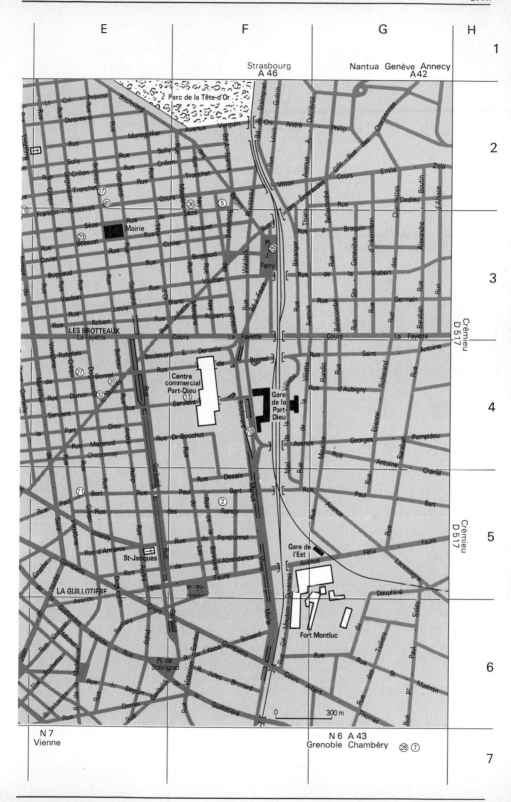

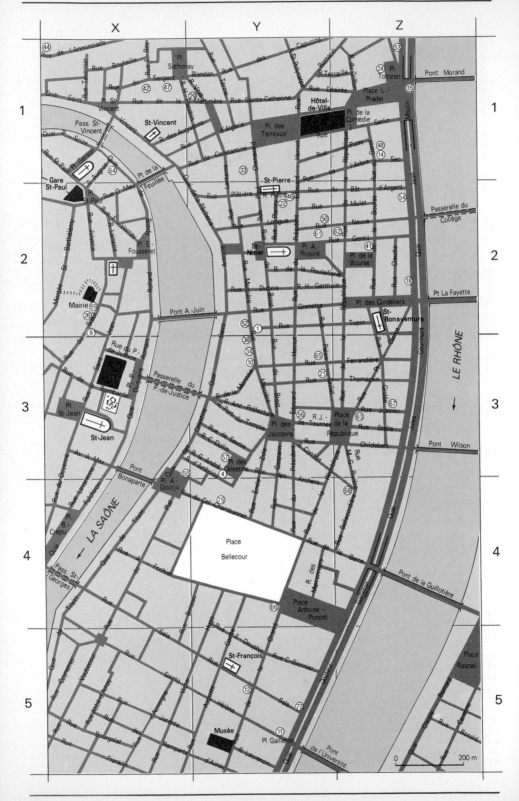

1 - Le Tupinier (2e) **R**
2 - Chez Pino (3e) **R**
3 - Le Moulin à Poivre (2e) **R**
4 - Christian Bourillot (2e) **R**
5 - L'Helvétie (6e) **R**
6 - Au Temps Perdu (1er) **R**
7 - Altea Park Hôtel (8e) **H**
    et Laennec **H**
8 - La Mère Brazier (1er) **R**
9 - Comptoir du Bœuf (5e) **R**
10 - Le Bistrot de Lyon (2e) **R**
11 - Le Vivarais (2e) **R**
12 - La Tassée (2e) **R**
13 - L'Arc-en-Ciel
    (Pullman
    Part-Dieu) (3e) **RH**
14 - Le Petit Flore (1er) **R**
15 - Le Saint-Alban (1er) **R**
16 - Bristol (2e) **H**
    La Mère Vittet **R**
    et Brasserie Georges **R**
17 - Cazenove (6e) **R**
18 - Nandron (2e) **R**
19 - Le Restaurant
    des Gourmets
    (Chez Luigi) (6e) **R**
20 - Le Bistrot
    de la Mère (2e) **R**
21 - Le Sarto (2e) **R**
22 - Léon de Lyon (1er) **R**
23 - Le Roosevelt (6e) **H**
24 - L'Assiette
    Lyonnaise (1er) **R**
25 - Le Gourmandin (6e) **R**
26 - La Tour Rose (La Maison
    de la Tour) (5e) **R**
27 - Holiday Inn
    Crowne Plaza (3e) **H**
28 - Auberge
    Savoyarde (8e) **R**
29 - Henry (1er) **R**
30 - Le Fédora (7e) **R**
31 - Mercure
    Pont-Pasteur (7e) **H**
32 - L'Alexandrin (3e) **R**
33 - Café
    des Fédérations (1er) **R**
34 - Le Bouchon
    aux Vins (2e) **R**
35 - Le Bistrot
    des Halles (3e) **R**
36 - La Romanière (6e) **R**
37 - La Romanée (1er) **R**
38 - Le Mercière (2e) **R**
39 - Charlemagne (2e) **H**
40 - Au Petit Col
    (Junet) (2e) **R**
41 - Les Fantasques (2e) **R**
42 - La Gousse d'Ail (1er) **R**
43 - Le Champiet (1er) **R**
44 - La Mandarine (1er) **R**
45 - Pierre Orsi (6e) **R**
46 - Le Passage (1er) **R**
47 - Chevallier (1er) **R**
48 - Le Garet (1er) **R**
49 - L'Estragon (1er) **R**
50 - La Meunière (1er) **R**
51 - Gervais (6e) **R**

52 - Le Layon (2e) **R**
53 - Boname (1er) **R**
54 - Têtedoie (2e) **R**
55 - La Voûte (2e) **R**
56 - Grand Hôtel
    des Beaux-Arts (2e) **H**
57 - Chez
    Jean-François (2e) **H**
58 - La Soupière (6e) **R**
59 - Le Quatre
    Saison (6e) **R**
60 - Les Belles Saisons
    (Pullman Perrache)
    (2e) **RH**
61 - Le Nord (2e) **R**
62 - Kun Yang (2e) **R**
63 - Carlton (2e) **H**
64 - Les Saisons (5e) **R**
65 - Guy Garioud (2e) **R**
66 - Royal (2e) **H**
67 - Grand Hôtel
    Concorde (2e) **H**
68 - Eriksen (2e) **H**

69 - Cour des Loges (5e) **H**
70 - Mercure (3e) **R**
71 - J.-C. Péquet (3e) **R**
72 - Les Trois Dômes
    (Sofitel) (2e) **RH**
73 - Hôtel de Lyon
    Métropole (4°) **H**
74 - A Ma Vigne (3e) **H**
75 - La Table
    en Périgord (2e) **R**
76 - Le Bouchon de Fourvière (5e) **R**
77 - Jean-Pierre Bergier (6e) **R**
78 - Le Jardin Romain (6e) **R**
79 - Auberge de l'Ile (9e) **R**

chef Jean-Paul Lacombe does best. On the contrary, his genius resides in his magnificent blendings of yesterday's rich flavours with today's lighter tastes, a talent amply demonstrated by his hot sausages and potatoes in olive oil, salad of Lyonnais charcuterie, gras-double (tripe) with onions, pig's trotters and ears, frogs' leg ravioli and a wild-mushroom flan coated with a heavenly raw watercress sauce, baked John Dory with garlic mayonnaise, blanquette de veau aux asperges, and sautéed leg of lamb with fresh, tender broad beans. These are the dishes we prefer for a leisurely meal in the first-floor dining room, cosily furnished with dark-wood panelling, paintings of banquets, and scale-model kitchens behind glass. Relais et Châteaux. See also Le Petit Léon listed under the 'And also...' heading.

A la carte: 400-550 F. Menus: 220 F, 420 F.

🍴13 La Mandarine
10, rue Rivet — 78.28.01.74
M. Perrier. Closed Sat lunch, Sun and Aug. Open until 10.30 pm. Private room: 30. V AE DC.   X1-44

Daniel Perrier's cooking reveals a strong personality and a fondness for contrasting flavours which always result in pleasant surprises. His latest creations include chitterling sausages and cabbage, watercress salad with scorpion fish goujonnettes seasoned with walnut oil, and pork tenderloin in an onion cream sauce served with an artichoke flan. Bistro décor and a warm welcome.

A la carte: 300 F. Menus: 90 F (lunch only), 120 F, 170 F, 200 F.

🍴16 La Mère Brazier   〇
12, rue Royale — 78.28.15.49
Mmes Brazier. Closed Sat lunch, Sun and 28 July-28 Aug. Open until 9.45 pm. Private room: 20. Valet parking. V AE DC.   D2-8

New customers would do well to order the dishes that have made this attractive restaurant famous. A change of chef has done nothing to alter the traditions in the kitchen, or in the dining room, where Jacotte Brazier continues to greet you as if she's known you all your life. To start with, the best rosette (the local dried pork sausage) available anywhere, followed by artichoke hearts stuffed with foie gras, crêpes aux truffes, and Bresse chicken served with vegetables, gherkins, and cherries preserved in vinegar. Last but not least comes the flambé Chabraninof of apples and vanilla ice cream. Excellent selection of Beaujolais and Côtes-du-Rhônes.

A la carte: 300-350 F. Menus: 280 F, 330 F.

12/20 La Meunière
11, rue Neuve — 78.28.62.91
M. Debrosse. Closed Sun, Mon, holidays and 14 July-15 Aug. Open until 9.45 pm. V AE DC.   Y2-50

This restaurant boasts a large central table laden with hors d'œuvres, desserts, and house selections of Beaujolais by the jug. The unchanging *carte* contains old favourites like tablier de sapeur, roast veal kidneys, and boudin sausages at old-fashioned prices.

A la carte: 160 F. Menus: 70 F, 85 F, 125 F.

🍴15 Le Passage
8, rue du Plâtre — 78.28.11.16
M. Carteron. Closed Sat lunch and Sun. Open until 9.45 pm. Air cond. V AE DC.   Y2-46

This trendy bistro caters to a chic set who come for Daniel Ancel's interpretation of the city's traditional dishes. Try his lamb's kidneys with marrow purée, lobster and lentil stew, braised

oxtail, and young pigeon with pears. A real *pâtissier* was taken on recently, which means the desserts are now as good as the rest. The décor, with its bench seats and subdued lighting, is enlivened by some 'old masters' painted by a friend of the chef.

A la carte: 320-370 F. Menus: 160 F (lunch only), 230 F, 290 F.

12/20 Le Petit Flore
19, rue du Garet — 78.27.27.51
M. Bonnin. Closed Sun, Mon and 12-27 Aug. Open until 9.45 pm. V.   Z1-14

Hardly anyone looks at the limited *carte*, preferring Maurice Bonnin's delectable set menu suggestions such as saddle of hare à la beaujolaise, tablier de sapeur, and andouillette sausage.

A la carte: 150 F. Menus: 80 F, 110 F.

La Romanée
19, rue Rivet — 72.00.80.87
M. Denis. Closed Mon off-season, and 15 Jan-15 Feb. Open until 9.30 pm. V AE DC.   B2-37

Elisabeth and Daniel Denis have just arrived in Lyon and promise to feature the same good dishes that earned them a toque at their Restaurant du Moulin at Châtillon-en-Diois. Past specialities included truffled trout mousse, baron of lamb with black-olive purée, and pear terrine with strawberries.

A la carte: 200 F. Menus: 68 F (weekdays lunch only), 98 F, 135 F, 175 F, 225 F.

🍴15 Le Saint-Alban
2, quai J.-Moulin — 78.30.14.89
M. Lechevalier. Closed Sat lunch and Sun. Annual closings not available. Open until 9.30 pm. Air cond. V.   Z1-15

Jean-Paul Lechevalier was pleased to return to a small restaurant. This one on the banks of the Rhône seats 30 or so and it's always full because you can enjoy a really good meal here for 130 F or 170 F. This award-winning chef still has the master's touch, and knows how to reinvent classic dishes like a liver pâté cooked to pink perfection and served with vegetable confit, prawn and leek cannelloni garnished with fresh morels, and perfectly cooked lamb noisettes with rosemary. His deliciously refreshing desserts include pistachio cream with apricot coulis, honey-roast peaches, and pralines with redcurrant sorbet. The wine list concentrates on northern Côtes-du-Rhône, and the reception and service are faultless.

A la carte: 300 F. Menus: 130 F, 170 F.

12/20 Au Temps Perdu
2, rue des Fantasques
78.39.23.04
M. Bellouere. Closed 12-26 Aug. Open until midnight. Private room: 40. V AE.   C2-6

Located on the Croix-Rousse slope, this small bistro boasts one of the finest views of Lyon, as well as fresh, intelligent cooking that compensates for the dull décor. The young owner-chef's calf's tongue sliced over a bed of salad greens is superb, his braised sweetbreads with cèpes perfectly cooked, and the praline tart extremely smooth. Very good value.

A la carte: 160 F. Menus: 65 F (weekdays lunch only), 85 F, 150 F.

12/20 Les Belles Saisons
12, cours de Verdun
78.37.58.11
M. Delubac. Open every day. Open until 10.30 pm. Private room: 48. Air cond. Valet parking. Telex 330500. V AE DC.   B6-60

Despite this hotel-restaurant's comfortable wood-panelled interior, lovely china, and perfect service, the cooking remains resolutely uninspired: artichoke hearts with smoked salmon, freshwater perch steamed with cucumber, and fresh fruit gratin.

A la carte: 220-260 F. Menus: 115 F (weekdays only, wine inc), 160 F.

Pullman Perrache
(See restaurant above)
Open every day. 2 stes 1,000 F. 124 rms 410-670 F. TV. Air cond. Conference facilities.

Next to Lyon-Perrache railway station, this excellent, modern, and fully equipped hotel features large, air-conditioned, soundproofed rooms. Shops, piano bar, winter garden, and efficient service.

12/20 Le Bistrot de la Mère
26, cours de Verdun — 78.42.16.91
M. Vittet. Closed 1 May. Open until 2 am. Terrace dining. Air cond. Telex 305559. V AE DC.   B6-20

This sparkling new, white-lacquered bistro offers overcooked poached eggs à la bourguignonne, good egg-and-breadcrumbed tripe, superb St-Marcellin cheese, and shellfish in season. Half a dozen wines are available by the jug. Rapid service.

A la carte: 140-300 F. Menus: from 75 F to 120 F.

Le Bistrot de Lyon
64, rue Mercière — 78.37.00.62
MM. Caro and Lacombe. Closed 1 May and 25 Dec. Open until 1.30 am. Private room: 30. Terrace dining. Air cond. V.   Y3-10

This restaurant is the subject of a lot of mud-slinging in Lyon—a sure indication of its continuing success. Crowds of customers gather here at lunchtime and after the theatre to enjoy typical bistro fare like oysters, roast pigeon, gras-double, beef tartare, and ravioli in chicken bouillon, all well worth the toque. Good wines by the jug, charming turn-of-the-century décor, and attentive service.

A la carte: 250 F.

Le Bouchon aux Vins
62, rue Mercière — 78.42.88.90
M. Caro. Closed Sun. Open until midnight. Terrace dining. Air cond. V.   Y3-34

Jean-Claude Caro's archetypal bistro overflows on to the pavement at the first hint of spring, and there's a counter for tardy customers when the place is packed. Thirty-odd wines are available by the glass, and dishes include assorted charcuterie, spinach salad with rabbit fillets, lotte in bilberry sauce with fresh pasta, duck pot-au-feu, and praline tarts. Skilled service.

A la carte: 250 F. Menu: 82 F (weekdays only).

Christian Bourillot
8, pl. des Célestins — 78.37.38.64
M. Bourillot. Closed Sun, holidays, 29 June-29 July and 24 Dec-2 Jan. Open until 10 pm. Private room: 25. Air cond. V AE DC.   Y3-4

The comfortable décor with mahogany panelling, white damask tablecloths, and silver chandeliers has not changed over the years, and

the quenelles, oysters gratin, and poultry pot-au-feu are still on the menu. But you can also sample new versions of classic Lyonnais dishes like lotte with split-pea flan, and tournedos steak with morels and truffles. There's a magnificent selection of wines and spirits, and Anne-Marie Bourillot and her staff treat you like an old friend.

A la carte: 400-450 F. Menus: 200 F, 310 F and 390 F (weekdays only).

12/20 Brasserie Georges
30, cours de Verdun — 78.37.15.78
M. Rinck. Closed 1 May. Open until 11 pm. Private room: 100. Terrace dining. V AE DC.   B6-16

Founded in 1836, this busy restaurant has had some famous visitors over the years to admire its six hundred square metres of painted ceiling. Chef Alain Corui prepares hearty brasserie dishes like pike quenelles, salmon tartare, choucroute, and duck breast. Excellent draught beer and efficient service.

A la carte: 180 F. Menus: 75 F, 90 F and 110 F (weekdays only), 150 F (w-e and holidays lunch only).

Bristol
28, cours de Verdun — 78.37.56.55
Closed 21 Dec-2 Jan. 134 rms 155-360 F. TV 123 rms. Air cond. Conference facilities. Telex 330584. V AE DC.   B6-16

Centrally located and next to Lyon-Perrache station, this hotel has neat, soundproofed rooms. Fitness centre, sauna, Jacuzzi.

Carlton
4, rue Jussieu — 78.42.56.51
Open every day. 83 rms 310-580 F. TV. Air cond 52 rms. Garage parking. V AE DC.   Z3-63

A distinguished hotel offering soundproofed rooms, 20 of which have just been redecorated. Friendly welcome. Meals on trays available.

Charlemagne
23, cours Charlemagne — 78.92.81.61
Open every day. 119 rms 350-440 F. Restaurant. TV. Conference facilities. Parking. Telex 380401. V AE DC.   B7-39

Two hotels (Charlemagne and Résidence) in one, with contemporary or period rooms, recently renovated and well-equipped. Lyon-Perrache station and the pedestrian precinct are within easy reach. Gift shop and bar.

12/20 Eriksen
28, rue L.-Pauflque — 78.38.01.90
M. Biehe. Closed Sun and Mon. Open until 10.30 pm. Terrace dining. Air cond. V AE DC.   Z4-68

A modern restaurant featuring Scandinavian smoked fish, pickled herrings, salmon cooked on one side, and smörgasbord in the evenings. Two copious lunch menus keep the customers coming.

A la carte: 250 F. Menus: 69 F (weekdays lunch only, beer inc), 98 F (weekdays lunch only), 185 F (dinner only), 168 F.

Les Fantasques
53, rue de la Bourse — 78.37.36.58
M. Gervais. Closed Sun and 5-26 Aug. Open until 10 pm. Private room: 12. Air cond. V AE DC.   Z2-41

This friendly and comfortable restaurant is known for its fresh seafood, and the bouillabaisse is as good as any on the Côte d'Azur. Other dishes include fish soup, artichoke hearts with foie gras, and conventional desserts (pastries, œufs à la

neige, sorbets). Warm, chatty reception.
A la carte: 400 F. Menu: 200 F.

Guy Garioud
14, rue du Palais-Grillet
78.37.04.71
*M. Garioud. Closed Sat lunch and Sun. Open until
10 pm. Private room: 60. Terrace dining. Air cond. V
AE.*   Y3-65

Now we've had time to get used to the ultra-realistic paintings, we're happy to report that the warm atmosphere, moderate prices, and reliable cooking haven't changed. It's a pleasure to rediscover the John Dory in aspic with fennel-flavoured cream, braised salmon, and spiced duck in a sweet-and-sour sauce.
A la carte: 250-300 F. Menus: 124 F, 169 F, 242 F.

Grand Hôtel Concorde
11, rue Grôlée – 72.40.45.45
*Open every day. 3 stes 1,300-1,700 F. 140 rms 490-
790 F. Restaurant. TV. Air cond. Conference facilities. Garage parking. V AE DC.*   Z3-67

This huge structure on the banks of the Rhône offers large and remarkably well-soundproofed rooms. Traditional reception and service, numerous conference facilities.

Grand Hôtel des Beaux-Arts
73, rue du Président-Herriot
78.38.09.50
*Open every day. 79 rms 310-540 F. TV. Air cond
62 rms. Conference facilities. TV AE DC.*   Y3-56

Right next to Jacobins square, this large hotel combines modern comfort with tradition, and features recently renovated, 1930s–style rooms.

12/20 Chez Jean-François
2, pl. des Célestins – 78.42.08.26
*M. Courtois. Closed Sun, 29 March-7 April and
26 July-26 Aug. Open until 10 pm. V.*   Y3-57

The more popular the show at the theatre next door, the better the business in Jean-François Courtois' restaurant. Traditionally prepared specialities include pike quenelles with wine sauce, giblet salad with mushrooms, and a slightly overcooked calf's liver. We'd still like to be made to feel more welcome, though.
A la carte: 230-250 F. Menus: 75 F, 135 F.

Kun Yang
12, rue Neuve – 78.39.98.12
*MM. Kan. Open every day. Open until 10.30 pm.
Private room: 24. Air cond. V AE DC.*   Y2-61

The best Asian restaurant in Lyon, which has precious few good ones. Try the spring rolls, chicken with bamboo shoots and black mushrooms, scampi with fresh pineapple, or one of the steamed specialities. Exemplary service.
A la carte: 250-300 F. Menus: 80 F, 110 F, 145 F, 165 F.

12/20 Le Layon
52, rue Mercière – 78.42.94.08
*M. Leger. Open every day. Open until 11.30 pm. Ter-
race dining. V.*   Y2-52

The Rue Mercière's most recent bistro, Le Layon is already appreciated for its warm reception, brisk service, comfortable seating, and good, straightforward food. Eggs in a well-seasoned wine sauce, rabbit with mustard on a bed of straw potatoes, and lemon sorbet with marc go well with the Beaujolais and Côtes-du-Rhône sold by the jug. The *patron* also proposes some Côteaux-du-Layon

from his native region, including a 1947 at 1,200 F!
A la carte: 200 F. Menus: 68 F (weekdays lunch only), 89 F, 115 F, 148 F.

Le Mercière
56, rue Mercière – 78.37.67.35
*M. Manoa. Open every day. Open until 11.30 pm.
Terrace dining. V AE DC.*   Y3-38

It's best to book at this bustling, top-value restaurant. The 69 F lunch menu includes a garlicky pork sausage salad, tablier de sapeur with a gutsy sauce gribiche, and fromage blanc à la crème. Jean-Louis Manoa also prepares more personal dishes like escargots with sliced artichokes, and lotte baked with spices and mussel stock. Excellent Beaujolais and Côtes-du-Rhône.
A la carte: 250 F. Menus: 69 F (weekdays lunch only), 80 F (dinner only).

11/20 La Mère Vittet
26, cours de Verdun – 78.37.20.17
*M. Vittet. Open 24 hours. Closed 1 May. Private
room: 45. Terrace dining. Air cond. Telex 305559. V
AE DC.*   B6-16

The atmosphere of this huge 24-hour brasserie, its displays of oysters, charming service, and time-honoured reputation all contribute to its lasting success, despite the uneventful cooking and off-putting prices. We liked the sautéed frogs' legs à la provençale and turbot in a potato crust.
A la carte: 350 F. Menus: from 110 F to 320 F.

12/20 Le Moulin à Poivre
11, quai de Perrache – 78.37.36.86
*M. Révillon. Closed Sat, Sun and Aug. Open until
9 pm. Air cond. V.*   C6-3

Customers are ill-advised to arrive here unexpectedly, for the owners are apt to be out cultivating their kitchen garden or wringing a duck's neck. But should they be in, they will serve you robust food from the South-west like foies gras, confits, and civets. Good Cahors wines and hot apple tarts.
A la carte: 270 F. Menu: 200 F.

Nandron
26, quai J.-Moulin – 78.42.10.26
*M. Nandron. Closed Sat and 29 July-27 Aug. Open
until 9.45 pm. Private room: 20. Air cond. Valet
parking. V AE DC.*   Z2-18

Lyon's political and business leaders gather under the low ceilings of this culinary institution perched above the Rhône to feast on the pike quenelles, Bresse chicken in vinegar, oxtail daube, rabbit in aspic, roast lambs' tongues, and braised frogs' legs with herbs. To claim that chef Gérard Nandron is a great innovator would be something of an exaggeration. His originality lies more in his talent for turning towards the past and adding the personal touch to forgotten recipes. For instance, how about Bresse chicken wings en papillote, stuffed with dried morels and coated with a chervil-scented cream sauce? Superb Burgundies and Côtes-du-Rhônes. Odette Nandron is a most welcoming hostess.
A la carte: 350-550 F. Menus: 190 F (weekdays only), 280 F, 380 F.

> *The new spiral-bound RAC Atlas France will
> help you to find your chosen restaurant of
> hotel, no matter how secluded.*

Le Nord
18, rue Neuve — 78.28.24.54
*M. Chassonnery. Open every day. Open until
10.30 pm. Private room: 60. Terrace dining. Air
cond. V.* Z2-62
This brightly decorated, 80-year-old brasserie
offers well-loved dishes prepared by Alain
Chassonnery: cassolette d'escargots aux morilles,
choucroute, baeckeoffe, stuffed chicken legs, and
veal knuckle pot-au-feu. Hearty local wines and
attentive service.
A la carte: 250-350 F. Menus: 90 F (weekdays
lunch only), 89 F and 190 F (weekdays only),
160 F, 200 F.

Au Petit Col
(Junet)
68, rue de la Charité — 78.37.25.18
*M. Junet. Closed Sun dinner and Mon. Annual
closings not available. Open until 10 pm. Air cond.
V AE.* C6-40
Robert Junet's restaurant, renovated and
redecorated from top to bottom, is now as fresh
and individual as his garlic-flavoured shredded
chicory and hot Lyon sausage cooked in wine,
scampi in stock with truffles and soft-boiled farm-
fresh eggs, cod fillet and shallots, and young pigeon casseroled with black turnips and carrots.
Well-chosen wines.
A la carte: 300 F. Menus: 120 F (weekdays only),
140 F, 170 F, 230 F.

Pullman Perrache
See restaurant Les Belles Saisons

Royal
20, pl. Bellecour — 78.37.57.31
*Open every day. 90 rms 400-810 F. Restaurant. Half-
board 530-950 F. TV. Air cond 80 rms. Conference
facilities. Garage parking. V AE DC.* Y4-66
A traditional hotel on the Place Bellecour with
well-equipped period rooms. Good service, quiet
bar, conference rooms.

Le Sarto
20, rue du Palais-Grillet — 78.37.49.64
*M. Battini. Closed Sun. Open until 10.15 pm. Private
room: 6. Terrace dining. Air cond. V.* Y3-21
Unoriginal but well-prepared dishes seem to be
the norm in Ange Battini's restaurant, but now that
he has completely redone the décor, we're looking
forward to something more inspired than the
grapefruit crèmes à la menthe poivrée, bass fillets
steamed with fennel, and freshwater perch with
crab coulis.
A la carte: 300-350 F. Menus: 95 F, 155 F, 230 F.

Sofitel
See restaurant Les Trois Dômes

12/20 La Table en Périgord 🔾
(Bistrot à Foie Gras)
4, pl. Bellecour — 78.42.74.49
*M. Cordonier. Closed Sun, Mon, holidays, 3-12 Feb
and 28 July-1 Sep. Open until 9.30 pm. Air cond. V
AE.* Y4-75
Numerous foies gras, a fricassée of giblets and
mushrooms, and an excellent cassoulet are served
in Pierre Champion's friendly and reasonably
priced bistro-cum-boutique.
A la carte: 180 F. Menus: 70 F (except Sat dinner),
88 F, 115 F.

La Tassée
20, rue de la Charité
78.37.02.35
*M. Borgeot. Closed Sun and 24 Dec-3 Jan. Open until
10.30 pm. Private room: 65. Air cond. Telex A76471.
V AE DC.* Y5-12
The Borgeot family's charming old bistro has
recently been redecorated, and now features a gift
shop and catering service. But the relaxed, cheerful atmosphere remains the same, and Jean-Paul
Borgeot continues to prepare good grilled
sausages, gras-double, and veal kidneys en cocotte
for the bankers, politicians, and civil servants who
gather here for lunch. His father Roger looks after
the excellent cellar.
A la carte: 300 F. Menus: from 105 F to 230 F.

Les Trois Dômes
20, quai du Dr-Gailleton
72.41.20.20
*M. Obeuf. Open every day. Open until 10 pm. Private
room: 220. Air cond. No pets. Valet parking.
Telex 330225. V AE DC.* Y5-72
The superb view of the Rhône from this eighth-
floor Sofitel restaurant is indisputably its major
attraction, for Eric Obeuf's cooking has not yet
settled down here. His turbot au gratin with chive
sauce has no real personality, the salmon with
caviar is slightly overcooked, and his sweet-and-
sour duck breast with ginger and mushrooms well
beneath the standards of his predecessor's cuisine.
The wines are good but expensive, like the set
menus and the *carte*. Efficient service. There's also
a snack bar, 'Le Sofishop'.
A la carte: 350-400 F. Menus: 225 F (wine inc),
295 F.

Sofitel
(See restaurant above)
*Open every day. 17 stes 995-1,800 F. 183 rms 785-
950 F. TV. Air cond. Conference facilities.*
Conveniently located in the centre of town, this
hotel is in the process of renovating all its rooms.
Good breakfasts. Piano bar.

11/20 Le Tupinier
2, rue Tupin
78.37.49.98
*M. Léron. Closed Mon lunch, Sun and Aug. Open
until 11 pm. Terrace dining. Air cond.* Y2-1
In a dimly lit dining room or out on the terrace,
customers tuck into rascasse terrine with crab and
à tarragon-flavoured tomato coulis, lotte
bouillabaisse with baby vegetables, and hot apple
tarts. Wines are available by the jug. Lukewarm
service.
A la carte: 150-200 F.

12/20 Le Vivarais
1, pl. du Dr-Gailleton
78.37.85.15
*M. Duffaud. Closed Sun, 14-31 July and 25 Dec-
2 Jan. Open until 10.30 pm. Private room: 16. Air
cond. V AE DC.* Y5-11
Robert Duffaut prepares light, classic dishes in
the friendly atmosphere of his popular Lyonnais
bouchon. Highly recommended are the young
rabbit salad, lotte with baby onions, and lamb's
tongue and brains. Good Mâcon and Beaujolais.
A la carte: 180-200 F. Menus: 90 F, 110 F.

12/20 La Voûte
(Chez Léa)
11, pl. A.-Gourju — 78.42.01.33
M. Rabatel. Closed Sun and 7-30 July. Open until 9.30 pm. Private room: 40. Terrace dining. Air cond. V AE DC.　　　　　X3-55

Popular with tourists, this timeless bistro offers honest, reasonably priced dishes: terrines, grasdouble, tablier de sapeur.

A la carte: 180 F. Menus: 98 F, 118 F, 160 F.

LYON　　　　　　　　3rd

  L'Alexandrin
83, rue Moncey
72.61.15.69
M. Alexanian. Closed Sun, Mon, 24 Dec-2 Jan and 5-27 Aug. Open until 9.15 pm. Terrace dining. Air cond. No pets. V.　　　　　E4-32

Talent like this should be rewarded, so we're giving Alain Alexanian two toques this year. His outstanding, moderately priced, and inventive cuisine includes a delicious chilled consommé with wild mushrooms, perfectly cooked fresh cod with mild garlic and cauliflower fritters, and heavenly desserts like the rhubarb and apple feuillantine with a blackcurrant coulis. Véronique Alexanian provides prompt, affable service, and the wine list has some fine Côtes-du-Rhônes.

A la carte: sbClosed Menus: 115 F, 160 F.

L'Arc-en-Ciel
129, rue Servient — 78.62.94.12
Mlle Vignat. Closed Sun dinner and 15 July-16 Aug. Open until 10 pm. Private room: 40. Air cond. Valet parking. Telex 380088. V AE DC.　　　　F4-13

Up on the 32nd floor of the Crédit Lyonnais building, this is one of the highest restaurants in France. Everyone seems to enjoy the classic, technically sound cooking, served in a modern, greyand-pink décor. The chef tends to employ rich and costly ingredients in preparing his lobster pie, turbot steamed with coriander, and pigeon pastilla with scampi and early vegetables. For smaller budgets, typical Lyonnais fare like andouillette sausages and sheep's trotters are available next door in the La Ripaille grill-room.

A la carte: 350-400 F. Menus: 220 F (weekdays lunch only), 430 F (dinner only), 195 F.

Pullman Part-Dieu
(See restaurant above)
Open every day. 2 stes 1,025-1,200 F. 245 rms 595-690 F. TV. Air cond. Conference facilities.

Europe's tallest hotel, the Pullman Part-Dieu has some magnificent, well-furnished rooms with aweinspiring views of the city.

11/20 Le Bistrot des Halles
101, rue Moncey — 78.60.90.23
M. Berry. Closed Sat lunch, Sun and 3-26 Aug. Open until 10.30 pm. Private room: 30. Terrace dining. Air cond. V AE DC.　　　　E4-35

This restaurant's success may well have contributed to the sharp decline in the quality of the food: the smoked salmon is deplorable and the chitterling sausage drowned in sauce. One point less this year.

A la carte: 160-180 F.

Some establishments change their closing times without warning. It is always wise to check in advance.

Holiday Inn Crowne Plaza
29, rue de Bonnel — 72.61.90.90
Open every day. 2 stes 1,500-2,800 F. 156 rms 810-1,350 F. Restaurant. TV. Air cond. Conference facilities. Valet parking. Telex 330703. V AE DC.　　E4-27

The newest chain hotel in town, with its American-style décor, boasts a formidable list of amenities: a boardroom for business meetings, sauna, Turkish baths, rooms reserved for non-smokers and others adapted for the disabled, piano-bar, American-style restaurant. Free shuttle service to Lyon Part-Dieu station.

Mercure
(Lyon Part-Dieu)
47, bd Vivier-Merle — 72.34.18.12
Open every day. 124 rms 315-530 F. Restaurant. TV. Air cond. Conference facilities. Parking. Telex 306469. V AE DC.　　　　F4-70

Next to Part-Dieu station, this hotel features comfortable, soundproofed and air-conditioned rooms. Conference facilities.

J.-C. Péquet
59, pl. Voltaire — 78.95.49.70
M. Péquet. Closed Sat, Sun, 14 July-1 Aug and 25 Dec-2 Jan. Open until 9.30 pm. Air cond. V AE DC.　　E5-71

Jean-Claude Péquet's charming restaurant with its tightly packed tables offers good, reliable food like the warm salad of lamb's lettuce and sweetbreads, fisherman's platter with saffron, and pigeon with turnips. Burgundy and Côtes-duRhône wines at reasonable prices, with numerous half-bottles.

A la carte: 250 F. Menus: 120 F, 155 F, 200 F.

12/20 Chez Pino
21, rue de la Rize — 78.60.09.37
M. Criado. Closed Mon dinner, Sun and 5-20 Aug. Open until 10 pm. Air cond. V AE DC.　　　F5-2

A far cry from the average pizzeria, Chez Pino is decked out with marble, wall hangings, and gorgeous table linen. A warm Italian welcome heralds a meal featuring marvellous Feta cheese crêpes, fresh gnocchi with four cheeses in a delicious sauce, good osso buco, and a superb cheese board. Eclectic wine list with an Italian accent.

A la carte: 240 F. Menus: 100 F, 130 F, 160 F.

Pullman Part-Dieu
See restaurant L'Arc-en-Ciel

12/20 A Ma Vigne
23, rue J.-Larrivé — 78.60.46.31
Mme Giraud. Closed Sun and Aug. Open until 9 pm. V.　　　　D5-74

This tiny, bustling restaurant offers the best chips in town, as well as delicious mussels, andouillette sausages, tripe, and a chocolate marquise. Côteaux-du-Lyonnais sold by the jug.

A la carte: 130-150 F.

LYON　　　　　　　　4th

Hôtel de Lyon Métropole
85, quai J.-Gillet — 78.29.20.20
Open every day. 30 stes 470-510 F. 119 rms 410-510 F. Restaurant. Half-board 410-510 F. TV. Air

cond. Conference facilities. Pool. Tennis. Garage parking. Telex 380198. V AE DC. A2-73

Large new building in a sports complex next to the Saône. The rooms are modern, tastefully furnished and spacious. Delectable breakfasts.

Le Bouchon de Fourvière
9, rue de la Quarantaine – 72.41.85.02
M. Borgeot. Closed Sat lunch, Sun dinner and 27 July-27 Aug. Open until 11 pm. Private room: 60. V AE. B5-76

Much in favour with local journalists, this bistro comprises three dining rooms in which to stoke up on scrambled eggs with wild mushrooms, calf's liver with parsley, generously served, delicious fresh pasta with basil, and a flawless lemon meringue pie. Typical, tasty, and not too expensive.

A la carte: 200 F. Menus: 60 F (weekdays lunch only), 90 F and 140 F (weekdays only).

LYON   5th

12/20 Comptoir du Bœuf
2, pl. Neuve-Saint-Jean
78.92.82.35
M. Chavent. Closed Sun. Open until midnight. Terrace dining. V. X3-9

Wine sold by the glass and a delightful terrace draw the crowds to this friendly annexe of La Tour Rose. The simply prepared dishes include tunny carpaccio and a seaweed salad, tomatoes stuffed with snails, and game pies.

A la carte: 200 F.

Cour des Loges
6, rue du Bœuf – 78.42.75.75
Open every day. 10 stes 1,900-2,900 F. 53 rms 1,000-1,500 F. Restaurant. TV. Air cond. Conference facilities. Heated pool. Valet parking. Telex 330831. V AE DC. X2-69

In the heart of the old town, Yves Boucharlat and Pierre Vurpas have created a masterpiece by combining four buildings from the fourteenth, seventeenth and eighteenth centuries into a 63-room hotel. The unique interior courtyard with its Florentine arcades and hanging gardens, the lounges, covered pool, contemporary paintings and lithographs, and tapas bar all contribute to a tasteful, harmonious whole. Natural light in the perfectly equipped rooms is somewhat diminished by the narrowness of the surrounding streets. Bar open until 2 am, gym, sauna, Jacuzzi.

12/20 Les Saisons
8, quai de Bondy – 78.28.47.55
Mme Hardy. Closed Sun, Mon, 24 Dec-3 Jan and 14 July-16 Aug. Open until 10 pm. Air cond. X1-64

Though the owner's West Indian origins account for some good, spicy specialities, people come here mainly for well-prepared Lyonnais dishes like the local hot sausage, and Beaujolais sold by the jug. Excellent reception.

A la carte: 180 F. Menus: 59 F, 79 F and 145 F (weekdays only).

La Tour Rose
22, rue du Bœuf – 78.37.25.90
M. Chavent. Closed 15 days in Aug. Open until 10.30 pm. Garden dining. Air cond. No-smoking section. Valet parking. V AE DC. X2-26

Philippe Chavent's La Tour Rose is now installed in a magnificently restored Renaissance convent, much sunnier than his former restaurant in a narrow street nearby. Were you to follow him up the slope to his herb garden you could take in a view of the whole building, with its monumental staircases and inner courtyards and a sea of old Lyon's red-tiled roofs beyond. The dining room in the former chapel is a showcase for the city's weaving industry, displaying fine silks and velvets. Nowadays Chavent masters his creative impulses better than in the past, and he concentrates on balancing flavours in each and every dish. The young vegetables in jelly scented with lemon leaves are fresh and tasty, and the skate served with a superb shallot-flavoured seaweed salad and oyster coulis offers a bouquet of savoury sensations. Equally subtle are the fresh pea cream soup with mushrooms, red-mullet fillets combined with hot duck foie gras and garlic-scented lentils, and roast pigeon stuffed with 'lardons de foie gras' in truffle juice—one of his best ideas ever. The cheeses are always a delight, and the strawberry gratin with almonds makes a perfect partner for the honey ice cream and warm madeleines. The glorious wines include Condrieu, Côte-Rôtie, Hermitage, and a delightfully fresh Viognier from the Domaine St-Estève. Now that work on his new restaurant is completed, we'd like to see Chavent renew his repertoire a little. Maybe he could slip in a cheaper menu at the same time?

A la carte: 500-700 F. Menus: 320 F, 420 F, 495 F.

La Maison de la Tour

(See restaurant above)
Open every day. 6 stes 1,500-2,200 F. 6 rms 950-1,200 F. TV. Air cond. Conference facilities.

In the heart of the old town, this hotel's delightful rooms and suites, all with terrace, are named after Lyonnais silk firms whose fabrics were used for the furnishings. Three hanging gardens contribute to the restful atmosphere.

LYON   6th

12/20 Jean-Pierre Bergier
20, rue Sully – 78.89.07.09
M. Bergier. Closed Sat lunch, Sun and 1-26 Aug. Open until 10 pm. Air cond. V AE DC. D2-77

Fortunately, Jean-Pierre Bergier has heeded our reviews and done away with his fussy, kiwi-with-everything cooking. The oysters gratinéed with spinach, and the baked calf's liver with raspberry vinegar were good, and the desserts are improving. The décor is rather dismal, and the reception could be warmer.

A la carte: 300 F. Menus: 110 F, 155 F, 230 F.

Cazenove
75, rue Boileau – 78.89.82.92
M. Orsi. Closed Sat, Sun and Aug. Open until 10 pm. Air cond. Telex 305965. V AE. E2-17

In the ten years since it opened, this annexe to Pierre Orsi's restaurant has become a smart spot, almost as expensive as Orsi itself. A distinguished clientele enjoys superior-quality bistro dishes like spinach salad with chicken livers, duck breast and green peppercorns, and roast young rabbit with thyme. Superb wines, all rather expensive.

A la carte: 350-400 F. Menus: 190 F (lunch only), 280 F.

Gervais
42, rue P.-Corneille – 78.52.19.13
M. Lescuyer. Closed Sat (except dinner off-season), Sun, holidays and July. Open until 10 pm. Private room: 20. Air cond. V AE DC. D3-51

Gervais Lescuyer's customers are as faithful as his cooking is consistent. The veal sweetbread salad, hot foie gras, stuffed turbot in Champagne, and scampi gratin continue to delight.

A la carte: 300-350 F. Menus: 130 F, 165 F.

Le Gourmandin
Gare des Brotteaux
14, pl. Jules-Ferry
78.52.02.52
M. Abattu. Closed Sun. Open until 10 pm. Private room: 30. Terrace dining. Air cond. Valet parking. V AE DC. F3-25

No sooner had work finished on converting this old railway station than Jean-Paul Lechevalier decided the undertaking was too large for his liking and left to open his own restaurant (Le Saint-Alban in the first arrondissement). The new chef, Frédéric Paquette, fresh from Alsace, prepares classic dishes like lobster lasagne with truffles, galette of young pigeon, and a petite nage de la mer (seafood poached with aromatics). Charles-André Charrier proposes a magnificent selection of wines and owner Daniel Abattu provides a businesslike reception. Superb terrace.

A la carte: 500 F and up. Menus: 189 F, 245 F, 395 F.

L'Helvétie
4, bd des Brotteaux — 78.24.38.18
M. Souvignet. Closed Sun and 24 Dec-3 Jan. Open until 11.30 pm. Terrace dining. V DC. F2-5

Through the popular ground-floor brasserie and up the stairs you'll find a good-value restaurant decorated with mirrors, pink walls, and potted plants. We recommend the 140 F set menu featuring quails in port sauce, and veal crépinette with watercress and superb fresh tagliatelle. Excellent shellfish is available too. Well-stocked wine cellar. A toque is deserved this year.

A la carte: 280-300 F. Menus: 140 F, 195 F, 260 F.

12/20 Le Jardin Romain
47, av. du Maréchal-Foch
78.89.58.73
M. Coret. Closed Sun and 11-31 Aug. Open until 11 pm. Terrace dining. V. D2-78

No pizzas are served within the stone walls of this authentic Italian restaurant featuring tomato salad with mozzarella, homemade lotte ravioli, and tiramisù. Italian wines and a warm welcome.

A la carte: 200 F. Menus: 98 F, 159 F.

Pierre Orsi
3, place Kléber
78.89.57.68
M. Orsi. Closed Sun dinner. Open until 9.30 pm. Private room: 60. Air cond. Valet parking. Telex 305965. V AE. E2-45

Pierre Orsi's restaurant now opening on to the Place Kléber, has been equipped with huge new kitchens, a superb terrace, and a dining room with a glass roof. The cooking remains highly conventional and impeccably prepared. Specialities include a generously served crab galette with a light lobster sauce, home-smoked salmon, crisp duck confit and slices of breast garnished with freshly made crisps, baked freshwater perch with potatoes à la Maxime, and an assortment of desserts based on crêpes, berries, and sorbets. Marie-Pierre Gauthier has taken competent charge of the cellar, and Geneviève Orsi provides the warmest of welcomes when her health permits.

A la carte: 450-500 F. Menus: 240 F and 350 F (weekdays only), 450 F.

Le Quatre Saisons
15, rue Sully — 78.93.76.07
M. Bertoli. Closed Sat lunch, Sun and 1-16 Aug. Open until 9.30 pm. Private room: 20. Air cond. V. D2-59

The restaurant's lovely flower-laden façade is most inviting, and once you're inside Lucien Bertoli, formerly maître d'hôtel for Paul Bocuse, will make you feel at home. The emphasis in the kitchen is on fine ingredients and consistent preparation. Try the hot foie gras, prawns sautéed with thyme, veal kidney baked in its fat, and marvellous little crêpes Suzette.

A la carte: 350-400 F. Menus: 170 F, 220 F, 290 F.

Le Restaurant des Gourmets
(Chez Luigi)
14, rue de Godefroy — 78.89.37.13
M. Ricci. Closed Sat lunch, Sun (except hols), 2-12 Jan, 5-25 Aug. Open until 10 pm. V AE DC. D2-19

Classic dishes, attentive service, and an intimate décor help to make this restaurant popular, and owner Luigi Ricci's personality does the rest. Stick to the good-value set menus offering lotte with foie gras, veal sweetbread feuilleté, and black-truffle soup.

A la carte: 350 F. Menus: 70 F (lunch only), 85 F, 135 F and 170 F (wine inc), 190 F, 260 F.

12/20 La Romanière
129, rue de Sèze — 78.24.23.42
M. Rossignol. Closed Wed dinner, Sun, 1 week in Feb, 15 days in Aug. Open until 10 pm. V AE. F2-36

This friendly, simply decorated restaurant in the heart of the Brotteaux district features honest and often imaginative dishes like hot crab turnover with mint, lotte and red mullet in Chiroubles sauce, and walnut tart with custard.

A la carte: 230 F. Menus: from 88 F to 168 F.

Le Roosevelt
25, rue Bossuet — 78.52.35.67
Open every day. 3 stes 453-566 F. 87 rms 333-466 F. TV. Air cond. Conference facilities. Garage parking. Telex 300295. V AE DC. E3-23

A modern, neat hotel offering many amenities for business travellers. Efficient room service and good conference facilities.

La Soupière
14, rue Molière — 78.52.75.34
M. Peyrard. Closed Sun, Mon and Aug. Open until 10 pm. Private room: 20. Air cond. V. D3-58

On our last visit to this restaurant, the prices had increased dramatically, the reception was indifferent, the service inept and pretentious, and the cuisine hastily prepared. We hope all this was exceptional, and maintain our rating in view of the fond memories we have of this restaurant. But they have been warned.

A la carte: 350 F. Menus: 170 F, 220 F, 350 F.

LYON **7th**

Le Fédora
249, rue M.-Mérieux
78.69.46.26
M. Judéaux. Closed Sat lunch, Sun and 22 Dec-3 Jan. Open until 10 pm. Private room: 20. Garden dining. Air cond. V AE DC. D7-30

The Judéaux family concentrates on providing superior seafood at reasonable prices in this rather drab office district. Daniel Judéaux offers a wonderful buffet at 120 F and a generous set menu for 160 F. Or order the lobster and bone marrow, cinnamon-scented red mullet, white truffle salad

with a perfectly seasoned tunny tartare, or brill with chanterelles, available à la carte. Excellent desserts and superb white wines.
A la carte: 400 F. Menus: 160 F, 240 F.

🏨 Mercure Pont-Pasteur
70, av. Leclerc — 78.58.68.53
Open every day. 194 rms 315-550 F. Restaurant. TV. Air cond. Conference facilities. Heated pool. Garage parking. Telex 305484. V AE DC.　　　　C7-31
Near the confluence of the Rhône and the Saône, this modern hotel offers comfortable rooms with double glazing. Good conference facilities. Boat trips are available.

LYON　　　　　　　　8th

🏨 Altea Park Hôtel
4, rue du Pr-Calmette — 78.74.11.20
Open every day. 1 ste 530 F. 72 rms 340-380 F. Restaurant. TV. Conference facilities. Garage parking. Telex 380230. V AE DC.　　　　G7-7
This huge hotel has newly renovated rooms and pleasant lounges. Meals served on the terrace in summer.

12/20 Auberge Savoyarde
72, av. des Frères-Lumière
78.00.77.64
M. Blache. Closed Sun. Open until 9.15 pm. Private room: 40. Air cond. No pets. V AE DC.　　　G7-28
Copious, well-crafted dishes served in a simple, country-style décor. We enjoyed the sweetbread terrine, pike soufflé, and duck confit. Cheese fondues and raclettes are available as well.
A la carte: 200 F. Menus: 80 F and 95 F (weekdays dinner only), 110 F (weekdays lunch only).

🏠 Laennec
36, rue Seignemartin — 78.74.55.22
Open every day. 14 rms 250-340 F. TV. Garage parking. V.　　　　G7-7
A fine little hotel in a quiet district. Meals on trays.

LYON　　　　　　　　9th

12/20 Auberge de l'Ile
Ile Barbe — 78.83.99.49
M. Ansanay-Alex. Closed Sun dinner, Mon and Feb school holidays. Open until 9.30 pm. Private room: 30. No pets. Parking. V.　　　A1-79
Quite costly, but ideal for family outings. In a cosy setting of stone, beams, and copperware, the chef offers personalised dishes like boned frogs' legs in a chive cream sauce, veal sweetbreads braised with gentian liqueur, and dried apricot soufflé with bilberry coulis.
A la carte: 350 F. Menus: 130 F, 210 F, 270 F.

In nearby Caluire
(5 km N on D 48)
69300 Lyon — (Rhône)

🍴 Auberge de Fond-Rose
23, quai Clemenceau — 78.29.34.61
M. Brunet. Closed Mon off-season and Sun dinner. Open until 9.30 pm. Private room: 30. Terrace dining. Parking. V AE DC.
Christophe Brunet has joined his father Michel in the kitchen of their restaurant, nestled in a pleasant garden alongside the Saône. We're hoping this will mean some new dishes to join the sea bream with capers and lime, young pigeon with garlic and

artichokes, and larded fillet of lamb en croûte. Efficient service.
A la carte: 350 F. Menus: 190 F (weekdays lunch only), and 240 F to 420 F.

In nearby Champagne-au-Mont-d'Or
(9 km N)
69410 Lyon — (Rhône)

🍴 Les Grillons
18, rue D.-Vincent — 78.35.04.78
M. Duthion. Closed Sun dinner and Mon. Annual closings not available. Open until 9.30 pm. Private room: 48. Garden dining. V AE DC.
Smiling is not the staff's strong point, but this restaurant is delightful in summer when the tables are set up in the garden. Fernand Duthion's expensive but well-crafted dishes include poultry and artichoke terrine with duck foie gras, freshwater perch in lentil cream sauce with mirabelle plums, and stuffed saddle of lamb. The cheapest menu, available on weekdays only, offers plaice with red chicory, kidneys with mustard, cheese, and dessert.
A la carte: 380-400 F. Menus: 135 F (weekdays only), 185 F, 245 F, 325 F.

In nearby Collonges-au-Mont-d'Or
(9 km N on N 51)
69660 Lyon — (Rhône)

🍴 Paul Bocuse
50, quai de la Plage
78.22.01.40
M. Bocuse. Open every day. Open until 9.45 pm. Private room: 50. Air cond. Telex 375382. V AE DC.
Recently named 'chef of the century' (along with two others, to his great indignation), Paul Bocuse continues his travels and business ventures, leaving his restaurant in the capable hands of Roger Jaloux and Christian Bouvarel (in the kitchen) and Jean Fleury (reception and service). Their task is to perpetuate the Bocuse legend without too many excursions into individual creativity. So fine ingredients are still the point of departure, and certain dishes, like the famous black-truffle soup with a pastry crust which Bocuse prepared for Valéry Giscard d'Estaing when he was president, are fixtures of the *carte*. Just as delicious are the green bean and artichoke salad with foie gras, asparagus and frogs' leg soup garnished with watercress, and fillet of sole flavoured with coriander and vanilla-scented butter. And it's worth taking a day trip by TGV to taste the Bresse chicken, cooked either en vessie à la sauce fleurette, or spit-roasted over a wood fire. Mère Richard provides the wonderful cheeses, and the superb desserts include a crème brûlée à la cassonade, chocolate mousse with œufs à la neige, and lovely heart-shaped waffles. The excellent selection of Beaujolais, Burgundy, and Bordeaux wines is the domain of the excellent sommelier, Yann Eon. What we admire most about Bocuse is his remarkable consistency, faithful to his inimitable style 365 days a year.
A la carte: 550-800 F. Menus: 390 F (weekdays lunch only), 570 F, 630 F, 660 F.

🏨 Mapotel Lyon Nord
Aire de la Porte-de-Lyon — 78.35.70.20
Open every day. 3 stes 975-1,015 F. 100 rms 375-415 F. Restaurant. Half-board 505-565 F. TV. Air cond. Conference facilities. Heated pool. Parking. Telex 900006. V AE DC.
This hotel offers simple, comfortable, and recently renovated rooms. Amenities include a

INDEX OF LYON RESTAURANTS AND HOTELS

> *Red toques signify modern cuisine; black toques signify traditional cuisine.*

fitness centre, solarium, sauna, French billiards, and conference facilities.

Le Panorama
Pl. du Gal-Brosset — 78.47.40.19
M. Léron. Closed Sun dinner, Mon, Feb and 18-30 Aug. Open until 10 pm. Private room: 30. Terrace dining. V AE DC.

The new owners of this fine Beaujolais restaurant 'with Alpine views in clear weather' are Denise and Daniel Léron. Market-fresh produce is the highlight of Daniel's cooking, though he has a slight tendency to over-sauce dishes. Try his duck carpaccio in raspberry vinegar served with warm foie gras, and sole with crayfish and mushrooms. A fine cheese board follows, and there are impressive wines to drink with it, like a robust 1988 Gigondas.

A la carte: 350 F. Menus: 168 F, 248 F, 360 F.

In nearby **Mionnay**

(19 km N on N 83)
01390 Lyon — (Rhône)

Alain Chapel
N 83
78.91.82.02
19.5
Mme Chapel. Closed Tue lunch and Mon (except holidays), and Jan. Open until 10 pm. Private room: 40. Garden dining. Valet parking. Telex 305605. V AE DC.

A few months ago, at the height of his powers, the retiring, warm, and generous master chef Alain Chapel was struck down by a heart attack. He had just begun an ambitious renovation programme of his old family-style *auberge*, including a shady park, swimming pool, and arcaded car park. The loss sent shock waves through the culinary community.

Courageously, his wife Suzanne, supported by his faithful and skilful team, decided to carry on his work, following the master's principles. His right-hand man, Maurice Lacharme, still produces flawless dishes. Should he decide to move on, Philippe Jousse, the next in line, and utterly devoted to Chapel's cooking, will take over. In any case, the prodigiously talented pastry chef Jean Audouze, a 30-year veteran, will remain, as will Hervé Duronzier, the supremely civil maître d'hôtel, and Pierre Eguizabal, the witty and charming sommelier who presides over the fabulous wine cellar.

No one can say what the future holds for Alain Chapel without Alain Chapel. But this year, in homage to the man, his team, and his life's work, we stick by our rating of four toques and 19.5 points.

A la carte: 600 F and up. Menus: 600 F, 750 F.

Alain Chapel
(See restaurant above)
Closed Mon (except holidays) and Jan. 13 rms 675-800 F. TV.

If respected, Alain Chapel's original plan to add luxurious new rooms and suites, and create a park and swimming pool, should be finished by summer 1991. In the meantime, the hotel offers thirteen comfortable rooms. Admirable breakfasts. Relais et Châteaux.

> *Remember to reserve your table or your room in advance, and please let the restaurant or hotel know if you cannot honour your reservation.*

In nearby **La Mulatière**

(SW)
69350 Lyon (Rhône)

Roger Roucou
(La Mère Guy)
35, quai J.-J.-Rousseau — 78.51.65.37
M. Roucou. Closed Sun dinner, Mon and Aug. Open until 9.30 pm. Private room: 200. Terrace dining. Air cond. Parking. Telex 310241. V AE DC.

The nostalgic few who remember those delightful days when Lyon was the unrivalled capital of French gastronomy may confidently make their pilgrimage to La Mulatière. For today, Roger Roucou's restaurant on the banks of the Saône, glowing with grand chandeliers, carries on the tradition. That doesn't mean the cooking is fusty, or smothered under leaden sauces. Roucou's credo calls above all for the freshest ingredients. He transforms them into marvellously light dishes, such as scallop salad with sherry vinegar, redolent with the aroma of truffles, and peerless lobster gratin cooked with port. Not to mention the perennial sole soufflée Escoffier, tournedos Cendrillon (with artichoke hearts and foie gras—make sure you eat it before midnight!), and, for dessert, soufflé glacé au Grand Marnier. The wine cellar is superb, the sommelier a true professional. Jacqueline, Roucou's daughter, provides the pleasantly dignified welcome. She plans to open a luxury hotel soon. That would be welcome indeed in Lyon.

A la carte: 400-600 F. Menus: 250 F, 320 F, 400 F.

In nearby **Rillieux-la-Pape**

(7 km N on N 83 and N 84)
69140 Lyon   (Rhône)

Larivoire
on the Rhône shore, ch. des Iles
78.88.50.92
M. Constantin. Closed Mon dinner, Tue, 1-25 Feb and 1-7 Sep. Open until 10 pm. Private room: 60. Garden dining. Garage parking. V.

The rose-coloured décor is luxurious yet weightlessly elegant. Reflected in the mirrors you'll see the contented countenances of countless food-lovers, who've been flocking here for decades—for generations even. The throng has swollen under chef Bernard Constantin—the third to bear that proud name since 1904—whose stewardship has made Larivoire one of the great gastronomic establishments of the region. A highly imaginative and skilful all-rounder, Constantin III has won an admiring public with his constantly changing *carte*. Never a slip, even in summer, when the fine weather fills the lovely terrace with hordes clamouring for foie gras sautéed with orange and rhubarb, scallops with coriander and fried celery, grilled pageot (a Mediterranean fish) with tiny shrimps and bacon, veal sweetbreads in artichoke butter with black olives and hazelnuts, followed by tasty cheeses and desserts like the chocolate mousse with candied oranges. The fine Beaujolais and Côtes-du-Rhônes are the domain of learned sommelier Arnaud Chambost.

A la carte: 350-400 F. Menus: 190 F, 300 F, 380 F.

In nearby **Villeurbanne**

(NE)
69100 Lyon — (Rhône)

Hôtel des Congrès
Pl. du Cdt-Rivière — 78.89.81.10
Open every day. 2 stes 660 F. 136 rms 325-355 F. Restaurant. Half-board 475 F. TV. Air cond. Confer-

ence facilities. Garage parking. Telex 370216. V AE DC.

Near Lyon Part-Dieu railway station and the Tête d'Or park, this fine modern hotel has well-equipped meeting rooms and an American bar.

See also: **Vonnas (Georges Blanc)**

LYONS-LA-FORÊT

27480 Lyons-la-Forêt — (Eure)
Paris 107 - Rouen 36 - Les Andelys 20

Le Grand Cerf
Place du Marché
32.49.60.44

M. Colignon. Closed Tue, Wed and 15 Jan-18 Feb. Open until 9.30 pm. Hotel: 8 rms 250-300 F, half-board oblig in seas. V AE DC.

Philippe Colignon, a dedicated professional and lover of fine ingredients, is no quack: he has just been named *maître canardier* (master duck chef). His best dish is pressed duck rouennaise, but the Atlantic fish stew and magnificent steamed fish are also well worth trying. Colignon makes everything himself, from the delicious bread to the ambrosial ice cream.

A la carte: 300 F. Menu: 150 F.

In nearby Rosay-sur-Lieure

(6 km SW on D 321)
27790 Lyons-la-Forêt — (Eure)

Château de Rosay
32.49.66.51

Open every day. 3 stes 550-600 F. 23 rms 250-500 F. Conference facilities. Heated pool. Valet parking.

This elegant Louis XIII château rises up from the heart of the forest. The rooms are spacious, the suites handsome. Guests may fish in a stream on the property. Catering service available for conferences.

MACINAGGIO

See CORSICA

MÂCON

71000 Mâcon — (Saône/Loire)
Paris 395 - Lyon 68 - Bourg 34 - Chalon-sur-S. 58

Laurent Couturier
70, rue de Lyon
85.38.16.16

M. Couturier. Closed Sat lunch, Sun, 1-9 Jan and Aug. Open until 9 pm. Private room: 25. V.

We've had a revelation of sorts. True, we had a foretaste of Laurent Couturier's talents last year, when we discovered his pleasantly modern restaurant in a sombre suburb, tucked away between the railway line and a supermarket. But we certainly didn't expect him to zip from 12/20 skywards, wearing two toques! And there's no reason to believe he won't continue climbing. His abilities are manifest in the diced foie gras and red mullet served with a celery pancake on a bed of chopped fresh herbs, luscious lobster with rosemary, venison with pine-nuts and raisins, and imaginative desserts such as gingerbread bavarois with crème caramel, or feuillantine with bitter chocolate and vanilla sauce. As might be expected in a new establishment, the cellar is not too well stocked yet. But what magnificently low prices! Let's hope success doesn't send them skywards too.

A la carte: 300 F. Menus: 95 F (weekdays only), 145 F, 185 F, 275 F.

Mercure
Aire de St-Albain
71260 Saint-Albain — 85.33.19.00

Open every day. 3 stes 900 F. 98 rms 340-490 F. Restaurant. TV. Air cond. Conference facilities. Heated pool. Garage parking. Telex 800881. V AE DC.

Just off a motorway rest area, the Mercure is hidden by greenery. The hotel is modern and graceless, but the rooms are handsome, spacious and functional. Good conference facilities.

12/20 Au Rocher de Cancale
393, quai J.-Jaurès — 85.38.07.50

M. Mabon. Closed Sat lunch, Sun dinner, Mon, Feb school holidays, 10 June-1 July and 25 Nov-2 Dec. Open until 9.30 pm. Air cond. V AE DC.

This sleepy, but worthy restaurant sits above the noisy road that follows the Saône. The first-floor dining room overlooks the river; it is here that food-loving locals savour the terrines, pike mousseline, and chicken grilled with herbs. Excellent Mâcon wines.

A la carte: 250-300 F. Menus: 90 F, 145 F, 195 F.

In nearby la Croix-Blanche

(14 km W on N 79)
71960 Mâcon — (Saône/Loire)

Le Relais du Mâconnais
85.36.60.72

M. Lannuel. Closed off-season Sun dinner and Mon, and 5 Jan-5 Feb. Open until 9 pm. Terrace dining. Hotel: 12 rms 145-250 F. Tennis. Parking. V AE DC.

Don't be put off by the outside of this reconverted filling station. The dining room is cheery and full of flowers, the welcome warm. Christian Lannuel's honest cooking demonstrates his great skill, and his flair for flavourful marriages: perfectly seasoned and startlingly fresh prawn salad with (unneeded) rounds of polenta, Bresse chicken with snails in succulently thick juices, and a tasty, imaginative banana and chicory cake. A second toque is on the horizon.

A la carte: 350 F. Menus: 115 F (weekdays only), 180 F, 230 F, 320 F.

In nearby Replonges

(4 km E Mâcon)
01750 Mâcon — (Saône/Loire)

La Huchette
on N 79
85.31.03.55

Closings not available. 1 ste 850 F. 14 rms 300-600 F. TV. Heated pool. Parking. Telex 800787. V AE DC.

The spacious, well-equipped, rustic rooms are very attractive. Excellent service.

See also: **Vonnas (Georges Blanc)**

MADIRAN

65700 Madiran — (H.-Pyrénées)
Paris 700 - Tarbes 39 - Maubourguet 13

Le Prieuré
62.31.92.50

M. Cuenot. Closed Sun dinner and Mon. Annual closings not available. Open until 9 pm. Garden dining. Parking. V AE DC.

This tastefully renovated priory is an excellent place for a restful meal. The white-and-grey dining room, exposed timbers, and stone walls are a fine backdrop for Michel Cuenot's precise cooking, which follows the seasons with care. His quail pâté with Armagnac, warm asparagus with two sauces, and pheasant with green cabbage are very good indeed. And if he were a bit bolder, he could go on to greater things. Divine desserts (flaky apple pie), good selection of regional wines. Warm welcome, competent service.

A la carte: 250 F. Menus: 80 F (weekdays only), 115 F, 150 F, 250 F.

▲▲ Le Prieuré

(See restaurant above)

Closed off-season Sun and Mon. Annual closings not available. 10 rms 230-270 F. Half-board 325 F. TV. Conference facilities.

Far from prying eyes, the priory's former cells have been transformed into very comfortable, well-equipped rooms. Ideal for rest and relaxation. Copious breakfasts.

MAGESCQ

40140 Magescq — (Landes)
Paris 698 - Soustons 10 - Bayonne 42 - Castets 12

Relais de la Poste

58.47.70.25

MM. Coussau. Closed Mon dinner and Tue (except July-Aug), and 12 Nov-24 Dec. Open until 9.30 pm. Private room: 30. Air cond. Garage parking. Telex 571349. V AE DC.

The festival of regional favourites continues year-round at the Coussaus' old coaching inn, now a chic restaurant-hotel with modernised rooms and décor. The strongest suit here: cèpes, truffles, foie gras, confit, and game. Young vegetables provide the back-up (Magescq asparagus is available in season). And the 240 F menu of duck specialities is alone worth a detour (off the N 10 between Dax and the sea). Try also the fillet of turbot stuffed with leeks, lamb sweetbreads braised with wild mushrooms, and caramelised pear feuillantine with whipped cream. Young sommelier Jacques Coussau will find you the perfect wine (avoid the exceptional Armagnacs, unless you don't mind spending a fortune). The reasonable prices—given the quality—will help you forgive the rare slip of the chef's hand.

A la carte: 400 F. Menus: 350 F (lunch w-e and holidays only), 260 F.

▲▲ Relais de la Poste

(See restaurant above)

Closed Mon and Tue (except July-Aug), and 12 Nov-24 Dec. 2 stes 700-800 F. 12 rms 480-550 F. TV 10 rms. No pets. Conference facilities. Heated pool. Tennis.

This huge, peaceful inn gives onto a park and pine forest. All rooms have been thoroughly refurbished recently.

MAGNY-COURS

58470 Magny-Cours — (Nièvre)
Paris 251 - Moulins 42 - Nevers 12 - Bourges 80

La Renaissance

former N 7 — 86.58.10.40

M. Dray. Closed Sun dinner, Mon, end Jan-beg March and first weeks of July. Open until 9.30 pm. Private room: 35. Air cond. Garage parking. V AE.

The opulence of this roadside restaurant has been toned down of late, with a new, light, and sunny décor, and a more spacious dining room. More good news: Michel Dray's enticing repertoire boasts several new dishes (duck foie gras with pineapple preserve, veal sweetbreads baked with artichokes and oranges). And the old favourites are so well prepared, with such top-quality in-

gredients, that we wouldn't dream of criticising them: lobster and foie gras buisson, chicken breast with morel mushroom sauce, or Charollais beef with bone marrow. Berthe Dray manages the dining room with tireless efficiency. Varied, reliable wines.

A la carte: 600 F and up. Menus: 200 F, 280 F, 350 F, 430 F.

▲▲ La Renaissance

(See restaurant above)

Closed Sun, Mon, end Jan-beg March and first week of July. 3 stes 500-700 F. 8 rms 300-450 F. TV 9 rms. Conference facilities.

The country inn *par excellence*, La Renaissance offers quiet, smartly decorated rooms. Exceptionally good breakfasts, served on the terrace in summer.

MAILLANE

See Saint-Rémy-de-Provence

MAISONS-LAFFITTE

See PARIS Suburbs

MALÈNE (LA)

48210 Malène (La) — (Lozère)
Paris 619 - Mende 42 - Florac 41 - Millau 42

▲▲ Château de la Caze

5.5 km on D 907 bis — 66.48.51.01

Open every day. 7 stes 790-950 F. 20 rms 480-740 F. Restaurant. Half-board 600-790 F. TV. Parking. V AE DC.

Set at the foot of the Sauveterre cliffs, this fairytale château has comfortable, adequately equipped rooms whose décor is rather more nineteenth-century than medieval (the Louis-Philippe beds aren't king size, either!). Some suites are located in 'La Ferme', overlooking meadows sloping down towards the River Tarn.

MALLEMORT-PONT-ROYAL

13370 Mallemort-Pont-Royal — (B./Rhône)
Paris 721 - Avignon 43 - Salon-de-Provence 8

12/20 Moulin de Vernègues

N 7, Sénas exit on motorway — 90.59.12.00

M. Ventre. Open every day. Open until 9.45 pm. Private room: 300. Garden dining. Valet parking. Telex 401645. V AE DC.

Pheasant, wild boar, and partridge shot on the 500-hectare estate make their appearance on the *carte* during the season, alongside shellfish lasagne, spiced veal kidneys, and a cake made with three kinds of chocolate. Marvellous terrace, spectacular dining room. Professional service.

A la carte: 400-500 F. Menus: 300 F, 340 F.

▲ Moulin de Vernègues

(See restaurant above)

Open every day. 34 rms 700-1,100 F. Half-board 800-1,000 F. TV. Conference facilities. Heated pool. Tennis.

This handsome old coaching inn has been luxuriously remodelled, and offers attractive rooms, superb salons, and a pretty park. A golf course is scheduled to open in June. Dogs allowed. Clay pigeon shooting and hunting expeditions organised.

MALNOUE

See PARIS Suburbs

06210 Mandelieu — (Alpes-Mar.)
Paris 850 - Cannes 8 - Nice 38 - La Napoule 2

La Cuisine d'Antan
Le Suffren, entrance G
Cannes Marina — 93.49.50.48
Mlle Tilmant. Closed Sun dinner and Mon. Annual closings not available. Open until 9 pm. Pool. Parking. V.
The unusual welcoming committee of this pleasant little restaurant is headed by two vivacious ladies and their dog Nancy. The family dishes are made from top-quality ingredients: three different terrines with homemade pickles, good *plats du jour* (calf's head, navarin d'agneau), and a dark, creamy, chocolate mousse. Short, well-balanced wine list.
A la carte: 220-240 F. Menus: 65 F (weekdays lunch only), 85 F, 135 F, 165 F.

Domaine d'Olival
778, av. de la Mer — 93.49.31.00
Closed 30 Oct-15 Jan. 10 stes 665-1,750 F. 8 rms 425-900 F. TV. Air cond. Conference facilities. Pool. Tennis. Parking. Telex 460000. V AE DC.
On the banks of the Siagne, this handsome hotel-residence is just a few hundred yards from the Mandelieu golf course. The comfortable, pleasantly decorated rooms and suites are furnished with antiques and have fully equipped, large kitchens. Very fine breakfasts. Catering service on request. Boat berths.

Hostellerie du Golf
780, bd de la Mer — 93.49.11.66
Open every day. 16 stes 550-780 F. 39 rms 300-590 F. Restaurant. Half-board 400-830 F. TV. Conference facilities. Pool. Tennis. Parking. Telex 470948. V AE DC.
The golfing greens spread beyond the trees that surround this large, single-storey hotel built in the neo-Provençal style. The spacious rooms are decorated with pretty fabrics and modern furnishings. Each has a loggia.

Plaza
308, av. de Cannes — 93.49.41.03
Closed 21 Dec-15 Jan. 51 rms 240-350 F. TV. Air cond 10 rms. Parking. Telex 461592. V.
Modern, smart, and unpretentious, the Plaza's frequently refurbished rooms are soundproofed. Hydrotherapy. Snacks served in your room or on the terrace.

See also: **Cannes, La Napoule**

04100 Manosque — (Alpes/H.-P.)
Paris 767 - Aix-en-P. 53 - Digne 57 - Sisteron 52

Hostellerie de la Fuste
92.72.05.95
M. Jourdan. Closed off-season Sun dinner and Mon (except holidays), and 3-18 Jan. Open until 9.30 pm. Private room: 40. Garden dining. Air cond. Garage parking. V AE DC.
Daniel Jourdan made a wise move when he decided to redecorate this old *auberge*. Work is continuing, but the improvement is already remarkable. Jourdan deserves a setting worthy of his delightful, supremely authentic Provençal cooking. His secret: he nips out to his kitchen garden to pluck the freshest herbs and vegetables, which he combines with other carefully chosen local ingredients to create highly flavourful dishes.

Sample the stuffed baby vegetables served with pistou (basil pounded with garlic and olive oil), young rabbit in jelly with spiced vegetables, or cervelle d'agneau on a bed of freshly dug potatoes with a garlicky anchovy jus. There's just the occasional lapse, like the bland stuffed lamb, reprieved by an exquisite gratin dauphinois. Enjoy them to the full before the merciless bill brings you down to earth.
A la carte: 500-550 F. Menus: from 230 F to 390 F.

Hostellerie de la Fuste
(See restaurant above)
Closed off-season Sun and Mon (except holidays), and 3-18 Jan. 3 stes 850 F. 9 rms 500-750 F. Half-board 620-780 F. TV. Air cond 4 rms. Conference facilities. Heated pool.
This attractive *bastide* has comfortable, spacious rooms. The reception is excellent. Fine covered swimming pool. Outstanding breakfasts.

(14 km N on N 96 and D 13)
04300 Manosque — (Alpes/H.-P.)

Le Bois d'Asson
D 13, rte de Forcalquier — 92.79.51.20
M. Michel. Closed Tue, 15 Feb-15 March and 30 Aug-8 Sep. Open until 9.30 pm. Garden dining. Parking. V AE.
Chef Robert Michel works by inspiration, and there's no predicting when that elusive quality will be present in his cooking. He prepares foie gras like nobody else, and his meat dishes (ox jowls in red wine, agneau à l'orientale, rib steak with Châteauneuf-du-Pape and bone marrow) can be excellent. The reception also works by inspiration. Fresh, simple décor.
A la carte: 300 F and up. Menus: 130 F (weekdays only), 180 F, 275 F.

72000 Mans (Le) — (Sarthe)
Paris 216 - Rennes 145 - Tours 81 - Angers 88

Arcade
40, rue du Vert-Galant — 43.24.47.24
Open every day. 95 rms 275-300 F. Restaurant. Half-board 377-400 F. TV. Air cond. Conference facilities. Garage parking. Telex 722967. V.
This five-storey modern hotel sits on the banks of the Sarthe, five minutes from the town centre. The smallish rooms (those on the upper floors are roomier) overlook the embankment or a courtyard. Bar.

11/20 Auberge du Pont Rouge
Ch. des Perrays — 43.85.05.87
M. Robin. Closed Sat lunch, Sun and holidays, 24 July-25 Aug and 23 Dec-6 Jan. Open until 9 pm. Air cond. No pets. V
A la carte: 300 F.
Set between two forks of the Sarthe River, this former tram station is steeped in nostalgia. The cooking is tasty and simple: duck breast with garlic butter, fresh sea bass au beurre blanc. Friendly service. The son of the household looks after the wines. Stiff prices.
A la carte: 250 F. Menus: 92 F (weekdays only), 165 F (wine inc), 180 F, 235 F, 270 F.

Central Hôtel
5, bd R.-Levasseur — 43.24.08.93
Open every day. 37 rms 160-300 F. Restaurant. TV. Conference facilities. Telex 722878. V AE.
The comfortable rooms with period furniture overlook a quiet courtyard. Wine bar. Sauna and weightlifting facilities.

Chantecler
50, rue de la Pelouse — 43.24.58.53
Open every day. 3 stes 360-470 F. 32 rms 230-280 F. Restaurant. Half-board 220-320 F. TV. Parking. Telex 722941. V.
Centrally located near the station, this recently redecorated hotel has double glazing. A veranda has been added. Pleasant welcome.

12/20 La Ciboulette
14, rue de la Vieille-Porte — 43.24.65.67
M. Desmats. Closed Sat, Sun, 1-5 Jan and 1-26 Aug. Open until 10.30 pm. V AE.
Near the Place de l'Eperon, the Ciboulette's charming, bistro-style dining room is a late-night favourite. The proprietors are eager to please, and manage marvellously with well-prepared fish dishes (sea bass with sweet peppers and olives, tartare de lotte aux aromates, John Dory with oysters). Rather expensive wines. The service could be looser.
A la carte: 280 F. Menu: 140 F.

12/20 Concorde
16, av. du Gal-Leclerc — 43.24.12.30
Mme Batifoulier. Open every day. Open until 10 pm. Private room: 200. Terrace dining. Garage parking. Telex 720487. V AE DC.
Chandeliers, Louis XVI chairs, and staff standing to attention set the tone of the dining room. Though the cooking is skilful, it too can give itself airs: fillet of sole with a tomato mould, veal roll with Parma ham and Roquefort sauce. Excellent desserts.
A la carte: 300 F and up. Menus: 130 F, 200 F.

Concorde
(See restaurant above)
Open every day. 68 rms 180-515 F. Half-board 305-425 F. TV. Conference facilities.
Halfway between the station and the historic centre of town, the Concorde has handsome, well-restored rooms, and a pleasant courtyard. Ask about the special rates.

La Feuillantine
19 bis, rue Foisy — 43.28.00.38
M. Adam. Closed Sat lunch, Sun, 22 Dec-2 Jan and 30 March-7 April. Open until 10 pm. V.
Huge mirrors, mosaics, and potted plants give this restaurant a 1930s feel. The cooking is classic and full of good intentions, but suffers an occasional slip (watch the toque!). Try the oysters with Champagne sabayon sauce, grilled salmon with fresh spinach, and poached pear with caramel. Wide choice of wines. Brisk service.
A la carte: 250-300 F. Menus: 68 F and 88 F (weekdays only), 290 F (wine inc), 135 F.

12/20 Le Flambadou
14 bis, rue St-Flaceau — 43.24.88.38
M. Jouy. Closed Sun, Easter week and 15 Aug. Open until 10.30 pm. V DC.
Patrick Jouy has migrated to this discreet restaurant in old Le Mans from his native Landes, bringing with him sunny specialities such as foie gras terrine, pot-au-feu with chicken leg confit, cassoulet,

magret aux fruits rouges, and other delights from the South-west. The cellar has many fine wines from Pécharmant, Bergerac, and Cahors.
A la carte: 250 F.

Green 7
447, av. G.-Durand — 43.85.05.73
Open every day. 40 rms 250 F. Restaurant. Half-board 235-345 F. TV. Parking. Telex 711948. V AE.
A former hunting lodge, this American-style, modernised hotel is near the race track. Well-equipped rooms painted in bold colours. English breakfasts. Slightly hesitant service.

Le Grenier à Sel
26, pl. de l'Eperon — 43.23.26.30
M. Godefroy. Closed Sun, Mon, Feb school holidays and 1-21 Aug. Open until 10 pm. Air cond. V.
This former salt storehouse makes a handsome restaurant. Recently remodelled, it has an elegant, flower-filled décor, and widely spaced tables set under a mirrored ceiling. The cooking is a medley of chic and rustic (good salade landaise, excellent baked prawns, hearty tête de veau). The only thing missing is a bit of verve, a better wine cellar, and more rigour when seasoning dishes. This is still the best restaurant in the centre of town. Prices are rising, but slowly.
A la carte: 280-300 F. Menus: 110 F (weekdays only), 170 F, 240 F.

Moderne
14, rue du Bourg-Belé — 43.24.79.20
Open every day. 32 rms 157-302 F. Restaurant. Half-board 256-362 F. TV 17 rms. Conference facilities. Parking. Telex 722113. V AE DC.
A good hotel in the centre, the Moderne has comfortable, well-kept rooms.

Novotel Le Mans
Bd R.-Schumann — 43.85.26.80
Open every day. 94 rms 365-440 F. Restaurant. Half-board 510-550 F. TV. Conference facilities. Pool. Parking. Telex 720706. V AE DC.
This fine, modern hotel located near a sports ground has huge rooms and good conference facilities.

In nearby **Arnage**
(9 km SE on D 147 and N 23)
72230 Mans (Le) — (Sarthe)

Auberge des Matfeux
(500 m near the village)
by D 147 then N 23 — 43.21.10.71
M. Souffront. Closed Mon, dinner Sun and holidays, Jan and 15-27 July. Open until 9 pm. Private room: 45. Parking. V AE DC.
The Le Mans race track seems a million miles away from this grand old restaurant surrounded by pine trees. Chef Alain Souffront, assisted by his son Xavier and another young cook, presides over the modern interpretation of classic dishes made from quality ingredients. He learned the trade by the inside route—what he calls 'industrial espionage', that is, eating out often *chez* the greats and learning via the palate. The tasty results include Stroganoff with vegetable pot-au-feu, saddle of young rabbit stuffed with veal sweetbreads and morels, and boned pigeon flavoured with foie gras. Rather ostentatious décor, which a touch of simplicity wouldn't hurt. The same goes for the service.
A la carte: 350 F. Menus: 198 F (w-e and holidays only), 248 F and 325 F (wine inc), 98 F, 158 F, 275 F, 315 F.

Campanile
Bd P.-Lefaucheux — 43.21.81.21
Open every day. 43 rms 239 F. Restaurant. Half-board 198-298 F. TV. Conference facilities. Parking. Telex 722803. V.
This is a good, modern, functional chain hotel with could-be-anywhere décor, set on the edge of a lake.

In nearby Changé
(7 km E on N 223)
72560 Mans (Le) — (Sarthe)

Le Cheval Blanc
25, pl. de l'Eglise — 43.40.02.62
M. Bonneville. Closed Wed, dinner Tue and Sun, Feb school holidays and 29 July-26 Aug. Open until 9 pm. Private room: 30. V AE.
This charming village hostelry with its unpromising façade stands on the church square. Chantal Bonneville and her husband Patrick, the chef, late of Maître Corbeau (in Paris), have feathered their nest with a comfortable, elegant rusticity that fits the cooking to a T. Patrick is an old hand with fish and shellfish, and a wine expert to boot (excellent Bordeaux). A steadier hand with the seasonings and all would be perfect. Try the delicious caramel cake.
A la carte: 250-280 F. Menus: 205 F (wine inc), 125 F, 175 F.

MARÇAY
See Chinon

MARCQ-EN-BARŒUL
See Lille

MARGAUX
33460 Margaux — (Gironde)
Paris 598 - Bordeaux 22 - Lesparre-Médoc 20

Le Relais de Margaux
Ch. de l'Ile-Vincent — 56.88.38.30
M. Reymond. Closed 21 Dec-31 Jan. Open until 10.15 pm. Private room: 30. Garden dining. No pets. Valet parking. Telex 572530. V AE DC.
Peace, luxury, and good taste overflow from this former wine cellar. The tables are laid before a grand terrace. The service is equally grand (rather starchy, really). And what of the boggling array of bottlings and half-bottles, at even more boggling prices! The cooking is improving: fresh oyster tartare with salmon (heavy on the chives), calf's liver with onions (slightly overdone), and enjoyable pistachio profiteroles with apricot sabayon (but why add raspberries?). We'd appreciate a simpler atmosphere all round. Flawless welcome.
A la carte: 350 F and up. Menus: 150 F (weekdays lunch only), 200 F.

Le Relais de Margaux
(See restaurant above)
Closed 21 Dec-31 Jan. 3 stes 1,200-1,800 F. 28 rms 775-1,300 F. TV. Air cond 11 rms. Conference facilities. Pool. Tennis.
This sumptuous hotel set in the heart of the wine-growing region is surrounded by 55 hectares of grounds, with swimming pool, tennis courts, and heliport. The elegantly decorated rooms are extremely handsome, and have admirably equipped bathrooms. Service and breakfasts improving.

MARGUERITTES
See Nîmes

MARIGNANE
See Marseille

MARIGNY
50570 Marigny — (Manche)
Paris 315 - Carentan 27 - Coutances 16 - St-Lô 12

La Poste
Pl. Wesport — 33.55.11.08
M. Meslin. Closed Sun dinner, Mon, 4-16 March and 22 Sep-4 Oct. Open until 9.15 pm. V AE DC.
Joël Meslin is wild about oysters, which he prepares in six different ways (the latest involves smoked ham and apple brandy). His other dishes use all the region's favourite ingredients: cream, cider, Calvados, fish, cheese. Try also his perfect canard à l'orange. Remarkable wine cellar.
A la carte: 230-250 F. Menus: 100 F (weekdays only), 135 F, 200 F, 250 F, 330 F.

MARLENHEIM
67520 Marlenheim — (Bas-Rhin)
Paris 437 - Strasbourg 20 - Saverne 19 - Molsheim 12

Hostellerie du Cerf ✧
30, rue du Gal-de-Gaulle — 88.87.73.73
M. Husser. Closed Tue, Wed and Feb school holidays. Open until 9 pm. Private room: 25. Terrace dining. Parking. V AE.
You might think you'd stepped into the scenery of a light opera, but everything about this old coaching inn is absolutely authentic: the cobbled courtyard, the well, the flower-covered balconies. So, too, is the warm, welcoming Husser family, who've run the Cerf for over six decades, and recently remodelled it, installing state-of-the-art kitchens.
Michel Husser has taken over from his father, Robert, who now presides over the dining room. Michel trained with Alain Senderens, then came home to Alsace to don his toques. After a hesitant start, he has now found a perfect balance between Parisian sophistication and rich, country flavours. Witness the herring terrine with potatoes and tiny tart pickles, topped with crème de caviar. Or the bass with pommes boulangère, freshwater perch with cabbage and horseradish cream, and crispy salmon with potatoes and white radish in a sweet-and-sour sauce. The revisited Alsace specialities are particularly fine (divine choucroute with smoked foie gras, suckling pig caramelised in honey). True, the desserts are not always up to scratch, but the wine list is matchless (try Jean Heywang's frisky Klevner de Heilgenstein). Fierce à la carte prices.
A la carte: 400-650 F. Menus: 210 F (weekdays lunch only, wine inc), 320 F, 450 F.

Hostellerie du Cerf 🌲
(See restaurant above)
Closed Tue, Wed and Feb school holidays. 2 stes 500-550 F. 15 rms 275-420 F. TV 7 rms. Conference facilities.
This charming village hotel is built around a garden-like courtyard. The sunny, carpeted, thoughtfully equipped rooms have been skilfully updated. Delightful welcome with a feminine touch. Good breakfasts. Pity the nearby noisy road is so intrusive.

Red toques signify modern cuisine; black toques signify traditional cuisine.

MARMANDE

47200 Marmande — (Lot/Garonne)
Paris 684 - Agen 58 - Bordeaux 89 - Bergerac 58

Thierry Arbeau

10, av. Ch.-Baylac — 53.64.24.03
*M. Arbeau. Closed Sun dinner and Mon. Open until
10 pm. Private room: 18. Terrace dining. V.*

Thierry Arbeau, pupil of Darroze and Guérard,
has made his mark in Marmande, serving fine fish
dishes and country produce (at city prices). Taste
the lotte in herb vinaigrette, grilled young pigeon
with spices, and the house speciality, lamprey eel
from the Garonne, with leeks. Intimate décor,
charming welcome.
A la carte: 350 F. Menus: 120 F, 180 F, 250 F.

Le Capricorne

Rte d'Agen, N 113 — 53.64.16.14
*Closed 20 Dec-6 Jan. 34 rms 220-255 F. Restaurant.
Half-board 190-290 F. TV. Conference facilities. Pool.
Parking. V.*

A modern, comfortable stopover on the outskirts
of town. The rooms at the back, overlooking the
swimming pool, are especially quiet.

MARNES-LA-COQUETTE

See PARIS Suburbs

MARSANNAY-LA-CÔTE

See Dijon

MARSEILLAN

See Agde

MARSEILLE

13000 Marseille — (B./Rhône)
Paris 771 - Lyon 315 - Nice 188 - Toulouse 400

Altea

See restaurant L'Oursinade

12/20 Les Arcenaulx ❍

25, cours d'Estienne-d'Orves (1er)
91.54.39.37
*Mmes Laffitte. Closed Mon dinner and Sun. Open
until 0.30 am. Private room: 100. Garden dining.
Air cond. V AE DC.*   D5-6

Ten years ago, publisher Jeanne Laffitte dreamed
of combining literature, art, and good food. Now
her bookshop with its exhibition room and
restaurant is a must for Marseille intellectuals, who
gather here to put the world to rights and to tuck
into mussel gratin with fennel, baby quail
Provençal-style, and scrambled eggs with black
olives. Outstanding selection of wines at reasonable prices.
A la carte: 200-250 F.

Bompard

2, rue des Flots-Bleus (7e) — 91.52.10.93
*Open every day. 47 rms 285-375 F. Restaurant. TV.
Conference facilities. Parking. Telex 400430. V AE
DC.*   F7-29

This quiet residence, set in quiet grounds, is just
minutes from the Old Port and city centre. Large,
sunny, functional and comfortable rooms (avoid
those overlooking the car park at the back). Wide,
flower-filled balconies.

Maurice Brun ❍

(Aux Mets de Provence)
18, quai Rive-Neuve (7e) — 91.33.35.38
*M. Brun. Closed Sun, Mon, holidays. Annual closings
not available. Open until 9.30 pm. V AE DC.*   D6-16

The wind of change has finally tickled even this
bastion of tradition perched above the Old Port: it
now has a *carte*. It's short, but at least you can read
it and make your choice. We know, however, that
the faithful will shun it, and instal themselves for
the perennial two-hour repast, which revolves
around hors-d'œuvres, perfect fish dishes, bœuf en
daube, and Provençal desserts.
A la carte: 250-350 F. Menu: 315 F.

Calypso

3, rue des Catalans (7e) — 91.52.64.00
M. Visciano. Information not available.   D7-20

Cooled by sea breezes, this sunny spot specialises
in perfectly grilled or poached fish (avoid the more
sophisticated dishes), which you choose yourself
fresh from great wicker baskets. The smartly
decorated, traditional dining room gives on to Le
Frioul. Moderately priced wines help to temper the
bill.
A la carte: 300-450 F.

12/20 Le Chaudron Provençal

48, rue de la Caisserie (2e) — 91.91.02.37
*Mme Paul. Closed Sat lunch and Sun. Open until
10.15 pm. Air cond. V AE.*   C6-41

The heart of every true Marseillais beats warmly
at the mention of this wonderful family restaurant,
which is ruled by the rhythms of the Old Port's
rocking boats. Sample the startlingly fresh red-mullet salad, fish baked in a salt crust, bouillabaisses,
and bourrides. Sunny welcome, brutal bill.
A la carte: 320-370 F.

Concorde Palm Beach

2, prom. de la Plage (8e) — 91.76.20.00
*Open every day. 1 ste 1,595 F. 145 rms 622-692 F.
Restaurant. TV. Air cond. Conference facilities. Pool.
Garage parking. Telex 401894. V AE DC.*   G7-17

This huge, modern hotel complex offers spacious, recently redecorated rooms with loggias
looking out to sea. Auditorium.

Concorde Prado

11, av. de Mazargues (8e) — 91.76.51.11
*Open every day. 100 rms 555-616 F. Restaurant. TV.
Air cond. Conference facilities. Garage parking.
Telex 420209. V AE DC.*   G4-7

This modern hotel is near the conference centre.
Pleasant, office-style rooms. The Prado shares the
swimming pool and seashore of the nearby Palm
Beach. Shops, conference rooms.

Cousin Cousine

102, cours Julien (6e) — 91.48.14.50
*M. Sellam. Closed Sun and Mon. Open until
10.30 pm. Terrace dining. Air cond. Parking. V AE
DC.*   E3-9

Jean-Luc Sellam's restaurant, set before the plas-
hing fountains of the cours Julien, offers cooking
full of freshness and good ideas. Try the tempting
set menus; the 'menu gourmand' includes scallop
salad, prawns with pistou, frogs' leg soup with
fresh tomatoes, and young pigeon and potato galette. Simple and delicious desserts. Exceptional
value.
A la carte: 280 F. Menus: 135 F, 225 F.

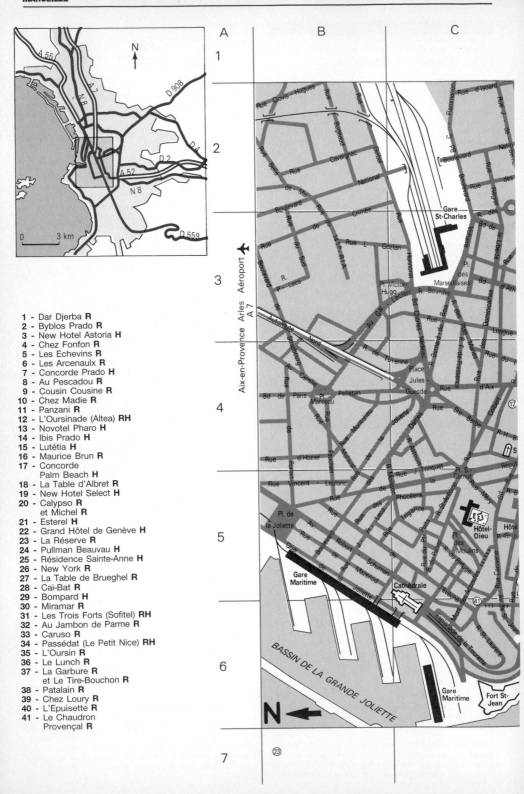

1 - Dar Djerba **R**
2 - Byblos Prado **R**
3 - New Hotel Astoria **H**
4 - Chez Fonfon **R**
5 - Les Echevins **R**
6 - Les Arcenaulx **R**
7 - Concorde Prado **H**
8 - Au Pescadou **R**
9 - Cousin Cousine **R**
10 - Chez Madie **R**
11 - Panzani **R**
12 - L'Oursinade (Altea) **RH**
13 - Novotel Pharo **H**
14 - Ibis Prado **H**
15 - Lutétia **H**
16 - Maurice Brun **R**
17 - Concorde
     Palm Beach **H**
18 - La Table d'Albret **R**
19 - New Hotel Select **H**
20 - Calypso **R**
     et Michel **R**
21 - Esterel **H**
22 - Grand Hôtel de Genève **H**
23 - La Réserve **R**
24 - Pullman Beauvau **H**
25 - Résidence Sainte-Anne **H**
26 - New York **R**
27 - La Table de Brueghel **R**
28 - Cai-Bat **R**
29 - Bompard **H**
30 - Miramar **R**
31 - Les Trois Forts (Sofitel) **RH**
32 - Au Jambon de Parme **R**
33 - Caruso **R**
34 - Passédat (Le Petit Nice) **RH**
35 - L'Oursin **R**
36 - Le Lunch **R**
37 - La Garbure **R**
     et Le Tire-Bouchon **R**
38 - Patalain **R**
39 - Chez Loury **R**
40 - L'Epuisette **R**
41 - Le Chaudron
     Provençal **R**

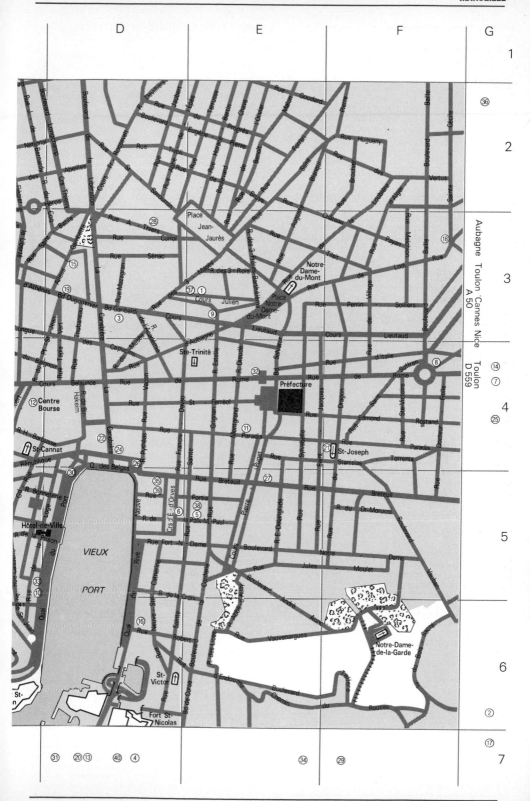

Les Echevins
44, rue Sainte (1er) — 91.33.08.08
M. Moréni. Closed Sat lunch, Sun and 1-25 Aug. Open until 10.30 pm. Air cond. V AE DC. E5-5

The new décor underlines the handsome beamed ceiling. Chef Jeanne Moreni has reintroduced several favourites from La Table d'Albret (duck stew, cassoulet), and created a shortish fish menu (grilled or en papillote). You'll even find the tasty lake fish omble chevalier here. Interesting wines, good desserts, pleasant service.
A la carte: 220-250 F. Menus: 140 F (lunch only), 180 F, 280 F.

L'Epuisette
Vallon des Auffes (7e) — 91.52.17.82
M. Bonnet. Closed Sat, Sun and 21 Dec-28 Jan. Open until 10 pm. Parking. V AE DC. D7-40

The view from L'Epuisette's grand veranda takes in the Planier lighthouse, while the dining room is decorated with elegant and original touches (chandeliers and parquet floor). Henri Bonnet manages his team with great professionalism, serving fresh grilled fish (netted live from a tank) and dishes redolent of the perfumes of Provence: salmon in a salt crust, fish soup, crab cocktail, bouillabaisse, and bourride. Fine wines, attentive service.
A la carte: 350 F. Menus: 150 F, 280 F.

Esterel
124 and 125, rue Paradis (6e) — 91.37.13.90
Open every day. 28 rms 87-283 F. TV. Air cond 20 rms. Conference facilities. Parking. Telex 430300. V AE DC. F4-21

Set in a residential neighbourhood, the rooms here are pleasant, well-kept and soundproofed. Many services.

Chez Fonfon
140, vallon des Auffes (7e) — 91.52.14.38
M. Mounier. Closed Sat, Sun and Oct. Open until 10.30 pm. Private room: 60. Terrace dining. Air cond. V AE DC. D7-4

Time stopped at Chez Fonfon over 50 years ago, when Fonfon was twenty. Do people come to this homely restaurant tucked away in a rocky inlet for the food, or to pay homage to the patriarch of Marseille's chefs? Both, decidedly. For the bouillabaisse and bourrides are generous and authentic, the fish luminously fresh. Fonfon selects them from the fishermen at the mouth of the creek. Adequate wine list.
A la carte: 300 F and up.

La Garbure ✪
9, cours Julien (6e) — 91.47.18.01
M. Lafargue. Closed 27 July-20 Aug. Open until 11 pm. Private room: 18. Terrace dining. Air cond. V DC. E3-37

Arnaud Lafargue simmers and serves his Gascon-Béarnaise specialities in this charming cellar restaurant, lit by chandeliers and the smiles of satisfied customers. Outstanding foie gras, hearty confits and cassoulets, wood pigeon salmis with cèpes, and prune ice cream with Armagnac. Reasonably priced Madiran and Buzet wines.
A la carte: 220-270 F.

> *Some establishments change their closing times without warning. It is always wise to check in advance.*

Grand Hôtel de Genève
3 bis, rue de la Reine-Elisabeth (1er) 91.90.51.42
Open every day. 6 stes 450-550 F. 43 rms 300-410 F. Restaurant. Half-board 419-648 F. TV. Telex 440672. V AE DC. D4-22

This old hotel, in a fairly quiet pedestrian precinct near the Canebière, has been modernised. Classic, comfortable rooms.

Chez Loury ✪
(Le Mistral)
3, rue Fortia (1er) — 91.33.09.73
M. Loury. Closed Sun. Open until 11 pm. Terrace dining. V AE DC. D5-39

The Loury husband-and-wife team are pleased as punch with their charming, freshly redecorated and remodelled restaurant. The ultra-traditional cooking has perked up too: baked sea urchins with herbs, conger eel stew, lamb sweetbreads with artichokes, and extraordinary herb sorbets. Disappointing desserts. Unbeatable prices.
A la carte: 180-250 F.

12/20 Le Lunch
Calanque de Sormiou (9e) — 91.25.05.37
M. Benkemoun. Closed 15 Oct-31 March. Open until 11 pm. Terrace dining. G2-36

The fish are grilled to perfection, the starters improving (scorpion fish with garlicky mayonnaise), and the prices still low.
A la carte: 220-260 F.

Lutétia
38, allées L.-Gambetta (1er) — 91.50.81.78
Open every day. 29 rms 200-260 F. TV. V DC. D3-15

Set in a quiet street near the Canebière and the station, this hotel has good, sunny, modern, recently renovated rooms.

12/20 Chez Madie ✪
138, quai du Port (2e) — 91.90.40.87
Mme Minassian. Closed Sun dinner, Mon and 1-21 Aug. Open until 10.30 pm. Terrace dining. Parking. V AE DC. C5-10

Madie's terrace and market-based cooking are fixtures of the Old Port district. Try the generous, sunny fish soup, bouillabaisse, clams seasoned with thyme, and red-mullet mousse with crab sauce. Pleasant wines.
A la carte: 220 F. Menus: 95 F, 120 F.

12/20 Michel
(Les Catalans)
6, rue des Catalans (7e) — 91.52.64.22
M. Visciano. Information not available. D7-20

The new décor here is smart and comfortable, the cooking as good as ever: flambéed fish with fennel, bouillabaisse, and bourrides. Affordable prices, if you avoid the rock lobster.
A la carte: 300-450 F.

Miramar
12, quai du Port (2e) — 91.91.10.40
MM. Minguella. Closed Sun, 23 Dec-6 Jan and 31 July-25 Aug. Open until 10 pm. Terrace dining. Air cond. Parking. V AE DC. D5-30

The Minguella brothers' efforts to keep down prices are less successful than their restaurant. But customers are prepared to pay for the fabulously fresh fish dishes, skilfully prepared by Jean-Michel Minguella: sea urchins with quail eggs and ginger cream, sea anemone flan with oyster sauce, and sea bass stew. The menu is bewildering and difficult

to read. Pierre Minguella and his team of serving staff are models of smiling efficiency.
A la carte: 350-400 F.

New Hotel Astoria
10, bd Garibaldi (1er)
91.33.33.50
Open every day. 58 rms 260-310 F. TV. Air cond. No pets. Telex 402175. V AE DC.   D3-3
Near the Canebière, this turn-of-the-century hotel has been thoroughly and pleasantly modernised. It has huge, sunny, well-equipped rooms, and an attractive entrance hall.

New Hotel Select
4, allées L.-Gambetta (1er) — 91.50.65.50
Open every day. 60 rms 260-310 F. TV. Air cond. No pets. Conference facilities. V AE DC.   D3-19
A central hotel with a handsome, classic façade and comfortable, modern, soundproofed rooms.

New York
7, quai des Belges (1er) — 91.33.60.98
Mme Venturini. Open every day. Open until 11.30 pm. Private room: 100. Terrace dining. Air cond. V AE DC.   D4-26
The chef has been here for nearly 30 years—quite an achievement in Marseille. His cooking was threatening to become routine, but he has managed to inject new life into the brasserie fare (poutargue, sole meunière) and the market-based dishes that have made the New York popular with Marseille high society. Warm welcome for regulars and visitors alike.
A la carte: 250 F.

Novotel Pharo
36, bd Ch.-Livon (7e) — 91.59.22.22
Open every day. 93 rms 460-520 F. Restaurant. TV. Air cond. Conference facilities. Pool. Garage parking. Telex 402937. V AE DC.   D7-13
Well situated in the Vieux-Port area, the Pharo's rooms are comfortable, functional, and especially spacious, with fine views.

L'Oursinade
Centre Bourse
Rue Neuve-St-Martin (1er) — 91.39.20.00
Closed Sun, holidays and 28 July-2 Sep. Open until 10 pm. Terrace dining. Air cond. Telex 401886. V AE DC.   C4-12
This prestigious restaurant is divided up by a profusion of pot plants. The skilful, rigorous cuisine of chef Denis Enfedaque has a personal touch. Try the foie gras with Sauternes, baked sea bass wrapped in a fresh seaweed crust, and outstanding desserts. Flawless service.
A la carte: 350-400 F. Menus: 195 F, 230 F, 270 F.

Mercure
(See restaurant above)
Open every day. 1 ste 1,050 F. 199 rms 540-650 F. TV. Air cond. Conference facilities.
The new Mercure's aim is to become the city's best hotel in its category. Thorough remodelling is under way to make the rooms more spacious and comfortable. First-class service.

Panzani
17, rue Montgrand (6e) — 91.54.72.72
M. Panzani. Open for lunch only. Closed Sat, Sun, 15 June-30 Aug and 15 Dec-5 Jan. Open until 9.30 pm. Air cond. No pets. V.   E4-11
The authentic market-based menu changes often, reflecting daily finds or seasonal specialities. Chef Dominique Panzani picks fine vegetables to accompany his confit, or saddle of rabbit with

pepper sauce. And be sure to try the loin of veal with fried potatoes. Truly marvellous.
A la carte: 250-300 F.

Passédat
Corniche Kennedy
Anse de Maldormé (7e) — 91.59.25.92
M. Passédat. Closed Sun off-season (except holidays) and Sat lunch. Open until 10 pm. Private room: 25. Garden dining. Air cond. No pets. Valet parking. Telex 401565. V AE.   E7-34
We think Gérald Passédat is the best chef in Marseille, despite the fact that high prices and innovative cooking have limited his success among local gourmets, who are renowned for their conservatism where food is concerned. His learned style is highly personal, but perfectly Mediterranean. He rejects artifice and is moving towards greater simplicity, even minimalism, which allows the flavours to shine through.
Settle down in the dining room, which has sweeping views, or the shady garden looking out at the Château d'If, and savour the lobster and ratatouille terrine, prawn, brain, and bone-marrow kebabs, sea bream with fennel and lightly caramelised juices flavoured with cumin and ginger, and duck foie gras with a Sauternes-flavoured fig syrup. The remarkable desserts include a warm berry tart.
The cellar is outstanding, and the young staff helps create a relaxed atmosphere. You can eat less expensively with the help of one of the well-balanced set menus.
A la carte: 650-800 F. Menus: 290 F (weekdays lunch only), 390 F, 520 F, 590 F.

Le Petit Nice
(See restaurant above)
Open every day. 2 stes 3,500 F. 15 rms 1,000-1,700 F. Half-board 1,610-2,300 F. TV. Air cond. Conference facilities. Pool.
Set in a breathtakingly beautiful and peaceful spot overlooking the sea, Le Petit Nice has a handful of lovely, comfortable rooms and suites done in 'designer' style (which you'll either love or hate), and superbly equipped bathrooms. Salt-water swimming pool, sun room, water skiing, and sea fishing. For the Robinson Crusoes among you, one luxury suite is located on an island, facing the hotel. Relais et Châteaux.

Patalain
49, rue Sainte (1er) — 91.55.02.78
Mme Quaglia. Closed Sat lunch, Sun, holidays and 14 July-5 Sep. Open until 11 pm. Private room: 12. V AE DC.   E5-38
Many a Marseillais considers this the best address in town, and Suzanne Quaglia's sincere, tasty cooking has convinced us to offer her a second toque this year. In addition to her market-based dishes and new game menu, she offers chicken wings coated with sesame seeds and served with cold vegetables à la grecque, firm-fleshed sea bream baked with spices, and incomparable young pigeon with boudin d'abats. Never content to rest on her laurels, she has expanded her cellar, added more exotic liqueurs to her list, and stocked her humidor with fresh cigars.
A la carte: 300-350 F. Menus: 140 F (lunch only), 195 F, 300 F.

For all the essential motoring information when driving in Europe, refer to the RAC European Motoring Guide.

Au Pescadou

13

19, pl. de Castellane (6e) — 91.78.36.01
*M. Mennella. Closed Sun dinner, July and Aug. Open
until 11 pm. Private room: 55. Air cond.
Telex 402417. V.*   F4-8
The arrival of a new chef hasn't revolutionised
this Marseille institution, whose décor features
mirrors and polished woodwork. And a good thing
too. For the faithful flock here to feast on the
outstandingly good oysters and shellfish, the
classic fish dishes (grouper with mustard sauce,
daurade à la crème de menthe), and the fresh
desserts. Attentive service.
A la carte: 250-300 F. Menu: 210 F (wine inc).

Le Petit Nice

See restaurant Passédat

Pullman Beauvau

4, rue Beauvau (1er) — 91.54.91.00
*Open every day. 1 ste 1,500 F. 71 rms 550-710 F. TV.
Air cond. Conference facilities. Telex 401778. V AE
DC.*   D4-24
Though remodelled in 1985, this grand hotel
situated near the Old Port maintains the charm of
bygone days, when George Sand and Chopin
stayed here and pianist-composer Francis Poulenc
tickled the ivories on the grand piano he had taken
up to the fifth floor. The sunny, restful,
soundproofed rooms are furnished with handsome antiques, but they are not always perfectly
kept or appointed. Bar open until 1 a.m. Room
service on weekdays.

12/20 La Réserve

151, plage de l'Estaque (16e) — 91.46.11.19
*M. Gonzalez. Closed Wed. Open until 9.30 pm. Gar-
den dining. Parking. V AE DC.*   B7-23
The skilful Jean-Noël Gonzalez has taken over
from his mother, carrying on the tradition of quality at this beachfront restaurant. The authentic,
generous, regional food is very reasonably priced
(bouillabaisse, bourrides, and grilled sea bass,
bream, and other local fish). Attentive service.
A la carte: 270 F. Menu: 130 F.

Résidence Sainte-Anne

50, bd Verne (8e) — 91.71.54.54
*Open every day. 45 rms 297-335 F. Restaurant. Half-
board 335 F. TV. Air cond. Conference facilities.
Parking. Telex 441082. V AE DC.*   G4-25
Near the Prado beaches, this modern, comfort-
able hotel sits in a quiet garden.

Sofitel

See restaurant Les Trois Forts

La Table d'Albret

13

5, rue Ste-Cécile (5e) — 91.80.07.93
*M. Souchon. Closed Sat lunch, Sun and Aug. Open
until 10 pm. Private room: 25. Air cond. V AE.*   F3-18
This cosy little restaurant with its floral, beamed
décor has changed hands. The new owners, true
professionals, have maintained the menu and the
quality of the foie gras, duck breasts, Gascon
daube, and cassoulet.
A la carte: 230-280 F. Menus: 100 F (weekdays
lunch only), 141 F.

12/20 La Table de Brueghel

57, rue Breteuil (6e) — 91.37.46.11
*Mme Lelièvre. Closed Mon dinner, Sat lunch, Sun,
July and Aug. Open until 10.30 pm. V AE DC.* E5-27
Wash down the hearty meals with carafes of
Costières-du-Gard, and enjoy the comfort and
warmth of this bustling, friendly restaurant. The
menu, chalked up on the slate, includes andouill-
ette à la ficelle, grilled veal kidneys, and veal
knuckle stew.
A la carte: 180-230 F.

Le Tire-Bouchon

13

11, cours Julien (6e) — 91.42.49.03
*M. Richard. Closed Sun and Mon. Open until 11 pm.
Terrace dining. Air cond. V DC.*   E3-37
The surrounding neighbourhood is on the decl-
ine, but Catherine Richard's warm welcome and
her husband's reliable cooking make this an address worth noting. Sample the grilled squid in a
sweet-pepper salad, trout millefeuille seasoned
with Thai basil, and roast duckling with orange and
ginger. The toque is back!
A la carte: 220-250 F.

Les Trois Forts

36, bd Ch.-Livon (7e) — 91.52.90.19
*M. Bouclet. Open every day. Open until 10 pm. Priv-
ate room: 120. Air cond. Valet parking.
Telex 401270. V AE DC.*   D7-31
Serge Devesa, the new chef, may be the Prince
Charming who will awaken this Sleeping Beauty of
a hotel-restaurant. No rating as yet, but we were
impressed by the promising warm scallop salad
with grapefruit, cabbage stuffed with king prawns,
and brilliant desserts. The décor and à la carte
prices are as unattractive as ever.
A la carte: 350-400 F. Menus: 175 F (weekdays
lunch only, wine inc), 175 F (weekdays dinner
only), 260 F (w-e and holidays only).

Sofitel

(See restaurant above)
*Open every day. 3 stes 1,750-2,100 F. 130 rms 650-
920 F. TV. Air cond. Conference facilities.*
The newly equipped bathrooms are an improvement, but the décor of the bedrooms is rather
impersonal. The view of the town across the Old
Port is superb.

And also...

Our selection of places for inexpensive, quick, or
late-night meals and smaller places to stay.
Al Dente (91.81.67.45 - 10, rue E.-Rostang, 6e.
Open until 11 pm): Tasty pasta dishes served with
a flourish in a bright décor. Near the antique
dealers' district (80-100 F).
Chez Angèle (91.90.63.35 - 50, rue Caisserie, 2e.
Open until 11 pm): Corridor-style dining room
renowned for its huge pizzas, pasta, and pleasant,
inexpensive wines (100-130 F).
Anh-Em (91.33.22.82 - 28, rue du Musée, 1er. Open
until 10 pm): In the middle of the Capucins
market, a spotless little restaurant where you can
stop for a Vietnamese snack from 10 am onwards
(60-100 F).
L'Art et les Thés (91.56.01.39 ext 359 - 2, rue de la
Charité, 1er. Open until 7 pm): Salads, sorbets, and
fruit juice served in the shadow of the Vieille
Charité chapel (60-90 F).
L'Artisan du Chocolat (91.33.55.00 - 43, cours Estienne-d'Orves. Lunch only): A master *pâtissier*
makes fresh salads and *plats du jour*, as well as
marvellous chocolates (00 F).
Byblos Prado (91.22.80.66 - 61, prom. de la Plage,

8e. Open until 10.30 pm): On the edge of a beach, Samir Chagouri and his daughters dish up succulent Lebanese specialities at low prices (150-200 F).

Le Café de Provence (42.78.42.78 - in Marignane, Sofitel Aéroport. Open until midnight): Good selection of hors d'œuvres and a 1,000-calorie menu (120 F).

Cai-Bat (91.42.33.78 - 43, rue A.-Thiers, 1er. Open until 11 pm): Try the delicious Asian dishes (glazed quail, spicy soup with tamarind and pineapple, and steamed specialities) in the pleasant garden (150 F).

Castelmuro (91.54.32.30 - 37, rue F.-Davso, 1er. Lunch only): Ugly décor, but a wide choice of fresh sandwiches and salads (80 F).

Caruso (91.90.94.04 - 158, quai du Port, 2e. Open until 10 pm): Perennial Italian favourites (ravioli, osso buco, saltimbocca) are served on a terrace overlooking the Old Port. Unchanging prices (200 F).

Le Cigalon (91.43.03.63 - 5, bd Pasteur, La Treille, 11e. Open until 10 pm. Lunch only Nov-April): A perfectly Marseillais menu (daube, paupiettes, tripe), served on a panoramic terrace (150 F).

La Coupole (91.54.88.57 - 5, rue Haxo, 1er. Open until 11 pm): Brasserie fare and *plats du jour* in the heart of the shopping district (150 F).

Dar Djerba (91.48.55.36 - 15, cours Julien, 6e. Open until 11 pm): This year's menu proposes North African specialities like couscous saharien. Charming welcome (180 F).

La Gentiane (91.42.88.80 - 9, rue des Trois-Rois, 6e. Open until 11 pm): Light, steamed dishes full of the scents and savours of Provence (100-130 F).

Ibis Prado (91.25.73.73 - 6, rue de Cassis, 8e. 118 rms 260-288 F): Near the conference centre, this modern hotel has recently remodelled, well-equipped rooms.

Au Jambon de Parme (91.54.37.98 - 67, rue de la Palud, 6e. Open until 10.15 pm): Favoured by businessmen and a society crowd, this classic, comfortable restaurant serves Italian and French specialities (vitello tonnato, salmon with corail sauce, fresh, locally caught fish), (300 F).

La Kahena (91.90.61.93 - 2, rue de la République, 2e. Open until 10.15 pm): The place to feast on couscous. Near the Old Port (100-120 F).

Chez Louis (91.79.89.79 - 80, av. de la Capelette, 10e. Dinner only, until 11 pm): A tiny neighbourhood bistro with baroque décor, famed for its incomparable, freshly made ravioli (170 F).

Manzi (91.62.37.19 - 129, rue Belle-de-May, 3e. Open until 11 pm): You have to queue on the pavement for the best pizzas in town (in the world, the locals will tell you), (90 F).

O'Stop (91.33.85.34 - 14, rue Saint-Saëns, 1er. Open until 6 am): The favourite late-night trattoria of singers, musicians and opera-goers: pizzas, pasta, meat dishes (140-170 F).

L'Oursin (91.33.34.85 - 14, cours J.-Ballard, 1er. Open until 11 pm): Superb seafood and shellfish, fried and grilled fish, accompanied by Gros-Plant and Entre-Deux-Mers (200 F).

Pasta Quick (91.91.10.40 - 6, quai du Port, 2e. Lunch only): On the Old Port. Try the fish soup, pasta, and excellent pâtisserie (80-120 F).

Le Poussin Bleu (91.33.34.83 - 17, rue Armény, 6e. Lunch only): A new menu every day at this successful caterer's fast-food outlet. Superb pastries too (90 F).

Taverne de Maître Kanter (91.33.84.85 - 38, cours Estienne-d'Orves, 1er. Open until 12.30 am): Oysters, choucroute, or good-but-expensive fish, and beer to go with them (120-150 F).

(28 km NW)
13700 Marseille (B./Rhône)

Le Clipper
at the airport — 42.78.42.78
M. Daugreilh. Closed Sat, Sun, holidays and Aug. Open until 10.30 pm. Terrace dining. Air cond. Valet parking. Telex 401980. V AE DC.

At the airport, in the centre of an industrial zone, the Clipper is singularly lacking in charm. Thank goodness for Jean-Pierre Artilland's carefully crafted cooking: snail and scallop millefeuille with sorrel, ricotta ravioli cooked in prawn stock, and saddle of young rabbit with mango. The price of the excellent business lunch hasn't gone up since last year. Fast, efficient service.

A la carte: 280 F. Menu: 165 F.

Sofitel
(See restaurant above)
Open every day. 3 stes 1,100 F. 180 rms 580 F. TV. Air cond. Conference facilities. Pool. Tennis.

More than half the spacious, soundproofed rooms in this modern hotel complex have been renovated recently, as well as the Pipper bar, and all the lounges. Well-designed sports facilities (sauna, gym). Large-capacity reception and conference halls.

MARTIN-EGLISE
See Dieppe

MASSANA (LA)
See Andorre (Principauté d')

MAUSSANE-LES-ALPILLES
13520 Maussane-les-Alpilles — (B./Rhône)
Paris 717 - Marseille 85 - Arles 18 - Salon 28

Le Pré des Baux
Rue du Vieux-Moulin — 90.54.40.40
Closed 31 Oct at Easter. 10 rms 380-580 F. TV. Pool. Parking. V.

In a quiet setting, this new hotel has sunny, modern rooms with terraces that give onto a swimming poool. Attentive service.

Ou Ravi Provençau
34, av. de la Vallée-des-Baux — 90.54.31.11
M. Richard. Closed Mon dinner off-season, Tue, 1-15 June and 25 Nov-20 Dec. Open until 10.30 pm. Private room: 16. Garden dining. V AE.

Jean-François Richard's cheerily decorated, Provençal restaurant is warm and welcoming. So is his cooking. In summer, Mme Richard dons local costume and flits about under a leafy arbour, serving delicious home-smoked ham, hearty lamb stew with spices, a fine cheese board, and superb sorbets (skip the chocolate cake). A toque and an extra point this year.

A la carte: 300 F. Menus: 95 F and 125 F (weekdays only), 220 F.

MAUZAC
24150 Mauzac — (Dordogne)
Paris 545 - Périgueux 62 - Bergerac 29 - Brive 95

La Métairie
Rte du Cingle-de-Trémolat — 53.22.50.47
Mme Vigneron and M. Culis. Closed Tue lunch and 15 Nov-29 March. Open until 9 pm. Garden dining. Parking. Telex 572717. V.

The spectacular, meandering Dordogne snakes away before you from this lovely old Perigord dwelling. The cooking, however good, has not improved since last year's promotion. Though generous and tasty, it has some faults: the onion confit that accompanies the delicious fresh cod was too sweet, and the copious veal sweetbreads were overcooked. Prices, meanwhile, are sky-rocketing. Smiling reception and good wines.

A la carte: 300 F. Menus: from 95 F to 300 F.

La Métairie
(See restaurant above)
Closed 15 Nov-29 March. 1 ste 920-1,170 F. 9 rms 470-780 F. Half-board 450-740 F oblig in seas. TV. Pool.

This delightful old inn is lost in a leafy park that opens onto peaceful countryside. The air is sweet and clean. The uniformly neat, well-equipped rooms are elegant and comfortable (some have modern, others rustic, décor). Polite staff.

MEGÈVE
74120 Megève — (H.-Savoie)
Paris 613 - Annecy 60 - Chamonix 35 - Lyon 197

Chalet du Mont d'Arbois
Rte du Mont-d'Arbois — 50.21.25.03
M. Vincent-Genod. Closed 8 Nov-8 Dec and mid-April to mid-June. Open until 10 pm. Private room: 14. Garden dining. Valet parking. Telex 309335. V AE DC.

The split-level dining room holds a score of beautifully laid tables in a baroque wood-panelled décor reminiscent of a pre-war hunting lodge, alleviated by the picture-postcard view of Megève in the distance. The cuisine carefully aims to please and absolutely never to surprise: gratin of turbot in Champagne with fresh pasta, braised veal kidney, grilled Bresse poussin.

A la carte: 400 F. Menus: 260 F, 340 F, 440 F.

Chalet du Mont d'Arbois
(See restaurant above)
Closed 8 Nov-8 Dec and mid-April to mid-June. 1 ste 2,560-4,180 F. 20 rms 600-1,700 F. Half-board 610-1,060 F oblig in seas. TV. Conference facilities. Pool. Tennis.

A lovely mountain chalet, tastefully decorated in regional style. Uncommonly pretty furnishings of dark wood. Hospitable welcome.

11/20 La Cote 2000
at the airport — 50.21.31.84
M. Lamblin. Closed Easter-mid-July and end Aug-Christmas. Open until 9.30 pm. Terrace dining. V.

Part of a venerable roadside farm, this restored chalet offers a concise menu of simple, bountiful dishes. Friendly service and tasty house wine round out the pleasures, for which it is a good idea to book in advance (obligatory for dinner).

A la carte: 200 F. Menu: 105 F (lunch only).

Le Fer à Cheval
36, rte du Crêt-d'Arbois — 50.21.30.39
M. Sibuet. Dinner only in summer. Closed beg April-end June and 10 Sep-15 Dec. Open until 9.30 pm. Garden dining. No pets. Garage parking. V.

The vintage wood décor and the hearty mountain ambience of this pretty chalet is as warm and cosy as you could wish. Enjoy the duck foie gras served with a tender brioche, a handsome joint of beef roasted to a turn and appetisingly presented with shallot confit, and a fresh-tasting croustillant de fruits au coulis d'abricots. Swift, gracious service (but the welcome is inexplicably starchy).

A la carte: 350 F.

Le Fer à Cheval
(See restaurant above)
Closed end April-end June and 10 Sep-15 Dec. 7 stes. 38 rms 740-1,490 F (per pers, half-board oblig). TV. Conference facilities. Heated pool.

Two connected mountain chalets share a fresh, comfortable décor as well as a swimming pool, sauna, Jacuzzi, and a cosy fireplace.

Ferme Hôtel Duvillard
Plateau du Mt-d'Arbois — 50.21.14.62
Closed 20 April-1 July and 15 Sep-20 Dec. 19 rms 490-790 F. Restaurant. Half-board 434-534 F oblig in seas. TV. Conference facilities. Heated pool. Parking. V.

A large old chalet just opposite the ski lifts. The décor is rudimentary, but the view of the valley is very pleasant. Sauna.

Les Fermes de Marie
Ch. de Riante-Colline — 50.93.03.10
Closed 20 April-20 June. 4 stes. 42 rms 600-1,300 F. Restaurant. Half-board 550-750 F oblig in seas. TV. Conference facilities. Heated pool. Garage parking. V AE.

For a storybook winter's holiday in Megève: an old hamlet of ten farmhouses has been restored as a luxury resort. The interiors are all in floral fabrics, regional antiques, naïve art, etc. Slimming and beauty facilities are on hand, as well as a covered swimming pool. Individual chalets for families.

Les Loges du Mont-Blanc
Pl. de l'Eglise — 50.21.20.02
Open every day. 3 stes 1,500-2,800 F. 41 rms 750-1,320 F (per pers, half-board oblig). Restaurant. TV. Air cond. Conference facilities. Heated pool. Valet parking. Telex 385854. V AE DC.

Luxurious, thoroughly renovated accommodation in the middle of town. This establishment is a traditional favourite for its large rooms with balconies, and the indoor terrace for sun-dappled lunches. Sauna, billiards.

Hôtel le Manège
Rd-Pt de Rochebrune — 50.21.21.08
Open every day. 19 stes 1,800-4,500 F. 13 rms 525-2,800 F. Restaurant. TV. Conference facilities. Heated pool. Valet parking. V AE DC.

A modern chalet near the centre of the resort offers nicely decorated rooms—each one different, and modern equipment including sauna, exercise room, and a small swimming pool.

Le Mont-Joly
Rue du Crêt-du-Midi — 50.21.26.14
M. Philippe. Closed 15 April-15 June and 15 Sep-20 Dec. Open until 9.30 pm. Terrace dining. No pets. Parking. Hotel: Hotel: 22 rms 600 F, half-board 500-600 F oblig in seas. V AE DC.

It's hard not to notice that the décor has faded badly, especially in contrast to the elegant, stylish reception and service. But the setting surely won't interfere with the delight you'll take in this short menu of seasonal suggestions prepared with care and imagination. Taste, for example, the sweetbread ravioli with wild mushrooms in a truffled sauce, the mould of frogs' legs with almonds and baby morels, and the noisettes of lamb with parsley purée, accompanied by ravioli filled with wild mushrooms and goat cheese. Justified high prices.

A la carte: 350 F. Menus: 260 F, 290 F.

Princesse de Megève
Demid-Quartier — 50.93.08.08
Closed 15 Nov-15 Dec. 11 rms 680-1,550 F. Restaurant. TV. Conference facilities. Heated pool. Garage parking. V AE.

In a peaceful little hamlet outside town stands this beautiful chalet with eleven sunny, spacious, tastefully decorated rooms. All have either a balcony or a patio overlooking the mountains. Sumptuous breakfasts, Jacuzzi, beauty centre. A swimming pool is planned.

La Résidence
Rte du Bouchet — 50.21.43.69
Closed 16 April-27 June and 10 Sep-15 Dec. 56 rms 750-1,950 F. Restaurant. Half-board 920-2,270 F. TV. Conference facilities. Heated pool. Tennis. Garage parking. Telex 385164. V AE DC.

At the bottom of the Roquebrune ski runs you'll find this big chalet, which resembles a block of flats. The rooms are sunny, quiet, and well equipped. Unenthusiastic reception.

La Rotonde
100, rue d'Arly — 50.93.05.03
M. Aubrun. Closed 22 April-15 June and 15 Sep-15 Dec. Open until 10.30 pm. Air cond. Valet parking. Telex 385854. V AE DC.

Several multi-toque French chefs have invested in this splendidly renovated grand luxury hotel and restaurant, which has roused this still chic but rather sleepy ski resort. François Galabert presides in the kitchen, over the fine (and ever-improving) cuisine. In the bright rotunda dining room, treat yourself to the suave gratinéed shellfish cream soup, grilled sea bream, spit-roasted mallard duck and its potato croustillant, and the unforgettable tarte Tatin made with nectarines. Delightful service. The hotel's second restaurant, Le Grand Café, offers a tempting selection of meats and spit-roasted poultry.

A la carte: 400 F. Menus: 160 F, 290 F.

Parc des Loges
(See restaurant above)
Closed 22 April-1 June and 15 Sep-15 Dec. 13 stes. 40 rms 750-10,000 F (per pers, half-board oblig). TV. Air cond. Conference facilities. Heated pool.

A true 'snow palace' from the 1930's has been sumptuously restored to its art deco glory, right down to the authentic room furnishings. The opulent amenities even include the rarest of all: sunlit bathrooms. The huge rooms are simply beautiful, the personnel attends to every little detail, and the breakfasts are memorable. A great success.

Saint-Jean
97, boucle des Houilles — 50.21.24.45
Closed Easter-1 July and 10 Sep-20 Dec. 15 rms 230-380 F. Restaurant. Half-board 300-315 F. TV. No pets. Parking.

Near the centre of town, yet blessedly quiet, this big chalet contains lovely wood-panelled rooms that look out over the great outdoors.

Au Coin du Feu
Rte de Rochebrune — 50.21.04.94
Closed 15 April-1 July and 31 Aug-15 Dec. 4 stes 580-650 F. 19 rms 650-780 F. Half-board 400-545 F oblig in seas. Restaurant. TV.

These warm, cosy rooms are almost over-decorated with floral prints and carved wood. Sauna; whirlpool baths.

Le Triolet
Rte du Bouchet — 50.21.08.96
Closed in summer. 3 stes 1,000-1,800 F. 10 rms 700-1,100 F. Restaurant. Half-board 650-1,000 F oblig in seas. TV. Valet parking. Telex 309545. V AE.

A kilometre from the centre of the resort, near the Roquebrune lifts, sits this luxurious chalet with huge bay windows that afford a superb view.

Au Vieux Moulin
4, rue A.-Martin — 50.21.22.29
Closed 15 April-1 June and 15 Sep-15 Dec. 4 stes 650-850 F. 33 rms 320-650 F. Restaurant. Half-board 360-510 F oblig in seas. TV. Conference facilities. Heated pool. Garage parking. Telex 385532. V.

A good old-fashioned mountain chalet with pretty rooms and a big garden.

MÉJANNES-LÈS-ALÈS
See Alès

MELUN
77000 Melun — (Seine/Marne)
Paris 55 - Meaux 57 - Sens 66 - Orléans 104

Grand Monarque
in Melun-la-Rochette
Av. de Fontainebleau — 64.39.04.40
M. Tribouillier. Closed at Christmas. Open until 9.30 pm. Private room: 35. Garden dining. Parking. Telex 690140. V AE DC.

This inviting little luxury hotel on the edge of the forest boasts a dining terrace with a view of the swimming pool and the lawns. A fine meal can be made of such rigorously fresh and well-prepared dishes as crab terrine, prawn ravioli, and a fillet of bass in a golden crust, or rich pot-au-feu à la ficelle. Decent cellar.

A la carte: 350 F. Menu: 170 F.

Grand Monarque
(See restaurant above)
Open every day. 5 stes 650-700 F. 45 rms 395-480 F. Half-board 610-630 F. TV. Conference facilities. Pool. Tennis.

The rooms are small but newly revamped and look over the peaceful grounds. Refinement and courtesy are the watchwords of this lovely hotel.

MÉNARS
See Blois

MÉNERBES
84560 Ménerbes — (Vaucluse)
Paris 713 - Cavaillon 16 - Apt 21 - Bonnieux 12

Le Roy Soleil
Rte des Beaumettes, Le Fort — 90.72.25.61
Closed 15 Nov-15 March. 2 stes 1,100 F. 14 rms 380-780 F. Restaurant. Half-board 460-700 F oblig in seas. TV. Conference facilities. Pool. Tennis. Parking. V.

A traditional Provençal homestead in the heart of the Lubéron, set amidst fragrant *garrigue* at the foot of a fortified village. It is tastefully decorated in rustic style (white walls, antiques), and offers quality service and delicious poolside breakfasts.

The prices quoted in this guide are those which we were given by the restaurants and hotels concerned. Increases in prices are beyond our control.

MENTON

06500 Menton — (Alpes-Mar.)
Paris 961 - Nice 31 - San-Remo 34 - Cannes 63

L'Aiglon
🏨 7, av. de la Madone — 93.57.55.55
Annual closings not available. 3 stes 720-1,275 F. 32 rms 290-605 F. Restaurant. Half-board 342-647 F. Heated pool. Parking. V AE DC.

A beautiful nineteenth-century mansion situated not far from the centre, and just 50 metres from the sea, presents big, well-outfitted rooms and delightful gardens. Some rooms are air-conditioned and soundproofed.

Chambord
🏨 6, av. Boyer — 93.35.94.19
Open every day. 40 rms 350-500 F. TV. Air cond. Garage parking. Telex 306022. V AE DC.

Close to the sea, this hotel features big, sunny rooms next to the municipal gardens.

Europ Hôtel
🏨 35, av. de Verdun — 93.35.59.92
Open every day. 33 rms 350-450 F. TV. Air cond. Garage parking. Telex 470673. V AE DC.

A modern hotel in the centre of town with huge, comfortable rooms that offer double-glazing and minibars.

Méditerranée
🏨 5, rue de la République — 93.28.25.25
Open every day. 90 rms 350-450 F. Restaurant. Half-board 230-565 F. TV. Conference facilities. Garage parking. Telex 461361. V.

A fairly new hotel in the centre of town, featuring a modern décor and good leisure and conference facilities.

Napoléon
🏨 29, porte de France — 93.35.89.50
Closed 1 Nov-16 Dec. 40 rms 340-570 F. Restaurant. Half-board 320-450 F oblig in seas. TV. Air cond. Conference facilities. Heated pool. Parking. Telex 470312. V AE DC.

You will enjoy a view either of the mountains or the sea, depending on which of these well-outfitted rooms you occupy. Panoramic restaurant.

12/20 L'Oursin
3, rue Trenca — 93.28.33.62
M. Casademont. Closed Wed, 18 Dec-11 Jan and 1-15 July. Open until 10 pm. Terrace dining. Air cond. V AE.

Everybody who is anybody in Menton gathers at this lively bistro for fine, fresh, unpretentious fare: shellfish assortments, bouillabaisse, bourride, and grilled fish from local waters. Reasonable (for the Riviera) prices.
A la carte: 250-300 F.

Viking
🏨 2, av. du Gal-de-Gaulle — 93.57.95.85
Closed 12 Nov-15 Dec. 34 rms 300-490 F. Restaurant. Half-board 270-355 F oblig in seas. TV. Air cond 12 rms. Pool. Garage parking. Telex 970331. V AE DC.

This big, white hotel opposite the beach is built around a salt-water swimming pool. Bright, well-equipped rooms give onto the sea or the mountains.

12/20 Les Viviers Bretons
Pl. du Cap — 93.35.24.24
Mme Geille. Closed Tue. Annual closings not available. Open until 10 pm. Terrace dining. V.

You can practically taste the salty sea spray sweeping in from St-Malo as you sample the Cancale oysters, the mussels à la bretonne, the huge sole served for two, or the Breton lobster prepared by Breton native Renaud Geille.
A la carte: 300 F. Menus: 150 F, 250 F, 350 F.

In nearby **Bordighera**

(12 km E, in Italie)
18012 Menton — (Alpes-Mar.)

Mistral
⑭ Via Aurelia, 23 — (184) 26.23.06
MM. Giordano and Graziano. Closed Wed, 21 Jan-11 Feb and 18 June-9 July. Open until 10 pm. Air cond. V AE DC.

The simple cooking served at this convivial, flower-decked restaurant fairly bursts with Southern flavours. Signor Graziano regales his international clientele with artichoke salad with scampi and prawns, shellfish sauté, perfectly cooked pasta with broccoli and clams, potato gnocchi with smoked mullet roe, and good Italian wines chosen by Romolo Giordano.
A la carte: 350 F. Menus: 150 F (weekdays lunch only), 290 F.

In nearby **Grimaldi Inferiore**

(5 km E, in Italie)
18036 Menton — (Alpes-Mar.)

Baia Beniamin
⑮ Corso Europa, 63 — (184) 38.002
MM. Brunelli and Falsiroli. Closed Mon. Annual closings not available. Open until 10 pm. Garden dining. No pets. Parking. AE.

The oleanders, eucalyptus trees, and the sunsets conspire to make this seaside terrace seem like a dream. No wonder it is considered one of the most seductive restaurants on the Riviera. Carlo Brunelli adds to the pleasure with his fresh, pure, precise cooking: try his cuttlefish à la vénitienne, or the prawns with fines herbes, baked or grilled Mediterranean fish, fillet of trout with fresh tomato and basil, John Dory with asparagus, the best pasta this side of Marseille, and the lightest of desserts. Stylish, witty service and fabulous wines from northern Italy.
A la carte: 400 F.

Baia Beniamin
🏨 (See restaurant above)
Closed Mon. Annual closings not available. 6 rms 1,000 F. No pets.

Half a dozen bright, inviting rooms open onto a veranda between the garden and the beach. The ambience is pure tropical Eden.

In nearby **Ponte San Ludovico**

(1 km E, in Italie)
18039 Menton (Alpes-Mar.)

Balzi Rossi
⑯ (Les Rochers Rouges)
Piazzale de Gasperi — (184) 38.132
M. Beglia. Closed Sun dinner, Mon, 2-18 March and 14 Nov-5 Dec. Open until 10.30 pm. Private room: 40. Terrace dining. Air cond. V AE.

It would be hard to find a border town more romantic than this one. The red rocky coast (*balzi rossi* in Italian) is on one side, the bay of Cap Martin on the other. Giuseppina Beglia's cuisine also straddles the border, inspired by Italian and Provençal muses. Avoid by all means the rich classical dishes that seem like anomalies on a menu that offers divine beignets filled with rice and courgettes, ravioli stuffed with rabbit and borage leaves, fillet of striped bass with tiny local courgettes, rockfish soup, and pasta with prawns and courgette flowers. The cellar holds treasures of local wines (Dolceacqua, Vermentino, Pigato). Refined service, magnificent setting, soaring prices.

A la carte: 600 F. Menus: 225 F (lunch only), 450 F.

MÉNUIRES (LES)

73440 Ménuires (Les) – (Savoie)
Paris 650 - Chambéry 100 - Moûtiers 27

Le Ménuire
79.00.60.33
Closed 1 May-30 June and 1 Sep-15 Dec. 3 stes 600-900 F. 41 rms 350-550 F. Restaurant. Half-board 250-380 F. TV. Conference facilities. Garage parking. V AE DC.

This modern, impersonal hotel provides well-equipped rooms and a lovely view of the valley. Buffet breakfasts.

MERCUÈS

See Cahors

MÉRIBEL-LES-ALLUES

73550 Méribel-les-Allues – (Savoie)
Paris 637 - Chambéry 93 - Albertville 45 - Annecy 90

Allodis
Le Belvédère – 79.00.56.00
M. Front. Closed 10 May-15 June and 15 Sep-15 Dec. Open until 10 pm. Private room: 35. Terrace dining. No pets. Valet parking. Telex 309949. V.

Everything about this place, from the warm welcome, zealous service, and the big, comfortable, flower-filled dining room to the goujonettes of striped bass, the shellfish fricassée with chanterelles, and the moist roast veal kidneys will make you want to come back again and again. But the prices are so stiff that you probably won't.

A la carte: 350 F and up. Menus: 140 F (lunch only), 220 F and 350 F (dinner only).

Allodis
(See restaurant above)
Closed 10 May-15 June and 15 Sep-15 Dec. 12 stes 830-980 F. 29 rms 710-1,200 F. Half board 680-980 F. TV. No pets. Conference facilities. Heated pool.

On the slopes above the resort area, these spacious wood-panelled rooms enjoy a great view of the Olympic runs.

Altiport Hôtel
79.00.52.32
Closed 30 April-23 June and 30 Sep-20 Dec. 8 stes 800-1,000 F. 41 rms 500-900 F. Half-board 450-750 F oblig in seas. Restaurant. TV. No pets. Conference facilities. Heated pool. Tennis.

This modern, attractively appointed chalet provides beautiful rooms decorated in rustic style, and a programme of summer activities (tennis, golf) as well as winter sports. Sauna, Jacuzzi.

12/20 Le Chalet
79.00.55.71
M. Bisac. Closed 12 May-29 June and 15 Sep-15 Dec. Open until 9.30 pm. Private room: 25. Terrace din-

ing. No-smoking section. No pets. Valet parking. Telex 309992. V AE DC.

The 140 F prix-fixe luncheon begins with such a generous and varied hors-d'œuvre buffet that the sporty types who frequent Le Chalet can hardly do justice to the main dishes and the dessert trolley. In the evening, chef Patrick Orain offers simple French home-style cooking (sweetbreads with sorrel, chicken fricassée, marmite de bœuf au pied de veau). A more regionally rooted repertoire and a bit more finesse in the execution would be welcome.

A la carte: 250-300 F. Menus: 140 F (lunch only), 250 F (dinner only).

Le Chalet
(See restaurant above)
Closed 12 May-29 June and 15 Sep-15 Dec. 6 stes 2,800-4,200 F. 29 rms 1,300-1,400 F. Half-board 950-1,050 F oblig in seas. TV. Conference facilities. Heated pool.

Michel and Dominique Bisac have built the ski chalet that they—and perhaps you—have always dreamed of. Above the resort, facing the trails, this all-pine structure is a stunning marriage of modern and traditional Savoyard elements. Every one of the huge rooms boasts a fireplace, a balcony, thick carpet, beautiful fabrics, and a superb bathroom. Amenities include a heated swimming pool with Jacuzzi and a ski-prep service that works while you sleep!

Le Grand Cœur
79.08.60.03
M. Buchert. Closed 10 April-18 Dec. Open until 10 pm. Terrace dining. No pets. Valet parking. Telex 309623. V AE DC.

Chef Patrick Beekes, who spends his summers on the Mediterranean at Le Club in Cavalière, in winter regales the patrons of this Savoie institution with the best food in Méribel. Taste his fresh pasta with duck foie gras and truffles, the char trout from Lake Geneva simply sautéed meunière, the thyme-smoked half-wild duckling, and the roast pheasant hen with spinach and pears. Expect an attentive reception, and first-rate service. The cellar has improved considerably of late.

A la carte: 450-500 F. Menus: 155 F (lunch only), 265 F (dinner only).

Le Grand Cœur
(See restaurant above)
Closed 10 April-18 Dec. 10 stes. 40 rms 650-1,050 F (per pers, half-board oblig). TV. Heated pool.

This fine hotel has added a fitness programme to its list of attractions. The large, comfortable rooms that look out over the mountain tops. Relais et Châteaux.

In nearby au Mottaret

(6 km S)
73550 Méribel-les-Allues – (Savoie)

Mont Vallon
79.00.44.00
Closed 15 April-15 Dec. 6 stes. 58 rms 850-1,500 F (per pers, half-board oblig). Restaurant. TV. No pets. Conference facilities. Heated pool.

An immense, sumptuous chalet with an intimate, warmly elegant décor. Wonderfully comfortable rooms, superb facilities (fitness club, squash, solarium, etc.).

MÉRIGNAC

See Bordeaux

MERVILLE-FRANCEVILLE-PLAGE

See Cabourg

MESNULS (LES)

See Montfort-l'Amaury

METZ

57000 Metz — (Moselle)
Paris 313 - Strasbourg 157 - Luxembourg 60

Le Crinouc
[14]
79-81, rue du Gal-Metman — 87.74.12.46
M. Lamaze. Closed Sat lunch, Sun dinner, Mon, first 2 weeks of Jan and 3 weeks in Aug. Open until 9.30 pm. Private room: 40. No pets. Hotel: 9 rms 230 F. Parking. V AE DC.
Lots of foie gras, truffles, and lobster find their way into Jean-Claude Lamaze's opulent cuisine. But this talented *saucier* possesses a sure, precise technique that keeps such dishes as navarin de homard et d'asperges aux nouilles fraîches, gourmandise de ris de veau et foie gras chaud, chicken fillets with truffles, and frozen chocolate-mint soufflé from weighing too heavily. Top-drawer service in a comfortable, contemporary décor.
A la carte: 400 F. Menus: 160 F (weekdays only), 230 F.

La Dinanderie
[15]
2, rue de Paris — 87.30.14.40
M. Piergiorgi. Closed Sun dinner, Mon and Feb school holidays. Open until 9.30 pm. Private room: 35. V AE.
On the one hand, there is a remarkable 160 F prix-fixe menu of turbot and fresh salmon 'brawn' in vinaigrette, roast lamb chops with mangetout peas, grilled chèvre atop mixed greens, and nougat glacé with rhubarb. On the other is a long *carte* of inviting, seasonal dishes that highlight chef Claude Piergiorgi's creative bent. Depending on his mood and the time of year, you might encounter chunks of salmon simmered with garlic 'almonds', a spiced ragoût of chicken morsels and veal kidney, stuffed pig's trotter cooked in local rosé wine, and a delicious chocolate croquant and mousse combination. Superb but expensive cellar.
A la carte: 320-350 F. Menus:160 F, 240 F, 320 F.

12/20 La Gargouille
29, pl. de Chambre — 87.36.65.77
M. Nachon. Closed Mon lunch, Sun and 24 Dec-2 Jan. Open until 9.30 pm. V.
This friendly little restaurant smiles back at the cathedral's grimacing gargoyles overhead, and serves bountiful prix-fixe menus that include everything—liquid and solid—from apéritif to coffee. Offerings run to hearty dishes like boudin de pied de porc, lamb kidneys in port, bay scallops with saffron.
A la carte: 250-300 F. Menus: 155 F and 180 F (wine inc).

La Goulue
[13]
24, pl. St-Simplice — 87.75.10.69
M. François. Closed Sun, Mon and 2 weeks in July. Open until 9.30 pm. Air cond. V AE.
Yves François's handwritten and oft-revised bill of fare features such market-fresh dishes as cèpes poached with garlic, red mullet with leeks, saddle of rabbit in truffle jus, or cod with morels. Follow up this good, uncomplicated cooking with one of the delicious pastries; beware, though, of the expensive cellar.
A la carte: 300 F. Menu: 240 F.

Novotel Metz Centre
Centre St-Jacques
Pl. des Paraiges — 87.37.38.39
Open every day. 3 stes 820 F. 112 rms 430-470 F. Restaurant. TV. Air cond. Conference facilities. Pool. Garage parking. Telex 861815. V AE DC.
This recently renovated hotel in the centre of Metz provides spacious, comfortable rooms, including one designed for the disabled.

Altea Saint-Thiébault
29, pl. St-Thiébault — 87.36.17.69
Open every day. 112 rms 415-600 F. TV. Air cond. Conference facilities. Restaurant.
In the centre of town between the railway station and the pedestrian precinct, this chain hotel offers modern, pleasant rooms that are very well kept and provided with all the usual amenities.

Royal Concorde
23, av. Foch — 87.66.81.11
Open every day. 12 stes 750-960 F. 75 rms 435-510 F. Restaurant. Half-board 558-648 F. TV. Conference facilities. Telex 860425. V AE DC.
Modern and period rooms are provided in this magnificent, completely renovated turn-of-the-century building. Fine soundproofing. Two restaurants.

A la Ville de Lyon
[13]
7, rue des Piques — 87.36.07.01
Mme Abadie-Vaur. Closed Sun dinner, Mon, Feb school holidays and 30 July-27 Aug. Open until 10 pm. Private room: 50. Air cond. Parking. V AE DC.
An arm of the Moselle laps the ancient walls of Metz's cathedral quarter, where you'll find this old coaching inn, a jewel in the charming maze of narrow streets. The somewhat heavy-handed décor does not detract from the generous, attractively presented cuisine prepared by the owner-chef: sample his lotte in verjuice, or the basil-scented lamb noisette. The prix-fixe menus provide relief from the pricey *carte*. Very good cellar.
A la carte: 300 F and up. Menus: 98 F, 170 F, 270 F.

And also...
Our selection of places for inexpensive, quick, or late-night meals.
L'Antartic (87.36.80.20 - 5, rue des Huiliers. Open until midnight): The clean-lined blue décor is a backdrop for all manner of fish dishes, familiar and exotic (100-150 F).
La Baraka (87.36.33.92 - 25, pl. de Chambre. Open until 11.30 pm): Metz's best for couscous, tajines, and pigeon pastilla (100-120 F).
Le Breg Much (87.74.39.79 - 22, pl. des Charrons. Open until 10 pm): French family-style cooking at unbeatable prices (80-100 F).
Le Piccolo (87.75.65.51 - 21, rue Mazelle. Open until 11.30 pm): Fresh pasta in myriad forms (100 F).

In nearby Chailly-lès-Ennery

(13 km N on D 2 and D 52)
57640 Metz (Moselle)

Auberge de Chailly
[13]
Rue Principale — 87.77.83.20
Mme Chapuis. Closed Sat lunch, Mon, 1-8 Jan and 16 Aug-10 Sep. Open until 10 pm. Terrace dining. V.
This quiet and appealing country restaurant on the edge of the village houses a bright, inviting dining room. The owner knows his ingredients, and only top-quality foodstuffs go into the dishes

which he prepares with conscientious care. Enjoy his fragrant foie gras de canard, the bountiful marinated salmon flanked by beef and shellfish tartares, and tender spiced salmon steaks. Desserts are not up to much, however. Cheerful, attentive service.

A la carte: 250-270 F. Menus: 70 F (weekdays only),115 F, 156 F, 195 F, 250 F.

MEUDON

See PARIS Suburbs

MEURSAULT

See Beaune

MEYLAN

See Grenoble

MEYRUEIS

48150 Meyrueis — (Lozère)
Paris 630 - Millau 42 - Florac 35 - Mende 58

Château d'Ayres
66.45.60.10

M. de Montjou. Closed 15 Nov-25 March. Open until 10.30 pm. Private room: 15. Garden dining. V AE DC.
Disappointed by too many lacklustre chefs, Chantal de Montjou has taken over the kitchen herself, where she is assisted by her son Thibaud, an enthusiastic chef. The result is a sincere, creative, personal menu that features salade de cuisses de pigeon confit, salmon heightened with the heady flavours of pastis and shallots, fillet of lamb with a coulis of broad beans, attractive desserts, and wonderful home-baked breads. A first toque for their efforts.

A la carte: 220-290 F. Menus: 115 F, 260 F.

Château d'Ayres
(See restaurant above)

Closed 15 Nov-25 March. 4 stes 700 F. 22 rms 300-700 F. Half-board 320-460 F oblig in seas. TV. Conference facilities. Pool. Tennis.
The Montjou family lovingly cares for this architecturally eclectic château; it is a delightful place to stay, with its period furnishings, sequoia grove, and the calm beauty that reigns everywhere. Horse riding.

MILLAU

12100 Millau — (Aveyron)
Paris 640 - Béziers 125 - Albi 113 - Rodez 71

International
1, pl. de la Tine — 65.60.20.66

M. Pomarède. Closed off-season Sun dinner and Mon. Open until 9.30 pm. V AE DC.
With unassailable technique the Pomarèdes (both father and son are in the kitchen) turn out a conservative menu of red mullet in truffle butter, salmon and foie gras en papillote, marsh duck with green apples, and spice cake with pears and honey ice cream. Now that they have redecorated the elegant little dining room, why don't they go on to rejuvenate their immutable repertoire? They certainly possess the expertise.

A la carte: 250-300 F. Menus: 160 F (wine inc), 98 F,125 F, 325 F.

International
(See restaurant above)

Open every day. 8 stes 465-495 F. 110 rms 192-412 F. Half-board 207-345 F. TV. Air cond 5 rms.
The dining room and terrace on the top floor of this large, modern building afford a splendid view,

while the rooms are comfortable and remarkably maintained. Very good breakfasts, with home-baked rolls.

Jacques Jannet
15, rue St-Martin — 65.60.74.89

M. Jannet. Closed Tue off-season and holidays. Open until 9 pm. Terrace dining. V AE.
Local gourmets visit this fine restaurant regularly for—in ascending order of attraction—the modern dining room, the delightful terrace overlooking the old quarter of Millau, and the pleasures of Jacques Jannet's appetising cuisine. When Jannet holds his penchant for rich foods in check, he produces such treats as a superb potato and foie gras tarte renversée flavoured with walnut oil and coarse salt, or a croustillant of veal in a crisp rye-crumb crust, or roast pigeon in a reduced sauce of Syrah wine with a hint of orange zest. A second toque this year, and a sigh of contentment both for the meal and for the very reasonable prices.

A la carte: 250-300 F. Menus:95 F, 160 F, 200 F.

MILLES (LES)

See Aix-en-Provence

MIMIZAN

40200 Mimizan — (Landes)
Paris 676 - Bordeaux 108 - Dax 73 - Arcachon 65

Au Bon Coin du Lac
34, av. du Lac — 58.09.01.55

M. Caule. Closed Sun dinner, Mon and Feb. Open until 10 pm. Private room: 15. Garden dining. Air cond. No pets. Garage parking. V AE.
A very peaceful sort of luxury reigns over this lakeside establishment. Either in the plush dining room with bay windows giving onto the grounds and the lake, or on the terrace shaded by plane trees, the surroundings conspire to heighten one's enjoyment of Jean-Pierre Caule's delicious little stuffed crabs, the striped bass with foie gras and truffles, or the croustillant d'agneau en surprise. The cellar features good Bordeaux and Madirans.

A la carte: 400-450 F. Menus: 120 F (weekdays only), 250 F, 320 F.

Au Bon Coin du Lac
(See restaurant above)

Closed Sun, Mon, Feb. 4 stes 280-300 F. 5 rms 340-550 F. Half-board 400-550 F. TV. Air cond. No pets.
This idyllic lakeside setting is complemented by perfectly comfortable rooms.

MIONNAY

See Lyon

MIRAMAR

See Théoule-sur-Mer

MOËLAN-SUR-MER

29116 Moëlan-sur-Mer — (Finistère)
Paris 514 - Concarneau 26 - Lorient 25

Manoir de Kertalg
Rte de Riec-sur-Belon — 98.39.77.77

Closed 12 Nov-28 March. 1 ste 940 F. 8 rms 390-820 F. TV. Conference facilities. Parking. V AE DC.
The stables of this old Breton manor house have recently been turned into a hotel with spacious, comfortable rooms set in extensive grounds. The decoration is no great shakes, but there are many amenities (hairdresser, massage...), and the staff is most pleasant.

82200 Moissac — (Tarn/Gar.)
Paris 710 - Agen 43 - Montauban 31 - Toulouse 71

 Le Pont Napoléon ۞
2, allées Montebello
63.04.01.55

M. Peyre. Closed Mon (except dinner in seas), Sun dinner, Jan and 5-20 June. Open until 9.30 pm. Private room: 60. Terrace dining. Air cond. No-smoking section. Garage parking. Hotel: 1 ste 340 F, 13 rms 170-250 F, half-board 260-330 F. V.

Don't go for the nondescript brick building, or for the stiff, pinched service; but this restaurant is surely worth a visit for Edmond Peyre's generous, painstaking cooking. This year taste the warm foie gras feuilleté, the civet of goose and prunes, the stewed pig's trotters with cèpes, and a heroic South-western choucroute. Astutely composed cellar; terrific set menus.

A la carte: 300 F. Menus: 80 F, 120 F, 165 F, 240 F.

See Bayeux

66500 Molitg-les-Bains — (Pyrénées-O.)
Paris 978 - Quillan 53 - Prades 7 - Perpignan 50

 Château de Riell
on D 116 — 68.05.04.40
Mlle Barthélemy. Closed 4 Nov-28 March. Open until 10 pm. No pets. Valet parking. Telex 500705. V AE.
The departure of yet another chef had an unexpected happy ending when the talented Marc Baudry, formerly chef here as well, wisely decided to return to his post. The spectacular dining room of this mountain fortress now glories in Baudry's stunning, polished cuisine (palpably influenced by Michel Guérard); the currrent menu features foie gras terrine layered with lentils, red mullet in olive oil, truffled duckling crépinette, and a divine hot apple tart.
A la carte: 350-400 F. Menus: 260 F (weekdays only, wine inc), 280 F, 415 F.

Château de Riell 🌲
(See restaurant above)
Closed 4 Nov-28 March. 3 stes 1,368-1,410 F. 18 rms 900-1,072 F. Half-board 1,082-1,186 F. TV. Conference facilities. Heated pool. Tennis.
In a marvellous wooded setting that towers above the thermal spa, this fantastic nineteenth-century version of a medieval castle contains charming, romantic rooms that contrast markedly with the heavy-handed exterior. Exceptional facilities including two swimming pools. Relais et Châteaux.

See Bergerac

84430 Mondragon — (Vaucluse)
Paris 646 - Avignon 46 - Bollène 6 - Pont-St-Esprit 8

 **La Beaugravière** ۞
N 7 — 90.40.82.54
M. Jullien. Closed Sun dinner and 15-30 Sep. Open until 9.30 pm. Private room: 30. Garden dining. Hotel: 3 rms 225-295 F. Parking. V.
Behind this large and unimpressive exterior, Guy Jullien, the king of Côtes-du-Rhône wines and of the truffle in all its forms unveils his treasures to a faithful clientele. Although it is present on the

menu year-round, when the fabled tuber is in season, an entire prix-fixe feast is designed in its honour. If you prefer an untruffled cuisine, the menu is rich in such savoury traditional fare as striped bass in olive oil, thyme-roasted saddle of rabbit stuffed with its liver, and beef fillet pan-roasted with Syrah wine. Circumstances permitting, book a table under the big maple tree on the terrace, and treat yourself to the generous set menu that includes a glass of a fine Côtes-du-Rhône with every course.

A la carte: 250 F (400 F with truffles). Menus: 280 F (wine inc), 92 F, 170 F.

See Auxerre

See Serre-Chevalier

82150 Montaigu-de-Quercy — (Tarn/Gar.)
Paris 613 - Montauban 54 - Agen 40 - Moissac 33

(10 km W)
82150 Montaigu-de-Quercy — (Tarn/Gar.)

 Château de l'Hoste ۞
63.95.25.61
M. Naulet. Closed Mon off-season and Feb. Open until 10 pm. Private room: 24. Terrace dining. Parking. Hotel: 1 ste 350-430 F, 32 rms 170-220 F, half-board 220 F. V.
Situated in dignified isolation at the end of a long tree-lined drive, this little manor house opens its rustic dining room to fans of South-western country cooking. Christian Naulet celebrates this robust cuisine with a menu of stuffed goose necks, baked shad, cassoulet, lamprey bordelaise, rack of Quercy lamb, and apple feuilleté laced with Armagnac. Good cellar, friendly service—an excellent address.

A la carte: 200 F. Menus: 110 F, 240 F.

45200 Montargis — (Loiret)
Paris 113 - Orléans 71 - Fontainebleau 50

(5 km S on D 943)
45200 Montargis — (Loiret)

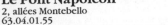 **Auberge de l'Ecluse**
Rue des Ponts
38.85.44.24
M. Girault. Closed Sun dinner, Mon and 23 Dec-14 Jan. Open until 9 pm. Private room: 20. Garden dining. No pets. Parking. V.
Until the scheduled face-lift of the dining room is complete, direct your gaze beyond the windows to the lovely Canal de Briare. And given the pace of the service, you'll have plenty of time to examine the view! Though his creativity seems to be flagging, the professionalism of chef Jean-Luc Girault, a former pupil of Robuchon, certainly is not. Try his salad of spinach and warm salmon, or the grilled freshwater perch with beurre rouge, or grouper fillets enlivened with ginger and lime. The otherwise appealing and nicely balanced wine list offers virtually no half-bottles.

A la carte: 300 F. Menus: 135 F and 180 F (weekdays only), 165 F and 225 F (w-e and holidays only).

(13 km N on N 7)
45210 Montargis — (Loiret)

Domaine de Vaugouard

Ch. des Bois — 38.95.71.85

M. Didier. Closed Sun dinner, Mon and 2-7 Jan. Open until 10 pm. Private room: 100. Air cond. No pets. Parking. Telex 783582. V AE DC.

A wedding-cake château from the Empire period squats near a noisy arterial road, on grounds that it shares with a former farmhouse that is now a deluxe motel. If all that seems a bit jarring, rest assured that one's nerves are soothed by the château's pretty grey-blue interior and attractively set tables. The chef is searching for a personal style, and his cooking still lacks simplicity and precision: lobster lasagne with parsley, sea bass en nid d'abeille, duck tourte with truffle jus. Classy service.

A la carte: 300-350 F. Menus: 155 F, 250 F, 350 F.

Domaine de Vaugouard

(See restaurant above)

Open every day. 11 stes 450-545 F. 32 rms 290-390 F. TV. No pets. Conference facilities. Heated pool. Tennis. Golf.

Spacious, motel-style rooms that are well equipped and prettily decorated. Facilities include an eighteen-hole golf course, horse riding, tennis, a fitness centre, and a sauna.

82000 Montauban — (Tarn/Gar.)
Paris 665 - Albi 72 - Cahors 60 - Toulouse 53

Arcade

Pont de Chaume
East rocade — 63.20.20.88

Open every day. 40 rms 270 F. Restaurant. TV. Air cond. Conference facilities. Heated pool. Tennis. Parking. V AE DC.

This tidy modern hotel offers functional rooms.

La Cuisine d'Alain

in front of the station — 63.66.06.66

M. Blanc. Closed Mon lunch, Sun, 1-15 July and 23 Dec-7 Jan. Open until 10 pm. Terrace dining. Air cond. Garage parking. Telex 520362. Hotel: 20 rms 200-300 F. V AE DC.

Jean Farge, the voluble maître d'hôtel/sommelier, is also the pastry chef; he invariably puts in a good word for his sweets as he wheels the dessert trolley around the pleasantly posh dining room. Indeed, his handiwork is a perfect finish to a feast of Alain Blanc's terrine of asparagus and foie gras, generous joint of beef in a (slightly over-reduced) wine sauce, escalope of lotte beaumontoise, and delicious grilled Cabécou goat cheese. Good regional cellar. An extra point this year.

A la carte: 300 F. Menus: 95 F, 145 F, 180 F and 250 F (weekdays only).

Hostellerie Les Coulandrières

3 km W on D 958, Rte de Castelsarrasin
82290 Montbeton — 63.67.47.47

Open every day. 22 rms 290-390 F. Half-board 285-415 F. TV. Restaurant. Air cond. Heated pool.

Pleasant, sunny rooms give onto the garden or a terrace.

Hôtel Ingres

10, av. de Mayenne — 63.63.36.01

Open every day. 2 stes 600-700 F. 33 rms 260-400 F. TV. Air cond. Conference facilities. Pool. Garage parking. Telex 520319. V AE DC.

A good hotel with big rooms and a little garden at the back, situated between the Pont Vieux and the railway station.

(10 km S on N 20)
82700 Montauban — (Tarn/Gar.)

Jacques Depeyre

N 20 — 63.02.13.13

M. Depeyre. Closed Sun dinner and Mon. Annual closings not available. Open until 9.30 pm. Private room: 50. Garden dining. Air cond. No-smoking section. Garage parking. V AE DC.

Chef-owner Jacques Depeyre turned his pockets inside out to finance a charming, luxurious, and tasteful setting for his opulent cuisine. The lawns, the gardens, and the elegant pale-grey-and-green dining room help erase the memory of the nearby motorway and the Nationale 20; and Depeyre will charm you with his technically proficient, flamboyant cooking: salmon and oysters in a fragrant aspic, a delicate feuilleté garnished with a ragoût of cockscombs, kidneys, and quenelles, bass in Sauternes with Chinese artichokes, and casserole-roasted pigeon with grapefruit and a touch of ginger. The cellar is huge, with plenty of affordable local wines.

A la carte: 350-400 F. Menus: 100 F (weekdays lunch only), 190 F (lunch only, wine inc), 320 F (wine inc), 195 F.

37250 Montbazon — (Indre/Loire)
Paris 247 - Chinon 41 - Tours 12 - Loches 32

La Chancelière

1, pl. des Marronniers — 47.26.00.67

MM. Hatet and de Pous. Closed Sun dinner (and lunch in summer), Mon (except holidays), 3 Feb-5 March, 1-10 Sep. Open until 9.30 pm. Air cond. V.

The good people of Touraine have some fine restaurants of which they are justly proud, but this one, we're sure, is their heart's favourite. Discreet but exacting taste rules over everything from the jewel-box décor of the new blue-and-beige dining room to the precise and delicate flavours of Michel Gagneux's polished cuisine. The menu does not change with dizzying frequency, but no one really minds having more than one opportunity to sample the oyster ravioli in Champagne, lobster sautéed with bits of bacon, or souffléed blinis with orange butter. Or try the flavoursome pig's trotters with cèpes (much less interesting when garnished with shiitake mushrooms), the honey-glazed prawns in turtle consommé, or sweetbreads sautéed with lobster coral. An intelligent selection of Loire Valley wines complements the food. Delightful, diligent service.

A la carte: 400-470 F. Menus: 270 F (weekdays only), 380 F, 460 F.

Château d'Artigny

Rte d'Azay-le-Rideau — 47.26.24.24

M. Rabier. Closed 1 Dec-11 Jan. Open until 9.15 pm. Private room: 100. Garden dining. Valet parking. Telex 750900. V.

You might as well find out from us: this eighteenth-century château seemingly steeped in history is in fact a bit of megalomania built in the 1920's by perfumer René Coty. Revived at huge expense by René Traversac, the décor is a spectacular—if not always harmonious—jumble of antiques, tapestries, and all the other trappings of Château Life. As you might expect, the menu strikes rich, full chords but it avoids the heaviness that often marks this genre. Chef Francis Maignaut's menu offers a sturdy salad of beef jowls and croûtons of roast chèvre, turbot with new potatoes and basil jus, veal kidneys with sweet peppers, and a berry chaud-froid with a lush vanilla granité. The cellar is one of the finest in France.

A la carte: 400 F. Menus: 240 F (weekdays lunch only, wine inc), 250 F, 300 F, 350 F.

Château d'Artigny

(See restaurant above)

Closed 1 Dec-11 Jan. 7 stes 750-1,400 F. 46 rms 500-1,250 F. Half-board 650-1,025 F. TV. Conference facilities. Heated pool. Tennis.

An immense terrace overlooking the River Indre, vast grounds and French gardens unrolling to the horizon compose a magnificent setting for the luxuriously appointed, overdecorated rooms and suites. Exercise room; golf; musical weekends. Relais et Châteaux.

MONTCHENOT

See Reims

MONT-DORE (LE)

63240 Mont-Dore (Le) — (Puy-de-Dôme)
Paris 436 - Aubusson 90 - Ussel 57

Carlina

Les Pradets — 73.65.04.22

Open every day. 2 stes 456-504 F. 49 rms 220-290 F. Restaurant. Half-board 220-350 F oblig in seas. TV 10 rms. Conference facilities. Garage parking. V AE DC.

The modern rooms of this tall hotel (great view from the fourth storey up) face the Puy de Sancy and the waterfall.

11/20 Le Castelet

Av. M.-Bertrand — 73.65.05.29

M. Pilot. Closed 1 April-15 May and 1 Oct-22 Dec. Open until 8.45 pm. No pets. Parking. Telex 283155. V DC.

This airy, flower-filled restaurant with a terrace facing manicured lawns serves delicious regional dishes like freshwater perch with gentian liqueur and magret aux cèpes.

A la carte: 160-180 F. Menu: 107 F.

Le Castelet

(See restaurant above)

Closed 1 April-15 May and 1 Oct-22 Dec. 37 rms 219-269 F. Half-board 247-290 F. TV. Conference facilities. Heated pool.

The neat rooms all have pleasant views and impeccable bathrooms. The perfect address for a quiet family holiday.

Le Puy Ferrand

4 km S on D 983
at the bottom of puy de Sancy — 73.65.18.99

Closed 15 Oct-20 Dec. 40 rms 210-350 F. Restaurant. Half-board 225-320 F. TV. Conference facilities. Parking. Telex 990147. V AE DC.

Ramblers and sports lovers appreciate this hotel's amenities. Quiet, simple rooms, shops, and sauna.

MONTE-CARLO

26200 Monte-Carlo
Paris 955 - Nice 18 - Menton 9 - San-Remo 44

Abela Hôtel

Quartier Fontvieille
23, av. des Papalins — 92.05.90.00

Open every day. 18 stes 800-1,350 F. 174 rms 425-975 F. Restaurant. TV. Air cond. Conference facilities. Pool. Parking. Telex 489307. V AE DC.

One of the latest hotels belonging to the Abela group, which also owns the Gray d'Albion in Cannes and the Beach Regency in Nice. The very attractive and comfortable rooms overlook the Princess Grace rose garden and the harbour. Excellent reception and delicious breakfasts.

Balmoral

12, av. de la Costa
93.50.62.37

Open every day. 77 rms 350-650 F. TV 45 rms. Air cond 30 rms. No pets. Telex 479436. V AE DC.

The rooms of this old hotel near the port are gradually being renovated and a seventh floor has been added. Small snack bar.

Beach Plaza

22, av. Princesse-Grace
93.30.98.80

Open every day. 9 stes 2050-4,550 F. 304 rms 645-1,850 F. Restaurant. TV. Air cond. Conference facilities. Heated pool. Garage parking. Telex 479617. V AE DC.

This elegant hotel has a private beach, three swimming pools and a 'sea club' offering a range of sporting activities. The rooms are spacious and prettily decorated. Two restaurants.

12/20 Belle Epoque

Square Beaumarchais
93.50.67.31

M. Rauline. Open every day. Open until 10 pm. Private room: 200. Terrace dining. Air cond. No pets. Valet parking. Telex 479432. V AE DC.

You can sample the salad of bass with coriander or magret with truffles in two splendid settings: the terrace opposite the palace, or the dining room with its pink marble columns, chandeliers, and astonishing ceiling. Conscientious, unsurprising cooking and prices fit for a prince.

A la carte: 500-550 F. Menus: 290 F, 390 F.

Hermitage

(See restaurant above)

Open every day. 16 stes 5,000-9,000 F. 246 rms 1,000-2,400 F. TV. Air cond. Conference facilities. Heated pool.

Perched on a cliff, this is an outstanding example of Belle Epoque architecture. Huge rooms, large swimming pool. Fitness centre.

12/20 Café de la Mer

(Hôtel Loews)
Av. de Spélugues — 93.50.65.00

M. Lorenzi. Open every day. Open until 10.30 pm. Private room: 40. Air cond. No pets. Heated pool. Valet parking. Telex 479435. V AE DC.

Flooded with light from the sea and sky, this good-value brasserie has a varied and amusingly designed menu. Try the superb charcuterie and fine grilled meat and fish. The desserts are less good and the wine list quite inappropriate for this style of establishment.

A la carte: 220 F.

11/20 Café de Paris
Pl. du Casino — 93.50.57.75
M. Grenier. Open every day. Open until 4 am. Garden dining. Air cond. Parking. Telex 469925. V AE DC.

The enormous brasserie has been totally rebuilt in Belle Epoque style and fitted with futuristic, computer-controlled kitchens. The aptly named chef, Roger Cuisinier, and his brigade of 30 cooks can dish up over a thousand meals a day. Specialities include grilled pavé de saumon, Charollais beef fillet with morels en croûte, and millefeuille au chocolat. Another point this year.
A la carte: 250-270 F.

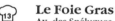

La Coupole
1, av. Princesse-Grace — 93.25.45.45
M. Siri. Closed lunch in July-Aug. Open until 10.30 pm. Terrace dining. Air cond. No pets. Valet parking. Telex 479413. V AE DC.

Yves Garnier's careful cooking, more remarkable for the high quality of its ingredients than for its personality, is solemnly served in an overblown décor of floral silk fabrics, opulent tableware, and fine silver. Mosaic of lotte with leeks in sauce vierge (a dressing of olive oil, basil, and fresh tomatoes) and risotto of ris de veau with black morels are examples. Weak wine list.
A la carte: 450 F. Menus: 240 F and 365 F (except holidays).

Mirabeau
(See restaurant above)
Open every day. 10 stes 2,850-3,500 F. 103 rms 850-1,800 F. Half-board 1,200-1,650 F. TV. Air cond. Conference facilities. Heated pool.

The well-equipped rooms have individual air-conditioning and terraces overlooking the sea. Heated swimming pool.

Le Foie Gras
Av. des Spélugues — 93.50.65.00
M. Lorenzi. Dinner only. Open until 11.30 pm. Private room: 10. Air cond. No pets. Valet parking. Telex 479435. V AE DC.

If you can forget the prices, you'll relish the light, original dishes prepared by a true professional and served in plush, comfortable surroundings. Half a dozen different kinds of foie gras, both hot and cold preparations, are a highlight of the menu, or you could sample soy-steamed salmon served with vermicelli spiced with ginger. Superb, classic desserts.
A la carte: 500 F and up. Menu: 490 F.

Loews
(See restaurant above)
Open every day. 69 stes 1,540-9,460 F. 650 rms 840-1,710 F. TV. Air cond. Conference facilities. Heated pool.

As well as its luxurious suites and bright, welcoming rooms, this hotel offers a host of facilities: five restaurants, bars, cabaret, casino, boutiques, swimming pool, and a superbly equipped fitness club.

Le Grill
de l'Hôtel de Paris
Place du Casino
93.50.80.80
M. Dario dell'Antonia. Closed 2-21 Dec. Open until 10.30 pm. Private room: 32. Terrace dining. Air cond. No pets. Heated pool. Tennis. Golf. Valet parking. Telex 469925. V AE DC.

Packed in the evenings, deserted in daytime, this restaurant with views of the sea and coast over the roofs of the casino is best enjoyed at lunchtime.

The sight of the bill is harder on the eyes, but Bruno Caironi's cooking sparkles with sunshine and flavour. The baked scampi with crudités in anchovy dressing, Provençal vegetables in prawn stock, and fillet of Sisteron lamb with truffles are all the more to his credit because the starchily dressed staff and high-society customers don't seem to appreciate them.
A la carte: 700-800 F.

Le Louis XV
(Alain Ducasse)
Pl. du Casino — 93.50.80.80
M. Ducasse. Closed Wed (except dinner in summer), Tue, 19 Feb-6 March and 26 Nov-25 Dec. Open until 10 pm. Terrace dining. Air cond. No pets. Valet parking. Telex 469925. V AE DC.

The civilised peasant cooking of Alain Ducasse is totally at odds with this ostentatious establishment, frequented for the most part by a flashy and affected clientele who apparently haven't a clue about the merits of the cuisine. But Ducasse can scarcely be blamed for taking advantage of this golden opportunity. Maybe he is only waiting for the day he can use his energy and talents in his own restaurant, where the décor and cooking would doubtless be in harmony. With supreme artistry, he combines the sensual, keen flavours of Provence and the Italian provinces of Liguria and Tuscany to produce the most delicate dishes ever offered in this shrine to the showy and extravagant. How about his baby peas and onions, new potatoes and asparagus cooked with country bacon? Or the John Dory baked on a bed of pommes boulangère? For the meat course, there's spit-roast baby lamb with its succulent juices and tiny stuffed vegetables, casseroled chop and trotter of suckling pig, or young pigeon and duck liver cooked over charcoal and served simply with new potatoes in their skins and gros sel. The restaurant's fourth toque would have been forthcoming last year if the standard of desserts had not been way below that of the rest of the cooking, but the new head *pâtissier* has put this right with delights such as wild strawberries served in their warm juices, and nectarine tart. And the two sommeliers will introduce you to the wine list, which has treasures from all corners of France.
A la carte: 700-1,200 F and up. Menus: 540 F, 635 F.

Hôtel de Paris
(See restaurant above)
Open every day. 39 stes 5,800-12,500 F. 255 rms 1,400-2,800 F. TV. Air cond. Conference facilities. Heated pool. Tennis.

The last of Europe's really grand hotels has been welcoming the rich and famous since it opened in 1865. Now completely modernised, it has divinely comfortable rooms, luxury shops, and a fine indoor pool.

10/20 Le Pinocchio
30, rue Comte-F.-Gastaldi — 93.30.96.20
M. Franceschini. Dinner only 15 June-15 Sep. Closed Wed off-season, and 8 Dec-31 Jan. Open until midnight. Garden dining. Air cond. V.

The tiny terrace, near a small square with a well, provides an attractive setting for supping on ravioli with sage or carpaccio with Parmesan. Two short-and-sweet set menus offer a starter and main course for 160 F or 200 F.
A la carte: 200 F.

11/20 Polpetta
2, rue Paradis — 93.50.67.84
*M. Guasco. Closed Sat lunch, Tue, 3 wks Feb-March,
2 wks in Oct. Open until 11 pm. Terrace dining. V.*
The Guasco brothers' simple, Italian-style cooking at reasonable prices is as popular as ever with Monaco's upper crust.
A la carte: 200 F. Menu: 130 F.

12/20 La Potinière
Av. du Bord-de-Mer, St-Roman
06190 Roquebrune-Cap-Martin
93.78.21.40
*M. Farina. Closed 16 Sep-7 June. Open until 9.30 pm.
Terrace dining. No pets. Valet parking. Telex 462010.
V AE DC.*
Reliable, professional cooking served in a splendid dining room with sea views. Choose the fine local fish grilled over a wood fire or the sauté of fillet of veal and sweet peppers—and try not to think about the bill. Excellent service.
A la carte: 450-500 F.

 ## Monte-Carlo Beach Hôtel
(See restaurant above)
*Closed 7 Oct-11 April. 1 ste 3,300-4,000 F. 46 rms
1,650-2,100 F. TV. Air cond. Conference facilities.
Heated pool.*
Billionaires lurk behind the splendid curved façade of this luxury hotel with its Olympic swimming pool and service from a more leisurely age. The magnificently restored rooms all have loggias overlooking the sea.

12/20 Le Rendez-Vous
2, rue des Iris — 93.30.95.23
*M. Dogramaciyan. Closed Sat lunch. Open until
11 pm. Terrace dining. V AE.*
An assortment of excellent Lebanese mezes opens a meal that also lets you sample Turkish and North African cooking (good couscous). Carefully chosen Greek wines and a charming welcome.
A la carte: 180-220 F. Menu: 98 F.

11/20 Restaurant du Port
Quai Albert-Ier — 93.50.77.21
*M. Ghiselli. Closed Mon and 5 Nov-5 Dec. Open until
11 pm. Terrace dining. Air cond. V AE DC.*
The world's most luxurious yachts provide the view while Dino Ghiselli resolutely steers his menu in the direction of Italy. Dishes include gnocchi with rabbit liver, sole with a mussel and saffron ragoût, veal chop with white beans, and mascarpone au café. Good Italian wines, especially from Tuscany and Piedmont.
A la carte: 300 F.

12/20 Le Saint-Benoît
10 ter, av. de la Costa — 93.25.02.34
*M. Athimond. Closed Mon and 3 Dec-7 Jan. Open
until 10.30 pm. Terrace dining. Air cond. V AE DC.*
One of the principality's finest views and the prices are still fairly reasonable. The food is skilfully prepared with fresh produce: scallops à la provençale, salmon steak, bouillabaisse, and iced bitter-chocolate truffles.
A la carte: 250-400 F. Menus: 155 F, 220 F.

12/20 Roger Vergé Café
Galerie du Sporting d'Hiver — 93.25.86.12
*M. Vergé. Closed Sun. Open until 11 pm. Air cond. V
AE DC.*
The young chef of Roger Vergé's snack bar has had to hand over to his second-in-command while he does his national service. The cooking has suffered slightly, although the salads, sandwiches, and the speciality, tartare of salmon, are still good.
A la carte: 250-300 F. Menus: 110 F, 130 F.

26200 Montélimar — (Drôme)
Paris 604 - Valence 46 - Marseille 182 - Lyon 145

 ## Relais de l'Empereur
1, pl. M.-Dormoy — 75.01.29.00
*Closed 10-20 Nov. 4 stes 500-650 F. 38 rms 280-
450 F. Restaurant. TV 20 rms. Conference facilities.
Valet parking. Telex 345537. V AE DC.*
The Emperor Napoleon did indeed spend the night here, in the middle of Montélimar, on 24 April 1814. Spacious, well-kept rooms. Porter; bar.

See Carpentras

See Besançon

See Avignon

78490 Montfort-l'Amaury — (Yvelines)
Paris 50 - Mantes 35 - Rambouillet 19 - Versailles 27

In nearby Mesnuls
(4 km SE)
78490 Montfort-l'Amaury — (Yvelines)

La Toque Blanche
12, Grande-Rue
34.86.05.55
*M. Philippe. Closed Sun dinner, Mon, 22 Dec-4 Jan
and Aug. Open until 10 pm. Private room: 30. Garden dining. Parking. V AE.*
Opposite the church on the main square of this pretty village, Jean-Pierre Philippe, a sturdy Breton, produces classic cooking with a light touch, using excellent seafood from his native province. The calf's head with six sauces, lobster with artichokes, and chocolate charlotte are masterful, lacking nothing but a small pinch of imagination.
A la carte: 450-500 F. Menu: 330 F.

See Chantilly

See Verdun

See CORSICA: Ile-Rousse (L')

24290 Montignac — (Dordogne)
Paris 496 - Brive 38 - Sarlat 25 - Limoges 102

Château de Puy Robert
1.5 km S on D 65
53.51.92.13
*M. Parveaux. Closed mid-Oct to mid-May. Open until
9.30 pm. Private room: 50. Parking. Telex 550616.
V AE DC.*
Albert Parveaux has chosen another talented young chef from his nearby Castel Novel to head the team at this charming little château. He already

deserves a toque for the John Dory on a bed of crispy courgettes and potatoes, half-smoked pigeon with young garlic, lamb 'sausages' with mint, and pineapple fritters with coconut-milk sauce. The delightful dining room has nine French windows opening on to the garden. A wider choice of regional wines would be welcome.

A la carte: 300-400 F. Menus: 215 F, 315 F, 430 F.

Château de Puy Robert
(See restaurant above)

Closed mid-Oct to mid-May. 5 stes 945-1,400 F. 33 rms 330-945 F. Half-board 585-1,045 F. TV. Air cond 8 rms. Conference facilities. Pool.

A quiet, woodland setting only a few minutes from Lascaux and its renowned cave paintings. The comfortable rooms are divided between the château itself and an attractive annexe.

See Tours

MONTLUÇON

03100 Montluçon — (Allier)
Paris 320 - Bourges 93 - Lyon 227 - Limoges 154

Château Saint-Jean
Parc St-Jean
70.05.04.65

Open every day. 7 stes 900-1,800 F. 17 rms 480-580 F. Restaurant. Half-board 700-900 F. TV 19 rms. Conference facilities. Heated pool. Garage parking. Telex 392339. V AE DC.

This former commandery of the Knights Hospitallers is set in grounds planted with century-old trees. Elegant décor.

Le Grenier à Sel
8, rue Sainte-Anne
70.05.53.79

M. Corlouër. Closed Sun dinner and Mon. Open until 9.30 pm. Private room: 16. Garden dining. V AE DC.

Michel Corlouër has large, well-designed kitchens at his new restaurant in the heart of Montluçon, plus space that will soon accommodate guest rooms. The cooking is skilful and reliable: attractive potatoes and scallops with a cider vinegar-dressed salad, pigeon en croûte, foie gras cooked to perfection with chanterelles, and a refreshing clementine and lime soufflé. Maryse Corlouër will give you a delightful welcome.

A la carte: 280-300 F. Menus: 120 F (weekdays only), 230 F, 320 F.

MONTMORENCY

See PARIS Suburbs

MONTMORILLON

86500 Montmorillon — (Vienne)
Paris 360 - Poitiers 48 - Châteauroux 84 - Limoges 83

Mercier
(Hôtel de France)
2, bd de Strasbourg — 49.91.00.51

MM. Mercier. Closed Sun dinner, Mon, 2-31 Jan, 11-17 June and 8-14 Oct. Open until 9 pm. Private room: 50. Hotel: 29 rms 140-240 F. V AE DC.

The father-and-son Mercier team have been together in the kitchen for over twenty years now, and are still devoted to good local foodstuffs served with generosity and a pinch of personality. The recent redecoration has given the place a breath of fresh air, but you will still receive the same warm welcome. Dishes not to be missed this year include foie gras de canard with vanilla, noisette d'agneau montmorillonnaise, and an exquisite dark-chocol-

ate feuilleté with orange sauce. Fine wines and good set menus.

A la carte: 280-300 F. Menus: 100 F, 180 F, and from 215 F to 290 F.

MONTPELLIER

34000 Montpellier — (Hérault)
Paris 760 - Marseille 164 - Perpignan 161 - Nîmes 51

Altea Antigone
(Le Polygone)
218, rue du Bastion-Ventadour — 67.64.65.66

Open every day. 1 ste 650 F. 115 rms 350-535 F. Restaurant. Half-board 410-500 F. TV. Air cond. Conference facilities. Garage parking. Telex 480362. V AE DC.

This hotel in the heart of Montpellier's business district offers a wide range of services. Attractive, well-equipped rooms.

Le Chandelier
3, rue Leenhardt — 67.92.61.62

M. Forest. Closed Mon lunch and Sun. Open until 9.30 pm. Air cond. V AE DC.

Gilbert Furlan's cooking is a constant quest for new marriages of flavour, backed up by sound technical knowledge that ensures balance and harmony. The menu resounds with rich descriptions: prime-cut salmon macerated in herbs and aromatics, beef with violet shallot juice and French-fried gnocchi with baby chestnuts. The desserts are in a similar vein and the wine list, which has a wide choice of half-bottles, is remarkable. Neo-classic décor provides a serene atmosphere, punctuated only by the splash of a tiny fountain. Jean-Marc Forest takes charge of the service with cheerful efficiency.

A la carte: 330-430 F. Menus: 120 F and 180 F (weekdays lunch only), 245 F and 320 F (weekdays only).

Grand Hôtel du Midi
22, bd V.-Hugo — 67.92.69.61

Open every day. 2 stes 690-790 F. 47 rms 315-690 F. TV. Air cond 37 rms. Telex 490752. V AE DC.

Here is an attractive, town-centre hotel in a nineteenth-century building. The spacious rooms, furnished in period style, have all modern comforts. Piano-bar.

Le Guilhem
18, rue J.-J.-Rousseau — 67.52.90.90

Open every day. 24 rms 270-500 F. TV. V AE DC.

The charming and comfortable rooms have views over the garden to the heart of the old town. Delightful reception and good breakfasts served on a sunny terrace.

12/20 Isadora
6, rue du Petit-Scel — 67.66.25.23

MM. Marty and Saugo. Closed Sat lunch and Sun. Annual closings not available. Open until 9.30 pm. Private room: 15. Air cond. V AE DC.

This vaulted cellar provides an intimate setting for romantic meals. The food is honest and well presented, but lacks personality (bland oyster flan, turbot with meadow mushrooms swimming in a buttery sauce), and the staff's smiles seem pasted on.

A la carte: 220 F. Menu: 110 F.

Some establishments change their closing times without warning. It is always wise to check in advance.

Le Jardin des Sens

11, av. St-Lazare — 67.79.63.38
MM. Pourcel and Château. Closed Mon lunch, Sun, 2-15 Jan and 16 June-7 July. Open until 10 pm. Private room: 15. Air cond. V AE.

Twin brothers Jacques and Laurent Pourcel belong to the new generation of young chefs for whom fine cooking is not just a matter of technique, but a means of expression to be explored and shared. Along with Olivier Château, who is in charge of the cellar and service, they have made Le Jardin des Sens, opened just two years ago, one of Montpellier's most popular restaurants. Surprising combinations of tastes, contrasting textures, and well-finished sauces distinguish cooking designed to show off the best produce of the Languedoc, and in which we detect the influence of Michel Bras, for whom the three have worked. Examples of the twins' prowess are the exquisite baked young turbot with garlic and a discreet black-olive purée, fillet of bass with almonds and tomato, or even the gratin of sea urchins stuffed with chopped mussels that add rather too much of their own taste (in our opinion, sea urchins are best served fresh, and on their own). The wine list offers only the best of each region, and one of the excellent local wines (like the Faugères of Estanilles) will help to keep the bill reasonable.

A la carte: 450 F. Menus: 150 F (weekdays lunch only), 230 F, 350 F.

12/20 Le Kashmir

6, rue de la Vieille — 67.52.98.67
M. Khan. Open every day. Open until midnight. Private room: 150. Terrace dining. Air cond. No-smoking section. V.

Classic North Indian dishes such as chicken tikka and lamb biryani are served until late at night in an amazingly kitsch setting. The lassi is better than the wines.

A la carte: 150-170 F. Menu: 105 F (wine inc).

Le Louvre ۞

2, rue de la Vieille — 67.60.59.37
M. Pillard. Closed Sun, Mon, May and 28 Oct-20 Nov. Open until 10 pm. Terrace dining. Air cond. V DC.

A pleasant bistro near the covered market where faithful customers enjoy the freshwater perch in white wine, sorbet of bitter oranges with chocolate sauce, and good wines, moderately priced.

A la carte: 200-250 F. Menu: 120 F.

Le Mas

Demeure des Brousses
Rte de Vauguières — 67.65.52.27
M. Loustau. Closed Sun dinner, Mon, 2 weeks in Jan and 1 week beg Sep. Open until 9.30 pm (10 pm in summer). Private room: 30. Garden dining. Parking. V AE DC.

Eighteenth-century stables have been transformed to create a dining room overlooking the attractive garden, and there's also a room with just one large table surrounded by greenery. Michel Loustau earns another point for his prawns in a bacon crust, braised bass with basil, excellent desserts, fine wines, and a superb collection of Armagnacs. We only wish Josette Loustau wouldn't fade away after greeting her customers.

A la carte: 340-400 F. Menus: 170 F (weekdays only), 200 F (w-e and holidays only), 320 F.

Métropole

3, rue du Clos-René — 67.58.11.22
Open every day. 8 stes 800-1,000 F. 85 rms 400-1,000 F. Restaurant. Half-board 600-1,300 F. TV. Air cond. Conference facilities. Valet parking. Telex 480410. V AE DC.

Thoroughly modernised last year, this hotel near the pedestrian precinct has retained a certain olde-worlde charm. Quiet, pleasant garden.

Noailles

2, rue des Ecoles-Centrales — 67.60.49.80
Closed 21 Dec-13 Jan. 30 rms 225-450 F. TV. V AE DC.

A listed seventeenth-century residence. The décor works well in some rooms, less well in others, but all are comfortable and well equipped.

L'Olivier ۞

12, rue A.-Ollivier — 67.92.86.28
M. Breton. Closed Sun, Mon, holidays and end July-end Aug. Open until 9.30 pm. Air cond. V AE DC.

We can only encourage Michel Breton to give us more of the same. His mosaic of confit with liver in its jelly is delicious, his John Dory with artichoke hearts and cockles is perfectly cooked, and the homemade sorbets are a subtle delight. Fresher décor (scheduled soon) might well be enough to merit another point.

A la carte: 260 F. Menus: 120 F, 168 F, 180 F.

Résidentiale

70-72, av. du Pont-Juvénal — 67.22.74.74
Open every day. 28 stes 490-650 F. 106 rms 350-480 F. TV. Air cond. Conference facilities. Pool. Tennis. Garage parking. V AE DC.

The rooms are pleasant and comfortable, especially those overlooking the garden, pool, and tennis courts. All have kitchenette and long-stay residential rates. Buffet breakfast and numerous convenient services.

Sofitel

Le Triangle, allée J.-Milhau — 67.58.45.45
Open every day. 2 stes 750-950 F. 96 rms 510-530 F. TV. Air cond. Conference facilities. Valet parking. Telex 480140. V AE DC.

Half the rooms have been redecorated in this modern building near the Place de la Comédie. One floor is reserved for non-smokers. Copious breakfasts and meals may be served in your room.

And also...

Our selection of places for inexpensive, quick, or late-night meals.

L'Aromate (67.66.06.27 - 8, rue Puits-des-Equilles. Open until 10.30 pm): Young, convivial atmosphere and Italian cooking. Try the excellent bresaola, lasagne with tunny, or osso buco in winter (120-150 F).

Le Bec de Jazz (67.66.22.40 - 9, rue Gagne-Petit. Dinner only until 11 pm): Salads that go with a swing, such as the Duke which includes confit de canard and pélardon (a local goat cheese). Wines by the glass (120-170 F).

Brasserie Saint-Germain (67.22.27.98 - Av. Pirée. Open until 11 pm): New Paris-style brasserie (so say the locals), with a menu at lunchtime and short à la carte formula in the evening (80-120 F).

Le Cerdan (67.60.86.96 - 8, rue Collot. Open until 11.30 pm): Dishes from Normandy and Algeria, served to the strains of classical music (an odd contrast with boxer Marcel Cerdan's enshrined photo...), (100-150 F).

Fazenda do Brazil (67.92.90.91 - 5, rue Ecole-de-Droit. Open until 11 pm): South American wines and dishes such as churrasco, comprising meat, bananas, red kidney beans, and chips. Salads available for smaller appetites (90-140 F).

Les Fines Gueules (67.64.67.67 - Centre commercial Polygone. Open until 7.30 pm): In the Polygone shopping centre, this bistro offers low-calorie dishes as well as homemade desserts (150 F).

Chez Marceau (67.66.08.04 - 7, pl. Chapelle. Open until 11 pm): You can enjoy the good, fish-centred cooking on the comfortable banquettes or outside on the pleasant terrace. Well-chosen wines by the glass (100-130 F).

The Quest (67.60.72.71 - 3, rue de Sœurs-Noires. Lunch only): Mixed salads and onion or salmon flan, plus sandwiches, scones, and brunch (80-100 F).

Le Summertime (67.65.65.25 - 98 bis, av. du Pont-Juvenal. Open until 11.30 pm): Pasta, salads, and grilled meats figure among the 30 dishes available in the evenings. There's live music at weekends and *plats du jour* for lunch (100-150 F).

Le Tire-Bouchon (67.66.26.50 - 2, pl. Jean-Jaurès. Open until 11 pm): Some tasty steaks and various kinds of kebabs. Good, fresh desserts (120-150 F).

Le Vieux Four (67.60.55.95 - 59, rue Aiguillerie. Dinner only until 11.30 pm): The *patron* cuts, trims, and grills some of the best meat in Montpellier for his vaulted restaurant and tiny terrace. Very good regional wines by the carafe (100-130 F).

MONTPINCHON

50210 Montpinchon — (Manche)
Paris 312 - Carentan 50 - Saint-Lô 22 - Coutances 12

14) Château de la Salle
33.46.95.19
Mme Lemesle. Closed 5 Nov-20 March. Open until 9.30 pm. No pets. Parking. V AE DC.

Much time and care has gone into the conversion of this very old residence on wooded grounds. A huge fireplace occupies one wall of the restaurant, which is richly decorated in Louis XIII style. Claude Esprabens lends a light, personal touch to dishes such as navarin of lobster with morels, braised sweetbreads, and Normandy farm chicken. Ethereal pastry desserts and fine wines.

A la carte: 350-450 F. Menus: 100 F (weekdays only), 155 F, 230 F.

Château de la Salle
(See restaurant above)
Closed 5 Nov-20 March. 11 rms 728 F (per pers, half-board oblig). TV. Conference facilities.

Deep in the countryside and surrounded by attractive grounds, the château offers large, elegant rooms furnished in an old-fashioned style, sometimes overdone.

MONTPON-MÉNESTEROL

24700 Montpon-Ménesterol — (Dordogne)
Paris 531 - Bergerac 42 - Ste-Foy-la-Grande 23

14) Auberge de l'Eclade
2 km N on D 730 — 53.80.28.64
M. Martin. Closed Tue dinner, Wed, 1-15 March and 15-30 Sep. Open until 9 pm. Parking. V.

In this simple, rustic setting between Bordeaux and Périgueux, you can enjoy a feast at a most delectable price. Christian Martin's cooking is ridding itself of frills and convention to concentrate on the skilful treatment of superb produce. His seafood terrine, scallops simply sautéed and served with a purée of chicory, and thick, tender tournedos steak with morels can be washed down with a good selection of affordably priced wines.

A la carte: 200 F. Menus: 55 F (weekdays lunch only), 100 F, 130 F, 160 F.

MONTREUIL

See Dreux

MONTREUIL-SUR-MER

62170 Montreuil-sur-Mer — (P./Calais)
Paris 204 - Le Touquet 18 - Boulogne 37 - Lille 114

15) Château de Montreuil
4, chaussée des Capucins — 21.81.53.04
M. Germain. Closed Mon off-season, Thu lunch and mid-Dec-1 Feb. Open until 9.30 pm. Garden dining. No pets. Valet parking. Telex 135205. V AE DC.

Christian Germain has carried out a complete renovation of his château attractively situated near the town ramparts. The décor has been rejuvenated, with white-painted beams and pillars now setting off the bright, old-fashioned blues and yellows. The food is resolutely regional. The local potato, the ratte du Touquet, crops up in a salad with asparagus, prawns, and truffle dressing, and beef jowls are braised in beer, Flemish-style. For dessert, try the vanilla soufflé with fresh pineapple. One cavil: we wish the cooking smells could be kept out of the dining room! Attentive service.

A la carte: 300-350 F. Menus: 250 F (lunch only, wine inc), 330 F.

Château de Montreuil
(See restaurant above)
Closed Mon off-season, and mid-Dec-1 Feb. 1 ste 850-950 F. 13 rms 400-650 F. Half-board 650-750 F. TV. No pets. Conference facilities.

The spacious, comfortable rooms have well-equipped bathrooms. Pleasant if rather affected service.

MONTREVEL-EN-BRESSE

01340 Montrevel-en-Bresse — (Ain)
Paris 402 - Mâcon 26 - Bourg 17 - Tournus 36

13) Léa
74.30.80.84
M. Monnier. Closed Wed, dinner Sun and holidays, 1 week in Feb and July. Open until 9 pm. No pets. Parking. V.

Louis Monnier's faithful clients relish the superb local ingredients he uses to produce his array of chicken liver terrines, fatted hen with morels, and roast duck with herb butter. But the chef also likes to surprise them with a salad of scallops and mangetout peas, or fillets of sole steeped in an infusion of garden herbs.

A la carte: 300 F. Menus: 120 F (weekdays only), 180 F, 260 F.

MONTRICHARD

41400 Montrichard — (Loir/Cher)
Paris 204 - Tours 44 - Blois 32 - Loches 31

In nearby Chissay-en-Touraine

(4 km W on N 76)
41400 Montrichard — (Loir/Cher)

Château de Chissay
54.32.32.01
Closed 3 Jan-15 March. 10 stes 920-1,400 F. 19 rms 450-1,000 F. Restaurant. Half-board 680-930 F. Conference facilities. Heated pool. Parking. Telex 750393. V AE DC.

The building was constructed in the twelfth and fifteenth centuries among wooded grounds and gardens. The rooms, luxuriously decorated, have eighteenth-century furniture and mosaic bathrooms. Magnificent public rooms.

42210 Montrond-les-Bains — (Loire)
Paris 441 - St-Etienne 28 - Lyon 68 - Montbrison 14

 ### Hostellerie La Poularde
2, rue de St-Etienne — 77.54.40.06

M. Etéocle. Closed Mon dinner and Tue lunch (except holidays), and 2 Jan-15 Feb. Open until 10 pm. Private room: 40. Air cond. Valet parking. Telex 307002. V AE DC.

Gilles Etéocle is a chef of the old school, and he attracts plenty of regional restaurant-goers with a yearning for the way things used to be. This huge corner house has all the tradition they could desire: comfortable, rather overburdened décor, faultless service, wines of repute, and a style of cooking locked into the certainty of its own perfection. There's nothing to take your tastebuds by surprise, but you have to take your hat off to dishes such as mosaic of freshwater perch and salmon in cream sauce, lamb from the Vaucluse hills, the chausson of black truffles and hot foie gras, or caramelised pain d'épice with baked pineapple. And you'll be delighted to discover a reasonably priced, well-constructed weekday set menu.

A la carte: 500 F. Menus: 165 F (weekdays only), 235 F, 345 F, 400 F.

Hostellerie La Poularde
(See restaurant above)

Closed Mon and 2-15 Jan. 3 stes 700 F. 11 rms 280-450 F. TV. Air cond 3 rms. Conference facilities.

The cosy, restful rooms with rather outmoded décor have good soundproofing and the suites overlook a revamped internal courtyard. The breakfast is remarkable, with wonderful brioches and jam, and perfectly served. Relais et Châteaux.

50116 Mont-Saint-Michel (Le) — (Manche)
Paris 323 - Rennes 66 - St-Malo 52 - Fougères 47

Altea-K-Motel
33.60.14.18

Closed 2 Nov-1 Feb. 100 rms 270-410 F. Restaurant. Half-board 280-355 F. TV. No pets. Conference facilities. Parking. Telex 772529. V AE.

Modern, functional hotel on the way to Mont-St-Michel. The bright, spacious rooms look out on to trees.

La Mère Poulard
33.60.14.01

Open every day. 1 ste 950 F. 26 rms 610-750 F. Restaurant. Half-board 610-780 F. TV. Garage parking. Telex 170197. V AE DC.

The comfortable rooms offer views over the bay and salt meadows.

11/20 Saint-Pierre
Grande-Rue — 33.60.14.03

Mme Gaulois. Closed 15 Nov-15 March. Open until 9 pm. Terrace dining. Air cond. Telex 772094. V.

A listed fifteenth-century building beneath the ramparts that offers good-value set menus of brasserie-style food, pizzas, and pasta.

A la carte: 180 F. Menus: 80 F, 105 F, 150 F.

Saint-Pierre
(See restaurant above)

Closed 15 Nov-15 March. 21 rms 400-650 F. Half-board 360-560 F. TV. Conference facilities.

This comfortable hotel simply oozes character. Eleven new rooms have been added this year.

Les Terrasses Poulard
Rue Principale — 33.60.14.09

Open every day. 29 rms 300-750 F. Restaurant. Half-board 260-525 F. TV. Conference facilities. Telex 170197. V AE DC.

Of recent vintage, this hotel fits admirably into its historic setting, a fair step away from the restaurant. The elegant rooms are on the small side. Excellent service.

See Villefranche-sur-Saône

See PARIS Suburbs

See Avignon

See Etampes

29210 Morlaix — (Finistère)
Paris 532 - Brest 60 - St-Brieuc 84 - Quimper 83

 ### Restaurant de l'Europe
1, rue d'Aiguillon — 98.62.11.99

M. Feunteuna. Open every day. Open until 9.30 pm. Private room: 80. Telex 941676. V AE DC.

The excellent Patrick Jeffroy has opened a new restaurant in Plounérin, leaving his former pupil, Olivier Brignou, to take over the reins here. The quality is not the same, but the new young chef is well on the way to imposing his personality with the tender pig's jowls accompanied by fresh pasta with basil, an interesting pigeon sautéed in the brown ale of Morlaix, and a flavoursome strawberry mousse. Pleasantly old-fashioned décor.

A la carte: 260 F. Menus: 95 F, 135 F, 215 F.

Hôtel d'Europe
(See restaurant above)

Open every day. 3 stes 560 F. 67 rms 130-380 F. Half-board 230-290 F. TV 57 rms. Conference facilities.

This large corner building with bright, modernised rooms is in the town centre.

17113 Mornac-sur-Seudre — (Charente-M.)
Paris 504 - Royan 13 - Saintes 37 - Rochefort 36

 ### La Gratienne
Rte de Breuillet — 46.22.73.90

Mlle Forgerit and M. Marono. Closed Wed and Thu (except July-Aug), and 1 Oct-24 March. Open until 10 pm. Garden dining. Hotel: 11 rms 200-300 F. Parking.

Alongside the railway line that ferries tourists from Tremblade to Saujon stands this restaurant with its enormous fireplace. Mireille Forgerit has forged quite a reputation as an exponent of Saintongeais specialities: chaudrée (an Atlantic version of bouillabaisse), caillebotte (a fresh farmhouse cheese) with lightly braised cabbage and smoked duck breast. There's also a creamy leek tart, fine pike fillets with asparagus, and a rich marquise au chocolat. Astonishing wine list with some excellent Bordeaux and Burgundy.

A la carte: 250 F. Menus: 100 F, 160 F.

85290 Mortagne-sur-Sèvre — (Vendée)
Paris 358 - Bressuire 40 - Nantes 56

La Taverne
4, pl. du Dr-Pichat — 51.65.03.37
M. Jagueneau. Closed Sat and 28 July-11 Aug. Open until 9.30 pm. Private room: 22. Air cond. Telex 711403. V AE DC.

This elegant *auberge* has managed to retain the gentle atmosphere of days gone by while introducing the best of modern comfort. In his ultramodern kitchen, Guy Jagueneau produces dishes that are often brilliant, always true to the seasons, and firmly rooted in regional traditions. The little eels with young leeks, oyster soup with Coteaux-du-Layon wine, or the leg of baby lamb with steamed white kidney beans are good examples. The cheapest menu is generous, and you'll easily track down some fine wines for under 100 F.
A la carte: 350 F. Menus: 145 F, 210 F, 298 F.

Hôtel de France
(See restaurant above)
Closed Sat and 28 July-11 Aug. 1 ste 300-380 F. 25 rms 210-330 F. Half-board 409-459 F. TV. Air cond 9 rms. Conference facilities. Heated pool.

These peaceful rooms are decorated in classic style and some boast a terrace. Well-equipped for small conferences, the hotel also offers a sauna, fitness centre, and magnificent covered pool.

60520 Mortefontaine — (Oise)
Paris 42 - Survilliers 7 - Ermenonville 8 - Senlis 14

L'Empire
3, rue G.-de-Nerval — 44.54.30.94
M. Stockl. Open every day. Open until 10 pm. Private room: 200. Garden dining. Parking. Telex 145766. V AE DC.

All the ingredients of success are present in this eighteenth-century château near Charles de Gaulle airport and the Villepinte exhibition centre. The imposing setting matches the elegant if unoriginal preparation of quality ingredients by a highly professional chef. You might like to try the tasty smoked duck breast and pear salad, pleasant but slightly overcooked pan-roasted cod, the prawn consommé made with basil stock, or the delicious 'chocophile's' dessert (apples in cane sugar, pâtisseries, and chocolate ice cream). So why the lingering feeling of dissatisfaction? Because of the skeletal wine list, unworthy of a restaurant of this calibre, the practically non-existent reception, and the slow if professional service.
A la carte: 400 F. Menus: 200 F, 260 F.

Château de Mortefontaine 🌲🍴
(See restaurant above)
Open every day. 2 stes 950-2,300 F. 44 rms 390-500 F. Half-board 450-640 F. TV. Tennis.

Huge, handsome rooms overlooking the forest. The reception is as offhand as in the restaurant.

74110 Morzine — (H.-Savoie)
Paris 602 - Lyon 230 - Chamonix 71 - Evian 42

Les Airelles
50.79.15.24
Closed 20 April-20 May and 20 Sep-1 Dec. 3 stes 490-750 F. 54 rms 290-750 F. Restaurant. Half-board 390-550 F oblig in seas. TV. Conference facilities. Heated pool. Valet parking. Telex 385178. V DC.

At the heart of the resort, this opulent chalet offers secretarial and laundry services. All the rooms have terraces, some overlooking the pool, others the mountains and forest. Sauna and fitness room.

La Bergerie
50.79.13.69
Closed 15 April-30 June and 10 Sep-15 Dec. 4 stes 500-850 F. 23 rms 230-620 F. TV. Air cond. Conference facilities. Heated pool. Garage parking. Telex 309066. V.

Most of the well-designed rooms and flats have a kitchenette and nearly all have a terrace. Pleasant reception and service in a restful, relaxed atmosphere. There's also a sauna, gym, and games room.

Le Carlina
Av. de Joux-Plane — 50.79.01.03
Closed 31 March-1 July and 20 Sep-20 Dec. 2 stes 480-650 F. 20 rms 300-480 F. Restaurant. Half-board 300-400 F oblig in seas. TV 12 rms. Conference facilities. Garage parking. V.

This renovated chalet at the foot of the Pleney ski slopes has spacious yet cosy rooms.

La Chamade
50.79.13.91
M. Thorens. Closed 10 May-10 June and 15 Sep-15 Oct. Open until 10 pm. Parking. V AE DC.

Thierry Thorens adds to the extravagant draped décor with his works of art in ice or sugar, trundled from table to table by the excellent serving staff to gasps of admiration all round. The meal itself is a feast of ideas, skilfully executed and beautifully presented by this talented young chef. His latest creations include quick-cooked tunny and salmon with basil, ballottin de volaille with two sauces (a creamy vegetable one and the other with tomato and fennel seeds), and a hearty but delicate fondue made with tomme cheese and onion. The delightful desserts include fried apples with ginger, apple and liquorice mousse, and grapefruit crêpes. The cellar is not yet up to the same lofty standard.
A la carte: 350 F. Menus: 230 F and 360 F (weekdays only).

Les Côtes
50.79.09.96
Closed 15 April-29 June and 7 Sep-21 Dec. 11 stes 240-510 F. 12 rms 220-280 F. Restaurant. Half-board 220-280 F. TV. Conference facilities. Heated pool. Parking. V.

This traditional chalet in a magnificent setting has a health club and Jacuzzi. Comfortable and welcoming.

Le Dahu 🌲🍴
50.79.11.12
Closed 15 April-15 June and 15 Sep-15 Dec. 2 stes 710 F. 42 rms 320-710 F. Restaurant. Half-board 325-610 F oblig in seas. TV. Conference facilities. Heated pool. Garage parking. Telex 309514. V.

Standing on a sunny slope with a garden, Le Dahu has undergone major improvements and now boasts a sauna and fitness centre. The well-kept rooms are decorated in period style. Free shuttle service to the ski lifts.

(5 km NE, access by cable-car)
74110 Morzine — (H.-Savoie)

 Les Dromonts
50.74.08.11
Mme Sirot. Closed 5 May-20 Dec. Open until 9.30 pm. Terrace dining. V AE DC.
Patrick Egreteau has taken over from Jean-Paul Hartmann in the kitchen and he's doing a creditable job with the smoked fish and blinis, the potato cake with tamié (a soft Savoie cheese), and a perfectly grilled steak which deserves better than the accompanying cubes of fried potato. Bottles from the well-stocked go for high—'resort'—prices. The décor, with its woodwork and softly lit nooks and corners, is warm and welcoming.
A la carte: 400 F. Menus: 170 F, 290 F.

Les Dromonts
(See restaurant above)
Closed 5 May-20 Dec. 40 rms 410-1,190 F. Half-board 540-785 F. TV.
Well-equipped rooms and brand-new bathrooms in a 1970s décor that is growing old gracefully. Cheerful and attentive service.

11/20 La Grignotte
Pl. du Téléphérique — 50.74.02.66
M. Breteau. Closed 30 April-23 Dec. Open until 10 pm. Terrace dining. No-smoking section. V DC.
Fresh, imaginative dishes such as tomatoes stuffed with snails, tourte aux cèpes with walnut sauce, and a hot apple tarte Tatin with cream are prepared by the *patronne*. Attractive, chalet-style décor.
A la carte: 220-260 F.

12/20 Les Hauts Forts
50.74.09.11
M. Yanez. Closed mid-April to beg July and 1 Sep-14 Dec. Open until 2 am. Terrace dining. V AE DC.
Reliable cooking with fresh produce is served in a large, multi-level dining room. Try the superb tournedos steak or the apple tart. Short wine list. You'll find an affable welcome and professional service.
A la carte: 300-350 F. Menus: 75 F (lunch only, wine inc), 160 F, 300 F.

Les Hauts Forts
(See restaurant above)
Closed 15 April-beg July and 1 Sep-14 Dec. 50 rms 360-1,860 F. TV. Conference facilities. Heated pool.
This spacious, modern hotel is well equipped for winter holidays. Sauna, bar, boutiques.

See Pons

See Méribel-les-Allues

06250 Mougins — (Alpes-Mar.)
Paris 902 - Nice 32 - Grasse 11 - Cannes 8

 L'Amandier de Mougins
Pl. du Cdt-Lamy — 93.90.00.91
M. Vergé. Closed Sat lunch, Wed and 2-9 Jan. Open until 10.30 pm. Private room: 40. Terrace dining. Telex 970732. V AE DC.
The vine-covered farmhouse perched atop the old village has lost none of its charm; nor has the vaulted dining room laid out by Denise and Roger Vergé with its millstone centrepiece and antique furniture. But Joël Manson is not as brilliant as his predecessor; and while the food may have lost some of its subtlety, the prices have become positively oppressive. The bass with fennel and the duckling with cinnamon are worth trying.
A la carte: 600 F. Menus: 220 F (lunch only), 330 F.

12/20 Le Bistrot de Mougins
Pl. du Village — 93.75.78.34
MM. Ballatore and Giordano. Closed off-season Tue and Wed, and 2 Dec-20 Jan. Dinner only in July-Aug. Open until 10 pm. Air cond. V AE.
Only one menu, but it's fresh and generous with a timbale of salt cod and spinach, rascasse with anchovies and olives, cheese, and delicious chocolate cake. A smiling reception and efficient service.
Menu: 150 F.

12/20 Brocherie Saint-Basile
427, av. St-Basile — 93.90.04.06
MM. Dupuy. Closed Jan. Open until 10 pm. Private room: 45. Garden dining. Parking. V.
The simple, generous style of the young owner-chef pervades the prix-fixe menus of this country restaurant with its enormous terrace. Try the courgette flowers with basil, the excellent smoked salmon served lukewarm with Bandol wine, or the garlic-flavoured confit de canard. Affable service.
A la carte: 300 F. Menus: 138 F, 160 F, 210 F.

La Ferme de Mougins
10, av. St-Basile — 93.90.03.74
M. Sauvanet. Closed off-season Sat lunch and Thu, 4-22 Feb and 25 Nov-13 Dec. Open until 9.30 pm (10 pm in summer). Private room: 180. Garden dining. Parking. Telex 970643. V AE DC.
This restaurant regains its two toques following the arrival of the new chef, Jean-Louis Vosgien, whose talents we recognised when he was at the Mas des Langoustiers in Porquerolles. A sensitive and imaginative cook, he has learned to blend the flavours of Provence with the spices of the Orient. After some disappointing, overcooked local asparagus, we were delighted by the sea bream served with a sesame crêpe and julienne of vegetables, and the more classic tian of lamb, attractively presented with a cardamom sauce. Less confidence comes through in the desserts, but we enjoyed the coffee mousse with toasted hazelnuts and liquorice ice cream. The knowledgeable young wine waiter will introduce you to the superb cellar, which has some especially fine Burgundies. Attentive service.
A la carte: 500 F. Menus: 230 F (until 9 pm only), 380 F.

Le Manoir de l'Etang
66, allée du Manoir — 93.90.01.07
Closed off-season Sun and Tue, and Feb. 2 stes 1,000-1,250 F. 15 rms 450-750 F. Restaurant. Half-board 420-820 F. TV 10 rms. No pets. Conference facilities. Pool. Parking. V AE.
This luxury establishment is set in attractive grounds near the municipal golf course. The comfortable rooms are decorated in traditional style.

Le Mas Candille
(See restaurant above)
Open every day. 2 stes 1,250-1,500 F. 21 rms 750-820 F. Air cond 8 rms. Conference facilities. Pool.
Bright, comfortable rooms look out on to delightful green landscape. Absolute, blessed quiet.

Le Moulin de Mougins
Quartier Notre-Dame-de-Vie
424, ch. du Moulin — 93.75.78.24

M. Vergé. Closed Thu lunch, Mon (except dinner 15 July-31 Aug) and 27 Jan-25 March. Open until 10.30 pm. Private room: 40. Garden dining. Air cond. Valet parking. Telex 970732. V AE DC.

Roger Vergé must take some credit for the fact that there are so many good cooks on the Côte d'Azur nowadays. It all began twenty years ago with his *cuisine du soleil* exalting the sunlit savours of Provence. There's still only one Moulin des Mougins, a green haven of peace and beauty, but it is now home to two distinct styles of cooking—one wonderful, the other puzzling. On the one hand, there are the clear, shimmering flavours of a fricassée of mushrooms and asparagus tips with virgin olive oil, crayfish with basil butter, sea bass on a purée of sweet peppers with sage leaves, or grilled fillet of baby veal with a purée of basil-scented fresh tomatoes: pure, luminous Nature on a plate! But a less pleasant contrast is provided by rich, heavy stocks and sauces, dry, breaded fillets of John Dory, the delicacy of young pigeon flesh dulled by a wine sauce, and a sorbet of grapefruit and vermouth which tends to block the appetite rather than stimulate it. Vergé is of course entitled to like this cooking from another age which stifles the natural taste of the ingredients, just as we are entitled not to share his view. It's up to you to decide which of his styles you prefer. In any case, you will fall under the spell of the lovely garden, the shady terrace and the dining room that displays some of Mühl's best paintings. The experience of eating here in the company of real and bogus stars from all over the world is priceless—as the bill amply proves.

A la carte: 800-1,200 F and up. Menu: 650 F.

Le Moulin de Mougins
(See restaurant above)

Closed 27 Jan-25 March. 2 stes 1,300 F. 3 rms 800-900 F. TV. Air cond.

The three rooms and two small suites are delightful and much cheaper than a grand hotel, but harder to obtain than a place in Paradise.

Les Muscadins
18, bd Courteline — 93.90.00.43

Mlle Charrier. Closed Wed lunch, Tue, 1 Feb-1 April and 1-15 Dec. Open until 10 pm. Terrace dining. Parking. V AE DC.

This restaurant has retained its rural character with a fireplace, garden furniture and pretty printed fabrics in the two dining rooms. The atmosphere is restful and the cooking lively, by a team of young chefs who have worked with Provençal maestros Chibois and Ducasse, among others. Only a hint of assertiveness is missing from the crumb-coated turbot with asparagus tips, roast young pigeon with petals of garlic and celery crisps, and the fruit compote with honey. Wines include a good choice of Coteaux-d'Aix and Champagnes, lovingly presented by the new sommelier, Stéphane Le Flammanc. Service is diligent, but slow.

A la carte: 400 F. Menus: 190 F (weekdays only), 310 F.

Les Muscadins
(See restaurant above)

Closed 1 Feb-1 April and 1-15 Dec. 1 ste 1,275 F. 7 rms 850 F. TV. Air cond. Conference facilities.

Eight delightful rooms, each one individually decorated and attractively furnished.

Le Relais à Mougins
Pl. de la Mairie — 93.90.03.47

M. Surmain. Closed Tue lunch, Mon, 3 weeks end Nov-beg Dec and 2 weeks in Feb. Open until 10.30 pm. Private room: 20. Terrace dining. Telex 462559. V.

This charming spot in the village centre has become the scene of savoury, creative cooking. Dominique Louis's talent has become more individual, and his classic baby pigeon in a potato crust, and lobster prepared three ways (fricassée, soufflé, and salad) have been joined this year by a marbled terrine of foie gras with artichokes and a prime cut of salmon with Guérande sea salt. Rich, far-ranging wine list.

A la carte: 450 F. Menus: 165 F (weekdays only), 235 F, 360 F.

MOULINS

03000 Moulins — (Allier)
Paris 292 - Vichy 57 - Nevers 54 - Bourges 98

Jacquemart
10, pl. de l'Hôtel-de-Ville — 70.44.32.58

M. Rauch de Roberty. Closed Sun dinner, Mon, 5-18 March and 29 July-18 Aug. Open until 9 pm. Private room: 25. Air cond. V AE DC.

The young chef is a pupil and admirer of Alain Senderens, but the long menu is the product of his own distinctive personality and discoveries. Here, in the cheerful dining room with its admirable ceiling, you can discover his consommé of beef with scallops and bone marrow, fillet of sole in courgette dressing with truffles, slices of roast duck with ginger, apples, and cinnamon, fillet of pigeon with spices and mushrooms, and banana feuillantine with rum ice cream. The prices may dampen your enthusiasm, but the wine list reveals a constant concern for good value along with some excellent white Burgundies, red Bordeaux, Beaujolais, and wines from the Loire. Delightful reception.

A la carte: 400-500 F. Menus: 140 F (weekdays only), 190 F, 290 F, 390 F.

Hôtel de Paris
21, rue de Paris — 70.44.00.58

M. Lefoll. Closed 2-31 Jan. Open until 9.30 pm. Private room: 50. Air cond. Garage parking. Telex: 394853. V AE DC.

Jean-Claude Lefoll is moving away from the heavily regional style of his predecessors (the marvellous potato pâté studded with plump escargots is still, thank heavens, on the menu!), though he makes creative use of fine local produce, especially in the game season. Try the lobster with potatoes and fresh truffles, young pigeon with pickled lemon and almonds, and the delicious desserts. The cellar is superb; the lovely provincial décor is warm and lavished with flowers.

A la carte: 350 F. Menus: 100 F (lunch only), 200 F, 250 F, 340 F.

Hôtel de Paris
(See restaurant above)

Closed 2-31 Jan. 6 stes 700-900 F. 21 rms 280-700 F. Half-board 550-900 F oblig in seas. TV. Conference facilities.

Some of the attic rooms are tiny, but all have been tastefully renovated and attractively furnished. Attentive service and good breakfasts. Special prices for hunting breaks in season.

MULATIÈRE (LA)

See Lyon

MULHOUSE

68100 Mulhouse — (Haut-Rhin)
Paris 537 - Belfort 44 - Colmar 41 - Strasbourg 116

L'Alsace

4, pl. Ch.-de-Gaulle — 89.46.01.23
M. Vincent. Open every day. Open until 10 pm. Private room: 150. Terrace dining. Garage parking. Telex 881807. V AE DC.

On the ground floor of this modern hotel or on its pleasant terrace, you'll enjoy classic cooking with just enough individual flavour. Venison and sweetbread pâté with hazelnuts, lotte with smoked bacon and Sauternes, and rabbit tournedos with red-cabbage purée are good choices.

A la carte: 250-280 F. Menus: 140 F (wine inc), 85 F, 160 F.

Altea

(See restaurant above)
Open every day. 96 rms 260-430 F. Half-board 385-525 F. TV. Conference facilities.

Comfortable, functional rooms that should be better soundproofed here in the town centre. The reception could be improved. Good breakfasts.

Hôtel du Parc

26, rue de la Sinne — 89.66.12.22
Open every day. 3 stes 1,950-2,850 F. 76 rms 680-950 F. Half-board 945-1,065 F. Restaurant. TV. Air cond. Conference facilities. Valet parking. Telex 881790. V AE DC.

The former hotel of the Schlumpf Brothers (the noted car collectors), has been modernised with meticulous attention to detail, restoring the décor to its full art deco glory. Superbly equipped. The service is excellent but the breakfasts need attention.

Au Quai de la Cloche

5, quai de la Cloche — 89.43.07.81
M. Michel. Closed Sat lunch, Sun dinner, Mon and 24 July-15 Aug. Open until 9.30 pm. Private room: 8. Parking. V.

A comfortable, slightly dreary restaurant looking out on the marketplace. Jacques Michel's regional-based cooking is intelligent, but can be strangely lacking in finishing touches. We enjoyed the lobster salad with celeriac rémoulade and shellfish vinaigrette, but the macaroon stuffed with cream and raspberries had little flavour. A cheery reception and efficient service.

A la carte: 320 F. Menus: 150 F, 220 F, 300 F.

Wir

1, porte de Bâle — 89.56.13.22
Mme Wir. Closed Fri and July. Open until 10 pm. Private room: 25. Hotel: 39 rms 150-285 F. Telex 881720. V AE DC.

Raymond Wir, a knowledgeable cook and master of sauces, is happier with classic cuisine than with regional dishes. The salad of foie gras is generously served, the ham and salmon are rather too heavily smoked, while the blanquette of veal tenderloin is paired with flamed (incinerated!) prawns. Excellent sorbets and homemade pâtisseries, and an exceptional choice of good local wines.

A la carte: 350 F. Menus: 160 F, 200 F, 265 F.

And also...

Our selection of places for inexpensive, quick, or late-night meals.

Airport Brasserie (89.69.77.48 - at the airport. Open until 11.30 pm): The German border runs through the airport, and this restaurant is on the French side with its fine range of well-chosen local produce: smoked and unsmoked charcuterie, farmhouse Munster cheese.

Aux Belles Fleurs (89.42.01.82 - 15, rue Madeleine. Open until 1 am): The cooking is less picturesque than the clientele, which is composed of journalists, eternal students, and so on (80-200 F).

Biniou (89.43.54.95- 88, av. de Colmar. Open until midnight): Buckwheat crêpes with bacon and a score of sweet crêpes, plus some grilled meat dishes (150 F).

Bucherie (89.42.12.51 - 2, av. Kennedy. Open until 9.30 pm): A good 50 F menu and *plats du jour* are offered alongside the meats you cook yourself on a hot stone brought to your table.

Obernois (89.59.03.75 - 1, rue du Siphon. Open until 10 pm): Cooking as local as you'll find, from the traditional Alsace stew, baeckeoffe, to the flamed apple tart (60-180 F).

Restaurant du Musée de l'Automobile (89.42.22.48 - 192, av. de Colmar. Lunch only): Forget the 'gastronomical' restaurant, and head for the self-service instead; the brasserie-style dishes priced from 90 to 200 F are best. The museum houses 500 of the most beautiful vintage cars in the world (90-200 F).

In nearby Illzach

(6 km N)
68110 Mulhouse — (Haut-Rhin)

La Closerie

6, rue H.-de-Crouzas — 89.61.88.00
M. Beyrath. Closed Sat lunch, Sun, 13-28 July and 22 Dec-3 Jan. Open until 9.15 pm. Private room: 20. Parking. V.

Two more points for this gentleman's residence decorated in tones of salmon-pink where Hubert Beyrath creates increasingly individual and engaging dishes. Among the best are the young pigeon cooked to rosy perfection with curly cabbage, carefully cooked and seasoned prawns with green beans, and the fillets of red mullet cooked with wine and a rich bone-marrow sauce. Well-balanced wine list and cheerful service.

A la carte: 320 F. Menus: 185 F, 215 F.

Le Parc

8, rue V.-Hugo — 89.56.61.67
M. Huffschmitt. Closed 2 weeks in Aug and Christmas week. Open until 9 pm. Private room: 40. Terrace dining. Parking. V.

Jean-Pierre Huffschmitt's cooking may be less adventurous than in previous years, but it's still thoroughly modern. The style is reminiscent of Fredy Girardet, with whom he has worked, but Huffschmitt needs to concentrate on coaxing more flavour from his excellent raw materials. The young rabbit with prawns and purslane is pleasant but insufficiently seasoned, and the poached fish with pistou (a basil and garlic sauce) needs more pistou. Good Munster cheese salad and an attractive array of fruit sorbets. Some of the fine wines are served by the glass. Very friendly reception and service.

A la carte: 350 F. Menus: 180 F (weekdays lunch only), 250 F (weekdays dinner only, wine inc), 350 F.

The new spiral-bound RAC Atlas France will help you to find your chosen restaurant of hotel, no matter how secluded.

(4 km N on D 20)
68260 Mulhouse — (Haut-Rhin)

Pierre Burger

163, fg de Mulhouse — 89.52.76.12
M. Burger. Closed Sun dinner and Mon. Open until 10 pm. Garden dining. Parking. V AE DC.
An unpromising setting in a suburban business area and rather dull décor, but the lady of the house soon dispels any gloom with her cheerful welcome. In the kitchen, the arrival of Pierre Burger's son, Frédéric, may give his father's skilful, traditional style just the youthful boost it needs. Already excellent are the medley of fish with sweet-pepper vinaigrette, stuffed veal, and the breads (try the sesame rolls). Appealing cellar.
A la carte: 350-400 F. Menus: 125 F and 180 F (weekdays lunch only) and from 185 F to 330 F.

(2 km E)
68400 Mulhouse — (Haut-Rhin)

Auberge de la Tonnelle

61, rue du Mal-Joffre — 89.54.25.77
M. Hirtzlin. Closed Sat lunch, Sun, 10-25 Feb and 15 Aug-3 Sep. Open until 9.30 pm. Private room: 16. Parking. V.
Resolutely modern, market-based, and bursting with ideas, Jean-Marie Hirtzlin's cooking makes his the best restaurant in this dingy suburb. Salad of grilled prawns and red beet, skate with watercress and chunks of fried bacon, and fillet of sole cooked in leek bouillon with caviar are served in a modern setting full of lush green plants.
A la carte: 400 F and up.

(8 km S on D 21)
68440 Mulhouse — (Haut-Rhin)

Moulin du Kaegy

89.81.30.34
M. Bégat. Closed Sun dinner, Mon and Jan. Open until 10.30 pm. Private room: 45. Parking. V AE DC.
Bernard Bégat came to this delightful wattle-and-daub mill thirty years ago to pioneer *la nouvelle cuisine* and he is still combining the best of old, new, and regional styles to produce some of the finest food in Alsace. After paying homage to the incomparable goose liver confit, you'll discover Bégat's stimulating style in the tartare of duck marinated with sage, bass with mace butter, breast of guinea fowl with fresh figs and elderberry vinegar. Or try the marvellous homely dishes such as pork and wine stew or bœuf à la mode. A few gorgeous desserts and a high-class wine list.
A la carte: 400 F. Menus: 180 F (weekdays lunch only), 310 F (wine inc), 250 F, 420 F.

68530 Murbach — (Haut-Rhin)
Paris 480 - Gérardmer 65 - Guebwiller 6 - Colmar 31

Hostellerie Saint-Barnabé

25, rue de Murbach — 89.76.92.15
M. Orban. Closed off-season Sun dinner and Mon, 30 Jan-7 March and 30 June-9 July. Open until 9.30 pm. Private room: 120. Terrace dining. Garage parking. Telex 881036. V AE DC.
Since leaving the Château d'Isenbourg at Rouffach, Eric Orban seemed to be groping around in search of a style, but now he is back on form and gains another point. His prawns with morels are delicious and perfectly prepared, and while the foie gras in a Gewurztraminer jelly may be a trifle overcooked, it still provides a very pleasant start to a meal. All the dishes are made with quality produce, the desserts are good (apart from the uninteresting pears in wine), and the wines above reproach. Unfortunately the prices are progressing along with the cooking.
A la carte: 350 F. Menus: 110 F, 200 F, 260 F.

Hostellerie Saint-Barnabé

(See restaurant above)
Closed off-season Sun and Mon, 30 Jan-7 March and 30 June-9 July. 3 stes 560 F. 24 rms 230-680 F. Half-board 375-575 F. TV 17 rms. Conference facilities. Tennis.
A delightful, perfectly quiet setting. Most of the rooms have been modernised and are very comfortably furnished.

22530 Mur-de-Bretagne — (Côtes/Armor)
Paris 455 - Saint-Brieuc 45 - Pontivy 16

Auberge Grand'Maison

1, rue L.-le-Cerf — 96.28.51.10
M. Guillo. Closed Sun dinner and Mon, Feb school holidays and 30 Sep-20 Oct. Open until 9 pm. Private room: 16. V AE DC.
Jacques Guillo has been hanging on in this lost corner of Brittany for over ten years now, despite the difficulty of filling his attractive stone-walled dining room in winter. This year carpeting makes for a cosier atmosphere and Guillo earns another point for his constant quest for perfection. This can lead him to unnecessary complexity, as in the lobster with five flavours presented in five tiny individual dishes, but if that's what he enjoys, his customers would be the last to complain. They'll also appreciate his prawn feuillantine with sesame seeds, the subtly spiced breast of duck à la rouennaise, and the excellent pâtisseries. Brigitte Guillo greets guests with a smile, the service is attentive, and the wine list, one of the finest in Brittany, offers some real bargains.
A la carte: 350 F. Menus: 160 F (weekdays only), 220 F, 350 F, 400 F.

Auberge Grand'Maison

(See restaurant above)
Closed Sun, Mon, Feb school holidays and 30 Sep-20 Oct. 12 rms 220-600 F. Half-board 420-650 F. TV 6 rms. Conference facilities.
All the rooms have just been attractively redecorated. Try the wonderful gourmet breakfast at 70 F.

24400 Mussidan — (Dordogne)
Paris 530 - Bergerac 25 - Angoulême 84

(9 km W on N 89)
24400 Mussidan — (Dordogne)

Le Clos Joli

7 km E on N 89 — 53.81.10.01
M. Latourte. Closed Tue, dinner off-season Sun and Mon, 3-15 June and 16-28 Sep. Open until 9 pm. Private room: 15. Garden dining. Parking. V AE DC.
Jean-Paul and Sigrid Latourte have spent four years lovingly restoring this former presbytery, a stone's throw from the main Bordeaux to Périgueux road. Sigrid welcomes customers and provides rapid, professional service, while Jean-Paul dishes up good local confit, foie gras terrine,

and bœuf Stroganoff. On the minus side there's a rather mundane cheese board, the desserts need improvement, and more local wines could be added to the wide range of Bordeaux.

A la carte: 260-280 F. Menus: 74 F (weekdays only), 109 F, 129 F, 169 F, 199 F.

NAJAC

12270 Najac — (Aveyron)
Paris 640 - Rodez 86 - Albi 50 - Villefranche-de-R. 24

L'Oustal del Barry
65.29.74.32

M. Miquel. Closed Mon off-season (except holidays), and 4 Nov-22 March. Open until 9 pm. Private room: 20. Terrace dining. No-smoking section. Garage parking. V AE.

Jean-Marie Miquel's vegetable and herb garden has become the cornerstone of his skilful and highly personal cooking, sometimes sophisticated, always balanced. Green beans and fennel accompany the prawns and foie gras, pumpkin juice with dill and courgette flowers enliven the baked salmon, and peas and turnips escort the duck braised in walnut-flavoured wine. Scrumptious desserts follow, and Catherine Miquel dispenses enthusiastic advice on the fine choice of wines.

A la carte: 350-400 F. Menus: 115 F, 200 F, 280 F.

L'Oustal del Barry
(See restaurant above)

Closed Mon off-season (except holidays), and 4 Nov-22 March. 4 stes 280 F. 17 rms 200-380 F. Half-board 270-300 F. TV.

The comfortable, well-equipped rooms are furnished in rustic style. Large garden.

In nearby La Fouillade

(7 km NE on D 39)
12270 Najac (Aveyron)

Longcol
65.29.63.36

Closed Tue off-season and Jan. 15 rms 380-700 F. Restaurant. Half-board 365-525 F. TV. Conference facilities. Pool. Tennis. Parking. V AE.

Restored from the remains of a twelfth- and thirteenth-century farm, this delightful hotel on the Aveyron is set in 25 hectares of wooded grounds surrounded by hills. The small rooms are decorated with impeccable taste and boast superb furniture and carpets.

NANCY

54000 Nancy — (Meurthe/M.)
Paris 307 - Metz 57 - Epinal 69 - Dijon 201

Les Agaves
2, rue des Carmes — 83.32.14.14

M. Durand. Closed Mon dinner, Sun, 18-26 Feb and 28 July-19 Aug. Open until 10.30 pm. V AE DC.

Gilles Durand has gradually improved the décor of this huge restaurant since he moved in seven years ago, adding attractive lighting and pale-green panelling. The classic dishes, brought diligently up to date, make this one of the best restaurants in Nancy. The prices à la carte have gone up (perhaps due to an excessive use of 'luxury' foodstuffs), but the set menus are still good value and the portions generous. Try the prawns with artichoke hearts, fisherman's casserole with aïoli, or the young pigeon with baby vegetables and foie gras ravioli.

A la carte: 300 F. Menus: 95 F, 125 F, 180 F.

Hôtel Américain
Pl. A.-Maginot — 83.32.28.53

Open every day. 51 rms 195-300 F. TV. Conference facilities. Telex 961831. V AE DC.

A well kept and equipped hotel in the town centre offering good, brunch-style breakfasts. Half-board possible.

Le Ban des Vendanges
104, rue Stanislas
83.37.42.20

Mme Mutel. Closed Sun, Mon and week of 15 Aug. Open until 10.30 pm. Air cond. V.

This former wine bar has been transformed into a real restaurant with a young, cheerful atmosphere. You can still taste an impressive range of wines by the glass, but now you can accompany them with fried small squid, and more original dishes like fritters of sole and vegetables, or foie gras in pastry with turnips and potatoes. The service sometimes seems overstretched.

A la carte: 250 F.

Le Capucin Gourmand
31, rue Gambetta
83.35.26.98

M. Veissière. Closed Sun, Mon and 1-18 Aug. Open until 10 pm. Private room: 26. Air cond. V.

The décor, which was beginning to show its age, has been renewed this year, but unfortunately the same cannot be said of the cooking. Not that Gérard Veissière lacks talent, far from it, but he does have a tendency to rest on his laurels. Maybe it's because what his customers appreciate most is the cheerful, relaxed atmosphere maintained by his wife Yolande, but we feel the stagnation has gone on for too long and Veissière loses his second toque this year. The cooking is classic but uneven; the desserts, on the other hand, are remarkable. Frédéric, the son of the household, is turning out to be a very talented pâtissier, and his crêpes Alaska (with vanilla ice cream, marmalade, and orange zest) are enchanting. With the help of the moderately priced wines and pleasant service, it shouldn't take long for Le Capucin Gourmand to scale the heights of gastronomy once more.

A la carte: 350-400 F. Menus: 180 F, 250 F, 400 F.

12/20 La Chaumière
60, rue Stanislas
83.37.05.03

M. Antoine. Closed Sat lunch, Sun and 28 July-18 Aug. Open until 10 pm. Private room: 40. Air cond. V AE DC.

Here you'll enjoy generous servings of carefully cooked but uninspired fare, such as warm salad of pigeon breast with wild mushrooms, red mullet in olive oil with courgette mousse, and whole grilled calf's liver. High prices.

A la carte: 300-350 F. Menus: 110 F, 185 F.

La Chine
31, rue des Ponts — 83.30.13.89

M. Ltm. Closed Sun dinner, Mon and 4-25 Aug. Open until 10.30 pm. Air cond. V AE DC.

A stone dragon guards the entrance to this good-value Chinese restaurant. We've awarded another point for the fresh, precise cooking: prettily presented chicken salad with ginger, delicious sole with sweet-and-sour sauce, glazed duck breast, and melting mandarin fritters. Charming service. Be sure to try the Chinese white wine 'La Grande Muraille' (the Great Wall).

A la carte: 200-300 F. Menus: 135 F, 175 F.

Comptoir du Petit Gastrolâtre

1, pl. de Vaudémont – 83.35.51.94
M. Tanesy. Closed Mon lunch, Sun, 1 week in Jan and at Easter, and 15 Aug-1 Sep. Open until 11 pm. Terrace dining. V.

Patrick Tanesy, who for some time ran one of Nancy's best restaurants, Le Gastrolâtre, has turned his talents to bistro cooking. The tripe terrine, baeckeoffe (regional stew) with foie gras, and iced gingerbread parfait are served with a smile. Terrific little wines.

A la carte: 250-280 F. Menus: 75 F and 145 F (weekdays only).

Le Goéland

27, rue des Ponts – 83.35.17.25
M. Mengin. Closed Sun dinner and Mon. Open until 10 pm. Private room: 25. Air cond. V AE.

In just a few years, Jean-Luc Mengin's imaginative fish cookery has become one of the best in France. His style is reflected in the elegant, modern, beige-and-pink décor, which will give you an appetite as surely as the Gewurztraminer that Danièle Mengin, a confirmed *sommelière*, will suggest as an apéritif. The meal is a voyage of discovery, from the seafood minestrone with pistou, frogs' legs and smoked salmon salad with warm baby potatoes, and eel with fresh noodles, to the orange salad in saffron jelly. Varied wines; perfect service.

A la carte: 400 F and up. Menus: 155 F, 220 F.

Le Stanislas

2, pl. Stanislas – 83.35.03.01
M. Algan. Open every day. Open until 10 pm. Private room: 90. Terrace dining. Valet parking. Telex 960367. V AE DC.

It was obviously impossible to impose too modern a décor on the dining room of this listed hotel situated on Nancy's sublime eighteenth-century Place Stanislas, but the new look strikes a balance between simplicity and elegance. Michel Douville's classic, pleasantly regional cooking is in perfect harmony, as the steamed freshwater perch in herb vinaigrette, pot-au-feu of chicken breast with truffles, and frozen nougat perfumed with bergamot amply demonstrate. Excellent service.

A la carte: 350-400 F. Menus: 160 F (weekdays lunch only), 185 F, 220 F, 250 F.

Grand Hôtel de la Reine

(See restaurant above)
Open every day. 8 stes 950-1,450 F. 51 rms 450-950 F. TV. Conference facilities.

This luxuriously equipped hotel occupies one of the historic buildings on the beautiful Place Stanislas and has a listed staircase and public rooms. The bedrooms are decorated in Louis XV style.

La Toison d'Or

11, rue R.-Poincaré – 83.39.75.75
M. Navarre. Open every day. Open until 10.30 pm. Private room: 200. Air cond. Telex 960034. V AE DC.

The cooking has grown more consistent of late, and you can enjoy top-drawer ingredients like the Angus steak with bone marrow in the comfortable, inviting dining room. The 'Toison d'Or' set menu, includes wine and coffee, offers asparagus and smoked-salmon salad, roast leg of lamb with thyme, and whisky-spiked crêpes stuffed with chestnuts.

A la carte: 300 F. Menus: 150 F (wine inc), 170 F (w-e and holidays only, wine inc), 126 F.

Altea Thiers

(See restaurant above)
Open every day. 190 rms 270-430 F. TV. Air cond. Conference facilities.

Extensive renovation has added 80 new rooms, a luxury floor, new bar, and breakfast lounge. Sauna and mini-gym.

12/20 Le Wagon

57, rue de Chaligny
83.32.32.16
M. Martin. Closed Sat, Sun, holidays and 12 July-12 Aug. Open until 9.30 pm. Air cond. Parking. V.

A genuine 1927 railway carriage with its original brass fittings, banquettes and marquetry, Le Wagon now stands on a car park offering salads, charcuteries, and uncomplicated cooked dishes.

A la carte: 200 F. Menus: 70 F, 120 F, 170 F.

And also...

Our selection of places for inexpensive, quick, or late-night meals.

L'Aiglon (83.32.21.43 - 5, rue Stanilas. Open until 11 pm): Hearty food (choucroute, trout with almonds) at reasonable prices (100-150 F).
Bonnie and Clyde (83.35.26.32 - 29, rue des Ponts. Open until 10.30 pm): Massive portions of American-style cooking. Good quality (150 F).
Chez Bagot (Le Chardon Bleu) (83.37.42.43 - 49, Grande-Rue. Open until 11 pm): Fish dishes served in a family atmosphere (200 F).
Flo (L'Excelsior) (83.35.24.57 - 50, rue H.-Poincaré. Open until 12.30 am): Open later than all the rest. Flo has succeeded in giving some personality to this exceptional setting.
Rôtisserie Le P'tit Cuny (83.32.85.94 - 97-99, Grande-Rue. Open until 10.30 pm): Good value and a warm atmosphere (150-200 F).
La Toque Blanche (83.30.17.20 - 1, rue Mgr-Trouillet, Pl. St-Epvre. Open until 10.30 pm): Well-prepared foie gras and fish (200-250 F).

In nearby Flavigny-sur-Moselle

(16 km S on N 57)
54630 Nancy (Meurthe/M.)

Le Prieuré

3, rue du Prieuré
83.26.70.45
M. Roy. Closed Wed, dinner Sun and holidays, Feb and Nov, and 10 days end Aug-beg Sep. Open until 9.30 pm. Private room: 60. Garden dining. Parking. V AE DC.

Slowly but surely, Joël Roy has transformed this mundane restaurant in an ordinary village into a place that tempts passers-by to stop and people from Nancy to leave town. And the bill remains reasonable even if you sample dishes like the smoked salmon and prawns with a truffle sorbet, breaded turbot with fresh tomatoes, pigeon poached in red wine and served with foie gras ravioli, or the iced nougat flavoured with bergamot.

A la carte: 330-380 F. Menus: 210 F (lunch only), 270 F (weekdays only), 320 F.

Le Prieuré

(See restaurant above)
Closed Wed, Feb and Nov school holidays, and 10 days end Aug-beg Sep. 4 rms 500 F. TV.

Four huge, comfortable rooms overlook the new cloistered garden. Fine bathrooms and breakfasts that will make you jump out of bed.

NANS-LES-PINS

83860 Nans-les-Pins — (Var)
Paris 811 - Toulon 61 - Aix 43 - Marseille 41

Domaine de Châteauneuf

N 560, Logis de Nans — 94.78.90.06
Mme Malet. Closed Mon off-season, and 30 Nov-24 March. Open until 10 pm. Private room: 30. Garden dining. Valet parking. Telex 400747. V AE DC.

Pierre Bagatta, who once worked with Jacques Maximin, has regained his former popularity since moving from the Old Port of Marseille to this delightful country house 40 kilometres away. His latest creations show a new maturity as well as his uncontested talent: remarkable foie gras and Aosta raw ham served with sultanas, herb-coated chicken breast, frozen beetroot and cucumber mousse. The service still seems ill at ease in the airy, opulent dining room.
À la carte: 300-400 F. Menu: 190 F.

Domaine de Châteauneuf

(See restaurant above)
Closed 30 Nov-24 March. 6 stes 1,200-2,000 F. 26 rms 480-980 F. Half-board 480-1,200 F. TV. Conference facilities. Pool. Tennis. Golf.

Surrounded by a superb eighteen-hole golf course, this seventeenth-century residence has been redecorated with clear, bright colours, fine antique furniture, and infinite taste. Excellent breakfasts and perfect reception.

NANTERRE

See PARIS Suburbs

NANTES

44000 Nantes — (Loire-Atlantique)
Paris 392 - Rennes 106 - Vannes 109 - Angers 87

Astoria

11, rue de Richebourg — 40.74.39.90
Closed 27 July-26 Aug. 45 rms 250-330 F. TV 43 rms. Conference facilities. Garage parking. Telex 700615. V.

Set in a quiet street near the station and botanical gardens. The comfortable rooms are regularly redecorated.

Auberge du Château

5, pl. de la Duchesse-Anne — 40.74.05.51
M. Bourhis. Closed Sun, Mon, 3-26 Aug and Christmas week. Open until 9.30 pm. V.

The produce is chosen with care and cooked simply and skilfully at this restaurant near the station. Try the paupiette of fresh and smoked salmon with parsley purée, duck breast with spices, scallops with vegetable jus, and wind up with an orange-scented fruit gratin. Good wines, especially from the Loire valley.
À la carte: 240 F. Menus: 115 F, 165 F.

La Cigogne

16, rue J.-J.-Rousseau — 40.69.72.65
MM. Bénard and Lacomère. Closed Sat, Sun, 1-7 April and 27 July-26 Aug. Open until 10.30 pm. V.

This small restaurant has new décor, but the menu is still faithful to fine basic ingredients and the hearty cooking of Lyon. Friendly staff will serve you tripe, andouillette sausage, and reasonably priced wines with a particularly good choice of Muscadets.
À la carte: 250 F. Menu: 210 F (wine inc).

Le Gavroche

139, rue des Hauts-Pavés — 40.76.22.49
MM. Parry and Hilaire. Closed Sun dinner, Mon and 15 July-15 Aug. Open until 10.30 pm. Private room: 35. Terrace dining. Air cond. Parking. V.

A small terrace has been added to the modern dining room and the unpretentious cooking has won over the locals. Hervé Hilaire's most reliable dishes include the sweetbread terrine, crêpes stuffed with saffron-spiced bay scallops and prawns, coquilles St-Jacques with cream and vermouth, and an excellent chocolate cake. Good value.
À la carte: 280-350 F. Menus: 185 F (weekdays lunch only, wine inc), 135 F, 175 F, 250 F.

L'Hôtel

6, rue Henri-IV — 40.29.30.31
Open every day. 31 rms 290-415 F. TV. Parking. Telex 701569. V AE DC.

The rooms are pretty and elegantly decorated; some boast a terrace overlooking the garden, others have views of the château of the Dukes of Brittany. Excellent breakfasts.

12/20 La Mangeoire

16, rue des Petites-Écuries — 40.48.70.83
M. Plisson. Closed Sun, Mon and 1-23 Sep. Open until 10 pm. Terrace dining. V.

The food is as conventional as can be—trout with almonds, entrecôte bordelaise, peach Melba—but conscientiously prepared. The set menus offer superb value.
À la carte: 200 F. Menus: 58 F (except dinner in summer), 75 F, 90 F, 140 F.

Le Manoir de la Régate

Gachet - Port Brégeon — 40.30.02.97
M. Hillenmeyer. Closed Sun dinner, Mon, 11-18 Feb and 18 Aug-8 Sep. Open until 10 pm. Private room: 20. Garden dining. Parking. V DC.

This vine-covered building on the banks of the Erdre houses a charming restaurant with beams, pastel décor, and gentle lighting. Alain Hillenmeyer emphasises quality ingredients in his classic cooking. Specialities include cassolette d'escargots in spiced fumet, freshwater perch in butter sauce, duck breast with sea salt, and iced praline dessert. More than 100 fine wines to choose from.
À la carte: 300 F. Menus: 85 F (weekdays lunch only), 150 F (weekdays only, wine inc), 190 F, 290 F.

Les Maraîchers

21, rue Fouré — 40.47.06.51
Mme Chan and M. Pacreau. Closed Sat lunch (except groupes), Sun and week 15 Aug. Open until 11 pm. Private room: 30. V AE DC.

Serge Pacreau has joined forces with the energetic Cécile Chan to give renewed vigour to his flagging establishment. The results are already visible, from the quality of the reception to the menu, which now changes every other day. Our last meal consisted of some especially good smoked salmon, crab soufflé with a hot, bitter-sweet dressing, turbot baked to a turn in a potato crust and served with spicy carrot jus, feuillantine of apricots, and a delicious berry gratin. It made us sorry that Philippe Tisserat is leaving, even though a top-class chef is expected to replace him. The next change should be redecoration of the dog-eared dining room, not forgetting the loos and the noisy serving hatch.
À la carte: 450 F. Menus: 120 F (summer only), 185 F, 245 F.

12/20 Margotte
2, rue Santeuil – 40.73.27.40
M. Bernard. Closed Sat lunch, Sun and 3-19 Aug. Open until 10.30 pm. Private room: 20. V AE DC.
The *patron* will tell you all about the local wines he serves by the bottle or the glass while his wife prepares prawn and fish casserole, roast rabbit with honey, and soufflés.
A la carte: 250 F. Menus: 150 F (weekdays lunch only, wine inc), 120 F, 230 F.

13 Le Pressoir
11, allée Turenne – 40.35.31.10
M. Bachelet. Closed Sun, dinner Sat (in summer) and Mon, and Aug. Open until 10 pm. V.
The kind of address you would rather share only with a few close friends. Michel Bachelet will talk for hours about his cellar, where he keeps some unusual bottles at prices that are always moderate and sometimes rock bottom. The food is excellent value too, with traditional dishes like Lyon sausage, tripes à la mode de Caen, and calf's head with sauce gribiche.
A la carte: 175 F.

Pullman Beaulieu
See restaurant Le Tillac

13 Le San Francisco
3, ch. des Bateliers – 40.49.59.42
Mme Brigoni-Biloré. Closed Sun dinner, Mon and Aug. Open until 10 pm. Private room: 25. Terrace dining. Parking. V AE DC.
The Loire flows past the terrace, reflected in strategically placed mirrors in the dining room; and from Franck Dronneau's kitchen comes reliable cooking with loads of personality and lots of local flavours. Tuck into his fish spirals in an asparagus charlotte, an escalope of bass flanked by hot oysters, and fragrantly herbal sweetbread crépinettes. Impeccable service and a well-designed wine list.
A la carte: 320 F. Menus: 150 F (weekdays lunch only, wine inc), 140 F, 185 F, 230 F.

Sofitel
Bd A.-Millerand – 40.47.61.03
Open every day. 2 stes 1,300 F. 100 rms 535-595 F. TV. Air cond. Restaurant. Conference facilities. Heated pool. Tennis. Valet parking. Telex 710990. V AE DC.
Quiet, comfortable rooms with neutral décor. The hotel is pleasantly situated on Beaulieu Island, with fine views of the Loire. Perfect for conferences.

13 Le Tillac
3, rue du Dr-Zamenhof – 40.41.30.00
M. Pelaud. Open every day. Open until 10.30 pm. Private room: 250. Air cond. Garage parking. Telex 711440. V AE DC.
Greenery surrounds this attractive restaurant on Beaulieu Island, and soft shades of grey and salmon pink brighten the interior. Marc Lebreton brings his talents to bear on top-notch local ingredients, for a repertoire of satisfying seasonal dishes: prawns with a warm salad of crisp cabbage, noisettes de lotte with bacon, roast young pigeon with petals of garlic. There's good Muscadet to go with them, plus a charming welcome and diligent service.
A la carte: 250-280 F. Menus: 85 F, 160 F, 190 F.

Pullman Beaulieu
(See restaurant above)
Open every day. 1 ste 1,100-1,200 F. 150 rms 340-620 F. TV. Conference facilities.
Situated in the business centre, this is one of the town's finest establishments. The rooms are large, comfortable, well equipped, and soundproofed. Various conference rooms and business services are available.

16 Torigaï
Ile de Versailles – 40.37.06.37
M. Torigaï. Closed Sun and 11-26 Aug. Open until 10 pm. Private room: 35. Garden dining. V.
There are two kinds of cooking at this riverside restaurant because Shigeo Torigaï is two chefs in one. Pure Japanese, he proposes a pure Japanese menu, but he also has a French wife, he trained under Michel Guérard and Alain Senderens, and has integrated their principles with his native gastronomy. The result is dishes that have minimal cooking times, meticulously measured flavours, and no fat whatsoever. The basic ingredients, all obviously flawless, stand out in all their simplicity, exalted by a hint of the exotic. This was how we judged the oysters in Muscadet jelly, the barely smoked roulade of salmon with seaweed stuffed with a single prawn, the extraordinary shellfish ravioli with crayfish juice served with asparagus and tiny mushrooms, turbot with thyme and chanterelles in prawn juice, Challans duck with sesame seeds and cèpes accompanied by a cashew nut and almond sauce, and a sweet, juicy roast peach enhanced with peach sorbet. The wine list has been greatly improved and offers many bargains. And the waiters are Japanese—in other words, courteous, unobtrusive, and efficient.
A la carte: 400 F. Menus: 150 F (lunch only, wine inc), and from 210 F to 380 F.

Le Jules Verne
3, rue du Couëdic – 40.35.74.50
Open every day. 65 rms 375 F. TV. Air cond. No pets. Telex 701166. V AE DC.
Seven storeys of well-equipped, soundproofed rooms in the town centre. The staff is very friendly. Good breakfasts.

And also...
Our selection of places for inexpensive, quick, or late-night meals.
L'Antartic (40.73.81.01 - 21, rue Scribe. Open until midnight): Behind the theatre, this new restaurant proposes very fresh fish at good-value prices (100-180 F).
Le Cortina (40.89.57.12 - 10, rue A.-Brossard. Open until 11 am): You'll taste the best pizzas in Nantes here. Lunchtimes are very busy (80-120 F).
Chez Georges (40.74.25.43 - 87, rue du Mal-Joffre. Open until 10.30 pm): Good, cheap food from the Indian Ocean island of La Réunion (80-150 F).
La Méditerranée (40.48.48.50 - 20, allée d'Orléans. Open until 11 pm): Classic cooking plus a low-calorie menu. Reasonable prices (70-130 F).
Le Molière (40.73.20.53 - pl. Graslin. Open until midnight): The young and chic flock to this centrally located restaurant (60-120 F).
Les Petits Saints (40.20.24.48 - 1, pl. St-Vincent. Open until 10.30 pm): A superb former cloister serving good-value meals (80-160 F).
Phileas Fogg (40.89.03.99 - 2, rue du Château. Open until 11 pm): A gastronomic world tour. Different, and not too expensive (100-180 F).
Le Pont-Levis (40.35.10.20 - 1, rue du Château. Open until 10.30 pm): A former butcher proposes

excellent meat in this pleasant setting opposite the château (80-160 F).

Le Vieux Quimper (40.20.46.09 - 10, rue de la Bâclerie. Open until 10.30 pm): Very good crêperie in an attractive old building (60-80 F).

In nearby Basse-Goulaine

(8 km E on D 119)
44115 Nantes (Loire-Atlantique)

⌂14 Mon Rêve ✿
Rte des Bords-de-Loire — 40.03.55.50
M. Ryngel. Closed off-season Tue dinner and Wed, Feb and Nov school holidays. Open until 9.30 pm. Private room: 40. Garden dining. No-smoking section. Parking. V AE DC.

Gérard Ryngel's baroque set menus are something like a treasure hunt, and while you may not find your fortune here you're bound to enjoy his fine, straightforward cooking. The freshwater perch with Muscadet butter, shad with buttery cabbage, and roast Challans duck are everything they promise. There are some good children's menus too, and swings in the garden. Wide range of Loire wines.

A la carte: 280-350 F. Menus: 120 F (weekdays lunch only), 148 F (weekdays lunch only, wine inc), 148 F (weekdays only), and from 182 F to 268 F.

In nearby Bouguenais

(9 km SW on D 723)
44340 Nantes — (Loire-Atlantique)

12/20 Lardeux
55, rue J.-Vallès — 40.84.14.17
M. Lardeux. Open every day. Open until 10 pm. Private room: 25. Air cond. Parking. V AE.

Lotte with lobster butter, rib of beef with Gamay and shallot butter, and frozen nougat with tuiles (almond biscuits) are served in a comfortable, pink-and-wine-coloured setting. The reception is rather cool, but the service very well organised. Good wine list, on the expensive side.

A la carte: 250 F. Menus: 160 F (weekdays only), 165 F (weekdays lunch only), 97 F, 220 F.

In nearby La Haie-Fouassière

(15 km SE)
44690 Nantes — (Loire-Atlantique)

⌂13 Le Cep de Vigne
Pl. de la Gare — 40.36.93.90
M. Teboul. Closed Wed, dinner Tue and Sun, 5-20 Feb and 6-27 Aug. Open until 9.15 pm. Private room: 50. V.

The first surprise is the décor of one of the three dining rooms: sequin-covered walls and a ceiling of pink pleated satin. The second is that Bruno Teboul has no canard au Muscadet or frogs' legs on his menu, which in this area is quite an achievement. What he does offer are light, regional dishes like fillet of sole with oysters and saffron sauce, guinea fowl with truffles, and hot crêpes with orange and honey butter. Rapid, attentive service.

A la carte: 350-400 F. Menus: from 95 F to 300 F.

We are always interested to hear about your discoveries, and to receive your comments on ours. Please feel free to write to us, stating your opinions clearly.

In nearby Orvault

(7 km NW on N 137 and D 42)
44700 Nantes — (Loire-Atlantique)

⌂15 Le Domaine d'Orvault
Ch. des Marais-du-Cens — 40.76.84.02
M. Bernard. Closed Feb. Open until 9.30 pm. Private room: 20. Garden dining. Parking. Telex 700454. V AE DC.

A breath of fresh air would be welcome in the heavily classic dining room with its red patterned carpet and brown curtains, as well as in the kitchen. While it would be churlish not to acknowledge Jean-Yves Bernard's superb ingredients and precise cooking, we feel his sophisticated style would benefit from some paring down. The excellent marinated turbot, for instance, is dominated by the taste of limes and spiced oil, and the superb foie gras does not need the mango salad served with it. The cheese board is excellent, as is the rhubarb tart with honey sorbet, but on the whole the desserts are not up to standard. The wine list will point you to some of the best bottles in the region—if you can read the tiny calligraphy. Professional, distant reception and service.

A la carte: 400-500 F. Menus: 195 F (weekdays only), 250 F, 305 F, 400 F.

🏠 Le Domaine d'Orvault
(See restaurant above)
Open every day. 1 ste 600-850 F. 29 rms 310-570 F. Half-board 505-705 F. TV. Conference facilities. Tennis.

Set in wooded grounds in a residential area. The huge, comfortable rooms are richly decorated. Cordial welcome and generous, tasty breakfasts.

In nearby Saint-Jean-de-Boiseau

(15 km SW)
44640 Nantes — (Loire-Atlantique)

⌂13 L'Enclos de la Cruaudière
40.65.66.10
M. Durand. Closed Sun (except holidays), Mon, 20 Dec-3 Jan and 2-27 Aug. Open until 9 pm. Private room: 20. Garden dining. Parking. V.

Tucked away in a village near Nantes, this small restaurant with its old regional furniture has a glorious garden and veranda for warmer days. Guy Durand's ultraclassic cooking is authentic but almost backward-looking: turbot with oyster sauce, calf's kidneys with meat essence, baby pigeon with spices, and feuilleté of fruit in season. Smiling reception.

A la carte: 300 F. Menus: 170 F, 240 F.

In nearby Sorinières

(12 km S on N 137 and D 178)
44400 Nantes — (Loire-Atlantique)

🏠 Abbaye de Villeneuve
Rte des Sables-d'Olonne — 40.04.40.25
Open every day. 3 stes 980-1,225 F. 17 rms 462-872 F. Half-board 577-840 F. Restaurant. TV 7 rms. Conference facilities. Pool. Garage parking. Telex 710451. V AE DC.

An atmosphere of harmony reigns in the spacious grounds and the luxurious, prettily decorated rooms. Ten minutes by car from the centre of town.

(16 km N on D 69)
44240 Nantes (Loire-Atlantique)

 ### La Châtaigneraie
(Delphin)
156, rte de Carquefou – 40.77.90.95
M. Delphin. Closed Mon (except dinner in seas), Sun dinner, Jan and 29 July-12 Aug. Open until 9.30 pm. Private room: 30. Terrace dining. Parking. V AE DC.

Fashionable 1930s décor in shades of beige and grey complement the peaceful setting in wooded grounds leading down to the River Erdre. Joseph Delphin has an able deputy in his son Jean-Louis, who has worked with Bocuse, Chapel, Robuchon, and the Troisgros brothers, and who produces his own menus for the business meals. The cooking is classic and rich: frogs' legs and sweetbreads with parsley (melted down like spinach), rabbit with onion confit, apples, and tarragon mousse. Excellent cheese board and good but costly wines. The service is rather formal and the restaurant provides a heliport for its rich and busy customers.

A la carte: 350-400 F. Menus: 170 F (weekdays lunch only), 270 F (weekdays lunch only, wine inc), 225 F, 290 F.

See also: Champtoceaux

06210 Napoule (La) – (Alpes-Mar.)
Paris 850 - St-Raphaël 34 - Cannes 8 - Mandelieu 2

 ### Ermitage du Riou
Av. H.-Clews – 93.49.95.56
Open every day. 2 stes 910-1,470 F. 40 rms 465-1,240 F. Restaurant. Half-board 475-800 F. TV. Air cond 22 rms. Conference facilities. Pool. Valet parking. Telex 470072. V AE DC.

This Provençal-style hotel has a delightful setting and pretty garden. The rooms and suites, some with large terraces, overlook the sea, harbour, golf course, or pool.

12/20 Chez Loulou
Bd H.-Clews – 93.49.90.00
M. Cipolla. Open every day. Open until 4 am. Private room: 650. Terrace dining. Air cond. No pets. Valet parking. Telex 469820. V AE DC.

The cooking is not wildly original and prices à la carte are high, but the fish—which you choose yourself—are always pristinely fresh. Try the baked salmon with celery tagliatelle, or the fricassée of sole with meadow mushrooms. The desserts are also good in this rather showy restaurant overlooking the bay of Cannes.

A la carte: 450-500 F. Menus. 135 F (lunch only), 240 F (dinner only).

 ### Loews
(See restaurant above)
Open every day. 29 stes 1,900-6,000 F. 211 rms /55-1,600 F. Half-board 920-2,100 F. TV. Air cond. Conference facilities. Heated pool. Tennis.

The contemporary rooms with sea views sport a fresh, attractive décor. The hotel provides an hourly shuttle service to Cannes and excellent facilities for conferences. Piano-bar.

See also: Cannes, Mandelieu

11100 Narbonne – (Aude)
Paris 850 - Perpignan 62 - Béziers 27

L'Alsace
2, av. P.-Sémard – 68.65.10.24
M. Sinfreu. Closed Mon dinner, Tue and 18 Nov-18 Dec. Open until 10 pm. Air cond. V AE DC.

The Sinfreu family rolls out the red carpet for the region's upper crust and serves them their rich and reliable cooking. The shellfish, red meats, and desserts are all first-rate.

A la carte: 300-400 F. Menus: 100 F (weekdays only), 140 F, 250 F, 320 F.

Hôtel du Languedoc
22, bd Gambetta – 68.65.14.74
Open every day. 6 stes 380-460 F. 40 rms 240-380 F. Restaurant. Half-board 235-540 F oblig in seas. TV 2 rms. Air cond 4 rms. Conference facilities. Valet parking. Telex 505167. V AE DC.

Well-kept hotel with plain rooms and posh lounges. Pub with pianist.

12/20 Le Léonard
34, av. P.-Sémard – 68.65.29.36
Mlle Carbonell and M. Senty. Closed Sun and Mon. Open until 10 pm. Air cond. V AE.

More plants and flowers would brighten up the square dining room. In any case, Bernard Senty's cooking (scallops simmered in vermouth, fillet of beef with vintage wine) is well rounded and affordably priced.

A la carte: 230-280 F. Menus: 84 F, 115 F, 165 F.

Hôtel d'Occitanie
Av. de la Mer – 68.65.23.71
Open every day. 55 rms 350-440 F. Restaurant. Half-board 480-520 F. TV. Conference facilities. Pool. Tennis. Parking. Telex 505562. V AE DC.

A modern complex on the way to the beach. The huge rooms have a terrace but the atmosphere, alas, is dismal.

La Résidence
6, rue 1er-Mai – 68.32.19.41
Closed 3 Jan-3 Feb. 1 ste 450 F. 25 rms 275-395 F. TV. Air cond 10 rms. No pets. Valet parking. V.

This attractive nineteenth-century hotel is set in a quiet street in the town centre. Charming reception, limited service.

(15 km E on D 168)
11100 Narbonne – (Aude)

Hôtel de la Clape
Rue des Flots-Bleus – 68.49.80.15
Closed 4 Nov-29 March. 12 rms 170-300 F. TV 1 rm

Twelve comfortable rooms, one adapted for the disabled. The likeable owners maintain a relaxed atmosphere.

 ### Les Flots Bleus
Pl. des Karantes – 68.49.83.47
Mme Marty. Closed Mon (except holidays) and 1 Oct-1 March. Open until 10.30 pm. Terrace dining. V.

The rule here is simple cooking to show off the excellent fresh fish to best advantage. Didier Marty, owner, chef, and fisherman, prepares an increasing number of eel dishes as well as lotte with tarragon, traditional grilled fish, and an assortment of sparkling raw shellfish. The desserts are improving and the whole meal represents good value.

A la carte: 200-250 F. Menus: 95 F, 150 F.

(14 km W on N 113 and D 24)
11200 Narbonne – (Aude)

 Relais du Val d'Orbieu

D 24 – 68.27.10.27

M. Gonzalvez. Dinner only (and lunch Sun 5 Nov-16 March). Closed 30 Dec-6 Jan and 4 Feb-3 March. Open until 9.30 pm. Private room: 25. Garden dining. Parking. Telex 505572. V AE DC.

Jean-Pierre Gonzalvez, the knowledgeable wine waiter, and Jean-Pierre Robert, the imaginative chef, fill this old mill surrounded by vineyards with their boundless enthusiasm. They are true professionals, whose restaurant attracts customers from far and wide and deserves closer attention from the locals. The iced tomato soup with mint-flavoured whisked egg white, baked fish with fennel and vegetables picked fresh from the restaurant garden, oxtail mould, and hot feuilleté of caramelised pears with sabayon sauce may be fairly expensive, but there can be no doubting their quality. The wine list is well worth lingering over.

A la carte: 350-400 F. Menus: 195 F, 275 F.

 Relais du Val d'Orbieu

(See restaurant above)

Closed Sun off-season, 30 Dec-6 Jan and 4 Feb-3 March. 7 stes 720-1,050 F. 15 rms 440-725 F. Half-board 600-950 F. TV. Conference facilities. Pool. Tennis.

Spacious, comfortable suites and rooms overlook the kitchen garden and vines in this picturesque village.

(18 km E)
11560 Narbonne (Aude)

 La Floride

1, pl. L.-Madaule – 68.49.81.31

M. Peralta. Closed Sun dinner and Mon (except July-Aug), and Jan. Open until 9.30 pm. Terrace dining. V DC.

Sylvain Peralta is back in his family's restaurant, accompanied by Pascale, a young cook from Lorraine who is winning hearts with her crab bisque, raw salmon ravioli with mushroom oil, and young rabbit with a red-wine and rosemary sauce. Interesting cellar, but the desserts need to be improved.

A la carte: 220-250 F. Menus: 85 F, 145 F, 160 F, 250 F.

See Sainte-Maxime

See Schirmeck

See Pontchartrain

77140 Nemours – (Seine/Marne)
Paris 79 - Orléans 87 - Fontainebleau 17

 Altea

on A 6, aire de service – 64.28.10.32

Open every day. 102 rms 325-430 F. TV. Conference facilities. Parking. Telex 690243. V AE DC.

Easily accessible from the motorway, a modern hotel with large, soberly decorated rooms.

 Les Roches

1, av. L.-Pelletier – 64.28.01.43

M. Paillassa. Closed Sun dinner and Mon lunch. Open until 9.45 pm. Private room: 40. Terrace dining. No-smoking section. Hotel: 15 rms 100-265 F. Garage parking. V AE DC.

If you took away half the dishes on the menu, there would still be more than enough to give the measure of the chef's meticulous, reliable cooking. As well as the moules marinière with vegetables, fillet of sole with morels, and quick-cooked duck breast with buttery, juniper-flavoured cabbage, there's a good regional menu. Excellent service and new, brighter décor this year.

A la carte: 300-320 F. Menus: 85 F (weekdays only), 120 F, 180 F, 250 F.

See Dijon

See PARIS Suburbs

See Lille

58000 Nevers – (Nièvre)
Paris 239 - Dijon 190 - Bourges 68 - Auxerre 112

 La Botte de Nevers

Rue du Petit-Château
86.61.16.93

M. Vernay. Closed Sun dinner, Mon, Feb school holidays and Aug. Open until 10 pm. V AE DC.

Hidden in an alleyway in the old town, this attractive restaurant with its imposing beams and restrained prices wins a toque this year. The cooking has been skilfully simplified, and makes the best of traditional dishes: poached eggs with finnan haddock, three fillets with meadow-mushroom juice, and an ingenious crêpe terrine. Magalie is a graceful hostess.

A la carte: 250-280 F. Menus: 98 F, 135 F, 160 F, 220 F.

 Château de la Rocherie

6 km N on N 7
58640 Varennes-Vauzelles – 86.38.07.21

MM. Reparet and Brunat. Closed Sun. Open until 9.30 pm. Private room: 15. Terrace dining. Parking. V AE DC.

Pierre Reparet's succinct seasonal menus are a model of simplicity, though he sometimes sacrifices the details in his efforts to make his cooking ever lighter and more modern. We enjoyed the prawns in young cabbage aspic, sole with broad beans, freshwater perch pan-roasted with fresh parsley, and duck breast with a fricassée of radishes. The reception is delightful, and makes you want to linger in the elegant dining room overlooking the gardens.

A la carte: 300 F. Menus: 95 F, 170 F, 225 F.

Château de la Rocherie

(See restaurant above)

Closed Sun. 15 rms 160-300 F. TV. 9 rms. Conference facilities.

This Napoleon III château is set back from the road in extensive grounds. The rooms are large and have been gracefully modernised. Friendly staff and good breakfasts.

Hôtel de Diane
38, rue du Midi — 86.57.28.10
Closed 20 Dec-10 Jan. 30 rms 330-460 F. Restaurant. TV. Conference facilities. Garage parking. Telex 801021. V AE DC.
A well-kept hotel in a quiet but central street with a small garden at the back. The décor is rather outdated and the quality of the service varies.

La Porte du Croux
17, rue de la Porte-du-Croux — 86.57.12.71
M. Gély. Closed Fri dinner and Sun (except holidays), and 12-31 Aug. Open until 9.30 pm. Private room: 100. Terrace dining. Hotel: 2 rms 150-180 F. V AE DC.
The well-lit dining room overlooks the ramparts, the fourteenth-century Croux gate, and the cathedral. The good-value cooking is at ease in this historic setting, putting the emphasis on fresh produce to offer a well-balanced salad of prawns and scallops, and delicious baked lobster with artichokes, but with never a hint of innovation. The daughter of the family has studied to be a *sommelière* and promises to add interest to the wine list.
A la carte: 300 F. Menus: 85 F, 125 F, 250 F.

12/20 Le Puits Saint-Pierre
21, rue Mirangron — 86.59.28.88
M. Machebeuf. Closed Sun dinner and Mon. Open until 9.30 pm. Private room: 40. V AE.
Just reopened, this small restaurant with its pink décor and cane-seated chairs is restful and inviting. The cooking is still rather hesitant, but now and again shows a stroke of brilliance. Our good scrambled eggs were punctuated by insipid morels, uninteresting sweetbreads came accompanied by a succulent garnish of julienne carrots with candied orange and spinach, and the strawberry bavarian was perfectly honest.
A la carte: 250 F. Menus: 95 F (weekdays only), 190 F (wine inc), 135 F.

See also: Magny-Cours

NEYRAC-LES-BAINS
07380 Neyrac-les-Bains — (Ardèche)
Paris 648 - Le Puy 76 - Aubenas 17 - Vals-les-Bains 13

Hôtel du Levant
75.36.41.07
Closed off-season Fri, Sat and Sun. 20 rms 110-210 F. Restaurant. Half-board 140-190 F. No pets. Conference facilities. Parking. V.
Meals are served on the shady terrace overlooking the valley of the Ardèche. Warm, family atmosphere.

NICE
06000 Nice — (Alpes-Maritimes)
Paris 943 - Lyon 475 - Marseille 188 - Turin 222

Altea Masséna
(ex-Continental Masséna)
58, rue Gioffredo — 93.85.49.25
Open every day. 116 rms 405-700 F. TV. Air cond. Conference facilities. Garage parking. Telex 470192. V DC. D5-3
This fine traditional hotel 500 metres from the sea has just had its rooms redecorated. Modern facilities, various services, and meals served in your room at all hours. Special prices for wine tastings and visits to the opera.

L'Ane Rouge
7, quai des Deux-Emmanuel — 93.89.49.63
M. Vidalot. Closed Sat, Sun and 20 July-1 Sep. Open until 9.30 pm. Terrace dining. V. F5-47
Quality produce, careful cooking, and prohibitive prices are still the rule in this restaurant overlooking the harbour. The specialities include oysters in Champagne, stuffed mussels, lobster, crayfish, and bass with orange. Good wines, with some interesting claret.
A la carte: 500 F.

Antoine
26, bd V.-Hugo — 93.88.49.75
M. Villa. Closed Sat lunch and Sun. Annual closings not available. Open until 10 pm. Private room: 12. Terrace dining. Air cond. V. C4-20
Last year's fire is the reason for the attractive new blue décor. The kitchens have been brought up to date too, but Antoine Villa's cooking still has the same Southern accent: delicious herring salad, superb fricassée of veal kidneys in a creamy sauce, tagliatelle with shellfish and vegetables. Mme Villa provides a spirited welcome.
A la carte: 350 F and up. Menus: 160 F (lunch only), 190 F and 240 F (dinner only).

12/20 Asia
12, rue Cassini — 93.56.80.83
M. Vu-Van. Closed Sun dinner and Mon. Open until 10.30 pm. Air cond. V. E5-29
The classic Vietnamese and Chinese dishes such as chicken with saté or Chinese dumplings are carefully cooked and fashioned of fine, fresh ingredients. Eating à la carte is rather expensive but there's a new lunchtime prix-fixe menu. Dishes to take away.
A la carte: 200-250 F. Menu: 70 F (lunch only).

Atlantic
12, bd V.-Hugo — 93.88.40.15
Open every day. 2 stes 750-850 F. 123 rms 370-800 F. Restaurant. Half-board 540-580 F. TV. Air cond. Conference facilities. Valet parking. Telex 460840. V AE DC. C4-18
This traditional hotel with pleasant, well-equipped rooms has a bar and solarium.

Barale
39, rue Beaumont — 93.89.17.94
Mme Barale. Dinner only (except upon reserv). Closed Sun and Mon (except groupes), and Aug. Open until 9 pm. F4-4
Such a rigid menu would be inadmissible anywhere else. But in Hélène Barale's restaurant—an academy of *la cuisine niçoise*—it's a guarantee of consistent quality. Here you can sample a real salade niçoise, ravioli stuffed with three kinds of meat cooked en daube, alouettes sans tête (rolled and stuffed sliced beef), socca (the local crêpe made with chickpea flour), and the typical dessert, sweet Swiss chard tart. Served on checked tablecloths around a pianola, they make for an unforgettable evening.
Menu: 185 F (wine inc).

Beach Regency
223, prom. des Anglais — 93.83.91.51
Open every day. 12 stes 1,500-6,000 F. 332 rms 600-1,090 F. TV. Air cond. Conference facilities. Pool. Valet parking. Telex 461635. V AE DC. A6-25
Huge, ultra-comfortable rooms with wonderful views over the bay.

1 - L'Eridan **R**
2 - Le Gourmet
  Lorrain **R**
3 - Altea Masséna **H**
4 - Barale **R**
5 - Le Bistrot de Nice **R**
6 - Bong-Laï **R**
7 - Westminster
  Concorde **H**
8 - La Mérenda **R**
9 - Relais de Rimiez **H**
10 - Windsor **H**
11 - La Rive Gauche **R**
12 - Plaza-Concorde **H**
13 - Hôtel-Club
  des Fleurs **H**
14 - Méridien **H**
15 - Café Léost **R**
16 - Christian Breton **R**
17 - Cicion-Mallen **R**
18 - Atlantic **H**
19 - Le Ciel d'Azur **R**
20 - Le Bistrot
  d'Antoine **R**
21 - Ruffel **R**
22 - Au Passage **R**
23 - Don Camillo **R**
24 - Chantecler
  et La Rotonde
  (Hôtel Negresco) **RH**
25 - Beach Regency **H**
  et Campanile **H**
26 - La Toque Blanche **R**
27 - Le Floride **RH**
28 - Gounod **H**
29 - Asia **R**
30 - Les Dents
  de la Mer **R**
31 - Mac Mahon **R**
32 - Le Grand Pavois
  (Chez Michel) **R**
33 - La Malmaison **H**
34 - Novotel Nice
  Centre Acropolis **H**
35 - La Pérouse **H**
36 - Boccaccio **R**
37 - L'Olivier **R**
38 - West End **H**
39 - Frantour Napoléon **H**
40 - Georges **H**
41 - Grand Hôtel Aston **RH**
42 - Palais Maeterlinck **RH**
43 - Park Hôtel **H**
44 - Holiday Inn **H**
45 - Sofitel-Splendid **H**
46 - Relais Beau
  Rivage
  (Beau Rivage) **RH**
47 - L'Ane Rouge **R**
  et L'Esquinade **R**
48 - Côte d'Azur **H**
49 - Pullman **H**
50 - L'Oasis **H**

51 - Relais Elysée
  (Elysée Palace) **RH**
52 - Le Cadaqués **R**

53 - Le Florian **R**
54 - Petit Palais **H**
55 - Mercure **H**

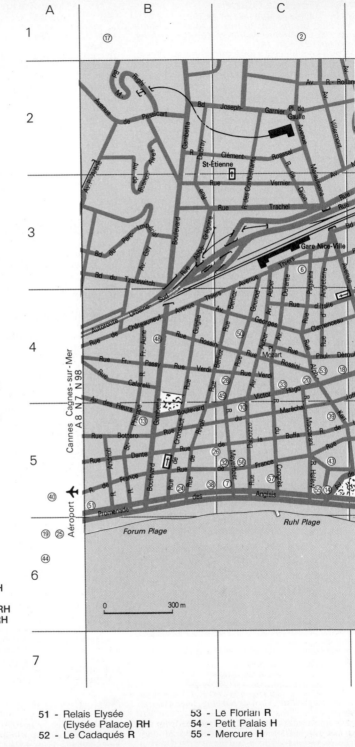

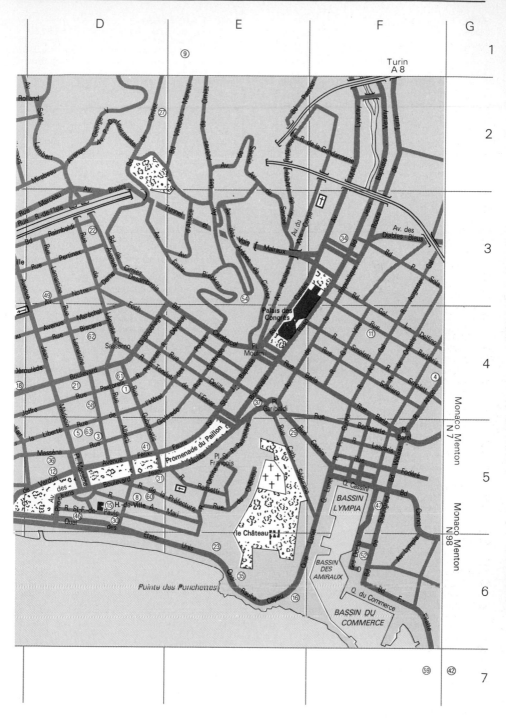

56 - Le Pot d'Etain **R**
57 - Le Saint-Moritz **R**
58 - Au Coin Breton **R**

59 - Coco Beach **R**
60 - Les Préjugés du Palais **R**
61 - Vendôme **H**

62 - Le Jardin
Gourmand **R**
63 - Jacques Maximin **R**

Beau Rivage

24, rue St-François-de-Paule — 93.80.80.70
Open every day. 10 stes 1,300-1,500 F. 110 rms 760-1,000 F. Restaurant. Half-board 865-1,065 F. TV. Air cond. Conference facilities. Valet parking. Telex 462708. V AE DC.   D5-46

Near the opera and favoured by prima donnas. The rooms are charming, and have good bathrooms. Attentive service.

Le Bistrot de Nice

2-4, rue S.-Guitry — 93.80.68.00
M. Maximin. Open every day. Open until 11.30 pm. Air cond. Telex 462794. V.   D5-5

In the same former theatre as his four-toque restaurant, Jacques Maximin has created a welcoming bistro serving hearty Niçois and Provençal cooking, sun-kissed dishes like salt-cod terrine with sweet peppers, tripe with Parmesan, and deep-fried baby red mullet. Reasonably priced, but the wines are rather expensive.
A la carte: 250 F.

12/20 Boccaccio

7, rue Masséna — 93.87.71.76
M. Cannatella. Open every day. Open until 11 pm. Terrace dining. Air cond. V AE DC.   D5-36

The new décor mixes mahogany, sky-blue fabrics and glass engravings of Mediterranean ports. The kitchen now aims for greater simplicity to show off the fine produce: crêpes with prawns, fillets of red mullet with violet artichokes, and fish baked en papillote. Superb shellfish. Prices are high, but not exorbitant.
A la carte: 300-400 F.

12/20 Bong-Laï

14, rue d'Alsace-Lorraine — 93.88.75.36
M. Costa. Closed Mon, Tue and 6-26 Dec. Open until 10 pm. Air cond. V AE DC.   C3-6

Authentic Vietnamese cooking, with specialities like steamed dumplings, fish and tamarind soups, and beef with vermicelli noodles, lettuce, and peanuts. The prices look expensive at first, but one dish will serve two or even three people. The owner says the full flavours don't emerge with smaller servings.
A la carte: 250 F. Menu: 185 F.

12/20 Christian Breton

4, pl. Guynemer — 93.56.62.06
M. Breton. Closed Sun dinner and Mon. Open until 9.30 pm. V.   E6-16

An unpretentious restaurant where you can enjoy fish and vegetable soup flavoured with garlic and basil, sea bream baked in flaky pastry with fennel, and feuillantine of pears.
A la carte: 300 F. Menus: 160 F, 240 F.

12/20 Le Cadaqués

8, quai des Docks — 93.89.41.76
M. Font-Puigferrer. Closed Tue. Open until 10.30 pm. Terrace dining. V DC.   F6-52

This welcoming Spanish *auberge* offers Catalan dishes such as gambas (jumbo prawn), paella, zarzuela (a fish soup), and veal kidneys in sherry. The cellar harbours some fine Riojas; excellent coffee. Charming reception.
A la carte: 300 F. Menu: 130 F.

11/20 Café Léost

12, rue St-François-de-Paule — 93.80.87.60
M. Baeta. Closed Sat lunch in summer. Open until 12.30 am. Terrace dining. Air cond. V AE.   D5-15

Brasserie-style cooking with a hint of sophistication, but rather inconsistent. The pretty peach-coloured dining room is busy at lunchtime.
A la carte: 250 F. Menu: 135 F.

Campanile

459-461, prom. des Anglais — 93.21.20.20
Open every day. 170 rms 325 F. Restaurant. TV. Air cond. Conference facilities. Garage parking. Telex 461640. V AE DC.   A6-25

Small, functional rooms with good air-conditioning.

Chantecler ✧

37, prom. des Anglais — 93.88.39.51
Mme Augier. Closed 19 Nov-17 Dec. Open until 10.30 pm. Private room: 50. Valet parking. Telex 460040. V AE DC.   B5-24

You won't find the limpid clarity of the Mediterranean in the weightily opulent new décor, but it is omnipresent in Dominique Le Stanc's refined regional cooking. The delights that await your palate here include a lamb's trotter stuffed with ratatouille, sardines marinated in olive oil, porchetta (suckling pig stuffed with offal and flavoured with herbs), fillets of red mullet with onions and olives, risotto with squid and peas, bass cooked in a rosemary fumet, veal kidneys with polenta, and roast pigeon with cumin served with honey-glazed baby turnips. Le Stanc also creates festive dishes using local vegetables: artichokes, tomatoes, and olives cooked in veal stock with anchovies, a potato mould with peas, and broad beans with butter and thyme. The desserts are exceptional, and wine waiter Patrick Millereau will steer you around the Provençal wines and the *grands crus*.
A la carte: 450-700 F. Menus: 260 F (weekdays lunch only), 390 F, 490 F, 550 F.

Hôtel Negresco

(See restaurant above)
Open every day. 25 stes 2,800-6,800 F. 150 rms 1,200-2,100 F. TV. Air cond. Conference facilities.

Witness to turn-of-the-century wealth and extravagance, the Negresco still oozes opulence and style. The fine old paintings and period furniture would fill an auction room several times over, and there's even a huge chandelier that is listed as an historic monument and a similar example of which hangs in the Kremlin. The 6,000 square metres of rooms and suites require constant maintenance, and the owners spare no efforts to keep them freshly decorated. The riot of colour in the 'Napoleon' rooms may not be to everyone's taste but they provide a glimpse of a more leisured era, like the much-photographed gentleman in a plumed hat who parks your car.

12/20 Cicion-Mallen

496, rte de Pessicart — 93.84.49.29
M. Mallen. Lunch only (except July-Aug and groupes). Closed Wed and 7 Jan-9 Feb. Open until 9.15 pm. Garden dining. Parking.   B1-17

Five generations of cooks have kept this restaurant near the old vineyards of Bellet. There's a wonderful plate of hors-d'œuvres (charcuterie and vegetables with anchovy sauce) and the meat is of excellent quality: only a touch of imagination is lacking. Warm welcome.
Menus: from 140 F to 175 F.

12/20 Le Ciel d'Azur

Aéroport de Nice (2nd floor) – 93.21.36.36
M. Poutz. Open every day. Open until 9.45 pm. Private room: 200. Air cond. No-smoking section. Telex 970011. V AE DC. A6-19
The dessert trolley is sheer delight, but otherwise our last meal here was disappointing and the wine list practically non existent. Maybe it's best to stick to tea and cakes in this pleasant dining room with sea views. Very professional service.
A la carte: 350 F. Menus: from 190 F to 300 F.

Coco Beach

2, av. J.-Lorrain – 93.89.39.26
Mme Cauvin. Closed off-season Sun and Mon. Dinner only in July-Aug. Annual closings not available. Open until 9 pm (10 pm in summer). Terrace dining. V AE DC. F7-59
The best grilled fish on the Riviera, plus the most delicate, juicy mussels, and the tastiest fish soup. Go out of season and you may be lucky enough to find the pageot (a kind of cold-water bream) on the menu.
A la carte: 400 F and up.

12/20 Au Coin Breton

5, rue Blacas – 93.85.17.01
MM. Banton and Deschamps. Closed Sun dinner, Mon and Aug. Open until 10 pm. V AE DC. D4-58
Despite the name, there's nothing here that might remind you of Brittany, from the restrained décor to the pot-au-feu of lotte with ravioli, and the fricassée of lamb's kidneys. Good, inexpensive set menus.
A la carte: 250 F. Menus: 85 F, 125 F, 160 F.

Côte d'Azur

57, bd Gambetta – 93.96.10.10
Open every day. 35 rms 310-370 F. TV. Parking. Telex 970225. V AE DC. B4-48
Between the station and the beach, this typical local hotel has been totally renovated. Pleasant rooms and a bar.

12/20 Les Dents de la Mer

2, rue St-François-de-Paule – 93.80.99.16
M. Bertoni. Open every day. Open until 11 pm. Terrace dining. Air cond. V AE DC. D5-30
An upturned boat and tanks full of fish provide the décor of this chic, popular restaurant serving lobster, crab, skate salad with orange, and mixed fish with tagliatelle. Expensive.
A la carte: 350 F. Menus: 135 F, 190 F, 255 F.

Don Camillo ✿

5, rue des Ponchettes – 93.85.67.95
M. Cerutti. Closed Sun, Mon, Feb school holidays and last 2 weeks of Aug. Open until 9.30 pm. V. E6-23
Franck Cerutti continues to dazzle customers with his inspired reinvention of the cooking of Nice. After working with Maximin and Ducasse and at the Enoteca in Florence, he has brought his talents to this fresh, simple restaurant, reviving long-forgotten flavours and combinations. The Swiss chard and artichoke tart, risotto of courgette flowers with crispy bacon, anchovy bouillabaisse, veal T-bone steak with capers, onions and panisse (chickpea flour pancake) highlight his respect for local ingredients. To end the meal, there are some admirable desserts inspired by the nearby Piedmont region of Italy. All at amazingly low prices for so much pleasure.
A la carte: 270-360 F.

Elysée Palace

59, prom. des Anglais – 93.86.06.06
Open every day. 2 stes 2,200-2,500 F. 144 rms 760-1,100 F. Restaurant. Half-board 865-1,065 F. TV. Air cond. Conference facilities. Pool. Garage parking. Telex 970336. V AE DC. B5-51
The façade features a female giant, 26 metres tall and 15 across, fashioned in bronze by the sculptor Sosno. Inside there are luxury rooms, a piano bar, gym, sauna, and conference rooms. And on the roof, a swimming pool.

L'Eridan

6, pl. Wilson – 93.92.43.75
M. Guenoux. Closed Sat lunch, Sun, 4-25 Aug and 22-27 Dec. Open until 10 pm. Terrace dining. Air cond. V AE DC. D4-1
Tasty duck with olives, delicious coppa (smoked pork charcuterie), but why are they so mean with the vegetables? Eric Guenoux is a talented cook (the apple and pear tart with caramel is sublime) and Catherine provides generous portions of good humour. Horribly expensive wines.
A la carte: 300-350 F. Menus: 145 F (weekdays lunch only), 280 F (weekdays only).

L'Esquinade

5, quai des Deux-Emmanuel – 93.89.59.36
M. Béraud. Closed Mon lunch, Sun, 5-31 Jan. Open until 11 pm. Terrace dining. Air cond. No-smoking section. Valet parking. V AE. F5-47
Philippe Gaillot's quality cooking draws on the best of local traditions but is occasionally inconsistent. Try the courgettes with their flowers and a tomato and basil dressing, crunchy mixed salad with seafood, and the excellent salmon 'sausage'. Prohibitive prices.
A la carte: 450-500 F. Menus: 180 F, 300 F.

Hôtel-Club des Fleurs

3, av. des Fleurs – 93.96.84.29
Open every day. 50 rms 230-295 F. Restaurant. Half-board 315-450 F. TV. Telex 470498. B5-13
The only establishment of its kind in Nice, comfortable and close to the sea. Various entertainments and excursions are offered.

Le Florian

22, rue A.-Karr – 93.88.86.60
M. Gillon. Closed Sat lunch and Sun. Annual closings not available. Open until 9.30 pm. Air cond. V. C4-53
Claude Gillon must make more of an effort. During our last visit, we were served a heavy rosette of quails stuffed with foie gras and some woolly-textured prawns cooked in lobster butter. On the other hand, the roast Bresse pigeon was absolutely perfect.
A la carte: 400 F and up. Menus: 230 F, 315 F.

Le Floride

52, bd de Cimiez – 93.53.11.02
M. Térèse. Open for lunch only. Closed Sat, Sun and Aug. Parking. V. D2-27
Here under the trees of this fashionable boulevard you'll find incredibly low prices compared to the rest of the area, a décor dotted with lush green plants, and a smiling welcome from Pierre and Robert. On the excellent-value menu: scrambled eggs with tomato, beef-jowl stew or veal chop with cream, and delicious tarte Tatin.
A la carte: 150-200 F. Menu: 80 F.

Le Floride

(See restaurant above)
Open every day. 20 rms 185-295 F. Half-board 270-340 F. TV.
Simple rooms at remarkable prices. This is the kind of clean, family hotel you can recommend to anyone.

Frantour-Napoléon

6, rue Grimaldi — 93.87.70.07
Open every day. 83 rms 340-650 F. TV. Air cond. Telex 460949. V AE DC. C5-39
This imposing 1930 hotel offers huge, modernised rooms and various services.

Georges

3, rue H.-Cordier — 93.86.23.41
Open every day. 18 rms 290-410 F. TV. Air cond 10 rms. Garage parking. V AE. A5-40
Just 200 metres from the sea, with a family atmosphere. You can have breakfast and admire the view on the third-floor terrace.

Gounod

3, rue Gounod — 93.88.26.20
Open every day. 5 stes 650 F. 47 rms 380-520 F. TV. Air cond. Garage parking. V AE DC. C4-28
This stylish hotel of the Belle Epoque has attractive décor and minibar in all the rooms. Excellent reception. Guests benefit from free access to the pool, sauna, restaurant, and other facilities of the nearby Sofitel-Splendid.

12/20 Le Gourmet Lorrain

7, av. Santa-Fior — 93.84.90.78
M. Leloup. Closed Sun dinner, Mon. Open until 9.30 pm. Hotel: 11 rms 300-350 F. V AE DC. C1-2
If we were judging his wine list (one of the finest in France) or his cheeses, Alain Leloup would rank among the country's great chefs. Sadly, our last meal did not even justify last year's toque: average foie gras de canard, tournedos steak with an original but bland Livarot cheese sauce, and nondescript apple tart. Slow, haughty service.
A la carte: 300-350 F. Menus: 100 F (weekdays lunch only), 180 F, 200 F.

Grand Hôtel Aston

12, av. F.-Faure — 93.80.62.52
Open every day. 160 rms 400-1,000 F. Restaurant. Half-board 550-1,200 F. TV. Air cond. Conference facilities. Garage parking. V AE DC. D5-41
Some of the rooms overlook a square with floodlit fountains. The superb garden-terrace on the roof affords a view of the Mediterranean.

12/20 Le Grand Pavois

(Chez Michel)
11, rue Meyerbeer — 93.88.77.42
M. Marquise. Closed Mon (except holidays) and 1 July-15 Aug. Open until 10.30 pm. Air cond. V. C5-32
The new owner will have changed the décor by the time you read this, but we hope he keeps the same supplier because such fresh fish is a rare treat in the centre of Nice. Try the carpaccio of rascasse (scorpion fish) with mint, fillet of sole with hollandaise sauce, and a selection of doughnut-style desserts with seven kinds of home-made jam. It's a pity so many of the dishes are only for two people and that the prices are so off-putting. Good choice of white wines.
A la carte: 350 F and up.

Holiday Inn

Aéroport de Nice
179, bd R.-Cassin — 93.83.91.92
Open every day. 1 ste 2,000 F. 151 rms 775-875 F. Restaurant. TV. Air cond. Conference facilities. Pool. Garage parking. Telex 970202. V AE DC. A6-44
Everything you expect from this huge American chain, plus a free bus to the airport and the station. The rooms are huge, comfortable, and well equipped. Good conference facilities. Piano bar.

Mac Mahon

50, bd J.-Jaurès — 93.62.30.71
M. Gamus. Open every day. Open until midnight. Terrace dining. Air cond. V AE DC. D5-31
This newly decorated brasserie, whose chef used to work at the Negresco, is famous for its shellfish from Brittany and its lobsters, crabs, and prawns. Also good are the grilled fish, John Dory poached with sea-urchin coral, and a mixture of red mullet and grouper topped with olive purée. The desserts are more mundane.
A la carte: 350 F. Menu: 170 F.

La Malmaison

48, bd V.-Hugo — 93.87.62.56
Open every day. 50 rms 390-880 F. Restaurant. Half-board 520-570 F. TV. Air cond. Conference facilities. Valet parking. Telex 470410. V AE DC. C4-33
A late nineteenth-century corner building with up-to-date facilities. The rooms are comfortable, with soundproofing and air-conditioning, and are redecorated regularly. Satellite television.

Jacques Maximin

2-4, rue S.-Guitry
93.80.70.10
M. Maximin. Annual closings not available. Open until 10.30 pm. Private room: 40. Air cond. Valet parking. Telex 462794. V AE DC. D5-63
For maximum business, Maximin might have been more sensible to turn this huge old theatre into a high-class brasserie and keep the small dining room for his more exclusive clientele. But this is a chef who does things his way, relishing the challenge to succeed against the odds in what the trade knows as a difficult town. Although the restaurant may be difficult to fill at lunchtime, there are enough customers in the evening to keep afloat these 3,600 square metres scattered with modern sculpture, where you can watch the chefs working behind a glass partition. Despite his occasional weaknesses, Maximin has shown enough strokes of genius to regain his fourth toque this year. He delighted us with a dish of local prawns, bone marrow, and rock salt, served with cumin-flavoured gnocchi, a marbled cucumber terrine with a peppery thyme sauce, a whole baked young hake à la niçoise, John Dory with chanterelles, a mixture of tiny anchovies and sardines in a reduced herb sauce, a plump duck with garlic and a turnip gratin, and Bresse chicken with tarragon and melting carrots. Not to mention an iced sabayon mousse with port and a dollop of melon purée, or the flaky caramelised pastries with wild strawberries. Obviously all these good things make a considerable hole in the pocket, but at lunchtime there's an excellent choice of dishes on the 280 F menu, which includes wine.
A la carte: 500 F and up. Menus: 280 F (weekdays lunch only, wine inc), 350 F, 500 F, 600 F, 700 F.

Mercure
2, rue Halévy – 93.82.30.88
Open every day. 124 rms 360-820 F. TV. Air cond. Conference facilities. V AE DC. C5-55
Looking bright and new following a series of face-lifts, this hotel has cheerful, well-equipped rooms. Good buffet breakfasts.

La Mérenda ☺
4, rue de la Terrasse — (no phone)
M. Giusti. Closed Sat, Sun, Mon, Feb and Aug. Open until 9.30 pm. D5-8
You can't book a table because there's no telephone, the bar stools are uncomfortable, and there's only one sort of wine. But Jean Giusti's small restaurant is packed all year with customers eager to taste the best courgette flower fritters in the world, the trulle (Niçois blood sausage), stockfish (dried salt cod), pasta with pistou (basil and garlic sauce), and daube, the local beef and wine stew. Authentic cooking at bargain prices.
A la carte: 180 F.

Méridien
1, prom. des Anglais — 93.82.25.25
Open every day. 9 stes 2,200-5,000 F. 305 rms 850-1,400 F. Restaurant. TV. Air cond. Conference facilities. Pool. Valet parking. V AE DC. C5-14
The modern, well-furnished rooms all overlook the sea. There's a piano bar, tea rooms, admirably appointed fitness centre, and the service is perfect.

Negresco
See restaurant Le Chantecler

Novotel Nice Centre Acropolis
8, espl. du Parvis-de-l'Europe — 93.13.30.93
Open every day. 2 stes 700 F. 173 rms 460-520 F. Restaurant. TV. Air cond. Conference facilities. Pool. Garage parking. Telex 460243. V AE DC. F3-34
Situated in the city's new shopping and cultural centre. The rooms are clean and practical, with minimal décor. Pleasant reception and a free shuttle service to the airport.

L'Oasis
23, rue Gounod — 93.88.12.29
Open every day. 1 ste 400 F. 38 rms 290-380 F. TV. Parking. Telex 462705. V AE DC. C4-50
An oasis of greenery in the centre of Nice. The rooms are simply decorated, well equipped, and very comfortable.

L'Olivier
2, pl. Garibaldi — 93.26.89.09
M. Musso. Closed Sun, Mon lunch, 1-21 Aug and 1-15 Dec. Open until 9.30 pm. No pets. V AE. E4-37
Eighteen customers is the most the Musso brothers can squeeze into their popular, pocket-sized restaurant. Christian provides perfect reception and service, while Franck prepares all his own bread, pasta, chocolate, as well as a highly personalised repertoire. Try the foie gras with apples served with a spinach-flavoured brioche, tasty roast pigeon with fresh pasta, and the delicious fondant au chocolat. The wine list is short but most pertinent.
A la carte: 300 F. Menus: 87 F (weekdays lunch only), 135 F.

12/20 Palais Maeterlinck
30, bd M.-Maeterlinck — 93.56.21.12
M. Buschiazzo. Closed Sun dinner, Mon and 6 Jan-12 Feb. Open until 10 pm. Private room: 12. Terrace dining. Air cond. No-smoking section. No pets. Valet parking. V AE. G7-42
Jean-Marc Thivet has managed to avoid the trap of conventional luxury, but his skilful cooking still lacks that touch of sparkle needed for a toque. The set menu has an appealing Provençal flavour, but the snail ravioli with garlicky butter sauce, turbot with lobster sauce and courgettes, and stuffed saddle of lamb with garlic cloves don't have the clear, uncomplicated tastes we expect from this region's dishes. The elegant dining room is decorated with large nineteenth-century paintings and fine furniture which, curiously, blocks the view of the sea.
A la carte: 420-500 F. Menus: 250 F (lunch only), 400 F (dinner only).

Palais Maeterlinck
(See restaurant above)
Closed 6 Jan-12 Feb. 11 stes 2,000-2,400 F. 8 rms 1,300-1,800 F. TV. Air cond. No pets. Conference facilities. Pool.
Designed by a Swiss financier for his friends and the occasional rich customer bored by the average luxury hotel. Here you can admire a profusion of murals and *trompe-l'œil* paintings by Serge Megter. Huge terraces, and a private beach, landing stage, and helipad.

Park Hôtel
6, av. de Suède — 93.87.80.25
Open every day. 2 stes 1,000 F. 130 rms 550-850 F. Restaurant. TV. Air cond. Conference facilities. Garage parking. Telex 970176. V AE DC. C5-43
This exceptionally well-equipped hotel overlooks gardens and the sea.

Au Passage
11 bis, bd Raimbaldi — 93.80.23.15
Mme N'Guyen. Closed Sun and Aug. Open until 10.30 pm. Terrace dining. Air cond. V. D3-22
The subtle, original flavours of this unusual cuisine are what attract customers to the small, graceless dining room. Henriette N'Guyen is French, of Dutch origin, she has a Vietnamese husband, and her cooking reflects the same diversity of tastes and techniques. First-rate fresh produce goes into her steamed salmon with fresh coriander, scallops sautéed with ginger, Cantonese grilled duck breast, and sesame nougat.
A la carte: 250-300 F. Menu: 70 F (lunch only, wine inc).

La Pérouse
11, quai Rauba-Capeu — 93.62.34.63
Open every day. 3 stes 1,200-1,800 F. 62 rms 310-1,050 F. TV. Air cond. Conference facilities. Pool. Parking. Telex 461411. V AE DC. E6-35
One of the town's most pleasant hotels, La Pérouse has magnificent rooms with loggia or terrace and sea views. Sun room with panoramic views, sauna and hydrotherapy pool. Bar and grill in summer.

Petit Palais
10, av. E.-Bieckert — 93.62.19.11
Open every day. 25 rms 320-500 F. Restaurant. Half-board 350-375 F. TV. Parking. V AE. E3-54
The interior décor borrows from the superb Belle Epoque style of the building, which sits on a hilltop overlooking the town. The attractive, well-equipped rooms—with terrace or private garden—boast fine paintings, comfortable armchairs, and superb bathrooms. Very attentive service.

Plaza-Concorde
12, av. de Verdun — 93.87.80.41
Open every day. 8 stes 1,500-2,500 F. 200 rms 500-1,200 F. Half-board 710-1,410 F. TV. Air cond. Conference facilities. Valet parking. V AE DC. D5-12
Wonderful rooftop terrace and well-equipped, air-conditioned conference rooms. The rooms are modern and attractive. Bar, grill, and various shops and services.

Le Pot d'Etain
12, rue Meyerbeer — 93.88.25.95
M. Régnier. Closed 2-30 Jan. Open until 11 pm. Terrace dining. Air cond. V AE DC. C5-56
Eric Régnier, a talented, ambitious young chef, offers traditional cooking from the South-west in this convivial restaurant with its varnished wood and mirrors. Dishes like the young pigeon with Périgord stuffing and fillet of beef with morels are all fresh and deftly prepared. Cheerful service and well-chosen wines.
A la carte: 250-300 F. Menus: 88 F (weekdays lunch only, wine inc), 140 F, 198 F.

Les Préjugés du Palais
1, pl. du Palais — 93.62.37.03
M. Scoffier. Closed Sat lunch and Sun dinner. Open until 11 pm. Terrace dining. Air cond. V AE. D5-60
Jean-Pierre Scoffier's delicious traditional cooking is studded with Oriental flavours, a legacy of the time he spent working as a doctor in Cambodia. His father welcomes guests to his intimate restaurant full of mirrors and flowers, or the pretty terrace on the Place du Palais. Here you can savour chicken with chilli sauce in brik pastry, perfect young turbot with butter sauce, fricassée of lamb with coconut, and a warm fruit tart served with exquisite vanilla ice cream. The cheapest set menu is a real bargain. Having moved to Nice from Montfort-l'Amaury only last year, Jean-Pierre Scoffier does not yet have a selection of mature wines, but there are some good bottles available at reasonable prices. One of the best and most original addresses in Nice.
A la carte: 300 F. Menus: 120 F (weekdays and holidays lunch only), 250 F (dinner only).

Pullman
28, av. Notre-Dame — 93.80.30.24
Open every day. 1 ste 1,300-1,600 F. 201 rms 550-1,050 F. TV. Air cond. Conference facilities. Pool. Telex 470662. V AE DC. D3-49
A remarkably soundproofed modern hotel in the centre of town. The comfortable rooms have various amenities that can be conveniently operated by remote control from the bed. The rooftop terrace offers a bar, swimming pool and sauna, with a poolside grill from May to September.

Relais de Rimiez
128, av. de Rimiez — 93.81.18.65
Closed 5 Jan-12 Feb. 24 rms 180-320 F. TV. Air cond. Conference facilities. Parking. V AE. E1-9
Quiet, comfortable rooms with terraces. A regular bus service runs to the beach and central Nice.

12/20 La Rive Gauche
27, rue Ribotti — 93.89.16.82
Closed Sun. Open until 10 pm. V AE. F4-11
Generous Provençal cooking in a cheerful, bistro atmosphere. Grouper en papillote with basil, sliced sole with fresh pasta, and calf's liver with baby onions are served at moderate prices. Swift service.
A la carte: 200 F. Menus: 109 F, 139 F.

12/20 La Rotonde
(Hôtel Negresco)
37, prom. des Anglais — 93.88.39.51
Mme Augier. Open every day. Open until midnight. Terrace dining. Air cond. Valet parking. Telex 460040. V AE DC. B5-24
The smoked-fish salad, compote of baby rabbit, and bass with fennel butter attract a young clientele to the Negresco's lower-priced restaurant.
A la carte: 150-250 F.

Ruffel
10, bd Dubouchage — 93.62.05.45
M. Lumeau. Closed off-season Sun dinner and Mon. Open until 11 pm. Garden dining. V. D4-21
Pierre Gay, who has worked with Joël Robuchon and Marc Meneau, has taken over from Ruffel in the kitchen. His cooking is promising but as yet lacks the personal touch: liver with fennel and crispy sesame-seed topping, remarkable fillet of beef served with undercooked vegetables, and ordinary desserts. Not enough half-bottles on the wine list.
A la carte: 350 F. Menus: 150 F (weekdays lunch only), 220 F, 395 F.

12/20 Le Saint-Moritz
5, rue des Congrès — 93.88.54.90
M. Martel. Closed Wed off-season, and 3 Nov-18 Dec. Open until 10.30 pm. V AE. C5-57
The affable staff does its utmost to cheer up the dark, dismal décor and the kitchen offers traditional, nicely crafted dishes like cheese soufflé, sole cooked in Champagne, and iced nougat with honey. Limited cellar with few regional wines.
A la carte: 320 F. Menus: 92 F, 135 F, 195 F.

Sofitel-Splendid
50, bd V.-Hugo — 93.88.69.54
Open every day. 13 stes 850-1,400 F. 128 rms 570-980 F. Restaurant. Half-board 480-680 F. TV. Air cond. Conference facilities. Pool. Valet parking. Telex 460938. V AE DC. C4-45
The rooms are air-conditioned and well equipped, and one floor is reserved for non-smokers. There's an excellent range of services including baby-sitting, hairdresser, sauna, beauty salon, solar-heated pool and solarium. Satellite television with fourteen channels.

La Toque Blanche
40, rue de la Buffa — 93.88.38.18
M. Sandelion. Closed Sun dinner, Mon and 15-31 July. Open until 9.30 pm. Air cond. V. B5-26
Denise Sandelion welcomes guests warmly to this pretty pastel dining room, where they enjoy sparkling fresh fish cooked with precision by her husband Alain. He deserves his self-awarded toque for the John Dory with sweet peppers, lotte soup coiffed with a pastry crust, and lobster in its own rich stock.
A la carte: 350 F. Menus: 130 F (except Sun), 160 F, 260 F.

Vendôme
26, rue Pastorelli — 93.62.00.77
Open every day. 5 stes 550-750 F. 57 rms 320-520 F. Half-board 280-565 F. TV. Air cond. Conference facilities. Valet parking. V AE DC. D4-61
This former town house with its superb staircase has been restored in the best of taste. The pleasant rooms are decorated in attractive colours and have handsomely designed furniture. Room service.

West End

31, prom. des Anglais – 93.88.79.91
Open every day. 7 stes 900-1,800 F. 130 rms 350-1,600 F. Restaurant. Half-board 530-1,000 F. TV. Air cond. Conference facilities. Garage parking. Telex 460879. V AE DC. B5-38

Close to the sea, a traditional hotel with oustanding views. Services include laundry, a safe, and a sauna.

Westminster Concorde

27, prom. des Anglais – 93.88.29.44
Open every day. 4 stes 1,100-2,200 F. 105 rms 600-1,100 F. Restaurant. TV. Air cond. No pets. Conference facilities. Telex 460872. V AE DC. C5-7

This 1880 hotel was renovated in 1986 and had air-conditioning installed recently, but the service has remained soothingly old-fashioned. Bar and discothèque.

Windsor

11, rue Dalpozzo – 93.88.59.35
Open every day. 60 rms 360-540 F. Restaurant. Half-board 350-600 F. TV. Air cond 5 rms. Conference facilities. Pool. Parking. V AE DC. C5-10

A lovely garden and moderate prices. This elegant hotel with superb frescoes in the rooms also boasts modern facilities like offices and a fitness club.

And also...

Our selection of places for inexpensive, quick, or late-night meals.
L'Auberge de Théo (93.81.26.19 - 52, av. Cap-de-Croix. Open until 10.30 pm): Set in the hills above Nice, popular with fans of pizzas, pasta, and grilled meats (140 F).
L'Avion Bleu (93.87.77.47 - 10, rue A.-Karr. Open until midnight): Aeroplanes abound, with posters and models everywhere in the smart, American-style décor. You'll enjoy the salads and grilled meats. Air-conditioned (100-120 F).
Lou Balico (93.85.93.71 - 20, av. St-Jean-Baptiste. Open until midnight): The whole repertoire of regional dishes can be found here, mostly well prepared. Relaxed atmosphere (180 F).
Castel Plage (93.85.22.66 - quai des Etats-Unis. Open until 11 pm): A fashionable spot where you'll dine on pizza and pasta (100-150 F).
L'Escalinada (93.62.11.71 - 22, rue Pairolière. Open until 11 pm): This family restaurant is set in one of the old town's prettiest streets. Dishes include ravioli, pasta, and daube (beef and wine stew) (140 F).
Fjord (93.26.20.20 - 21, rue F.-Grisol. Lunch only): A corner with tables where you can sample the Scandinavian products sold in the shop: the Nordic version of caviar with eggs from the lavaret (a member of the salmon family), marinated herrings, and gravad lax (pickled salmon with dill) (130 F).
Grand Café de Turin (93.62.29.52 - 5, pl. Garibaldi. Open until 10 pm): The freshest shellfish served from 8.30 am onwards (100 F).
Icardo (93.83.17.30 - 234, rte de Grenoble. Lunch only): This timeless bar has a good range of typical dishes (100 F).
Chez Nino (93.88.07.71 - 50, rue Trachel. Open until 10.30 pm): For beer lovers. It crops up in the duck, andouillette sausage, and sorbet, as well as out of the barrel (100 F).
Prince de Prusse (93.80.75.11 - pl. du Jésus. Open until midnight): A convivial restaurant in the heart of the old town. Try the shin of veal or choucroute with pineapple, washed down with Rhine wines or German beer (180 F).

Le Safari (93.80.18.44 - 1, cours Saleya. Open until 11 pm): A costly and popular terrace serving grilled peppers, pizza, roast rabbit, and shellfish in winter (200 F).
Ville de Siena (93.80.12.45 - 10, rue St-Vincent. Open until 11 pm): Good fresh pasta cooked to order and served in a lively, Italian-style setting (140 F).

In nearby **Saint-Martin-du-Var**

(27 km N on N 202)
06670 Nice (Alpes-Maritimes)

Issautier

(Auberge de la Belle Route)
on N 202 – 93.08.10.65
M. Issautier. Closed Sun dinner (and lunch in seas), Mon, mid-Feb to mid-March and 5-13 Nov. Open until 9.30 pm. Parking. V AE DC.

Jean-François Issautier has needed all his determination to make this rather isolated restaurant a success, and all his enthusiasm to breathe life into it. His cooking has matured gradually, casting aside rigid classicism to reveal his true personality and earn a third toque. The best of Provençal flavours are still present in the salmon with artichokes stuffed with ham and mushrooms and served forth napped with a basil sauce, or duck steak sautéed with Szechuan peppercorns and red cherries, or veal kidney casseroled with red onions. And then there are the fabulous desserts like guanaja chocolate jelly, or rich, smooth coffee and pine honey cream. Comfortable décor, to which Nicole Issautier adds her smiling presence and some magnificent flower arrangements.

A la carte: 500 F and up. Menus: 245 F (weekdays lunch only), 400 F.

Servotel

6 km S on N 202
in Castagniers-les-Moulins – 93.08.22.00
Open every day. 43 rms 240-320 F. Restaurant. Half-board 230-260 F oblig in seas. TV. Air cond. Conference facilities. Pool. Tennis. Garage parking. Telex 461547. V AE.

Set on two hectares of grounds, this is just the place for a relaxing or sporting break. Pool, games room, hairdresser.

In nearby **Saint-Pancrace**

(8 km N on D 914)
06100 Nice – (Alpes-Maritimes)

Rôtisserie de Saint-Pancrace

92.09.94.94
M. Teillas. Closed Mon (except July-Aug) and 5 Jan-5 Feb. Open until 10 pm. Private room: 50. Garden dining. Parking. V.

The chef, Pascal Roche, is not quite at home yet in the classic mode that the owner wishes him to adopt. The millefeuille of half-smoked salmon with lotte liver, grouper studded with anchovies and served with a basil, tomato, and citrus-fruit sauce, and lamb chops wrapped in caul fat succeed admirably, but they need a more individual touch. Jean-Charles Nivoix crafts the luscious desserts and Antoine Luciano unearths marvellous wines from all corners of France. Expensive, especially if you dine à la carte.

A la carte: 400-500 F. Menus: 180 F and 280 F (except holidays).

NIEUIL

16270 Nieuil — (Charente)
Paris 430 - Limoges 65 - Ruffec 36 - Confolens 25

Château de Nieuil ♻
Rte de Fontafie — 45.71.36.38
M. Bodinaud. Closed 4 Nov-25 April. Open until 9 pm. Private room: 30. Garden dining. Valet parking. Telex 791230. V AE DC.

A hotchpotch restoration job in the last century grafted pseudo-medieval elements onto this luxurious Renaissance château. As a result, the dining room is handsome but rather austere. Not so Luce Bodinaud's modern cooking, which tastes best when savoured on the sunny summer terrace.

A la carte: 350-400 F. Menus: 210 F, 245 F, 275 F.

Château de Nieuil
(See restaurant above)
Closed 4 Nov-25 April. 3 stes 1,100-1,600 F. 11 rms 450-1,100 F. Half-board 565-805 F. TV. Air cond 4 rms. Conference facilities. Pool. Tennis.

Nice 'n' easy, château-style, might be the motto here. The regal elegance of the décor matches the sybaritic comforts offered. Stroll around the vast grounds, fish in the private pond, and take rides in a horse-drawn carriage. Relais et Châteaux.

NÎMES

30000 Nîmes — (Gard)
Paris 712 - Lyon 249 - Marseille 123 - Montpellier 52

L'Enclos de la Fontaine
Quai de la Fontaine
66.21.90.30
M. Créac'h. Closed Sat lunch. Open until 9.30 pm. Private room: 60. Garden dining. Air cond. Valet parking. Telex 490635. V AE DC.

Chef Jean-Michel Nigon juggles classic cooking and bolder, modern dishes. Try his very successful feuilleté of quail and oyster mushrooms, sea bass in lemon-butter served with a gaufrette, rack of lamb stuffed with rice and spinach, and semi-sweet chocolate tart. These delicacies suit the discreet charm of the dining room, which opens onto a glorious garden. The wine list is unoriginal.

A la carte: 400 F. Menus: 195 F (weekdays lunch only), 230 F and 260 F (dinner only), 420 F.

Impérator Concorde
(See restaurant above)
Open every day. 2 stes 1,200-1,500 F. 62 rms 450-780 F. Half-board 550-745 F. TV. Air cond. Conference facilities.

A major renovation has freshened up this handsome old hotel, set between the Maison Carrée and the Jardins de la Fontaine. Charming, well-equipped rooms. This is the best address in town.

Le Magister
5, rue Nationale — 66.76.11.00
M. Hocquart. Closed Sat lunch, Sun and 1-17 Aug. Open until 10.30 pm. Air cond. V AE DC.

Considered by many to be the best restaurant in Nîmes, Le Magister has been redecorated and is more comfortable and expensive than ever. Chef Martial Hocquart's highly personal cooking derives its inspiration from luscious local ingredients. Witness the round, richly flavoured brandade (without garlic), baked skate with olive purée, and excellent desserts. Another point this year.

A la carte: 300 F. Menus: 150 F (weekdays lunch only), 180 F, 210 F.

Novotel Atria
Espl. Ch.-de-Gaulle — 66.76.56.56
Open every day. 7 stes 740 F. 112 rms 430-480 F. Restaurant. TV. Air cond. Conference facilities. Garage parking. Telex 485618. V AE DC.

Just 100 metres from the Roman arena, the rooms here are quite spacious, soundproofed, and sunny. Office and secretarial services available.

Le P'tit Bec
87 bis, rue de la République — 66.38.05.83
M. Beldio. Closed Sun dinner and Mon. Open until 9.30 pm. Garden dining. No pets. V.

Despite his move to this handsome new location, which boasts a pretty interior garden, Serge Beldio has kept his prices down. His three menus follow the seasons, and though they are somewhat less original than before, they are all skilfully made using excellent ingredients. Try the sensationally good value 130 F menu, featuring skate with fennel vinaigrette, saddle of rabbit stuffed with liver and wrapped in a cabbage leaf, fine cheeses, and perfect desserts.

A la carte: 250-300 F. Menus: 90 F (lunch only), 130 F, 190 F.

Plazza
10, rue Roussy — 66.76.16.20
Open every day. 28 rms 210-360 F. TV. Air cond. No pets. Valet parking. Telex 485727. V AE DC.

A few streets away from the Roman arena and Maison Carrée, this hotel has been entirely rebuilt behind its nineteenth-century façade. The quiet rooms are furnished and decorated in 1930s style.

Relais du Moulin
1973, av. P.-Mendès-France — 66.84.30.20
M. Nuris. Closed Sun dinner, Mon and Nov. Open until 10 pm. Garden dining. Air cond. Parking. V AE.

Bernard Trouiler, a pupil of Paul Bocuse, has come to the Moulin after a stint at the Méridien in Rio de Janeiro, bringing with him a pinch of the exotic. His repertoire is classic, but not boring or bourgeois, the fruit of careful seasoning and a sure hand. We're glad to award him two toques for his prawns in aspic with artichoke hearts, lotte stew with tiny pickles, stuffed and boned young pigeon, and iced mousse of guanaja (a south American chocolate) with Colombian brandy. Let's hope he also brings some warmth and charm to the spartan décor.

A la carte: 320-380 F. Menus: 150 F (lunch only), 240 F, 320 F.

Relais du Moulin
(See restaurant above)
Closed Sun, Mon and Nov. 2 stes. 21 rms 320-480 F. TV. Air cond. Conference facilities.

This old mill fit for an operetta set on the outskirts of Nîmes has comfortable rooms with smart Provençal furniture, elegant bathrooms, loggias, terraces, and a garden that opens onto the Gard countryside. Golf practice, horse riding.

And also...
Our selection of places for inexpensive, quick, or late-night meals and smaller places to stay.
Le Jardin d'Hadrien (66.21.86.65 - 11, rue Enclos-Rey. Open until 10.30 pm): Modest, tasty food served in a sunny terrace-garden (lotte salad with hazelnut oil, fresh cod with chopped parsley and garlic), (220 F).
Novotel Nîmes Ouest (66.84.60.20 - W exit on motorway, 124, ch. de l'Hostellerie. 4 stes 550-650 F. 98 rms 390-430 F): This modern hotel near the motorway has good facilities for conferences.

Golf practice, children's playground, weight-lifting, bar, restaurant (open 6 am-midnight).
Le San Francisco (66.21.00.80 - 33, rue Roussy. Open until midnight: Tex-Mex specialities and good steaks prepared by a former butcher, Hollywood film star décor (200 F).

(9 km S on D 42 and D 442)
30128 Nîmes – (Gard)

Alexandre
2, rue X.-Tronc – 66.70.08.99

M. Kayser. Closed Sun dinner, Mon and Feb school holidays. Open until 9.30 pm. Air cond. Parking. V.

A welcome, flower-filled dining room near the airport, Alexandre's dining room–veranda has been nicely remodelled. Michel Kayser's skilful, savoury cooking is as worthy as ever. Sample the snail and cèpes ravioli with mild garlic, scallops in a lotte papillote and sea-urchin cream sauce, breast of duckling seasoned with saffron, and fine desserts. Good choice of wines, served by a knowledgeable sommelier. Stiff prices.

A la carte: 300-400 F. Menus: 170 F (weekdays lunch only), 225 F, 280 F.

(8 km NE on N 86)
30320 Nîmes – (Gard)

L'Hacienda
Mas de Brignon – 66.75.02.25

Open every day. 11 rms 250-450 F. Restaurant. Half-board 350-420 F. TV. Conference facilities. Pool. Garage parking. Telex 480146. V AE DC.

This grand old country farmhouse, set around a swimming pool and patio, has elegantly decorated rooms with handsome solid-wood furniture. Outstanding facilities and services. Charming welcome.

79000 Niort – (Deux-Sèvres)
Paris 412 - Angers 149 - Angoulême 111 - Nantes 144

Altea
17, rue de Bellune – 49.24.29.29

Open every day. 1 ste 800-920 F. 60 rms 400-920 F. Restaurant. Half-board 535 F. TV. Conference facilities. Pool. Parking. Telex 793120. V AE DC.

A new and outwardly graceless hotel, the Altea is situated in a hectare of grounds in the centre of town. The snug rooms have perfect bathrooms.

12/20 La Belle Etoile
115, quai M.-Métayer – 49.73.31.29

M. Guignard. Closed Sun dinner, Mon and 5-25 Aug. Open until 9.30 pm. Private room: 120. Garden dining. Parking. V AE DC.

Anglers and *boules* players dot the banks of the Sèvre Niortaise next to the leafy garden of this regional restaurant. The tasty cooking is well-prepared: luscious lobster ravioli with prawn coulis, young pigeon breast in a peppery St-Hubert sauce, and pear chaud-froid.

A la carte: 250-280 F. Menus: 365 F (wine inc), 115 F, 170 F, 225 F.

Le Relais Saint-Antoine
Pl. de la Brèche – 49.24.02.76

M. Cardin. Closed Sat lunch, Feb school holidays and 16-29 July. Open until 10 pm. Private room: 55. Terrace dining. V AE DC.

The ultra-trendy, neo-1930s décor features halogen lamps, peach-coloured walls hung with

photographs, and round tables. Even the toilets follow the same style. We like it. Diners who prefer a more classic ambience should choose the terrace. Either way, you'll enjoy Kaline Cardin's warm welcome and her husband Patrick's cooking, which he learned with Robuchon, among others. Customers love green-olive purée, served as an appetiser, and the outstanding chicken liver terrine with raisins and Armagnac. His mastery comes through in classic dishes as well: veal kidneys with wild mushrooms, perfectly grilled sea bass, and excellent pastries. Well-balanced wine list (140 varieties, including some from California and Spain).

A la carte: 300-350 F. Menus: 130 F, 175 F, 200 F.

Hôtel des Rocs
Rte de Paris
79260 Chavagné – 49.25.50.38

Open every day. 51 rms 335-370 F. Restaurant. Half-board 330-460 F. TV. Conference facilities. Pool. Tennis. Parking. Telex 790632. V AE DC.

Extensive grounds surround this hotel complex of recent vintage. The décor is rather dull, but the rooms are quite spacious and well equipped. Many services and leisure activities are available (fitness centre planned). The staff is impersonal.

12/20 La Tuilerie
2 km SW on N 11
in Bessines – 49.09.12.45

M. Beaufils. Closed Sun dinner. Open until 10 pm. Private room: 300. Garden dining. Air cond. Heated pool. Tennis. Parking. V.

The tasty caterer's cooking holds no surprises—except when the bill comes. True, La Tuilerie's garden-cum-swimming pool setting, high above Niort, is worth a supplement. Try the crab croustillant with Pineau de Charente, baked sea bass in a salt crust with beurre rouge, and saddle of lamb with herbs.

A la carte: 300-350 F. Menus: 168 F, 215 F.

(11 km W on D 9)
79510 Niort (Deux-Sèvres)

Au Marais
46-48, quai L.-Tardy
49.35.90.43

Mme Mathé. Closed Mon (except July-Aug), Sun dinner and 1 Nov-15 March. Open until 9.30 pm. Hotel: 11 rms 240-280 F, half-board 400 F oblig in seas. V.

The talented young chef is a stickler for regional specialities. When he acquires a little more polish, this handsomely rustic restaurant will doubtless become one of the area's best. Excellent goat cheeses, and well-chosen wines. Flawless service (but very noisy kitchen!).

A la carte: 280 F. Menus: 95 F (weekdays lunch only, wine inc), 150 F.

(13 km S on N 150)
79360 Niort (Deux-Sèvres)

Domaine du Griffier
Le Griffier 49.32.62.62

Open every day. 29 rms 290-450 F. Restaurant. TV. Conference facilities. Heated pool. Parking. V AE.

This fortified farmhouse built of white stone is surrounded by lawns and trees. The comfortable, sunny, smartly furnished rooms are slightly sterile. Large, well-equipped bathrooms. Golf course nearby.

NOGENT-SUR-MARNE

See PARIS Suburbs

NOIRMOUTIER (ILE DE)

85 Noirmoutier (Ile de) – (Vendée)
access by Fromentine

In nearby Bois-de-la-Chaize

85330 Noirmoutier (Ile de) – (Vendée)

12/20 L'Anse Rouge
51.39.05.63
M. Buron. Closed 3 Nov-15 March. Open until 9.30 pm. Private room: 60. Garden dining. V AE.
Stick to the regional specialities and seafood, served in a quiet, flower-filled garden (the dining room is joyless).
A la carte: 300 F and up. Menus: 200 F (w-e and holidays only), 158 F, 250 F.

Saint-Paul
(See restaurant above)
Closed 3 Nov-15 March. 4 stes. 35 rms 350-550 F (per pers, half-board oblig). TV. Conference facilities. Heated pool. Tennis.
Set in green grounds, this comfortable, family-style hotel is just 150 metres from the beach. The rooms are being modernised. Fitness classes.

In nearby La Guérinière

85680 Noirmoutier (Ile de) – (Vendée)

Punta Lara
Bois des Eloux – 51.39.11.58
Closed 10 Oct-25 March. 1 ste 1,100 F. 60 rms 660-880 F. Restaurant. Half-board 540-570 F oblig in seas. Conference facilities. Heated pool. Tennis. Parking. Telex 701892. V AE DC.
Each of the seafront bungalows has a terrace or balcony, and direct access to the beach.

La Volière
D 948 – 51.39.82.77
Closed 15 Nov-15 March. 37 rms 200-350 F. Restaurant. Half-board 220-400 F. TV 10 rms. Conference facilities. Heated pool. Tennis. Parking. Telex 710111. V AE DC.
Of recent vintage, this pleasant holiday hotel is situated 200 metres from the sea, and has well-equipped, soundproofed rooms. Grill restaurant.

In nearby L' Herbaudière

85330 Noirmoutier (Ile de) – (Vendée)

Bord à Bord
6, rue de la Linière – 51.39.27.92
Open every day. 2 stes 470-590 F. 22 rms 280-320 F. TV. Conference facilities. Heated pool. Parking. V.
This pleasant, modern hotel faces the harbour. The rooms have kitchenettes and look out on the sea. Sixteen have mezzanines. Bar. Sauna.

In nearby Noirmoutier-en-l'Ile

85330 Noirmoutier (Ile de) – (Vendée)

Fleur de Sel
Rue des Saulniers – 51.39.21.59
M. Wattecamps. Closed 5 Nov-13 Feb. Open until 10 pm.Garden dining. Parking. Telex 701229. V.
Set between the beaches and salt flats, and with a view of the Noirmoutier church, this is the island's best restaurant and it's getting better all the time. Chef Hervé Robin polishes his technique each winter by training with a top chef. His highly flavourful dishes rely on fine fish and shellfish: oyster feuilleté with spinach, baked sea bass au beurre rouge, and fresh fruit terrine for dessert.
A la carte: 250 F. Menus: 90 F (weekdays lunch only), 138 F, 200 F.

Fleur de Sel
(See restaurant above)
Closed 5 Nov-13 Feb. 35 rms 310-470 F. Half-board 320-420 F oblig in seas. TV. No pets. Conference facilities. Heated pool.
Ideal for stopovers or holidays, this hotel has modern, pleasant rooms with English furniture. Most give onto a lawn. Sauna and tanning machine.

Général d'Elbée
Pl. d'Armes – 51.39.10.29
Closed 30 Sep-1 April. 27 rms 285-800 F. Restaurant. Conference facilities. Pool. Telex 701892. V AE DC.
This eighteenth-century townhouse near the port has old-fashioned rooms decorated in good taste. Interior garden, terrace.

NOIZAY

37210 Noizay – (Dordogne)
Paris 230 - Tours 18 - Amboise 9 - Blois 43

Château de Noizay
47.52.11.01
Closed 12 Nov-15 March. 14 rms 600-950 F. Half-board 600-1,250 F. Restaurant. TV. Conference facilities. Pool. Tennis. Garage parking. Telex 752715. V AE.
This delightful spot groans with history (it was the arsenal of Castelnau, one of the leaders of the Amboise conspiracy). The rooms are very comfortable (number five has a four-poster bed), and open onto the garden. Professional reception. Good breakfasts with homemade pastries.

NONZA

See CORSICA

NOVES

13550 Noves – (B./Rhône)
Paris 700 - St-Rémy-de-Provence 16 - Avignon 14

Auberge de Noves
2.5 km NW on D 28 – 90.94.19.21
M. Lalleman. Closed Wed lunch (and dinner off-season), and 2 Jan-20 Feb. Open until 10 pm. Garden dining. Parking. Telex 431312. V AE DC.
André Lalleman's prodigiously talented son Robert has returned from a long apprenticeship with famous names like Troisgros, Chapel, and Pic. So the good times are back in this dreamy old inn lost among the pines and cypresses. Try the cold artichoke and asparagus tip salad with truffes d'été, red-mullet fillets with olive oil, herbs, and dried garlic, and medallions of lamb with tapenade. Needless to say, the desserts are exquisite too.
A la carte: 400-500 F. Menus: 235 F (weekdays lunch only), 280 F (weekdays lunch only, wine inc), 325 F, 380 F, 435 F.

Auberge de Noves
(See restaurant above)
Closed 2 Jan-15 Feb. 2 stes 1,500 F. 23 rms 1,000-1,250 F. TV. Air cond. Pool. Tennis.
The recent renovation has exposed the handsome timbers and stone façade of this farmhouse. It is now less austere, and the perfectly equipped rooms are more comfortable and spacious than ever. There are two new 'junior suites', equipped with Jacuzzi. Fabulous breakfasts. Impeccable welcome and service. Relais et Châteaux.

NUITS-SAINT-GEORGES
21700 Nuits-Saint-Georges — (Côte-d'Or)
Paris 330 - Beaune 16 - Dijon 22 - Chalon-sur-Saône 48

La Côte d'Or
37, rue Thurot — 80.61.06.10
M. Guillot. Closed Thu lunch and Wed. Open until
9.30 pm. Private room: 25. Air cond. V AE DC.
Thierry Guillot's scallops in slightly sparkling
wine, fillets of sole with coriander and fried celery,
veal with raspberry vinegar, and fine desserts are
laudable indeed. But some sauces could be more
flavourful, and the quality of the ingredients isn't
always the highest. The wine cellar is superb, and
the décor pleasant. Prices are getting out of line.
A la carte: 350-500 F. Menus: 140 F, 240 F, 380 F.

La Côte d'Or
(See restaurant above)
Closed Wed. 1 ste 600 F. 7 rms 320-600 F. TV 6 rms.
Some of the rooms in this old hotel are very
spacious. All have been nicely restored in various
styles. Good soundproofing.

La Gentilhommière
13, vallée de la Serrée — 80.61.12.06
M. Vanroelen. Closed Tue lunch, Mon and end Dec-
end Jan. Open until 9 pm. Private room: 30. Terrace
dining. Parking. V AE DC.
Chef Jack Vanroelen is a tried-and-true pro with
solid references. He seems to be leaning towards
luxury cooking, which suits his sumptuously
restored old hunting lodge down to the ground.
No question: the fine ingredients are skilfully handled. But we prefer the simple country soup and
pigeon pot-au-feu to the overly elaborate turbot
Waleska and saumon en vessie. Excellent desserts.
A la carte: 300 F. Menus: 160 F, 220 F.

La Gentilhommière
(See restaurant above)
Closed end Dec-end Jan. 20 rms 350 F. Half-board
500-600 F. Conference facilities.
This modern, motel-like structure blends into the
greenery of the surrounding countryside. The spacious rooms give onto large grounds. Swimming
pool and tennis courts under construction.

In nearby Gilly-lès-Cîteaux
(6 km NE on N 74 and D 25)
21640 Nuits-Saint-Georges — (Côte-d'Or)

Château de Gilly
80.62.89.98
M. Bottigliero. Closed 1 Feb-10 March. Open until
9.30 pm. Private room: 200. Terrace dining. No pets.
Parking. Telex 351467. V.
Lost among the vineyards between Dijon and
Beaune, this former Cistercian monks' retreat has
been very well restored by the Traversac group.
The château is handsome, and though the décor of
the cellar restaurant is rather cold, the traditional
cooking is warming and well executed. Sample the
Burgundy snails with sorrel, salmon in truffle juice,
Charollais beef with blackcurrants, and soufflé
glacé.
A la carte: 350 F. Menus: 240 F (weekdays lunch
only, wine inc), 190 F, 250 F, 380 F.

Château de Gilly
(See restaurant above)
Closed 1 Feb-10 March. 7 stes 1,200-1,500 F. 36 rms
440-950 F. Half-board 775-1,285 F. TV. Conference
facilities. Tennis.
A blend of the aristocratic and the bourgeois, this
hotel has large and extremely well equipped
rooms with lovely furnishings, and breathtaking

bathrooms. Four new rooms have been added this
year. Sumptuous breakfasts. Several luxury suites
are available, as are simpler rooms in the former
stables. Relais et Châteaux.

NYONS
26110 Nyons — (Drôme)
Paris 660 - Montélimar 51 - Orange 42 - Carpentras 44

In nearby Aubres
(4 km E on D 94)
26110 Nyons — (Drôme)

Auberge du Vieux Village
Route de Gap
75.26.12.89
Open every day. 4 stes 1,100 F. 19 rms 420-780 F.
Restaurant. Half-board 452-657 F oblig in seas. TV.
Conference facilities. Heated pool. Parking. V AE DC.
Built on the ruins of an old château, this handsome group of buildings enjoys a spectacular setting, overlooking a fragrant valley and the distant
Alps. Each room has a character of its own, with a
small balcony and rustic furniture. Terraced garden. Gym and sauna. The restaurant is for non-
smokers only. Low out-of-season rates.

OBERNAI
67210 Obernai — (Bas-Rhin)
Paris 486 - Strasbourg 27 - Sélestat 23 - Erstein 16

In nearby Ottrott-le-Haut
(4 km W)
67530 Obernai (Bas-Rhin)

Beau Site
Place de l'Eglise
88.95.80.61
MM. Schreiber. Closed Feb school holidays. Open
until 9.30 pm. Private room: 18. Terrace dining. No-
smoking section. Garage parking. V AE DC.
The setting, at the foot of the Mont St Odile, is
handsome indeed, and so is the cheerful dining
room. But after last year's excellent meal, we were
taken aback by the poor service, apparently ill-in-
formed sommelier, the zestless sauces, and dreary
desserts. In short, by the humdrumness of it all. An
off night, perhaps.
A la carte: 300-400 F. Menus: 195 F, 280 F, 360 F.

Beau Site
(See restaurant above)
Closed Feb school holidays. 8 stes 450-650 F. 7 rms
250-400 F. Half-board 300-450 F. TV 5 rms.
Lost among woods and meadows, the Beau Site's
traditional rooms, recently redecorated, are comfortable and well equipped.

OFFEMONT
See Belfort

OLÉRON (ILE D')
Oléron (Ile d') — (Charente-M.)
Paris 500 - Marennes 10

In nearby Boyardville
(17 km pont d'Oléron)
17190 Oléron (Ile d') — (Charente-M.)

La Perrotine
46.47.01.01
M. Paque. Closed Tue. Open until 10 pm. Terrace
dining. Parking. V.
The fish are fabulously fresh and perfectly
cooked. Witness the succulent warm lotte salad

425

with artichokes and a hint of saffron, fillet of bass with seaweed, and sole goujonettes with green cabbage. Rather disappointing desserts, though the caramelised pear tart is good. Flawless service.

A la carte: 300-350 F. Menus: 100 F (weekdays lunch only, wine inc), 130 F, 170 F.

In nearby La Cotinière

(16 km pont d'Oléron)
17310 Oléron (Ile d') — (Charente-M.)

12/20 L'Ecailler
65, rue du Port
46.47.10.31

M. Coligneaux. Closed Sun dinner, Mon and 15 Nov-1 Feb. Open until 10 pm. Garden dining. Hotel: 8 rms 280-370 F. Parking. V AE DC.

Enjoy seafood at reasonable prices on the terrace overlooking the port, or in the flower-filled garden. Attentive service.

A la carte: 300 F. Menus: 90 F (weekdays only), 100 F and from 129 F to 320 F.

Motel Ile de Lumière
46.47.10.80

Closed 1 Oct-1 April. 3 stes 1,220-1,380 F. 45 rms 340-550 F. TV. Heated pool. Tennis. Parking. V.

The surf will rock you to sleep in this quiet motel with comfortable rooms on the island's west coast.

In nearby Dolus-d'Oléron

(6 km pont d'Oléron)
17550 Oléron (Ile d') — (Charente-M.)

Floratel
Rte de Boyardville — 46.75.46.40

Open every day. 50 rms 210-350 F. Restaurant. TV. Conference facilities. Heated pool. Parking. Telex 793454. V AE DC.

A few kilometres from the beach, the Floratel is a new hotel far from noisy roads, with well-equipped, comfortable rooms.

In nearby La Rémigeasse

(10 km pont d'Oléron)
17550 Oléron (Ile d') — (Charente-M.)

Amiral
46.75.37.89

Mme Moreau and M. Lemoine. Closed end Sep-Easter. Open until 9.15 pm. Private room: 30. Parking. Telex 790395. V.

The Amiral sails stoically on. Its steamship-style décor is stolid, and its cooking solid as the proverbial rock. Sample the succulent prawns with bacon and fennel fondue, delightful John Dory with nettle mousse, and fabulous fricaséed quails with morels in port sauce. Slightly starchy service. Fine but rather costly wines.

A la carte: 400 F. Menus: 220 F, 320 F.

Le Grand Large
(See restaurant above)

Closed end Sep-Easter. 5 stes 1,130-1,700 F. 21 rms 520-1,430 F. Half-board 590-1,055 F oblig in seas. TV. Conference facilities. Heated pool. Tennis.

A big, modern, rather graceless hotel, the Grand Large is very comfortable and ideally situated facing the open sea. Relais et Châteaux.

In nearby Saint-Pierre-d'Oléron

(14 km pont d'Oléron)
17310 Oléron (Ile d') (Charente-M.)

La Campagne
46.47.25.42

M. Nicolas. Closed off-season Sun dinner and Mon, and Oct-March (except Nov school holidays). Open until 10 pm. Terrace dining. Parking. V AE DC.

Bernard Nicolas is on the right track with his highly personal, seasonal cooking, which features exotic Thai marrows to accompany the duck breast, as well as lobster tian with a vin jaune sabayon, and sea bass with sea-urchin cream sauce. The islands' best desserts end the meal in style. Neat, well-kept dining room with rustic décor. Friendly, attentive service.

A la carte: 350 F. Menus: 130 F (lunch only), 190 F.

OLETTA
See CORSICA

ONZAIN
41150 Onzain — (Loir/Cher)
Paris 199 - Tours 45 - Blois 16 - Amboise 20

Domaine des Hauts de Loire
Rte d'Herbault — 54.20.72.57

M. Bonnigal. Closed off-season Tue lunch and Mon (except holidays), and 3 Dec-3 March. Open until 9 pm. Private room: 70. Garden dining. No pets. Parking. Telex 751547. V AE DC.

Rémy Giraud's cooking is light, original and professional, and made from top-quality ingredients. Try the salad of young pigeon in fennel-flavoured jelly and raw vegetables, red-mullet terrine with foie gras and asparagus, grapefruit and skate mould, and rhubarb crêpe bundles with strawberries. Well-balanced cellar (but too few half-bottles). Smiling welcome and service.

A la carte: 450 F. Menus: 230 F (weekdays lunch only), 275 F.

Domaine des Hauts de Loire
(See restaurant above)

Closed 3 Dec-3 March. 6 stes 1,575-1,680 F. 23 rms 525-1,680 F. Half-board 750-950 F. TV. Air cond 4 rms. No pets. Conference facilities. Tennis.

With impeccable taste, Mme Bonnigal has had decorated the immense, elegant rooms, suites and bathrooms of this enchanting domain. The best suites are in the Sologne-style annexe. Fishing in the lake. Relais et Châteaux.

In nearby Chouzy-sur-Cisse

(6 km NE on D 58)
41150 Onzain — (Loir/Cher)

La Carte
Nationale 152
54.20.49.00

M. Wayaffe. Closed 15 Nov-1 March. Open until 9.45 pm. Garden dining. No pets. Parking. V AE.

Skilled staff serve Eric Bourreau's outstanding cooking in the delightful dining room, or on the summer terrace. Seven years at Taillevent taught Bourreau many a marvel. His mouthwatering repertoire includes prawn ravioli with spiced butter, pike mousseline with morels, and young pigeon wrapped in green cabbage.

A la carte: 350 F. Menus: 85 F and 150 F (weekdays lunch only), 210 F.

La Carte

(See restaurant above)
*Closed 15 Nov-1 March. 5 stes 510-600 F. 20 rms
450-600 F. Half-board 685-835 F oblig in seas. TV.
Conference facilities. Heated pool. Tennis. Golf.*
Perfectly quiet in its 80-hectare estate, La Carte
has fifteen rooms and five suites with all modern
comforts.

ORANGE

84100 Orange — (Vaucluse)
Paris 660 - Avignon 31 - Nîmes 55 - Carpentras 23

 ### Altea Orange

80, rte de Caderousse
90.34.24.10
*Open every day. 99 rms 340-440 F. Restaurant. Half-
board 380-450 F. TV. Air cond. Conference facilities.
Pool. Parking. Telex 431550. V AE DC.*
This modern hotel is located just outside town,
and offers well-designed, sunny, practical rooms,
good for business trips.

Arène

Pl. de Langes — 90.34.10.95
*Closed 1 Nov-15 Dec. 30 rms 260-350 F. TV 22 rms.
Air cond. Valet parking. V AE DC.*
Located on a leafy square in the heart of the
historic city centre, this marvellous, peaceful hotel
is regularly improved.

12/20 Le Parvis

3, cours Pourtoules — 90.34.82.00
*M. Berengier. Closed Mon, 15 Jan-1 Feb and 24 Nov-
1 Dec. Open until 9.30 pm. Terrace dining. Air cond.
V AE DC.*
The ceiling of this former blacksmith's shop feels
a mile high, and the décor is terribly twee. But the
cooking, though on the expensive side, is worth a
stop. Try the mussel ravioli with spinach, local
asparagus, and lamb stew with young vegetables.
Fine selection of wines from Châteauneuf-du-Pape.
A la carte: 300 F. Menus: 98 F, 130 F, 160 F.

In nearby Rochegude

(14 km NW on D 976, D 11 and D 117)
26790 Orange — (Vaucluse)

 ### Château de Rochegude

75.04.81.88
*M. Chabert. Closed 1 Jan-3 March. Open until 9 pm.
Garden dining. Air cond. No pets. Valet parking.
Telex 345661. V AE DC.*
Chef Eric Coisel, a disciple of Alain Senderens,
has blended local inspiration with the tang of
truffles and the perfumes of Provençal herbs. Uncork a bottle of Tricastin, Côtes du Ventoux or
Châteauneuf-du-Pape and savour the truffle
turnover, turbot braised with mustard, and young
rabbit tian with toasted poppy seeds. Fine cheese
board. The lengthy wine list also includes a welcome selection of Burgundies and Bordeaux.
A la carte: 500-600 F. Menus: 180 F (weekdays
lunch only), 200 F (weekdays lunch only, wine
inc), 400 F (w-e and holidays only), 300 F.

 ### Château de Rochegude

(See restaurant above)
*Closed 1 Jan-3 March. 4 stes 1,800-2,500 F. 25 rms
500-1,500 F. Half-board 800-2,800 F. TV. Air cond.
Conference facilities. Heated pool. Tennis.*
Mont Ventoux and the Tricastin stare back as you
wander in the château's enormous grounds. This
extremely elegant and charming hotel offers huge
rooms furnished with rare antiques. Exemplary
staff. Relais et Châteaux.

ORCINES

See Clermont-Ferrand

ORLÉANS

45000 Orléans — (Loiret)
Paris 116 - Chartres 72 - Tours 113 - Blois 56 - Bourges 105

Les Antiquaires

2-4, rue au Lin — 38.53.52.35
*M. Pipet. Closed Sun, Mon, 3rd week of April and
3 first weeks of Aug. Open until 9.30 pm. Private
room: 15. Air cond. V AE DC.*
You're sure to enjoy the original cooking that
respects the seasons, served with flawless flair at
unbeatable prices. We recommend the smoked
salmon blinis with leek fondue, smoked prawn
'sausage' with cabbage, grilled mullet with crispy
potatoes, veal kidney baked with horseradish, and
fine game dishes. No great flights of fancy, but no
flops either. Good set menus. The well-stocked
cellar includes many bottles for under 100 F.
A la carte: 280-300 F. Menus: 100 F (weekdays
only), 190 F (wine inc), 290 F.

12/20 Le Bigorneau

54, rue des Turcies — 38.68.01.10
*M. Garnon. Closed Sun, Mon, 5-18 Feb and 7-22 July.
Open until 10.30 pm. Private room: 20. Air cond. V
AE DC.*
The chef knows the tides and times like the
Ancient Mariner. Seafood, absolutely fresh and sim-
ply prepared, is all you'll find here.
A la carte: 280 F.

12/20 La Chancellerie

27, place du Martroi
38.53.57.54
*MM. Erta. Closed Sun and Feb school holidays. Open
until midnight. Terrace dining. Parking. V AE.*
From her pedestal, Joan of Arc stares down at
diners on this brasserie's terrace. The proprietor is
an award-winning sommelier, and his wines, available by the glass or the bottle, are all delicious,
some rare and exotic, others bargains from nearby.
The cooking is simple but tasty (Loire salmon,
pheasant with wild mushrooms). An extension is
planned this year.
A la carte: 300 F.

12/20 Le Florian

70, bd A.-Martin — 38.53.08.15
*M. Viron. Closed Sun, 1-15 April and 15-31 Aug.
Open until 10 pm. Garden dining. Air cond. V AE.*
The owners are attentive to the slightest detail,
and the cooking is getting better all the time. Try
the cressonnette d'escargots en feuilleté, and quail
pie with morels. Another point.
A la carte: 260-280 F. Menus: 100 F, 120 F and
170 F (weekdays only).

Le Lautrec

26, pl. du Châtelet — 38.54.09.54
*M. Boulais. Closed Wed, Sun, 23 Dec-5 Jan and last 2
weeks of July. Open until 10 pm. Private room: 10.
Terrace dining. V AE DC.*
South-west cooking in Orléans: it's not what you
expect, is it? But then again, why not? True, the
décor is rather drab, but improvements are
planned. And Bruno Boulais, who cut his teeth
under Daguin, successfully transmits the heady
savours of his region in dishes such as quail eggs
with foie gras, duck magret, and salmon confit.
Excellent local wines (but not one half-bottle!).
Fabulous selection of vintage Armagnacs.
A la carte: 300 F. Menus: 120 F, 230 F.

La Loire
6, rue J.-Hupeau — 38.62.76.48
M. Servais. Closed Sat lunch, Sun, 7-12 Jan and 12-26 Aug. Open until 9.30 pm. V AE.
The prices are reasonable, given the quality and freshness of the ingredients. You can easily eat for less than 300 F, including a good Muscadet or Bourgeuil, if you avoid the lobster feuilleté with morels, and shellfish pot-au-feu with truffle juice. Try instead the tasty oysters, braised freshwater perch with morels and green cabbage, and sole cooked in sweet wine with leeks. Good desserts.
A la carte: 280-300 F. Menus: 120 F (weekdays only), 170 F, 260 F.

12/20 Le Lyonnais
82, rue des Turcies — 38.53.15.24
M. Payraudeau. Closed Sat lunch, Sun and 14 July-15 Aug. Open until 10.30 pm. Air cond. V.
Besieged at lunchtime, this bistro-style restaurant serves Lyonnais classics like pork charcuterie, calf's head, and chicken liver terrine, with jugs of Beaujolais.
A la carte: 210 F. Menu: 105 F.

Novotel Orléans La Source
11 km S on N 20
2, rue H.-de-Balzac — 38.63.04.28
Open every day. 119 rms 390-450 F. Restaurant. TV. Air cond. Conference facilities. Pool. Tennis. Parking. Telex 760619. V AE DC.
Modern, well-maintained, and comfortable, this chain hotel has sports facilities and a children's playground. Set in wooded grounds.

La Poutrière
8, rue de la Brèche — 38.66.02.30
M. Thomas. Closed Sun dinner and Mon. Open until 10 pm. Private room: 18. Garden dining. Heated pool. V AE DC.
A smart, conservative clientele comes here for the smoked-salmon salad with grapefruit, lotte papillote with semi-smoked salmon, and roast saddle of lamb. Fine wine cellar (but the Bordeaux are over-priced). Professional service to match the cooking.
A la carte: 300 F. Menus: 150 F (weekdays lunch only, wine inc), 160 F, 200 F.

Sofitel
(See restaurant above)
Open every day. 1 ste 1,500 F. 109 rms 525-595 F. TV. Air cond. Conference facilities. Heated pool.
A quality chain hotel with all modern comforts (free locked car park, satellite TV). The rooms have been thoroughly refurbished. Pool with terrace overlooking the Loire.
A la carte: 250-300 F. Menu: 130 F.

OUISTREHAM
14150 Ouistreham — (Calvados)
Paris 251 - Caen 14 - Cabourg 19 - Bayeux 35

11/20 Le Métropolitain
1, route de Lion — 31.97.18.61
M. Jacquot. Closed off-season Tue dinner and Wed. Open until 9 pm. Terrace dining. Parking. V AE DC.
Here you'll find an amusing Paris *métro* décor, and unoriginal but reliable cooking.
A la carte: 175-200 F. Menus: 87 F, 120 F, 145 F, 180 F.

Hôtel Rivabella
68, av. du Commandant-Kieffer
31.96.40.40
Open every day. 5 stes 1,060 F. 51 rms 550-810 F. Restaurant. Half-board 650 F. TV. Conference facilities. Parking. V.
Spanking-new and handsome, this long, modern building on the beach comprises a hotel, terrace-restaurant, and sea water therapy centre. Comfortable rooms decorated in restful colours.

PACY-SUR-EURE
27120 Pacy-sur-Eure — (Eure)
Paris 84 - Rouen 62 - Evreux 18 - Vernon 13

In nearby **Cocherel**

(6 km NW on D 836)
27120 Pacy-sur-Eure (Eure)

La Ferme de Cocherel
Route de la Vallée d'Eure
32.36.68.27
M. Delton. Closed Tue, Wed and 2-24 Jan. Open until 9.15 pm. Private room: 15. Parking. V AE DC.
Pierre Delton's Norman cooking sometimes borders on the extravagant, but is constantly improving in terms of execution. This year savour the enormous, fresh morels with veal sweetbreads, succulent baked lotte with truffle juice, and a fabulous raspberry dessert with berry coulis.
A la carte: 400 F. Menu: 200 F (wine inc).

In nearby **Douains**

(par D 181)
27120 Pacy-sur-Eure — (Eure)

Château de Brécourt
32.52.40.50
M. Charpentier. Open every day. Open until 9.30 pm. Private room: 120. Parking. Telex 172250. V AE DC.
Refinement and elegance are the watchwords, with prices to match, but the food is skilfully prepared. Choose the truffle turnover, duck confit salad with prawns, and roast farm pigeon with mild garlic.
A la carte: 400 F. Menus: 460 F (champagne inc), 225 F, 345 F.

Château de Brécourt 🏕️🍴
(See restaurant above)
Open every day. 25 rms 400-1,300 F. Half-board 650-950 F. Conference facilities. Heated pool. Tennis.
The Brécourt's hotel has huge, comfortable, smartly furnished rooms (the bathrooms are rather small, though). Those under the eaves are much less appealing and far too expensive. Good breakfasts. The lovely grounds include a covered swimming pool with adjacent Jacuzzi.

PAIMPOL
22500 Paimpol — (Côtes/Armor)
Paris 491 - St-Brieuc 45 - Guingamp 28

Le Relais des Pins
4 km W on D 786
Pont de Lézardrieux — 96.20.11.05
Mme Jacquemet and M. Laurent. Closed Tue lunch and Mon. Open until 9.30 pm. Private room: 40. Terrace dining. No-smoking section. Parking. Telex 740676. V AE DC.
The cooking is always excellent, even on those rare occasions when Laurent isn't there. Enjoy the rich yet ethereal crème de moules, fresh and flavourful artichoke heart salad, and mouthwatering boned pigeon.
A la carte: 350-400 F. Menus: from 140 F to 440 F.

Le Relais des Pins 🏕️🍴
(See restaurant above)
Open every day. 3 stes 1,350-2,900 F. 19 rms 550-800 F. Half-board 500-1,200 F oblig in seas. TV.
Admirably situated above the mouth of the Trieux, and surrounded by a flower-filled garden that sweeps down to the water's edge, the Relais has spacious, sunny, well-soundproofed rooms with luxurious bathrooms.

Repaire de Kerroc'h
29, quai Morand — 96.20.50.13
M. Broc. Open every day. Open until 9.30 pm. Private room: 50. Terrace dining. V.
André Morel's cooking features spicy poached prawns, Breton artichoke terrine with foie gras, turbot with shellfish, and pear and coffee croustillant. Rather cool reception.
A la carte: 280 F. Menus: 110 F, 165 F.

Repaire de Kerroc'h 🏕️🍴
(See restaurant above)
Open every day. 1 ste 580 F. 12 rms 200-480 F. Half-board 400 F. TV 5 rms. Conference facilities.
All twelve rooms are spotlessly clean, with hessian wallcoverings. Ask for the third-floor attic room known as 'l'île Tudy', which has a fine sea view through a bull's-eye window.

La Vieille Tour
13, rue de l'Eglise — 96.20.83.18
M. Rosec. Closed Sun dinner and Wed (except July-Aug), Feb school holidays and 13-30 Nov. Open until 9 pm. V DC.
Alain Rosec skilfully produces many a bold dish and lets his imagination run free. Sometimes too free: the warm prawn and veal sweetbread salad was a bit heavy on the accompanying meat stock; the John Dory in aromatic herbs was also rather swamped in juice. But the young pigeon with fresh ginger was good, and the caramelised apple millefeuille marvellous. Sprightly service.
A la carte: 300-350 F. Menus: 90 F (weekdays only), 95 F (w-e and holidays only), 180 F, 290 F, 320 F.

(9 km S on D 7 and D 79)
22290 Paimpol — (Côtes/Armor)

Château de Coatguelen 🥇
96.22.31.24
M. de Boisgelin. Closed off-season Mon lunch and Tue, and 1-21 Feb. Open until 9.30 pm. Garden dining. No-smoking section. No pets. Parking. Telex 741300. V AE DC.
Louis Leroy's highly professional cooking is a happy blend of Breton specialities and personal finds. Try the flavourful consommé d'ormeaux, spiny lobster braised with potatoes and truffles, lobster with veal sweetbreads, foie gras millefeuille with artichokes, and succulent shellfish. The cellar has some very old, very expensive Bordeaux and Burgundies (plus more affordable Loire wines). Special weekend rates include dinner, room, and breakfast.
A la carte: 450-500 F. Menus: 280 F, 400 F.

Château de Coatguelen 🏕️🍴
(See restaurant above)
Closed 1-21 Jan. 17 rms 435-1,200 F. Half-board 655-890 F. TV. Pool. Tennis. Golf.
A charming little château set in extensive grounds, Coatguelen has very comfortable rooms furnished with antiques, and excellent bathrooms. Delicious breakfasts. Horse riding, fishing, nine and eighteen-hole golf courses. Golf lessons and cookery classes with Louis Leroy are available. Wavering welcome, but friendly service.

PALAGACCIO
See CORSICA: Bastia

PAS-DE-LA-CASE
See Andorre (Principauté d')

PAU
64000 Pau — (Pyrénées-Atlantiques)
Paris 759 - Bordeaux 195 - Toulouse 195

L'Agripaume
14, rue Latapie — 59.27.68.70
M. Rodolphe. Closed Sat lunch and Sun (except holidays). Annual closings not available. Open until 10.30 pm. Private room: 30. No-smoking section. V.
Young and impetuous, François Rodolphe got off to a bumpy start here but is now creating refined, authentic dishes. The flavourful foie gras with beetroot and spiced juices, delicious duck fillet à la ficelle, and a good choice of desserts help to forgive the odd unsuccessful experiment. Fine wines at affordable prices.
A la carte: 200 F. Menus: 95 F, 145 F, 195 F.

Continental
2, rue du Mal-Foch — 59.27.69.31
Open every day. 2 stes 700-900 F. 80 rms 270-480 F. Restaurant. Half-board 310-480 F. TV. Air cond 5 rms. Valet parking. Telex 570906. V AE DC.
The Continental is Pau's prestige hotel, centrally located. Five of the rooms are luxurious; all are well equipped, smartly decorated, and soundproofed. Attentive welcome and service.

Paris
80, rue E.-Garet — 59.27.34.39
Open every day. 41 rms 300-450 F. TV. V AE DC.
In the centre of town near the Beaumont park, the rooms here are fairly quiet (all overlook the courtyard). Buffet breakfasts included in the cost of a room.

Pierre
16, rue L.-Barthou – 59.27.76.86
M. Casau. Closed Sat lunch, Sun (except holidays) and last 2 weeks of Feb. Open until 10 pm. Private room: 40. Air cond. V AE DC.
Raymond Casau's cooking is authentic, refined, and refreshing. Witness the duck confit with sautéed potatoes, and rack of lamb, or the exquisite prawn ravioli with a delicate curry sauce. The divine desserts include the much-copied gâteau des Prélats (invented by Raymond's father, Roland Casau), and mouthwatering fruit-filled crêpes flambéed with Grand Marnier. Fine Bordeaux and Burgundies flank worthy regional wines (the Madiran, especially).
A la carte: 300 F.

12/20 Les Pyrénées
9, pl. Royale – 59.27.07.75
M. Bouchet. Closed Sun and 1-22 Aug. Open until 10 pm. Terrace dining. Air cond. V AE DC.
This Pau institution is popular with both young people and town councillors. The atmosphere is warm, and the succulent cooking swiftly served. Take a mezzanine table above the bar and sample the fresh foie gras with apples, and veal sweetbreads with chanterelles. Courteous welcome, sturdy à la carte prices.
A la carte: 250 F. Menus: 92 F, 160 F.

Roncevaux
25, rue L.-Barthou – 59.27.08.44
Open every day. 44 rms 100-320 F. TV. Parking. Telex 570849. V AE DC.
Near the château's lovely park and the casino, this large hotel is in the city centre. Pleasant, comfortable rooms.

La Table d'Hôte
1, rue du Hédas – 59.27.56.06
M. Sicard. Closed Mon lunch and Sun. Open until 10 pm. Terrace dining. V.
The *patron* welcomes customers to his old stone restaurant decorated in modern style. The cooking is refreshing and tasty, specialising in fish: tiny squid in brioche, salmon tartare, and scallops in Champagne. Good local wines.
A la carte: 220-250 F. Menus: 80 F and 150 F (weekdays only).

Trespoey
71, av. du Gal-Leclerc – 59.30.64.77
M. Peyrou. Closed Fri dinner, Sat and 20 Dec-10 Jan. Open until 9.30 pm. Hotel: 20 rms 110-230 F. V AE.
Philippe Maré, the new chef, has been busy renewing the menu, and our last meal showed great promise. A pupil of Dutournier, Vergé and Issautier, Maré prepares luscious lightly cooked duck foie gras, succulent fresh salmon with chives and Jurançon-flavoured cream, and ambrosial honey gratin with a redcurrant coulis. The wine list includes many flavourful Jurançons. We're eager to award Maré another point, but let's give him time to settle in.
A la carte: 250 F. Menus: 65 F (weekdays only), 55 F, 90 F, 100 F.

Le Viking
33, bd Tourasse – 59.84.02.91
M. David. Closings not available. Open until 9.15 pm. Garden dining. No pets. Parking. V AE.
Hubert David keeps down the number of dishes, the better to lavish care and attention on each one. Last year's shortcomings have been remedied, and we were most pleased with the fresh stuffed mussels with a flavourful sauce, exquisite sole and oyster sauce, and mouthwatering homemade vanilla ice cream. Dare we now suggest that this conscientious chef should renew his *carte* more often? Short wine list with good Bordeaux.
A la carte: 350-400 F. Menu: 150 F.

In nearby **Artiguelouve**
(10 km W on D 2 and D 146)
64230 Pau (Pyrénées-Atlantiques)

Alain Bayle
59.83.05.08
M. Bayle. Closed Wed (except July-Aug) and Sun dinner. Open until 9.30 pm. Garden dining. Parking. V AE DC.
Alain Bayle's skilfully lightened cooking is authentic and refined, and based on local, seasonal ingredients. Savour the sea bream fillets with sweet peppers, and kidneys and sweetbreads in a creamy sauce. Efficient service.
A la carte: 250 F. Menus: 90 F (weekdays only), 132 F, 190 F.

In nearby **Jurançon**
(2 km SW on N 134))
64110 Pau – (Pyrénées-Atlantiques)

Castel du Pont d'Oly
2, av. Rausky – 59.06.13.40
Open every day. 7 rms 350-400 F. Restaurant. Half-board 500 F. TV. Conference facilities. Pool. Parking. V.
On the outskirts of Pau, this handsome hotel is on the ski resort route. Very comfortable, welcoming and flawlessly maintained. Some rooms overlook the swimming pool and pretty garden.

Ruffet
3, av. Ch.-Touzet
59.06.25.13
M. Larrouy. Closed Sun dinner and Mon. Open until 10 pm. V AE DC.
Milou Larrouy's personal, inventive, regional cooking is as appealing as ever. We enjoyed the delicate scrambled eggs with smoked salmon, assiette béarnaise (magret, confit, fresh foie gras, and duck heart), and duck in every delectable sauce imaginable. Polite welcome and fast, competent service.
A la carte: 250 F. Menu: 120 F.

33250 Pauillac – (Gironde)
Paris 570 - Bordeaux 50 - Lesparre-Médoc 20 - Blaye 13

Château Cordeillan-Bages
Rte des Châteaux – 56.59.24.24
M. Paillardon. Closed Sun dinner, Mon and 24 Dec-23 Jan. Open until 9.30 pm. Private room: 18. Garden dining. Parking. Telex 573050. V AE DC.
Proprietor—and award-winning sommelier—Pierre Paillardon will gently try to persuade you to organise your meal around the 1,001 wines in his sumptuous cellar. The young chef, François Tillier, trained by the Troisgros brothers, is skilful, and improving all the time.
A la carte: 280-320 F. Menus: 140 F and 190 F (weekdays only), 160 F and 220 F (w-e and holidays only).

Château Cordeillan-Bages
(See restaurant above)
Closed 24 Dec-23 Jan. 3 stes 620-770 F. 18 rms 490-630 F. Half-board 580 F. TV. Conference facilities.
Latour's round tower is a stone's throw away. But why go further? The rooms of this glorious castle

are elegant, airy, and comfortable. They give onto a small vineyard where the proprietor grows the eight major varieties of Bordeaux grape. Wine-tasting courses. Relais et Châteaux.

PÉRIGNAT-LÈS-SARLIÈVE

See Clermont-Ferrand

PÉRIGUEUX

24000 Périgueux — (Dordogne)
Paris 528 - Bordeaux 120 - Limoges 101 - Angoulême 85

L'Oison
31, rue St-Front — 53.09.84.02
M. Chiorozas. Closed Sun dinner, Mon, 10 Feb-10 March and 23 June-7 July. Open until 9.30 pm. Private room: 40. Air cond. V AE DC.
Trained by Guy Girard and Michel Peignaud in Paris, Chiorozas has a simple secret: excellent ingredients, perfectly cooked, and sauces of rare finesse. His specialities include a copious potato salad with truffles, seasoned with just a hint of vinegar, terrine sarladaise (composed of sliced potatoes and foie gras, and served sprinkled with truffles), the perfect pig's trotter crépinette, and scrumptious cold barigoule seasoned with coriander, herbs, and fresh tomatoes. The cheeses are less brilliant, but most of the desserts (and especially the chocolate selection) deserve three toques. The wine list is also excellent, abounding in quality Bordeaux and also including some bargains.
A la carte: 350-400 F. Menus: 135 F (weekdays only), 175 F, 275 F, 380 F.

In nearby Antonne-et-Trigonant
(10 km NE on N 21)
24420 Périgueux — (Dordogne)

Les Chandelles
Le Parc — 53.06.05.10
Closed Mon off-season, and mid-Jan to mid-Feb. 7 rms 180-340 F. Restaurant. Half-board 300-400 F. TV 3 rms. Pool. Tennis. Parking. V AE DC.
This converted fifteenth-century residence has pleasantly furnished, well-appointed rooms. A river runs through the grounds.

PÉROUGES
01800 Pérouges — (Ain)
Paris 454 - Bourg 37 - Lyon 36 - Saint-André-de-Corcy 20

Ostellerie du Vieux Pérouges
Pl. du Tilleul — 74.61.00.88
Closed Wed off-season. 3 stes 900 F. 25 rms 390-790 F. Restaurant. TV 8 rms. Conference facilities.
Embraced by massive fourteenth-century walls, the Ostellerie's huge, comfortable, well-modernised rooms are furnished with regional antiques and are breathtakingly beautiful. Family atmosphere. Breakfast is served on a covered terrace perched on top of the tower.

PERPIGNAN
66000 Perpignan — (Pyrénées-O.)
Paris 908 - Toulouse 208 - Béziers 93 - Foix 137

Athéna

1, rue Queya — 68.34.37.63
Open every day. 1 ste 380 F. 40 rms 120-250 F. TV. Conference facilities. Pool. Valet parking. V AE DC.
In the heart of the old town, this recently restored fourteenth-century residence has quiet, comfortable rooms set around a patio. Meal service, cafeteria.

Le Bourgogne
63, av. du Mal-Leclerc — 68.34.96.05
M. Morlans. Closed Sat lunch, Sun dinner and 11-25 Feb. Open until 10 pm. Air cond. V AE DC.
Teresa Morlans refuses to limit herself to regional cookery, preferring to let her imagination run free. Marinated sardines wrapped in vine leaves, sea bass with lettuce and asparagus, and magret and foie gras with apple nougatine in a Banyuls sauce are examples of her repertoire.
A la carte: 250-350 F. Menus: 170 F, 280 F.

Le Chapon Fin
18, bd J.-Bourrat — 68.35.14.14
M. Fernandez. Closed Sat dinner, Sun, 1-14 Jan and 11 Aug-1 Sep. Open until 9.30 pm. Private room: 100. Air cond. Garage parking. V AE DC.
The faithful include many well-off French and Spanish gourmets. Chef Claude Patry manages to please them all, while managing to avoid the trap of ultra-classic cooking. His creativity comes through in such unconventional dishes as shellfish soup with seaweed, fresh cod with oyster fritters, and John Dory picada with an olive-studded potato purée. The desserts are as original as they are delicious. Outstanding wine list.
A la carte: 330-400 F. Menus: 180 F, 260 F, 350 F.

Park Hôtel
(See restaurant above)
Open every day. 67 rms 230-500 F. TV. Air cond. Conference facilities.
Some rooms are remarkably spacious, others are cramped, but all are very well maintained and equipped. Dull breakfasts.

Festin de Pierre
7, rue du Théâtre — 68.51.28.74
M. Bellaton. Closed Tue dinner, Wed, last 2 weeks of Feb and June. Open until 9.30 pm. Air cond. V AE DC.
Catalan high society gathers under the Festin's gorgeous Renaissance coffered ceiling to enjoy Michel Bellaton's flavourful cooking. Excellent desserts. Flawless wine list.
A la carte: 280-330 F. Menu: 150 F.

La Loge
1, pl. de la Loge — 68.34.54.84
Open every day. 22 rms 270-350 F. TV. Air cond. Conference facilities. Telex 506116. V AE DC.
Part of this hotel is listed as an historic monument from the sixteenth century. Cosy rooms, bar.

Mas des Arcades
Av. d'Espagne — 68.85.11.11
Closed 23 Dec-15 Jan. 3 stes 700-800 F. 140 rms 240-400 F. Restaurant. TV. Air cond. No pets. Conference facilities. Pool. Tennis. Garage parking. Telex 500176. V.
On the road to Spain, the Arcades is a modern, comfortable hotel. The large, well-equipped rooms with bathrooms are air-conditioned.

12/20 Le Vauban
29, quai Vauban — 68.51.05.10
M. Authié. Closed Sun. Open until 10.30 pm. Terrace dining. Air cond. V.
The young chef prepares a limited number of dishes with real attention to detail. His gazpacho is authentically Andalusian, his carpaccio as good as the Italian original, and his pastries worth their weight in sugar. Competent maître d', friendly service, and quality wines served by the glass.
A la carte: 190 F.

PERREUX (LE)

See PARIS Suburbs

PERROS-GUIREC

22700 Perros-Guirec — (Côtes/Armor)
Paris 521 - St-Brieuc 76 - Lannion 12

Grand Hôtel de Trestraou
Bd J.-Le Bihan — 96.23.24.05
Open every day. 10 stes 474-750 F. 68 rms 267-375 F. Restaurant. Half-board 265-364 F oblig in seas. TV. Conference facilities. Garage parking. Telex 741261. V AE DC.
Set between the tennis club and casino, and with direct access to the sea-water therapy centre, the Trestraou offers nicely updated rooms.

Printania
Hauteurs de Trestraou
12, rue des Bons-Enfants — 96.23.21.00
Closed 16 Dec-14 Jan. 1 ste 750-1,000 F. 33 rms 450-590 F. Restaurant. Half-board 405-470 F oblig in seas. TV. No pets. Conference facilities. Tennis. Parking. Telex 741431. V AE DC.
The newly remodelled rooms look out to sea, with a marvellous view of the Sept-Iles bird reserve. Beach just 250 metres away. Attentive reception and service. Sea fishing expeditions.

12/20 Le Sphinx
67, ch. de la Messe — 96.23.25.42
M. Levergé. Closed Mon lunch and 6 Jan-15 March. Open until 9.30 pm. Private room: 24. Garage parking. Telex 740637. V.
Ask for a table near the window: the view of the sea and coastline are preferable to the dreary décor. Nothing overwhelming is cooking here, but at least the food is fresh and generously served: baked turbot, grilled lamb, and tulipe de fruits rouges for dessert. Pleasant welcome, approximate service.
A la carte: 270 F. Menus: 110 F, 160 F, 210 F.

Le Sphinx
(See restaurant above)
Closed 6 Jan-15 March. 11 rms 370-385 F (per pers, half-board oblig). TV. Air cond. Conference facilities.
Along with the fabulous sea view, Le Sphinx offers huge, comfortable, but poorly decorated rooms. Attentive service.

In nearby Ploumanach

(6 km W on D 788)
22700 Perros-Guirec (Côtes/Armor)

Les Rochers
(Chez Justin)
Port de Ploumanach — 96.91.44.49
Mme Justin. Closed Wed off-season, and end Sep-Easter. Open until 9 pm. No pets. V.
The à la carte prices are as high as the view of Ploumanach harbour is pleasant. The carefully executed dishes show great respect for their ingredients: crab terrine, John Dory with spinach, and millefeuille glacé au Grand Marnier. Some excellent wines are available too.
A la carte: 300 F. Menus: 130 F, 185 F, 360 F.

Les Rochers
(See restaurant above)
Closed Wed and end Sep-Easter. 15 rms 275-375 F. Half-board 340-400 F.
The seafront rooms are spacious and quite pleasant. The owner and staff bend over backwards to serve and inform guests. Fine breakfasts.

PERTUIS

84120 Pertuis — (Vaucluse)
Paris 747 - Manosque 20 - Aix-en-Provence 20

L'Olivier
Av. de Verdun — 90.09.60.11
M. Tantini. Closed Tue off-season, and Jan. Open until 10 pm. Private room: 40. Terrace dining. Hotel: 36 rms 328-538 F Pool. Tennis. Parking. Telex 431470. V AE.
Michel Tantini's highly personal repertoire (shellfish brochettes with coconut served on a bed of squid 'tagliatelle', for instance) hasn't been a great success in this far-flung corner of the Lubéron. So he's switching back to a simpler style, familiar to those who discovered and appreciated him several years ago.
A la carte: 280-350 F. Menus: 125 F, 150 F, 220 F, 300 F.

Sévan
Av. de Verdun — 90.79.19.30
Closed Jan. 36 rms 368-496 F. Restaurant. Half-board 535-570 F oblig in seas. TV. Air cond 4 rms. Pool. Tennis. Parking. Telex 431470. V AE DC.
The Sévan's façade may be unattractive, but the interior garden is utterly charming, and the rooms are comfortable and adequately decorated.

PESSAC

See Bordeaux

PETIT-PRESSIGNY (LE)

See Grand-Pressigny (Le)

PEYRELEAU

12720 Peyreleau — (Aveyron)
Paris 655 - Mende 80 - Rodez 85 - Millau 14

Grand Hôtel Muse et Rozier
65.62.60.01
Closed Jan and Feb. 3 stes 590-660 F. 35 rms 290-520 F. Restaurant. Half-board 350-540 F oblig in seas. TV. Conference facilities. Tennis. Garage parking. V AE DC.
One of the most spectacular hotels on the banks of the Tarn, the Muse et Rozier is modern yet blends well into the surrounding greenery. From the verandas and windows you'll enjoy a sweeping view of the leafy landscape and rushing river. The rooms are sunny and soberly decorated. A little more enthusiasm from the staff would be welcome. Swimming pool under construction.

PHALSBOURG

57370 Phalsbourg — (Moselle)
Paris 430 - Sarrebourg 16 - Saverne 11 - Strasbourg 57

Au Soldat de l'An II
1, rte de Saverne — 87.24.16.16
M. Schmitt. Closed Sun dinner, Mon, 2-17 Jan and 4-18 Nov. Open until 9.30 pm. Private room: 16. Terrace dining. Parking. Telex 890555. V.
Former decorator Georges Schmitt has transformed this old barn into a luxurious hostelry. The stone walls and exposed beams contrast with a pleasant, muted décor filled with rustic Alsace antiques. Entirely self-taught, Schmitt has learned his craft well and chooses his rich ingredients with care. Though his dishes are dependable, he's been led astray of late by fashion and preciosity (maraîchère d'homard à la crème d'or, young pigeon with foie gras and almond feuilleté, aumônière croustillante en surprise). Excellent

selections of fine Alsace wines (120 kinds), liqueurs (40), and cigars (400).

A la carte: 350-400 F. Menus: 145 F (weekdays only), 240 F (weekdays only, wine inc), 255 F, 285 F.

PIANA

See CORSICA: Porto

PIEDICROCE

See CORSICA

PIOGGIOLA

See CORSICA

PISCIATELLO

See CORSICA: Porticcio

PLAGNE (LA)

73210 Plagne (La) — (Savoie)
Paris 653 - Moûtiers 34 - Val-d'Isère 24 - Chambéry 109

12/20 La Boule de Neige

in Montchavin — 79.07.83.30
M. Pasquette. Open every day. Open until 9.30 pm. Terrace dining. Parking. V DC.

The mezzanine dining room is light and gay, with bright napery, artificial flowers, and some windows that offer a clear view over the mountain. The cooking is simple and not expensive: veal escalope with melted cheese, meats cooked on a hot stone, and freshwater perch fillet pepped up with lime. Good house wines.

A la carte: 180 F. Menus: from 65 F to 145 F.

11/20 La Galerne

Plagne Centre — 79.09.04.42
M. L'Hostis. Closed 1 June-28 June and 1 Sep-15 Dec. Open until midnight. Terrace dining. V AE DC.

Opposite the ski slopes and always full of lively, hungry skiers, this little spot serves crêpes and pancakes (150 kinds) at lunchtime, and in the evening cheese fondues and raclette (melted cheese served with ham, potatoes and condiments).

A la carte: 160 F. Menu: 60 F (lunch only).

Graciosa

79.09.00.18
Closed end April-beg July and end Aug-beg Dec. 3 stes 650-770 F. 14 rms 400-450 F. Restaurant. Half-board 370-460 F oblig in seas. TV. Parking. Telex 309626. V AE DC.

A good little hotel overlooking the resort opposite the Biolley run. The rooms and suites have mountain views. Chilly welcome.

11/20 Piano-Bar

in Plagne-Bellecôte — 79.09.03.07
M. Penasa. Closed 15 May-30 June and 1 Sep-1 Dec. Open until 11 pm. Terrace dining. No pets. V AE.

This place is a great success—it now seats twice the number of patrons it served before. Every evening the owner leads the musicians and singers to entertain the resort's in-crowd. The food is a harmless diversion (salmon with dill, guinea fowl with cocoa).

A la carte: 250-350 F. Menus: 79 F (lunch only), 105 F, 119 F and 147 F (dinner only).

COL DE PLAINPALAIS (LE)

See Chambéry

PLAISANCE-DU-GERS

32160 Plaisance-du-Gers — (Gers)
Paris 740 - Condom 64 - Auch 54 - Tarbes 44 - Pau 64

16 Ripa-Alta

3, pl. de l'Eglise — 62.69.30.43
M. Coscuella. Closed off-season Sun dinner and Mon lunch, and 4 Nov-5 Dec. Open until 9.30 pm. Hotel: 14 rms 95-300 F. Garage parking. V AE DC.

The stained-glass windows and rustic charm give the impression of an Alsace inn, an impression that dissipates immediately one enters the flowered-filled dining room and hears the patron's rich South-western accent. All the serious food lovers in the region jostle with the tourists (English in particular) to taste the passionate cooking of Maurice Coscuella. His menu changes weekly, and there are always unexpected discoveries to be made. Besides the dishes always in demand—the famous goose tripe stew or the extraordinary lobster pastilla with foie gras—you will find rarities like smooth chestnut soup with foie gras, goose hearts pan-roasted with fines herbes, or duck with pink peppercorns, and the best apple- and prune-filled pastry in the world. You may also expect an admirable selection of local wines, and a bill that won't give you indigestion after such an excellent meal.

A la carte: 250-300 F. Menus: 75 F (wine inc), 140 F, 195 F, 300 F.

PLANCOËT

22130 Plancoët — (Côtes/Armor)
Paris 385 - Dinard 14 - Dinan 17 - St-Brieuc 47

15 Chez Crouzil

Les Quais — 96.84.10.24
M. Crouzil. Closed Sun dinner (except July-Aug), Mon, 10-24 June and 11-25 Nov. Open until 9.15 pm. Private room: 15. Terrace dining. Parking. V.

Twenty years of dedicated work have transformed an unremarkable bistro into a luxury restaurant with a charming atmosphere. The new dining room is a jewel, with beautiful place settings and fresh flowers, with a pleasant quay-front terrace beyond. A worthy setting for the delicious and generous cooking of Jean-Pierre Crouzil, a fanatic for fabulously fresh and fine ingredients. Taste his hot and cold oysters with a Vouvray sabayon, or a whole, sumptuous Périgord truffle steamed in Monbazillac wine, a gratin of sole and lobster flavoured with cider and crocus pistils, or sautéed sweetbreads with morels and lemon confit. The wine cellar gets better every time we visit; impeccable service.

A la carte: 350-400 F. Menus: 110 F (weekdays lunch only), 185 F, 275 F, 380 F.

L'Ecrin

(See restaurant above)
Closed Sun, Mon, 10-24 June and 11-25 Nov. 7 rms 260-550 F. Half-board 400-450 F. TV. No pets. Conference facilities.

The hotel was completely renovated last year and the large rooms are prettily decorated with English furniture and have huge, comfortable bathrooms with antique taps. The welcome is faultless, the service excellent and breakfasts incredible (oysters, charcuterie, boiled eggs, fresh fruit juice, etc.). There is a sauna and a solarium. One of the best hotels in the region.

PLÉHÉDEL

See Paimpol

See Saint-Brieuc

PLEURT
See Dinard

PLOUNÉRIN
22780 Plounérin — (Côtes/Armor)
Paris 510 - Morlaix 23 - St-Brieuc 60

 Patrick Jeffroy   ✿✿
96.38.61.80
M. Jeffroy. Closed off-season Sun dinner and Mon. Annual closings not available. Open until 9.30 pm. Hotel: 3 rms 250-280 F. Parking. V AE.

In a little granite village a stone's throw from the Rennes-Brest expressway, Patrick Jeffroy is on the brink of recapturing the third toque he held at the Hôtel de l'Europe in Morlaix. A passionate, exuberant chef, Jeffroy has constructed a *carte* that reflects his wide-ranging tastes and interests. We were bowled over by his salmon cooked on flat stones (a technique borrowed from Antiquity!), and his turbot with mango, made more exotic by a vinaigrette touched with vanilla and ginger. And then there is his sole in cider with fried apples, cooked with split-second precision (as is all the seafood, be it lobster, prawns, or rock lobster). Not forgetting a full-flavoured Roquefort pâté, and, for dessert, a tender millefeuille layered with ripe, fragrant seasonal fruit. Along with these delights comes his excellent apple-cider bread, and a whole cellar full of interesting wines chosen and recommended by Christine Tollemer. Even better, the prices are as friendly as can be. Meals here are served by a deft, swift staff, but if you're not in a hurry to continue your journey, three simple, cosy rooms are available, giving you the chance to sample an excellent breakfast the next morning.

A la carte: 320-350 F. Menus: 120 F (weekdays only, wine inc), 150 F, 250 F, 320 F.

POËT-LAVAL (LE)
See Dieulefit

POISSY
78300 Poissy — (Yvelines)
Paris 38 - Pontoise 17 - Mantes-la-Jolie 29

 L'Esturgeon
6, cours 14-Juillet
39.65.00.04
M. Soulat. Closed Thu, 1-9 Feb and Aug. Open until 9.30 pm. Private room: 60. V AE DC.

This renovated former dance hall and outdoor café was a favourite haunt of the Impressionists. Its continued success owes in part to the graceful indoor terrace bathed in light, curiously traversed by tree trunks. And then there is the famous koulibiac de saumon served with beurre blanc, which is almost as popular as the other house speciality, duck with cherries.

A la carte: 350-400 F.

POITIERS
86000 Poitiers — (Vienne)
Paris 338 - Tours 104 - Angoulême 109 - Niort 74

 **Hôtel Continental**
2, bd Solférino — 49.37.93.93
Open every day. 39 rms 218-254 F. TV. V AE DC.

A classic construction in the town centre; pleasant, soundproofed rooms with every comfort.

 Maxime
4, rue Saint-Nicolas
49.41.09.55
M. Rougier. Closed Sat, Sun, 5-15 Jan, 10-20 July and 10-20 Aug. Open until 10 pm. V AE.

Christian Rougier's exceptional set menus and *carte* include generous warm lobster and sprouted-lentil salad, John Dory simmered in chicken bouillon with sea salt, tender duck breast with a sauce of Hungarian Tokay wine, and an exquisite triple-chocolate dessert, served with a glass of suave Banyuls wine.

A la carte: 280-300 F. Menus: 140 F (weekdays lunch only, wine inc), 95 F, 175 F, 220 F.

In nearby Buxerolles
(4 km N on D 4)
86180 Poitiers — (Vienne)

Auberge de la Cigogne
20, rue du Planty
49.45.61.47
M. Kress. Closed Sun, Mon, Easter school holidays and 21 July-12 Aug. Open until 9.15 pm. Private room: 25. Garden dining. No pets. Parking. V AE.

Charles Kress won't tire you with an unending list of specialities from his native Alsace. Apart from a good choucroute, and some starters enlivened with horseradish, his menu offers classic, seasonal dishes of no particular provincial provenance. Good cellar.

A la carte: 220-250 F. Menus: 95 F and 120 F (weekdays lunch only), 170 F.

In nearby Chasseneuil-du-Poitou
(8 km N on N 10)
86360 Poitiers — (Vienne)

Clos de la Ribaudière   ♠♣
Rue du Champ-de-Foire
49.52.86.32
Open every day. 2 stes 500 F. 17 rms 300-580 F. Restaurant. Half-board 530 F. TV. V AE DC.

It has taken several months (and probably several million francs) to restore its former lustre to this nineteenth-century residence, superbly situated in a delightful park. There are eleven spacious, fresh, comfortable rooms (as well as eight others in the caretaker's lodge next door), all with marble bathrooms. Undistinguished breakfasts.

In nearby Croutelle
(6 km S on N 10)
86240 Poitiers — (Vienne)

Pierre Benoist
N 10 - A 10, Poitiers South exit
49.57.11.52
M. Benoist. Closed Sun dinner, Mon, Feb school holidays and 1st week of Aug. Open until 9.30 pm. Garden dining. Parking. V AE DC.

For a quarter of a century Pierre Benoist has devoted himself to good, classic cooking, with a marked taste for offal (his old-fashioned calf's head is exemplary, as is the pig's head simmered in a spiced broth). He is equally at ease, however, with fish, lobster or pigeon with shallot confit. The pastries do not seem up to quite the same standard, but the selection of goat cheeses is sensational. Excellent but expensive wines.

A la carte: 300 F and up. Menus: 155 F (lunch only), 175 F (dinner only).

PONS

17800 Pons — (Charente-M.)
Paris 495 - Bordeaux 96 - Cognac 23 - Saintes 22

In nearby Mosnac

(11 km S on N 137 and D 134)
17240 Pons — (Charente-M.)

Le Moulin de Marcouze
46.70.46.16

M. Bouchet. Closed off-season Wed lunch and Tue (except holidays), and Feb. Open until 9.30 pm. Private room: 15. Air cond. Parking. V AE DC.

Philippe Bouchet's cooking is supremely intelligent; he draws every nuance of flavour from his first-rate ingredients: just taste his duck and fresh pear salad topped with curly endive, or the sole fillet napped with shellfish cream given depth by a touch of Cognac and spiced with a pinch of Cayenne pepper, or lemon crêpes filled with airy meringue and drizzled with strawberry coulis. The wine list is sumptuous, with a superb array of Bordeaux. On the down side, customers suffer from the lack of staff (the services of a sommelier would be particularly welcome); the coffee is inexplicably bad; and noisy groups are not (as they should be) seated so as not to disturb other guests. But such problems are easily remedied. To heighten your enjoyment and appreciation of the region, a helicopter is available for trips to the Bordeaux and Cognac vineyards.

A la carte: 400 F. Menus: 135 F (weekdays only), 180 F, 250 F, 400 F.

Le Moulin de Marcouze
(See restaurant above)

Closed Tue off-season (except holidays). 1 ste 900-1,200 F. 9 rms 550-650 F. TV. Air cond. Pool.

Choice large rooms looking over the river or the lawn. The bathrooms are rather small.

PONTAUBERT

See Avallon

PONT-AUDEMER

27500 Pont-Audemer — (Eure)
Paris 168 - Rouen 52 - Honfleur 24 - Lisieux 36 - Evreux 68

Auberge du Vieux Puits
6, rue Notre-Dame-du-Pré — 32.41.01.48

M. Foltz. Closed Mon dinner, Tue, 1-10 July and 17 Dec-17 Jan. Open until 9 pm. Private room: 18. Hotel: 12 rms 150-360 F. V.

Tourists adore it, and while the young owners greet guests with a smile, in the kitchen the chef produces lovely classic (but never boring) cuisine. We recommend the fragrant local duck liver with fried apples, trout Bovary in Champagne sauce, duck with sour cherries, and a Norman dumpling—an apple swathed in pastry. The cellar is small but choice, and the cider is excellent.

A la carte: 300 F and up. Menus: 155 F (weekdays lunch only), 250 F.

Belle Isle-sur-Risle
1.5 km on N 175
112, rte de Rouen — 32.56.96.22

Closed 15 Jan-15 Feb. 3 stes 1,000-1,300 F. 12 rms 490-1,000 F. Half-board 600-830 F oblig in seas. Restaurant. TV. Heated pool. Tennis. V AE DC.

This aristocratic house on pleasant grounds has undeniable charm, shown to advantage in the spacious and elegant rooms, as well as by the perfectly polished service.

PONTAULT-COMBAULT

See PARIS Suburbs

PONT-AVEN

29930 Pont-Aven — (Finistère)
Paris 522 - Lorient 36 - Concarneau 15 - Quimper 38

Moulin de Rosmadec
98.06.00.22

M. Sébilleau. Closed Sun dinner off-season, Wed, Feb and 2 last weeks of Oct. Open until 9.15 pm. V.

The welcome is extremely kind, and the cooking intelligent and lively. Try the feuilleté of prawns and asparagus, pan-roasted red mullet scented with basil, or tian d'agneau. All these dishes could be shown to better advantage with lighter sauces, but that is a very small detail. The cheese selection is most appealing, and the desserts are beautifully prepared. The cellar offers some surprising vintages (notably from Alsace), of which the prices are faithfully brought up to date.

A la carte: 300 F and up. Menus: 110 F, 240 F.

Moulin de Rosmadec
(See restaurant above)

Closed Feb and 2 last weeks of Oct. 4 rms 420 F. TV.

There are only four bedrooms, but they are charmingly decorated in fresh, simple tones, and perfectly comfortable.

La Taupinière
Rte de Concarneau — 98.06.03.12

M. Guilloux. Closed Mon dinner (except July-Aug), Tue and 20 Sep-20 Oct. Open until 9.15 pm. Air cond. No pets. Parking. V.

Brittany's wonderful seafood is featured in crab crépinettes, in the tender buckwheat crêpe stuffed with shellfish and morels, and the lightly cooked prawn tails swaddled in feathery pastry with chicory and mushrooms. Or one could plump instead for the lovely rack of farm-reared suckling pig, cooked to a turn, and then finish with magnificent hot strawberries served with a warm coulis and a dash of crème fraîche. From the peach-coloured dining room guests can see and hear the busy kitchen brigade at work.

A la carte: 300-350 F. Menus: 220 F, 320 F, 420 F.

PONTCHARTRAIN

78760 Pontchartrain — (Yvelines)
Paris 40 - Rambouillet 21 - Versailles 17 - Montfort 10

In nearby Neauphle-le-Château

(2 km N on D 13e)
78640 Pontchartrain — (Yvelines)

La Griotte
58, av. de la République — 34.89.19.98

M. Faucon. Closed Sun dinner, Mon, 4 Feb-4 March and 12-19 Aug. Open until 10 pm. Garden dining. No-smoking section. V AE DC.

The restrainedly elegant dining room opens onto an exquisite terrace overlooking flowers and woods. Despite a slight tendency to complicate what could be supremely simple, chef Jacky Duval will satisfy the most demanding gourmet with his sesame-crusted red-mullet fillets, lamb with artichokes, and crêpe 'beggar's purses' filled with mango and oranges.

A la carte: 300-350 F. Menus: 125 F (weekdays lunch only), 170 F.

PONT-DE-BRIQUES

See Boulogne-sur-Mer

PONT-DE-BUIS-LÈS-QUIMERCH

See Châteaulin

PONT-DE-L'ISÈRE

See Valence

PONT-D'OUILLY

See Falaise

PONTE SAN LUDOVICO

See Menton

PONTET (LE)

See Avignon

PONT-L'EVÊQUE

14130 Pont-l'Evêque — (Calvados)
Paris 190 - Deauville 11 - Lisieux 17 - Rouen 79

In nearby **Saint-André-d'Hébertot**

(9 km E on N 175)
14130 Pont-l'Evêque — (Calvados)

Auberge du Prieuré
31.64.03.03

M. Millet. Closed Wed. Open until 10.30 pm. Garden dining. Parking. Hotel: 1 ste 540 F, 7 rms 310-540 F, half-board 440-550 F. V.

This adorable, romantic hideaway was once a priory. The friendly *patron* seats you at pretty wooden tables set against a backdrop of old stone, massive beams, period furniture, and a monumental fireplace. Thanks to her kitchen garden and the farm next door as well as fish from the not-too-distant sea, his wife Ursula produces tasty, admirably fresh cooking. Try the terrine of young duck with truffles, the tender andouillette with a chive-flavoured cream sauce, or the crunchy feuilleté of apples and sultanas. The cellar is poorly stocked and expensive, so why not try the cider?

A la carte: 250 F. Menu: 130 F.

FONTONX-SUR-L'ADOUR

See Dax

PORNIC

44210 Pornic — (Loire-Atl.)
Paris 428 - Nantes 51 - Saint-Nazaire 29

12/20 Beau Rivage
Plage de la Birochère — 40.82.03.08

M. Corchia. Closed off-season Thu dinner and Mon, and 2-31 Jan. Open until 9.30 pm. Terrace dining. Air cond. V AE DC.

Tuck in, me hearties, to Gérard Corchia's fresh and down-to-earth cooking.

A la carte: 260-300 F. Menus: 98 F (weekdays only), 150 F (wine inc), 135 F, 220 F.

PORNICHET

44380 Pornichet — (Loire-Atl.)
Paris 457 - St-Nazaire 11 - La Baule 6 - Nantes 72

12/20 La Piscine
42, bd de la République — 40.61.02.68

M. Bardouil. Closed 15 Nov-15 Dec. Open until 10 pm. Garden dining. Garage parking. V AE DC.

The statues and columns give a Greek feel to the place, and the prices for the good seafood dishes served around the pool are as high as Olympus.

A la carte: 300 F and up. Menus: 230 F, 350 F, 400 F.

Le Sud-Bretagne
(See restaurant above)

Closed 15 Nov-15 Dec. 5 stes 800-1,400 F. 30 rms 350-800 F. Half-board 400-550 F oblig in seas. TV. Conference facilities. Heated pool. Tennis.

A large, amusing, and eccentric establishment about 200 metres from the beach. Very pleasant rooms and bathrooms. There are two swimming pools, tennis court, and billiards.

PORQUEROLLES (ILE DE)

83400 Porquerolles (Ile de) — (Var)
Boarding: Cavalaire, Hyères, Toulon

Mas du Langoustier
94.58.30.09

Mme Richard. Closed Nov-April. Open until 9 pm. Garden dining. V AE DC.

A complete renovation has given it a new wing with rooms opening onto glorious views, and a large, half-covered terrace under the pine trees. There's also a big, bright dining room around a patio with a gnarled, centuries-old olive tree. The kitchen is presided over by chef Michel Sarran, a cheerful Gascon who trained under Michel Guérard and is happy as a sandboy under Provençal skies. His cooking is laced with sunshine and powerful flavours. Try his aïoli, salad of red mullet with tapenade in a robust vinaigrette, numerous fish dishes which are the result of the island fishermen's daily catches, and a bouillabaisse beloved of the yachting community. Finish with a gratin of raspberries and honey, and linger under a canopy of umbrella pines over one of the island's delectable little wines.

A la carte: 350-600 F. Menus: 300 F, 360 F.

Mas du Langoustier
(See restaurant above)

Closed Nov-April. 4 stes 1,335 F. 60 rms 872-1,121 F. TV 55 rms. Conference facilities. Tennis.

For all you lovers of the Mas, a terrible thing has happened: there is now colour television in nearly all the rooms. Close your eyes, stop up your ears and concentrate instead on the paradisaical tranquillity of the island, pierced only by the sound of the wind murmuring in the pines or the cicadas' creaking song. The 60 rooms and suites have been upgraded. Air-conditioning is provided by the sea breezes, and there's a sandy beach instead of a pool. Two tennis courts.

PORTA (LA)

See CORSICA

PORT-CAMARGUE

See Grau-du-Roi (Le)

PORT-CROS (ILE DE)

83400 Port-Cros (Ile de) — (Var)
Boarding: Cavalaire, Le Lavandou, Hyères

Le Manoir
94.05.90.52

M. Buffet. Closed 8 Oct-4 May. Open until 9.15 pm. Private room: 20. Garden dining. No pets.

As we write, chef Gérard Ré has left the Manoir and not yet been replaced. However, it shouldn't be hard to find someone to take charge of this lovely establishment devoted to a cosmopolitan clientèle from all over Europe. Stay tuned.

Menus: 200 F, 250 F.

Le Manoir

(See restaurant above)
Closed 8 Oct-4 May. 25 rms 600-830 F (per pers, half-board oblig). No pets.

A charming white hotel with large, quiet rooms (cars are banned on the island).

PORT-EN-BESSIN

14520 Port-en-Bessin — (Calvados)
Paris 280 - Bayeux 9 - Caen 37 - Cherbourg 91

In nearby Escures

(2 km S on D 6)
14520 Port-en-Bessin — (Calvados)

La Chenevière

31.21.47.96
Mme Verly. Closed Mon off-season, and 1 Jan-1 March. Open until 9.30 pm. Private room: 10. Garden dining. Parking. Telex 171997. V AE DC.

This venerable manor surrounded by century-old trees is nurturing the talent of young François Laurent. His filet mignon with honey and black pepper, and tartare of salmon with Indian spices deserved another point or two, but a number of dishes need to catch up before we award them. Impeccable welcome.

A la carte: 280-330 F. Menus: 150 F (weekdays lunch only), 190 F, 290 F.

La Chenevière

(See restaurant above)
Closed Mon off-season, and 1 Jan-1 March. 4 stes 750-850 F. 11 rms 550-950 F. Half-board 700-1,100 F. TV. Conference facilities.

A sumptuous house with a slate roof not far from the beaches. It is set in extensive grounds with a tennis court, helipad, and golf course nearby. The rooms are huge with superb bathrooms.

PORTES-EN-RÉ (LES)

See Ré (Ile de)

PORT-GRIMAUD

83310 Port-Grimaud — (Var)
Paris 871 - Ste-Maxime 13 - St-Tropez 10 - Grimaud 6

L'Amphitrite

Grand-Rue
94.56.31.33
M. Allemand. Closed Oct-March. Open until 10 pm. Private room: 60. Terrace dining. Air cond. Valet parking. Telex 470494. V AE DC.

The wonderfully light, summery offerings include a capon stuffed with langoustines, and sea bass in a caviar cream sauce. The croustillant of lamb with tender vegetables, and the young Maures pigeon with pine-nuts and chestnuts are equally successful. Round off with a nougat glacé with Provençal honey, or a bitter-chocolate pavé.

A la carte: 350-500 F. Menus: 235 F, 345 F.

Giraglia

(See restaurant above)
A very attractive set of Provençal-style buildings which blend in well with the village. Rooms are spacious, comfortable and remarkably well-appointed. A fine sandy beach, water sports, and excursions into the hills.

See also: Grimaud

PORTICCIO

See CORSICA

PORTICCIOLO

See CORSICA

PORT-MARLY (LE)

See PARIS Suburbs

PORTO

See CORSICA

PORTO-POLLO

See CORSICA

PORTO-VECCHIO

See CORSICA

PORT-VILLEZ

See Vernon

POUDENAS

47170 Poudenas — (Lot/Garonne)
Paris 659 - Nérac 17 - Barbotan 23

A la Belle Gasconne

53.65.71.58
M. Gracia. Closed off-season Sun dinner and Mon, 2-15 Jan and 1-15 Dec. Open until 9.30 pm. Private room: 40. Garden dining. Valet parking. V AE DC.

Marie-Claude Gracia, who has plucked a lot of ducks and geese in her time, finally plucked up the courage to produce a cookery book. But when she's not writing, this Gascon cook still stirs her stews and daubes in a tiny village of 300 inhabitants, at the foot of a castle where French King Henri IV used to tumble a damsel or two. The book's success has made no impact on the good humour or basic simplicity of this country cook who listens to Verdi while concocting her sauces. Her repertoire includes river pike, grilled pork, her own foie gras, farm pigeon with garlic, and other modest regional marvels, served in a setting filled with antiques, flowers, and pets.

A la carte: 280-350 F. Menus: 165 F, 240 F.

A la Belle Gasconne

(See restaurant above)
Closed off-season Sun and Mon, 2-15 Jan and 1-15 Dec. 1 ste 590-650 F. 7 rms 390-490 F. Half-board 495-685 F. TV. Conference facilities.

Madame Gracia has at last managed to acquire a mill across the street that she's had her eye on for some time. On the banks of the romantic Gélise River, it has seven rooms and one suite. There's a fine terrace on the river, cookery demonstrations, visits to wine growers, tennis in the village, and golf fifteen kilometres away.

POULIGNY-NOTRE-DAME

See Châtre (La)

POULIGUEN (LE)

See Baule (La)

PRA-LOUP

See Barcelonnette

PRÉ-SAINT-GERVAIS (LE)

See PARIS Suburbs

PROPRIANO

See CORSICA

77160 Provins — (Seine/Marne)
Paris 85 - Sens 47 - Fontainebleau 53 - Melun 48

12/20 Quat'Saisons

44, rue du Val — 64.08.99.44
M. Courtois. Closed Sun dinner, Mon and 1-15 Aug.
Open until 9 pm. V.

An agreeably fresh décor matches the unpretentious cooking made from market-fresh ingredients and charmingly presented.

A la carte: 180-200 F.

21190 Puligny-Montrachet — (Côte-d'Or)
Paris 327 - Autun 43 - Beaune 12 - Chagny 5

Le Montrachet

Pl. des Marronniers — 80.21.30.06
M. Gazagnes. Closed Wed and 26 Nov-8 Jan. Open
until 9.30 pm. Terrace dining. V AE DC.

The regionally inspired cooking reaches some high peaks but also sinks to some regrettable lows: the three langoustines which make up the salad of the same name could easily do without their 'decorative' sweet-pepper coulis, the generous coq au vin is a bit dull, and the warm apple tart, which can be marvellous, is frequently too sweet. The service is pleasant and highly professional. As you might expect, the cellar is exceptional, but so are some of the prices. Wine tastings and sales.

A la carte: 400-450 F. Menus: 150 F, 220 F, 350 F.

Le Montrachet

(See restaurant above)
Closed 26 Nov-8 Jan. 1 ste 800 F. 32 rms 350-475 F.
TV 3 rms. Conference facilities.

Airy, comfortable rooms, some of which have pretty country furniture. You can visit local wine growers with the house sommelier. There are ten new rooms in a fine house next to the hotel.

See PARIS Suburbs

See Agen

See Arcachon

56230 Questembert — (Morbihan)
Paris 423 - Redon 33 - Vannes 26 - Rennes 88

Georges Paineau

13, rue St-Michel — 97.26.11.12
M. Paineau. Closed Sun dinner off-season, Mon (ex-
cept dinner in July-Aug) and 2 Jan-15 Feb. Open
until 10 pm. Private room: 35. Garden dining. Valet
parking. Telex 951801. V AE.

You'll love the delectable oyster tart which is slipped onto your plate the moment you sit down, and the mouthwatering casserole of *rattes* potatoes with truffles, sprinkled with a clear veal gravy, not to mention the ravioli of baby scallops with honey and ginger, in which each element comes together in a rare harmony. And then there's the marvellously subtle Muscadet-steamed turbot and its divine shallot galette, and bass with a watercress purée, plus, for dessert, the fondant of dark chocolate, and a 'rich' vanilla sorbet with an artemisia coulis, which is a real masterpiece.

Georges Paineau labours to make the most of Breton ingredients, which gives his essentially classic style a youthfulness and a special dimension, although it seems to us that this highly talented chef has not yet used his imagination to the full. He is certainly never lacking in praise for his second-in-command, his son-in-law Claude Corlouer, to whom he owes much of his success. As he does to his wife Michèle, who creates a wonderfully happy atmosphere and knows how to direct you to the dishes and wines which will make your meal complete.

A la carte: 350-550 F. Menus: 150 F (weekdays dinner only), 268 F, 305 F, 450 F.

Le Bretagne

(See restaurant above)
Closed Sun and Mon (except July-Aug and holidays),
and 2 Jan-15 Feb. 6 rms 330-580 F. Half-board 680-
780 F. TV. Conference facilities.

A mother-and-daughter team watch over the friendly and warm atmosphere of this little hotel with its hotchpotch décor. The cosy rooms are perched over an attractive garden. Breakfasts are sublime and there are pretty knick-knacks to be had in the boutique. Relais et Châteaux.

56170 Quiberon — (Morbihan)
Paris 498 - Lorient 52 - Vannes 46 - Auray 28

12/20 Compagnie du Poisson

5, bd d'Hœdic — 97.30.55.62
M. Carn. Closed Wed and 2 Jan-Easter. Open until
10 pm. Terrace dining. Parking. V.

Jean-Jacques Carn, himself a fishmonger, easily nets the best of the day's catch for his marinated fish flavoured with olive oil and a touch of fennel, or a perfect medallion of lobster in mousseline sauce. The desserts are slightly cloying. Nice wine list, but low on half-bottles. Best terrace in Quiberon.

A la carte: 280 F. Menus: 186 F, 280 F.

Le Gulf Stream

17, bd Chamard — 97.50.16.96
Closed 15 Nov-31 Jan. 27 rms 200-400 F TV. Park-
ing. V AE.

This charming small hotel was created in an old house. Most rooms have a fine view over the extensive beach. All are comfortable and full of character, with antique furniture and ornaments.

Hôtel Ker-Noyal

Route St-Clément — 97.50.08.41
Closed end Oct-beg March. 102 rms 420-460 F.
Restaurant. Half-board 420-445 F oblig in seas. TV.
No pets. Conference facilities. Valet parking. V AE.

A comfortable, roomy, holiday hotel not far from the sea. Classic breakfasts, friendly service.

Le Thalassa

Pointe de Goulvars
97.50.20.00
M. Schuhler. Closed Jan. Open until 9.30 pm. Private
room: 20. No pets. Parking. Telex 730712. V AE DC.

Angelo Orilieri uses excellent ingredients with precision, as in his artichoke and prawn salad with truffle-flavoured oil, or brill steamed with basil, but we were less enthusiastic about the turbot baked with meat juice—far too watery. The wine list is informative and includes some very affordable bottles. The service is courteous and well managed, but mistakes sometimes occur. There's a well-thought-out 520-calorie menu for 195 F.

A la carte: 350-400 F. Menus: 200 F, 250 F.

Sofitel Thalassa
(See restaurant above)

Closed Jan. 16 stes 1,600-2,050 F. 117 rms 655-1,290 F. Half-board 770-1,120 F. TV. Conference facilities. Heated pool. Tennis.

The hotel is right at the end of the Quiberon headland, linked to the sea-water cure centre by an interior corridor. A private pedestrian street ensures a quiet stay. Facilities are luxurious, the rooms have all been renovated (some have terraces or private patios).

29000 Quimper — (Finistère)
Paris 552 - Rennes 207 - Brest 79 - Lorient 68

Les Acacias
88, bd Créach-Gwen — 98.52.15.20

M. Hatté. Closed Sun dinner. Open until 9 pm. Private room: 15. Parking. V AE.

Philippe Hatté is having a few problems with his cooking times and sauces, but his ingredients are top-notch and generously prepared: fillets of red mullet with chanterelles (slightly overcooked), sweetbreads (definitely overcooked) with insipid truffle juice, but a good warm apple tart.

A la carte: 250-270 F. Menus: 98 F (weekdays only), 120 F,155 F, 210 F.

12/20 L'Ambroisie
49, rue E.-Fréron — 98.95.00.02

M. Guyon. Closed Mon off-season, and 7-18 Jan. Open until 9.30 pm. V AE DC.

This is simple, unpretentious food, well cooked and served in an agreeable setting: steamed cod with new potatoes, noisette of lamb with thyme, and banana gratin with a Creole sauce.

A la carte: 270 F. Menus: 115 F, 170 F.

Le Capucin Gourmand
29, rue des Reguaires — 98.95.43.12

M. Conchon. Closed Sun and holidays. Annual closings not available. Open until 9.30 pm. V DC.

Christian Conchon is rapidly becoming Quimper's best chef. A bit more imagination please, but the home-smoked salmon served with blinis is outstanding, the feuilleté de langoustines generous and well prepared, the turbot with verjuice and fried leeks of very high quality.

A la carte: 300 F. Menus: 140 F (except Sat), 180 F.

Le Gradlon
30, rue de Brest — 98.95.04.39

Closed 20 Dec-16 Jan. 1 ste 430 F. 25 rms 225-324 F. TV 22 rms. No pets. V AE DC.

A centrally located hotel built around a courtyard-cum-garden where you can have breakfast. The rooms are quiet and comfortable and are currently being modernised.

Le Griffon
131, route de Bénodet — 98.90.33.33

Open every day. 49 rms 260-340 F. Restaurant. TV. Heated pool. Parking. Telex 940063. V AE DC.

This is a modern building off the beaten track with biggish, bright, functional rooms and double glazing. Sauna.

Novotel
Route de Bénodet — 98.90.46.26

Open every day. 92 rms 370-430 F. Restaurant. TV. Air cond. Heated pool. Parking. V AE DC.

A good hotel, part of the chain, on the outskirts of Quimper. The rooms are spacious and breakfasts average.

29130Quimperlé — (Finistère)
Paris 513 - Concarneau 32 - Lorient 20 - Quimper 48

Le Bistro de la Tour
2, rue Dom-Morice — 98.39.29.58

M. Cariou. Closed Sat lunch, Sun dinner and Mon. Annual closings not available. Open until 9.30 pm. Private room: 12. No pets. V AE.

Takeaway dishes, fine wines and bric-a-brac are all for sale at Bernard and Bernadette Cariou's restaurant. Choose a table on the ground floor among the knick-knacks or on the much neater upper floor to order the *patron's* latest inventions: plump prawns, magret de canard, bass with bone marrow and Chinon wine. A well-deserved toque.

A la carte: 300 F. Menus: 54 F (weekdays lunch only),89 F, 139 F, 210 F.

L'Hermitage
Manoir de Kerroch
Rte du Pouldu — 98.96.04.66

Open every day. 3 stes 350-750 F. 28 rms 250-350 F. Restaurant. Half-board 235-285 F. TV. Conference facilities. Heated pool. Parking. V AE.

The hotel and its annexes are set in parkland overlooking the river. The largish rooms have rustic furniture and functional bathrooms. Choice of breakfasts.

83350 Ramatuelle — (Var)
Paris 892 - Hyères 54 - St-Tropez 10 - Draguignan 53

12/20 Auberge des Vieux Moulins
Quartier des Moulins
Rte des Plages — 94.97.17.22

M. Ugo. Dinner only. Closed Oct-March. Open until midnight. Private room: 25. Garden dining. Hotel: 5 rms 440-540 F (for 2 pers). Parking. V AE.

This charming *mas* covered with virginia creeper is on the way to the beach. Locals and holidaymakers alike gather in the lush garden to enjoy fresh fish, roast lamb, and good pastries.

Menu: 250 F.

The Beaches
Open generally from Easter to mid-November.

Les Catamarans (94.97.10.80): For a daurade royale or a bouillabaisse in pleasant surroundings (200-250 F).

Club 55 (94.79.80.14): Bring your tan for a warm welcome from Jean and Patrice de Colmont and some fresh-caught fish (200-300 F).

Liberty Plage (94.79.84.17): Admirably grilled fish near the nudist colony (250-300 F).

Mooréa (94.97.18.17): A youthful atmosphere and good cooking, especially the seafood dishes (200-250 F).

Le Nioulargo (94.79.84.21): Lovely beach, adequate cooking. Its sister restaurant, the Key Largo, offers good Asian dishes.

La Plage des Jumeaux (94.79.84.21): Palm trees, a terrace, and simple, pleasing food (200-250 F).

Tahiti (94.97.18.02): Once a showbiz hot-spot, the Tahiti still has good meat and local fish dishes (250-300 F).

Tropicana (94.79.83.96): Pampelonne's best address (along with the Sénéquier below), run by a family from Marseille. Try the stuffed baby vegetables, daubes, and other Provençal specialities (250-300 F).

La Voile Rouge (94.79.84.34): Very fashionable. La Mamma Tomaselli prepares Italian-Provençal food (250-300 F).

Les Bergerettes
Rte des Plages — 94.97.40.22
Closed Oct-Easter. 29 rms 650-940 F. Restaurant. TV. Pool. Parking. Telex 460037. V AE.

This charming hotel, which looks rather like a Provençal *bastide*, is set in a pine wood, facing the beach. The rooms are very appealing, and some have terraces.

Les Bouis
Rte des Plages — 94.79.87.61
Closed 15 Nov-15 March. 4 stes 1,000-1,300 F. 11 rms 700-900 F. TV. Air cond 6 rms. Pool. Parking. V.

A group of luxurious buildings dotted around the swimming pool. The attractive rooms have cane furniture, tiled floors and private terraces with a sea view. Poolside snacks available.

11/20 Chez Camille
Quartier de Bonne-Terrasse — 94.79.80.38
M. Bérenguier. Closed Tue off-season, and 1 Oct-31 March. Open until 9.30 pm. Parking. V.

A standard bouillabaisse and perfectly good grilled fish are sufficient reason to stop for a meal and a view of the Bonne-Terrasse bay. It's not great gastronomy, but the holiday hordes keep coming, so do reserve.

Menus: from 150 F to 390 F.

La Figuière
Le Pinet, rte de Tahiti — 94.97.18.21
Closed 7 Oct-23 March. 45 rms 420-800 F. Restaurant. TV 31 rms. Air cond. Pool. Tennis. Parking. V.

An old farmhouse set among vineyards, 300 metres from the sea. Peace, comfort, and an elegant clientele of regulars.

La Garbine
Rte de Tahiti — 94.97.11.84
Closed 31 Oct-27 Dec and 3 Jan-1 April. 20 rms 450-950 F. TV. No pets. Pool. Tennis. Parking. V AE.

A brand new, Provençal-style hotel on a stream, surrounded by vines and not far from Tahiti beach. The décor is sparsely modern, bright and attractive; the rooms are well equipped (minibars), all with private terraces giving onto the pool.

Karikal
Quartier des Marres
Rte des plages — 94.97.32.26
Closed 15 Jan-15 March. 2 stes 2,400 F. 14 rms 850-1,500 F. TV. Pool. Tennis. Garage parking. V AE.

A colonial-style hillside hotel set among pines and overlooking the Bay of St-Tropez. The rooms are spacious (some at garden level with terraces), and there are also two luxurious bungalows.

Chez Madeleine
Rte de Tahiti — 94.97.15.74
Mme Serra. Closed Tue off-season, and 31 Oct-25 March. Open until 11 pm. Garden dining. Parking. V AE DC.

Madeleine Serra's children somehow manage to grab the best of the catch from their fishermen friends, even at the height of summer.

A la carte: 250-400 F. Menu: 170 F (weekdays lunch only).

Dei Marres
Rte des Plages — 94.97.26.68
Closed 15 Oct-15 March. 15 rms 450-800 F. TV. Pool. Tennis. Parking. V AE DC.

This Provençal château in its flower-filled grounds at the foot of the Ramatuelle hills is a must for tennis fans (four courts for hire).

Saint-Vincent
Rte de Tahiti — 94.97.36.90
Closed end Oct-Easter. 4 stes 1,450 F. 16 rms 630-950 F. Restaurant. TV. Pool. Parking. V.

Bright, comfortable rooms among the vines, giving onto a garden, with individual terraces and nice bathrooms.

12/20 Sénéquier
Plage de Pampelonne
Rte de l'Epi — 94.79.82.04
M. Sénéquier. Closed Sun dinner and 1 Oct-1 April. Open until 10.30 pm. Terrace dining. Pool. Parking.

These former wine growers have left the beach for an attractive garden where they've installed a swimming pool. Try the delicious courgette fritters and the local fish, grilled to perfection. The warm welcome, pleasing prices, and family feel of this *auberge* make it popular with the locals.

A la carte: 180-250 F. Menus: 100 F, 200 F.

La Terrace du Baou
Av. G.-Clemenceau — 94.79.20.48
M. Bourgoin. Closed 15 Nov-1 March. Open until 11 pm. Terrace dining. Garage parking. V AE DC.

With its daytime view of the sea and countryside behind St-Tropez or the twinkling lights of Ramatuelle by night, the Baou would be a magical spot if its successive proprietors would only do something about the dining room and reception area's horrid décor. In the meantime, choose a terrace table to sample the well-prepared, Provençal-style cooking: shellfish consommé and pistou ravioli, little stuffed vegetables with basil juice, pink sea bream with tapenade, or fillet of beef in Barbeyrolles wine sauce. Desserts include a nougat glacé made with Provençal honey, and melon soup laced with Beaumes-de-Venise. This fine-tasting cuisine deserves a more gracious environment and more experienced staff.

A la carte: 400-500 F. Menus: 295 F, 400 F.

Le Baou
(See restaurant above)
Closed 15 Nov-1 March. 11 stes 1,400-1,700 F. 41 rms 620-1,700 F. Half-board 1,010-2,330 F. TV. Conference facilities. Heated pool.

An outstanding location overlooking the sea. Some rooms are small; new décor would be welcome. Terraced garden.

RAMBOUILLET

78120 Rambouillet — (Yvelines)
Paris 52 - Orléans 90 - Versailles 31 - Etampes 44

12/20 Le Cheval Rouge
78, rue du Gal-de-Gaulle
34.85.80.61
M. Garric. Open every day. Open until 9.30 pm. Garden dining. Air cond. V AE DC.

Boulogne, La Rochelle, and the Rungis food market near Paris all furnish this establishment with its excellent fish, which is carefully cooked in a traditional manner.

A la carte: 300 F. Menus: 110 F (weekdays only), 180 F.

Resthôtel Primevère
ZA du Bel-Air,
Rue J.-Jacquard — 34.85.51.02
Open every day. 44 rms 215-235 F. Restaurant. Half-board 330-351 F. TV 31 rms. Conference facilities. V.

A new building off the N 10 and not far from the famous forest. The rooms are bright and pleasing.

RAPHÈLE-LÈS-ARLES

See Arles

RÉ (ILE DE)

Ré (Ile de) — (Charente-M.)
access by La Palice

In nearby **Bois-Plage-en-Ré**

17580 Ré (Ile de) — (Charente-M.)

Les Gollandières
46.09.23.99

Closed mid-Nov to mid-March. 32 rms 250-400 F. Restaurant. Conference facilities. Heated pool. Parking. V AE DC motel devant la plage. Discothèque.
Simple and agreeably rustic rooms in a hotel-motel on the beach. Discothèque.

In nearby **La Couarde-sur-Mer**

17670 Ré (Ile de) — (Charente-M.)

La Salicorne
16, rue de l'Olivette
46.29.82.37

M. Dumond. Closed Nov-Easter (except holidays). Open until 11 pm. Terrace dining. Hotel: 5 rms 140-155 F. V.
Luc Dumond prepares simple, authentic, and inexpensive food. Try his classic prawns with fresh pasta, or on a more personal note, salmon with a green tea sauce, duck breast with vanilla and honey, and young rabbit stuffed with black olives. Interesting list of Loire wines.
A la carte: 240 F. Menus: 85 F (lunch only), 120 F.

In nearby **La Flotte-en-Ré**

17630 Ré (Ile de) — (Charente-M.)

L'Ecailler
3, quai de Sénac
46.09.56.40

Mme Lagord and M. Rabeux. Closed 31 Oct-31 March (except w-e and school holidays). Open until 11 pm. Garden dining. V DC.
Marie-Josée Lagord, who has a degree in oyster-farming, is in the kitchen preparing seafood and shellfish. Her repertoire also includes a tartare of very fresh bass and salmon, clamboy (clams, mussels, potatoes and charcuterie), and spiced, poached fruit to finish with. Attentive service.
A la carte: 220 F. Menu: 95 F (lunch only).

Le Lavardin
5, rue H.-Lainé — 46.09.68.32

M. Barbet. Closed Tue off-season, 15 Jan-14 Feb and 12 Nov-12 Dec. Open until 9.30 pm (10.30 pm in summer). Private room: 40. Air cond. V.
Georges Barbet's stint as maître d'hôtel at the Maison du Danemark accounts for some Danish specialities like gravlax—marinated salmon with dill—which go well with local dishes. Prices are not bad for the island and the restaurant is charmingly situated near the delightful harbour.
A la carte: 230 F. Menus: 370 F (for 2 pers), 150 F, 205 F.

Le Richelieu
44, av. de la Plage
46.09.60.70

M. Gendre. Closed 5 Jan-15 Feb. Open until 9.30 pm. Private room: 150. Garden dining. Air cond. Parking. Telex 791492. V.
The prices keep the riff-raff away from this terrace overlooking the harbour. Those who can afford to pay 450 to 600 F à la carte can be sure of peace and tranquillity in which to feast on brill with green parsley butter, (a better choice than the cassolette de langoustines, overwhelmed by the taste of ginger), an impeccable young pigeon, cooked rare, and a souffléed crêpe with orange coulis. There's a superb cellar with ten-year-old wines at affordable prices, but it's a shame there aren't more whites to go with the fish. The service is first-rate.
A la carte: 450-600 F. Menus: 295 F (wine inc), 210 F, 380 F.

Le Richelieu
(See restaurant above)

Closed 5 Jan-15 Feb. 32 rms 450-1,300 F (per pers, half-board oblig). TV. Air cond 1 rm. Conference facilities. Heated pool. Tennis.
All the rooms have been renovated, and redecorated with period furniture. The bathrooms have been enlarged and there's now a magnificent terrace overlooking the sea. Good breakfasts.

In nearby **Portes-en-Ré**

17880 Ré (Ile de) — (Charente-M.)

Auberge de la Rivière
D 101 - La Rivière
27, av. des Salines — 46.29.54.55

M. Massé. Closed Tue (except school holidays) and 15 Nov-10 Dec. Open until 9.30 pm. Private room: 100. Garden dining. Parking. V AE.
The Massés have used the winter months to revamp their inn. All the more reason to come and try the langoustines au naturel, very slightly over-cooked, or the turbot with Ile de Ré oysters which is light and well balanced with its fine oyster sauce and beetroot purée. The feuillantine of warm apples served with cinnamon ice cream rounds off the meal nicely. Warm welcome. A toque this year.
A la carte: 270-300 F. Menus: 80 F (weekdays only), 155 F, 220 F, 320 F.

In nearby **Saint-Clément-des-Baleines**

17590 Ré (Ile de) — (Charente-M.)

Le Chat Botté
2, rue de la Mairie
Hotel: pl. de l'Eglise — 46.29.42.09

M. Massé. Closed Wed and 5 Jan-15 March. Open until 9 pm. Private room: 25. Terrace dining. Hotel: 23 rms 120-245 F. V.
Enjoy Daniel Massé's speciality: bass en croûte served with beurre blanc (for two). New dishes on the short menu show that this pleasing holiday address is trying hard.
A la carte: 250-300 F. Menus: 75 F (weekdays only), 145 F, 290 F.

In nearby **Saint-Martin-de-Ré**

17740 Ré (Ile de) — (Charente-M.)

La Baleine Bleue
Quai Launay-Razilly
46.09.03.30

M. Bodart. Closed Mon off-season and 5 Jan-10 Feb. Open until 9.30 pm (10.30 pm in summer). Terrace dining. No-smoking section. No pets. V.
The chef uses a light Japanese style to bring out the subtle flavours of dishes like his original carpaccio de langoustines with a vanilla sauce, or his baked red mullet off the bone. The wine list is short but quite adequate.
A la carte: 300 F. Menus: 120 F, 160 F, 220 F.

Le Galion

Allée de la Guyane — 46.09.03.19
Open every day. 31 rms 400-465 F. TV. Garage parking. Telex 793583. V AE DC.
On a quiet square near the little harbour, this hotel has recently been modernised. The rooms are small, but airy and well equipped. Sea views.

REIMS

51100 Reims — (Marne)
Paris 145 - Lille 212 - Metz 187 - Verdun 118

L'Assiette Champenoise

40, av. P.-Vaillant-Couturier
51430 Tinqueux — 26.04.15.56
M. Lallement. Open every day. Open until 10 pm. Garden dining. Parking. Telex 830267. V AE DC.
We were worried about Jean-Pierre Lallement; his technique was perfect but his creativity had disappeared. Now Lallement is getting back on form, and we recently tasted a remarkable John Dory with hazelnut sauce, and a pleasing potato galette with prawns. Desserts, once his weak point, are improving (the chocolate pastries are the best choice), and the wine list, dominated by Champagne, is superb but expensive. The enormous dining room, which offers a pleasant view in summer, is managed by a smiling Colette Lallement.
A la carte: 450 F. Menus: 250 F, 410 F.

Château de la Muire

(See restaurant above)
Open every day. 2 stes 750-950 F. 62 rms 460-750 F. Half-board 580-640 F. TV. Conference facilities. Pool.
Comfortable, well-appointed rooms in large grounds along an avenue on the outskirts of Reims.

Boyer

(Les Crayères)
64, bd H.-Vasnier — 26.82.80.80
M. Boyer. Closed Tue lunch, Mon and 22 Dec-14 Jan. Open until 9.30 pm. Private room: 24. Terrace dining. Air cond. Valet parking. Telex 830959. V AE DC.
'Luxe, calme et volupté' wrote Baudelaire, three words which perfectly describe a stay chez Gérard and Elyane Boyer. For one thing, here you are practically in the middle of town in an English garden of some seven hectares, in a hotel whose rooms and suites are on a rare level of luxury and refinement. Push a button and you have the most courteous and efficient personnel in the world at your beck and call. To say nothing of the fine pictures, period furniture, and general elegance of a grand house which is never stuffy. You are treated so kindly and with such ease that you can actually enjoy château living without all the pomp and ceremony it usually entails. And then there are the delights of a wonderful table and the treasures of a stupendous cellar—all for the cost, or almost, of an impersonal four-star chain hotel.
This very French *art de vivre* is fast disappearing, as Les Crayères' customers are well aware. They trek halfway across Europe for a taste of this particular *dolce vita* and Gérard Boyer's admirable cuisine, which is great in every sense of the word. He's never flashy, but nor is he conventional; his technique is at the service of the ingredients and not vice versa. Personal touches do come through, but without needless complications. Try his feuilleté of shellfish with saffron, his plump Glénans langoustine ravioli and coral sauce, the sensational grilled bass with its crispy skin on a delectable mixture of artichokes and celery in a velvety sauce made with Graves wine, the croustillant of sweetbreads with hazelnuts, or baby veal with basmati rice and a buckwheat galette. The dessert menu is dedicated to Boyer's two daughters, whose job it is to taste and approve all his creations. After trying the assiette tout chocolat, florentin biscuits with a walnut mousse and almond milk, the crème brûlée, or the pineapple feuillantine, you will understand their enthusiasm.
The Champagnes, excellent Burgundies and Bordeaux, and well-chosen, less-known wines are the province of the irreplaceable Werner, who watches jealously over his stock. Once he has poured you a glass, you can be sure it is just right for drinking.
A la carte: 480-800 F.

Boyer

(See restaurant above)
Closed 22 Dec-14 Jan. 3 stes 1,590 F. 16 rms 980-1,590 F. TV. Air cond. Conference facilities. Tennis.
Gérard and Elyane Boyer have turned a dilapidated pavilion in the grounds of their hotel into an island of charm and comfort with one suite and two duplexes. As for the château itself, we've said it all above. The rooms are elegantly decorated in period style (classic French, English, romantic, or exotic), and you'll find incomparable comfort and service for about what you would pay in a luxury chain hotel. On the edge of the grounds is a tennis court and on the other side of the wall, an experimental vine. There's an English bar and you may request a hairdresser or masseur in your room. Relais et Châteaux.

Bristol

76, pl. Drouet-d'Erlon — 26.40.52.25
Open every day. 40 rms 190-265 F. TV. Telex 842155. V AE DC.
Fairly elegant, centrally located hotel, entirely renovated with well-kept, comfortable rooms.

Le Chardonnay

184, av. d'Epernay — 26.06.08.60
M. Lange. Closed Sat lunch, Sun, 22 Dec-13 Jan and 3-18 Aug. Open until 9.30 pm. Parking. V AE DC.
Dominique Giraudeau is in the kitchen manipulating his pans with unfailing technical skill. It would be nice to see more imagination and less caviar, foie gras, and Champagne on the menu, but his regulars seem quite happy with the terrine of salmon with an oyster and caviar jelly, poached red mullet in Champagne, and the ravioli with confit, cèpes, and warm foie gras. Lovely welcome.
A la carte: 350-380 F. Menus: 160 F, 230 F, 380 F.

Le Florence

43, bd Foch — 26.47.12.70
M. Maillot. Closed Sun (except holidays), Feb school holidays and 1-19 Aug. Open until 9.30 pm. Private room: 30. Garden dining. V AE DC.
Large paintings and armfuls of flowers have added a splash of colour to the dining room where customers can discover the cooking of new chef Jos Bergman, fresh from La Truffe Noire in Brussels (where he earned 17 points). For the time being, he has retained some of his predecessor's most successful dishes but he is already demonstrating his own inventiveness; witness the smoked salmon roll with prawns served with creamed caviar, or the sublime fillet of turbot stuffed with black truffles, sweetbreads wrapped in a cabbage leaf and served with chanterelles, and an irresistible chocolate mousse surrounded by dark-chocolate 'Champagne corks'. Our last meal, a month after Bergman's arrival, deserved another point but we have withheld it—solely to give him time to spread

his wings. All the best Champagnes, of course, and efficient, smiling service.

A la carte: 400-450 F. Menus: 200 F (weekdays only), 280 F, 400 F.

12/20 La Forêt Noire
2, bd Jules-César — 26.47.63.95
M. Flamant. Closed Sun dinner and Mon. Open until 10 pm. Terrace dining. No-smoking section. V.

Specialities from Alsace served in a neat décor with shiny wood panelling.

A la carte: 140-160 F. Menus: 51 F (weekdays lunch only), 69 F, 98 F.

Grand Hôtel des Templiers
22, rue des Templiers — 26.88.55.08
Open every day. 2 stes 1,600 F. 17 rms 950-1,400 F. TV. Air cond 6 rms. Conference facilities. Heated pool. Valet parking. Telex 830088. V AE DC.

The nineteenth-century building has superb lounges, a dark wood staircase, and huge rooms, each decorated in a different style and remarkably well-equipped—hairdryer, bathrobe, slippers, magnifying make-up mirror. Marble bathrooms. The hotel also has a swimming pool, Turkish bath, sauna, and Jacuzzi. The reception and service are pleasant and efficient. Meals on trays upon request.

Hôtel Liberté
55, rue Boulard — 26.40.52.61
Open every day. 81 rms 380-410 F. Restaurant. TV. Garage parking. Telex 841103. V AE DC.

A huge, modern construction near the cathedral and the motorwa.

La Paix
9, rue Buirette — 26.40.04.08
Open every day. 105 rms 330-435 F. Restaurant. TV. Conference facilities. Pool. V AE DC.

In a perfect setting near the imposing Sube fountain, this hotel is also near the railway station and cathedral.

12/20 Le Paysan
16, rue de Fismes — 26.40.25.51
M. Arnould. Open every day. Open until 10.30 pm. Parking. V AE.

A convivial restaurant in a quiet district, where Jean-Michel Champenois prepares hearty country cooking. A good choice of lesser Bordeaux and lots of affordable Champagnes.

A la carte: 200 F. Menus: from 68 F to 150 F, 190 F.

12/20 Au Petit Comptoir
17, rue de Mars — 26.40.58.58
Mme Boyer. Closed Sat lunch, Sun, 5-19 Aug and 21 Dec-15 Jan. Open until 10.30 pm. Terrace dining. Air cond. V.

This is Gérard Boyer's bistro, complete with green banquettes and a jostling crowd enjoying tête de veau sauce gribiche, tripes à l'ancienne, paupiettes of veal with carrots, and an excellent chocolate cake. Boyer trained the young chef, Fabrice Maillot.

A la carte: 150-200 F.

12/20 Les Relais Bleus
12, rue G.-Voisin — 26.82.59.79
Mme Piedagnel. Closed Sun dinner. Open until 10 pm. Garden dining. Hotel: 40 rms 260-350 F. V.

The cooking is generous and well-prepared: salade gourmande with foie gras, lobster, and truffles,

freshwater perch with an artichoke coulis, ris de veau aux cèpes. It's expensive though, and so are the wines.

A la carte: 250-280 F. Menus: 75 F and 95 F (weekdays only), 99 F (w-e and holidays only), 159 F, 199 F.

12/20 Le Vigneron
Pl. P.-Jamot — 26.47.00.71
M. Liégent. Closed Sat lunch, Sun and 23 Dec-2 Jan. Open until 10 pm. Terrace dining. V.

The exceptional cellar of this restaurant with its fine collection of Belle Epoque posters has over 800 different Champagnes, including some 1892 vintages. The cooking too digs deep into regional traditions: feuilleté of local ham, salmon with a shrimp and Champagne bisque, warm pear tart.

A la carte: 230 F.

Vonelly Gambetta
9, rue Gambetta — 26.47.22.00
M. Géraudel. Closed Sun dinner, Mon and 3 weeks in Aug. Open until 9.45 pm. No pets. Hotel: 14 rms 200-250 F. V AE.

Make yourself comfortable to taste Pascal Géraudel's excellent home-smoked salmon, succulent beef in a foie gras sauce, delicious Brie with hazelnuts, and a most enjoyable chocolate charlotte. The cellar is well stocked and expensive.

A la carte: 350 F. Menus: 100 F (weekdays only), 150 F, 220 F, 250 F.

And also...
Our selection of places for inexpensive, quick, or late-night meals.

Le Colibri (26.47.50.67 - 12, rue Chanzy. Open until 10.30 pm): Near the cathedral, one of three establishments (the others are Le Notre-Dame and Le Flamm'Steack) offering varied, cheap menus (45-60 F and up).

La Grappa (26.08.66.78 - 49, rue du Col.-Fabien. Open until 11 pm): Good choice of pizzas, trattoria style (140 F).

L'Impromptu (26.08.44.73 - 18, av. de Paris. Open until 10.30 pm): Don't miss the foie gras and raw salmon served in this pleasant bistro. Shady terrace (160 F).

New China (26.47.45.15 - 39, rue de Châtivesle. Open until 10.30 pm): Very good Chinese and Thai specialities (150 F).

Le Palanquin (26.88.39.32 - 61, rue Chanzy. Open until 10.30 pm): A warm welcome awaits you here, and the Chinese and Vietnamese food is good value (140 F).

Le Petit Bacchus (26.47.10.05 - 11, rue de l'Université. Open until 9.30 pm): Inexpensive, traditional cooking (120-150 F).

Quorum (26.88.26.02 - 14, rue de Thillois. Open until 10 pm): Pastel décor, quick service, and good fresh pasta (160 F).

La Taverne de Maître Kanter (26.47.00.45 - 25, pl. d'Erlon. Open until 11.45 pm): A brasserie offering good shellfish right in the centre of town (180 F).

In nearby Champigny
(6 km NW on N 31 and D 275)
51370 Reims — (Marne)

La Garenne
Rte de Soissons — 26.08.26.62
M. Laplaige. Closed Sun dinner, Mon, 28 Jan-4 Feb and 29 July-19 Aug. Open until 10 pm. Private room: 15. Parking. V AE.

Laurent Laplaige, who used to work with Boyer, is a rigorous professional and some of his dishes are worthy of the very best tables. His lobster salad with tiny crunchy vegetables, accompanied by caramelised leeks, is absolutely fresh, and his fricassée of kidneys with Bouzy wine is a delight. An ultra-classic dessert like the very well prepared nougat glacé shows how far his desserts have come. All this earns an extra point. The welcome and service are also excellent and the cellar is filled with Champagne, and lots of half-bottles, well chosen and moderately priced.

A la carte: 300-350 F. Menus: 290 F (w-e and holidays only), 130 F, 210 F.

In nearby Montchenot

(11 km S on N 51)
51500 Reims — (Marne)

Auberge du Grand Cerf

N 51 — 26.97.60.07
M. Guichaoua. Closed Sun dinner, Wed, Feb school holidays and 13-29 Aug. Open until 9.30 pm. Private room: 40. Garden dining. Parking. V AE.

Before he pulled in his sails to coast into this nineteenth-century inn, Breton Alain Guichaoua did a lot of travelling, which could account for the numerous influences on his cooking. The sea predominates: salade trilogie (lobster, foie gras, salmon), but also try his roast farm chicken with truffle juice. There are some remarkable Champagnes and a pretty garden for summer eating.

A la carte: 400 F. Menus: 170 F (weekdays only), 265 F, 335 F.

RÉMIGEASSE (LA)

See Oléron (Ile d')

RENNES

35000 Rennes — (Ille-et-Vilaine)
Paris 348 - Brest 245 - Nantes 106 - Le Mans 153

Altea

See restaurant Le Goëlo

Anne de Bretagne

12, rue Tronjolly — 99.31.49.49
Open every day. 42 rms 298-350 F. TV. Conference facilities. Garage parking. Telex 741255. V.

In the centre of town, but quiet. The modern rooms are bright and well appointed.

Le Corsaire

52, rue d'Antrain — 99.36.33.69
M. Luce. Closed Sun dinner and 15 days in Aug. Open until 9.45 pm. Private room: 40. V AE DC.

Reliability and freshness are the watchwords in this elegant dining room lacquered in midnight blue. The Luces are real professionals who are completely in control of service and cooking. Antoine Luce, whose experience includes Lasserre and Le Grand Véfour, is capable of cooking that is as delicious as it is personal, as in the buckwheat crêpe with scallops, sole with beetroot and spinach, or oxtail braised with foie gras. A fine cellar and good homemade bread.

A la carte: 280-300 F. Menus: 90 F (weekdays only), 160 F.

Du Guesclin

5, pl. de la Gare — 99.31.47.47
Open every day. 68 rms 290-320 F. TV. Conference facilities. Telex 740748. V AE DC.

An old establishment in the heart of town with agreeable, modern rooms.

L'Escu de Runfao

5, rue du Chapitre — 99.79.13.10
M. Duhoux. Closed Sat lunch, Sun dinner, Feb school holidays and 4-19 Aug. Open until 10 pm. No pets. V AE DC.

The Duhouxs have completely renewed the décor and maintained a policy of nothing but top quality ingredients in the kitchen. In addition, Alain Duhoux has amply demonstrated his talent with perfectly cooked fish accompanied by light, flavourful sauces. But why is the service so slow to take off? Even though it picks up, it does discourage even the most patient palate. An interesting and varied wine list. An extra point this year.

A la carte: 350 F. Menus: 95 F (weekdays only), 175 F, 225 F, 370 F.

Le Four à Ban

4, rue St-Mélaine — 99.38.72.85
M. Marx. Closed Sun dinner, Mon, 2-8 Jan and 2 first weeks of Aug. Open until 10 pm. V AE DC.

A cosy atmosphere, static prices, high quality ingredients and a seasonally based menu show that the chef has everything under control. Enjoy original dishes like the crêpe with creamed crab, a timbale of sole with an artichoke purée, pot-au-feu minute accompanied by a salad of tiny vegetables, and pineapple sorbet. A good address.

A la carte: 200-240 F. Menus: 98 F, 138 F, 198 F.

Garden Hotel

3, rue Duhamel — 99.65.45.06
Open every day. 24 rms 110-260 F. TV 13 rms. Conference facilities. Parking. Telex 730772. V AE.

Between the quays and the Maison de la Culture. The rooms are simple and quiet, and there are some family-sized duplexes. Interior garden. Cafeteria.

Altea

(See restaurant above)
Open every day. 140 rms 395-625 F. TV.

Not far from the town centre in the new Colombier district. The rooms are functional and well equipped (video). Excellent welcome from one of the best hotels in this chain.

12/20 Lecoq-Gadby

156, rue d'Antrain — 99.38.05.55
M. Valeau. Closed 1-22 Aug. Open until 9.15 pm. Garden dining. Parking. V AE DC.

This venerable address is a haven for politicians who like to gather under the chandeliers for a good meal made from fine ingredients. Nothing too adventurous is the rule for this crowd, so the chef sticks to dishes like turbot au beurre blanc, rib of beef, and soufflé for dessert. Good value.

A la carte: 220 F. Menus: 88 F and 135 F (weekdays only).

Mercure

Rue P.-L.-Courier — 99.78.32.32
Open every day. 104 rms 320-455 F. TV. Conference facilities. Telex 741850. V AE DC.

This new addition to the chain is set in a garden. The medium-sized rooms have comfortable beds and pleasant bathrooms.

L'Ouvrée

18, pl. des Lices — 99.30.16.38
MM. Langlais and Jehannin. Closed Mon, Easter school holidays, 14 Juil. and 15 Août. Open until 10.30 pm. Private room: 80. Terrace dining. No-smoking section. No pets. Garage parking. V AE DC.

Only market-fresh produce is used in Gérard Jehannin's generously served and reasonably priced hot asparagus flan with baked prawns, sole fillets with grapefruit, sauvageon baked in lime juice. Marvellous sorbets.

A la carte: 280 F. Menus: 120 F, 152 F.

Le Palais

7, place du Parlement — 99.79.45.01

M. Tizon. Closed Sun dinner, Mon, Feb school holidays and last 3 weeks of Aug. Open until 9.45 pm. Private room: 20. V AE DC.

We were absolutely thrilled by our last visit to this cosy restaurant facing Rennes's seventeenth-century law courts. Tizon has a natural gift for using the right ingredients in the correct quantities, as his carefully balanced sauces show. Specialities include sweet-and-sour drumsticks lightly flavoured with coriander, lobster enlivened with a hint of ginger and saffron, an outstanding duck—fed on honey and figs for three weeks to make its flesh tender—in a sauce flavoured with allspice, sage and cocoa, a superb bilberry gratin, and a wild strawberry millefeuille, all worthy of our two-toque rating. Distinguished, efficient service.

A la carte: 300-350 F. Menus: 110 F (weekdays only), 180 F.

Le Piano Blanc

Route de Ste-Foix — 99.31.20.21

M. Piette. Closed Sat lunch, Sun and 11-22 Aug. Open until 10 pm. Garden dining. Parking. V AE.

The chef's bold combinations (creamed tarragon with the red mullet, and a vanilla-flavoured sauce on the turbot) are quite successful, due in part to his use of top-quality produce. We have recently noticed a tendency to more classic dishes: scampi in crab juice, and John Dory fillet with chanterelles and cèpes. A well-deserved toque.

A la carte: 220-250 F. Menus: 92 F (lunch only), 158 F.

Le Piré

18, rue du Mal-Joffre — 99.79.31.41

M. Angelle. Closed Sat lunch, Sun, 15-30 Aug and 23 Dec-5 Jan. Open until 9.45 pm. Private room: 12. Valet parking. V AE DC.

Marc Angelle obviously delights in combining superior quality produce with rustic ingredients. During our last visit, for instance, we sampled a refined and savoury blend of cockles and truffles, wild rice with coriander juice and crab, tasty buckwheat pancakes and creamed caviar, a superb lobster baked with truffles and served with green beans, sweetbreads with herb ravioli, and delicious gingerbread with caramel ice cream. Madame Angelle glides with smiling ease among the tables of the bright, comfortable dining room and garden-courtyard. The wine list is filling out and now features some extraordinary bottles from the Loire and Bordeaux.

A la carte: 350 F. Menus: 110 F (weekdays only), 160 F, 380 F.

Le Président

27, av. Janvier — 99.65.42.22

Closed 20 Dec-6 Jan. 34 rms 276-330 F. TV. Valet parking. V AE DC.

Next to the railway station, this contemporary hotel offers comfortable rooms furnished in various period styles. Attractive bar.

Le Sévigné

47, av. J.-Janvier — 99.67.27.55

Open every day. 46 rms 155-290 F. TV. Conference facilities. Parking. Telex 741058. V AE DC.

Comfortable, well-soundproofed and recently redecorated rooms with perfectly equipped bathrooms. Friendly reception. Light meals are available.

Ti-Koz

3, rue St-Guillaume — 99.79.33.89

Mme Leleu. Closed Sun (except holidays). Open until 11 pm. Private room: 12. V AE DC.

Ranked among the town's loveliest buildings, Nicole Leleu's restaurant has beamed ceilings, beautiful furniture, curios, and a superb fireplace. Her new chef is sometimes heavy-handed with the seasonings, but his cooking times are well judged.

A la carte: 250 F. Menus: 120 F (weekdays lunch only, wine inc), 98 F, 148 F.

And also...

Our selection of places for inexpensive, quick, or late-night meals.

Le Black-Jack (99.36.88.38 - 38, rue de la Visitation. Open until 11 pm): This trendy new establishment in the town centre offers fine meat dishes at reasonable prices (60-100 F).

Les Cantines (99.79.22.52 - 8, galerie des Arcades. Open until 10.30 pm): A friendly, good-natured bistro featuring good home cooking (60-100 F).

La Chope (99.79.34.54 - 3, rue de La Chalotais. Open until midnight): Fine brasserie-style meals served in a picturesque décor. Rapid service (80-120 F).

Le Cortez (99.78.12.83 - 11, pl. du Champ-Jacquet. Open until 11.30 pm): Salads and fine grilled foods, served on the loveliest square in the old town (60-120 F).

Durand (99.78.10.00 - 5, quai Chateaubriand. Open until 10.30 pm): A tastefully decorated restaurant where you'll find salads, savoury flans, and excellent cakes (60-90 F).

Le Grain de Sable (99.30.78.18 - 2, rue des Dames. Open until 10 pm): Andouillette sausages and kebabs are cooked over a wood fire here in the heart of the old town (60-90 F).

Le Kerlouan (99.36.83.02 - 17, rue Saint-Georges. Open until 10.30 pm): One of Rennes's best crêperies, near Parlement de Bretagne square (50-80 F).

Le Serment de Vin (99.30.99.30 - 20, bd de La Tour-d'Auvergne. Open until midnight): Good brasserie-style dishes and an interesting choice of wines (50-100 F).

In nearby La Bouëxière

(16 km NE on N 12 and D 27)
35340 Rennes — (Ille-et-Vilaine)

La Fontaine aux Perles

6, rue J.-M.-Pavy — 99.00.91.50

M. Gesbert. Closed Sun dinner, Mon. Annual closings not available. Open until 9.30 pm. Private room: 30. Parking. V.

The chef is never short of ideas or fine ingredients. Try the potato cake with brawn, sole simmered with Chinese vermicelli, tian of vanilla-flavoured young pigeon with artichokes, and iced liquorice mousse. Many wines at reasonable prices, friendly reception.

A la carte: 200 F. Menus: 65 F (weekdays lunch only), 80 F and 105 F (weekdays only), 130 F, 160 F, 200 F.

> *Red toques signify modern cuisine; black toques signify traditional cuisine.*

In nearby Pacé

(10 km NW on N 12 and D 287)
35740 Rennes — (Ille-et-Vilaine)

La Griotte

[13] 42, rue du Dr-Léon — 99.60.62.48
M. Morand. Closed dinner Sun and Tue, Wed, 15-28 Feb and 24 July-28 Aug. Open until 9.45 pm. Private room: 30. V AE DC.

The cooking in this attractive, elegantly converted farmhouse is light and subtle. Noteworthy dishes include an excellent salad of sweetbreads and shallots, brill with beetroot, and chocolate truffles with cherries. Superb wines, relaxed service. The set menus are excellent value.

A la carte: 220-250 F. Menus: 80 F (weekdays lunch only), 98 F, 140 F, 200 F.

REPLONGES

See Mâcon

RETHONDES

See Compiègne

RIBAUTE-LES-TAVERNES

See Alès

RIBEAUVILLÉ

68150 Ribeauvillé — (Haut-Rhin)
Paris 434 - Colmar 15 - Sélestat 15 - Mulhouse 57

Clos Saint-Vincent

[13] Rte de Bergheim — 89.73.67.65
M. Chapotin. Closed Tue, Wed and 15 Nov-15 March. Open until 8.30 pm. Terrace dining. Parking. Telex 871377. V.

Bernard Chapotin is beginning to assert himself in the kitchen and now offers appealing and personalised dishes like scrambled eggs with anchovies, lotte with horseradish, rib steak in a wine sauce, and a rich chocolate cake. Impeccable service.

A la carte: 350 F. Menus: 150 F (lunch only), 250 F.

Clos Saint-Vincent

(See restaurant above)
Closed 15 Nov-15 March. 3 stes 880-1,115 F. 12 rms 540-845 F. TV. Heated pool.

The quiet, spacious, and recently redecorated rooms overlook a park and surrounding vineyards.

Les Vosges

[14] 2, Grande-Rue — 89.73.61.39
M. Matter. Closed Tue lunch, Mon, 14-31 Jan, 25 Feb-12 March and 24-30 June. Open until 9.30 pm. V AE.

Joseph Matter's individual cuisine gives him a particular niche in the region's gastronomy, even if his search for subtlety sometimes results in overcomplicated dishes. We enjoyed the baby pig's jowl and foie gras with horseradish-flavoured lentils, seafood casserole perfumed with cardamom, crab-stuffed river perch, and a gratin of berries and melon with almonds. Excellent fruit liqueurs and a magnificent wine list.

A la carte: 350-400 F. Menus: 150 F (weekdays only), 270 F, 360 F.

Les Vosges

(See restaurant above)
Closed Mon, 14-31 Jan, 25 Feb-12 March and 24-30 June. 2 stes 455-480 F. 18 rms 245-385 F. Half-board 310-355 F oblig in seas. TV. No pets.

A large, turn-of-the-century hotel with spacious, quiet, well-modernised rooms. Attentive service.

RIEC-SUR-BELON

29340 Riec-sur-Belon — (Finistère)
Paris 518 - Quimper 42 - Concarneau 19 - Quimperlé 13

Auberge de Kerland

[14] 3 km S on D 24
Domaine de Kerstinec — 98.06.42.98
M. Chatelain. Open every day. Open until 10 pm. Private room: 90. Terrace dining. Parking. V.

Since our previous visit, chef Christian Chatelain's cooking has become much lighter, and though he continues to cherish sauces made with curry, ginger, and cinnamon, he now uses much less cream in them. And his desserts are still just as remarkable, particularly the strawberry soup with Champagne. Respectable cellar, with some reasonably priced Loire wines.

A la carte: 300 F. Menus: 120 F, 165 F, 215 F, 270 F.

Auberge de Kerland

(See restaurant above)
Open every day. 2 stes 560-600 F. 17 rms 380-496 F. Half-board 410-468 F. TV. Conference facilities.

The old stone building has been entirely restored to provide large, well-equipped, and soundproofed rooms giving onto the river.

RIEDISHEIM

See Mulhouse

RIGNAC

See Gramat

RILLIEUX-LA-PAPE

See Lyon

ROANNE

42300 Roanne — (Loire)
Paris 390 - Lyon 88 - St-Etienne 77 - Mâcon 97

Troisgros

Pl. de la Gare
77.71.66.97
19.5 *MM. Troisgros. Closed Wed lunch, Tue and 12 Feb-12 March. Open until 9.30 pm. Private room: 25. Air cond. Valet parking. Telex 307507. V AE DC.*

As other great restaurateurs followed the trend for extensive grounds with swimming pools, the Troisgros had to decide whether to move out of town or make the most of what they had. They decided to stay put and, judging by the steady flow of customers, the latest investments have been right on target. What is more, the changes have had a beneficial effect on Michel, who is now in complete control of the kitchen and has virtually abandoned the 'decorative' cuisine that once tempted him for deeper, more intense flavours. His latest dishes leave no doubt that Michel is the equal of his father, grandfather, and his late uncle, the sadly missed Jean Troisgros: snails in herb juice delicately dominated by tarragon, a crab quenelle garnished with diced potatoes and leeks in a slightly creamy chive sauce, crisp red-mullet fillets with hot céleri-rémoulade and a hint of mustard, perfectly cooked freshwater perch in a delicious Roanne wine sauce, served with smoked bone marrow, lentils, diced carrots, and green beans, bass with violet artichokes, spatchcocked young pigeon, whose juices permeate the accompaniment of garlic cloves, button mushrooms, peas, and bacon cubes, and an incredible calf's ear with gherkins.

The desserts, once Michel's weak point, have improved. Try the chocolate fondant with caramel and custard sauces, or the extremely light feuilleté filled with walnut cream. And to accompany the feast there's a dazzling selection of Burgundy, Côtes-du-Rhône, Bordeaux, and Beaujolais wines, with great bottles costing barely more than mediocre ones elsewhere. Highly recommended: the Côte-Rôtie La Viaillère 1971.

A la carte: 560-750 F. Menus: 440 F, 550 F.

Troisgros
(See restaurant above)

Closed Tue and 12 Feb-12 March. 6 stes 1,300-2,500 F. 15 rms 650-1,100 F. TV. Air cond.

The hotel has two wings: the old one, completely transformed, offers ultra-modern, superbly equipped rooms overlooking either the garden or the station square. The new wing features five suites and three rooms, luxuriously decorated with contemporary furnishings, and overlooking an interior garden and the room where the outstanding breakfasts are served. Relais et Châteaux.

ROCAMADOUR

46500 Rocamadour — (Lot)
Paris 522 - Figeac 46 - Brive 54 - Gramat 9 - Cahors 61

Jehan de Valon
Rue R.-le-Preux — 65.33.63.08

M. Menot. Closed 12 Nov-23 March. Open until 9 pm (10 pm00 in summer). Private room: 20. Terrace dining. Valet parking. Telex 520421. V AE DC.

Didier Menot's superbly located establishment features meticulously prepared, aromatic dishes from the South-west like crayfish salad with a delicate vinaigrette, lamb cooked with violet mustard and garnished with baby vegetables, and a delicious red fruit dessert. Good selection of Cahors wine, friendly atmosphere. A toque this year.

A la carte: 250-300 F. Menus: 89 F, 150 F, 220 F.

Le Beau Site
(See restaurant above)

Closed 12 Nov-23 March. 50 rms 250-390 F. Half-board 250-450 F. TV 20 rms. Conference facilities.

This fine, family-owned hotel offers a variety of well-kept rooms. Splendid valley views.

ROCHE-BERNARD (LA)

56130 Roche-Bernard (La) — (Morbihan)
Paris 441 - La Baule 31 - St-Nazaire 35 - Nantes 70

Auberge Bretonne
2, pl. Du Guesclin — 99.90.60.28

M. Thorel. Closed Fri lunch, Thu and 15 Nov-15 Dec. Open until 9 pm. Private room: 20. Garden dining. Hotel: 1 ste. 11 rms 250-650 F (per pers, half-board oblig). Garage parking. V.

Chef Jacques Thorel is making a name for himself in this lovely restored stone building with its large dining area and some comfortable rooms around an enclosed garden of aromatic herbs.

Inspired by the produce of his beloved Brittany, Thorel brims over with ideas that inject new life into traditional cooking, leaving plenty of room for personal touches. Try his sea urchins with curly endive and scallops, small sole and hazelnuts, red mullet casseroled in wine with sage fritters, lobster braised in its shell with delicious little potatoes, sole with cabbage and a garnish of chopped capers and winkles, and a marvellous combination of milk-fed veal and stewed morels. To follow there are excellent local goat cheeses and delectable desserts like apples in puff pastry with cherries, or

baked peaches with almond-milk ice cream. The superb wine list has more than 1,500 entries. Friendly, efficient service. If you find other menus offering such excellent value, let us know.

A la carte: 250-450 F. Menus: 100 F (weekdays only), 250 F, 350 F, 400 F.

ROCHEGUDE

See Orange

ROCHELLE (LA)

17000 Rochelle (La) — (Charente-M.)
Paris 475 - Niort 63 - Bordeaux 188 - Angoulême 128

Les Brises
17, ch. de la Digue-Richelieu — 46.43.89.37

Open every day. 48 rms 260-510 F. V.

In a quiet location away from the centre, this square, utterly charmless residence has a vast terrace looking out on the water, and large, attractively decorated rooms with balconies. TV upon request.

Le Champlain
(France et Angleterre)
20, rue Rambaud — 46.41.23.99

Open every day. 4 stes 530 F. 33 rms 280-420 F. TV. Conference facilities. Garage parking. V AE DC.

Ranked among the city's finest, this beautiful former town house has comfortable, stylishly furnished rooms. Lovely flower garden; bar.

Richard Coutanceau
Plage de la Concurrence — 46.41.48.19

M. Coutanceau. Closed Mon dinner and Sun. Open until 9.30 pm. Private room: 45. Air cond. V AE DC.

Only the choicest ingredients are used by this talented chef; he can turn a mundane sole meunière into a gastronomical feast (it was the best we've ever eaten) so fine is the fish, so sure is his technique. The same simplicity and authentic flavours characterise his bass carpaccio with green peppercorns, his salad of roast prawns and oysters, the turbot with artichokes, or sea bream roasted with aromatics, a marvellous local duckling, and skilfully composed desserts, like the pear roasted with pralines served with vanilla ice cream. While the menu may not be wildly innovative, it is flawlessly executed, surely deserving of the third toque we award this year.

A la carte: 350-400 F. Menus: 180 F, 390 F.

La Marmite
14, rue St-Jean-du-Pérot — 46.41.17.03

M. Marzin. Closed Wed and Feb school holidays. Open until 10 pm. Air cond. V AE DC.

Badly calculated cooking times sometimes spoil otherwise fine dishes like the rousing prawn aïoli garnished with slices of (undercooked!) potatoes, but the sauté of coquilles St-Jacques and fresh foie gras, the John Dory fillet with artichokes, the assortment of original and ingeniously displayed sorbets, and bright-flavoured crêpes à l'orange make this one of the best addresses in La Rochelle. Superb but expensive cellar (the Loire wines are the most affordable).

A la carte: 350 F. Menus: 160 F, 260 F, 350 F.

Yachtman
23, quai Valin — 46.21.20.68

M. Le Divellec. Closed Mon off-season. Open until 10 pm. Garden dining. Garage parking. V AE DC.

Here's the best—and most charming—of La Rochelle's portside establishments. In comfortable surroundings diners enjoy the fresh, light cooking of Frédéric Layez presented in the form of a generous 140 F set menu. On a given day, the chef might offer a salade terre-mer (lightly cooked liver, sole fillets, diced salmon), luminously fresh prawns pan-roasted to perfection, roast turbot with a deftly prepared winkle cream sauce, and to wind things up, a moreish succès praliné. The cellar offers a small but worthwhile range of local growths, and the service manages to be both relaxed and efficient. A toque this year!

Menus: 90 F (lunch only, wine inc), 80 F (lunch only), 140 F and 180 F (dinner only).

Yachtman

(See restaurant above)
Open every day. 3 stes 650 F. 46 rms 310-650 F. Half-board 315-570 F. TV. Heated pool.

A very comfortable hotel ideally located on the old harbour.

In nearby Aytré

(5 km S on D 937)
17440 Rochelle (La) (Charente-M.)

La Maison des Mouettes

Rte de la Plage — 46.44.29.12
M. Pouget. Closed Mon (except holidays and July-Aug). Open until 9 pm. Private room: 100. Terrace dining. Parking. V AE DC.

Jacques Pouget's cooking relies on pristine ingredients, and most of the food served in this agreeable, beachfront restaurant is very good indeed; garnishes, however, need a bit more attention. Our rock lobster salad was both generous and delicious, and so was the roast lotte with green lentils; the floating island with pink pralines and diced fresh fruit was excellent, but the profiteroles were stale and the cheese board barely presentable. Impeccable reception and service.

A la carte: 300 F. Menus: 110 F, 178 F, 350 F.

RODEZ

12000 Rodez — (Aveyron)
Paris 608 - Brive-la-Gaillarde 156 - Albi 78 - Aurillac 96

Le Parc Saint-Joseph

4 km W, rte de Rignac — 65.67.03.30
Closed Jan. 2 stes 420 F. 18 rms 270-390 F. Restaurant. Half-board 410 F. TV. Parking. V AE.

This classic dwelling, set on the edge of a splendid park dotted with noble cedars and sequoias, was once the summer residence of the Bishop of Rodez. Good breakfasts.

Le Saint-Amans

12, rue de la Madeleine — 65.68.03.18
M. Amat. Closed Sun dinner, Mon and 5 Feb-5 March. Open until 9.30 pm. Air cond. V.

In a sophisticated décor of black-lacquer panelling and smoked mirrors, Jacques Amat displays his considerable skill with a lengthy menu of somewhat complicated fare. But we're not complaining; neither will you when you taste his cassolette de fruits de mer with aniseed-flavoured courgettes, sautéed prawns with tagliatelle, pigeon roasted with Banyuls wine and a touch of bitter cocoa, and wonderful desserts. The less expensive set menu is a marvel of generosity.

A la carte: 220-260 F. Menus: 115 F, 245 F.

The prices quoted in this guide are those which we were given by the restaurants and hotels concerned. Increases in prices are beyond our control.

ROISSY-EN-FRANCE

See PARIS Suburbs

ROMAINVILLE

See PARIS Suburbs

ROMORANTIN

41200 Romorantin — (Loir/Cher)
Paris 183 - Tours 92 - Bourges 65 - Blois 41

Grand Hôtel du Lion d'Or

69, rue G.-Clemenceau
54.76.00.28
M. Barrat. Closed beg Jan to mid-Feb. Open until 9 pm. Private room: 40. Garden dining. Valet parking. Telex 750990. V AE DC.

Chef Didier Clément, a fervent collector of ancient recipes and connoisseur of arcane plants and herbs, orchestrates the aromas of his garden and culinary lore compiled over centuries to create one of the most exciting, intelligent, and sensual cuisines in France. After a cool apéritif—one of the cellar's remarkable Loire wines, for example—enjoyed (weather permitting) beneath a white parasol out of doors, guests are ushered into the distinguished wood-panelled dining room decorated in tones of blue, with watercolours on the walls and a huge Dutch brass chandelier.

And then the feast begins. Why not try the outstanding duck liver in chilled bouillon with tiny vegetables (brilliantly accompanied by a glass of sherry)? But there is also a thick slice of salmon with a garland of pink radishes; or prawn risotto to which the addition of balsamic vinegar lends mysterious depth; an ethereal vol-au-vent filled with fresh morels and sprightly spring onions; snails and artichokes flavoured with liquorice; or a plump young duck, cooked to pink and tender perfection, its savour heightened with candied rosemary. But if you are making a first visit to the Lion d'Or, we urge you to try the fat prawns roasted with half a score of freshly ground spices, a mixture that confers a subtle flavour that lingers long on the palate....

Didier Clément's mother-in-law, Colette Barrat, will introduce you to the region's superb goat cheeses, perfect partners for a last swallow of Loire Valley wines. But do save room, for the magnificent, utterly original desserts are too tempting to skip: strawberries glazed in red wine with iced milk, rhubarb pie flattered with caramel and ginger, a frozen cherry-peach sablé, or—Clément's masterpiece—angelica sorbet with a subtly perfumed Muscat jelly.

A la carte: 470-750 F. Menus: 330 F (weekdays only), 550 F.

Grand Hôtel du Lion d'Or

(See restaurant above)
Closed beg Jan-mid-Feb. 3 stes 2,000 F. 13 rms 600-1,600 F. TV.

What was formerly a dilapidated post house is now an elegant country inn with luxurious rooms and suites overlooking a Renaissance fountain at the centre of a medieval courtyard. A pianist plays on Friday evenings in the delightful lounge by the garden. Relais et Châteaux.

ROSAY-SUR-LIEURE

See Lyons-la-Forêt

ROSBRUCK

See Forbach

29680 Roscoff — (Finistère)
Paris 561 - Brest 63 - Morlaix 28 - Landivisiau 27

Le Yachtman
Bd Ste-Barbe — 98.69.70.78
Mme Chapalain. Closed off-season Sun dinner and Mon, and 15 Nov-15 March. Open until 9.30 pm. Private room: 30. Parking. Telex 940397. V AE.
  Loïc Le Bail's knack for wedding flavours comes across in a salad of plaice with good, slightly tart leeks, cod with smoked bacon, and his spicy John Dory à l'orientale. Limited wine cellar; the staff is young and eager to please.
A la carte: 300-400 F. Menus: 145 F, 250 F, 380 F.

Brittany
(See restaurant above)
Closed off-season Sun and Mon, and 15 Nov-15 March. 3 stes 480-720 F. 22 rms 310-480 F. Half-board 390-450 F. TV. Heated pool.
  This beautiful yet stern seventeenth-century mansion provides comfortable, nicely fitted rooms that overlook a beach. Indoor heated swimming pool, a fitness centre, Jacuzzi, and sauna.

59100 Roubaix — (Nord)
Paris 231 - Lille 12 - Tourcoing 14 - Tournai 19

Altea Grand Hôtel
22, av. J.-B.-Lebas — 20.73.40.00
Open every day. 92 rms 278-415 F. TV. V AE DC.
  A splendid turn-of-the-century hotel, renovated with care. Rooms are functional, the decoration absolutely mundane. Good conference facilities; bar.

Le Caribou
8, rue Mimerel — 20.70.87.08
M. Siesse. Closed dinner (except Fri and Sat), Mon, 1 week at Easter and mid-July to end Aug. Open until 9 pm. Private room: 20. Parking. V.
  This restaurant's anachronistic and tired décor seems to affect the reception, and even the youthful staff; fortunately chef Christian Siesse has not succumbed to the morose ambience, for his straightforward, seasonal cuisine is as fine as ever. The foie gras, noted as one of the best in the region, is worthy of your attention, as is a herbed terrine of prawns and veal sweetbreads, sole in parsley-flavoured cream, and rosemary-scented lamb noisettes.
A la carte: 350 F. Menus: 190 F, 300 F.

76000 Rouen   (Seine-Mar.)
Paris 139 - Caen 124 - Amiens 116 - Le Havre 88

Le Beffroy
15, rue du Beffroy — 35./1.55.27
Mme Engel. Closed Sun dinner. Annual closings not available. Open until 9.30 pm. V AE DC.
  Odile Engel, who had made an enviable reputation for herself in her charming restaurant in Beuvron-sur-Auge, has decided to try her luck in the big city. Guests seated in the pleasant, flower decked dining room of this half-timbered house, will enjoy the sensual, generous cuisine focussed on seafood and Normandy's finest produce. You must try the divincly fragrant salmon which she smokes herself, the panaché de poisson drizzled with a lemon-flavoured olive oil emulsion, or the roast duck with an apple brandy sauce, and her delicious traditional chocolate cake. Superb Alsace wines selected by Marcel Engel; cheerful welcome.
A la carte: 300-350 F. Menus: 155 F, 250 F.

Hôtel de Dieppe
Pl. B.-Tissot — 35.71.96.00
Open every day. 42 rms 340-500 F. Restaurant. Half-board 375-525 F. TV 40 rms. V AE DC.
  Recently renovated, comfortable, soundproofed rooms are provided by this pleasant hotel just next to the station.

L'Ecaille
26, rampe Cauchoise — 35.70.95.52
Mme Tellier. Closed Sun, Mon, Feb school holidays and 4-23 Aug. Open until 9.30 pm. V.
  In his subterranean dining room (note the thirteenth-century vaulting), Marc Tellier offers carefully crafted seafood specialities. Each day he goes off to procure the freshest fish from his suppliers on the coast, then turns his purchases into fine dishes like skate with tomato coulis, or sole fillet in chive-flavoured cream with fragrant chanterelles. When he strays from the traditional path, however, his inventions are not always successful. The atmosphere is cosy, the service amiable and efficient; prices are steep.
A la carte: 350 F. Menus: 130 F (except Sat dinner), 220 F.

Gill
9, quai de la Bourse — 35.71.16.14
M. Tournadre. Closed Mon (except dinner in seas), Sun, holidays, Feb school holidays and 25 Aug-10 Sep. Open until 9.45 pm. Air cond. No pets. V DC.
  Though he is not a 'regional chef' in the accepted sense—his cooking is not traditional—Gilles Tournadre makes excellent use of local produce: fresh fish, ducks, cider, apples. Apart from an over-elaborate pigeon and sweetbreads pie with sauce rouennaise, we were pleased as punch with everything we sampled: there was fresh duck liver with Cox's Orange Pippin apples, a salad of sweetbreads with watercress dressed with meat juices pepped up with vinegar (his salads are alway terrific), pearly-fleshed turbot roasted with fresh herbs, sole pan-braised in crab juices, wild duckling roasted with cider and turnips, calf's tongue and beef jowls braised in red wine, and lush desserts like gingerbread croustillant with raisin-and prune-studded ice cream. Prices are neither low nor terrifying, but keep in mind that Gill proposes a great prix-fixe lunch that includes a robust duck terrine, the catch of the day, a meat or poultry dish, dessert, and petits fours.
A la carte: 350-500 F. Menus: 170 F (lunch only), 300 F.

Pullman Albane
Rue de la Croix-de-Fer — 35.98.06.98
Open every day. 4 stes 770-990 F. 121 rms 430-670 F. Restaurant. Half-board 580-820 F. TV. Air cond. Garage parking. Telex 180949. V AE DC.
  This modern three-storey building, set in the heart of old Rouen, features spacious, thoughtfully appointed rooms with excellent soundproofing. Air-conditioning; garage; bar.

Pascal Saunier
12, rue du Belvédère
76130 Mont-St-Aignan — 35.71.61.06
M. Saunier. Closed Sun dinner, Mon and 1-12 Aug. Open until 9.15 pm. Private room: 25. Garden dining. Air cond. Parking. V AE.
  Pascal Saunier, a picture-perfect Normandy native (complete with a thatch of blond hair and a local accent) is nonetheless the principal practitioner of Provençal cooking in these northerly parts. His 1930s–style restaurant, with its sweeping view of the Seine, is redolent of the rich, herbal scents

of the South. Rouen will feel like Ramatuelle when you taste Saunier's salad of prawns and sweetbreads dressed with wine vinaigrette, tiny red mullet grilled with rosemary, roast salmon served atop multicoloured lasagne, veal kidney roasted with cabbage and turnips in a Banyuls wine sauce, lamb rosace heightened with an aubergine jus, and for dessert, succulent roast pineapple with honey-rum ice cream, or frozen nougat with raspberry coulis.

A la carte: 400 F. Menus: 160 F (weekdays lunch only, wine inc), 215 F, 275 F.

And also...

Our selection of places for inexpensive, quick, or late-night meals.
Les Halles du Vieux Marché (35.71.03.58 - pl. du Vieux-Marché. Open until 10.30 pm): Good family-style meals in an authentic country inn (120-150 F).
La Mer (35.89.95.96 - 14, pl. du Vieux-Marché. Open until 11 pm): For seafood-fanciers; the décor is reminiscent of yesteryear's great ocean liners (120-150 F).
Le Queen Mary (35.71.52.09 - 1, rue du Cercle. Open until 11 pm): Brasserie-style fare, in a dining room done up like a 1930s transatlantic liner (130-160 F).

ROUFFACH

68250 Rouffach — (Haut-Rhin)
Paris 458 - Mulhouse 28 - Colmar 15 - Guebwiller 10

Les Tommeries
89.49.63.53
MM. Traversac and Dalibert. Closed mid-Jan to mid-March. Open until 9.15 pm. Private room: 150. Terrace dining. Valet parking. Telex 880819. V.

The Prince de Traversac's château is hard to date, owing to the many transformations and additions it has undergone over the years. But that fact won't interfere with your enjoyment of the spacious rooms, the splendid view of the village, or the antique-filled dining room, nor will it prevent you from delighting in Alain Finkbeiner's savoury millefeuille de foie gras with celery and apples, lotte roasted with slab bacon with a Pinot Noir sauce, pigeon façon Isenbourg, and frozen chestnut parfait. Superb, far-ranging cellar; fleet, elegant service.

A la carte: 500 F. Menus: 620 F (champagne c.), 240 F, 330 F.

Château d'Isenbourg
(See restaurant above)
Closed mid-Jan to mid-March. 2 stes 1,380-1,600 F. 38 rms 620-1,250 F. Half-board 680-995 F. TV. Conference facilities. Heated pool. Tennis.

The hotel pampers guests with large, very agreeable, comfortable and stylish rooms. Every care has been taken for the clients' well-being and pleasure: there's tennis, an indoor swimming pool with sauna, a whirlpool, and a fitness centre. Provisions can be made for horse riding and bicycle rentals. Relais et Châteaux.

ROYAN

17200 Royan — (Charente-M.)
Paris 490 - Bordeaux 124 - Saintes 37

Family Golf Hôtel
Grande-Conche
28, bd Garnier — 46.05.14.66
Closed 30 Sep-Easter. 33 rms 310-450 F. TV. V.

Located opposite Royan's main beach, this small, recently updated holiday hotel enjoys a fine view of the port and Gironde estuary.

Grand Hôtel de Pontaillac
195, av. de Pontaillac — 46.39.00.44
Closed 1 Oct-1 May. 50 rms 280-400 F. TV 23 rms. Garage parking. V.

A beachfront hotel with pleasant, constantly renovated, soundproofed rooms. Shaded garden; bar.

La Jabotière
in Pontaillac — 46.39.91.29
M. Auger. Closed off-season Sun dinner and Mon, and 2 Jan-2 Feb. Open until 10 pm. Private room: 50. Terrace dining. V AE DC.

Jean Auger is smiling now that his beachfront restaurant has been completely redone, and so are his customers, eager to rediscover Patrick Bachelard's delectable dishes. An extra point for the tarragon-flavoured ravioles of young rabbit with a drizzle of pistachio oil, sole goujonnettes bathed in prawn essence with a hint of coriander, and a crisp apple gratin dusted with maple sugar.

A la carte: 300-350 F. Menus: 150 F, 250 F, 350 F.

Résidence de Rohan
3 km, in Vaux-sur-Mer
Parc des Fées, rte de St-Palais — 46.39.00.75
Closed 15 Nov-23 March. 41 rms 250-600 F. TV. Tennis. Parking. V AE.

An elegant hotel, set apart by its shaded park with direct access to the beach, offering rooms furnished with English, Empire, or rustic pieces. Twenty additional rooms in an annexe.

ROYAT

See Clermont-Ferrand

ROYE

80700 Roye — (Somme)
Paris 105 - Amiens 41 - Compiègne 38 - Péronne 29

La Flamiche
20, pl. de l'Hôtel-de-Ville — 22.87.00.56
Mme Klopp and M. Borck. Closed Sun dinner, Mon, 8-16 July and 22 Dec-14 Jan. Open until 9.30 pm. Private room: 25. Air cond. V AE DC.

Pascal Charreyras is now the man in control of the kitchen, seconded by a brilliant sous-chef. Co-owners Mme Klopp and Mr Borck actively partake in the restaurant's success: she as a most gracious hostess, he as a fine connoisseur of wines and spirits. And with their attentive and prompt staff at the ready, we happily tucked away one of our year's best meals in this (alas, drab and weary) dining room.

We began with a stirring foie gras set upon a bed of fragrant vegetables (escorted by a velvety sweet Juraçon wine), followed by three dazzling roast prawns in a cauliflower cream (with a remarkable Riesling), a croustillant of freshwater perch in a tasty veal jus (the accompanying Chinon was a trifle oaky), a fabulous young pigeon perfumed with cumin (helped along by an elegant St-Emilion), and very good (if not thrilling) desserts—chocolate tart, strawberry soup—cleverly paired with a glass of white Lillet. The menu was thoroughly thought out, and yet seemed brilliantly self-evident: in short, it was high art.

A la carte: 500 F. Menus: from 190 F to 595 F.

Motel des Lions
Rte de Rosières — 22.87.20.61
Open every day. 43 rms 260-300 F. Restaurant. Half-board 240-310 F. TV. Parking. V AE DC.

Set in green surroundings not far from a motorway exit, this sparsely decorated hotel offers modern, bright, thoroughly soundproofed rooms.

RUEIL-MALMAISON
See PARIS Suburbs

RUNGIS
See PARIS Suburbs

RUY
See Bourgoin-Jallieu

SABLES-D'OLONNE (LES)

85100 Sables-d'Olonne (Les) — (Vendée)
Paris 450 - Nantes 90 - La Roche-sur-Yon 35

Atlantic' Hôtel
5, prom. G.-Godet — 51.95.37.71
Open every day. 30 rms 298-656 F. Restaurant. Half-board 478-537 F oblig in seas. TV. Conference facilities. Heated pool. Telex 710474. V AE DC.

A beachfront hotel, quiet and clean, with rooms that are a trifle small for the price; all have loggias (some with a view of the sea). Gorgeous covered pool with sliding roof, and many amenities: laundry service, photo shop, hair salon, bar.

Beau Rivage
40, prom. G.-Clemenceau — 51.32.03.01
M. Drapeau. Closed off-season Sun dinner and Mon (except holidays), 6-17 Oct and 22 Dec-22 Jan. Open until 9.30 pm. Private room: 8. Air cond. V AE DC.

The best restaurant on the Vendée coast has customers vying hotly for tables next to the dining room's bay windows, with a view of the beach. Joseph Drapeau, a chef with a weakness for truffles and foie gras, treated us to a wonderfully flavourful, well-balanced prawn timbale with leeks and truffle butter, sea bream cooked to perfection with a simple garnish of butter-braised sorrel, generously apportioned red mullet with foie gras (rich but most harmonious), a pig's trotter with Swiss chard—a marvel of rustic sophistication, and a delicious giboulée de fruits rouges: hot berries on vanilla ice cream sweetened with demerara sugar. The superb cellar, well-stocked with Bordeaux and Loire wines, is actually more affordable than the food.... Mme Drapeau greets guests with cheerful attentiveness.

A la carte: 400 F. Menus: 160 F (weekdays only), 280 F (wine inc), 195 F, 260 F and 420 F.

Le Navarin
18, pl. Navarin — 51.21.11.61
M. Privat. Closed off-season Sun dinner. Open until 9.30 pm. Terrace dining. V.

They are serving classical dishes that give the ingredients the starring role. Taste the gratin of crunchy vegetables and fresh shellfish.

A la carte: 250 F. Menus: 85 F (weekdays lunch only, wine inc), 105 F (weekdays only), 170 F, 155 F (wine inc), 260 F.

Les Roches Noires
12, prom. Clemenceau — 51.32.01.71
Open every day. 37 rms 218-607 F. TV. V AE DC.
The sunny, pleasant rooms look out to sea. Well-equipped bathrooms and friendly service

SACLAY
See PARIS Suburbs

SAGONE
See CORSICA

SAINT-AGNAN-EN-VERCORS
See Chapelle-en-Vercors (La)

SAINT-ANDRÉ-D'HÉBERTOT
See Pont-l'Evêque

SAINT-ARNOULT
See Deauville

SAINT-BEAUZEIL
See Montaigu-de-Quercy

SAINT-BONNET-LE-FROID

43290 Saint-Bonnet-le-Froid — (Haute-Loire)
Paris 558 - St-Etienne 59 - Annonay 26 - Tournon 53

Auberge des Cimes
71.59.93.72
M. Marcon. Closed Sun dinner, Wed and 15 Nov-Easter. Open until 9.30 pm. Parking. Hotel: 7 rms 280-380 F, half-board 280-340 F oblig in seas. V DC.

Revel for yourself in the full flavours of Régis Marcon's cooking, which now rates three toques and is firmly rooted in local ingredients: salad of warm cèpes on lamb's lettuce and and apple quarters, salmon trout with citrus peel, duckling with green lentils flavoured with garlic and bacon, pigeon with fennel, citronella-scented vegetable ragoût, and fine desserts based on roast chicory, almonds, and verveine.

A la carte: 300-400 F. Menus: 120 F (weekdays only), 180 F, 250 F, 380 F.

SAINT-BRIEUC

22000 Saint-Brieuc — (Côtes/Armor)
Paris 445 - Brest 146 - Rennes 99 - Dinan 59

L'Amadeus
22, rue du Gouet — 96.33.92.44
M. Malotaux. Closed Sun. Open until 9.30 pm. V AE.
First, the compliments: good ingredients cooked in interesting ways and not too expensive.

A la carte: 280 F. Menus: 70 F (except Sat dinner), 85 F, 120 F, 180 F.

La Croix Blanche
61, rue de Genève — 96.33.16.97
M. Mahé. Open every day. Open until 9.30 pm. Private room: 100. Parking. V AE.
While the décor is getting spruced up, the cooking has raced ahead with a fine salad of skate and fresh goat cheese, turbot braised in Madeira with morels.

A la carte: 230 F. Menus: 85 F, 98 F, 148 F, 185 F.

12/20 Le Griffon
Rue de Guernesey — 96.94.57.62
Mme Horel. Closed 22 Dec-6 Jan. Open until 10 pm. Garage parking. Telex 950701. V AE DC.
Try the warm oysters in Riesling, lotte medallions in cider vinegar, and duck fillet with Breton mead. The *patronne* provides a pleasant welcome.

A la carte: 280-300 F. Menus: 85 F (weekdays only), 135 F, 195 F.

Le Griffon
(See restaurant above)
Closed 22 Dec-6 Jan. 3 stes 370 F. 42 rms 255-330 F. Half-board 375-395 F. TV. Tennis.
A large modern hotel on the edge of town containing quiet, comfortable rooms which show signs of needing the promised refurbishment.

Ker Izel
20, rue du Gouet — 96.33.46.29
Open every day. 22 rms 205-270 F. TV. Air cond. No pets. Garage parking. Telex 741811. V.
Small rooms with modern equipment in the heart of the pedestrian precinct.

Aux Pesked
59, rue du Légué — 96.33.34.65
M. Martin. Closed Sat lunch, Sun dinner, Mon and Feb school holidays. Open until 10 pm. Private room: 15. Parking. V.
Thierry Martin has kept it full ever since with his charming welcome, astonishingly low prices, and the tasty, modern cuisine of chef Pascal Hervé.
A la carte: 230 F. Menus: 280 F (wine inc), 78 F, 98 F.

Le Quatre Saisons
61, ch. des Courses — 96.33.20.38
M. Faucon. Closed Sun dinner, Mon (except holidays and groupes). Open until 9.30 pm. Private room: 120. Garden dining. V.
You can enjoy there a quiet lunch under the weeping willow. Smiling welcome.
A la carte: 300 F. Menus: from 80 F to 260 F.

In nearby Plérin-sous-la-Tour

(3 km NE on D 24)
22190 Saint-Brieuc — (Côtes/Armor)

La Vieille Tour
Port de St-Brieuc - Le Légué
75, rue de la Tour — 96.33.10.30
M. Hellio. Closed Sat lunch off-season, Sun dinner and Mon (except holidays). Annual closings not available. Open until 9.30 pm. Private room: 30. V.
Chef Michel Hellio combs garden, market, field, and farmyard to search out the best local produce. Then it's down to the docks for the best seafood with which to produce his fish-based menu. From the upper dining room you can watch the boats come in while you sample duck foie gras with rhubarb, lotte cooked with diced lobster, precisely roasted lamb, fillet of brill with baby vegetables, and a remarkable strawberry millefeuille. The wine list is expanding and offers excellent value. Pleasing floral decor.
A la carte: 280-300 F. Menus: 110 F (weekdays only), 165 F, 230 F, 320 F.

SAINT-CAPRAISE-DE-LALINDE
See Lalinde

SAINT-CIRQ-LAPOPIE

46330 Saint-Cirq-Lapopie — (Lot)
Paris 628 - Cahors 33 - Villefranche-de-Rouergue 36

12/20 Auberge du Sombral
65.31.26.08
M. Hardeveld. Closed Tue dinner and Wed (except school holidays), and 11 Nov-1 April. Open until 9 pm. Terrace dining. V.
The rustic décor of this country inn reflects the charms of the medieval village. The prices are more up to date.
A la carte: 220-300 F. Menus: 85 F, 150 F, 280 F.

Auberge du Sombral
(See restaurant above)
Closed Tue and Wed (except school holidays), and 11 Nov-1 April. 8 rms 180-300 F.
The renovated, rustic rooms look onto the Place du Sombral.

SAINT-CLÉMENT-DES-BALEINES
See Ré (Ile de)

SAINT-CLOUD
See PARIS Suburbs

SAINT-CYPRIEN

66750 Saint-Cyprien — (Pyrénées-O.)
Paris 920 - Perpignan 15 - Port-Vendres 20

L'Almandin
Les Capellans — 68.21.01.02
M. Lormand. Annual closings not available. Open until 10 pm. Private room: 14. Terrace dining. No pets. Garage parking. V.
We have been astonished by the speed with which this talented young chef from Alsace, trained in the best of his region's kitchens, has made the transition to a completely new set of local traditions and ingredients. The proof is in the anchovy blinis with tapenade, bourride de lotte with pickled broom buds, salmon and prawn andouillette in a star-anise sauce, roast rack of lamb and creamed lamb's lettuce, or any of his other intelligent interpretations of Catalan cuisine.
A la carte: 350 F. Menus: 160 F, 190 F, 280 F.

L'Ile de la Lagune
(See restaurant above)
Open every day. 4 stes 700-830 F. 22 rms 500-650 F. Half-board 470-520 F. TV. Air cond. Pool.
This beautifully designed hotel has large terraces overlooking the lagoon. The comfortable rooms have fresh, pretty décor but the banal furniture spoils the effect. Wonderful little bathrooms and a delightful reception.

SAINT-DENIS
See PARIS Suburbs

SAINT-DIDIER
See Châteaubourg

SAINT-DIDIER
See Carpentras

SAINT-EMILION

33330 Saint-Emilion — (Gironde)
Paris 549 - Bordeaux 38 - Libourne 7 - Langon 49

Hostellerie de Plaisance
Place du Clocher
57.24.72.32
M. Quilain. Closed 2-31 Jan. Open until 9.15 pm. Private room: 70. Telex 573032. V AE DC.
A plush provincial interior with tall windows offering a fine view of the roofs of the old city. The cooking is organised around excellent ingredients and careful technique, leaving little room for imagination: foie gras in several forms, bass fillet and orange. The wine list is impressive, and not just in St-Emilions.
Menus: 125 F and 145 F (weekdays only), 205 F, 260 F.

Hostellerie de Plaisance
(See restaurant above)
Closed 2-31 Jan. 1 ste 900-1,100 F. 11 rms 470-720 F. Air cond 7 rms. Conference facilities.
These beautifully appointed rooms range from spacious down to tiny, some with terraces. The soundproofing could be improved.

11/20 Logis de la Cadène

Pl. du Marché-au-Bois — 57.24.71.40

Mme Mouliérac-Maarfi. Closed Sun dinner, Mon, Jan, 24 June-2 July and 2-10 Sep. Open until 9 pm. Terrace dining. V.

The uncomplicated dishes include fish and meat grilled on a wood fire, saumon sauce gribiche, and a good almond gâteau. The family wine is Château La Clotte, Grand Cru Classé.

A la carte: 200 F. Menus: 90 F (weekdays lunch only), 120 F, 150 F, 180 F.

SAINT-ESTEBEN

See Hasparren

SAINT-ETIENNE

42000 Saint-Etienne — (Loire)
Paris 520 - Lyon 59 - Le Puy 78 - Clermont-F. 150

Altea Parc de l'Europe

Rue de Wuppertal — 77.25.22.75

Open every day. 120 rms 550 F. Restaurant. TV.

These well-equipped rooms benefit from their location on a sunny hillside. The hotel has been recently redecorated in soothing pink and grey.

Astoria

Le Rond-Point, rue H.-Déchaud
77.25.09.56

Open every day. 33 rms 250-330 F. TV. Conference facilities. Garage parking. Telex 307237. V AE DC.

This small modern hotel with a garden is easy to find, just off the motorway.

André Barcet

19 bis, cours V.-Hugo — 77.32.43.63

M. Barcet. Closed Wed and last 2 weeks of July. Open until 9.30 pm. Private room: 25. Air cond. V AE DC.

Discouragement is in the air, and in the kitchen as well judging from the lack of sparkle in the salad of young rabbit, chicory, and beetroot, the duck legs in a wine sauce, and the so-so desserts. Balanced wine list at moderate prices. The reception is rather distant.

A la carte: 300-350 F. Menus: from 160 F to 300 F.

Le Bouchon

7, rue Robert — 77.32.93.32

M. Lejeune. Closed Sat lunch and Sun (except holidays), 20 Dec-5 Jan and 12 July-5 Aug. Open until 9.30 pm. No pets. V AE DC.

The market dictates what will appear on the *carte*, which changes every day.

A la carte: 300 F. Menus: 110 F (weekdays only), 160 F, 220 F, 320 F.

12/20 Le Chantecler

5, cours Fauriel — 77.25.48.55

M. Berna. Closed Sat, Sun and 27 July-27 Aug. Open until 10 pm. Private room: 25. V AE DC.

All the comfort of a fine bourgeois establishment awaits you here.

A la carte: 300 F. Menus: 120 F, 170 F.

Le Clos des Lilas

28, rue Virgile — 77.25.28.13

M. Ploton. Closed Tue dinner, Mon, Feb school holidays and Aug. Open until 9.15 pm. Private room: 45. Terrace dining. V.

This is fast becoming one of St-Etienne's favourite restaurants for classical cooking.

A la carte: 300 F. Menus: from 170 F to 310 F.

12/20 Les Colonnes

17, pl. J.-Jaurès — 77.32.66.76

M. Cherbland. Closed Sun and holidays. Open until midnight. Terrace dining. Air cond. V AE DC.

A chic and even luxurious version of a brasserie.

A la carte: 300 F. Menus: from 76 F to 265 F.

12/20 La Coquille

1, rue du Pdt-Wilson — 77.32.15.13

M. Berna. Closed Sun and 13-19 Aug. Open until midnight. Air cond. V AE DC.

Shellfish, seafood salads, and good grilled fish are available here at very reasonable prices.

A la carte: 260-300 F. Menus: 100 F, 160 F.

12/20 Les Deux Gosses

16, rue Ph.-Blanc — 77.32.84.81

MM. Marcellier. Dinner only. Closed Sun and Aug. Open until 11 pm. V.

A plain, welcoming little restaurant in which to sample a generous seafood salad (which didn't need the lumpfish roe), duck breast with bilberries, and apple tarte Tatin.

A la carte: 230 F. Menus: 60 F, 80 F, 115 F.

Pierre Gagnaire

3, rue G.-Teissier
77.37.57.93

M. Gagnaire. Closed Sun, Mon, 2-14 Jan and 11 Aug-2 Sep. Open until 9.45 pm. Private room: 12. Valet parking. V AE DC.

We can no longer ignore the huge and rising talent that is contained—barely!—in the person of Pierre Gagnaire. A visit to his restaurant leaves you sitting in a whirlwind of ideas, tastes and surprises. You may have chosen what you want to eat but this laughing giant may change your mind, and then there's no stopping the torrent of dishes that pour forth from his imagination. We must make it clear that his ability to astonish his customers from one year's end to the next is not done for effect. The goal is never to be different or to be new; Gagnaire's sole concern is to do justice to the bonfire of inspiration that so clearly burns within him.

In a lesser chef this attitude would not necessarily lead to anything worth eating. But in Gagnaire's hands the most unlikely combinations become exquisite. Relais et Châteaux.

A la carte: 450-650 F. Menus: 220 F, 365 F, 495 F.

Midi

19, bd Pasteur — 77.57.32.55

Closed Aug. 33 rms 245-330 F. TV. Garage parking. Telex 300012. V AE DC.

Modern and functional.

Le Parc Fauriel

106, cours Fauriel — 77.41.13.94

M. Cartal. Closed Sun dinner, Mon and Aug. Open until 9.30 pm. Private room: 55. Garden dining. V.

Jean-Paul Cartal's cooking is above reproach: duck and goose foies gras on toasted brioche, sea-bream fillets with a curry sauce and toasted rice, and heavenly desserts like the chocolate, coffee and rum cakes. Well-chosen wines at competitive prices.

A la carte: 280-300 F. Menus: 110 F, 150 F, 170 F, 230 F.

Some establishments change their closing times without warning. It is always wise to check in advance.

Terminus du Forez
29, av. Denfert-Rochereau — 77.32.48.47
Open every day. 1 ste 275-365 F. 66 rms 245-315 F. Restaurant. TV. Conference facilities. Garage parking. Telex 307191. V AE DC.
A lot of effort has been put into renovating this big hotel near the railway station. Equipped for conferences.

SAINT-FLORENT
See CORSICA

SAINT-FLOUR
15100 Saint-Flour — (Cantal)
Paris 490 - Le Puy 93 - Mende 83 - Aurillac 74 - Issoire 71

Grand Hôtel des Voyageurs ✿
25, rue du Collège — 71.60.34.44
Mlle Promayrat. Closed 4 Jan-15 March and 4 Nov-Easter. Open until 9.30 pm. Private room: 15. No pets. Garage parking. Hotel: 33 rms 120-300 F, half-board 160-260 F oblig in seas. V AE DC.
The young chef, Diego Quinonero, has the technique to back up his ideas and the results are tempting and tasty.
A la carte: 220 F. Menus: 85 F (weekdays only), 110 F (w-e and holidays only), 140 F, 200 F.

Grand Hôtel L'Etape
18, av. de la République — 71.60.13.03
Open every day. 23 rms 280-300 F. Restaurant. Half-board 250-280 F. TV. Garage parking. V AE DC.
A modern building offering comfortable rooms with period furniture. Half of them have mountain views.

SAINT-FORT-SUR-LE-NÉ
See Cognac

SAINT-GERMAIN-DU-PLAIN
See Chalon-sur-Saône

SAINT-GERMAIN-EN-LAYE
See PARIS Suburbs

SAINT-HILAIRE-DE-BRETHMAS
See Alès

SAINT-JEAN
See Toulouse

SAINT-JEAN-AUX-BOIS
See Compiègne

SAINT-JEAN-CAP-FERRAT
06230 Saint-Jean-Cap-Ferrat — (Alpes-Mar.)
Paris 945 - Nice 14 - Monte-Carlo 11 - Menton 23

Brise Marine
58, av. J.-Mermoz — 93.76.04.36
Closed end Oct-1 Feb. 15 rms 254-584 F. TV. Air cond 4 rms. V.
This hotel, 100 metres from the sea, has large rooms, a garden and terraces for summer breakfasts.

Bel Air Cap Ferrat
Bd du Gal-de-Gaulle — 93.76.00.21
M. Maissen. Closed 2 Jan-22 March. Open until 10 pm (10.30 pm in summer). Garden dining. Air cond. No pets. Valet parking. V AE DC.
You can sample on the terrace the featherlight dishes of the talented Jean-Claude Guillon: rock lobster ravioli in shellfish broth, crispy-skinned bass with a fennel and olive oil sauce
A la carte: 500 F and up. Menu: 450 F.

Bel Air Cap Ferrat
(See restaurant above)
Closed 2 Jan-22 March. 11 stes 2,600-7,900 F. 47 rms 950-4,150 F. TV. Air cond. Conference facilities. Heated pool. Tennis.
This grand hotel from the Belle Epoque is hidden away in six hectares of lawns, copses and flower beds. A funicular takes you down to the Olympic pool.

Jean-Jacques Jouteux
(Le Provençal)
2, av. D.-Semeria — 93.76.03.97
MM. Jouteux and Salmon. Closed Feb. Open until 11 pm. Garden dining. Air cond. V.
The talent of Jean-Jacques Jouteux doesn't come cheap of course, but once you taste his latest creations the sacrifice seems slight: potato and anchovy tart, asparagus with prawns, lobster in a 'shell' of violet artichokes (almost too pretty to eat), baked John Dory with bone-marrow sauce, saddle of Pauillac lamb surrounded by a tart sautéed salad, and delicious pigeon with cinnamon.
A la carte: 500 F and up. Menus: 150 F (weekdays lunch only), 250 F, 450 F.

12/20 Panorama
3, av. J.-Monnet — 93.01.20.20
Mlle Van Driessche. Closed 3 Nov-15 Dec. Open until 10.30 pm. Private room: 100. Garden dining. Air cond. No pets. Valet parking. Telex 470302. V AE DC.
The views of the bay and the Greek villa Kerylos are so spectacular, especially at night, that it is easy to be distracted from your food. Which would be a pity, because Yves Merville's cooking is classic and reliable.
A la carte: 500 F and up. Menus: 250 F (lunch only), 300 F (w-e and holidays only).

Royal Riviera
(See restaurant above)
Closed 3 Nov-15 Dec. 1 ste 2,800-6,350 F. 76 rms 650-3,850 F. Half-board 1,040-2,240 F oblig in seas. TV. Air cond. Conference facilities. Heated pool.
The best of these luxuriously appointed rooms overlook the garden and pool. Expensive.

Le Sloop
Port de plaisance — 93.01.48.63
M. Therlicocq. Closed off-season Sun dinner and Wed, and 15 Nov-20 Dec. Open until 11 pm. Garden dining. V AE DC.
Alain Therlicocq has the happy knack of marrying regional dishes with his modern style.
A la carte: 300-350 F. Menu: 155 F.

La Voile d'Or
Port de plaisance — 93.01.13.13
M. Lorenzi. Closed 31 Oct-1 March. Open until 10.15 pm. Private room: 30. Garden dining. Air cond. Valet parking. Telex 470317. V.
This bastion of tradition has decided, against all expectations, to accept credit cards, but that's the only concession to modern times you'll find here. The geraniums have been cascading over the terrace for decades, and Jean Crépin's classic cooking is reminiscent of another age: baked prawns on a bed of ratatouille, fillet of bass with two kinds of caviar, saddle of lamb in a pancake wrapping with truffled vegetables, and superb desserts.
A la carte: 600-800 F. Menus: 400 F, 500 F.

La Voile d'Or
(See restaurant above)
Closed 31 Oct-1 March. 4 stes. 46 rms 600-2,950 F. Half-board 1,300-1,990 F oblig in seas. TV. Air cond. Conference facilities. Heated pool.
An Italian villa and its luxuriant gardens overlooking the harbour. The interior is highly decorative, with *trompe-l'œil* paintings and white-leaded wood furniture.

SAINT-JEAN-DE-BOISEAU
See Nantes

SAINT-JEAN-DE-BRAYE
See Orléans

SAINT-JEAN-DE-LUZ
64500 Saint-Jean-de-Luz — (Pyrénées-A.)
Paris 760 - Biarritz 15 - Hendaye 13 - Pau 128

 ## Chantaco
Golf de Chantaco — 59.26.14.76
M. Libouban. Closed 1 Nov-1 April. Open until 10 pm. Garden dining. No pets. Valet parking. Telex 540016. V AE DC.
The attraction is delicate, inventive, and beautifully presented food like the spiced prawns, crab gratin, and apple pie, plus some good, moderately priced Bordeaux to go with them.
A la carte: 300 F. Menus: 145 F (weekdays lunch only), 160 F and 280 F (w-e and holidays in summer dinner only), 245 F (weekdays dinner only).

 ## Chantaco
(See restaurant above)
Closed 1 Nov-1 April. 4 stes 1,400-1,800 F. 20 rms 700-1,450 F. Half-board 750-1,000 F. TV. Pool.
Superb rooms, mostly modernised, overlook a garden and the famous golf course.

 ## La Devinière
5, rue Loquin — 59.26.05.51
Open every day. 8 rms 450-550 F. No pets. Garage parking. V.
This hotel has eight delightfully decorated and furnished rooms in the heart of town. Pleasant welcome and quiet garden.

12/20 La Fontaine de Jade
Pl. du Midi — 59.26.02.76
Mme Tao. Closed Mon and 15 Feb-15 March. Open until 10 pm (10.30 pm summer). Terrace dining. V.
A smiling welcome awaits you in this Chinese décor where you will be served sam-sin (lotte, king prawns, and scallops with courgettes.
A la carte: 150-180 F.

 ## Le Grand Hôtel
43, bd Thiers — 59.26.35.36
M. Touati. Closed Nov-March. Open until 10 pm. Private room: 80. Terrace dining. Air cond. No pets. Valet parking. Telex 571810. V AE DC.
The lobster gazpacho, and the John Dory in a shrimp sauce, spit-roasted young pigeon, and a wild strawberry millefeuille are definitely worth a toque and we're sure the best is yet to come.
A la carte: 350 F. Menu: 185 F.

 ## Le Grand Hôtel
(See restaurant above)
Closed Nov-March. 6 stes 454-1,208 F. 44 rms 854-1,208 F. TV. Air cond. Heated pool.
The former nightclub of this small luxury hotel is now, tellingly, a fitness centre. Other signs of rebirth include new décor.

 ## Kaïku
17, rue de la République
59.26.13.20
M. Ourdanabia. Closed Mon lunch in sais, Wed off-season, and 13 Nov-21 Dec. Open until 11 pm. Terrace dining. V AE.
Rich, lively dishes like prawns with cabbage, cuttlefish and fresh pasta, and duck breast with apples are served by amiable staff in a pleasing pale stone setting.
A la carte: 300 F.

 ## Léonie
6, rue Garat — 59.26.37.10
MM. Etchenic. Closed Mon lunch in seas and Feb. Open until 10 pm. V AE DC.
The Basque traditions that suffuse the menu benefit from the chef's modern inspiration.
A la carte: 270 F. Menus: 108 F, 140 F.

 ## Le Mallet-Stevens
Pl. M.-Ravel — 59.51.51.51
M. Lawton. Open every day. Open until 10 pm. Private room: 250. Terrace dining. Air cond. No-smoking section. Valet parking. Telex 573415. V AE DC.
You can still enjoy an assortment of foies gras, bass in Madiran butter, and a medley of chocolate desserts, alongside the calorie-counted menus.
A la carte: 280-350 F. Menu: 175 F.

 ## L'Hélianthal
(See restaurant above)
Open every day. 5 stes. 100 rms 375-1,170 F. Half-board 615-1,650 F. TV. Air cond.
The rooms of this hotel set back from the beach glory in a perfect art deco style, right down to the mahogany trim, curved windows, and Hopper lithographs. Excellent reception.

 ## La Marée
Plage de Socoa-Ciboure — 59.47.06.88
M. Vivensang. Closed Mon and Jan. Open until 11 pm. Terrace dining. V AE DC.
This popular restaurant earns a toque after our last meal of perfectly grilled cuttlefish, cod-stuffed sweet peppers, scallops and cabbage in a light saffron sauce, and an expertly prepared chocolate cake. The cellar is still the weak spot here.
A la carte: 200 F and up.

 ## La Réserve
(Hôtel Basque)
Rd-pt de Ste-Barbe — 59.26.04.24
Mme Boutin. Open every day. Open until 10 pm. Private room: 120. Terrace dining. Hotel: 1 ste 630-780 F. 35 rms 325-550 F. Golf. Garage parking. V AE DC.
The classic Basque repertoire includes sweet peppers stuffed with salt cod, and spicy stuffed crab Txangurro. The cheese and desserts are disappointing. Good selection of Bordeaux.
A la carte: 260-300 F. Menus: 130 F (weekdays only), 160 F (w-e and holidays only), 220 F.

 ## Le Tourasse
25, rue Tourasse
59.51.14.25
M. Basset. Closed Tue dinner and Wed. Open until 10.30 pm. Air cond. V AE.
Savour the terrine of foie gras confit, crisp spider-crab turnover, and braised sweetbreads à l'ancienne. Dreamy desserts (roasted pear with honey and spices, chocolate truffles). Sturdy cellar. Smiling welcome.
A la carte: 270-300 F. Menu: 110 F (weekdays only).

In nearby Ciboure

(1 km SW)
64500 Saint-Jean-de-Luz – (Pyrénées-A.)

12/20 Arrantzaleak
Av. J.-Poulou – 59.47.10.75
M. Courdé. Closed off-season Mon dinner and Tue (Mon in seas), and 15 Dec-20 Jan. Open until 10 pm. V AE DC.
This is the seafront bistro of your dreams, with a lovely view, fresh fish, and chummy atmosphere.
A la carte: 200-230 F. Menu: 130 F (weekdays only).

La Marine
in Socoa
39, bd du Cdt-Passicot – 59.47.98.60
MM. Germain and de la Iglesia. Closed Sun dinner, Thu and 15 Dec-15 Jan. Open until 9.45 pm. Terrace dining. V.
Eric Germain shuns the shackles of purely regional cuisine and offers instead a selection of light, delectable 'marketplace' fish dishes.
A la carte: 250-300 F. Menu: 105 F (weekdays only).

12/20 Pantxua
59.47.13.73
M. Hou. Closed Mon dinner, Tue, Dec and Jan. Open until 10 pm. Terrace dining. V.
Handsomely situated on the Socoa harbour—a favourite among locals and tourists alike—this popular bistro is perpetually thronged.
A la carte: 200-250 F. Menu: 110 F (except Sun).

In nearby Urrugne

(3 km W on La Corniche)
64122 Saint-Jean-de-Luz – (Pyrénées-A.)

Chez Maïté
Pl. de la Mairie – 59.54.30.27
M. Tardieu. Closed Sun dinner, Mon and 13-29 Jan. Open until 9.30 pm. Terrace dining. Hotel: 7 rms 150-180 F. V AE.
Maman Tardieu welcomes you into her handsome, beamed dining room, then regales you with her son Guy's skilful, fresh-flavoured cuisine.
A la carte: 250 F. Menus: 80 F (weekdays lunch only), 100 F.

SAINT-JEAN-PIED-DE-PORT

64220 Saint-Jean-Pied-de-Port – (Pyrénées-A.)
Paris 793 - Pau 102 - Bayonne 54 - Dax 86

Les Pyrénées
19, pl. du Gal-de-Gaulle
59.37.01.01
M. Arrambide. Closed Tue (except holidays and in summer), Mon dinner off-season, 5-28 Jan and 15 Nov-22 Dec. Open until 9 pm. Private room: 40. Terrace dining. Air cond. Parking. TV AE.
Pack your toothbrush and slippers, and gird up your gastronomical loins: At long last, Firmin Arrambide's dream has come true. He's got three toques, a swimming pool, a gorgeous garden that slopes sweetly towards the river, and a charming, comfortable inn with eighteen cosy rooms. True, the garage and handsome seventeenth-century stone house still want some fixing. And perhaps some day he'll convert the disused hangar to house his dining room, for it would command a spectacular panorama of sheep-dotted hills and snow-capped Pyrenees. But all in good time.
Just now, let's settle into the elegant salmon-hued salle with enamelled ceilings and soft lighting, or onto the flower-filled terrace. Shepherds and farmers, all sporting berets, file past with their cargo of cured ham and tangy cheese. And while VIPs and grand gastronomes spend lavishly à la carte, in the back room commercial travellers and groups of merry regulars order the eminently reasonable prix-fixe menus. For Firmin, despite his triple toques and fame, is still close to the local folk, and the authentic traditions of his land.
Though he transforms them with a personal touch, regional recipes remain the backbone of Firmin's freestyle cuisine. Take, for example, the lamb's head salad 'à ma façon', an exemplary dish comprising a divine croustillant de cervelle, tongue with ravigote sauce, spiced lamb cheeks, and a truffled salad. Then there is Firmin's peerless Adour salmon, so tender you'd think it had been raised on mother's milk or manna. Why? The quality of the fish, of course. But the preparation, too: three or four minutes on each side, then a dab of béarnaise. Voilà. Perfection.
We could go on about the Pyrenees lamb 'délices'—sweetbreads, trotters, kidneys, and stuffed fillet—flanked by a heavenly purée of white haricot beans. And the homemade foie gras. And the prawn salad with sun-dried tomatoes. And the pan-roasted spiced duck fillet. Or the maddeningly mouthwatering desserts (nougat glacé with honey and almonds). But we'd soon run out of room. Besides, we must mention the Bordeaux and Jurançons, the rare Spanish bottlings, and the tasty local Irouléguy white and red, made by the neighbouring Brana family from vines that grow just across the fields.
A la carte: 400-600 F. Menus: 180 F (weekdays only), 260 F, 340 F, 420 F.

Les Pyrénées
(See restaurant above)
Closed Tue (except holidays and in summer), Mon off-season, 5-28 Jan and 15 Nov-22 Dec. 2 stes 800-880 F. 18 rms 480-750 F. Half-board 500-600 F. TV. No pets. Conference facilities. Heated pool.
The breathtaking view of countryside and mountains is enjoyed, alas, not from the hotel's hallways, not its smart and comfortable rooms or suites. Delicious breakfasts. Anne-Marie Arrambide's welcome is charming and disarmingly shy. Relais et Châteaux.

SAINT-JORIOZ
See Annecy

SAINT-JULIEN-DE-CREMPSE
See Bergerac

SAINT-LAMBERT-DES-BOIS
See Chevreuse

SAINT-LAURENT-DU-VAR

06700 Saint-Laurent-du-Var – (Alpes-Mar.)
Paris 925 - Nice 10 - Cannes 27 - Antibes 16

12/20 Le Centurion
Port St-Laurent – 93.07.99.10
M. Melzer. Closed Wed and 15 Oct-15 Nov. Open until 10 pm. Terrace dining. Air cond. V AE.
Taste the marmite du pêcheur, choucroute aux poissons, and salt-cod blanquette with mussel juices.
A la carte: 270 F. Menus: 65 F (weekdays lunch only), 98 F, 139 F, 245 F.

Hôtel Galaxie
Av. Maréchal-Juin
93.07.73.72
Open every day. 28 rms 360-500 F. TV. Air cond. Parking. Telex 470431. V AE DC.
The sea is a stone's throw from this modern hotel with perfectly designed rooms.

 Le Mas Saint-Laurent 🌲🌳
Magnolias
rue Plateau-Calliste — 93.31.93.31
Open every day. 2 stes 680-730 F. 13 rms 300-480 F. TV. Valet parking. V AE DC.
This nineteenth-century Provençal-style hotel has several modern annexes that blend nicely with the old house and with the surrounding greenery.

 SAINT-LOUIS

68300 Saint-Louis — (Haut-Rhin)
Paris 556 - Mulhouse 29 - Bâle 5 - Altkirch 28

In nearby **Buschwiller**

(7 km SW on D 419 and D 12b)
68220 Saint-Louis — (Haut-Rhin)

 La Couronne
6, rue du Soleil — 89.69.12.62
M. Lacour. Closed Sun dinner, Mon, 11-24 Feb and 12-25 Aug. Open until 9 pm. Private room: 30. Parking. V.
Renaissance tapestries and silk flowers help enliven the large, dour dining room of this simple village restaurant. The proprietor's cuisine is skilful and creative: snail ravioli in a crispy pastry shell seasoned with herb cream, pan-roasted scallops with coriander and ginger served with hard-wheat semolina and al dente sweet peppers, and yummy chocolate fondant with (unfindable) grapes. Irresistible welcome and smiling service (the *patronne* is English).
A la carte: 250 F and up. Menus: 75 F (weekdays lunch only), and from 150 F to 310 F.

SAINT-MAIME

See Manosque

SAINT-MALO

35400 Saint-Malo — (Ille/Vil.)
Paris 366 - Rennes 69 - Dinan 34 - St-Brieuc 76

 Robert Abraham
4, chaussée du Sillon
99.40.50.93
M. Abraham. Closed Sun dinner, Mon, 25 Nov-5 Dec and 18 Feb-5 March. Open until 9.30 pm. Private room: 25. No-smoking section. V AE DC.
The guinea fowl chaponnée, specially raised for Abraham, is a must. Sommelier Hervé Camus need only add a few whites, and few more half-bottles, to his cellar, and we shall whine no more. Lyliane Abraham's welcome is reserved but attentive. Stylish service.
Menus: 120 F (weekdays only), 160 F, 230 F, 310 F.

 Alexandra
138, bd Hébert — 99.56.11.12
Open every day. 15 rms 240-550 F. TV. Parking. Telex 740802. V AE DC.
This large hotel on the dike is thoughtfully decorated; some rooms overlook the sea from small terraces. The other rooms are quieter.

Le Cap Horn
100, bd Hébert — 99.40.75.75
M. Raulic. Closed 6-27 Jan. Open until 9 pm. Air cond. No pets. Garage parking. V AE DC.
Try the lobster salade exotique, the mould of jellied oxtail and shin, the braised brill with tiny vegetables and mushrooms, and farm chicken with sweetbreads en roulade in chive-flavoured cream. The modern, flower-filled, sunny dining room facing the dike and sea is more pleasant than ever. Wine cellar improving.
A la carte: 300-350 F. Menus: 110 F (weekdays lunch only), 165 F, 240 F.

Le Grand Hôtel des Thermes
(See restaurant above)
Closed 6-27 Jan. 3 stes. 194 rms 480-1,780 F (per pers, half-board oblig). TV. Heated pool.
This hotel caters for guests taking health cures at the spa. It has been remodelled in a tasteful, pseudo-1920s–style.

Le Chalut
8, rue de la Corne-du-Cerf — 99.56.71.58
M. Foucat. Closed Sun dinner off-season and Mon. Open until 9.30 pm. Air cond. V AE.
The fresh, inventive seafood cuisine is readily accessible with a prix-fixe menu at 100 F. The cellar is rich in fine bottles from the Loire. Béatrice Foucat supervises the courteous staff.
A la carte: 250-300 F. Menus: 100 F (weekdays lunch only), 160 F.

Hôtel de la Cité
26, rue Ste-Barbe — 99.40.55.40
Open every day. 2 stes 600-800 F. 41 rms 330-600 F. TV. Conference facilities. Garage parking. V AE.
Spanking-new, this five-storey hotel in the oldest part of town has huge, charming rooms.

Hôtel Du Guesclin
8, pl. Du Guesclin — 99.56.01.30
Open every day. 22 rms 190-390 F. TV. Conference facilities. Parking. Telex 740802. V AE.
Located on the Duguay-Trouin bassin, this corner building provides small, well-soundproofed rooms with tinyl bathrooms.

Elizabeth
2, rue des Cordiers
(ville close) — 99.56.24.98
Open every day. 17 rms 280-485 F. TV. Garage parking. Telex 949000. V AE DC.
This extremely well-appointed little hotel behind a sixteenth-century façade has rooms decorated in various styles.

Central
6, Grande-Rue — 99.40.87.70
Open every day. 46 rms 200-600 F. Half-board 330-440 F. Restaurant. TV. Conference facilities.
Located just a stone's throw from the ramparts, and bathed in the dark charm of the old town's narrow alleys, this modest hotel has smallish but comfortable rooms. Good service.

Manoir de la Grassinais
12, rue de la Grassinais — 99.81.33.00
M. Bouvier. Closed Tue lunch and Mon. Open until 9.30 pm. Terrace dining. Air cond. Garage parking. V.
We applaud Christophe Bouvier's 'herring-style' marinated salmon, his lotte with bacon and green lentils, and buckwheat galette with rosemary-scented sweetbreads. Far-ranging cellar. Exemplary prices.
A la carte: 300 F. Menus: 90 F, 140 F.

Manoir de la Grassinais
(See restaurant above)
Closings not available. 29 rms. Rates not available. TV. Conference facilities.
The space here is used to the utmost. Set around an inner court and insulated from the surrounding industrial district, the rooms have a modern, sober décor.

In nearby **Saint-Servan**

(SE on N 137)
35400 Saint-Malo – (Ille/Vil.)

La Korrigane
39, rue Le Pomellec – 99.81.65.85
Closed 1 Jan-15 March and 15 Nov-31 Dec. 10 rms 350-550 F. TV. Conference facilities. Parking. Telex 740802. V AE DC.
Smart, comfortable, well-soundproofed rooms.

La Métairie de Beauregard
2 km S on La Grassinais
in Saint-Etienne – 99.81.37.06
M. Gonthier. Closings not available. Open until 10 pm. Terrace dining. Parking. V AE DC.
Marie-Claire and Jacques Gonthier serve highest-quality ingredients skilfully transformed into dishes such as scallops with fresh pasta, John Dory with mussels, and roast saddle of young rabbit. For dessert, try the original strawberry tulipe. Gracious and efficient service.
A la carte: 250-300 F. Menus: 90 F (weekdays lunch only), 150 F, 180 F.

Saint-Placide
6, pl. Poncel – 99.81.70.73
M. Lempérière. Closed off-season Tue dinner and Wed. Annual closings not available. Open until 9.30 pm. V.
Didier Lempérière continues to regale diners with a 95 F menu of rare generosity.
A la carte: 250 F. Menus: 90 F (weekdays lunch only), 95 F, 150 F, 220 F.

Le Valmarin
7, rue Jean-XXIII – 99.81.94.76
Closed 24 Dec-1 March. 10 rms 380-480 F. TV. Parking. V AE.
Outside the town walls, this handsome eighteenth-century residence rises before a pretty park.

12/20 Le Moderne
46, rue d'Anjou – 40.22.55.88
Closed Sun dinner and Mon. Open until 9.30 pm. Private room: 50. V AE DC.
Though the dull décor leaves much to be desired, the cuisine sings: smoked salmon with a curious sour-cherry cream sauce, and delectable pot-au-feu. Friendly welcome, fledgling service.
A la carte: 250 F. Menus: 65 F (weekdays only), 70 F, 85 F, 110 F, 150 F.

12/20 Le Best
2, pl. du Vainquai – 21.38.25.78
M. Beauvalot. Closed Sun dinner, Sat and holidays. Annual closings not available. Open until 9.30 pm. Private room: 90. Parking. Telex 133290. V AE.
Though unoriginal, the cuisine is likeable, featuring foie gras and fish, as well as buffet starters and desserts. Stiff prices.
A la carte: 330 F. Menus: 180 F (wine inc), 160 F.

Le Bretagne
(See restaurant above)
Open every day. 43 rms 200-400 F. TV 24 rms. No pets. Conference facilities.
The Bretagne's two- and three-storey buildings are laid out in a horseshoe. Spacious, well-equipped rooms.

La Baronnie
86, rue Grande – 93.32.65.25
Mme d'Alessandro. Dinner only in July-Aug. Open until 10.30 pm (midnight in summer). Garden dining. Air cond. Valet parking. V AE DC.
Szanco will regale you with red-mullet fillets flavoured with olive oil and herbs in an artichoke barigoule, and sweetbreads en paupiette with smoked bacon and morel juices, herbs, and broad beans, followed by a wonderful selection of local cheeses, and a scrumptious strawberry sablé biscuit for dessert. Capacious cellar, but short on half-bottles and wines from Provence. The young waiters in monkey jackets are a mite mournful.
A la carte: 450-500 F. Menus: 275 F, 375 F.

Le Saint-Paul
(See restaurant above)
Open every day. 4 stes 1,550-2,100 F. 15 rms 650-1,250 F. TV. Air cond. Conference facilities.
This hotel has been taken over by Régis Bulot (owner of the Abbaye in Brantôme) and will be run by his wife.

12/20 La Brouette
830, rte de Cagnes — 93.58.67.16
M. Bornemann. Dinner only. Closed Tue and 1 Nov-15 Dec. Open until 11 pm. Private room: 12. Garden dining. Air cond. Parking. V.
Ole and Brigitte Bornemann serve authentic Danish specialities in a lively, pleasant atmosphere. Stunning garden setting with a view of town. Expansive welcome.
A la carte: 250 F. Menus: 148 F, 195 F.

Climat
Les Fumerates — 93.32.94.24
Open every day. 15 stes 450-500 F. 4 rms 350 F. Restaurant. Half-board 300-370 F. TV. Pool. Parking. V AE.
Surrounded by greenery, the Climat offers nineteen comfortable rooms and suites with terraces or loggias that give onto a swimming pool.

12/20 La Colombe d'Or
Pl. du Gal-de-Gaulle — 93.32.80.02
M. Roux. Closed 5 Nov-20 Dec. Open until 10 pm. Private room: 40. Terrace dining. Valet parking. V AE DC.
Picture a paradise for art lovers, with works by Picasso, Rouault, Léger, Miró and others adorning the walls. Yves Montand pops in sometimes to enjoy the leafy terrace and garden and tuck into Sisteron lamb or turbot fillet, washed down with Côtes-de-Provence.
A la carte: 300-400 F.

La Colombe d'Or
(See restaurant above)
Closed 5 Nov-20 Dec. 10 stes 1,100 F. 15 rms 950 F. Half-board 650 F. TV. Air cond. Heated pool.
This warmly welcoming Provençal hotel is very tastefully decorated. The rooms are delightful and the rates reasonable for so much comfort. Attractive pool.

La Corbeille
838, rte de La Colle — 93.32.80.13
M. Mendjisky. Closed Mon off-season and 5 Nov-15 Dec. Open until 10.15 pm. Terrace dining. Air cond. Valet parking. V AE.
Cyril Mendjisky's garden restaurant is dotted with olive trees, as well as intellectuals and artists. The recent departure of talented chef Philippe Marc was regrettable, but the new team, also from the Vista Palace, is doing almost as good a job. Proof: the seasonal salad (with Japanese-sculpted vegetables), perfectly fresh and flavourful red-mullet fillets served with baby broad beans in rosemary-perfumed butter, and banana tart spiced with cinnamon. No lack of originality.
A la carte: 350 F. Menus: 185 F (lunch only), 350 F (dinner only).

Le Hameau
528, rte de La Colle — 93.32.80.24
Closed 6 Jan-15 Feb and 16 Nov-22 Dec. 2 stes 600-650 F. 14 rms 280-480 F. Pool. Garage parking. V AE.
Almost all the attractively furnished rooms open onto the sea and citrus groves. Beautiful terrace.

Mas d'Artigny
Rte de La Colle — 93.32.84.54
M. Scordel. Open every day. Open until 9.30 pm. Private room: 160. Terrace dining. Garage parking. V AE.
An occasional unnecessary taste intrudes on the Provençal flavours, but many an agreeable meal is had on the long veranda overlooking the swimming pool. Sample, for example, the snails with aromatic herbs, cod brandade with prawns, truffle-scented foie gras 'lasagne', and chicken casserole with bitter orange zest. Rich, conventional cellar. Excellent service.
A la carte: 400-600 F. Menus: 285 F, 380 F.

Mas d'Artigny
(See restaurant above)
Open every day. 26 stes 1,460-2,480 F. 59 rms 450-1,720 F. Half-board 795-2,620 F. TV. Air cond 77 rms. Heated pool. Tennis.
The rooms and poolside suites have all it takes to make you feel like a millionaire. There are several marvellous multi-room villas scattered among the eight hectares of pines. Relais et Châteaux.

Mas des Gardettes
Ch. de la Vieille-Bergerie — 93.32.63.00
Open every day. 1 ste 520-680 F. 10 rms 450-580 F. TV. Parking. AE DC.
Just 100 metres from the Fondation Maeght, this little hotel offers peaceful rooms with independent access. Full bathrooms, sheltered terraces, kitchenettes.

Les Orangers
Ch. des Fumerates — 93.32.80.95
Open every day. 2 stes 460-580 F. 7 rms 390-460 F. Parking.
Set in a handsome park planted with olive and orange trees, the rooms here are smartly furnished. Some have terraces with fine views of the old village.

In nearby La Colle-sur-Loup
(3 km SW on D 7)
06480 Saint-Paul-de-Vence — (Alpes-Mar.)

12/20 Bacchus
Rte de Grasse — 93.32.83.53
Mlles Bigot and Moulinier. Closed Sun dinner and Mon, and Jan. Open until 10 pm. Garden dining. Pool. Tennis. Parking. V AE.
On the shady banks of the River Loup, this is a good place to stop for lunch. The décor is stunning, and Jean-Jacques Moulinier's skilful, traditional cooking features dishes such as canard sarladaise, veal kidneys with morels, fruit tart, and crème brûlée.
A la carte: 300 F. Menus: 110 F (weekdays only), 170 F.

12/20 La Belle Epoque
2 km S on D 6
1634, rte de Cagnes — 93.20.10.92
M. Frédéric. Closed Tue lunch and Wed off-season, and Jan. Open until 10 pm. Garden dining. Parking. V AE DC.
Rich, flavourful food served by the sprightly *patronne* on a pleasant summer terrace: warm foie gras with redcurrants, stuffed morels in a chicken cream sauce, and finely sliced truffles with cream. The set menus are good value.
A la carte: 350 F and up. Menus: 98 F, 140 F, 190 F.

Hostellerie de l'Abbaye
Rte de Grasse — 93.32.66.77
M. Picciochi. Closed Wed. Annual closings not available. Open until 9.30 pm. Terrace dining. Parking. V AE DC.

Christian Plumail, late of the Auberge de l'Estérel in Juan-les-Pins, has found a forum worthy of his talent: a marvellous medieval abbey, whose chapel dates from the tenth century (and is still used for weddings). As for the cuisine, it is light and imaginative: pea soup with baby morels and foie gras, lobster with pistou (basil sauce) and new vegetables, and John Dory baked with tapenade and served with extremely tasty artichoke hearts and puréed fennel. For dessert, rhubarb soup with a cherry sorbet. These are most promising beginnings. Surprisingly low prices for the area.
A la carte: 330 F. Menus: 180 F, 290 F.

Hostellerie de l'Abbaye
(See restaurant above)
Open every day. 13 rms 450-700 F. Half-board 630-830 F. TV 11 rms. Pool.

No trace of monkish austerity is left in this former winter residence of the Lérins order, built between the tenth and twelfth centuries. Elegance is everywhere, from the superb rooms to the pretty garden-patio.

Marc-Hély
535, route de Cagnes
93.22.64.10
Open every day. 3 stes 390-610 F. 14 rms 250-390 F. TV. Parking. V AE.

All the rooms here have a terrace overlooking St-Paul-de-Vence. Double glazing and flower-filled garden.

La Strega
1260, rte de Cagnes — 93.22.62.37
M. Stella. Closed Sun dinner off-season, Mon and 2 Jan-1 March. Open until 9.30 pm. Garden dining. Parking. V.

Summer is the best time to savour Gilbert Stella's cooking, served in a leafy garden: delicious baby courgettes whose flowers are stuffed with a lotte and basil mousse, succulent sirloin steak in red wine sauce with sautéed potatoes, and an airy strawberry feuillantine, itself worth more than this year's well-earned toque! Warm welcome, efficient service.
A la carte: 250-300 F. Menus: 120 F, 160 F.

SAINT-PÈRE-SOUS-VÉZELAY
See Vézelay

SAINT-PIERRE-D'OLÉRON
See Oléron (Ile d')

SAINT-PIERRE-LA-MER
See Narbonne

SAINT-QUENTIN
02100 Saint-Quentin — (Aisne)
Paris 155 - Amiens 73 - Lille 116 - Reims 96

Le Château
3 km SE on D 12
In Neuville-St-Amand — 23.68.41.82
M. Meiresonne. Closed Sun dinner, Sat, Feb school holidays, 5-25 Aug and 24-31 Dec. Open until 9 pm. 100. Hotel: 6 rms 310-370 F. Parking. V AE DC.

Much of the Château's success is due to its pretty setting. Jean-François Meiresonne's classic cooking is pleasant (young rabbit terrine with foie gras,

grilled salmon with fennel butter, beef with morel mushroms), but the prices leave a bad taste in the mouth.
A la carte: 350 F. Menus: 150 F and 260 F (weekdays only), 250 F and 300 F (w-e and holidays only).

Diamant
14, pl. de la Basilique — 23.64.19.19
Open every day. 7 stes 480 F. 43 rms 335-385 F. Restaurant. TV. V AE.

This spanking-new hotel with all the modern conveniences is opposite the basilica. Some suites with kitchenette are available. Good value.

Le Président
6-8, rue Dachery — 23.62.69.77
M. Roupioz. Closed Sun dinner, Mon, 29 July-26 Aug and 23 Dec-2 Jan. Open until 10 pm. Garage parking. V AE DC.

Chef Jean-Marc Le Guennec is a young Breton trained by Robuchon and Cussac who has recently taken over the kitchen of this elegant hotel-restaurant to make Le Président a must.
As simplicity often unmasks true talent, we chose to order the frequently changing 195 F menu, and we were delighted. It amply demonstrates Le Guennec's subtle skill: firm, flavourful lotte in a salad dressed with meat juices, wonderful roast pigeon and lightly spiced artichokes, and orange jelly with lemon-scented apple slices and blackberry sauce.
A la carte: 450 F. Menus: 195 F, 330 F.

Grand Hôtel
(See restaurant above)
Open every day. 24 rms 380-550 F. TV.

The Grand Hôtel's 24 newly remodelled, well-designed, and tastefully decorated rooms are set around a glassed-in patio with a panoramic lift. Excellent breakfasts.

SAINT-RAPHAËL
83700 Saint-Raphaël — (Var)
Paris 892 - Cannes 44 - Toulon 96 - Draguignan 33 - Aix 119

Golf-Hôtel de Valescure
Av. P.-Lhermite — 94.82.40.31
Closed 7 Jan-31 Jan and 15 Nov-20 Dec. 40 rms 460-720 F. Restaurant. Half-board 435-475 F oblig in seas. TV. Air cond. Pool. Tennis. Parking. V AE DC.

Comfortable, sunny rooms (some facing the golf course) are available here. Golf and tennis lessons.

L'Ile Bleue
Port Santa-Lucia — 94.82.22.26
M. Petit. Closed off-season Tue and 15 Dec-15 Feb. Open until 10 pm (11 pm in summer). Terrace dining. Air cond. V AE.

This pretty little restaurant looks towards the sea from the new marina. Everything is pleasantly blue, and the dining room is an island of comfort and charm, dotted with exotic plants.
A la carte: 300 F. Menus: 160 F, 250 F.

L'Orangerie
Prom. René-Coty
94.83.10.50
Mme Porro. Closed Sun dinner and Mon, lunch in July-Aug from Mon to Thu. Annual closings not available. Open until 10 pm (11 pm in summer). Terrace dining. V AE DC.

We love Thierry Bernard's finely balanced, lively and fresh cuisine: baked Atlantic fish with onion juices, prawn gratin and a sabayon sauce, rabbit stew with olives and polenta, and good desserts.
A la carte: 280-320 F. Menus: 160 F, 270 F.

Pastorel
54, rue de la Liberté – 94.95.02.36
M. Floccia. Closed Sun dinner, Mon and 15 Nov-15 Dec. Open until 9.30 pm. Terrace dining. V AE.

Take a terrace table if you can. There you'll enjoy even more Charles Floccia's marinated sardines with aubergine purée, young rabbit sautéed with capers and anchovies (too salty), and a good choice of desserts. A la carte prices are climbing but the set menus are a bargain. Flawless service.
A la carte: 350 F. Menus: 140 F, 195 F, 240 F.

La Potinière
5 km E on N 98
in Boulouris – 94.95.21.43
Open every day. 4 stes 480-708 F. 25 rms 320-580 F. Restaurant. Half-board 410-530 F oblig in seas. TV. Pool. Tennis. Parking. V AE DC.

The Potinière's well-equipped, modern rooms have terraces that give onto extensive grounds dotted with pines, mimosas, and eucalyptus trees.

San Pedro
Av. du Colonel-Brooke
94.40.57.40
M. Wateau. Open every day. Open until 9.45 pm. Garden dining. Air cond. Parking. V AE DC.

Opt for the flower-filled terrace shaded by umbrella pines, next to the golf course and swimming pool. Chef Philippe Troncy, a disciple of Michel Guérard, creates inventive, appealing dishes such as lobster ravioli, duck breast grilled with lavender, thinly sliced lamb with summer savory and puréed garlic, and minty bitter-chocolate millefeuille.
A la carte: 350 F. Menus: 160 F, 300 F.

San Pedro
(See restaurant above)
Closed Jan. 28 rms 550-690 F. TV. Air cond. Pool.

Near the Valescure golf course and tennis club, this imposing building is in questionable taste, but the garden and pine-wood setting are pleasant. Good, recently remodelled rooms.

And also...
Our selection of places for inexpensive, quick, or late-night meals.
La Bouillabaisse (94.95.03.57 - Pl. V.-Hugo. Open until 10 pm): As the name suggests, fish soup is the speciality. Also tasty house wines (220 F).
Le Sirocco (94.95.39.99 - 35, quai Albert-Ier. Open until 9.30 pm): A newly decorated brasserie on the old harbour, serving perfectly cooked fish dishes (250 F).
La Voile d'Or (94.95.17.04 - 1, bd du Gal-de-Gaulle. Open until 10 pm): A beach-front institution serving perennial favourites such as marinated anchovies, scallops with sea urchins, and bourride (fish soup), (250 F).

SAINT-RÉMY-DE-PROVENCE
13210 Saint-Rémy-de-Provence — (B./Rhône)
Paris 710 - Marseille 91 - Arles 24 - Avignon 21
Hôtel des Antiques
15, av. Pasteur
90.92.03.02
Closed 20 Oct-25 March. 27 rms 320-415 F. Pool. Parking. V AE DC.

In the heart of town, this romantic establishment sits in three hectares of grounds.

Château de Roussan
2 km on N 99, Rte de Tarascon – 90.92.11.63
Closed 15 Nov-20 Dec. 20 rms 210-750 F. Restaurant. Half-board 400-790 F. Valet parking. V AE.

This delightful eighteenth-century residence is surrounded by a huge park dotted with rare trees, flower beds and ponds.

Château des Alpilles
D 31 – 90.92.03.33
Closed 4 Jan-20 March and 12 Nov-20 Dec. 2 stes 1,100-1,300 F. 16 rms 670-890 F. TV. Air cond 2 rms. Pool. Tennis. Parking. V AE DC.

Serene and lovely, this early nineteenth-century château is surrounded by majestic trees. The rooms are huge and have been redecorated with impeccable taste. Enjoy a true change of scenery at one of the most refined hotels in Provence. Sauna. Poolside grill in summer.

Domaine de Valmouriane
5 km on N 99 and D 27
Petite route des Baux – 90.92.44.62
Mlle McHugo. Closed off-season Tue lunch and Mon, and 7 Jan-8 Feb. Open until 10 pm. Terrace dining. Parking. V AE.

Chef Jean-Claude Aubertin has just left the Domaine, opening his own restaurant in Villeneuve-lès-Avignon. We look forward to trying it, as well as the one Catherine McHugo plans to open here.
A la carte: 250-350 F. Menus: 220 F (weekdays only), 380 F.

Domaine de Valmouriane
(See restaurant above)
Closed 7 Jan-8 Feb. 12 rms 750-1,250 F. Half-board 795-1,025 F. TV. Air Cond. Heated pool. Tennis.

This luxurious little hotel has spacious rooms (some with sun rooms and terraces), equipped with all modern amenities and decorated with rare attention to detail. Tennis, archery, a putting green.

Vallon de Valrugues
Ch. de Canto Cigalo – 90.92.04.40
M. Gallon. Closed Feb. Open until 9.30 pm. Private room: 30. Garden dining. Air cond. No-smoking section. Valet parking. V AE DC.

We always enjoy Jacky Morlon's polished and updated Provençal cooking. Trained by Guérard and Lorain, Morlon is a thorough professional. Try his scorpion fish fillets and garlic mayonnaise, red mullet scented with basil, young pigeon with glazed onions, and a crispy millefeuille for dessert. We only wish Morlon would renew the menu once in a while. Superb wine cellar.
A la carte: 400-450 F. Menus: 190 F, 230 F, 290 F.

Vallon de Valrugues
(See restaurant above)
Closed Feb. 14 stes 980-1,120 F. 35 rms 680-780 F. Half-board 650-750 F oblig in seas. TV. Air cond. Heated pool. Tennis.

Quiet, well equipped, and graced with terraces overlooking the olive groves or Alpilles, the rooms here are rather small and soberly decorated. Good breakfasts. Faultless staff. Sauna, golf practice.

And also...
Our selection of places for inexpensive, quick, or late-night meals, and smaller hotels.
Le Café des Arts (90.92.08.50 - Hôtel des Arts, 30, bd V.-Hugo. Open until 9.30 pm): An intellectual's café hung with paintings.(150 F).
Le Castelet des Alpilles (90.92.07.21 - 6, pl. Mireille.

18 rms 210-410 F): Comfortable rooms, some with period furniture and all with attractive views. Family atmosphere, garden, terrace restaurant.

In nearby **Maillane**

(7 km NW on D 5)
13910 Saint-Rémy-de-Provence — (B./Rhône)

12/20 L'Oustalet Maïanen
90.95.74.60
Mme Garino. Closed Sun dinner, Mon and 1 Nov-1 March. Open until 9.45 pm. Terrace dining. V.
René Garino and his wife have been running this friendly roadside inn for a quarter of a century. Their sons Christian and Jean-Pierre are responsible for the original, flavourful cuisine.
A la carte: 220 F. Menus: 98 F (weekdays only), 125 F, 180 F.

SAINT-SAVIN
See Argelès-Gazost

SAINT-SERNIN-SUR-RANCE
12380 Saint-Sernin-sur-Rance — (Aveyron)
Paris 702 - Albi 50 - Saint-Affrique 32 - Lacaune 30

Carayon
Pl. du Fort — 65.99.60.26
M. Carayon. Closed off-season Sun dinner and Mon. Open until 9.30 pm. Private room: 60. Garden dining. Garage parking. Hotel: 2 stes 309-400 F, 40 rms 119-300 F, half-board 189-279 F. V AE DC.
Pierre and Claudette Carayon are warm-hearted and eager to please. And please they do, with such authentically regional dishes as crayfish and leek feuilleté, boudin with apples and onions, and chocolate and pear soufflé. Well-chosen wines. Cheerful décor, and a delightful setting in the south of the Aveyron.
A la carte: 200-270 F. Menus: from 62 F to 149 F, 250 F.

SAINT-SERVAN
See Saint-Malo

SAINT-SYLVAIN-D'ANJOU
See Angers

SAINT-SYMPHORIEN-LE-CHÂTEAU
28700 Saint-Symphorien-le-Château — (Eure-et-Loir)
Paris 69 - Rambouillet 23 - Chartres 26

Château d'Esclimont
37.31.15.15
M. Spitz. Open every day. Open until 9.30 pm. Parking. Telex 780560. V.
The Château d'Esclimont is a fief of luxury, with scintillating silverware, Cordovan leather wall-hangings, and handsome furnishings. The service, of course, purrs like the proverbial well-oiled machine. Sample the scallop carpaccio with fines herbes, truffled brandade, and saddle of hare cooked in Pomerol, served with crunchy cabbage. Divine desserts. Huge cellar with a wide range of well-chosen wines.
A la carte: 400-500 F. Menus: 290 F, 460 F.

Château d'Esclimont
(See restaurant above)
Open every day. 6 stes 1,570-2,400 F. 48 rms 545-1,350 F. Half-board 960-1,150 F. TV. Heated pool. Tennis.
Some 60 hectares of luxuriant landscape between the forest of Rambouillet and the Beauce

foothills. All the rooms and the six suites are supremely comfortable. And every imaginable distraction is available. Relais et Châteaux.

SAINT-TROPEZ
83990 Saint-Tropez — (Var)
Paris 890 - Cannes 75 - Toulon 69 - Sainte-Maxime 14

Les Arcades
Av. P.-Signac — 94.97.00.04
M. Virot. Closed mid-Oct to mid-March. Open until 11 pm. Garden dining. Air cond. Valet V AE DC.
This candlelit, luxury establishment linked to the Byblos hotel offers peace and comfort on its poolside terrace. Unfortunately, the Provençal-style dishes don't always live up to the descriptions on the *carte*.
A la carte: 350-500 F.

Byblos
(See restaurant above)
Closed mid-Oct to mid-March. 47 stes 1,880-3,900 F. 59 rms 950-2,190 F. TV. Air cond. Heated pool.
Each year, some of the Byblos' often cramped rooms and more spacious suites are redecorated. The layout is so skilful that customers are not bothered by the bustling attendance of St-Tropez's gilded set. Extremely luxurious appointments and a magnificent pool.

La Bastide des Salins
Rte des Salins — 94.97.24.57
Closed 13 Nov-20 March. 4 stes 1,100-1,500 F. 9 rms 800 F. TV. Pool. Parking. V.
This is one of the most pleasant hotels in town. A fortified farmhouse built during the last century, it has huge, stunningly handsome, well-kept rooms and superb grounds. Delicious poolside breakfasts.

The Beaches
See Ramatuelle

Les Bigorneaux
Pl. de la Garonne — 94.97.51.00
M. Chauvet. Closed Mon off-season. Open until 11.30 pm. Garden dining. V.
Gérard Chauvet went to work at the Bistrot des Lices and Baron before returning as to this delightful little bistro in a green garden, this time as the *patron*. His new style focuses on grilled meat and fish, as well as regional dishes like fricasséed squid, stuffed capon, and artichauts à la barigoule with (unnecessary) scallops.
A la carte: 300-400 F. Menus: 180 F (in winter only, wine inc), 240 F (in summer only).

12/20 Brasserie de la Renaissance
Pl. des Lices — 94.97.02.00
M. de Colmont. Open every day. Open until 11 pm. Terrace dining. V AE DC.
The owner of the Club 55 recently took over this brasserie, which had fallen on hard times. Suddenly the terrace and dining room are filled with customers eager to enjoy the good-value brasserie fare.
A la carte: 150-250 F.

Les Capucines
Domaine du Treizain — 94.97.70.05
Closed 30 Oct-15 March. 24 rms 380-880 F. TV. Air cond 8 rms. Heated pool. Parking. V AE DC.
This group of pretty Provençal buildings is two kilometres from town, lost among pine trees near the sea (100 metres away). Jacuzzi. Snack bar and modest meals.

Chabichou

Av. Foch – 94.54.80.00

M. Rochedy. Dinner only in July-Aug. Closed 15 Oct-15 April. Open until 10 pm. Garden dining. Air cond. Valet parking. V AE DC.

Talented chef Michel Rochedy will pay any price to get the best ingredients available. His rich repertoire embraces the lusty flavours and subtle nuances of Provençal cuisine. We enjoyed the rock lobster risotto with garlic butter, prawn and red-mullet tempura flavoured with saffron, artichoke barigoule and red-mullet fillets, baby rock lobster aïoli with vegetable tabbouleh, and duck with fresh figs. The desserts are equally exquisite and expensive: liquorice parfait, apricots baked with pistachios, and peach soup made with Beaumes-de-Venise sweet wine. The cellar includes the best wines of Provence, and the service and welcome are worthy of a great restaurant.

A la carte: 500-800 F. Menus: 185 F, 480 F.

Château de la Messardière

Rte de la Belle-Isnarde – 94.97.56.57

M. Marinacce. Closed 1 Nov-15 Feb. Open until 11 pm. Private room: 40. Terrace dining. Air cond. Valet parking. V AE DC.

Leroy is from Normandy, but he's plucked his inspiration from Provence. The short but sunny *carte* features updated classics such as anchovy tartlets, iced potato soup with summer truffles (everyone clamours for a second helping), local king prawns marinated with slivered garlic, a delicate crayfish risotto, braised fish from the bay with baby vegetables, spit-roast young pigeon, and tempting desserts, made by Leroy's younger brother (croustillant de chocolat au praliné and a superb tiramisù).

More than 50 kinds of Provençal wine—from a mere 90 F—are available.

A la carte: 350-450 F (at the Grill: 200-350 F). Menus: 190 F, 380 F (at the Grill: 150 F, 220 F).

Château de la Messardière

(See restaurant above)

Closed 1 Nov-15 Feb. 55 stes 2,500-18,000 F. 82 rms 950-2,800 F. TV. Air cond. Heated pool.

Sir Walter Scott might have set a novel in the crumbling nineteenth-century castle that was the Château de la Messardière until recently. But he wouldn't recognise the newly renovated version with its over-the-top decorations in questionable taste. But the setting is spectacular, offering views of two bays, huge gardens, and soothing countryside. The large, comfortable rooms and suites are decorated in a more restrained style with colonial touches. Two heated swimming pools, shuttle service to private beaches. Conference rooms.

Le Domaine de l'Astragale

Ch. de Gassine – 94.97.48.98

Closed 15 Nov-15 Feb. 34 rms 1,500-2,100 F. Restaurant. TV. Air cond. Heated pool. Tennis. Parking. V AE DC.

This new hotel is on the edge of St-Tropez. On either side of a swimming pool are 34 luxurious, quiet, and costly rooms, some with balconies. The style is an odd mix of Alpine chalet and Provençal (the developer is from Savoie). Excellent service.

Ermitage

Av. P.-Signac – 94.97.52.33

Open every day. 2 stes 880-920 F. 27 rms 400-920 F. Parking. V AE DC.

At the foot of the citadel and with a sweeping view of old St-Tropez, this big, white hotel with green shutters is surrounded by gardens. Attractive rooms, all with minibar.

12/20 Chez Fuchs

7, rue des Commerçants – 94.97.01.25

M. Fuchs. Closed Mon off-season, and beg Nov to mid-Dec. Open until 10.30 pm (11.30 pm in summer). Terrace dining. Air cond. V AE.

The cigar cellar gives this restaurant a chic atmosphere that attracts the locals. The food is generously served but not cheap: ravioli, beef stew, fresh fish, and generous cuts of meat.

A la carte: 250-300 F.

Les Lauriers

Rue du Temple – 94.97.04.88

Closed 11 Nov-30 Nov. 18 rms 350-700 F. TV. V AE

Near the Place des Lices, this small hotel has eighteen reasonably comfortable, quiet rooms with TV. Garden. Low rates (for St-Tropez).

Le Levant

Rte des Salins – 94.97.33.33

Closed 13 Oct-22 March. 26 rms 455-850 F. Restaurant. TV 7 rms. Air cond. Pool. Parking. V AE DC.

Scattered around the garden are a handful of small bungalows with charming, quiet, thoroughly remodelled rooms. Direct access to the sea.

La Maison Blanche

Pl. des Lices – 94.97.52.66

Open every day. 1 ste 1,200-1,500 F. 7 rms 790-1,500 F. TV. Air cond. Valet parking. V AE DC.

This turn-of-the-century residence in the centre of town is flanked by a tiny garden. Pleasant, posh décor and atmosphere, antique furniture. Very attentive service.

La Mandarine

Rte de Tahiti – 94.97.21.00

M. Jaggi. Closed 11 Nov-27 March. Open until 10.30 pm. Terrace dining. Parking. V AE DC

Chirping birds and a peaceful country setting are part of the attraction of this modern, Provençal hotel-restaurant just three minutes from central St-Tropez. Of an evening, the terrace fills with a quiet clientele who appreciate the refined, authentic cooking: fresh pasta, rascasse ravioli, grilled fish, and good sauces. Considerate service, stout but fair prices.

A la carte: 350-400 F. Menus: 230 F and 350 F (dinner only).

La Mandarine

(See restaurant above)

Closed 11 Nov-27 March. 4 stes 2,000-2,800 F. 38 rms 750-1,900 F. Half-board 490-980 F. TV. Air cond 13 rms. Heated pool.

This clump of neo-Provençal buildings painted pink houses about 40 sunny, modern rooms with fine terraces. Minibar. Private beach at nearby Pampelonne.

12/20 La Marine

22, quai J.-Jaurès – 94.97.04.07

M. Cassini. Closed 11 Nov-20 Dec. Open until 12.15 am. Terrace dining. Air cond. V AE DC.

Throughout the season, the sparkling white dining room of this restaurant on the harbour is packed. The tasty, simple dishes include tapenade, grilled fish, and bourride. Stiff prices.

A la carte: 350-400 F.

Le Mas de Chastelas
Quartier Bertaud, rte de Gassin — 94.56.09.11
*Closed Oct-Easter. 10 stes 1,750-1,950 F. 20 rms 900-
1,400 F. Restaurant. TV. Conference facilities.
Heated pool. Tennis. Parking. V AE DC.*

Those who remember the old Mas de Chastelas
will be surprised to discover some 30 new villas
scattered round the grounds of what used to be
St-Tropez's most charming hotel, the result of estate development. But the hotel and restaurant
carry on, and Patrick Cartier, manager and chef,
promises us that he will safeguard the spirit and
beauty of the place.

L'Olivier
Rte des Carles, 1 km — 94.97.58.16
*M. Neutelings. Closed off-season Tue lunch and Wed,
and 15 Nov-20 Dec. Open until 10.30 pm. Private
room: 30. Garden dining. Air cond. Valet parking.
Telex 461275. V AE DC.*

Just minutes away from the Place des Lices you
find yourself among verdant fields and vineyards,
in a lush garden with a swimming pool surrounded
by palm, olive, and fig trees. This is the realm of
Francis Cardaillac, a Gascon by birth, whose sunny
and flavourful cooking has won us over.
Menus: 200 F, 250 F, 300 F.

Bastide de Saint-Tropez
(See restaurant above)
*Open every day. 8 stes 2,100-3,000 F. 19 rms 1,000-
2,000 F. TV. Air cond. Conference facilities. Pool.*

The rooms—some rather cramped— are divided
among three charming buildings around the pool.
The décor is rather heavy-handed, but comfort is
guaranteed. For the trifling sum of 6,000 F a day
you can hire a speedboat, complete with skipper
and free Champagne.

11/20 La Ponche
Pl. du Révelin — 94.97.02.53
*Mme Barbier. Closed mid-Oct-Easter. Open until mid-
night. Private room: 30. Terrace dining. Air cond.
Valet parking. Telex 461516. V AE.*

A cosmopolitan clientele haunts La Ponche's terrace overlooking the old fishing port. Try the warm
lotte salad with shrimps and artichokes, lamb
tournedos with butter and mint sauce, duck breast
with thyme, and nougat glacé.
A la carte: 280-300 F. Menus: 110 F (lunch only),
180 F (dinner only).

La Ponche
(See restaurant above)
*Closed mid-Oct-Easter. 1 ste 1,300-1,600 F. 20 rms
650-1,100 F. TV. Air cond. Conference facilities.*
Charming, remodelled rooms with sea views.

La Ramade
Rue du Temple — 94.97.00.15
*M. Aurelly. Dinner only. Closed Wed (except July-
Aug) and Nov-Easter. Open until 10.30 pm. Garden
dining. V.*

You can't fool Pierrot Aurelly, a former fisherman, about the freshness of the day's catch. And
he loves to show you his fish—stuffed with herbs,
glistening with olive oil and sprinkled with pine-
nuts—before cooking them over vine-wood.
A la carte: 300-400 F.

Le Rascasson III
40, rue Portail-Neuf — 94.97.77.41
*M. de Montbarban. Open every day. Open until mid-
night. Terrace dining. V AE DC.*

No fancy presentation or complex sauces either:
just perfectly cooked bass, red mullet, sea bream,
and other Mediterranean delights with a dab of
local olive oil. Voilà. Exceptionally tasty.
A la carte: 250-350 F.

Résidence de la Pinède
Plage de la Bouillabaisse — 94.97.04.21
*M. Delion. Closed 25 Oct-20 March. Open until
10.30 pm. Terrace dining. Air cond. Valet parking.
Telex 470489. V AE DC.*

Reputedly, the Résidence de la Pinède is now the
most consistently popular and constantly booked
of the Relais et Châteaux group hotels. True or not,
its success is beyond question. Why? Manager Jean-
Claude Delion came down from the Alps to revive
this catatonic turn-of-the-century hotel-restaurant
and achieved the miracle in record time. He
certainly had his work cut out: a busy road passes
in front, and the Bouillabaisse beach—just below—
is no longer as chic as it was. With a wave of his
magic wand, Delion spruced up the Pinède, transforming it into a luxurious Italian-style villa. Meals
are served on a glorious terrace above the beach.
A dream setting, in short.
We loved the huge, firm prawns baked to perfection and flanked by a crisp vegetable salad, Swiss
chard cannelloni in tasty daube juices, courgette
risotto dressed with veal gravy, baked lobster in its
shell bathed in a vinegar sauce with walnut overtones, and young pigeon with green lentils
flavoured with crushed truffles and crispy bacon.
A la carte: 500-800 F. Menus: 450 F and 470 F
(dinner only), 250 F, 350 F.

Résidence de la Pinède
(See restaurant above)
*Closed 25 Oct-20 March. 6 stes 2,000-4,200 F. 36 rms
700-2,700 F. Half-board 950-1,850 F. TV. Air cond.
Conference facilities. Heated pool.*

A screen of greenery keeps road noise out, and
the Bay of St-Tropez spreads seductively below
(direct access to the beach). Umbrella pines shade
the huge, extremely comfortable rooms, all of
which have been recently remodelled and
redecorated. Kidney-shaped swimming pool.
Relais et Châteaux.

12/20 La Romana
Ch. des Conquettes — 94.97.15.50
*M. Siri. Closed end Sep-beg April. Open until
11.30 pm. Garden dining. Hotel: 12 rms 380 F. V AE.*

Brigitte Bardot and the *beau monde* no longer
haunt La Romana, but the food, served in a charming garden, is as generous and good as ever: many
kinds of fresh pasta of course, grilled fish, and
other Italian favourites. Smiling welcome and
service.
A la carte: 250-350 F.

Hôtel Sube Continental
at the harbor — 94.97.30.04
*Open every day. 29 rms 500-1,400 F. TV. Air cond
5 rms. Valet parking. V AE DC.*

The Sube Continental's restaurant has been
wound up and replaced by six new rooms offering
a spectacular view of the port and wharf. Regulars
are relieved that the bar, a St-Tropez institution, is
still in operation and open all winter.

La Tartane
Ch. des Salins — 94.97.21.23
*Closed 5 Nov-15 March. 12 rms 600-875 F. Restaur-
ant. TV. Air cond. Pool. Parking. Telex 461516. V.*

La Tartane's dozen handsome bungalows,
nestled in the greenery, form a sort of hamlet, with
superb, well-equipped rooms and comfortable terraces.

Lou Troupelen

Chemin des Vendanges
94.97.44.88

Closed 4 Nov-21 March. 44 rms 290-440 F. No pets. Parking. V DC.

These two hefty, neo-Provençal buildings are located between the shore and the town centre. The rooms are comfortable and pleasantly decorated, with attractive views. Breakfasts served in the garden.

Le Yaca

1, bd d'Aumale
94.97.11.79

Closed 15 Oct-20 Dec and 10 Jan-10 April. 1 ste 2,500 F. 23 rms 800-1,650 F. Restaurant. TV. Air cond. Heated pool. Valet parking. Telex 462140. V AE DC.

In the heart of St-Tropez, Le Yaca is a delightful little hotel with well-decorated rooms that overlook the inner garden. Fine bed linen. Welcome and service with a personal touch.

And also...

Our selection of places for inexpensive, quick, or late-night meals, and smaller hotels.

Bar à Vins (94.97.46.10 - 13, rue des Féniers. Open 1 am): Wine by the glass, and a convivial atmosphere in the *salle de billard*. The food served in the white-tiled dining room is tasty and popular with the locals: duck carpaccio, entrecôte steak with bone marrow, tarte Tatin (200 F).

La Barlière (94.97.41.24 - Rte du Pinet. 22 rms 480-550 F): This smart little farmhouse-style hotel is sited away from the summer crowds. Comfortable, tasteful rooms with fine bathrooms.

Bistrot des Lices (94.97.29.00 - 3, pl. des Lices. Open until 10.30 pm, in seas 12.30 am): Regulars come for the friendly atmosphere on the fashionable Place des Lices. Pleasant terrace, charming interior garden. We'll wait to rate the new chef (300 F).

Café des Arts (94.97.02.25 - Pl. des Lices. Dinner only in seas): If you don't mind the crush, you can enjoy filling dishes like rabbit with mustard sauce while the trendy types watch the world go by (175 F wine inc).

La Flo (94.54.85.85 - 5, rue des Féniers. Open until midnight): Go with the Flo if you're young, hip, and only mildly hungry—the atmosphere counts for more than the cuisine (170 F).

Le Girelier (94.97.03.87 - at the harbour. Open until 11.30 pm): Paying 160 F for the menu—crudités, breaded veal escalope, cheese or dessert—lets you sit under a parasol and admire the yachts of visiting millionaires (300 F).

Leï Mouscardins (94.97.01.53 - Rue Portalet. Open until 10.45 pm): Once the best restaurant in town, this venerable establishment serves perennial classics (Provençal omelette, bouillabaisse, fish grilled with fennel) to a touristy clientele. Superb terrace above the harbour (500 F).

See also: **Cogolin, Gassin, Grimaud, Port-Grimaud, Ramatuelle**

SAINTE-ADRESSE

See Havre (Le)

SAINTE-ANNE-D'AURAY

See Auray

SAINTE-ANNE-LA-PALUD

29127 Sainte-Anne-la-Palud — (Finistère)
Paris 569 - Quimper 25 - Châteaulin 19 - Douarnenez 16

La Plage

98.92.50.12

Mme Le Coz. Closed 12 Oct-29 March. Open until 8.45 pm. Private room: 50. No pets. Parking. Telex 941377. V AE DC.

Follow the gorse bushes past the last chapel, all the way down to where the land ends and the Atlantic crashes against the cliffs of Finistère. There you'll find the spirit and substance of Jean-Pierre Gloanec's authentic regional cooking, a marvellous marriage of *Armor* (sea, in Breton) and *Argoat* (land). The results are excellent, as in the spider crab and lamb's lettuce terrine delicately perfumed with orange oil, the John Dory casserole with oyster juice subtly underscored with a pinch of coriander, and the inventive desserts.

A la carte: 300-350 F. Menus: 250 F and 350 F (w-e and holidays only), 180 F.

La Plage

(See restaurant above)

Closed 12 Oct-29 March. 4 stes 950-1,150 F. 26 rms 400-800 F. Half-board 600-750 F oblig in seas. TV. Conference facilities. Heated pool. Tennis.

All the rooms of this Relais et Châteaux hotel are sunny and spacious. The delicious breakfasts include fresh fruit and wonderful pain au chocolat. Excellent service, charming welcome. Fine collection of paintings by Mathurin Méheust.

STE-GEMME-MORONVAL

See Dreux

SAINTE-MARINE

See Bénodet

SAINTE-MAXIME

83120 Sainte-Maxime — (Var)
Paris 880 - Toulon 63 - St-Raphaël 23 - Cannes 61 - Aix 122

Amiral

Le Port — 94.43.99.36

M. Guerre. Closed off-season Sun dinner and Mon, and 15 Nov-15 Dec. Open until 10 pm. Terrace dining. Air cond. V AE.

André Jacoulot, formerly the 'first mate' here, has donned Bernard Mathis' toque and is carrying on admirably as before. Try the delicious soup of rock fish and tiny crabs, large prawns with potatoes, snail ravioli in truffle stock, saddle of veal with polenta, and the many fresh, perfectly cooked fish dishes (lotte provençale with artichauts à la barigoule, and John Dory topped with creamed raw cress).

A la carte: 300-350 F. Menus: 165 F, 245 F.

Calidianus

Bd J.-Moulin — 94.96.23.21

Closed Jan. 33 rms 490-690 F. TV. Pool. Tennis. Parking. V.

Nestled in leafy grounds near the sea, the Calidianus is a group of small buildings in the local style. The rooms are spacious and well furnished, most with terraces giving onto the swimming pool. All have minibars. The reception and service are somewhat lacking. Lunches available in summer.

12/20 La Croisette
2, bd des Romarins
94.96.17.75
Mme Bluntzer. Dinner only. Closed Wed off-season, 1 Nov-15 Dec and 3 Jan-28 Feb. Open until 10 pm. Terrace dining. Parking. V DC.
The son of the house has taken over in the kitchen and is already producing some interesting dishes: succulent salmon tartare, a light fish mousse with a tasty crab sauce, remarkable baked turbot, and grilled pepper steak.
A la carte: 200 F. Menu: 98 F.

La Croisette
(See restaurant above)
Closed 1 Nov-15 Dec and 3 Jan-28 Feb. 20 rms 280-390 F. Half-board 325-360 F oblig in seas
This recently built hotel has a pretty garden and charming staff, but the rooms are poorly soundproofed and amenities vary.

La Gruppi
Av. du Gal-de-Gaulle – 94.96.03.61
Mme Lindemann. Closed Mon (except July-Aug and holidays), and 10-25 Oct. Open until 9.30 pm. Terrace dining. Air cond. V.
Skip the more complicated dishes and go straight for those made with fish from the morning's catch. They're delicious and cooked with care.
A la carte: 330-400 F. Menu: 159 F.

Hostellerie de Beauvallon
in Beauvallon – 94.43.81.11
Closed end Sep-Easter. 28 rms 500-700 F. Restaurant. TV. Pool. Tennis. Parking. V AE DC.
Laid out around a large swimming pool, the Beauvallon's buildings have modern, bright, spacious rooms. The beaches are just 200 metres away.

Hostellerie de la Belle Aurore
4, bd J.-Moulin – 94.96.02.45
M. Morandi. Closed Wed lunch and 15 Nov-15 March. Open until 10 pm. Terrace dining. Air cond. Parking. V AE DC.
After a few hiccups, the new, young team that took over and refurbished this sleepy old inn (with a wonderful view of the bay) has found its cruising speed. The chef's Provençal cooking plays on sharply defined, rich flavours. Try the anchovies stuffed à la provençale, scampi with shellfish juices, brandade, tasty Barjols tripe, sage-scented potato gnocchi, and crispy sea bream with herbs.
A la carte: 300-450 F. Menus: 210 F (weekdays only), 330 F.

Hostellerie de la Belle Aurore
(See restaurant above)
Closed 15 Nov-15 March. 2 stes 1,300-1,600 F. 17 rms 600-1,200 F. Half-board 750-1,250 F oblig in seas. TV. Pool.
Dawn's rosy fingers reach across the bay into the rooms of this thoroughly remodelled inn perched above the sea. Provençal-style furniture, handsome fabrics, cane chairs. Swimming pool with diving board.

Hôtel de la Poste
7, bd F.-Mistral – 94.96.18.33
Closed 25 Oct-25 March. 24 rms 330-550 F. Restaurant. Half-board 340-490 F oblig in seas. Pool. V AE DC.
Just 100 metres from the harbour, in the centre of town, this outstanding, newly built hotel is elegant and bright, with handsome rooms (some have connecting rooms, for families). Breakfast is served on the poolside terrace. Sun-room, garden.

12/20 Le Sarrazin
7, place Colbert
94.96.10.84
M. Quatrevaley. Closed Tue, 2 Jan-5 Feb. Dinner only July-Aug. Open until 10 pm. Terrace dining. V.
Classic, reliable cooking served in a fetchingly rustic setting: pink walls and a magnificent seventeenth-century sideboard as a centrepiece.
A la carte: 200-230 F. Menus: 110 F, 200 F.

In nearby La Nartelle
(3 km E on N 98)
83120 Sainte-Maxime – (Var)

Hostellerie de La Nartelle
N 98 – 94.96.58.00
M. Collignon. Closed off-season Sun and Mon. Open until 10 pm. Garden dining. Parking. V AE DC.
Garden furniture and bright colours give this new, Provençal-style inn a summery feel. Chef Etienne Colignon is not particularly innovative but he knows his craft and skilfully summons the flavours from his fine ingredients. Try the tasty fish soup with rouille sauce, warm foie gras cooked with spinach, and crème brûlée. Superb cellar with wines from all over France at prices for every pocket. Warm welcome.
A la carte: 350 F. Menu: 180 F.

Hostellerie de La Nartelle
(See restaurant above)
Open every day. 16 rms 400-500 F. Half-board 760-980 F. TV. Conference facilities. Pool.
The small but comfortable and functional rooms have loggias and face either the main coast road or the pool.

SAINTES
17100 Saintes – (Charente-M.)
Paris 465 - Bordeaux 118 - Royan 37 - Rochefort 42

Le Logis Santon
54, cours Genêt – 46.74.20.14
M. Sorillet. Closed Sun dinner, Mon, and 15-30 Sep. Open until 9.30 pm. Private room: 25. Terrace dining. Parking. V AE DC.
Creative chef Alain Sorillet has just hired a young assistant to bring more ideas into the kitchen. The ingredients in the oyster cressonnette with lobster cream sauce, John Dory cooked in Riesling, and caramelised pear feuillantine are already excellent. Charming service led by Mme Sorillet. Well-chosen wines.
A la carte: 300 F. Menus: 230 F (w-e and holidays lunch only), 120 F, 170 F.

Mancini
Rue A.-Lemoine
46.93.06.61
M. Baty. Closed off-season Sat lunch and Sun. Open until 9.30 pm. Private room: 60. Garage parking. Telex 791012. Hotel: 7 stes 270-380 F, 32 rms 130-360 F. V AE DC.
Third generation owner-chef François Baty prepares food to fit the comfortable setting of crystal chandeliers, Tudor-style windows, and moulded ceiling. Though skilful and reliable, Baty could be bolder. Sample his spiny lobster ballottine served with a light avocado mousseline, oyster and scallop blanquette, garlic-studded roast kid, and pear turnover with blackberry jelly. Respectable cellar. Smiling, efficient service.
A la carte: 300-350 F. Menus: 120 F, 220 F, 380 F.

Relais du Bois Saint-Georges
1.5 km W on D 137
Rue de Royan-Cours Genêt — 46.93.50.99
M. Emery. Open every day. Open until 9.30 pm. Private room: 80. Garden dining. No-smoking section. Valet parking. Telex 790488. V.

We think Gérard Vial's classic, unpretentious cooking deserves another point this year: foie gras terrines, prawns with a salad of lettuce and red cabbage, stuffed pig's trotter en crépine, and delicate pastries (tarte Tatin, petits fours). Superb cellar.

A la carte: 350 F. Menus: 150 F (weekdays only), 220 F (weekdays only, wine inc), 430 F (wine inc).

Relais du Bois Saint-Georges
(See restaurant above)
Open every day. 3 stes 900-1,400 F. 27 rms 290-900 F. Half-board 520-690 F. TV. Conference facilities. Heated pool. Tennis.

Tucked away in a seven-hectare park on the edge of Saintes, the Relais is scented by the sweet smell of century-old magnolia trees. The setting is peaceful, the hotel elegantly decorated, and the spacious rooms fetchingly finished with modern touches.

SAINTES-MARIES-DE-LA-MER (LES)
13460 Saintes-Maries-de-la-Mer (Les) — (B./Rhône)
Paris 777 - Marseille 129 - Nîmes 53 - Arles 38

12/20 Le Brûleur de Loups
Av. G.-Leroy — 90.97.83.31
M. Van Hoed. Closed Tue dinner and Wed (except Aug and Sep), and 11 Nov-15 March. Open until 9.30 pm. V AE DC.

Bracing sea air wafts across the beach-front terrace as holidaymakers feast on delicate, generously served fish dishes.

A la carte: 350-450 F. Menus: 175 F, 205 F.

L'Estelle
4 km on D 38 — 90.97.89.01
Closed 2 Jan-22 March and 12 Nov-20 Dec. 3 stes 640 F. 17 rms 600-640 F. TV. Conference facilities. Heated pool. Garage parking. V AE DC.

Set on the edge of the Camargue marshes on the site of an old farmhouse, this new hotel has smart, spacious rooms with pleasant décor, and terraces and private gardens where you can sunbathe in peace. There is a gym, and poolside snacks are available.

L'Etrier Camarguais
2 km N on N 570
Ch. bas des Launes — 90.97.81.14
Closed 15 Nov-1 April. 27 rms 630 F (per pers, half-board oblig). Restaurant. TV. Conference facilities. Pool. Tennis. Parking. Telex 403144. V AE DC.

A group of small houses in a verdant setting outside Saintes-Maries. The nicely furnished rooms are spacious and decorated in bold colours. All have fine terraces opening onto a garden. Horse riding.

Mas de la Fouque
Rte d'Aigues-Mortes, 4 km — 90.97.81.02
M. Cochat. Closed Tue (except holidays), 4 Jan-14 March and 15 Nov-1 Dec. Open until 9.30 pm. Private room: 15. Terrace dining. No-smoking section. Parking. Telex 403155. V AE DC.

Owner Jean-Paul Cochat has finally found a team to suit the tastes of his high-flying clientele (helicopters deliver some diners to the nearby beaches of the Petite Camargue). Chefs Nadine Tetrel and Christian Bourret, late of the two-toque

Abbaye de Pomier, turn out perfectly cooked dishes with light, refined sauces like the red mullet with perfumed oil, salmon fillet and a creamy prawn sauce, and some fine desserts. The atmosphere is one of relaxed luxury. The weakest link is the wine.

A la carte: 350 F. Menus: 220 F (dinner only), 245 F, 350 F.

Mas de la Fouque
(See restaurant above)
Closed 4 Jan-14 March and 15 Nov-1 Dec. 1 ste. 14 rms 1,500-1,890 F (per pers, half-board oblig). TV. Conference facilities. Heated pool. Tennis.

Enjoy your breakfast on a sheltered poolside patio or a terrace facing the Etang des Launes. The rooms have original, elegant décor and dream bathrooms. Smiling service and welcome. Golf practice, and shooting on the large estate.

Mas du Clarousset
7 km N on D 85A
Rte de Cacharel — 90.97.81.66
Mme Eyssette. Closed Tue and 16 Nov-15 Dec. Open until 10 pm. Private room: 10. Garden dining. Garage parking. V AE DC.

The rather costly charm of the Clarousset springs from a blend of gipsy guitar music and the simple yet satisfying cooking: eel pâté, leg of lamb and kid à la ficelle, meat and fish grilled over vine-cuttings. Not to mention Henriette Eyssette's enchanting welcome.

Menus: 220 F, 300 F.

Mas du Clarousset
(See restaurant above)
Closed 16 Nov-15 Dec. 15 rms 950-1,030 F (per pers, half-board oblig). TV. Conference facilities. Pool.

From the terraces of the huge, bright, recently redecorated rooms, the view over the Etang de Gines seems boundless.

SALON-DE-PROVENCE
13300 Salon-de-Provence — (B./Rhône)
Paris 730 - Marseille 55 - Avignon 46 - Arles 40 - Nîmes 71

L'Abbaye de Sainte-Croix
3 km NE on D 16
Rte du Val-de-Cuech — 90.56.24.55
Mlle Bossard. Closed Mon lunch and 31 Oct-28 Feb. Open until 9.30 pm. Private room: 150. Terrace dining. No pets. Parking. Telex 401247. V AE DC.

After a brilliant reign under the toques of former chef Yves Sauret, the Abbaye is on its way to becoming one of the finest restaurants in Provence. Former second-in-command Pascal Morel, who trained under Roger Vergé, Georges Blanc, and others, has taken over in the kitchen, and with the encouragement of owner Catherine Bossard his dishes are becoming lighter and more imaginative all the time. For example, we tasted an artichoke fondant accompanied by chopped tomatoes with basil and purslane, red-mullet fillets enhanced by an unusual pistachio-perfumed cream sauce, and young pigeon breasts with morels.

A la carte: 450-500 F. Menus: 220 F (wine inc), and from 185 F to 490 F.

L'Abbaye de Sainte-Croix
(See restaurant above)
Closed 31 Oct-28 Feb. 5 stes 1,040-1,630 F. 19 rms 490-920 F. Half-board 570-1,190 F oblig in seas. TV. 7 rms. Conference facilities. Pool. Tennis.

The modern additions to this twelfth-century abbey are remarkably faithful to the original. Relais et Châteaux.

11/20 Domaine Roquerousse
N 538 — 90.59.50.11

M. Maurel. Open every day. Open until 9 pm. Private room: 40. Terrace dining. No pets. Parking. Telex 403881. Hotel: 30 rms 220-350 F, half-board 255-310 F. V AE DC.

Meat, meat, and more meat—all of it tender and tasty—make this old *bastide* a carnivore's paradise. At weekends, tourists turn up to hunt on the 550-hectare estate, then retire here for a relaxed meal. Approximate service.

A la carte: 250-280 F. Menus: 68 F (weekdays only), 160 F (w-e and holidays only), 100 F, 130 F.

In nearby Cornillon-Confoux

(5 km S on D 19)
13250 Salon-de-Provence — (B./Rhône)

Le Devem de Mirapier
5 km N on D 19 on D 70
90.55.99.22

Closed off-season Sat and Sun, and 15 Dec-15 Jan. 16 rms 350-570 F. Restaurant. Half-board 460-500 F. TV. Air cond. Conference facilities. Pool. Tennis. Parking. V AE DC.

The surrounding *garrigue* and pine wood makes a lovely backdrop for this farmhouse-style hotel.

SANCERRE

18300 Sancerre — (Cher)
Paris 201 - Bourges 46 - Nevers 50 - La Charité 26

La Tour
31, pl. de la Halle — 48.54.00.81

M. Fournier. Closed Mon dinner and Tue (except July-Aug and holidays), 24 Dec-13 Jan and 4-15 March. Open until 10 pm. Private room: 16. Terrace dining. Air cond. V AE.

La Tour is an address to remember, with enjoyable, inventive cooking served at reasonable prices. The décor is deliciously rustic (timbers, pretty curtains, but hideous pictures), and the first-floor dining room has a wonderful view of the vineyards.

A la carte: 300-400 F. Menus: 98 F (weekdays only), 165 F, 220 F, 280 F.

SAN SEBASTIAN

See Hendaye

SANSSAT

See Lapalisse

SAPPEY-EN-CHARTREUSE (LE)

See Grenoble

SARI-DI-PORTO-VECCHIO

See CORSICA: Solenzara

SARREBOURG

57400 Sarrebourg — (Moselle)
Paris 378 - Epinal 84 - Sarreguemines 53 - Nancy 83

Restaurant Mathis
7, rue Gambetta — 87.03.21.67

M. Mathis. Closed Sun dinner, Mon and 1-24 Aug. Open until 9 pm. Private room: 12. Parking. V.

This excellent restaurant deserves more attention than it gets. The welcome is exemplary, the service always fleet of foot, and the salmon-pink décor sweetly seductive. Owner-chef Ernest Mathis is a true professional who tirelessly updates his classic cuisine.

A la carte: 350 F. Menus: 135 F (weekdays lunch only), 210 F, 275 F, 330 F.

Au Soleil
5, rue des Halles — 87.03.21.71

Closings not available. 6 stes 190 F. 10 rms 88-190 F. Restaurant. Half-board 185-220 F. TV. Air cond. Conference facilities. Parking. V AE.

Spotlessly clean, the Soleil has modest but pleasant little rooms.

SARREGUEMINES

57200 Sarreguemines — (Moselle)
Paris 383 - Saverne 61 - Sarrebruck 18 - Metz 69

Auberge Saint-Walfrid
2 km W on N 61, in Welferding
58, rue de Grosbliederstroff — 87.98.43.75

M. Schneider. Closed Sun, Mon, 1-15 Jan and 1-15 Aug. Open until 9 pm.Garden dining. Parking. V.

The décor is remarkably elegant and tasteful, and the summer terrace charming. Along with the flawless service and welcome, these are the St-Walfrid's strongest suits. For the cooking, though sincere, generous, and reliable, often lacks finesse.

A la carte: 350 F. Menus: 100 F, 168 F, 290 F.

Hôtel d'Alsace
10, rue Poincaré — 87.98.44.32

Closed Good Fri and 24 Dec. 2 stes 585 F. 26 rms 270-330 F. TV 20 rms. Restaurant. No pets.

Comfortable, convenient, discreet, and centrally located, the Alsace offers very simple, very clean, and very dull rooms. Minimal service.

SARTÈNE

See CORSICA

SASSETOT-LE-MAUCONDUIT

76540 Sassetot-le-Mauconduit — (Seine-Mar.)
Paris 210 - Rouen 64 - Fécamp 15 - Bolbec 28

Domaine du Château
(See restaurant above)
35.28.00.11

Closed Jan. 2 stes 750-800 F. 30 rms 335 F. Half-board 455-550 F. TV. Conference facilities. Parking. V.

Set in extensive grounds dotted with ancient trees, this handsome eighteenth-century château offers spacious rooms with period furniture.

SATILLIEU

See Annonay

SAULIEU

21210 Saulieu — (Côte-d'Or)
Paris 255 - Dijon 73 - Autun 41 - Avallon 39

La Côte d'Or
(Bernard Loiseau)
2, rue d'Argentine — 80.64.07.66

19.5   *M. Loiseau. Open every day. Open until 10 pm. Valet parking. Telex 350778. V AE DC.*

After spending a small fortune on improvements and additions to his old *auberge*, Bernard Loiseau is watching the customers pour in, giving the lie to critics who warned he would come a cropper if he continued with his ambitious programme.
In its earlier incarnation, La Côte d'Or was a decrepit little roadside establishment unworthy of Loiseau's talent. Seeing his star on the rise—or rather his toques accumulating—backers and bankers stepped in. La Côte d'Or's new kitchen and the dining room overlooking the garden should be ready by the time you read this. Then it will be time to refit the adjoining hotel.

In any case, we can't speak highly enough of Loiseau's resolutely original, bold, and featherlight cuisine. In a region where rich, greasy food is the rule, Loiseau keeps fat to an absolute minimum with water-based sauces, light fish stocks, and simple meat and vegetable juices. He continues to astound and delight us with dishes such as oyster and sea-urchin soup, frogs' leg jambonnettes with garlic purée, humble fillets of whiting ennobled by a lentil cream sauce and a nest of crispy fried onions, sea bass cooked in a sea-urchin emulsion, Morvan salmon with a potato croustillant, red mullet with olive compote, honeyed duck served on a bed of melting turnips, and steamed chicken with truffled basmati rice—the aromas turn every head when the dish is brought to table.

As you might expect, the cheeses are extraordinarily good, the desserts divine, and young sommelier Lionel's list crowded with Burgundies of all sorts. Hubert, the discreet maître d'hôtel, manages the service with rare diplomacy. All this excellence doesn't come cheap, of course. But what a wonderful way to spend money!

A la carte: 550-850 F. Menus: 350 F (weekdays lunch only), 680 F (dinner only).

La Côte d'Or
(See restaurant above)
Open every day. 8 stes 1,500-1,800 F. 23 rms 260-950 F. TV 18 rms. Conference facilities.

The garden is lovely at last. And the red décor suits the eight new suites that give onto the surrounding greenery. The other rooms are smaller and simpler, but all are pleasantly decorated and perfectly comfortable. Copious breakfasts. Relais et Châteaux.

La Poste
1, rue Grillot — 80.64.05.67
M. Virlouvet. Open every day. Open until 10 pm. Air cond. Valet parking. Telex 350540. V AE DC.

The proprietors of this former coaching inn have wisely conserved its traditional, rustic charm, while carefully updating the cooking: sole and turbot terrine in bouillabaisse jelly, sea bass in a potato crust, and pigeon in truffle juice. Fine but rather expensive wines bottled by the growers.
A la carte: 300 F. Menus: from 128 F to 298 F.

La Poste
(See restaurant above)
Open every day. 48 rms 160-395 F. Half-board 300-400 F. TV. Air cond. Conference facilities.

This former post house is the oldest hotel in Saulieu, dating from the seventeenth century. The décor is rather heavy, but the rooms are comfortable and well soundproofed.

See Clermont-Ferrand

49400 Saumur — (Maine/Loire)
Paris 300 - Angers 53 - Tours 65 - Nantes 127

Anne d'Anjou
32-33, quai Mayaud — 41.67.30.30
Closed 23 Dec-4 Jan. 3 stes 430-570 F. 50 rms 230-570 F. Restaurant. TV. Air cond. No pets. Conference facilities. Parking. V AE DC.

At the foot of the château and overlooking the Loire, this wonderful eighteenth-century hotel is in part an historic monument (the façade and grand staircase). Recently remodelled, the rooms are pleasant and well equipped. Restaurant: see Les Ménestrels, below.

Le Clos des Bénédictins
3 km NW on D 751
in St-Hilaire - St-Florent — 41.67.28.48
Closed off-season Sun and Mon, and 4 Jan-28 Feb. 1 ste 500 F. 23 rms 210-340 F. Restaurant. Half-board 300-360 F oblig in seas. TV. Conference facilities. Pool. Parking. V AE.

This quiet hotel looks down on the town and the Loire. The welcoming rooms are modern, well-equipped, spacious, and considerably more comfortable than in the past. Special tasting package, featuring 380 kinds of Loire wine.

Les Délices du Château
Les Feuquières — 41.67.65.60
M. Millon. Closed off-season Sun dinner and Mon, and 15 Dec-Jan. Open until 10.30 pm. Private room: 45. Garden dining. Parking. V AE DC.

Savour the lotte braised with radishes and green onions, calf's sweetbreads with Japanese shiitake mushrooms and baby broad beans, and caramelised pear feuillantine. Millon, the son of a local wine grower, has one of the best cellars around.
A la carte: 300-350 F. Menus: 120 F (weekdays lunch only), 160 F, 250 F, 300 F.

Les Ménestrels
11, rue Raspail — 41.67.71.10
M. Hosselet. Closed off-season Mon lunch and Sun, and 2-14 Jan. Open until 9.30 pm. Private room: 35. Terrace dining. V AE DC.

In record time, Catherine and Christophe Hosselet have made a huge success of their handsome restaurant with its pretty garden at the foot of the château. No surprise then that their repertoire has grown to embrace truffles and caviar, and that prices have rocketed accordingly.
A la carte: 350 F. Menus: 154 F (weekdays only), 200 F, 280 F.

12/20 La Serre
94, av. du Gal-de-Gaulle — 41.67.45.30
M. Leclerc. Open every day. Open until 10 pm. Private room: 20. Garage parking. Telex 723266. V AE.

Lit by the river's reflections, the salmon-pink dining room is discreetly modern. The cooking, while rather rich, is well executed: oyster gratin with avocado, sandre au beurre blanc et aux pleurotes, and duck breast croustillant cooked in a honey infusion.
A la carte: 250 F. Menus: from 90 F to 170 F.

Hôtel du Roi René
(See restaurant above)
Open every day. 38 rms 240-330 F. Half-board 270-290 F. TV. Conference facilities.

On the island near the centre of town, the Roi René's rooms are soundproofed and well equipped, with fine views of the river and castle.

(8 km NW)
49350 Saumur (Maine/Loire)

Le Prieuré
D 751 — 41.67.90.14
M. Traversac. Closed 6 Jan-2 March. Open until 9.30 pm. Terrace dining. Parking. V AE.

Take a table in the terrace-dining room and taste the asparagus feuilleté with watercress, baked turbot and artichokes, and sweetbreads with baby vegetables. The cheese board is particularly fine, and the long, varied wine list has many of the Loire's best bottles, often at affordable prices.
A la carte: 350 F. Menus: 200 F (weekdays lunch only), 280 F, 340 F, 400 F.

Le Prieuré
(See restaurant above)
Closed 6 Jan-2 March. 2 stes 1,000-1,700 F. 33 rms
500-1,500 F. Half-board 650-1,150 F. TV. Conference
facilities. Heated pool. Tennis.

This former priory has been remarkaby restored and modernised. The huge, opulent rooms—sometimes too 'opulent—overlook the Loire. Simpler bungalow accommodation is available in the grounds. Delicious breakfasts. Relais et Châteaux.

SAUZE
See Barcelonnette

SCEAUX
See PARIS Suburbs

SCHIRMECK
67130 Schirmeck — (Bas-Rhin)
Paris 405 - Strasbourg 49 - St-Dié 39 - Molsheim 25

In nearby Natzwiller
(11 km SE on N 420, D130 and D 530)
67130 Schirmeck — (Bas-Rhin)

Auberge Metzger
88.97.02.42
M. Metzger. Closed Sun dinner, off-season, Mon, 2-22 Jan and 24-30 June. Open until 9 pm.Terrace dining. Hotel: 10 rms 180-185 F. Garage parking. V DC.

The quintessential country inn, with attractive décor and smiling, relaxed service.

A la carte: 180-200 F. Menus: 50 F (weekdays only), 87 F, 120 F, 150 F.

SCIEZ
See Thonon-les-Bains

SECLIN
See Lille

SEDAN
08200 Sedan — (Ardennes)
Paris 237 - Metz 139 - Reims 96

In nearby Bazeilles
(4 km SW on N 43 and D 764)
08140 Sedan — (Ardennes)

Château de Bazeilles
24.27.09.68
Open every day. 20 rms 280-310 F. Restaurant. V.

Far from noisy roads, the Bazeilles is a luxurious hotel set on the edge of a large estate with ancient trees.

SÉGOS
See Aire-sur-l'Adour

SÉGURET
See Vaison-la-Romaine

SENLIS
60300 Senlis — (Oise)
Paris 50 - Chantilly 15 - Soissons 60 - Lille 172

Les Gourmandins
3, pl. de la Halle — 44.60.94.01
M. Knecht. Closed Mon dinner and Tue (except holidays), and 5-25 Aug. Open until 10 pm. V.

The old marketplace setting is striking, the décor rather dull, but the real attraction is Sylvain

Knecht's mouthwatering cooking and tempting set menus. We enjoyed the oxtail compote cooked in Chinon wine, salad of tiny scallops, fricasséed fish flavoured with saffron (Knecht is a fish specialist), and roast duck breast cooked on the bone.

Menus: 100 F (weekdays only), 190 F, 290 F.

In nearby Fleurines
(6.5 km N on N 17)
60700 Senlis — (Oise)

Le Vieux Logis
105, rue de Paris — 44.54.10.13
Mme Nivet. Closed Sun dinner and Mon. Open until 9.30 pm. Hotel: 2 rms 250 F. Parking. V AE DC.

Yann Nivet's cooking is of a classic cast and ignores regional produce, including the fine game. His bolder creations include avocado mousse with baked prawns, sweetbread fritters in Muscat, and veal kidney with star anise. There's nothing reticent about the prices. Very fine cellar.

A la carte: 400-500 F. Menu: 350 F.

SÉREILHAC
See Limoges

SERRE-CHEVALIER
05240 Serre-Chevalier — (H.-Alpes)
Paris 674 - Grenoble 110 - Col du Lautaret 22

In nearby Chantemerle
05330 Serre-Chevalier — (H.-Alpes)

Hôtel Plein Sud
92.24.17.01
Closed 21 April-15 June and 15 Sep-14 Dec. 1 ste 550-730 F. 40 rms 250-410 F. TV 20 rms. No pets. Heated pool. Garage parking. V

It offers bright, spacious rooms with small terraces overlooking the ski slopes. Jacuzzi, gym, heated indoor pool.

In nearby Monêtier-les-Bains
05220 Serre-Chevalier — (H.-Alpes)

Auberge du Choucas
17, rue de la Fruitière — 92.24.42.73
M. d'Arsine. Closed 20 April-15 June and 30 Sep-20 Dec. Open until 9 pm. Garden dining. V.

This is a handsome, family-run hotel and restaurant. Yves Gattechaut's generous cooking is somewhat out of the ordinary: fresh foie gras cooked with apples in cider, poached salmon and sweetbreads with cucumber and ginger, and fish barely cooked in thyme oil. On the expensive side.

A la carte: 400 F. Menus: 145 F (weekdays lunch only), 210 F, 290 F.

Auberge du Choucas
(See restaurant above)
Closed 15 Nov-20 Dec. 4 stes 850-980 F. 8 rms 480-530 F. Half-board 410-470 F oblig in seas. TV.

The new décor makes heavy use of wood. The rooms are comfortable, with pleasant sun terraces and large bathrooms. Family atmosphere. The breakfasts are perfect.

SERRIÈRA
See CORSICA: Porto

34200 Sète — (Hérault)
Paris 790 - Béziers 53 - Montpellier 35 - Lodève 72

12/20 Le Chalut
38, quai de la Marine — 67.74.81.52
M. Coulon. Closed Wed and mid-Dec-beg Feb. Open until 10 pm. Air cond. No pets.
The sublimely hideous amusement-park décor is rather more amusing than the proprietor's witticisms or the ploddingly honest seafood cooking. Moderate prices.
À la carte: 200-280 F. Menus: 80 F, 120 F.

Le Grand Hôtel
17, quai de Lattre-de-Tassigny — 67.74.71.77
Closed 20 Dec-5 Jan. 1 ste 950-1,150 F. 51 rms 189-550 F. TV 44 rms. Air cond 22 rms. V AE DC.
This turn-of-the-century hotel has a breathtaking view of Sète and the Mt St-Clair. Very comfortable rooms, with elegant décor and outstanding amenities, at reasonable rates.

La Palangrotte
1, rampe P.-Valéry — 67.74.80.35
M. Gémignani. Closed Sun dinner, Mon, Jan and 1 week in Nov. Open until 10 pm. Terrace dining. V.
Alain Gémignani prepares subtly modernised Languedoc dishes: seafood spaghettini with rock lobster juice, red-mullet and squid stew with young leeks, and firm-fleshed turbot with mild, melting onions. Some of the set menus offer outstanding value.
À la carte: 300-350 F. Menus: 120 F (weekdays only), 170 F, 250 F, 280 F.

12/20 La Rascasse 🙂
27, quai du Gal-Durand — 67.74.38.46
Mme Britto. Closed Tue and 3 Jan-3 Feb. Open until 10.30 pm. Terrace dining. Air cond. V DC.
All the local favourites are to be found here: thon à la sétoise, fish soup with lotte, turbot en eau de sel, and a seafood assortment featuring stuffed mussels and two kinds of squid with rouille (spicy garlic mayonnaise). Fine regional wines like Faugères and Picpoul.
À la carte: 250-300 F. Menus: 68 F, 96 F, 165 F.

Les Saveurs Singulières
5, quai Lemaresquier — 67.74.14.41
Mlle Sabatino. Closings not available. Open until 9.30 pm. Air cond. V AE DC.
Valérie Sabatino's restaurant has all the ingredients for success: a charming proprietor, bright décor, and fine food oozing originality. So it's no wonder the locals turn out in force to do justice to the scallop tempura with basil and fresh tomatoes, foie gras en papillote with tart citrus fruits, fine fish stew, tian of veal fillet with Muscat, and caramelised fruit kebabs with a cinnamon-scented mango coulis.
À la carte: 280-330 F. Menus: 125 F (weekdays lunch only), 175 F, 290 F.

Les Terrasses du Lido
Le Corniche
Rd-pt de l'Europe — 67.51.39.60
Closed 28 Jan-28 Feb. 1 ste 600 F. 8 rms 300-400 F. Half-board 300-400 F. Restaurant. TV. Air cond. Conference facilities. Pool.
Extremely comfortable, pleasant and perfectly equipped rooms by the sea.

See PARIS Suburbs

51120 Sézanne — (Marne)
Paris 110 - Meaux 75 - Troyes 60 - Châlons-sur-Marne 57

12/20 La Croix d'Or
53, rue Notre-Dame — 26.80.61.10
M. Dufour. Closed Mon and 2-17 Jan. Open until 9.30 pm. Hotel: 13 rms 100-240 F. V AE DC.
This typically provincial hotel-restaurant offers classic, high-quality cooking at very attractive prices. We've awarded an extra point this year for the warm foie gras tart, and the sweetbreads with cockles accompanied by a cauliflower salad.
À la carte: 230 F. Menus: 55 F (weekdays only), 85 F, 135 F, 285 F.

Hôtel de France
25, rue L.-Jolly — 26.81.41.48
Closed Sun off-season. 25 rms 220-320 F. Restaurant. Half-board 250 F. TV. Garage parking. V AE DC.
In the centre of town, this hotel provides pleasant rooms with period furniture.

24170 Siorac-en-Périgord — (Dordogne)
Paris 533 - Bergerac 45 - Sarlat 29 - Périgueux 57

In nearby au Buisson-de-Cadouin
(7 km NW on D 25)
24480 Siorac-en-Périgord — (Dordogne)

Manoir de Bellerive 🍴🌳
53.27.16.19
Closed 1 Nov-15 April. 16 rms 270-550 F. TV. Pool. Tennis. Parking. V.
Surrounded by lovely grounds on the banks of the Dordogne, this handsome little Napoleon III château boasts fine period furniture and pretty fabrics. Windows open onto the park or the river. Satisfying breakfasts served on a glorious terrace overlooking the Dordogne Valley.

See Nantes

See CORSICA

See Grasse

See Mulhouse

67000 Strasbourg — (Bas-Rhin)
Paris 488 - Colmar 69 - Bâle 137 - Lyon 489

12/20 L'Alsace à Table
8, rue des Francs-Bourgeois — 88.32.50.62
M. Baumann. Open every day. Open until 12.30 am. Private room: 100. Air cond. V AE DC. D4-4
Parisian restaurateur Monsieur Baumann has opened another temple to choucroute, with a décor of etched glass, cascades of indoor plants, and mahogany panelling. The result is immense, amusing, and rather good. Alongside the classic cabbage repertoire you'll find magnificent shellfish, and many tartares. Excellent choice of regional wines, and attentive service.
À la carte: 250-300 F. Menus: 100 F (lunch only), 143 F.

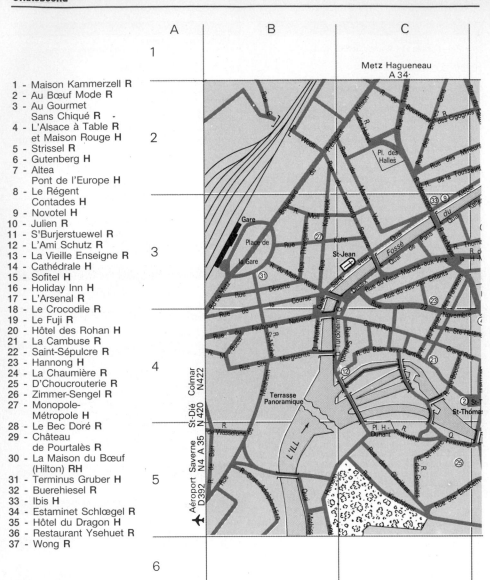

Altea Pont de l'Europe
Parc du Rhin — 88.61.03.23
Open every day. 5 stes 585-605 F. 88 rms 390-425 F.
Restaurant. TV. Conference facilities. Parking.
Telex 870833. V AE DC. G5-7
  This imposing group of modern, rather charm-
less buildings, is surrounded by a large estate on
the banks of the Rhine. The functional rooms are
well equipped. Good reception.

12/20 L'Arsenal
11, rue de l'Abreuvoir — 88.35.03.69
M. Bader. Closed Sat lunch, Sun and 22 July-18 Aug.
Open until 11 pm. V AE DC. F5-17
  The new chef has broken away from the strictly
regional house repertoire, adding elaborately

named (and often less elaborately flavourful) dishes such as duck rillettes with rhubarb sorbet,
quail egg croustillant with fennel, prawns and
sweetbreads with bone marrow and capers. Euro
MPs are among the regulars. Warm welcome,
reasonable prices.
  A la carte: 250-300 F. Menus: 120 F (lunch only),
165 F.

12/20 Le Bec Doré
8, quai des Pêcheurs — 88.35.39.57
M. Maria. Closings not available. Open until 10 pm.
Air cond. V AE DC. F4-28
  This little blue jewel box of a restaurant is bright
as a button. The house speciality is poultry: boned
rooster cooked in Chambertin wine lees, and

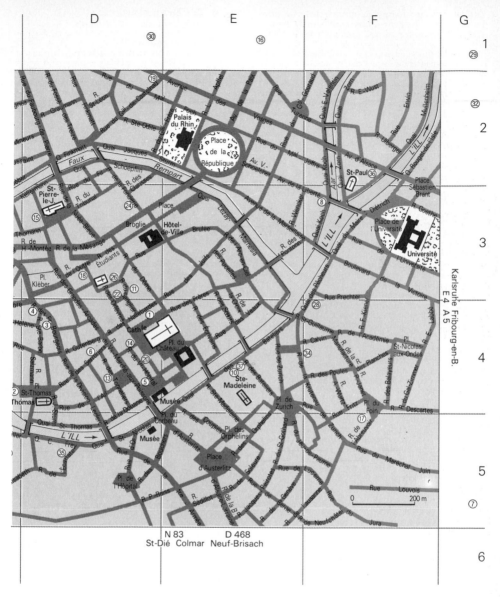

mixed grilled poultry. Generous fish dishes are also available. Charming, enthusiastic owner. The lunch menu is good and served rapidly.

A la carte: 280 F. Menus: (weekdays lunch only, wine inc), 130 F, 250 F.

12/20 Au Bœuf Mode
2, pl. St-Thomas – 88.32.39.03
M. Letzter. Closed Sun. Annual closings not available. Open until 11 pm. Private room: 20. Terrace dining. V AE DC. C4-2

To make room for more customers, this popular establishment has added a bistro annexe with a pretty terrace (serving typical Alsace food). The main dining room continues to cater for carnivores, specialising in outstanding beef from

Aberdeen: beef fillet carpaccio, prime rib, and Kobe-style fillet.

A la carte: 300 F. Menus: 140 F (weekdays only), 190 F.

Buerehiesel
4, parc de l'Orangerie – 88.61.62.24
M. Westermann. Closed Tue (except lunch in seas), Wed, 23 Dec-3 Jan, beg March and 8-22 Aug. Open until 9.30 pm. Private room: 50. Terrace dining. Air cond. Parking. V AE DC. G2-32

Proprietor-chef Antoine Westermann has successfully grafted a winter garden onto his farmhouse, which stands proudly among the hedges and flowers of a fabulous landscaped garden. Three centuries have mellowed this wooden wonder, so we are happy to report that the new conservatory's décor—glass and natural wood, shades of salmon pink and green plants—holds its own.

We must confess, however, to an abiding affection for the snug little dining rooms, where technocrats and Euro MPs draw up blueprints for the future over foie gras and venison. Here intimacy reigns. For even when it is bursting at the seams, the Buerehiesel remains peaceful and civilised, no doubt due to Westermann's gentle, sensitive touch.

Nowhere is this more apparent than in the cuisine. With masterly skill, Westermann breathes new life into classic dishes. His own creations never fall into the trap of frivolous fashion: well-balanced flavours always come through. We were enchanted most recently by the foie gras sautéed with poppy seeds, rocket salad and wine vinegar, eel galette with potatoes and white cabbage, perfectly prepared perch accompanied by celeriac in a Pinot Noir sauce, Barbary duck breast stuffed with foie gras and vegetables, and freshwater fish ravioli in a Riesling wine stew. And let's not forget the nutty-flavoured Munster cheese and desserts like kouglof (raisin brioche) with cherries and spicy Kirsch ice cream, or the best vanilla ice-cream in the world.

The remarkable cellar has some of the very best Alsace wines (including a fine selection of magnums and half-bottles). Relais et Châteaux.

A la carte: 500-700 F. Menus: 260 F (weekdays lunch only), 290 F (dinner only), 470 F.

12/20 S'Burjerstuewel ۞

(Chez Yvonne)
10, rue du Sanglier — 88.32.84.15
Mme Haller. Closed Mon lunch, Sun, 14 July-12 Aug and 23 Dec-2 Jan. Open until 0.30 am. Private room: 15. V.   D3-11

This is the most popular winstube in Strasbourg. Despite the crowds, the authentic cuisine and smiling service are excellent. Sample the famous saümawe (stuffed pig's stomach), sauerkraut salad with duck breast, the cheesecake, and Alsace wines by the carafe. Delightful, picturesque décor.

A la carte: 140-180 F.

🍴14 La Cambuse

1, rue des Dentelles — 88.22.10.22
M. Lefebvre. Closed Sun and Mon. Annual closings not available. Open until 10 pm. V.   C4-21

Shellfish and fish, full stop. But that's perfectly adequate in the capable hands of chef Elisabeth Lefebvre. Her varied repertoire is rivalled only by that of La Table Gourmande at nearby Fegersheim. Marvellous fish soup, crab ravioli, raw fish with herbs, sea bass fillet with coconut served on a banana leaf, and turbot with spinach and sesame, have earned another point this year. Sumptuous selection of white wines (Alsace, Graves). Simple, charming décor.

A la carte: 280-300 F.

🏠 Cathédrale

12, pl. de la Cathédrale — 88.22.12.12
Open every day. 3 stes 600-700 F. 32 rms 340-650 F. TV. No pets. Conference facilities. Telex 871054. V AE DC.   D4-14

Superbly situated opposite the cathedral (the booming bells wake you up on Sundays) this comfortable hotel's soberly decorated, well-equipped rooms have fine views. The breakfasts are average. Fitness club.

12/20 D'Choucrouterie

20, rue St-Louis — 88.36.52.87
M. Siffer. Dinner only. Open until 1 am. Private room: 70. Terrace dining. V.   C5-25

This converted choucroute factory continues to serve the Strasbourg speciality prepared with salmon, smoked beef and garlic sausages. Also on offer: sürbrode (beef marinated in vinegar and herbs). Actors, musicians and theatre-goers enjoy the convivial atmosphere, lubricated with tasty, low-priced Alsace wines. Bohemian décor (musical instruments, caricatures, and original paintings).

A la carte: 150-200 F. Menus: from 110 F to 180 F.

🍴18 Le Crocodile ۞

10, rue de l'Outre — 88.32.13.02
M. Jung. Closed Sun, Mon, 7 July-5 Aug and 22 Dec-1 Jan. Open until 10 pm. Private room: 40. Air cond. V AE DC.   D3-18

During the many years we've frequented Le Crocodile we haven't always been swept off our feet by Emile Jung's cuisine. Yes, it's never been anything but excellent, made from the best ingredients and skilfully prepared, but sometimes the magic has been missing. Our latest meal was totally enchanting.

True, the mixed salad with truffles, sweetbreads and foie gras dressed with hazelnut oil would have been better served warm. But from there on our enthusiasm was boundless. Jung's uncontested masterpiece was a feuilleté of scallops in sweet pepper purée, followed by a simple dish of veal whose juices enriched a potato pancake. For dessert, wonderful wild rose and prune-flavoured waffles topped with spiced cream. Sommelier Gilbert Mestrallet outdid himself, selecting for us a 1988 Viognier from the Château Saint-Estève, and other rare delights from the magnificent cellar.

But don't let these magnificent memories stop you from exploring the rest of the *carte*, which features four new dishes each day. There's something for all tastes: foie gras, jugged hare with horseradish, crayfish in tarragon jelly, and roast goose with sauerkraut for traditionalists, and turbot and vermicelli with oysters, pigeon and sweetbreads with green cabbage, or duck consommé with beetroot for the more adventurous. Monique Jung and Bernard Epp welcome the anonymous visitor with the same exquisite courtesy as Eurocrats and local dignitaries. Relais et Châteaux.

A la carte: 500-700 F. Menus: 250 F (weekdays lunch only), 350 F (dinner only).

🏠 Hôtel du Dragon

2, rue de l'Ecarlate — 88.35.79.80
Open every day. 32 rms 380-500 F. TV. No pets. Conference facilities. Telex 871102. V AE DC.   D5-35

In 1987 this hotel was created within the walls of a seventeenth-century town house in a quiet cul-de-sac in the historic centre. The rooms are very neat and comfortable, with resolutely modern décor in shades of grey. Friendly service by a refined, multilingual staff.

🍴13 Estaminet Schlœgel

19, rue de la Krutenau — 88.36.21.98
M. Deprez. Closed Sun, Mon, 16-31 July and 22 Dec-7 Jan. Open until 10 pm. Private room: 30. Air cond. V.   F4-34

This warm and welcoming restaurant has a pleasantly relaxed atmosphere. Gérard Deprez's cooking, though not overly imaginative, is professionally prepared and copiously served. Drawing inspiration from regional recipes, he lightens and personalises such dishes as sweetbreads cooked in shellfish stock, lamb fillet with a poppy seed crust, and ravioli filled with chanterelles and snails. Simple wines at reasonable prices.

A la carte: 300 F. Menus: 140 F (weekdays lunch only), 190 F, 220 F, 250 F.

Au Gourmet Sans Chiqué
15, rue Ste-Barbe – 88.32.04.07
M. Klein. Closed Mon lunch, Sun, 17 March-29 April and 11-29 Aug. Open until 10 pm. Air cond. No pets. V DC. D4-3

The prices are climbing gradually, but Daniel Klein's cooking hasn't budged. This is his policy of course: to produce reliable, no-nonsense meals. Discreet, professional staff will serve you frogs' legs in a parsley cream sauce, fillet of sole baked with spices, and marquise of coffee and bitter chocolate. Superb Alsace wines at painful prices.

A la carte: 300 F and up. Menus: 180 F, 240 F, 300 F.

Hannong
15, rue 22-Novembre – 88.32.16.22
Closed 23-30 Dec. 70 rms 310-460 F. Restaurant. TV. Conference facilities. Parking. Telex 890551. V AE DC. C3-23

Just minutes from the heart of the old town, this fine classic hotel bears the name of the famous eighteenth-century Hannong earthenware with which it is decorated. Half the rooms have been thoroughly restored. There are top facilities for small conferences. Wine bar.

Holiday Inn
20, pl. de Bordeaux – 88.37.80.00
Open every day. 1 ste 1,300-1,410 F. 170 rms 665-855 F. Restaurant. TV. Air cond. Conference facilities. Heated pool. Parking. V AE DC. E1-16

This modern, functional hotel features a solarium, sauna, Turkish bath, and gym. Other facilities include a discotheque, bank, and travel agency.

Julien
22, quai des Bateliers – 88.36.01.54
M. Schaller. Closed Sat lunch, Sun, Feb school holidays and 3 first weeks of Aug. Open until 10 pm. Private room: 20. Air cond. V AE DC. E4-10

The choice of dishes is bewildering and the prices daunting. But this cosy little restaurant, just right for business lunches and romantic dinners, treats its customers so well that it is always busy. The cooking sometimes sacrifices good, simple tastes on the altar of elegance. Try the salmon millefeuille with caviar, crêpe stuffed with lobster in a coral sauce, and Numidie hen stuffed with foie gras.

A la carte: 350 F. Menus: 145 F (lunch only), and from 180 F to 250 F.

La Maison du Bœuf
Av. Herrenschmidt – 88.37.10.10
M. Zimmermann. Closed Sat, Sun, 26 Jan-10 Feb and 13 July-25 Aug. Open until 10.15 pm. Private room: 300. Terrace dining Air cond. No pets. Parking. Telex 890363. V AE DC. D1-30

A favourite haunt of business people and politicians in search of a quiet corner. The restaurant has two strong points: the prices are now more reasonable and the cooking has been kept simple. Dishes include American rib steak baked with coarse salt, lamb tournedos cooked in garlicky juices, and poached hen with a creamy sauce.

A la carte: 300-350 F. Menus: 270 F (dinner only), 170 F.

Hilton
(See restaurant above)
Open every day. 5 stes 1,900-4,750 F. 241 rms 720-950 F. TV. Air cond. Conference facilities.

Set in leafy greenery off a busy avenue, the Hilton offers functional, well-soundproofed, large and perfectly furnished (though charmless) rooms. Some have a fine view of the town and cathedral, and all have individual air conditioning. Excellent welcome. Sauna, solarium, piano bar, shops, and round-the-clock room service.

Maison Kammerzell
16, pl. de la Cathédrale – 88.32.42.14
M. Baumann. Open every day. Open until 1 am. Private room: 150. Terrace dining. Air cond. Hotel: 9 rms 420-630 F. Telex 891012. V AE DC. D4-1

This culinary institution is a must for tourists, but also attracts the local citizenry, thanks to its warm brasserie-style atmosphere. Nestling at the foot of the cathedral, this fairytale medieval building features frescoes, wood panelling, stained-glass windows and polished furniture. Guy-Pierre Baumann regales customers with his famous fish choucroute, hearty Alsace specialities and other, more inventive dishes such as sea bream baked with red pepper purée. Try the local wines or Shutzenberger beer.

A la carte: 300 F. Menus: 180 F, 250 F.

Maison Rouge
4, rue des Francs-Bourgeois – 88.32.08.60
Open every day. 2 stes 800-950 F. 140 rms 350-510 F. TV. Conference facilities. Telex 880130. V AE DC. D4-4

The Place Kléber is just down the road from this hotel, built between the wars and recently renovated. The modern décor is mellowed by period furniture and stained-glass windows, luxurious fabrics, handsome paintings, splendid marble bathrooms, and comfortable lounges. Buffet breakfasts.

Monopole-Métropole
16, rue Kuhn – 88.32.11.94
Closed 21 Dec-6 Jan. 94 rms 330-535 F. TV. Conference facilities. Valet parking. V AE DC. B3-27

Situated near the Petite France district, this fine traditional hotel has both rustic and modern rooms (minibar, twelve television channels).

Novotel
Quai Kléber – 88.22.10.99
Open every day. 97 rms 480-540 F. Restaurant. TV. Air cond. Conference facilities. Telex 880700. V AE DC. C3-9

Perched above a large shopping centre within walking distance of the Place Kléber, this is a modern hotel with functional, recently refurbished rooms. Bar open 6 am to midnight.

Le Régent Contades
8, av. de la Liberté – 88.36.26.26
Closed 23 Dec-22 Jan. 16 stes 1,300-1,800 F. 45 rms 600-1,800 F. TV. Air cond. Conference facilities. Valet parking. Telex 890641. V AE DC. F3 8

Reigning princes (in the guise of Euro MPs) like to stay at this imposing, handsome hotel built during the Prussian era and set on the green banks of the Ill. The reception is exceptionally friendly. The rooms are huge, and soberly but tastefully decorated in a restrained modern manner that blends in well with the Bismarck-style mouldings. Fourteen suites and a meeting room have just been added. Round-the-clock room service. Bar, sauna, solarium.

Hôtel des Rohan
17-19, rue du Maroquin — 88.32.85.11
Open every day. 36 rms 280-570 F. TV. Air cond 12 rms. No pets. Telex 870047. V. D4-20

Located fifty metres from the cathedral in the pedestrian precinct, this is one of Strasbourg's finest hotels. The rooms are elegant and peaceful, and the equipment and facilities are regularly refurbished.

Sofitel
Pl. St-Pierre-le-Jeune — 88.32.99.30
Open every day. 3 stes 950-3,700 F. 158 rms 700-850 F. Restaurant. TV. Air cond. Conference facilities. Valet parking. Telex 870894. V AE DC. D3-15

This hotel is extremely well situated on a quiet, leafy square in the centre of town. The rooms are rather small but well equipped. There is a pleasant patio, shops, hairdresser and room service. Free rooms for children at weekends and during school holidays.

Terminus Gruber
10, pl. de la Gare — 88.32.87.00
Open every day. 10 stes 550-650 F. 68 rms 250-550 F. Restaurant. Half-board 400-475 F. TV 65 rms. Conference facilities. V AE DC. B3-31

The well-soundproofed rooms of this fine traditional hotel are gradually being modernised. Outstanding comfort, attentive service and a brasserie.

La Vieille Enseigne
9, rue des Tonneliers — 88.32.58.50
M. Langs. Closed Sat lunch, Sun and 15 July-4 Aug. Open until 10 pm. Private room: 20. Air cond. V AE DC. D4-13

For over sixteen years, Franz and Jeannine Langs have been running this delightful historic monument of a restaurant, located between the cathedral and the Petite France district. They've managed to preserve its original charm while introducing understated elegance, comfort and gaiety. Though the prices are high, the cooking lives up to its ambitions: outstanding foie gras terrine, perch cooked in sweet wine, lamb fillets coated with with black pepper, and stunningly good veal brawn. Very good desserts, especially the sorbets.
A la carte: 350-400 F. Menus: 165 F (lunch only), 230 F, 240 F.

Wong
13, quai des Bateliers — 88.36.36.64
M. Wong. Closed Mon lunch. Open until 10.30 pm. Air cond. V AE DC. E4-37

We've decided to award a toque to this excellent Chinese restaurant on the banks of the Ill. The cooking is flavourful and skilfully adapted to European tastes. Harmonious blends of ingredients and seasoning go into specialities such as succulent shrimp salad, and glazed duck served Peking-style. Good choice of wines and delicious jasmine tea. Professional service.
A la carte: 170-220 F. Menus: 90 F and 125 F (lunch only, except Sun).

Zimmer-Sengel
8, rue du Temple-Neuf — 88.32.35.01
M. Sengel. Closed 1-6 Jan and 5-25 Aug. Open until 9.30 pm. Terrace dining. V AE DC. D3-26

Chef-proprietor Georges Sengel's well-crafted, conscientious cooking is enlivened by a pinch of imagination. This year we enjoyed his duck foie gras and mixed mushroom ravioli, baked perch served on a bed of sauerkraut with smoked salmon, and prawn croustillant with creamed leeks. The

setting is a warm and welcoming sixteenth-century town house, built on a site once occupied by the Templars. Though friendly and discreet, the service is not always attentive. The well-chosen wines won't break the bank. Parking is difficult, as the cathedral is close by.
A la carte: 350 F. Menus: 130 F and 360 F (weekdays only).

And also...
Our selection of places for inexpensive, quick, or late-night meals.
L'Ami Schutz (88.32.76.98 - 1, rue des Ponts-Couverts. Open until midnight): Traditional dishes served in a picturesque setting: pot-au-feu, pork cooked in beer, choucroute), (200 F).
Château de Pourtalès (88.31.37.40 - 161, rue Mélanie. Open until 10 pm): Looking out over the leafy municipal park, you can enjoy seasonal dishes like duck tartare with basil, snail strudel, and red mullet pot-au-feu. Fine cellar (200 F).
La Chaumière (88.32.35.23 - 12, rue de la Fonderie. Open until 10 pm): The *patronne* prepares the food in the middle of the dining room's homely disorder. Grilled chicken, home-made confit, pot-au-feu, and excellent Munster (180 F).
Le Coucou des Bois (88.39.76.19 — 44, allée D.-Goldschmidt. Open until 9.30 pm): Located on the edge of the woods. The Alsace specialities include an excellent tarte flambée (130-150 F).
Jean dit Carolis (88.37.04.44 - 5, rue de Zurich. Open until 11.30 pm): A tiny, amusing *winstube* serving quiches, ham, presskopf, and grilled meat, at reasonable prices (100 F).
Kirn (88.32.10.00 - 17, rue 22-Novembre. Open until 6 pm): On the first floor of the famous Kirn butcher's shop. Modest dishes and top-quality meat.
Le Mille Pâtes (88.35.55.23 - 8, pl. St-Etienne. Open until 11 pm): Popular with the locals, who come for the *patron*'s marvellous pasta (100-150 F).
Olivier (88.32.74.13 - 5, rue de la Mésange. Lunch only): A pastry-shop/confectioner's serving a handful of updated traditional dishes for lunch (150 F).
L'Osthof (88.69.55.94 - 7, rue du Gal-de-Gaulle, in Eckwersheim. Open until 10.30 pm): A handsome, leafy terrace and generous, homely food (120-140 F).
Pizzeria des Théâtres (88.35.59.64 - 23, rue Brûlée. Open until 11.30 pm): Big pizzas, tiny dining room. The service is friendly. (150 F).
La Tartine Cosmopolite (88.25.07.89 - 10, rue de la Croix. Open until 10.30 pm): A quiet, shady square is the setting for fresh salads and delicious sandwiches (130 F).
A la Tête de Lard (88.32.13.56 - 3, rue Hannong. Open until 11 pm): Traditional, simple Alsace food, pleasantly served. Close to the cinemas (120-150 F).

In nearby Fegersheim
(13 km S on N 83)
67640 Strasbourg — (Bas-Rhin)

La Table Gourmande
43, rte de Lyon — 88.68.53.54
M. Reix. Closed Sun dinner, Mon, 24-30 Dec and end July- mid-Aug. Open until 9.30 pm. V AE DC.

One of the finest fish restaurants in France, and definitely the best in Alsace. Owner-chef Alain Reix's repertoire pays tribute to the very best fish, bought straight off the boats, while he invents daring dishes that successfully marry the flavours of land and sea. An equally bold vein blends regional specialities with seafood: cod and calf's foot baeckeoffe cooked in chicken stock, or larded freshwater perch with tiny spätzle dumplings. Marvellous wine cellar.

A la carte: 400-500 F. Menus: 190 F (weekdays lunch only), 370 F.

In nearby La Wantzenau

(13 km NE on D 468)
67610 Strasbourg — (Bas-Rhin)

A la Barrière
3, rte de Strasbourg — 88.96.20.23
M. Aeby. Closed Tue dinner, Wed, Feb school holidays and 7-30 Aug. Open until 9.30 pm. Terrace dining. Parking. V AE DC.

In fine weather, the hungry day-trippers who head out of Strasbourg into the countryside often end up on the flower-filled terrace here. The cooking is rich and conventional, with no regional overtones. All the same, chef Claude Sutter is skilful enough to pull off dishes like sole and spiny lobster gratin, salad of frogs' legs and calf's sweetbreads with broad beans, and terrine of lamb sweetbreads with calf's tongue cooked in port. Very pleasant service.

A la carte: 350 F. Menus: 250 F, 400 F.

Le Moulin de la Wantzenau
27, rte de Strasbourg — 88.96.27.83
Closed 24 Dec-2 Jan. 1 ste 450 F. 20 rms 247-341 F. Restaurant. TV. Conference facilities. Garage parking. V AE.

Opposite the restaurant of the same name, this converted mill offers twenty lovely rooms. Breakfast and apéritifs are served on the terrace next to the mill race.

12/20 Le Moulin de la Wantzenau
25, rte de Strasbourg — 88.96.20.01
M. Clauss. Closed Wed, dinner Sun and holidays, 4-19 Jan and 27 June-22 July. Open until 9.15 pm. Private room: 70. Garden dining. Air cond. No-smoking section. Garage parking. V AE DC

Le Moulin's enormous success is mostly due to the beautiful setting, charming country-style dining rooms, and lovely summer terrace. A few interesting dishes dot the otherwise dull menu: salad of garlicky sautéed eels, and fillet of baby boar with red fruit. Very well chosen wines.

A la carte: 300-350 F. Menus: 140 F, 210 F, 280 F.

Relais de la Poste
21, rue du Gal-de-Gaulle — 88.96.20.64
M. Daull. Closed Sun dinner and Jan. Open until 10 pm. Private room: 25. Terrace dining. Air cond. Garage parking. V AE DC.

The exquisite dining room with its handsome wood panelling leads to a delightful winter garden. Understated elegance wafts about this laudably rejuvenated old coaching inn. The staff is extremely attentive, and proprietor Jérôme Daull's cooking features finely crafted traditional dishes such as warm lobster à la parisienne, stuffed quail with morel mushroom sauce, and young pigeon turnover with foie gras. Stiff prices.

A la carte: 350 F. Menus: 200 F, 250 F, 350 F.

Relais de la Poste
(See restaurant above)
Closed Jan. 2 stes 450-650 F. 19 rms 250-650 F. Half-board 450-600 F. TV. Air cond. Conference facilities.

This old coaching inn's rooms are comfortable and elegantly decorated. Those at the back are quieter. Exemplary reception and service.

Zimmer
23, rue des Héros — 88.96.62.08
M. Bengel. Closed Sun dinner, Mon, 27 Jan-10 Feb and 14 July-5 Aug. Open until 9.15 pm. Private room: 60. Garden dining. Parking. V AE DC.

Zimmer is a culinary institution assiduously frequented by local gourmets. Tourists sometimes feel less than cordially treated, but that's the way they do things round here. The service is nonetheless attentive, and the cooking of the highest quality. We suggest the lamb fillet en feuilletage, salad of boned quail and frogs' legs, and salmon in brik pastry with a tarragon-scented sabayon sauce.

A la carte: 300-350 F. Menus: 130 F (weekdays only), 185 F.

SUCÉ-SUR-ERDRE
See Nantes

SUPER-BESSE
See Besse-en-Chandesse

SUPER-SAUZE
See Barcelonnette

SURVILLIERS
See PARIS Suburbs

TAIN-L'HERMITAGE
26600 Tain-l'Hermitage — (Drôme)
Paris 550 - Grenoble 99 - Saint-Etienne 75 - Valence 18

Reynaud
82, av. du Pdt-Roosevelt — 75.07.22.10
M. Reynaud. Closed Sun dinner, Mon, Jan and 16-24 Aug. Open until 9.30 pm. Private room: 30. Garden dining. Air cond. No pets. Parking. V AE DC.

Whether you're seated in the restaurant's lovely enclosed terrace or its elegant beamed dining room, you'll notice Jean-Marc Reynaud's *joie de vivre* spilling over into his inventive, intelligent cooking. We were delighted by his duck terrine garnished with the bird's perfectly cooked fillets, foie gras and egg in a crêpe (a welcome break from the ubiquitous brik pastry), and crisp asparagus tips with crushed olives (a clever alternative to truffles). Good Côtes-du-Rhône wines, impeccable reception and service, splendid views of the Rhône.

A la carte: 300 F. Menus: 150 F, 200 F, 300 F.

Reynaud
(See restaurant above)
Closed Sun, Mon, Jan and 16-24 Aug. 1 ste 500 F. 10 rms 320 F. TV. Air cond. Heated pool.

Despite its austere décor, this hotel offers comfortable, inexpensive rooms looking onto a swimming pool. Ideal for short stays.

TALENCE
See Bordeaux

TALLOIRES
See Annecy

We are always interested to hear about your discoveries, and to receive your comments on ours. Please feel free to write to us, stating your opinions clearly.

TANCARVILLE

76430 Tancarville — (Seine-Mar.)
Paris 200 - Rouen 70 - Deauville 43 - Le Havre 29

 La Marine
D 984 — 35.39.77.15
*M. Sedon. Closed Sun dinner, Mon, Feb school
holidays and 16 July-10 Aug. Open until 8.45 pm.
Private room: 45. Garden dining. Hotel: 2 stes.
7 rms. Rates not available. Parking. V.*
The views of Tancarville bridge and the steady
flow of barges are this restaurant's two major
attractions. We'd gladly include its fresh and copious cooking, but certain fish (the house specialities, no less) were carelessly cooked.
A la carte: 350 F. Menus: 130 F (except holidays),
285 F (holidays only), 300 F (Fri dinner and Sat
only), 185 F.

TARASCON

13150 Tarascon — (B./Rhône)
Paris 710 - Avignon 23 - Arles 18 - Marseille 96

 Les Mazets des Roches
Rte de Fontvieille
90.91.34.89
*Closed 15 Oct-Easter. 24 rms 340-560 F. Restaurant.
Half-board 450-530 F. TV. 4 rms. Air cond. Confer-
ence facilities. Pool. Tennis. Parking. V AE DC.*
Set in a thirteen-hectare park at the foot of the
Baux, this agreeable residence features comfort-
able, perfectly equipped, air-conditioned rooms
with beautiful bathrooms.

TARBES

65000 Tarbes — (Hautes-Pyrénées)
Paris 778 - Toulouse 155 - Auch 72 - Lourdes 19

 Hôtel Président
1, rue G.-Fauré — 62.93.98.40
*Open every day. 9 stes 500 F. 57 rms 260-350 F.
Restaurant. TV. Conference facilities. Heated pool.*
This hotel offers modern, recently renovated,
functional rooms with lovely views of the
mountains and town. Terrace, swimming pool,
grill.

In nearby Juillan

(6 km SW on N 21)
65290 Tarbes — (Hautes-Pyrénées)

 La Caravelle
Tarbes airport — 62.32.99.96
*M. Rouzaud. Closed Sun dinner, Mon, 1-17 July and
6-30 Jan. Open until 10 pm. Private room: 150. Air
cond. Parking. Telex 532968. V AE DC.*
The local smart set enjoys gathering here for the
cold stuffed duckling à l'orange, duck breast with
green peppercorns, and grilled grouper with red-
pepper butter, all served by a friendly and efficient
staff.
A la carte: 300 F. Menus: 155 F (weekdays only),
200 F and 220 F (weekends and holidays only).

TAVERS

See Beaugency

TENDU

See Argenton-sur-Creuse

TESTE (LA)

See Arcachon

TETEGHEM

See Dunkerque

THÉOULE-SUR-MER

06590 Théoule-sur-Mer — (Alpes-Mar.)
Paris 895 - Saint-Raphaël 36 - Cannes 10 - Nice 41

In nearby Miramar

(6 km S on N 98)
06590 Théoule-sur-Mer — (Alpes-Mar.)

 Père Pascal
16, av. du Trayas — 93.75.40.11
*M. Cozzolino. Closed Thu (except holidays), 1 Nov-
31 Jan. Open until 10 pm. Garden dining. No-smoking section. Parking. V AE DC.*
We were impressed by the red-mullet terrine, the
mousseline de mostelle (a Mediterranean fish)
with a crab coulis, the ginger-flavoured lobster,
and lovely desserts like the crêpes with almond
butter.
A la carte: 400-500 F. Menu: 180 F.

Saint-Christophe
on La Corniche d'Or
47, av. de Miramar — 93.75.41.36
*Open every day. 40 rms 295-950 F. Restaurant. Half-
board 335-615 F oblig in seas. TV. Conference facilities. Pool. Garage parking. Telex 470878. V AE DC.*
Conveniently located, with direct access to a
private beach, this modern hotel offers functional
rooms with terraces and loggias

THIONVILLE

57100 Thionville — (Moselle)
Paris 342 - Luxembourg 32 - Metz 29 - Nancy 83

Le Concorde
6, pl. du Luxembourg — 82.53.83.18
*M. Nachon. Closed Sun dinner. Open until 10 pm.
Hotel: 25 rms 260-310 F. Telex 861338. V AE.*
Daniel Nachon's cooking is as robust as it is
classic, and his sweetbread and lobster terrine,
orange-flavoured onion compote, and fish lasagne
in a prawn and cream sauce all have a personal
touch.
A la carte: 320 F. Menus: 180 F (weekdays only),
220 F (weekends and holidays only), 290 F, 330 F.

L'Horizon
50, rte du Crève-Cœur — 82.88.53.65
*Closed Jan. 10 rms 360-640 F. Half-board 600-900 F.
Restaurant. TV. Conference facilities.*
All the rooms in this hotel have been provided
with thick carpets and curtains and lovely Lorraine
furniture. Sweeping valley views. Relais et
Châteaux.

THOIRY

See Saint-Genis-Pouilly

THOMERY

See Fontainebleau

THONON-LES-BAINS

74200 Thonon-les-Bains — (H.-Savoie)
Paris 575 - Genève 33 - Evian 9 - Annecy 72

 Le Prieuré
68, Grande-Rue
50.71.31.89
*M. Plumex. Closed Sun dinner and Mon. Open until
10.30 pm. Private room: 40. V AE DC.*
Comfortably ensconced at the stylishly set tables,
you'll be impressed by the inventive dishes (ex-

pensive, but well worth it): prawns pan-roasted with a ginger infusion, lightly salted fresh salmon in whipped sour cream, quail in a peppery sauce, and exceptional desserts.

A la carte: 350-400 F. Menus: 200 F (weekdays lunch only, wine inc), 180 F, 250 F, 350 F.

In nearby Sciez

(10 km SW)
74140 Thonon-les-Bains — (H.-Savoie)

Château de Coudrée
50.72.62.33

Closed end Oct-end April. 18 rms 650-1,450 F. Half-board 680-1,180 F. Restaurant. TV 10 rms.

The quiet of the extensive grounds, a fine view of Lake Geneva, and the sumptuously decorated rooms are some of the reasons why this hotel is one of the most pleasant Relais et Châteaux. Sauna, disco, private beach.

TIGNES

73320 Tignes — (Savoie)
Paris 690 - Bourg-St-Maurice 30 - Val-d'Isère 13

Les Campanules
Lac de Tignes
79.06.34.36

Closed 12 May-28 June and 31 Aug-9 Nov. 36 rms 350-550 F. Restaurant. Half-board 400-450 F oblig in seas. TV. No pets. V.

This large modern chalet with bright, well-equipped rooms, enjoys magnificent views of Tignes lake and the Grande Motte glacier.

11/20 Le Clin d'Œil
Quartier du Rosset
75.06.59.10

M. Lacan. Closed 5 May-5 July and 30 Aug-25 Oct. Open until 11 pm. Terrace dining. V AE DC.

A lively, family-style atmosphere pervades this little restaurant opposite the Grande Motte glacier.

A la carte: 160-200 F.

Curling
in Val-Claret — 79.06.34.34

Closed 12 May-30 June and 2 Sep-26 Oct. 35 rms 400-680 F. TV. Telex 309605. V AE DC.

A hotel near the ski-lifts, with attractively decorated, perfectly comfortable rooms, and a bar reputed for its cocktails. Half-board possible (meals at one of three neighbouring restaurants).

Le Ski d'Or
2 km SE
in Val-Claret — 79.06.51.60

M. Bréchu. Closed 1 May-1 Dec. Open until 9.30 pm. Parking. Telex 306254. V.

We like especially the hot oysters and salmon eggs, turbot fillet with asparagus, sliced kidney with truffles, and the tempting duck pot-au-feu. Perfect service.

A la carte: 350-400 F. Menus: 100 F (lunch only), 215 F (dinner only), 285 F.

Le Ski d'Or
(See restaurant above)

Closed 1 May-1 Dec. 21 rms 700-900 F. Half-board 900 F oblig in seas. TV. Conference facilities.

Renovation of this lovely Val Claret residence has been completed and all the rooms are now spacious and excellently equipped. Relais et Châteaux.

Le Terril Blanc
Lac de Tignes — 79.06.32.87

Closed May, June and 30 July-15 Dec. 25 rms 400-460 F. Restaurant. Half-board 380-400 F oblig in seas. TV. Parking. V.

A small lakeside hotel with recently renovated, well-kept rooms with lovely views. Seven are brand-new.

TONNERRE

89700 Tonnerre — (Yonne)
Paris 196 - Troyes 57 - Avallon 52 - Sens 73 - Auxerre 35

L'Abbaye Saint-Michel
Montée de St-Michel
86.55.05.99

M. Cussac. Closed 1 Jan-7 Feb. Open until 9.15 pm. Private room: 30. Garden dining. No-smoking section. Parking. Telex 801356. V AE DC.

Few chefs have so astutely interpreted the repertoire of Burgundian dishes as Christophe Cussac, whether it's simmered beef jowls, meurette d'escargots, or a delicious tête de veau. But his multiple talents extend far beyond the region, as he amply demonstrates with an excellent, crisp feuilleté of foie gras in a shallot butter sauce. His desserts are of slightly lower quality. There's a huge choice of northern Burgundy wines (try the little-known Epineuil and Irancy).

A la carte: 500 F. Menus: 250 F (weekdays lunch only, wine inc), 290 F, 420 F, and 490 F.

L'Abbaye Saint-Michel
(See restaurant above)

Closed 1 Jan-7 Feb. 5 stes. 10 rms 1,050-1,400 F (per pers, half-board oblig). TV. Tennis.

We can't say we like everything about the highly stylised, ultramodern suites, but we do, unlike others, find the blend of old and new on this hotel's exterior tasteful. Relais et Châteaux.

TOUL

54200 Toul — (Meurthe/M.)
Paris 283 - Bar-le-Duc 61 - Metz 74 - Nancy 23

Le Dauphin
Rte de Villey-St-Etienne — 83.43.13.46

M. Vohmann. Closed Sun dinner, Mon, 8-28 Feb and 5-15 Nov. Open until 10 pm. Private room: 40. Garden dining. Parking. V.

Christophe Volmann has pared down his *carte* to focus his fertile imagination on a limited choice of perfectly balanced, expertly prepared dishes. We urge you to sample his creamed cèpes with spring cabbage, oyster and red-mullet salad with fried celery, fricassée of pig's jowls with truffles, and a lightly spiced dried-apricot crumble. Exceptionally amiable staff, very full and varied cellar (white Burgundy, Graves, Côtes-de-Toul, Alsace).

A la carte: 350-400 F. Menus: 130 F (weekdays lunch only), 210 F, 320 F.

TOULON

83000 Toulon — (Var)
Paris 833 - Nice 152 - Aix 81 - Marseille 66 - St-Raphaël 96

America
51, rue Jean-Jaurès
94.92.32.19

Open every day. 30 rms 177-247 F. TV 26 rms. Conference facilities. Telex 400479. V AE DC.

A small, friendly, and well-modernised hotel not far from the station.

Le Bistro des Princes
449, av. F.-Roosevelt – 94.42.45.31
M. Matheron. Closed Sun and holidays. Open until 11 pm. Private room: 85. Air cond. V AE DC.

Jean Matheson dishes up generous portions of chateaubriand en feuilletage, sliced duckling in verjuice, and hearty andouillette sausage.
A la carte: 240-320 F. Menus: 150 F (wine inc), 100 F, 135 F.

La Corniche
Corniche du Mourillon
1, littoral F.-Mistral – 94.41.39.53
M. Suère. Closed Sun dinner (except July-Aug), Mon and 12-26 Feb. Open until 10.30 pm. Private room: 20. Garden dining. Garage parking. V AE DC.

How can Eric Berthier, a remarkable chef who loves spices and knows how to use them, prepare food so lacking in spirit? A puzzle of sorts, considering the talent so evidently displayed in his chilled oysters in creamed cauliflower, red-mullet fillets with orange-scented butter and artichokes, and veal kidneys with melting apples. His desserts are less good, the wine list remarkable.
A la carte: 350-400 F. Menus: 140 F, 230 F, 320 F.

La Corniche
(See restaurant above)
Open every day. 4 stes 380-520 F. 18 rms 320-450 F. TV. Air cond.

This hotel provides well-equipped, distinctive, comfortable rooms, half of which have balconies or terraces overlooking the sea.

12/20 Le Dauphin
21 bis, rue J.-Jaurès – 94.93.12.07
M. Biles. Closed Sat lunch, Sun, holidays and 13-29 July. Open until 9.45 pm. Air cond. V.

Alain Biles appreciates fine produce and prepares it to best advantage in this restaurant on the edge of the old town.
A la carte: 250-280 F. Menus: 132 F, 192 F.

Le Gros Ventre
Corniche du Mourillon
In front of Fort St-Louis – 94.42.15.42
M. Audibert. Closed Thu lunch and Wed. Open until 11 pm. Private room: 40. Terrace dining. V AE DC.

Alain Audibert and Dominique Hollyck have two particularly successful specialities: seafood (excellent oysters gratinéed with almonds, rascasse fish in a crab coulis) and dishes in a pastry crust.
A la carte: 250-300 F. Menus: 95 F, 116 F, 184 F.

Résidence du Cap Brun
Chemin du Petit Bois – 94.41.29.46
Closed Feb. 20 rms 250-600 F. Restaurant. Half-board 315-465 F oblig in seas. TV. Conference facilities. Pool. Garage parking. V AE.

A lovely manor in a wooded park above the sea, with huge rooms furnished with antiques.

Le Saint Nicolas
49, rue J.-Jaurès – 94.91.02.28
Open every day. 40 rms 196-286 F. TV. Air cond 6 rms. Conference facilities. Telex 400479. V AE DC.

Conveniently located near the theatre and shops, this large colourful hotel has been restored to its original 1930s style.

La Tour Blanche
Bd de l'Amiral-Vence – 94.24.41.57
M. Engelhardt. Open every day. Open until 10 pm. Terrace dining. Parking. V AE DC.

This young professional is capable of more spirited stuff, but try his salade armoricaine with king prawns, blanquette de lotte à la sauge, and lamb cooked in a salt crust. Stiff service, limited wine list.
A la carte: 350 F. Menus: 125 F, 165 F.

Altea La Tour Blanche
(See restaurant above)
Open every day. 92 rms 340-690 F. Half-board 400-440 F. TV. Air cond. Conference facilities. Pool.

Bright, well-equipped rooms and comfortable bathrooms. Entirely renovated.

La Véranda
29, rue A.-Daumas – 94.92.81.46
M. Rocher. Closed off-season dinner Mon and Wed, in seas Sat lunch and Sun. Open until 10 pm. Private room: 22. Air cond. V AE DC.

It's still a pleasure to sit down in one of his two snug dining rooms for a meal of red-mullet fillet with tomatoes and anchovies, sliced sweetbreads with morels, and seasonal fruit zabaglione. Gracious reception.
A la carte: 280-330 F. Menus: 120 F (weekdays lunch only), 180 F.

In nearby **Cuers**

(20 km NE on N 97)
83390 Toulon – (Var)

Le Lingousto
Rte de Pierrefeu – 94.28.69.10
M. Ryon. Closed Sun and Mon (except July-Aug), and Feb. Open until 9.30 pm. Private room: 30. Terrace dining. Parking. V AE DC.

Local gourmets gather here to savour the region's rich supply of beautiful vegetables, excellent poultry and succulent fruit which Alan Ryon, trained by Georges Blanc and Roger Vergé, prepares with finesse.
A la carte: 380-500 F. Menus: 195 F, 350 F.

TOULOUSE

31000 Toulouse – (H.-Garonne)
Paris 681 - Lyon 534 - Marseille 400 - Bordeaux 249

12/20 L'Abbaye
20, rue Peyrolières
61.22.72.40
M. Gleyses. Closed Sat lunch, Sun, 1-7 Jan, 30 March-8 April and 27 July-19 Aug. Open until 10.30 pm. Air cond. V AE DC. D4-7

The agreeable beamed décor affords a glimpse of the wine and cheese cellars. The menu of cheese-based specialities (blue cheese soufflé, tournedos au Pont-l'Evêque with morels) has been enlarged to include grilled red mullet, and duck breast in a tart sauce. Good choice of wines, excellent reception.
A la carte: 250 F. Menus: 67 F and 87 F (weekdays lunch only), 115 F.

Airport Hotel
176, route de Bayonne
61.49.68.78
Open every day. 3 stes 309-319 F. 48 rms 279-309 F. TV. Air cond 26 rms. Conference facilities. Garage parking. Telex 521752. V AE DC. A2-29

The rooms here are modern, entirely renovated, soundproofed and carefully equipped. Free shuttle service to the airport, a sauna, fitness centre, and meals served on trays.

Altea Les Capitouls
29, allées J.-Jaurès – 61.62.63.33
Open every day. 1 ste 980 F. 52 rms 380-575 F. TV.
Air cond. Conference facilities. Parking.
Telex 533363. V AE DC. E3-3
Centrally placed on the Allées Jean-Jaurès (the 'Champs-Elysées' of Toulouse), this recently built hotel offers stylish, well-soundproofed and excellently equipped rooms, most of which enjoy views of the Place Wilson. The young, efficient staff provide a pleasant welcome.

Altea Matabiau
Gare SNCF Matabiau – 61.62.84.93
Open every day. 1 ste 650 F. 62 rms 300-450 F. TV.
Air cond. Conference facilities. Garage parking.
Telex 533888. V AE DC. F2-16
A good, functional hotel, with comfortable, air-conditioned rooms. Light meals available.

Altea Wilson
7, rue Labéda (corner pl. Wilson)
61.21.21.75
Open every day. 2 stes 850 F. 95 rms 390-685 F. TV.
Air cond. Conference facilities. Garage parking.
Telex 530550. V AE DC. E4-13
An excellent, centrally located hotel with many amenities and recently redecorated rooms. Children under eighteen are offered free accommodation during school holidays and at weekends. Piano bar, room service until 10 pm.

12/20 L'Astarac
(Le Cahuzac)
21, rue Perchepinte – 61.53.11.15
M. Dussin. Closed Sat lunch, Sun and 15 July-15 Aug.
Open until 11 pm. Air cond. V AE. E5-19
The brick-walled dining room is irresistible in the evenings, with its blazing fireplace and elegantly set, candle-lit tables. The owner-chef tries hard to personalise his classic Gascon cooking and succeeds with an aubergine flan and stuffed duck, paupiettes of duck fillet with wild mushrooms, and a fine assortment of foies gras and confits.
A la carte: 250 F. Menus: 65 F (lunch only), 105 F, 160 F, 230 F.

Hôtel Athénée
13, rue Matabiau – 61.63.10.63
Open every day. 35 rms 310-400 F. TV. Air cond.
Conference facilities. Parking. Telex 530955. V AE
DC. E2-2
Set between the railway station and the conference centre, this hotel offers modern, attractively decorated rooms that are well equipped and perfectly soundproofed. Room service, dry cleaning, meals served on trays.

La Barigoude
8, rue Mage – 61.53.07.24
M. Tanguy. Closed Sun, Mon, holidays and 20 July-20 Aug. Open until 10.30 pm. Private room: 15. V AE
DC. E5-33
The décor is not what you'd call elegant, but the warm black and pink tones and the *patronne*'s tireless good humour make it extremely welcoming. Her husband, a master sauce chef, is fond of sweet and savoury associations. Sample his brand-ade with leeks, saumon au caramel, duck breast with honey and cinammon, and a delicious chocolate marquise. Inexpensive Fronton wines.
A la carte: 250-280 F. Menus: 80 F (lunch only, wine inc, except holidays), 140 F and 220 F (dinner only).

Hôtel des Beaux-Arts
1, pl. du Pont-Neuf – 61.23.40.50
Open every day. 20 rms 310-520 F. TV. Air cond.
Telex 532451. V AE DC. D5-23
A friendly, recently renovated hotel, with well-equipped, soundproofed rooms that are pleasantly decorated. Fine views of the Garonne, meals served on trays. Restaurant (see Brasserie des Beaux-Arts, below).

La Belle Epoque
3, rue Pargaminières
61.23.22.12
Mme Roudgé. Closed Sat lunch, Sun, holidays, 13-22 July and 12-19 Aug. Open until 11 pm. Private room: 20. Air cond. V AE DC. C4-10
In this newly renovated bistro-style restaurant, Pierre-Jean Ferrié provides customers with the same fine specialities served at his former place of work, Les Magnolias at Le Perreux. Now, as then, he regales us with his sliced, dried duck breast in paprika, crab fondant with avocado (it could almost pass for a dessert), fricassée of lotte and poultry livers (an admirable land-and-sea blend), veal kidney with shellfish, and a deliciously melting apricot tart accompanied by a sorbet. Charming reception, gourmet boutique.
A la carte: 400-500 F. Menus: 190 F (wine inc), 270 F.

12/20 Benjamin
7, rue des Gestes – 61.22.92.66
M. Lemercier. Open every day. Open until 11 pm. Air cond. V. D4-28
The city's late-night crowd loves this bistro for its *trompe-l'œil* décor, good prices, and generous all-encompassing cooking. Try the courgette tart, rabbit confit with prunes, and pork tenderloin with Roquefort.
Menus: 75 F (lunch only), 116 F.

12/20 Brasserie des Beaux-Arts
1, quai de la Daurade – 61.21.12.12
M. Noizet. Open every day. Open until 1 am. Terrace dining. Air cond. V AE DC. D5-23
This brasserie's art nouveau décor (walnut panelling, mirrors), its brisk and efficient staff, the reliable cooking, the late-night menu after 11 pm and the queue waiting to be seated are reminiscent of the Brasserie Flo in Paris. A most successful cloning. Sample the fine oysters, salmon with sorrel, knuckle of veal with potatoes in olive oil, choucroute, and house Riesling (by the carafe).
A la carte: 250 F. Menus: 88 F (weekdays lunch only, wine inc), 132 F.

Hôtel de Brienne
20, bd du Mal-Leclerc – 61.23.60.60
Open every day. 3 stes 590-790 F. 68 rms 395-480 F.
TV. Air cond. Conference facilities. Garage parking.
Telex 533031. V AE DC. B3-37
Contemporary, not to say futuristic, architecture for this hotel with functional, well-equipped rooms, most of which look onto a patio. Meals on trays available.

Le Brucelles
84, allées J.-Jaurès – 61.10.23.10
M. Merelle. Open every day. Open until 11.30 pm.
Private room: 200. Air cond. Valet parking.
Telex 533361. V AE DC. F3-24
You'll enjoy Francis Dulucq's promising cooking in this bright pastel-toned restaurant in the heart of Toulouse. Though the *carte* isn't stunningly original, he does come up with some nice ideas,

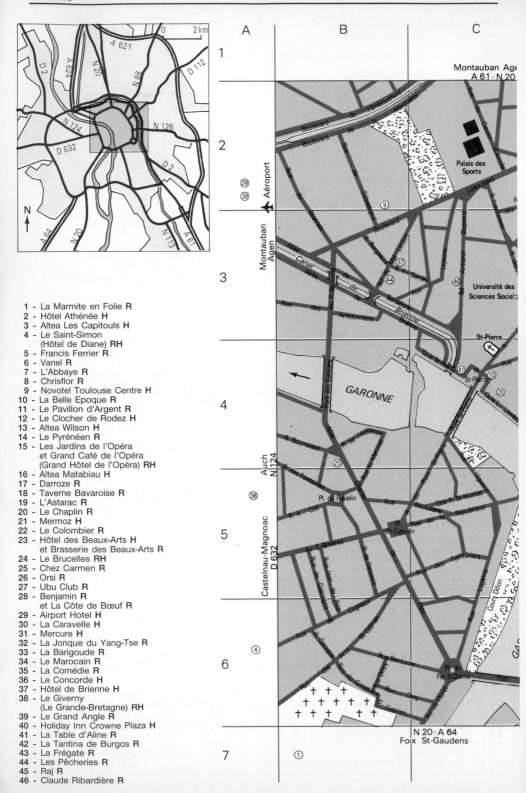

1 - La Marmite en Folie **R**
2 - Hôtel Athénée **H**
3 - Altea Les Capitouls **H**
4 - Le Saint-Simon
   (Hôtel de Diane) **RH**
5 - Francis Ferrier **R**
6 - Vanel **R**
7 - L'Abbaye **R**
8 - Chrisflor **R**
9 - Novotel Toulouse Centre **H**
10 - La Belle Epoque **R**
11 - Le Pavillon d'Argent **R**
12 - Le Clocher de Rodez **H**
13 - Altea Wilson **H**
14 - Le Pyrénéen **R**
15 - Les Jardins de l'Opéra
   et Grand Café de l'Opéra
   (Grand Hôtel de l'Opéra) **RH**
16 - Altea Matabiau **H**
17 - Darroze **R**
18 - Taverne Bavaroise **R**
19 - L'Astarac **R**
20 - Le Chaplin **R**
21 - Mermoz **H**
22 - Le Colombier **R**
23 - Hôtel des Beaux-Arts **H**
   et Brasserie des Beaux-Arts **R**
24 - Le Brucelles **RH**
25 - Chez Carmen **R**
26 - Orsi **R**
27 - Ubu Club **R**
28 - Benjamin
   et La Côte de Bœuf **R**
29 - Airport Hotel **H**
30 - La Caravelle **R**
31 - Mercure **H**
32 - La Jonque du Yang-Tse **R**
33 - La Barigoude **R**
34 - Le Marocain **R**
35 - La Comédie **R**
36 - Le Concorde **H**
37 - Hôtel de Brienne **H**
38 - Le Giverny
   (Le Grande-Bretagne) **RH**
39 - Le Grand Angle **R**
40 - Holiday Inn Crowne Plaza **H**
41 - La Table d'Aline **R**
42 - La Tantina de Burgos **R**
43 - La Frégate **R**
44 - Les Pêcheries **R**
45 - Raj **R**
46 - Claude Ribardière **R**

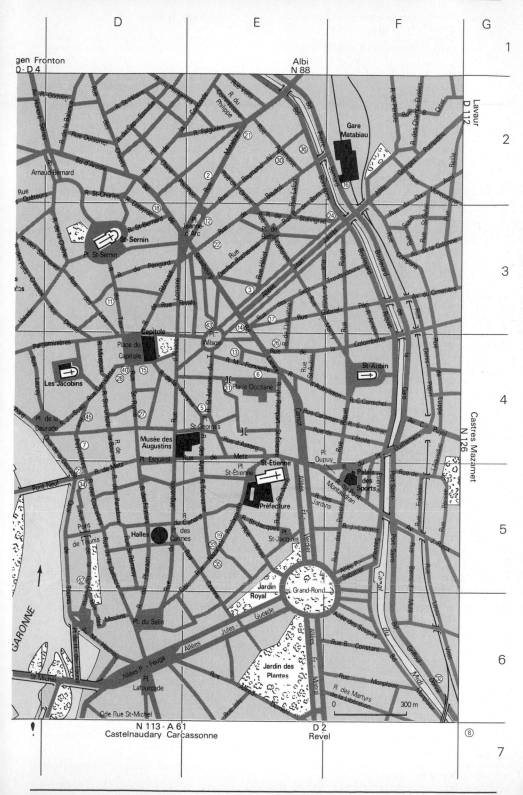

like the crab and shrimp ravioli with mangoes. Fine desserts, limited but well-presented wine list, affordable prices.

A la carte: 250 F. Menus: 160 F and 180 F (lunch only).

Le Brucelles
(See restaurant above)
Open every day. 14 stes 1,250 F. 105 rms 750 F. Half-board 950 F. TV. Air cond. Conference facilities.

A classic chain-owned hotel, centrally located, offering comfortable rooms and various services.

La Caravelle
62, rue Raymond-IV – 61.62.70.65
Open every day. 30 rms 300-360 F. TV. Air cond. Garage parking. Telex 530438. V AE DC. E2-30

A well-kept hotel near the station, with air-conditioned, soundproofed rooms. Bar, cold meals.

11/20 Chez Carmen
(Café des Abattoirs)
97, allées Ch.-de-Fitte – 61.42.04.95
M. Carmen. Closed Mon dinner, Sun and Aug. Open until 10.30 pm. Private room: 35. Terrace dining. Air cond. V. B4-25

This very popular and lively bistro features the same menu all year round. Try the rib steak with bone marrow, homemade pot-au-feu, and the calf's head with tangy ravigote sauce.

A la carte: 200 F. Menus: 70 F (lunch only, wine inc), 85 F (wine inc).

Le Chaplin
56, rue des Blanchers – 61.22.82.25
M. Belkadi. Dinner only. Closed Mon and week of 15 Aug. Open until 11 pm. V AE. C4-20

If you appreciate bold cooking, a new set of flavours, and a lively assortment of dishes, you too will love Yacine Belkadi's popular restaurant. We enjoyed his oyster ragoût with dandelion leaves, oxtail with leeks, foie gras sautéed with fresh pasta and soy sauce, and poached pear with chocolate cream. Excellent set menus.

A la carte: 300 F. Menus: 105 F, 180 F, 250 F.

Chrisflor
26, av. St-Exupéry – 61.53.12.86
M. Martin. Closed Sat lunch, Sun dinner (and lunch in summer), 25 March-1 April and 12-26 Aug. Open until 10 pm. No pets. V. G7-8

Jean-François Martin has a gift for devising seafood dishes that retain all their natural freshness and fragrance. Try his scampi soup with foie gras, courgette flowers stuffed with lobster, omble chevalier au Madiran, and bass with pistou, followed by Xavier's famous cheeses and delicious desserts (strawberry gratin with peaches).

A la carte: 250-300 F. Menus: 240 F and 280 F (dinner only), 130 F, 180 F.

Le Clocher de Rodez
14-15, pl. Jeanne d'Arc – 61.62.42.92
Open every day. 46 rms 180-300 F. Restaurant. TV. Conference facilities. Garage parking. Telex 531508. V AE DC. E3-12

Among the city's oldest, this recently renovated hotel features pleasantly decorated, comfortable rooms. Bar.

Red toques signify modern cuisine; black toques signify traditional cuisine.

Le Colombier
14, rue Bayard – 61.62.40.05
M. Zasso. Closed Sat, Sun, 24 Dec-1 Jan, 1 week at Easter and 1-21 Aug. Open until 10 pm. Air cond. V AE. E3-22

Gérard Zasso's cassoulet—the best in town—is only the tip of his culinary iceberg. He also regaled us with a tasty salad of foie gras seasoned with raspberry vinegar, a beautiful braised sole with morels, and perfectly cooked magret aux cèpes, all served in a friendly, brick-and-wood dining room with an imposing fireplace. One toque this year.

A la carte: 300 F. Menus: 80 F, 100 F, 190 F.

12/20 La Comédie
1, rue Vélane – 61.53.51.71
M. de Lepinay. Dinner only. Closed Sun, 23 Dec-6 Jan and 28 July-18 Aug. Open until 0.30 am. V. E5-35

The late-night, up-market set gathers under the vaulted ceiling to see and be seen—and to sample the chef's generous, simply prepared dishes: assortment of specialities from the Gers, cod cassoulet, and leg of lamb with garlic. Good local wines for around 50 F.

A la carte: 200 F.

Le Concorde
16, bd Bonrepos – 61.62.48.60
Open every day. 97 rms 400-520 F. Restaurant. Half-board 530-550 F. TV. Air cond. Conference facilities. Garage parking. Telex 531686. V AE DC. E2-36

Opposite the station and the Canal du Midi, this recently renovated hotel provides spacious, comfortable, and well-equipped luxury rooms.

12/20 La Côte de Bœuf
12, rue des Gestes – 61.21.19.61
Mme Gagnard. Closed Sun. Open until 10.30 pm. V. D4-28

The *patronne*'s huge rib steaks seem to dominate all other items on this friendly restaurant's menu. If you're in the mood for something else, try the fresh foie gras with coarse salt, goat-cheese salad with honey, duck breast, and her good homemade desserts.

A la carte: 200-230 F. Menus: 60 F (weekdays only), 110 F (dinner only).

Darroze
19, rue de Castellane
61.62.34.70
M. Darroze. Closed Sat lunch, Sun, holidays and 28 July-18 Aug. Open until 9.30 pm. Air cond. No pets. V AE DC. E3-17

The menu's elegantly penned entries are so numerous and tempting that it's a shame to have only one stomach to sample Viviane Darroze's dazzling cooking. So come along with a party of friends to relish her grilled lamb's sweetbreads with salt-water crayfish, piperade, cassoulet, sautéed wild mushrooms with foie gras, superb grilled salmon simply seasoned with olive oil and coarse salt, pigeon and green cabbage in a velvety smooth mixture of truffles and foie gras, jambonnette de canard à la paysanne, mint-chocolate marquise, and outstanding fresh chocolate profiteroles. Everything here is made from the freshest ingredients, prepared with skill, imagination and a light touch. Viviane's sister-in-law, Françoise, oversees the pleasant service. Fabulous collection of Armagnacs.

A la carte: 350-400 F. Menus: 170 F (lunch only), 260 F, 330 F.

Hôtel de Diane
See restaurant Le Saint-Simon

Francis Ferrier ☼
(Chez Emile)
13, place St-Georges
61.21.05.56
M. Ferrier. Closed Sun, Mon and 23 Dec-3 Jan. Open until 10.30 pm. Private room: 35. Terrace dining. Air cond. V AE DC. E4-5

This entreprising Toulousain (he also owns La Jonque du Yang-Tsé) has partitioned his delightful establishment into three. Seafood is served on the ground floor, Gascon cooking on the first, and in summer a special menu is offered on the terrace overlooking the square. The seafood is bracing (zarzuela, grouper Rossini), and the cassoulet generously served. Superb cellar, full of excellent finds.

A la carte: 220-350 F. Menus: 98 F and 129 F (lunch in summer only), 175 F, 195 F.

12/20 La Frégate
1, rue d'Austerlitz – 61.21.59.61
M. Fernandez. Open every day. Open until 10 pm. Private room: 80. Air cond. TV AE DC. E3-43

This Frégate (frigate) had sunk, but has now been refloated and is back up to cruising speed. The décor is pompous and the staff rather affected, but the chef offers good sweet red peppers in their oil, smoked salmon papillote with spinach, and pigeon with truffles and mushrooms. Good wines.

A la carte: 300 F. Menu: 145 F (wine inc).

12/20 Le Giverny
298-300, av. de Grande-Bretagne
61.31.84.85
M. Dupuy. Open every day. Open until 10 pm. Private room: 100. Air cond. Parking. Telex 533116. V AE DC. A5-38

An elegantly furnished hotel-restaurant, and an overly stylish cuisine with no more than the odd allusion to regional food. But it's carefully prepared and the calf's liver with grapes is most successful. Good-value lunch menu. Diligent service.

A la carte: 250 F. Menu: 85 F.

Le Grande-Bretagne
(See restaurant above)
Open every day. 2 stes 650 F. 41 rms 280-440 F. Half-board 320 F. TV. Air cond. Conference facilities.

A modern, left-bank hotel with tastefully decorated, functional and perfectly soundproofed rooms. Free shuttle service to the airport (in a London taxi!).

11/20 Le Grand Angle
156, allée de Barcelone
61.21.89.89
M. Castagna. Open every day. Open until 11.30 pm. Terrace dining. Parking. V AE DC. A2-39

This restaurant-terrace overlooking the Canal du Midi is always so packed that it now has a new rôtisserie specialising in shoulder of lamb and suckling pig. Other dishes to try include Creole-style fish, sole in anchovy butter, and veal kidneys with mustard). Jazz and spaghetti all night in the pub downstairs.

A la carte: 200-230 F.

12/20 Grand Café de l'Opéra
1, pl. du Capitole – 61.21.37.03
M. Heuillet. Closed 29 July-18 Aug. Open until 0.30 am. Private room: 10. Terrace dining. Air cond. No pets. Telex 521998. V AE DC. D4-15

Local notables love to congregate on the terrace for fine brasserie-style cooking. We recommend the seafood (in season), calf's head, pig's trotters, and numerous grilled dishes (salmon, rabbit with fresh pasta, steak). Fine wines.

A la carte: 230-250 F.

Grand Hôtel de l'Opéra
See restaurant Les Jardins de l'Opéra

Grande-Bretagn
See restaurant Le Giverny

Holiday Inn Crowne Plaza
7, pl. du Capitole – 61.61.19.19
Open every day. 2 stes 1,200-1,800 F. 162 rms 650-850 F. Restaurant. Half-board 825 F. TV. Air cond. Conference facilities. Valet parking. Telex 520348. V AE DC. D4-40

This beautiful building on the Place du Capitole offers spacious, sophisticated rooms. Some are reserved for non-smokers and some are designed for the disabled. Excellent reception, New Orleans-style bar, many lounges. The health club includes a sauna and Jacuzzi.

Les Jardins de l'Opéra
1, pl. du Capitole – 61.23.07.76
M. Toulousy. Closed Sun, holidays, 2-6 Jan and 15 Aug-1 Sep. Open until 10 pm. Private room: 80. Garden dining. Air cond. No-smoking section. Valet parking. Telex 521998. V AE DC. D4-15

Located in the Grand Hôtel's magnificent courtyard, this restaurant has all the fittings of a Florentine opera décor, with its glass ceilings, fine fabrics, and sensuous lighting. The elegantly set tables, glorious flowers, and competent, friendly staff are perfectly tailored to the outstanding cooking of Dominique Toulousy, who is as comfortable preparing full-flavoured Gascon foods as he is creating more modern and subtle marriages. The delicate vegetables à la crème de caviar, wild salmon and oyster tartare, and fresh foie gras ravioli with truffle juice bear little resemblance to the earthy roast lamb with garlic croquettes, young pigeon casserole with green cabbage, and the superb cassoulet, with its large, melting beans, confit de canard, and Toulouse sausages—but the same ease, the same straightforward flavours come through in these two different styles. The desserts are equally dazzling: caramelised lemon feuillantine, chaud-froid of wild strawberries, figs baked in Banyuls wine and filled with delicious vanilla ice cream. Sommelier Patrick Guiral is as knowledgeable about vintage Bordeaux as he is about wines from the South-west. The lunch club helps to lighten the only thing you may find heavy-handed here—the bill.

A la carte: 500-750 F. Menus: 300 F, 440 F.

Grand Hôtel de l'Opéra
(See restaurant above)
Open every day. 15 stes 1,050-1,400 F. 63 rms 400-1,050 F. TV. Air cond. Conference facilities. Pool.

This charming hotel with a garden and pool has tastefully decorated, restful, air-conditioned rooms that are extremely comfortable. Some of them are sparkling new and have balconies overlooking the city's old tiled roofs. Excellent reception. Facilities include a Jacuzzi, sauna, Turkish baths, gym and relaxation room.

La Jonque du Yang-Tsé
Canal du Midi
Bd Griffoul-Dorval – 61.20.74.74
M. Ferrier. Closed Mon lunch and Sun. Open until 10.30 pm. Private room: 50. Terrace dining. Air cond. V AE DC. F6-32

Francis Ferrier has transformed on old barge on the Canal du Midi into one of the finest and most original Chinese restaurants in France. A team of chefs from Szechwan prepare dishes you won't find anywhere else, like chicken breast with mandarin peel, sun-maï steamed in a basket, and grilled pork with prunes. Fine wine list. Menus only, all excellent value.
Menus: 99 F and 132 F (lunch only, wine inc), 198 F (dinner only, wine inc).

La Marmite en Folie
28, rue P.-Painlevé – 61.42.77.86
M. Brandolin. Closed Sat lunch and Sun. Open until 10 pm. Private room: 15. Garden dining. Air cond. Parking. V. B7-1

Partisans of tradition will prefer the duck salad, blanquette de lotte with creamed garlic, and veal kidneys with sherry that now figure regularly on the menu. Every now and then, though, Marc Brandolin surprises customers with innovative dishes like smoked cod and mild pepper salad, capon fillet with sorrel, or oysters accompanied by duck ham. His little suburban restaurant has an elegant dining room and a tiny garden for summer meals.
A la carte: 300 F.

12/20 Le Marocain
47, rue des Couteliers – 61.53.28.01
M. Boualami. Closed Mon. Open until 11 pm. Private room: 16. Air cond. No pets. V DC. D5-34

With its décor straight out of the *Thousand and One Nights*, this Moroccan restaurant satisfies the locals' cravings for exotic cuisine. Try Madame Zohra's grilled pepper salad, couscous, tajines, and pastilla. Wide choice of Moroccan wines, friendly reception and service.
A la carte: 250 F.

Mercure
Rue St-Jérôme – 61.23.11.77
Open every day. 170 rms 405-560 F. Restaurant. TV. Air cond. Conference facilities. Telex 520760. V AE DC. E4-31

Set above a shopping centre, this modern and centrally located hotel offers recently renovated, well-equipped rooms (though those opposite the Place Occitane are poorly soundproofed). Excellent breakfasts.

Mermoz
50, rue Matabiau – 61.63.04.04
Open every day. 1 ste 850 F. 52 rms 460-490 F. TV. Air cond. Conference facilities. Garage parking. Telex 532427. V AE DC. E2-21

Near the station and built round a peaceful interior courtyard, this modern hotel has 1930s-style rooms that are original and well-equipped. Wonderful breakfasts. Meals served on trays around the clock.

Novotel Toulouse Centre
5, pl. A.-Jourdain – 61.21.74.74
Closed Tue, Wed and Thu (Sep, Oct, Nov and June). 6 stes 800 F. 131 rms 470-510 F. Restaurant. Half-

board 195-295 F. TV. Air cond. Conference facilities. *Garage parking. Telex 532400. V AE DC.* B2-9

Recently built, this well-designed hotel offers numerous amenities. Five rooms are reserved for non-smokers. Underground car park. Superb breakfasts.

Orsi
(Le Bouchon Lyonnais)
13, rue de l'Industrie – 61.62.97.43
M. Orsi. Closed Sun (except holidays). Open until 11 pm. Private room: 60. Air cond. V AE DC. E4-26

Although its 1930s brasserie décor is fashioned after Pierre Orsi in Lyon and its menu features the same chitterling sausages and saucisson chaud, the cooking here tends to be more modern or based on regional ingredients. Unfortunately, success seems to have marred the quality of the food, and though the young pigeon in honey vinegar was tasty and well-balanced, we were frankly disappointed by the prawns with tarragon mousseline, and the lasagne of (barely visible) turbot and tomato coulis. The service works smoothly despite the crush. Splendid choice of wines and brandies.
A la carte: 350 F. Menu: 192 F.

12/20 Le Pavillon d'Argent
43, rue du Taur – 61.23.36.48
M. Nguyen. Closed Mon lunch, Sun and Aug. Open until 10 pm. Private room: 50. Air cond. No pets. V AE DC. D3-11

The service is laconic to say the least, but the Saigon specialities are pleasant enough: unusual crab nems, chicken fritters in a delicious sweet-and-sour sauce, classic flambéed banana. Efficient service.
A la carte: 150 F. Menu: 59 F (lunch only).

Les Pêcheries
30, bd du Mal-Leclerc – 61.23.62.72
M. Sabeyses. Open every day. Open until 11.30 pm. Garden dining. Air cond. V AE DC. B3-44

The new chef, an old hand at preparing meat and game, is doing a great job at this seafood restaurant owned by a major fish wholesaler. The menu offers the widest choice of fish dishes in town, and one of the most original: oyster parmentier, prawn casserole with wine and sweet peppers, lotte with 40 cloves of garlic, and grouper fish piperade. Superb shellfish is also available. Contemporary décor, attractive wines, reasonable prices.
A la carte: 270-340 F. Menus: 88 F (lunch only), 160 F.

11/20 Le Pyrénéen
14, allées F.-Roosevelt – 61.23.38.88
M. di Pietro. Open every day. Open until midnight. Air cond. V DC. E3-14

Leather banquettes and a wrought-iron and glass ceiling give an old-fashioned feel to this lively, late-night establishment featuring fine shellfish platters and brasserie cooking.
A la carte: 200-250 F.

Raj
48, rue Peyrolières – 61.21.84.44
M. Miah. Dinner only (lunch weekends). Open until midnight. Air cond. V AE DC. D4-45

The Mayor of Toulouse is said to have a weakness for the tandoori chicken. He's one of many contented regulars who come here to sample Bengali dishes served with extreme courtesy in the large, blue-tinted dining room. The only drawback is that the tables are too close together. As you might expect, the wine list is not this restaurant's strong point (many customers drink tea with their meal), but the coffee could be improved.

A la carte: 200 F. Menus: 69 F (until 8.30 pm), 98 F, 105 F, 148 F.

Claude Ribardière
21, bd A.-Duportal — 61.13.91.12
M. Ribardière. Closed Sun. Open until 10.15 pm. Garden dining. Air cond. V AE DC. C3-46

The owner and all the staff from his previous restaurant in Tarbes have just moved into what looks destined to be Toulouse's new business district when the conference centre is ready. We're reserving judgment about his restaurant and cooking to give him time to settle in, and wish him well in this city endowed with many a fine chef.

A la carte: 300-350 F. Menus: 145 F (lunch only, wine inc), 170 F, 260 F.

12/20 Le Saint-Simon
3, rte de St-Simon — 61.07.59.44
M. Chagnon. Open every day. Open until 10 pm. Garden dining. Air cond. No pets. Parking. Telex 530518. V AE DC. A6-4

Whether you're seated next to the fireplace in winter, or out on the terrace in summer, you're bound to enjoy René Pollentier's simple, constantly renewed, seafood dishes: mussel and avocado cassolette, salmon escalope with seaweed butter, and bitter-chocolate marquise with a minty sauce. Wide choice of wines, friendly service.

A la carte: 260 F. Menus: 125 F and 160 F (weekdays only).

🏠 Hôtel de Diane
(See restaurant above)
Open every day. 35 rms 345-450 F. Half-board 350-420 F. TV. Conference facilities. Pool. Tennis.

This hotel sits in two hectares of parkland especially suited for sports-minded guests (tennis, swimming pool, minigolf). Well-equipped, comfortable rooms.

12/20 La Table d'Aline
7, quai St-Pierre — 61.23.24.07
M. Escudero. Closed Sat lunch, Sun, Mon and 10-25 Aug. Open until 11 pm. V AE DC. C4-41

Charming, rustic, and slightly nostalgic, this pleasant little restaurant offers good cooking at affordable prices. Sample the lapin à la tapenade, duck breast, cassoulet, and île flottante with redcurrant sauce.

A la carte: 150 F. Menus: 50 F (lunch only), 70 F, 90 F, 130 F.

11/20 La Tantina de Burgos
27, rue de la Garonnette — 61.55.59.29
M. Boury. Closed Sun, Mon, 24 Dec-3 Jan and 10-20 Aug. Open until midnight. Terrace dining. No pets. V. D5-42

A good cross-section of customers frequent this typical Spanish *bodega* with its large communal tables, festive atmosphere, countless tapas, and of course, its paella and zarzuela. Brisk service.

A la carte: 150 F.

12/20 Taverne Bavaroise
59, bd de Strasbourg — 61.21.54.46
M. Chaffre. Closed at Christmas. Open until 11 pm. Terrace dining. Air cond. V. D3-18

Pop into this convivial brasserie for inexpensive oysters, excellent charcuterie from Germany and the nearby Ariège, the best choucroute in

Toulouse, and draught German beer. Terrace under the plane trees, pleasant service.

A la carte: 160-180 F.

🍷 Ubu Club
16, rue St-Rome — 61.23.26.75
M. Blanc. Dinner only. Closed Sun. Open until 2 am. Private room: 40. Air cond. No pets. Telex 530955. V AE DC. D4-27

You go through the adjacent night-club to reach the vaulted restaurant, which celebrates its thirtieth birthday this year. Superior quality produce is used to produce classic food with a regional flavour: foie gras in peppery aspic, young pigeon, sweetbreads with crayfish, and strawberry millefeuile. Excellent range of Bordeaux, amiable service.

A la carte: 350-400 F.

🍷 Vanel ۞
22, rue M.-Fonvielle — 61.21.51.82
M. Roudgé. Closed Sun, holidays, 12-22 July and 9-19 Aug. Open until 11 pm. Private room: 25. Air cond. V AE DC. E4-6

Pierre Roudgé has taken Lucien Vanel's place in the kitchen, and now faces the difficult task of being accepted as the successor to this master of Gascon cuisine. Roudgé has sufficient sincerity, skill, and breadth to impose his personality in this shrine to regional food, and we look forward to awarding him three toques that will be all his own. He also benefits from the backing of André Solomiac, who takes professional charge of the service, the superb cellar, and the fine collection of Armagnacs and Cognacs.

A la carte: 400-450 F. Menus: 200 F (weekdays lunch only, wine inc), 330 F, 450 F.

And also...
Our selection of places for inexpensive, quick, or late-night meals.

La Bascule (61.52.09.51 - 14, av. M.-Hauriou. Open until 10.30 pm): New décor, charming staff, and rising prices, fuelled by the arrival on the menu of costly ingredients like rock lobster. But you'll still find fine regional food, such as the excellent cassoulet (200 F).

Le Bistrot des Vins (61.52.02.89 - 5, rue Riguepels. Open until 2 am): From 6 pm onwards, wines are available by the glass (sixteen featured each day from a cellar boasting 400). Plus an increasing number of Champagnes and spirits from near (Armagnac, Cognac) and far (Scotch whisky, Kentucky bourbon). A variety of cheeses, charcuterie, and bistro dishes provide the solids (150 F).

La Camargue (61.23.82.28 - 5, rue Cujas. Open until 10.30 pm): You'll need to make reservations at this lively and popular restaurant, where the menu changes often (120 F).

Les Caves de la Maréchale (61.23.89.88 - 3, rue J.-Chalande. Open until 11 pm): The chef's greeting is as lively as his cuisine: salmon tartare, duck breast with peaches, home-prepared foie gras (180 F).

Le Flambadou (61.32.94.53 - 5, bd de la Méditerranée. Open until 11 pm): A friendly establishment offering young rabbit, farm poultry, and game in season (sometimes grouse), all cooked 'au flambadou' (in bacon fat) (150-200 F).

Chez Jeannette (61.62.44.90 - 59, rue Riquet. Open until midnight): Oddly decorated with ladies' underwear hanging from the ceiling, this restaurant proposes a wide range of dishes: tajine with prunes, sauerkraut, charcuterie, and a market-

based *plat du jour*. Vodka and foie gras are always available. Popular with intellectuals (150 F).
La Plancha (61.21.50.30 - 16, rue d'Austerlitz. Open until midnight): Typical Spanish fare like tapas, parillada, zarzuela, and paella, plus a pleasant surprise menu. And Spanish wines of course (160 F).

In nearby **Blagnac**

(7 km W)
31700 Toulouse (H.-Garonne)

12/20 Le Caouec
at the airport — 61.71.11.25
M. Mornat. Open every day. Open until 11 pm. Private room: 120. Air cond. Parking. V AE DC.
Pierre-François Dreneau is quite capable of producing reliable, tasty food: sole fillets with wild mushrooms, and 'gourmet' sweetbreads.
A la carte: 300-350 F. Menus: 140 F, 160 F, 180 F.

Sofitel
(See restaurant above)
Open every day. 100 rms 680-780 F. TV. Air cond. Conference facilities. Heated pool. Tennis.
This hotel provides spacious, well-equipped rooms, and a number of amenities.

12/20 Le Gabriel
1, bd F.-Pons — 61.71.18.17
Mme Guiblain. Closed Sat lunch, Sun and 12-19 Aug. Open until 10 pm. Terrace dining. V.
Le Gabriel boasts vigorous and tasty bistro cooking prepared by a team of professionals.
A la carte: 280-300 F. Menus: 75 F (lunch only), 110 F, 190 F.

Pujol
21, av. du Gal-Compans — 61.71.13.58
M. Pujol. Closed Sun dinner, Sat. Open until 9.30 pm. Private room: 36. Garden dining. Parking. V DC.
Cassoulet is among the best in Toulouse, the fricassée of lamb sweetbreads with chanterelles subtly tasty, and classic desserts (soufflé au Grand Marnier) are consistently perfect. A little more audacity would be welcome....
A la carte: 400 F.

In nearby **Bouloc**

(22 km N on D 14 and D 4)
31620 Toulouse — (H.-Garonne)

Le Lord
1, rue du Fontanas — 61.82.09.34
M. Vidal. Closed Sat lunch and Sun dinner. Open until 10 pm. Air cond. V.
You'll love René Vidal's foie gras, duck aiguillettes in Montauriol wine, seafood medley with sage, fine cheeses, and inviting pastries. Pleasant regional wines at moderate prices.
A la carte: 300 F. Menus: 70 F (weekdays only), 89 F (weekends and holidays only), 120 F, 165 F.

In nearby **Garidech**

(17 km NE on N 88)
31380 Toulouse — (H.-Garonne)

12/20 Le Club
61.84.20.23
M. Delsol. Closed Tue dinner (except July-Aug), Wed, Feb school holidays and 23 Aug-beg Sep. Open until 10 pm. Terrace dining. Tennis. Parking. V.
This suburban house produces consistent, enjoyable cooking: mussel gratin with spinach, cassou-

let au confit de canard, and warm apple and honey tartlets. Well-balanced wine list and a wide choice of Armagnacs. Friendly, efficient service.
A la carte: 200-240 F. Menus: 75 F (weekdays lunch only), 110 F, 160 F, 220 F.

In nearby **Labarthe-sur-Lèze**

(12 km on N 20)
31860 Toulouse — (H.-Garonne)

Le Poêlon
Place de la Mairie
61.08.68.49
M. Autebon. Closed Mon, dinner Sun and holidays, 3 weeks end Aug-beg Sep and 2-15 Jan. Open until 9.30 pm. Garden dining. No pets. V AE.
Try the lime-scented skate salad, perfectly cooked freshwater perch in a grapefruit infusion, and lamb sweetbreads and veal kidney garnished with buttery cabbage.
A la carte: 300 F. Menus: 100 F (weekdays lunch only, wine inc), 150 F, 200 F.

In nearby **Purpan**

(3 km W)
31300 Toulouse — (H.-Garonne)

Novotel
23, rue Maubec — 61.49.34.10
Open every day. 123 rms 420 F. Restaurant. TV. Air cond. Conference facilities. Pool. Tennis. Parking. Telex 520640. V AE DC.
The modern, well-equipped rooms (two adapted for the disabled) look onto pleasant grounds. There's a play area, and tennis court.

In nearby **Ramonville-St-Agne**

(8 km SE on N 113)
31520 Toulouse — (H.-Garonne)

12/20 La Chaumière
102, av. Tolosane (N 113) — 61.73.02.02
M. Maurel. Open every day. Open until 10 pm. Garden dining. Garage parking. Telex 520646. V AE DC.
This large suburban restaurant caters mainly for the business community at lunchtime, and to chattering academics in the evening. Professional welcome and service.
A la carte: 300 F. Menus: 65 F, 150 F, 200 F.

La Chaumière
(See restaurant above)
Open every day. 43 rms 300-330 F. Half-board 510-550 F. TV. Air cond. Conference facilities. Pool.
Set in a park, this large, modern building offers pleasant, comfortable, air-conditioned rooms.

In nearby **Saint-Jean**

(9 km NE on N 98)
31240 Toulouse — (H.-Garonne)

Horizon 88
Rte d'Albi — 61.74.34.15
Open every day. 38 rms 195-270 F. TV. Conference facilities. Pool. Garage parking. Telex 533071. V DC.
A modern building with comfortable, well-equipped rooms and loggias. Laundry service.

The new spiral-bound RAC Atlas France will help you to find your chosen restaurant of hotel, no matter how secluded.

In nearby **Tournefeuille**

(8.5 km W on D 632)
31170 Toulouse — (H.-Garonne)

Les Chanterelles
279, ch. Ramelet-Moundi — 61.86.21.86
Open every day. 10 stes 260-350 F. TV 3 rms. No pets. Garage parking.
Well-equipped chalets (living room, covered terrace, garage) in pleasant and restful grounds.

In nearby **Vieille-Toulouse**

(8.5 km S on D 4)
31320 Toulouse — (H.-Garonne)

La Flânerie
Rte de Lacroix-Falgarde — 61.73.39.12
Closed 23 Dec-6 Jan. 12 rms 200-450 F. TV 9 rms. Pool. Garage parking. V AE DC.
A lovely hilltop house, with sweeping views of the Garonne. Charming reception.

In nearby **Vigoulet-Auzil**

(12 km S exit Ramonville and D 35)
31320 Toulouse — (H.-Garonne)

Auberge de Tournebride
near the riding club — 61.73.34.49
M. Nony. Closed Sun dinner, Mon, 3 weeks in Jan and 2 weeks in Aug. Open until 10 pm. Private room: 100. Terrace dining. Parking. V AE DC.
Though Pierre Nony is known to be grumpy, but his wife Gilberte and her staff are always good-humoured. Try his asparagus flan with tomato vinaigrette, freshwater perch cooked in crab broth, and kid blanquette with sorrel. The superb view of the Pyrenees is as soothing as the generous desserts.
A la carte: 300-370 F. Menus: 170 F (weekdays only), and from 220 F to 240 F (Sun and holidays only).

TOUQUES

See Deauville

TOUQUET (LE)

62520 Touquet (Le) — (P./Calais)
Paris 222 - Abbeville 61 - Boulogne 32 - Lille 132

11/20 Bistro de la Charlotte
36, rue St-Jean — 21.05.32.11
M. Beurton. Closed Jan. Open until 9.30 pm (11 pm in seas). Air cond. V.
In this restaurant just 100 metres from the sea, you'll find a steady stream of customers relishing scallops with tagliatelle, seafood curry with tart berries, brik of ginger-flavoured salmon, and a fine chocolate tart.
A la carte: 150-180 F. Menu: 78 F.

Le Café des Arts
80, rue de Paris — 21.05.21.55
M. Panni-Rousseau. Closed off-season Mon and Tue lunch. Annual closings not available. Open until 10 pm (10.30 pm in summer). V AE DC.
If Jérôme Panni keeps having such great ideas for his carefully selected ingredients, he'll end up with the best restaurant in town. Customers in his bright and charming two-tiered restaurant enjoy red-mullet fillet in beetroot juice with parslied mushrooms, prawns in their shells and tomato purée, and cod bouillabaisse. The delicious desserts include a raspberry gratin with chocolate. Increasingly well-stocked cellar.
A la carte: 300-350 F. Menus: 135 F, 260 F.

12/20 Le Chalut
7, bd J.-Pouget
21.05.22.55
MM. Caput and Thiriez. Closed off-season Tue and Wed, and Jan. Open until 10 pm. Terrace dining. V
The best reasons for coming to this restaurant are its view of the sea and incredibly varied wine list. The careful cooking concentrates primarily on seafood: scampi, lotte, seafood pot-au-feu.
A la carte: 300-350 F. Menus: 110 F, 220 F.

Flavio-Club de la Forêt

1, av. du Verger
21.05.10.22
M. Flavio. Closed Wed and 6 Jan-1 March. Open until 10 pm. Private room: 20. Garden dining. V AE DC
Flavio's enthusiastic conversation and Danièle Delmotte's smiling welcome are the perfect foil for the duo of salmon (smoked and raw with coarse salt), perfectly cooked brill steamed with sea kale, and lamb with fresh morels.
A la carte: 500-600 F. Menus: 200 F (lunch only), 350 F, 620 F.

Manoir Hôtel
Av. du Golf
21.05.20.22
Open every day. 2 stes 1,200-1,250 F. 40 rms 550-1,050 F. Restaurant. Half-board 720-1,220 F. TV. Heated pool. Tennis. Golf. Parking. V AE.
An inviting, Normandy-style residence with beautiful, comfortable rooms, some of which have been renovated. Golf course (reduced rates for guests), billards.

Novotel-Thalamer
Beach front — 21.09.85.00
Closed 6-27 Jan. 104 rms 375-720 F. Restaurant. TV. Conference facilities. Heated pool. Parking. Telex 160480. V AE DC.
This large, contemporary seafront hotel provides bright, functional rooms with superb views. Direct access to the salt-water spa. Sauna.

Westminster
Av. du Verger — 21.05.48.48
Closed 2 Jan-15 Feb. 2 stes 1,250-1,700 F. 115 rms 480-905 F. Restaurant. TV. Conference facilities. Heated pool. Tennis. Valet parking. V AE DC.
Within easy reach of the casino and forest, this last of Le Touquet's grand hotels from the period between the wars features entirely refurbished, perfectly comfortable rooms, as well as numerous amenities (covered swimming pool, sauna, solarium, squash courts).

In nearby **Etaples**

(5 km E on N 39)
62630 Touquet (Le) — (P./Calais)

11/20 Les Pêcheurs d'Etaples
Quai de la Canche
21.94.06.90
M. Rup. Closed Jan. Open until 10 pm. Air cond. Parking. V.
Unfortunately, this restaurant's tendency to over-cook dishes doesn't do justice to the freshness of its seafood: shellfish platters, lobster bisque, lotte with turnips, bouillabaisse étaploise.
A la carte: 230 F. Menus: 85 F, 110 F.

59200 Tourcoing — (Nord)
Paris 234 - Lille 14 - Roubaix 4 - Gand 61 - Ostende 66

12/20 La Baratte
395, rue du Clinquet
20.94.45.63

*M. Bajeux. Closed Sat and Sun, Feb school holidays
and 3-26 Aug. Open until 9.30 pm. Air cond. V AE.*

This restaurant in an out-of-the-way district is
well worth finding, particularly for its subtly prepared salmon in orange brine with truffled cream,
veal sweetbreads with baked shallots, and chocolate feuilleté. Reasonably priced Bordeaux.

A la carte: 270 F. Menus: from 94 F to 280 F.

Ibis
Centre Gal-de-Gaulle — 20.24.84.58

*Open every day. 1 ste 350 F. 102 rms 265-285 F.
Restaurant. Half-board 370-420 F. TV. Conference
facilities. Garage parking. Telex 132695. V.*

Opposite a municipal park, this hotel provides
recently refurbished rooms in the heart of town.

Au P'tit Bedon
5, bd de l'Egalité — 20.25.00.51

*M. Ferlin. Closed Mon, 15-31 July and 1-15 Sep. Open
until 11 pm. V AE DC.*

Dany Ferlin has access to the best seafood
suppliers in Morbihan, and his brother Bruno is an
expert at cooking fish. Together, they've developed a remarkable repertoire that features colombo
de coquilles St-Jacques, lotte with lemon grass,
rack of lamb in a peppery sauce, and an iced
strawberry and lemon croquantine. Excellent wine
list.

A la carte: 350 F. Menus: 180 F (weekdays only,
wine inc), 250 F (wine inc).

La Saucière
189, bd Gambetta
20.26.67.90

*M. Legrand. Closed Sun dinner, Mon, 25 Feb-
5 March and Aug. Open until 9 pm. V.*

Chef Legrand, formerly of the Maxim's outpost
at Charles de Gaulle airport, has taken over this
posh, flower-decked dining room. His polished
cuisine is pricey: 400F for a lobster salad with
avocado and mango, a crumb-coated turbot with
horseradish, kidneys in a mustardy cream sauce,
and a generously apportioned fruit gratin with
frothy sabayon. Absent-minded staff.

A la carte: 400 F. Menus: 180 F, 250 F.

See Deauville

See Toulouse

71700 Tournus — (Saône/Loire)
Paris 360 - Mâcon 30 - Chalon 27 - Bourg-en-B. 53

Hôtel de Greuze
5-6, pl. de l'Abbaye — 85.40.77.77

*Open every day. 2 stes 1,780 F. 21 rms 595-1,150 F.
Restaurant. TV. Air cond. Valet parking. V AE DC.*

A former townhouse facing the abbey has been
transformed into a hotel containing a score of
magnificently upholstered, curtained, and carpeted guest rooms.

Greuze
1, rue A.-Thibaudet — 85.51.13.52

*M. Ducloux. Closed 1-10 Dec. Open until 9.45 pm.
Air cond. V AE.*

Jean Ducloux is a living monument to all that is
best about fine traditional French cuisine, and in
his forty-fourth year at the hob he still manages to
hone his magnificent technique, ever more closely
approaching perfection. Single-handedly he is
keeping alive a style of dining that the world has
nearly forgotten. Even if there were the tiniest
hope of convincing him that the world had
changed, would we want to? For where else can
one taste the likes of his pâté en croûte Alexandre
Dumaine—the best pâté on earth—or the astonishing frogs' legs (where does he get such beauties?)
en persillade, or the wonderfully rich and delicate
pike quenelles?

. The parade of nostalgic dishes whisks us back to
a more expansive era: truffle galette in sauce
Périgueux; opulent lobster timbale (the crustacean
ceremoniously presents his claws for your appro-
val); sautéed Bresse chicken (for two), its juices
sublimely, simply deglazed with white wine. And
the desserts—easily worth four toques—like pear
feuilleté au caramel, matchless profiteroles, or
sorbets that are pure-fruit wonders.

This year we could no longer withhold Ducloux's
third toque, which he has earned, not for
'seniority' or old times' sake, but for his pure,
vibrant homage to a great tradition.

A la carte: 500 F. Menus: 255 F (weekdays only),
470 F.

37000 Tours — (Indre/Loire)
Paris 234 - Angers 105 - Orléans 113

Hôtel Alliance
292, av. de Grammont — 47.28.00.80

*Open every day. 6 stes 655 F. 119 rms 440-515 F.
Restaurant. Half-board 335-450 F. TV. Air cond.
Pool. Tennis. Parking. V AE DC.*

This recent hotel was built in the traditional Loire
style, with white freestone walls and a slate roof.
It's near the lake and offers comfortable,
soundproofed rooms.

Jean Bardet
57, rue Groison
47.41.41.11

*M. Bardet. Closed Sun dinner off-season, Mon (except
dinner in seas and holidays) and 19 Feb-9 March.
Open until 9.30 pm. Garden dining. Valet parking.
V AE DC.*

If the French government were ever to appoint
a minister of the palate, Jean Bardet is unquestionably the most qualified candidate. Sneak into the
kitchen one evening after the last service, and
you're likely to catch him and his wife eagerly
tucking into one of the evening's productions, or
nose-deep in an old Vouvray.

Their passion for matters gustatory, their drive for
perfection, spreads to the whole staff, and even to
the patrons, who are seduced by the subtle
harmonics of a velvety cream of turkey enhanced
with chervil, an oyster ragoût with a watercress
mousse spiked with a drop of Muscadet, a bosky
fricassée of asparagus and morels, or baby eels
from Vendée simmered with garlic and Loire wine
vinegar, or a remarkable lobster poached in broth
with goose fat, prawns, and truffles, a dish that
brings the sea and the land together to make...
heaven. And when truffle season arrives, Bardet's
passion for the tuber spurs him to truffle an entire
menu: scallops and leeks, brandade de morue,

pot-au-feu of cockscombs and cocks' kidneys, and a thick tournedos of capon all receive a touch of the black magic.

What can't be listed, besides the many layers of taste and subtlety that characterise the art of Bardet's table, are the 62 vintages of Vouvray that are just a small part of the dazzling wine list.

A la carte: 550-800 F. Menus:250 F, 470 F, 620 F.

Jean Bardet
(See restaurant above)
Closed 19 Feb-9 March. 6 stes 1,300-1,600 F. 9 rms 550-850 F. TV. Heated pool.

A high wall encloses the wide, romantic, stream-fed grounds that surround this grand Directoire-period villa. The rooms and suites are furnished in an attractive mix of period and contemporary charm. Fabulous marble bathrooms; breakfasts must be tasted to be believed.

Barrier
101, av. de la Tranchée – 47.54.20.39
M. Barrier. Closed Sun dinner. Open until 9.45 pm. Private room: 20. Air cond. Parking. V.

The nearly immortal Charles Barrier will soon be 77 years old, and it is hard to tell how much he is still involved in the day-to-day running of the kitchen. when one thinks back on his triumphs: the terrine of Loire fish in a caviar cream, the eel stewed in Chinon wine with plump prunes, the young Touraine pigeon cooked in a bladder, or the feuilleté of Loire Valley strawberries, there's no question that things are slipping. Can the old gentleman crack the whip and win back his third toque? It wouldn't be the first time that Charles Barrier has astonished us.

A la carte: 500 F and up. Menus: 245 F (weekdays only), 435 F.

12/20 Les Gais Lurons
15, rue Lavoisier – 47.64.75.50
MM. Libreau and Halm. Closed Sat lunch, Sun and 15-31 Aug. Open until 10 pm. V AE DC.

This spot is already well known, at least among the owners' friends, for its medallions of trout and smoked salmon (overcooked, oversalted in our opinion), good tournedos Rossini, and an excellent morello cherry dessert.

A la carte: 250 F. Menus: 98 F, 130 F, 180 F.

Hôtel Harmonie
15, rue Fr.-Joliot-Curie – 47.66.01.48
Open every day. 6 stes 600-730 F. 54 rms 350-730 F. Restaurant. Half-board 475-510 F. TV. Garage parking. V AE.

Located on a quiet street not far from the railway station, these modern rooms are beautifully appointed in a bright, art deco spirit.

Le Jardin du Castel
10, rue Groison – 47.41.94.40
MM. Lironville, Tricon and André. Closed Sat lunch and Wed. Annual closings not available. Open until 9.30 pm. Garden dining. Valet parking. V.

Assortment of raw fish in coarse salt, authentic Touraine farm hen cooked in a bacon shell and carved tableside, saddle of young rabbit with mild garlic: the explicit menu hardly needs commentary. Except to point out that the tableside carving takes forever, portions are shrinking, and the announced accompaniments are sometimes barely noticeable.

A la carte: 350-400 F. Menus: 210 F (weekdays lunch only, wine inc), 210 F, 420 F.

Hôtel de Groison
(See restaurant above)
Open every day. 10 rms 440-680 F. Half-board 520-650 F. TV.

A garden of delights, from the reception to the spacious rooms, the superb breakfasts, and... the garden.

Le Lys
63, rue Bl.-Pascal – 47.05.27.92
MM. Aubrun and Jimenez. Closed Sun dinner, Mon and 2-15 Jan. Open until 10.30 pm. Private room: 30. V.

The two young owner-chefs had just finished fixing up their restaurant when fire destroyed the attractive contemporary dining room now redone in Louis XV style. Meanwhile the kitchen has been set ablaze by the imagination of these very intelligent cooks; taste their pan-roasted prawns covered with blanched sliced ginger, then floated in a tasty bouillon with tiny diced vegetables, or the pigeon with lemony couscous, or the sea bream and salmon fillets with spiced shredded chicory. The only thing lacking is a sommelier to administrate an enriched cellar.

A la carte:300 F. Menus:95 F, 145 F, 280 F.

La Roche Le Roy
55, rte de St-Avertin – 47.27.22.00
M. Couturier. Closed Sat lunch, Sun and 3-25 Aug. Open until 9.45 pm. Garden dining. Parking. V AE.

Alain Couturier is one the most exciting up-and-coming chefs in the formerly sleepy Val de Loire. Local foodies, who don't want to miss a bit of the action, keep Couturier's dining room full day and evening. They love savoury, seasonal dishes that are brought to them. For example: lightly breaded frogs' legs accompanied by a little carrot custard, aïoli de sole sauce vierge, and a rabbit grenadin with morel mushroom cream (a country dish fit for a palace). Local chèvres grace the cheese board, and desserts include an enticing warm sablé topped with apples and raspberries. The fine cellar features wonderful Loire wines and claret, mercifully priced.

A la carte: 300-350 F. Menus: 150 F (lunch only), 190 F, 250 F.

Rôtisserie Tourangelle
23, rue du Commerce – 47.05.71.21
M. Féron. Closings not available. Open until 10 pm. Terrace dining. V AE DC.

A well-deserved first toque to new chef Claude Gautier, for his salad of rabbit and carrot confit dressed with a delicate sauce hinting of paprika, the duo of fresh cod and sea trout with a creamy avocado sauce, a pretty and delicious rosette of lamb with chanterelles (and too much basil sauce). Overdosed, omnipresent sauces, indeed, are the problem Gautier must resolve if he wants to win back the extra point he had at his previous restaurant. Delectable homemade sorbets; short, balanced wine list.

A la carte: 280-300 F. Menus: from 140 F to 245 F.

Le Royal
65, av. de Grammont – 47.64.71.78
Open every day. 50 rms 292-344 F. TV. Garage parking. V AE DC.

A hideous modern building conceals beautiful, well-equipped rooms with period furnishings. Private garage.

La Touraine

5, bd Heurteloup — 47.05.37.12

M. Faury. Closed Sat. Open until 9.15 pm. Garage parking. V AE DC.

Enjoy Gilles Millard's soft-boiled eggs with foie gras, (slightly overgrilled) salmon fillet on a bed of fresh spinach, and the sumptuous mango tarte Tatin with coconut sauce. The wine list is an odd mishmash, with few local bottlings.

A la carte: 200-250 F. Menus: 170 F, 200 F.

L'Univers

(See restaurant above)

Open every day. 89 rms 400-690 F. TV.

Almost all the rooms give onto the courtyard and are therefore quiet. Facilities for conferences and banquets.

Les Tuffeaux

19, rue Lavoisier — 47.47.19.89

M. Marsollier. Closed Mon lunch and Sun. Open until 9.30 pm. Air cond. V.

The charm of old Tours is everywhere present in this attractive beamed dining room. A trifle more rigour would surely make Gildas Marsollier's interesting cuisine even better. The generous saffron-yellow mussel and chard soup is tasty, but lacks finesse, and the cooking juices of the duckling in Bourgueil wine needed further reduction. Good pastries; fine selection of local wines.

A la carte: 250 F. Menus: 110 F (weekdays lunch only), 150 F, 200 F.

In nearby **Montlouis-sur-Loire**

(12 km E on D 751)
37270 Tours — (Indre/Loire)

Roc en Val

Pl. Courtemanche — 47.50.81.96

M. Régnier. Closed Sun dinner, and Mon (except dinner 15 April-15 Oct). Open until 10 pm. Garden dining. Parking. V AE.

Reflections from the Loire light up the opulent dining room as the passion for fine cuisine, shared by chef Thierry Marx and owner Thierry Régnier, lights up a sophisticated but savoury menu. Taste the adroit chaud-froid of red mullet with a sweet-pepper coulis, the hot oyster and foie gras flan, or the homely pot-au-feu aux trois viandes with a bright tomato coulis. The cellar boasts treasures from Montlouis, Vouvray, and Bourgueil.

A la carte: 350-400 F. Menus: 220 F (weekdays lunch only, wine inc), 165 F, 245 F, 310 F.

83690 Tourtour — (Var)
Paris 860 - Draguignan 20 - Aups 10 - Salernes 11

Bastide de Tourtour

94.70.57.30

Closed 31 Oct-9 March. 25 rms 560-930 F (per pers, half-board oblig). Restaurant. TV. Heated pool. Tennis. Parking. V AE DC.

You can take in a hundred kilometres of Var scenery from this luxurious mountain fastness among the pines. Jacuzzi, exercise room. Relais et Châteaux.

Les Chênes Verts

2 km, rte de Villecroze — 94.70.55.06

M. Bajade. Closed Tue dinner, Wed and 1 Jan-20 Feb. Open until 9 pm. Parking.

We happily report that last year's second toque is still firmly in place. See for yourself when you taste Paul Bajade's marinade of fish adorned with a courgette blossom, the lobster and lemon salad

with mixed greens, and the delicious duckling roast with a red-wine fumet, the thighs served with a delicate salad glistening with fruity olive oil. The house steadfastly refuses to honour credit cards.

A la carte: 400-500 F. Menus: 200 F, 340 F, 650 F.

22560 Trébeurden — (Côtes/Armor)
Paris 519 - Perros-Guirec 13 - St-Brieuc 72

Manoir de Lan Kerellec

Allée Centrale — 96.23.50.09

M. Daubé. Closed Mon lunch and Tue (except in summer), and 15 Nov-15 March. Open until 10 pm. Garden dining. No-smoking section. Valet parking. Telex 741172. V AE DC.

This huge turn-of-the-century manor perched on a rocky point above the sea has welcomed a new chef, François Reverdy. His light, precise style coaxes out the full flavour of fine ingredients in dishes like lobster and prawn salad with a truffle dressing, prawn cassolette with (a trifle too much) tarragon, John Dory and apples in a creamy cider sauce, a hearty calf's head ragoût with olives, and a tasty hot apple tart enhanced by a remarkable Calvados cream. The dining room has a nautical motif. Thoughtful service.

A la carte: 350-400 F. Menus: 130 F (weekdays lunch only), 200 F, 250 F, 320 F.

Manoir de Lan Kerellec

(See restaurant above)

Closed 15 Nov-15 March. 8 stes 1,080-1,500 F. 18 rms 500-880 F. Half-board 500-1,000 F oblig in seas. TV. Tennis.

Thanks to the polished taste of the lady of the house, this beautiful seafront establishment has become luxurious while preserving its family ambience. There are mahogany bathrooms, water-massage bathtubs and private patios where guests may enjoy delicious breakfasts.

24510 Trémolat — (Dordogne)
Paris 530 - Périgueux 54 - Sarlat 46 - Bergerac 34

Le Vieux Logis

53.22.80.06

M. Giraudel-Destord. Closed Wed lunch, Tue and 7 Jan-18 Feb. Open until 10 pm. Garden dining. Valet parking. V AE DC.

Rarely in this world does it happen that a setting, service, and food conspire to create such a heavenly impression of well-being. Here one sits among glowing antiques to feed upon Pierre-Jean Duribreux's vibrant, light yet earthy repertoire. Pinch yourself as you pull up to a feast of foie gras with fig compote, an omelette paysanne, stuffed trout in a potato crust with Bergerac wine sauce, and bœuf à la ficelle. The stunning wine list is rich in superb regional bottlings and rare vintages and does nothing to restore one's sense of reality!

A la carte: 350-500 F. Menus: 210 F, 300 F.

Le Vieux Logis

(See restaurant above)

Closed 7 Jan-18 Feb. 8 stes 930-960 F. 14 rms 595-900 F. Half-board 630-750 F. TV. Pool.

These remarkably comfortable rooms, so tastefully decorated, are surrounded by an exuberant garden. Blessedly quiet. Relais et Châteaux.

See CORSICA: Porto-Vecchio

56470 Trinité-sur-Mer (La) — (Morbihan)
Paris 482 - Auray 12 - Vannes 30 - Quiberon 22

 L'Azimut
1, rue du Men-Dû — 97.55.71.88
M. Le Calvez. Closed Christmas and 2 Jan-15 Feb. Open until 10 pm (11 pm in seas). Terrace dining. Parking. V.

The new ownerswho are former two-toque veterans—are very slowly steering the menu towards more regional interest. On the harbour-view terrace, taste the oysters grilled with rillettes (an amusing local recipe that doesn't seem to hurt the oysters), red mullet au Pinot Noir with leeks and fresh peas, and an original strawberry gratin. Fish and lobsters are also simply grilled in the rustic fireplace.

A la carte: 300 F. Menus: 95 F (weekdays lunch only), 190 F, 360 F.

 Les Hortensias
4, pl. Y.-Sarcey — 97.55.73.69
MM. Flé and Bellance. Closed off-season Tue and Wed, and from beg Jan to mid-Feb. Open until 9.30 pm. Terrace dining. No-smoking section. Parking. V AE.

A good vantage point from which to witness chef Jacques Pichon's attempt to capture a second toque. Urge him on by trying the anise-scented scallops in a buttery jus with mangetout peas, bass and red mullet pan-braised in olive oil with a Cabernet wine sauce, the nicely cooked rack of lamb in a salt crust, and the caramelised apple croustillant with a subtle liquorice coulis. Professional service.

A la carte: 350 F and up. Menus: 150 F (lunch only), 200 F, 250 F.

68410 Trois-Epis (Les) — (Haut-Rhin)
Paris 450 - Munster 17 - Colmar 12 - Orbey 12

 Le Grand Hôtel
Pl. de l'Eglise — 89.49.80.65
Open every day. 4 stes 1,050-2,100 F. 46 rms 480-980 F. Half-board 590-840 F. Restaurant. TV. Heated pool.

A sophisticated mountain theme runs through these thoroughly modern rooms. Among the amenities are a covered pool, solarium, sauna, and verandas that afford a stunning view of the Vosges.

14360 Trouville — (Calvados)
Paris 206 - Le Havre 76 - Caen 43 - Lisieux 29

 Beach Hotel
Quai Albert-Ier
31.98.12.00
Closed 2 Jan-22 Feb. 6 stes 750-1,020 F. 112 rms 390-520 F. Restaurant. Half-board 340-420 F. TV. Pool. Garage parking. V AE DC.

Guests may go directly from their big, well-equipped rooms to the casino. Or they can stay put and enjoy the harbour view. Good breakfasts. Solarium; bar.

 La Régence
132, bd Moureaux
31.88.10.71
M. Enée. Closed Wed. Open until 10.30 pm. V AE DC.
The speciality here is freshness. Enjoy the balanced flavours of oysters and sole fricasséed in cider, a blanquette of sole with mushrooms and shellfish, and the other delights of this fine new seafood restaurant. Good selection of white

Burgundies. Cheerful reception.
A la carte: 300-350 F. Menus: 120 F (weekdays only), 290 F (wine inc), 165 F.

12/20 Les Vapeurs
160, bd F.-Moureaux
31.88.15.24
M. Bazire. Closed off-season Tue dinner and Wed, and 7 Jan-9 Feb. Open until 1 am. Terrace dining. V.
As many as eight hundred hearts and tummies each day are warmed by the tasty mussels in cream, hot shrimps, tartares of salmon or bass, and sole normande. Rivers of cool white wine serve as irrigation, and the service is friendly.
A la carte: 200 F.

10000 Troyes — (Aube)
Paris 158 - Amiens 276 - Dijon 151 - Nancy 186 - Reims 121

 La Poste
1-3, rue Raymond-Poincaré
25.73.05.05
Open every day. 2 stes 600-900 F. 26 rms 280-490 F. Restaurant. TV. V AE.
Everything about this renovated hotel is right: the tasteful luxury, the elaborate bathrooms, the attractive furnishings, and the fine breakfasts.

 Le Valentino
11, cour de la Rencontre
25.73.14.14
M. Vattier. Closed Sun dinner, Mon, Feb school holidays and 16 Aug-6 Sep. Open until 9.45 pm. Terrace dining. V AE DC.
Ten years ago, the owner of this half-timbered beauty in the old quarter of Troyes decided he would become the king of seafood. The long bet he placed a few years ago on a young chef with slim credentials proved to be a winner. Joël Lejeune has developed a sincere, personal repertoire based on the superb seafood Alain Vattier procures from the docks. Taste the delicately fragrant raw salmon marinated in olive oil and sprinkled with dill seed, the turbot steak in a superb wine sauce with saffron rice, the truffled Brie cheese, and a fine nougat glacé—for once not too sweet. Fine cellar, attractively priced.
A la carte: 350 F. Menus: 145 F, 320 F.

See Ax-les-Thermes

See Bayonne

See Saint-Jean-de-Luz

See Bayonne

See Brive-la-Gaillarde

See Bayonne

30700 Uzès — (Gard)
Paris 706 - Avignon 38 - Alès 33 - Nîmes 25 - Arles 54

In nearby Collias

(8 km SE on D 981 and D 3)
30210 Uzès — (Gard)

Le Castellas
[14]
Grand-Rue — 66.22.88.88
M. Aparis. Closed Wed off-season, and 6 Jan-10 March. Open until 9.30 pm. Garden dining. Parking. V AE DC.
In his first year in charge of the kitchen, the young former sous-chef has proven his mettle with inventive, perfectly executed dishes like foie gras with apples and caramelised turnips, tian of roast lotte with meadow mushrooms and chicken jus, and saddle of rabbit wrapped in a cabbage leaf. Desserts and pastries are tops. Good cellar; high prices à la carte.
A la carte: 350-450 F. Menus: 140 F, 205 F.

Le Castellas
(See restaurant above)
Closed Wed off-season, and 6 Jan-10 March. 14 rms 405-620 F. Half-board 390-490 F. TV.
Two nineteenth-century village houses and a garden comprise this tastefully decorated hotel.

84110 Vaison-la-Romaine — (Vaucluse)
Paris 670 - Avignon 46 - Montélimar 65 - Carpentras 28

11/20 Le Bateleur
1, pl. Th.-Aubanel — 90.36.28.04
M. Montagné. Closed Sun dinner, Mon and Oct. Open until 9 pm. V.
This tidy, family-run restaurant offers only set menus which feature, for example, terrines or red-mullet soufflé, grilled lamb with herbs, or freshwater perch in beurre blanc, followed by lemon meringue pie.
Menus: 180 F (weekends and holidays only), 105 F.

La Fête en Provence
[13]
Pl. du Vieux-Marché — 90.36.36.43
M. Christiansen. Closed Tue dinner off-season, Wed (except July-Aug) and 15 Nov-15 Dec. Open until 10 pm. Terrace dining. Hotel: 7 rms 250-550 F. V.
A self-taught chef of Nordic origin has created a lovely, tranquil restaurant serving unpretentious regional fare. Good options are the caillettes (a sort of rissole) à l'ancienne, saffron-scented mussel soup, grilled salmon, and duck confit. Four rooms are available for overnight stays.
A la carte: 250 F. Menu: 98 F.

Hostellerie Le Beffroi
Rue de l'Evêché — 90.36.04.71
Closed 5 Jan-15 March. 1 ste 550 F. 20 rms 270-550 F. Restaurant. Half-board 350-450 F oblig in seas. TV 18 rms. Parking. V AE DC.
Here's a beautiful sixteenth-century dwelling, in the heart of old Vaison. Rooms are huge, furnished with antiques; there is a garden, a terrace, and lovely views.

In nearby Entrechaux

(7 km SE on D 938 and D 54)
84340 Vaison-la-Romaine — (Vaucluse)

La Manescale
Rte de Faucon — 90.46.03.80
Closed end Oct-Easter. 1 ste 550-780 F. 5 rms 275-450 F. Half-board 335-460 F. TV. Pool. Parking. V AE DC.
Book well in advance to reserve one of these six pretty rooms in a charmingly converted sheepfold.

In nearby Séguret

(10 km SW on D 88)
84110 Vaison-la-Romaine — (Vaucluse)

Auberge de Cabasse
90.46.91.12
Closed 3 Nov-15 March. 10 rms 400-470 F (per pers, half-board oblig). Restaurant. TV. Pool. Parking. V.
These pleasant rooms in vineyard country are made all the more agreeable by patios that lead out to the swimming pool.

La Table du Comtat
[14]
Le Village — 90.46.91.49
M. Gomez. Closed Tue dinner and Wed (except Christmas, Easter and in summer), Feb and end Nov-beg Dec. Open until 9 pm. Air cond. Parking. Hotel: 8 rms 400-600 F. Pool. V AE DC.
True, it's a drain on the finances, but what a pleasure it is to dine in this wonderfully tranquil sixteenth-century Provençal dining room. The splendid ingredients and expert cooking of chef Franck Gomez will delight you with, for example, a soufflé of julienned truffles in an eggshell, a thick slice of sea bass roasted with bone marrow, or pan-roasted fillet of lamb. The cellar holds a treasure trove of fabulous wines from Châteauneuf-du-Pape.
A la carte: 450-550 F. Menus: 210 F and 285 F (except holidays), 420 F.

06560 Valbonne — (Alpes-Mar.)
Paris 913 - Cannes 13 - Grasse 9 - Nice 30

12/20 Le Bistro de Valbonne
11, rue de la Fontaine — 93.42.05.59
M. Purgato. Closed Sun, Mon, March and Nov. Open until 9.30 pm. Terrace dining. Air cond. V.
Lively service, the hostess's radiant smile, and two appealing prix-fixe offerings attract crowds to this little restaurant and its even smaller patio.
Menus: 138 F, 210 F.

12/20 Le Cadran Solaire
4, rue E.-Giraud — 93.42.13.30
MM. Dartois and Manganaro. Closed Wed, Thu and 12 Nov-1 Jan. Open until 10.30 pm. Terrace dining. Air cond. V AE.
The cool dining room, the excellent fish dishes on the à la carte menu, and—especially—the 98 F prix-fixe meal that includes fish soup, a Provençal daube, and hot apple tart, all perfect company for the tasty local wines.
A la carte: 250-280 F. Menus: 98 F, 165 F.

Problems with French? The RAC France language pack will help you to converse with confidence.

12/20 Cave Saint Bernardin

8, rue des Arcades — 93.42.03.88

Mme Averbeke and M. Sénéclauze. Closed Sun, Mon and 2 Jan-15 Feb. Open until 9.30 pm. Terrace dining. Air cond. V AE.

The generous set menus offer, for instance, warm turbot salad, a choice between sole with basil cream sauce or a mixed grill, gratin dauphinois, cheese, and poire Belle-Hélène.

Menus: 120 F, 140 F.

Novotel

Sophia-Antipolis

Rue Dostoïevski — 93.65.40.00

Open every day. 97 rms 435-540 F. Restaurant. TV. Air cond. Pool. Tennis. Parking. V AE DC.

In front of the big Sophia-Antipolis park, this is an excellent hotel for conferences.

12/20 Le Val Martin

Domaine de Val Martin

93.42.07.10

M. Jehanno. Closed Sun dinner and Mon. Open until 9.30 pm. Private room: 18. Garden dining. Heated pool. Tennis. Golf. Parking. V AE DC.

Nature's charms abound here, in the form of mountains, lakes, rural landscapes... and the neighbouring golf course. Maurice Jehenno and his son produce a superb grilled beef fillet with green peppercorns, and the memorable hot apple tart.

Menus: 100 F (lunch only), 140 F, 180 F.

VAL-D'ISÈRE

73150 Val-d'Isère — (Savoie)

Paris 690 - Chambéry 133 - Albertville 85 - Briançon 158

Altitude

79.06.12.55

Closed 12 May-30 June and 30 Aug-1 Dec. 40 rms 400-720 F. Restaurant. Half-board 370-460 F. TV. Heated pool. Parking. V.

A modern chalet at the foot of the ski trails. The rooms face south, and are perfectly comfortable. Amenities include a fireside lounge, sauna, solarium, and a bar.

Bellier

Altitude 1850

79.06.03.77

Closed 10 May-1 Dec. 2 stes 800-900 F. 22 rms 220-650 F. Restaurant. Half-board 330-580 F oblig in seas. TV. Heated pool. Parking. V AE DC.

A huge chalet overlooking the Olympic runs, offering simple, comfortable rooms.

Le Blizzard

Rue de la Banque

79.06.02.07

Closed 13 May-1 Dec. 70 rms 450-900 F Restaurant. TV. Valet parking. V AE DC.

This is one of the resort's most reputable hotels, complete with refurbished rooms that are cosy and bright, and a fitness centre. Discothèque.

Christiana

79.06.08.25

Closed 2 May-1 Dec. 4 stes 2,500-3,600 F. 45 rms 950-1,350 F Restaurant. TV. Heated pool. V.

Here is Val-d'Isère's most concentrated glitter. Lovely rooms, with fine appointments. Sauna.

12/20 El Cortijo

Rue Principale — 79.06.03.25

M. Henrypierre. Open every day. Open until 10.30 pm. V AE DC.

The Breton proprietor loves nothing so much as his native seafood. Which is why he ought to prune his overlong menu and stick with the likes of fish soup, mussels in cream, grilled turbot, poached bass, and the grilled sea bream royale, all cooked with split-second accuracy. Convivial atmosphere.

A la carte: 350 F.

12/20 Grand Paradis

79.06.11.73

M. Korosec. Closed 12 May-30 June and 25 Aug-24 Nov. Open until 10 pm. Private room: 25. Terrace dining. Valet parking. V AE DC.

From the Austrian-style, wood-panelled dining room, try the mint-scented striped bass tartare, the fillet of sole in Calvados, and the crêpes à la Chartreuse. Warm welcome; excessive prices.

A la carte: 300-350 F. Menu: 220 F.

Grand Paradis

(See restaurant above)

Closed 12 May-30 June and 25 Aug-24 Nov. 4 stes 440-1,200 F. 40 rms 210-1,050 F. Half-board 310-720 F oblig in seas. TV. Tennis.

The trail-side location is truly exceptional. Some of the huge rooms are cosy and charming, and some are emphatically not.

Le Kern

79.06.06.06

Closed 12 May-1 Aug and 25 Aug-1 Dec. 18 rms 250-490 F. Restaurant. Half-board 365-390 F oblig in seas. TV 10 rms. Valet parking. V.

A dear little family-run chalet, smothered in flowers, right in the middle of the resort. Friendly welcome and service.

Mercure

79.06.12.93

Closed 11 May-9 June. 4 stes 780-1,160 F. 41 rms 440-940 F. Restaurant. Half-board 620-850 F oblig in seas. TV. Heated pool. Valet parking. V AE DC.

Regular clients of the Mercure chain are going to be really taken by this one; its huge, functional rooms are right on the slopes. Bistro-bar.

Savoyarde

79.06.01.55

Closed 3 May-11 Aug and 25 Aug-1 Dec. 2 stes 1600-2,600 F. 44 rms 560-780 F. Restaurant. Half-board 510-640 F oblig in seas. TV. Valet parking. V AE DC.

Here's a traditional mountain chalet, just 100 metres from the lifts, with attractive rooms, pine furnishings, and wainscotted bathrooms.

Sofitel

79.06.08.30

Closed 4 May-6 July and 24 Aug-2 Dec. 5 stes 1,300-3,100 F. 48 rms 650-1,150 F. Restaurant. Half-board 650-770 F oblig in seas. TV. Heated pool. Garage parking. V AE DC.

These fine modern rooms located in the heart of the resort wide bay windows. Bathing-cure centre with up-to-date equipment.

Les Sorbiers

79.06.23.77

Closed 8 May-1 July. 2 stes 1,200-1,400 F. 26 rms 580-780 F. TV. Garage parking. V.

A new chalet with traditional fittings, this pretty hotel provides sunny pleasant accommodation.

Tsanteleina
79.06.12.13
*Closed 12 May-28 June and 1 Sep-1 Dec. 40 stes 470-
700 F. 20 rms 450-700 F. Restaurant. Half-board
470-560 F oblig in seas. TV. Tennis. Parking. V AE
DC.*

You can rest up from all that downhill skiing in
your comfortable room, or take in the view of the
resort from the beautiful terrace. Solarium; sauna.

VALENÇAY
36600 Valençay — (Indre)
Paris 230 - Châteauroux 41 - Issoudun 44 - Vierzon 49

Hôtel d'Espagne
9, rue du Château
54.00.00.02
*Closed off-season Sun and Mon, and Jan. 6 stes 850-
1,050 F. 14 rms 400-600 F. Half-board 600-800 F.
Restaurant. TV.*

We wish the management would take a critical
look at the wallpaper and the upholstery of the
rooms and lounges, for the grand old décor is
nearly exhausted. Comfort is assured, however,
and the service is wonderfully attentive. Relais et
Châteaux.

VALENCE
26000 Valence — (Drôme)
Paris 560 - Lyon 100 - Grenoble 99 - Marseille 215

Pic
285, av. V.-Hugo
75.44.15.32
*M. Pic. Closed Sun dinner, Wed and Aug. Open until
9.30 pm. Garden dining. Air cond. Garage parking.
V AE DC.*

New efforts have been made to restore the perfection of this brilliant old establishment and as
always, Pic is worth the detour for the marvellous
welcome, and of course for the sublime cuisine.
Representing the very best of the grand provincial
dining tradition, the cooking effortlessly embraces
all tendencies and trends. Jacques Pic's stunning
galette de truffes et céleri au foie gras cleverly and
deftly blends courgettes, tomatoes, and a smooth
cream of beetroot; and then there's the perfectly
arranged marriage of beef fillet and sweetbreads
braised with rosemary; or the richly aromatic
'braid' of striped bass and salmon with caviar; or
the harmonious salad of lobster in a basil-scented
vinaigrette. In short, though the selection of pastries is (we repeat) a trifle conventional, Pic is still
an admirable restaurant. And one which glories as
well in a fabulous list of Côtes-du-Rhône wines.
A la carte: 600-900 F. Menus: 280 F (weekdays
lunch only), 450 F, 550 F.

Pic
(See restaurant above)
*Closed Wed, Sun and Aug. 2 stes 600-800 F. 2 rms
450-480 F. TV. Air cond.*
The house offers a grand total of two suites and
two guestrooms. Expect to spend a very comfortable night and to waken to birdsong and a sumptuous breakfast. Relais et Châteaux.

> *RAC Regional Maps of France at 4 miles to
> 1 inch are the ideal touring companion. Avail-
> able from RAC offices and all good bookshops.*

In nearby Pont-de-l'Isère
(9 km N on N 7)
26600 Valence — (Drôme)

Chabran
Av. 45e-Parallèle (N 7)
75.84.60.09
*M. Chabran. Closed off-season Sun dinner and Mon,
and 18 Nov-9 Dec. Open until 10 pm. Garden dining. Air cond. No-smoking section. Parking. V AE.*

Now that the infinitely long-awaited new interior
is complete, the heavenly memories we cherish of
Michel Chabran's fillets of sole simmered in a
shellfish broth and flanked by fried oysters, or his
marvellous croûtons topped with sautéed snails,
or the freshwater perch from the Rhône with little
vegetables in a perfect, mustardy beurre blanc can
be recollected without the dismal thought that to
taste them again, we'd have to endure the same
ugly, dated 'modern' setting.
Thus encouraged, Chabran is back at work con-
structing a short, brilliant menu that displays rare
balance, skill, and overflowing personality. A note
on the *carte* encourages guests to share dishes, and
taste a bit of everything. By all means take the
advice, and savour *à deux* the lush marinated
salmon with its salad of tiny, firm potatoes and
shallots, a Breton lobster with a shredded potato
'crique', local guinea hen with the region's
celebrated cheese-filled ravioles, and the refined
yet rustic vol-au-vent filled with veal sweetbreads
and kidneys. The desserts still fail to fire our imagination. Perhaps that's next year's surprise?
A la carte: 450-500 F. Menus: 210 F, 320 F, 430 F.

Chabran
(See restaurant above)
*Closed off-season Sun and Mon, and 18 Nov-9 Dec.
12 rms 350-660 F. TV. Air cond.*
All the modern rooms are luxuriously comfort-
able, but some are considerably more charming
than others. The breakfasts are delicious. Relais et
Châteaux.

VALENCIENNES
59300 Valenciennes — (Nord)
Paris 205 - Bruxelles 102 - Cambrai 32 - St-Quentin 70

L'Albéroi
(Buffet de la Gare)
Place de la Gare
27.46.86.30
*M. Benoist. Closed Sun dinner. Open until 10 pm. V
AE DC.*

Inside and out, this place looks like a railway
station buffet in a struggling region—and that's just
what it is. But L'Alberoi is also home to one of the
area's better tables, and we salute the jovial
François Benoist for his dedication to maintaining
the tradition of fine cuisine: perfectly grilled lamb
chops, red mullet in olive oil, and a smooth crème
brûlée with demerara sugar.
A la carte: 350-400 F. Menus: 300 F (weekends
and holidays only), 130 F, 180 F, 250 F.

Grand Hôtel
de Valenciennes
8, pl. de la Gare
27.46.32.01
*Open every day. 5 stes 490-540 F. 92 rms 330-420 F.
Restaurant. TV. V AE DC.*
You will be welcomed warmly into this huge,
classic hotel opposite the railway station, and to its
modernised, well-equipped rooms.

In nearby Haulchin

(10 km SW on N 30)
59121 Valenciennes — (Nord)

Le Clos Saint-Hugues
3, rue P.-Vaillant-Couturier — 27.43.80.83
Mme Devries. Closed Sat lunch, Sun and Mon dinner. Open until 9.15 pm. Garden dining. Parking. V AE.
The wife of the town's doctor had the bright idea of opening a restaurant in this old brick buildinge. The kitchen is run by a young well-trained female chef, an even younger woman is in charge of the cellar, and a service staff of you guessed correctly. We liked our mixed salad of smoked fish, the cucumbers stuffed with fresh cod, and the vanilla crème brûlée. The prices are frankly less appealing.
A la carte: 300-400 F. Menus: 230 F (weekends only), 120 F, 170 F, 290 F.

VALLAURIS

See Cannes

VALLE-DI-MEZZANA

See CORSICA: Ajaccio

VALS-LES-BAINS

07600 Vals-les-Bains — (Ardèche)
Paris 636 - Privas 34 - Montélimar 50 - Le Puy 87

Runel
43, rue J.-Jaurès — 75.37.48.57
M. Runel. Closed Sun dinner and Mon (except July-Aug) and Feb. Open until 9.30 pm. Terrace dining. V.
Maurice Runel's cuisine is clever, generous, and highly appetising: sample his terrine of duck breast and local lentils, John Dory braised with celery, celeriac, and truffles, the delicious foie gras 'marbled' with chestnuts, and a crépinette of trout with cèpes and Chardonnay butter. Interesting cellar, with bottles from the region and farther afield.
A la carte: 250 F. Menus: 60 F (weekdays lunch only), 118 F, 155 F, 240 F.

Le Vivarais
5, rue Cl.-Expilly — 75.94.65.85
Open every day. 40 rms 260-380 F. Restaurant. Half-board 300-350 F. TV. Pool. Parking. Telex 345866. V AE DC.
Charming spa hotel surrounded by trees next to a park. Rooms are stylish and comfortable, decorated with their original 1930s furniture. Attentive welcome.

VAL-SUZON

See Dijon

VAL-THORENS

73440 Val-Thorens — (Savoie)
Paris 670 - Chambéry 110 - Albertville 70 - Moûtiers 36

Bel Horizon
79.00.04.77
Closed 11 May-15 Dec. 8 stes 400-1,300 F. 23 rms 300-900 F. Restaurant. Half-board 390-600 F oblig in seas. TV. Valet parking. V.
A nice modern chalet on the mountainside with a view over the ski slopes. Rooms have attractive light-wood furniture. Kind service and copious breakfasts. For your leisure hours, there is a sauna, a gym, and billiards.
A la carte: 200 F. Menus: from 75 F to 200 F.

11/20 La Chaumière
Centre de Caron
79.00.01.13
Mme Albouy. Closed 10 May-1 Dec. Open until 11.30 pm. Terrace dining.
The owner is a ski instructor, full of useful advice for his guests. Cooking here is simple with a rustic flavour: mountain charcuterie, charcoal-grilled meats, fondues, and raclettes, served in a snug panelled dining room. At lunch there is an 'express menu' for 62F, with starter and main course.
A la carte: 200 F (dinner only). Menu: 76 F (lunch only).

Le Sherpa
79.00.00.70
Closed 1 May-13 Dec. 40 rms 290-430 F (per pers, half-board oblig). Restaurant.
A modern building in a quiet setting on the ski slopes. Lovely rooms with balcony. Good amenities, including a sauna, Jacuzzi, solarium, and lounge-bar.

12/20 La Table du Roy
79.00.04.78
Mme Loubet. Closed 6 May-1 Nov. Open until 10 pm. Terrace dining. Air cond. Valet parking. V AE DC.
A crackling blaze warms the wood panelling and caramel hues of the décor. The chef is self-taught, and though his cooking may lack simplicity, it is full of laudable enthusiasm. Taste the brill stuffed with prawns and oysters, kebabs of calf's liver and kidneys flavoured with vermouth, and warm duck pâté in a potato crust.
A la carte: 350 F. Menus: from 250 F to 500 F (dinner only).

Fitz Roy
(See restaurant above)
Closed 10 May-28 Oct. 6 stes. 30 rms 850-1,500 F (per pers, half-board oblig). TV. Air cond. Heated pool.
A huge, modern, luxury chalet with spacious and cosily panelled rooms. Panoramic lift. For fitness worshippers, there's a swimming pool and superb exercise and slimming equipment. Relais et Châteaux.

11/20 Le Val Thorens
79.00.04.33
M. Perkov. Closed 4 May-1 Nov. Open until 10.30 pm. Terrace dining. Air cond. Hotel: 74 rms 400-1,050 F, half-board 390-643 F. V AE DC.
One face of this mountainside restaurant serves fondues and regional specialities, the other is rather more chic and pleasantly partitioned, offering pan-roasted lotte with cucumbers, and veal in a creamy sauce with wild mushrooms.
A la carte: 300 F. Menus: 84 F (lunch only), 160 F and 190 F (dinner only).

VANNES

56000 Vannes — (Morbihan)
Paris 454 - Lorient 56 - Nantes 109 - Rennes 106

Aquarium'Hôtel
Le Parc du Golfe — 97.40.44.52
Open every day. 48 rms 310-380 F. Restaurant. TV. Conference facilities. Garage parking. V AE DC.
A futuristic construction in a verdant setting near the Gulf of Morbihan. Functional rooms, all with sea view.

Régis Mahé
(Le Richemont)
Pl. de la Gare — 97.42.61.41
M. Mahé. Closed Sun dinner and Mon (except holidays), 18 Feb-4 March and 18 Nov-2 Dec. Open until 9.30 pm. V AE.

Yet Régis Mahé, a wildly talented chef (already a three-toque winner in Paris, at Le Bourdonnais) has captured the hearts and tummies of his native Vannes with vivacious, polished, delicious cuisine. Mahé puts a personal, exciting spin on every dish that comes out of his kitchen. Now as much at home with Breton flavours as he once was with the tastes of Provence (he worked side by side with Jacques Maximin for years), he takes local sardines and creates a marvellous biscuit accented with an olive tapenade (a nod to the Mediterranean), or adds an intriguing spicy note to red mullet in vinaigrette, or gives sea bass and tiny Breton potatoes a vibrant touch of pepper.... And then there is the incredible lobster with saffron and rum, the noisettes of local lamb with glazed baby vegetables and a zesty dose of Szechuan pepper, or a pigeon galette with bell peppers and prawns, or a farm veal kidney with crushed potatoes drizzled with balsamic vinegar.
Desserts are a dream: caramel de bananes et citron au kirsch, chocolate fondant with morello cherries, buttery gâteau breton with rhubarb and apples.
A la carte: 250-350 F. Menus: 98 F (weekdays only), 160 F, 250 F, 300 F.

Manche-Océan
31, rue du Lt-Col.-Maury — 97.47.26.46
Open every day. 42 rms 185-260 F. TV. V AE DC.
Not far from the railway station and the town hall. Rooms are well soundproofed, constantly updated, with good sanitation. Excellent breakfasts.

Le Pressoir
5 km N on D 767
7, rue de l'Hôpital
56890 Saint-Avé — 97.60.87.63
M. Rambaud. Closed Sun dinner, Mon, 4-14 March and 1-18 Oct. Open until 9.30 pm. Private room: 20. Air cond. Parking. V AE DC.
Bernard Rambaud is a proficient and inventive cook, talents he shows to advantage with an asparagus and crab charlotte, a galette of red mullet perfumed with rosemary, or more classic dishes like beef jowls stewed with bone marrow and carrots, its rich sauce thickened with a calf's foot.
A la carte: 300 F and up. Menus: 100 F (weekdays lunch only), 150 F, 240 F, 290 F.

In nearby **Arradon**

(7 km SW on N 165)
56610 Vannes — (Morbihan)

L'Arlequin
Parc de Botquelen — 97.40.41.41
M. Tournaire. Closed Sun dinner. Open until 9.30 pm. Garden dining. Parking. V AE.
Subtle lighting plays off garnet-hued walls and beautifully set round tables to create a most appealing atmosphere. As for the food, it is in tune with the setting—you'll like the light, skilfully executed prawn croustillant with poached vegetables, mould of roast lotte with a zesty splash of shellfish oil, breast of pigeon with chanterelles, and moist chocolate cake. Genuinely charming welcome and service.
A la carte: 250 F. Menus: 78 F (weekdays only), 128 F, 180 F.

See also: **Questembert**

VARCES
See Grenoble

VARENNE-ST-HILAIRE (LA)
See PARIS Suburbs

VARENNES-JARCY
See PARIS Suburbs

VARETZ
See Brive-la-Gaillarde

VAUDRAMPONT
See Compiègne

VÉLIZY
See PARIS Suburbs

VELLERON
See Isle-sur-la-Sorgue (L')

VENASQUE
See Carpentras

VENCE
06140 Vence - (Alpes-Mar.)
Paris 925 - Nice 22 - Antibes 19 - Grasse 27

Auberge des Templiers
39, av. Joffre — 93.58.06.05
M. Lopez. Closed off-season Sun dinner and Mon, 20 Dec-10 Jan and 8-20 March. Open until 9.30 pm. Garden dining. V.
Patrice Lopez favours Provençal produce, which he handles with a pleasing personal touch: we like his rock fish and crab soup, rock lobster salad with morel dressing, sea bream with citrus, and roast rack of Sisteron lamb. You can savour these treats in a rustic dining room or in a leafy garden. Well-chosen wines; cheerful, dynamic service.
A la carte: 350 F. Menus: 110 F, 180 F, 250 F.

Château des Arômes
2618, rte de Grasse — 93.58.70.24
M. Mosiniak. Closed Sun dinner, Mon and 31 Oct-29 Feb. Open until 9.30 pm. Private room: 120. Garden dining. Air cond. Parking. V AE.
Gérard Mosiniak possesses a range of some forty essences which add marvellous aromas to his Provençal recipes. An astonishing millefeuille d'aubergines et de saint-pierre (John Dory) aux tomates is scented with essence of dill; lobster swaddled in seaweed is embellished with bitter-orange butter and tarragon; scallop petals are marinated in lime juice with pink peppercorns; and hot goat cheese is escorted by spicy cumin jelly. The cellar is succinct but balanced, with a fine selection of Mediterranean wines.
Menus: 150 F (lunch only), 220 F, 260 F, 320 F.

Château Saint-Martin
Rte de Coursegoules — 93.58.02.02
Mlle Brunet. Closed Wed off-season and 15 Nov-15 March. Open until 9.30 pm. Private room: 20. Garden dining. Valet parking. V AE DC.
The food is rich (rich! rich!) and ably prepared, but it lacks sparkle. There's a fresh house salad, generous tournedos in wine with sliced seasonal vegetables, flavourful but oily fresh pasta with salmon; the dessert trolley is not wildly tempting—

basic chocolate-mocha cake and good strawberry genoise. The cellar is short on half-bottles; lots of fleet-footed waiters whirl round the dining room.

A la carte: 600 F and up, Menus: 300 F (weekdays lunch only), 390 F, 450 F.

Château Saint-Martin
(See restaurant above)
Closed 15 Nov-15 March. 10 stes 2,620-3,200 F. 15 rms 1,560-2,210 F. Half-board 2,035-3,675 F. TV. Conference facilities. Heated pool. Tennis.

Guests are housed in little villas whose richly decorated rooms have an uninterrupted view over the hills. Lovely swimming pool; beautiful grounds. Relais et Châteaux.

11/20 La Farigoule
15, rue H.-Isnard — 93.58.01.27
Mme Gastaud. Closed off-season Sat lunch and Fri, and 10 Nov-15 Dec. Open until 9 pm (10 pm in summer). Private room: 10. Terrace dining.

Georgette Gastaud cooks up tasty regional dishes: fish soup, rabbit Farigoule with lots of herbs, salt cod and vegetables with garlicky aïoli, winey beef daube, and aniseed tart. A nice patio and friendly prices.

Menus: 100 F, 120 F, 130 F.

Hôtel Floréal
440, av. Rhin-et-Danube — 93.58.64.40
Annual closings not available. 1 ste 750-850 F. 43 rms 445-540 F. TV. Pool. Parking. V.

A recent building set in pretty grounds. The modern rooms are bright and cosy, with tasteful decoration and a view over the countryside. Snacks are served round the swimming pool.

Miramar
Plateau St-Michel — 93.58.01.32
Closed 31 Oct-1 March. 17 rms 260-350 F. Parking. Telex 470673. V AE.

Situated just 300 metres from the centre, surrounded by exotic trees and plants, this elegantly simple hotel affords views of the sea and the Alps. Pleasant rooms, regularly refurbished. Bar.

Relais Cantemerle
258, ch. Cantemerle — 93.58.08.18
Mlle Igou. Closed Wed off-season, and 15 Oct-15 March. Open until 10 pm. Terrace dining. Parking. V AE DC.

Chef Robert Cesbron is a talented chap with a knack for light, flavourful cooking. Do try his salmon feuilleté with chicory confit, suprême of sea bass with vegetable 'pearls' and prawns, beef fillet in a sauce of wine lees and tiny onions. Pleasant service.

A la carte: 400 F. Menus: 250 F (weekends and holidays only), 200 F.

Relais Cantemerle
(See restaurant above)
Closed 15 Oct-15 March. 19 stes 830 F.1 rm 550 F. Half-board 525-665 F. TV. Pool.

Lovely split-level rooms, perfectly quiet, that open right onto the swimming pool and grounds with masses of flowers. Decoration and furnishings in 1930s style.

La Roseraie
Av. H.-Giraud — 93.58.02.20
M. Ganier. Closed Tue lunch and Wed, and Jan. Open until 9.30 pm. Garden dining. Hotel: 12 rms 260-380 F. Pool. Parking. V AE.

Maurice Ganier is the local defender of the caloric South-western tradition (good confit, magret, foie gras) but he's been exploring new horizons of

late, with his lobster and walnut salad, sea bream with scallop coulis, and beef fillet with a rich 'sauce gourmande'. Good wines from the South-west; attentive service.

A la carte: 300 F. Menus: 180 F, 260 F.

Le Vieux Couvent
37, av. A.-Toreille — 93.58.78.58
M. Bissières. Closed Wed and 15 Nov-15 Dec. Open until 10 pm. V.

Jean-Jacques Bissière's virtuosity is apparent even in simple dishes like a delicious basil-scented rabbit fricassée served in a phyllo-pastry 'purse', fresh sea bream on a bed of bright spinach, and flawless triple-chocolate mousse. The cellar is still a trifle thin, but there are some good finds at reasonable prices.

A la carte: 300-350 F. Menus: 170 F, 240 F, 330 F.

55100 Verdun — (Meuse)
Paris 265 - Metz 78 - Nancy 120 - Châlons-sur-Marne 88

Le Coq Hardi
8, av. de la Victoire — 29.86.36.36
M. Leloup. Closed Fri (except holidays) and Jan. Open until 9.30 pm. Private room: 60. Garage parking. Telex 860464. V AE DC.

This impressive institution takes pride of place among the region's restaurants. No cost, no pains have been spared to create the opulent provincial setting or the excellent cuisine based on choice ingredients.

A la carte: 350-400 F. Menus: 160 F, 370 F.

Le Coq Hardi
(See restaurant above)
Closed Jan. 5 stes 525-680 F. 40 rms 160-400 F. TV 38 rms. Conference facilities.

Renovation has been in progress for some time and four junior suites and seven bedrooms are now complete. There is still more work to be done before this grand old house recovers its former glory. Warm welcome.

In nearby **Monthairons**

(13 km S on D 334)
55320 Verdun (Meuse)

Château des Monthairons
29.87.78.55
Closed Feb. 3 stes 750-900 F. 11 rms 280-600 F. Restaurant. TV. Conference facilities.

The rooms and bathrooms are huge, with very high ceilings and a marvellous view over the park.

See CORSICA: Porticcio

27200 Vernon — (Eure)
Paris 82 - Evreux 31 - Rouen 63 - Mantes-la-Jolie 25

Les Jardins de Giverny
Ch. du Roy
27620 Giverny — 32.21.60.80
M. Pirault. Closed Tue, dinner Sun and Mon, and Feb. Open until 9 pm. Parking. V AE DC.

A few minutes from Monet's famous gardens, this large turn-of-the-century house also has lovely lawns and a rose garden. Serge Pirault's delicious classic menu changes every month: poached lotte with rock salt, magret with citrus zests and fresh pasta, and the famous house cassoulet. Excellent little cellar.

A la carte: 300-350 F. Menus: 130 F, 190 F.

Normandy
1, av. P.-Mendès-France — 32.51.97.97
*Open every day. 3 stes 980 F. 50 rms 385-420 F.
Restaurant. Half-board 460 F. TV. Conference facilities. Valet parking. V AE.*
A modern hotel with all amenities, which has just opened in the town centre. Rooms are comfortable but unoriginal; those at the back are quiet.

12/20 Le Relais Normand
11, pl. d'Evreux — 32.21.16.12
Mme El-Baze. Closed Sun. Open until 9 pm. Private room: 15. Garden dining. Garage parking. V AE DC.
The cooking lacks creativity, but the gourmet salad is fresh (too much dressing), the oxtail pastry generous, and the pear tart well prepared. Smiling service.
A la carte: 200-250 F. Menus: 75 F (weekdays lunch only), 145 F, 195 F.

Le Relais Normand
(See restaurant above)
Open every day. 18 rms 170-340 F. TV.
An old rustic hotel in the town centre. The rooms are panelled from stem to stern, and have been recently refurbished.

In nearby **Port-Villez**

(5 km SE on N15)
78270 Vernon (Eure)

La Gueulardière
at Le Village — 34.76.22.12
M. Marguerite. Closed dinner Sun and Mon. Open until 9.30 pm. Private room: 20. Garden dining. Air cond. Garage parking. V DC.
This attractive Norman inn with a warm rustic atmosphere is a favourite haunt of visitors to Giverny. Unfortunately the second toque was swept away this year by the avalanche of mustard in the 'Assiette de monseigneur' (raw salmon, lobster, tomatoes, raisins, etc.) and the mediocre lamb fillet—despite its deft seasoning of basil and orange zest. But we know that chef Claude Marguerite is capable of rectifying the problems, as he proves with an excellent Normandy-style John Dory and a delicious caramel apple tart. Impeccable service.
A la carte: 350 F. Menus: 150 F (except holidays), 230 F.

VERSAILLES
See PARIS Suburbs

VER-SUR-LAUNETTE
See Senlis

VERTUS
51130 Vertus — (Marne)
Paris 140 - Châlons-sur-Marne 30 - Fère-Champenoise 17

In nearby **Bergères-les-Vertus**

(4 km S on D 9, on N 33)
51130 Vertus — (Marne)

12/20 Le Mont Aimé
4-6, rue de Vertus — 26.52.21.31
M. Sciancalepore. Open every day. Open until 9 pm. Private room: 40. Garden dining. Parking. Hotel: 29 rms 150-290 F, half-board 200-240 F. V AE DC.
The proprietors of this attractive inn at the foot of Mt Aimé are renovating in all directions. It is now an excellent place to spend the night after dining in the garden (the interior is comfortable but uni-

nspiring): thin tart of sweetbreads and snails, grilled turbot in a Bouzy wine sauce, and herbed roast lamb.
A la carte: 300 F. Menus: 75 F (weekdays only), 120 F, 150 F, 195 F.

VÉSINET (LE)
See PARIS Suburbs

VEYRIER-DU-LAC
See Annecy

VÉZELAY
89450 Vézelay — (Yonne)
Paris 221 - Clamecy 23 - Avallon 13 - Auxerre 52

In nearby **Saint-Père-sous-Vézelay**

(3 km SE)
89450 Vézelay — (Yonne)

Marc Meneau
86.33.20.45
*M. Meneau. Closed Wed lunch and Tue (ex-
19.5   cept holidays), and beg Jan-beg Feb. Open
until 9.30 pm. Private room: 50. Parking.
Telex 800005. V AE DC.*
A huge greenhouse full of mature trees with a stream running through it—that's where customers could be eating soon if Marc Meneau's latest project comes to fruition. The architect Pierre Parat (responsible for the Bercy sports complex in Paris) plans to bring specially adapted trees from California to a meadow with a stream between the main building and the converted mill. Here, next to the vegetable garden, the revolutionary new annexe will be constructed.
Meanwhile, Marc Meneau is still delighting customers with his inspired cooking in the glassed-in dining rooms that don't really go with the style of the nineteenth-century building. He possesses the signal talent of making simple what, in the hands of other chefs, would fatally become complicated, creating apparently seamless dishes that are actually the result of a great deal of work. The point is proved once more by the new pleasures he plied us with this year: a masterpiece of a soup in which chunks of skate, sautéed in plaice stock, absorb the flavours of tarragon and fresh coriander; an ethereal tourte of green asparagus and foie gras; and chicken marinated in white wine and herbs before being browned and then covered in a cold cream sauce flavoured with meat juices, tarragon, and fried onions.
Meneau puts this same magic to work on plain food like baked turbot with onions, sweetbreads with watercress, or an exemplary leg of lamb, coaxing from them nuances that are all his own. Add to this the delectable desserts—sautéed pear with liquorice ice cream, gâteau of orange-scented caramelised apples, bananas with peppery ice cream—and a fine Burgundy, or even a lesser regional wine, and the bill will be enormous; but so will your enjoyment.
A la carte: 600-900 F. Menus: 290 F (weekdays lunch only), 540 F, 750 F.

L'Espérance
(See restaurant above)
Closed beg Jan-beg Feb. 4 stes 1,280-2,500 F. 18 rms 500-900 F. TV. Conference facilities.
Guests can choose between charming little rooms in fresh colours overlooking the garden or enchanting suites in the converted mill. The break-

fasts are so good you'll leap out of bed. Françoise Meneau's welcome is flawless.

VICHY

03200 Vichy — (Allier)
Paris 348 - Clermont-Ferrand 59 - Lyon 160 - Roanne 74

L'Alambic
[15] 8, rue N.-Larbaud — 70.59.12.71
M. Barbot. Closed Tue lunch, Mon, 4-26 Feb and 19 Aug-3 Sep. Open until 10 pm. Air cond. V.
Jean-Jacques Barbot was anxious to earn back the two toques he had at the Château d'Ombremont, and the perfect produce cooked with talent and precision have convinced us to award them. No overwhelming innovations, just the best cuisine in Vichy: ravioli of frogs' legs with herbs, prawn ragoût with wild mushrooms, roast young pigeon wrapped in Swiss chard leaves. The lady of the house, Marie-Ange, produces excellent desserts like the gratin of pears with toasted almonds.
A la carte: 350 F. Menus: 160 F, 280 F.

12/20 Brasserie du Casino
4, rue du Casino — 70.98.23.06
M. Dechassat. Closed Thu lunch, Wed, 15 Feb-1 March and Nov. Open until 10 pm. Terrace dining. V.
Vichy's best and prettiest brasserie with its genuine 1920s wood panelling and copperware. Pianist in the evenings.
A la carte: 200-220 F. Menu: 95 F (weekdays lunch only).

Grignan
7, pl. Sévigné — 70.32.08.11
Closed 18 Oct-11 Nov. 121 rms 190-320 F. Restaurant. Half-board 253-293 F. TV. No pets. Conference facilities. Parking. Telex 392357. V AE DC.
One of the biggest hotels in Vichy, the Grignan was thoroughly modernised in 1986. Well-equipped rooms.

Pavillon Sévigné
[15] 10-12, pl. Sévigné — 70.32.16.22
Mme Potter. Closed 2 Jan-1 March. Open until 10 pm. Private room: 30. Terrace dining. No pets. Valet parking. Telex 392370. V AE DC.
Here—at a price—you can savour the smoked-salmon ravioli with caviar cream, pot-au-feu made with beef fillet and foie gras, and a chocolate assortment with warm madeleines that have earned Jean-François Delanné his second toque this year. Expensive wines, too.
A la carte: 450 F. Menus: 140 F (weekdays lunch only), 260 F, 330 F.

Pavillon Sévigné
(See restaurant above)
Closed 2 Jan-1 March. 2 stes 1,450-1,680 F. 40 rms 510-765 F. Half-board 700-835 F. TV.
A charming hotel with magnificent lounges and some elegant rooms. Special long-stay rates.

Hôtel du Portugal
121, bd des Etats-Unis — 70.31.90.66
Closed 1 Dec-15 March. 50 rms 190-410 F. Restaurant. Half-board 298-506 F. TV. V AE.
Pleasant, well kept, and conveniently situated near the River Allier and the spa.

Régina
4, av. Thermale — 70.98.20.95
Closed 15 Oct-15 April. 1 ste 500-700 F. 80 rms 240-500 F. Restaurant. Half-board 340-540 F. TV. V AE.
This charming, old-fashioned hotel has all modern amenities and a garden.

Thermalia
1, av. Thermale — 70.31.04.39
Open every day. 128 rms 370-510 F. Restaurant. Half-board 543-638 F. TV. Air cond. Conference facilities. Pool. Parking. Telex 990547. V AE DC.
A modern building in the town centre, with spacious, comfortable rooms and direct access to the spa. Bar and restaurant.

In nearby Abrest
(4 km S on D 906)
03200 Vichy — (Allier)

12/20 La Colombière
1 km SE on D 906 — 70.98.69.15
M. Sabot. Closed off-season Sun dinner and Mon, and mid-Jan to mid-Feb. Open until 9 pm. Hotel: 4 rms 130-240 F. Parking. V AE DC.
Looking out onto the green banks of the Allier from this charming converted dovecote, you can sample cockscombs en salade, tender roast fillet of lamb with honey, and chocolate sorbet with mint coulis, or choose one of the good-value menus. Very pleasant service.
A la carte: 230 F. Menus: 85 F (weekdays only), 100 F (weekends and holidays only), 160 F, 250 F.

10/20 Aux Eperons
5, av. d'Hauterive — 70.32.24.86
M. Barla. Closed 1 Nov-2 Jan. Open until 9.30 pm. Terrace dining. Hotel: 6 rms 90-110 F. Parking.
Terrines, stuffed mussels, and *plats du jour* are to be found on a generous set of menus. Large riverside terrace.
A la carte: 150 F. Menus: 60 F, 85 F, 105 F.

In nearby Bellerive-sur-Allier
(Left bank)
03700 Vichy — (Allier)

Marcotel
Rue de la Grange-aux-Grains — 70.32.34.00
Closed Sun (Oct-Easter) and 20-30 Dec. 3 stes 465-587 F. 38 rms 280-392 F. Restaurant. Half-board 316-383 F. TV. Garage parking. V AE DC.
The well-equipped rooms overlook a park in the newest part of town.

VIEILLE-TOULOUSE

See Toulouse

VIENNE

38200 Vienne — (Isère)
Paris 488 - Grenoble 86 - Lyon 31 - Valence 70

La Pyramide
[18] 14, av. F.-Point — 74.53.01.96
M. Henriroux. Closed Thu lunch, Wed and 27 Jan-7 March. Open until 9.30 pm. Private room: 30. Terrace dining. Air cond. Valet parking. Telex 308058. V AE DC.
A gastronomic legend under Fernand Point and then his widow, La Pyramide had gone downhill in recent years. Although we rewarded Patrick Henriroux's talent with 16 points when he opened here last year, we didn't give much for his chances

of survival. However, the new Pyramide, luxuriously renovated around an interior garden full of roses, is now in full swing and deserves two more points and another toque.

Henriroux has brought with him from Mougins all the sunny flavours of Provence, which shine through in the lamb's trotter and prawn salad dressed with sherry vinegar and mixed with fresh herbs and young leeks, the cod with aubergine and oregano purée, and the roast kid stuffed with strips of red pepper and served on a bed of baby broad beans and courgette flowers. He also pays tribute to his new region, with ravioles de Romans floating in a chicken consommé, and the lake fish omble chevalier, its delicate flesh cooked to perfection. There are dishes from the old days of La Pyramide, greatly improved by Henriroux's light touch, as well as excellent cheeses, homemade bread, delicious chocolate desserts, and aromatic coffee. Let the enthusiasm of Jean-Claude Ruet guide you through a wine list that boasts some astonishing bottles of Condrieu, Côte-Rôtie, Hermitage, and Châteauneuf-du-Pape, not to mention the freshness and charm of the Viognier Château St-Estève. And if you arrive feeling down in the dumps, the relaxed good humour with which Christian Allandrieu takes charge of the service is highly infectious.

A la carte: 450-600 F. Menus: 250 F, 360 F, 460 F.

La Pyramide
(See restaurant above)
Closed 27 Jan-7 March. 4 stes 1,100 F. 24 rms 750 F. TV. Air cond. Conference facilities.
The twenty-four rooms and four suites overlooking the garden provide the perfect place to stop halfway between Paris and the Riviera. The décor is bright and modern, although the bathrooms are on the small side. Breakfast, coffee, and the wonderful collection of old port and liqueurs are served in the pleasant conservatory.

In nearby **Chonas-l'Amballan**

(9 km S on N 7)
38121 Vienne — (Isère)

Le Marais Saint-Jean
74.58.83.28
M. Heugas. Closed Tue dinner, Wed, 5 Feb-6 March and 11 Nov-1 Dec. Open until 8.45 pm. Terrace dining. Parking. V AE DC.
Christian Heugas pays close attention to the seasons in preparing sweetbread and asparagus salad, grilled salmon with baby broad beans, and stuffed calf's liver with mustard seeds. Good Côtes-du-Rhônes.

A la carte: 300 F. Menus: 150 F, 260 F, 320 F.

Le Marais Saint-Jean
(See restaurant above)
Closed Tue, Wed, 5 Feb-6 March and 11 Nov-1 Dec. 10 rms 480-520 F. TV. Conference facilities.
Quiet, comfortable rooms in a small Provençal-style hotel.

VIEUX-MAREUIL

24340 Vieux-Mareuil — (Dordogne)
Paris 500 - Périgueux 45 - Angoulême 45 - Brantôme 15

Château de Vieux-Mareuil
Mareuil-sur-Belle
53.60.77.15
M. Lefranc. Closed off-season Sun dinner and Mon, and 15 Jan-28 Feb. Open until 9.30 pm. Private

room: 40. Terrace dining. No-smoking section. Garage parking. V AE DC.
Set on a hillside among wooded valleys, this five-century-old château is more like a private residence turned into an hotel-restaurant. In the pretty pastel dining room you can sample some of Bernard Plancher's tasty and unusual creations: mushroom salad with confit de canard, lamb with mustard seeds, and a Monbazillac-flavoured walnut cake served with crème brûlée. The wine list has good Cahors and Bergerac, but the serving staff is too chatty and rather inattentive.

A la carte: 300 F. Menus: 100 F (weekdays only), 180 F, 280 F.

Château de Vieux-Mareuil
(See restaurant above)
Closed off-season Sun and Mon, and 15 Jan-28 Feb. 1 ste 800-1,200 F. 14 rms 380-500 F. Half-board 380-450 F. TV. Conference facilities. Heated pool. Tennis.
The rooms of the château and the fifteenth-century tower have been tastefully decorated with white furniture and brightly coloured fabrics. Excellent breakfasts with homemade pastries.

VIGERIE (LA)

See Angoulême

VIGOULET-AUZIL

See Toulouse

VILLANDRY

37510 Villandry — (Indre/Loire)
Paris 252 - Tours 20 - Chinon 32 - Langeais 13

Manoir de Foncher
47.50.02.40
Closed 1 Oct-15 April. 1 ste 750 F.1 rm 500 F. Parking.
There's space for four people at most in this historic manor house's single suite.

VILLARD-DE-LANS

38250 Villard-de-Lans — (Isère)
Paris 590 - Lyon 125 - Valence 70 - Grenoble 35 - Die 68

Grand Hôtel de Paris
76.95.10.06
Closed 13 April-11 May and 5 Oct-22 Dec. 60 rms 300-446 F. Restaurant. Half-board 320-386 F. TV. Conference facilities. Tennis. Garage parking. Telex 308448. V AE DC.
Well equipped for conferences and skiing holidays. The spacious rooms overlook the three hectares of grounds and the mountains.

Le Tétras
Av. du Pr-Nobécourt — 76.95.12.51
M. Buisson. Dinner only in winter. Closed 17 April-1 June and 30 Sep-15 Dec. Open until 9.30 pm. Private room: 30. Garden dining. No pets. Garage parking. Telex 320125. V AE DC.
The chef, trained by Troisgros and Loiseau, is becoming more adventurous, and he wins a toque this year for original dishes like the feuillantine of prawns with sesame seeds, and the duck breast with spicy apricots. Good wines and professional service.

A la carte: 300 F. Menus: 142 F, 179 F, 240 F.

> *Red toques signify modern cuisine; black toques signify traditional cuisine.*

Le Christiania
(See restaurant above)

Closed 17 April-1 June and 30 Sep-15 Dec. 24 rms 250-390 F. Half-board 305-390 F oblig in seas. TV. Conference facilities. Heated pool.

Here's an appealing mountain hotel opposite the municipal tennis courts. Almost all the comfortable rooms have a south-facing balcony, but the quality of the soundproofing varies.

VILLE-BLANCHE (LA)
See Lannion

VILLEBON-SUR-YVETTE
See PARIS Suburbs

VILLEFORT
48800 Villefort — (Lozère)
Paris 607 - Mende 59 - Le Puy 91 - Aubenas 60 - Alès 55

Balme
Pl. du Portalet — 66.46.80.14

M. Gomy. Closed off-season Sun dinner and Mon, 1-6 Oct and 12 Nov-31 Jan. Open until 9 pm. Private room: 20. Terrace dining. Hotel: 22 rms 100-220 F. Garage parking. V AE DC.

Michel Gomy's numerous trips to the Far East have contributed exotic variations to his light, delicious cooking. His repertoire includes some low-calorie dishes and he shows the same concern for keeping down prices. The fine 220 F menu includes home-prepared foie gras, assortment of three freshwater fish with chicory and saffron, pigeon with fresh pea purée, cheese, and dessert. The dining room overlooks the attractive garden.
Menus: from 90 F to 220 F.

VILLEFRANCHE-DE-ROUERGUE
12200 Villefranche-de-Rouergue — (Aveyron)
Paris 620 - Albi 72 - Cahors 61 - Montauban 73

Lagarrigue
Pl. B.-Lhez — 65.45.01.12

Closed Sun off-season and 1 week mid-Feb. 20 rms 100-250 F. Restaurant. Half-board 160-310 F. TV 10 rms. Garage parking. V AE DC.

Over a hundred years old, this simple, charming hotel has peaceful rooms.

Le Relais de Farrou
3 km, rte de Figeac
65.45.18.11

Closed 7-19 Feb, 7-17 Oct and 16-27 Dec. 1 ste 375 F. 26 rms 220-335 F. Restaurant. Half-board 225-290 F. TV. Conference facilities. Pool. Tennis. Garage parking. V.

The more pleasant rooms overlook the garden and swimming pool; others are on the main road. Turkish baths.

11/20 L'Univers
2, pl. de la République
65.45.15.63

M. Cancé. Closed Fri dinner and Sat (except 10/7-20/9), 8-19/3, 14-23/6 and 29/11-14/12. Open until 9 pm. Private room: 30. Terrace dining. V AE.

Seventy-nine next birthday, and the *patron* is still dishing up huge portions of foie gras terrine, moules marinière, and duck breasts. There's space on the terrace for a few tables overlooking the River Aveyron.
A la carte: 220-250 F. Menus: 65 F, 70 F, 80 F, 130 F, 210 F, 270 F.

L'Univers
(See restaurant above)

Open every day. 31 rms 115-280 F. Half-board 210-270 F. TV 24 rms. Conference facilities.

The owners have brought the décor and amenities of the rooms attractively up to date. Views over the old town and the hills across the river. Pleasant reception and service.

VILLEFRANCHE-DU-PÉRIGORD
24550 Villefranche-du-Périgord — (Dordogne)
Paris 570 - Cahors 40 - Périgueux 85 - Sarlat 45

10/20 La Clé des Champs
8 km NW on D 660
in Mazeyrolles — 53.29.95.94

M. Pinche. Open every day. Open until 10 pm. Terrace dining. Garage parking. V.

The self-taught *patronne* serves plentiful, homely dishes in the rustic, beamed dining room: scrambled eggs with cèpes and snails, quails stewed in Pécharmant wine, apple tart.
A la carte: 180-220 F. Menus: 80 F, 150 F, 230 F.

La Clé des Champs
(See restaurant above)

Open every day. 13 rms 225-245 F. Half-board 205-245 F. Pool. Tennis.

Sunny, welcoming rooms with views of the woods on one side, the pool and gardens on the other.

VILLEFRANCHE-SUR-MER
06230 Villefranche-sur-Mer — (Alpes-Mar.)
Paris 935 - Monte-Carlo 15 - Nice 6 - Cannes 39

12/20 Langoustine's
10, rue du May
93.01.91.86

Mlle Cattet. Dinner only (and lunch Sun and holidays). Closed Nov-end March. Open until midnight. Terrace dining. Air cond. V AE DC.

The *patronne* shows you the fresh local fish before sending it to the kitchen to be grilled to a turn by the young chef. There's also an assortment of shellfish and prawns prepared eight different ways. Only a few Provençal wines are available.
A la carte: 250 F.

12/20 Le Massoury
Avenue Léopold-II
93.01.03.66

M. Haussy. Closed Mon and 2 Jan-2 Feb. Open until 10.15 pm. Private room: 40. Terrace dining. Parking. V AE DC.

The new chef's cooking is costly and inconsistent: excellent fillets of red mullet, but mediocre young pigeon with pine-nuts and pumpkin. He loses his toque. The reception is very pleasant, but the service needs improvement.
A la carte: 400-500 F. Menus: 210 F (weekdays lunch only, wine inc), 330 F, 400 F, 440 F.

Welcome
1, quai de l'Amiral-Courbet
3.76.76.93

Closed 20 Nov-20 Dec. 32 rms 360-800 F. Restaurant. Half-board 370-580 F. TV. Air cond. Garage parking. Telex 470281. V AE DC.

This former convent where the writer Jean Cocteau liked to stay has recently been modernised. The rooms are comfortable and air-conditioned, with some spectacular ones on the fifth floor overlooking the sea.

VILLEFRANCHE-SUR-SAÔNE

69400 Villefranche-sur-Saône — (Rhône)
Paris 436 - Lyon 31 - Mâcon 41 - Bourg-en-Bresse 51

Château de Chervinges

3 km W on D 38, in Chervinges — 74.65.29.76
*Closed Sun and Mon (except in summer), Jan and
Feb. 5 stes 1,000-1,250 F. 10 rms 650-950 F. Restaurant. Half-board 700 F. TV 8 rms. Conference facilities. Pool. Tennis. Parking. Telex 380772. V AE DC.*
Rebuilt in the eighteenth century on the site of a
medieval mansion, this luxury hotel is surrounded
by Beaujolais vineyards. Its suites and huge rooms
are attractively furnished.

In nearby Anse

(6 km S on N 6)
69480 Villefranche-sur-Saône — (Rhône)

12/20 Hôtel Saint-Romain

Rte de Graves — 74.68.05.89
*M. Levet. Closed Sun dinner off-season, and 2-9 Dec.
Open until 9.30 pm. Garden dining. Hotel: 1 ste 230-
397 F. 22 rms 186-230 F. Garage parking. V AE DC.*
Good and inexpensive dishes are veal with three
meats, carp fillet with raspberry vinegar, and
scallops in pastry. Fine Beaujolais.
A la carte: 250 F. Menus: 75 F (weekdays only),
105 F, 142 F, 186 F.

VILLEFRANQUE

See Bayonne

VILLEMAGNE

11310 Villemagne — (Aude)
Paris 740 - Carcassonne 40 - Castelnaudary 16 - Saissac 6

Castel de Villemagne

68.94.22.95
*Closed 15 Nov-15 March. 7 rms 220-385 F. Restaur-
ant. Half-board 255-310 F oblig in seas. Parking. V.*
Four hundred metres up, this delightful fifteenth-
century manor restored in the eighteenth century
has quiet rooms with fine antique furniture.

VILLEMATIER

31340 Villematier — (H.-Garonne)
Paris 688 - Toulouse 32 - Montauban 27 - Albi 61

Auberge de la Braise

61.35.35.64
*Mme Bertin. Closed Sun dinner, Mon, Tue, 5-26 Feb
and 20 Sep-5 Oct. Open until 9.30 pm. Private
room: 21. Terrace dining. Parking. V.*
Francis Bertin, a jovial ex-wrestler with a superb
moustache, serves hearty regional cooking in this
rustic *auberge* surrounded by vineyards. We enjoyed the baby eels in a basquaise sauce of
tomatoes and peppers, sanquette of chicken and
garlic (cooked with blood and bacon), and salmon
with tomato 'flowers', but the menu changes
frequently as the market varies.
A la carte: 350-400 F. Menu: 130 F.

VILLEMUR-SUR-TARN

31340 Villemur-sur-Tarn — (H.-Garonne)
Paris 671 - Albi 62 - Toulouse 33 - Montauban 26

12/20 La Ferme de Bernadou

Av. du Gal-Leclerc — 61.09.02.38
*M. Voisin. Closed Sun dinner off-season, Mon and
2-15 Jan. Open until 10.30 pm. Private room: 50.
Garden dining. Parking. V AE.*
The décor is charming and the dishes precisely
prepared, but a little less foie gras, lobster, and

truffles would help curb the ever-rising prices.
You'll appreciate the baked lotte with bacon and
glazed onions, sweetbreads with truffles and a
crunchy topping, and chocolate and orange
millefeuille.
A la carte: 350-400 F. Menus: 85 F (weekdays
lunch only), 130 F, 165 F, 210 F, 250 F.

VILLENAVE-D'ORNON

See Bordeaux

VILLENEUVE-DE-MARSAN

40190 Villeneuve-de-Marsan — (Landes)
Paris 690 - Mont-de-Marsan 17 - Aire-sur-l'Adour 21

Francis Darroze

Grand-Rue — 58.45.20.07
*M. Darroze. Closed off-season Sun dinner and Mon
(except holidays), and 1-22 Jan. Open until 9.30 pm.
Private room: 25. Telex 560164. V AE DC.*
Resolutely regional cooking that knows when to
be bold. Francis Darroze lets his chef get on with
the lamb sweetbreads with Sauternes stock,
salmon with cream and fresh herbs, and good
game in season, while he looks after his astonishing cellar where the best Bordeaux rub shoulders
with a wonderful collection of Armagnacs. The
comfortable dining room looks out over a garden
planted with pines and lime trees.
A la carte: 350-450 F. Menus: 150 F (weekdays
lunch only), 250 F, 320 F.

Francis Darroze

(See restaurant above)
*Closed off-season Sun and Mon (except holidays),
and 1-22 Jan. 3 stes 750-950 F. 25 rms 400-750 F.
TV. Conference facilities. Pool.*
This very pleasant hotel has a well-tended gar-
den, swimming pool, and bright, modern rooms.

VILLENEUVE-LA-GARENNE

See PARIS Suburbs

VILLENEUVE-LÈS-AVIGNON

See Avignon

VILLENEUVE-LOUBET

06270 Villeneuve-Loubet — (Alpes-Mar.)
Paris 920 - Nice 16 - Antibes 12 - Cannes 23

Bahia

Rte du Bord-de-Mer — 93.20.21.21
*Open every day. 48 rms 365-620 F. TV. Air cond.
Pool. Garage parking. Telex 970922. V AE DC.*
This modern hotel is set in its own grounds and
has a private beach. The rooms, decorated in lively
colours, have contemporary wood furniture.

VILLENEUVE-SUR-LOT

47300 Villeneuve-sur-Lot — (Lot/Garonne)
Paris 614 - Bergerac 60 - Agen 29 - Cahors 76

12/20 Aux Berges du Lot

3, rue de l'Hôtel-de-Ville — 53.70.84.41
*M. Delpeyroux. Closed off-season Sun dinner, Mon,
11-24 Nov. Open until 10 pm. Garden dining. V DC.*
A charming welcome in this pretty but slightly
chilly dining room overlooking the River Lot. The
cassolette of snails is good but the wine sauce is a
little thin, and a fine tournedos steak with cream
of chives is served with a disappointing potato
gratin. Silky-smooth chocolate mousse.
A la carte: 200-250 F. Menus: 69 F (weekdays
lunch only), 95 F, 135 F, 190 F.

12/20 Hostellerie du Rooy
Ch. de Labourdette — 53.70.48.48
M. Brouat. Closed Wed (except July-Aug). Open until 9.30 pm. Private room: 60. Garden dining. No-smoking section. No pets. Parking. V AE DC.

Modern cuisine with a local flavour is served amid pastel tones under the barrel vaulting. The fricassée of sole and scallops is perfectly cooked and you should try the best end of lamb roasted with garlic cloves. The cellar is well stocked.

A la carte: 320 F. Menus: 98 F (weekdays only), 148 F, 198 F.

Hôtel des Remparts
1, rue E.-Marcel — 53.70.71.63
Open every day. 9 rms 85-159 F. TV 3 rms. Garage parking. V AE.

An 'office-hotel' with unpretentious rooms. Good breakfasts.

VILLEPINTE

See PARIS Suburbs

VILLERÉAL

47210 Villeréal — (Lot/Garonne)
Paris 590 - Bergerac 35 - Agen 59 - Marmande 57

Le Lac
Rte de Bergerac — 53.36.01.39
Closed 1 Oct-31 March. 28 rms 190-205 F. Restaurant. Half-board 185-200 F oblig in seas. Conference facilities. Pool. Garage parking. V.

For fishermen and bathers staying at this unpretentious hotel with a pretty garden and honest cooking, the lake is 300 metres away through the trees.

VILLERS-BOCAGE

14310 Villers-Bocage — (Calvados)
Paris 266 - Caen 26 - Vire 34 - Bayeux 25 - St-Lô 35

Le Relais Normand
9 km NE on N 175acro
14210 Noyers-Bocage — 31.77.97.37
Closed Wed, 25 Jan-8 Feb and 15 Nov-8 Dec. 8 rms 150-220 F. Restaurant. Half-board 250-300 F. TV. Conference facilities. Parking. V Michel.

Well-modernised, comfortable, quiet rooms for an overnight stop on the way to Mont-Saint-Michel.

11/20 Les Trois Rois
Rte de Vire — 31.77.00.32
M. Martinotti. Closed Sun dinner and Mon (except holidays), Feb and 25 June-1 July. Open until 9.30 pm. Private room: 25. Parking. V AE DC.

The *patron* of this pleasant inn keeps his customers happy with his excellent speciality, tripes à la mode de Caen, fresh lobster salad, and iced nougat with Cointreau. Good cellar and a warm welcome.

A la carte: 250 F. Menus: 115 F, 200 F.

Les Trois Rois
(See restaurant above)
Closed Sun and Mon (except holidays), Feb and 25 June-1 July. 14 rms 185-300 F. TV.

The simple, comfortable and well-soundproofed rooms have pretty little bathrooms. Manned car park.

Some establishments change their closing times without warning. It is always wise to check in advance.

VILLERS-COTTERÊTS

02600 Villers-Cotterêts — (Aisne)
Paris 75 - Soissons 23 - Château-Thierry 48 - Compiègne 29

Château d'Oigny en Valois
23.96.01.11
Mme Pétrel. Closed Tue dinner, Wed and 1-22 Jan. Open until 10 pm. Private room: 50. Garden dining. Parking. V AE DC.

This superbly restored fifteenth-century château set in formal gardens deserves to be better known, even if the medieval mummery is laid on a bit thick. In the two dining rooms with oak panelling and delightful furniture you will discover classic, careful cooking. There is perfectly cooked veal kidney, an assortment of three foies gras—excellent texture but too salty—and good cheeses featuring an interesting Roquefort mousse with slices of pear. The price of the wines will make your head spin.

A la carte: 350-400 F. Menus: 150 F, 250 F, 350 F.

Le Commerce
17, rue du Gal-Mangin — 23.96.19.97
M. Lepage. Closed Sun, Mon, 18 Jan-10 Feb and 12-26 Aug. Open until 9 pm. Garden dining. Hotel: 7 rms 95-160 F. V.

A new chef has taken over, but we hope this will not affect the repertoire of delicious boudin blanc of rabbit, flambéed veal kidney, and prune vacherin traditionally served in this welcoming family restaurant. We'll award points next year.

A la carte: 220-250 F. Menus: 80 F (except holidays), 120 F.

Le Régent
26, rue du Gal-Mangin — 23.96.01.46
Open every day. 1 ste 570 F. 17 rms 139-295 F. TV 15 rms. Conference facilities. Garage parking. Telex 150747. V AE DC.

Perfectly equipped period-style rooms grace this well-kept hotel in a magnificent sixteenth-century post house. Laundry service and bicycle hire.

VILLERS-LE-LAC

25130 Villers-le-Lac — (Doubs)
Paris 459 - Besançon 72 - Salin-les-Bains 79 - Morteau 6

Hôtel de France
8, place M.-Cupillard
81.68.00.06
M. Droz. Closed Sun dinner, Mon and 18 Nov-11 Jan. Open until 9 pm. Private room: 60. V AE DC.

The calm harmony of this family hotel is based on the father's scrupulous craftsmanship and the son's urge to innovate. The result is honest, aware cooking using good produce, such as the braised fillets of trout, lobster ravioli, and chicken 'ham' stuffed with morels, all served with a smile. Good choice of Jura wines.

A la carte: 270 F. Menus: from 120 F to 300 F.

Hôtel de France
(See restaurant above)
Closed 18 Nov-11 Jan. 14 rms 220-300 F. Half-board 240-260 F. TV. Conference facilities.

This small hotel gets better every year. The rooms are well equipped, a little noisy and old-fashioned, but good value.

VILLEURBANNE

See Lyon

VILLIERS-LE-BÂCLE

See PARIS Suburbs

VINAY
See Epernay

VINON-SUR-VERDON
83560 Vinon-sur-Verdon — (Var)
Paris 777 - Aix-en-Provence 43 - Manosque 16

12/20 Olivier
Rte de Manosque — 92.78.86.99
*M. Berton. Closed Sat off-season, and 23 Dec-15 Jan.
Open until 10 pm. Terrace dining. Air cond. Parking.
V AE DC.*
In the sunny dining room or on the terrace by the
pool, you can enjoy cooking that is fresh, balanced
and, if you eat à la carte, expensive. Choose
marinated salmon with dill, bass cutlet with baby
vegetables, lamb sweetbreads with cèpes—or go
for one of the good-value menus.
A la carte: 350 F. Menus: 90 F (weekdays only),
125 F, 160 F.

Olivier
(See restaurant above)
*Closed 23 Dec-15 Jan. 5 stes 400-550 F. 26 rms 270-
325 F. Half-board 300 F. TV. Conference facilities.
Pool. Tennis.*
Comfortable rooms looking out over the terraces
or the lawns shaded by olive trees near the pool.

VIOLÈS
84150 Violès — (Vaucluse)
Paris 670 - Avignon 31 - Orange 13 - Carpentras 17

11/20 Château Le Martinet
Rte de Vaison-la-Romaine — 90.70.94.98
*M. Boursier. Closed Tue off-season. Open until
10 pm. Terrace dining. Parking. V.*
Copious, unpretentious dishes like fillets of red
mullet with sweet peppers or rib of beef with
Gigondas are served in a cosy dining room, or on
the terrace in summer. The desserts are less good.
A la carte: 260 F. Menus: 100 F, 150 F, 210 F.

Château Le Martinet
(See restaurant above)
*Closed Tue off-season. 2 stes 400-450 F. 8 rms 180-
350 F. Half-board 280-350 F oblig in seas. TV. Conference facilities. Pool.*
This old family residence has just been converted
into a relaxed and comfortable hotel, complete
with pool, extensive grounds, and attractively
furnished rooms.

Le Mas de Bouvau
Rte de Cairanne — 90.70.94.08
*M. Hertzog. Closed Sun dinner and Mon, Feb school
holidays, 28 Aug-9 Sep and 20-30 Dec. Open until
8.45 pm. Garden dining. Hotel: 5 rms 240-325 F.
Parking. V.*
A family atmosphere, fine, fresh food, and good
local wines are the strong points of this country
restaurant. Try the snail stew, salmon with asparagus, or roast pigeon with garlic. You might
even be lucky enough to stay in one of the plain
rooms with glorious views that are much in
demand.
A la carte: 230 F. Menus: 105 F (weekdays only),
165 F, 220 F.

> *The prices quoted in this guide are those which
> we were given by the restaurants and hotels
> concerned. Increases in prices are beyond our
> control.*

VIRE
14500 Vire — (Calvados)
Paris 272 - Caen 59 - Fougères 67 - St-Lô 39

Hôtel de France
4, rue d'Aignaux — 31.68.00.35
*Closed 23 Dec-13 Jan. 20 rms 140-250 F. Restaur-
ant. Half-board 210-240 F oblig in seas. TV. Air cond.
Conference facilities. Garage parking. V AE.*
Centrally situated by a busy crossroads, this hotel
nonetheless has quiet rooms.

12/20 Manoir de la Pommeraie
2 km SE (from Paris road)
in Roullours — 31.68.07.71
*M. Lesage. Closed Sun dinner, Mon and Feb school
holidays. Open until 9.30 pm. Private room: 35. Garden dining. Parking. V AE DC.*
This well-renovated manor is set in wooded
grounds. In the flower-filled dining room you can
enjoy traditional dishes like the scallop salad with
Champagne and truffle vinegar, sweetbread
turnover with foie gras, or brill with leeks. Good
wines.
A la carte: 300 F. Menus: 102 F (weekdays only),
205 F (weekdays lunch only, wine inc), and from
153 F to 280 F.

VIRY-CHÂTILLON
See PARIS Suburbs

VITRÉ
35500 Vitré — (Ille/Vil.)
Paris 311 - Rennes 37 - Laval 37 - Fougères 30

Le Pichet
17, bd de Laval — 99.75.24.09
*M. Levillain. Closed Sun dinner, Mon, Feb school
holidays and 4-19 Aug. Open until 9 pm. Private
room: 20. V.*
You'll receive a charming welcome to this
beamed dining room with large bay windows overlooking the garden. The *carte* is as short as ever,
offering light dishes prepared from carefully
chosen produce: raw salmon marinated in lime
juice, turbot with vegetables, braised sweetbreads,
and hot apple tart. A well-deserved toque.
A la carte: 250-270 F. Menus: 90 F, 150 F, 180 F.

VITTEL
88800 Vittel — (Vosges)
Paris 334 - Epinal 43 - Nancy 70 - Belfort 129

L'Aubergade
265, av. des Tilleuls
29.08.04.39
*M. Meresse. Closed Sun dinner and Mon (except July-
Aug), and 23 Dec-8 Jan. Open until 9.30 pm. Private
room: 45. Air cond. Parking. V AE.*
You will appreciate the owner's three kinds of
foie gras, fisherman's platter, and veal kidneys and
sweetbreads, cheerfully served in the elegant dining room.
A la carte: 300-350 F. Menus: 180 F, 240 F and
285 F (weekdays only).

L'Aubergade
(See restaurant above)
*Closings not available. 9 rms 250-390 F. Half-board
471-581 F. TV. Air cond. Conference facilities.*
Very close to the spa, with rooms that vary in size
but are all well equipped. Poor soundproofing and
mundane breakfasts.

66400 Vivès — (Pyrénées-O.)
Paris 939 - Amélie-les-Bains 15 - Céret 8

11/20 Hostalet de Vivès ✪
Rue de la Mairie — 68.83.05.52
M. Girones. Closed Tue off-season, Wed and 10 Jan-9 March. Open until 9 pm. Air cond. V.
A typically Catalan establishment, from the furniture to the serving staff, wines, and food: local ham and charcuterie, pig's jowls, and cargolade (grilled snails served with a garlic sauce).
A la carte: 160 F. Menu: 70 F (weekdays lunch only).

52160 Vivey — (Haute-Marne)
Paris 328 - Langres 31 - Auberive 8 - Dijon 57

12/20 Relais du Lys
25.84.81.01
M. Robolin. Closed 15 Nov-1 April. Open until 9 pm. Private room: 15. Garden dining. Valet parking. V AE DC.
Major improvements to the château and garden were going on during our last visit. The modernised kitchens can only improve the beef with foie gras, snail soup with parsley juice, and duckling with green peppercorns.
A la carte: 300 F.

🏠 Relais du Lys 🌲
(See restaurant above)
Closed 15 Nov-1 April. 2 stes 665-740 F. 7 rms 390-550 F. Half-board 350-400 F oblig in seas. Conference facilities.
Wonderfully quiet and isolated. The huge, comfortable rooms are furnished in old-fashioned style and overlook the peaceful countryside.

38500 Voiron — (Isère)
Paris 520 - Bourg 108 - Grenoble 27 - Valence 80

🍳 Le Baron de Cheny
(Philippe Serratrice)
3, av. des Frères-Tardy — 76.05.29.88
M. Serratrice. Closed Sun dinner, Mon and 22 June-12 Sep. Open until 10 pm. Private room: 28. V AE DC.
This restaurant fitted out like the cabin of a boat provides the ideal setting in which to sample Philippe Serratrice's magnificent assortment of shellfish, prawns cooked in their own stock, and grilled salmon. Excellent value with a moderately priced Muscadet or white Chinon. During the summer, Serratrice organises gastronomic cruises on his catamaran.
A la carte: 300 F. Menus: 89 F (weekdays lunch only, wine inc), 119 F, 168 F.

12/20 Castel Anne
exit Voiron, towards Valence
73, av. du Dr-Valois — 76.05.86.00
M. Charvet. Closed Feb school holidays. Open until 9.30 pm. Private room: 60. Garden dining. Garage parking. Telex 320149. V AE DC.
The attractive dining room has a glass roof and overlooks the grounds. The cooking, with a bias towards seafood, is nicely prepared and nimbly served. Try the salad of warm chèvre with confit of rabbit, fillet of sole with ravioles de Royans, and the iced chocolate dessert with orange sauce.
A la carte: 300 F. Menus: 108 F, 160 F, 255 F.

🏠 Castel Anne
(See restaurant above)
Closed Feb school holidays. 18 rms 275-315 F. TV. Conference facilities.
Peaceful rooms furnished in period style and set in two acres of grounds.

63530 Volvic — (Puy-de-Dôme)
Paris 380 - Clermont-Ferrand 21 - Riom 7 - Aubusson 85

🏠 La Rose des Vents 🌲
3 km on N 686
in Luzet — 73.33.50.77
Closed Mon. 28 rms 190-240 F. Restaurant. Half-board 210-250 F oblig in seas. TV 12 rms. Pool. Tennis. Garage parking. V AE DC.
Everything you need to make the most of a spa cure or just to relax: tennis, swimming pool, and other sports facilities. Good rooms.

01540 Vonnas — (Ain)
Paris 419 - Bourg 24 - Mâcon 19 - Lyon 66 - Villefranche 39

🍳 Georges Blanc
(La Mère Blanc)
74.50.00.10
19.5 *M. Blanc. Closed Thu (except dinner in summer), Wed (except holidays) and 2 Jan-8 Feb. Open until 9.30 pm. Private room: 60. Air cond. No-smoking section. Valet parking. Telex 380776. V AE DC.*
Those who accuse Georges Blanc of megalomania forget that he has helped his native village prosper while remaining as unassuming and eager to please as he was in his youth. The square named after him with its fountain and flowers, the renovated family hotel, the shop selling Blanc food products, the exhibition gallery, the new white wine (blanc de Blanc), are all down to him—and paid for out of his own pocket. And it's no coincidence if the Bresse chickens he helps to promote are enjoying a huge commercial success. What is really astonishing is that Georges Blanc's cooking does not suffer from all this activity; on the contrary, we find it is scaling new heights of harmony and finesse.
When it was said he was not very inventive, Blanc took up the challenge and produced a 'menu découverte' with an achingly appetising choice of dishes. Judge for yourself: first there's Bresse duck marinated in a black-olive purée, crisp-tender green beans with foie gras, or spicy eel in a Beaujolais sauce, followed by frogs' legs stewed with cèpes, potato pancake with salmon and caviar, or a white-bean soup garnished with truffles sautéed just enough to magnify their flavour. Next, tomato with snails, artichokes, and fennel, or lake trout and omble chevalier (another lake fish) with a purée of aubergine and sweet peppers, or fillets of freshwater perch with tomatoes, potatoes, and anchovy sauce. Then you can choose among guinea fowl with onions and mushrooms, lobster in a Savagnin wine sauce, or a Bresse pigeon accompanied by ravioli stuffed with a purée of garlic-scented peas and meadow mushrooms, before moving on to the cheese board piled high with Mâcon goat cheeses, among many others. There are two hot desserts and then a large selection of petits fours to linger over....
Would all this leave you feeling peckish, as one of our readers claimed? Hundreds of hungry customers turn up every day, and we have only noticed those lucky enough to get a place in the dining rooms filled with bouquets and antique

porcelain, looking very content. All the same, should you hear any stomachs rumbling, do let us know! Jacqueline Blanc, ever watchful and attentive, supervises the excellent staff, and the wines, from the greatest to the most humble, provide the sweetest of temptations.

A la carte: 580-800 F. Menus: 380 F, 580 F.

 La Mère Blanc
(See restaurant above)
Closed 2 Jan-8 Feb. 6 stes 1,500-2,700 F. 30 rms 470-1,300 F. TV. Air cond. Conference facilities. Heated pool. Tennis.
On the banks of the romantic River Veyle, the supremely comfortable Mère Blanc has 30 rooms and six suites. The breakfasts are exquisite, there's a helipad on the grounds, and within ten kilometres you'll find three eighteen-hole golf courses. A covered bridge across the road provides access to La Cour aux Fleurs, built in the traditional style with ten rooms and a suite.

VOREPPE

See Grenoble

VOUILLÉ

86190 Vouillé — (Vienne)
Paris 343 - Parthenay 32 - Poitiers 19 - Thouars 52

 Château de Périgny
49.51.80.43
M. Keates. Closed Jan and March. Open until 9.30 pm. Private room: 200. Garden dining. Parking. Telex 791400. V AE DC.
The Danish owner has installed yet another new team, under Danish management. The serving staff are English, German, Spanish and Italian, and the result is as confusing as certain directives from Brussels. The French chef, Bernard Lafuente, is still finding his feet but his cooking is confident and skilful. We liked the salmon roll with cabbage leaves, bass with two sauces, and spiced croquant of guinea fowl.

A la carte: 320-400 F. Menus: 95 F (weekdays lunch only), 160 F, 230 F, 310 F.

 Château de Périgny
(See restaurant above)
Closed Jan and Feb. 3 stes 1,000-1,450 F. 42 rms 350-1,000 F. TV 25 rms. Conference facilities. Heated pool. Tennis.
Set in open green countryside, this fourteenth-century castle has even older outbuildings. The comfortable rooms have been recently decorated in mock-medieval. Excellent sports facilities, riding centre, and helipad.

VOULTE-SUR-RHÔNE (LA)

07800 Voulte-sur-Rhône (La) — (Ardèche)
Paris 590 - Valence 19 - Privas 20 - Crest 33

 Le Musée
Place 4-Septembre
75.62.40.19
Closed Sat off-season and Feb. 15 rms 140-280 F. Restaurant. Half-board 210-280 F. TV 8 rms. Conference facilities. Garage parking. V.
Good small hotel with pretty rooms and an attractive terrace.

VOUVRAY

37210 Vouvray — (Indre/Loire)
Paris 233 - Blois 49 - Tours 10 - Amboise 16

12/20 Auberge du Grand Vatel
8, rue Brûlé — 47.52.70.32
M. Copin. Closed Sun dinner off-season, Mon, 1-15 March and 1-15 Dec. Open until 9 pm. Terrace dining. Hotel: 7 rms 230-280 F (per pers, half-board oblig). Parking. V.
We think Bernard Copin is capable of greater things, judging by his good foie gras, salmon with crunchy bacon (a bit too salty), an honest duck leg with olives, and a nondescript mousse laced with sparkling Vouvray. Rabelaisian frescoes decorate the pleasant dining room, where the service is still hesitant.

A la carte: 230 F. Menus: 120 F (weekdays only), 200 F (weekends and holidays only), 160 F.

VOUZIERS

08400 Vouziers — (Ardennes)
Paris 200 - Reims 56 - Rethel 31

 **A la Ville de Rennes**
18, rue Chanzy — 24.71.84.03
Open every day. 20 rms 100-230 F. Restaurant. Half-board 140-190 F. TV 6 rms. Garage parking. V.
A family atmosphere reigns in this simple village hotel with a pleasant garden.

VOVES

28150 Voves — (Eure-et-Loir)
Paris 97 - Ablis 34 - Chartres 24 - Orléans 58

 Au Quai Fleuri
15, rue Texier-Gallas — 37.99.11.20
Closed off-season Fri and Sun, and 20 Dec-9 Jan. 15 rms 115-290 F. Restaurant. Half-board 215-290 F. TV 8 rms. Conference facilities. Parking. V AE.
Cheery, well-equipped bungalows set deep in wooded grounds. Amenities include games room and rides in a horse-drawn carriage.

WANGENBOURG

67710 Wangenbourg — (Bas-Rhin)
Paris 465 - Strasbourg 41 - Saverne 20 - Molsheim 29

Parc Hôtel
88.87.31.72
Closed 5 Nov-22 Dec. 34 rms 215-306 F. Restaurant. Half-board 257-268 F. No pets. Conference facilities. Heated pool. Tennis. Valet parking. V.
Fine spacious rooms and bedsitters with kitchenette. Various leisure activities are available, including a giant outdoor chessboard. Fitness centre.

Hôtel Scheidecker-Fruhauff
35, rue du Gal-de-Gaulle — 88.87.30.89
Closed off-season Mon and Tue, and 1-25 Dec. 26 rms 100-200 F. Restaurant. Half-board 150-180 F. Conference facilities. Garage parking. V.
The warm welcome and magnificent views are ample compensation for the building's lack of charm. Full board a possibility.

WANTZENAU (LA)

See Strasbourg

WIMILLE

See Boulogne-sur-Mer

CITIES INDEX
CLASSIFIED BY *DEPARTEMENTS*

R : restaurants with or without toques - **H:** hotels

	R		H
Urcuit *(see Bayonne)*	R		
Urrugne *(see Saint-Jean-de-Luz)*	R	⌂	
Urt *(see Bayonne)*	R	⌂	
Ustaritz *(see Bayonne)*	R	⌂	H
Villefranque *(see Bayonne)*	R		

65 Hautes-Pyrénées

	R		H
Argelès-Gazost	R	⌂	H
Asté *(see Bagnères-de-Bigorre)*	R		
Bagnères-de-Bigorre			H
Cauterets	R		
Juillan *(see Tarbes)*	R	⌂	
Lourdes	R	⌂	H
Madiran	R	⌂	H
Saint-Savin *(see Argelès-Gazost)*	R	⌂	
Tarbes	R	⌂	H

66 Pyrénées-Orientales

	R		H
Amélie-les-Bains			H
Arles-sur-Tech *(see Amélie-les-Bains)*	R		
Banyuls-sur-Mer	R	⌂	H
Canet-Plage	R		H
Céret	R	⌂	H
Collioure	R	⌂	H
Enveitg			H
Molitg-les-Bains	R	⌂	H
Perpignan	R	⌂	H
Saint-Cyprien	R		H

67 Bas-Rhin

	R		H
Baldenheim	R	⌂	
Colroy-la-Roche	R	⌂	H
Fegersheim *(see Strasbourg)*	R	⌂	
Haguenau	R	⌂	
Landersheim	R		
Lauterbourg	R		
Lembach	R	⌂	H
Marlenheim	R	⌂	H
Natzwiller *(see Schirmeck)*	R	⌂	
Obernai	R		H
Ottrott-le-Haut *(see Obernai)*	R	⌂	H
Strasbourg	R	⌂	H
Wantzenau (La) *(see Strasbourg)*	R	⌂	H

68 Haut-Rhin

	R		H
Ammerschwihr	R	⌂	H
Artzenheim	R	⌂	H
Bartenheim	R	⌂	
Buschwiller *(see Saint-Louis)*	R	⌂	
Colmar	R	⌂	H
Diefmatten	R	⌂	
Eguisheim *(see Colmar)*	R	⌂	
Husseren-les-Châteaux *(see Colmar)*			H
Illhaeusern	R	⌂	H
Illzach *(see Mulhouse)*	R	⌂	
Kaysersberg	R	⌂	
Kingersheim *(see Mulhouse)*	R	⌂	
Mulhouse	R	⌂	H
Murbach	R	⌂	H
Ribeauvillé	R	⌂	H
Riedisheim *(see Mulhouse)*	R	⌂	
Rouffach	R	⌂	H
Steinbrunn-le-Bas *(see Mulhouse)*	R	⌂	
Trois-Epis (Les)	R	⌂	

69 Rhône

	R		H
Anse *(see Villefranche-sur-Saône)*	R		
Caluire *(see Lyon)*	R	⌂	
Champagne-au-Mont-d'Or *(see Lyon)*	R	⌂	
Chénas	R	⌂	
Collonges-au-Mont-d'Or *(see Lyon)*	R	⌂	
Condrieu	R	⌂	H
Dardilly *(see Lyon)*	R	⌂	H
Fleurie	R	⌂	
Halles (Les)	R		

	R		H
Lyon	R	⌂	H
Mulatière (La) *(see Lyon)*	R	⌂	
Rillieux-la-Pape *(see Lyon)*	R	⌂	
Villefranche-sur-Saône	R		H
Villeurbanne *(see Lyon)*			H

70 Haute-Saône

	R		H
Fougerolles	R	⌂	
Gray	R		H

71 Saône-et-Loire

	R		H
Autun	R	⌂	H
Bourbon-Lancy	R	⌂	H
Chagny	R	⌂	H
Chalon-sur-Saône	R	⌂	H
Chassey-le-Camp *(see Chagny)*			H
Cluny	R	⌂	H
Croix-Blanche (La) *(see Mâcon)*	R	⌂	
Digoin	R	⌂	
Igé	R	⌂	H
Mâcon	R	⌂	H
Saint-Germain-du-Plain *(see Chalon-sur-Saône)*			H
Saint-Marcel *(see Chalon-sur-Saône)*	R	⌂	
Solutré *(see Mâcon)*	R		H
Tournus	R	⌂	H

72 Sarthe

	R		H
Arnage *(see Mans, Le)*	R	⌂	
Changé *(see Mans, Le)*	R	⌂	
Château-du-Loir			H
Loué	R	⌂	
Mans (Le)	R	⌂	H

73 Savoie

	R		H
Aiguebelette (Lac d')			H
Aix-les-Bains	R	⌂	H
Albertville	R	⌂	
Arcs (Les)	R	⌂	H
Bourget-du-Lac (Le)	R	⌂	H
Bourg-Saint-Maurice			H
Challes-les-Eaux *(see Chambéry)*			H
Chambéry	R	⌂	H
Courchevel	R	⌂	H
Crest-Volant			H
Ménuires (Les)			H
Méribel-les-Allues	R	⌂	H
Mottaret (Le) *(see Méribel-les-Allues)*	R		H
Plagne (La)	R		H
Tignes	R	⌂	H
Val-d'Isère	R		H
Val-Thorens	R		H

74 Haute-Savoie

	R		H
Abondance			H
Allonzier-la-Caille			H
Amphion-les-Bains *(see Evian)*			H
Annecy	R	⌂	H
Annemasse			H
Argentière			H
Avoriaz *(see Morzine)*	R	⌂	H
Bonneville	R	⌂	H
Carroz-d'Araches (Les)	R	⌂	H
Chamonix	R	⌂	H
Chapelle-d'Abondance (La)			H
Clusaz (La)	R	⌂	H
Combloux			H
Contamines-Montjoie (Les)			H
Cordon	R		H
Evian	R	⌂	H
Flaine	R	⌂	H
Gaillard *(see Annemasse)*			H
Gets (Les)			H
Megève	R	⌂	H
Morzine	R	⌂	H
Saint-Jorioz *(see Annecy)*			H
Talloires *(see Annecy)*	R	⌂	H
Thonon-les-Bains	R	⌂	H

76 Seine-Maritime

	R		H
Cany-Barville	R	⌂	
Caudebec-en-Caux	R	⌂	H

	R		H
Clères	R	⌂	
Dieppe	R	⌂	H
Elbeuf	R		
Etretat	R		H
Eu	R		H
Fécamp	R		
Fontaine-le-Dun	R	⌂	
Forges-les-Eaux	R	⌂	H
Harfleur *(see Havre, Le)*			
Havre (Le)	R	⌂	H
Hode (Le) *(see Havre, Le)*	R	⌂	
Jumièges	R	⌂	
Martin-Eglise *(see Dieppe)*			
Rouen	R	⌂	H
Sainte-Adresse *(see Havre, Le)*	R	⌂	
Sassetot-le-Mauconduit	R		
Tancarville	R		H

77 Seine-et-Marne

	R		H
Barbizon	R	⌂	H
Bussy-Saint-Georges *(see Lagny-sur-Marne)*	R		H
Croissy-Beaubourg *(see Paris Suburbs)*	R	⌂	
Ecrennes (Les)	R	⌂	
Ferté-sous-Jouarre (La)	R	⌂	
Flagy	R		H
Fontainebleau	R	⌂	H
Fontenay-Trésigny	R	⌂	H
Lagny-sur-Marne	R	⌂	
Malnoue *(see Paris Suburbs)*	R		
Meaux	R	⌂	H
Melun	R	⌂	H
Nemours	R	⌂	H
Ozoir-la-Ferrière *(see Paris Suburbs)*	R		
Pontault-Combault *(see Paris Suburbs)*	R		
Provins	R		
Rozay-en-Brie	R	⌂	H
Thomery *(see Fontainebleau)*	R	⌂	H

78 Yvelines

	R		H
Bailly *(see Paris Suburbs)*	R		
Bougival *(see Paris Suburbs)*	R		
Buc *(see Paris Suburbs)*	R	⌂	
Celle-Saint-Cloud (La) *(see Paris Suburbs)*			
Cernay-la-Ville	R	⌂	H
Châteaufort *(see Paris Suburbs)*	R	⌂	
Chesnay (Le) *(see Paris Suburbs)*	R	⌂	
Coignières	R	⌂	
Dampierre-en-Yvelines	R	⌂	
Garancières	R	⌂	
Jouy-en-Josas *(see Paris Suburbs)*	R	⌂	
Loges-en-Josas (Les) *(see Paris Suburbs)*	R	⌂	H
Louveciennes *(see Paris Suburbs)*	R		
Maisons-Laffitte *(see Paris Suburbs)*	R	⌂	
Mesnuls (Les) *(see Montfort-l'Amaury)*	R	⌂	H
Neauphle-le-Château *(see Pontchartain)*	R	⌂	
Poissy	R	⌂	
Port-Marly (Le) *(see Paris Suburbs)*	R	⌂	
Port-Villez *(see Vernon)*	R	⌂	
Rambouillet	R		H
Saint-Germain-en-Laye *(see Paris Suburbs)*	R	⌂	H
Saint-Lambert-des-Bois *(see Chevreuse)*	R	⌂	
Vélizy *(see Paris Suburbs)*			H
Versailles *(see Paris Suburbs)*	R	⌂	H
Vésinet (Le) *(see Paris Suburbs)*	R		H

79 Deux-Sèvres

	R		H
Coulon *(see Niort)*	R	⌂	H

continued page 516

● Restaurant with
   3 or 4 toques

— Département
   boundary

79 Département
   number

Restaurants and hotels
can be approximately
located by means of
their département
number, which may be
found both in the main
entry and, in numerical
order, in the index.

In order to establish a
more precise location
for a particular
establishment, refer to
the *RAC Atlas France,*
or to the relevant map
in the RAC Regional
Maps of France series,
all at a scale of
1:250,000
(4 miles to 1 inch).